HOLLYWOOD
REPRESENTATION
DIRECTORY

33RD EDITION
SUMMER 2007

FROM THE PUBLISHERS OF

THE REPORTER®

In print.
Online.
All the time.

EDITORIAL OFFICES

5055 Wilshire Blvd., Los Angeles, CA 90036
Phone 323.525.2369 or 800.815.0503
Fax 323.525.2393
www.hcdonline.com

Jeff Black ....VP, Information Services

EDITORIAL

Cary Tusan................................Sr. Research Editor
L. M. Siegel ....Research Editor
Ben Taylor ....Research Associate
Jill Sherwin ....Research Assistant
Carla Green ....Production Manager

SALES AND MARKETING

Valencia McKinley ....Sr. Director, Sales
Jia-Juh Yuh ....Coordinator, Sales

Aleks Horvat ....Founder

John Kilcullen ....Publisher
Paula Parisi...............................VP, Executive Editor
Evan Atkinson.............................Advertising Sales
          eatkinson@hollywoodreporter.com

Nielsen Business Media

Robert L. Krakoff ....President & CEO
Greg Farrar ....COO
Kirk Miller ....CFO
Michael Alicea................................Sr. VP, Human Resources
Bill Cooke......Sr. VP, Travel, Performance & Marketing Services
John Kilcullen ....Sr. VP, Music & Literary
Tom Kuczynski ....Sr. VP, Corporate Development & Planning
David Loechner................................Sr. VP, Retail
Toni Nevitt ....Sr. VP, eMedia Strategy & Technology
Mike Parker ....Sr. VP, Marketing & Media
Joe Randall ....Sr. VP, Building Design
Mary Kay Sustek.......................Sr. VP, Central Services
Deborah Patton ....VP, Corporate Communications
Howard Applebaum..............................VP, Licensing & Events
John Lerner ....VP, eMedia/Digital Strategy
Jennifer Grego ....VP, Manufacturing & Distribution
Joanne Wheatley.........................VP, Information Marketing
Drew DeSarle ....VP, Marketing Services
Sid Holt ....Editorial Director

33RD EDITION • SPRING 2007

CONTENTS

The companies listed in the *Hollywood Representation Directory* are broken into the following categories:

AGENTS: Individuals or companies who represent clients and negotiate their contracts for a standard fee – usually ten percent. Agents solicit work on behalf of clients by obtaining interviews, auditions, handling request bookings, as well as negotiating and collecting fees. Agents usually deduct a union or agreed-upon commission and generally assist in the development of the client's career.

MANAGERS: Individuals or companies that advise, counsel, guide, and develop the professional careers of talent for an agreed-upon percentage of earnings – usually between ten and fifteen percent. Managers may also serve as a liaison between clients and other service providers. Managers may not legally negotiate contracts. Most of the managers listed in this directory are personal managers, as opposed to business managers whose job is to provide accounting, investment, and other financial services.

ENTERTAINMENT ATTORNEYS: Individuals and companies providing a variety of legal services for clients in the film, television and music industries. Services may include contract negotiation and drafting, intellectual property law, contract dispute and litigation.

BUSINESS & LEGAL AFFAIRS DEPARTMENTS: Attorneys and business affairs executives for studios, networks and major representation firms.

PUBLICITY COMPANIES: Individuals, companies or divisions providing marketing and promotional support, often responsible for press, press junkets, satellite and media tours, celebrity appearances, product placement and special events.

CASTING DIRECTORS: Individuals or companies hired by producers, directors and studios to compile lists of talent and organize the casting process to meet the criteria of a given project or production. Casting Directors coordinate and run auditions and provide the producers and directors with ideas regarding what the characters should look and sound like.

The types of talent are defined as follows:

BELOW-THE-LINE TALENT: Technical talent working in motion pictures, commercials and television, including cinematographers, composers, film editors, production designers and sound editors.

COMMERCIAL TALENT: Acting talent for on-camera and voice-over work in commercials.

FILM/TV TALENT: Talent working in the motion picture and television industry, including actors, animals, broadcast journalists/newscasters, children, choreographers, comedians, dancers, directors, hosts/MCs, infants, martial artists/stunts, producers, seniors and teens/young adults.

LITERARY TALENT: Writers working in motion pictures, television, theatre, interactive game development and publishing.

MODELING TALENT: Models working in print, runway and television.

MUSIC TALENT: Talent working in the music industry, on soundtracks, live concerts and/or personal appearance, including composers, music artists, music editors, music producers and music supervisors. Magicians, speakers/lecturers, sports personalities and variety artists fall under the category of personal appearance.

THEATRE TALENT: Talent working in both legitimate and musical theatre, including actors, choreographers, comedians, dancers, directors, musical theatre performers and playwrights.

The following terms are commonly used in submission policies:

DEMO: A short tape or recording showcasing musical or voice-over abilities.

HEADSHOT: An 8x10 black and white photograph, taken by a professional photographer and used by actors in order to secure representation and find work.

INDUSTRY REFERRAL ONLY: Will only accept materials with a personal recommendation from someone in the business.

LOGLINE: A one line summary of a literary project.

NO UNSOLICITED SUBMISSIONS: Materials will only be considered if sent through an agent, manager or attorney.

OUTLINE: A detailed description covering the main points of a literary project.

QUERY: A one page letter including a brief pitch of the story concept or literary project, explanation of qualifications and request for a release form.

REEL: A short videotape or DVD showcasing an artist's best work in film, television and commercials.

RESUMÉ: A brief written account of industry related work experience and qualifications.

SASE: Acronym for self-addressed, stamped envelope.

The following abbreviations are used to represent their respective guilds, unions and associations:

AAR	Association of Authors' Representatives
AEA	Actors' Equity Association
AFM	American Federation of Musicians
AFTRA	American Federation of Radio & Television Artists
AGVA	American Guild of Variety Artists
ATA	Association of Talent Agents
CCDA	Commercial Casting Directors Association
CSA	Casting Society of America
DGA	Directors Guild of America
NCOPM	National Conference of Personal Managers
SAG	Screen Actors Guild of America
TMA	Talent Managers Association
WGA	Writers Guild of America

GUILDS, UNIONS AND ASSOCIATIONS

Academy of Country Music (ACM)

www.acmcountry.com

Supports, promotes and enhances the advancement of country music worldwide.

5500 Balboa Blvd., Ste. 200
Encino, CA 91316
Phone   818-788-8000
Fax   818-788-0999
Email   info@acmcountry.com
Tiffany Davis, Director,
    Membership & Creative Services

The Academy of Dance on Film (DOF)

www.danceonfilm.org

Nonprofit research library for the preservation, documentation and advancement of popular filmed dance.

798 Shadowgrove St.
Brea, CA 92821
Phone   714-529-0828
Fax   714-529-1406
Email   info@danceonfilm.org

Mailing address
PO Box 68
Brea, CA 92822-0068
Saadia Byram, Administrator

Academy of Motion Picture Arts and Sciences (AMPAS)

www.oscars.org

Honorary organization of motion picture professionals founded to advance the arts and sciences of motion pictures.

8949 Wilshire Blvd.
Beverly Hills, CA 90211-1972
Phone   310-247-3000
Fax   310-859-9619
Email   publicity@oscars.org
Sid Ganis, President
Bruce Davis, Executive Director
Leslie Unger, Director,
    Communications

Academy of Television Arts & Sciences (ATAS)

www.emmys.tv

Nonprofit corporation for the advancement of telecommunications arts and sciences.

5220 Lankershim Blvd.
North Hollywood, CA 91601
Phone   818-754-2800
Fax   818-761-2827
Alan Perris, Chief Operating
    Officer
Terri Clark, Executive Director
John Leverence, Sr.VP, Awards
Laurel Whitcomb, VP, Marketing
Gregory Sims, Director, Human
    Resources
Barbara Chase, Director,
    Membership
Juan Morales, Director,
    Membership Publications
Lisa Fike, Controller
Ava Surrena, Manager, Corporate
    Relations
Scott Buford, Art Director
Karalee Vint, Director, Board
    Relations
Stephen Laughlin, Director,
    Information Technology

Actors' Equity Association (AEA)

www.actorsequity.org

Labor union representing US actors and stage managers working in the professional theatre.

New York
165 W. 46th St., 15th Fl.
New York, NY 10036
Phone   212-869-8530
Fax   212-719-9815

Chicago
125 S. Clark St., Ste. 1500
Chicago, IL 60603
Phone   312-641-0393
Fax   312-641-6365

Orlando
10319 Orangewood Blvd.
Orlando, FL 32821
Phone   407-345-8600
Fax   407-345-1522

Los Angeles
5757 Wilshire Blvd., Ste. 1
Los Angeles, CA 90036
Phone   323-634-1750
Fax   323-634-1777

San Francisco
350 Sansome St., Ste. 900
San Francisco, CA 94104
Phone   415-391-3838
Fax   415-391-0102

Mark Zimmerman, President
John Connolly, National Executive
    Director

Actors' Fund of America

www.actorsfund.org

Nonprofit organization providing for the social welfare of entertainment professionals.

New York
729 Seventh Ave., 10th Fl.
New York, NY 10019
Phone   212-221-7300
         800-221-7303
Fax   212-764-0238
Email   info@actorsfund.org

Los Angeles
5757 Wilshire Blvd., Ste. 400
Los Angeles, CA 90036
Phone   323-933-9244
Fax   323-933-7615

Alliance of Canadian Cinema, Television & Radio Artists (ACTRA)

www.actra.ca

Labor union founded to negotiate, safeguard, and promote the professional rights of Canadian performers working in film, television, video, and all recorded media.

625 Church St., 3rd Fl.
Toronto, ON M4Y 2G1 Canada
Phone   800-387-3516
         416-489-1311
Fax   416-489-8076
Email   national@actra.ca
         info@actratoronto.com

American Academy of Dramatic Arts (AADA)

www.aada.org

Offers a two-year professional actor's training program, a third year advanced performance program and a six-week summer program. Nonprofit and accredited.

Los Angeles
1336 N. La Brea Ave.
Los Angeles, CA 90028
Phone   323-464-2777
         800-463-8990
Fax   323-464-1250

New York
120 Madison Ave.
New York, NY 10016
Roger Croucher, President
Marguerite Artura, President,
    Los Angeles Division

American Booksellers Association (ABA)

www.bookweb.org

Nonprofit organization of independently owned bookstores with retail storefront locations.

200 White Plains Rd. 6th Fl.
Tarrytown, NY 10591
Phone   800-637-0037
         914-591-2665
Fax   914-591-2720
Email   info@bookweb.org

American Cinema Editors, Inc. (ACE)

www.ace-filmeditors.org
www.americancinemaeditors.com

Honorary society made up of editors deemed to be outstanding in their field.

100 Universal City Plaza, Verna
Fields Bldg. 2282, Rm. 190
Universal City, CA 91608
Phone   818-777-2900
Fax   818-733-5023
Email   amercinema@earthlink.net
Alan Heim, President
Jennifer McCormick, Managing
    Director

American Federation of Musicians (AFM)

www.afm.org

Labor union representing professional musicians.

National Headquarters
1501 Broadway, Ste. 600
New York, NY 10036
Phone   212-869-1330
Fax   212-764-6134

Los Angeles
3550 Wilshire Blvd., Ste. 1900
Los Angeles, CA 90010
Phone   213-251-4510
Fax   213-251-4520

American Federation of Television & Radio Artists (AFTRA)

www.aftra.org

Labor organization representing broadcast performers.

Los Angeles
5757 Wilshire Blvd., Ste. 900
Los Angeles, CA 90036
Phone   323-634-8100
Fax   323-634-8246
Email   losangeles@aftra.com
         aftrany@aftra.com

New York
260 Madison Ave., 7th Fl.
New York, NY 10016
Phone   212-532-0800
Fax   212-545-1238
Stephen Burrow, Executive Director,
    New York Chapter
Mathis L. Dunn Jr., Interim
    Executive Director, Los Angeles
    Chapter

American Film Institute (AFI)

www.afi.com

Organization dedicated to preserving and advancing the art of the moving image through events, exhibitions and education.

2021 N. Western Ave.
Los Angeles, CA 90027
Phone   323-856-7600
Fax   323-467-4578
Email   ldevilla@afi.com

Jean Picker Firstenberg, Director/CEO
Jonathan Estrin, Executive VP
Liza deVilla, Chief Communications Officer

American Guild of Musical Artists (AGMA)

www.musicalartists.org

Labor organization that represents the men and women who create America's operatic, choral and dance heritage.

1430 Broadway, 14th Fl.
New York, NY 10018
Phone   212-265-3687
Fax   212-262-9088
Email   agma@musicalartists.org

Linda Mays, President
Alan S. Gordon, National Executive Director

American Guild of Variety Artists (AGVA)

Labor union representing performers in Broadway, off-Broadway, and cabaret productions, as well as theme park and nightclub performers.

Los Angeles
4741 Laurel Canyon Blvd., Ste. 208
Valley Village, CA 91607
Phone   818-508-9984
Fax   818-508-3029
Email   agvawest@earthlink.net

New York
363 Seventh Ave., 17th Fl.
New York, NY 10001
Phone   212-675-1003
Fax   212-633-0097

Allison Donnelly, West Coast Representative
Steve Rosen, West Coast Representative

American Humane Association (AHA) Film & TV Unit

www.americanhumane.org/film

Watchdog organization dedicated to preventing cruelty to animal actors performing in films and television.

15366 Dickens St.
Sherman Oaks, CA 91403
Phone   818-501-0123
Fax   818-501-8725

Marie Belew Wheatley, President/CEO, AHA

American Screenwriters Association (ASA)

www.goasa.com

Nonprofit professional association dedicated to the promotion and encouragement of the art and craft of screenwriting, with members in 40 countries and 2,000 cities worldwide.

269 S. Beverly Dr., Ste. 2600
Beverly Hills, CA 90212-3807
Phone   866-265-9091
Email   asa@goasa.com

John E. Johnson, Executive Director

American Society of Cinematographers (ASC)

www.theasc.com

Society representing professional cinematographers, dedicated to improving the quality of motion picture presentation.

1782 N. Orange Dr.
Hollywood, CA 90028
Phone   323-969-4333
           800-448-0145
Fax   323-882-6391

Daryn Okada, President
Kim Weston, Administrative Assistant

American Society of Composers, Authors & Publishers (ASCAP)

www.ascap.com

Performing rights organization representing composers, lyricists, songwriters, and music publishers. Additional offices in New York, Nashville, Chicago, Miami, Atlanta, Puerto Rico, and London.

7920 W. Sunset Blvd., 3rd Fl.
Los Angeles, CA 90046
Phone   323-883-1000
           212-621-6000
           615-742-5000
Fax   323-883-1049
           212-724-9064
           615-742-5020
Email   info@ascap.com

American Society of Journalists & Authors (ASJA)

www.asja.org

Organization of independent nonfiction writers.

1501 Broadway, Ste. 302
New York, NY 10036
Phone   212-997-0947
Fax   212-937-2315

Anne Peace, Executive Director

American Society of Media Photographers (ASMP)

www.asmp.org

Trade organization dedicated to protecting and promoting the interests and high professional standards of photographers whose work is for publication.

150 N. Second St.
Philadelphia, PA 19106
Phone   215-451-2767
Fax   215-451-0880

Eugene Mopsik, Executive Director

American Society of Young Musicians (ASYM)

www.asymusicians.org

National nonprofit organization committed to the enrichment of young musicians. Sponsor of the annual ASYM Spring Benefit Concert and Awards.

6100 Wilshire Blvd., Ste. 230
Los Angeles, CA 90048
Phone   310-358-8300
Fax   310-358-8304
Email   info@asymusicians.org

American Women in Radio & Television (AWRT)

www.awrt.org

National organization supporting the advancement of women in the communications industry.

8405 Greensboro Dr., Ste. 800
McLean, VA 22102
Phone   703-506-3290
Fax   703-506-3266
Email   info@awrt.org

Maria Brennan, Executive Director

Animal Content in Entertainment (ACE)

www.ace-tvfilm.com

Develops and supports film and TV productions featuring storylines that raise awareness of animal issues. A program of The Humane Society of the United States (HSUS); Presenter of the annual Genesis Awards.

5551 Balboa Blvd.
Encino, CA 91316
Phone   818-382-6565
Fax   818-501-2226
Email   contact@ace-tvfilm.com

Beverly Kaskey, Director, Hollywood Office, HSUS
Julie Lofton, Producer/TV & Film Development
Sue Blackmore, Marketing/Publicity
Jen Tait, Writer/TV & Film Resources
Leigh O'Bryan, Database Administration
Monica Tiller, Office Coordinator
Gretchen Wyler, Executive Producer

Art Directors Guild & Scenic, Title and Graphic Artists

www.artdirectors.org

Organization representing production designers, art directors, assistant art directors and scenic, title and graphic designers.

c/o Local 800 I.A.T.S.E.
11969 Ventura Blvd., Ste. 200
Studio City, CA 91604
Phone   818-762-9995
Fax   818-762-9997

Tom Walsh, President
Lydia Zimmer, Office Manager

Association of American Publishers, Inc. (AAP)

www.publishers.org

Trade association for the book publishing industry.

Washington, DC
50 F St., NW, Ste. 400
Washington, DC 20001-1564
Phone   202-347-3375
Fax   202-347-3690
Email   dhuntington@publishers.org

New York
71 Fifth Ave., 2nd Fl.
New York, NY 10003-3004
Phone   212-255-0200
Fax   212-255-7007

Patricia S. Schroeder, President/CEO

Association of Authors' Representatives (AAR)

www.aar-online.org

Nonprofit organization of independent literary and dramatic agents.

676A 9th Avenue #312
New York, NY 10036
Phone   212-840-5777
Email   aarinc@mindspring.com

Association of Independent Commercial Producers (AICP)

www.aicp.com

Organization representing interests of US companies that specialize in producing commercials in various media (film, video, Internet, etc.) for advertisers and agencies.

Los Angeles
650 N. Bronson Ave., Ste. 223-B
Los Angeles, CA 90004
Phone   323-960-4763
Fax   323-960-4766
Email   info@aicp.com

New York
3 W. 18th St., 5th Fl.
New York, NY 10011
Phone   212-929-3000
Fax   212-929-3359

Steve Caplan, Executive VP
Christine Allen, Events Regional Events Manager

Association of Talent Agents (ATA)

www.agentassociation.com
www.actorsagentsearch.com
Nonprofit trade association for talent agencies representing clients in the motion picture and television industries, as well as literary, theatre, radio and commercial clients.
9255 Sunset Blvd., Ste. 930
Los Angeles, CA 90069
Phone   310-274-0628
Fax   310-274-5063
Shellie Jetton, Administrative Director

The Authors Guild

www.authorsguild.org
Society dedicated to advocacy for fair compensation, free speech, and copyright protection for published authors.
31 E. 32nd St., 7th Fl.
New York, NY 10016
Phone   212-563-5904
Fax   212-564-5363
Email   staff@authorsguild.org
Paul Aiken, Executive Director

Axis of Justice

www.axisofjustice.org
Nonprofit organization whose purpose is to bring together musicians, fans of music, and grassroots political organizations to fight for social justice together.
1275 N. Wilton Pl., Ste. B
Los Angeles, CA 90038
Email   politics@axisofjustice.org
Jake Sexton, Media Director

The Black Filmmaker Foundation (BFF)

www.dvrepublic.org
Nonprofit organization which administers an online community and a filmmaker lab.
11 W. 42nd St., 9th Fl.
New York, NY 10036
Phone   212-253-1690
Fax   718-407-0608
Email   hudlin@dvrepublic.org
Warrington Hudlin, Founder/Chief

BMI (Los Angeles)

www.bmi.com
8730 Sunset Blvd., 3rd Fl. West
Los Angeles, CA 90069
Phone   310-659-9109
Fax   310-657-6947
Doreen Ringer Ross, VP, Film & TV Relations
Michael Crepezzi, Sr. Director, Performing Rights
Linda Livingston, Sr. Director, Film & TV Relations
Ray Yee, Sr. Director, Film & TV Relations
Anne Cecere, Associate Director, Film & TV Relations (310-289-6300)
Delia Orjuela, Assistant VP, Publisher Relations, Latin Music

BMI (New York)

www.bmi.com
320 W. 57th St.
New York, NY 10019
Phone   212-586-2000
Fax   212-246-2163
Del R. Bryant, President/CEO
Alison Smith, Sr. VP, Performing Rights
Phillip R. Graham, Sr. VP, Writer/Publisher Relations
Richard Conlon, VP, New Media & Strategic Development
Mark Barron, Assistant VP, Corporate Marketing
John Coletta, Assistant VP, Legal Affairs
Ben Tischker, Associate Director, Writer/Publisher Relations
Rick Garza, Director, Legal & Business Affairs
Wardell Malloy, Director, Writer/Publisher Relations

Breakdown Services

www.breakdownservices.com
Communications network and casting system providing integrated tools for casting directors and talent representatives, as well as casting information for actors.
2140 Cotner Ave.
Los Angeles, CA 90025
Phone   310-276-9166
            212-869-2003
            604-943-7100

California Arts Council (CAC)

www.cac.ca.gov
State organization encouraging artistic awareness, expression, and participation reflecting California's diverse cultures.
1300 I St., Ste. 930
Sacramento, CA 95814
Phone   916-322-6555
            800-201-6201
Fax   916-322-6575
Email   info@caartscouncil.com
Mary Beth Barber, Communications Director

Casting Society of America

www.castingsociety.com
Trade organization of professional film and television casting directors.

Los Angeles
606 N. Larchmont Blvd., Ste. 4B
Los Angeles, CA 90004
Phone   323-463-1925
Fax   323-463-5753

New York
C/O Bernard Telsey
311 W. 43rd St. 10th Fl.
New York, NY 10036
Phone: 212-868-1260
Fax: 212-868-1261
Larry Raab
Alice S. Cassidy

CineStory

www.cinestory.com
Nonprofit organization for emerging screenwriters.
PO Box 3736
Idyllwild, CA 92549
Phone   800-6STORY6
            951-659-1180
Fax   951-659-1176
Email   csa@cinestory.com

Cinewomen

www.cinewomen.org
Nonprofit organization dedicated to supporting the advancement of women within the motion picture industry.

Los Angeles
PO Box 691637
Los Angeles, CA 90069
Phone   310-288-1160
Email   info@cinewomen.com

New York
PO Box 1477
Cooper Station
New York, NY 10276
Phone   212-604-4264
Email   info@cinewomenny.org

Commercial Casting Directors Association (CCDA)

Organization dedicated to providing a level of professionalism for casting directors within the commercial industry.
c/o Jeff Gerard/Chelsea Studios
11340 Moorpark St.
Studio City, CA 91604
Phone   818-782-9900

Costume Designers Guild (CDG)

www.costumedesignersguild.com
Union representing motion picture, television, and commercial costume designers. Promotes research, artistry and technical expertise in the field of film and television costume design.
4730 Woodman Ave., Ste. 430
Sherman Oaks, CA 91423
Phone   818-905-1557
Fax   818-905-1560
Email   cdgia@earthlink.net
Deborah Landis, President
Rachael Stanley, Assistant Executive Director

Directors Guild of America (DGA)

www.dga.org
Labor union representing film and television directors, unit production managers, first assistant directors, second assistant directors, technical coordinators, tape associate directors, stage managers and production associates.

Los Angeles
7920 Sunset Blvd.
Los Angeles, CA 90046
Phone   800-421-4173
            310-289-2000
Fax   310-289-2029

New York
110 W. 57th St.
New York, NY 10019
Phone   212-581-0370
Fax   212-581-1441

Chicago
400 N. Michigan Ave., Ste. 307
Chicago, IL 60611
Phone   312-644-5050
Fax   312-644-5776

The Dramatists Guild of America, Inc.

www.dramatistsguild.com
Professional association of playwrights, composers and lyricists.
1501 Broadway, Ste. 701
New York, NY 10036
Phone   212-398-9366
Fax   212-944-0420
Email   director@dramatistsguild.com
Ralph Sevush, Executive Director

Entertainment Industries Council, Inc.

www.eiconline.org

Nonprofit organization founded in 1983 by leaders in the entertainment industry to provide information, awareness and understanding of major health and social issues among the entertainment industries and to audiences at large.

2600 W. Olive St., Ste. 574
Burbank, CA 91505
Phone   818-333-5001
Fax   818-333-5005
Email   eicwest@eiconline.org

Film Independent

www.filmindependent.org

Nonprofit service organization providing resources and information for independent filmmakers and industry professionals. Produces the Independent Spirit Awards and Los Angeles Film Festival.

9911 West Pico Blvd.
Los Angeles, CA 90035
Phone   310-432-1200
Fax   310-432-1203
Dawn Hudson, Executive Director

Filmmakers Alliance (FA)

www.filmmakersalliance.com

Community of film artists bound by a commitment to realize the full creative potential of independent film; Hosts monthly meetings, screenings, seminars, discussion forums, writers groups and staged readings.

10920 Ventura Blvd.
Studio City, CA 91604
Phone   818-980-8161
Fax   213-228-1156
Email   info@
            filmmakersalliance.com

Gospel Music Association (GMA)

www.gospelmusic.org

Organization founded for the purpose of supporting, encouraging and promoting the development of all forms of Gospel music.

1205 Division St.
Nashville, TN 37203
Phone   615-242-0303
Fax   615-254-9755

Hispanic Organization of Latin Actors (HOLA)

www.hellohola.org

Arts service organization committed to projecting Hispanic artists and their culture into the mainstream of Anglo-American industry and culture. Publishes an online photo and resumé directory of Hispanic talent on Web site.

107 Suffolk St., Ste. 302
New York, NY 10002
Phone   212-253-1015
Fax   212-253-9651
Email   holagram@hellohola.org
Manny Alfaro, Executive Director

Hollywood Radio & Television Society (HRTS)

www.hrts.org

Recognized as the entertainment industry's premiere networking and information forum. Through the signature Newsmaker Luncheon Series and other HRTS events, provides industry executives the opportunity to stay abreast of current trends while also staying connected to other key entertainment industry leaders.

13701 Riverside Dr., Ste. 205
Sherman Oaks, CA 91423
Phone   818-789-1182
Fax   818-789-1210
Email   info@hrts.org
*Andy Friendly, President, Board of
    Directors*
Dave Ferrara, Executive Director

Horror Writers Association

www.horror.org

Worldwide organization of horror and dark fantasy writers and publishing professionals.

244 Fifth Ave., Ste. 2767
New York, NY 10001
Email   hwa@horror.org
Gary Braunbeck, President

The Humanitas Prize

www.humanitasprize.org

Prestigious prizes awarded to film and television writers whose produced scripts communicate values which most enrich the human person.

17575 Pacific Coast Highway
PO Box 861
Pacific Palisades, CA 90272
Phone   310-454-8769
Fax   310-459-6549
Email   humanitasmail@aol.com
Frank Desiderio C.S.P., President
Chris Donahue, Executive Director
*Cara D'Antoni, Assistant to
    Executive Director*

Independent Feature Project (IFP)

www.ifp.org

Notprofit organization designed to foster a more sustainable infrastructure that supports independent filmmaking, and ensures opportunities for the public to see films more accurately reflecting the full diversity of American culture; Presents the IFP Market, Gotham Awards and Filmmaker Magazine.

104 W. 29th St., 12th Fl.
New York, NY 10001
Phone   212-465-8200
Fax   212-465-8525
Email   newyorkmembership@
            ifp.org
Michelle Byrd, Executive Director

Independent Film & Television Alliance (IFTA)

www.ifta-online.org

Non-profit trade association for the independent film and television industries.

10850 Wilshire Blvd., 9th Fl.
Los Angeles, CA 90024-4321
Phone   310-446-1000
Fax   310-446-1600
Email   info@ifta-online.org
Jean Prewitt, President/CEO

Independent Writers of Southern California

www.iwosc.org

Brings together journalists, business writers, authors, copywrights, playwrights, poets, screenwriters and others for networking and professional development.

PO Box 34279
Los Angeles, CA 90034
Phone   877-799-7483
Email   info@iwosc.org
Alice Campbell Romano, President

International Alliance of Theatrical Stage Employees (IATSE)

www.iatse-intl.org

Union representing technicians, artisans and craftpersons in the entertainment industry including live theatre, film and television production and trade shows.

<u>Los Angeles</u>
10045 Riverside Dr.
Toluca Lake, CA 91602
Phone   818-980-3499
Fax   818-980-3496

<u>New York</u>
1430 Broadway, 20th Fl.
New York, NY 10018
Phone   212-730-1770
Fax   212-730-7809

International Press Academy

www.pressacademy.com

Association of professional entertainment journalists.

9601 Wilshire Blvd., Ste. 755
Beverly Hills, CA 90210
Phone   310-271-7041
            818-989-1589
Fax   818-787-3627
Email   info@pressacademy.com

International Thriller Writers, Inc.

www.thrillerwriters.org

Created by thriller authors to celebrate the genre. Awards prizes to outstanding thriller novels, screenplays and authors, and creates opportunities for collegiality within the thriller community.

PO Box 311
Eureka, CA 95502
Fax   707-442-9251
Email   info@thrillerwriters.org

Motion Picture Association of America (MPAA)

www.mpaa.org

Trade association for the US motion picture, home video and television industries.

15503 Ventura Blvd.
Encino, CA 91436
Phone   818-995-6600
Fax   818-382-1799
Dan Glickman, Chairman/CEO

Motion Picture Editors Guild

www.editorsguild.com

Union representing motion pictures, television, and commercial editors, sound technicians and story analysts.

<u>Los Angeles</u>
7715 Sunset Blvd., Ste. 200
Hollywood, CA 90046
Phone   323-876-4770
Fax   323-876-0861
Email   mail@editorsguild.com

<u>New York</u>
145 Hudson St., Ste. 201
New York, NY 10013
Phone   212-302-0700
Fax   212-302-1091

<u>Chicago</u>
6317 N. Northwest Hwy.
Chicago, IL 60631
Phone   773-594-6598
Fax   773-594-6599
*Serena Kung, Director,
    Membership Services*

Multicultural Motion Picture Association (MMPA)

www.thediversityawards.org
Association promoting and encouraging diversity of ideas, cultures and perspectives in film and television. Sponsor of the annual Diversity Awards.
6100 Wilshire Blvd., Ste. 230
Los Angeles, CA 90048
Phone   310-358-8300
Fax   310-358-8304
Email   jammpa@sbcglobal.net

Music Managers Forum (MMF)

www.mmfus.org
Organization dedicated to furthering the interests of managers and their artists in all fields of the music industry including live performance, recording and publishing.
PO Box 444, Village Station
New York, NY 10014
Phone   212-213-8787
Fax   212-213-9797
Email   info@mmfus.org

Music Video Production Association (MVPA)

www.mvpa.com
Nonprofit trade organization made up of music video production and post production companies, as well as editors, directors, producers, cinematographers, choreographers, script supervisors, computer animators and make-up artists involved in the production of music videos.
201 N. Occidental Blvd.,
Bldg. 7, Unit B
Los Angeles, CA 90026
Phone   213-387-1590
Fax   213-385-9507
Email   info@mvpa.com
Andrea Clark, Executive Director
Amy E, Executive

Mystery Writers of America (MWA)

www.mysterywriters.org
Organization of published mystery authors, editors, screenwriters, and other professionals in the field. Sponsors symposia, conferences and The Edgar Awards.
17 E. 47th St., 6th Fl.
New York, NY 10017
Phone   212-888-8171
Fax   212-888-8107
Email   mwa@mysterywriters.org

Nashville Association of Talent Directors (NATD)

www.n-a-t-d.com
Professional entertainment organization comprised of industry professionals involved in all aspects of the music and entertainment industries.
PO Box 23903
Nashville, TN 37202-3903
Phone   615-297-0100
Email   info@n-a-t-d.com

National Academy of Recording Arts & Sciences (NARAS)

www.grammy.com
Organization dedicated to improving the quality of life and cultural condition for musicians, producers, and other recording professionals. Provides outreach, professional development, cultural enrichment, education and human services programs. Sponsors The Grammy Awards.
The Recording Academy
3402 Pico Blvd.
Santa Monica, CA 90405
Phone   310-392-3777
Fax   310-399-3090
Email   grammyfoundation@
          grammy.com

National Association of Latino Independent Producers (NALIP)

www.nalip.org
Organization of Latino/Latina, television and documentary film makers.
Los Angeles
1323 Lincoln Blvd., Ste. 220
Santa Monica, CA 90401
Phone   310-395-8880
Fax   310-395-8811
Email   membership@nalip.info
          naliped@msn.com
New York
32 Broadway, 14th Fl.
New York, NY 10004
Phone   646-336-6333
Fax   212-727-0549
Kathryn Galán, Executive Director
Octavio Marin, Signature Programs Director
Monica Espinosa, Membership Coordinator

National Association of Talent Representatives (NATR)

www.agentassociation.com
c/o Cunningham, Escott, Slevin, Doherty
257 Park Ave South
Ste 900
New York, NY 10010
Phone   212-277-1666
Email   natrmail@gmail.com
Ken Slevin, President

National Association of Television Program Executives (NATPE)

www.natpe.org
Global, nonprofit organization dedicated to the creation, development and distribution of televised programming in all forms, across all platforms. Develops and nurtures opportunities for the buying, selling and sharing of content and ideas.
5757 Wilshire Blvd., Penthouse 10
Los Angeles, CA 90036-3681
Phone   310-453-4440
Fax   310-453-5258
Email   info@natpe.org
Rick Feldman, President/CEO

National Conference of Personal Managers (NCOPM)

www.ncopm.com
Association for the advancement of personal managers and their clients.
Los Angeles
1440 Beaumont Ave., Ste. A2-360
Beaumont, CA 92223
Phone   310-492-5983
New York
330 W. 38th St., Ste. 904
New York, NY 10018
Phone   212-245-2063
Fax   212-245-2367
Daniel Abrahamsen, Executive Director, Eastern Division
Candee Barshop, Executive Director, Western Division

National Council of La Raza (NCLR)

www.nclr.org
Private, nonprofit, nonpartisan, tax-exempt organization dedicated, in part, to promoting fair, accurate, and balanced portrayals of Latinos in film, television and music. Sponsor of the ALMA Awards.
c/o Raul Yzaguirre Bldg.
1126 16th St. NW
Washington, DC 20036
Phone   202-785-1670
Fax   202-785-7620
Email   comments@nclr.org

Nosotros/Ricardo Montalban Foundation

www.nosotros.org
Organization established to improve the image of Latinos/Hispanics as they are portrayed in the entertainment industry, both in front of and behind the camera, as well as to expand employment opportunities within the entertainment industry. Producers of The Golden Eagle Awards.
1615 N. Vine St.
Hollywood, CA 90028
Phone   323-465-4167
          (General Information)
          323-463-0089
          (Nosotros/Theatre Office)
Fax   323-466-8540
Email   info@nosotros.org

Organization of Black Screenwriters (OBS)

www.obswriter.com
Nonprofit organization developing and supporting Black screenwriters.
1968 W. Adams Blvd.
Los Angeles, CA 90018
Phone   323-735-2050
Email   sfranklin@obswriter.com
Sylvia Franklin, President

PEN

www.pen.org
Nonprofit organization made up of poets, playwrights, essayists, novelists, television writers, screenwriters, critics, historians, editors, journalists, and translators. Dedicated to protecting the rights of writers around the world, to stimulate interest in the written word and to foster a vital literary community.
Pen American Center
568 Broadway, Ste. 303
New York, NY 10012-3225
Phone   212-334-1660
Fax   212-334-2181
Email   pen@pen.org

Players Directory

www.playersdirectory.com
Casting directory published every six months as a cooperative service to the players and production studios of Hollywood.
2210 W. Olive Ave., Ste. 320
Burbank, CA 91506
Phone   310-247-3058
Fax   310-601-4445
Email   info@playersdirectory.com
Keith Gonzales, Editor
Brooke Boles, Managing Editor

PR Newswire

www.prnewswire.com

Electronic satellite newswire for media dissemination

865 S. Figueroa St., Ste. 2500
Los Angeles, CA 90017-2565
Phone   800-321-8169
Fax   800-473-5152

Producers Guild of America (PGA)

www.producersguild.org

Organization representing the interests of all members of the producing team.

8530 Wilshire Blvd., Ste. 450
Beverly Hills, CA 90211
Phone   310-358-9020
Fax   310-358-9520
Vance Van Petten, Executive Director

Professional Electronic Entertainment Recruiters (PEER)

www.peer-org.com

Professional Electronic Entertainment Recruiters (PEER) is an interactive entertainment software industry trade association comprised of recruiters committed to better serving the gaming industry.

Email   join@peer-org.com
David Musgrove, President

Recording Musicians Association (RMA)

www.rmala.org

Nonprofit organization of studio musicians and composers.

817 Vine St., Ste. 209
Hollywood, CA 90038-3716
Phone   323-462-4762
Fax   323-462-2406
Neil Stubenhaus, President

The Reporters Committee for the Freedom of the Press

www.rcfp.org

A nonprofit organization dedicated to providing free legal assistance to journalists.

1101 Wilson Blvd., Ste. 1100
Arlington, VA 22209
Phone   800-336-4243
          703-807-2100
Email   rcfp@rcfp.org
Lucy Dalglish, Executive Director

Rock the Vote

www.rockthevote.com

Dedicated to protecting freedom of expression and mobilizing young people to get out and vote.

Los Angeles
409 N. Pacific Coast Hwy., #589
Redondo Beach, CA 90277
Phone   310-234-0665
Email   info@rockthevote.org

Washington, DC
1313 L St., NW, 1st Fl.
Washington, DC 20005
Phone   202-962-9710
Fax   202-962-9715

Romance Writers of America (RWA)

www.rwanational.org

National nonprofit genre writers' association providing networking and support to published aspiring romance writers.

16000 Stuebner Airline Rd., Ste. 140
Spring, TX 77379
Phone   832-717-5200
Email   info@rwanational.org

Screen Actors Guild (SAG)

www.sag.org

Union representing actors in feature films, short films and digital projects.

Los Angeles
5757 Wilshire Blvd.
Los Angeles, CA 90036
Phone   323-954-1600

New York
360 Madison Ave., 12th Fl.
New York, NY 10017
Phone   212-944-1030

Scriptwriters Network

www.scriptwritersnetwork.org

Organization providing information and career counseling for film and television writers.

11684 Ventura Blvd., Ste. 508
Studio City, CA 91604
Phone   323-848-9477
Email   info@
          scriptwritersnetwork.org

Society of Children's Book Writers & Illustrators (SCBWI)

www.scbwi.org

Professional organization for writers and illustrators of children's books.

8271 Beverly Blvd.
Los Angeles, CA 90048
Phone   323-782-1010
Fax   323-782-1892
Email   scbwi@scbwi.org

The Society of Composers & Lyricists

www.thescl.com

Nonprofit volunteer organization advancing the professional interests of lyricists and composers of film and television music.

400 S. Beverly Dr., Ste. 214
Beverly Hills, CA 90212
Phone   310-281-2812
Fax   310-284-4861

Society of Illustrators (SOI)

www.societyillustrators.org

Society made up of professional illustrators, art directors, art buyers, creative supervisors, instructors and publishers, dedicated to the well-being of individual illustrators and the industry of illustration.

128 E. 63rd St.
New York, NY 10021-7303
Phone   212-838-2560
Fax   212-838-2561
Email   info@societyillustrators.org

Society of Operating Cameramen (SOC)

www.soc.org

Organization promoting excellence in the fields of camera operation and the allied camera crafts.

PO Box 2006
Toluca Lake, CA 91610
Phone   818-382-7070
Email   info@soc.org

Society of Stage Directors & Choreographers (SSDC)

www.ssdc.org

Union representing directors and choreographers of Broadway national tours, regional theatre, dinner theatre and summer stock, as well as choreographers for motion pictures, television and music videos.

1501 Broadway, Ste. 1701
New York, NY 10036-5653
Phone   212-391-1070
          800-541-5204
Fax   212-302-6195

Stunts-Ability, Inc.

www.stuntsability.com

Nonprofit organization training amputees and other disabled persons for stunts, acting and effects for the entertainment industry.

PO Box 600711
San Diego, CA 92160-0711
Phone   619-542-7730
Fax   619-542-7731
Email   info@stuntsability.com

Talent Managers Association (TMA)

www.talentmanagers.org

Nonprofit organization promoting and encouraging the highest standards of professionalism in the practice of talent management.

4804 Laurel Canyon Blvd., Ste. 611
Valley Village, CA 91607
Phone   310-205-8495
Fax   818-765-2903
Steven Nash, President
Betty McCormick Aggas, Marketing & Benefits Director

US Copyright Office

www.copyright.gov

Promotes progress of the arts and protection for the works of authors; Web site serves the copyright community of creators and users, as well as the general public.

Library of Congress
101 Independence Avenue S.E.
Washington, D.C. 20559
Phone   202-707-5959
          202-707-3000

Women In Film (WIF)

www.wif.org

Organization dedicated to empowering, promoting and nurturing women in the film and television industries.

8857 W. Olympic Blvd., Ste. 201
Beverly Hills, CA 90211-3605
Phone   310-657-5144
Fax   310-657-5154
Email   info@wif.org
Jane Fleming, President
Gayle Nachlis, Executive Director

Women's Image Network (WIN)

www.winfemme.com
www.thewinawards.com

Nonprofit corporation encouraging positive portrayals of women in theatre, television and film.

2118 Wilshire Blvd., Ste. 144
Santa Monica, CA 90403
Phone   310-229-5365
Email   info@winfemme.com
Phyllis Stuart, President

**Writers Guild of America
(WGA)**
www.wga.org
www.wgaeast.org
*Union representing writers in the
motion pictures, broadcast cable
and new technologies industries.*

Los Angeles
7000 W. Third St.
Los Angeles, CA 90048-4329
Phone 323-951-4000
Fax   323-782-4800

New York
555 W. 57th St., Ste. 1230
New York, NY 10019
Phone 212-767-7800
Fax   212-582-1909
Patric Verrone, President

LIBRARIES AND MUSEUMS

**Academy of Motion Picture
Arts & Sciences - Margaret
Herrick Library**
www.oscars.org
*Extensive and comprehensive
research and reference
collections documenting film as
an art form and an industry.*
333 S. La Cienega Blvd.
Beverly Hills, CA 90211
Phone 310-247-3020
Fax   310-657-5193
Linda Harris Mehr, Director

Library of Congress
www.loc.gov/rr/mopic
*Acquisition, cataloging and
preservation of the motion picture
and television collections.
Operates the Motion Picture and
Television Reading Room to
provide access and information
services to an international
community of film and television
professionals, archivists, scholars
and researchers.*
c/o Motion Pictures & Television
Reading Room
101 Independence Ave., SE
James Madison Bldg., Ste. 336
Washington, DC 20540
Phone 202-707-8572
Fax   202-707-2371
Email   mpref@loc.gov
*Rosemary Hanes, Reference
   Librarian
Zoran Sinobad, Reference
   Librarian
Josie Walters-Johnson, Reference
   Librarian*

**The Library of Moving
Images, Inc.**
www.libraryofmovingimages.com
*Independent film archives
including 19th Century
experimental film footage, silent
film footage, 20th Century
newsreel footage, short subjects,
education and industrial films,
classic documentaries, vintage
cartoons, home movies and
world news feeds.*
6671 Sunset Blvd., Bungalow 1581
Hollywood, CA 90028
Phone 323-469-7499
Fax   323-469-7559
Email   mylmi@pacbell.net
Michael Peter Yakaitis, President

**Lillian Michelson
Research Library**
c/o DreamWorks SKG
1000 Flower St.
Glendale, CA 91201
Phone   818-695-6445
Fax   818-695-6450

**Los Angeles County Museum
of Art (LACMA)**
collectionsonline.lacma.org
www.lacma.org
*Holdings include entertainment-
related photographs, prints,
costumes and costume sketches.
Museum also has film department
and film series.*
5905 Wilshire Blvd.
Los Angeles, CA 90036
Phone   323-857-6000
              323-857-0098 (TDD)
Email   library@lacma.org

Louis B. Mayer Library
www.afi.com
*Books, periodicals and other
special collections covering
various aspects of motion
pictures and television. Serves
the research needs of the
American Film Institute's staff,
faculty and students. Library is
available on a non-circulating
basis to visiting scholars,
researchers, and advanced
graduate students, as well as
members of the entertainment
industry.*
c/o American Film Institute
2021 N. Western Ave.
Los Angeles, CA 90027
Phone   323-856-7600

**Museum of the
Moving Image**
www.movingimage.us
*Dedicated to educating the
public about the art, history,
technique, and technology of
film, television, and digital media
and to examining their impact on
culture and society. Nation's
largest permanent collection of
moving image artifacts.*
35th Avenue at 36th St.
Astoria, NY 11106
Phone   718-784-4520
              718-784-0077
Fax   718-784-4681
Rochelle Slovin, Director

**New York Public Library for
the Performing Arts**
www.nypl.org
*Extensive combination of
circulating, reference and rare
archival collections in the
performing arts.*
40 Lincoln Center Plaza
New York, NY 10023-7498
Phone   212-870-1630
Email   performingarts@nypl.org

**Warner Bros. Studio
Research Library**
2777 N. Ontario St.
Burbank, CA 91504
Phone   818-977-5050
Fax   818-567-4366
*Steve Bingen, Research Librarian
Linda Cummings, Research
   Librarian*

**Writers Guild Foundation
Shavelson Webb Library**
www.wgfoundation.org
*Collection dedicated to the art,
craft, and history of writing for
motion pictures, radio, television
and new media. Open to the
public and Guild members.*
7000 W. Third St.
Los Angeles, CA 90048-4329
Phone   323-782-4544
Karen Pedersen, Library Director

WORKSHEET

FREQUENTLY CALLED PHONE NUMBERS			
NAME	**COMPANY**	**PHONE #**	**FAX #**

WORKSHEET

DATE	PROJECT	CONTACT	NOTES

WORKSHEET

NAME	COMPANY	PHONE #	FAX #

WORKSHEET

DATE	PROJECT	CONTACT	NOTES

SECTION **A**

AGENTS

- Below-the-Line Talent
- Commercial Talent
- Film/TV Talent
- Literary Talent
- Modeling Talent
- Music Talent
- Talent & Literary Packaging
- Theatre Talent

FOR SALE

Film Rights

May 31 - June 3, 2007 | Jacob Javits Convention Center, NY, NY | bookexpoamerica.com

What equals more than one billion dollars?

The DaVinci Code + The Devil Wears Prada + The Good German + The Last King of Scotland + Running With Scissors + The Pursuit of Happyness + A Scanner Darkly = $1,000,000,000.00 in total Box Office. Great movies come from great books — find your next project at BookExpo America — the largest English language publishing event in the world.

Conference/Educational Program | May 31 - June 3, 2007
International Rights Center | June 1-3, 2007
Exhibition Halls | June 1-3, 2007

Sponsored by:

BookExpo America

ABA AMERICAN BOOKSELLERS ASSOCIATION

aap ASSOCIATION OF AMERICAN PUBLISHERS INC

Produced by:

Reed Exhibitions

A...LIST ARTISTS
2217 Berkeley Ave.
Los Angeles, CA 90026
PHONE 213-484-3800
FAX 213-484-4200
EMAIL .agent@alistartists.com
WEB SITE . . . . .www.alistartists.com
TYPES   Below-the-Line Talent
REPRESENTS   Cinematographers
SUBMISSION POLICY   Send reel
COMMENTS   TV, Episodic, Features, Commercials, Documentaries, Underwater, Aerial; IATSE Talent Only

Debbie Martone . . . . .Owner/Agent
Anne Wilde . . . . .Marketing

ABA - AMATRUDA BENSON & ASSOCIATES
9107 Wilshire Blvd., Ste. 500
Beverly Hills, CA 90210
PHONE 310-276-1851
FAX 310-276-3517
TYPES   Commercial Talent - Film/TV Talent
AFFILIATIONS   SAG
REPRESENTS   Actors - Children - Teens/Young Adults
SUBMISSION POLICY   No phone calls; Via mail only
COMMENTS   Specializes in children, teens and young adults

Kimberley Gola . . . . .Owner/Agent, Print/Commercial
Joseph Le . . . . .Agent, Feature Film/TV
Chris Ledford . . . . .Agent, Commercial, Adult/Theatrical

ABC MODEL/TALENT/SPORT MANAGEMENT
12708 Northup Way, Ste. 201
Bellevue, WA 98005
PHONE 425-861-8712
FAX 425-861-8713
EMAIL . . . . .info@abcmgmt.com
WEB SITE . . . . .www.abcmgmt.com
TYPES   Commercial Talent - Film/TV Talent - Modeling Talent - Music Talent
REPRESENTS   Actors - Broadcast Journalists/Newscasters - Children - Choreographers - Comedians - Dancers - Directors - Hosts/MCs - Infants - Martial Artists/Stunts - Music Artists - Music Producers - Print Models - Runway Models - Seniors - Speakers/Lecturers - Sports Personalities - Teens/Young Adults - Variety Artists - Voice-Over Artists
SUBMISSION POLICY   Submit demo reels or press kits by mail or email (one photo only); No faxes; No follow-up

David Van Maren . . . . .President
Chersti Bray . . . . .Agent
Jennifer Weller . . . . .Agent
Lacey Langmade . . . . .Director
Leah Beauchamp . . . . .Scout
Donna Seals . . . . .Scout
Tami Wakasugi . . . . .Scout
Amanda Duford . . . . .Assistant

CAROLE ABEL LITERARY
160 W. 87th St.
New York, NY 10024
PHONE 212-724-1168
TYPES   Literary Talent
REPRESENTS   Book Authors
SUBMISSION POLICY   Send outline and sample chapter only
COMMENTS   No screenplays or children's books

Carole Abel . . . . .Owner/Agent

ABOUT ARTISTS AGENCY
1650 Broadway, Ste. 1406
New York, NY 10019
PHONE 212-581-1857
TYPES   Commercial Talent - Film/TV Talent - Music Talent - Theatre Talent
AFFILIATIONS   AEA - AFTRA - SAG
REPRESENTS   Actors - Comedians - Dancers - Hosts/MCs - Music Artists - Musical Theatre Performers - Seniors
SUBMISSION POLICY   Do not call or drop in; Mail picture and tape only
COMMENTS   Actors and actresses eighteen years old and up

Renee Glicker . . . . .President/Agent
Chase Jennings . . . . .Assistant

ABOVE THE LINE AGENCY
468 N. Camden Dr., Ste. 200
Beverly Hills, CA 90210
PHONE 310-859-6115
TYPES   Literary Talent
AFFILIATIONS   DGA - WGA
REPRESENTS   Directors - Producers - Screenwriters
SUBMISSION POLICY   Mail query letter only; Include logline and synopsis no longer than one and a half pages

Rima Bauer Greer . . . . .President
Bruce Bartlett . . . . .VP

ABRAMS ARTISTS AGENCY (LOS ANGELES)
9200 Sunset Blvd., 11th Fl.
Los Angeles, CA 90069
PHONE 310-859-0625
FAX 310-276-6193
WEB SITE .www.abramsartists.com
TYPES   Commercial Talent - Film/TV Talent - Literary Talent - Modeling Talent - Talent & Literary Packaging - Theatre Talent
AFFILIATIONS   AEA - AFTRA - ATA - SAG
REPRESENTS   Actors - Book Authors - Broadcast Journalists/Newscasters - Children - Comedians - Composers - Directors - Hosts/MCs - Infants - Musical Theatre Performers - Playwrights - Print Models - Screenwriters - Seniors - Speakers/Lecturers - Sports Personalities - Teens/Young Adults - TV Writers - Voice-Over Artists
SUBMISSION POLICY   By mail only; Do not phone or visit

Harry Abrams . . . . .President/Motion Pictures/TV/Commercials
Jeremy Apody . . . . .Commercials/Youth Division
Juan Bagnell . . . . .Commercials/Voice Division
Bradford Bricken . . . . .Commercials/Voice Division
Valerie Chiovetti . . . . .Commercials
Brad Diffley . . . . .Commercials/Youth Division
Mark Measures . . . . .Head, Commercials/Voice Division
Kristin Nava . . . . .Commercials
Peter Novick . . . . .Commercials
Wendi Green . . . . .Head, Youth Division/Motion Pictures/TV
Jennifer Millar . . . . .Youth Division/Motion Pictures/TV
Harold Augenstein . . . . .Motion Pictures/TV
Eric Emery . . . . .Motion Pictures/TV
Lauren Fishman .Motion Pictures/TV
Gregg A. Klein .Motion Pictures/TV
Joe Rice . . . . .Head, Motion Pictures/TV
Marni Rosenzweig . . . . .Motion Pictures/TV
Alec Shankman . . . . .Hosting/MCs/Reality/Broadcast Journalism
Brian Cho . . . . .Business Affairs
Nathan Schwam . . . . .Business Affairs
Sunny Valencia . . . . .Business Affairs

ABRAMS ARTISTS AGENCY (NEW YORK)

275 Seventh Ave., 26th Fl.
New York, NY 10001
PHONE 646-486-4600
FAX 646-486-0100
WEB SITE .www.abramsartists.com

TYPES	Below-the-Line Talent - Commercial Talent - Film/TV Talent - Literary Talent - Modeling Talent - Music Talent - Talent & Literary Packaging - Theatre Talent
AFFILIATIONS	AEA - AFTRA - DGA - SAG - WGA
REPRESENTS	Actors - Book Authors - Broadcast Journalists/Newscasters - Children - Choreographers - Comedians - Composers - Directors - Hosts/MCs - Infants - Musical Theatre Performers - Print Models - Screenwriters - Seniors - Speakers/Lecturers - Sports Personalities - Teens/Young Adults - TV Writers - Voice-Over Artists
SUBMISSION POLICY	By mail only; Do not phone or visit
COMMENTS	All talent for all areas

Harry Abrams . . . . .President/Motion Pictures/TV/Commercials
Neal Altman . . . . .Sr. VP/Voice-Over
Robert Attermann . . . . .VP/Theatrical/Motion Pictures/TV
Tracey Goldblum . . . . .VP/Commercials
J.J. Adler . . . . .Voice-Over
Beth Blickers . . . . .Literary
Sarah Douglas . . . . .Literary
Genine Esposito . . . . .Print
Jessica Felrice . . . . .Voice-Over
Richard Fisher . . . . .Theatrical/Motion Pictures/TV
Ellen Gilbert . . . . .Children/Theatrical/Motion Pictures/TV
Morgan Jenness . . . . .Literary
Charles Kopelman . . . . .Literary
Amy Mazur . . . . .Commercials
Jill McGrath . . . . .Theatrical/Motion Pictures/TV
Kate Navin . . . . .Literary
Alison Quartin . . . . .Commercials
Paul Reisman . . . . .Theatrical/Motion Pictures/TV
Jonathan Saul . . . . .Voice-Over Promos
Billy Serow . . . . .Voice-Over
Bonnie Shumofsky . . . . .Children/Commercials
Maura Teitelbaum . . . . .Literary
Joe Thompson . . . . .Print
Mark Turner . . .Celebrities/Hosting/MCs/Broadcast Journalists/Reality TV

ACCESS TALENT

171 Madison Ave., Ste. 910
New York, NY 10016
PHONE 212-331-9600/212-684-7795
FAX 212-684-8553
EMAIL . . . . .chascowing@accesstalent.com
WEB SITE . . . . .www.accesstalent.com

TYPES	Commercial Talent
AFFILIATIONS	AFTRA - SAG
REPRESENTS	Voice-Over Artists
SUBMISSION POLICY	CD preferred
COMMENTS	Voice-over and spoken word only

Chas Cowing . . . . .Co-Owner
Linda Weaver . . . . .Co-Owner
Todd Kijanka . . . . .Broadcast Promotions Agent
Marge Tate . . . . .Talent Payment
Chris Davis . . . . .Studio Manager

ACME TALENT & LITERARY

4727 Wilshire Blvd., Ste. 333
Los Angeles, CA 90010
PHONE 323-954-2263
FAX 323-954-2262
WEB SITE . . . . .www.acmetalentagents.com

TYPES	Commercial Talent - Film/TV Talent - Literary Talent - Modeling Talent - Theatre Talent
AFFILIATIONS	AEA - AFTRA - ATA - DGA - SAG - WGA
REPRESENTS	Actors - Book Authors - Children - Comedians - Directors - Musical Theatre Performers - Print Models - Producers - Screenwriters - Teens/Young Adults - TV Writers - Voice-Over Artists

Adam Lieblein .Agent/President (LA)
Matt Fletcher . . . . .Theatrical, Children/Young Adults/Adults (LA)
Mickey Freiberg . . . . .Head, Literary (LA)
Emily Hope . . . . .Head, Commercial, Adults (LA)
Eddie Winkler . . . . .Head, Commercial, Children (LA)
Eileen Haves . . . . .Commercial (NY)
Brian Duensing . . . . .Commercial, Adults (LA)
Matt Taylor . . . . .Commercial/Adult (LA)
Portia Scott-Hicks . . . . .Voice-Over (LA)

ACTORS & OTHERS TALENT AGENCY

6676 St. Elmo Rd.
Bartlett, TN 38135
PHONE 901-384-6464
FAX 901-373-3364

TYPES	Commercial Talent - Film/TV Talent
AFFILIATIONS	AFTRA - SAG
REPRESENTS	Actors - Children - Teens/Young Adults - Voice-Over Artists
SUBMISSION POLICY	Mail head shot and resumé; No drop-ins
COMMENTS	Talent of all ages

Pat West . . . . .Owner/Agent

ACTORS ETC., INC.

c/o Denise Coburn
2620 Fountainview, Ste. 210
Houston, TX 77057
PHONE 713-785-4495
FAX 713-785-2641
EMAIL . . . . .actorsetc@birch.net
WEB SITE . . . . .www.actorsetc.net

TYPES	Commercial Talent - Film/TV Talent - Theatre Talent
AFFILIATIONS	AFTRA - SAG
REPRESENTS	Actors - Children - Comedians - Hosts/MCs - Infants - Magicians - Martial Artists/Stunts - Musical Theatre Performers - Print Models - Seniors - Sports Personalities - Teens/Young Adults - Variety Artists - Voice-Over Artists
SUBMISSION POLICY	By mail only; Include photo, letter and phone number
COMMENTS	Also affiliated with ITVA (International Television Association), ASMP

Denise A. Coburn . . . . .Owner/Agent
Edwin Johnson . . . . .Assistant
Judy Kay . . . . .Assistant

ACTORS LA AGENCY
12435 Oxnard St.
North Hollywood, CA 91606
PHONE 818-755-0026
FAX 818-755-0027
EMAIL . . . . .agentpdh2@att.net
SECOND EMAIL . . . . .actorsla@gmail.com
TYPES   Commercial Talent
AFFILIATIONS   SAG
REPRESENTS   Actors - Print Models - Runway Models -
                         Teens/Young Adults

Bonita E. Hart . . . . .Owner
Patrick Hart . . . . .Theatrical/Commercial
Kali Chung . . . . .Assistant
Brooke Harker . . . . .Assistant
Ming Wang . . . . .Assistant

BRET ADAMS, LTD.
448 W. 44th St.
New York, NY 10036
PHONE 212-765-5630
FAX 212-265-2212
EMAIL . . . . .bretadamsltd.bal@varizon.net
TYPES   Film/TV Talent - Literary Talent - Theatre
                         Talent
AFFILIATIONS   AEA - AFTRA - SAG - WGA
REPRESENTS   Actors - Choreographers - Composers -
                         Directors - Musical Theatre Performers -
                         Playwrights - TV Writers

Ken Melamed . . . . .Partner
Bruce Ostler . . . . .Partner
Margi Rountree . . . . .Partner
Michael Golden . . . . .Assistant
Antje Oegel . . . . .Assistant
Mark Orsini . . . . .Assistant

ADVANCE LA
7904 Santa Monica Blvd., Ste. 200
West Hollywood, CA 90046
PHONE 323-650-5022
FAX 323-650-6749
EMAIL . . . . .info@advancela.com
WEB SITE . . . . .www.advancela.com
TYPES   Commercial Talent - Film/TV Talent -
                         Modeling Talent
AFFILIATIONS   AFTRA - ATA
REPRESENTS   Actors - Children - Comedians - Dancers -
                         Hosts/MCs - Infants - Playwrights - Print
                         Models - Producers - Runway Models -
                         Speakers/Lecturers - Sports Personalities -
                         Teens/Young Adults
SUBMISSION POLICY   Mail headshots and resumés; No drop-ins

Vance Peyton . . . . .President/CEO
Daniel Farr . . . . .CFO
Sean Maurer . . . . .VP
Isabel Arias . . . . .Commercial Agent
Cory Matteo . . . . .Jr. Agent
Erica Russell . . . . .Assistant
Nan Mann . . . . .Assistant

AFFINITY MODEL & TALENT AGENCY
8721 Santa Monica Blvd., Ste. 27
West Hollywood, CA 90069
PHONE 323-525-0577
EMAIL . . . . .info@affinitytalent.com
WEB SITE . . . . .www.affinitytalent.com
SECOND WEB SITE . . . . .www.affinitymodels.com
TYPES   Commercial Talent - Film/TV Talent -
                         Modeling Talent
REPRESENTS   Actors - Broadcast Journalists/Newscasters
                         - Children - Comedians - Dancers -
                         Hosts/MCs - Print Models - Runway Models
                         - Sports Personalities - Teens/Young Adults
COMMENTS   Full-service agency

Ross Grossman . . . . .Director

AGAPE PRODUCTIONS
3375 State Rd. 252
PO Box 147
Flat Rock, IN 47234
PHONE 812-587-5654
TYPES   Film/TV Talent - Literary Talent - Music
                         Talent - Talent & Literary Packaging
AFFILIATIONS   WGA
REPRESENTS   Actors - Book Authors - Composers - Music
                         Producers - Producers - Screenwriters -
                         Songwriters - TV Writers - Voice-Over
                         Artists
COMMENTS   Member: Christian Film & Television
                         Commission, National Literary Foundation,
                         Flatrock Records

Terry D. Porter . . . . .Agent/Owner/Manager
David Ruiz . . . . .Literary Agent
Carol McDaniel . . . . .Sub-Agent

AGENCY FOR THE PERFORMING ARTS, INC.
(LOS ANGELES)
405 S. Beverly Dr.
Beverly Hills, CA 90210
PHONE 310-888-4200
FAX 310-888-4242
EMAIL . . . . .firstinitiallastname@apa-agency.com
WEB SITE . . . . .www.apa-agency.com
TYPES   Film/TV Talent - Literary Talent - Music
                         Talent - Talent & Literary Packaging -
                         Theatre Talent
AFFILIATIONS   AEA - AFM - AFTRA - ATA - DGA - WGA
REPRESENTS   Actors - Book Authors - Comedians -
                         Composers - Directors - Hosts/MCs -
                         Music Artists - Music Producers -
                         Playwrights - Producers - Screenwriters -
                         Teens/Young Adults - TV Writers - Variety
                         Artists

Jim Gosnell . . . . .President/CEO
Roger Vorce . . . . .Chairman Emeritus
Jeff Witjas . . . . .Sr. VP, Talent
Ryan Martin . . . . .VP, Talent
Barry McPherson . . . . .VP, Talent
Paul Santana . . . . .VP, Talent

(Continued)

AGENCY FOR THE PERFORMING ARTS, INC. (LOS ANGELES) (Continued)

Dan Baron . . . . .Talent
Todd Eisner . . . . .Talent
Karen Forman . . . . .Talent
Tyler Grasham . . . . .Talent
Josh Pollack . . . . .Talent
Scott Simpson . . . . .Talent
Mike Wilson . . . . .Talent
David Saunders . . . . .Executive VP, Feature Literary
Steven Fisher . . . . .VP, Feature Literary
David Boxerbaum . . . . .Feature Literary
Lee Dinstman .Executive VP, TV Literary
Beth Bohn . . . . .VP, TV Literary
Matt Ochacher . . . . .VP, TV Literary
Debbie Deuble-Hill . . . . .Literary
Lindsay Howard . . . . .Literary
Jack Leighton . . . . .Literary
Michael Pelmont . . . . .Literary
Sheryl Petersen . . . . .Literary
Hayden Meyer . . . . .Alternative TV
Troy Blakely . . . . .Executive VP, Concert
Josh Humiston . . . . .VP, Concert
Andrew Buck . . . . .Concert
Jaime Kelsall . . . . .Concert
Craig Newman . . . . .Concert
Shane Shuhart . . . . .Concert
Brett Stair . . . . .Concert
Danny Robinson . . . . .Sr. VP, Comedy Department
Jackie Miller-Knobbe . . . . .Comedy
Eric Murphy . . . . .Comedy
Tim Scally . . . . .Comedy
Tony Villa . . . . .Assistant Controller, Accounting
Joanne Johnson . . . . .Director, Administration
Ron Rewald . . . . .Director, Operations
Liz Cooper . . . . .Marketing
Miranda Inganni . . . . .Marketing

AGENCY FOR THE PERFORMING ARTS, INC. (NASHVILLE)

3017 Poston Ave.
Nashville, TN 37203
PHONE 615-297-0100
FAX 615-297-5434
EMAIL . . . . .firstinitiallastname@apanashville.com
WEB SITE . . . . .www.apa-agency.com
TYPES   Music Talent
AFFILIATIONS   AEA - AFM - AFTRA - SAG
REPRESENTS   Hosts/MCs - Music Artists
COMMENTS   Also affiliated with IAFE, NATD, IEBA,
                         CMA, ACM, NARAS, GMA, WFA, APAP;
                         Nashville office handles music talent only;
                         Alliance with Christian agency Jeff Roberts
                         & Associates; Los Angeles office handles
                         casting and literary, as well as musical
                         artists and comedians

Steve Lassiter . . . . .Sr. VP, Personal Appearance/Agent/Co-Head
Bonnie Sugarman . . . . .Sr. VP, Personal Appearance/Agent/Co-Head
Scott Galloway . . . . .VP, Personal Appearance/Agent
Rob Battle . . . . .Personal Appearance/Agent
John Dotson .Personal Appearance/Agent
Mark Guynn .Personal Appearance/Agent
Jeff Howard .Personal Appearance/Agent
Stu Walker . . . . .Personal Appearance/Agent
Angie W. Osburn . . .Office Administrator/Assistant to Bonnie Sugarman

AGENCY FOR THE PERFORMING ARTS, INC. (NEW YORK)

250 W. 57th St., Ste. 1701
New York, NY 10107
PHONE 212-687-0092
FAX 212-245-5062
EMAIL . . . . .firstinitiallastname@apa-agency.com
WEB SITE . . . . .www.apa-agency.com
TYPES   Music Talent - Theatre Talent
AFFILIATIONS   AEA - AFM - AFTRA - ATA - DGA - WGA
REPRESENTS   Comedians - Music Artists

Christine Barkley . . . . .Music/Performing Arts Centers
Michael Berkowitz . . . . .Comedy
Avi Gilbert . . . . .Comedy
Fred Hansen . . . . .Music/Performing Arts Centers
Simon Shaw . . . . .Music/Performing Arts Centers
Christianne Weiss . . . . .Music/Performing Arts Centers

THE AGENCY GROUP LTD. (LOS ANGELES)

1880 Century Park East, Ste. 711
Los Angeles, CA 90067
PHONE 310-385-2800
FAX 310-385-1220
WEB SITE . . . . .www.theagencygroup.com
TYPES   Literary Talent - Music Talent - Talent &
                         Literary Packaging - Theatre Talent
REPRESENTS   Book Authors - Comedians - Composers -
                         Music Artists - Music Supervisors - Sports
                         Personalities - TV Writers
COMMENTS   Additional offices: Toronto, London,
                         Scandinavia, New York

Andy Somers . . . . .Sr. VP
Bruce Solar . . . . .VP
Omar Al-Joulani . . . . .Agent, Music
Brian Blumer . . . . .Agent, Music
Corrie Christopher . . . . .Agent, Music
Ian Fintak . . . . .Agent, Music
Marc Gerald . . . . .Agent, Literary
Caroline Greeven . . . . .Agent, Literary
Donovan Hebard . . . . .Agent, Music
Linda Kordek . . . . .Agent/TV & Film Licensing & Composers
Keith Naisbitt . . . . .Agent, Music
Dave Shapiro . . . . .Agent, Music
Val Wolfe . . . . .Agent, Music
Gabe Apodaca . . . . .Assistant to Corrie Christopher
Will Evans . . . . .Assistant to Dave Shapiro
Courtney Hyatt . . . . .Assistant to Andy Somers
J.J. Italiano . . . . .Assistant to Andy Somers & Bruce Solar
Sarah Kesselman . . . . .Assistant to Donovan Hebard & Omar Al-Joulani
Jenny McPhee .Assistant to Val Wolfe
Tawny Mitchell . . . . .Assistant to Linda Kordek
Sarah Stephens . . . . .Assistant to Marc Gerald
David Strunk . . . . .Assistant to Bruce Solar

THE AGENCY GROUP LTD. (NEW YORK)
1775 Broadway, Ste. 515
New York, NY 10019
PHONE 212-581-3100
FAX 212-581-0015
WEB SITE . . . . .www.theagencygroup.com
TYPES   Literary Talent - Music Talent - Talent &
                                 Literary Packaging - Theatre Talent
REPRESENTS   Book Authors - Comedians - Composers -
                                 Music Artists - Music Editors - Music
                                 Producers - Music Supervisors - Sports
                                 Personalities - TV Writers
COMMENTS   Additional offices: Toronto, London,
                                 Scandinavia, Los Angeles

Neil Warnock . . . . .Chairman (London)
Steve Herman . . . . .CEO
Steve Martin . . . . .President
Ken Fermaglich . . . . .Sr. VP
Steve Kaul . . . . .VP
Peter Schwartz . . . . .VP
Tim Borror . . . . .Agent, Music
Jordan Burger . . . . .Agent, Music
David Galea . . . . .Agent, Music
Jeremy Holgersen . . . . .Agent, Music
Dave Kaplan . . . . .Agent, Music
Mike Mori . . . . .Agent, Music
Seth Rappaport . . . . .Agent, Music
Nick Storch . . . . .Agent, Music
Marc Bauer . . . . .Assistant to Dave Kaplan
Justin Bridgewater . . . . .Assistant to Nick Storch
Doug Croy . . . . .Assistant to Jeremy Holgersen
Kelly Di Stefano . . . . .Assistant to Seth Rappaport
Joshua Dick . . . . .Assistant to Steve Martin
Megan Kesler . . . . .Assistant to Ken Fermaglich
Anthony Paolercio . . . . .Assistant to Steve Kaul
Meredith Peters . . . . .Assistant to Mike Mori
Leah Peterson . . . . .Assistant to Tim Borror
David Poe . . . . .Assistant to Steve Martin
Zach Quillen . . . . .Assistant to Peter Schwartz
Bryan Vastano . . . . .Assistant to Jordan Burger & David Galea

AGENTS FOR THE ARTS, INC.
203 W. 23rd St., 3rd Fl.
New York, NY 10011
PHONE 212-229-2562
TYPES   Film/TV Talent - Music Talent - Theatre
                                 Talent
AFFILIATIONS   AEA - AFTRA - AGVA - SAG
REPRESENTS   Actors - Dancers - Musical Theatre
                                 Performers - Seniors - Teens/Young Adults
SUBMISSION POLICY   Pictures/resumés by mail; Videos by request
                                 only; No phone calls; No drop-ins

Carole J. Russo . . . . .Agent

AIMÉE ENTERTAINMENT AGENCY
15840 Ventura Blvd., Ste. 215
Encino, CA 91436
PHONE 818-783-3831
FAX 818-783-4447
WEB SITE . . . . .www.aimeeentertainment.com
TYPES   Commercial Talent - Film/TV Talent -
                                 Literary Talent - Modeling Talent
AFFILIATIONS   AFTRA - SAG - WGA
REPRESENTS   Actors - Book Authors - Children -
                                 Comedians - Dancers - Infants - Martial
                                 Artists/Stunts - Screenwriters - Seniors -
                                 Sports Personalities - Teens/Young Adults -
                                 Variety Artists
SUBMISSION POLICY   No phone calls; Mailed submissions only

Joyce Aimée . . . . .President
Sharif Ali . . . . .Sr. Partner

AKA TALENT AGENCY
6310 San Vicente Blvd., Ste. 200
Los Angeles, CA 90048
PHONE 323-965-5600
FAX 323-965-5601
EMAIL . . . . .aka@akatalent.com
WEB SITE . . . . .www.akatalent.com
TYPES   Commercial Talent - Film/TV Talent
AFFILIATIONS   AFTRA - ATA
REPRESENTS   Actors - Children - Hosts/MCs -
                                 Teens/Young Adults

Mike Abrams . . . . .Owner/Agent, Commercial
Doug Ely .Owner/Agent, Commercial
Pamela Porter . . . . .Owner/Agent, Commercial
Patrick Welborn . . . . .Head, Theatrical
Jason Doran . . . . .Agent, Youth Theatrical
Joel McKenna . . . . .Agent, Youth Commercial
Mike Schibel . . . . .Agent, Hosting/Broadcasting
David Stieve . . . . .Agent, Adult Theatrical
Jeremy Jones . . . . .Jr. Agent, Commercial
Larry Israel . . . . .Director, Business Affairs
Shannon Bobo . . . . .Assistant
Chip Hooley . . . . .Assistant, Theatrical
Noreen Konkle . . . . .Assistant, Business Affairs
Amy Stofferahn . . . . .Assistant, Theatrical

ALEXA MODEL & TALENT MANAGEMENT, INC.
4100 W. Kennedy Blvd., Ste. 228
Tampa, FL 33609
PHONE 813-289-8020
FAX 813-286-8281
EMAIL .alexa@alexamodels.com
WEB SITE . . . . .www.alexamodels.com
TYPES   Below-the-Line Talent - Commercial Talent
                                 - Film/TV Talent - Modeling Talent
AFFILIATIONS   SAG
REPRESENTS   Actors - Children - Print Models - Runway
                                 Models - Seniors - Teens/Young Adults -
                                 Voice-Over Artists
SUBMISSION POLICY   Pictures or headshot and resumé

Susan Schwabinger . . . . .President/Booker
Matt Angelo . . . . .Booker
Chris Tesoriero . . . . .Booker

ALL CREW AGENCY
2920 W. Olive Ave., Ste. 201
Burbank, CA 91505
PHONE 818-206-0144
FAX 818-206-0169
WEB SITE . . . . .www.allcrewagency.com
TYPES   Below-the-Line Talent
AFFILIATIONS   DGA
REPRESENTS   Cinematographers - Film Editors -
                                 Producers - Production Designers
COMMENTS   Formerly the Dinedor Agency; Currently
                                 looking for below-the-line talent for world-
                                 wide representation for motion pictures, TV,
                                 commercials and music videos

Brian Ellis . . . . .Managing Partner (US)
James Little . . . . .UK Affiliate
Lisa Hogan . . . . .Associate
Kristy Tantillo . . . . .Associate

THE ALPERN GROUP

15645 Royal Oak Rd.
Encino, CA 91436
PHONE 818-528-1111
FAX 818-528-1110
EMAIL . . . . .mail@alperngroup.com
TYPES   Literary Talent - Talent & Literary Packaging
AFFILIATIONS   ATA - DGA - WGA
REPRESENTS   Directors - Producers - Screenwriters - TV
                         Writers

Jeff Alpern . . . . .President
Jeff Aghassi . . . . .Agent
Elana Trainoff . . . . .Agent
Hilary Swett . . . . .Assistant

MIRIAM ALTSHULER LITERARY AGENCY

53 Old Post Rd. North
Red Hook, NY 12571
PHONE 845-758-9408
TYPES   Literary Talent
AFFILIATIONS   AAR
REPRESENTS   Book Authors
SUBMISSION POLICY   Does not accept faxed or emailed queries
                         or unsolicited manuscripts; Send query with
                         brief synopsis and SASE; If no SASE includ-
                         ed, no response will be sent
COMMENTS   Commercial fiction and nonfiction; No sci-
                         ence fiction, fantasy, horror, romance, mys-
                         tery, westerns, self-help, techno thrillers,
                         metaphysical, how-to, poetry or screenplays

Miriam Altshuler .Literary Agent
Emily Katz . . . . .No Title

THE ALVARADO REY AGENCY

8455 Beverly Blvd., Ste. 410
West Hollywood, CA 90048
PHONE 323-655-7978
TYPES   Commercial Talent - Film/TV Talent -
                         Modeling Talent - Theatre Talent
AFFILIATIONS   AFTRA - ATA
REPRESENTS   Actors - Hosts/MCs - Print Models
SUBMISSION POLICY   Mail only; Theatrical clients by referral only;
                         Direct submissions to Nick Roses; Looking
                         to represent young children/talent of all
                         ages and ethnicities; Teens/young adults
                         for on-camera commercials, voice-over,
                         theatrical, musical theater and print
COMMENTS   Specializing in ethnic diversity

Nikkolas Rey . . . . .Owner/Agent
Philippe Macridis . . . . .Print/TV Hosting Associate
Alex Lara . . . . .Commercial Associate
Nick Roses . . . . .Associate, Young Talent

MICHAEL AMATO AGENCY

1650 Broadway, Ste. 307
New York, NY 10019
PHONE 212-247-4456
FAX 212-664-0641
EMAIL . . . . .phfxdesign@aol.com
TYPES   Commercial Talent - Film/TV Talent -
                         Literary Talent - Modeling Talent
AFFILIATIONS   AAR - AFM - AGVA - DGA - WGA
REPRESENTS   Actors - Broadcast Journalists/Newscasters
                         - Children - Hosts/MCs - Infants -
                         Magicians - Martial Artists/Stunts - Print
                         Models - Runway Models - Screenwriters -
                         Seniors - Teens/Young Adults - Voice-Over
                         Artists
SUBMISSION POLICY   Send headshot by US Mail or email

Michael Amato . . . . .Agent
Andrea Dasilva . . . . .Talent Manger

AMBASSADOR TALENT AGENTS, INC.

333 N. Michigan Ave., Ste. 910
Chicago, IL 60601
PHONE 312-641-3491
TYPES   Commercial Talent - Film/TV Talent -
                         Literary Talent - Modeling Talent - Music
                         Talent
AFFILIATIONS   AFM - AFTRA - SAG
REPRESENTS   Actors - Animals - Book Authors - Children
                         - Comedians - Dancers - Hosts/MCs -
                         Infants - Magicians - Print Models - Runway
                         Models - Seniors - Teens/Young Adults -
                         Variety Artists - Voice-Over Artists
SUBMISSION POLICY   By mail only
COMMENTS   Infants two months old and up

Susan A. Sherman . . . . .Director

AMBITION TALENT INC.

70 High Park Ave., Ste. 2003
Toronto, Ontario M6P1A1, Canada
PHONE 416-629-3023
FAX 416-850-0618
EMAIL . . . . .info@ambitiontalent.com
TYPES   Commercial Talent - Film/TV Talent -
                         Literary Talent
REPRESENTS   Actors - Broadcast Journalists/Newscasters
                         - Cinematographers - Directors - Producers
                         - Screenwriters - TV Writers
SUBMISSION POLICY   Established artists or referral only
COMMENTS   Can operate as a management company
                         within other countries

David Ritchie . . . . .Owner

AMERICAN PROGRAM BUREAU

36 Crafts St.
Newton, MA 02458
PHONE 617-965-6600
FAX 617-965-6610
EMAIL . . . . .apb@apbspeakers.com
SECOND EMAIL . . . . .firstinitiallastname@apbspeakers.com
WEB SITE . . . . .www.apbspeakers.com
TYPES   Film/TV Talent - Literary Talent - Music
                         Talent - Theatre Talent
REPRESENTS   Actors - Book Authors - Broadcast
                         Journalists/Newscasters - Comedians -
                         Composers - Dancers - Directors -
                         Producers - Speakers/Lecturers - Sports
                         Personalities - Variety Artists
COMMENTS   Specializing in Speakers/Lecturers

Tammy Choquette . . . . .Agent (617-614-1608)
Heather Colburn . . . . .Agent (617-614-1626)
Bob Davis .Agent (617-614-1618)
Ken Eisenstein . . . . .Agent (617-614-1612)
Nancy Eisenstein . . . . .Agent (617-614-1616)
Brenda Kane . . . . .Agent (617-614-1607)
Flip Porter .Agent (617-614-1624)
Trinity Ray .Agent (617-614-1614)
Michael Rosenberg . . . . .Agent (617-614-1617)
Harry Sandler . . . . .Agent (617-614-1627)
Dan Schlossberg . . . . .Agent (617-614-1601)
Jan Tavitian . . . . .Agent (617-614-1631)
Andrew Walker . . . . .Agent (617-614-1611)

AMSEL, EISENSTADT & FRAZIER, INC.
5055 Wilshire Blvd., Ste. 865
Los Angeles, CA 90036
PHONE 323-939-1188
FAX 323-939-0630
TYPES   Commercial Talent - Film/TV Talent
AFFILIATIONS   AEA - AFTRA - ATA
REPRESENTS   Actors - Children - Comedians -
                    Teens/Young Adults

Mike Eisenstadt . . . . .Co-Owner/Theatrical
John Frazier . . . . .Co-Owner/Theatrical
Gloria Hinojosa . . . . .Theatrical/Commercial
Nicole Jolley . . . . .Youth Theatrical/Commercial
Milton Perea .Youth Theatrical/Commercial
Carolyn Thompson-Goldstein . . . . . .Youth Theatrical/Commercial

MARCIA AMSTERDAM AGENCY
41 W. 82nd St., Ste. 9A
New York, NY 10024
PHONE 212-873-4945
TYPES   Literary Talent
AFFILIATIONS   WGA
REPRESENTS   Book Authors - TV Writers
SUBMISSION POLICY   Query letter with SASE

Marcia Amsterdam . . . . .Principal/Literary

BEVERLY ANDERSON AGENCY
1501 Broadway, Ste. 2008
New York, NY 10036
PHONE 212-944-7773
FAX 212-944-1034
EMAIL . . . . .bandersontalent@aol.com
TYPES   Film/TV Talent - Theatre Talent
AFFILIATIONS   AEA - AFTRA - AGVA - SAG
REPRESENTS   Actors - Dancers - Musical Theatre
                    Performers - Seniors
SUBMISSION POLICY   No calls, visits; Attends showcases; Accepts
                    picture/resumé submissions from union tal-
                    ent only; Will contact if interested
COMMENTS   Also affiliated with NATRA, WIF; Teens
                    eighteen years old and up

Beverly Anderson . . . . .Owner/President

ANDREADIS TALENT AGENCY, INC.
119 W. 57th St., Ste. 711
New York, NY 10019
PHONE 212-315-0303
FAX 212-315-0311
EMAIL . . . . .andreadis@verizon.net
TYPES   Commercial Talent - Film/TV Talent -
                    Theatre Talent
AFFILIATIONS   AEA - AFTRA
REPRESENTS   Actors - Children - Choreographers -
                    Dancers - Musical Theatre Performers -
                    Seniors - Teens/Young Adults
SUBMISSION POLICY   No audio or video tapes unless requested
COMMENTS   Also affiliated with NATR

Barbara Andreadis . . . . .Owner/Agent
Jim Daly . . . . .No Title
Amanda Gabhard . . . . .No Title

ANGEL CITY TALENT
4741 Laurel Canyon Blvd., Ste. 101
Valley Village, CA 91607
PHONE 818-760-9980
TYPES   Commercial Talent - Film/TV Talent -
                    Literary Talent - Theatre Talent
AFFILIATIONS   AFTRA - ATA - WGA
REPRESENTS   Actors - Broadcast Journalists/Newscasters
                    - Children - Comedians - Hosts/MCs -
                    Magicians - Martial Artists/Stunts - Print
                    Models - Seniors - Speakers/Lecturers -
                    Sports Personalities - Teens/Young Adults -
                    Variety Artists - Voice-Over Artists
SUBMISSION POLICY   Referrals only; No walk-ins

Mimi Mayer . . . . .Owner, MP/TV/Legit Agent
Lincoln Dabagia . .Agent, Commercial On-Camera & Voice-Over, Adults
Vicki Miller . . . . .Agent, Youth & Teen Film, TV, & Commercial
Lori Peters . . . . .TV & Screenwriters
Kim Saunders . . . . .Kids Print

DOUG APATOW AGENCY
12049 W. Jefferson Blvd., Ste. 200
Culver City, CA 90230
PHONE 310-821-4800
FAX 310-821-2211
EMAIL . . . . .doug@apatowagency.com
TYPES   Below-the-Line Talent
AFFILIATIONS   DGA
REPRESENTS   Cinematographers - Film Editors -
                    Production Designers
COMMENTS   Features only; Exclusively reps Feature Line
                    Producers and Key Production Artists; Also
                    represents First Assistant Directors, Line
                    Producers, Costume Designers and
                    Production Sound Mixers

Doug Apatow . . . . .Below-the-Line Agent/Owner/Agent
Erica Grimm . . . . .Associate Agent/Assistant

AQUA
9000 Sunset Blvd., Ste. 515
Los Angeles, CA 90069
PHONE 310-859-8889
FAX 310-859-8898
EMAIL . . . . .jkolinofsky@aquatalent.com
SECOND EMAIL .aqua@aquatalent.com
TYPES   Commercial Talent - Film/TV Talent -
                    Modeling Talent - Music Talent - Theatre
                    Talent
AFFILIATIONS   AFTRA - SAG
REPRESENTS   Actors - Children - Comedians - Dancers -
                    Hosts/MCs - Infants - Martial Artists/Stunts
                    - Music Artists - Print Models - Runway
                    Models - Seniors - Sports Personalities -
                    Teens/Young Adults

Lawrence Har . . . . .Owner
John Kolinofsky . . . . . . .Associate, Adult/Youth Division, Hosting Division
Babo Hong .Associate, Adult/Youth Division

ARCIERI & ASSOCIATES, INC.
305 Madison Ave., Ste. 2315
New York, NY 10165
PHONE 212-286-1700
FAX 212-286-1110
EMAIL . . . . .talent@arcieritalent.com
WEB SITE . . . . .www.arcieritalent.com
TYPES   Commercial Talent - Modeling Talent
AFFILIATIONS   AFTRA - SAG
REPRESENTS   Actors - Hosts/MCs - Print Models - Voice-
                       Over Artists

Steven Arcieri . . . . .Agent
Carmen Marrufo . . . . .Agent
Brooke Barnett . . . . .Agent
Michele Bianculli . . . . .Agent

ARIA TALENT
1017 W. Washington, Ste. 2C
Chicago, IL 60607
PHONE 312-850-9671
FAX 312-226-5523
WEB SITE . . . . .www.ariatalent.com
TYPES   Commercial Talent - Film/TV Talent -
                       Modeling Talent - Theatre Talent
AFFILIATIONS   AEA - AFTRA - SAG
REPRESENTS   Actors - Children - Comedians -
                       Hosts/MCs - Teens/Young Adults
SUBMISSION POLICY   Send headshot and resumé

Robert Schroeder . . . . .Director, TV/Film
Lisa Barston . . . . .Children's TV/Film
Daria Grubb . . . . .TV/Film

IRVIN ARTHUR ASSOCIATES
350 E. 79th St., Ste. 18C
New York, NY 10021
PHONE 212-570-0051
FAX 212-535-2501
TYPES   Music Talent
REPRESENTS   Comedians - Magicians -
                       Speakers/Lecturers - Variety Artists
COMMENTS   Personal Appearance

Irvin Arthur . . . . . . .Principal, Personal Appearance/Theatrical/Packaging

ARTIST MANAGEMENT AGENCY
261 Bush St.
Santa Ana, CA 92701
PHONE 714-972-0311/619-233-6655
EMAIL . . . . .david@artistmanagementagency.com
SECOND EMAIL . . . . .nanci@artistmanagementagency.com
WEB SITE . . . . .www.artistmanagementagency.com
TYPES   Commercial Talent - Film/TV Talent -
                       Modeling Talent - Theatre Talent
AFFILIATIONS   AFTRA - SAG
REPRESENTS   Actors - Children - Print Models - Runway
                       Models - Teens/Young Adults - Voice-Over
                       Artists
SUBMISSION POLICY   No walk-ins; No phone calls; No open
                       calls; No email submissions, snail mail
                       only; No children under five
COMMENTS   Corporate Spokespeople; San Diego and
                       Orange County markets exclusively; San
                       Diego office: 835 Fifth Ave., Ste. 411, San
                       Diego, CA 92101

Nanci Washburn . . . . .President (San Diego)
David Lipton . . . . .VP (Santa Ana)

ARTISTS AGENCY, INC.
230 W. 55th St., Ste. 29D
New York, NY 10019
PHONE 212-245-6960
FAX 212-333-7420
TYPES   Commercial Talent - Film/TV Talent -
                       Literary Talent
AFFILIATIONS   AFTRA - DGA - WGA
REPRESENTS   Book Authors - Directors - Producers - TV
                       Writers
SUBMISSION POLICY   By referral only; No unsolicited material;
                       Do not call or fax

Jonathan Russo . . . . .Talent
Nikole Tsabasis . . . . .Talent
Barry Weiner . . . . .Talent

THE ARTISTS AGENCY
1180 S. Beverly Dr., Ste. 400
Los Angeles, CA 90035
PHONE 310-277-7779
FAX 310-785-9338
TYPES   Film/TV Talent - Literary Talent
AFFILIATIONS   AEA - AFTRA - ATA - DGA - SAG - WGA
REPRESENTS   Actors - Directors - Producers -
                       Screenwriters - Teens/Young Adults - TV
                       Writers
COMMENTS   Recently merged with Marc Bass Agency,
                       Inc. (MBA)

Jim Cota . . . . .Partner/Talent
Michael Livingston . . . . .Partner/Talent
Richard Shepherd . . . . .Partner/Literary
Bruce Tufeld . . . . .Talent
Freddie Miller . . . . .Office Manager
Jaime Smith . . . . .Talent Assistant
Christine De Martin . . . . .Assistant to Michael Livingston & Bruce Tufeld

THE ARTISTS GROUP, LTD.
3345 Wilshire Blvd., Ste. 915
Los Angeles, CA 90010
PHONE 310-552-1100/212-586-1452
FAX 213-531-0006
TYPES   Film/TV Talent - Theatre Talent
AFFILIATIONS   AEA - AFTRA - DGA - SAG
REPRESENTS   Actors
COMMENTS   East Coast office: 1650 Broadway, Ste.
                       610, New York, NY 10019

Robert Malcolm . . . . .Owner/Agent, Theatrical/Literary (LA/NY)
Gabraella King . . . . .Assistant

ARTISTS LITERARY GROUP (ALG)
27 West 20th St., 10th Fl.
New York, NY 10011
PHONE 212-675-6400
FAX 212-675-6406
EMAIL . . . . .jv@algmedia.com
SECOND EMAIL .db@algmedia.com
WEB SITE . . . . .www.algmedia.com
TYPES   Literary Talent
REPRESENTS   Book Authors
SUBMISSION POLICY   Fiction: Query letter with two sample chap-
                       ters and SASE; Nonfiction: Query letter with
                       proposal and SASE

Joe Veltre . . . . .Founder/Literary Agent
Diane Bartoli . . . . .Literary Agent

ASSOCIATED BOOKING CORPORATION (ABC)
501 Madison Ave., Ste. 603
New York, NY 10022
PHONE 212-874-2400
FAX 212-769-3649
EMAIL . . . . .musicbiz@mindspring.com
WEB SITE . . . . .www.abcbooking.com
TYPES   Commercial Talent - Film/TV Talent - Music
                         Talent
AFFILIATIONS   AFM - AFTRA - SAG
REPRESENTS   Comedians - Music Artists

Oscar Cohen . . . . .President
Lisa Cohen . . . . .Agent/Director, Marketing & Public Relations

ATLANTA MODELS & TALENT, INC.
3091 Maple Dr. NE, Ste. 201
Atlanta, GA 30305
PHONE 404-261-9627
TYPES   Commercial Talent - Film/TV Talent -
                         Modeling Talent
AFFILIATIONS   AFTRA - SAG
REPRESENTS   Actors - Children - Print Models - Seniors -
                         Teens/Young Adults - Voice-Over Artists
SUBMISSION POLICY   Do not mail original photo; Mail comp,
                         headshot and resumé

Kathy Hardegree . . . . .Owner/Sr. Agent, All Media
Sarah Carpenter . . . . .Agent, Commercial/Industrial, Voice-Over

ATLAS TALENT AGENCY
15 E. 32nd St., 6th Fl.
New York, NY 10016
PHONE 212-730-4500
FAX 212-730-5820
WEB SITE . . . . .www.atlastalent.com
TYPES   Commercial Talent - Modeling Talent
AFFILIATIONS   AEA - AFTRA - ATA - DGA - SAG
REPRESENTS   Actors - Broadcast Journalists/Newscasters
                         - Hosts/MCs - Print Models - Voice-Over
                         Artists

Hoss . . . . .Partner/Promo Agent
Lisa Marber-Rich . . . . .Partner/Promo Agent
Jonn Wasser . . . . .Partner/Promo Agent
Eric Faber . . . . .On-Camera Agent
Michael Guy . . . . .On-Camera Agent
David Lyerly . . . . .Promo Agent
Marilyn McAleer . . . . .Promo Agent
David Coakley . . . . .Voice-Over Agent
Rachel Sackheim . . . . .Voice-Over Agent

THE AUSTIN AGENCY
6715 Hollywood Blvd., Ste. 204
Hollywood, CA 90028
PHONE 323-957-4444
FAX 323-957-4311
EMAIL . . . . .jlyons@theaustinagency.com
WEB SITE . . . . .www.theaustinagency.com
TYPES   Commercial Talent - Film/TV Talent -
                         Theatre Talent
AFFILIATIONS   AEA - AFTRA - SAG
REPRESENTS   Actors
SUBMISSION POLICY   Referrals only; No unsolicited mail; Strong
                         theatrical background required

John Lyons . . . . .Owner/Agent

BAIER/KLEINMAN INTERNATIONAL
3575 Cahuenga Blvd. West, Ste. 500
Los Angeles, CA 90068
PHONE 323-874-9800
FAX 323-874-4828
EMAIL . . . . .bki@anet.net
TYPES   Film/TV Talent - Theatre Talent
AFFILIATIONS   AEA - AFTRA - SAG
REPRESENTS   Actors
COMMENTS   Includes International talent division

Joel Kleinman . . . . .Owner

DONNA BALDWIN TALENT
2237 W. 30th Ave.
Denver, CO 80211
PHONE 303-561-1199
FAX 303-561-1337
EMAIL . . . . .info@donnabaldwin.com
WEB SITE . . . . .www.donnabaldwin.com
TYPES   Commercial Talent - Film/TV Talent -
                         Modeling Talent
AFFILIATIONS   AFTRA - SAG
REPRESENTS   Actors - Children - Comedians - Print
                         Models - Runway Models - Teens/Young
                         Adults - Voice-Over Artists
SUBMISSION POLICY   Actors: Send media headshot and resumé
                         to Kathleen; Models: Open call every
                         Wednesday 2:30-3:30 pm for women
                         5'8"-5'11" and men 5'11"-6'3"

Donna Baldwin . . . . .Owner/Agent, Fashion
Amy Gibson . . . . .Agent, Print
Kathleen Ham . . . . .Agent, Acting
Brad Baldwin . . . . .Promotions

BALDWIN TALENT, INC.
8055 W. Manchester Ave., Ste. 550
Playa del Rey, CA 90293
PHONE . . . . .310-827-2422/310-823-4708 (after hours)
TYPES   Commercial Talent
AFFILIATIONS   AFTRA - SAG
REPRESENTS   Actors - Comedians - Martial Artists/Stunts
                         - Seniors - Sports Personalities -
                         Teens/Young Adults
SUBMISSION POLICY   By mail only; No unsolicited tapes;
                         Currently not accepting new clients
COMMENTS   Primarily represents circus stunt men, rodeo
                         stunt men, gymnastic performers and
                         extreme athletes

Lyn Baldwin . . . . .Owner/Agent

BARON ENTERTAINMENT
5757 Wilshire Blvd., Ste. 659
Los Angeles, CA 90036-3600
PHONE 323-936-7600
FAX 323-936-8600
EMAIL . . . . .rod@baronentertainment.com
WEB SITE . . . . .www.baronentertainment.com

TYPES	Commercial Talent - Film/TV Talent - Modeling Talent - Music Talent - Theatre Talent
AFFILIATIONS	AFTRA - SAG
REPRESENTS	Actors - Book Authors - Broadcast Journalists/Newscasters - Children - Choreographers - Comedians - Dancers - Hosts/MCs - Infants - Magicians - Martial Artists/Stunts - Music Producers - Print Models - Producers - Runway Models - Seniors - Speakers/Lecturers - Sports Personalities - Teens/Young Adults - Variety Artists
SUBMISSION POLICY	Mail only

Rod Baron . . . . .Agent

LORETTA BARRETT BOOKS, INC.
101 Fifth Ave., 11th Fl.
New York, NY 10003
PHONE 212-242-3420
WEB SITE . . . . .www.lorettabarrettbooks.com

TYPES	Literary Talent
AFFILIATIONS	AAR
REPRESENTS	Book Authors
COMMENTS	Books only

Loretta Barrett . . . . .President
Nick Mullendore . . . . .Agent/Rights Coordinator

BARRY HAFT BROWN ARTISTS AGENCY
249 E. 48th St., Ste. 5J
New York, NY 10017
PHONE 212-869-9310
FAX 212-759-7209
EMAIL . . . . .bhbaa@aol.com

TYPES	Film/TV Talent - Theatre Talent
AFFILIATIONS	AEA - AFTRA - SAG
REPRESENTS	Actors
COMMENTS	Call first before sending fax

Bob Barry . . . . .Owner/Agent

BASKOW & ASSOCIATES, INC.
2948 E. Russell Rd.
Las Vegas, NV 89120
PHONE 702-733-7818
FAX 702-733-2052
EMAIL . . . . .jaki@baskow.com
WEB SITE . . . . .www.baskow.com

TYPES	Commercial Talent - Film/TV Talent - Literary Talent - Modeling Talent - Music Talent - Talent & Literary Packaging
AFFILIATIONS	AEA - AFM - AGVA - SAG
REPRESENTS	Actors - Book Authors - Children - Choreographers - Comedians - Dancers - Hosts/MCs - Magicians - Music Artists - Print Models - Runway Models - Screenwriters - Speakers/Lecturers - Sports Personalities - TV Writers - Variety Artists
COMMENTS	Also affiliated with Destination Management Company; Event planning; Location scouting; Print and video production; Produces segments for TV shows about Las Vegas; Also represents extras and celebrities

Jaki Baskow . . . . .CEO

MARC BASS AGENCY, INC. (MBA)
9171 Wilshire Blvd., 3rd Fl., Ste. 380
Beverly Hills, CA 90210
PHONE 310-278-1900
FAX 310-281-0900
EMAIL . . . . .info@mba-agency.com
WEB SITE . . . . .www.mba-agency.com
SECOND WEB SITE . . . . .www.mba-newyork.com

TYPES	Film/TV Talent - Literary Talent - Talent & Literary Packaging - Theatre Talent
AFFILIATIONS	AEA - AFTRA - SAG
REPRESENTS	Directors - Screenwriters - TV Writers
SUBMISSION POLICY	Accepted on a requested or referral basis only; No drop-offs or mail submissions accepted; Established motion picture, TV and legitimate theatre artists
COMMENTS	Recently merged with The Artists Agency

Marc L. Bass . . . . .President/CEO
Greg McGee . . . . .Theatrical/Literary
Jon A. Cassir . . . . .Theatrical/Literary
Sheida F. Pisheh . . . . .Theatrical/Literary
Anthony DeMichele . . . . .Theatrical/Literary
Natalie Goodwin . . . . .Controller

BAUMAN, REDANTY, & SHAUL AGENCY
5757 Wilshire Blvd., Ste. 473
Los Angeles, CA 90036
PHONE 323-857-6666/212-757-0098
FAX 323-857-0368/212-489-8531

TYPES	Film/TV Talent - Theatre Talent
AFFILIATIONS	AEA - AFTRA - ATA - SAG
REPRESENTS	Actors - Choreographers
SUBMISSION POLICY	No unsolicited submissions
COMMENTS	East Coast office: 250 W. 57th St., Ste. 2223, New York, NY 10019

Mark Redanty . . . . .Partner (NY)
David Shaul . . . . .Partner (LA)
Charles Bodner . . . . .Talent Representative (NY)
Adam Lazarus . . . . .Talent Representative (LA)
Tim Marshall . . . . .Talent Representative (NY)
Colleen Schlegel . . . . .Talent Representative (LA)
Naveen Kumar . . . . .Assistant (NY)
Chris Manno . . . . .Assistant (LA)
Amy Rafa . . . . .Assistant (NY)

BEACHFRONT BOOKINGS
PO Box 13218
Portland, OR 97213-0218
PHONE 503-281-3874
FAX 503-281-3881
EMAIL . . . . .tammartin@aol.com
WEB SITE .www.beachfrontbookings.com

TYPES	Music Talent - Talent & Literary Packaging - Theatre Talent
REPRESENTS	Comedians - Music Artists
COMMENTS	Clients include Bob Smith, Suede, Kate Clinton, Holly Near and Suzanne Westenhoefer

Tam Martin . . . . .Owner/Agent

BEACON ARTISTS AGENCY
120 E. 56th St., Ste. 540
New York, NY 10022
PHONE 212-736-6630
FAX 212-588-1592
TYPES   Literary Talent
AFFILIATIONS   AAR - WGA
REPRESENTS   Directors - Playwrights - Screenwriters
SUBMISSION POLICY   By referral only
COMMENTS   Small agency; Musical theatre writers; No
                           actors

Patricia McLaughlin . . . . .President

BEAUTY MODELS/BC4
6565 W. Sunset Blvd., Ste. 415
Hollywood, CA 90028
PHONE 323-466-0600
FAX 323-466-1605
EMAIL .jose@beautymodelsla.com
WEB SITE .www.beautymodelsla.com
TYPES   Commercial Talent - Modeling Talent
REPRESENTS   Actors - Print Models - Teens/Young Adults
COMMENTS   California Talent License and Member of
                           Better Business Bureau

Jose Cuellar . . . . .Agent

THE SANDI BELL TALENT AGENCY, INC.
2582 S. Maguire Rd., Ste. 171
Ocoee, FL 34761
PHONE 407-445-9221
FAX 407-445-0549
WEB SITE .www.sandibelltalent.com
TYPES   Commercial Talent - Film/TV Talent
AFFILIATIONS   SAG
REPRESENTS   Actors - Children - Teens/Young Adults -
                           Voice-Over Artists
SUBMISSION POLICY   Referrals only, by mail

Sandi Bell . . . . .Owner/Agent

BELOW THE LINE ARTISTS
4430 Irvine Ave.
Studio City, CA 91602
PHONE 818-284-6423
FAX 818-755-0708
EMAIL . . . . .info@btlartists.com
WEB SITE . . . . .www.btlartists.com
TYPES   Below-the-Line Talent
REPRESENTS   Cinematographers - Film Editors -
                           Production Designers
COMMENTS   Also represents make-up artists, steadicam
                           operators and costume designers

Moe Montoya . . . . .Agent

MEREDITH BERNSTEIN LITERARY AGENCY
2095 Broadway, Ste. 505
New York, NY 10023
PHONE 212-799-1007
FAX 212-799-1145
TYPES   Literary Talent
AFFILIATIONS   AAR
REPRESENTS   Book Authors

Meredith Bernstein .President/Owner/Agent

BERZON TALENT AGENCY
336 E. 17th St.
Costa Mesa, CA 92627
PHONE 949-631-5936
FAX 949-631-6881
EMAIL . . . . .marian@berzon.com
WEB SITE . . . . .www.berzontalent.com
TYPES   Commercial Talent - Film/TV Talent -
                           Literary Talent - Modeling Talent - Theatre
                           Talent
AFFILIATIONS   AEA - AFTRA - ATA - SAG - WGA
REPRESENTS   Actors - Book Authors - Children -
                           Comedians - Hosts/MCs - Martial
                           Artists/Stunts - Playwrights - Print Models -
                           Screenwriters - Seniors - Sports Personalities
                           - Teens/Young Adults - TV Writers - Voice-
                           Over Artists

Marian Berzon . . . . .Owner
Mark Pavlovich . . . . .Sub-Agent

THE BETHEL AGENCY
PO Box 21043
Park West Station
New York, NY 10025
PHONE 212-864-4510
TYPES   Commercial Talent - Film/TV Talent -
                           Literary Talent - Music Talent - Talent &
                           Literary Packaging - Theatre Talent
AFFILIATIONS   AEA - AFTRA - SAG
REPRESENTS   Actors - Book Authors - Broadcast
                           Journalists/Newscasters - Children -
                           Choreographers - Comedians - Composers
                           - Dancers - Directors - Hosts/MCs - Infants
                           - Interactive Game Developers - Magicians
                           - Martial Artists/Stunts - Music Artists -
                           Musical Theatre Performers - Playwrights -
                           Producers - Production Designers -
                           Screenwriters - Seniors - Speakers/Lecturers
                           - Teens/Young Adults - TV Writers - Variety
                           Artists - Voice-Over Artists
SUBMISSION POLICY   Actors: Headshot and resumé by mail only;
                           Literary: Query letter and brief synopsis

Lewis Chambers . . . . .Owner/Agent

BEVERLY HILLS INTERNATIONAL TALENT AGENCY
1360 Sierra Bonita Ave.
Pasadena, CA 91104-2647
PHONE 310-980-4242
EMAIL .bevhillsprop@yahoo.com
WEB SITE . . . . .www.bhtalent.com
TYPES   Commercial Talent - Film/TV Talent -
                           Literary Talent - Modeling Talent - Music
                           Talent - Talent & Literary Packaging
AFFILIATIONS   SAG
REPRESENTS   Actors - Book Authors - Comedians -
                           Composers - Directors - Music Artists - Print
                           Models - Seniors - Teens/Young Adults
SUBMISSION POLICY   Hard copy sent via US mail only
COMMENTS   Boutique, full-service agency specializing in
                           SAG and non-union talent

Tracy Turner . . . . .Talent Agent

BICOASTAL TALENT
210 North Pass Ave., Ste. 204
Burbank, CA 91505
PHONE 818-845-0150/818-559-6422
FAX 818-845-0152/818-559-7222
EMAIL . . . . .britagirl@aol.com
SECOND EMAIL .liz@bicoastaltalent.com
WEB SITE . . . . .www.bicoastaltalent.com
TYPES   Commercial Talent - Film/TV Talent - Literary Talent - Theatre Talent
AFFILIATIONS   AFTRA - SAG - WGA
REPRESENTS   Actors - Children - Comedians - Screenwriters - Teens/Young Adults - TV Writers
SUBMISSION POLICY   Theatrical: SAG and credits only; Commercial: Ethnic actors ages eighteen to ninety; Writers: Email queries to literary@bicoastaltalent.com

Greta Hanley . . . . .Owner/Motion Pictures/TV Agent
Samantha Daniels . . . . .Agent, Commercial
Liz Hanley . . . . .Agent, Motion Pictures/TV/Literary
Niche Martin . . . . .Youth Agent
Diane McGee . . . . .Agent, Literary

VICKY BIJUR LITERARY AGENCY
333 West End Ave., Ste. 5B
New York, NY 10023
PHONE 212-580-4108
FAX 212-496-1572
TYPES   Literary Talent
AFFILIATIONS   AAR
REPRESENTS   Book Authors
SUBMISSION POLICY   No screenplays
COMMENTS   Authors Guild, Women's Media Group, Mystery Writers of America, PEN

Vicky Bijur . . . . .Agent
Claire Dunnington . . . . .Assistant

BONNIE BLACK TALENT & LITERARY AGENCY
12034 Riverside Dr., Ste. 103
Valley Village, CA 91607
PHONE 818-753-5424
EMAIL . . . . .bbtphotosub@yahoo.com
TYPES   Commercial Talent - Film/TV Talent - Literary Talent - Modeling Talent
AFFILIATIONS   AFTRA - SAG - WGA
REPRESENTS   Actors - Children - Comedians - Directors - Print Models - Producers - Screenwriters - Speakers/Lecturers - Teens/Young Adults - TV Writers
SUBMISSION POLICY   Referral only for talent; Query letter only for writers; Do not seal mail submissions; Submit photo and resumé by email; Do not fax, email or mail screenplays

Bonnie Black . . . . .President
Frank Black . . . . .Executive Director

THE BLAKE AGENCY
c/o Merritt Blake
1327 Ocean Ave., Ste. J
Santa Monica, CA 90401
PHONE 310-899-9898
FAX 310-899-3858
EMAIL . . . . .blakeagency@aol.com
WEB SITE . . . . .www.theblakeagency.com
TYPES   Commercial Talent - Film/TV Talent - Talent & Literary Packaging - Theatre Talent
AFFILIATIONS   AFTRA - SAG
REPRESENTS   Actors
SUBMISSION POLICY   No unsolicited submissions
COMMENTS   Handles stars and established name talent only

Merritt Blake . . . . .Owner/Agent

BLEU MODEL MANAGEMENT
8564 Wilshire Blvd.
Beverly Hills, CA 90211
PHONE 310-854-0088
FAX 310-854-0033
EMAIL . . . . .info@bleumodels.com
WEB SITE . . . . .www.bleumodels.com
TYPES   Modeling Talent
REPRESENTS   Print Models
SUBMISSION POLICY   Submit photos by regular mail or email
COMMENTS   High-Fashion Models

Rosie Niku . . . . .Owner
Shabi Shahryar . . . . .Agent

BLOC TALENT AGENCY, INC.
5651 Wilshire Blvd., Ste. C
Los Angeles, CA 90036
PHONE 323-954-7730/212-924-6200
FAX 323-954-7731/212-924-6280
EMAIL . . . . .firstname@blocagency.com
WEB SITE . . . . .www.blocagency.com
TYPES   Commercial Talent - Film/TV Talent
AFFILIATIONS   AEA - AFTRA - SAG
REPRESENTS   Choreographers - Dancers - Martial Artists/Stunts - Sports Personalities
SUBMISSION POLICY   Referral preferred
COMMENTS   Skateboarders; East Coast office: 137 Varick St., 6th Fl., New York, NY 10013

Brendan Filuk . . . . .Head of Agency/Agent
Laney Filuk . . . . .Head of Agency/Agent
Todd Cameron . . . . .Talent Representative, Choreography
Alison Diaz . . . . .Talent Representative, Kids, Commercial, Sports, Dance
Anastasia Miller . . . . . .Talent Representative, Kids, Commercial, Dance
Nefertiti Robinson . . . . .Talent Representative (Atlanta)
Sindy Schneider . . . . .Talent Representative (Atlanta)
Steve Chetelat . . . . .Assistant
Jennifer Musgrove . . . . .Assistant

BLUE RIDGE ENTERTAINMENT
41 Union Square West, Ste. 809
New York, NY 10003
PHONE 646-638-1745
FAX 646-638-2036
TYPES   Film/TV Talent - Theatre Talent
AFFILIATIONS   AEA - SAG
REPRESENTS   Actors - Comedians - Dancers
SUBMISSION POLICY   By mail only

Tony Cloer . . . . .Owner/Agent
Elena Berger . . . . .Associate

JUDY BOALS, INC.
307 W. 38th St., Ste. 812
New York, NY 10018
PHONE 212-500-1424
FAX 212-500-1426
EMAIL . . . . .info@judyboals.com
WEB SITE .www.judyboals.com
TYPES   Film/TV Talent - Literary Talent - Theatre
                          Talent
AFFILIATIONS   AEA - SAG
REPRESENTS   Actors - Comedians - Composers -
                          Dancers - Directors - Hosts/MCs - Musical
                          Theatre Performers - Playwrights
SUBMISSION POLICY   Established talent only
COMMENTS   Dramatist's Guild

Judy Boals . . . . .Talent & Literary Agent
Kevin Thompson . . . . .Talent Agent

BOBBY BALL TALENT AGENCY
4605 Lankershim Blvd., Ste. 721
Universal City, CA 91602
PHONE 818-506-8188
FAX 818-506-8588
WEB SITE . . . . .www.bobbyballagency.com
SECOND WEB SITE . . . . .www.bbamodels.com
TYPES   Commercial Talent - Film/TV Talent -
                          Modeling Talent - Music Talent - Theatre
                          Talent
AFFILIATIONS   AEA - AFTRA - ATA
REPRESENTS   Actors - Children - Directors - Hosts/MCs -
                          Infants - Martial Artists/Stunts - Music Artists
                          - Print Models - Screenwriters - Seniors -
                          Sports Personalities - Teens/Young Adults
SUBMISSION POLICY   Via mail only; No phone calls; Not accept-
                          ing adult theatrical at this time

Patty Grana-Miller . . . . .President
Christine Tarallo . . . . .Director, Operations/Print Models
Isabel Fajardo .Director, Accounting
Darci Price . . . . .Agent, Kids Commercial & Theatrical
Mike O'Dell . . . . .Agent, Commercial
Dina Shapiro . . . . .Agent, Adult Theatrical
Shana Randell . . . . .Agent, Commercial & Adult Theatrical
Denice Duff . . . . .Print Models

BOCA TALENT & MODEL AGENCY
829 SE Ninth St.
Deerfield Beach, FL 33441
PHONE . . . . .954-428-4677/954-428-2010 (Print)
FAX 954-429-9203
EMAIL . . . . .hannah@bocamodels.com
WEB SITE . . . . .www.bocamodels.com
TYPES   Commercial Talent - Film/TV Talent -
                          Modeling Talent - Theatre Talent
AFFILIATIONS   AFTRA - SAG
REPRESENTS   Actors - Broadcast Journalists/Newscasters
                          - Children - Comedians - Dancers - Martial
                          Artists/Stunts - Print Models - Runway
                          Models - Seniors - Teens/Young Adults -
                          Variety Artists - Voice-Over Artists
SUBMISSION POLICY   Mail and email submissions accepted; Kids
                          submissions should be sent to Tammy or
                          Natalie
COMMENTS   No infants

Natalie Kahn Toewe . . . . .Owner
Hannah Edwards . . . . .Booker
Tammy Tarlton Gomez . . . . . . .Booker (Kids) (tammy@bocamodels.com)

THE BOHRMAN AGENCY
8899 Beverly Blvd., Ste. 811
Los Angeles, CA 90048
PHONE 310-550-5444
TYPES   Film/TV Talent - Literary Talent - Theatre
                          Talent
AFFILIATIONS   DGA - WGA
REPRESENTS   Book Authors - Directors - Playwrights -
                          Producers - Screenwriters - TV Writers
SUBMISSION POLICY   No phone calls; Referral only; Queries via
                          regular mail must include SAS (U.S.
                          postage only) postcard for response

Caren Bohrman . . . . .President/Partner
Michael Hruska . . . . .CEO/Partner

BOOM MODELS & TALENT
2325 Third St., Ste. 223
San Francisco, CA 94107
PHONE 415-626-6591
FAX 415-626-6594
EMAIL . . . . .boomagency@sbcglobal.net
WEB SITE . . . . .www.boomagency.com
TYPES   Below-the-Line Talent - Commercial Talent
                          - Film/TV Talent - Modeling Talent
AFFILIATIONS   AFTRA - SAG
REPRESENTS   Actors - Broadcast Journalists/Newscasters
                          - Children - Comedians - Dancers -
                          Hosts/MCs - Infants - Martial Artists/Stunts
                          - Print Models - Runway Models - Seniors -
                          Sports Personalities - Teens/Young Adults -
                          Variety Artists - Voice-Over Artists
COMMENTS   Full-service agency representing models
                          and talent from six months old to seniors

Kristen Usich . . . . .Co-Owner
John E. Hutcheson . . . . .Co-Owner

GEORGES BORCHARDT, INC.
136 E. 57th St.
New York, NY 10022
PHONE 212-753-5785
TYPES   Literary Talent
AFFILIATIONS   AAR - WGA
REPRESENTS   Book Authors
SUBMISSION POLICY   No unsolicited query letters or manuscripts

Georges Borchardt . . . . .President
Anne Borchardt . . . . .VP, Film/TV Rights
Valerie Borchardt . . . . .VP, Foreign Rights
Alexandra Dumont . . . . .Assistant
Barbara Galletly . . . . .Assistant
Kate Johnson . . . . .Assistant

BOUTIQUE
10 Universal City Plaza, Ste. 2000
Universal City, CA 91608
PHONE 818-753-2385
FAX 818-753-2386
EMAIL . . . . .boutiquetalent1@sbcglobal.net
TYPES   Film/TV Talent - Literary Talent - Theatre
                          Talent
AFFILIATIONS   AEA - AFTRA - SAG
REPRESENTS   Actors - Musical Theatre Performers
SUBMISSION POLICY   Referral only for film/TV talent; Literary sub-
                          missions via email

Nancy Schmidt Sanford . . . . .Owner
Staci Greason . . . . .Associate

BRADY, BRANNON & RICH
5670 Wilshire Blvd., Ste. 820
Los Angeles, CA 90036
PHONE 323-852-9559
FAX 323-852-9579
TYPES   Commercial Talent
AFFILIATIONS   AFTRA - ATA - SAG
REPRESENTS   Actors - Comedians - Hosts/MCs - Voice-
                         Over Artists
SUBMISSION POLICY   By mail

David Brady . . . . .Partner/Celebrity Division
Pat Brannon . . . . .Partner/Commercial
Judy Rich . . . . .Partner/Commercial
Gary Bornstein .Agent/Talent Payment
Sally Kadison . . . . .Sub-Agent, On-Camera/Commercial
Tim Kessler . . . . .Sub-Agent, Hosting Division
Jennifer Bernardi . . . . .Assistant, On-Camera
Jill Johnson .Assistant, On-Camera

BRAND MODEL AND TALENT AGENCY, INC.
1520 Brookhollow Dr., Ste. 39
Santa Ana, CA 92705
PHONE 714-850-1158
FAX 714-850-0806
EMAIL . . . . .info@brandtalent.net
WEB SITE . . . . .www.brandmodelandtalent.com
TYPES   Commercial Talent - Modeling Talent
AFFILIATIONS   AFTRA - SAG
REPRESENTS   Actors - Children - Infants - Print Models -
                         Runway Models - Seniors -
                         Speakers/Lecturers - Teens/Young Adults -
                         Voice-Over Artists
COMMENTS   Also represents plus-size models

Patty Brand . . . . .President
Lisa Burdick . . . . .Children
Crystal Anderson . . . . .Trade Shows/Runway
Lisa Audiss . . . . .Plus Size/Commercial/Industrial/Voice-Over
Linda Robards . . . . .Print Director
Katrina/Runway Attaman . . . . .Fittings/Runway
Phyllis Brand . . . . .Accounting
Aubrey Green .President's Assistant
Susan DeBrynne . . . . .Kids Assistant
Andrea Johnson . . . . .Commercial Assistant
Claudia Sanchez . . . . .Tradeshow Runway Assistant
Rita Sehmi . . . . .New Faces Print Assistant

BRANDS-TO-BOOKS, INC.
419 Lafayette St.
New York, NY 10003
PHONE 646-723-4583
FAX 212-228-3547
EMAIL . . . . .kspinelli@brandstobooks.com
WEB SITE .www.brandstobooks.com
TYPES   Literary Talent
REPRESENTS   Book Authors
SUBMISSION POLICY   Email inquiry first; Proposals upon request
COMMENTS   Develops original content for brands, as
                         well as providing representation to the liter-
                         ary marketplace

Robert Allen . . . . .Principal
Kathleen Spinelli . . . . .Principal

BRANDT & HOCHMAN LITERARY AGENTS
1501 Broadway, Ste. 2310
New York, NY 10036
PHONE 212-840-5760
FAX 212-840-5776
TYPES   Literary Talent
AFFILIATIONS   AAR
REPRESENTS   Book Authors

Gail Hochman . . . . .President
Carl Brandt . . . . .VP
Bill Contardi . . . . .Agent
Marianne Merola . . . . .Agent
Charles Schlessiger . . . . .Agent

BRASS ARTISTS & ASSOCIATES
9025 Wilshire Blvd., Ste. 450
Beverly Hills, CA 90211
PHONE 310-246-3486
FAX 310-246-1879
EMAIL . . . . .info@thebrassagency.com
TYPES   Commercial Talent - Film/TV Talent
AFFILIATIONS   AFTRA - SAG
REPRESENTS   Actors - Comedians - Seniors -
                         Teens/Young Adults
SUBMISSION POLICY   Mail only; Referral preferred
COMMENTS   Eighteen years and older

Randy Cabrera . . . . .Agent, Theatrical & Commercial
Tony Ferrar . . . . .Agent, Theatrical & Commercial
Jack Iannaci . . . . .Agent, Commercial
Michelle Pitts .Agent, Commercial & Print

BRESLER KELLY & ASSOCIATES
11500 W. Olympic Blvd., Ste. 352
Los Angeles, CA 90064
PHONE 310-479-5611
TYPES   Film/TV Talent - Theatre Talent
AFFILIATIONS   AEA - AFTRA - ATA - DGA - SAG
REPRESENTS   Actors
SUBMISSION POLICY   No unsolicited submissions

Sandy Bresler . . . . .Partner/Agent
John S. Kelly . . . . .Partner/Agent
Colleen Dina . . . . .Agent Trainee

BREVARD TALENT GROUP, INC.
301 E. Pine St., Ste. 175
Orlando, FL 32801
PHONE 407-841-7775
FAX 407-841-7716
WEB SITE . . . . .www.brevardtalentgroup.com
TYPES   Commercial Talent - Film/TV Talent
AFFILIATIONS   AEA - SAG
REPRESENTS   Actors - Children - Teens/Young Adults
SUBMISSION POLICY   Mail only; No fax or email submissions

Traci Danielle . . . . .President

BRICK ENTERTAINMENT
13321 Ventura Blvd.
Sherman Oaks, CA 91423
PHONE 818-784-2000
FAX 818-986-8739
EMAIL . . . . .mail@brickentertainment.com
WEB SITE . . . . .www.brickentertainment.com
TYPES   Commercial Talent - Film/TV Talent - Music
                         Talent - Theatre Talent
AFFILIATIONS   ATA
REPRESENTS   Actors - Broadcast Journalists/Newscasters
                         - Children - Comedians - Hosts/MCs -
                         Martial Artists/Stunts - Runway Models -
                         Seniors - Sports Personalities
COMMENTS   Intimate talent agency dedicated to helping
                         clients secure work throughout the industry

Barry Rick . . . . .Head, Theatrical Department
Jacob Ponder . . . . .Head, Commercial Department
Gordon Duke . . . . .Recruiting Director

THE BROGAN AGENCY
1517 Park Row
Venice, CA 90291
PHONE 310-450-9700
FAX 310-450-0058
EMAIL .info@thebroganagency.com
WEB SITE .www.thebroganagency.com
TYPES   Commercial Talent - Film/TV Talent -
                         Modeling Talent - Music Talent - Theatre
                         Talent
AFFILIATIONS   AFTRA - ATA
REPRESENTS   Actors - Children - Comedians -
                         Hosts/MCs - Infants - Magicians - Martial
                         Artists/Stunts - Music Artists - Music
                         Producers - Musical Theatre Performers -
                         Print Models - Seniors - Teens/Young Adults

Shawn Brogan . . . . .Owner/Theatrical Agent
Michael Daly .Commercial Department
Belle Bromfield . . . . .Director, Youth Division
Linda Lee . . . . .New Talent
Natalie Martin . . . . .New Talent
Liza Karakashian .Accounting Department

BROWNE & MILLER LITERARY ASSOCIATES LLC
410 S. Michigan Ave., Ste. 460
Chicago, IL 60605
PHONE 312-922-3063
FAX 312-922-1905
EMAIL .mail@browneandmiller.com
WEB SITE .www.browneandmiller.com
TYPES   Literary Talent
AFFILIATIONS   AAR
REPRESENTS   Book Authors
SUBMISSION POLICY   Absolutely no screenplays; Book authors
                         only; Do not fax or email query
COMMENTS   Also affiliated with MWA, RWA, Authors
                         Guild

Danielle Egan-Miller . . . . .President/Agent
Joanna McKenzie . . . . .Associate Agent
Paul Samuelson . . . . .Editorial Associate

MARCUS BRYAN & ASSOCIATES
1500 Skokie Blvd., Ste. 310
Northbrook, IL 60062
PHONE 847-412-9394
FAX 847-412-9396
EMAIL .mba3308@aol.com
WEB SITE .www.marcusbryan.com
TYPES   Literary Talent
AFFILIATIONS   WGA
REPRESENTS   Book Authors - Screenwriters - TV Writers
SUBMISSION POLICY   Query letter via email

Marsha Cook . . . . .President
Alison Hopkins . . . . .Literary Agent
Vicki Russo . . . . .Literary Agent
Marcus Cook . . . . .Editor
Jeff Fleischer . . . . .Editor
Lawrence Dictor . . . . .Management
Roberta Chess . . . . .Assistant

DON BUCHWALD & ASSOCIATES, INC. (LOS ANGELES)
6500 Wilshire Blvd., Ste. 2200
Los Angeles, CA 90048
PHONE 323-655-7400
FAX 323-655-7470
WEB SITE .www.buchwald.com
TYPES   Commercial Talent - Film/TV Talent -
                         Literary Talent - Modeling Talent - Talent &
                         Literary Packaging - Theatre Talent
AFFILIATIONS   AEA - AFTRA - DGA - SAG - WGA
REPRESENTS   Actors - Book Authors - Broadcast
                         Journalists/Newscasters - Children -
                         Comedians - Directors - Hosts/MCs -
                         Martial Artists/Stunts - Musical Theatre
                         Performers - Playwrights - Print Models -
                         Producers - Screenwriters - Seniors - Sports
                         Personalities - Teens/Young Adults - TV
                         Writers - Variety Artists - Voice-Over Artists

Tim Angle . . . . .President, LA Office
Neil Bagg . . . . .Agent, Talent
Julia Buchwald . . . . .Agent, Talent
Tracy Christain . . . . .Agent, Talent
Michael Greenwald . . . . .Agent, Talent
Gayla Nethercott . . . . .Agent, Literary
Hannah Roth . . . . .Agent, Theatre
David Swift . . . . .Agent, Broadcast
Spencer Willis . . . . .Agent, Talent
Peter Young . . . . .Agent, Talent

DON BUCHWALD & ASSOCIATES, INC. (NEW YORK)
10 E. 44th St.
New York, NY 10017
PHONE 212-867-1200
FAX 212-867-2434/212-972-3209
TYPES   Commercial Talent - Film/TV Talent -
     Literary Talent - Modeling Talent - Talent &
     Literary Packaging - Theatre Talent
AFFILIATIONS   AEA - AFTRA - DGA - SAG - WGA
REPRESENTS   Actors - Book Authors - Broadcast
     Journalists/Newscasters - Children -
     Comedians - Directors - Hosts/MCs -
     Martial Artists/Stunts - Musical Theatre
     Performers - Playwrights - Print Models -
     Producers - Screenwriters - Seniors - Sports
     Personalities - Teens/Young Adults - Variety
     Artists - Voice-Over Artists

Don Buchwald . . . . .All Areas
Robyn Stecher . . . . .Executive VP
Richard Basch . . . . .Executive VP, Business Affairs, Film/TV/Theatre
Ricki Olshan . . . . .Executive VP, Film/TV/Theatre
Stephen Fisher . . . . .VP, Finance
Lisa Roina . . . . .Director, Celebrity Endorsements
David Elliott . . . . .Agent, Commercials/On-Camera
Christian Gesue . . . . .Agent, Promotional
David Katz . . . . .Agent, Broadcast
Victoria Kress . . . . .Agent, Children
David Lewis . . . . .Agent, Film/TV/Theatre
Joanne Nici . . . . .Agent, Film/TV/Theatre
Michael Raymen . . . . .Agent, Commercials/On-Camera
Rae Ruff . . . . .Agent, Beauty
Katherine Ryan . . . . .Agent, Voice-Over
Rachel Sheedy . . . . .Agent, TV/Theatre/Film
Robyn Starr . . . . .Agent, Commercials/Voice-Over
Robin Steinfeld . . . . .Agent, Voice-Over/Promotional
Alan Willig . . . . .Agent, Film/TV/Theatre

BUCHWALD TALENT GROUP, LLC
6500 Wilshire Blvd., Ste. 2210
Los Angeles, CA 90048
PHONE 323-852-9555
FAX 323-852-9577
TYPES   Commercial Talent - Film/TV Talent
AFFILIATIONS   AEA - AFTRA - SAG
REPRESENTS   Actors - Children - Teens/Young Adults -
     Voice-Over Artists
COMMENTS   Youth division; Seeking all talent

Matt Jackson .Agent/Head, Theatrical Youth
Julie Balfour .Head, Commercial & Voice

THE BURNS AGENCY, INC.
1255 Marlborough Ln.
Winston-Salem, NC 27105
PHONE 336-744-5037
FAX 336-744-5039
EMAIL . . . . .rona@theburnsagency.com
WEB SITE .www.theburnsagency.com
TYPES   Commercial Talent - Film/TV Talent
AFFILIATIONS   AFTRA - SAG
REPRESENTS   Actors - Hosts/MCs - Teens/Young Adults -
     Voice-Over Artists
SUBMISSION POLICY   Mail and email submissions
COMMENTS   Exclusive representation only; Georgia
     office: 3800 Bretton Woods Rd., Decatur,
     GA 30032

Rona L. Burns . . . . .President
Carrie Miller . . . . .Assistant

SHEREE BYKOFSKY ASSOCIATES, INC.
16 W. 36th St., 13th Fl.
New York, NY 10018
PHONE 212-244-4144/212-244-3353
EMAIL . . . . .shereebee@aol.com
SECOND EMAIL . . . . .submitbee@aol.com
WEB SITE . . . . .www.shereebee.com
TYPES   Literary Talent
AFFILIATIONS   AAR
REPRESENTS   Book Authors
SUBMISSION POLICY   Query with SASE; No unsolicited manu-
     scripts or phone calls

Sheree Bykofsky . . . . .President
Janet Rosen . . . . .Associate
Caroline Woods . . . . .Associate

THE CALLAMARO LITERARY AGENCY
427 N. Canon Dr., Ste. 202
Beverly Hills, CA 90210
PHONE 310-274-6783
FAX 310-274-6536
TYPES   Literary Talent
AFFILIATIONS   WGA
REPRESENTS   Book Authors - Directors - Screenwriters
SUBMISSION POLICY   Does not accept unsolicited queries or
     manuscripts

Lisa Callamaro . . . . .Agent
Angela Berliner . . . . .Assistant

CALLIOPE TALENT, MODEL & ARTIST MANAGEMENT, LLC
1802 NE Loop 410, Ste. 107
San Antonio, TX 78217
PHONE 210-804-1055
FAX 210-804-2008
EMAIL .calliopesa@sbcglobal.net
WEB SITE . . . . .www.calliopetalent.com
TYPES   Commercial Talent - Film/TV Talent -
     Modeling Talent - Music Talent
REPRESENTS   Actors - Children - Choreographers -
     Comedians - Dancers - Hosts/MCs -
     Martial Artists/Stunts - Music Artists - Music
     Producers - Musical Theatre Performers -
     Print Models - Runway Models - Seniors -
     Speakers/Lecturers - Sports Personalities -
     Teens/Young Adults - Variety Artists - Voice-
     Over Artists
SUBMISSION POLICY   See Web site or call 210-244-1744
COMMENTS   Affiliated with Los Angeles-based Calliope
     Talent Management, LLC

Kristy Martin . . . . .CEO/Manager
Mike Britton . . . . .VP, Business & Finance
Michael Druck . . . . .Agent/Development Coordinator
Amanda Rivas . . . . .Agent/Development Coordinator
Max Parra . . . . .Business Administrator/Website Coordinator

CAMBRIDGE LITERARY ASSOCIATES, INC.
135 Beach Rd., Unit C3
Salisbury, MA 01952
PHONE 978-499-0374
EMAIL . . . . .cambridgelit@aol.com
WEB SITE .www.cambridgeliterary.com
TYPES   Literary Talent
AFFILIATIONS   AAR
REPRESENTS   Book Authors - Screenwriters - TV Writers
SUBMISSION POLICY   Mail only, currently not seeking new clients
COMMENTS   Actively sells novels for film

Michael R. Valentino . . . . .President
Ralph D. Valentino . . . . .VP
Joyce Quinn . . . . .Executive Assistant

SUZANNA CAMEJO & ASSOCIATES: ARTISTS FOR THE ENVIRONMENT
520 Broadway, Ste. 350, #105
Santa Monica, CA 90401
PHONE 310-479-4470
EMAIL . . . . .scamejo@earthlink.net
TYPES   Below-the-Line Talent - Commercial Talent - Film/TV Talent - Literary Talent - Talent & Literary Packaging
REPRESENTS   Actors - Book Authors - Cinematographers - Directors - Film Editors - Producers - Production Designers - Screenwriters - Teens/Young Adults - TV Writers
COMMENTS   Also reps line producers

Suzanna Camejo . . . . .Agent
Emily Bloom . . . . .Associate
Mariana Delgado . . . . .Associate
Alejandro Medina . . . . .Associate

THE CAMPBELL AGENCY
3906 Lemmon Ave., Ste. 200
Dallas, TX 75219-3760
PHONE 214-522-8991
FAX 214-522-8997
EMAIL . . . . .nancycampbell@thecampbellagency.com
WEB SITE . . . . .www.thecampbellagency.com
TYPES   Commercial Talent - Film/TV Talent - Modeling Talent - Music Talent
AFFILIATIONS   AFTRA - SAG
REPRESENTS   Actors - Children - Comedians - Print Models - Teens/Young Adults - Voice-Over Artists

Nancy Campbell . . . . .President
Bob Campbell . . . . .VP
Nancy Tasker Johnson . . . .Director, Broadcast/Theatrical, Adult Division
Sharon Hendricks Howell . . . . .Broadcast/Theatrical, Adult Division
Barbara Blanchette . . . . .Print/Broadcast, Kids
Diana Dyer . . . . .Kids/Print/Broadcast
Peter John . . . . .Fashion/Commercial Print Division
Kate Lazar . . . . .Fashion/Commercial Print Division
Cactus McCallum . . . . .Fashion/Commercial/Artist Print Division
Laura Gene . . . . .Business Manager
Elizabeth Upton . . . . .Receptionist

CARMICHAEL TALENT
PO Box 884, 337 N. Railroad Ave.
Johnsonville, SC 29555
PHONE 843-386-3320
FAX 843-386-3893
EMAIL . . . . .sherman@acmenet.net
TYPES   Below-the-Line Talent - Commercial Talent - Film/TV Talent - Theatre Talent
REPRESENTS   Actors - Children - Comedians - Dancers - Hosts/MCs - Martial Artists/Stunts - Music Artists - Musical Theatre Performers - Teens/Young Adults - Variety Artists - Voice-Over Artists
SUBMISSION POLICY   Mail only
COMMENTS   Nationwide talent representation

Sherman Carmichael . . . . .Owner

CONAN CARROLL & ASSOCIATES
11350 Ventura Blvd., Ste. 200
Studio City, CA 91604
PHONE 818-760-4730
TYPES   Commercial Talent - Film/TV Talent - Literary Talent - Theatre Talent
AFFILIATIONS   AEA - AFTRA - ATA - WGA
REPRESENTS   Actors - Children - Print Models - Screenwriters - Teens/Young Adults - TV Writers
SUBMISSION POLICY   Mail only; No drop-offs; No follow-up calls

Conan Carroll . . . . .Agent

THE CARRY CO.
3875 Wilshire Blvd., Ste. 402
Los Angeles, CA 90010
PHONE 213-388-0770/212-768-2793
FAX 646-349-2250
WEB SITE . . . . .www.carrycompany.com
TYPES   Commercial Talent - Film/TV Talent - Music Talent - Theatre Talent
AFFILIATIONS   AEA - AFTRA - SAG - WGA
REPRESENTS   Actors - Broadcast Journalists/Newscasters - Children - Comedians - Dancers - Hosts/MCs - Music Artists - Print Models - Teens/Young Adults
SUBMISSION POLICY   By mail only; No phone calls, No visits please
COMMENTS   East Coast address: 20 W. 20th St., 2nd Fl., New York, NY 10011

Sharon Carry . . . . .Owner
Amanda Keith . . . . .Assistant

THE CARSON ORGANIZATION, LTD.
419 Park Ave. South, Ste. 606
New York, NY 10016
PHONE 212-221-1517
TYPES   Below-the-Line Talent - Commercial Talent - Film/TV Talent - Modeling Talent - Theatre Talent
AFFILIATIONS   AEA - AFTRA
REPRESENTS   Actors - Animals - Children - Comedians - Dancers - Hosts/MCs - Infants - Interactive Game Developers - Playwrights - Print Models - Runway Models - Seniors - Sports Personalities - Teens/Young Adults - Variety Artists - Voice-Over Artists
SUBMISSION POLICY   Mail only
COMMENTS   Also affiliated with NATR

Barry Kolker . . . . .Agent/Owner, Head, Legitimate Theatre Department, Film, TV
Jenevieve Brewer . . . . . .Commercials, Hosting, Industrials, Trade Shows, Voice-Over, Animals (Print Division, About Face)
Alice Skiba . . . . .Assistant
Keith Williston . . . . .Assistant

CARSON-ADLER AGENCY, INC.
250 W. 57th St., Ste. 2030
New York, NY 10107
PHONE 212-307-1882
TYPES   Commercial Talent - Film/TV Talent - Theatre Talent
AFFILIATIONS   AEA - AFTRA
REPRESENTS   Actors - Children - Comedians - Music Artists - Musical Theatre Performers - Teens/Young Adults
SUBMISSION POLICY   Referral preferred; Accepts general submissions by mail
COMMENTS   Also affiliated with NATR

Nancy Carson . . . . .Company Owner (x202)
Bonnie Deroski . . . . .Agent (x201)
Shirley Faison . . . . .Agent (x203)

AGENTS

CASALA, LTD.
6539 Colbath Ave.
Valley Glen, CA 91401
PHONE 818-780-7180
FAX 818-780-8262
EMAIL . . . . .casala@childreninfilm.com
WEB SITE .www.childreninfilm.com
TYPES   Below-the-Line Talent
REPRESENTS   Children
COMMENTS   Studio teachers and baby wranglers; Child
                             labor law experts; Entertainment work per-
                             mit services

Toni Casala . . . . .President
Trisha Noble . . . . .Permit Services

CASSELL-LEVY, INC. (DBA CLINC)
843 N. Sycamore Ave.
Los Angeles, CA 90038-3316
PHONE 323-461-3971
FAX 323-461-1134
EMAIL . . . . .clincvoices@earthlink.net
TYPES   Commercial Talent
AFFILIATIONS   AFTRA - ATA
REPRESENTS   Actors - Broadcast Journalists/Newscasters
                             - Children - Comedians - Dancers - Infants
                             - Martial Artists/Stunts - Seniors -
                             Teens/Young Adults - Voice-Over Artists

Leanna Levy . . . . .President/Commercials/Voice-Over
Richard Ohanesian . . . . .On-Camera Agent
Terre Worhach . . . . .Children's Division

CAST IMAGES TALENT AGENCY
2530 J St., Ste. 330
Sacramento, CA 95816
PHONE 916-444-9655
FAX 916-444-2093
EMAIL .chandra@castimages.com
WEB SITE . . . . .www.castimages.com
TYPES   Commercial Talent - Film/TV Talent -
                             Modeling Talent
REPRESENTS   Actors - Children - Print Models - Runway
                             Models - Teens/Young Adults - Voice-Over
                             Artists
SUBMISSION POLICY   Submit photos and resumés by mail, email
                             or drop-off; See Web site

Chandra Bourne . . . . .Owner/Booking (chandra@castimages.com)
Bret Cota . . . . .Booking (bret@castimages.com)
Melissa Martinston . . . . .Booking (melissa@castimages.com)

CASTIGLIA LITERARY AGENCY
1155 Camino del Mar, Ste. 510
Del Mar, CA 92014
PHONE 858-755-8761
FAX 858-755-7063
TYPES   Literary Talent
AFFILIATIONS   AAR
REPRESENTS   Book Authors
SUBMISSION POLICY   Mail query letter only
COMMENTS   Member, PEN

Julie Castiglia . . . . .President/Agent
Winifred Golden . . . . .Agent
Sally Van Haitsma . . . . .Associate Agent
Robert Bridge . . . . .Assistant

CASTLE HILL TALENT AGENCY
1101 S. Orlando Ave.
Los Angeles, CA 90035
PHONE 323-653-3535
EMAIL . . . . .leigh@castlehill.net
WEB SITE . . . . .www.castlehill.net
TYPES   Commercial Talent - Film/TV Talent - Music
                             Talent - Theatre Talent
AFFILIATIONS   AEA - AFM - AFTRA - SAG
REPRESENTS   Actors - Animals - Children - Comedians -
                             Hosts/MCs - Infants - Martial Artists/Stunts
                             - Seniors - Teens/Young Adults - Variety
                             Artists - Voice-Over Artists
COMMENTS   Across the board representation

Leigh Castle . . . . .Owner/Agent

CAVALERI & ASSOCIATES
178 S. Victory Blvd., Ste. 205
Burbank, CA 91502
PHONE 818-955-9300
FAX 818-955-9399
EMAIL . . . . .cavaleri@hotmail.com
SECOND EMAIL . . . . .cavakids@charterinternet.com
TYPES   Commercial Talent - Film/TV Talent -
                             Literary Talent - Music Talent - Talent &
                             Literary Packaging - Theatre Talent
AFFILIATIONS   AEA - AFTRA - DGA - SAG
REPRESENTS   Actors - Children - Comedians - Directors -
                             Martial Artists/Stunts - Screenwriters -
                             Teens/Young Adults
SUBMISSION POLICY   Mail only; No drop-ins
COMMENTS   Established talent only; Six years old and
                             up

Ray Cavaleri . . . . .Owner/Agent
Cinthia Becks .Children/Young Adults
Al Choi . . . . .Literary

CEDAR GROVE AGENCY ENTERTAINMENT
PO Box 1692
Issaquah, WA 98027-0068
PHONE 425-837-1687
FAX 425-391-7907
EMAIL . . . . .cedargroveagency@msn.com
TYPES   Literary Talent - Music Talent
REPRESENTS   Music Artists - Screenwriters
SUBMISSION POLICY   Send one-page synopsis; Do not send
                             email attachment or call; Presently does not
                             represent Horror, Erotic Thrillers or Period
                             Pieces
COMMENTS   Screenwriters only; Cinema Seattle,
                             Bellevue Community College Film Advisory
                             Board

Amy B. Taylor . . . . .President
Samantha Powers . . . . .VP
Linda Runge . . . . .Story Editor

CELEBRITY SUPPLIERS/SPORTS STAR SUPPLIERS
2756 N. Green Valley Pkwy., Ste. 449
Las Vegas, NV 89014
PHONE 702-451-8090
EMAIL . . . . .info@entertainmentservices.com
WEB SITE . . . . .www.celebritysuppliers.com
REPRESENTS   Actors - Book Authors - Broadcast
                  Journalists/Newscasters - Comedians -
                  Music Artists - Sports Personalities - Variety
                  Artists
COMMENTS   Supplies TV, movie and sports celebrities for
                  appearances, autographs and product
                  endorsements worldwide

A.J. Sagman . . . . .President
S. Schneider . . . . .Sales Director
Steve Rosenthal . . . . .Account Manager
D. Manning . . . . .No Title

CELESTINE AGENCY
1548 16th St.
Santa Monica, CA 90404
PHONE 310-998-1977
FAX 310-998-1978
EMAIL . . . . .info@celestineagency.com
WEB SITE . . . . .www.celestineagency.com
TYPES   Below-the-Line Talent
COMMENTS   Represents Hair & Make-Up Artists; Fashion
                  and Prop Stylists

Angelika Schubert . . . . .President/Owner
Anita Castillo . . . . .Agent
Frank Moore . . . . .Agent
Chip Adams . . . . .Agent
Melanie Clark . . . . .Agent
Angela Guidry . . . . .Artist Relations
Lara Smiley . . . . .Art Director
Linda Wong . . . . .Accounting Assistant

NANCY CHAIDEZ AGENCY & ASSOCIATES
6818 Longridge Ave.
North Hollywood, CA 91605
PHONE 323-467-8954
FAX 323-467-8963
TYPES   Commercial Talent - Film/TV Talent -
                  Modeling Talent - Music Talent - Theatre
                  Talent
AFFILIATIONS   SAG
REPRESENTS   Actors - Broadcast Journalists/Newscasters
                  - Children - Comedians - Dancers - Martial
                  Artists/Stunts - Print Models - Producers -
                  Runway Models - Sports Personalities -
                  Teens/Young Adults - TV Writers - Variety
                  Artists - Voice-Over Artists

Nancy Chaidez . . . . .Agent
Maria Chaidez .Director, General Talent

THE CHARACTERS
1505 W. Second Ave., Ste. 200
Vancouver, BC V6H 3Y4, Canada
PHONE 604-733-9800
FAX 604-733-6000
EMAIL . . . . .characters.office@canadafilm.com
WEB SITE . . . . .www.slfa.com
TYPES   Below-the-Line Talent - Commercial Talent
                  - Film/TV Talent - Literary Talent - Talent &
                  Literary Packaging - Theatre Talent
REPRESENTS   Actors - Broadcast Journalists/Newscasters
                  - Children - Cinematographers - Directors -
                  Film Editors - Hosts/MCs - Musical Theatre
                  Performers - Playwrights - Producers -
                  Production Designers - Screenwriters -
                  Teens/Young Adults - TV Writers - Voice-
                  Over Artists
SUBMISSION POLICY Via mail; Attn: Submissions

Leonard Bonnell . . . . .President (leonardb@canadafilm.com)
Tyman Stewart .VP (tyman@canadafilm.com)
Barbara Bird . . . . .Production Agent (barbarab@canadafilm.com)
Murray Gibson . . . . .Theatrical Agent (murrayg@canadafilm.com)
Ben Silverman . . . . . .Literary Agent (characters.office@canadafilm.com)
Gail Murphy . . . . .Voice Agent/Manager (gailm@canadafilm.com)
Wendy Shobe . . . . .Associate to Tyman Stewart
                  (wendyshobe@canadafilm.com)
Stacey Ando . . . .Assistant to Murray Gibson (staceya@canadafilm.com)
Louise Green . . . .Assistant to Gail Murphy (louiseg@canadafilm.com)
Ryan Stewart . . .Assistant to Leonard Bonnell (rstewart@canadafilm.com)

CHARLES TALENT AGENCY
11950 Ventura Blvd., Ste. 3
Studio City, CA 91604
PHONE 818-761-2224
FAX 818-761-5761
EMAIL . . . . .charlestalentagency@yahoo.com
TYPES   Commercial Talent - Film/TV Talent -
                  Theatre Talent
AFFILIATIONS   AFTRA - SAG
REPRESENTS   Actors
SUBMISSION POLICY Mail only; Industry referral only
COMMENTS   Talent eighteen years old and up

Bert Charles . . . . .Owner/Agent
James Kelley . . . . .Agent

THE CHASIN AGENCY
8899 Beverly Blvd., Ste. 716
Los Angeles, CA 90048
PHONE 310-278-7505
FAX 310-275-6685
TYPES   Film/TV Talent - Literary Talent - Talent &
                  Literary Packaging
AFFILIATIONS   AFTRA - DGA - SAG - WGA
REPRESENTS   Actors - Book Authors - Comedians -
                  Directors - Producers - Screenwriters
SUBMISSION POLICY Query letters accepted; Talent department
                  accepts referrals only; No drop-offs

Tom Chasin . . . . .President/Talent, Directors, Producers
Kelly Duncan-Joiner . . . . .Talent
Scott Penney . . . . .Literary
Brett Bynane . . . . .Assistant

AGENTS

CHATEAU BILLINGS TALENT AGENCY

8489 W. Third St., Ste. 1032
Los Angeles, CA 90048
PHONE 323-965-5432
TYPES   Commercial Talent - Film/TV Talent -
                     Modeling Talent - Theatre Talent
AFFILIATIONS   AFTRA - SAG
REPRESENTS   Actors - Broadcast Journalists/Newscasters
                     - Children - Print Models - Producers -
                     Seniors - Teens/Young Adults
SUBMISSION POLICY   Established actors or industry referral;
                     Currently not accepting new clients
COMMENTS   Interested in young, ethnic talent, over
                     eighteen to play younger

Kay Billings . . . . .Owner/Theatrical/Commercials
Jessica Biscardi . . . . .Print
Guy Chateau . . . . .Commercials

STACY CHERIFF AGENCY

2901 Dunleer Pl.
Los Angeles, CA 90064
PHONE 310-314-2606
EMAIL .stacy@stacycheriffagency.com
WEB SITE .www.stacycheriffagency.com
TYPES   Below-the-Line Talent - Commercial Talent
                     - Theatre Talent
REPRESENTS   Cinematographers

Stacy Cheriff . . . . .Agent/Partner

CHIC MODELS & TALENT AGENCY

5353 Paoli Way
Long Beach, CA 90803
PHONE 562-433-8097
FAX 562-433-2224
WEB SITE . . . . .www.chicmodels.com
TYPES   Commercial Talent - Modeling Talent
AFFILIATIONS   SAG
REPRESENTS   Actors - Children - Print Models - Runway
                     Models - Seniors - Teens/Young Adults

Patty Mezin . . . . .Agent

THE CHRISTENSEN GROUP

4395 St. John's Pkwy.
Sanford, FL 32771
PHONE 407-302-2272
FAX 407-302-2285
EMAIL . . . . .jamato@thechristensengroup.com
WEB SITE .www.thechristensengroup.com
TYPES   Commercial Talent - Film/TV Talent -
                     Modeling Talent
AFFILIATIONS   AFTRA - SAG
REPRESENTS   Actors - Broadcast Journalists/Newscasters
                     - Children - Comedians - Dancers - Print
                     Models - Runway Models - Teens/Young
                     Adults - Voice-Over Artists

Steven Shea . . . . .Agent
Joey Amato . . . . .Director, Talent
Kristen Koldenhoven . . . . .Agent

CIAO! TALENT AGENCY

1310 E. University Ave.
Georgetown, TX 78626
PHONE 512-930-9301
FAX 512-930-9302
EMAIL . . . . .liz@ciaoagency.com
WEB SITE . . . . .www.ciaoagency.com
TYPES   Commercial Talent - Film/TV Talent -
                     Modeling Talent
REPRESENTS   Actors - Children - Comedians -
                     Hosts/MCs - Print Models - Teens/Young
                     Adults - Voice-Over Artists
COMMENTS   Experienced talent only

Liz Atherton . . . . .Owner

CIRCLE TALENT ASSOCIATES

433 N. Camden Dr., Ste. 400
Beverly Hills, CA 90210
PHONE 310-279-5155
TYPES   Commercial Talent - Film/TV Talent -
                     Theatre Talent
AFFILIATIONS   AFTRA - ATA
REPRESENTS   Actors - Children - Seniors
SUBMISSION POLICY   Photo and resumé by mail only

Jennifer Lee Garland . . . . .Principal/Theatrical/Commercial Agent

WM. CLARK ASSOCIATES

154 Christopher St., Ste. 3C
New York, NY 10014
PHONE 212-675-2784
FAX 646-349-1658
EMAIL . . . . .query@wmclark.com
SECOND EMAIL . . . . .general@wmclark.com
WEB SITE . . . . .www.wmclark.com
TYPES   Literary Talent
AFFILIATIONS   AAR
REPRESENTS   Book Authors
SUBMISSION POLICY   Query via text email only with no attach-
                     ment; Queries via other means will not be
                     read
COMMENTS   Handles film and TV rights for books writ-
                     ten by clients only

William Clark . . . . .President

MARY ANNE CLARO TALENT AGENCY, INC.

1513 W. Passyunk Ave.
Philadelphia, PA 19145
PHONE 215-465-7788
FAX 215-465-2747
EMAIL . . . . .rocco1513@aol.com
WEB SITE . . . . .www.clarotalent.com
TYPES   Commercial Talent - Film/TV Talent -
                     Theatre Talent
AFFILIATIONS   AEA - AFTRA - SAG
REPRESENTS   Actors - Children - Hosts/MCs
SUBMISSION POLICY   No phone calls; Send in headshots and
                     resumés for review

Mary Anne Claro . . . . .Agent

CLEAR TALENT GROUP
10950 Ventura Blvd.
Studio City, CA 91604
PHONE .818-509-0121/212-840-4100
FAX 818-509-7729
EMAIL . . . . .lainfo@cleartalentgroup.com
SECOND EMAIL . . . . .nyinfo@cleartalentgroup.com
WEB SITE . . . . .www.cleartalentgroup.com
TYPES   Below-the-Line Talent - Commercial Talent - Film/TV Talent - Modeling Talent - Theatre Talent
AFFILIATIONS   AEA - AFTRA - ATA - SAG
REPRESENTS   Actors - Children - Choreographers - Dancers - Directors - Print Models - Teens/Young Adults - Variety Artists
SUBMISSION POLICY Send pictures, resumés and/or reels, attention appropriate department; No phone calls
COMMENTS   Latino/Spanish Commercial Market; East Coast office: 440 Ninth Ave., 8th Fl., New York, NY 10001

Tim O'Brien . . . . .Owner/President/Choreography Agent
Wendy Bogdon . . . . .Print Agent
Indra Armstrong Clark . . . . .Commercial Agent
Peter Engle . . . . .Dance Agent
Jamie Harris . . . . .Dance Department
Brooklyn Lavin . . . . .Choreography Agent
Brianna Barcus . . . . .Director, Dance & Theatrical Agent
Christopher Freer . . . . .Director, Equity & Dance Agent (NY)
Thomas Scott . . . . .Dance & Equity Assistant (NY)
Joel Wiggins . . . . .Commercial Agent

COLLEEN CLER TALENT AGENCY
178 S. Victory Blvd., Ste. 108
Burbank, CA 91502
PHONE 818-841-7943
FAX 818-841-4541
EMAIL . . . . .agent@colleencler.com
SECOND EMAIL . . . . .alana@colleencler.com
WEB SITE . . . . .www.colleencler.com
TYPES   Commercial Talent - Modeling Talent
AFFILIATIONS   AFTRA - SAG
REPRESENTS   Actors - Children - Infants - Print Models - Seniors - Teens/Young Adults
COMMENTS   All ages

Colleen Cler . . . . .Owner/Agent
Craig Schulze . . . . .CFO
Alana Antolak . . . . .Booker

CLIENT FIRST AGENCY
2134 Fairfax Ave., Ste. A3
Nashville, TN 37212
PHONE 615-463-2388
TYPES   Literary Talent
AFFILIATIONS   WGA

Robin Swensen . . . . .Agent

COAST TO COAST TALENT GROUP, INC.
3350 Barham Blvd.
Los Angeles, CA 90068
PHONE 323-845-9200
FAX 323-845-9212
EMAIL . . . . .coast2c@pacbell.net
TYPES   Commercial Talent - Film/TV Talent
AFFILIATIONS   AFTRA - ATA - DGA - SAG - WGA
REPRESENTS   Actors - Book Authors - Children - Directors - Producers - Screenwriters - Sports Personalities - Teens/Young Adults - TV Writers
SUBMISSION POLICY Mail preferred; No follow-up calls

Jeremiah Doryon . . . . .Principal/Business Affairs
Elyah Doryon . . . . .Principal/Motion Pictures/TV, Adult
Hugh Leon . . . . .Head, Adult Commercials/Celebrity Athletes
Meredith Fine .Director, Children's Division
Renata Dobrucki . . . . .Commercials, Children
Dana Edrick . . . . .Theatrical, Children
Petrina Herman . . . . .Print, Teen & Adult
Sydel Lisi . . . . .Commercials, Children
Tana Loy . . . . .Print, Teen & Adult
Amber Raitz . . . . .Theatrical, Adult
Kevin Turner . . . . .Theatrical, Adult
Aimee Rivers . . . . .Assistant, Adult Commercials
Reagan Wallace .Assistant, Children

FRANCES COLLIN LITERARY AGENT
PO Box 33
Wayne, PA 19087-0033
PHONE 610-254-0555
TYPES   Literary Talent
AFFILIATIONS   AAR
REPRESENTS   Book Authors
SUBMISSION POLICY Query by mail with SASE only; No email or telephone queries
COMMENTS   Commercial fiction and nonfiction; No screenplays

Frances Collin . . . . .Owner/Agent
Sarah Yake . . . . .Assistant

COMMERCIAL TALENT, INC.
9255 Sunset Blvd., Ste. 505
Los Angeles, CA 90069
PHONE 310-247-1431
FAX 310-247-1327
TYPES   Commercial Talent
AFFILIATIONS   AEA - AFTRA - SAG
REPRESENTS   Actors - Children - Comedians - Print Models - Seniors - Sports Personalities - Teens/Young Adults

Sheila Di Marco . . . . .Agent
Neil Kreppel . . . . .Agent
Blair Taylor . . . . .Agent
Rebecca Brunson . . . . .Print
Bill Naoum . . . . .Assistant

DON CONGDON ASSOCIATES

156 Fifth Ave., Ste. 625
New York, NY 10010-7002
PHONE 212-645-1229
FAX 212-727-2688
EMAIL . . . . .dca@doncongdon.com
TYPES   Literary Talent
AFFILIATIONS   AAR
REPRESENTS   Book Authors
SUBMISSION POLICY   Query letter with SASE only
COMMENTS   No screenplays; Also affiliated with Authors
                       Guild

Don Congdon . . . . .Owner/Agent
Michael Congdon . . . . .VP/Agent
Susan Ramer . . . . .Agent
Cristina Concepcion . . . . .Agent

CONTEMPORARY ARTISTS, LTD.

610 Santa Monica Blvd., Ste. 202
Santa Monica, CA 90401
PHONE 310-395-1800
TYPES   Film/TV Talent - Literary Talent
AFFILIATIONS   DGA - WGA
REPRESENTS   Directors - Producers - Screenwriters - TV
                       Writers
SUBMISSION POLICY   Not accepting new clients
COMMENTS   Does not represent actors

Ronnie Leif . . . . .President

CORALIE JR. THEATRICAL AGENCY

907 S. Victory Blvd.
Burbank, CA 91502
PHONE 818-766-9501/818-842-5513
TYPES   Commercial Talent - Film/TV Talent -
                       Literary Talent - Modeling Talent - Music
                       Talent - Theatre Talent
AFFILIATIONS   AEA - AFM - AFTRA - SAG - WGA
REPRESENTS   Actors - Animals - Children - Comedians -
                       Dancers - Hosts/MCs - Magicians - Music
                       Artists - Print Models - Screenwriters -
                       Seniors - Teens/Young Adults - TV Writers -
                       Variety Artists
COMMENTS   Specializes in actors and actresses of eth-
                       nicity, celebrity look-alikes, circus acts and
                       little people 2'8 to 5'

Coralie Jr. . . . . .Owner/Agent
Stuart Edward . . . . .Commercial/Theatrical Agent

CORNERSTONE LITERARY, INC.

4525 Wilshire Blvd., Ste. 208
Los Angeles, CA 90010
PHONE 323-930-6039
FAX 323-930-0407
WEB SITE . . . . .www.cornerstoneliterary.com
TYPES   Literary Talent
AFFILIATIONS   AAR
REPRESENTS   Book Authors
SUBMISSION POLICY   Mail query with bio only; No unsolicited
                       manuscripts; No screenplays
COMMENTS   Also affiliated with Authors Guild, PEN,
                       MWA, RWA

Helen Breitwieser . . . . .Owner/Agent
Diane Frank . . . . .Assistant/Office Manager

CORNERSTONE TALENT AGENCY

37 W. 20th St., Ste. 1108
New York, NY 10011
PHONE 212-807-8344
FAX 212-807-8662
TYPES   Film/TV Talent - Theatre Talent
AFFILIATIONS   AEA - AFTRA - SAG
REPRESENTS   Actors
SUBMISSION POLICY   Do not phone or visit
COMMENTS   Also affiliated with NATR

Steve Stone . . . . .Agent
Mark Schlegel . . . . .Agent
Shannon Kelly . . . . .Assistant

CORSA AGENCY

11704 Wilshire Blvd., Ste. 204
Los Angeles, CA 90025
PHONE 310-231-7010
FAX 310-231-7013
TYPES   Commercial Talent - Film/TV Talent
AFFILIATIONS   ATA
REPRESENTS   Actors - Children - Teens/Young Adults
SUBMISSION POLICY   By mail only; No drop-offs

Larry Corsa . . . . .Owner
Thomas Richards . . . . .Associate

CREATIVE ARTISTS AGENCY - CAA

2000 Avenue of the Stars
Los Angeles, CA 90067
PHONE 424-288-2000
FAX 424-288-2900
TYPES   Film/TV Talent - Literary Talent - Music
                       Talent - Theatre Talent
AFFILIATIONS   AEA - AFTRA - ATA - DGA - SAG - WGA
REPRESENTS   Actors - Book Authors - Broadcast
                       Journalists/Newscasters - Comedians -
                       Composers - Directors - Hosts/MCs -
                       Music Producers - Music Supervisors -
                       Musical Theatre Performers - Playwrights -
                       Producers - Screenwriters -
                       Speakers/Lecturers - Sports Personalities -
                       TV Writers - Video Game Designers -
                       Voice-Over Artists
COMMENTS   New York office: 162 Fifth Ave., 6th Fl.,
                       New York, NY 10010, Phone: 212-277-
                       9000; Nashville office: 3310 West End
                       Ave., Ste. 500, Nashville, TN 37203,
                       phone: 615-383-8787; China office:
                       Dong Yu Building, Ste. 803, No. 1 Jia,
                       Shuguang Xili, Chaoyang District, Beijing,
                       China 100028, phone: 8610-5822-0376;
                       London office: 2 Queen Caroline St.,
                       Hammersmith, London, W6 9DX, United
                       Kingdom, phone: 020-8323-8016; fax:
                       020-8323-8317

Richard Lovett . . . . .President
Lee Gabler . . . . .Co-Chairman
Rick Nicita . . . . .Co-Chairman
Kevin Huvane . . . . .Motion Picture Talent, Managing Director
Rob Light . . . . .Head of Music Department, Managing Director
Bryan Lourd . . . . .Motion Picture Talent, Managing Director
David O'Connor . . . . .Motion Picture Literary, Managing Director
Michael Mand . . . . .Head of Communications
Sophie Duong .Communications
Lisa Holloway .Communications
Alison Lehrer .Communications
Beth McClinton . . . . .Communications
Lawrence Rubin . . . . .Communications
Peter Jacobs . . . . .Speakers
Amie Yavor . . . . .Speakers
Gabe Kleinman . . . . .Foundation
Michelle Kydd Lee .Foundation
Ryan Tarpley . . . . .Foundation

(Continued)

CREATIVE ARTISTS AGENCY - CAA (Continued)

Judee Ann Williams . . . . .Foundation
Steve Alexander . . . . .Motion Picture Talent
Chris Andrews .Motion Picture Talent
Martin Baum . . . . .Motion Picture Talent
Darren Boghosian . . . . .Motion Picture Talent
Tracy Brennan .Motion Picture Talent
David Bugliari . . . . .Motion Picture Talent
Jimmy Darmody . . . . .Motion Picture Talent
Matthew DelPiano . . . . .Motion Picture Talent
Jason Heyman .Motion Picture Talent
Kimberly Hodgert . . . . .Motion Picture Talent
Brandt Joel . . . . .Motion Picture Talent
Ara Keshishian .Motion Picture Talent
Rick Kurtzman .Motion Picture Talent
Peter Levine . . . . .Motion Picture Talent
Josh Lieberman . . . . .Motion Picture Talent
Tony Lipp . . . . .Motion Picture Talent
Joel Lubin . . . . .Motion Picture Talent
Michael Nilon .Motion Picture Talent
Emanuel Nuñez . . . . .Motion Picture Talent
Jeremy Plager .Motion Picture Talent
Hylda Queally .Motion Picture Talent
Fred Specktor .Motion Picture Talent
Jeffery Speich .Motion Picture Talent
Nick Styne . . . . .Motion Picture Talent
Mick Sullivan .Motion Picture Talent
Kelly Tiffan . . . . .Motion Picture Talent
Jim Toth . . . . .Motion Picture Talent
Jack Whigham .Motion Picture Talent
Megan Crawford . . . . .Motion Picture, Marketing
Marissa Garcia . . . . .Motion Picture, Marketing
Roger Batchelder . . . . .Motion Picture, Business Affairs
Steven Brookman . . . . .Motion Picture, Business Affairs
Jenna Gambaro . . . . .Motion Picture, Business Affairs
Matthew Leaf . . . . .Motion Picture, Business Affairs
Charles Melniker . . . . .Motion Picture, Business Affairs
Glen Meredith . . . . .Motion Picture, Business Affairs
Joanna Mulas . . . . .Motion Picture, Business Affairs
Eileen Rapke . . . . .Motion Picture, Business Affairs
Keith Sears . . . . .Motion Picture, Business Affairs
Sheldon Sroloff . . . . .Motion Picture, Business Affairs
Marc Von Arx . . . . .Motion Picture, Business Affairs
Dan Aloni . . . . .Motion Picture Literary
Rowena Arguelles . . . . .Motion Picture Literary
Jay Baker . . . . .Motion Picture Literary
Spencer Baumgarten . . . . .Motion Picture Literary
Christina Bazdekis . . . . .Motion Picture Literary (NY)
John Campisi . . . . .Motion Picture Literary
Maha Dakhil . . . . .Motion Picture Literary
J.P. Evans . . . . .Motion Picture Literary
Todd Feldman . . . . .Motion Picture Literary
Craig Gering . . . . .Motion Picture Literary
Risa Gertner . . . . .Motion Picture Literary
Micah Green . . . . .Motion Picture Literary
Scott Greenberg . . . . .Motion Picture Literary
Billy Hawkins . . . . .Motion Picture Literary
Rick Hess . . . . .Motion Picture Literary, Film Finance
Rand Holston . . . . .Motion Picture Literary
Kevin Iwashina . . . . .Motion Picture Literary
Adam Kanter . . . . .Motion Picture Literary
Brian Kavanaugh-Jones . . . . .Motion Picture Literary
Brian Kend .Motion Picture Literary
Michael Kives . . . . .Motion Picture Literary
Christopher Lawson . . . . .Motion Picture Literary
Jon Levin . . . . .Motion Picture Literary
Byrdie Lifson-Pompan . . . . .Motion Picture Literary
Gregory McKnight . . . . .Motion Picture Literary
Victoria Metzger . . . . .Motion Picture Literary
Michael Peretzian . . . . .Motion Picture Literary
Carin Sage .Motion Picture Literary
Brian Siberell . . . . .Motion Picture Literary
Martin Spencer . . . . .Motion Picture Literary
Ken Stovitz .Motion Picture Literary
David Styne .Motion Picture Literary
Roeg Sutherland . . . . .Motion Picture Literary
Elizabeth Swofford . . . . .Motion Picture Literary
Bart Walker . . . . .Motion Picture Literary (NY)
Robert Bookman . . . . .Motion Picture Literary, Books

(Continued)

CREATIVE ARTISTS AGENCY - CAA (Continued)

Richard Green . . . . .Motion Picture Literary, Books
Shari Smiley . . . . .Motion Picture Literary, Books
Matthew Snyder . . . . .Motion Picture Literary, Books
Sally Willcox . . . . .Motion Picture Literary, Books
Seamus Blackley . . . . .Games
Ophir Lupu . . . . .Games
Larry Shapiro . . . . .Games
Steven Lafferty . . . . .Head of Television
Matt Altman . . . . .TV
Janine Argiriou . . . . .TV
Omid Ashtari . . . . .TV
Roy Ashton . . . . .TV
Alan Berger . . . . .TV
Adam Berkowitz . . . . .TV
Glenn Bickel . . . . .TV
Pierre Brogan . . . . .TV
Michael Camacho . . . . .TV
Greg Cavic . . . . .TV
Joseph Cohen . . . . .TV
Kevin Cooper . . . . .TV
Andy Elkin . . . . .TV
Nancy Etz . . . . .TV
Tony Etz . . . . .TV
Bryan Geers . . . . .TV
Sean Grumman . . . . .TV
Chris Harbert . . . . .TV
Alix Hartley . . . . .TV
Jeffrey Jacobs . . . . .TV
Nancy Jones . . . . .TV
Michael Katcher . . . . .TV
Rob Kenneally . . . . .TV
Grant Kessman . . . . .TV
Joe LaBracio . . . . .TV
Rick Lefitz . . . . .TV
Martin Lesak . . . . .TV
Brett Loncar . . . . .TV
Peter Micelli . . . . .TV
Ted Miller . . . . .TV
Andrew Miller . . . . .TV
Tracey Murray . . . . .TV
Brian Pike . . . . .TV
Michael Rosenfeld . . . . .TV
Sonya Rosenfeld . . . . .TV
Andrea Ross . . . . .TV
Chris Simonian . . . . .TV
Steve Smooke . . . . .TV
Andy Stabile . . . . .TV
Catherine Stellin . . . . .TV
Steve Tellez . . . . .TV
Jaclyn Travers . . . . .TV
Bruce Vinokour . . . . .TV
Tiffany Ward . . . . .TV
Kathy White . . . . .TV
Tom Young . . . . .TV
Bill Zotti . . . . .TV
Teri Eaton . . . . .TV, Business Affairs
Daniel Grover .TV, Business Affairs
Gregory Pulis .TV, Business Affairs
Jon Ringquist .TV, Business Affairs
Jason Cooper . . . . .Theatre (NY)
George Lane . . . . .Theatre (NY)
Olivier Sultan . . . . .Theatre, Business Affairs (NY)
Mitch Rose . . . . .Department Head, Music (LA)
Jenna Adler . . . . .Music
Christine Belden . . . . .Music
Erin Culley . . . . .Music
Christopher Dalston . . . . .Music
Darryl Eaton . . . . .Music
Jeff Frasco . . . . .Music
Kevin Gelbard . . . . .Music
Brian Greenbaum . . . . .Music
Carole Kinzel . . . . .Music
Jim Lewi . . . . .Music
Jbeau Lewis . . . . .Music
Brian Loucks . . . . .Music
Brian Manning . . . . .Music
Allison McGregor . . . . .Music
Don Muller . . . . .Music

(Continued)

CREATIVE ARTISTS AGENCY - CAA (Continued)

Candy Nguyen	Music, Artist Relations
Robert Norman	Music
Nick Nuciforo	Music, Comedy Touring
Jon Pleeter	Music
Rick Roskin	Music
LaPrial Runkel	Music
Joanna Scott	Music
Brett Steinberg	Music
Marlene Tsuchii	Music
Emma Banks	Music (London)
Mike Greek	Music (London)
Rebecca Wedlake	Music (London)
Paul Wilson	Music (London)
Rod Essig	Department Head, Music (Nashville)
John Huie	Department Head, Music (Nashville)
Stan Barnett	Music (Nashville)
Tim Beeding	Music (Nashville)
Brad Bissell	Music (Nashville)
Scott Clayton	Music (Nashville)
Marc Dennis	Music (Nashville)
Nancy Gent	Music (Nashville)
Jeff Gregg	Music (Nashville)
Jeff Hill	Music (Nashville)
Tony Johnsen	Music (Nashville)
Blake McDaniel	Music (Nashville)
Darin Murphy	Music (Nashville)
Bryan Myers	Music (Nashville)
Risha Rodgers	Music (Nashville)
Joe Brauner	Music (NY)
Nat Farnham	Music (NY)
Mario Tirado	Music (NY)
David Zedeck	Music (NY)
Angie Rho	Music, Business Affairs
J.P. Barry	Sports
Pat Brisson	Sports
Casey Close	Sports
Tom Condon	Sports
Ben Dogra	Sports
Ken Kremer	Sports
Howard Nuchow	Sports
David Rone	Sports
Leon Rose	Sports
Jim Steiner	Sports
Michael Levine	Sports (NY)
Christian Carino	Endorsement, Sponsorship, Commercials
John Eckel	Endorsement, Sponsorship, Commercials
Lauren Hale	Endorsement, Sponsorship, Commercials (NY)
Peter Hess	Endorsement, Sponsorship, Commercials (NY)
Steven Lashever	Endorsement, Sponsorship, Commercials
Jim Nicolay	Endorsement, Sponsorship, Commercials
Lenny Stern	Head of Marketing (NY)
Andrew Ault	Marketing
Lori Cloud	Marketing
Jesse Coulter	Marketing
Nathan Coyle	Marketing
Lori Golay	Marketing
Jae Goodman	Marketing
Mark Grundland	Marketing
Tera Hanks	Marketing
Christy Haubegger	Marketing
Eric Hunter	Marketing
John Kaplan	Marketing
Christopher King	Marketing
David Kung	Marketing
Aubree Lynch	Marketing
Seth Matlins	Marketing
Hilary Meserole	Marketing
David Messinger	Marketing
Robin Moraetes	Marketing (NY)
Haeran Park	Marketing
Roy Peters	Marketing
Scott Pruitt	Marketing
Crystal Rocabado	Marketing
Mark Sacks	Marketing
Mark Shambura	Marketing
Chuck Shorter	Marketing
Jennifer Stanley	Marketing
Andrea Wade	Marketing

(Continued)

CREATIVE ARTISTS AGENCY - CAA (Continued)

Adam Devejian	Corporate Development
Jigar Thakarar	Corporate Development
Brian Weinstein	Corporate Development
Maggie Dumais	Lifestyle
John Frierson	Lifestyle
Lisa Shotland	Lifestyle
Michael Yanover	Lifestyle, Corporate Development
Jane Buckingham	Marketing/President of The Intelligence Group
Kristen Bennett	Marketing, The Intelligence Group (NY)
Tristan Coopersmith	Marketing, The Intelligence Group
Barbara Coulon	Marketing, The Intelligence Group (NY)
Cynthia Engelke	Marketing, The Intelligence Group (NY)
Amanda Freeman	Marketing, The Intelligence Group (NY)
Elizabeth Gray	Marketing, The Intelligence Group (NY)
Jillian Hertzman	Marketing, The Intelligence Group (NY)
Melissa Lawrence	Marketing, The Intelligence Group (NY)
Dianne McGunigle	Marketing, The Intelligence Group (NY)
Margot Nason	Marketing, The Intelligence Group (NY)
Clare Ramsey	Marketing, The Intelligence Group (NY)
Jessica Chen	China
Long Yin Fan	China
Jonah Greenberg	China
Linda Liu	China
HS Liu	China
Peter Loehr	China
Dong Hui Wang	China

THE CRITERION GROUP, INC.
4842 Sylmar Ave.
Sherman Oaks, CA 91423-1716

PHONE	818-995-1485
FAX	818-995-1085
EMAIL	info@criterion-group.com
WEB SITE	www.criterion-group.com
TYPES	Below-the-Line Talent - Film/TV Talent - Literary Talent
AFFILIATIONS	DGA - WGA
REPRESENTS	Cinematographers - Directors - Film Editors - Screenwriters
SUBMISSION POLICY	Literary: Mail query letter, no calls; Below-the-Line: Submit resumés by fax or email
COMMENTS	Make-up Artists; Hair Artists; Also affiliated with IATSE, ACE, Costume Guild, Make-up and Hair Guilds, AFI

Susan Wright	Partner/CEO, Literary/Below-the-Line

THE CROFOOT GROUP, INC.
23632 Calabasas Rd., Ste. 104
Calabasas, CA 91302-1553

PHONE	818-223-1500
TYPES	Film/TV Talent
AFFILIATIONS	AFTRA
REPRESENTS	Broadcast Journalists/Newscasters - Hosts/MCs - Producers - Sports Personalities

Andrew Crofoot	No Title
Terry Crofoot	No Title

CRYSTAL AGENCY
4237 Los Nietos Dr.
Los Angeles, CA 90027
PHONE .323-906-9600/323-788-1336
FAX 323-443-3752/323-913-0900
EMAIL . . . . .bookings@crystalagency.com
SECOND EMAIL . . . . .crystal@crystalagency.com
WEB SITE . . . . .www.crystalagency.com
SECOND WEB SITE . . . . .www.makeuphairandstyling.com
TYPES   Below-the-Line Talent
REPRESENTS   Print Models
SUBMISSION POLICY   Please forward a link to your Web site for
                       review to crystal@crystalagency.com;
                       Otherwise, send 2-3 jpegs of no greater
                       than 500k of best work along with a
                       resumé
COMMENTS   Represents Make-up Artists, Hair Stylists,
                       Fashion/Wardrobe Stylists, Manicurists and
                       Photographers

Crystal Wright . . . . .Creative Director
Andrea Stradford . . . . .Creative Coordinator/Booker

THE CULBERTSON GROUP, LLC
8430 Santa Monica Blvd., Ste. 210
West Hollywood, CA 90069
PHONE 323-650-9454
TYPES   Commercial Talent - Theatre Talent
AFFILIATIONS   AFTRA - ATA
REPRESENTS   Actors - Teens/Young Adults

Eddie Culbertson . . . . .Partner/Theatrical
Lorri Herman .Partner/Commercial

**CUNNINGHAM-ESCOTT-SLEVIN-DOHERTY TALENT
AGENCY (LOS ANGELES)**
10635 Santa Monica Blvd., Stes. 130, 135, 140
Los Angeles, CA 90025
PHONE 310-475-2111/310-475-7573
FAX 310-475-1929/310-475-3362
EMAIL . . . . .info@cesdtalent.com
WEB SITE . . . . .www.cesdtalent.com
SECOND WEB SITE . . . . .www.cesdvoices.com
TYPES   Commercial Talent - Film/TV Talent -
                       Modeling Talent
AFFILIATIONS   AEA - AFTRA - ATA
REPRESENTS   Actors - Broadcast Journalists/Newscasters
                       - Children - Comedians - Dancers - Print
                       Models - Runway Models - Sports
                       Personalities - Teens/Young Adults - Variety
                       Artists - Voice-Over Artists
SUBMISSION POLICY   Do not call or fax; Mail photo/resumé only;
                       Mail voice-over demo on CD or via your
                       Web site or an FTP site, email link to
                       lavoices@cedtalent.com

Ken Slevin . . . . .President/Partner
Paul Doherty . . . . .Secretary/Treasurer/Partner
T.J. Escott . . . . .Chairman/Partner
Carol Scott . . . . .VP, Print/Fashion Division
Peter Varano . . . . .VP, Voice-Over/Commercial Division
Mitchell Gossett . . . . .Director, Theatrical Division
David Ziff . . . . .Director, On-Camera Commercials
Beau Berdahl . . . . .Print Agent
Adrienne Berg .On-Camera Agent
Melissa Berger . . . . .Young Talent Agent
Pat Brady . . . . .Voice-Over/Puppetry Agent

(Continued)

**CUNNINGHAM-ESCOTT-SLEVIN-DOHERTY TALENT
AGENCY (LOS ANGELES) (Continued)**
Stephanie Casequin . . . . .Print Agent
Trisha Esposito . . . . .Voice-Over Promo Trailer Agent
Alex Fox . . . . .Print/Beauty On-Camera Agent
Dedra Galiher . . . . .On-Camera Agent
Margot Klar . . . . .Theatrical Agent
Cathey Lizzio . . . . .Voice-Over/Animation Agent
Jerry Ryba . . . . .Voice-Over Agent
Carol Lynn Sher . . . . .Young Talent Commercials Agent
Sumeet Iyengar .Booth Director
Mark McIntyre . . . . .Booth Director

**CUNNINGHAM-ESCOTT-SLEVIN-DOHERTY TALENT
AGENCY (NEW YORK)**
257 Park Ave. South, Stes. 900 & 950
New York, NY 10010
PHONE 212-477-1666
FAX 212-979-2011
EMAIL . . . . .info@cesdtalent.com
WEB SITE . . . . .www.cesdtalent.com
SECOND WEB SITE . . . . .www.cesdvoices.com
TYPES   Commercial Talent - Film/TV Talent -
                       Modeling Talent - Theatre Talent
AFFILIATIONS   AEA - AFTRA - ATA
REPRESENTS   Actors - Children - Choreographers -
                       Comedians - Dancers - Hosts/MCs -
                       Martial Artists/Stunts - Print Models -
                       Seniors - Sports Personalities - Teens/Young
                       Adults - Voice-Over Artists
SUBMISSION POLICY   Mail photo/resumé only; Mail voice-over
                       demo on CD or via your Web site or
                       an FTP site, email link to
                       nyvoices@cedtalent.com
COMMENTS   Print children's department: 257 Park Ave.
                       South, Ste. 950, New York, NY 10010

Ken Slevin . . . . .President/Partner
Paul Doherty . . . . .Secretary/Treasurer/Partner
T.J. Escott . . . . .Chairman/Partner
Stephanie Bellarosa . . . . .Director, Print Division
Halle Madia . . . . .Director, Youth Division
Jason Bercy . . . . .Young Talent Agent
Tom Celia . . . . .Voice-Over Agent
William Collura . . . . .Voice-Over Agent
Mara Glauberg . . . . .Young Talent Theatrical Agent
Jessie Krysko . . . . .Beauty On-Camera Agent
Maura Maloney . . . . .On-Camera Agent
Anita Reilly . . . . .Voice-Over Agent
Lindsay Sestanovich . . . . .Young Talent Print Agent
Kirsten Walther . . . . .On-Camera Agent
Lakey Wolff . . . . .Dance Agent
Nate Zeitz . . . . .Voice-Over Promo Agent/Affiliates
Jennifer Lee . . . . .Voice-Over Promo Agent
Diana Lote . . . . .Booth Director
Donna Mancino . . . . .Director, Voice-Over Promo Division
Jill Reiling . . . . .Director, Beauty Division
Oscar Garnica . . . . .Print Booker
Danielle Russo . . . . .Print Booker

CURTIS BROWN, LTD.
10 Astor Pl.
New York, NY 10003
PHONE 212-473-5400
TYPES   Film/TV Talent - Literary Talent
AFFILIATIONS   AAR - WGA
REPRESENTS   Book Authors - Screenwriters
SUBMISSION POLICY   One-page query letters with SASE; No
                       unsolicited works

Timothy Knowlton . . . . .CEO
Holly Frederick . . . . .Film Agent
Ed Wintle . . . . .Film Agent
Dave Barbor . . . . .Translation Rights
Sylvie Flatow . . . . .Film Assistant

AGENTS

D4EO LITERARY AGENCY
7 Indian Valley Rd.
Weston, CT 06883
PHONE 203-544-7180
FAX 203-544-7160
EMAIL . . . . .d4eo@optonline.net
WEB SITE www.publishersmarketplace.com/members/d4eo/
TYPES   Literary Talent
REPRESENTS   Book Authors
COMMENTS   Specializes in commercial fiction and non-
                         fiction; Manuscripts only; No screenplays

Robert G. Diforio . . . . .Principal

DATTNER DISPOTO AND ASSOCIATES
10635 Santa Monica Blvd., Ste. 165
Los Angeles, CA 90025
PHONE 310-474-4585
FAX 310-474-6411
EMAIL . . . . .talent@dattnerdispoto.com
WEB SITE . . . . .www.dattnerdispoto.com
TYPES   Below-the-Line Talent
REPRESENTS   Cinematographers - Producers - Production
                         Designers
COMMENTS   DPs for film, TV and music videos only in
                         below-the-line category

Fay Dattner . . . . .Partner/Agent
Bill Dispoto . . . . .Partner/Agent
Richard Caleel . . . . .Agent, Motion Pictures/TV
Lisa Holguin . . . . .Agent, Commercials/Music Videos
Juanita Tiangco . . . . .Agent, Commercials/Music Videos
Dan Burnside . . . .Agent, Commercials/Music Videos/Motion Pictures/TV
David Agell .Operations Manager

KIM DAWSON TALENT
1645 Stemmons Fwy., Ste. B
Dallas, TX 75207
PHONE 214-638-2414
FAX 214-638-2446
EMAIL . . . . .talent@kimdawsonagency.com
WEB SITE . . . . .www.kimdawsonagency.com
TYPES   Commercial Talent - Film/TV Talent -
                         Modeling Talent
AFFILIATIONS   AFTRA - SAG
REPRESENTS   Actors - Children - Infants - Print Models -
                         Runway Models - Teens/Young Adults -
                         Voice-Over Artists
COMMENTS   Texas license #216

Sylvia Gill . . . . .Director, Talent/Agent, Voice-Over
Susan Karr . . . . .Agent, Adults
Jennifer Patredis .Agent, Youth Division

DDO ARTISTS AGENCY
8322 Beverly Blvd., Ste. 301
Los Angeles, CA 90048
PHONE 323-782-0070/212-379-6314
FAX 323-782-0111/212-379-6356
EMAIL . . . . .reception@ddoagency.com
WEB SITE .www.ddoagency.com
TYPES   Commercial Talent - Film/TV Talent -
                         Modeling Talent - Theatre Talent
AFFILIATIONS   AEA - AFTRA - SAG
REPRESENTS   Actors - Children - Choreographers -
                         Dancers - Hosts/MCs - Infants - Musical
                         Theatre Performers - Print Models - Seniors
                         - Sports Personalities - Teens/Young Adults
SUBMISSION POLICY   Submit by mail only; Do not fax or call;
                         Interviews by appointment only
COMMENTS   Miami office: 46 N. West 36th St., 2nd Fl.,
                         Miami, FL 33127, Phone: 305-573-5995,
                         Fax: 305-402-0380; Las Vegas office:
                         2850 Horizon Ridge Pkwy., Ste. 200,
                         Henderson, NV 89052, Phone: 702-430-
                         4588, Fax: 702-430-4501; New York
                         office: 116 W. Houston St., 3rd Fl., New
                         York, NY 10012

Abigail Girvin . . . . .President
Bill Bohl . . . . .President, Dance
Marlene Sutton . . . . .President, Commercials
Corey Smith . . . . . . .VP/Agent, Musical Dance/Choreography/TV/Film/
                         Commercials/Print (NY)
Kat Akra . . . . .Agent, Dance/Choreography/TV/Film/
                         Commercials/Print (Miami)
Karen Jensen . . . . .Sports/Print/Hosting
Janet Jones . . . . .Agent, Dance/Choreography/TV/Film/
                         Commercials/Print (Miami)
Jennifer Lamaj . . . . . . .Agent, Musical Dance/Choreography/TV/Film/
                         Commercials/Print (NY)
Joy Sharp . . . . .Agent, Dance/Choreography/Specialty (Las Vegas)
Bernalyn Dalo . . . . .Commercials
Maria Walker . . . . .Commercials
Chantelle Ameli . . . . .Dance/Musical Theatre
Remy Crane . . . . .Director, Kids/Commercials & Theatrical
Jim Keith . . . . .Director, Dance/Choreography

RICHARD DE LANCY & ASSOCIATES TALENT AGENCY
4741 Laurel Canyon Blvd., Ste. 100
Valley Village, CA 91607
PHONE 818-760-3110
EMAIL . . . . .rdelancy@mindspring.com
TYPES   Commercial Talent - Film/TV Talent -
                         Modeling Talent - Theatre Talent
REPRESENTS   Actors - Animals - Children -
                         Cinematographers - Comedians - Directors
                         - Hosts/MCs - Music Artists - Print Models -
                         Runway Models - Seniors - Teens/Young
                         Adults - Voice-Over Artists
SUBMISSION POLICY   No drop-offs
COMMENTS   Affiliated with NATAS; Seeking male/female
                         talent eighteen to twenty-two years old;
                         Grooms non-union and new talent

Richard De Lancy . . . . .Owner
Eric Castro . . . . .Associate

DEFINING ARTISTS
10 Universal City Plaza, 20th Fl.
Universal City, CA 91608
PHONE 818-753-2405
FAX 818-753-2403
EMAIL . . . . .definingartists@yahoo.com
TYPES   Film/TV Talent
AFFILIATIONS   AFTRA - ATA
REPRESENTS   Actors
SUBMISSION POLICY   Referrals only; No unsolicited tapes accept-
                       ed

Dede Binder-Goldsmith . . . . .Agent, Film & TV/Co-Owner
Kim Dorr . . . . .Agent, Film & TV/Co-Owner
Breanna Bell . . . . .Jr. Associate

DEITER LITERARY AGENCY
6207 Fushsimi Ct.
Burke, VA 22015-3451
PHONE 703-440-8920
FAX 703-440-8929
EMAIL . . . . .sjph@cox.net
TYPES   Literary Talent
AFFILIATIONS   WGA
REPRESENTS   Book Authors - Broadcast
                       Journalists/Newscasters - Playwrights -
                       Screenwriters
SUBMISSION POLICY   Query letters only
COMMENTS   Graphic artists, illustrators and writers of
                       fiction and nonfiction

James Carlson . . . . .Partner/Business Administrator
Mary A. Deiter . . . . .Agent

MARLA DELL TALENT AGENCY
2124 Union St., Ste. C
San Francisco, CA 94123
PHONE 415-563-9213
FAX 415-563-8734
EMAIL . . . . .marla@marladell.com
WEB SITE .www.marladell.com
TYPES   Commercial Talent - Modeling Talent
AFFILIATIONS   AFTRA - SAG
REPRESENTS   Actors - Children - Comedians - Infants -
                       Musical Theatre Performers - Print Models -
                       Seniors - Teens/Young Adults - Voice-Over
                       Artists
SUBMISSION POLICY   No walk-ins or email submissions; See Web
                       site for submission procedure
COMMENTS   Fit Models; Specializes in children and
                       adult commercial talent; Real families

Marla Dell . . . . .Owner
Lu Freeman . . . . .Adult Print/Commercial/Voice Over
Rebecca Jonas . . . . .Children's Fit Modeling
Iris Safar .Children's Print/Commercial

DESANTI TALENTS, INC.
700 N. Green, Ste. 503
Chicago, IL 60622
PHONE 312-666-1677
FAX 312-666-1681
EMAIL . . . . .dtalents@ameritech.net
WEB SITE . . . . .www.desantimodels.com
TYPES   Commercial Talent - Film/TV Talent -
                       Modeling Talent - Music Talent - Theatre
                       Talent
AFFILIATIONS   AEA - AFTRA - SAG
REPRESENTS   Actors - Children - Choreographers -
                       Comedians - Dancers - Hosts/MCs -
                       Infants - Music Artists - Print Models -
                       Teens/Young Adults - Voice-Over Artists
COMMENTS   All ethnicities welcome; Casting;
                       Production; Creative translations

Susana DeSantiago . . . . .President/Agent
Martha Flores . . . . .Sub-Agent
Martha Favela . . . . .Assistant

GINGER DICCE TALENT AGENCY
56 W. 45th St., Ste. 1100
New York, NY 10036
PHONE 212-869-9650
TYPES   Commercial Talent - Film/TV Talent -
                       Theatre Talent
AFFILIATIONS   AEA - AFTRA - SAG
REPRESENTS   Actors - Voice-Over Artists
SUBMISSION POLICY   Do not send CDs; No phone calls
COMMENTS   On-camera and legit talent

Ginger Dicce . . . . .Owner

DIGITAL ARTISTS AGENCY (DAA)
13323 W. Washington Blvd., Ste. 304
Los Angeles, CA 90066
PHONE 310-788-3918
FAX 310-788-3415
EMAIL . . . . .bcoleman@d-a-a.com
WEB SITE . . . . .www.d-a-a.com
TYPES   Below-the-Line Talent
COMMENTS   Representation, career management and
                       development sources for digital visual
                       effects artists; Specializes in feature film,
                       entertainment TV, commercials, music
                       videos; Affiliated with VES

Bob Coleman . . . . .President
Jennifer Heusser . . . . .Executive Assistant

DIMENSIONS III TALENT AGENCY
2827 Cullen Lake Shore Dr.
Orlando, FL 32812
PHONE 407-851-2575
FAX 407-855-2455
EMAIL . . . . .dimensionsIIIorl@aol.com
TYPES   Commercial Talent - Film/TV Talent -
                       Modeling Talent
AFFILIATIONS   AFTRA - SAG
REPRESENTS   Actors - Children - Comedians - Dancers -
                       Print Models - Teens/Young Adults - Voice-
                       Over Artists

Edna Byers . . . . .Owner/Agent

DIVERSE TALENT GROUP

1875 Century Park East, Ste. 2250
Los Angeles, CA 90067
PHONE 310-201-6565
FAX 310-201-6572
EMAIL . . . . .info@diversetalentgroup.com
WEB SITE . . . . .www.diversetalentgroup.com
TYPES   Below-the-Line Talent - Commercial Talent
                         - Film/TV Talent - Literary Talent - Talent &
                         Literary Packaging
AFFILIATIONS   AEA - AFTRA - DGA - SAG - WGA
REPRESENTS   Actors - Children - Cinematographers -
                         Directors - Film Editors - Playwrights -
                         Producers - Production Designers -
                         Screenwriters - Sound Editors - Sports
                         Personalities - Teens/Young Adults - TV
                         Writers
SUBMISSION POLICY   By referral only

Christopher Nassif .Partner/Agent, Packaging
Susan Sussman . . . . .Partner/Agent, Literary
Tom Harrison . . . . .Head, Theatrical
Sandra Bernath . . . . .Agent, Theatrical
Amanda Brammall . . . . .Agent, Literary
Nicole Cataldo . . . . .Agent, Talent
Courtney Hanlon . . . . .Agent, Commercial
Suzanne Bennett Harrison . . . . .Agent, Theatrical
Leland LaBarre . . . . .Agent, Theatrical
Jackie Lewis . . . . .Agent, Youth Theatrical/Commercial
Owen Massey . . . . .Agent, Literary/Below-the-Line
Wendy Morrison . . . . .Agent, Commercial
Natalie Burke . . . . .Jr. Agent, Literary
Janaya Crudup . . . . .Jr. Agent, Talent
Rochelle Hartson . . . . .Jr. Agent, Theatrical
Lori Mason . . . . .Jr. Agent, Literary
Zachary Solov . . . . .Jr. Agent, Packaging
Gina DiBella . . . . .Accounting/Business Affairs
Lori Smaller . . . . .Contracts
Chrissy Metz . . . . .Assistant, Youth Theatrical/Commercial

DOMAIN

9229 Sunset Blvd., Ste. 415
Los Angeles, CA 90069
PHONE 310-888-8500
FAX 310-888-8879
EMAIL . . . . .reception@domainla.org
TYPES   Film/TV Talent
REPRESENTS   Actors

Gabrielle Krengel . . . . .Agent/Partner
Melisa Spamer . . . . .Agent/Partner
Joe Vance . . . . .Agent/Partner
Tom Legath . . . . .Assistant
Jonathan Ripp . . . . .Assistant

DOUBBLE TROUBBLE ENTERTAINMENT, INC.

7251 W. Lake Mead Blvd., Ste. 300
Las Vegas, NV 89128
PHONE 702-257-2350
FAX 702-257-9078
EMAIL . . . . .info@doubbletrouble.com
WEB SITE . . . . .www.doubbletrouble.com
TYPES   Modeling Talent - Theatre Talent
REPRESENTS   Comedians - Dancers - Music Artists -
                         Variety Artists

Nicholas D. Karvounis . . . . .President/Sr. Agent
Alex D. Karvounis . . . . .VP, Sr. Agent
Barbara Berlin . . . . .Director, Marketing
Andrea Dashiell .Director, Operations
Stephanie Depensmith . . . . .Marketing Manager

DOUGLAS, GORMAN, ROTHACKER & WILHELM, INC.

1501 Broadway, Ste. 703
New York, NY 10036
PHONE 212-382-2000
FAX 212-719-2878
EMAIL . . . . .dgrwinc@aol.com
TYPES   Film/TV Talent - Theatre Talent
AFFILIATIONS   AEA - AFTRA - AGVA
REPRESENTS   Actors - Dancers - Directors - Musical
                         Theatre Performers
SUBMISSION POLICY   By mail only
COMMENTS   Also affiliated with SSDC, AGMA and NATR

Jim Wilhelm . . . . .Owner
Michael Rodriguez . . . . .Agent
Joel Carlton . . . . .Agent
Nicole Wichinsky . . . . .Assistant

DUNHAM LITERARY, INC.

156 Fifth Ave., Ste. 625
New York, NY 10010-7002
PHONE 212-929-0994
FAX 212-929-0904
WEB SITE . . . . .www.dunhamlit.com
TYPES   Literary Talent
AFFILIATIONS   AAR
REPRESENTS   Book Authors
SUBMISSION POLICY   Query letter
COMMENTS   Also represents Illustrators

Jennie Dunham . . . . .President
Melanie Klesse . . . . .Assistant

THE E S AGENCY

6612 Pacheco Way
Citrus Heights, CA 95610
PHONE 916-723-2794
FAX 916-723-2796
EMAIL . . . . .edley07@cs.com
WEB SITE .www.edsilveragency.com
TYPES   Literary Talent
AFFILIATIONS   AFTRA - WGA
REPRESENTS   Book Authors - Screenwriters - TV Writers
SUBMISSION POLICY   Query letter only with SASE; No unsolicited
                         manuscripts or screenplays

Ed Silver . . . . .President
Barbara Bitela . . . . .Assistant

EC MODEL & TALENT AGENCY (ENTERTAINMENT CATERERS, INC.)

8022 Office Court, Ste. 200
Orlando, FL 32809
PHONE 407-926-1840/800-709-7469
FAX 407-926-1841
EMAIL . . . . .info@entertainmentcaterers.com
SECOND EMAIL . . . . .sean@entertainmentcaterers.com
WEB SITE . . . . .www.entertainmentcaterers.com
TYPES   Commercial Talent - Film/TV Talent -
                         Modeling Talent - Music Talent
REPRESENTS   Actors - Comedians - Dancers - Hosts/MCs
                         - Magicians - Martial Artists/Stunts - Music
                         Artists - Print Models - Runway Models -
                         Sound Editors - Speakers/Lecturers - Variety
                         Artists
COMMENTS   World class talent and full production serv-
                         ices

Sean McCabe . . . . .President
Eric Rung . . . . .Technical Director
Antonio J. Lane . . . . .Talent Casting Director

EDNA TALENT MANAGEMENT (ETM) LTD.
318 Dundas St. West
Toronto, ON M5T 1G5, Canada
PHONE 416-413-7800/800-390-4027
FAX 416-413-7804
EMAIL . . . . .edna@etmltd.com
WEB SITE . . . . .www.etmltd.com
TYPES   Commercial Talent - Film/TV Talent -
     Theatre Talent
REPRESENTS   Actors - Voice-Over Artists

Edna Khubyar . . . . .President
Paul Hemrend . . . . .Sr. On-Camera Agent
Paul Smith . . . . .Voice Agent
Angela Wright . . . . .On-Camera Agent
David Dunston . . . . .Assistant

DULCINA EISEN ASSOCIATES
154 E. 61st St.
New York, NY 10021
PHONE 212-355-6617
TYPES   Film/TV Talent - Theatre Talent
AFFILIATIONS   AEA - AFTRA - SAG
REPRESENTS   Actors - Comedians - Dancers -
     Teens/Young Adults
SUBMISSION POLICY   Mail submissions only while performing
     locally
COMMENTS   Represents actors who sing

Dulcina Eisen . . . . .Owner
Margaret Emory . . . . .Agent
Barry P. Katz . . . . .Agent

ELECTRIC TALENT
172-13 Hillside Ave., Ste. 202
Jamaica Estates, NY 11432
PHONE 718-883-1940
EMAIL .electrictalent@aol.com
TYPES   Commercial Talent - Film/TV Talent -
     Modeling Talent
AFFILIATIONS   AFTRA
REPRESENTS   Actors - Print Models
SUBMISSION POLICY   Picture and resumé by mail only; No visits;
     Do not call
COMMENTS   Also represents look-alike talent

Robert Persad . . . . .Agent

ELEGANCE TALENT AGENCY
2763 State St.
Carlsbad, CA 92008
PHONE 760-434-3397
FAX 760-434-1406
EMAIL . . . . .eletalent@aol.com
WEB SITE . . . . .www.eletalent.com
TYPES   Below-the-Line Talent - Commercial Talent
     - Film/TV Talent - Modeling Talent
AFFILIATIONS   AFTRA - SAG
REPRESENTS   Actors - Children - Hosts/MCs - Print
     Models - Runway Models - Seniors -
     Teens/Young Adults - Variety Artists - Voice-
     Over Artists
SUBMISSION POLICY   Mail photo, resumé and SASE; Do not fol-
     low up
COMMENTS   Children two years old and up

Pam Pahnke . . . . .Owner/Agent

ELITE MODEL MANAGEMENT
345 N. Maple Dr., Ste. 397
Beverly Hills, CA 90210
PHONE 310-274-9395
FAX 310-278-7520
WEB SITE . . . . .www.elitemodel.com
TYPES   Modeling Talent
AFFILIATIONS   SAG
REPRESENTS   Print Models - Teens/Young Adults
SUBMISSION POLICY   Open call Mondays and Thursdays, 3-3:30
     pm
COMMENTS   Fashion and print for women thirteen to
     twenty-one years old

Sven Gruber . . . . .No Title
Jacqueline Salem . . . . .No Title
Jason Stafford . . . . .No Title
Vavine Tahapehi . . . . .No Title
Tia Talbott . . . . .No Title

ELLIS TALENT GROUP
4705 Laurel Canyon Blvd., Ste. 300
Valley Village, CA 91607
PHONE 818-980-8072
WEB SITE . . . . .www.ellistalentgroup.com
TYPES   Film/TV Talent - Theatre Talent
AFFILIATIONS   AEA - SAG
REPRESENTS   Actors - Comedians
SUBMISSION POLICY   No unsolicited demo reels from actors

Pamala Ellis-Evenas . . . . .President/Owner/Agent
Gabrielle Allabashi . . . . .Agent

THE NICHOLAS ELLISON AGENCY
55 Fifth Ave., 15th Fl.
New York, NY 10003
PHONE 212-206-6050
FAX 212-463-8718
WEB SITE . . . . .www.greenburger.com
TYPES   Literary Talent
REPRESENTS   Book Authors
SUBMISSION POLICY   One page query letter including synopsis,
     author bio and SASE

Nicholas Ellison . . . . .President
Sarah Dickman . . . . .Agent/Director, Foreign Rights
Arija Weddle .Associate Agent
Marissa Matteo . . . . .Agent's Assistant

EMPIRE TALENT AGENCY
468 N. Camden Dr., Ste. 301H
Beverly Hills, CA 90210
PHONE 310-860-5691/323-654-4046
FAX 323-654-4037
EMAIL . . . . .info@empiretalentagency.com
TYPES   Commercial Talent - Modeling Talent -
     Theatre Talent
REPRESENTS   Actors - Children - Print Models -
     Teens/Young Adults
COMMENTS   Full-service agency

Michael Gentry . . . . .Theatrical
Nathan Giles . . . . .Commercial

ENCORE TALENT AGENCY

1732 W. Hubbard St.
Chicago, IL 60622
PHONE 312-738-0230
FAX 312-738-0233
EMAIL . . . . .encoretalentagency@yahoo.com
WEB SITE . . . . .www.encoretalentagency.net
TYPES   Commercial Talent - Film/TV Talent -
                    Modeling Talent - Music Talent - Theatre
                    Talent
AFFILIATIONS   AEA - AFTRA - SAG
REPRESENTS   Actors - Children - Comedians - Dancers -
                    Martial Artists/Stunts - Print Models -
                    Teens/Young Adults - Variety Artists - Voice-
                    Over Artists
COMMENTS   Emphasis on minorities; A large diverse tal-
                    ent pool

Susan Acuna . . . . .President
Dawn Gray . . . . .Agent

ENDEAVOR AGENCY, LLC

9601 Wilshire Blvd., 3rd Fl.
Beverly Hills, CA 90210
PHONE 310-248-2000/646-278-2900
FAX 310-248-2020/646-278-2902
TYPES   Film/TV Talent - Literary Talent
AFFILIATIONS   AAR - AFTRA - ATA - DGA - SAG - WGA
REPRESENTS   Actors - Book Authors - Cinematographers
                    - Directors - Film Editors - Producers -
                    Production Designers - Screenwriters -
                    Sports Personalities - TV Writers - Voice-
                    Over Artists
COMMENTS   Affiliated with Buddy Lee Attractions, Inc.;
                    East Coast office: 152 W. 57th St., 25th
                    Fl., New York, NY 10019

Adriana Alberghetti . . . . .Partner/Motion Picture Literary
Michelle Bohan . . . . .Partner/Talent
Chris Donnelly . . . . .Partner, Motion Picture Literary
Ariel Emanuel . . . . .Partner/TV Literary
Ari Greenburg . . . . .Partner/TV Literary
Paul Haas . . . . .Partner/TV Literary
Greg Hodes . . . . .Partner, TV Literary
Adam Isaacs . . . . .Partner/Talent
Nancy Josephson .Partner/TV Literary
Robert Newman . . . . .Partner/Motion Picture Literary
Sean Perry . . . . .Partner/Alternative TV
Philip Raskind . . . . .Partner/Motion Picture Literary
Richard Rosen . . . . .Partner/TV Literary
Elyse Scherz . . . . .Partner/Talent
Matt Solo . . . . .Partner/TV Literary
Jason Spitz . . . . .Partner/Motion Picture Literary
Tom Strickler . . . . .Partner/Motion Picture Literary
Brian Swardstrom . . . . .Partner/Talent
Adam Venit . . . . .Partner/Talent
Richard Weitz . . . . .Partner/TV Literary
Patrick Whitesell . . . . .Partner/Talent
Richard Abate . . . . .Motion Picture Literary (NY)
Bryan Besser .Motion Picture Literary
Philip d'Amecourt . . . . .Motion Picture Literary
Elia Infascelli-Smith . . . . .Motion Picture Literary
Sarah Lemkin . . . . .Motion Picture Literary
Adam Levine . . . . .Motion Picture Literary
Brian Lipson . . . . .Motion Picture Literary
Lisbeth Rowinski . . . . .Motion Picture Literary
Dawn Saltzman . . . . .Motion Picture Literary
Susan Solomon . . . . .Motion Picture Literary
Bill Weinstein . . . . .Motion Picture Literary
Graham Taylor . . . . .Head, Endeavor Independent
Mark Ankner . . . . .Endeavor Independent
Devin Mann . . . . .Physical Production
Jonathan Silverman . . . . .Physical Production
Zachary Druker . . . . .TV Literary
Hugh Fitzpatrick . . . . .TV Literary
Lisa Harrison . . . . .TV Literary
Jessica Hawthorne-Castro . . . . .TV Literary
Erin Junkin . . . . .TV Literary
Theresa Kang . . . . .TV Literary

(Continued)

ENDEAVOR AGENCY, LLC (Continued)

Melissa Myers . . . . .TV Literary
Scott Seidel . . . . .TV Literary
Karyn Smith . . . . .TV Literary
Julie Weitz . . . . .TV Literary
Thomas Wellington . . . . .TV Literary
Ivo Fischer . . . . .Alternative TV
Greg Horangic . . . . .Alternative TV
Lance Klein . . . . .Alternative TV
Amanda Kogan .Alternative TV
Bonnie Bernstein . . . . .Talent (NY)
Eric Bevans . . . . .Talent (NY)
Jonathan Bluman . . . . .Talent
Leanne Coronel . . . . .Talent
Sean Elliott . . . . .Talent
Craig Gartner . . . . .Talent
Douglas Lucterhand . . . . .Talent
Boomer Malkin . . . . .Talent
Scott Melrose . . . . .Talent
Brent Morley . . . . .Talent
Kami Putnam-Heist . . . . .Talent
Jennifer Rawlings . . . . .Talent
Stephanie Ritz . . . . .Talent
Matt Shaffer . . . . .Talent
Greg Siegel . . . . .Talent
Megan Silverman . . . . .Talent
Lee Stollman . . . . .Talent
Kevin Volchok . . . . .Talent
Andrew Weitz . . . . .Talent
Daisy Wu . . . . .Talent
Conan Smith . . . . .Personal Appearance (NY)
Brittany Balbo . . . . .Commercials
Jessica Thomas . . . . .Commercials
Will Ward . . . . .Commercials
Carole Katz . . . . .VP, Human Resources
Michael Donkis . . . . .Director, Corporate Communications
Tom McGuire . . . . .General Counsel
Catherine Sugar . . . . .Head, TV Business Affairs
Ann Du Val . . . . .Business Affairs
Vikki Karan . . . . .Business Affairs
Deb Shuwarger .Business Affairs

EQUINOX MODELS/EQUINOX TALENT/ZOO MODELS

8455 Beverly Blvd., Ste. 308
Los Angeles, CA 90048
PHONE 323-951-7100
FAX 323-951-7101
EMAIL .zoomtalent@zoomtalent.net
WEB SITE .www.zoomtalent.net
TYPES   Commercial Talent - Modeling Talent
AFFILIATIONS   SAG
REPRESENTS   Actors - Print Models - Runway Models

Jeanette Agaronoff . . . . .President
Robert Abrams . . . . .Agency Director/Commercial Agent
Bill Iannone . . . . .Agency Director/Print Booker/Agent
Tracy Mikolas . . . . .Print Booker
Kristen Noelle . . . . .Agent, Commercials
Marina Masowietsky . . . . . .International Scout & International Bookings
                    for Print
Betsy Johnson . . . . .Office Manager

ESQ. MANAGEMENT

PO Box 469
Hollywood, CA 90078
PHONE 310-252-9879
WEB SITE .www.esqmanagement.biz
TYPES   Below-the-Line Talent - Film/TV Talent -
                    Literary Talent
REPRESENTS   Cinematographers - Composers - Directors
                    - Film Editors - Music Editors - Production
                    Designers - Sound Editors
COMMENTS   Also represents motion picture and TV edi-
                    tors, DPs, storyboard artists and script
                    supervisors; Affiliated with the Motion
                    Picture Editors Guild

Patricia E. Lee, Esq. . . . . .Agent/Attorney
Elizabeth Walsh . . . . .Administrative Services

EVOLUTION MUSIC PARTNERS, LLC
9100 Wilshire Blvd., Ste. 201, East Tower
Beverly Hills, CA 90212
PHONE 310-623-3388
FAX 310-623-1897
EMAIL . . . . .firstname@evolutionmusicpartners.com
WEB SITE . . . . .www.evolutionmusicpartners.com
TYPES   Music Talent
REPRESENTS   Composers - Music Artists - Music Editors -
                         Music Producers - Music Supervisors
COMMENTS   Music publishing catalogs; Copyright hold-
                         ers; Licensing

Seth Kaplan . . . . .Partner
Christine Russell . . . . .Partner

EXPRESSIONS MODEL & TALENT
220 Church St.
Philadelphia, PA 19106
PHONE 215-923-4420
FAX 215-440-7179
TYPES   Commercial Talent - Film/TV Talent -
                         Modeling Talent
AFFILIATIONS   AEA - AFTRA - SAG
REPRESENTS   Actors - Children - Hosts/MCs - Print
                         Models - Runway Models - Seniors -
                         Teens/Young Adults - Voice-Over Artists
SUBMISSION POLICY   No drop-ins; Mail headshot

Pamela Lankford . . . . .President
Lisa Askins . . . . .Director
Diana Juliano . . . . .Talent Director

FARBER LITERARY AGENCY, INC.
14 E. 75th St.
New York, NY 10021
PHONE 212-861-7075
FAX 212-861-7076
EMAIL . . . . .farberlit@aol.com
WEB SITE . . . . .www.donaldfarber.com
TYPES   Literary Talent
REPRESENTS   Book Authors - Playwrights

Ann Farber . . . . .Owner/Agent
Donald C. Farber . . . . .Agent/Attorney
Seth Farber . . . . .Aquisitions Agent

SYLVIA FERGUSON & ASSOCIATES TALENT & LITERARY AGENCY
15303 Ventura Blvd., 9th Fl.
Sherman Oaks, CA 91403
PHONE 818-380-3024
FAX 818-380-3025
EMAIL . . . . .info@sfatalent.com
WEB SITE . . . . .www.sfatalent.com
TYPES   Commercial Talent - Film/TV Talent -
                         Literary Talent - Modeling Talent
REPRESENTS   Actors - Children - Comedians - Dancers -
                         Infants - Martial Artists/Stunts -
                         Screenwriters - Seniors - Teens/Young
                         Adults - TV Writers - Variety Artists
SUBMISSION POLICY   Open call once a week for commercial tal-
                         ent only; Call for time and date

Sylvia Ferguson . . . . .Owner/Commercial & Literary
Annie Dersrochers . . . . .Commercial
Danielle Hartley . . . . .Youth Theatrical
Kimberly Roberts . . . . .Print

JFA/JAIME FERRAR AGENCY
4741 Laurel Canyon Blvd., Ste. 110
Valley Village, CA 91607
PHONE 818-506-8311
FAX 818-506-8334
WEB SITE . . . . .www.jfala.com
TYPES   Commercial Talent - Film/TV Talent -
                         Theatre Talent
AFFILIATIONS   AEA - AFTRA - SAG
REPRESENTS   Actors - Children - Comedians - Seniors -
                         Teens/Young Adults
SUBMISSION POLICY   Mail only
COMMENTS   Referral

Jaime Ferrar . . . . .CEO
Irma Villalvazo . . . . .Commercials
David Tamez . . . . .Assistant

FILM ARTISTS ASSOCIATES
21044 Ventura Blvd., #215
Woodland Hills, CA 91364
PHONE 818-883-5008
TYPES   Commercial Talent
AFFILIATIONS   SAG
REPRESENTS   Actors - Comedians - Variety Artists
SUBMISSION POLICY   Submit pictures and resumés for commer-
                         cials only
COMMENTS   Celebrity endorsements

Cris Dennis . . . . .CEO/Commercials
Penrod Dennis . . . . .President/Overscale Celebrities

FIRST ARTISTS MANAGEMENT
16000 Ventura Blvd., Ste. 605
Encino, CA 91436
PHONE 818-377-7750
FAX 818-377-7760
EMAIL . . . . .fam-info@firstartistsmgmt.com
SECOND EMAIL . . . . .firstinitiallastname@firstartistsmgmt.com
WEB SITE . . . . .www.firstartistsmgmt.com
TYPES   Music Talent
REPRESENTS   Composers - Music Editors - Music
                         Supervisors
SUBMISSION POLICY   No unsolicited material of any kind;
                         Industry referral only

Vasi Vangelos . . . . .Partner/Agent
Robert Messinger . . . . .Partner/Agent
Rich Jaocobellis . . . . .Agent
Randy Gerston . . . . .Agent
Dan Davis . . . . .Operations

FLICK EAST-WEST TALENTS, INC.
9057 Nemo St., Ste. A
West Hollywood, CA 90069
PHONE 310-271-9111
TYPES   Commercial Talent
AFFILIATIONS   AFTRA - SAG
REPRESENTS   Actors - Comedians - Hosts/MCs - Print
                         Models - Runway Models - Seniors - Sports
                         Personalities
COMMENTS   Mail submissions only; No phone calls

Tina Kiratsoulis .Commercial Agent
Chris Bonk . . . . .Assistant

JIM FLYNN AGENCY
307 W. 38th St., Ste. 801
New York, NY 10018
PHONE 212-868-1068
TYPES   Film/TV Talent - Theatre Talent
AFFILIATIONS   AEA - AFTRA - SAG
REPRESENTS   Actors
SUBMISSION POLICY   Established talent only

Jim Flynn Esq. . . . . .Agent

FOLIO LITERARY MANAGEMENT, LLC
505 Eighth Ave., Ste. 603
New York, NY 10018
PHONE 212-400-1494
WEB SITE . . . . .www.foliolit.com
TYPES   Literary Talent
AFFILIATIONS   AAR
REPRESENTS   Book Authors
SUBMISSION POLICY   Refer to website for individual submission
                    policies
COMMENTS   DC office: 1627 K St. NW, Ste. 1200,
                    Washington, DC 20006

Scott Hoffman . . . . .Partner/Agent (shoffman@foliolit.com)
Jeff Kleinman . . . . .Partner/Agent (DC) (jkleinman@foliolit.com)
Paige Wheeler . . . . .Partner/Agent (pwheeler@foliolit.com)
Laney K. Becker . . . . . .Marketing Director/Agent (lkbecker@foliolit.com)
Erin Cartwright-Niumata . . . . .Agent (ecniumata@foliolit.com)
Celeste Fine .Agent (cfine@foliolit.com)

FORD MODELS AT THE RALEIGH HOTEL
1775 Collins Ave.
Miami Beach, FL 33139
PHONE 305-534-7200
FAX 305-534-8220
WEB SITE . . . . .www.fordmodels.com
TYPES   Modeling Talent
AFFILIATIONS   SAG
REPRESENTS   Print Models
SUBMISSION POLICY   Accepted via mail only; No email submis-
                    sions accepted; No walk-ins

Robert Iglesias . . . . .Women's Division
Marie Luce . . . . .Women's Division
Lily Manzano . . . . .Women's Division
Heike Wiese . . . . .Women's Division
Sebastian McWilliams .Men's Division
Barbara Neuman . . . . .Men's Division
Paula Espinoza . . . . .Artist Division, Hair & Make-Up
Ben Simpson . . . . .Artist Division, Hair & Make-Up
Dianne Kimball . . . . .Office Manager

FORD/ROBERT BLACK AGENCY
4032 N. Miller Rd., Ste. 104
Scottsdale, AZ 85251
PHONE 480-966-2537
FAX 480-967-5424
EMAIL . . . . .info@fordrba.com
WEB SITE . . . . .www.fordrbatalent.com
SECOND WEB SITE . . . . .www.fordmodels.com
TYPES   Commercial Talent - Film/TV Talent -
                    Modeling Talent
AFFILIATIONS   AFTRA - SAG
REPRESENTS   Actors - Hosts/MCs - Print Models -
                    Runway Models - Teens/Young Adults -
                    Voice-Over Artists
SUBMISSION POLICY   By mail only

Sheree Kirkeby . . . . .Owner/Director/Runway/Fashion/Print/
                                        Editorial/Catalog/Promotions
Matt Englehart . . . .TV/Film/Commercials/Voice-Over/Commercial Print
Arianna Sinclair . . . . .Assistant

FOSI'S MODELING & TALENT AGENCY
2777 N. Campbell Ave., Ste. 209
Tuscon, AZ 85719
PHONE 520-795-3534/520-795-3602
FAX 520-795-3602
EMAIL . . . . .warnertrips@cs.com
TYPES   Below-the-Line Talent - Commercial Talent
                    - Film/TV Talent - Modeling Talent
AFFILIATIONS   AFTRA - SAG
REPRESENTS   Actors - Children - Martial Artists/Stunts -
                    Print Models - Seniors - Teens/Young Adults
                    - Voice-Over Artists
SUBMISSION POLICY   Pictures and resumés, audio and video
                    tapes

Fosi Costello . . . . .Owner/Agent
Warner McKay Burritt . . . . .Secretary

ROBERT A. FREEDMAN DRAMATIC AGENCY, INC.
1501 Broadway, Ste. 2310
New York, NY 10036
PHONE 212-840-5760
TYPES   Literary Talent
AFFILIATIONS   AAR - WGA
REPRESENTS   Playwrights - Screenwriters - TV Writers
SUBMISSION POLICY   Query letter with SASE

Robert A. Freedman .Owner/Agent
Selma Luttinger . . . . .Agent
Robin Kaver . . . . .Agent
Marta Praeger . . . . .Agent

FRESH FACES AGENCY, INC.
2911 Carnation Ave.
Baldwin, NY 11510
PHONE 516-223-0034
FAX 516-379-0353
EMAIL . . . . .ffagent@aol.com
WEB SITE .www.freshfacesagency.com
TYPES   Film/TV Talent - Music Talent - Theatre
                    Talent
AFFILIATIONS   AEA - AFTRA - SAG
REPRESENTS   Actors - Children - Musical Theatre
                    Performers - Teens/Young Adults

Aggie Gold . . . . .President

FRONTIER BOOKING INTERNATIONAL, INC.
1560 Broadway, Ste. 1110
New York, NY 10036
PHONE 212-221-0220
WEB SITE .www.frontierbooking.com
TYPES   Commercial Talent - Film/TV Talent
AFFILIATIONS   AEA - AFTRA
REPRESENTS   Actors - Children - Dancers - Hosts/MCs -
                    Infants - Magicians - Print Models -
                    Teens/Young Adults - Voice-Over Artists
COMMENTS   Talent three to thirty years old

John Shea . . . . .Department Head, Theatrical/Commercial
Heather Finn .Agent, Commercial
Marion Falk . . . . .Assistant

FRP LITERARY - TALENT AGENCY
14044 Ventura Blvd., Ste. 201
Sherman Oaks, CA 91423
PHONE 818-763-6365
FAX 818-763-2920
TYPES   Commercial Talent - Film/TV Talent -
                    Literary Talent
REPRESENTS   Book Authors - Playwrights - Screenwriters -
                    TV Writers - Voice-Over Artists
SUBMISSION POLICY   Call before sending query letters

Fred R. Price . . . . .President/CEO

THE GAGE GROUP, INC. (LOS ANGELES)
14724 Ventura Blvd., Ste. 505
Sherman Oaks, CA 91403
PHONE 818-905-3800
FAX 818-905-3322
TYPES   Commercial Talent - Film/TV Talent -
                         Literary Talent - Theatre Talent
AFFILIATIONS   AEA - AFTRA - ATA - DGA - SAG - WGA
REPRESENTS   Actors - Children - Choreographers -
                         Directors - Hosts/MCs - Musical Theatre
                         Performers - Playwrights - Producers -
                         Screenwriters - Seniors - Teens/Young
                         Adults - TV Writers - Voice-Over Artists
SUBMISSION POLICY   Headshots and queries by mail only; No
                         unsolicited scripts or reels

Martin Gage . . . . .Principal/Talent/Literary
Mark Fadness . . . . .Talent, Commercials
Denton Heaney . . . . .Talent
Gerry Koch . . . . .Talent
Kitty McMillan . . . . .Talent
Josh Orenstein . . . . .Literary/Voice-Over

THE GAGE GROUP, INC. (NEW YORK)
450 Seventh Ave., Ste. 1809
New York, NY 10123
PHONE 212-541-5250
TYPES   Commercial Talent - Film/TV Talent -
                         Theatre Talent
AFFILIATIONS   AEA - AFTRA - ATA
REPRESENTS   Actors - Musical Theatre Performers
COMMENTS   Member, NATR

Wendie Adelman . . . . .Agent
Philip Adelman . . . . .Agent
Steven Unger . . . . .Agent
Erika Karneil . . . . .Associate Agent
Tyler Cohn . . . . .Assistant to Philip Adelman
Chris Foster . . . . .Assistant to Wendie Adelman

GAGE TALENT, INC.
c/o Barbizaon Agency
6711 Kingston Pike, Ste. 201
Knoxville, TN 37919
PHONE 865-588-8336
FAX 865-588-8816
EMAIL . . . . .agency@barbizonknox.com
WEB SITE . . . . .www.gagetalent.com
TYPES   Commercial Talent - Modeling Talent
REPRESENTS   Actors - Print Models - Runway Models

Jaime Hatcher . . . . .Agency Director
Susie West . . . . .Agent

GARBER TALENT AGENCY
2 Pennsylvania Plaza, Ste. 1910
New York, NY 10121
PHONE 212-292-4910
TYPES   Commercial Talent - Film/TV Talent -
                         Music Talent - Theatre Talent
AFFILIATIONS   AEA - AFTRA - SAG
REPRESENTS   Actors - Broadcast Journalists/Newscasters
                         - Choreographers - Dancers - Directors -
                         Hosts/MCs - Musical Theatre Performers
SUBMISSION POLICY   Referral preferred
COMMENTS   Full-service agency

Karen S. Garber . . . . .Owner

DALE GARRICK INTERNATIONAL AGENCY
1017 N. La Cienega Blvd., Ste. 109
West Hollywood, CA 90069
PHONE 310-657-2661/310-854-6753
TYPES   Commercial Talent - Film/TV Talent
AFFILIATIONS   AEA - AFTRA - DGA - SAG
REPRESENTS   Actors - Children - Comedians - Directors -
                         Teens/Young Adults
SUBMISSION POLICY   Not taking on new clients; Referrals only

Dale Garrick . . . . .Principal/Talent/Theatrical
Alexander Dale . . . . .Theatre
Cynthia Lynn . . . . .Youth/Commercials
Tony Teneceli . . . . .Theatrical

MAX GARTENBERG LITERARY AGENCY
912 N. Pennsylvania Ave.
Yardley, PA 19067
PHONE 215-295-9230
FAX 215-295-9240
EMAIL . . . . .gartenbook@att.net
WEB SITE . . . . .www.maxgartenberg.com
TYPES   Literary Talent
REPRESENTS   Book Authors
SUBMISSION POLICY   Query by letter with SASE; Submissions only
                         at agent's request
COMMENTS   Focus on adult fiction and nonfiction

Max Gartenberg . . . . .President/Agent
Anne G. Devlin . . . . .Agent (agdevlin@aol.com)
Will Devlin . . . . .Agent (wad411@hotmail.com)

THE GARY-PAUL AGENCY
1549 Main St.
Stratford, CT 06615-7057
PHONE 203-345-6167
EMAIL . . . . .maynard@optonline.net
WEB SITE . . . . .www.thegarypaulagency.com
TYPES   Literary Talent
AFFILIATIONS   WGA
REPRESENTS   Screenwriters
SUBMISSION POLICY   Query by email only through Web site

Garret C. Maynard .President/Literary Agent

THE GATSBY GROUP, INC.
PO Box 1127
Boston, MA 02117
PHONE 617-847-4430
FAX 617-847-0050
EMAIL . . . . .gatsbygrp@aol.com
TYPES   Below-the-Line Talent - Commercial Talent
                         - Film/TV Talent - Literary Talent - Music
                         Talent
REPRESENTS   Actors - Book Authors - Cinematographers
                         - Directors - Music Producers - Producers -
                         Screenwriters - TV Writers
COMMENTS   Affiliated with Law Offices of Weischadle &
                         Weischadle

Douglas E. Weischadle Esq. . . . . .President
David E. Weischadle II Esq. . . . . .VP

THE GEDDES AGENCY (CHICAGO)
1633 N. Halsted, Ste. 300
Chicago, IL 60614
PHONE 312-787-8333
FAX 312-787-6677
EMAIL . . . . .chagents@geddes.net
WEB SITE . . . . .www.geddes.net
TYPES   Commercial Talent - Film/TV Talent -
                               Modeling Talent - Theatre Talent
AFFILIATIONS   AEA - AFTRA - SAG
REPRESENTS   Actors - Children - Comedians - Infants -
                               Print Models - Seniors - Teens/Young Adults
                               - Voice-Over Artists
SUBMISSION POLICY   Mail only

Elizabeth Geddes . . . . .Agent
Katie Richter . . . . .Jr. Agent
Tanisha Tyler . . . . .Assistant

THE GEDDES AGENCY (LOS ANGELES)
8430 Santa Monica Blvd., Ste. 200
West Hollywood, CA 90069
PHONE 323-848-2700
EMAIL . . . . .smile@geddes.net
WEB SITE . . . . .www.geddes.net
TYPES   Film/TV Talent - Theatre Talent
AFFILIATIONS   AEA - AFTRA - SAG
REPRESENTS   Actors - Hosts/MCs - Seniors -
                               Teens/Young Adults
SUBMISSION POLICY   No phone calls

Ann Geddes . . . . .Principal/Theatrical
Richard Lewis . . . . .Theatrical
Nancy Moon-Broadstreet . . . . .Theatrical

LAYA GELFF AGENCY
16133 Ventura Blvd., Ste. 700
Encino, CA 91436
PHONE 818-996-3100
TYPES   Film/TV Talent - Literary Talent - Theatre
                               Talent
AFFILIATIONS   AEA - AFTRA - DGA - SAG - WGA
REPRESENTS   Actors - Directors - Screenwriters - TV
                               Writers
SUBMISSION POLICY   WGA writers only, send query letter with
                               SASE; SAG adult actors only, send head-
                               shot and resumé; Do not send unsolicited
                               VHS, DVD, CD, etc.
COMMENTS   No children; No models; SAG Adults only;
                               Do not call

Laya Gelff . . . . .President

GELFMAN SCHNEIDER LITERARY AGENTS, INC.
250 W. 57th St.
New York, NY 10107
PHONE 212-245-1993
FAX 212-245-8678
EMAIL . . . . .mail@gelfmanschneider.com
TYPES   Literary Talent
AFFILIATIONS   AAR
REPRESENTS   Book Authors
SUBMISSION POLICY   Mail query with SASE; No fax or email
                               queries; No screenplays; Book authors only
COMMENTS   Also affiliated with Authors Guild

Jane Gelfman . . . . .Director/Agent
Deborah Schneider . . . . .Director/Agent

THE GELLER AGENCY
1547 Cassil Pl.
Los Angeles, CA 90028
PHONE 323-856-3000
FAX 323-856-3009
WEB SITE . . . . .www.thegelleragency.com
TYPES   Below-the-Line Talent
AFFILIATIONS   ATA - DGA
REPRESENTS   Cinematographers - Directors - Film Editors
                               - Production Designers
COMMENTS   Below-the-line talent for features and TV

Maureen Toth .Owner/Agent, Features/TV
Jen McKnight . . . . .Jr. Agent

GENERATION TV
20 W. 20th St., Ste. 1008
New York, NY 10011
PHONE 646-230-9491
FAX 212-727-7147
TYPES   Commercial Talent - Film/TV Talent -
                               Theatre Talent
AFFILIATIONS   AFTRA - SAG
REPRESENTS   Children - Teens/Young Adults - Voice-
                               Over Artists
SUBMISSION POLICY   Young children to adults in mid-twenties

Patti Fleischer . . . . .Owner
Dina Torre . . . . .Commercial Agent

GENERATIONS MODEL & TALENT AGENCY
340 Brannan St., Ste. 302
San Francisco, CA 94107
PHONE . . . . .415-777-9003/650-366-5301 (info hotline)
FAX 415-777-5055
WEB SITE . . . . .www.generationsagency.com
TYPES   Commercial Talent - Film/TV Talent
AFFILIATIONS   AFTRA - SAG
REPRESENTS   Actors - Children - Infants - Print Models -
                               Runway Models - Seniors - Teens/Young
                               Adults - Voice-Over Artists
SUBMISSION POLICY   Photo via US mail; Follow procedures indi-
                               cated on hotline or Web site

Jennifer Jorgl . . . . .Agent

PAUL GERARD AGENCY
PO Box 1959
Studio City, CA 91614
PHONE 818-769-7015
TYPES   Below-the-Line Talent
AFFILIATIONS   DGA - SAG
REPRESENTS   Cinematographers - Directors
COMMENTS   Line Producers; Not accepting new writers
                               at this time

Steve England . . . . .President
Tracy Downes . . . . .VP/Office Administration

DON GERLER AGENCY
3349 Cahuenga Blvd. West, Ste. 1
Los Angeles, CA 90068
PHONE 323-850-7386
TYPES   Film/TV Talent
AFFILIATIONS   AEA - AFTRA - SAG
REPRESENTS   Actors
SUBMISSION POLICY   Open to new talent

Don Gerler . . . . .Owner/Agent
Doug Bennett . . . . .Agent

THE GERSH AGENCY (LOS ANGELES)
232 N. Canon Dr.
Beverly Hills, CA 90210
PHONE 310-274-6611
FAX 310-274-3923
WEB SITE . . . . .www.gershagency.com
SECOND WEB SITE . . . . www.gershsports.com
TYPES   Below-the-Line Talent - Commercial Talent
                         - Film/TV Talent - Literary Talent
AFFILIATIONS   AEA - AFTRA - ATA - DGA - SAG - WGA
REPRESENTS   Actors - Book Authors - Comedians -
                         Directors - Producers - Screenwriters -
                         Sports Personalities - TV Writers
COMMENTS   Includes Gersh Sports

Bob Gersh . . . . .Co-President/Talent
David Gersh . . . . .Co-President/Literary
Leslie Siebert . . . . .Sr. Managing Partner/Co-Head, Talent
Rick Greenstein . . . . .Sr. Partner/VP, Comedy/Personal Appearance
Richard Arlook . . . . .Partner/Head, Motion Picture Literary
Lorrie Bartlett . . . . .Partner, Talent
David DeCamillo . . . . .Partner/Co-Head, Talent
Jack Dytman . . . . .Partner/Sr. VP, Literary
Chuck James . . . . .Partner, Talent
Ken Kaplan . . . . .Partner, Talent
Gary Loder . . . . .Partner/Sr. VP, Head, TV Literary
Frank Wuliger . . . . .Partner, Literary
Stephen M. Kravit . . . . .Executive VP, Business Affairs
Matthew Blake . . . . .VP, Comedy/Personal Appearance
Rob Golenberg . . . . .VP, Head, TV Packaging
Barbara Halperin . . . . .VP, Below-the-Line
Abram Nalibotsky .VP/Co-Head, Talent
Amy Schiffman . . . . .VP, Books & Literary Properties
Ethan Antonucci . . . . .Literary
John Bauman . . . . .TV Literary
Todd Christopher . . . . .TV Literary
Jennifer Craig . . . . .Talent
Douglas Edley . . . . .Comedy/Personal Appearance
Lynn Fimberg . . . . .TV Literary
Chris Fioto . . . . .Talent
Carlos Gonzalez . . . . .Talent
Lee Keele . . . . .Literary
David Kopple . . . . .Literary
Barry Kotler . . . . .TV Literary
Bradley Lefler . . . . .Talent
Sandra Lucchesi . . . . .Literary
Brett Norensberg . . . . .Talent
Greg Pedicin . . . . .Literary
Sandy Pepe . . . . .Reality TV
Melanie Ramsayer . . . . .Below-the-Line/Literary
Amy Retzinger . . . . .TV Literary
Paul Rosicker . . . . .Talent
Sara Sheragy . . . . .Comedy/Personal Appearance
Sarah Shyn . . . . .Talent
Bernie Spektor . . . . .Comedy
Nate Steadman . . . . .Talent
Alex Yarosh . . . . .Talent
Warren Zavala . . . . .Talent
Jonathan Zimelis . . . . .TV Literary
Steve Feldman . . . . .Sr. VP, Gersh Sports
Toi Cook . . . . .Sr. VP, Business Development, Gersh Sports
Josh Luchs . . . . .VP, Gersh Sports
Elita T. Bray . .Director, Player Public Relations & Marketing, Gersh Sports
Steve Rossmann . . . . .Marketing & New Media

THE GERSH AGENCY (NEW YORK)
41 Madison Ave., 33rd Fl.
New York, NY 10010
PHONE 212-997-1818
FAX 212-391-8459
WEB SITE . . . . .www.gershagency.com
TYPES   Below-the-Line Talent - Commercial Talent
                         - Film/TV Talent - Literary Talent - Music
                         Talent - Talent & Literary Packaging -
                         Theatre Talent
AFFILIATIONS   AEA - AFTRA - DGA - SAG - WGA
REPRESENTS   Actors - Book Authors - Comedians -
                         Directors - Producers - Screenwriters - TV
                         Writers

William Butler .Sr. Partner/VP/Talent
John Buzzetti . . . . .Partner/Literary/Theatrical
Stephen Hirsh . . . . .Partner/Talent
Rhonda Price . . . . .Partner/Talent
Earl Penney . . . . . . .Administration/Office Manager/Human Resources
Christopher Highland . . . . .Assistant to William Butler
Kara Baker-Young . . . . .Below-the-Line/Film/TV
Randi Goldstein . . . . .Talent
Jason Gutman . . . . .Talent
Peter Hagan .Literary/Theatrical
Joyce Ketay .Literary/Theatrical
Jennifer Konowal . . . . .Talent
Carl Mulert .Literary/Theatrical
Lindsay Porter . . . . .Talent
Sarah Self . . . . .Literary
Sally Ware . . . . .Talent
Scott Yoselow . . . . .Literary/Below-the-Line/Theatrical
Kyetay Beckner .Talent Coordinator
Adam Draves . . . . .Assistant to Kara Baker-Young
Chris Eleftheriades . . . . .Assistant to Jason Gutman
Christy Franklin . . . . .Assistant to Stephen Hirsh
Joshua Harmon . . . . .Assistant to Peter Hagan
Ernie Klein . . . . .Assistant to Jennifer Konowal
Sara Lichterman . . . . .Assistant to Sally Ware
Alex Reveliotty . . . . .Assistant to Scott Yoselow
Joseph Rosswog . . . . .Assistant to John Buzzetti
Carrie Sansone . . . . .Assistant to Carl Mulert
Jessica Sarbo . . . . .Assistant to Joyce Ketay
Sam Sibble . . . . .Assistant to Lindsay Porter

GESTE, INC.
3366 Wichita Falls Ave.
Simi Valley, CA 93063
PHONE 805-527-2680
FAX 801-416-5376
EMAIL . . . . .gesteinc@aol.com
TYPES   Literary Talent
REPRESENTS   Composers - Producers - Screenwriters
SUBMISSION POLICY   Query first by email; Do not call
COMMENTS   Assists producers in seeking funding;
                         Affiliated with ATAS

Norma Brody . . . . .President

GILLA ROOS, LTD.
16 W. 22nd St., 3rd Fl.
New York, NY 10010
PHONE 212-727-7820
FAX 212-727-7833
EMAIL .talent@gillaroos.com
WEB SITE . . . . .www.gillaroos.com
TYPES   Commercial Talent - Film/TV Talent -
                           Modeling Talent
AFFILIATIONS   AEA - AFTRA - SAG
REPRESENTS   Actors - Children - Musical Theatre
                           Performers - Print Models - Runway Models
                           - Teens/Young Adults
SUBMISSION POLICY   Mail photo and resumé; Do not call or visit
COMMENTS   All types, ages and ethnicities

David Roos . . . . .President
Nigel Pembroke-Sloan . . . . .Director, Fashion Division
Ramona Pitera . . . . .Director, Adult Print, On Camera
Alison Swift . . . . .Director, Print, Kids, On Camera
Jillian Hassett . . . . .Adult Commercial Print Agent
Laura Hearn . . . . .Agent, Adult Print/On-Camera
Marvin A. Josephson . . . . .Motion Pictures/TV/Theatre
Evelyn Rijos-Ortiz . . . . .Agent, Fashion Division
Ninna Sexsmith .Agent, Children

THE GLICK AGENCY, LLC
1250 Sixth St., Ste. 100
Santa Monica, CA 90401
PHONE 310-593-6500
FAX 310-593-6505
TYPES   Film/TV Talent - Literary Talent
AFFILIATIONS   AFTRA - ATA - DGA - WGA
REPRESENTS   Actors - Directors - Producers -
                           Screenwriters - TV Writers

Steve Glick . . . . .Agent
Barbara Pollans .Executive Assistant

GLOBAL ARTISTS AGENCY
1648 N. Wilcox Ave.
Los Angeles, CA 90028
PHONE 323-836-0320
FAX 323-836-0325
EMAIL . . . . .assistant@globalartistsagency.net
WEB SITE . . . . .www.globalartistsagency.net
TYPES   Film/TV Talent - Literary Talent - Theatre
                           Talent
AFFILIATIONS   AFTRA - ATA
REPRESENTS   Actors - Comedians - Directors -
                           Screenwriters - Teens/Young Adults - TV
                           Writers
SUBMISSION POLICY   Unsolicited material not accepted

April Lim . . . . .Agent
Monica Barkett . . . . .Agent
Angela Hutchison . . . . .Assistant

MICHELLE GORDON & ASSOCIATES
260 S. Beverly Dr., Ste. 308
Beverly Hills, CA 90212
PHONE 310-246-9930
TYPES   Commercial Talent - Film/TV Talent -
                           Literary Talent - Theatre Talent
AFFILIATIONS   AEA - AFTRA - SAG
REPRESENTS   Actors - Screenwriters
SUBMISSION POLICY   Industry referral only and mail only
COMMENTS   Established talent with prior lead roles in
                           feature films or series only; Eighteen years
                           old and up, all ethnicities welcome

Michelle Gordon .Owner/Talent Agent

GORFAINE/SCHWARTZ AGENCY, INC.
4111 W. Alameda Ave., Ste. 509
Burbank, CA 91505
PHONE 818-260-8500
FAX 818-260-8522
WEB SITE . . . . .www.gsamusic.com
TYPES   Music Talent
REPRESENTS   Composers - Music Artists - Music
                           Producers - Songwriters

Michael Gorfaine .Partner/Agent
Samuel H. Schwartz . . . . .Partner/Agent
Maria Machado . . . . .Agent
Cheryl Tiano . . . . .Agent

GRAHAM AGENCY
311 W. 43rd St.
New York, NY 10036
PHONE 212-489-7730
TYPES   Literary Talent - Theatre Talent
AFFILIATIONS   WGA
REPRESENTS   Playwrights
SUBMISSION POLICY   Query by mail only

Earl Graham . . . . .Owner/Agent

GRANT, SAVIC, KOPALOFF AND ASSOCIATES
6399 Wilshire Blvd., Ste. 414
Los Angeles, CA 90048
PHONE 323-782-1854
FAX 323-782-1877
EMAIL .contact@gsktalent.com
WEB SITE . . . . .www.gsktalent.com
TYPES   Below-the-Line Talent - Film/TV Talent -
                           Literary Talent
AFFILIATIONS   AFTRA - DGA - SAG - WGA
REPRESENTS   Actors - Cinematographers - Directors -
                           Film Editors - Producers - Production
                           Designers - Screenwriters - TV Writers
COMMENTS   Also represents costume designers, line
                           producers/UPMs, VFX producers/supervi-
                           sors and assistant directors

Susan Grant . . . . .Partner/Agent, Below-the-Line/Literary
Ivana Savic . . . . .Partner/Agent, Below-the-Line
Larry Metzger . . . . .Agent, Talent

ASHLEY GRAYSON LITERARY AGENCY
1342 18th St.
San Pedro, CA 90732
PHONE 310-514-0267
FAX 310-514-1148
EMAIL . . . . .graysonagent@earthlink.net
TYPES   Literary Talent
AFFILIATIONS   AAR
REPRESENTS   Book Authors
SUBMISSION POLICY   Query first with first ten pages of a novel
                           and short synopsis; No screenplays or
                           poetry

Ashley Grayson . . . . .Agent

AGENTS

SANFORD J. GREENBURGER ASSOCIATES
55 Fifth Ave., 15th Fl.
New York, NY 10003
PHONE 212-206-5600
FAX 212-463-8718
WEB SITE . . . . .www.greenburger.com
TYPES . . . . Literary Talent
AFFILIATIONS . . . . AAR
REPRESENTS . . . . Book Authors

Francis Greenburger . . . . .Owner
Heide Lange . . . . .VP/Literary Agent
Matthew Bialer . . . . .Literary Agent
Tricia Davey . . . . .Literary Agent
Faith Hamlin . . . . .Literary Agent
Jeremy Katz . . . . .Literary Agent
Daniel Mandel . . . . .Literary Agent
Peter McGuigan . . . . .Literary Agent
Carol Frederick . . . . .Foreign Scout

GREENE & ASSOCIATES
190 N. Canon Dr., Ste. 200
Beverly Hills, CA 90210
PHONE 310-550-9333
FAX 310-550-9334
TYPES . . . . Commercial Talent - Film/TV Talent -
                        Theatre Talent
AFFILIATIONS . . . . AEA - AFTRA - SAG
REPRESENTS . . . . Actors - Comedians - Teens/Young Adults
SUBMISSION POLICY . . . Pictures and resumés by industry referral
                        only

Michael Greene .Owner/Agent, Film/TV
Azeem Chiba . . . . .Agent, Film/TV
Joy Keller . . . . .Agent, Film/TV
Abbie Waters . . . . .Agent, Film/TV/Commercials
Jim Lighte . . . . .Assistant to Michael Greene
Jim Victor . . . . .Assistant

GREER LANGE MODEL & TALENT AGENCY, INC.
3 Bala Plaza West, Ste. 201
Bala Cynwyd, PA 19004
PHONE 610-747-0300
FAX 610-747-0330
EMAIL . . . . .info@greerlange.com
WEB SITE . . . . .www.greerlange.com
TYPES . . . . Commercial Talent - Film/TV Talent -
                        Modeling Talent
AFFILIATIONS . . . . AEA - AFTRA - SAG
REPRESENTS . . . . Actors - Print Models - Seniors - Voice-
                        Over Artists

Greer Lange . . . . .Agent

GROSSMAN & JACK TALENT
230 E. Ohio St., Ste. 200
Chicago, IL 60611
PHONE 312-587-1155
FAX 312-587-2122
WEB SITE . . . . .www.grossmanjack.com
TYPES . . . . Commercial Talent - Film/TV Talent -
                        Theatre Talent
AFFILIATIONS . . . . AEA - AFTRA - SAG
REPRESENTS . . . . Actors - Children - Comedians - Infants -
                        Musical Theatre Performers - Print Models -
                        Teens/Young Adults - Voice-Over Artists
SUBMISSION POLICY . . . By mail only

Linda Jack . . . . .Owner/Voice-Over Agent
Mickey Grossman . . . . .Owner/On-Camera Agent
Jenny Knuepfer . . . . .On-Camera Agent
Vanessa Lanier . . . . .Voice-Over Agent
Amie Richardson . . . . .Children's Department
Richard Shoff . . . . .Voice-Over Agent
Nell Wasserstrom . . . . .Agent

THE SUSAN GURMAN AGENCY, LLC
865 West End Ave., Ste. 15-A
New York, NY 10025-8403
PHONE 212-749-4618
FAX 212-864-5055
TYPES . . . . Literary Talent - Music Talent - Theatre
                        Talent
AFFILIATIONS . . . . WGA
REPRESENTS . . . . Composers - Directors - Playwrights
SUBMISSION POLICY . . . Referral only
COMMENTS . . . . Live theatre only; Also reps stage designers
                        and touring stage shows

Susan R. Gurman .Principal/Agent
Kate Prascher . . . . .Associate Agent

THE CHARLOTTE GUSAY LITERARY AGENCY
10532 Blythe Ave.
Los Angeles, CA 90064
PHONE 310-559-0831
FAX 310-559-2639
EMAIL . . . . .gusay1@ca.rr.com
WEB SITE . . . . .www.gusay.com
TYPES . . . . Literary Talent
REPRESENTS . . . . Book Authors - Playwrights - Screenwriters
SUBMISSION POLICY . . . One-page query with SASE only
COMMENTS . . . . Affiliated with Authors Guild and PEN West;
                        Fiction and nonfiction books; Books to film;
                        Young Adult book projects with film poten-
                        tial

Charlotte Gusay . . . . .Owner/Agent

GVA TALENT AGENCY, INC.
9229 Sunset Blvd., Ste. 320
Los Angeles, CA 90069
PHONE 310-278-1310
FAX 310-888-1290
EMAIL .alexstewart@gvatalent.com
TYPES . . . . Film/TV Talent - Theatre Talent
AFFILIATIONS . . . . AEA - AFTRA - ATA - SAG
REPRESENTS . . . . Actors - Directors - Hosts/MCs -
                        Screenwriters
SUBMISSION POLICY . . . Referral only

Geneva V. Bray . . . . .Theatrical/Owner
Brett Carducci . . . . .Theatrical/Television
Tony Martinez . . . . .Theatrical/Television
Gwenn Pepper . . . . .Theatrical/Television
Bradie Steinlauf . . . . .Theatrical/Television
Alex Stewart . . . . .Executive Assistant

GWYN FOXX TALENT AGENCY (GFTA)
3500 W. Olive Ave., Ste. 300
Burbank, CA 91505
PHONE 818-973-2732
FAX 818-973-2779
TYPES . . . . Commercial Talent - Film/TV Talent
AFFILIATIONS . . . . AFTRA - ATA
COMMENTS . . . . Full-Service talent agency

Gwyn Foxx . . . . .Agent

PEGGY HADLEY ENTERPRISES, LTD.
250 W. 57th St., Ste. 2317
New York, NY 10107-2317
PHONE 212-246-2166
EMAIL . . . . .phadleyent@aol.com
TYPES   Film/TV Talent - Theatre Talent
AFFILIATIONS   AEA - AFTRA - SAG
REPRESENTS   Actors - Dancers - Musical Theatre
                        Performers - Seniors

Peggy Hadley . . . . .Owner
Dani Seacrest . . . . .No Title
Marlene Williams . . . . .No Title

BUZZ HALLIDAY & ASSOCIATES
PO Box 481275
Los Angeles, CA 90048
PHONE 310-275-6028
EMAIL . . . . .buzzagent@earthlink.net
TYPES   Film/TV Talent - Theatre Talent
AFFILIATIONS   AEA - AFTRA - ATA
REPRESENTS   Actors - Directors
SUBMISSION POLICY   Do not phone or drop-off; Mail only
COMMENTS   Theatre and musical directors

Buzz Halliday . . . . .President

NEAL HAMIL AGENCY
7887 San Felipe, Ste. 227
Houston, TX 77063
PHONE 713-789-1335
FAX 713-789-6163
EMAIL . . . . .acting@nealhamilmodels.com
WEB SITE . . . . .www.nealhamilagency.com
TYPES   Commercial Talent - Film/TV Talent -
                        Modeling Talent - Talent & Literary
                        Packaging
AFFILIATIONS   AFTRA - SAG
REPRESENTS   Actors - Children - Choreographers -
                        Hosts/MCs - Music Artists - Print Models -
                        Runway Models - Teens/Young Adults -
                        Voice-Over Artists
SUBMISSION POLICY   Send non-returnable photo or headshot
                        and resumé or submit via email

Jeff Shell . . . . .Director
Ally Shell . . . . .Booking/Placement

THE MITCHELL J. HAMILBURG AGENCY
149 S. Barrington Ave., #732
Los Angeles, CA 90049
PHONE 310-471-4024
FAX 310-471-9588
TYPES   Literary Talent
AFFILIATIONS   DGA - SAG - WGA
REPRESENTS   Book Authors - Screenwriters
COMMENTS   MOW writers; Mostly fiction and nonfiction
                        book authors

Michael Hamilburg . . . . .Principal/Literary
Joanie Kern . . . . .Principal/Literary

HANNS WOLTERS INTERNATIONAL, INC.
211 E. 43rd St., Ste. 505
New York, NY 10017
PHONE 212-714-0100
FAX 212-643-1412
EMAIL . . . . .hannsw@aol.com
TYPES   Below-the-Line Talent - Commercial Talent
                        - Film/TV Talent - Literary Talent - Theatre
                        Talent
AFFILIATIONS   AEA - SAG
REPRESENTS   Actors - Broadcast Journalists/Newscasters
                        - Comedians - Directors - Hosts/MCs -
                        Musical Theatre Performers - Playwrights -
                        Producers - Screenwriters - Seniors -
                        Teens/Young Adults - TV Writers - Variety
                        Artists - Voice-Over Artists
COMMENTS   Specializes in foreign talent, offbeat New
                        York talent and film financing; Represents
                        German Film Service & Marketing GmbH

Oliver Mahrdt . . . . .Owner
Bill Duey . . . . .Assistant

HARDEN-CURTIS ASSOCIATES
850 Seventh Ave., Ste. 903
New York, NY 10019
PHONE 212-977-8502
FAX 212-977-8420
WEB SITE . . . . .www.hardencurtis.com
TYPES   Film/TV Talent - Literary Talent - Theatre
                        Talent
AFFILIATIONS   AEA - AFTRA - ATA
REPRESENTS   Actors - Choreographers - Composers -
                        Dancers - Directors - Musical Theatre
                        Performers - Playwrights - Screenwriters -
                        TV Writers

Nancy Curtis . . . . .Owner
Mary Harden . . . . .Owner
Michael Kirsten . . . . .Agent
Diane Riley . . . . .Agent
Scott D. Edwards . . . . .Agent
Joanna Brett Bell . . . . .Assistant
Sarah McLellan . . . . .Assistant
Amanda Reeves . . . . .Assistant

HARMONY ARTISTS, INC. artists' managers

HARMONY ARTISTS
8455 Beverly Blvd., Ste. 400
Los Angeles, CA 90048
PHONE 323-655-5007
FAX 323-655-5154
EMAIL . . . . .contact_us@harmonyartists.com
WEB SITE . . . . .www.harmonyartists.com
TYPES   Commercial Talent - Film/TV Talent - Music
                        Talent - Theatre Talent
REPRESENTS   Dancers - Hosts/MCs - Magicians - Music
                        Artists - Musical Theatre Performers -
                        Variety Artists

Mike Dixon . . . . .Agent/President
Jerry Ross . . . . .Agent/VP
Adrienne Crane . . . . .Agent

THE JOY HARRIS LITERARY AGENCY
156 Fifth Ave., Ste. 617
New York, NY 10010
PHONE 212-924-6269
FAX 212-924-6609
TYPES   Literary Talent
AFFILIATIONS   AAR
REPRESENTS   Book Authors
SUBMISSION POLICY   Does not accept screenplay submissions

Joy Harris . . . . .President (joyharris@jhlitagent.com)
Adam Reed . . . . .Assistant to Joy Harris (adamreed@jhlitagent.com)

HARTIG HILEPO AGENCY, LTD.
54 W. 21st St., Ste. 610
New York, NY 10010
PHONE 212-929-1772
FAX 212-929-1266
EMAIL . . . . .info@hartighilepo.com
TYPES   Film/TV Talent - Theatre Talent
AFFILIATIONS   AEA - AFTRA - SAG
REPRESENTS   Actors

Paul Hilepo . . . . .Owner/Agent
Nancy Clarkin . . . . .Agent
Liz Rosier . . . . .Agent

JOHN HAWKINS & ASSOCIATES
71 W. 23rd St., Ste. 1600
New York, NY 10010
PHONE 212-807-7040
FAX 212-807-9555
WEB SITE . . . . .www.jhalit.com
TYPES   Literary Talent
AFFILIATIONS   AAR
REPRESENTS   Book Authors

John Hawkins . . . . .Owner/Agent
Warren Frazier . . . . .Agent
Anne Hawkins . . . . .Agent
William Reiss . . . . .Agent
Moses Cardona . . . . .Agent

HAYS MEDIA LLC
59 Stratford Ln.
Hastings-on-Hudson, NY 10706
PHONE 914-478-5110/323-377-6230
FAX 914-478-4899
EMAIL . . . . .tim@haysmedia.net
SECOND EMAIL . . . . .chuck@haysmedia.net
WEB SITE . . . . .www.haysmedia.net
TYPES   Commercial Talent - Literary Talent - Talent
                          & Literary Packaging
REPRESENTS   Book Authors - Screenwriters -
                          Speakers/Lecturers - Sports Personalities
SUBMISSION POLICY   Query first by USPS or email

Tim Hays . . . . .President
Chuck Novack . . . . .VP, West Coast

BEVERLY HECHT AGENCY
3500 W. Olive Ave., Ste. 1180
Burbank, CA 91505
PHONE 818-559-5600
FAX 818-559-7485
WEB SITE .www.beverlyhecht.com
TYPES   Commercial Talent - Film/TV Talent
AFFILIATIONS   AFTRA - SAG - WGA
REPRESENTS   Actors - Children - Comedians -
                          Teens/Young Adults
SUBMISSION POLICY   New talent encouraged to send picture and
                          resumé; Do not call
COMMENTS   Talent ages six and up

Teresa Valente . . . . .Owner/Agent
Mary Dangerfield . . . . .Commercial & Print
Robert Depp . . . . .Theatrical Agent
Samantha Weisman . . . . .Jr. Agent, Theatrical

HENDERSON/HOGAN AGENCY
850 Seventh Ave., Ste. 1003
New York, NY 10019
PHONE 212-765-5190/310-854-0160
FAX 212-586-2855/310-854-0794
EMAIL . . . . .info@hendersonhogan.com
TYPES   Commercial Talent - Film/TV Talent -
                          Literary Talent - Music Talent - Theatre
                          Talent
AFFILIATIONS   AEA - AFM - AFTRA - AGVA - ATA - SAG
REPRESENTS   Actors - Comedians - Dancers - Hosts/MCs
                          - Musical Theatre Performers
SUBMISSION POLICY   West Coast office: 8929 Wilshire Blvd.,
                          Ste. 312, Beverly Hills, CA 90211
COMMENTS   No children under twelve

E. Jerry Hogan . . . . .Principal/Advisor
George Lutsch . . . . .President
Alex Butler . . . . .Agent
David Cash . . . . .Agent
Peter Kaiser . . . . .Agent
Fran Tolstonog . . . . .Agent
Jameson Lamarca . . . . .Assistant

JEFF HERMAN AGENCY, LLC
PO Box 1522
Stockbridge, MA 01262
PHONE 413-298-0077
FAX 413-298-8188
EMAIL . . . . .jeff@jeffherman.com
WEB SITE . . . . .www.jeffherman.com
TYPES   Literary Talent
REPRESENTS   Book Authors
SUBMISSION POLICY   Query letter with SASE
COMMENTS   Subjects: self-help, how-to, nonfiction, spir-
                          itual, business

Jeff Herman . . . . .Owner/Agent
Deborah Herman . . . . .Agent, Psychology/Spirituality

SUSAN HERNER RIGHTS AGENCY
PO Box 57
Pound Ridge, NY 10576
PHONE 914-234-2864
FAX 914-234-2866
EMAIL . . . . .sherneragency@optonline.net
TYPES   Literary Talent
REPRESENTS   Book Authors
COMMENTS   Licenses film rights to books

Susan Herner . . . . .President

HERVEY/GRIMES TALENT AGENCY
10561 Missouri Ave., Ste. 2
Los Angeles, CA 90025
PHONE 310-475-2010/818-340-8402
FAX 310-475-5851
TYPES   Commercial Talent - Film/TV Talent -
                         Modeling Talent - Theatre Talent
AFFILIATIONS   AFTRA - SAG
REPRESENTS   Actors - Children - Comedians -
                         Hosts/MCs - Print Models - Seniors -
                         Teens/Young Adults - Voice-Over Artists
SUBMISSION POLICY   No unsolicited tapes

Pam Grimes . . . . .Agent
Marsha Hervey . . . . .Agent
Amy B. Karlin . . . . .Associate
Susannah Brown . . . . .Associate

DANIEL HOFF AGENCY
5455 Wilshire Blvd., Ste. 1100
Los Angeles, CA 90036
PHONE 323-932-2500
FAX 323-932-2501
WEB SITE . . . . .www.danielhoffagency.com
TYPES   Commercial Talent - Film/TV Talent -
                         Modeling Talent - Music Talent - Theatre
                         Talent
AFFILIATIONS   AEA - AFM - AFTRA - SAG
REPRESENTS   Actors - Children - Comedians - Dancers -
                         Infants - Music Artists - Musical Theatre
                         Performers - Print Models - Runway Models
                         - Seniors - Teens/Young Adults - Voice-
                         Over Artists

Daniel Hoff .Owner/Commercial & Print Agent
Nancy Abt . . . . .Head Motion Picture & Musical Theatre Agent
Debra Manners . . . . .Head Youth Agent
Jarett Wilkins . . . . .Motion Picture Agent
Lynda McCarrell . . . . .Voice-Over/Department Head
Laura Molina .Assistant to Daniel Hoff
Anna Leigh Simmons . . . . .Assistant to Daniel Hoff
Annie Mayo .Assistant to Nancy Abt
Mari Ueda . . . . .Assistant to Debra Manners
Kyra Dixon . . . . .Assistant to Jarett Wilkens
Barbara Niles . . . . .Assistant

BARBARA HOGENSON AGENCY, INC.
165 West End Ave., Ste. 19-C
New York, NY 10023
PHONE 212-874-8084
FAX 212-362-3011
AFFILIATIONS   AAR - WGA
REPRESENTS   Book Authors - Directors - Playwrights
SUBMISSION POLICY   Query letter with SASE; No manuscripts;
                         Not accepting actor submissions

Barbara Hogenson . . . . .Owner/Agent
Nicole Verity . . . . .Contract Manager

HOHMAN MAYBANK LIEB
9229 Sunset Blvd., Ste. 700
Los Angeles, CA 90069
PHONE 310-274-4600
FAX 310-274-4741
EMAIL . . . . .info@hmllit.com
WEB SITE . . . . .www.hmllit.com
TYPES   Literary Talent
AFFILIATIONS   DGA - WGA
REPRESENTS   Directors - Screenwriters
SUBMISSION POLICY   Referral only

Robert Hohman . . . . .Partner/Agent
Bayard Maybank . . . . .Partner/Agent
Devra Lieb . . . . .Partner/Agent

HOLLANDER TALENT GROUP
14011 Ventura Blvd., Ste. 202 W
Sherman Oaks, CA 91423
PHONE 818-382-9800
TYPES   Commercial Talent - Film/TV Talent
AFFILIATIONS   AFTRA - SAG
REPRESENTS   Actors - Children - Voice-Over Artists

Vivian Hollander . . . . .Agent, Voice-Over/Theatrical/Commercial

HOLLYWOOD VIEW
5255 Veronica St.
Los Angeles, CA 90008
PHONE 323-290-0950
EMAIL .dj@hollywood-view.com
WEB SITE .www.hollywood-view.com
TYPES   Below-the-Line Talent - Literary Talent -
                         Talent & Literary Packaging
AFFILIATIONS   DGA - SAG - WGA
REPRESENTS   Book Authors - Directors - Screenwriters -
                         TV Writers
SUBMISSION POLICY   Mail or email queries with loglines only;
                         No phone calls

David J. Freedman . . . . .Agent

Models & Talent Agency

HOP MODELS & TALENT AGENCY
5825 Glenridge Dr., Ste. 2-218
Atlanta, GA 30328
PHONE 404-297-6638/404-297-6738
FAX 404-297-6858
EMAIL . . . . .info@hopmodels.com
WEB SITE . . . . .www.hopmodels.com
TYPES   Below-the-Line Talent - Commercial Talent
                         - Film/TV Talent - Modeling Talent - Theatre
                         Talent
REPRESENTS   Actors - Children - Comedians - Magicians
                         - Print Models - Runway Models -
                         Teens/Young Adults
SUBMISSION POLICY   See Web site for open call details; Do not
                         fax or visit; Accepts photos and resumés by
                         US mail only; Photos non-returnable;
                         Attends showcases
COMMENTS   Boutique agency known for signature style
                         of diverse ethnic and foreign models

Lyndon Winchester . . . . .Director/Agent
Kenea Yancey . . . . .Women's Director
Renee Froboese . . . . .New Faces

HOT SHOT KIDS/TEENS
195 W. Pike St., NW, Ste. 200
Lawrenceville, GA 30045
PHONE 770-237-3245
FAX 770-237-3246
EMAIL .jpervis@bellsouth.net
SECOND EMAIL . . . . .jayme@hotshotkidsinc.net
WEB SITE .www.hotshotkids.net
TYPES | Commercial Talent - Film/TV Talent - Modeling Talent - Theatre Talent
AFFILIATIONS | AFTRA - ATA
REPRESENTS | Actors - Children - Musical Theatre Performers - Print Models - Runway Models - Teens/Young Adults - Voice-Over Artists
SUBMISSION POLICY | See Web site or submit hard copy non-returnable photo, headshot or composite card
COMMENTS | Three to nineteen years old

Joy Pervis . . . . .Owner/Agent
Jayme Osburn . . . . .Agent
Julie Pye . . . . .Assistant/Receptionist

HOTCHKISS & ASSOCIATES
611 Broadway, Ste. 741
New York, NY 10012
PHONE 212-253-0161
FAX 212-253-0519
TYPES | Literary Talent
REPRESENTS | Book Authors - Screenwriters

Jody Hotchkiss . . . . .Agent
Sean T. Daily . . . . .Associate

THE HOUSE OF REPRESENTATIVES
400 S. Beverly Dr., Ste. 101
Beverly Hills, CA 90212
PHONE 310-772-0772
FAX 310-772-0998
TYPES | Film/TV Talent - Theatre Talent
AFFILIATIONS | AEA - AFTRA - ATA - DGA - SAG
REPRESENTS | Actors - Children - Comedians - Hosts/MCs - Seniors - Teens/Young Adults
SUBMISSION POLICY | Unsealed envelopes; No unsolicited tapes

Pam Braverman . . . . .Agent
Ginger Lawrence . . . . .Agent
Denny Sevier . . . . .Agent
Tim Weissman . . . . .Agent
Matthew Sanchelli . . . . .Assistant

HOWARD TALENT WEST
10657 Riverside Dr.
Toluca Lake, CA 91602
PHONE 818-766-5300
FAX 818-760-3328
EMAIL . . . . .me10u90@pacbell.net
TYPES | Commercial Talent - Film/TV Talent - Theatre Talent
AFFILIATIONS | AEA - AFTRA - ATA - DGA
REPRESENTS | Actors - Children - Comedians - Dancers - Directors - Hosts/MCs - Infants - Print Models - Seniors - Teens/Young Adults
SUBMISSION POLICY | Mail only; Do not follow up

Bonnie Howard . . . . .Owner/Agent, Theatrical Department
Lynn Eriks . . . . .Commercial Department, Youth & Adult

HUDSON AGENCY
3 Travis Ln.
Montrose, NY 10548
PHONE 914-737-1475
FAX 914-736-3064
EMAIL . . . . .hudflicks@juno.com
WEB SITE . . . . .www.hudsonagency.net
TYPES | Literary Talent
AFFILIATIONS | WGA
REPRESENTS | Screenwriters
SUBMISSION POLICY | Does not represent R-rated material or anything to do with the occult; Not taking new clients
COMMENTS | See Web site for credits of represented writers

Susan Giordano . . . . .Agent, Features/TV
Kelly Olenik . . . . .Assistant

THE I GROUP MODEL & TALENT MANAGEMENT
29540 Southfield Rd., Ste. 200
Southfield, MI 48076
PHONE 248-552-8842
FAX 248-552-9866
EMAIL .igroup@theigroup.com
WEB SITE . . . . .www.theigroup.com
TYPES | Commercial Talent - Film/TV Talent - Modeling Talent
AFFILIATIONS | AFTRA - SAG
REPRESENTS | Actors - Broadcast Journalists/Newscasters - Children - Comedians - Hosts/MCs - Infants - Magicians - Martial Artists/Stunts - Print Models - Runway Models - Seniors - Sports Personalities - Teens/Young Adults - Voice-Over Artists
COMMENTS | Auto shows, conventions, corporate, special events, fashion, promotions

Phillip DiMambro . . . . .Owner/Agent
Ryan Hill . . . . .Agent
Tony DiMambro . . . .Director, Talent/Actors/Voice-Over/Print/Sub-Agent
Cyndi Bock . . . . .Film & Broadcast/Sub-Agent
Teresa Omari . . . . .Office Manager
Matthew Ward . . . . .Assistant

IDENTITY TALENT AGENCY
9107 Wilshire Blvd., Ste. 500
Hollywood, CA 90028
PHONE 310-461-1975
EMAIL . . . . .erik@idtalent.com
WEB SITE . . . . .www.idtalent.com
TYPES | Commercial Talent - Film/TV Talent - Modeling Talent - Talent & Literary Packaging
AFFILIATIONS | ATA
REPRESENTS | Actors - Children - Hosts/MCs - Seniors - Speakers/Lecturers - Sports Personalities - Teens/Young Adults
COMMENTS | Product placement and integration; Celebrity appearances and promotion

Erik DeSando . . . . .President
Jimmy Villarreal . . . . .Specialty Talent & Events

IFA TALENT AGENCY
8730 Sunset Blvd., Ste. 490
Los Angeles, CA 90069
PHONE 310-659-5522
FAX 310-659-3344
TYPES   Film/TV Talent - Theatre Talent
AFFILIATIONS   AEA - AFTRA - DGA - SAG - WGA
REPRESENTS   Actors - Directors
SUBMISSION POLICY   No submissions accepted

Ilene Feldman . . . . .Agent
David Lillard . . . . .Agent
Wendy Murphey . . . . .Agent
Christy Hall . . . . .Agent
Toni Zimmerman . . . . .Agent
Scott Benson . . . . .Assistant to Ms. Hall
Tee McKnight . . . . .Assistant to Mr. Lillard
Tara Nostramo . . . . .Assistant to Ms. Feldman
Megan Senior . . . . .Assistant to Ms. Zimmerman
Matt Shepherd . . . . .Assistant to Ms. Murphey

IMAGE MODEL & TALENT
44 W. Flagler St., Ste. 2450
Miami, FL 33130
PHONE 305-375-0448
FAX 305-375-0449
EMAIL .info@imagemodel-talent.com
WEB SITE . . . . .www.imagemodel-talent.com
TYPES   Commercial Talent - Film/TV Talent -
                         Modeling Talent - Music Talent - Theatre
                         Talent
REPRESENTS   Actors - Children - Dancers - Hosts/MCs -
                         Infants - Print Models - Runway Models -
                         Seniors - Teens/Young Adults - Voice-Over
                         Artists

Jerry Babij . . . . .CEO/President
Blake Fisher . . . . .Print
Heidi Rivera . . . . .TV/Film
Joel Woodes . . . . .Director, New Faces
Katia Jiras . . . . .Women's & Men's Board
Dan Nita . . . . .Children's Board
Jose Wong . . . . .Accounting

IMG/BROADCASTING
1640 S. Sepulveda Blvd., Ste. 216
Los Angeles, CA 90025
PHONE 310-966-5940
FAX 310-966-5949
WEB SITE . . . . .www.imgworld.com
TYPES   Commercial Talent - Film/TV Talent -
                         Modeling Talent - Music Talent
REPRESENTS   Book Authors - Broadcast
                         Journalists/Newscasters - Directors -
                         Hosts/MCs - Print Models - Producers -
                         Runway Models - Speakers/Lecturers -
                         Sports Personalities
COMMENTS   Also represents non-scripted producers

Babette Perry . . . . .VP, Broadcasting, West Coast
Julie Fisher . . . . .Sr. Departmental Assistant
Chris Kettler . . . . .Assistant

IMPACT TALENT GROUP
4401 Wilshire Blvd., Ste. 250
Los Angeles, CA 90010
PHONE 323-933-8709
FAX 323-933-8710
TYPES   Film/TV Talent - Music Talent - Theatre
                         Talent
AFFILIATIONS   AEA - AFTRA - SAG
REPRESENTS   Actors - Children - Comedians - Sports
                         Personalities - Teens/Young Adults
SUBMISSION POLICY   Mail only; No phone calls

Sheila Morrow .Sr. Youth Agent
Sheba L. Williams . . . . .Principal Agent

IMPERIUM 7 TALENT AGENCY (i7)
9911 W. Pico Blvd., Ste. 1290
Los Angeles, CA 90035
PHONE 310-203-9009
FAX 310-203-9099
EMAIL . . . . .admin@imperium-7.com
TYPES   Commercial Talent - Film/TV Talent -
                         Theatre Talent
AFFILIATIONS   AFTRA - SAG
REPRESENTS   Actors - Broadcast Journalists/Newscasters
                         - Children - Comedians - Hosts/MCs -
                         Music Artists - Musical Theatre Performers -
                         Seniors - Speakers/Lecturers - Sports
                         Personalities - Teens/Young Adults - Voice-
                         Over Artists
SUBMISSION POLICY   Send headshot, resumé and demo CD by
                         US Mail

Joy Tom . . . . .Agent
Steven Neibert . . . . .Agent
Marni Anhalt . . . . .Jr. Agent
Cary DeGraff . . . . .Assistant
Chase Heinrich . . . . .Assistant
Alanna Miller . . . . .Assistant

INDEPENDENT ARTISTS AGENCY INC.
330 W. 38th St., Ste. 709
New York, NY 10018
PHONE 646-486-3332
TYPES   Film/TV Talent - Theatre Talent
AFFILIATIONS   AEA - AFTRA - SAG
REPRESENTS   Actors - Comedians - Dancers - Music
                         Artists - Runway Models - Seniors -
                         Teens/Young Adults
SUBMISSION POLICY   Mail only; No calls or drop-ins
COMMENTS   Tapes only by request

Jack Menashe .Agent/Owner
Cyd Levin . . . . .Agent
Lauren Ress . . . . .Agent, Commercials
Clay Smith . . . . .Agent
Rachel L. Cohen . . . . .Assistant

INDEPENDENT ARTISTS AGENCY, INC.
9601 Wilshire Blvd., Ste. 750
Beverly Hills, CA 90210
PHONE 310-550-5000
FAX 310-550-5005
TYPES   Commercial Talent - Modeling Talent
AFFILIATIONS   AFTRA - ATA
REPRESENTS   Actors - Comedians - Print Models - Voice-
                         Over Artists
SUBMISSION POLICY   Mail only; No drop-ins

Laura Fogelman . . . .President/Agent, Celebrity/On-Camera/Voice-Over
Beverly Kline . . . . .Sr. VP/Agent, Celebrity/On-Camera/Voice-Over
Jenine Leigh . . . . .Agent, On-Camera/Beauty
Elizabeth Pine . . . . .Booth Director
Dhyani Niedelman . . . . .Assistant
Erica Powell . . . . .Assistant

INGBER & ASSOCIATES
274 Madison Ave., Ste. 1104
New York, NY 10016
PHONE 212-889-9450
TYPES   Commercial Talent
AFFILIATIONS   AEA - AFTRA - SAG
REPRESENTS   Actors - Voice-Over Artists
SUBMISSION POLICY   Photos and resumés by mail only; No calls
                         or drop-ins
COMMENTS   Industrials

Carole Ingber . . . . .Commercials/Voice-Over/Industrials
Amy Davidson . . . . .Commercials/Voice-Over/Industrials

INKWELL MANAGEMENT
521 Fifth Ave., 26th Fl.
New York, NY 10175
PHONE 212-922-3500
FAX 212-922-0535
WEB SITE . . . . .www.inkwellmanagement.com
TYPES   Literary Talent
REPRESENTS   Book Authors
SUBMISSION POLICY   Query letter, outline or synopsis of book
                         and SASE

Michael Carlisle . . . . .Agent/Co-Owner
Richard Pine . . . . .Agent/Co-Owner
Kim Witherspoon . . . . .Agent/Co-Owner
Catherine Drayton . . . . .Agent
David Forrer . . . . .Agent
George Lucas . . . . .Agent
Pilar Queen . . . . .Agent
Alexis Hurley . . . . .Rights Director
Nathaniel Jacks . . . . .Rights Associate
Celine Texler-Rose . . . . .Contracts Manager
Jenny Witherell . . . . .Business Manager

INNOVATIVE ARTISTS (CHICAGO)
541 N. Fairbanks Ct., 27th Fl.
Chicago, IL 60611
PHONE 312-832-1113
FAX 312-832-1124
EMAIL . . . . .vu@voicesunlimited.com
WEB SITE . . . . .www.voicesunlimited.com
TYPES   Commercial Talent
AFFILIATIONS   AFTRA - SAG
REPRESENTS   Voice-Over Artists
SUBMISSION POLICY   Send CD with address and phone number;
                         No walk-ins

Sharon Wottrich . . . . .President/Agent
Linda Bracilano . . . . .Agent
Sue Geraghty . . . . .Manager
Laurie Lambert . . . . .Agent
Sandy Norman . . . . .Agent

INNOVATIVE ARTISTS (LOS ANGELES)
1505 Tenth St.
Santa Monica, CA 90401
PHONE 310-656-0400
FAX 310-656-0456
TYPES   Below-the-Line Talent - Commercial Talent
                         - Film/TV Talent - Literary Talent
AFFILIATIONS   AEA - AFTRA - ATA - DGA - WGA
REPRESENTS   Actors - Broadcast Journalists/Newscasters
                         - Children - Directors - Producers -
                         Screenwriters - Teens/Young Adults - TV
                         Writers - Voice-Over Artists

Scott Harris . . . . .Owner
Debbie Haeusler . . . . .Head, Below-the-Line
Marcia Hurwitz . . . . .Head, Commercials & Voice-Over
Amy Abell . . . . .Young Talent
Marci Alter-Polzin . . . . .Commercials & Voice-Over
Abby Bluestone . . . . .Young Talent
Bruce Brown . . . . .Literary
Kim Byrd . . . . .Beauty
Kimberly Carver . . . . .Literary
Jimmy Cundiff . . . . .Talent
Thomas Cushing . . . . .Talent
Michele De La Riva . . . . .Beauty
Nevin Dolcefino . . . . .Talent
Heather Griffith . . . . .Below-the-Line
Robert Haas . . . . .Talent
Melissa Hirschenson . . . . .Talent
Jonathan Howard . . . . .Talent
Stephen LaManna . . . . .Talent
David Lederman . . . . .Talent
Jeff Mahoney . . . . .Below-the-Line
Michael McConnell . . . . .Talent
Craig Mizrahi . . . . .Below-the-Line
Steve Muller . . . . .Talent
Nancy Nigrosh . . . . .Literary
Mike Packenham . . . . .Talent
Ben Press . . . . .Talent
David Rose . . . . .Talent
Art Rutter . . . . .Literary
Luanne Salandy-Regis . . . . .Commercials & Voice-Over
Shari Shankewitz .Below-the-Line
Craig Shapiro . . . . .Talent
Marnie Sparer . . . . .Talent
Jim Stein . . . . .Literary
Brad Sterling . . . . .Literary
Cher Van Amburg . . . . .Commercials
Louise S. Ward . . . . .Talent
Sheila Wenzel . . . . .Talent

AGENTS

INNOVATIVE ARTISTS (NEW YORK)
235 Park Avenue South, 7th Fl.
New York, NY 10003
PHONE 212-253-6900
FAX 212-253-1198
TYPES   Commercial Talent - Film/TV Talent -
                         Theatre Talent
AFFILIATIONS   AEA - AFTRA - ATA - SAG
REPRESENTS   Actors - Children - Teens/Young Adults -
                         Voice-Over Artists
SUBMISSION POLICY   No drop-offs

Gary Gersh ....Talent
Brian C. Davidson ....Talent
Kenneth Lee ....Talent
Allison Levy ....Talent
Lisa Lieberman ....Talent
Bill Veloric ....Talent
Ali Denholtz ....Young Talent
Jana Kogen ....Young Talent
Marla Haut ....On-Camera
Michael Shera ....On-Camera
Heather Stewart ....On-Camera
Barbara Coleman ....Young Talent, On-Camera
Maury DiMauro ....Beauty
Ross Haime ....Beauty
Bonnie Osborn ....Beauty
Nipa Parikh ....Beauty
Allan G. Duncan ....Voice-Over
Eileen Schellhorn ....Voice-Over
Debra Sherry ....Voice-Over
Jewel Chandler ....Voice-Over/Promos
Shari Hoffman ....Voice-Over/Promos
Max Roman ....Feature Film Literary
Lola Richardson ....Business Affairs

INTERNATIONAL ARTISTS GROUP, INC.
2121 N. Bayshore Dr., Ste. 1007
Miami, FL 33137
PHONE 305-576-0001
TYPES   Commercial Talent - Film/TV Talent -
                         Literary Talent - Modeling Talent - Talent &
                         Literary Packaging - Theatre Talent
REPRESENTS   Actors - Broadcast Journalists/Newscasters
                         - Children - Comedians - Dancers -
                         Directors - Martial Artists/Stunts - Print
                         Models - Screenwriters - Sports
                         Personalities - TV Writers - Voice-Over
                         Artists
COMMENTS   Focus on Hispanic talent; Crossover;
                         Novellas

Meris Zittman ....President

INTERNATIONAL CREATIVE MANAGEMENT, INC. - ICM (LOS ANGELES)
10250 Constellation Blvd.
Los Angeles, CA 90067
PHONE 310-550-4000
FAX 310-550-4100
WEB SITE ....www.icmtalent.com
TYPES   Below-the-Line Talent - Commercial Talent
                         - Film/TV Talent - Literary Talent - Music
                         Talent - Talent & Literary Packaging -
                         Theatre Talent
AFFILIATIONS   AEA - AFM - AFTRA - AGVA - ATA - DGA -
                         WGA
REPRESENTS   Actors - Book Authors - Broadcast
                         Journalists/Newscasters - Children -
                         Cinematographers - Comedians -
                         Composers - Dancers - Directors -
                         Hosts/MCs - Interactive Game Developers
                         - Music Artists - Music Producers - Music
                         Supervisors - Musical Theatre Performers -
                         Playwrights - Producers - Production
                         Designers - Screenwriters -
                         Speakers/Lecturers - Sports Personalities -
                         Teens/Young Adults - TV Writers - Variety
                         Artists - Voice-Over Artists
COMMENTS   Also affiliated with AGMA

Jeffrey Berg ....Chairman/CEO
Robert Broder ....Vice Chairman
Ed Limato ....Vice Chairman/Co-President
Chris Silbermann ....Co-President/Co-Head, Worldwide TV
Richard B. Levy, Esq. ....Chief Business Development Officer/
                              General Counsel, Office of the Chairman
David Shane ....Sr. VP, Corporate Communications
Karen Abrams ....VP, Human Resources
Greg Chun ....Chief Information Officer
Greg Arvesen ....Head, Finance & Accounting
Lori Sale ....Head, Global Branded Entertainment
John Burnham ......Executive VP/Head, Motion Picture Administration,
                                                    West Coast
Dan Donahue ....Executive VP
Elliot Webb ....Executive VP
Carol Bodie ....Head, Motion Picture Talent
Hal Sadoff ....Head, International/Independent Film Division
Brian Bunnin ....Motion Picture Talent
Carter Cohn ....Motion Picture Talent
Joe Funicello ....VP, Motion Picture Talent
Jack Gilardi ....Executive VP, Motion Picture Talent
Guido Giordano ....Motion Picture Talent
Chris Hart ....Motion Picture Talent
Toni Howard ....Executive VP, Motion Picture Talent
Richard Konigsberg ....Motion Picture Talent
Matt Eskander ....Motion Picture Talent
Martha Luttrell ....Sr. VP, Motion Picture Talent
Andrea Nelson Meigs ....Motion Picture Talent
Jim Osborne ....Motion Picture Talent
Scott Schachter ....Motion Picture Talent
Risa Shapiro ....Sr. VP, Motion Picture Talent
Evan Tripoli ....Motion Picture Talent
Meredith Wechter ....Motion Picture Talent
Eddy Yablans ....Executive VP, Motion Picture Talent
Lars Theriot ....Sr. Data Coordinator, Motion Picture Department
Doug MacLaren ....Co-Head, Motion Picture Literary
Nick Reed ....Co-Head, Motion Picture Literary
Ron Bernstein ....VP, Sr. Subsidiary Rights, Motion Picture Literary
Nicole Clemens ....Motion Picture Literary
Harley Copen ....Motion Picture Literary
Josie Freedman ....Motion Picture Literary
Jenny Fritz ....Motion Picture Literary
Emile Gladstone ....Motion Picture Literary
Todd Hoffman ....Motion Picture Literary

(Continued)

INTERNATIONAL CREATIVE MANAGEMENT, INC. - ICM (LOS ANGELES) (Continued)

Sophy Holodnik .Motion Picture Literary
Josh Hornstock .Motion Picture Literary
Ava Jamshidi . . . . .Motion Picture Literary
Bruce Kaufman .Motion Picture Literary
Brian Levy . . . . .Motion Picture Literary
Eva Lontscharitsch . . . . .Motion Picture Literary
Barbara Mandel .Motion Picture Literary
Dan Rabinow . . . . .Motion Picture Literary
Nathan Ross . . . . .Motion Picture Literary
Brian Sher . . . . .Motion Picture Literary
Ben Smith . . . . .Motion Picture Literary
Paul Alan Smith .Motion Picture Literary
Renee Tab . . . . .Motion Picture Literary
D.J. Talbot . . . . .Motion Picture Literary
David Unger . . . . .Motion Picture Literary
Jessica Lacy . . . . .International & Independent Film
Bic Tran . . . . .International & Independent Film
Paul Hook . . . . .Executive VP/Head, Motion Picture Production
Dan Baime . . . . .Motion Picture Production
Craig Bernstein . . . . .Motion Picture Production
Janet Carol Norton . . . . .Motion Picture Production
Tad Lumpkin . . . . .Motion Picture Production
Tom Marquardt . . . . .Motion Picture Production
Ted Chervin . . . . .Co-Head, Worldwide TV
Bob Levinson . . .Executive VP/Worldwide Head, TV/Head, TV Packaging
Greg Lipstone . . . . .Sr. VP/Head, Reality Packaging & International Format Sales
Steve Wohl   Sr. VP/Head, Reality Packaging & International Format Sales
Leigh Brillstein . . . . .Sr. VP, Head, TV Talent
Brian Mann . . . . .VP, TV Talent
Tom Burke . . . . .TV Talent
Andy Cohen . . . . .TV Talent
Lisa Gallant . . . . .TV Talent
Iris Grossman . . . . .TV Talent
Mike Jelline . . . . .TV Talent
Heather Nunn . . . . .TV Talent
Dar Rollins . . . . .TV Talent
Mickey Berman . . . . .TV Literary
Kevin Crotty . . . . .TV Literary
Carel Cutler . . . . .TV Literary
Sean Freidin . . . . .TV Literary
Mark Gordon . . . . .TV Literary
Robert Lazar . . . . .TV Literary
Burrad Marsh . . . . .TV Literary
Michael Rizzo . . . . .TV Literary
Pete Stone . . . . .TV Literary
Chris von Goetz . . . . .TV Literary
Cindy Mintz . . . . .TV Longform
Greg Shephard . . . . .TV Longform
Susan A. Simons . . . . .Head, TV, Alternative Programming
Michael Kagan . . . . .TV, Alternative Programming
Marc Kamler . . . . .TV, Alternative Programming
Kimberly Oelman . . . . .TV, Alternative Programming
Steve Levine   Executive VP/Head, Comedy & West Coast Music/Concerts
Chris Smith . . . . .VP, Concerts
Dennis Ashley . . . . .Concerts
Marty Beck . . . . .Concerts
Natalka Dudynsky . . . . .Concerts
Rick Farrell . . . . .Concerts
Robert Gibbs . . . . .Concerts
Scott Mantell . . . . .Concerts
Scott Pang . . . . .Concerts
William Rodriguez . . . . .Concerts
Michelle Scarbrough .Concerts
Brice Gaeta . . . . .Composers
Andy Barzvi . . . . .Publications
Nick Khan . . . . .Sports
Jeremy Tefft . . . . .Voice-Over
Karen Sellars . . . . .Head, Celebrity/Endorsement
Jason Pinyan . . . . .Celebrity/Endorsement
Penny Reiss . . . . .Global Branded Entertainment
Randy Smith . . . . .Global Branded Entertainment
Pam Brockie . . . . .Sr. VP/Head, Motion Picture Business Affairs
Michael Tenzer . . . . .Sr. VP/Head, Business Affairs, TV
Janet Kaye . . . . .VP, Business Affairs, TV
Michael Kernan . . . . .VP, Business Affairs, TV
Anne Pedersen . . . . .VP, Business Affairs, TV

(Continued)

INTERNATIONAL CREATIVE MANAGEMENT, INC. - ICM (LOS ANGELES) (Continued)

Michael Runnels . . . . .VP, Business Affairs, Motion Picture Production
Sara Stimac . . . . .VP, Legal Affairs
George Ruiz . . . . .Business Affairs, Motion Pictures
Jacqui Schock . . . . .Business Affairs, Motion Pictures
Cecelia Andrews . . . . .Business Affairs
Robin Weitz . . . . .Corporate Secretary
Joe Friedman . . . . .Controller
Alison Keeny . . . . .Paralegal, Business & Legal Affairs
Erin Oremland . . . . .VP, Contract Administration
Doug Turski . . . . .Director, Tax

INTERNATIONAL CREATIVE MANAGEMENT, INC. - ICM (NEW YORK)

40 W. 57th St.
New York, NY 10019

PHONE	212-556-5600
FAX	212-556-5665
WEB SITE	. . . . .www.icmtalent.com
TYPES	Commercial Talent - Film/TV Talent - Literary Talent - Music Talent - Talent & Literary Packaging - Theatre Talent
AFFILIATIONS	AEA - AFM - AFTRA - AGVA - ATA - DGA - WGA
REPRESENTS	Actors - Book Authors - Broadcast Journalists/Newscasters - Choreographers - Cinematographers - Comedians - Composers - Dancers - Directors - Hosts/MCs - Interactive Game Developers - Music Artists - Music Producers - Music Supervisors - Musical Theatre Performers - Playwrights - Producers - Screenwriters - Speakers/Lecturers - Teens/Young Adults - TV Writers - Variety Artists
COMMENTS	Personal Appearance, Concerts; London office: 4-6 Soho Square, London, W1D 3PZ, United Kingdom, phone: 44-207-432-0800

Esther Newberg . . . . .Co-Head, Publications
Sloan Harris . . . . .Co-Head, Publications
Amanda Urban . . . . .Executive VP, Publications
Sam Cohn . . . . .Vice Chairman/Motion Pictures
Boaty Boatwright .Consultant
Andrea Eastman . . . . .Consultant
Paul Martino .Motion Pictures
Patrick Herold . . . . .Sr. VP, Theater
Mala Mosher . . . . .Theater
Thomas Pearson . . . . .Theater
Lisa Bankoff . . . . .Literary
Herb Cheyette . . . . .Literary
Katherine Cluverius . . . . .Literary
Kristine Dahl . . . . .Literary
Buddy Thomas . . . . .Theater
Elizabeth Farrell . . . . .Literary
Margaret Halton . . . . .Literary, Foreign Rights (London Office)
Elizabeth Iveson . . . . .Literary, Foreign Rights (London Office)
Jennifer Joel . . . . .Literary
Kate Jones . . . . .Literary (London Office)
Jill Jones . . . . .Literary
Pippa Lambert . . . . .TV (London Office)
Kate Lee . . . . .Literary
Daisy Meyrick . . . .(London Office)
Heather Schroder . . . . .Literary
Adam Schweitzer . . . . .Motion Picture Talent
Karolina Sutton . . . .(London Office)
Helen Shabason . . . . .VP, News & Public Affairs
Terry Rhodes . . . . .VP/Head, East Coast Music/Concerts
Craig Bruck . . . . .Concerts
Lucia Chang . . . . .Concerts
Kristine Marshall . . . . .Concerts
Scott Morris . . . . .Concerts
Mark Siegel . . . . .Concerts
Bob Zievers . . . . .Concerts
Mark Cheatham . . . . .VP, Urban Contemporary Music

(Continued)

AGENTS

INTERNATIONAL CREATIVE MANAGEMENT, INC. - ICM
(NEW YORK) (Continued)
Maarten Kooij . . . . .Sr. VP, Business Affairs
John DeLaney . . . . .Business Affairs, Literary
Colin Graham . . . . .Business Affairs, Literary
Steven David . . . . .Business Affairs, Theater

IRISHVOX
149 Washington St., Ste. E
Rutherford, NJ 07070
PHONE .201-340-2110/201-456-2162
FAX 201-683-0217
EMAIL . . . . .irishvox@irishvox.com
SECOND EMAIL . . . . .seanmccarthy@irishvox.com
WEB SITE . . . . .www.irishvox.com
TYPES   Commercial Talent - Theatre Talent
REPRESENTS   Actors - Voice-Over Artists
COMMENTS   Provides access to America's premier Irish
                       voice-over artists

Sean McCarthy . . . . .CEO
Bob Gallico . . . . .Managing Director

JACOB & KOLE AGENCY
c/o Julia Kole
6715 Hollywood Blvd., Ste. 216
Los Angeles, CA 90028
PHONE 323-460-4767
FAX 323-460-4804
EMAIL . . . . .info@jacobandkole.com
WEB SITE . . . . .www.jacobandkole.com
TYPES   Below-the-Line Talent
AFFILIATIONS   ATA
REPRESENTS   Cinematographers - Film Editors -
                       Production Designers
COMMENTS   Commercial Production Designers,
                       Directors of Photography and Costume
                       Designers

Steven Jacob . . . . .Owner
Julia Kole . . . . .Owner
Alex Khan . . . . .Agent
Ian Schluder . . . . .Agent
Namarata Tandon . . . . .Agent

JAMES PETER ASSOCIATES, INC.
PO Box 358
New Canaan, CT 06840
PHONE 203-972-1070
FAX 203-972-1759
EMAIL . . . . .gene_brissie@msn.com
TYPES   Literary Talent
REPRESENTS   Book Authors

Eugene F. Brissie . . . . .President
Bert Holtje . . . . .Agent

JANKLOW & NESBIT ASSOCIATES
445 Park Ave.
New York, NY 10022
PHONE 212-421-1700
FAX 212-980-3671
EMAIL . . . . .postmaster@janklow.com
TYPES   Literary Talent
REPRESENTS   Book Authors
SUBMISSION POLICY   No unsolicited manuscripts or screenplays

Morton L. Janklow . . . . .Sr. Partner
Lynn Nesbit . . . . .Partner
Anne Sibbald . . . . .Sr. VP
Cecile Barendsma . . . . .Agent, Foreign Rights
Tina Bennett . . . . .Agent, Domestic Rights
Priscilla Gilman . . . . .Agent, Domestic Rights
Rebecca Gradinger . . . . .Agent, Domestic Rights
Lucas W. Janklow . . . . .Agent, Domestic Rights
Richard Morris . . . . .Agent, Film/Domestic Subsidiary Rights
Kate Schafer . . . . .Agent, Foreign Rights
Eric Simonoff . . . . .Agent, Domestic Rights
Cullen Stanley . . . . .Agent, Foreign Rights
Dorothy Vincent .Agent, Foreign Rights

JE TALENT, LLC/JE MODEL, INC.
323 Geary St., Ste. 302
San Francisco, CA 94102
PHONE . . . . .415-395-9475 (Talent)/415-395-4777 (Model)
FAX . . . . .415-395-9301(Talent)/415-395-9678 (Model)
WEB SITE . . . . .www.jetalent.com
SECOND WEB SITE . . . . .www.jemodel.com
TYPES   Commercial Talent - Film/TV Talent -
                       Modeling Talent - Theatre Talent
AFFILIATIONS   AEA - AFTRA - SAG
REPRESENTS   Actors - Children - Comedians -
                       Hosts/MCs - Infants - Print Models -
                       Runway Models - Teens/Young Adults -
                       Voice-Over Artists
SUBMISSION POLICY   Modeling submissions can be sent to
                       phillip@jemodel.com; Open calls for
                       modeling Fridays 2:30-3:30 pm
COMMENTS   Industrials; Corporate trade shows

John Erlendson . . . . .Owner/Theatrical
Phillip Gums . . . . .Co-Owner/Women's Booker (JE Model)
Emily Clark . . . . .Voice-Over Agent (JE Talent)
Shannon Malloy . . . . .Kid's Booker (JE Model)
Eddie Sassin . . . . .Men's Booker (JE Model)
Dee Dee Shaughnessey . . . . . . .Commercial Agent/Theatrical (JE Talent)

JET SET MANAGEMENT GROUP, INC.
2160 Avenida De La Playa
La Jolla, CA 92037
PHONE 858-551-9393
FAX 858-551-9392
EMAIL . . . . .info@jetsetmodels.com
WEB SITE . . . . .www.jetsetmodels.com
SECOND WEB SITE .www.jetsetagency.com
TYPES   Commercial Talent - Film/TV Talent -
                       Modeling Talent
AFFILIATIONS   AFTRA - SAG
REPRESENTS   Actors - Children - Hosts/MCs - Infants -
                       Martial Artists/Stunts - Print Models -
                       Runway Models - Speakers/Lecturers -
                       Sports Personalities - Teens/Young Adults
SUBMISSION POLICY   Call or see Web site

Cindy Kauanui . . . . .President/CEO, Special Bookings
Lindsay Stewart . . . . .Director, Children's Division
Jessica Brown . . . . .Director, Theatrical Department
Corrina Lewis .Adult Commercial Agent
Paloma Jackson . . . . .Director, Baby Division
Amanda Lewis . . . . .Adult Print Division

JKA TALENT & LITERARY AGENCY
8033 Sunset Blvd., Ste. 115
Los Angeles, CA 90046
PHONE 818-980-2093
FAX 818-980-4092
TYPES   Film/TV Talent - Literary Talent - Talent &
                         Literary Packaging
AFFILIATIONS   AFTRA - ATA - DGA - WGA
REPRESENTS   Actors - Book Authors - Comedians -
                         Directors - Producers - Screenwriters - TV
                         Writers
SUBMISSION POLICY   No unsolicited submissions

James Kellem . . . . .President

JLA TALENT
9151 Sunset Blvd.
West Hollywood, CA 90069
PHONE 310-276-5677
FAX 310-276-2559
WEB SITE . . . . .www.jlatalent.com
TYPES   Commercial Talent - Film/TV Talent
AFFILIATIONS   AFTRA - SAG
REPRESENTS   Actors - Children

Gar Lester . . . . .Agent, Adult Commerical/Theatrical Talent
Curtis Hayes . . . . .Agent, Adult Commercial/Theatrical Talent
Christa Agustanovich . . . . .Agent, Adult Commercial
Kendall Park . . . . .Agent, Kids Commercial

JORDAN, GILL & DORNBAUM
1133 Broadway, Ste. 623
New York, NY 10010
PHONE 212-463-8455
TYPES   Commercial Talent - Film/TV Talent -
                         Theatre Talent
AFFILIATIONS   AEA - AFTRA - SAG
REPRESENTS   Actors - Children - Comedians - Dancers -
                         Martial Artists/Stunts - Teens/Young Adults -
                         Variety Artists
SUBMISSION POLICY   Submit picture or press material
COMMENTS   Theatrical talent from four to thirty years
                         old only; Specialty is representation for
                         commercials

Robin Dornbaum . . . . .Owner/Commercials
Jeffrey Gill . . . . .Owner/Commercials
Jan Jarrett . . . . .Theatrical
David McDermott . . . . .Commercials (Over 18 & Specialties)

JS REPRESENTS
6815 Willoughby Ave., Ste. 102
Los Angeles, CA 90038
PHONE 323-462-3246
FAX 805-566-3942
EMAIL . . . . .jsreps@veizon.net
WEB SITE . . . . .www.jsrepresents.com
TYPES   Commercial Talent
AFFILIATIONS   SAG
REPRESENTS   Actors
SUBMISSION POLICY   Mail photos and resumés; No phone calls
                         or drop-offs

Paul Jon Strotheide . . . . .Owner
Anne Mulles . . . . .Agent
M.K. Taupin . . . . .Agent

MERRILY KANE AGENCY
857 S. Bundy Dr.
Los Angeles, CA 90049
PHONE 310-820-0020
FAX 310-820-0404
TYPES   Film/TV Talent - Literary Talent
AFFILIATIONS   ATA - DGA - WGA
REPRESENTS   Book Authors - Directors - Playwrights -
                         Producers - Screenwriters - TV Writers
SUBMISSION POLICY   No unsolicited material

Merrily Kane . . . . .Agent

STANLEY KAPLAN TALENT
139 Fulton St., Rm. 503
New York, NY 10038
PHONE 212-385-4400
TYPES   Commercial Talent - Film/TV Talent -
                         Modeling Talent - Music Talent - Theatre
                         Talent
AFFILIATIONS   AEA - AFTRA - SAG
REPRESENTS   Actors - Children - Comedians - Dancers -
                         Hosts/MCs - Infants - Magicians - Martial
                         Artists/Stunts - Music Artists - Print Models -
                         Runway Models - Seniors - Teens/Young
                         Adults - Variety Artists - Voice-Over Artists

Stanley Kaplan . . . . .Agent
Janet Swabey . . . . .Agent, Children's Department

THE KAPLAN-STAHLER-GUMER-BRAUN AGENCY
8383 Wilshire Blvd., Ste. 923
Beverly Hills, CA 90211
PHONE 323-653-4483
TYPES   Literary Talent
AFFILIATIONS   AFTRA - DGA - SAG - WGA
REPRESENTS   Directors - Producers - TV Writers
COMMENTS   Reality

Mitch Kaplan . . . . .TV Literary
Elliot Stahler . . . . .TV Literary
Robert Gumer . . . . .TV Literary
Alan Braun . . . . .TV Literary
Bradley Glenn . . . . .TV Literary
Ra Kumar . . . . .TV Literary
Gordon Hvolka . . . . .TV Literary

THE KAUFMAN AGENCY
12007 Laurel Terrace Dr.
Studio City, CA 91604-3617
PHONE 818-506-6013
FAX 818-506-7270
EMAIL . . . . .jhk@pacbell.net
WEB SITE . . . . .www.kaufmanagency.net
TYPES   Music Talent
AFFILIATIONS   AFM
REPRESENTS   Composers - Music Artists - Music
                         Producers
COMMENTS   Handles talent worldwide with a focus on
                         film and TV composers

Jeff H. Kaufman . . . . .Film Music Agent/Consultant
Debi Kaufman . . . . .Associate

KAZARIAN/SPENCER & ASSOCIATES

11969 Ventura Blvd., 3rd Fl., Box 7409
Studio City, CA 91604
PHONE 818-769-9111/212-582-7572
FAX .818-769-9840/212-582-7448
WEB SITE . . . . .www.ksawest.com
TYPES   Commercial Talent - Film/TV Talent -
                         Modeling Talent - Theatre Talent
AFFILIATIONS   AEA - AFTRA - ATA
REPRESENTS   Actors - Children - Choreographers -
                         Comedians - Composers - Dancers -
                         Hosts/MCs - Infants - Martial Artists/Stunts
                         - Music Supervisors - Musical Theatre
                         Performers - Print Models - Runway Models
                         - Seniors - Sports Personalities -
                         Teens/Young Adults - Variety Artists - Voice-
                         Over Artists
COMMENTS   East Coast office: Carnegie Plaza, 162 W.
                         56th St., Ste. 307, New York, NY, 10019

Cindy Kazarian . . . . .President/On-Camera
Tory Preston . . . . .VP, Finance
Alicia Ruskin . . . . .VP/On-Camera
Brooke Nuttall . . . . .Agent, On-Camera
Mara Santino . . . . .Agent, Theatrical
Ryan Daly . . . . .Agent, Theatrical
Leslie Stokoe . . . . .Agent, Theatrical
Victoria Morris . . . . .Director, Equity/Dance/Choreography (NY)
Lori Swift . . . . .Agent, Film/TV/Theatre (NY)
Greg Marrero . . . . .Director, Sports/Stunts
Fred Wostbrock . . . . .Director, Hosts & Variety
Jenny Vavra . . . . .Director, Print
Jody Alexander . . . . .Co-Director, Young People
Bonnie Ventis . . . . .Co-Director, Young People
Philip Marcus . . . . .Agent, Young People
Donn Murret . . . . .Assistant, On-Camera
Kelly Thomas .Assistant, Theatrical
Jacole Kitchen . . . . .Assistant, Equity/Dance/Choreography
Adam Fox . . . . .Assistant, Equity/Dance/Choreography
Eileen Priboy . . . . .Assistant (NY)
Nancy Yearing . . . . .Assistant, Sports/Stunts
Rose Marston . . . . .Assistant, Print
Casey Vandeventer . . . . .Assistant, Young People
John Thompson . . . . .Executive Assistant/Office Manager
Dana Bennett . . . . .Assistant/Office Manager (NY)
Marie Bagnell . . . . .Receptionist
Jacqueline Rodriguez .Receptionist

GLYN KENNEDY, MODELS TALENT

16 Willow Bend Dr.
Cartersville, GA 30121
PHONE 770-607-2863
EMAIL . . . . .glynkennedy@msn.com
WEB SITE . . . . .www.glynkennedytalent.com
TYPES   Commercial Talent - Film/TV Talent
AFFILIATIONS   AFTRA - SAG
REPRESENTS   Actors - Children - Teens/Young Adults
COMMENTS   Twenty-five years experience; Full-service

Glyn Kennedy . . . . .President
Darlene McCrary . . . . .Broadcast Director

KERIN-GOLDBERG & ASSOCIATES

155 E. 55 St., Ste. 5D
New York, NY 10022
PHONE 212-838-7373
FAX 212-838-0774
TYPES   Film/TV Talent - Theatre Talent
AFFILIATIONS   AEA - AFTRA - SAG
REPRESENTS   Actors

Charles Kerin . . . . .Owner
Ellison K. Goldberg . . . . .Owner
Michael Legg . . . . .Agent
Ronald Ross . . . . .Agent

WILLIAM KERWIN AGENCY

1605 N. Cahuenga Blvd., Ste. 202
Hollywood, CA 90028
PHONE 323-469-5155
TYPES   Commercial Talent - Film/TV Talent -
                         Literary Talent - Theatre Talent
AFFILIATIONS   AEA - AFTRA - ATA - DGA - SAG - WGA
REPRESENTS   Actors - Producers - Screenwriters - Seniors
SUBMISSION POLICY   Send SASE with tapes; Follow-up by phone
COMMENTS   No children

William Kerwin . . . . .President/Theatrical
Albert Woods . . . . .Literary

ARCHER KING, LTD.

1650 Broadway, Ste. 407
New York, NY 10019
PHONE 212-765-3103
FAX 212-765-3107
EMAIL . . . . .akingltd@yahoo.com
TYPES   Film/TV Talent - Literary Talent - Music
                         Talent - Talent & Literary Packaging -
                         Theatre Talent
AFFILIATIONS   AEA - AFTRA - DGA - SAG - WGA
REPRESENTS   Actors - Book Authors - Choreographers -
                         Comedians - Dancers - Directors - Musical
                         Theatre Performers - Playwrights -
                         Producers - Screenwriters - Seniors -
                         Teens/Young Adults - TV Writers - Variety
                         Artists
COMMENTS   Focus on film

Archer King . . . . .Agent
Sophia Robbins . . . . .No Title

HARVEY KLINGER, INC.

300 W. 55th St.
New York, NY 10019
PHONE 212-581-7068
EMAIL . . . . .queries@harveyklinger.com
WEB SITE . . . . .www.harveyklinger.com
TYPES   Literary Talent
AFFILIATIONS   AAR
REPRESENTS   Book Authors
SUBMISSION POLICY   Submit query by mail or email only

Harvey Klinger . . . . .President
Sara Crowe . . . . .Agent
David Dunton .Agent & Rights
Andrea Somberg . . . . .Agent
Anna Cory-Watson .Associate

KNEERIM & WILLIAMS AT FISH & RICHARDSON, PC

225 Franklin St.
Boston, MA 02110
PHONE 617-542-5070
FAX 617-542-8906
EMAIL . . . . .erogers@fr.com
WEB SITE . . . . .www.fr.com
TYPES   Literary Talent
REPRESENTS   Book Authors - Producers - Screenwriters
COMMENTS   Represents life story rights and teleplay writ-
                         ers; Law firm; Additional office in New York

Jill Kneerim . . . . .Director
Steve Wasserman . . . . .Director, Literary
John Taylor Williams . . . . .Director/Attorney
Elaine M. Rogers Esq. . . . . . . .Director, Subsidiary Rights/Attorney
Brettne Bloom . . . . .Agent
Leslie Kaufmann . . . . .Assistant
Cara Shiel . . . . .Assistant
Hope Denekamp .Administrator

PAUL KOHNER, INC.
9300 Wilshire Blvd., Ste. 555
Beverly Hills, CA 90212
PHONE 310-550-1060
FAX 310-276-1083
TYPES   Film/TV Talent - Literary Talent - Theatre
                         Talent
AFFILIATIONS   AEA - AFTRA - DGA - SAG - WGA
REPRESENTS   Actors - Book Authors - Directors -
                         Producers - Screenwriters - TV Writers

Pearl Wexler . . . . .President
Stephen Moore . . . . .Head, Literary
Sheree Cohen . . . . .Agent
Samantha Crisp . . . . .Agent
Amanda Glazer . . . . .Agent
Missy Masters . . . . .Literary Agent

KOLSTEIN TALENT AGENCY (KTA)
247 W. 38th St., Ste. 1001
New York, NY 10018
PHONE 212-937-8967
FAX 212-937-8937
EMAIL . . . . .submissions@kolsteintalent.com
WEB SITE . . . . .www.kolsteintalent.com
TYPES   Commercial Talent - Film/TV Talent -
                         Modeling Talent - Theatre Talent
AFFILIATIONS   AEA - AFTRA - SAG
REPRESENTS   Actors - Comedians - Hosts/MCs - Runway
                         Models - Speakers/Lecturers - Teens/Young
                         Adults - Voice-Over Artists
SUBMISSION POLICY   New clients through industry referral only;
                         No tapes; No phone calls
COMMENTS   Also affiliated with NATR; West Coast
                         office: 8499 W. Sunset Blvd., 2nd Fl., West
                         Hollywood, CA 90069

Naomi Kolstein . . . . .Owner/Agent, Theatre & Commercials
Jeremy Zall . . . . .Owner/Agent, Film, TV & Commercials
Judilin Bosita . . . . .No Title
Tara Greenfield . . . . .No Title
Victoria Katz . . . . .No Title
Mia Labar . . . . .No Title

BARBARA S. KOUTS
PO Box 560
Bellport, NY 11713
PHONE 631-286-1278
FAX 631-286-1538
TYPES   Literary Talent
AFFILIATIONS   AAR
REPRESENTS   Book Authors
COMMENTS   Children's book authors only

Barbara S. Kouts . . . . .Literary Agent

OTTO R. KOZAK LITERARY & MOTION PICTURE AGENCY
114 Coronado St.
Atlantic Beach, NY 11509
PHONE 516-371-4922
FAX 516-371-4922
EMAIL . . . . .literaryagent1@hotmail.com
TYPES   Literary Talent
AFFILIATIONS   WGA
REPRESENTS   Book Authors - Screenwriters - TV Writers
SUBMISSION POLICY   Material accepted by referral and recom-
                         mendation only; No unsolicited submis-
                         sions
COMMENTS   Specializes in representing screenplays and
                         manuscripts by professionals in various
                         fields of their expertise; Branch office in the
                         Czech Republic; Additional address: PO
                         Box 152, Long Beach, NY 11561

Yitka Kozak . . . . .Manager/Agent
Lynne Cirr . . . . .Agent
Robert Kozak . . . . .Agent
Milada Simova . . . . .Agent (Czech Republic)

CARY KOZLOV LITERARY REPRESENTATION
16000 Ventura Blvd., Ste. 1000
Encino, CA 91436
PHONE 818-501-6622
FAX 818-708-0299
EMAIL .ckozlov@carykozlov.com
TYPES   Literary Talent
AFFILIATIONS   WGA
REPRESENTS   Directors - Screenwriters
SUBMISSION POLICY   No unsolicited material

Cary Kozlov . . . . .Principal/Literary

KRAFT-ENGEL MANAGEMENT
15233 Ventura Blvd., Ste. 200
Sherman Oaks, CA 91403
PHONE 818-380-1918
FAX 818-380-2609
TYPES   Music Talent
REPRESENTS   Composers - Music Artists - Music
                         Supervisors
SUBMISSION POLICY   Referral only

Richard Kraft . . . . .Agent
Laura Engel . . . . .Agent
David Klane . . . . .VP, Operations
Amanda Bramall . . . . .Executive Coordinator
Julie Michaels . . . . .Executive Coordinator

THE KRASNY OFFICE, INC.
1501 Broadway, Ste. 1303
New York, NY 10036
PHONE 212-730-8160
FAX 212-768-9379
TYPES   Commercial Talent - Film/TV Talent -
                         Theatre Talent
AFFILIATIONS   AEA - AFTRA - SAG
REPRESENTS   Actors - Comedians

Gary Krasny . . . . .Owner
Norma Eisenbaum . . . . .Agent
B. Lynne Jebens . . . . .Agent
Tom Kammer . . . . .Agent

KRISTINE KRUPP TALENT AGENCY
PO Box 6556
San Rafael, CA 94903
PHONE 415-479-5404
EMAIL . . . . .kktalent@mindspring.com
TYPES   Literary Talent
REPRESENTS   Screenwriters
SUBMISSION POLICY   Email subject line "Query and Synopsis"
                        only, with title and one-page synopsis in
                        body of email; No email attachments; First-
                        time writers OK; Include contact info and
                        synopsis with all queries

Kristine Krupp . . . . .Owner/Agent

L.A. TALENT
7700 W. Sunset Blvd.
Los Angeles, CA 90046
PHONE 323-436-7777
FAX 323-436-7788
WEB SITE . . . . .www.latalent.com
TYPES   Commercial Talent - Film/TV Talent -
                        Theatre Talent
AFFILIATIONS   AEA - AFTRA - ATA
REPRESENTS   Actors - Children - Infants - Seniors -
                        Teens/Young Adults
SUBMISSION POLICY   Photos and resumes by mail only; Attends
                        showcases

Patsy Beattie . . . . .Agent, Adult
Mike Casey . . . . .Agent, Adult
Tracy Dwyer . . . . .Agent, Children
Pam Loar . . . . .Agent, Adult

THE LA LITERARY AGENCY
PO Box 46370
Los Angeles, CA 90046
PHONE 323-654-5288
FAX 323-654-5388
TYPES   Literary Talent
REPRESENTS   Book Authors

Eric Lasher . . . . .Principal/Agent
Ann Cashman . . . . .Agent

LALLY TALENT AGENCY (LTA)
630 Ninth Ave., Ste. 800
New York, NY 10036
PHONE 212-974-8718
TYPES   Film/TV Talent - Literary Talent - Music
                        Talent - Talent & Literary Packaging -
                        Theatre Talent
AFFILIATIONS   AEA - AFTRA - SAG
REPRESENTS   Actors - Book Authors - Choreographers -
                        Music Artists - Playwrights - Screenwriters

Dale R. Lally . . . . .Owner
Stephen Laviska . . . . .Owner
Barry Axelrod . . . . .Assistant

PETER LAMPACK AGENCY, INC.
551 Fifth Ave., Ste. 1613
New York, NY 10176-0187
PHONE 212-687-9106
FAX 212-687-9109
EMAIL . . . . .lampackag@verizon.net
TYPES   Literary Talent
REPRESENTS   Book Authors
SUBMISSION POLICY   Query letters only; Will request a partial or
                        complete manuscript if interested

Peter Lampack . . . . .President
Andrew Lampack . . . . .Agent
Rema Dilanyan . . . . .Agent (Foreign Rights)
Tatsiana Karankevich . . . . .Officer Manager

AL LAMPKIN ENTERTAINMENT, INC.
1817 W. Verdugo Ave.
Burbank, CA 91506
PHONE 818-846-4951
FAX 818-846-5908
EMAIL . . . . .info@allampkin.com
WEB SITE . . . . .www.allampkin.com
TYPES   Commercial Talent - Film/TV Talent - Music
                        Talent
AFFILIATIONS   AFTRA - SAG
REPRESENTS   Comedians - Magicians - Variety Artists
COMMENTS   Full-service entertainment agency providing
                        bands, DJs, karaoke, and other variety acts
                        for special events, movies, TV and wrap
                        parties

Al Lampkin . . . . .President
Matt Kabel . . . . .Assistant Manager
Amy Lucas . . . . .Executive Assistant

LANE AGENCY
9903 Santa Monica Blvd., Ste. 756
Beverly Hills, CA 90212
PHONE 310-275-1455
FAX 310-284-8896
EMAIL . . . . .info@laneagency.com
WEB SITE .www.laneagency.com
TYPES   Below-the-Line Talent - Commercial Talent
                        - Film/TV Talent - Modeling Talent - Music
                        Talent
AFFILIATIONS   SAG
REPRESENTS   Actors - Comedians - Dancers - Hosts/MCs
                        - Infants - Magicians - Martial Artists/Stunts
                        - Music Artists - Print Models - Teens/Young
                        Adults - Variety Artists
COMMENTS   Fortune 500 clients; Bookings worldwide;
                        Models and talent for every event

Judith Feinstein . . . . .CEO
Bruce Feinstein . . . . .President
Stella Archer . . . . .Agent
Amanda Sandoval . . . . .Assistant

THE LANTZ OFFICE
200 W. 57th St., Ste. 503
New York, NY 10019
PHONE 212-586-0200
FAX 212-262-6659
EMAIL . . . . .rlantz@lantzoffice.com
TYPES   Literary Talent - Theatre Talent
AFFILIATIONS   ATA - DGA - SAG - WGA
REPRESENTS   Composers - Directors - Playwrights -
                        Screenwriters
COMMENTS   Focus on writer/directors

Robert Lantz . . . . .Owner/Agent
Dennis Aspland . . . . .Agent

LARCHMONT LITERARY AGENCY
444 N. Larchmont Blvd., Ste. 200
Los Angeles, CA 90004
PHONE 323-856-3070
TYPES   Literary Talent
AFFILIATIONS   DGA - WGA
REPRESENTS   Directors - Screenwriters
SUBMISSION POLICY   Referral only

Joel Millner . . . . .Agent
Marianne Moore . . . . .Agent

LE PAWS
12211 W. Washington Blvd., #100
Los Angeles, CA 90066
PHONE .310-397-3143, x113
FAX 310-397-1877
EMAIL . . . . .casting@lepaws.tv
WEB SITE . . . . .www.lepaws.tv
TYPES   Commercial Talent - Film/TV Talent
REPRESENTS   Animals
SUBMISSION POLICY   See Web site
COMMENTS   Works with studio trained dogs only

Stuart Kinzey . . . . .Owner
Michelle Zahn . . . . .Owner/Booking Agent
April Baker . . . . .Booking Agent
Nick Ferrara . . . . .New Talent
Aly Hartmen . . . . .New Talent
Anya Heron . . . . .Office Manager
Megan Fleming . . . . .Office Coordinator

SUSANNA LEA ASSOCIATES
28, rue Bonaparte
Paris 75006, France
PHONE 33-1-5310-2840
FAX 33-1-5310-2849
EMAIL . . . . .postmaster@susannalea.com
WEB SITE . . . . .www.susannaleaassociates.com
TYPES   Literary Talent
REPRESENTS   Book Authors
COMMENTS   Offices in New York

Susanna Lea . . . . .Agent/Owner
Katrin Hodapp . . . . .Agent
Mark Kessler . . . . .Agent
Marion Millet . . . . .Agent
Marie Garnero . . . . .Assistant

LEADING ARTISTS, INC.
145 W. 45th St., Ste. 1000
New York, NY 10036
PHONE 212-391-4545
FAX 212-354-4941
TYPES   Film/TV Talent - Theatre Talent
AFFILIATIONS   AEA - AFTRA - SAG
REPRESENTS   Actors
COMMENTS   Also affiliated with NATR; Sister agency in
                      Los Angeles: SMS Talent

Dianne Busch . . . . .Agent/Owner
Stacy Baer . . . . .Agent
Michael Kelly Boone . . . . .Agent
Mike Francis . . . . .Assistant
Mat Hollis . . . . .Assistant

BUDDY LEE ATTRACTIONS, INC.
38 Music Square East, Ste. 300
Nashville, TN 37203-4396
PHONE 615-244-4336
FAX 615-726-0429
EMAIL . . . . .tconway@blanash.com
WEB SITE . . . . .www.buddyleeattractions.com
TYPES   Commercial Talent - Film/TV Talent - Music
                      Talent - Theatre Talent
AFFILIATIONS   AFM - AFTRA - AGVA - SAG
REPRESENTS   Actors - Book Authors - Comedians -
                      Composers - Hosts/MCs - Music Artists -
                      Music Editors - Music Producers - Music
                      Supervisors - Musical Theatre Performers -
                      Speakers/Lecturers - Sports Personalities
COMMENTS   Affiliated with Endeavor Agency, LLC

Joey Lee . . . . .CEO
Tony Conway . . . . .President
Joan Saltel . . . . .Executive VP
Kevin Neal . . . . .VP
Jon Folk . . . . .Agent
Bob Kinkead . . . . .Agent
Gary Kirves . . . . .Agent
David Kiswiney . . . . .Agent
Tony Lee . . . . .Agent

LEIGHTON AGENCY, INC.
10049 E. Dynamite Blvd., #D125
Scottsdale, AZ 85262
PHONE 480-704-8800
WEB SITE . . . . .www.leightonagency.com
TYPES   Commercial Talent - Film/TV Talent -
                      Modeling Talent
AFFILIATIONS   AFTRA - SAG
REPRESENTS   Actors - Children - Hosts/MCs - Print
                      Models - Runway Models - Seniors -
                      Teens/Young Adults - Voice-Over Artists

Ruth Leighton . . . . .Owner/Agent

LEMODELN MODEL & TALENT AGENCY
7536 Market St.
Boardman, OH 44512
PHONE 330-758-4417/330-726-6441
FAX 330-758-0076
EMAIL . . . . .lemodeln@aol.com
SECOND EMAIL . . . . .lemodeln@sbcglobal.net
WEB SITE . . . . .www.lemodeln.com
TYPES   Below-the-Line Talent - Commercial Talent
                      - Film/TV Talent - Literary Talent - Modeling
                      Talent - Music Talent - Talent & Literary
                      Packaging - Theatre Talent
AFFILIATIONS   WGA
REPRESENTS   Actors - Animals - Book Authors -
                      Broadcast Journalists/Newscasters -
                      Children - Cinematographers - Comedians
                      - Composers - Dancers - Directors -
                      Hosts/MCs - Infants - Martial Artists/Stunts
                      - Music Artists - Music Producers - Musical
                      Theatre Performers - Print Models -
                      Producers - Runway Models - Screenwriters
                      - Seniors - Speakers/Lecturers - Sports
                      Personalities - Teens/Young Adults - TV
                      Writers - Variety Artists - Voice-Over Artists
COMMENTS   Also represents extras, lyricists and photog-
                      raphers

Linda Weaver . . . . .President
Vincent Richards . . . . .Tech Support/Music Consultant
Helene Mavar . . . . .Bookkeeper
John Holowach . . . . .Tech Support
Denise Weaver . . . . .Administrative Assistant

LENHOFF & LENHOFF

830 Palm Ave.
West Hollywood, CA 90069
PHONE 310-855-2411
FAX 310-855-2412
WEB SITE ....www.lenhoff.com
TYPES   Below-the-Line Talent - Literary Talent
AFFILIATIONS   ATA - DGA - WGA
REPRESENTS   Book Authors - Cinematographers -
                     Directors - Producers - Screenwriters - TV
                     Writers
SUBMISSION POLICY   By referral only

S. Charles Lenhoff ....President
Lisa Helsing Lenhoff ....CFO
Jennifer Derkitt ....Agent Trainee

LENZ AGENCY

1591 E. Desert Inn Rd.
Las Vegas, NV 89109
PHONE 702-733-6888
FAX 702-731-2008
EMAIL ....tena@lenztalent.com
WEB SITE ....www.lenztalent.com
SECOND WEB SITE ....www.destinationvegas.com
TYPES   Commercial Talent - Film/TV Talent -
                     Modeling Talent - Theatre Talent
AFFILIATIONS   AEA - AFTRA - SAG
REPRESENTS   Actors - Broadcast Journalists/Newscasters
                     - Comedians - Dancers - Hosts/MCs -
                     Martial Artists/Stunts - Print Models -
                     Runway Models - Sports Personalities -
                     Teens/Young Adults - Variety Artists - Voice-
                     Over Artists

Richard Weber ....CEO/CFO/Agent
Tena Houser ....President/Agent

SID LEVIN AGENCY

8484 Wilshire Blvd., Ste. 750
Beverly Hills, CA 90211
PHONE 323-653-7073
FAX 323-653-0280
TYPES   Commercial Talent - Film/TV Talent -
                     Theatre Talent
AFFILIATIONS   AFTRA - SAG
REPRESENTS   Actors - Broadcast Journalists/Newscasters
                     - Children - Comedians - Dancers - Sports
                     Personalities - Teens/Young Adults - Variety
                     Artists - Voice-Over Artists
SUBMISSION POLICY   Mail only; No drop-offs or phone calls; No
                     unsolicited tapes

Sid Levin ....Owner/Agent
Patricia Levin ....Agent

LEVINE GREENBERG LITERARY AGENCY

307 Seventh Ave., Ste. 2407
New York, NY 10001
PHONE 212-337-0934
FAX 212-337-0948
EMAIL ....ledgecombe@levinegreenberg.com
WEB SITE ....www.levinegreenberg.com
TYPES   Literary Talent
AFFILIATIONS   AAR
REPRESENTS   Book Authors
SUBMISSION POLICY   Prefer online submissions through our Web
                     site

James Levine ....Principal
Daniel Greenberg ....Principal
Arielle Eckstut ....Agent
Stephanie Kip Rostan ....Agent
Jenoyne Adams ....Associate Agent
Elizabeth Fisher ....Rights & Contracts Manager
Melissa Rowland ....Business Manager
Danielle Svetcov ....Associate
Lindsay Edgecombe ....Editorial Assistant
Monika Verma ....Editorial Assistant

PAUL S. LEVINE LITERARY AGENCY

1054 Superba Ave.
Venice, CA 90291-3940
PHONE 310-450-6711
FAX 310-450-0181
EMAIL ....pslevine@ix.netcom.com
WEB SITE ....www.paulslevine.com
TYPES   Literary Talent
AFFILIATIONS   AAR
REPRESENTS   Book Authors - Directors - Playwrights -
                     Producers - Screenwriters - TV Writers
SUBMISSION POLICY   Query letter only
COMMENTS   Entertainment, copyright and trademark
                     attorney

Paul S. Levine ....Agent/Attorney

MICHAEL LEWIS & ASSOCIATES

2506 Fifth St., Ste. 100
Santa Monica, CA 90405
PHONE 310-399-1999
EMAIL ....mlewis2506@aol.com
TYPES   Below-the-Line Talent - Literary Talent -
                     Talent & Literary Packaging
AFFILIATIONS   DGA - WGA
REPRESENTS   Cinematographers - Directors - Film Editors
                     - Producers - Production Designers -
                     Screenwriters - TV Writers
SUBMISSION POLICY   Via recommendation only

Michael R. Lewis ....Agent

BERNARD LIEBHABER AGENCY

352 Seventh Ave.
New York, NY 10001
PHONE 212-631-7561
TYPES   Film/TV Talent - Theatre Talent
AFFILIATIONS   AEA - AFTRA - ATA - SAG
REPRESENTS   Actors - Musical Theatre Performers
SUBMISSION POLICY   Pictures and resumés received by mail will
                     be given respectful consideration
COMMENTS   Also affiliated with NATR

Bernard Liebhaber ....Owner

LILY'S TALENT AGENCY, INC.
1017 W. Washington Blvd., #4F
Chicago, IL 60607
PHONE 312-601-2345
FAX 312-601-2353
EMAIL . . . . .lily@lilystalent.com
SECOND EMAIL . . . . .gina@lilystalent.com
WEB SITE . . . . .www.lilystalent.com
TYPES   Commercial Talent - Film/TV Talent -
     Literary Talent - Modeling Talent - Music
     Talent - Theatre Talent
AFFILIATIONS   AEA - AFTRA - SAG - WGA
REPRESENTS   Actors - Broadcast Journalists/Newscasters
     - Children - Choreographers - Comedians
     - Dancers - Hosts/MCs - Infants -
     Magicians - Martial Artists/Stunts - Music
     Artists - Music Editors - Music Producers -
     Musical Theatre Performers - Playwrights -
     Print Models - Producers - Runway Models -
     Screenwriters - Seniors - Speakers/Lecturers
     - Teens/Young Adults - TV Writers - Voice-
     Over Artists
COMMENTS   Full-service agency; Representing a com-
     plete range of ethnic talents of all ages

Lily Liu . . . . .President/Agent
Gina Stevanovich . . .Agent, Film/Screenwriters/Adults & Kids/Voice-Over
Andrea Shipp . . . . .Agent, Print/Kids & Adults
Dan Tower . . . . .Marketing & Fashion Director
Pamela Kilgore . . . . .Accounting/Bookkeeping
Oliver Aldape . . . . .Agent Assistant

KEN LINDNER & ASSOCIATES, INC.
2049 Century Park East, Ste. 3050
Los Angeles, CA 90067
PHONE 310-277-9223
FAX 310-277-5806
EMAIL . . . . .info@klateam.com
WEB SITE .www.kenlindner.com
TYPES   Film/TV Talent
AFFILIATIONS   AFTRA - SAG
REPRESENTS   Broadcast Journalists/Newscasters -
     Hosts/MCs - Producers - Sports
     Personalities
COMMENTS   Focus on broadcasting and programming

Ken Lindner . . . . .CEO
Susan Levin . . . . .Executive VP
Rick Ramage . . . . .Executive VP/Agent
Karen Wang-Lavelle . . . . .VP
Kristin Allen . . . . .Chief Corporate Counsel/Agent
Shannon McLaughlin . . . . .Agent
Melissa Van Fleet . . . . .Agent
Tom Ragonnet . . . . .Director, Operations
Shari Freis . . . . .Assistant to Ken Lindner
C.J. Woods . . . . .Assistant to Ken Lindner
Raina Lewis . . . . .Assistant to Rick Ramage
Lexi Strumor . . . . .Assistant to Karen Wang-Lavelle

LITERARY AND CREATIVE ARTISTS, INC. (LCA, INC.)
3543 Albemarle St. NW
Washington, DC 20008
PHONE 202-362-4688
FAX 202-362-8875
EMAIL . . . . .muriel@lcadc.com
WEB SITE . . . . .www.lcadc.com
TYPES   Literary Talent
AFFILIATIONS   AAR
REPRESENTS   Book Authors
COMMENTS   Also affiliated with Authors Guild and
     American Bar Association, Women in
     Communications Division

Muriel G. Nellis . . . . .President
Jane Roberts . . . . .VP

THE LITERARY GROUP
51 E. 25th St., Ste. 401
New York, NY 10010
PHONE 212-274-1616
FAX 212-274-9876
EMAIL . . . . .fweimann@theliterarygroup.com
WEB SITE . . . . .www.theliterarygroup.com
TYPES   Literary Talent - Talent & Literary Packaging
AFFILIATIONS   AAR - WGA
REPRESENTS   Book Authors - Speakers/Lecturers - Sports
     Personalities
COMMENTS   Also represents illustrators; Affiliated with
     Authors Guild, ASJA

Frank Weimann . . . . .CEO/President
Anne DeWitt . . . . .Nonfiction & Fiction
Ian Kleinert . . . . .Nonfiction & Fiction

LOOK TALENT
166 Geary St., Ste. 1406
San Francisco, CA 94108
PHONE 415-781-2841
FAX 415-781-5722
WEB SITE . . . . .www.looktalent.com
TYPES   Commercial Talent - Film/TV Talent -
     Modeling Talent - Theatre Talent
AFFILIATIONS   AEA - AFTRA - SAG
REPRESENTS   Actors - Comedians - Print Models - Voice-
     Over Artists
SUBMISSION POLICY   Mail only

Joan Spangler . . . . .President/Agent/Owner
David Michael Silverman . . . . .Agent, Print

NANCY LOVE LITERARY AGENCY
250 E. 65th St., Ste. 4-A
New York, NY 10021
PHONE 212-980-3499
FAX 212-308-6405
EMAIL . . . . .nloveag@aol.com
TYPES   Literary Talent
AFFILIATIONS   AAR
REPRESENTS   Book Authors
SUBMISSION POLICY   Call or send written query or proposal; Do
     not fax or email; No unsolicited manu-
     scripts
COMMENTS   Also affiliated with Authors Guild

Nancy Love . . . . .Agent
Kelsey Osgood . . . . .Assistant

THE LUEDTKE AGENCY
1674 Broadway, Ste. 7A
New York, NY 10019
PHONE 212-765-9564
TYPES   Film/TV Talent - Literary Talent - Theatre
     Talent
AFFILIATIONS   AEA - AFTRA - AGVA - SAG - WGA
REPRESENTS   Actors - Directors - Playwrights -
     Screenwriters - TV Writers - Voice-Over
     Artists

Penny Luedtke . . . . .Owner

JANA LUKER AGENCY

1923-1/2 Westwood Blvd., Ste. 3
Los Angeles, CA 90025
PHONE 310-441-2822
FAX 310-441-2820
TYPES   Commercial Talent - Film/TV Talent
AFFILIATIONS   AEA - AFTRA - SAG - WGA
REPRESENTS   Actors - Children - Seniors - Teens/Young
                         Adults
SUBMISSION POLICY   Submit picture and resumé; Do not call

Jana Luker . . . . .Owner/Agent
Kathy Keeley . . . . .Agent
Gigi Schell . . . . .Assistant

M INTERNATIONAL TALENT AGENCY

1875 Century Park East, Ste. 700
Los Angeles, CA 90067
PHONE 310-284-3714/310-407-5105
FAX 310-284-3715
EMAIL . . . . .info@mmodels.com
SECOND EMAIL . . . . .john@mmodels.com
WEB SITE . . . . .www.mmodels.com
TYPES   Below-the-Line Talent - Commercial Talent
                         - Film/TV Talent - Modeling Talent - Music
                         Talent - Theatre Talent
REPRESENTS   Actors - Hosts/MCs - Print Models -
                         Teens/Young Adults - Voice-Over Artists

John Nguyen . . . . .President
Marc Ngoho . . . . .Creative Director
Sandro Gelke . . . . .Promotions, Industrial
Courtney Kahmbay . . . . .Commercial/Theatrical
Paul Kendall . . . . .Commercial
Kristen Van Dernoot . . . . .Fashion Print

GINA MACCOBY LITERARY AGENCY

PO Box 60
Chappaqua, NY 10514
PHONE 914-238-5630
TYPES   Literary Talent
AFFILIATIONS   AAR
REPRESENTS   Book Authors
SUBMISSION POLICY   Query first with SASE
COMMENTS   No screenplays; Also affiliated with Authors
                         Guild

Gina Maccoby . . . . .Principal

THE MACK AGENCY

4705 Laurel Canyon Blvd., Ste. 204
Valley Village, CA 91607
PHONE 818-753-6300
FAX 818-753-6311
WEB SITE .www.themackagency.net
TYPES   Below-the-Line Talent
AFFILIATIONS   DGA
REPRESENTS   Cinematographers - Interactive Game
                         Developers - Producers - Production
                         Designers
COMMENTS   Also affiliated with IATSE, AICP and MVPA

Patty Mack . . . . .Agent
Stacey Karp . . . . .Agent

MADEMOISELLE TALENT & MODELING AGENCY

10835 Santa Monica Blvd., Ste. 204A
Los Angeles, CA 90025
PHONE 310-441-9994
TYPES   Commercial Talent - Film/TV Talent -
                         Modeling Talent
AFFILIATIONS   SAG
REPRESENTS   Actors - Children - Comedians - Dancers -
                         Print Models - Teens/Young Adults - Variety
                         Artists - Voice-Over Artists

Won Lee . . . . .Owner
Alan Siegel . . . . .Agent
Ana Kim . . . . .Intern

MALAKY INTERNATIONAL

205 S. Beverly Dr., Ste. 211
Beverly Hills, CA 90212
PHONE 310-777-7560
TYPES   Commercial Talent - Film/TV Talent -
                         Modeling Talent - Music Talent - Theatre
                         Talent
AFFILIATIONS   AFTRA - SAG
REPRESENTS   Actors - Broadcast Journalists/Newscasters
                         - Children - Comedians - Dancers -
                         Hosts/MCs - Magicians - Martial
                         Artists/Stunts - Print Models - Seniors -
                         Teens/Young Adults
SUBMISSION POLICY   Mail only; No drop-ins

Virginia Dib . . . . .Agent
J.R. Dib . . . . .Agent

MARGARET MALDONADO AGENCY

8422 Melrose Pl.
Los Angeles, CA 90069
PHONE 323-556-3455
FAX 323-556-3456
EMAIL . . . . .mmainfo@margaretmaldonado.com
WEB SITE . . . . .www.margaretmaldonado.com
TYPES   Below-the-Line Talent
COMMENTS   Production Designers, Photographers,
                         Stylists, Hair and Make-up Artists

Margaret Maldonado . . . . .Agent
Kent Belden . . . . .Agent
Roderick Muhammad . . . . .Agent
Dani Brown-Walker . . . . .Agent
Mosha Katani . . . . .Agent
Mikko Koskinen .Accounting Manager
Meredith Goguen . . . . .Accounting
Stephen Spano . . . . .Production Coordinator
Noel Gordon . . . . .Assistant to Margaret Maldonado
Crystal Sanford . . . . .Office Manager

THE MANNEQUIN AGENCY
2021 San Mateo Blvd. NE
Albuquerque, NM 87110
PHONE 505-266-6823
FAX 505-266-6829
EMAIL . . . . .diana@dianahorneragency.com
WEB SITE . . . . .www.themannequinagency.com
TYPES   Commercial Talent - Film/TV Talent -
                         Modeling Talent
AFFILIATIONS   SAG
REPRESENTS   Actors - Children - Hosts/MCs - Infants -
                         Print Models - Runway Models - Seniors -
                         Speakers/Lecturers - Teens/Young Adults -
                         Voice-Over Artists
SUBMISSION POLICY   Photo submissions
COMMENTS   Union/non-union talent

Diana Horner . . . . .Owner/Agent

MANUS & ASSOCIATES LITERARY AGENCY, INC.
425 Sherman Ave., Ste. 200
Palo Alto, CA 94306
PHONE 650-470-5151
FAX 650-470-5159
EMAIL . . . . .manuslit@manuslit.com
WEB SITE . . . . .www.manuslit.com
TYPES   Literary Talent
AFFILIATIONS   AAR
REPRESENTS   Book Authors
SUBMISSION POLICY   No unsolicited manuscripts
COMMENTS   East Coast office: 444 Madison Ave., 39th
                         Fl., New York, NY 10022

Janet Wilkens Manus . . . . .Partner (NY)
Jillian Manus . . . . .Partner (CA)
Jandy Nelson . . . . .Sr. Agent (CA)
Stephanie Lee . . . . .Agent (CA)
Penny Nelson . . . . .Agent (CA)
Dena Fischer . . . . .Agent (CA)
Theresa Van Eeghen . . . . .Executive Assistant (CA)

MARKHAM & FROGGATT LTD.
4 Windmill St.
London W1T 2HZ, United Kingdom
PHONE 44-0-20-7636-4412
FAX 44-0-20-7637-5233
EMAIL . . . . .admin@markhamfroggatt.co.uk
WEB SITE . . . . .www.markhamfroggatt.com
REPRESENTS   Actors

Pippa Markham . . . . .Agent
Millie Chadbon . . . . .Agent, Commercial Voiceover & Radio
Alex Irwin . . . . .Agent
Stephanie Randall . . . . .Agent
Tracey Gittins . . . . .Business Affairs
Anna Dudley . . . . .Assistant to Stephanie Randall & Alex Irwin
Kristian Leven . . . . .Assistant to Millie Chadbon
Nicola Sandon . . . . .Assistant to Pippa Markham
Sarah Wolf . . . . .Assistant to Pippa Markham

JUDY MARKS AGENCY
606 N. Larchmont Blvd., Ste. 208
Los Angeles, CA 90004
PHONE 323-461-3555
FAX 323-962-0225
EMAIL . . . . .jrmarks@aol.com
WEB SITE . . . . .www.judymarks.com
TYPES   Below-the-Line Talent
REPRESENTS   Cinematographers
SUBMISSION POLICY   No unsolicited submissions
COMMENTS   No actors or models

Judy Marks . . . . .Agent
Kevin Koehler . . . . .Assistant

SANDRA MARSH MANAGEMENT
9150 Wilshire Blvd., Ste. 220
Beverly Hills, CA 90212
PHONE 310-285-0303
FAX 310-285-0218
EMAIL . . . . .info@sandramarsh.com
WEB SITE . . . . .www.sandramarsh.com
TYPES   Below-the-Line Talent - Commercial Talent
                         - Film/TV Talent - Music Talent
AFFILIATIONS   WGA
REPRESENTS   Cinematographers - Composers - Film
                         Editors - Martial Artists/Stunts - Music
                         Artists - Music Editors - Music Supervisors -
                         Producers - Production Designers - Sound
                         Editors
COMMENTS   Also represents production sound mixers,
                         set decorators, visual and special (physical)
                         effects designers, creature make-up effects
                         designers, second unit directors; Affiliated
                         with IATSE

Sandra Marsh . . . . .President/Agent
Claire Best . . . . .COO/Agent
Gary Roisentul . . . . .Financial Controller
Shawn Burns . . . . .Agent
Rocco Hindman . . . . .Agent
Rochelle Sharpe . . . . .Agent
Michael Vasquez . . . . .Agent
Wendi Hammock . . . . .Tracking Agent/Music Assistant
Lindsay Gray . . . . .Assistant
Jess Jaworski . . . . .Assistant

MARTIN & DONALDS TALENT AGENCY, INC.
2131 Hollywood Blvd., Ste. 308
Hollywood, FL 33020
PHONE . . . . .954-921-2427/866-694-1160 (North Carolina office)
FAX 954-921-7635
EMAIL . . . . .mdtalent@bellsouth.net
WEB SITE .www.martinanddonalds.com
TYPES   Commercial Talent - Film/TV Talent -
                         Modeling Talent - Music Talent - Theatre
                         Talent
AFFILIATIONS   SAG
REPRESENTS   Actors - Animals - Children -
                         Choreographers - Comedians - Dancers -
                         Hosts/MCs - Infants - Magicians - Martial
                         Artists/Stunts - Music Artists - Musical
                         Theatre Performers - Print Models -
                         Producers - Runway Models - Seniors -
                         Speakers/Lecturers - Teens/Young Adults -
                         Variety Artists - Voice-Over Artists
SUBMISSION POLICY   Mail headshot, composite card and resumé

Sharon F. Martin . . . . .Owner/Agent/President
Christine Donalds . . . . .Owner/Agent/VP
Joyce Glusman . . . . .Agent/Non-Union TV & Film

MAXINE'S TALENT AGENCY

4830 Encino Ave.
Encino, CA 91316
PHONE 818-986-2946
TYPES   Film/TV Talent - Literary Talent - Music
                         Talent
AFFILIATIONS   AFTRA - SAG
REPRESENTS   Actors - Book Authors - Comedians -
                         Screenwriters - Variety Artists
COMMENTS   Adults only, no children

Maxine . . . . .CEO/President
Chad . . . . .Agent
Tick One . . . . .Agent
Casey . . . . .Agent

THE MCCABE GROUP

8285 Sunset Blvd., Ste. 1
Los Angeles, CA 90046
PHONE 323-650-3738
FAX 323-650-6014
EMAIL . . . . .filmgirl323@aol.com
SECOND EMAIL . . . . .bmccabe@atalentagency.com
WEB SITE . . . . .www.atalentagency.com
TYPES   Film/TV Talent - Theatre Talent
AFFILIATIONS   AEA - AFTRA - ATA
REPRESENTS   Actors - Teens/Young Adults
SUBMISSION POLICY   By referral only; Tape required
COMMENTS   Established film and TV stars; Actors eight-
                         een and up

Brian McCabe . . . . .Theatrical
Rob Dee . . . . .Theatrical
Sandy Oroumieh . . . . .Assistant

MCCARTY TALENT, INC.

2600 W. Olive Ave., 5th Fl.
Burbank, CA 91505
PHONE 818-556-5410
FAX 800-494-7587
EMAIL . . . . .agent@mccartytalent.com
WEB SITE . . . . .www.mccartytalent.com
TYPES   Commercial Talent - Film/TV Talent -
                         Modeling Talent
AFFILIATIONS   SAG
REPRESENTS   Actors - Hosts/MCs - Print Models -
                         Runway Models - Voice-Over Artists
SUBMISSION POLICY   US Mail or email only
COMMENTS   Only actors with resumes co-star and
                         above

Cody Garden . . . . .President

MCCORMICK & WILLIAMS

37 W. 20th St., Ste. 606
New York, NY 10011
PHONE 212-691-9726
TYPES   Literary Talent
SUBMISSION POLICY   No email; Accompany query with SASE

David McCormick . . . . .Agent/Partner
Amy Williams . . . . .Agent/Partner
Leslie Falk . . . . .Managing Partner
PJ Mark . . . . .Sr. Agent/Director, Foreign Rights
Joy Gallagher . . . . .Editorial Assistant

MCDONALD/SELZNICK ASSOCIATES

1611A N. El Centro Ave.
Hollywood, CA 90028
PHONE 323-957-6680
FAX 323-957-6688
EMAIL . . . . .tony@mcdonaldselznick.com
WEB SITE . . . . .www.mcdonaldselznick.com
TYPES   Below-the-Line Talent - Commercial Talent
                         - Film/TV Talent - Theatre Talent
AFFILIATIONS   AEA - AFTRA - ATA
REPRESENTS   Actors - Choreographers - Dancers -
                         Martial Artists/Stunts - Musical Theatre
                         Performers - Producers - Production
                         Designers - Variety Artists
COMMENTS   Also represents stage directors and body
                         doubles; Affiliated with SSDC

Julie McDonald . . . . .Partner
Tony Selznick . . . . .Partner
Nicole Connor . . . . .Theatrical Agent
Lisa Coppola . . . . .Agent
Andrew Jacobs . . . . .Agent
Terry Lindholm . . . . .Agent
Lori Santalla . . . . .Office Manager
Karen Gersch . . . . .Dance Assistant
Gabriel Paige . . . . .Dance Assistant
Jenn Proctor .Commercial Assistant
Laura Savery . . . . .Dance Assistant
Stephanie Warren . . . . .Choreography Assistant

HELEN MCGRATH & ASSOCIATES

1406 Idaho Ct.
Concord, CA 94521
PHONE 925-672-6211
FAX 925-672-6383
EMAIL . . . . .hmcgrath_lit@yahoo.com
TYPES   Literary Talent
REPRESENTS   Book Authors
COMMENTS   Books to film only

Helen McGrath . . . . .Owner
Doris Johnson . . . . .Associate

MCINTOSH AND OTIS, INC.

353 Lexington Ave., 15th Fl.
New York, NY 10016
PHONE 212-687-7400
FAX 212-687-6894
TYPES   Literary Talent
AFFILIATIONS   WGA
REPRESENTS   Book Authors - Screenwriters
SUBMISSION POLICY   Letter of inquiry required with SASE

Gene Winick . . . . .President
Jonathan Lyons . . . . .Literary Agent/Foreign Rights
Edward Necarsulmer . . . . .Literary Agent, Juvenile/Young Adults
Evva Pryor . . . . .Motion Pictures/TV/Stage
Elizabeth Winick . . . . .Literary Agent, Adult/Audio
Ian Polonsky .Motion Pictures/TV/Stage

MEDIA ARTISTS GROUP
6300 Wilshire Blvd., Ste. 1470
Los Angeles, CA 90048
PHONE . . . . .323-658-5050/323-658-7434 (Literary)
FAX 323-658-7842
TYPES   Commercial Talent - Film/TV Talent -
                          Literary Talent - Theatre Talent
AFFILIATIONS   AEA - AFTRA - DGA - SAG - WGA
REPRESENTS   Actors - Children - Comedians - Producers
                          - Screenwriters - Sports Personalities -
                          Teens/Young Adults - TV Writers

Raphael Berko . . . . .President/Principal, Theatrical
Barbara Alexander . . . . .President/Principal, Media Artists Group Literary
Kyle Lawrence . . . . .Agent

MENDEL MEDIA GROUP LLC
115 West 30th St., Ste. 800
New York, NY 10001
PHONE 646-239-9896
FAX 212-685-4717
EMAIL . . . . .scott@mendelmedia.com
WEB SITE . . . . .www.mendelmedia.com
TYPES   Literary Talent
AFFILIATIONS   AAR
REPRESENTS   Book Authors

Scott Mendel . . . . .Managing Partner

MENZA-BARRON AGENCY
1170 Broadway, Ste. 807
New York, NY 10001
PHONE 212-889-6850
EMAIL . . . . .claudia@menzabarron.com
SECOND EMAIL . . . . .manie@menzabarron.com
TYPES   Literary Talent
AFFILIATIONS   AAR
REPRESENTS   Book Authors - Screenwriters - TV Writers
COMMENTS   Focus on book authors

Claudia Menza . . . . .President
Manie Barron . . . . .Partner

METROPOLIS
132 Lasky Dr.
Beverly Hills, CA 90212
PHONE 310-273-2764
FAX 310-273-2784
TYPES   Literary Talent
REPRESENTS   Book Authors - Interactive Game
                          Developers - Producers - Screenwriters
COMMENTS   Specializes in animation talent

John Goldsmith . . . . .President
Matthew Ellis . . . . .Agent

METROPOLITAN TALENT AGENCY (MTA)
4500 Wilshire Blvd., 2nd Fl.
Los Angeles, CA 90010
PHONE 323-857-4500
FAX 323-857-4599
WEB SITE . . . . .www.mta.com
TYPES   Commercial Talent - Film/TV Talent -
                          Literary Talent - Modeling Talent - Talent &
                          Literary Packaging - Theatre Talent
AFFILIATIONS   AEA - AFTRA - ATA - DGA - WGA
REPRESENTS   Actors - Book Authors - Directors -
                          Producers - Screenwriters - Teens/Young
                          Adults - TV Writers - Variety Artists

Christopher Barrett . . . . .President/Talent/Literary
Dino Carlaftes . . . . .Head, Literary
Alan Ellsweig . . . . .Talent
Jennifer Good . . . . .Literary
Christina King . . . . .Talent
Aaron Kogan . . . . .Talent
Ryan Saul . . . . .Literary
Sara Schedeen . . . . .Talent
Andrés Rigal . . . . .Talent Coordinator

THE DORIS S. MICHAELS LITERARY AGENCY, INC.
1841 Broadway, Ste. 903
New York, NY 10023
PHONE 212-265-9474
FAX 212-265-9480
EMAIL . . . . .query@dsmagency.com
WEB SITE . . . . .www.dsmagency.com
TYPES   Literary Talent
SUBMISSION POLICY   Email submissions preferred

Doris S. Michaels . . . . .President
Delia Berrigan . . . . .Subsidiary Rights Specialist

THE GILBERT MILLER AGENCY LLC
4535 W. Sahara Ave., Ste. 112-C
Las Vegas, NV 89102-3708
PHONE 702-365-9000/702-362-6334
FAX 702-362-6055
TYPES   Commercial Talent - Music Talent - Talent
                          & Literary Packaging - Theatre Talent
AFFILIATIONS   AFM - AGVA
REPRESENTS   Animals - Comedians - Dancers -
                          Hosts/MCs - Magicians - Martial
                          Artists/Stunts - Music Artists - Seniors -
                          Speakers/Lecturers - Sports Personalities -
                          Variety Artists

Gilbert Miller . . . . .President
Bernice Miller . . . . .VP

THE STUART M. MILLER CO.
11684 Ventura Blvd., Ste. 225
Studio City, CA 91604-2699
PHONE 818-506-6067
FAX 818-506-4079
EMAIL . . . . .smmco@aol.com
TYPES   Literary Talent
AFFILIATIONS   ATA - DGA - WGA
REPRESENTS   Book Authors - Directors - Interactive
                          Game Developers - Playwrights - Producers
                          - Screenwriters - TV Writers

Stuart M. Miller . . . . .Owner

MIRAMAR TALENT AGENCY
7400 Beverly Blvd., Ste. 220
Los Angeles, CA 90036
PHONE 323-934-0700
TYPES   Commercial Talent - Film/TV Talent -
                        Modeling Talent
AFFILIATIONS   SAG
REPRESENTS   Actors - Print Models
SUBMISSION POLICY   No drop-offs

Virgilio Guillen . . . . .Agent

THE MIRISCH AGENCY
1875 Century Park East, Ste. 2050
Los Angeles, CA 90067
PHONE 310-282-9940
FAX 310-282-0702
EMAIL . . . . .robin@mirisch.com
WEB SITE . . . . .www.mirisch.com
TYPES   Below-the-Line Talent - Commercial Talent
                        - Film/TV Talent
AFFILIATIONS   DGA
REPRESENTS   Cinematographers - Composers - Film
                        Editors - Producers - Production Designers

Lawrence A. Mirisch . . . . .Owner/Agent
Jamie Allen . . . . .Commercial Agent
Cecilia Banck . . . . .Agent
Robin Schreer . . . . .Agent
Winston Taylor . . . . .Controller
Sino Tour . . . . .Projects Coordinator

MODEL CLUB, INC.
329 Columbus Ave.
Boston, MA 02116
PHONE 617-247-9020/401-273-7120
FAX 617-247-9262
WEB SITE . . . . .www.modelclubinc.com
TYPES   Commercial Talent - Film/TV Talent -
                        Modeling Talent
AFFILIATIONS   AFTRA - SAG
REPRESENTS   Actors - Children - Infants - Print Models -
                        Runway Models - Seniors - Teens/Young
                        Adults
COMMENTS   Full-service talent and model agency

Ed Sliney . . . . .Agent

MODEL TEAM
PO Box 10363
Aspen, CO 81612
PHONE 970-925-2022
FAX 970-920-3139
EMAIL .angela@modelteam.com
WEB SITE . . . . .www.modelteam.com
TYPES   Commercial Talent - Film/TV Talent -
                        Modeling Talent - Theatre Talent
AFFILIATIONS   SAG
REPRESENTS   Actors - Animals - Children - Dancers -
                        Infants - Martial Artists/Stunts - Print Models
                        - Runway Models - Seniors - Sports
                        Personalities - Teens/Young Adults
SUBMISSION POLICY   Via mail

Angela Seaman . . . . .Director
Siobhan O'Harrow . . . . .Booker

MOMENTUM TALENT & LITERARY AGENCY
6399 Wilshire Blvd., Ste. 1010
Los Angeles, CA 90048
PHONE 323-951-1151
FAX 323-951-1119
WEB SITE .www.momentumtal.com
TYPES   Commercial Talent - Film/TV Talent -
                        Literary Talent - Theatre Talent
REPRESENTS   Actors - Children - Print Models
SUBMISSION POLICY   No phone calls; Send hard copy via US mail

Garry Purdy . . . . .Owner/Agent
Mike Baldridge . . . . .Theatrical
Patti Crosby . . . . .Youth Division

MONTANA ARTISTS AGENCY, INC.
7715 Sunset Blvd., 3rd Fl.
Los Angeles, CA 90046
PHONE 323-845-4144
FAX 323-845-4155
WEB SITE .www.montanartists.com
TYPES   Below-the-Line Talent
AFFILIATIONS   DGA
REPRESENTS   Cinematographers - Composers - Film
                        Editors - Music Supervisors - Producers -
                        Production Designers
COMMENTS   Also represents costume designers, hair
                        and make-up artists, first assistant directors
                        and second unit directors

Jon Furie . . . . .President/CEO
Karen Berch . . . . .Sr. Agent, Features & Television
Brady Torgeson . . . . .Agent, Features & Television
Leslie Alyson . . .Agent, Commercials & Music Videos, Make-Up Artists &
                                                        Hair Stylists
Mike Rosen . . . . .Agent, Composers & Music Supervisors
Maya Jakubowicz . . . . .VP, Finance & Operations
Eric Klein . . . . .VP, Business & Legal Affairs
Allison Shashok . . . . .Executive Assistant to Jon Furie
Claudio Barrientos . . . . .Executive Assistant to Karen Berch
Christina Lehmann   Executive Assistant to Brady Torgeson & Leslie Alyson
Julian Savodivker . . .Executive Assistant to Maya Jakubowicz & Eric Klein

MONTEIRO ROSE DRAVIS AGENCY, INC.
17514 Ventura Blvd., Ste. 205
Encino, CA 91316
PHONE 818-501-1177
FAX 818-501-1194
WEB SITE .www.monteiro-rose.com
TYPES   Literary Talent
AFFILIATIONS   WGA
REPRESENTS   Book Authors - Producers - Screenwriters -
                        TV Writers

Candy Monteiro . . . . .Partner
Fredda Rose . . . . .Partner
Jason Dravis . . . . .Partner
Andrew Batey . . . . .Jr. Agent
Allein Siwa .Executive Assistant

MONTGOMERY WEST LITERARY AGENCY, LLC
225 N. Valley View Dr., Bldg. 85
St. George, UT 84770
PHONE 435-688-0273
FAX 435-688-0273
EMAIL .mntgmywest@aol.com
TYPES   Literary Talent
REPRESENTS   Book Authors - Screenwriters
SUBMISSION POLICY   Prefers queries by email
COMMENTS   Seeking screenwriting contest winners, but
                        will consider talented newcomers

Dr. Carole Western . . . . .President/Agent
Mary Barnes . . . . .Agent
Judi Daggy . . . . .Agent
Nancy Gummery . . . . .No Title

THE MORGAN AGENCY

6222 Wilshire Blvd., Ste. 302
Los Angeles, CA 90048
PHONE 323-938-6250
FAX 323-938-6244
WEB SITE . . . . .www.themorganagency.com
TYPES   Commercial Talent - Film/TV Talent -
     Modeling Talent - Music Talent - Theatre
     Talent
AFFILIATIONS   AEA - AFTRA - ATA - WGA
REPRESENTS   Actors - Children - Comedians - Dancers -
     Hosts/MCs - Martial Artists/Stunts - Print
     Models - Runway Models - Seniors -
     Teens/Young Adults - Variety Artists

Keith Lewis . . . . .President
Patricia Dawson . . . . .Agent, Union Commercials, Adult
Pierre Gatling . . . . .Agent, Union Commercials, Adult
Rich Smith . . . . .Agent, Non-Union Commercials & Print, Adult
Lilly Colon . . . . .Assistant to Keith Lewis
Trina Martinez . . . . .Agent's Assistant

H. DAVID MOSS & ASSOCIATES

733 N. Seward St., PH
Hollywood, CA 90038
PHONE 323-465-1234
FAX 323-465-1241
TYPES   Commercial Talent - Film/TV Talent -
     Theatre Talent
AFFILIATIONS   AEA - AFTRA - AGVA - DGA - SAG - WGA
REPRESENTS   Actors - Broadcast Journalists/Newscasters
     - Comedians - Musical Theatre Performers
     - Print Models - Seniors - Teens/Young
     Adults
SUBMISSION POLICY   By mail; No calls

H. David Moss . . . . .President/Owner

N.S. BIENSTOCK, INC.

1740 Broadway, 24th Fl.
New York, NY 10019
PHONE 212-765-3040
FAX 212-757-6411
EMAIL . . . . .nsb@nsbienstock.com
WEB SITE . . . . .www.nsbienstock.com
TYPES   Commercial Talent - Film/TV Talent -
     Literary Talent - Talent & Literary Packaging
AFFILIATIONS   AFTRA
REPRESENTS   Broadcast Journalists/Newscasters -
     Producers - TV Writers

Carole Cooper . . . . .Agent
Peter Goldberg . . . . .Agent
Myles Hazleton . . . . .Agent
George Hiltzik . . . . .Agent
Adam Leibner . . . . .Agent
Richard Leibner . . . . .Agent
Ezra Marcus . . . . .Agent
Steve Sadicario . . . . .Agent
Eric Wattenberg . . . . .Agent
Stuart Witt . . . . .Agent
Lori S. York . . . . .Agent

JEAN V. NAGGAR LITERARY AGENCY, INC.

216 E. 75th St., Ste. 1-E
New York, NY 10021
PHONE 212-794-1082
EMAIL . . . . .jregel@jvnla.com
WEB SITE . . . . .www.jvnla.com
TYPES   Literary Talent
AFFILIATIONS   AAR
REPRESENTS   Book Authors
SUBMISSION POLICY   Query letter with SASE

Jean V. Naggar . . . . .President
Anne Engel . . . . .Agent
Mollie Glick . . . . .Agent
Alice Tasman . . . . .Agent
Jennifer Weltz . . . . .VP, Rights Director/Children & Adults Agent
Jessica Regel . . . . .Subsidiary Rights/Children & Adults Agent
Mark Ferguson .Assistant to President

NAPOLI MANAGEMENT GROUP

8844 W. Olympic Blvd., Ste. 100
Beverly Hills, CA 90211
PHONE 310-385-8222
FAX 310-385-8242
EMAIL . . . . .nmg@tvtalent.com
WEB SITE . . . . .www.tvtalent.com
TYPES   Film/TV Talent
REPRESENTS   Broadcast Journalists/Newscasters -
     Hosts/MCs - Sports Personalities
COMMENTS   Works extensively with TV news on-air tal-
     ent/hosts

Mendes J. Napoli . . . . .President
Kathy Lieske-Peterson . . . . .VP, Business Affairs
David Ahrendts . . . . .Representative
Liz Hart . . . . .Representative
Laurie Jacoby . . . . .Representative
Sue McInerney . . . . .Representative
Jean Sage . . . . .Representative
Liz Sherwin . . . . .Representative
Lynda Ruffino . . . . .Executive Assistant to Mendes J. Napoli

NASH-ANGELES, INC.

PO Box 363
Hendersonville, TN 37077-0363
PHONE 615-347-8258
EMAIL . . . . .nafilm1@aol.com
TYPES   Commercial Talent - Film/TV Talent -
     Literary Talent - Music Talent
AFFILIATIONS   AFM - AFTRA - SAG
REPRESENTS   Book Authors - Composers - Music Artists -
     Music Producers - Screenwriters -
     Songwriters - Voice-Over Artists
COMMENTS   Full-service, multimedia entertainment com-
     pany; NATD, CMA, IEBA; Artist manage-
     ment; Film and video production; Film
     scoring; Music library

Eddie Reasoner . . . . .CEO
Jack Edwards . . . . .General Manager

AGENTS

SUSAN NATHE & ASSOCIATES, CPC
8281 Melrose Ave., Ste. 200
Los Angeles, CA 90046
PHONE 323-653-7573
FAX 323-653-1179
TYPES   Commercial Talent
AFFILIATIONS   AFTRA - ATA
REPRESENTS   Actors - Children - Teens/Young Adults
SUBMISSION POLICY   Referral only

Susan Nathe . . . . .Principal
Liz Quintero . . . . .Agent
Lisa Frantz . . . . .Assistant
Joanne Gordon . . . . .Assistant
Claire Ross . . . . .Assistant

NATURAL TALENT, INC.
3331 Ocean Park Blvd., Ste. 203
Santa Monica, CA 90405
PHONE 310-450-4945
FAX 310-450-4140
EMAIL . . . . .naturalt@earthlink.net
REPRESENTS   Directors - Producers - TV Writers
COMMENTS   Animation agency

Kelly Calder . . . . .Agent
Donna Felten . . . . .Agent

NEW ENGLAND PUBLISHING ASSOCIATES
PO Box 361
Chester, CT 06412-0361
PHONE 860-345-7323
FAX 860-345-3660
EMAIL . . . . .nepa@nepa.com
WEB SITE . . . . .www.nepa.com
TYPES   Literary Talent
AFFILIATIONS   AAR
REPRESENTS   Book Authors
SUBMISSION POLICY   Include one to two-page summary of pro-
                         posed book, description of intended audi-
                         ence and competition, annotated chapter
                         outline, polished sample chapter, statement
                         of authorship credentials, writing samples,
                         list of prior publications

Edward Knappman . . . . .President
Elizabeth Frost-Knappman . . . . .VP

NEW YORK OFFICE
15 W. 26th St., 5th Fl.
New York, NY 10010
PHONE 212-545-7895/323-468-2240
FAX 212-545-7941/323-468-2244
EMAIL . . . . .info@nyoffice.net
SECOND EMAIL . . . . .tm@nyoffice.net
WEB SITE . . . . .www.nyoffice.net
TYPES   Below-the-Line Talent - Commercial Talent
                         - Literary Talent - Music Talent - Theatre
                         Talent
REPRESENTS   Cinematographers - Composers - Directors
                         - Film Editors - Producers - Production
                         Designers - Screenwriters
COMMENTS   West Coast office: 6605 Hollywood Blvd.,
                         Ste. 200, Los Angeles, CA 90028

Julianne Hausler . . . . .President (NY)
Britton Rizzio . . . . .Agent (LA)
Dan De Filippo . . . . .Agent (NY)
Leslie Nowinski . . . . .Agent (NY)
Tamara Menear . . . . .Finance (NY)

NICOLOSI & CO., INC.
150 W. 25th St., Ste. 1200
New York, NY 10001
PHONE 212-633-1010
FAX 212-633-0050
EMAIL . . . . .jnicolosi@nicolosi-co.com
SECOND EMAIL . . . . .rgregory@nicolosi-co.com
TYPES   Below-the-Line Talent - Film/TV Talent
AFFILIATIONS   AFTRA
REPRESENTS   Actors - Comedians - Musical Theatre
                         Performers - Teens/Young Adults
SUBMISSION POLICY   Industry referral preferred; Do not call, fax
                         or send tape
COMMENTS   Also affiliated with NATR

Jeanne Nicolosi . . . . .Agent
Russell Gregory . . . . .Agent
Michael Goddard . . . . .Assistant
Emi Irikawa . . . . .Assistant

BETSY NOLAN LITERARY AGENCY
214 W. 29th St., 10th Fl., Ste. 1002
New York, NY 10001
PHONE 212-967-8200
FAX 212-967-7292
TYPES   Literary Talent
REPRESENTS   Book Authors
COMMENTS   No screenplays or poetry

Donald Lehr . . . . .President
Carla Glasser . . . . .Agent

NOUVEAU MODEL & TALENT
909 Prospect St., Ste. 230
La Jolla, CA 92037
PHONE 858-456-1400
FAX 858-456-1969
EMAIL . . . . .nouveaumodels@pacbell.net
WEB SITE . . . . .www.nouveaumodels.com
TYPES   Commercial Talent - Film/TV Talent -
                         Modeling Talent - Theatre Talent
AFFILIATIONS   AFTRA - SAG
REPRESENTS   Actors - Children - Print Models - Runway
                         Models - Teens/Young Adults
SUBMISSION POLICY   Submit by mail or email

Tony Long . . . . . .Agency Director/Female Model Division/Men's Division
Peter Hamm . . . . .CEO/International Scout

NOUVELLE TALENT MANAGEMENT, INC.
302A W. 12th St., Ste. 327
New York, NY 10014
PHONE 212-645-0940
FAX 212-242-6466
TYPES   Commercial Talent - Modeling Talent
AFFILIATIONS   AFTRA - SAG
REPRESENTS   Actors - Hosts/MCs - Magicians - Print
                         Models - Runway Models - Variety Artists
COMMENTS   Trade show models; Specializes in trade
                         shows and corporate promotions; Chicago
                         office: PO Box 578100, Chicago, IL
                         60657

Toni Sipka . . . . .President

NTA TALENT AGENCY
1445 N. Stanley Ave., 2nd Fl.
Los Angeles, CA 90046
PHONE 323-969-0113
FAX 323-969-0115
EMAIL .nta@ntatalent.com
WEB SITE . . . . .www.ntatalent.com
TYPES   Commercial Talent - Modeling Talent
AFFILIATIONS   SAG
REPRESENTS   Actors - Children - Comedians - Dancers -
                     Hosts/MCs - Infants - Magicians - Martial
                     Artists/Stunts - Print Models - Runway
                     Models - Seniors - Sports Personalities -
                     Teens/Young Adults
SUBMISSION POLICY   By mail only; No phone calls or drop-offs

Nick Terzian . . . . .President/Owner
Nancy Luciano .Commercial Agent
Adam Reeves . . . . .Commercial Agent
James Delio . . . . .Print Agent (323-969-0114)
Stephanie Ryan . . . . .Assistant

NU TALENT AGENCY
117 N. Robertson Blvd.
Los Angeles, CA 90048
PHONE 310-385-6907
FAX 310-385-6910
TYPES   Commercial Talent - Modeling Talent
AFFILIATIONS   AFTRA - SAG
REPRESENTS   Actors - Comedians - Dancers - Hosts/MCs
                     - Interactive Game Developers - Magicians
                     - Martial Artists/Stunts - Music Artists - Print
                     Models - Runway Models - Sports
                     Personalities - Teens/Young Adults - Variety
                     Artists

Magdalena Sanoja Ping . . . . .Director, Commercial Division
Danielle Valencia . . . . .Assistant

NXT ENTERTAINMENT, INC.
121 S. Palm Canyon Dr.
Palm Springs, CA 92262
PHONE 760-327-6500/323-496-9891
FAX 760-327-6510
EMAIL . . . . .talent@nxtentertainmentinc.com
WEB SITE . . . . .www.nxtentertainmentinc.com
TYPES   Commercial Talent - Film/TV Talent -
                     Modeling Talent - Music Talent - Theatre
                     Talent
AFFILIATIONS   SAG
REPRESENTS   Actors - Children - Dancers - Directors -
                     Infants - Music Artists - Print Models -
                     Runway Models - Seniors - Teens/Young
                     Adults - Voice-Over Artists

Terri Carroll . . . . .President/CEO
Dawn Parr . . . . .VP

HAROLD OBER ASSOCIATES
425 Madison Ave.
New York, NY 10017-1110
PHONE 212-759-8600
FAX 212-759-9428
TYPES   Literary Talent
AFFILIATIONS   AAR
REPRESENTS   Book Authors
SUBMISSION POLICY   No scripts

Don Laventhall . . . . .Motion Pictures/TV Rights
Pamela Malpas .Foreign Rights/Literary
Craig Tenney . . . . .Permissions
Phyllis Westberg . . . . .Literary/Dramatic

OFRENDA, INC.
3467 N. Knoll Dr.
Los Angeles, CA 90068
PHONE 323-851-6145
FAX 323-851-9078
EMAIL . . . . .donna@ofrenda.com
WEB SITE . . . . .www.ofrenda.com
TYPES   Below-the-Line Talent - Literary Talent -
                     Talent & Literary Packaging
AFFILIATIONS   AFM - SAG
REPRESENTS   Book Authors - Directors - Screenwriters -
                     Speakers/Lecturers - TV Writers
SUBMISSION POLICY   Upon request only
COMMENTS   Also affiliated with NALIP

Luis Aira . . . . .Founder/Agent/Director
Donna Casey-Aira .Executive Producer
Rachel Johnson . . . . .Director, Operations

O'NEILL TALENT GROUP
4150 Riverside Dr., Ste. 212
Burbank, CA 91505
PHONE 818-766-7717
WEB SITE . . . . .www.oneilltalent.com
TYPES   Commercial Talent - Film/TV Talent
AFFILIATIONS   AFTRA - SAG
REPRESENTS   Actors
SUBMISSION POLICY   Not accepting submissions

Sheila Ellis . . . . .Agent

ORACLE CREATIVE MANAGEMENT
9 Desbrosses St., Ste. 516
New York, NY 10013
PHONE 212-371-6269/310-694-3819
FAX 212-371-6270/310-694-3815
EMAIL . . . . .novak@oraclecreative.com
SECOND EMAIL . . . . .agent@oraclecreative.com
WEB SITE . . . . .www.oraclecreative.com
TYPES   Below-the-Line Talent - Commercial Talent
                     - Theatre Talent
AFFILIATIONS   DGA - SAG
REPRESENTS   Animals - Cinematographers - Directors -
                     Martial Artists/Stunts - Producers -
                     Screenwriters - TV Writers
COMMENTS   Represents directors of photography, assis-
                     tant directors, steadicam operators, cos-
                     tume designers and EFX make-up artists; IA
                     600

Ari Novak . . . . .President
Danny Stern . . . . .Agent
Jessica Tuffley . . . . .Agent
James Wolf . . . . .Agent
Anthony Ramirez . . . . .Associate

AGENTS

THE ORANGE GROVE GROUP, INC.
12178 Ventura Blvd., Ste. 205
Studio City, CA 91604
PHONE 818-762-7498
FAX 818-762-7499
EMAIL . . . . .gregmayo@orangegroupgroup.com
SECOND EMAIL . . . . .agent@orangegrovegroup.com
WEB SITE . . . . .www.orangegrovegroup.com
TYPES   Film/TV Talent - Literary Talent - Music
                     Talent - Talent & Literary Packaging -
                     Theatre Talent
AFFILIATIONS   AEA - AFTRA - ATA - DGA - WGA
REPRESENTS   Actors - Screenwriters - Teens/Young Adults
                     - TV Writers - Variety Artists

Gregory D. Mayo . . . . .President

ORIGIN TALENT
4705 Laurel Canyon Blvd., Ste. 306
Studio City, CA 91607
PHONE 818-487-1800
FAX 818-487-9788
EMAIL . . . . .firstname@origintalent.com
TYPES   Commercial Talent - Film/TV Talent -
                     Theatre Talent
AFFILIATIONS   AFTRA - SAG
REPRESENTS   Actors - Children - Comedians -
                     Teens/Young Adults
SUBMISSION POLICY   Send photo and resumé; Send tape upon
                     request only

Marc Chancer . . . . .Agent/Owner
Annie Schwartz . . . . .Agent/Owner
Robin Spitzer . . . . .Origin Kids, Theatrical/Commercial
Janet Tscha .Commercial Agent
Casey Schlesinger . . . . .Assistant
Lito Villareal . . . . .Assistant
April Zufelt . . . . .Assistant

ORIGINAL ARTISTS
9465 Wilshire Blvd., Ste. 324
Beverly Hills, CA 90212
PHONE 310-275-6765
FAX 310-275-6725
TYPES   Literary Talent - Talent & Literary Packaging
AFFILIATIONS   DGA - WGA
REPRESENTS   Book Authors - Directors - Producers -
                     Screenwriters - TV Writers
SUBMISSION POLICY   By referral only; No unsolicited material

Jordan Bayer . . . . .Agent
Matt Leipzig . . . . .Agent
Chris Sablan . . . . .Agent
Andrea Spiegel . . . . .Executive Assistant

ORLANDO MANAGEMENT
15134 Martha St.
Sherman Oaks, CA 91411
PHONE 818-781-9233
EMAIL . . . . .kirk@orlandomanagement.com
WEB SITE . . . . .www.orlandomanagement.com
TYPES   Below-the-Line Talent
REPRESENTS   Cinematographers - Production Designers

Kirk Orlando .President/Owner

OSBRINK TALENT AGENCY
4343 Lankershim Blvd., Ste. 100
Universal City, CA 91602
PHONE 818-760-2488
FAX 818-760-0991
EMAIL . . . . .contact@osbrinkagency.com
WEB SITE . . . . .www.osbrinkagency.com
TYPES   Below-the-Line Talent - Commercial Talent
                     - Film/TV Talent - Modeling Talent - Theatre
                     Talent
AFFILIATIONS   AFTRA - ATA
REPRESENTS   Actors - Children - Infants - Print Models -
                     Runway Models - Seniors - Teens/Young
                     Adults - Voice-Over Artists
SUBMISSION POLICY   Via mail or online

Cindy Osbrink . . . . .Partner/Head, Youth Theatrical
Scott Wine .Partner/Brand Manager
Dawn Osbrink . . . . .VP/Head, Youth Commercial & Modeling
Angela Strange . . . . .VP, Operations
Marco Servetti . . . . .Head, Adult Modeling
Laura Soo Hoo . . . . .Head, Adult Commercial
Maureen Rose . . . . .Voice-Over
Emily Urbani . . . . .Agent, Youth Theatrical
Erica Stimac . . . . .Public Relations
Erica Dugas . . . . .Branding & Licensing
Erika Franco . . . . .Assistant, Youth Print
Meghan Kelly . . . . .Assistant, Youth Commercial
Lea Patrick . . . . .Assistant, Voice-Over
Peyton Stroud . . . . .Assistant, Adult Commercial
Jennifer Velez . . . . .Assistant, Youth Theatrical

FIFI OSCARD AGENCY, INC.
110 W. 40th St.
New York, NY 10018
PHONE 212-764-1100
FAX 212-840-5019
EMAIL . . . . .agency@fifioscard.com
WEB SITE . . . . .www.fifioscard.com
TYPES   Commercial Talent - Film/TV Talent -
                     Literary Talent - Music Talent - Theatre
                     Talent
AFFILIATIONS   AAR - AEA - AFTRA - DGA - WGA
REPRESENTS   Actors - Book Authors - Composers -
                     Directors - Playwrights - Producers -
                     Screenwriters - Sports Personalities - Voice-
                     Over Artists
COMMENTS   Creative services; Dramatist Guild

Peter Sawyer .Managing Partner
Carmen LaVia . . . . .VP
Frances Del Duca . . . . .Agent
Carolyn French .Literary Agent
Kevin McShane . . . . .Agent
Jerry Rudes . . . . .Literary Agent

PACIFIC WEST ARTISTS
12500 Riverside Dr., Ste. 202
Valley Village, CA 91607
PHONE 818-755-8544
FAX 818-755-8549
TYPES   Commercial Talent
AFFILIATIONS   DGA - SAG
REPRESENTS   Actors - Comedians - Seniors

Marjorie Sperling . . . . .Agent

PAKULA/KING & ASSOCIATES
9229 Sunset Blvd., Ste. 315
Los Angeles, CA 90069
PHONE 310-281-4868
FAX 310-281-4866
TYPES   Film/TV Talent - Theatre Talent
AFFILIATIONS   AEA - AFTRA - SAG
REPRESENTS   Actors - Teens/Young Adults
SUBMISSION POLICY   By referral only; Absolutely no walk-ins

Joel King . . . . .Owner
Hilary Steinberg . . . . .Agent
Dennis Gleason . . . . .Agent
Jessica Dallow . . . . .Assistant
Craig Gaynier . . . . .Assistant

DOROTHY PALMER TALENT AGENCY, INC.
235 W. 56th St., Ste. 24-K
New York, NY 10019
PHONE 212-765-4280
FAX 212-977-9801
WEB SITE . . . . .www.dorothypalmertalentagency.com
TYPES   Commercial Talent - Film/TV Talent -
                          Literary Talent - Modeling Talent - Music
                          Talent - Talent & Literary Packaging
AFFILIATIONS   AEA - AFTRA - SAG - WGA
REPRESENTS   Actors - Animals - Book Authors -
                          Broadcast Journalists/Newscasters -
                          Children - Comedians - Dancers -
                          Hosts/MCs - Magicians - Martial
                          Artists/Stunts - Music Artists - Musical
                          Theatre Performers - Playwrights - Runway
                          Models - Screenwriters - Seniors -
                          Speakers/Lecturers - Sports Personalities -
                          Teens/Young Adults - TV Writers - Variety
                          Artists - Voice-Over Artists
COMMENTS   Singers; All ages, all ethnicities; Beautiful,
                          handsome and character types

Dorothy Palmer . . . . .Talent & Literary Agent
Kate Guille . . . . .No Title

THE MEG PANTERA AGENCY, INC.
138 W. 15th St.
New York, NY 10011
PHONE .212-219-9330/212-219-9332
FAX 646-201-4119
TYPES   Film/TV Talent - Theatre Talent
AFFILIATIONS   AEA - AFTRA - AGVA - SAG
REPRESENTS   Actors - Dancers - Musical Theatre
                          Performers

Meg Pantera . . . . .Agent

PANTHEON
1900 Avenue of the Stars, 28th Fl.
Los Angeles, CA 90067
PHONE 310-201-0120
FAX 310-201-5958
TYPES   Film/TV Talent - Literary Talent
AFFILIATIONS   AFTRA - ATA - SAG
REPRESENTS   Actors - Directors - Screenwriters

Art Bortolini . . . . .Agent
Lance Crayon . . . . .Agent
Reva Duenas . . . . .Agent
Stephen Rice . . . . .Agent
Araceli Romero . . . . .Agent
Adrienne Spitzer . . . . .Agent

PARADIGM (LOS ANGELES)
360 N. Crescent Dr., North Bldg.
Beverly Hills, CA 90210
PHONE 310-288-8000
FAX 310-288-2000
TYPES   Below-the-Line Talent - Endorsements -
                          Film/TV Talent - Literary Talent - Music
                          Talent - New Media - Talent & Literary
                          Packaging
AFFILIATIONS   AEA - AFTRA - DGA - SAG - WGA
REPRESENTS   Actors - Cinematographers - Comedians -
                          Directors - Music Artists - Producers -
                          Screenwriters - Teens/Young Adults - TV
                          Writers - Voice-Over Artists
COMMENTS   Monterey office: 509 Hartnell St.,
                          Monterey, CA 93940, phone: 831-375-
                          4889, fax: 831-375-2623; Nashville
                          office: 124 12th Ave. South, Ste. 410,
                          Nashville, TN 37203, phone: 615-251-
                          4400, fax: 615-251-4401

Sam Gores . . . . .Chairman
Jim Caskey . . . . .CFO
Craig Wagner . . . . .Executive VP, Business Affairs
Bill Harrison . . . . .Head, Corporate Communications
Joel Wright . . . . .VP, Business Development, New Media
Robert Stein . . . . .Head, Motion Picture Department
Sarah Clossey . . . . .Co-Head, Motion Picture Talent
Michael Lazo . . . . .Co-Head, Motion Picture Talent
Marc Helwig . . . . .Motion Picture Talent
Rich Hueners . . . . .Motion Picture/TV Talent
Jack Kingsrud . . . . .Motion Picture Talent
Sara Ramaker . . . . .Motion Picture Talent
Stephanie Ramsey .Motion Picture Talent
Andrew Rogers . . . . .Motion Picture Talent
Andrew Ruf . . . . .Motion Picture Talent
Brad Schenck . . . . .Motion Picture Talent
Chris Schmidt . . . . .Motion Picture Talent
Steve Small . . . . .Motion Picture/TV Talent
Alisa Adler . . . . .Co-Head, TV Talent
Joel Rudnick . . . . .Co-Head, TV Talent
Jim Dempsey . . . . .TV Talent
Judith Moss . . . . .TV Talent
Arthur Toretzky . . . . .TV Talent
Jim Hess . . . . .Comedy/Personal Appearances
Jeff Benson . . . . .Co-Head, TV Literary Department
Debbee Klein . . . . .Co-Head, TV Literary Department
Bill Douglass . . . . .TV Literary
Doug Fronk . . . . .TV Literary
Jill Gillett . . . . .TV Literary
Ken Greenblatt . . . . .TV Literary
Ian Greenstein . . . . .TV Literary
Max Kisbye . . . . .TV Literary
Andy Patman . . . . .TV Literary
Stephen Rose . . . . .TV Literary
Michael Van Dyck . . . . .TV Literary
Cal Boyington . . . . .Head, Alternative Programming
Josh Levenbrown . . . . .Alternative Programming
Norman Aladjem . . . .Head, International & Independent Film Packaging
Valarie Phillips . . . . .Head, Motion Picture Literary
Trevor Astbury . . . . .Motion Picture Literary
Lee Cohen . . . . .Motion Picture Literary
Rich Freeman . . . . .Motion Picture Literary
Scott Henderson .Motion Picture Literary
Mark Ross . . . . .Motion Picture Literary
Christopher Smith .Motion Picture Literary
Lucy Stille . . . . .Motion Picture Literary
Frank Balkin . . . . .Co-Head, Physical Production
Jay Gilbert . . . . .Co-Head, Physical Production
Lesley Feinstein . . . . .Physical Production
Gil Harari . . . . .Physical Production
Jasan Pagni . . . . .Physical Production

(Continued)

PARADIGM (LOS ANGELES) (Continued)

Jeannine Angelique	Commercial/Music Video Production
Kris Frazier	Endorsements/Commercials & Voice-Over/Branding
Fred Bohlander	Music (Monterey)
Lynn Cingari	Music (Monterey)
Donald E. Hooper	Music (Monterey)
Jonathan Levine	Music (Monterey)
Duffy McSwiggin	Music (Monterey)
Jackie Nalpant	Music (Monterey)
Aaron Pinkus	Music (Monterey)
Hank Sacks	Music (Monterey)
Dan Weiner	Music (Monterey)
Bobby Cudd	Music (Nashville)
Steve Dahl	Music (Nashville)
Brian Hill	Music (Nashville)
Greg Janese	Music (Nashville)
Curt Motley	Music (Nashville)
Pete Olsen	Music (Nashville)
Ray Shelide	Music (Nashville)
Aaron Tannenbaum	Music (Nashville)
James Yelich	Music (Nashville)
Shauna Emmons	Director, Business & Legal Affairs
Larry Sheffield	Executive, Business & Legal Affairs

PARADIGM (NEW YORK)
500 Fifth Ave., 37th Fl.
New York, NY 10110

PHONE	212-703-7540
FAX	212-764-8941
TYPES	Commercial Talent - Endorsements - Film/TV Talent - Literary Talent - Modeling Talent - Music Talent - Theatre Talent
AFFILIATIONS	AEA - AFTRA - DGA - SAG
REPRESENTS	Actors - Book Authors - Choreographers - Directors - Music Artists - Playwrights - Print Models - Production Designers - Screenwriters - Voice-Over Artists
COMMENTS	Additional offices: 19 W. 44th St., Ste. 1410, New York, NY 10036, phone: 212-391-1112, fax: 212-575-6397; 1776 Broadway, Ste. 2010, New York, NY 10019, phone: 212-586-1000, fax: 212-586-1007; Little Big Man Booking Agency office: 155 Avenue of the Americas, 6th Fl., New York, NY 10013, phone: 646-336-8520, fax: 646-336-8522

Sarah Fargo	Theatrical/Motion Pictures/TV
Scott Metzger	Theatrical/Motion Pictures/TV
Thomas O'Donnell	Theatrical/Motion Pictures/TV
Rosanne Quezada	Theatrical/Motion Pictures/TV
Timothy Sage	Theatrical/Motion Pictures/TV
Richard Schmenner	Theatrical/Motion Pictures/TV
Clifford Stevens	Theatrical/Motion Pictures/TV
Ed Batchelor	Voice-Over/Commercials
Jeb Bernstein	Voice-Over/Commercials
Olivia Catt	Voice-Over/Commercials
Matt Ambrosia	Voice-Over/Promos
Vickie Barroso	Voice-Over/Promos
Douglas Kesten	Commercials
Stacye Mayer	Commercials
Vanessa Gringer	Models/Celebrity Endorsements
Lydia Wills	Literary/Books (44th St. Office)
Jason Yarn	Literary/Books (44th St. Office)
William Craver	Theatrical/Literary (44th St. Office)
Christopher Till	Theatrical/Literary (44th St. Office)
Stephanie Mahler	Music (44th St. Office)
Fleurette Vincent	Music (44th St. Office)
Bryan Billig	Comedy/Personal Appearances (Broadway Office)
Matt Frost	Comedy/Personal Appearances (Broadway Office)
Marty Diamond	President/CEO (Little Big Man)
Larry Webman	VP (Little Big Man)
Andy Adelewitz	Music/Publicity (Little Big Man)
Jonathan Adelmen	Music (Little Big Man)
Steve Ferguson	Music (Little Big Man)

THE PARADISE GROUP TALENT AGENCY
8721 Sunset Blvd., Ste. 209
Los Angeles, CA 90069

PHONE	310-854-6622
FAX	310-854-6665
EMAIL	info@theparadisegroup.com
WEB SITE	www.theparadisegroup.com
TYPES	Commercial Talent - Modeling Talent
AFFILIATIONS	AFTRA - SAG
REPRESENTS	Actors - Broadcast Journalists/Newscasters - Comedians - Hosts/MCs - Producers - Sports Personalities
COMMENTS	Hosting talent agency; Talent and producers for reality shows, entertainment/news programs, game shows, documentaries, talk shows, infomercials, trade shows, new media networks, commercial endorsements

John Paradise	President/Agent
Paul Barrutia	Agent
Joshua Johnson	Agent
Ben Toubia	Assistant to Joshua Johnson
Jonathan Yates	Assistant to Paul Barrutia

THE PARTOS COMPANY
227 Broadway, Ste. 204
Santa Monica, CA 90401

PHONE	310-458-7800
FAX	310-587-2250
WEB SITE	www.partos.com
TYPES	Below-the-Line Talent
AFFILIATIONS	DGA - SAG - WGA
REPRESENTS	Cinematographers - Production Designers
COMMENTS	Also represents wardrobe, prop stylist/set designers, and hair and make-up artists

Walter Partos	Owner/Agent
Martijn Hostetler	Agent
Tomoko Konami-Quinn	Agent

PASTORINI-BOSBY TALENT, INC.
3013 Fountainview, Ste. 240
Houston, TX 77057

PHONE	713-266-4488
FAX	713-266-3314
WEB SITE	www.pastorini-bosbytalent.com
TYPES	Commercial Talent - Film/TV Talent
AFFILIATIONS	AFTRA - SAG
REPRESENTS	Actors - Broadcast Journalists/Newscasters - Children - Comedians - Sports Personalities - Teens/Young Adults - Voice-Over Artists
COMMENTS	WIFT

Jenny Bosby	Owner/Agent
Beverly Pastorini	Owner/Agent

KATHI J. PATON LITERARY AGENCY
PO Box 2240
New York, NY 10101

PHONE	212-265-6586
EMAIL	kjplitbiz@optonline.net
TYPES	Literary Talent
REPRESENTS	Book Authors
COMMENTS	Books only; No screenplays

Kathi J. Paton	Agent

PEAK MODELS & TALENT
27955 Smyth Dr., Ste. 103
Valencia, CA 91355
PHONE 661-294-1100
FAX 661-294-9311
EMAIL . . . . .natasha@peakmodels.com
SECOND EMAIL . . . . .info@peakmodels.com
WEB SITE . . . . .www.peakmodels.com
TYPES   Commercial Talent - Film/TV Talent -
           Modeling Talent
AFFILIATIONS   SAG
REPRESENTS   Actors - Dancers - Print Models - Runway
           Models - Voice-Over Artists
COMMENTS   Also reps fit models

Natasha Duswalt . . . . .Agency Owner, Commercials/Print
Craig Duswalt . . . . .Agency Owner, Film/TV
Tammi Weaver . . . . .Sr. Booker
Sue Doran . . . . .Talent Coordinator
Melissa Brimigion .Account Manager
Shawn Nickerson . . . . .IT Specialist

BARRY PERELMAN AGENCY
1155 N. La Cienega Blvd., Ste. 412
West Hollywood, CA 90069
PHONE 310-659-1122
FAX 310-659-1122
TYPES   Literary Talent
REPRESENTS   Book Authors - Directors - Producers -
           Screenwriters - TV Writers
SUBMISSION POLICY   Mail query only

Barry A. Perelman . . . . .President/Literary

PERFECTLY PETITE, INC.
2500 W. County Rd. 42, Ste. 108
Burnsville, MN 55337
PHONE 952-882-9626
FAX 952-882-9618
EMAIL . . . . .models@perfectlypetite.com
SECOND EMAIL . . . . .info@perfectlypetite.com
WEB SITE . . . . .www.perfectlypetite.com
TYPES   Commercial Talent - Film/TV Talent -
           Modeling Talent - Music Talent - Theatre
           Talent
REPRESENTS   Actors - Animals - Broadcast
           Journalists/Newscasters - Children -
           Choreographers - Comedians - Dancers -
           Directors - Hosts/MCs - Infants - Magicians
           - Martial Artists/Stunts - Music Artists -
           Musical Theatre Performers - Print Models -
           Producers - Runway Models - Seniors -
           Speakers/Lecturers - Sports Personalities -
           Teens/Young Adults - Variety Artists - Voice-
           Over Artists
SUBMISSION POLICY   No faxed or emailed submissions accepted;
           Direct mail only

Dawn Parr . . . . .President

PERIWINKLE ENTERTAINMENT PRODUCTIONS
PO Box 2486
Anaheim, CA 92814-0486
PHONE 714-776-5820
FAX 714-635-1711
TYPES   Commercial Talent - Film/TV Talent - Music
           Talent
REPRESENTS   Animals - Magicians - Variety Artists
COMMENTS   Represents circus and sideshow talent

Bambi Burnes . . . . .Co-Owner
Chuck Burnes . . . . .Co-Owner

L. PERKINS AGENCY
5800 Arlington Ave.
Riverdale, NY 10471
PHONE 718-543-5344
EMAIL . . . . .lperkinsagency@yahoo.com
TYPES   Literary Talent
AFFILIATIONS   AAR
REPRESENTS   Book Authors
COMMENTS   Also affiliated with HWA

Lori Perkins . . . . .Owner/Agent
Jenny Rappaport . . . . .Agent (jrlperkinsagency@yahoo.com)

PETERS FRASER & DUNLOP (PFD)
373 Park Avenue South, 5th Fl.
New York, NY 10016
PHONE 917-256-0707
FAX 212-685-9635
WEB SITE . . . . .www.pfd.co.uk
TYPES   Below-the-Line Talent - Literary Talent
REPRESENTS   Book Authors

Zoe Pagnamenta . . . . .Agent
Mark Reiter . . . . .Agent

STEPHEN PEVNER, INC.
382 Lafayette St., 8th Fl.
New York, NY 10003
PHONE 212-674-8403
FAX 212-529-3692
EMAIL . . . . .spevner@aol.com
TYPES   Literary Talent
AFFILIATIONS   DGA
REPRESENTS   Book Authors - Directors - Playwrights -
           Screenwriters

Stephen Pevner . . . . .Founder/President
Elizabeth Romanski . . . . .Development Assistant

PHOENIX ARTISTS, INC.
311 W. 43rd St., Ste. 304
New York, NY 10036
PHONE 212-586-9110
FAX 212-586-8019
EMAIL . . . . .phoenixartistsinc@gmail.com
TYPES   Film/TV Talent - Literary Talent - Theatre
           Talent
AFFILIATIONS   AEA - AFTRA
REPRESENTS   Actors - Children - Teens/Young Adults
COMMENTS   Also affiliated with NATR

Gary Epstein . . . . .No Title
Randi Ross . . . . .No Title
Jayson Simmons . . . . .No Title

JOHN PIERCE AGENCY
800 S. Robertson Blvd., Ste. 5
Los Angeles, CA 90035
PHONE 310-358-0101
TYPES   Film/TV Talent
REPRESENTS   Actors

John Pierce . . . . .Agent

PINDER LANE & GARON-BROOKE ASSOCIATES, LTD.
159 W. 53rd St., Ste. 14-C
New York, NY 10019
PHONE 212-489-0880
FAX 212-489-7104
EMAIL . . . . .pinderl@rcn.com
TYPES   Literary Talent
AFFILIATIONS   AAR - AFM - AFTRA - SAG - WGA
REPRESENTS   Book Authors
SUBMISSION POLICY   Query only; No unsolicited manuscripts;
                         No screenplays

Dick Duane . . . . .Co-Owner/Sr. Agent
Robert Thixton . . . . .Co-Owner/Sr. Agent

PINNACLE COMMERCIAL TALENT
5055 Wilshire Blvd., Ste. 865
Los Angeles, CA 90036
PHONE 323-939-5440
FAX 323-939-0630
TYPES   Commercial Talent
AFFILIATIONS   AFTRA - ATA
REPRESENTS   Actors

Mike Eisenstadt . . . . .Owner
John Frazier . . . . .Owner
Joan Messinger . . . . .Agent
Kim Muir . . . . .Agent

PLAYERS TALENT AGENCY
16000 Ventura Blvd., Ste. 522
Encino, CA 91436
PHONE 818-379-1722
FAX 323-297-2877
TYPES   Commercial Talent - Film/TV Talent - Music
                         Talent - Theatre Talent
AFFILIATIONS   AFTRA - SAG
REPRESENTS   Actors - Broadcast Journalists/Newscasters
                         - Comedians - Hosts/MCs - Martial
                         Artists/Stunts - Seniors - Sports Personalities
                         - Teens/Young Adults
SUBMISSION POLICY   No drop-offs
COMMENTS   A division of Player Talent, dealing with
                         teens, Latin celebrities, professional athletes
                         and top collegiate athletes

Joe Kolkowitz . . . . .Owner/Agent

THE LYNN PLESHETTE LITERARY AGENCY
2700 N. Beachwood Dr.
Los Angeles, CA 90068
PHONE 323-465-0428
TYPES   Literary Talent
AFFILIATIONS   WGA
REPRESENTS   Screenwriters
SUBMISSION POLICY   Unsolicited submissions not accepted

Lynn Pleshette . . . . .Agent
Michael Cendejas . . . . .Agent
Rowan Riley . . . . .Assistant

PREFERRED ARTISTS
16633 Ventura Blvd., Ste. 1421
Encino, CA 91436
PHONE 818-990-0305
FAX 818-990-2736
TYPES   Literary Talent
AFFILIATIONS   DGA - WGA
REPRESENTS   Directors - Producers - Screenwriters - TV
                         Writers
SUBMISSION POLICY   Referrals only

Roger Strull . . . . .Principal
Brad Rosenfeld . . . . .Literary
Paul Weitzman . . . . .Literary
Lew Weitzman . . . . .Literary

JIM PREMINGER AGENCY
11111 Santa Monica Blvd., Ste. 530
Los Angeles, CA 90025
PHONE 310-231-7979
FAX 310-231-7970
TYPES   Literary Talent - Talent & Literary Packaging
AFFILIATIONS   DGA - WGA
REPRESENTS   Directors - Producers - Screenwriters - TV
                         Writers
SUBMISSION POLICY   By personal referral only

Jim Preminger . . . . .Principal/Literary
Dean A. Schramm .Agent, Literary
Joan Turner . . . . .Administrator
Christine Work . . . . .Assistant to Mr. Preminger
Michael Endler . . . . .Assistant to Mr. Schramm

THE PRICE GROUP LLC
280 Madison Ave., Ste. 705
New York, NY 10016
PHONE 212-725-1980
FAX 646-292-5110
EMAIL .lisa@thepricegroupllc.net
WEB SITE .www.thepricegroupllc.net
TYPES   Film/TV Talent - Theatre Talent
AFFILIATIONS   AEA
REPRESENTS   Actors - Dancers - Musical Theatre
                         Performers
SUBMISSION POLICY   No calls; No visits; Attends showcases;
                         Pictures, resumés and reels from union tal-
                         ent only; Will contact if interested
COMMENTS   Broadway, tours, stock and live appear-
                         ances; Talent over the age of eighteen

Lisa Price . . . . .President
Dominic Edlin . . . . .Assistant
Alyceson Reyman . . . . .Assistant

THE AARON M. PRIEST LITERARY AGENCY
708 Third Ave., 23rd Fl.
New York, NY 10017
PHONE 212-818-0344
FAX 212-573-9417
TYPES   Literary Talent
REPRESENTS   Book Authors
SUBMISSION POLICY   Email a one page query letter describing
                         your work as well as your background; Do
                         not attach portions of your work unless
                         requested; Please do not submit to more
                         than one agent at this agency; Agents will
                         respond within three weeks if interested
COMMENTS   No sci fi, horror, fantasy, screenplays or
                         poetry

Aaron Priest . . . . .Owner/Agent, Thrillers/Fiction
                         (querypriest@aaronpriest.com)
Lisa Erbach Vance . . . . .Agent, Mystery/Thriller/Historical Fiction/
                         Women's Fiction/Narrative Non-Fiction/Memoir
                         (queryvance@aaronpriest.com)
Lucy Childs . . . . .Agent, Literary & Commercial Fiction/Memoir/
                         Historical Fiction/Women's Fiction (querychilds@aaronpriest.com)

Nicole Kenealy . . . . . .Agent, Chick-Lit/Women's Fiction/Literary Fiction/
    Young Adult Fiction/Non-Fiction (querykenealy@aaronpriest.com)
Alexandra Ozeri . . . . .General Assistant

PRIME ARTISTS
20121 Ventura Blvd., Ste. 301
Woodland Hills, CA 91364
PHONE 818-888-5171
FAX 818-884-2402
EMAIL . . . . .info@primeartists.net
WEB SITE . . . . .www.primeartists.net
TYPES   Below-the-Line Talent
AFFILIATIONS   DGA
REPRESENTS   Cinematographers - Composers - Directors
                  - Film Editors - Music Supervisors -
                  Producers - Production Designers
COMMENTS   Also represents line producers, UPMs,
                  sound mixers, costume designers, first ADs

Darren A. Sugar . . . . .President
Dave Kensler . . . . .Agent
Carole Biggerstaff . . . . .Agent
Nancy Shawish . . . . .Agent

PRIVILEGE TALENT AGENCY
PO Box 260860
Encino, CA 91426
PHONE 818-386-2377
TYPES   Commercial Talent - Film/TV Talent -
                  Modeling Talent
AFFILIATIONS   AFTRA - SAG
REPRESENTS   Actors - Broadcast Journalists/Newscasters
                  - Children - Comedians - Dancers -
                  Hosts/MCs - Infants - Martial Artists/Stunts
                  - Print Models - Runway Models - Sports
                  Personalities - Teens/Young Adults
SUBMISSION POLICY By mail only; No follow-up calls

Carol Oleesky . . . . .Owner/President/Theatrical/Commercial
Melanie Raymundo . . . . .Print Division
Melissa Graf . . . . .Assistant

PROFESSIONAL ARTISTS
321 W. 44th St., Ste. 605
New York, NY 10036
PHONE 212-247-8770
FAX 212-977-5686
TYPES   Film/TV Talent - Literary Talent - Theatre
                  Talent
AFFILIATIONS   AEA - AFTRA - SAG - WGA
REPRESENTS   Actors - Directors
COMMENTS   No children; Directors for stage only

Sheldon Lubliner . . . . .Owner/Agent
Marilynn Scott Murphy . . . . .Owner/Agent
Ashley Williams . . . . .Sub-Agent
Paul Riley . . . . .Agent Assistant

PROGRESSIVE ARTISTS AGENCY
400 S. Beverly Dr., Ste. 216
Beverly Hills, CA 90212
PHONE 310-553-8561
FAX 310-553-4726
TYPES   Film/TV Talent - Theatre Talent
AFFILIATIONS   AEA - AFTRA - SAG
REPRESENTS   Actors - Comedians - Directors - Producers
                  - Teens/Young Adults
SUBMISSION POLICY By mail only

Bernard Carneol . . . . .Theatrical
Belle Zwerdling . . . . .Theatrical
Jillana Devine . . . . .Assistant

SUSAN ANN PROTTER LITERARY AGENT
110 W. 40th St., Ste. 1408
New York, NY 10018
PHONE 212-840-0480
FAX 212-840-1132
EMAIL . . . . .sapla@aol.com
WEB SITE . . . . .www.susanannprotter.com
TYPES   Literary Talent
AFFILIATIONS   AAR
REPRESENTS   Book Authors
SUBMISSION POLICY Query first by US Mail with SASE or brief
                  query by email to saprotter@aol.com
COMMENTS   Also affiliated with the Authors Guild

Susan Protter . . . . .Agent

PTI TALENT AGENCY, INC.
14724 Ventura Blvd., PH
Sherman Oaks, CA 91403
PHONE 818-386-1310
TYPES   Commercial Talent - Modeling Talent
AFFILIATIONS   SAG
REPRESENTS   Actors - Comedians - Print Models -
                  Seniors - Teens/Young Adults
SUBMISSION POLICY By mail only
COMMENTS   Actors and actresses of all types and ages

Danie Wulff . . . . .Owner/Agent

Q MODEL MANAGEMENT
8618 W. Third St.
Los Angeles, CA 90048
PHONE 310-205-2888/212-807-6777
FAX 310-205-6920/212-807-8999
WEB SITE .www.qmanagementinc.com
TYPES   Commercial Talent - Modeling Talent
AFFILIATIONS   SAG
REPRESENTS   Actors - Comedians - Print Models -
                  Seniors - Teens/Young Adults
SUBMISSION POLICY Commercial: mail only; Print: call for open
                  call times
COMMENTS   Sixteen years and up; New York office: 180
                  Varick, Fl. 13, New York, NY 10014

Jennifer Chandler . . . . .Talent
Cynthia Cheng . . . . .Print
Shelly Kolsrud . . . . .Print

Q6 MODEL & ARTIST MANAGEMENT
800 E. Burnside St., Studio 2
Portland, OR 97214
PHONE 503-274-8555
FAX 503-274-4615
EMAIL . . . . .justin@q6talent.com
WEB SITE www.q6talent.com
TYPES   Modeling Talent
AFFILIATIONS   SAG
REPRESENTS   Print Models - Runway Models
SUBMISSION POLICY Mail or email

Justin Habel . . . . .President/Manager
Mateo Harris . . . . .Booking Agent
Jon Shultz . . . . .Booking Agent

QUALITA DELL' ARTE: ARTISTS & WRITERS DI QUALITA
6303 Owensmouth Ave., 10th Fl.
Woodland Hills, CA 91367
PHONE 818-936-3566
TYPES   Commercial Talent - Film/TV Talent -
                       Literary Talent - Music Talent - Theatre
                       Talent
AFFILIATIONS   AEA - AFTRA - DGA - SAG - WGA
REPRESENTS   Actors - Book Authors - Broadcast
                       Journalists/Newscasters - Children -
                       Comedians - Composers - Dancers -
                       Directors - Martial Artists/Stunts - Music
                       Artists - Music Producers - Print Models -
                       Producers - Screenwriters - Sports
                       Personalities - Teens/Young Adults - TV
                       Writers - Variety Artists - Voice-Over Artists

Dan A. Bellacicco . . . . .Agent/President
Giovanni Fresco . . . . .Executive VP, Theater/TV/Commercials
Aida Buonarroti . . . . .Sr. VP, Young Adults/Teens
Julianna Di Fiori . . . . .Sr. VP, Literary/Directors
Pulci Nella . . . . .Sr. VP, Lyricists/Composers

QUILLCO AGENCY
3104 W. Cumberland Ct.
Westlake Village, CA 91362
PHONE 805-495-8436
FAX 805-373-9868
EMAIL . . . . .quillco22@verizon.net
TYPES   Literary Talent
AFFILIATIONS   WGA
REPRESENTS   Screenwriters - TV Writers
SUBMISSION POLICY   Referral only

Sandy Mackey . . . . .Principal/Owner/Agent

THE RABINEAU WACHTER SANFORD & HARRIS LITERARY AGENCY
522 Wilshire Blvd., Ste. L
Santa Monica, CA 90401
PHONE 310-587-2700
FAX 310-587-2710
EMAIL . . . . .firstname@rwshagency.com
TYPES   Literary Talent
REPRESENTS   Book Authors - Directors - Screenwriters

Sylvie Rabineau . . . . .Partner
Liza Wachter . . . . .Partner
Geoffrey Sanford . . . . .Partner
Nick Harris . . . . .Partner

RAINES & RAINES
c/o Theron Raines
103 Kenyon Rd.
Medusa, NY 12120
PHONE 518-239-8311
FAX 518-239-6029
TYPES   Literary Talent
AFFILIATIONS   AAR - WGA
REPRESENTS   Book Authors - Screenwriters
SUBMISSION POLICY   One-page queries only; Not accepting
                       screenplays at this time

Joan Raines . . . . .Partner
Theron Raines . . . . .Partner
Keith Korman . . . . .Associate

THE RAPPAPORT AGENCY
6311 Romaine St., Ste. 7204
Hollywood, CA 90038
PHONE 323-464-4481
FAX 323-464-5030
EMAIL . . . . .bungalow8@rappagency.com
WEB SITE . . . . .www.rappagency.com
TYPES   Below-the-Line Talent
REPRESENTS   Directors
COMMENTS   Represents photographers

Jodi Rappaport . . . . .Agent

READ.
8033 Sunset Blvd., Ste. 937
Los Angeles, CA 90046
PHONE 323-876-2800
FAX 323-876-2801
TYPES   Literary Talent
AFFILIATIONS   DGA - WGA
REPRESENTS   Directors - Producers - Screenwriters - TV
                       Writers
SUBMISSION POLICY   No unsolicited material; Referral only

Melissa Read . . . . .Agent/Principal (melissa@readagency.net)
Hilary Stern . . . . .Agent (hilary@readagency.net)

REBEL ENTERTAINMENT PARTNERS, INC.
5700 Wilshire Blvd., Ste. 456
Los Angeles, CA 90036
PHONE 323-935-1700
FAX 323-932-9901
EMAIL .frontdesk@reptalent.com
WEB SITE . . . . .www.reptalent.com
TYPES   Film/TV Talent - Talent & Literary Packaging
AFFILIATIONS   AFTRA - ATA - DGA - SAG
REPRESENTS   Actors - Directors - Hosts/MCs - Producers
COMMENTS   FKA Abrams-Rubaloff & Lawrence;
                       Celebrities and talent for reality TV, news,
                       game shows; Strong focus on packaging;
                       Selectively representing theatrical clients

Richard Lawrence . . . . .President
Debra Goldfarb . . . . .VP, TV Department
Bill Thompson . . . . .VP, TV Department
Philip Irven . . . . .Agent, TV Department
Seth Lawrence .Agent, TV Department
Jason Egenberg . . . . .Agent, Talent Department
Dana-Lee Schuman . . . . .Agent, Talent Department
Joyce Goertzen . . . . .CFO
Jason Corman . . . . .Human Resources
Tina Wlasick . . . . .Business Affairs
William McNeal . . . . .Talent Payments
Jeffrey Wank . . . . .Television Coordinator

REECE HALSEY NORTH
98 Main St., #704
Tiburon, CA 94920
PHONE 415-789-9191
FAX 415-789-9177
EMAIL . . . . .info@reecehalseynorth.com
WEB SITE . . . . .www.reecehalseynorth.com
TYPES   Literary Talent
AFFILIATIONS   AAR
REPRESENTS   Book Authors
SUBMISSION POLICY   Book authors only: Mail query with first ten
                       to fifty pages and SASE to Kimberley
                       Cameron

Kimberley Cameron . . . . .Agent, Reece Halsey North
Elizabeth Evans . . . . .Associate, Reece Halsey North
Phil Lang . . . . .Associate, Reece Halsey North

JODIE RHODES AGENCY
8840-315 Villa La Jolla Dr.
La Jolla, CA 92037
PHONE 858-625-0544
TYPES   Literary Talent
AFFILIATIONS   AAR
REPRESENTS   Book Authors
COMMENTS   Mainstream/commercial, multicultural,
                          political, fiction, nonfiction

Jodie Rhodes . . . . .President
Bob McCarter . . . . .Nonfiction Agent at Large
Clark McCutcheon . . . . .Fiction Agent at Large
Vicki Satlow .Foreign Rights Agent (Milan, Italy)

RIGHTS UNLIMITED
6 West 37th St.
New York, NY 10018
PHONE 212-246-0900
FAX 212-246-2114
WEB SITE .www.rightsunlimited.com
TYPES   Literary Talent
AFFILIATIONS   AAR
REPRESENTS   Book Authors
SUBMISSION POLICY   Query letter/email with SASE, synopsis or
                          sample chapters
COMMENTS   Affiliated with International Thriller Writers,
                          Inc. (ITW), Mystery Writers of America and
                          Women's National Book Association

John Sansevere . . . . .CEO
Raymond Kurman . . . . .Chairman
Diane Dreher . . . . .Director
Albert T. Longden . . . . .Director
Ben Salmon . . . . .Literary Agent

THE ANGELA RINALDI LITERARY AGENCY
PO Box 7877
Beverly Hills, CA 90212
PHONE 310-842-7665
FAX 310-837-8143
EMAIL . . . . .amr@rinaldiliterary.com
TYPES   Literary Talent
AFFILIATIONS   AAR
REPRESENTS   Book Authors
SUBMISSION POLICY   Brief email query only; Novels: brief synop-
                          sis and first three chapters; Nonfiction: out-
                          line and sample chapter; Include SASE,
                          allow 4-6 weeks for response
COMMENTS   Commercial and literary fiction and nonfic-
                          tion

Angela Rinaldi . . . . .Literary Agent
Lisa Cron . . . . .Associate

ANN RITTENBERG LITERARY AGENCY, INC.
30 Bond St.
New York, NY 10012
PHONE 212-684-6936
WEB SITE . . . . .www.rittlit.com
TYPES   Literary Talent
AFFILIATIONS   AAR
REPRESENTS   Book Authors
SUBMISSION POLICY   Mail query letters; Include SASE; No email
                          or fax queries
COMMENTS   No screenplays

Ann Rittenberg . . . . .President
Penn Whaling . . . . .Assistant

RLR ASSOCIATES
7 W. 51st St., 4th Fl.
New York, NY 10019
PHONE 212-541-8641
FAX 212-262-7084
EMAIL .info@rlrassociates.net
WEB SITE .www.rlrassociates.net
TYPES   Film/TV Talent - Literary Talent
REPRESENTS   Book Authors - Broadcast
                          Journalists/Newscasters - Directors -
                          Producers - Sports Personalities
SUBMISSION POLICY   See Web site

Robert L. Rosen . . . . .President
Gary I. Rosen . . . . .Executive VP
Craig C. Foster . . . . .VP
Jennifer Unter . . . . .VP, Literary Division
Tara Mark . . . . .Literary Agent
Michael Klein . . . . .Director, Business Development
Gail Lockhart .Executive Assistant

MICHAEL D. ROBINS & ASSOCIATES
23241 Ventura Blvd., Ste. 300
Woodland Hills, CA 91364
PHONE 818-343-1755
FAX 818-343-7355
EMAIL . . . . .mdr2@msn.com
TYPES   Below-the-Line Talent - Film/TV Talent -
                          Literary Talent - Music Talent
AFFILIATIONS   DGA - WGA
REPRESENTS   Book Authors - Cinematographers -
                          Comedians - Composers - Directors -
                          Music Producers - Producers - Screenwriters
                          - TV Writers
SUBMISSION POLICY   Send query letter with synopsis and contact
                          info; Will contact if interested

Michael D. Robins . . . . .Principal
Beverly S. Robins . . . . .Office Manager

THE ROISTACHER LITERARY AGENCY
545 W. 111th St.
New York, NY 10025
PHONE 212-222-1405
TYPES   Literary Talent
REPRESENTS   Book Authors
SUBMISSION POLICY   Serious nonfiction; Literary fiction only from
                          previously published authors; No screen-
                          plays

Robert Roistacher . . . . .President

CINDY ROMANO MODELING & TALENT AGENCY
PO Box 1951
Palm Springs, CA 92263
PHONE 760-323-3333
TYPES   Commercial Talent - Film/TV Talent -
                          Modeling Talent
AFFILIATIONS   SAG
REPRESENTS   Actors - Animals - Children - Comedians -
                          Martial Artists/Stunts - Print Models -
                          Runway Models - Screenwriters - Seniors -
                          Sports Personalities - Teens/Young Adults -
                          TV Writers - Voice-Over Artists
SUBMISSION POLICY   Headshot and resumé by mail
COMMENTS   Fitness models and bodybuilders

Cindy Romano . . . . .President
Charis Romano McFarlane . . . . .VP

THE BRANT ROSE AGENCY
6671 Sunset Blvd., Ste. 1584B
Los Angeles, CA 90028
PHONE 323-460-6464
FAX 323-460-6454
EMAIL . . . . .hub@brantroseagency.com
TYPES   Literary Talent - Talent & Literary Packaging
AFFILIATIONS   DGA - WGA
REPRESENTS   Directors - Producers - Screenwriters - TV
                     Writers
SUBMISSION POLICY   No unsolicited material

Brant Rose . . . . .Owner/Agent
Toochis Morin . . . . .Agent
John Strong . . . . .Assistant

THE ROSENBERG GROUP
23 Lincoln Ave.
Marblehead, MA 01945
PHONE 781-990-1341
FAX 781-990-1344
WEB SITE .www.rosenberggroup.com
TYPES   Literary Talent
AFFILIATIONS   AAR
REPRESENTS   Book Authors
SUBMISSION POLICY   Query letters only
COMMENTS   Adult fiction: women's, romance, main-
                     stream, literary; See Web site for areas of
                     interest in trade nonfiction

Barbara Collins Rosenberg . . . . .Agent

ROSENSTONE/WENDER
38 E. 29th St., 10th Fl.
New York, NY 10016
PHONE 212-725-9445
FAX 212-725-9447
TYPES   Literary Talent - Theatre Talent
AFFILIATIONS   AAR - DGA - WGA
REPRESENTS   Book Authors - Choreographers - Directors
                     - Playwrights - Screenwriters - TV Writers
SUBMISSION POLICY   No unsolicited material

Phyllis Wender . . . . .Partner
Ron Gwiazda . . . . .Agent
Sonia Pabley . . . . .Agent
Amy Wagner . . . . .Associate
Sheila Myrie . . . . .Accounting

THE ROTHMAN BRECHER AGENCY
9465 Wilshire Blvd., Ste. 840
Beverly Hills, CA 90212
PHONE 310-247-9898
FAX 310-247-9888
EMAIL . . . . .reception@rothmanbrecher.com
TYPES   Literary Talent - Talent & Literary Packaging
AFFILIATIONS   DGA - WGA
REPRESENTS   Directors - Producers - Screenwriters - TV
                     Writers
SUBMISSION POLICY   Referral only

Dan Brecher . . . . .Partner/TV Agent
Robb Rothman . . . . .Partner/TV Agent
Jim Rothman . . . . .CFO
Jim Ehrich . . . . .Feature Agent
Dennis Kim . . . . .TV Agent
Vanessa Livingston . . . . .TV Agent
Camran Shafii . . . . .TV Agent
Ariel Rubin . . . . .Assistant
Kyle Shimizu . . . . .Assistant
Josh Sussman . . . . .Assistant
Diana Metzger . . . . .Receptionist

JANE ROTROSEN AGENCY
318 E. 51st St.
New York, NY 10022
PHONE 212-593-4330
FAX 212-935-6985
TYPES   Literary Talent
AFFILIATIONS   AAR
REPRESENTS   Book Authors
SUBMISSION POLICY   No queries accepted from unpublished
                     authors or those not referred by client or
                     colleague

Jane Rotrosen Berkey . . . . .Owner/Director
Andrea Cirillo . . . . .Agent
Annelise Robey . . . . .Agent
Meg Ruley . . . . .Agent
Peggy Gordijn .Sub-Rights Director
Kelly Harms . . . . .Assistant to Andrea Cirillo
Christina Hogrebe . . . . .Assistant to Annelise Robey & Meg Ruley

PETER RUBIE LITERARY AGENCY
240 W. 35th St., Ste. 500
New York, NY 10001
PHONE 212-279-1282
FAX 212-279-0927
WEB SITE . . . . .www.prlit.com
TYPES   Literary Talent
AFFILIATIONS   AAR
REPRESENTS   Book Authors
SUBMISSION POLICY   See Web site
COMMENTS   No scripts, screenplays or short stories

Peter Rubie . . . . .President
June Clark . . . . .Sr. Associate
Bob Shuman . . . . .Agent at Large
Amy Tipton . . . . .Agent (assist@prlit.com)

RUSSELL & VOLKENING

50 W. 29th St., Ste. 7E
New York, NY 10001
PHONE 212-684-6050
FAX 212-889-3026
TYPES   Literary Talent
AFFILIATIONS   AAR
REPRESENTS   Book Authors

Tim Seldes . . . . .President/Literary Agent
Jesseca Salky . . . . .Agent

SAN DIEGO MODEL MANAGEMENT TALENT AGENCY

438 Camino del Rio South, Ste. 116
San Diego, CA 92108
PHONE 619-296-1018
FAX 619-296-3422
EMAIL . . . . .info@sdmodel.com
WEB SITE . . . . .www.sdmodel.com
TYPES   Commercial Talent - Film/TV Talent -
                       Modeling Talent
AFFILIATIONS   AFTRA - SAG
REPRESENTS   Actors - Children - Infants - Print Models -
                       Runway Models - Teens/Young Adults
COMMENTS   Largest agency south of Los Angeles

Fred Sweet . . . . .President
Linda Comer . . . . .Agency Director, Print/Talent/Runway
Jennifer Fite . . . . .Kids/Promo
Sarah Canton . . . . .Office Manager

SAN FRANCISCO TOP MODELS & TALENT

2261 Market St., Ste. 295
San Francisco, CA 94114
PHONE 415-391-1800
FAX 415-391-2012
EMAIL . . . . .sftoptalent@sbcglobal.net
WEB SITE . . . . .www.sftoptalent.com
TYPES   Commercial Talent - Film/TV Talent -
                       Modeling Talent - Theatre Talent
AFFILIATIONS   AFTRA - SAG
REPRESENTS   Actors - Broadcast Journalists/Newscasters
                       - Children - Comedians - Hosts/MCs -
                       Infants - Martial Artists/Stunts - Print Models
                       - Seniors - Sports Personalities -
                       Teens/Young Adults - Voice-Over Artists
SUBMISSION POLICY   Mail with SASE; Do not drop off

Belinda Irons . . . . .Owner/Agent

VICTORIA SANDERS & ASSOCIATES, LLC

241 Avenue of the Americas, Ste. 11H
New York, NY 10014
PHONE 212-633-8811
EMAIL .queriesvsa@hotmail.com
WEB SITE . . . . .www.victoriasanders.com
TYPES   Literary Talent
AFFILIATIONS   AAR - WGA
REPRESENTS   Book Authors
SUBMISSION POLICY   Query letter via email; If via regular mail,
                       include SASE
COMMENTS   No screenplays

Victoria Sanders . . . . .Member
Diane Dickensheid . . . . .Member

SANGER TALENT AGENCY

9911 W. Pico Blvd., 8th Fl.
Los Angeles, CA 90035
PHONE 310-284-2619
FAX 310-388-5422
EMAIL . . . . .sangertalent@aol.com
WEB SITE . . . . .www.sangertalent.com
TYPES   Commercial Talent - Literary Talent - Music
                       Talent - Talent & Literary Packaging -
                       Theatre Talent
AFFILIATIONS   SAG
REPRESENTS   Actors - Children - Comedians -
                       Composers - Dancers - Directors -
                       Hosts/MCs - Magicians - Martial
                       Artists/Stunts - Music Artists - Music
                       Producers - Print Models - Producers -
                       Screenwriters - Speakers/Lecturers -
                       Teens/Young Adults - TV Writers - Variety
                       Artists - Voice-Over Artists
COMMENTS   Affiliated with Little Studio Films; Owner of
                       Music Unlimited Talent Agency

Karl B. Sanger . . . . .Agent
Teresa Otteson . . . . .Agent

THE SARNOFF COMPANY, INC.

10 Universal City Plaza, Ste. 2000
Universal City, CA 91608
PHONE 818-753-2377
FAX 818-753-2378
TYPES   Film/TV Talent - Literary Talent - Modeling
                       Talent - Talent & Literary Packaging
AFFILIATIONS   AEA - AFTRA - DGA - SAG - WGA
REPRESENTS   Actors - Broadcast Journalists/Newscasters
                       - Directors - Print Models - Producers -
                       Screenwriters - TV Writers
SUBMISSION POLICY   No unsolicited material from writers

James Sarnoff . . . . .Owner
David Sarnoff . . . . .Agent

THE SAVAGE AGENCY

6212 Banner Ave.
Los Angeles, CA 90038-2802
PHONE 323-461-8316
FAX 323-461-2417
TYPES   Commercial Talent - Film/TV Talent - Music
                       Talent - Theatre Talent
AFFILIATIONS   AEA - AFTRA - SAG
REPRESENTS   Actors - Children - Teens/Young Adults
SUBMISSION POLICY   Submit by mail only; No follow-up calls
COMMENTS   Represents talent ages three to twenty-five

Judy Savage . . . . .Owner/Theatrical Agent
Stella Alex . . . . .Agent
Jason Barias . . . . .Agent
Jennifer Boyce . . . . .Commercial Agent
Mark Savage . . . . .Bookkeeper
Mark Smith . . . . .Office Assistant

JACK SCAGNETTI TALENT & LITERARY AGENCY

5118 Vineland, Ste. 102
North Hollywood, CA 91601
PHONE 818-762-3871/818-761-0580
WEB SITE . . . . .www.jackscagnetti.com
TYPES   Below-the-Line Talent - Commercial Talent
                        - Film/TV Talent - Literary Talent - Modeling
                        Talent - Talent & Literary Packaging -
                        Theatre Talent
AFFILIATIONS   AEA - AFTRA - SAG - WGA
REPRESENTS   Actors - Book Authors - Comedians -
                        Dancers - Hosts/MCs - Magicians - Martial
                        Artists/Stunts - Screenwriters - Seniors - TV
                        Writers - Voice-Over Artists
SUBMISSION POLICY   Mail only, do not call
COMMENTS   Seeking actors late teens to early twenties,
                        plus others; Focus on comics and charac-
                        ters of all ages

Jack Scagnetti . . . . .Principal

THE IRV SCHECHTER COMPANY

9460 Wilshire Blvd., Ste. 300
Beverly Hills, CA 90212
PHONE 310-278-8070
FAX 310-278-6058
EMAIL . . . . .asst@iscagency.com
TYPES   Below-the-Line Talent - Film/TV Talent -
                        Literary Talent - Talent & Literary Packaging
                        - Theatre Talent
AFFILIATIONS   AEA - AFTRA - ATA - DGA - SAG - WGA
REPRESENTS   Actors - Book Authors - Comedians -
                        Directors - Producers - Screenwriters -
                        Sports Personalities - TV Writers
COMMENTS   Animation

Irv Schechter . . . . .Principal/Literary/Directors/Producers
Mieke Schechter . . . . .Talent

SCHIOWITZ CONNOR ANKRUM WOLF, INC.

1680 N. Vine St., Ste. 1016
Los Angeles, CA 90028
PHONE 323-463-8355/212-840-6787
TYPES   Film/TV Talent - Theatre Talent
AFFILIATIONS   AEA - AFTRA - SAG - WGA
REPRESENTS   Actors
COMMENTS   Daytime soaps; Established adult clientele
                        and well-trained young adults eighteen and
                        up; East Coast office: 165 W. 46th St., Ste.
                        1210, New York, NY 10036

Josh Schiowitz . . . . .Partner, Theatrical/Equity (NY)
Teresa Wolf . . . . .Partner, Theatrical/Equity (NY)
David Ankrum . . . . .Partner, Theatrical/Literary
Erin Connor . . . . .Partner, Theatrical
Steven Dry . . . . .Equity
Caleigh Vancata . . . . .Theatrical

SANDIE SCHNARR TALENT

8500 Melrose Ave., Ste. 212
West Hollywood, CA 90069
PHONE 310-360-7680
FAX 310-360-7681
TYPES   Commercial Talent - Film/TV Talent
AFFILIATIONS   AFTRA - SAG
REPRESENTS   Actors - Voice-Over Artists
SUBMISSION POLICY   By referral only

Sandie Schnarr . . . . .Principal
Melissa Grillo . . . . .Agent
Mark Gura . . . . .Agent
Seth Podowitz . . . . .No Title

THE SCHNEIDER ENTERTAINMENT AGENCY

22287 Mulholland Hwy., Ste. 210
Calabasas, CA 91302-5157
PHONE 818-222-5200
FAX 818-222-5284
EMAIL . . . . .mail@schneiderentertainment.com
WEB SITE . . . . .www.schneiderentertainment.com
TYPES   Below-the-Line Talent
AFFILIATIONS   DGA
REPRESENTS   Cinematographers - Directors
SUBMISSION POLICY   Accepts general submissions for Below-the-
                        Line talent only
COMMENTS   Also reps hair stylists, make-up artists and
                        steadicam operators

Wendy Schneider . . . . .Agent/Owner
Teena Deocales . . . . .Associate Agent

JUDY SCHOEN & ASSOCIATES

606 N. Larchmont Blvd., Ste. 307
Los Angeles, CA 90004
PHONE 323-962-1950
TYPES   Film/TV Talent
AFFILIATIONS   AEA - AFTRA - ATA - SAG
REPRESENTS   Actors - Teens/Young Adults
SUBMISSION POLICY   By referral only

Michelle Mazurki . . . . .President
Jon Williams . . . . .Agent

SCHULLER TALENT/NY KIDS

276 Fifth Ave., Ste. 206
New York, NY 10001
PHONE 212-532-6005/917-747-6017
FAX 212-252-1256
EMAIL . . . . .margaret@schullertalent.com
WEB SITE . . . . .www.schullertalent.com
TYPES   Commercial Talent - Film/TV Talent -
                        Literary Talent - Modeling Talent - Music
                        Talent - Theatre Talent
AFFILIATIONS   AFTRA - SAG
REPRESENTS   Actors - Children - Choreographers -
                        Comedians - Composers - Dancers -
                        Directors - Hosts/MCs - Infants - Martial
                        Artists/Stunts - Music Artists - Musical
                        Theatre Performers - Print Models -
                        Producers - Teens/Young Adults - Variety
                        Artists - Voice-Over Artists

Margaret Matuka . . . . .Agent/President
Mark Smith . . . . .No Title
Cindy Snow . . . . .No Title

SUSAN SCHULMAN LITERARY AGENCY

454 W. 44th St.
New York, NY 10036
PHONE 212-713-1633
FAX 212-581-8830
EMAIL . . . . .schulman@aol.com
TYPES   Literary Talent
AFFILIATIONS   AAR - WGA
REPRESENTS   Book Authors - Playwrights - TV Writers
SUBMISSION POLICY   Send query letter and resumé with SASE
COMMENTS   Dramatists Guild; Fiction and nonfiction
                        authors including children's books;
                        Subsidary rights including foreign/transla-
                        tion, film and TV rights

Susan Schulman . . . . .Owner/Agent/Literary
Linda Migalti . . . . .Submissions Editor
Eleanora Tevis . . . . .Rights Director
Emily Uhry . . . . .Theater Department

AGENTS

KATHLEEN SCHULTZ ASSOCIATES
6442 Coldwater Canyon Ave., Ste. 206
Valley Glen, CA 91606
PHONE 818-760-3100
FAX 818-760-3125
EMAIL . . . . kschultzassoc@aol.com
TYPES   Film/TV Talent - Theatre Talent
AFFILIATIONS   AEA - AFTRA - SAG
REPRESENTS   Actors - Teens/Young Adults
SUBMISSION POLICY Mail photo and resumé

Kathleen Schultz . . . . .Owner
Jennifer Trendowski . . . . .Agent, Comericals/Print

SCREEN ARTISTS AGENCY, LLC
4361 Tujunga Ave.
Studio City, CA 91604
PHONE 818-487-8880
FAX 818-487-8883
TYPES   Below-the-Line Talent - Commercial Talent
                 - Film/TV Talent - Theatre Talent
AFFILIATIONS   AFTRA - SAG
REPRESENTS   Actors - Children - Teens/Young Adults
SUBMISSION POLICY Mail only, do not call

Cyndee Burditt . . . . .Owner/Agent
Erica Hunton . . . . .Agent
Arjon Flenoy . . . . .Assistant

THE SCREEN TALENT AGENCY, LTD.
58 Speed House, Barbican
London EC2Y 8AT, United Kingdom
PHONE 020-7628-5180
FAX 020-7681-3588
EMAIL . . . . info@screen-talent.com
WEB SITE . . . . .www.screen-talent.com
TYPES   Commercial Talent - Film/TV Talent -
                 Literary Talent - Modeling Talent
REPRESENTS   Cinematographers - Composers - Directors
                 - Musical Theatre Performers - Producers -
                 Screenwriters

James Little . . . . .President
Sue Williams . . . . .Associate

SCRIBBLERS HOUSE LLC LITERARY AGENCY
PO Box 1007
Cooper Station
New York, NY 10276-1007
PHONE 212-714-7747
WEB SITE . . . . .www.scribblershouse.net
TYPES   Literary Talent
REPRESENTS   Book Authors
SUBMISSION POLICY See web site

Stedman Mays . . . . .Agent
Garrett Gambino . . . . .Agent

SDB PARTNERS, INC.
1801 Avenue of the Stars, Ste. 902
Los Angeles, CA 90067
PHONE 310-785-0060
FAX 310-785-0071
EMAIL . . . . info@sdbpartners.com
TYPES   Film/TV Talent - Theatre Talent
AFFILIATIONS   AEA - AFTRA - SAG
REPRESENTS   Actors
SUBMISSION POLICY Industry referral only

Louis Bershad . . . . .Partner
Ro Diamond . . . . .Partner
Susie Schwarz . . . . .Partner
Steven Jang . . . . .Agent
Andrea Robinette .Assistant

SESLER & COMPANY
11840 Jefferson Blvd.
Culver City, CA 90230
PHONE 310-966-4005/416-504-1223
FAX 323-988-0930/416-504-3345
EMAIL . . . . .dora@seslercompany.com
SECOND EMAIL . . . . .info@seslercompany.com
TYPES   Below-the-Line Talent
REPRESENTS   Cinematographers
COMMENTS   Represents cinematographers worldwide for
                 Features, Commercials, TV and Music
                 Videos; Toronto office: 862 Richmond St.
                 West, Ste. 200, Toronto, ON, M6J 1C9
                 Canada

Dora Sesler .Owner/Agent
Michael Pepper . . . . .Agent
Samantha Mogan . . . . .Agent (Toronto)

SGM - SARA GAYNOR MANAGEMENT
433 N. Camden Dr., Ste. 600
Beverly HIlls, CA 90210
PHONE 310-994-2935
FAX 310-861-0103
EMAIL . . . . .sara@sgmmodels.com
WEB SITE . . . . .www.sgmmodels.com
TYPES   Commercial Talent - Modeling Talent
REPRESENTS   Actors - Hosts/MCs - Print Models -
                 Runway Models - Teens/Young Adults
COMMENTS   Emphasis on personal attention and man-
                 agement

Sara Gaynor Novick . . . . .Owner/Agent

SHAMON FREITAS MODEL & TALENT AGENCY
9606 Tierra Grande, Ste. 204
San Diego, CA 92126
PHONE 858-549-3955/949-582-3955
FAX 858-549-7028
EMAIL . . . . .carol@shamonfreitas.com
SECOND EMAIL . . . . .frank@shamonfreitas.com
WEB SITE . . . . .www.shamonfreitas.com
TYPES   Commercial Talent - Film/TV Talent -
                 Modeling Talent - Theatre Talent
AFFILIATIONS   AEA - AFTRA - SAG
REPRESENTS   Actors - Children - Hosts/MCs - Infants -
                 Print Models - Runway Models - Seniors -
                 Teens/Young Adults - Voice-Over Artists
SUBMISSION POLICY See Web site
COMMENTS   Office in Orange County

Carol S. Freitas . . . . .Owner/Agent
Frank DiPalermo . . . . .Agent
Jodie Bowman . . . . .Assistant

DAVID SHAPIRA & ASSOCIATES (DSA)
193 N. Robertson Blvd.
Beverly Hills, CA 90211
PHONE 310-967-0480
FAX 310-659-4177
EMAIL . . . . .sison@dsa-agency.com
TYPES   Literary Talent - Theatre Talent
AFFILIATIONS   AFTRA - SAG
REPRESENTS   Actors - Hosts/MCs

David Shapira .Owner/CEO
Ryan Karvola . . . . .Agent
Mark Scroggs . . . . .Agent
Matt Shapira . . . . .Agent
Michelle Sison . . . . .Assistant to David Shapira/Office Manager
Abbey Robertson . . . . .Assistant to Mark Scroggs & Ryan Karvola

SHAPIRO-LICHTMAN TALENT AGENCY, INC.

1010 Lexington Rd.
Beverly Hills, CA 90210
PHONE 310-859-8877
FAX 310-276-0630
EMAIL . . . . .mss@shapiro-lichtman.com
TYPES   Below-the-Line Talent - Film/TV Talent -
                      Literary Talent
AFFILIATIONS   AEA - AFTRA - DGA - SAG - WGA
REPRESENTS   Actors - Cinematographers - Directors -
                      Film Editors - Producers - Production
                      Designers - Screenwriters - TV Writers
SUBMISSION POLICY   Query letters only; No unsolicited material

Mark Lichtman . . . . .Principal
Martin Shapiro . . . . .Principal

SHELDON PROSNIT AGENCY

800 S. Robertson Blvd., Ste. 6
Los Angeles, CA 90035
PHONE 310-652-8778
FAX 310-652-8772
EMAIL . . . . .info@lspagency.net
WEB SITE . . . . .www.lspagency.net
TYPES   Below-the-Line Talent - Commercial Talent
                      - Film/TV Talent - Music Talent
AFFILIATIONS   DGA - WGA
REPRESENTS   Cinematographers - Directors - Film Editors
                      - Music Supervisors - Producers -
                      Production Designers - Sound Editors
COMMENTS   Also represents Make-Up Artists, First assis-
                      tant directors, Line Producers and Costume
                      Designers; Affiliated with AICP and MVPA

Robin Sheldon . . . . .Partner/Features & TV
Jane Prosnit . . . . .Partner/Features & TV
Gregg Dallesandro . . . . .Agent, Commercials & Music Videos
Rebecca Fayyad . . . . .Agent, Features & TV
Veronica Lombardo . . . . .Agent, Commercials & Music Videos
Joey Sabella . . . . .Features Assistant
Amanda Ross . . . . .Commercials & Music Videos Assistant

KEN SHERMAN & ASSOCIATES

9507 Santa Monica Blvd., Ste. 211
Beverly Hills, CA 90210
PHONE 310-273-8840
FAX 310-271-2875
EMAIL . . . . .ken@kenshermanassociates.com
TYPES   Literary Talent - Talent & Literary Packaging
REPRESENTS   Book Authors - Playwrights - Producers -
                      Screenwriters - TV Writers
SUBMISSION POLICY   By referral only
COMMENTS   Executive advisory board of the Christopher
                      Isherwood Foundation, BAFTA, TV
                      Academy; PEN International advisory
                      board; Fiction and nonfiction;
                      Commissioner of Arts & Cultural Affairs,
                      West Hollywood; Represents life rights and
                      film & TV rights to books

Ken Sherman . . . . .President
Helia Correia . . . . .Assistant
Todd Robbins . . . . .Assistant

BOBBE SIEGEL LITERARY AGENCY

41 W. 83rd St.
New York, NY 10024
PHONE 212-877-4985
FAX 212-877-4985
EMAIL . . . . .bobbesiegelagency@yahoo.com
TYPES   Literary Talent
REPRESENTS   Book Authors
SUBMISSION POLICY   No unsolicited manuscripts; Send query let-
                      ter with SASE; Absolutely no short stories,
                      humor, romance, science fiction, poetry,
                      religion or cooking material
COMMENTS   OAG

Bobbe Siegel . . . . .Owner/Agent
Sarah Jo Siegel . . . . .Agent

JEROME SIEGEL ASSOCIATES

1680 N. Vine St., Ste. 613
Hollywood, CA 90028
PHONE 323-466-0185
TYPES   Film/TV Talent - Literary Talent
AFFILIATIONS   AEA - DGA - SAG
REPRESENTS   Actors - Book Authors - Directors -
                      Producers - Screenwriters

Jerome Siegel . . . . .Owner

THE SKOURAS AGENCY

1149 Third St., 3rd Fl.
Santa Monica, CA 90403
PHONE 310-395-9550
FAX 310-395-4295
TYPES   Below-the-Line Talent - Commercial Talent
                      - Film/TV Talent
REPRESENTS   Cinematographers - Directors - Film Editors
                      - Producers - Production Designers

Spyros Skouras . . . . .Owner/Agent
Lara Polivka Sackett . . . . .Partner, Features
Hilary McQuaide . . . . .Partner, Commercials
Marie Perry . . . . .Agent, Commercials
Hillary Corinne Cook . . . . .Agent, Features

SKY TALENT AGENCY

1642 N. Cahuenga Blvd., #206
Hollywood, CA 90028
PHONE 323-469-4118
FAX 323-469-1790
EMAIL . . . . .info@skytalentagency.com
WEB SITE . . . . .www.skytalentagency.com
TYPES   Commercial Talent - Modeling Talent
AFFILIATIONS   SAG
REPRESENTS   Actors - Comedians - Infants - Runway
                      Models - Teens/Young Adults

Isam Duzzi . . . . .Agent
Ehab Duzzi . . . . .Agent

SMA, LLC

PMB 380, 8950 W. Olympic Blvd.
Beverly Hills, CA 90211
PHONE 310-203-8787
FAX 310-203-8742
EMAIL . . . . .sara@smaagency.com
WEB SITE . . . . .www.smaagency.com
TYPES   Film/TV Talent - Literary Talent
AFFILIATIONS   WGA
REPRESENTS   Directors - Producers - Screenwriters - TV
                      Writers
SUBMISSION POLICY   Industry referral preferred; Agency's release
                      form signed by applicant required before
                      reading material

Sara Margoshes . . . . .Literary Agent

CRAYTON SMITH AGENCY
15760 Ventura Blvd., 16th Fl.
Encino, CA 91436
PHONE 310-600-6171
TYPES   Below-the-Line Talent

Crayton Smith . . . . .Agent

SMS TALENT, INC.
8730 Sunset Blvd., Ste. 440
Los Angeles, CA 90069
PHONE 310-289-0909
TYPES   Film/TV Talent - Theatre Talent
AFFILIATIONS   AEA - AFTRA - ATA
REPRESENTS   Actors
SUBMISSION POLICY   No unsolicited submissions

Donna Massetti . . . . .Partner
Gregg Mehlman . . . . .Partner
Charles Silver . . . . .Partner
Marilyn Szatmary . . . . .Partner
Ian Roumain . . . . .Sub-Agent
Erin Cooper . . . . .Assistant
Danielle Henderson .Assistant
Esi Impraim . . . . .Assistant

THE SOHL AGENCY
935 Sanborn Ave.
Los Angeles, CA 90029
PHONE 323-644-0500
FAX 323-644-0544
TYPES   Commercial Talent - Film/TV Talent
AFFILIATIONS   SAG
REPRESENTS   Actors
SUBMISSION POLICY   Currently not accepting submissions for
                         representation

Sohl . . . . .Owner/Agent
Sarah Sorrell . . . . .Assistant

SOLID TALENT, INC.
6860 Lexington Ave.
Los Angeles, CA 90038
PHONE 323-978-0808
FAX 323-978-0810
EMAIL . . . . .mikesoliday@solidtalent.com
WEB SITE . . . . .www.solidtalent.com
TYPES   Commercial Talent - Film/TV Talent - Music
                         Talent - Theatre Talent
AFFILIATIONS   AFTRA - SAG

Mike Soliday . . . . .Agent

MICHAEL H. SOMMER LITERARY AGENCY
202 US Route 1, Ste. 123
Falmouth, ME 04105
PHONE 207-773-4859
FAX 207-773-4859
EMAIL . . . . .mhsmaine@yahoo.com
TYPES   Literary Talent
REPRESENTS   Book Authors - Directors - Producers -
                         Screenwriters - TV Writers
SUBMISSION POLICY   Via email only
COMMENTS   See listing for West Coast co-agent,
                         Warden McKinley Literary Agency

Michael H. Sommer . . . . .Owner

SONJA WARREN BRANDON'S COMMERCIALS UNLIMITED, INC.
190 N. Canon Dr., Ste. 302
Beverly Hills, CA 90210
PHONE 310-278-5123
FAX 310-278-4665
TYPES   Commercial Talent - Film/TV Talent
AFFILIATIONS   AFTRA - ATA - SAG
REPRESENTS   Actors - Children - Comedians - Seniors -
                         Teens/Young Adults
SUBMISSION POLICY   Mail or drop off picture and resumé

Sonja Warren Brandon . . . . .Agent
Randi Rubenstein . . . . .Agent
Richard Reiner . . . . .Agent
Paul Williams . . . . .Agent
Nora Zilz . . . . .Agent
Sheran Burke . . . . .Assistant

SPECIAL ARTISTS AGENCY
9465 Wilshire Blvd., #890
Beverly Hills, CA 90212
PHONE 310-859-9688
TYPES   Commercial Talent
AFFILIATIONS   AFTRA - SAG
REPRESENTS   Actors
SUBMISSION POLICY   Referral and SAG/AFTRA only; Voice-Over
                         demos and pictures

Elizabeth Dalling .Celebrities
Alix Gucovsky . . . . .Agent
Kylie MacKenzie . . . . .Agent
Lisa Reider . . . . .Agent

PHILIP G. SPITZER LITERARY AGENCY, INC.
50 Talmage Farm Lane
East Hampton, NY 11937
PHONE 631-329-3650
FAX 631-329-3651
EMAIL . . . . .spitzer516@aol.com
SECOND EMAIL . . . . .ortiz516@yahoo.com
TYPES   Literary Talent
AFFILIATIONS   AAR
REPRESENTS   Book Authors
SUBMISSION POLICY   Submit a synopsis and a sample chapter

Philip G. Spitzer .Owner/Agent
Lukas Ortiz . . . . .Literary Manager, Foreign Rights Director
Lucas Hunt . . . . .Assistant

SCOTT STANDER & ASSOCIATES, INC.
13701 Riverside Dr., Ste. 201
Sherman Oaks, CA 91423
PHONE 818-905-7000
FAX 818-990-0582
EMAIL . . . . .info@scottstander.com
WEB SITE . . . . .www.scottstander.com
TYPES   Commercial Talent - Film/TV Talent -
                         Modeling Talent - Music Talent - Theatre
                         Talent
AFFILIATIONS   AEA - AFTRA - SAG
REPRESENTS   Actors - Broadcast Journalists/Newscasters
                         - Children - Choreographers - Comedians
                         - Composers - Hosts/MCs - Magicians -
                         Martial Artists/Stunts - Music Artists -
                         Musical Theatre Performers - Playwrights -
                         Print Models - Producers - Runway Models -
                         Seniors - Speakers/Lecturers - Teens/Young
                         Adults - Variety Artists - Voice-Over Artists
COMMENTS   Seeking kids five to fifteen years old;
                         Commercial moms, dads and seniors;
                         Looking for celebrities who want more per-
                         sonal attention

Scott Stander . . . . .President
Tama Kennemer . . . . .Agent
Jacqueline Stander . . . . .Agent, Film/TV/Commercials

STARCRAFT TALENT AGENCY
265 E. Orange Grove, Ste. D
Burbank, CA 90512
PHONE 323-845-4784
TYPES   Commercial Talent - Film/TV Talent -
                         Modeling Talent
AFFILIATIONS   AFTRA - SAG
REPRESENTS   Actors - Children - Comedians - Infants -
                         Print Models - Runway Models - Seniors -
                         Teens/Young Adults
SUBMISSION POLICY   Via mail only or showcase invitation; By
                         appointment only

Paula McAfee . . . . .Agent

STARS, THE AGENCY
23 Grant Ave., 4th Fl.
San Francisco, CA 94108
PHONE 415-421-6272
FAX 415-421-7620
EMAIL .lynnc@starsagency.com
SECOND EMAIL . . . . .kristinc@starsagency.com
WEB SITE . . . . .www.starsagency.com
TYPES   Commercial Talent - Film/TV Talent -
                         Literary Talent - Modeling Talent - Music
                         Talent - Talent & Literary Packaging -
                         Theatre Talent
AFFILIATIONS   AEA - AFTRA - ATA - DGA - SAG - WGA
REPRESENTS   Actors - Book Authors - Broadcast
                         Journalists/Newscasters - Children -
                         Choreographers - Comedians - Dancers -
                         Hosts/MCs - Infants - Magicians - Martial
                         Artists/Stunts - Print Models - Runway
                         Models - Screenwriters - Seniors - Sports
                         Personalities - Teens/Young Adults - TV
                         Writers - Variety Artists - Voice-Over Artists
COMMENTS   Production services; Casting facilities; Trade
                         shows

Lynn Claxon . . . . .CEO
Kristin Claxon Stinnett . . . . .President, Talent Division
Scott Claxon . . . . .President, Model Management
Brian Burge . . . . .Director, Voice-Over
Teri Donner . . . . .Talent Division
Connie Hall . . . . .Literary Division
Amy Jones . . . . .Print
Amber Jones . . . . .Print & Runway
Elena Ng . . . . .Children's Division
(Continued)

STARS, THE AGENCY (Continued)
R.J. Owens . . . . .Entertainment
Nadia Potel . . . . .Print & Runway
Nate Tico . . . . .Talent Division
Colin Claxon . . . . .Legal & Business Affairs
Teresa Marley . . . . .Accounting
Karen Theusen . . . . .Accounting
Ryan Ung . . . . .Accounting

STARWIL TALENT
433 N. Camden Dr., 4th Fl.
Beverly Hills, CA 90210
PHONE 818-761-3213
EMAIL . . . . .starwil2@sbcglobal.net
TYPES   Commercial Talent - Film/TV Talent -
                         Theatre Talent
AFFILIATIONS   AFTRA - DGA - SAG - WGA
REPRESENTS   Actors - Children - Comedians - Dancers -
                         Hosts/MCs - Print Models - Seniors -
                         Teens/Young Adults - Variety Artists
SUBMISSION POLICY   Via email or US mail only
COMMENTS   Talent four years old and up

Starwil Reed . . . . .Agent
Gregory Porter . . . . .Agent
Gwen Reed . . . . .Agent

ANN STEELE AGENCY
330 W. 42nd St., 18th Fl.
New York, NY 10036
PHONE 212-629-9112
TYPES   Commercial Talent - Film/TV Talent -
                         Theatre Talent
AFFILIATIONS   AEA - AFTRA
REPRESENTS   Actors
SUBMISSION POLICY   Does not open unsolicited mail; Accepts
                         referrals from signed clients only
COMMENTS   Also affiliated with NATR

Ann Steele . . . . .Owner
Gene Jones . . . . .No Title

THE STEIN AGENCY
5125 Oakdale Ave.
Woodland Hills, CA 91364
PHONE 818-594-8990
FAX 818-594-8998
EMAIL . . . . .mail@thesteinagency.com
TYPES   Below-the-Line Talent - Literary Talent
AFFILIATIONS   DGA - WGA
REPRESENTS   Cinematographers - Directors - Film Editors
                         - Producers - Production Designers -
                         Screenwriters - TV Writers
SUBMISSION POLICY   Does not accept query letters or unsolicitied
                         materials

Mitchel E. Stein . . . . .Principal
Sarita Choy . . . . .Agent
Joy Houng . . . . .Associate

STEINBERG'S TALENT AGENCY
6399 Wilshire Blvd., Ste. 220
Los Angeles, CA 90048
PHONE 323-653-3146
EMAIL . . . . .steinbergsagency@sbcglobal.net
TYPES   Commercial Talent - Film/TV Talent
AFFILIATIONS   SAG
REPRESENTS   Actors
SUBMISSION POLICY   Mail only, no drop-offs; All ages and eth-
                         nicities; Professionals only

Barbara LeBaron . . . . .Owner

STELLAR MODEL & TALENT AGENCY
3001 W. Hallandale Beach Blvd., #303
Pembroke Park, FL 33009
PHONE 954-241-7376
FAX 954-241-7381
EMAIL . . . . .stlrtalent@aol.com
TYPES   Commercial Talent - Film/TV Talent -
                         Modeling Talent
AFFILIATIONS   AFTRA - SAG
REPRESENTS   Actors - Broadcast Journalists/Newscasters
                         - Children - Comedians - Infants - Martial
                         Artists/Stunts - Print Models - Teens/Young
                         Adults - Voice-Over Artists
SUBMISSION POLICY   Mail only

Cindy Schirmer . . . . .President/Commercial Division
Barbara Agozzino . . . . .Children's Division
Britt Geller . . . . .Print Division

THE STEVENS GROUP
14011 Ventura Blvd., Ste. 201
Sherman Oaks, CA 91423
PHONE 818-528-3674
TYPES   Commercial Talent - Film/TV Talent -
                         Modeling Talent
AFFILIATIONS   AFTRA - SAG
REPRESENTS   Actors - Seniors - Teens/Young Adults
SUBMISSION POLICY   Send picture, resumé and videotapes;
                         Tapes will not be returned
COMMENTS   Very limited client list

Steven Stevens . . . . .No Title
Steven Stevens Jr. . . . . .No Title

JOAN STEWART AGENCY
885 Second Ave., 35th Fl.
New York, NY 10017
PHONE 212-418-7255/212-832-3800
FAX 212-832-3809
TYPES   Literary Talent
REPRESENTS   Book Authors
SUBMISSION POLICY   Query letter by mail

Joan Stewart . . . . .Owner/Agent

STEWART TALENT
58 W. Huron St.
Chicago, IL 60610
PHONE 312-943-3131
FAX 312-943-5107/312-943-8512
WEB SITE . . . . .www.stewarttalent.com
TYPES   Commercial Talent - Film/TV Talent -
                         Literary Talent - Modeling Talent - Theatre
                         Talent
AFFILIATIONS   AEA - AFTRA - SAG - WGA
REPRESENTS   Actors - Children - Comedians - Directors -
                         Infants - Musical Theatre Performers - Print
                         Models - Seniors - Teens/Young Adults -
                         Voice-Over Artists

Jane Stewart . . . . .President
Wade Childress . . . . .Commercial Print
Sheila Dougherty . . . . .Voice-Over, Adults/Kids
Kathi Gardner . . . . .Print, Kids
Jenn Hall . . . . .Commercial Print, Adults/Kids
Nancy Kidder . . . . .Industrial/TV/Film, Adults
Sam Samuelson . . . . .TV/Film/Theater, Adults
Joan Sparks . . . . .Voice-Over
Todd Turina . . . . .TV/Film, Adults/Kids
Jenny Wilson . . . . .TV/Film, Adults/Kids
Kim Valkenberg . . . . .Business Manager/Voice-Over/Promo

IVETT STONE AGENCY
14677 Midway Rd., Ste. 113
Addison, TX 75001
PHONE 972-392-4951
FAX 972-392-7045
EMAIL . . . . .ivettstone@aol.com
WEB SITE . . . . .www.ivettstoneagency.com
TYPES   Commercial Talent - Film/TV Talent
AFFILIATIONS   AFTRA - SAG
REPRESENTS   Actors - Children - Print Models -
                         Teens/Young Adults - Voice-Over Artists
SUBMISSION POLICY   Nonreturnable pictures, resumé and/or
                         CDs

Ivett Stone . . . . .Owner/Agent
Elaine Napier . . . . .Commercial Print, Children

STONE MANNERS AGENCY
6500 Wilshire Blvd., Ste. 550
Los Angeles, CA 90048
PHONE 323-655-1313/212-505-1400
FAX 323-655-7676/212-505-1448
TYPES   Film/TV Talent - Literary Talent - Talent &
                         Literary Packaging - Theatre Talent
AFFILIATIONS   AEA - AFTRA - ATA - DGA
REPRESENTS   Actors - Directors - Hosts/MCs - Musical
                         Theatre Performers - Producers -
                         Screenwriters - Teens/Young Adults - TV
                         Writers
COMMENTS   East Coast office: 900 Broadway, Ste. 803,
                         New York, NY 10003

Scott Manners . . . . .Partner/Talent
Tim Stone . . . . .Partner/Talent (NY)
Kerim Ekonomi . . . . .Talent Agent
Laura Gibson . . . . .Talent Agent
Erin Grush . . . . .Talent Agent (NY)
Bobby Moses . . . . .Talent Agent
Glenn Salners . . . . .Talent Agent
Michael Sheehy . . . . .Literary Agent
Bianca Campos . . . . .Office Manager
Thomas Prochnow . . . . .Coordinator
Vicki York . . . . .Accountant

PETER STRAIN & ASSOCIATES, INC. (LOS ANGELES)
5455 Wilshire Blvd., Ste. 1812
Los Angeles, CA 90036
PHONE 323-525-3391
FAX 323-525-0881
TYPES   Film/TV Talent - Theatre Talent
AFFILIATIONS   AEA - AFTRA - ATA
REPRESENTS   Actors - Teens/Young Adults
SUBMISSION POLICY   Industry referral; No phone calls; No drop-
                         offs

Peter Strain . . . . .Owner
Davin Levenberg . . . . .Agent
Adel Nur . . . . .Agent
Susie Tobin . . . . .Agent
Larissa Szwast . . . . .Assistant

PETER STRAIN & ASSOCIATES, INC. (NEW YORK)
321 W. 44th St., Ste. 805
New York, NY 10036
PHONE 212-391-0380
FAX 212-391-1405
TYPES   Film/TV Talent - Theatre Talent
AFFILIATIONS   AEA - AFTRA - ATA
REPRESENTS   Actors - Teens/Young Adults

Peter Strain . . . . .Owner
Michelle Arst . . . . .Agent
Bill Timms . . . . .Agent
Merri Bracken . . . . .Executive Assistant
Jeffrey Lockhorn . . . . .Executive Assistant

MARIANNE STRONG LITERARY AGENCY

65 E. 96th St.
New York, NY 10128
PHONE 212-249-1000/917-439-8948
FAX 212-831-3241
EMAIL . . . . .stronglit@aol.com
TYPES   Literary Talent - Talent & Literary Packaging
REPRESENTS   Book Authors
COMMENTS   Authors Guild; Sports writers; Some screen-
                        plays and TV scripts mostly based on
                        books, or by produced writers with strong
                        credentials; Nonfiction, politics, history,
                        biography, memoir, some historical fiction,
                        pop culture, finance, health and fitness,
                        business, lifestyle, multi-cultural books
                        about and by authors from similar back-
                        grounds

Marianne Strong . . . . .President
Lord Colin Campbell . . . . .Agent/Associate
Jason Ashworth . . . . .Agent
Alexandra Lee . . . . .Agent

MITCHELL K. STUBBS & ASSOCIATES

8695 W. Washington Blvd., Ste. 204
Culver City, CA 90232
PHONE 310-838-1200
FAX 310-838-1245
EMAIL . . . . .mks@mksagency.com
WEB SITE . . . . .www.mksagency.com
TYPES   Commercial Talent - Film/TV Talent -
                        Theatre Talent
AFFILIATIONS   AEA - AFTRA - ATA - DGA - SAG - WGA
REPRESENTS   Actors - Directors - Teens/Young Adults

Mitchell K. Stubbs . . . . .President/Owner
Ray Moheet . . . . .Talent Agent
Judy Page . . . . .Talent Agent
Carrie Johnson .Commercial Agent
James Wenn . . . . .Accounting
Nathan Gabbard . . . . .Assistant
Gricelda Godinez . . . . .Assistant
Kemble Huang . . . . .Assistant
Sean Kotzin . . . . .Assistant

SUITE A MANAGEMENT TALENT & LITERARY AGENCY

120 El Camino Dr., Ste. 202
Beverly Hills, CA 90212
PHONE 310-278-0801/310-666-4333
FAX 310-278-0807
EMAIL . . . . .suite-a@juno.com
WEB SITE . . . . .www.suite-a-management.com
TYPES   Literary Talent
AFFILIATIONS   DGA - WGA
REPRESENTS   Book Authors - Directors - Playwrights -
                        Producers - Screenwriters
SUBMISSION POLICY   Fax one-page biography, including educa-
                        tion and credits; Screenplays should
                        include one-page title, logline and synopsis
COMMENTS   Specializes in MOWs and low to mid-
                        budget features; Authors' novels and stage
                        plays for adaptation to film and TV;
                        Completed films for distribution

Lloyd D. Robinson . . . . .Agent/Principal
Judith Jacobs . . . . .Assistant
Kevin Douglas . . . . .Receptionist

SUMMIT COMEDY, INC.

112 Old Statesville Rd. South, Ste. 209
Huntersville, NC 28078
PHONE 704-947-3057
FAX 704-947-7531
EMAIL .summitcomedy@aol.com
WEB SITE . . . . .www.summitcomedy.com
TYPES   Film/TV Talent
REPRESENTS   Comedians - Hosts/MCs - Magicians
COMMENTS   Agents and suppliers of comedy

Chuck Johnson . . . . .President/CEO

SUMMIT TALENT & LITERARY AGENCY

9454 Wilshire Blvd., Ste. 203
Beverly Hills, CA 90212
PHONE 310-205-9730
FAX 310-205-9734
TYPES   Film/TV Talent - Literary Talent
AFFILIATIONS   DGA - WGA
REPRESENTS   Book Authors - Directors - Producers -
                        Screenwriters - TV Writers
SUBMISSION POLICY   Referral only; No unsolicited submissions

Sandy Weinberg . . . . .President/Agent
Craigin Howland . . . . .Assistant

SUPER ARTISTS INC.

2910 Main St., 2nd Fl.
Santa Monica, CA 90405
PHONE 310-395-1113
FAX 310-395-1136
EMAIL . . . . .danielle@superartists.com
WEB SITE . . . . .www.superartists.com
TYPES   Theatre Talent
REPRESENTS   Comedians - Hosts/MCs - Musical Theatre
                        Performers - Speakers/Lecturers
SUBMISSION POLICY   Unsolicited materials will not be considered

Rich Super . . . . .President
Jonathan David . . . . .Agent
Danielle Stewart . . . . .Associate
Joseph Gussman . . . . .Accounting
Jennifer Hendrickson .Assistant

SUPERIOR TALENT AGENCY

11712 Moorpark St., Ste. 209
Studio City, CA 91604
PHONE 818-508-5627
FAX 818-508-5687
EMAIL . . . . .superiortalent@sbcglobal.net
TYPES   Commercial Talent - Film/TV Talent -
                        Modeling Talent
AFFILIATIONS   AFTRA - SAG
REPRESENTS   Actors - Broadcast Journalists/Newscasters
                        - Children - Comedians - Dancers -
                        Hosts/MCs - Infants - Martial Artists/Stunts
                        - Print Models - Seniors - Teens/Young
                        Adults - Variety Artists - Voice-Over Artists

Jody Edwards . . . . .Owner/Theatrical Agent
Debbie Palmer .Commercial Agent
Molly Sweet . . . . .Theatrical Agent

SUTTON, BARTH & VENNARI, INC.
145 S. Fairfax Ave., Ste. 310
Los Angeles, CA 90036
PHONE 323-938-6000
FAX . . . . .323-935-8671 (Voice-Over)
WEB SITE . . . . .www.sbvtalent.com
TYPES   Commercial Talent
AFFILIATIONS   AFTRA - ATA - SAG
REPRESENTS   Actors - Voice-Over Artists
SUBMISSION POLICY   On-Camera: submit headshot and resume
                     via mail; Voice-over: submissions by indus-
                     try referrals only

Rita Vennari . . . . .President & Voice-Over/Celebrity Agent
Anna Rodriguez .Voice-Over, Latin Department
Robin Lamel . . . . .Voice-Over
Mary Ellen Lord . . . . .Voice-Over
Cynthia McLean . . . . .Voice-Over
Kelli Wickline . . . . .Voice-Over
Pam Sparks . . . . .On-Camera
Kelley Thornton . . . . .On-Camera

TAG MODELS
4727 Wilshire Blvd., Ste. 333
Los Angeles, CA 90010
PHONE 323-602-0344
FAX 323-954-2262
EMAIL . . . . .tag@acmeagents.com
SECOND EMAIL . . . . .phillip@acmeagents.com
TYPES   Commercial Talent - Modeling Talent
REPRESENTS   Actors - Children - Dancers - Hosts/MCs -
                     Infants - Print Models - Runway Models -
                     Seniors - Teens/Young Adults
SUBMISSION POLICY   US mail or email only; No phone calls

Tag Turner .Head Agent/Director, Print
Phillip M. Espinoza . . . . .Adult Agent, Print
John Robertson . . . . .Children's Agent, Print
Tessy Garcia . . . . .Print Assistant

MARY M. TAHAN LITERARY AGENCY, LLC
PO Box 1015, Cooper Station
New York, NY 10276
PHONE 212-714-7798
FAX 212-714-7795
EMAIL .query@tahanliterary.com
WEB SITE . . . . .www.tahanliterary.com
TYPES   Literary Talent
AFFILIATIONS   AAR
COMMENTS   Currently not accepting new clients

Mary M. Tahan . . . . .Agent

TALENT & MODEL LAND
4516 Granny White Pike
Nashville, TN 37204
PHONE 615-321-5596
FAX 615-321-5497
EMAIL . . . . .tmlboop@earthlink.net
TYPES   Commercial Talent - Film/TV Talent
AFFILIATIONS   AEA - AFM - AFTRA - SAG
REPRESENTS   Actors - Children - Comedians -
                     Hosts/MCs - Infants - Seniors -
                     Teens/Young Adults - Voice-Over Artists
COMMENTS   Second mailing address: PO Box 40763,
                     Nashville, TN 37204

Betty Clark . . . . .Owner/Agent

THE TALENT GROUP
2820 Smallman St.
Pittsburgh, PA 15222
PHONE 412-471-8011/216-622-8011
FAX 412-471-0875/216-622-7551
EMAIL .talent.group@verizon.net
SECOND EMAIL . . . . .talentgroupcleveland@ameritech.net
WEB SITE . . . . .www.talentgroup.com
TYPES   Commercial Talent - Film/TV Talent -
                     Modeling Talent - Theatre Talent
AFFILIATIONS   AFTRA - SAG
REPRESENTS   Actors - Broadcast Journalists/Newscasters
                     - Children - Print Models - Runway Models
                     - Sports Personalities - Teens/Young Adults
                     - Voice-Over Artists
COMMENTS   Union/non-union talent; Extensive Voice-
                     Over clientele from all over the country;
                     Cleveland office: 2530 Superior Ave., Ste.
                     6C, Cleveland, OH 44114

Stephen Black . . . . .Owner/Agent (Pittsburgh)
Richard Kohn . . . . .Agency Director (Cleveland)
Brian Bowers . . . . .Head, Print Department (Cleveland)
Rebecca DiNapoli . . . . .Head, Film/TV/Voice-Over (Pittsburgh)
Doug Snyder . . . . .Head, Film/TV/Voice-Over (Cleveland)
Tom Watson . . . . .Head, Print Department (Pittsburgh)
Mark Pfeffer . . . . .Agent (Pittsburgh)
Mary Reid . . . . .Agent (Pittsburgh)
Steve Shakoske . . . . .Agent (Pittsburgh)
Beth Ann Helminiak . . . . .Agent (Cleveland)

TALENT HOUSE AGENCY
311 W. 43rd St., Ste. 602
New York, NY 10036
PHONE 212-957-5220
EMAIL . . . . .talenthousenyc@earthlink.net
TYPES   Below-the-Line Talent - Film/TV Talent -
                     Talent & Literary Packaging - Theatre Talent
AFFILIATIONS   AEA
REPRESENTS   Actors - Choreographers - Dancers - Music
                     Supervisors - Musical Theatre Performers -
                     Playwrights
SUBMISSION POLICY   By mail and with referral

Ari Cohn . . . . .Agent
Flora Johnstone . . . . .Agent

TALENT PLUS, INC./CENTRO MODELS

1222 Lucas Ave., Ste. 300
St. Louis, MO 63103
PHONE 314-421-9400
FAX 314-421-9440
EMAIL . . . . .info@talent-plus.com
SECOND EMAIL . . . . .info@centromodels.com
WEB SITE . . . . .www.talent-plus.com
SECOND WEB SITE . . . . .www.centromodels.com
TYPES   Commercial Talent - Film/TV Talent - Modeling Talent - Music Talent
AFFILIATIONS   AFTRA - SAG
REPRESENTS   Actors - Children - Comedians - Hosts/MCs - Magicians - Martial Artists/Stunts - Music Artists - Print Models - Runway Models - Seniors - Speakers/Lecturers - Sports Personalities - Teens/Young Adults - Variety Artists - Voice-Over Artists

Sharon Tucci . . . . .President/Owner
Chris Hansen . . . . .VP, Spotlight Entertainment, Music Division
Christina Klobe . . . . .Director, Centro Models
Lisa Laird . . . . .Director, Spotlight Division, Speakers & Corporate Entertainment
Jack White . . . . .Executive Consultant, Corporate Entertainment
Maureen O'Brien . . . . .Casting Coordinator
J. Kim Tucci . . . . .Chairman, Speakers & Corporate Entertainment
Victoria Satchell . . . . .Speakers & Corporate Entertainment, Research/Development
Diane Schorsch . . . . .Broadcast Agent
Mary Kruse . . . . .Manager, Accounting
Adria Spenser-Jones . . . . .Appointment Secretary
Eric Wenzelburger . . . . .Internet Guru

TALENT PLUS/LOS LATINOS TALENT AGENCY

2801 Moorpark Ave., Ste. 11
San Jose, CA 95128
PHONE 831-443-5542
WEB SITE . . . . .www.talentplusloslatinos.com
TYPES   Commercial Talent - Film/TV Talent - Modeling Talent
AFFILIATIONS   AFTRA - SAG
REPRESENTS   Actors - Broadcast Journalists/Newscasters - Children - Print Models - Seniors - Teens/Young Adults - Voice-Over Artists
SUBMISSION POLICY   Submit headshot, zedcard, resumé, CD or demo reel with dated cover letter and SASE
COMMENTS   Trade show models/spokespersons; Educational and corporate videos; Voice-over is secondary (Spanish, British, Mandarin, Cantonese, Japanese, Vietnamese); Los Latinos Agency specializes in Hispanic actors/models; Represents talent from five to eighty-five years old

Gail Jones . . . . .Director

TALENT REPRESENTATIVES, INC.

307 East 44th St., Ste. 1F
New York, NY 10017
PHONE 212-752-1835
TYPES   Film/TV Talent - Literary Talent - Theatre Talent
AFFILIATIONS   AEA - AFTRA - DGA - SAG - WGA
REPRESENTS   Actors - Composers - Directors - Producers - TV Writers
SUBMISSION POLICY   No unsolicited manuscripts
COMMENTS   NATR

Honey Raider . . . . .President
Liz Hart . . . . .Associate

THE TALENT SHOP

30400 Telegraph Rd., Ste. 141
Bingham Farms, MI 48025
PHONE 248-644-4877
FAX 248-644-0331
EMAIL . . . . .info@thetalentshop.com
WEB SITE . . . . .www.thetalentshop.com
TYPES   Commercial Talent - Film/TV Talent - Modeling Talent - Music Talent - Theatre Talent
AFFILIATIONS   AFTRA - ATA - SAG
REPRESENTS   Actors - Broadcast Journalists/Newscasters - Children - Choreographers - Comedians - Dancers - Hosts/MCs - Infants - Martial Artists/Stunts - Music Artists - Print Models - Runway Models - Seniors - Speakers/Lecturers - Sports Personalities - Teens/Young Adults - Variety Artists - Voice-Over Artists
SUBMISSION POLICY   By mail only
COMMENTS   Plus sizes; Print men and women

Jacquelin Kagan . . . . .Owner/Agent of Record
Marsha Bassi . . . . .Agent
Mary Fischioni . . . . .Agent
Ricka Fuger . . . . .Agent
Marce Haney . . . . .Agent
Ann Wilson . . . . .Agent
Linda Lange Davidson . . . . .Sub-Agent
Kathy Mooney . . . . .Sub-Agent
Peggy Okray . . . . .Sub-Agent
Constantina . . . . .All-Automotive Agent
Corale Richards . . . . .Automotive Agent

TALENT TREK AGENCY

5401 Kingston Pike, Ste. 450
Knoxville, TN 37919
PHONE 865-977-8735/615-279-0010
FAX 865-977-9200/615-279-0013
EMAIL . . . . .talentrek@mindspring.com
SECOND EMAIL . . . . .ttanash@aol.com
WEB SITE . . . . .www.talenttrek.com
TYPES   Below-the-Line Talent - Commercial Talent - Film/TV Talent - Modeling Talent
AFFILIATIONS   AFTRA - SAG
REPRESENTS   Actors - Children - Comedians - Dancers - Hosts/MCs - Infants - Print Models - Runway Models - Seniors - Teens/Young Adults - Voice-Over Artists
SUBMISSION POLICY   Photo submission necessary before interview
COMMENTS   Film principals; Nashville office: 2021 21st Ave. South, Ste. 102, Nashville, TN 37212

Charlotte Dennison . . . . .Owner
Juanell Walker . . . . .Owner
Courtney Rudisil . . . . .Agent, Nashville
Evelyn Foster . . . . .Office Manager, Nashville

TALENT UNLIMITED, INC.
4049 Pennsylvania, Ste. 400
Kansas City, MO 64111
PHONE 816-561-9040
FAX 816-756-3950
EMAIL . . . . .contactus@talentunlimited.net
SECOND EMAIL . . . . .jeanl@talentunlimited.net
WEB SITE . . . . .www.talentunlimited.net
TYPES   Commercial Talent - Film/TV Talent -
                         Modeling Talent
AFFILIATIONS   AFTRA - SAG
REPRESENTS   Actors - Broadcast Journalists/Newscasters
                         - Children - Comedians - Hosts/MCs -
                         Infants - Magicians - Print Models - Runway
                         Models - Seniors - Teens/Young Adults -
                         Variety Artists - Voice-Over Artists
SUBMISSION POLICY   By mail or email
COMMENTS   Specializes in on-camera narrators, voice-
                         over talent and models of all ages

Jean Liebau .Owner/Broadcast & Print Agent
Tracey Turner . . . . .Sub-Agent
Mary Bosch . . . . .Account Manager
Clinton Irey . . . . .Sub-Agent

TALENTWORKS
3500 W. Olive Ave., Ste. 1400
Burbank, CA 91505
PHONE 818-972-4300
FAX 818-955-6411
TYPES   Commercial Talent - Film/TV Talent
AFFILIATIONS   AEA - AFTRA - ATA - DGA - SAG - WGA
REPRESENTS   Actors - Children - Comedians -
                         Teens/Young Adults
SUBMISSION POLICY   Industry referrals only; Headshot and
                         resumé by mail; Attn: New Talent
COMMENTS   H.W.A. and TalentWorks have formed a
                         strategic alliance in Los Angeles under the
                         TalentWorks banner

Harry Gold . . . . .Partner/Theatrical, Adults
Bonnie Liedtke . . . . .Partner/Theatrical, Children
Suzanne Wohl . . . . .Theatrical, Adults
Thor Bradwell . . . . .Theatrical/TV/Film, Young Adults
Marion Campbell . . . . .Theatrical, Adults
Joel Dean . . . . .Theatrical, Children/Adults
Pamela Fisher . . . . .Commercial, Adults/Children
Brandy Gold . . . . .Theatrical, Adults
August Kammer . . . . .Theatrical, Adults
Hank Hedland . . . . .Operations Manager
Caitlin Ferrara . . . . .Assistant to Mr. Gold

TALENTWORKS NEW YORK
220 E. 23rd St., Ste. 303
New York, NY 10010
PHONE 212-889-0800
TYPES   Commercial Talent - Film/TV Talent -
                         Modeling Talent - Theatre Talent
AFFILIATIONS   AEA - AFTRA - ATA
REPRESENTS   Actors - Comedians - Hosts/MCs - Music
                         Artists - Print Models - Seniors - Voice-Over
                         Artists
COMMENTS   Also affiliated with NATR

Patty Woo . . . . .Owner
Philip Cassese . . . .On-Camera Commercials/Print/Voice-Overs, Beauty
Jay Kane . . . . .TV/Film/Theatrical
Anthony Calamita . . . . .TV/Film/Theatrical
Danielle Ippolito . . . . .TV/Film/Theatrical
Kendra Day . . . . .Assistant
Samara Gulrajani . . . . .Commercial Assistant
Nellie Gonzalez . . . . .Business Affairs/Office Manager
Raquel Kernyansky . . . . .Receptionist

ROSLYN TARG LITERARY AGENCY
105 W. 13th St., Ste. 15-E
New York, NY 10011
PHONE 212-206-9390
FAX 212-989-6233
EMAIL . . . . .roslyn@roslyntargagency.com
TYPES   Literary Talent
AFFILIATIONS   AAR - WGA
REPRESENTS   Book Authors
SUBMISSION POLICY   Query by mail preferred with SASE
COMMENTS   No plays or screenplays

Roslyn Targ . . . . .Owner/Agent

TDN ARTISTS (THE DIRECTOR'S NETWORK)
17071 Ventura Blvd., #105
Encino, CA 91316
PHONE 818-906-0006
FAX 818-301-2224
EMAIL . . . . .jeff@tdnartists.com
SECOND EMAIL .steve@tdnartists.com
WEB SITE . . . . .www.tdnartists.com
TYPES   Commercial Talent - Theatre Talent
AFFILIATIONS   DGA
REPRESENTS   Cinematographers - Directors -
                         Screenwriters

Jeff Lewis . . . . .Partner/Agent
Steve Lewis . . . . .Founder/Agent
Caroline Lewis . . . . .Business Affairs

TGMD TALENT AGENCY
6767 Forest Lawn Dr., Ste. 101
Los Angeles, CA 90068
PHONE 323-850-6767
FAX 323-850-7340
EMAIL . . . . .firstname@tgmdtalent.com
TYPES   Commercial Talent - Film/TV Talent
AFFILIATIONS   AFTRA - SAG
REPRESENTS   Voice-Over Artists
SUBMISSION POLICY   Represents only SAG and AFTRA clients;
                         For submission send a CD to agency
                         attention Voice-Over Department
COMMENTS   Voice-over talent, eighteen years old and up

Vanessa Gilbert . . . . .President/Agent
Kevin Motley . . . . .Partner/Agent
Ilko Drozdoski . . . . .Agent, Hispanic Voice-Over Department
Steve Tisherman . . . . .Agent
Christina Tropp . . . . .Assistant Agent
Steve Reisberg . . . . .Booth Director
Cyndi Raymond Solorio . . . . .Assistant to Vanessa Gilbert

THE THOMAS TALENT AGENCY
6709 La Tijera Blvd., Ste. 915
Los Angeles, CA 90045-2017
PHONE 310-665-0000
TYPES	Commercial Talent - Film/TV Talent
AFFILIATIONS	AEA - AFTRA - SAG
REPRESENTS	Actors - Teens/Young Adults
SUBMISSION POLICY	Mail photo and resumé, will call if interested; No VHS or DVDs; No personal deliveries
COMMENTS	Currently seeking submissions from adult talent of all ages and types for commercials; Small, carefully selected list of clients; SAG actors only

Venus Thomas .Owner/Agent

ARLENE THORNTON & ASSOCIATES
12711 Ventura Blvd., Ste. 490
Studio City, CA 91604
PHONE 818-760-6688
FAX 818-760-1165
EMAIL . . . . .arlene@arlenethornton.com
WEB SITE . . . . .www.arlenethornton.com
TYPES	Commercial Talent
AFFILIATIONS	AFTRA - SAG
REPRESENTS	Actors - Voice-Over Artists

Arlene Thornton . . . . .President
John Lohr . . . . .Booth Director
Larry Reiss . . . . .Booth Director
Lauren Adams .Booth Director
Tracy Mapes . . . . .On-Camera Agent
Stephanie Bloom . . . . .Voice Over Department
Jazmin Rangel . . . . .On-Camera Assistant

TILMAR TALENT AGENCY
4929 Wilshire Blvd., Ste. 1020
Los Angeles, CA 90010
PHONE 323-938-9815
TYPES	Commercial Talent

Elton Bolden . . . . .Agent

RUSSELL TODD AGENCY (RTA)
14859 Moorpark St., Ste. 108
Sherman Oaks, CA 91403
PHONE 818-808-0042
FAX 818-808-0043
EMAIL . . . . .rtamail@aol.com
WEB SITE . . . . .www.russelltoddagency.com
TYPES	Below-the-Line Talent
REPRESENTS	Cinematographers
COMMENTS	US, Puerto Rico, Canadian and Australian Steadicam/camera operators only

Russell Todd . . . . .Owner/Agent

TONRY TALENT
885 Bryant St., Ste. 201
San Francisco, CA 94103
PHONE 415-543-3797
FAX 415-957-9656
EMAIL . . . . .tonry@mindspring.com
WEB SITE .www.tonrytalent.com
TYPES	Commercial Talent - Film/TV Talent
AFFILIATIONS	AEA - AFTRA - SAG
REPRESENTS	Actors - Broadcast Journalists/Newscasters - Children - Hosts/MCs - Print Models - Seniors - Teens/Young Adults - Voice-Over Artists
SUBMISSION POLICY	Mail with SASE
COMMENTS	Full-service agency; Union/non-union talent

Mary Tonry . . . . .Owner/Agent
Tom Kelly . . . . .Sub-Agent

S©OTT TREIMEL NY
434 Lafayette St.
New York, NY 10003
PHONE 212-505-8353
FAX 212-505-0664
EMAIL . . . . .st.ny@verizon.net
TYPES	Literary Talent
AFFILIATIONS	AAR
REPRESENTS	Book Authors
COMMENTS	Exclusively represents authors and illustrators of books for children and teens

Scott Treimel . . . . .Agent
MaryLeigh Krasniewicz . . . . .Assistant

TRIDENT MEDIA GROUP, LLC
41 Madison Ave., 36th Fl.
New York, NY 10010
PHONE 212-262-4810
FAX 212-262-4849
WEB SITE . . . . .www.tridentmediagroup.com
TYPES	Literary Talent
REPRESENTS	Book Authors

Robert Gottlieb . . . . .Chairman
Daniel Strone . . . . .CEO
Sheldon Schultz . . . . .President, TMG Artists
Ellen Levine AAR . . . . .Executive VP
John Silbersack . . . . .Sr. VP
Kimberly Whalen . . . . .VP/Literary Agent
Claire Roberts . . . . .Managing Director, Foreign Rights
Lara Allen . . . . .Associate Director, Foreign Rights
Jenny Bent . . . . .Literary Agent
Eileen Cope .Literary Agent
Paul Fedorko .Literary Agent
Melissa Flashman . . . . .Literary Agent
Alex Glass . . . . .Literary Agent
Alyssa Eisner Henkin . . . . .Literary Agent
Scott Miller . . . . .Literary Agent
Elisabeth Weed . . . . .Literary Agent
Nicole Steen . . . . .Associate Agent, Foreign Rights
Holly Root . . . . .Audio Rights Agent
Daniel Harvey . . . . .Director, Marketing
Iazamir Gotta . . . . .Consultant

TROIKA

74 Clerkenwell Rd., 3rd Fl.
London EC1M 5QA, UK
PHONE 44-020-7336-7868
FAX 44-020-7490-7642
EMAIL . . . . .info@troikatalent.com
WEB SITE . . . . .www.troikatalent.com
REPRESENTS   Hosts/MCs

Michael Duff . . . . .Agent
Conor McCaughan . . . . .Agent
Melanie Rockcliffe . . . . .Agent

UNITED TALENT AGENCY - UTA

9560 Wilshire Blvd., Ste. 500
Beverly Hills, CA 90212
PHONE 310-273-6700
FAX 310-247-1111
WEB SITE . . . . .www.unitedtalentagency.com
TYPES   Below-the-Line Talent - Commercial Talent
                     - Film/TV Talent - Literary Talent - Music
                     Talent - Talent & Literary Packaging -
                     Theatre Talent
AFFILIATIONS   AEA - AFTRA - DGA - SAG - WGA
REPRESENTS   Actors - Book Authors - Cinematographers
                     - Directors - Film Editors - Interactive Game
                     Developers - Music Artists - Playwrights -
                     Producers - Production Designers -
                     Screenwriters - Sports Personalities - TV
                     Writers - Voice-Over Artists
SUBMISSION POLICY   Referral only

James Berkus . . . . .Chairman/Board Member/Agent
Peter Benedek . . . . .Board of Directors/Partner/Agent
Nick Stevens . . . . .Board of Directors/Partner/Agent
Jay Sures . . . . .Board of Directors/Partner/Agent
Jeremy Zimmer . . . . .Board of Directors/Partner/Agent
Blair Belcher . . . . .Partner/Agent
Andrew Cannava . . . . .Partner/Agent
Gary Cosay . . . . .Partner/Agent
Wayne Fitterman .Partner/Agent
David Guillod . . . . .Partner/Agent
Lisa Hallerman . . . . .Partner/Agent
Tracey Jacobs . . . . .Partner/Agent
Lisa Jacobson . . . . .Partner/Agent
Richard Klubeck . . . . .Partner/Agent
Marc Korman . . . . .Partner/Agent
David Kramer . . . . .Partner/Agent
Sue Naegle . . . . .Partner/Agent
Matt Rice . . . . .Partner/Agent
Howard Sanders . . . . .Partner/Agent
Sharon Sheinwold .Partner/Agent
Robert Arakelian . . . . .Agent
Tobin Babst . . . . .Agent
Allison Band . . . . .Agent
Jeremy Barber . . . . .Agent
Joel Begleiter . . . . .Agent
Brinda Bhatt . . . . .Agent
Jason Burns . . . . .Agent
Carlos Carreras . . . . .Agent
Stephanie Comer . . . . .Agent
James Degus . . . . .Agent
Marissa Devins . . . . .Agent
Barbara Dreyfus . . . . .Agent
Gueran Ducoty . . . . .Agent
Shana Eddy . . . . .Agent
Dan Erlij . . . . .Agent
Jacob Fenton . . . . .Agent
Charlie Ferraro . . . . .Agent
Pete Franciosa . . . . .Agent
Barrett D. Garese . . . . .Agent
Jay Gassner . . . . .Agent

(Continued)

UNITED TALENT AGENCY - UTA (Continued)

Nancy Gates . . . . .Agent
Brett Hansen . . . . .Agent
Lee Horvitz . . . . .Agent
Jon Huddle . . . . .Agent
Josh Katz . . . . .Agent
Keya Khayatian . . . . .Agent
Rob Kim . . . . .Agent
Billy Lazarus . . . . .Agent
Everly Lee . . . . .Agent
Stuart Manashil . . . . .Agent
Leslie Maskin . . . . .Agent
Jason U. Nadler . . . . .Agent
John Pantle . . . . .Agent
David Park . . . . .Agent
Jonathan Perry . . . . .Agent
Tim Phillips . . . . .Agent
Rob Prinz . . . . .Agent
Ashwin Rajan . . . . .Agent
Ryan Reber . . . . .Agent
Itay Reiss . . . . .Agent
Shani Rosenzweig . . . . .Agent
Larry Salz . . . . .Agent
Ruthanne Secunda . . . . .Agent
Steve Seidel . . . . .Agent
Jason Shapiro . . . . .Agent
Darren Statt . . . . .Agent
Lauren Stern . . . . .Agent
Kevin Stolper . . . . .Agent
Max Stubblefield . . . . .Agent
Geoff Suddleson . . . . .Agent
Jonathan Swaden . . . . .Agent
Feroz Taj . . . . .Agent
Julien Thuan . . . . .Agent
Sarah Warda . . . . .Agent
Brent Weinstein . . . . .Agent
Adam Weinstein . . . . .Agent
Nikki Wheeler . . . . .Agent
Haena Worthing . . . . .Agent
Jo Yao . . . . .Agent
Elizabeth Ziemska . . . . .Agent
Jeff Dalla Betta . . . . .CFO
Michael Conway . . . . .CAO
Chris Day . . . . .Head, Corporate Communications
Adam Ware . . . . .Head, Business Development
Gary Gradinger . . . . .Head, Business Affairs
Rene Jones . . . . .Director, UTA Foundation
Thora Leiken . . . . .Business Affairs
Lauren Menkes .Business Affairs
Mike Rubi . . . . .Business Affairs
Leroy Simmons .Business Affairs
Sarah Ebrahimi . . . . .Legal Affairs

UNIVERSAL TALENT INTELLIGENCE

PO Box 19575
Cincinnati, OH 45219
PHONE 513-369-3398
FAX 513-751-5949
EMAIL . . . . .majorstudios@hotmail.com
TYPES   Commercial Talent - Film/TV Talent -
                     Literary Talent - Music Talent
REPRESENTS   Actors - Book Authors - Comedians -
                     Composers - Dancers - Directors - Martial
                     Artists/Stunts - Music Producers - Producers
                     - Screenwriters - Sports Personalities - TV
                     Writers - Variety Artists - Voice-Over Artists

Chris Hutchins . . . . .Talent Agent
Calvin Poole . . . . .Talent Agent
Trace Harris . . . . .VP, TV Business Development

UPTOWN TALENT, INC.
PO Box 29388
Richmond, VA 23242
PHONE 804-740-0307
EMAIL . . . . .liz@uptowntalent.com
WEB SITE .www.uptowntalent.com
SECOND WEB SITE . . . . .www.lizmarkscasting.com
TYPES   Below-the-Line Talent - Commercial Talent
                       - Film/TV Talent - Modeling Talent - Theatre
                       Talent
AFFILIATIONS   AEA - AFTRA - SAG
REPRESENTS   Actors - Children - Comedians - Infants -
                       Print Models - Seniors - Teens/Young Adults
                       - Variety Artists - Voice-Over Artists

Billy Caldwell . . . . .Casting Agent
Liz Marks . . . . .Casting Director

ANNETTE VAN DUREN AGENCY
11684 Ventura Blvd., Ste. 235
Studio City, CA 91604
PHONE 818-752-6000
FAX 818-752-6985
EMAIL . . . . .avagency@pacbell.net
TYPES   Film/TV Talent - Literary Talent
AFFILIATIONS   DGA - WGA
REPRESENTS   Directors - Producers - Screenwriters - TV
                       Writers
SUBMISSION POLICY   Send short email
COMMENTS   Also represents animation artists

Annette van Duren . . . . .President

VERITAS LITERARY AGENCY
510 Sand Hill Circle
Menlo Park, CA 94025
PHONE 415-647-6964
FAX 415-647-7116
EMAIL .agent@veritasliterary.com
TYPES   Literary Talent
AFFILIATIONS   AAR
REPRESENTS   Book Authors
COMMENTS   Adult fiction and nonfiction

Katherine Boyle . . . . .Agent

VERITAS MEDIA, INC.
111 Euclid Ave.
Hastings-On-Hudson, NY 10706
PHONE 917-365-4435
EMAIL . . . . .veritasmedia@mac.com
TYPES   Literary Talent
REPRESENTS   Book Authors

Sam Pinkus . . . . .Agent

THE VICIOUS TREND AGENCY
3698 E. River Rd.
Grand Island, NY 14072
PHONE 716-604-7668
FAX 716-773-5308
EMAIL .vtproductions@msn.com
TYPES   Literary Talent - Music Talent
AFFILIATIONS   AFM
REPRESENTS   Composers - Music Artists - Screenwriters
SUBMISSION POLICY   Solicited material only

Steven Paul . . . . .President
Lynn Schriver . . . . .Creative Development, Music
Mark Susko . . . . .Creative Development, Writers

VISION ART MANAGEMENT
9200 Sunset Blvd., PH 1
Los Angeles, CA 90069-3502
PHONE 310-888-3288
FAX 310-888-2268
TYPES   Literary Talent
AFFILIATIONS   DGA - SAG - WGA
REPRESENTS   Actors - Directors - Producers -
                       Screenwriters - TV Writers

Scott Schwartz . . . . .Owner/Agent
Mark Woodvine . . . . .Agent
Melissa Cooper . . . . .Jr. Agent

VISION LOS ANGELES
8500 Steller Dr., Bldg. 8
Culver City, CA 90232
PHONE 310-733-4440
FAX 310-733-4441
EMAIL . . . . .models@visionlosangeles.com
SECOND EMAIL . . . . .info@visionlosangeles.com
WEB SITE . . . . .www.visionlosangeles.com
TYPES   Commercial Talent - Modeling Talent
AFFILIATIONS   AFTRA - ATA - SAG
REPRESENTS   Actors - Print Models - Runway Models
SUBMISSION POLICY   Photo and resumé by mail; Open call for
                       models Tuesdays through Thursdays, 3-4
                       pm

Francine Champagne . . . . .Owner/Agent
Victor Del Toro . . . . .Women's Print
Jennifer Manna . . . . .Women's Print Division
Allen Osborne . . . . .Men's Print Division
Pam Lyles . . . . .Talent Agent
Jaclyn Shanfeld . . . . .New Faces
David Folsom . . . . .Talent Associate

VOX, INC.
5670 Wilshire Blvd., Ste. 820
Los Angeles, CA 90036
PHONE 323-655-8699
FAX 323-852-1472
EMAIL . . . . .wstevens@voxusa.net
WEB SITE . . . . .www.voxusa.net
TYPES   Commercial Talent - Film/TV Talent
AFFILIATIONS   AFTRA - ATA
REPRESENTS   Voice-Over Artists

Wes Stevens . . . . .Owner/Agent
Tom Lawless . . . . .Agent
Jerome Titshaw . . . . .Agent
Jason Merrell . . . . .Audio Director

WALES LITERARY AGENCY, INC.
PO Box 9428
Seattle, WA 98109-0428
PHONE 206-284-7114
EMAIL .waleslit@waleslit.com
WEB SITE . . . . .www.waleslit.com
TYPES   Literary Talent
AFFILIATIONS   AAR
REPRESENTS   Book Authors
SUBMISSION POLICY   Send one-page query by email (no attach-
                     ments) or US Mail (with SASE)
COMMENTS   Mainstream and literary fiction and nonfic-
                     tion

Elizabeth Wales . . . . .President
Neal Swain . . . . .Assistant Agent

THE WALLIS AGENCY
210 N. Pass Ave., Ste. 205
Burbank, CA 91505
PHONE 818-953-4848
EMAIL .info@wallisagency.com
WEB SITE .www.wallisagency.com
TYPES   Commercial Talent - Film/TV Talent -
                     Theatre Talent
AFFILIATIONS   AFTRA - SAG
REPRESENTS   Actors - Seniors - Voice-Over Artists
SUBMISSION POLICY   Via Internet for all submissions; Seeking
                     native born foreign language speakers in
                     all languages for voice-overs

Kristene Wallis . . . . .Owner
Deidre Brumsey . . . . .Office Manager
Blake Clark . . . . .Assistant

WARDEN MCKINLEY LITERARY AGENCY
1275 Fourth St., Ste. 247
Santa Rosa, CA 95404
PHONE 707-538-9259
FAX 707-539-8757
EMAIL . . . . .wardenmckinley@sbcglobal.net
TYPES   Literary Talent
REPRESENTS   Book Authors - Producers - Screenwriters -
                     TV Writers
COMMENTS   See listing for East Coast co-agent,
                     Michael H. Sommer

Bob Warden . . . . .Owner
Skye Nicole Warden . . . . .Associate

WARDEN, WHITE & ASSOCIATES
8444 Wilshire Blvd., 4th Fl.
Beverly Hills, CA 90211
PHONE 323-852-1028
TYPES   Film/TV Talent - Literary Talent
AFFILIATIONS   DGA - WGA
REPRESENTS   Directors - Screenwriters
SUBMISSION POLICY   No unsolicited material

Dave Warden . . . . .Partner/Literary
Steve White . . . . .Partner/Literary

WARDLOW & ASSOCIATES
14000 Palawan Way, Ste. 36
Marina del Rey, CA 90292
PHONE 310-452-1292
FAX 310-452-9002
EMAIL .wardlowaso@aol.com
TYPES   Literary Talent - Talent & Literary Packaging
AFFILIATIONS   DGA
REPRESENTS   Book Authors - Directors - Producers -
                     Screenwriters - TV Writers
SUBMISSION POLICY   Referral only

David Wardlow . . . . .Partner/Literary/Theatrical
Jeff Ordway . . . . .Literary

JOHN A. WARE LITERARY AGENCY
392 Central Park West
New York, NY 10025
PHONE 212-866-4733
FAX 212-866-4734
TYPES   Literary Talent
REPRESENTS   Book Authors
SUBMISSION POLICY   Query letter (1-2 pages) with SASE only
COMMENTS   Fiction and nonfiction

John A. Ware . . . . .Agent

BOB WATERS AGENCY, INC.
4311 Wilshire Blvd., Ste. 622
Los Angeles, CA 90010
PHONE 323-965-5555
FAX 323-965-5565
TYPES   Film/TV Talent - Theatre Talent
AFFILIATIONS   AEA - AFTRA - SAG
REPRESENTS   Actors

Bob Waters . . . . .Owner

WATKINS/LOOMIS AGENCY INC.
133 E. 35th St., Ste. 1
New York, NY 10016
PHONE 212-532-0080
WEB SITE .www.watkinsloomis.com
TYPES   Literary Talent
REPRESENTS   Book Authors
SUBMISSION POLICY   No unsolicited submissions

Gloria Loomis . . . . .President
Jacqueline Hackett . . . . .Literary Agent

THE ANN WAUGH TALENT AGENCY
4741 Laurel Canyon Blvd., Ste. 200
North Hollywood, CA 91607
PHONE 818-980-0141
TYPES   Commercial Talent - Film/TV Talent -
                     Theatre Talent
AFFILIATIONS   AEA - AFTRA - SAG
REPRESENTS   Actors - Children - Teens/Young Adults
SUBMISSION POLICY   Industry referral for theatrical; Commercial
                     by mail

John Hugh . . . . .Owner/Theatrical
Connie Hamilton . . . . .Sub-Agent, Commercials/Theatrical
Shelley Pang . . . . .Sub-Agent, Theatrical/Print

DONNA WAUHOB AGENCY
2565 Chandler Ave., #30
Las Vegas, NV 89120
PHONE 702-795-1523
TYPES   Commercial Talent - Film/TV Talent -
                       Literary Talent - Modeling Talent - Music
                       Talent - Theatre Talent
AFFILIATIONS   AFM - AFTRA - SAG
REPRESENTS   Actors - Animals - Children -
                       Choreographers - Comedians - Composers
                       - Dancers - Directors - Infants - Martial
                       Artists/Stunts - Music Artists - Music
                       Producers - Print Models - Production
                       Designers - Runway Models - Screenwriters
                       - Seniors - Sports Personalities -
                       Teens/Young Adults - TV Writers - Variety
                       Artists - Voice-Over Artists
SUBMISSION POLICY   Accepts literary submissions from first-time
                       writers
COMMENTS   Modeling/finishing school from five years
                       and up

Donna Wauhob . . . . .Agent, Literary
Mel Wauhob . . . . .Literary
John Powers . . . . .Computer Technician

WAVING CLOUDS PRODUCTIONS
c/o JMM & Associates
309 College St.
Burlington, VT 05401
PHONE 888-283-1639/852-2834-8866
FAX .802-658-0103/852-2834-5300
EMAIL . . . . .info@wavingclouds.com
WEB SITE . . . . .www.wavingclouds.com
TYPES   Commercial Talent - Film/TV Talent -
                       Modeling Talent - Theatre Talent
REPRESENTS   Choreographers - Directors - Martial
                       Artists/Stunts - Print Models - Producers -
                       Production Designers - Screenwriters -
                       Sports Personalities
COMMENTS   Globally promotes and represents Chinese
                       martial artists; Provides talent, creative and
                       production expertise to the film and multi-
                       media industries; Hong Kong office: 1/F,
                       15B Wo Tong Kong, Lot No. 381 IN
                       DD239, Sai Kung, New Territories, Hong
                       Kong

David Schneider . . . . .Company Director
Ivy Yew . . . . .Company Director

IRENE WEBB LITERARY
1112 Montana Ave., #294
Santa Monica, CA 90403
PHONE 310-394-9024/310-722-7011
FAX 310-394-9024
EMAIL . . . . .webblit@verizon.net
WEB SITE . . . . .www.irenewebb.com
TYPES   Literary Talent
REPRESENTS   Book Authors
SUBMISSION POLICY   Email queries only
COMMENTS   Film and TV rights to books and screen-
                       plays; Publishing mainstream fiction, non-
                       fiction, memoirs, celebrity bios and inspira-
                       tional books

Irene Webb . . . . .Owner

THE WENDY WEIL AGENCY, INC.
232 Madison Ave., Ste. 1300
New York, NY 10016
PHONE 212-685-0030
FAX 212-685-0765
EMAIL . . . . .wweil@wendyweil.com
TYPES   Literary Talent
AFFILIATIONS   AAR
REPRESENTS   Book Authors
COMMENTS   No screenplays or children's books

Wendy Weil . . . . .President
Emily Forland . . . . .Associate
Emma Patterson . . . . .Assistant

WEINGEL-FIDEL AGENCY
310 E. 46th St., Ste. 21E
New York, NY 10017
PHONE 212-599-2959
FAX 212-286-1986
TYPES   Literary Talent
REPRESENTS   Book Authors

Loretta Weingel-Fidel . . . . .Owner

WILHELMINA WEST, INC./LW1 TALENT AGENCY
7257 Beverly Blvd., 2nd Fl., Ste. 200
Los Angeles, CA 90036
PHONE . . . . .323-655-0909 (Women)/323-655-6508 (Men)/
                                                   323-653-5700
FAX 323-653-2255
WEB SITE . . . . .www.wilhelminala.com
TYPES   Commercial Talent - Film/TV Talent -
                       Modeling Talent
AFFILIATIONS   SAG
REPRESENTS   Actors - Print Models - Runway Models
SUBMISSION POLICY   Open call every Wednesday from 3-4 pm
COMMENTS   Fashion Models; Fifteen years old and up

Dieter Esch . . . . .Owner (Wilhelmina)
Sean Patterson . . . . .President (Wilhelmina)
Sean Robinson . . . . .President (LW1)
Luc Brinker . . . . .Director, Women's Division (Wilhelmina)
Paul Nelson . . . . .Director, Men's Division (Wilhelmina)
Tricia Brink . . . . .Lifestyle & 10/20 Division Agent (Wilhelmina)
Laurie-Beth Little . . . . .Lifestyle & 10/20 Division Agent (Wilhelmina)
Charlotte Halford .Women (Wilhelmina)
Jill Sullivan . . . . .Men (Wilhelmina)

XXXX
WILLIAM MORRIS AGENCY

WILLIAM MORRIS AGENCY - WMA (LOS ANGELES)

One William Morris Pl.
Beverly Hills, CA 90212
PHONE 310-859-4000
FAX 310-859-4462
WEB SITE . . . . .www.wma.com
TYPES   Commercial Talent - Film/TV Talent - Literary Talent - Music Talent - Talent & Literary Packaging - Theatre Talent
AFFILIATIONS   AEA - AFM - AFTRA - ATA - DGA - WGA
REPRESENTS   Actors - Book Authors - Broadcast Journalists/Newscasters - Choreographers - Comedians - Composers - Directors - Hosts/MCs - Interactive Game Developers - Music Artists - Musical Theatre Performers - Playwrights - Producers - Screenwriters - Speakers/Lecturers - Sports Personalities - TV Writers - Variety Artists - Voice-Over Artists

Norman Brokaw . . . . .Chairman of the Board
Lou Weiss . . . . .Chairman Emeritus
Walter Zifkin . . . . .CEO Emeritus
Jim Wiatt . . . . .CEO
David Wirtschafter . . . . .President
Irv Weintraub . . . . .COO
Michael Dates . . . . .CFO
David Kekst . . . . .Sr. VP/General Counsel
Cecile Ablack . . . . .Sr. VP, Global Corporate Communications
Michael Page . . . . .VP, Treasury Management
Paul Bricault . . . . .Co-Head, William Morris Consulting
Johnny Levin . . . . .Co-Head, William Morris Consulting
Cody Alexander . . . . .William Morris Consulting
Frank Catapano . . . . .William Morris Consulting
Aaron Lenzini . . . . .William Morris Consulting
John Mass . . . . .William Morris Consulting
Kevin Murray . . . . .William Morris Consulting
Edward Ryan . . . . .William Morris Consulting
Bryan Thoensen . . . . .William Morris Consulting
Mark Itkin . . . . .Worldwide Head, Cable, Syndication & Non-Fiction Programming
Aaron Kaplan . . . . .Worldwide Head, Scripted TV & Programming
Lanny Noveck . . . . .Worldwide Co-Head, Scripted TV & Packaging
John Ferriter . . . . .Worldwide Head, Nonscripted TV & Packaging
Lewis Henderson . . . . .Head, Digital Media Group
Gaby Morgerman . . . . .Head, Talent
Holly Baril . . . . .Talent
Philip Button . . . . .Talent
Esther Chang . . . . .Talent
Julie Colbert . . . . .Talent
Michael Cooper . . . . .Talent
Brian DePersia . . . . .Talent
Ashley Franklin . . . . .Talent
Daniel Gabai . . . . .Talent
Kenny Goodman . . . . .Talent
Philip Grenz . . . . .Talent
Scott Henderson . . . . .Talent
Ashley Josephson . . . . .Talent
Jeff Kolodny . . . . .Talent
Scott Lambert . . . . .Talent
Theresa Peters . . . . .Talent
Dana Sims . . . . .Talent
Brad Slater . . . . .Talent
Jason Trawick . . . . .Talent
Joanne Wiles . . . . .Talent
Troy Zien . . . . .Talent
Scott Agostoni . . . . .TV
Erwin More . . . . .TV
Paul Nagle . . . . .TV
Chris Newman . . . . .TV
Laurie Pozmantier . . . . .TV
Joshua Pyatt . . . . .TV
Collin Reno . . . . .TV

(Continued)

WILLIAM MORRIS AGENCY - WMA (LOS ANGELES)
(Continued)

Hans Schiff . . . . .TV
Adam Sher . . . . .TV
Suzy Unger . . . . .TV
Evan Warner . . . . .TV
Cori Wellins .Head, TV Literary
Elana Barry . . . . .TV/Literary
Todd Berger . . . . .TV/Literary
Ann Blanchard . . . . .TV/Literary
Blake Fronstin . . . . .TV/Literary
Elise Hartley . . . . .TV/Literary
Renee Kurtz . . . . .TV/Literary
Dan Norton . . . . .TV/Literary
Marc Provissiero . . . . .TV/Literary
Alan Rautbort . . . . .TV/Literary
Steven Selikoff . . . . .TV/Literary
Darren Shewchuk . . . . .TV/Literary
Lauren Heller Whitney . . . . .TV/Literary
Marcus Wiley . . . . .TV/Literary
Jeffrey Wise . . . . .TV/Literary
Adam Gelvan . . . . .Cable, Syndication & Non-Fiction Programming
Steven Grossman . . . . . .Cable, Syndication & Non-Fiction Programming
John Fogelman . . . . .Co-Head, Worldwide Motion Pictures
David Lonner . . . . .Co-Head, Worldwide Motion Pictures
Mike Simpson . . . . .Co-Head, Worldwide Motion Pictures
Danny Greenberg . . . . .Head, Motion Picture Literary
Cassian Elwes . . . . .Co-Head, William Morris Independent
Rena Ronson . . . . .Co-Head, William Morris Independent
Nicole David . . . . .Motion Pictures
George Freeman .Motion Pictures
Craig Kestel . . . . .Motion Pictures
Roya Weiner . . . . .Motion Pictures
Kimberly Bialek . . . . .Motion Picture/Literary
Sara Bottfeld .Motion Picture/Literary
Rob Carlson .Motion Picture/Literary
Anna DeRoy .Motion Picture/Literary
Mike Eisner . . . . .Motion Picture/Literary
Michael Esola . . . . .Motion Picture/Literary
Ken Freimann . . . . .Motion Picture/Literary
Alan Gasmer .Motion Picture/Literary
Alicia Gordon . . . . .Motion Picture/Literary
Jeff Gorin . . . . .Motion Picture/Literary
Ava Greenfield . . . . .Motion Picture/Literary
Aaron Hart . . . . .Motion Picture/Literary
Ramses Ishak . . . . .Motion Picture/Literary
Charles King .Motion Picture/Literary
David Lubliner . . . . .Motion Picture/Literary
Steve Rabineau . . . . .Motion Picture/Literary
Cliff Roberts .Motion Picture/Literary
Michael Sheresky . . . . .Motion Picture/Literary
Jeff Shumway . . . . .Motion Picture/Literary
Carolyn Sivitz . . . . .Motion Picture/Literary
Phil Alberstat . . . . .William Morris Independent
Jerome Duboz . . . . .William Morris Independent
Cary Berman . . . . .Head, Commercials
Andrew Atkin . . . . .Commercials
Troy Bailey . . . . .Commercials
Tim Curtis . . . . .Commercials
Orly Agai Marley .Commercials
Erik Seastrand . . . . .Commercials
Brooke Slavik . . . . .Commercials
Jill Smoller . . . . .Head, Sports & Entertainment
Ross Berlin . . . . .Sports & Entertainment
Evan Levy . . . . .Sports & Entertainment
Lon Rosen . . . . .Sports & Entertainment
Carrie Wiener . . . . .Sports & Entertainment
Peter Grosslight . . . . .Worldwide Head, Personal Appearance
David Snyder . . . . .Head, Adult Contemporary Personal Appearance
Marc Geiger . . . . .Head, Contemporary Personal Appearance
Tony Goldring . . . . .Head, International Personal Appearance
Brian Ahern . . . . .Personal Appearance
Dick Alen . . . . .Personal Appearance
Ben Bernstein . . . . .Personal Appearance
Michele Bernstein . . . . .Personal Appearance
John Branigan . . . . .Personal Appearance
Chris Burke .Personal Appearance
Brian Cohen . . . . .Personal Appearance
Brian Edelman . . . . .Personal Appearance
Heidi Feigin . . . . .Personal Appearance

(Continued)

AGENTS

WILLIAM MORRIS AGENCY - WMA (LOS ANGELES)
(Continued)
Amy Flax . . . . .Personal Appearance
Robby Fraser .Personal Appearance
Bradley Goodman . . . . .Personal Appearance
Rob Heller . . . . .Personal Appearance
Gayle Holcomb . . . . .Personal Appearance
Tom Illius . . . . .Personal Appearance
Andrew Lanoie .Personal Appearance
David Levine . . . . .Personal Appearance
Stacy Mark . . . . .Personal Appearance
Rob Markus . . . . .Personal Appearance
John Marx . . . . .Personal Appearance
Stephanie Miles . . . . .Personal Appearance
Clint Mitchell . . . . .Personal Appearance
Craig Mogil . . . . .Personal Appearance
Ron Opaleski . . . . .Personal Appearance
Zachary Radoski . . . . .Personal Appearance
Marshall Reznick . . . . .Personal Appearance
Guy Richard . . . . .Personal Appearance
Akiko Rogers . . . . .Personal Appearance
Joel Roman . . . . .Personal Appearance
Keith Sarkisian .Personal Appearance
Larry Shields . . . . .Personal Appearance
Brent Smith . . . . .Personal Appearance
Kirk Sommer . . . . .Personal Appearance
Suchir Batra . . . . .Corporate Consulting
Susan Brooks . . . . .Worldwide Head, TV Business Affairs
June Horton Van Nort . . . . .Head, Motion Picture Business Affairs
Aron Baumel . . . . .Business Affairs
Jessica Drood . . . . .Business Affairs
Ruth Engelhardt .Business Affairs
Ruth Estrada . . . . .Business Affairs
Robyn Goldman .Business Affairs
Mary Harding . . . . .Business Affairs
Angela Petillo . . . . .Business Affairs
Brian Rabolli . . . . .Business Affairs
Berkeley Reinhold . . . . .Business Affairs
David Taghioff . . . . .Business Affairs
Stuart Tenzer . . . . .Business Affairs
Kelly Weiss . . . . .Business Affairs

WILLIAM MORRIS AGENCY - WMA (NEW YORK)
1325 Avenue of the Americas
New York, NY 10019
PHONE 212-586-5100
FAX 212-246-3583
WEB SITE . . . . .www.wma.com
TYPES   Commercial Talent - Film/TV Talent -
                    Literary Talent - Music Talent - Talent &
                    Literary Packaging - Theatre Talent
AFFILIATIONS   AAR - AEA - AFTRA - ATA - DGA - SAG -
                    WGA
REPRESENTS   Actors - Book Authors - Broadcast
                    Journalists/Newscasters - Choreographers -
                    Comedians - Composers - Directors -
                    Hosts/MCs - Musical Theatre Performers -
                    Playwrights - Producers - Screenwriters -
                    Speakers/Lecturers - Sports Personalities -
                    TV Writers - Variety Artists - Voice-Over
                    Artists

Wayne S. Kabak . . . . .Co-COO, New York/Literary/News
Cara Stein . . . . . . .Co-COO, New York/TV, Cable & Network Packaging
Randi Michel . . . . .Head, Motion Picture Talent, East Coast
Jeff Hunter . . . . .Motion Picture Talent
Leora Rosenberg . . . . .Motion Picture Literary
Jason Hodes . . . . .TV, Cable Packaging
Jonathan Rosen . . . . .TV, Cable Packaging
Scott Lonker . . . . .TV, Comedy
Brian Stern . . . . .TV, Comedy
Dan Shear . . . . .TV, Literary
Jason Fox . . . . .TV, News
Jim Griffin . . . . .TV, News
Jacqueline Harris . . . . .TV, News
Jim Ornstein . . . . .TV, News
Henry Reisch . . . . .TV, News
Ken Slotnick . . . . .TV, News

(Continued)

WILLIAM MORRIS AGENCY - WMA (NEW YORK)
(Continued)
Scott Wachs . . . . .TV, News
Ken DiCamillo .Personal Appearance
Sam Kirby . . . . .Personal Appearance
Cara Lewis . . . . .Personal Appearance
Seth Seigle . . . . .Personal Appearance
Barbara Skydel .Personal Appearance
Mel Berger . . . . .Literary
Bill Clegg . . . . .Literary
Raffaela De Angelis . . . . .Literary
Tracy Fisher . . . . .Literary
Suzanne Gluck . . . . .Literary
Lisa Grubka . . . . .Literary
Dorian Karchmar . . . . .Literary
Shana Kelly . . . . .Literary
Jay Mandel . . . . .Literary
Andy McNicol . . . . .Literary
Jennifer Rudolph Walsh . . . . .Literary
Val Day . . . . .Theatre
Peter Franklin . . . . .Theatre
Biff Liff . . . . .Theatre
Roland Scahill . . . . .Theatre
Jack Tantleff . . . . .Theatre
Susan Weaving . . . . .Theatre
David Kalodner .Theatre Talent
Brian Dubin . . . . .Commercials
Jeff Googel . . . . .Commercials
Marc Guss . . . . .Commercials
Andrew Muser . . . . .Commercials
Betsy Berg . . . . .Lectures
Paul Furia . . . . .Corporate Consulting
Patti Kim . . . . .Corporate Consulting
Sara Newkirk . . . . .Client Marketing
Don Aslan . . . . .Business Affairs
Catherine Bennett . . . . .Business Affairs
Richard Charnoff . . . . .Business Affairs
Annette Frankel . . . . .Business Affairs
David Schmerler .Business Affairs
Eric Zohn . . . . .Business Affairs

WILLIAM MORRIS AGENCY - WMA (NASHVILLE)
1600 Division St., Ste. 300
Nashville, TN 37203
PHONE 615-963-3000
FAX 615-963-3090/615-963-3091
WEB SITE . . . . .www.wmanashville.com
TYPES   Film/TV Talent - Music Talent
REPRESENTS   Comedians - Music Artists
COMMENTS   See Web site for full artist roster

Rick Shipp . . . . .Co-COO
Paul Moore . . . . .Co-COO
Rob Beckham . . . . .Sr. VP, Country Department
Charles Dorris . . . . .Sr. VP, Christian Department
Keith Miller . . . . .Sr. VP, Country Department
Greg Oswald . . . . .Sr. VP, Country Department
Steve Hauser . . . . .VP, Country Department
Barry Jeffrey . . . . .VP, Fair Department
Mark Roeder . . . . .VP, Country Department
Valerie Summers . . . . .VP, Adult Contemporary Department
Jay Williams . . . . .VP, Country Department
Lane Wilson . . . . .VP, Country Department
Kathy Armistead . . . . .Agent, Sponsorships
Becky Baughman . . . . .Club Agent, Country Department
Carey Nelson Burch . . . . .Agent, TV Department
Mark Claassen . . . . .Agent, Christian Department
Ryan Gardenhire . . . . .Club Agent, Country Department
John Gimenez . . . . .Agent, Fair Department
Gloria Green . . . . .Agent, Christian Department
Tinti Moffat . . . . .Club Agent & Canada, Country Department
Barrett Sellers . . . . .Club Agent, Country Department
Abby Wells . . . . .Agent, Country Department
Eric Arnold . . . . .Coordinator
Dana Burwell . . . . .Executive Assistant to Greg Oswald
Drew Burchfield . . . . .Assistant to Rick Shipp
Ramsey Casteel . . . . .Assistant to Barry Jeffrey
Laura Clark . . . . .Assistant to Paul Moore

(Continued)

WILLIAM MORRIS AGENCY - WMA (NASHVILLE)
(Continued)
Rush Davenport . . . . .Assistant to Valerie Summers
Annie Marie Gebel . . . . .Assistant to Paul Moore
Andy Goerlich . . . . .Assistant to Mark Claassen
Travis Gordon . . . . .Assistant to John Gimenez
Beth Hamilton . . . . .Assistant to Keith Miller
Brian Hannah . . . . .Assistant to Mark Roeder
Emily Hewson . . . . .Assistant to Carey Nelson Burch
Laura Hutfless . . . . .Assistant to Kathy Armistead
Kevin Meads . . . . .Assistant to Jay Williams
Matthew Miller . . . . .Assistant to Steve Hauser
Tammy Nichols .Assistant to Rick Shipp
Ryan Onan . . . . .Assistant to Tinti Moffat
Erin Pauling . . . . .Assistant to Becky Baughman
Kristen Pridgen . . . . .Assistant to Greg Oswald
Kristy Reeves . . . . .Assistant to Rob Beckham
Ember Rigsby .Assistant to Gloria Green
Nathan Towne .Assistant to Lane Wilson
Neil Vance . . . . .Assistant to Ryan Gardenhire
Lisa Whitaker . . . . .Assistant to Barrett Sellers
Anthony Wozniak . . . . .Assistant to Charles Dorris
Elizabeth Younger . . . . .Assistant to Abby Wells

WILLIAM MORRIS AGENCY - WMA (MIAMI BEACH)
119 Washington Ave., Ste. 400
Miami Beach, FL 33139
PHONE 305-938-2000
FAX 305-938-2002
WEB SITE . . . . .www.wma.com
TYPES   Commercial Talent - Film/TV Talent -
                         Literary Talent - Music Talent - Talent &
                         Literary Packaging - Theatre Talent
AFFILIATIONS   AEA - AFTRA - DGA - SAG
REPRESENTS   Actors - Book Authors - Broadcast
                         Journalists/Newscasters -
                         Cinematographers - Comedians - Directors
                         - Music Artists - Music Producers - Musical
                         Theatre Performers - Playwrights -
                         Producers - Screenwriters -
                         Speakers/Lecturers - Sports Personalities -
                         Teens/Young Adults - TV Writers - Variety
                         Artists - Voice-Over Artists

Raul Mateu . . . . .Agent/Sr. VP/Head, Miami Beach Office
Michel Vega . . . . .Agent/VP, Personal Appearance/Music
Pedro Bonilla . . . . .Agent, Commercials & Sponsorships
Jeremy Norkin . . . . .Agent, Personal Appearance/Music
Eric Rovner . . . . .Agent, TV
Albert Garcia Jr. . . . . .Agent Trainee/Assistant to Raul Mateu
Margarita Montilla . . . . .Agent Trainee/Assistant to Eric Rovner
Gabriela Pino . . . . .Agent Trainee/Assistant to Jeremy Norkin
Allison Seriani . . . . .Agent Trainee/Assistant to Pedro Bonilla
Mark Swartz . . . . .Agent Trainee/Assistant to Michel Vega
Faye Ibars .Agent Trainee/Mailroom
Paul Perez . . . . .Agent Trainee/Mailroom

WILLIAM MORRIS AGENCY - WMA (LONDON)
Centrepoint Tower
103 Oxford St.
London WC1A 1DD, United Kingdom
PHONE 44-20-7534-6800
FAX 44-20-7534-6900
WEB SITE . . . . .www.wma.com
TYPES   Commercial Talent - Film/TV Talent -
                         Literary Talent - Music Talent - Talent &
                         Literary Packaging - Theatre Talent
AFFILIATIONS   AEA - AFM - AFTRA - ATA - DGA
REPRESENTS   Actors - Book Authors - Broadcast
                         Journalists/Newscasters - Choreographers -
                         Comedians - Composers - Directors -
                         Hosts/MCs - Interactive Game Developers
                         - Music Artists - Musical Theatre Performers
                         - Playwrights - Screenwriters -
                         Speakers/Lecturers - Sports Personalities -
                         TV Writers - Voice-Over Artists

Caroline Michel . . . . .Managing Director
Ed Bicknell . . . . .Head, International Music Division
Nick Cave . . . . .Music
Hamish Crombie . . . . .Music
Eugenie Furniss . . . . .Literary
Steve Hogan . . . . .Music
Sophie Laurimore . . . . .TV
David Levy . . . . .Music
Solomon Parker . . . . .Music
Lucinda Prain . . . . .Literary/Motion Pictures
Holly Pye . . . . .TV
Diana Richardson . . . . .Music
Adele Slater . . . . .Music
Cathryn Summerhayes . . . . .Literary
Russell Warby . . . . .Music
Isabella Zottowski . . . . .TV

WILLIAM MORRIS AGENCY - WMA (SHANGHAI)
Suite 1858 Bund Center 222
Yan An Road East
Shanghai 200002, China
PHONE 86-21-6132-3848
FAX 86-21-6335-2120
WEB SITE . . . . .www.wma.com
TYPES   Commercial Talent - Film/TV Talent -
                         Literary Talent - Music Talent - Talent &
                         Literary Packaging - Theatre Talent
AFFILIATIONS   AEA - AFM - AFTRA - ATA - DGA
REPRESENTS   Actors - Book Authors - Broadcast
                         Journalists/Newscasters - Composers -
                         Directors - Hosts/MCs - Interactive Game
                         Developers - Music Artists - Musical
                         Theatre Performers - Playwrights -
                         Screenwriters - Speakers/Lecturers - Sports
                         Personalities - TV Writers

Grace Chen . . . . .Director

SHIRLEY WILSON & ASSOCIATES
5410 Wilshire Blvd., Ste. 510
Los Angeles, CA 90036
PHONE 323-857-6977
FAX 323-857-6980
EMAIL . . . . .son4shirl@aol.com
TYPES   Commercial Talent - Film/TV Talent
AFFILIATIONS   AEA - AFTRA - SAG
REPRESENTS   Actors - Children - Comedians -
                         Teens/Young Adults

Shirley Wilson . . . . .Principal/Theatrical/Commercials
Harold Gray .Theatrical/Commercials

WORLD CLASS SPORTS
840 Apollo St., Ste. 314
El Segundo, CA 90245-4752
PHONE 310-535-9120
FAX 310-535-9128
EMAIL . . . . .wcsagent@pacbell.net
TYPES   Commercial Talent
AFFILIATIONS   ATA
REPRESENTS   Sports Personalities
SUBMISSION POLICY   By mail only; No phone calls; No email
                               submissions
COMMENTS   Represents athletes with college or national
                               level experience only for commercials and
                               print; Sports celebrities for endorsements,
                               personal appearances and speaking
                               engagements

Don Franken . . . . .Agent
Andrew Woolf . . . . .Agent

ANN WRIGHT REPRESENTATIVES
165 W. 46th St., Ste. 1105
New York, NY 10036
PHONE 212-764-6770
FAX 212-764-5125
TYPES   Commercial Talent - Film/TV Talent -
                               Literary Talent - Theatre Talent
AFFILIATIONS   AEA - AFTRA - SAG - WGA
REPRESENTS   Actors - Book Authors - Playwrights -
                               Screenwriters - Voice-Over Artists
COMMENTS   Dramatists Guild

Ann Wright . . . . .Owner
Dan Wright . . . . .Head, Theatrical

WRITERS HOUSE
21 W. 26th St.
New York, NY 10010
PHONE 212-685-2400
FAX 212-685-1781
WEB SITE . . . . .www.writershouse.com
TYPES   Literary Talent - Talent & Literary Packaging
AFFILIATIONS   AAR
REPRESENTS   Book Authors
SUBMISSION POLICY   See Web site
COMMENTS   Authors of juvenile and adult books in all
                               markets including publishing, foreign, film,
                               TV, audio, magazines; Agents for book
                               club, reprint, foreign rights for independent
                               publishing; Agents of foreign publishers for
                               sales of US rights; Book illustrators

Al Zuckerman . . . . .Chairman
Jerry Butler . . . . .CFO
Amy Berkower . . . . .President
Merrilee Heifetz . . . . .Executive VP
Susan Cohen . . . . .Sr. Agent, Juvenile/Young Adults
Susan Ginsburg . . . . .Sr. Agent
Simon Lipskar . . . . .Sr. Agent
Steven Malk . . . . .Sr. Agent, Juvenile/Young Adult (San Diego)
                                                    (858-678-8767)
Jodi Reamer . . . . .Sr. Agent
Michele Rubin . . . . .Sr. Agent
Robin Rue . . . . .Sr. Agent
Daniel Lazar . . . . .Agent
Rebecca Sherman . . . . .Agent
Kenneth Wright Sr. . . . . .Agent
Maya Rock . . . . .Jr. Agent
Emily Saladino . . . . .Jr. Agent
Maja Nikolic . . . . .Director, Foreign Rights
Al Araneo . . . . .Contracts Manager

WRITERS' REPRESENTATIVES, LLC
116 W. 14th St., 11th Fl.
New York, NY 10011-7305
PHONE 212-620-9009
FAX 212-620-0023
EMAIL . . . . .transom@writersreps.com
WEB SITE . . . . .www.writersreps.com
TYPES   Literary Talent
REPRESENTS   Book Authors

Glen Hartley . . . . .Agent
Lynn Chu . . . . .Agent
Farah Peterson . . . . .Assistant Agent

CRAIG WYCKOFF & ASSOCIATES
11350 Ventura Blvd., Ste. 100
Studio City, CA 91604
PHONE 818-752-2300
FAX 818-752-2305
TYPES   Commercial Talent - Film/TV Talent -
                               Literary Talent - Theatre Talent
AFFILIATIONS   AEA - AFTRA - ATA - DGA - SAG
REPRESENTS   Actors - Children - Comedians - Directors -
                               Screenwriters - Teens/Young Adults - TV
                               Writers
SUBMISSION POLICY   Written queries only

Craig Wyckoff . . . . .President
Kate Kribel . . . . .Associate

THE WYLIE AGENCY
250 W. 57th St., Ste. 2114
New York, NY 10107
PHONE 212-246-0069/44-20-7908-5900
FAX .212-586-8953/44-20-7908-5901
EMAIL . . . . .mail@wylieagency.com
SECOND EMAIL . . . . .mail@wylieagency.co.uk
WEB SITE . . . . .www.wylieagency.com
TYPES   Literary Talent
REPRESENTS   Book Authors
SUBMISSION POLICY   No unsolicited manuscripts or screenplays
COMMENTS   London office: 17 Bedford Square, London
                               WC1B 3JA, United Kingdom

Andrew Wylie . . . . .President/Literary Agent
Sarah Chalfant . . . . .Literary Agent

NICK YELLEN CREATIVE AGENCY
1501 Broadway, Ste. 2310
New York, NY 10036
PHONE 212-840-5760
FAX 212-840-5776
EMAIL . . . . .nycagency@nyc.rr.com
TYPES   Literary Talent
REPRESENTS   Book Authors - Directors - Playwrights -
                               Producers - Screenwriters - TV Writers

Nick Yellen . . . . .No Title

ZACHARY SHUSTER HARMSWORTH AGENCY

1776 Broadway, Ste. 1405
New York, NY 10019

PHONE	212-765-6900/617-262-2400
FAX	212-765-6490/617-262-2468
WEB SITE	www.zshliterary.com
TYPES	Literary Talent
REPRESENTS	Book Authors
SUBMISSION POLICY	No unsolicited manuscripts are accepted
COMMENTS	Boston office: 535 Boylston St., Boston, MA 02116

Todd Shuster . . . . .Agent (NY)
Lane Zachary . . . . .Agent (Boston & NY)
Jason Anthony . . . . .Agent (NY)
Eve Bridburg . . . . .Agent (Boston)
Mary Beth Chappell . . . . .Agent (Boston)
Jennifer Gates . . . . .Agent (NY)
Esmond Harmsworth .Agent (Boston & NY)
Jessica Spradling . . . . .Agent (NY)
Rachel Sussman . . . . .Agent (NY)
Joanne Wyckoff . . . . .Agent (Boston)

ZANUCK, PASSON AND PACE, INC.

4717 Van Nuys Blvd., Atrium, Ste. 102
Sherman Oaks, CA 91403

PHONE	818-783-4890
FAX	818-501-4327/818-501-8857
EMAIL	agentpace@aol.com
TYPES	Commercial Talent - Film/TV Talent - Modeling Talent - Theatre Talent
AFFILIATIONS	AEA - AFTRA - SAG
REPRESENTS	Actors - Children - Hosts/MCs - Print Models - Teens/Young Adults
SUBMISSION POLICY	Via mail or email; Include return address
COMMENTS	Children ten and over

Michael Zanuck . . . . .Partner, Film/TV
Jerry Pace . . . . .Partner, Film/TV
Mellisa Cohen . . . . .Commercials & Print
Marcia Robbins . . . . .Commercials & Print

ZENOBIA AGENCY, INC.

130 S. Highland Ave.
Los Angeles, CA 90036

PHONE	323-937-1010/888-639-6917
FAX	323-937-1133
WEB SITE	www.zenobia.com
TYPES	Below-the-Line Talent
COMMENTS	Hair and make-up artists; Wardrobe and prop styling; Food styling; Set decorators; Location scouts; Artists available nationwide; Complete portfolios on Web site; San Francisco office: 415-621-7410

Keith Zenobia . . . . .President
Heidi Nielsen . . . . .Booking Agent

WORKSHEET

DATE	PROJECT	CONTACT	NOTES

WORKSHEET

NAME	COMPANY	PHONE #	FAX #

WORKSHEET

DATE	PROJECT	CONTACT	NOTES

WORKSHEET

FREQUENTLY CALLED PHONE NUMBERS			
NAME	**COMPANY**	**PHONE #**	**FAX #**

Hollywood Representation Directory
AGENTS AND MANAGERS

To submit your company for a free listing in the HOLLYWOOD REPRESENTATION DIRECTORY, complete and return this application form along with a <u>brief bio and/or company profile</u>. All listings are at the discretion of the Editor.

PHONE: 323-525-2376   FAX: 323-525-2393   www.hcdonline.com

COMPANY_____ C/O _____

STREET _____ CITY _____ STATE _____ ZIP _____

PHONE(S) _____ FAX(S) _____

PUBLISHED EMAIL _____ WEBSITE _____

NONPUBLISHED EMAIL _____ NONPUBLISHED FAX _____

AFFILIATIONS/GUILDS
(check all that apply)

- ❏ AAR
- ❏ AFTRA
- ❏ DGA
- ❏ TMA
- ❏ AEA
- ❏ AGVA
- ❏ NCOPM
- ❏ WGA
- ❏ AFM
- ❏ ATA
- ❏ SAG

YOU ARE...
(check one)

- ❏ AGENCY
- ❏ MANAGEMENT COMPANY

YOU REPRESENT...
(check all that apply)

- ❏ BELOW-THE-LINE
- ❏ COMMERCIAL
- ❏ MUSIC TALENT
- ❏ THEATRE
- ❏ MODELING
- ❏ FILM & TV
- ❏ LITERARY
- ❏ PACKAGING

TYPES OF CLIENTS REPRESENTED
(check all that apply)

- ❏ ACTORS
- ❏ ANIMALS
- ❏ BOOK AUTHORS
- ❏ BROADCAST/NEWSCASTERS
- ❏ CHILDREN
- ❏ CHOREOGRAPHERS
- ❏ CINEMATOGRAPHERS
- ❏ COMEDIANS
- ❏ COMPOSERS
- ❏ DANCERS
- ❏ DIRECTORS
- ❏ FILM EDITORS

- ❏ HOSTS/MCs
- ❏ INFANTS
- ❏ INTERACTIVE GAME DEVELOPERS
- ❏ MAGICIANS
- ❏ MARTIAL ARTISTS/STUNTS
- ❏ MUSIC ARTISTS
- ❏ MUSIC EDITORS
- ❏ MUSIC PRODUCERS
- ❏ MUSIC SUPERVISORS
- ❏ MUSICAL THEATRE PERFORMERS
- ❏ PLAYWRIGHTS
- ❏ PRINT MODELS

- ❏ PRODUCERS
- ❏ PRODUCTION DESIGNERS
- ❏ RUNWAY MODELS
- ❏ SCREENWRITERS
- ❏ SENIORS
- ❏ SOUND EDITORS
- ❏ SPEAKERS/LECTURERS
- ❏ SPORTS PERSONALITIES
- ❏ TEENS/YOUNG ADULTS
- ❏ TV WRITERS
- ❏ VARIETY ARTISTS
- ❏ VOICE-OVER ARTISTS

STAFF

NAME _____ TITLE _____

NAME _____ TITLE _____

NAME _____ TITLE _____

NAME _____ TITLE _____

NAME _____ TITLE _____

NAME _____ TITLE _____

NAME _____ TITLE _____

SUBMISSION POLICY _____

ADDITIONAL COMMENTS _____

_____

SUBMITTED BY _____ DATE _____

SECTION B

MANAGERS

- Below-the-Line Talent
- Commercial Talent
- Film/TV Talent
- Literary Talent
- Modeling Talent
- Music Talent
- Theatre Talent

UTAH FILM
C O M M I S S I O N

Supporting independent film for over 30 years.

MANAGERS

American Pastime, ShadowCatcher Entertainment

F I L M . U T A H . G O V

1 MANAGEMENT
9000 Sunset Blvd., Ste. 1550
West Hollywood, CA 90069
PHONE 310-270-4304/212-431-0054
EMAIL . . . . .info@1modelmanagement.com
WEB SITE www.1modelmanagement.com
TYPES   Film/TV Talent - Modeling Talent
REPRESENTS   Actors - Music Artists - Print Models
COMMENTS   East Coast Office: 424 West Broadway,
                         New York, NY 10012

Darren Goldberg . . . . .Partner
Scott Lipps . . . . .Partner
Jeb Brandon . . . . .Manager
Andrew Edwards . . . . .Manager
Sean Fay . . . . .Manager

3 ARTS ENTERTAINMENT, INC.
9460 Wilshire Blvd., 7th Fl.
Beverly Hills, CA 90212
PHONE 310-888-3200
FAX 310-888-3210
TYPES   Film/TV Talent - Literary Talent
AFFILIATIONS   DGA
REPRESENTS   Actors - Comedians - Directors -
                         Screenwriters - TV Writers
SUBMISSION POLICY   No unsolicited material

Howard Klein . . . . .Partner/Manager
Michael Rotenberg . . . . .Partner/Manager
Erwin Stoff . . . . .Partner/Manager
Dave Becky . . . . .Manager
Stephanie Davis . . . . .Manager
Nicholas Frenkel . . . . .Manager
Pam Kohl . . . . .Manager
Tom Lassally . . . . .Manager
Molly Madden . . . . .Manager
David Miner . . . . .Manager
Mark Schulman . . . . .Manager
Tucker Voorhees . . . . .Manager
Scott Wexler . . . . .Manager
Greg Walter . . . . .Manager
Brad Bertner . . . . .Executive Director, Development

6 PICTURES
14358 Magnolia Blvd., Ste. 135
Sherman Oaks, CA 91423
PHONE 818-789-7666
EMAIL. . . . . .6pictures@earthlink.net
TYPES   Literary Talent
REPRESENTS   Directors - Screenwriters

Peter Soby Jr. . . . . .Manager

777 GROUP, LTD
1015 Gayley Ave., Ste. 1128
Los Angeles, CA 90024
PHONE 310-824-0664
EMAIL . . . . .admin@777entgroup.com
WEB SITE www.the777group.com
TYPES   Film/TV Talent - Literary Talent
REPRESENTS   Actors - Directors - Producers -
                         Screenwriters - TV Writers

Marcello Robinson . . . . .CEO

A FEIN MARTINI
37 West 20th St., Ste. 1004
New York, NY 10001
PHONE 212-414-4041
FAX 212-414-4631
EMAIL . . . . .steve@afeinmartini.com
TYPES   Film/TV Talent - Modeling Talent - Music
                        Talent - Theatre Talent
REPRESENTS   Actors - Music Artists - Teens/Young Adults

Steven Feinberg . . . . .Owner/Manager (steve@afeinmartini.com)
Mike Martinovich . . . . .Owner/Manager (mike@afeinmartini.com)
Jamie Sampson . . . . .Manager (jamie@afeinmartini.com)
Matt Winkler . . . . .Manager (matt@afeinmartini.com)
Evange Livanos . . . . .Manager (evange@afeinmartini.com)
Matthew Gilbert . . . . .CFO (matthew@afeinmartini.com)
Jessica Savage . . . . .Assistant (jessica@afeinmartini.com)

A MANAGEMENT
500 S. Buena Vista St., Production Bldg., Ste. 355
Burbank, CA 91521-2290
PHONE 818-560-8150
FAX 818-560-6688
TYPES   Film/TV Talent
REPRESENTS   Actors - Teens/Young Adults
SUBMISSION POLICY   No unsolicited material

Abe Hoch . . . . .Owner/Manager
Charlton Blackburne . . . . .Manager
Lisa Bronitt . . . . .Coordinator

A WINK AND A NOD MANAGEMENT, INC.
843 12th St., Ste. 4
Santa Monica, CA 90403
PHONE 310-394-5752
WEB SITE . . . . .www.awinkandanod.com
TYPES   Literary Talent
REPRESENTS   Directors - Producers - Screenwriters
SUBMISSION POLICY   New clients via referral only

Wendy Winks . . . . .President
CJ Helm . . . . .Assistant

ABC MANAGEMENT GROUP
11271 Ventura Blvd., Ste. 510
Studio City, CA 91604
PHONE 818-789-3545
FAX 818-789-3539
EMAIL . . . . .abcmgmt@comcast.net
TYPES   Commercial Talent - Film/TV Talent - Music
                         Talent
REPRESENTS   Actors - Broadcast Journalists/Newscasters
                         - Children - Comedians - Dancers -
                         Hosts/MCs - Martial Artists/Stunts - Music
                         Artists - Music Producers - Print Models -
                         Speakers/Lecturers - Sports Personalities -
                         Teens/Young Adults - Voice-Over Artists
SUBMISSION POLICY   Photo, resumés or reels by mail only (no
                         returns); Do not phone, fax, email or visit
COMMENTS   Looking for established artists only

David Van Maren . . . . .Sr. Partner
Keri Murphy . . . . .Manager
Carol Lukens . . . . .Manager

ABSOLUTE TALENT MANAGEMENT, INC.
9713 Santa Monica Blvd., Ste. 219
Beverly Hills, CA 90210
PHONE 310-273-1373
FAX 310-273-1374
EMAIL .info@absolutetalent.net
WEB SITE . . . . .www.absolutetalent.net
TYPES   Commercial Talent - Film/TV Talent
REPRESENTS   Actors - Children - Print Models -
                         Teens/Young Adults - Voice-Over Artists

Pat O'Brien . . . . .President

ACE MEDIA
9200 Sunset Blvd., 10th Fl.
Los Angeles, CA 90069
PHONE 310-786-8975
FAX 310-777-2112
TYPES   Film/TV Talent - Literary Talent
REPRESENTS   Actors - Choreographers - Comedians -
                         Directors - Martial Artists/Stunts -
                         Screenwriters - TV Writers
SUBMISSION POLICY   No unsolicited material
COMMENTS   Also produces; Affiliated with PGA

Steven Chasman .Manager/CEO
David Shojai .Office Coordinator

A.C.T. MANAGEMENT
11684 Ventura Blvd., Ste. 441
Studio City, CA 91604
PHONE 818-752-4664
TYPES   Below-the-Line Talent - Commercial Talent
                         - Film/TV Talent - Theatre Talent
REPRESENTS   Actors - Children - Choreographers -
                         Comedians - Directors - Hosts/MCs -
                         Musical Theatre Performers - Playwrights -
                         Producers - Screenwriters -
                         Speakers/Lecturers - TV Writers - Variety
                         Artists - Voice-Over Artists
SUBMISSION POLICY   Not currently seeking clients; Rarely meets
                         without referrals; Occasionally attends
                         shows/showcases

Michelle Kirkhoff . . . . .Owner/Manager
Carol Lynne Convey . . . . .Owner/Manager
Lenny Moore . . . . .Assistant to Carol Lynne Convey

ACUNA ENTERTAINMENT
4130 Cahuenga Blvd., Ste. 200
Toluca Lake, CA 91602
PHONE 818-508-6462
FAX 818-508-0652
EMAIL . . . . .assistant@acunaentertainment.com
WEB SITE . . . . .www.acunaentertainment.com
TYPES   Literary Talent
REPRESENTS   Directors - Screenwriters - TV Writers

Marvin Acuna . . . . .No Title
Randy Becker . . . . .No Title
Tara Norris . . . . .No Title
Melissa Stone . . . . .No Title
Deborah Clifford . . . . .No Title

A.D.S. MANAGEMENT
269 S. Beverly Dr., Ste. 441
Beverly Hills, CA 90212
PHONE 310-745-1359
FAX 310-745-1358
EMAIL .stevi000@hotmail.com
TYPES   Commercial Talent - Film/TV Talent -
                         Literary Talent - Modeling Talent - Theatre
                         Talent
REPRESENTS   Actors - Broadcast Journalists/Newscasters
                         - Hosts/MCs - Martial Artists/Stunts -
                         Musical Theatre Performers - Print Models -
                         Producers - Seniors - Speakers/Lecturers -
                         Sports Personalities - Voice-Over Artists
SUBMISSION POLICY   Mail only; Union actors only

Andrew Stawiarski . . . . .Owner/Manager

AEI-ATCHITY/ENTERTAINMENT INTERNATIONAL
9601 Wilshire Blvd., Box 1202
Beverly Hills, CA 90210
PHONE 323-932-0407
FAX 323-932-0321
EMAIL . . . . .submissions@aeionline.com
WEB SITE . . . . .www.aeionline.com
TYPES   Film/TV Talent - Literary Talent
REPRESENTS   Book Authors - Screenwriters - TV Writers
SUBMISSION POLICY   Only accepts query letters with one to two-
                         page synopsis and SASE
COMMENTS   All productions are WGA signatory;
                         Signatures Network; Literary merchandising
                         and licensing

Ken Atchity . . . . .CEO
Chi-li Wong . . . . .President
Andrea McKeown . . . . .Executive VP, Editorial (KC)
Michael Kuciak . . . . .VP, Acquisitions & Marketing
Brenna Lui . . . . .Development Executive
Jennifer Pope . . . . .Submissions Coordinator

AK ASSOCIATES
8950 W. Olympic Blvd., Ste. 396
Beverly Hills, CA 90211
PHONE 310-854-4246
WEB SITE . . . . .www.aklit.com
TYPES   Film/TV Talent - Literary Talent
REPRESENTS   Producers - Screenwriters - TV Writers
SUBMISSION POLICY   No unsolicited material
COMMENTS   Represents writers/producers, TV format
                          creators, international production compa-
                          nies

Angela Kyle . . . . .Principal

ALCHEMY ENTERTAINMENT
9229 Sunset Blvd., Ste. 720
Los Angeles, CA 90069
PHONE 310-278-8889
TYPES   Film/TV Talent
REPRESENTS   Actors
COMMENTS   Also a production company

Jason Barrett .Manager/Producer
Angie Edgar . . . . .Development Associate

ALL THAT ENTERTAINMENT MANAGEMENT
2415 Courtland Ave.
Henderson, NV 89074
PHONE 702-429-7487
EMAIL .gems.gems@cox.net
TYPES   Commercial Talent - Film/TV Talent -
                          Modeling Talent
REPRESENTS   Actors - Children - Music Artists - Print
                          Models - Runway Models
SUBMISSION POLICY   Call for instructions

Gem Wiltshire . . . . .Manager

LESLIE ALLAN-RICE MANAGEMENT
1007 Maybrook Dr.
Beverly Hills, CA 90210
PHONE 310-247-1234
FAX 310-247-8505
TYPES   Film/TV Talent
REPRESENTS   Actors - Children - Teens/Young Adults
SUBMISSION POLICY   Accepts submissions by mail only
COMMENTS   Children six and over

Leslie Allan-Rice . . . . .Manager
Kara Fitzgerald . . . . .Assistant

ALLMAN/REA MANAGEMENT
141 S. Barrington Ave., Ste. E
Los Angeles, CA 90049
PHONE 310-440-5780
FAX 310-440-5779
EMAIL . . . . .allmanrea@aol.com
SECOND EMAIL . . . . .allmanrea@verizon.net
TYPES   Film/TV Talent
REPRESENTS   Actors

Danielle Allman-Del . . . . .Partner
Edith Rea . . . . .Partner
Traci Braddock . . . . .Associate

ALPHA CENTAURI MANAGEMENT
432 Ebony Tree Ave.
Galloway Township, NJ 08205
PHONE 609-404-1778
FAX 609-652-0542
EMAIL . . . . .closestar@aol.com
WEB SITE . . . . .www.alphacentaurimgmt.com
TYPES   Film/TV Talent - Literary Talent
AFFILIATIONS   NCOPM
REPRESENTS   Actors - Book Authors - Comedians -
                          Hosts/MCs - Magicians - Screenwriters - TV
                          Writers - Variety Artists

Al Caz . . . . .CEO
Jaqueline Coady . . . . .VP

AM PRODUCTIONS & MANAGEMENT
8899 Beverly Blvd., Ste. 713
Los Angeles, CA 90048
PHONE 310-275-9081
FAX 310-275-9082
TYPES   Film/TV Talent - Music Talent
REPRESENTS   Actors - Music Artists
SUBMISSION POLICY   No unsolicited submissions

Ann-Margret . . . . .No Title
Engelbert Humperdinck . . . . .No Title
Alan Margulies . . . . .No Title
Roger Smith . . . . .No Title

AMBITIOUS ENTERTAINMENT
15120 Hartsook St.
Sherman Oaks, CA 91403
PHONE 818-990-8993
EMAIL . . . . .ambitious1@sbcglobal.net
WEB SITE . . . . .www.ambitiousent.com
TYPES   Film/TV Talent
REPRESENTS   Cinematographers - Directors - Producers -
                          Production Designers
SUBMISSION POLICY   Not accepting writer submissions
COMMENTS   CGI/VFX for commercials, field producers,
                          DPs; See Web site for credits and full
                          streaming reels

Paul Addis . . . . .President

AMERICAN ARTISTS ENTERTAINMENT GROUP
1143 Fitzgerald St.
Philadelphia, PA 19148
PHONE 215-462-0115
FAX 215-462-2329
EMAIL .amessina@aaegec.com
SECOND EMAIL . . . . .ajmessina@hotmail.com
WEB SITE . . . . .www.aaeg.com
TYPES   Commercial Talent - Film/TV Talent -
                          Modeling Talent - Music Talent
AFFILIATIONS   AFM - NCOPM - TMA
REPRESENTS   Actors - Music Artists - Music Producers -
                          Print Models - Producers - Runway Models

Anthony J. Messina . . . . .President
Fred Cohen . . . . .Associate
Hal Kaye . . . . .Associate
Jay Michaels . . . . .Associate
Jay Raymond . . . . .Associate

AMERICAN ARTISTS GROUP MANAGEMENT
13321 Ventura Blvd., Ste. C
Sherman Oaks, CA 91423
PHONE 818-501-8917
FAX 818-464-2420
EMAIL . . . . .americanartists@earthlink.net
TYPES　　　　　　　　　Film/TV Talent
REPRESENTS　　　　　　Actors - Comedians - Directors -
　　　　　　　　　　　　Hosts/MCs - Producers - Teens/Young
　　　　　　　　　　　　Adults
COMMENTS　　　　　　　Open to established film and TV actors;
　　　　　　　　　　　　Teens and young adults with training

Sharon Nixon Kelly . . . . .Owner/Manager, Film/TV
Grazna Broucki . . . . .Manager, Commercial/Print
Donna Danthridge . . . . .Assistant
Rustie McCoy . . . . .Assistant

AMPERSAND MANAGEMENT GROUP
447 S. Robertson Blvd., Ste. 103
Beverly Hills, CA 90211
PHONE 310-274-7707/212-362-0421
TYPES　　　　　　　　　Film/TV Talent - Literary Talent
REPRESENTS　　　　　　Book Authors - Directors - Playwrights -
　　　　　　　　　　　　Screenwriters - TV Writers
COMMENTS　　　　　　　East Coast office: 12 W. 72nd St., Ste.
　　　　　　　　　　　　10D, New York, NY 10023

Joan Scott . . . . .Partner/Owner (NY) (jscott@ampersandmgmt.com)
Marti Blumenthal　Partner/Owner (mblumenthal@ampersandmgmt.com)
Jessie Blatt . . . . .Assistant to Marti Blumenthal
Corwin Neuse . . . . .Assistant to Joan Scott

ANONYMOUS CONTENT
3532 Hayden Ave.
Culver City, CA 90232
PHONE 310-558-3667/212-925-0055
FAX 310-558-4212/212-925-5030
WEB SITE . . . . .www.anonymouscontent.com
TYPES　　　　　　　　　Film/TV Talent - Literary Talent
AFFILIATIONS　　　　　　DGA
REPRESENTS　　　　　　Actors - Directors - Screenwriters - TV
　　　　　　　　　　　　Writers
COMMENTS　　　　　　　East Coast office: 588 Broadway, Ste.
　　　　　　　　　　　　1005, New York, NY 10012

Lenny Bekerman . . . . .No Title
Eric Black . . . . .No Title
Bard Dorros . . . . .No Title
Joy Gorman . . . . .No Title
David J. Kanter . . . . .No Title
Raelle Koota . . . . .No Title (NY)
Adam Krentzman . . . . .No Title
Jeff Okin . . . . .No Title
Keith Redmon . . . . .No Title
Eli Selden . . . . .No Title
Shawn Hopkins Simon . . . . .No Title
Beverly Strong . . . . .No Title
Michael Sugar . . . . .No Title
Doreen Wilcox-Little . . . . .No Title

ANTHEM ENTERTAINMENT
6100 Wilshire Blvd., Ste. 1170
Los Angeles, CA 90048
PHONE 323-939-4500
FAX 323-939-4520
EMAIL . . . . .dan@anthement.com
TYPES　　　　　　　　　Film/TV Talent - Literary Talent - Theatre
　　　　　　　　　　　　Talent
REPRESENTS　　　　　　Actors - Directors - Screenwriters -
　　　　　　　　　　　　Teens/Young Adults - Voice-Over Artists

Cynthia Campos-Greenberg . . . . .Owner/Manager
Adam Levine . . . . .Owner/Manager
Francis Okwu . . . . .Owner/Manager

ARCHETYPE
9100 Wilshire Blvd., Ste. 350W
Beverly Hills, CA 90212
PHONE 310-288-5882
FAX 310-276-5694
EMAIL .info@thearchetypegroup.com
WEB SITE . . . . .www.thearchetypegroup.com
TYPES　　　　　　　　　Literary Talent - Theatre Talent
REPRESENTS　　　　　　Actors - Directors - Screenwriters - TV
　　　　　　　　　　　　Writers

Ray Miller . . . . .Manager/Partner
Lincoln Gasking . . . . .Partner
Shepard Smith . . . . .Manager
David Server . . . . .Assistant

ARDENT ENTERTAINMENT
345 N. Maple Dr., Ste. 317
Beverly Hills, CA 90210
PHONE 310-308-6986
TYPES　　　　　　　　　Film/TV Talent
REPRESENTS　　　　　　Actors - Producers

Mitch Blumberg . . . . .Producer/Manager

ARIAS & ASSOCIATES INTERNATIONAL
6701 Center Drive West, 14th Fl.
Los Angeles, CA 90045
PHONE 310-645-0055
FAX 310-670-1231
EMAIL . . . . .marias@aogllp.com
WEB SITE . . . . .www.aogllp.com
REPRESENTS　　　　　　Sports Personalities
COMMENTS　　　　　　　Athletes only

Mike Arias . . . . .President
Mark Ozzello . . . . .General Counsel
Chip Oliver . . . . .Client Development

ARPIL ENTERTAINMENT
1680 N. Vine St., Ste. 503
Hollywood, CA 90028
PHONE 323-461-6612
EMAIL . . . . .arpil@arpil.com
WEB SITE . . . . .www.arpil.com
TYPES　　　　　　　　　Literary Talent
REPRESENTS　　　　　　Directors - Screenwriters
SUBMISSION POLICY　　Unsolicited scripts not accepted

Adam B. Finer . . . . .Manager

ART/WORK ENTERTAINMENT
5900 Wilshire Blvd., Ste. 2150
Los Angeles, CA 90036
PHONE 323-456-0333
FAX 323-456-0323
TYPES　　　　　　　　　Film/TV Talent - Literary Talent
REPRESENTS　　　　　　Actors - Directors - Screenwriters - TV
　　　　　　　　　　　　Writers

Julie Bloom . . . . .Partner/Literary
David K. Brownstein . . . . .Partner/Talent
Deweyne Lee . . . . .Literary
Charles P. Skouras IV . . . . .Talent Assistant

ARTIST INTERNATIONAL
9595 Wilshire Blvd., 9th Fl.
Beverly Hills, CA 90212
PHONE 310-358-9239
FAX 310-943-2230
WEB SITE . . . . .www.artistint.com
SECOND WEB SITE . . . . .www.hsifilms.com
TYPES   Commercial Talent - Film/TV Talent -
                         Literary Talent - Modeling Talent - Music
                         Talent - Theatre Talent
REPRESENTS   Actors - Book Authors - Comedians -
                         Composers - Directors - Hosts/MCs -
                         Music Artists - Music Producers - Print
                         Models - Producers - Screenwriters - Sports
                         Personalities - Teens/Young Adults - TV
                         Writers
COMMENTS   Packaging

Steven Saxton . . . . .CEO
Joel Newton . . . . .VP, Production
Stan Spry . . . . .VP, Management
Joseph Bovino . . . . .Manager
Joshy Ready . . . . .Talent Manager
Robbie Webb . . . . .Manager
Jason Gold .Jr. Manager/Story Editor
Mike Jones . . . . .Creative Executive

ARTIST MANAGEMENT
1119 Colorado Ave., Ste. 12
Santa Monica, CA 90401
PHONE 310-656-9600
TYPES   Film/TV Talent - Literary Talent
REPRESENTS   Actors
SUBMISSION POLICY   No faxes; No drop-offs; Industry referral
                         only

Cheri Barner . . . . .Manager
Carolyn Govers . . . . .Manager
Lauren Moore . . . . .Assistant

ARTISTS INTERNATIONAL
23151 Plaza Pointe Dr., Ste. 100
Laguna Hills, CA 92653
PHONE 800-350-1602/949-855-0880
EMAIL . . . . .artistsinternational@operamail.com
SECOND EMAIL . . . . .artistsinternational@yahoo.com
TYPES   Film/TV Talent - Modeling Talent
REPRESENTS   Actors - Teens/Young Adults
SUBMISSION POLICY   Accepts photos and resumés from young
                         adults

Diane C. Adams . . . . .Owner/President
Bob Shannon . . . . .Manager

ARTISTS MANAGEMENT
3761 Sunswept Dr.
Studio City, CA 91604
PHONE 818-506-8344
TYPES   Film/TV Talent - Music Talent
REPRESENTS   Composers - Music Producers

Austin Godsey . . . . .Manager

ARTISTS ONLY MANAGEMENT
c/o Crystal Sky Communications
10203 Santa Monica Blvd., 5th Fl.
Los Angeles, CA 90067
PHONE 310-843-0223
FAX 310-553-9895
TYPES   Film/TV Talent - Literary Talent
AFFILIATIONS   AFM - DGA
REPRESENTS   Actors - Directors - Screenwriters -
                         Teens/Young Adults

Hank Paul . . . . .Chairman
Steven Paul . . . . .Owner/President
Dorothy Koster . . . . .Co-Chairman
Patrick Ewald . . . . .Executive VP, Development
Allison Gorelik . . . .Development Assistant/Talent Management Assistant

ARTS AND LETTERS MANAGEMENT
7715 Sunset Blvd., Ste. 100
Los Angeles, CA 90046
PHONE 323-883-1070
EMAIL . . . . .steven.nash@talentmanagers.org
WEB SITE . . . . .www.artsandlets.com
TYPES   Commercial Talent - Film/TV Talent -
                         Literary Talent - Modeling Talent - Theatre
                         Talent
AFFILIATIONS   TMA
REPRESENTS   Actors - Children - Directors - Print Models
                         - Screenwriters - Teens/Young Adults -
                         Voice-Over Artists
SUBMISSION POLICY   Will review all submissions and make con-
                         tact if interested; No unsolicited scripts will
                         be accepted
COMMENTS   President of the Talent Managers
                         Association; Also produces features

Steven Nash . . . . .Manager
Toribio Torres . . . . .Manager

ASSOCIATED ARTISTS PR & MANAGEMENT
6404 Wilshire Blvd., Ste. 1575
Los Angeles, CA 90048
PHONE 323-758-1972/323-758-1991
TYPES   Below-the-Line Talent - Commercial Talent
                         - Film/TV Talent - Literary Talent - Modeling
                         Talent - Music Talent - Theatre Talent
AFFILIATIONS   AFM
REPRESENTS   Actors - Cinematographers - Comedians -
                         Directors - Hosts/MCs - Martial
                         Artists/Stunts - Music Artists - Musical
                         Theatre Performers - Playwrights - Print
                         Models - Producers - Screenwriters -
                         Seniors - TV Writers - Voice-Over Artists
SUBMISSION POLICY   Referral only
COMMENTS   AFI, IFP, WIF, Publicists Guild, Cinewomen;
                         Publicist

Erich C. Smith . . . . .Manager
Evan Jackson . . . . .Assistant
Cris Sommers . . . . .Assistant

ATHENA TALENT MANAGEMENT, LLC
427 N. Canon Dr., Ste. 107
Beverly Hills, CA 90210
PHONE 310-275-0273
FAX 310-275-0224
TYPES   Film/TV Talent
AFFILIATIONS   TMA
REPRESENTS   Actors
SUBMISSION POLICY   No unsolicited submissions; SAG actors
                    only

Gloria Tait . . . . .Manager
Joseph D'Onofrio . . . . .Manager

MARILYN ATLAS MANAGEMENT
8899 Beverly Blvd., Ste. 704
Los Angeles, CA 90048
PHONE 310-278-5047
FAX 310-278-5289
TYPES   Film/TV Talent - Literary Talent
REPRESENTS   Actors - Directors - Screenwriters -
                    Teens/Young Adults - TV Writers - Voice-
                    Over Artists
SUBMISSION POLICY   No unsolicited material, will not respond;
                    Send query letter with logline and industry
                    referral only by fax or mail, Attn: Elizabeth;
                    Credits and demo reel required
COMMENTS   Produces film, theatre and TV; Small client
                    list; Attends plays

Marilyn R. Atlas . . . . .Owner/President
S. Rosenthal . . . . .Literary
Elizabeth Lopez . . . . .Assistant, Talent & Literary Development

AVALON MANAGEMENT, INC.
5619 W. Fourth St., Ste. 7
Los Angeles, CA 90036
PHONE 323-930-6010/44-207-598-8000
FAX 323-930-6018/44-207-598-7300
WEB SITE . . . . .www.avalon-usa.com
TYPES   Film/TV Talent - Literary Talent
REPRESENTS   Actors - Comedians - Directors -
                    Hosts/MCs - Producers - Screenwriters - TV
                    Writers - Variety Artists
COMMENTS   All clients comedy-related; UK office: 4A
                    Exmoor St., London W10 6BD, United
                    Kingdom

Jon Thoday . . . . .President
Richard Allen-Turner .President
Julie James . . . . .Manager
Isaac Horne . . . . .Manager

AVERY MANAGEMENT
311 N. Robertson Blvd., Ste. 374
Beverly Hills, CA 90211
PHONE 310-289-7194
EMAIL . . . . .averymgt@aol.com
TYPES   Literary Talent
REPRESENTS   Book Authors - Directors - Producers -
                    Screenwriters - TV Writers
SUBMISSION POLICY   Queries accepted by email only

Dionell Guanco . . . . .Principal

AXIOM MANAGEMENT
1875 Century Park East, Ste. H3600
Los Angeles, CA 90067
PHONE 310-446-4498
FAX 310-446-9950
EMAIL . . . . .axiommanagement@aol.com
TYPES   Commercial Talent - Film/TV Talent
REPRESENTS   Actors - Hosts/MCs - Sports Personalities -
                    Teens/Young Adults
COMMENTS   Second office: 16302 Crowne Brook
                    Circle, Franklin, TN 37067

Kathy Carter . . . . .President/Manager
Leslie Moore . . . . .Manager
Janine Jackson . . . . .Jr. Manager
J.R. Little . . . . .Assistant

BAMBOO MANAGEMENT LLC
17 Buccaneer St.
Marina del Rey, CA 90292
PHONE 310-827-0930
EMAIL .hype2120@earthlink.net
TYPES   Commercial Talent - Film/TV Talent -
                    Literary Talent - Theatre Talent
REPRESENTS   Actors - Screenwriters - Teens/Young Adults
                    - TV Writers - Voice-Over Artists
SUBMISSION POLICY   Actors by industry referral only; Actors
                    should not contact company directly;
                    Literary queries must include an SASE; Do
                    not email loglines

Heidi L. Ifft . . . . .Manager
Patrick Kelly . . . . .Executive VP/Manager
Daniel Glazer . . . . .Manager
Lisa Padron . . . . .Manager
Kristin Wells . . . . .Manager
Fritz Werner . . . . .Literary Manager
Anita Cheng . . . . .Office Manager
Bernhard Strohman . . . . .Associate Manager
Emma Kreiger-Kahn . . . . .Assistant to Heidi Ifft
Christy Block . . . . .Assistant to Patrick Kelly
Maria Cedano . . . . .Assistant to Lisa Padron
David Goldberg . . . . .Assistant to Kristin Wells
Lukas Müller . . . . .Assistant to Fritz Werner
Sophie O'Donahue . . . . .Assistant to Danny Glazer

BANDWAGON ENTERTAINMENT
12930 Ventura Blvd., Ste. 114-633
Studio City, CA 91604
PHONE 818-762-0732
EMAIL . . . . .joshbandwagon@mail.com
TYPES   Commercial Talent - Film/TV Talent
REPRESENTS   Comedians
SUBMISSION POLICY   Mail resumé and cover letter; No calls or
                    drop-ins

Robert Longmuir . . . . .Partner
Frank Payne . . . . .Partner
Andrea Beck . . . . .Manager
Josh Silverstein . . . . .Manager
Aaron Gottlieb . . . . .Associate Manager
Bruce Longmuir . . . . .Associate Manager

BARKING DOG ENTERTAINMENT, INC.
9 Desbrosses St., 2nd Fl.
New York, NY 10013
PHONE 212-343-2117
FAX 212-343-9018
TYPES   Film/TV Talent - Theatre Talent
REPRESENTS   Actors - Comedians

Sue Leibman . . . . .President
Lauren Honig . . . . .Executive Assistant

THE BAUER COMPANY

9720 Wilshire Blvd., Mezzanine
Beverly Hills, CA 90212
PHONE 310-247-3880
FAX 310-247-3881
TYPES   Below-the-Line Talent - Film/TV Talent -
                               Literary Talent
REPRESENTS   Actors - Book Authors - Comedians -
                               Directors - Film Editors - Hosts/MCs -
                               Producers - Screenwriters - TV Writers -
                               Voice-Over Artists
SUBMISSION POLICY   No unsolicited submissions; Referral only

Martin R. Bauer . . . . .President
Tom Demko . . . . .Manager
Mario Garcia . . . . .Executive Assistant

BAUMGARTEN MANAGEMENT & PRODUCTION

9595 Wilshire Blvd., Ste. 1000
Beverly Hills, CA 90212
PHONE 310-445-1601
FAX 310-996-1892
EMAIL . . . . .craigbaumgarten@yahoo.com
TYPES   Literary Talent - Theatre Talent
REPRESENTS   Directors - Screenwriters - TV Writers
COMMENTS   PGA

Craig Baumgarten .Producer/Manager

BEATY FOUR ENTERTAINMENT

3470 Middle View Dr.
Las Vegas, NV 89129
PHONE 702-880-7911/702-808-9233
FAX 702-880-7911
EMAIL . . . . .frank@beatyfour.com
WEB SITE . . . . .www.beatyfour.com
TYPES   Below-the-Line Talent - Commercial Talent
                               - Film/TV Talent - Literary Talent - Modeling
                               Talent - Music Talent
REPRESENTS   Comedians - Music Artists - Music
                               Producers - Screenwriters -
                               Speakers/Lecturers

Frank M. Beaty . . . . .President
Lisa M. Beaty . . . . .CFO
Freeman Beaty . . . . .Music Director
Franklin Beaty . . . . .Artist Relations
Tony Reason . . . . .Director, Operations

BECKER ENTERTAINMENT GROUP

636 N. Sweetzer Ave., Ste. 4
Los Angeles, CA 90048
PHONE 323-655-1491
FAX 323-655-7811
EMAIL . . . . .beckerent@aol.com
TYPES   Below-the-Line Talent - Film/TV Talent -
                               Literary Talent - Music Talent
REPRESENTS   Actors - Cinematographers - Directors -
                               Music Artists - Producers - Screenwriters
COMMENTS   Also represents Line Producers

Michael Becker . . . . .Manager/Producer
Michelle Silver . . . . .Director, Development

THE BEDDINGFIELD COMPANY, INC.

13600 Ventura Blvd., Ste. B
Sherman Oaks, CA 91423
PHONE 818-285-7411
FAX 818-907-8127
TYPES   Film/TV Talent
REPRESENTS   Actors

Ric Beddingfield . . . . .President/Manager
Tash Moseley . . . . .Manager

DAVID BELENZON MANAGEMENT, INC.

PO Box 3819
La Mesa, CA 91944-3819
PHONE 619-462-6400
FAX 619-546-4535/619-462-2244
EMAIL . . . . .info@belenzon.com
WEB SITE . . . . .www.belenzon.com
TYPES   Film/TV Talent - Music Talent - Theatre
                               Talent
AFFILIATIONS   TMA
REPRESENTS   Hosts/MCs - Music Artists - Producers -
                               Speakers/Lecturers - Variety Artists
COMMENTS   Also affiliated with IEBA and IACEP;
                               Specializes in variety entertainment, pro-
                               duction shows and '50s-'60s musical
                               artists; Partial client list: Kevin Johnson -
                               Franz Harary - Michael Moschen - Max
                               Maven - Mark Wenzel - Jon 'Bowzer'
                               Bauman; Shows include: Bowzer's Ultimate
                               Doo Wop Party, Jungle Dreams, MTV Laser
                               Factory, Holiday in Motion, International
                               Festival of Magic

David Belenzon . . . . .President

CARL BELFOR ENTERTAINMENT MANAGEMENT COMPANY

PO Box 8388
Calabasas, CA 91372-8388
PHONE 818-224-3036
TYPES   Film/TV Talent - Literary Talent
AFFILIATIONS   TMA
REPRESENTS   Directors - Producers - Screenwriters - TV
                               Writers
SUBMISSION POLICY   Fax query letters; No phone calls; Does not
                               represent actors

Carl Belfor . . . . .Owner/Manager

MANAGERS

BENDERSPINK
110 S. Fairfax Ave., Ste. 350
Los Angeles, CA 90036
PHONE 323-904-1800
FAX 323-904-1802
EMAIL . . . . .info@benderspink.com
WEB SITE .www.benderspink.com
TYPES   Film/TV Talent - Literary Talent
REPRESENTS   Actors - Book Authors - Directors -
                           Screenwriters - TV Writers

Chris Bender . . . . .Manager
Christian Donatelli . . . . .Manager
Charlie Gogolak . . . . .Manager
Cory Hebenstreit . . . . .Manager
Courtney Kivowitz . . . . .Manager
Jill McElroy . . . . .Manager
Mason Novick . . . . .Manager
Brian Spink . . . . .Manager
J.C. Spink . . . . .Manager
Jake Weiner . . . . .Development
Jon Silk . . . . .Development
Neal Flaherty . . . . .Development
Amber DeFrancis .TV Coordinator
Langley Perer . . . . .Film Coordinator
Alex Kerr . . . . .TV
Andrea Castro . . . . .No Title
Peter Collins . . . . .No Title
Michael Klein . . . . .No Title
Andrew Mallett . . . . .No Title
Amanda Potts . . . . .No Title
Matthew Reis . . . . .No Title
Rachel Roberts . . . . .No Title

BENSKY ENTERTAINMENT
15030 Ventura Blvd., Ste. 343
Sherman Oaks, CA 91403
PHONE 818-830-3912
FAX 818-830-3914
EMAIL . . . . .lynbensky@aol.com
TYPES   Commercial Talent - Film/TV Talent -
                          Literary Talent - Theatre Talent
REPRESENTS   Actors - Book Authors - Broadcast
                          Journalists/Newscasters - Children -
                          Directors - Producers - Screenwriters -
                          Teens/Young Adults - TV Writers - Voice-
                          Over Artists
SUBMISSION POLICY   Does not accept unsolicited submissions;
                          Referrals only

Lynda Bensky . . . . .President
Jill Stribling . . . . .Assistant

MARTIN BERNEMAN MANAGEMENT
5820 Wilshire Blvd., Ste. 200
Los Angeles, CA 90036
PHONE 323-692-9214
FAX 323-692-0913
EMAIL . . . . .marina@bernemanmgmt.com
TYPES   Film/TV Talent
REPRESENTS   Actors - Directors

Martin Berneman . . . . .Manager/Producer
Marina D'Amico . . . . .Manager
Holly Shelton . . . . .Manager

SUE BERNSTEIN MANAGEMENT
2552 N. Vermont Ave.
Los Angeles, CA 90027
PHONE 818-502-8195/323-559-3945
FAX 818-502-8109/323-663-5949
EMAIL . . . . .bernsteinmgt@earthlink.net
SECOND EMAIL . . . . .bernsteinmgt@sbcglobal.net
TYPES   Commercial Talent - Film/TV Talent
REPRESENTS   Actors - Children
SUBMISSION POLICY   Accepts tapes with picture and resumé

Sue Bernstein . . . . .Owner
Max McFarlane . . . . .Assistant

BETWIXT TALENT MANAGEMENT
12655 Washington Blvd., Ste. 204
Los Angeles, CA 90066
PHONE 310-313-6442
WEB SITE . . . . .www.betwixttalent.com
TYPES   Commercial Talent - Film/TV Talent -
                        Modeling Talent
AFFILIATIONS   NCOPM - TMA
REPRESENTS   Actors - Directors - Print Models - Runway
                        Models
SUBMISSION POLICY   Union and non-union considered; Prefers
                        tapes from actors

Daniel Wojack . . . . .President

BINDER & ASSOCIATES
1465 Lindacrest Dr.
Beverly Hills, CA 90210
PHONE 310-274-9995
EMAIL . . . . .binderandassoc@earthlink.net
TYPES   Film/TV Talent
REPRESENTS   Actors

Chuck Binder .Manager/Producer
Tiffany Smith . . . . .Manager

MICHAEL BLACK MANAGEMENT, INC.
9701 Wilshire Blvd., Ste. 1000
Beverly Hills, CA 90212
PHONE 310-651-3081
FAX 310-651-3083
EMAIL . . . . .blackmb@aol.com
SECOND EMAIL . . . . .alexapag@aol.com
TYPES   Below-the-Line Talent - Film/TV Talent -
                        Literary Talent - Theatre Talent
REPRESENTS   Actors - Directors - Producers -
                        Screenwriters - TV Writers
SUBMISSION POLICY   By referral only

Michael Black . . . . .President
Alexa Pagonas . . . . .Manager

BLACKWOOD TALENT MANAGEMENT
8306 Wilshire Blvd., Ste. 1724
Beverly Hills, CA 90211
PHONE 310-295-0111
FAX 310-295-0110
EMAIL . . . . .lisa@blackwoodcompany.com
SECOND EMAIL . . . . .majorie@blackwoodcompany.com
WEB SITE . . . . .www.blackwoodcompany.com
TYPES	Commercial Talent - Film/TV Talent - Literary Talent - Modeling Talent - Music Talent
AFFILIATIONS	NCOPM - TMA
REPRESENTS	Actors - Choreographers - Comedians - Dancers - Directors - Music Artists - Music Producers - Print Models - Screenwriters - Teens/Young Adults - TV Writers - Voice-Over Artists

Horacio Blackwood . . . . .Manager (horacio@blackwoodcompany.com)
Raquel Blackwood . . . . . . .Associate (raquel@blackwoodcompany.com)
Lisa Blas . . . . .Assistant (lisa@blackwoodcompany.com)
Majorie Scott . . . . .Assistant (majorie@blackwoodcompany.com)

BLAIN & ASSOCIATES
8840 Wilshire Blvd.
Beverly Hills, CA 90211-2606
PHONE 310-358-3111
FAX 310-358-3181
EMAIL . . . . .tblain2004@hotmail.com
TYPES	Film/TV Talent - Literary Talent
REPRESENTS	Book Authors - Directors - Screenwriters - Sports Personalities - TV Writers
SUBMISSION POLICY	Industry referral preferred; Accepts one-page query letter with resume
COMMENTS	Entertainment law

Tony Blain . . . . .Principal
Brian Flaherty . . . . .Manager
Bob Jensen . . . . .Lawyer
Dire McCain . . . . .Creative Assistant

JANE BLOOM & ASSOCIATES
77-694 Calle Las Brisas N.
Palm Desert, CA 92211
PHONE 760-200-1199
TYPES	Commercial Talent - Film/TV Talent
REPRESENTS	Actors - Teens/Young Adults
SUBMISSION POLICY	Actors: Only accepting SAG/AEA/AFTRA actors with TV and feature film credits and industry referrals, do not send tapes

Jane Bloom . . . . .Manager

BLUBAY TALENT MANAGEMENT
9000 Sunset Blvd., Ste. 1101
West Hollywood, CA 90069
PHONE 310-288-0482
FAX 310-288-0470
EMAIL . . . . .submissions@blubaytalent.com
WEB SITE . . . . .www.blubaytalent.com
SECOND WEB SITE . . . . .www.guptapublishing.com
TYPES	Commercial Talent - Film/TV Talent - Literary Talent - Modeling Talent
AFFILIATIONS	TMA
REPRESENTS	Actors - Book Authors - Print Models - Producers - Runway Models - Screenwriters - Sports Personalities
SUBMISSION POLICY	Union, agent and industry referral only; Strong TV and motion picture credits (leads and principals, speaking roles); Send head shot and resume to: PO Box 629, Beverly Hills, CA 90213; Must have reels available and assortment of recent (color only) head-shots for submissions upon interview; No screenplays unless requested by management
COMMENTS	PGA, WIF; Owner of Zinkler Films; See Guptapublishing.com for Blubay Talent Publication info

Jessica Russell . . . . .President/Manager/Producer
Kate Miller . . . . .Manager
Karen Huges . . . . .Manager
Terry Ford . . . . .Submissions Coordinator
Dmitriy Katsel . . . . .No Title
Richard Ginsburg . . . . .Music Attorney
Dennis Holahan . . . . .Attorney
Michael Holtz . . . . .Attorney
Mike Favie . . . . .Jr. Associate
Cynthia Valley . . . . .Jr. Associate

BLUE TRAIN ENTERTAINMENT
798 Brooktree Rd.
Pacific Palisades, CA 90272
PHONE 310-285-7300
FAX 310-459-7848
TYPES	Film/TV Talent - Literary Talent - Theatre Talent
REPRESENTS	Actors - Directors - Producers - Screenwriters

Brian Gersh . . . . .Owner/Manager
John Myers . . . . .Associate Manager
Rebecca Escanio . . . . .Associate Manager

BLUEPRINT ARTIST MANAGEMENT
5670 Wilshire Blvd., Ste. 2525
Los Angeles, CA 90036
PHONE 323-330-0333
FAX 323-330-0330
TYPES	Film/TV Talent - Theatre Talent
REPRESENTS	Actors - Comedians - Directors - Hosts/MCs - Musical Theatre Performers - Producers - Teens/Young Adults
SUBMISSION POLICY	By mail only

Craig Dorfman . . . . .Manager
Liz York . . . . .Manager
Adam Lewis . . . . .Manager
Ryan Dibble . . . . .Assistant
Jon Goss . . . . .Assistant

BOHEMIA GROUP
8170 Beverly Blvd., Ste. 102
Los Angeles, CA 90048
PHONE 323-651-5001
FAX 323-651-3323
EMAIL . . . . .management@bohemiaent.com
TYPES   Film/TV Talent - Literary Talent
REPRESENTS   Actors - Children - Comedians - Music
                      Artists - Screenwriters - Teens/Young Adults

Susan Ferris . . . . .Partner
Adam Seid . . . . .Partner
Ali Carooso . . . . .Manager
Ryan Glasgow . . . . .Manager
Alison Buck . . . . .No Title

BARRY BOOKIN MANAGEMENT
4545 San Feliciano Dr.
Woodland Hills, CA 91364
PHONE 818-999-0622
FAX 818-999-6817
EMAIL . . . . .bbookin@bigfoot.com
TYPES   Film/TV Talent - Literary Talent - Music
                      Talent
REPRESENTS   Actors - Book Authors - Broadcast
                      Journalists/Newscasters - Comedians -
                      Directors - Hosts/MCs - Magicians - Music
                      Artists - Producers - Screenwriters -
                      Speakers/Lecturers - Sports Personalities
SUBMISSION POLICY   Referral only

Barry Bookin . . . . .Owner

BRAND X MANAGEMENT
2828 Waverly Dr.
Los Angeles, CA 90039
PHONE 323-660-8230/615-349-1169
FAX 919-640-8230
EMAIL . . . . .brandxmgmt@aol.com
WEB SITE .www.BrandXManagement.com
TYPES   Literary Talent - Music Talent
REPRESENTS   Composers - Directors - Music Artists -
                      Music Producers - Producers - Screenwriters
SUBMISSION POLICY   No phone calls; Professional submissions
                      welcome by post or email
COMMENTS   Nashville office: 2511 Natchez Trace,
                      Nashville, TN 37212

Charley Chartoff . . . . .Partner
Eric M. Griffin . . . . .Partner
Ian Faith . . . . .Assistant

THE BRAVERMAN/BLOOM CO., INC.
6399 Wilshire Blvd., Ste. 901
Los Angeles, CA 90048
PHONE 323-782-4900
FAX 323-782-4926
TYPES   Film/TV Talent - Literary Talent
REPRESENTS   Actors - Book Authors - Broadcast
                      Journalists/Newscasters - Hosts/MCs -
                      Martial Artists/Stunts - Producers -
                      Screenwriters - Sports Personalities - TV
                      Writers - Variety Artists

Barry Bloom . . . . .Partner/Manager
Michael Braverman . . . . .Partner/Manager
Colleen Maloney . . . . .Associate

BRIDGE FALLS ENTERTAINMENT
4811 Hillsdale Dr.
Los Angeles, CA 90032
PHONE 323-224-8990
FAX 323-224-8970
EMAIL . . . . .bfallsent@aol.com
TYPES   Literary Talent
REPRESENTS   Screenwriters - TV Writers
SUBMISSION POLICY   No unsolicited material; Send query letter
                      by fax or mail
COMMENTS   Member: IDA, ATAS, American Theatre
                      Wing

Steven Roche .Manager/Producer
John Machado . . . . .Associate

BRILLSTEIN-GREY MANAGEMENT
9150 Wilshire Blvd., Ste. 350
Beverly Hills, CA 90212
PHONE 310-275-6135
FAX 310-275-6180
TYPES   Film/TV Talent - Literary Talent
REPRESENTS   Actors - Book Authors - Comedians -
                      Directors - Producers - TV Writers
COMMENTS   TV and film production

Bernie Brillstein . . . . .Founding Partner/Consultant
Jonathan Liebman . . . . .CEO
Cynthia Pett-Dante . . . . .Partner
David Zwarg . . . . .CFO
Geoff Cheddy . . . . .Manager
JoAnne Colonna . . . . .Manager
Naren Desai . . . . .Manager
Todd Diener . . . . .Manager
Kassie Evashevski . . . . .Manager
Colton Gramm . . . . .Manager
Mary Putnam Greene . . . . .Manager
Marc Gurvitz . . . . .Manager
Lee Kernis . . . . .Manager
Aleen Keshishian . . . . .Manager
Jai Khanna . . . . .Manager
Missy Malkin . . . . .Manager
David McIlvain . . . . .Manager
Andrea Pett-Joseph . . . . .Manager
Margaret Riley . . . . .Manager
Tim Sarkes . . . . .Manager
Ezekiel Steiner . . . . .Manager
Danny Sussman . . . . .Manager
Amy Weiss . . . . .Manager
Sandy Wernick . . . . .Manager

ROBIN BROOKS MANAGEMENT
5619 N. Lankershim Blvd., Ste. 1104
North Hollywood, CA 91601
PHONE 949-589-0858
WEB SITE . . . . .www.robinbrooksmanagement.com
TYPES   Commercial Talent - Film/TV Talent -
                         Modeling Talent - Music Talent
AFFILIATIONS   TMA
REPRESENTS   Actors - Children - Dancers - Infants -
                         Music Artists - Print Models - Teens/Young
                         Adults - Voice-Over Artists
SUBMISSION POLICY   Via US Mail only; No phone calls, no
                         drop-ins accepted; Every piece of mail is
                         opened and performers will be contacted if
                         there is interest

Robin Brooks . . . . .Manager/Owner
Doug Murphy . . . . .Manager
Eric Stevens . . . . .Manager
Alison Mack . . . . .Assistant
Melinda Ruiz . . . . .Assistant

BROOKSIDE ▪ ARTIST ▪ MANAGEMENT

BROOKSIDE ARTIST MANAGEMENT
250 W. 57th St., Ste. 2303
New York, NY 10107
PHONE 212-489-4929
FAX 212-489-9056
TYPES   Film/TV Talent - Literary Talent - Music
                         Talent - Theatre Talent
REPRESENTS   Actors - Directors - Music Artists - Musical
                         Theatre Performers - Playwrights -
                         Screenwriters - Teens/Young Adults - TV
                         Writers

Emily Gerson Saines . . . . .Owner/Manager
Joan Fields . . . . .Manager
Greg Weiss . . . . .Manager
Kerin Nadler . . . . .Talent Coordinator

BROOM IN THE MOON PRODUCTIONS
4804 Laurel Canyon Blvd., Ste. 298
Valley Village, CA 91607
PHONE 818-769-6378
FAX 818-761-4321
EMAIL . . . . .broominmoon@aol.com
TYPES   Below-the-Line Talent - Literary Talent
REPRESENTS   Producers - Screenwriters - TV Writers
SUBMISSION POLICY   Fax inquires only

Trudy Davies .Manager/Development
Gibbi Tkatch . . . . .Manager
Anna Tkatch . . . . .Writer/Development
Dr. Mary Denk . . . . .Science Advisor
K.J. Keller . . . . .Production Specialist
Kimberly Sikman . . . . .Assistant

BROWN LEADER GROUP
9220 Sunset Blvd., #111
West Hollywood, CA 90069
PHONE 310-887-3818
FAX 310-887-3806
TYPES   Commercial Talent - Film/TV Talent
REPRESENTS   Actors - Children - Hosts/MCs -
                         Teens/Young Adults

Philip Leader . . . . .Owner/Manager
Patricia Brown . . . . .Owner/Manager
Jermaine Shelton . . . . .Manager

THE MICHAEL BRUNO GROUP LOS ANGELES
13576 Cheltenham Dr.
Sherman Oaks, CA 91423
PHONE 818-905-6168
FAX 818-905-6169
WEB SITE . . . . .www.mbgla.com
TYPES   Film/TV Talent
REPRESENTS   Actors
COMMENTS   Focus on soap opera talent

Michael Bruno . . . . .President
Karen Abouab . . . . .Associate

BRUSTEIN ENTERTAINMENT
2934-1/2 Beverly Glen Circle, Ste. 367
Bel Air, CA 90077
PHONE 310-571-3500
FAX 310-571-3505
EMAIL . . . . .nadinejon4@aol.com
TYPES   Film/TV Talent - Literary Talent - Music
                         Talent
REPRESENTS   Actors - Book Authors - Directors - Music
                         Artists - Producers - Screenwriters - TV
                         Writers - Variety Artists
SUBMISSION POLICY   Referral only
COMMENTS   Also a production company

Richard C. Brustein . . . . .Owner/President/Executive Producer
Nadine Kavanaugh . . . . .Manager/Producer/Executive Producer/Casting
Rhonda Young . . . . .Casting
Thom Vitale . . . . .Executive Assistant/Casting Associate
Cathy Gellis . . . . .Executive Assistant

BSC MANAGEMENT
PO Box 368
Tujunga, CA 91043
PHONE 818-487-9803
EMAIL . . . . .bscmgmt@sbcglobal.net
TYPES   Commercial Talent - Film/TV Talent -
                         Literary Talent - Music Talent
REPRESENTS   Actors - Legitimate Theater - Music Artists -
                         Producers - Teens/Young Adults - Variety
                         Artists
COMMENTS   Affiliated with Country Music Association
                         and Western Fairs Association

Kenn E. Kingsbury Jr. . . . . .President

BUMBERSHOOT ENTERTAINMENT
1433 Sixth St., Bldg. H
Santa Monica, CA 90401
PHONE 310-656-0626
WEB SITE .www.bumbershootent.com
TYPES   Literary Talent
REPRESENTS   Book Authors - Directors - Screenwriters -
                         TV Writers

Ariel Hauter . . . . .Manager
Paris Hauter . . . . .Manager

THE BURSTEIN COMPANY
15304 Sunset Blvd., Ste. 208
Pacific Palisades, CA 90272
PHONE 310-454-9462
FAX 310-454-9362
TYPES   Film/TV Talent - Literary Talent
REPRESENTS   Actors - Directors - Screenwriters - TV
                         Writers - Voice-Over Artists
SUBMISSION POLICY   By referral only; Not currently accepting
                         new clients

Joanna Burstein . . . . .Partner/Manager
Candice Blizzard . . . . .Associate
Yoni Ovadia . . . . .Associate
Andrew Besser . . . . .Business & Legal Affairs

CALLIOPE TALENT MANAGEMENT, LLC

101 N. Victory Blvd., Ste. L, #267
Burbank, CA 91502-1847
PHONE 323-343-9823
FAX 210-804-2008
EMAIL . . . . .calliopela@sbcglobal.net
WEB SITE . . . . .www.calliopetalent.com
TYPES   Commercial Talent - Film/TV Talent -
                          Modeling Talent - Music Talent
REPRESENTS   Actors - Children - Choreographers -
                          Comedians - Dancers - Hosts/MCs -
                          Martial Artists/Stunts - Music Artists - Music
                          Producers - Print Models - Runway Models -
                          Seniors - Speakers/Lecturers - Sports
                          Personalities - Teens/Young Adults - Variety
                          Artists - Voice-Over Artists
SUBMISSION POLICY   See Web site
COMMENTS   Affiliated with Texas-based Calliope Talent,
                          Model & Artist Management, LLC

Kristy Martin . . . . .CEO/Manager
Mike Britton . . . . .VP, Business & Finance
Michael Druck . . . . .Agent/Developmental Coordinator
Amanda Rivas . . . . .Agent/Developmental Coordinator
Max Parra . . . . .Business Administrator/Web site Coordinator

CANDY ENTERTAINMENT, INC.

8981 W. Sunset Blvd., Ste. 310
West Hollywood, CA 90069
PHONE 310-858-4999
FAX 310-858-7999
WEB SITE . . . . .www.candyentertainment.com
TYPES   Commercial Talent - Film/TV Talent
REPRESENTS   Actors
SUBMISSION POLICY   By referral only
COMMENTS   Specializes in ingenues

Denise Fisher . . . . .CEO/Manager
Dennis Duban . . . . .CFO
Lisa Galvin . . . . .Marketing/Public Relations Director
Diane Sarnoff . . . . .Business Affairs
Jessica Ruiz-Miller . . . . .Assistant to Denise Fisher

CAREYES ENTERTAINMENT

400 S. Beverly Dr., Ste. 219
Beverly Hill, CA 90212
PHONE 310-888-1240
FAX 310-281-0196
EMAIL . . . . .careyesent@aol.com
TYPES   Literary Talent
REPRESENTS   Directors - Producers - Screenwriters
SUBMISSION POLICY   Send inquiry/synopsis in a one-page letter,
                          fax or email

Alan M. Shafer . . . . .Owner/CEO

JOHN CARRABINO MANAGEMENT

100 N. Crescent Dr., Ste. G400
Beverly Hills, CA 90210
PHONE 310-385-4264
FAX 310-385-3673
EMAIL .ggonzalez@carrabinomgt.com
TYPES   Film/TV Talent
REPRESENTS   Actors

John Carrabino . . . . .Manager
Gladys Gonzalez . . . . .Manager

CASTING UNLIMITED & MANAGEMENT

PO Box 661185
Los Angeles, CA 90066-9585
PHONE 562-467-6155
FAX 562-981-7427
EMAIL . . . . .dictor@gte.net
TYPES   Commercial Talent - Literary Talent - Music
                          Talent
REPRESENTS   Book Authors - Directors - Music Artists -
                          Music Producers - Screenwriters - Sports
                          Personalities - TV Writers

Lawrence Dictor . . . . .Owner
Ian A. Cannell . . . . .Associate

CASTLEBRIGHT

10 Universal City Plaza
NBC/Universal Bldg., 20th Fl.
Universal City, CA 91608
PHONE 818-753-2319
FAX 818-753-2310
EMAIL . . . . .info@castlebright.com
SECOND EMAIL . . . . .submissions@castlebright.com
WEB SITE . . . . .www.castlebright.com
TYPES   Commercial Talent - Literary Talent
REPRESENTS   Actors - Directors - Producers -
                          Screenwriters
SUBMISSION POLICY   Accepts up to one-page query letter with
                          resumé via email only

Jay Douglas . . . . .Partner/Manager
Nav Gupta . . . . .Partner/Manager
Lorraine Lopez . . . . .Assistant to Mr. Douglas
Brianna Ramirez . . . . .Assistant to Mr. Gupta

CENTRAL ARTISTS

3310 W. Burbank Blvd.
Burbank, CA 91505
PHONE 818-557-8284
FAX 818-557-8348
EMAIL . . . . .centralartists@centralartists.com
WEB SITE . . . . .www.centralartists.com
TYPES   Commercial Talent - Film/TV Talent -
                          Modeling Talent
AFFILIATIONS   TMA
REPRESENTS   Actors - Children - Print Models - Seniors -
                          Sports Personalities - Teens/Young Adults
SUBMISSION POLICY   Mail or email only
COMMENTS   Also represents Native Americans, Little
                          People

Jean-Marc Carré . . . . .Commercial/Print
Laura Walsh . . . . .TV/Film
Harold Gray . . . . .TV/Film

CFB PRODUCTIONS, INC.

PO Box 50008
Henderson, NV 89016
PHONE 702-837-1170
EMAIL . . . . .cfbproductions@earthlink.net
WEB SITE . . . . .www.cfbproductions.biz
TYPES   Commercial Talent - Film/TV Talent -
                          Literary Talent - Music Talent
AFFILIATIONS   NCOPM
REPRESENTS   Book Authors - Comedians - Music Artists -
                          Variety Artists
COMMENTS   TV personalities

Clinton Ford Billups Jr. . . . . .Manager

CHACHKIN MANAGEMENT
824 Wright Dr.
Maple Glen, PA 19002
PHONE 800-649-9796
EMAIL . . . . .chachkin@aol.com
TYPES   Film/TV Talent - Music Talent
REPRESENTS   Actors - Choreographers - Music Producers
COMMENTS   Affiliated with ATAS

Margery Lee Chachkin . . . . .Owner/Manager

CHANCELLOR ENTERTAINMENT
10600 Holman Ave., Ste. 1
Los Angeles, CA 90024
PHONE 310-474-4521
FAX 310-470-9273
EMAIL . . . . .info@chancellorentertainment.com
WEB SITE . . . . .www.chancellorentertainment.com
TYPES   Commercial Talent - Film/TV Talent -
             Modeling Talent - Music Talent
AFFILIATIONS   TMA
REPRESENTS   Actors - Dancers - Hosts/MCs - Music
             Artists - Music Producers - Print Models -
             Runway Models - Teens/Young Adults
COMMENTS   Also affiliated with AMPAS, ATAS, NARAS
             and PGA

Robert P. Marcucci . . . . .President
DJ Marcucci . . . . .Talent Manager

DOUG CHAPIN MANAGEMENT, INC.
1416 Havenhurst Dr., Unit GF
West Hollywood, CA 90046
PHONE 310-360-0030
FAX 310-360-3952
TYPES   Film/TV Talent - Literary Talent
REPRESENTS   Actors - Directors - Producers -
             Screenwriters - Voice-Over Artists

Doug Chapin . . . . .President

JOYCE CHASE MANAGEMENT
2 Fifth Ave.
New York, NY 10011
PHONE 212-473-1234
TYPES   Film/TV Talent - Theatre Talent
AFFILIATIONS   NCOPM
REPRESENTS   Actors
SUBMISSION POLICY   By mail only; Must belong to SAG or Equity
COMMENTS   Experienced actors only

Joyce Chase . . . . .Sole Proprietor

CHEATHAM, GREENE & COMPANY
4470 Sunset Blvd., Ste. 469
Los Angeles, CA 90027
PHONE . . . . .323-463-0420/323-769-5561 (Voicemail)
FAX 323-469-1230
TYPES   Film/TV Talent - Literary Talent
REPRESENTS   Actors - Comedians - Directors -
             Teens/Young Adults - TV Writers
SUBMISSION POLICY   By referral only

Clearance Cheatham . . . . .Manager
Jeff R. Greene . . . . .Manager
Makeda Téne . . . . .Assistant
John Theelen . . . . .Assistant

CHIC PRODUCTIONS & MANAGEMENT (CPM)
12228 Venice Blvd., Ste. 499
Los Angeles, CA 90066
PHONE 310-391-2152
FAX 310-985-7329
EMAIL . . . . .steve@chicproductions.com
SECOND EMAIL . . . . .jessica@chicproductions.com
WEB SITE . . . . .www.chicproductions.com
TYPES   Literary Talent
REPRESENTS   Directors - Screenwriters
SUBMISSION POLICY   Must have financing or major talent
             attached
COMMENTS   Deal with Shoreline Entertainment for film
             and TV production

Steve Chicorel . . . . .Manager/Producer
Dan Chicorel . . . . .Associate
Jessica Miller . . . . .Production Assistant

CINE/LIT
PO Box 802918
Santa Clarita, CA 91380-2918
PHONE 661-513-0268
FAX 661-513-0951
EMAIL . . . . .cinelit@msn.com
TYPES   Film/TV Talent - Literary Talent
REPRESENTS   Book Authors
SUBMISSION POLICY   Queries with SASE accepted
COMMENTS   Affiliated with AAR, BAFTA, FIND

Anna Cottle . . . . .Partner
Mary Alice Kier . . . . .Partner

CIRCLE OF CONFUSION
107-23 71st Rd., Ste. 300
Forest Hills, NY 11375
PHONE 718-275-1012/310-253-7777
FAX 718-997-0521/310-253-9065
EMAIL . . . . .queries@circleofconfusion.com
WEB SITE . . . . .www.circleofconfusion.com
TYPES   Literary Talent
AFFILIATIONS   DGA
REPRESENTS   Directors - Producers - Screenwriters - TV
             Writers
COMMENTS   Also represents Comic Book and Video
             Game Creators; West Coast office: 8548
             Washington Blvd., Culver City, CA 90232

Lawrence Mattis . . . . .Manager/Partner
David Alpert . . . . .Manager/Partner (LA)
David Engel . . . . .Manager/Partner (LA)
Ashley Berns . . . . .Manager (LA)
Kemper Donovan . . . . .Manager (LA)
John Orlando . . . . .Manager (LA)
Noah Rosen . . . . .Manager (LA)
Nazia Boodram . . . . .Assistant to Lawrence Mattis
Shelly Narine . . . . .Assistant to Lawrence Mattis
Bryan Millard . . . . .Assistant (LA)
Noble Robinette . . . . .Assistant (LA)

VINCENT CIRRINCIONE ASSOCIATES, LTD.

1516 North Fairfax Ave.
Los Angeles, CA 90046
PHONE .323-850-8080/212-245-8632
FAX 323-850-5080/212-541-5345
WEB SITE . . . . www.vincentcirrincione.com
TYPES   Film/TV Talent - Literary Talent
REPRESENTS   Actors - Directors - Screenwriters
COMMENTS   East Coast office: 300 W. 55th St., New
                           York, NY 10019

Vincent Cirrincione . . . . .President/Owner
Anna Liza Recto . . . . .VP/Manager
Tobie Haggerty . . . . .VP/Manager (NY)
John Nila . . . . .Manager
Miguel Ellison . . . . .Assistant
DaVida Smith . . . . .Assistant
Brandi Welch . . . . .Assistant

CLARK MANAGEMENT COMPANY

c/o Vicki Clark
1115 Foothill Blvd.
La Cañada, CA 91011
PHONE 818-957-1952
FAX 818-790-8997
EMAIL . . . . .iampuresuccess@hotmail.com
TYPES   Literary Talent
AFFILIATIONS   AFM
REPRESENTS   Screenwriters
SUBMISSION POLICY   Email or written query
COMMENTS   Also affiliated with MMF, AIMP

Vicki Clark . . . . .Manager
Becky Harris . . . . .Marketing Director
Sara Muriello .Administrative Assistant

COASTAL ENTERTAINMENT PRODUCTIONS

32-31 35th St.
Astoria, NY 11106
PHONE 718-728-8581
FAX 718-728-2638
EMAIL . . . . .linda@coastalentertainment.com
WEB SITE . . . . .www.coastalentertainment.com
TYPES   Commercial Talent - Film/TV Talent -
                           Theatre Talent
AFFILIATIONS   NCOPM
REPRESENTS   Actors - Comedians - Hosts/MCs - Musical
                           Theatre Performers - Variety Artists - Voice-
                           Over Artists

Linda Rohe . . . . .Manager
Roe Valinoti . . . . .Assistant

CODE

9229 Sunset Blvd., Ste. 615
Los Angeles, CA 90069
PHONE 310-772-0008
FAX 310-772-0006
EMAIL .contact@codeentertainment.com
TYPES   Literary Talent
REPRESENTS   Book Authors - Directors - Screenwriters -
                           TV Writers

Larry Kennar . . . . .Manager/Producer
Rick Berg . . . . .Manager/Producer
Rogers Hartmann .Manager/Producer
Al Corley . . . . .Producer
Bart Rosenblatt . . . . .Producer
Kim Olsen . . . . .VP, Production Services
Karen Irvin . . . . .Story Editor
Reynolds Anderson . . . . .Manager Assistant
Robert Dmitri . . . . .Manager Assistant

COHEN/THOMAS MANAGEMENT

1888 N. Crescent Heights Blvd.
Los Angeles, CA 90069
PHONE 323-654-8800
FAX 323-654-8804
TYPES   Film/TV Talent
REPRESENTS   Actors
SUBMISSION POLICY   Mail photo and resumé; Demo reel on
                           request only
COMMENTS   Actors in mid to late teens; Established
                           actors

Paul Cohen . . . . .Owner
Sheri Anderson Thomas . . . . .Owner

THE COLLECTIVE

9100 Wilshire Blvd., Ste. 700 West
Beverly Hills, CA 90212
PHONE 310-288-8181
FAX 310-888-1555
TYPES   Film/TV Talent - Literary Talent
REPRESENTS   Actors - Comedians - Directors - Producers
                           - Screenwriters - Teens/Young Adults - TV
                           Writers - Variety Artists
SUBMISSION POLICY   Industry referrals only

Michael Green . . . . .Manager/Partner
Jeff Golenberg . . . . .Manager/Partner
Sam Maydew . . . . .Manager/Partner
Aaron Ray . . . . .Manager/Partner
Gary Binkow . . . . .Venture Partner
Max Burgos . . . . .Manager
Ashley Franklin . . . . .Manager
Aron Giannini . . . . .Manager
Michael Goldman . . . . .Manager
Allan Grifka . . . . .Manager
Al Hassas . . . . .Manager
Reza Izad . . . . .Manager
Shaun Redick . . . . .Manager
Alexis Nicholls . . . . .Office Manager
Kristin Fine . . . . .Assistant
Solomon Hinton . . . . .Assistant
Kottie Kreischer . . . . .Assistant
Karen Norman . . . . .Assistant
Brett Ruttenberg . . . . .Assistant
Christina Gualazzi . . . . .Assistant
Raymond Mansfield . . . . .Assistant
Lucy Mukerjee . . . . .Assistant
Davida Ross . . . . .Assistant

COLUMBIA ARTISTS MANAGEMENT LLC
1790 Broadway
New York, NY 10019-1412
PHONE 212-841-9500
FAX 212-841-9744
EMAIL . . . . .info@cami.com
WEB SITE . . . . .www.cami.com
TYPES   Music Talent - Theatre Talent
REPRESENTS   Choreographers - Composers - Dancers - Music Artists - Musical Theatre Performers - Production Designers - Variety Artists
COMMENTS   Classical, jazz and popular musicians; Orchestras and orchestral programs; Stage directors and designers; Instrumental ensembles; World music and dance; Dance companies; Theatrical productions; Offices in Europe

Ronald A. Wilford . . . . .Chairman, CEO (212-841-9502)
Tim Fox . . . . .President (212-841-9571)
Jean-Jacques Cesbron . . . . .CAMI Music (212-841-9564)
Mark Maluso . . . . .President, CAMI Ventures (212-841-9702)
Margaret Selby . . . . . . .President, CAMI Spectrum (212-841-9554)
Andrew S. Grossman . . . . .Sr. VP (212-841-9558)
Mark Z. Alpert . . . . .Booking (212-841-9568)
Andrea Anson . . . . .Manager (212-841-9549)
Anna Bacon-Silveira . . . . .Booking (212-841-9533)
Michael Benchetrit . . . . .Manager (212-841-9559)
Ken Benson .Manager (212-841-9545)
Matt Chinn . . . . .Theatricals (917-206-4606)
Elizabeth Crittenden . . . . .Manager (212-841-9682)
Matthew Epstein . . . . .Manager (212-841-9550)
Celina Guerrero . . . . .Booking (212-841-9566)
William G. Guerri . . . . .Manager (212-841-9680)
Judie Janowski . . . . .Manager (212-841-9507)
Jason Mainland . . . . .Booking (212-841-9737)
Gary McAvay . . . . .Theatricals (917-206-4609)
Pamela Ramsey McKean . . . . .Booking (415-252-5705)
Ron Merlino . . . . .Manager (212-841-9560)
Denise A. Pineau . . . . .Manager (212-841-9527)
Aldo Scrofani . . . . .Theatricals (917-206-4610)
R. Douglas Sheldon . . . . .Manager (212-841-9512)
Josh Sherman . . . . .Theatricals (917-206-4607)
Tara Troutman . . . . .Theatricals (917-206-4611)
Tobias Tumarkin . . . . .Manager (212-841-9563)
W. Seton Ijams . . . . .Associate Manager (212-841-9752)
Robert Scott . . . . .Associate Manager (212-841-9540)
Jann Simpson . . . . .Music Theatre Associate (917-206-4608)

COMMONWEALTH TALENT GROUP
5225 Wilshire Blvd., Ste. 509
Los Angeles, CA 90036
PHONE 323-935-3111
FAX 323-935-3311
EMAIL . . . . .info@commtalent.com
TYPES   Film/TV Talent - Literary Talent - Theatre Talent
REPRESENTS   Actors - Screenwriters

Nick Campbell . . . . .Partner
Christie Thomas . . . . .Partner

THE COMPANY ARTISTS
5000 S. Centinela Ave., Ste. 313
Los Angeles, CA 90066
PHONE 310-313-4003/310-529-1014
EMAIL . . . . .thecompanyartists@verizon.net
TYPES   Film/TV Talent - Literary Talent
REPRESENTS   Actors - Directors - Screenwriters
SUBMISSION POLICY   Industry referrals welcome

Nancy Scanlon . . . . .Manager/Producer
Grace Lynn . . . . .Assistant

CONCEPT ENTERTAINMENT
334-1/2 N. Sierra Bonita Ave.
Los Angeles, CA 90036
PHONE 323-937-5700
FAX 323-937-5720
EMAIL . . . . .enquiries@conceptentertainment.biz
WEB SITE . . . . .www.conceptentertainment.biz
TYPES   Film/TV Talent - Literary Talent
REPRESENTS   Directors - Screenwriters - TV Writers
SUBMISSION POLICY   No phone calls; Email query; If interested, will reply with release form to accompany script submission
COMMENTS   Represents writers and director in the US, UK and Canada

David Faigenblum . . . . .Producer/Manager
Melissa Goddard . . . . .Producer/Manager
Karina Wilson . . . . .Creative Executive/Jr. Manager

CONNECTION III ENTERTAINMENT CORP.
8489 W. Third St.
Los Angeles, CA 90048
PHONE 323-937-8700
EMAIL . . . . .info@connection3.com
WEB SITE www.connection3.com
TYPES   Film/TV Talent - Literary Talent
AFFILIATIONS   DGA
REPRESENTS   Actors - Children - Directors - Screenwriters - Teens/Young Adults
COMMENTS   PGA - WGA

Cleveland O'Neal . . . . .Manager/Producer

DIANE CONNORS MANAGEMENT
PO Box 83
Los Angeles, CA 90078
PHONE 323-274-8600/615-320-6000
TYPES   Film/TV Talent - Music Talent - Theatre Talent
REPRESENTS   Actors - Broadcast Journalists/Newscasters - Comedians - Directors - Music Artists - Music Producers - Producers - Sports Personalities - Variety Artists - Voice-Over Artists
COMMENTS   Primary operations in Nashville; Growing Los Angeles roster of TV and film stars; Producers Alliance

Diane Connors . . . . .President/CEO
Jim Kersey . . . . .VP/Operations Director
Alan Joyce . . . . .Client & Media Relations
Marie Thomas . . . . .Production Manager

CONTEMPORARY TALENT PARTNERS (CTP)
1800 Century Park East, Ste. 600
Los Angeles, CA 90067
PHONE 310-365-5485
TYPES   Film/TV Talent - Literary Talent - Theatre Talent
REPRESENTS   Actors - Book Authors - Comedians - Directors - Producers - Screenwriters - TV Writers
SUBMISSION POLICY   No unsolicited material, query only; No new clients at this time

Anita Haeggstrom . . . . .Manager/Partner
Doug Robbins . . . . .Manager/Partner

CONTENT HOUSE
2029 Century Park East, Ste. 2880
Los Angeles, CA 90067
PHONE 310-277-7701
FAX 310-277-7708
EMAIL . . . . .info@contenthousela.com
TYPES   Literary Talent
REPRESENTS   Book Authors - Directors - Screenwriters -
                         TV Writers
COMMENTS   Also represents comic book entities

Kevin Cleary . . . . .Partner
Josh Morris . . . . .Partner
Mark Safflan . . . . .Partner
Josh Goldsmith . . . . .Director, Special Projects
Tom Hastings . . . . .Executive
Ed McWilliams . . . . .Executive
Jeff Shelton . . . . .Executive
Ian Feller . . . . .Manager

THE CONVERSATION COMPANY, LTD.
1044 Northern Blvd., Ste. 304
Roslyn, NY 11576
PHONE 516-686-9000
FAX 516-686-9009
EMAIL . . . . .info@tccltd.com
WEB SITE . . . . .www.tccltd.com
TYPES   Commercial Talent - Film/TV Talent -
                         Literary Talent - Music Talent - Theatre
                         Talent
REPRESENTS   Actors - Comedians - Music Artists -
                         Screenwriters - TV Writers - Variety Artists -
                         Voice-Over Artists

Rory Rosegarten . . . . .President
Peter Rosegarten . . . . .Manager
Brian Friedman . . . . .Associate
Debbie Kneski . . . . .Associate
Yamari Reyes . . . . .Associate
Melissa Tempone . . . . .Associate

DAN COOPER & ASSOCIATES
333 Ovington Ave., Ste. B-47
Brooklyn, NY 11209-1413
PHONE 917-862-2239
FAX 815-550-1611
EMAIL .dcooper@dcamgmt.com
WEB SITE . . . . .www.dcamgmt.com
TYPES   Film/TV Talent
REPRESENTS   Actors - Broadcast Journalists/Newscasters
                         - Hosts/MCs
SUBMISSION POLICY   By referral only
COMMENTS   Attends performances

Daniel Cooper . . . . .Manager/Producer

THE COPPAGE COMPANY
PO Box 147
11902 Ventura Blvd.
Studio City, CA 91604
PHONE 818-980-8806
FAX 818-980-8824
EMAIL . . . . .coppage@aol.com
TYPES   Below-the-Line Talent - Film/TV Talent -
                         Literary Talent - Theatre Talent
REPRESENTS   Actors - Book Authors - Directors -
                         Playwrights - Producers - Screenwriters - TV
                         Writers
SUBMISSION POLICY   Referral only

Judy Coppage . . . . .Owner/Principal
Ron Leshem . . . . .Assistant
Michael Rose . . . . .Assistant

THE CORE
14724 Ventura Blvd., PH
Sherman Oaks, CA 91403
PHONE 818-986-8040
FAX 818-986-8041
TYPES   Film/TV Talent - Music Talent
REPRESENTS   Comedians - Composers - Hosts/MCs -
                         Music Artists

Howard Lapides . . . . .CEO
Bill Siddons . . . . .President
Andrew Lear . . . . .VP, Comedy & Development
Jackie Stern . . . . .VP/Manager
Brian Frank . . . . .Manager
Toni Profera . . . . .Manager
Jordan Yousem . . . . .Manager
Kesila Childers . . . . .Associate Manager
Brad Bilger . . . . .Executive Assistant
Barb Frederick .Executive Assistant

CORNERSTONE MANAGEMENT
944 County Line Rd.
Bryn Mawr, PA 19010
PHONE 610-525-5800
FAX 610-525-5585
WEB SITE . . . . .www.cornerstonemgmt.net
TYPES   Commercial Talent - Film/TV Talent - Music
                         Talent
REPRESENTS   Music Artists - Sports Personalities

Steve Mountain . . . . .President/Principal Agent/Founder
Debbi Collard . . . . .Director, Music Client Services
Chris McNelis . . . . .Director, Client Services
Nicole Brennan . . . . .Client Services/Finance

CORNICE ENTERTAINMENT
421 S. Beverly Dr., 8th Fl.
Beverly Hills, CA 90212
PHONE 310-279-4080
FAX 310-789-4791
TYPES   Film/TV Talent - Literary Talent
REPRESENTS   Directors - Screenwriters - TV Writers

Michael E. Marcus . . . . .No Title

COURSE MANAGEMENT
15159 Greenleaf St.
Sherman Oaks, CA 91403
PHONE 818-783-7747
FAX 818-784-6012
EMAIL . . . . .brandtco@aol.com
TYPES   Below-the-Line Talent - Film/TV Talent - Literary Talent
REPRESENTS   Actors - Book Authors - Directors - Producers - Screenwriters - TV Writers
SUBMISSION POLICY   Through a known third party industry referral only

Geoffrey Brandt . . . . .Partner
Jill Gordon . . . . .Partner
Katie Altman . . . . .Assistant to Mr. Brandt

EDNA COWAN MANAGEMENT
295 Central Park West, Ste. 17A
New York, NY 10024
PHONE 212-595-7969
FAX 212-595-7969
EMAIL . . . . .edna@ednacowanmanagement.com
TYPES   Commercial Talent - Film/TV Talent - Literary Talent
AFFILIATIONS   NCOPM
REPRESENTS   Actors - Comedians - Directors - TV Writers - Variety Artists
SUBMISSION POLICY   Photos, resumés and tapes accepted by mail; No phone calls; Attends showcases

Edna Cowan . . . . .Manager

CREATED BY
1041 N. Formosa Ave.
West Hollywood, CA 90046
PHONE 323-850-3555
FAX 323-850-3554
EMAIL . . . . .createdby@earthlink.net
TYPES   Literary Talent
REPRESENTS   Book Authors
SUBMISSION POLICY   No unsolicited submissions

Ralph M. Vicinanza .President
Vincent Gerardis . . . . .Manager
Eli Kirschner . . . . .Director, Development
Shelley Andagan . . . . .Story Editor

CREATIVE CONTENT MANAGEMENT
110 W. 26th St., 3rd Fl.
New York, NY 10001-6805
PHONE 212-645-3068
FAX 212-989-6459
EMAIL . . . . .creativecontentm@aol.com
WEB SITE . . . . .www.countdownentertainment.com
TYPES   Music Talent
REPRESENTS   Composers - Music Artists - Music Producers - Producers
SUBMISSION POLICY   Email queries preferred

James Citkovic . . . . .Partner
Al Brodie . . . . .Partner
David Brodie . . . . .Partner

CREATIVE CONVERGENCE
11040 Santa Monica Blvd., Ste. 200
Los Angeles, CA 90025
PHONE 310-954-8480
FAX 310-954-8481
EMAIL . . . . .info@creative-convergence.com
SECOND EMAIL . . . . .literary@creative-convergence.com
WEB SITE . . . . .www.creative-convergence.com
TYPES   Literary Talent
REPRESENTS   Directors - Screenwriters - TV Writers
COMMENTS   Also produces and consults

Bradley D. Kushner . . . . .Partner/Literary Management
Karen A. Hamilton . . . . .Partner/Production
Philippa Burgess . . . . .Partner/Business Development

CREATIVE ENTERPRISES MANAGEMENT
500 Avenue G
Redondo Beach, CA 90277
PHONE 310-316-8652
TYPES   Commercial Talent - Film/TV Talent - Literary Talent
AFFILIATIONS   DGA
REPRESENTS   Actors - Book Authors - Directors - Producers - Screenwriters - Sports Personalities - TV Writers
SUBMISSION POLICY   Call to pitch best story, then send 4-6 page synopsis via US Mail; If managers like synopsis they will call to request WGA registered screenplay

Anthony Ridio . . . . .Producer/Personal Manager
Maria Bain . . . . .Manager
Stephanie Nichols . . . . .Manager
Terry Anfuso .Literary Manager
Phillip Georgious . . . . .Literary Manager
Ed Golden . . . . .Literary Manager
Kelly Ridio . . . . .Literary Manager
Rosemary Torigian . . . . .Literary Manager

CREATIVE HAVEN ENTERTAINMENT
13554 Wyandotte St.
Van Nuys, CA 91405
PHONE 818-374-1380
FAX 818-374-1381
EMAIL . . . . .management@creativehaven.net
WEB SITE . . . . .www.creativehaven.net
TYPES   Commercial Talent - Film/TV Talent - Literary Talent - Music Talent
REPRESENTS   Actors - Dancers - Directors - Film Editors - Hosts/MCs - Playwrights - Producers - Production Designers - Screenwriters - TV Writers

Christopher Gauntt . . . . .Owner
Lana Ford . . . . .Literary Manager

CREATIVE MANAGEMENT ENTERTAINMENT GROUP (CMEG)

2050 S. Bundy Dr., Ste. 280
West Los Angeles, CA 90025
PHONE 310-207-7333
FAX 310-207-7373
EMAIL .cmeg2050@yahoo.com
WEB SITE . . . . .www.cmeg.com
TYPES   Commercial Talent - Film/TV Talent
REPRESENTS   Actors - Broadcast Journalists/Newscasters
                       - Comedians - Hosts/MCs - Sports
                       Personalities - Teens/Young Adults - Voice-
                       Over Artists
SUBMISSION POLICY   See Web site; Hard copy mailings preferred
COMMENTS   Specializes in on-air host talent manage-
                       ment

Marki Costello . . . . .Owner/President
Benjamin McCormick . . . . .Theatrical Division Manager
Brandon McCormick . . . . .Assistant
Tara Sinoker . . . . .Assistant

CREATIVE TALENT COMPANY

165 W. 46th St., Ste. 1210
New York, NY 10036
PHONE 212-957-5043/323-965-1175
TYPES   Commercial Talent - Film/TV Talent -
                       Theatre Talent
REPRESENTS   Actors - Children - Directors - Hosts/MCs -
                       Musical Theatre Performers - Teens/Young
                       Adults - Voice-Over Artists
SUBMISSION POLICY   Send picture, resumé, DVDs by mail
COMMENTS   Represents a small number of established
                       actors

Breanna Benjamin . . . . .Manager/Owner
Erick Price . . . . .Associate

CREATIVE TALENT MANAGEMENT

91-08 172nd St.
Jamaica, NY 11432
PHONE 718-658-0443
FAX 718-526-7347
TYPES   Commercial Talent - Film/TV Talent -
                       Literary Talent - Music Talent
AFFILIATIONS   NCOPM
REPRESENTS   Actors - Comedians - Composers -
                       Directors - Music Artists - Producers -
                       Screenwriters - Voice-Over Artists

Tanden R. Heyes . . . . .Manager

CREATIVE TALENT MANAGEMENT GROUP (CTMG)

433 N. Camden Dr., Ste. 600
Beverly Hills, CA 90210
PHONE 310-385-9200
FAX 310-385-9205
EMAIL . . . . .mail@ctmg.net
TYPES   Commercial Talent - Film/TV Talent - Music
                       Talent
REPRESENTS   Actors - Composers - Music Artists - Music
                       Producers

Steve C. Smith . . . . .President

JOHN CROSBY MANAGEMENT

1310 N. Spaulding Ave.
Los Angeles, CA 90046
PHONE 323-874-2400
FAX 323-874-2500
TYPES   Film/TV Talent
REPRESENTS   Actors

John Crosby . . . . .Manager
Jackie Tucker . . . . .Manager
Lucas Tanner . . . . .Assistant

CRYSIS MANAGEMENT

3800 Barham Blvd., Ste. 409
Los Angeles, CA 90068
PHONE 323-876-4000
FAX 323-876-4010
EMAIL . . . . .info@crysismanagement.com
WEB SITE . . . . .www.crysismanagement.com
TYPES   Film/TV Talent - Music Talent - Theatre
                       Talent
REPRESENTS   Actors

Gerry Cagle . . . . .Founder/Manager
David Rudy . . . . .Head, TV/Film

CTM ARTISTS

484 W. 43rd St., Ste. 11S
New York, NY 10036
PHONE 212-564-3536
FAX 212-629-7233
TYPES   Commercial Talent - Film/TV Talent -
                       Modeling Talent
REPRESENTS   Actors - Directors - Voice-Over Artists
SUBMISSION POLICY   Mail only, do not call
COMMENTS   Also represents animators

Charlene Turney . . . . .Manager

CUE11 ENTERTAINMENT

37 E. Cozza Dr.
Spokane, WA 99208
PHONE 509-464-0062
FAX 509-468-0622
EMAIL .shawnwest@cue11.com
WEB SITE www.cue11.com
TYPES   Below-the-Line Talent - Commercial Talent
                       - Film/TV Talent - Literary Talent - Modeling
                       Talent - Music Talent - Theatre Talent
AFFILIATIONS   NCOPM
REPRESENTS   Actors - Book Authors - Composers -
                       Directors - Hosts/MCs - Music Artists -
                       Music Editors - Music Producers - Music
                       Supervisors - Musical Theatre Performers -
                       Print Models - Producers - Runway Models -
                       Screenwriters - Speakers/Lecturers - Sports
                       Personalities - Teens/Young Adults - TV
                       Writers - Variety Artists - Voice-Over Artists
SUBMISSION POLICY   Via email or US Mail only; No phone calls

David Cebert . . . . .President/Composer
Shawn West .Executive VP, Manager
Joe Brasch . . . . .Producer/Composer
Kevin Dodson .Composer/Technician
Brent Oty . . . . .Accounting

CUTLER MANAGEMENT

13043 Sunset Blvd.
Los Angeles, CA 90049
PHONE 310-471-4400
TYPES   Film/TV Talent
REPRESENTS   Actors - Voice-Over Artists

Patricia Cutler . . . . .Manager

D/F MANAGEMENT
270 Lafayette St., Ste. 402
New York, NY 10012
PHONE 212-343-0069
TYPES   Film/TV Talent
REPRESENTS   Actors
SUBMISSION POLICY   Unsolicited submissions not accepted
COMMENTS   West Coast address: 8607 E. Washington
                         Blvd., #7, Culver City, CA 90232, phone:
                         310-558-3333

Steve Dontanville . . . . .Partner (LA)
Frank Frattaroli . . . . .Partner (NY)
Marnie Briskin . . . . .Associate (NY)
Charles Mastropietro . . . . .Associate (NY)
Daniel Pancotto . . . . .Associate (LA)
Eric Stein . . . . .Assistant (NY)

MARV DAUER MANAGEMENT
11661 San Vicente Blvd., Ste. 104
Los Angeles, CA 90049
PHONE 310-207-6884
FAX 310-207-4551
TYPES   Film/TV Talent - Literary Talent
REPRESENTS   Actors - Directors - Screenwriters
SUBMISSION POLICY   Mail only; Do not call

Marv Dauer . . . . .Owner/Personal Manager
Greg Strangis . . . . .Partner/Personal Manager
Alisa Collins . . . . .Office Manager

ALAN DAVID MANAGEMENT
8840 Wilshire Blvd., Ste. 200
Beverly Hills, CA 90211
PHONE 310-358-3155
FAX 310-358-3256
EMAIL . . . . .adavid@planbproductions.net
TYPES   Commercial Talent - Film/TV Talent -
                         Theatre Talent
REPRESENTS   Actors - Producers - Voice-Over Artists

Alan David . . . . .Owner
Ari Gottfried . . . . .Consultant
Miriam Kravitz . . . . .Assistant

DAVILA & CO.
9255 Sunset Blvd., Ste. 803
Los Angeles, CA 90069
PHONE 310-859-0153
FAX 310-859-3519
TYPES   Film/TV Talent - Literary Talent - Music
                         Talent - Theatre Talent
REPRESENTS   Actors - Book Authors - Comedians -
                         Directors - Music Artists - Musical Theatre
                         Performers - Playwrights - Screenwriters -
                         TV Writers

Juan Davila . . . . .Owner/Manager
Ethan Salter . . . . .Manager

DEAN LITERARY CONCEPTS
412 Emerald Pl.
Seal Beach, CA 90740-6223
PHONE 562-594-0665
TYPES   Film/TV Talent - Literary Talent - Theatre
                         Talent
REPRESENTS   Playwrights - Screenwriters
COMMENTS   Affiliated with Film Independent (FIND)

Liza A. Dean . . . . .Manager
Howard Kapp . . . . .Associate
Iris Larsen . . . . .Associate

RON DEBLASIO MANAGEMENT
740 N. La Brea Ave.
Los Angeles, CA 90038
PHONE 323-933-9977
FAX 323-933-0633
EMAIL . . . . .ron@sdmmusic.com
TYPES   Film/TV Talent - Music Talent
REPRESENTS   Actors - Comedians - Music Artists
COMMENTS   Partial client list: George Lopez - X - Exene
                         Cervenka - Forest for the Trees - Original
                         Sinners

Ron DeBlasio . . . . .Partner
Chetan Balachandra . . . . .A&R

DEJ MANAGEMENT COMPANY
4139 Via Marina, #204
Marina del Rey, CA 90292
PHONE 310-306-4541
EMAIL . . . . .wkdej@yahoo.com
TYPES   Commercial Talent - Film/TV Talent -
                         Literary Talent - Modeling Talent - Music
                         Talent - Theatre Talent
AFFILIATIONS   TMA
REPRESENTS   Actors - Book Authors - Broadcast
                         Journalists/Newscasters - Choreographers -
                         Cinematographers - Comedians -
                         Composers - Dancers - Directors - Film
                         Editors - Hosts/MCs - Music Artists - Music
                         Producers - Music Supervisors - Musical
                         Theatre Performers - Playwrights - Print
                         Models - Producers - Production Designers
                         - Runway Models - Screenwriters - Seniors -
                         Speakers/Lecturers - Sports Personalities -
                         TV Writers - Variety Artists - Voice-Over
                         Artists
SUBMISSION POLICY   Accepted via email and US Mail

Willia DeJarnett . . . . .Talent Manager
Marcus DeJarnett . . . . .Administrative Assistant

DELPHINIUS MANAGEMENT
6668 Apache Way
West Chester, OH 45069-1433
PHONE 513-755-3705
FAX 513-755-3705
EMAIL . . . . .delphiniuscbg@aol.com
WEB SITE . . . . .www.delphinius-management.com
TYPES   Film/TV Talent - Literary Talent - Music
                         Talent
REPRESENTS   Actors - Book Authors - Cinematographers
                         - Comedians - Composers - Directors -
                         Film Editors - Hosts/MCs - Interactive
                         Game Developers - Music Artists - Music
                         Editors - Music Producers - Music
                         Supervisors - Playwrights - Producers -
                         Screenwriters - Speakers/Lecturers - TV
                         Writers - Variety Artists - Voice-Over Artists
SUBMISSION POLICY   Submit query by email or US Mail

Cynthia 'Cy' Brohas-Gulacsy . . . . .Owner/Manager
John Bowker . . . . .Creative/Development Director
Kenn Hoekstra . . . . .Manager/Webmaster
Cy Roberts . . . . .Literary Manager
David Todd Adams . . . . .Promotions/Marketing Manager
Nick Gulacsy Jr. . . . . .A&R Manager

DENISE DENNY TALENT MANAGEMENT
PO Box 69A88
Los Angeles, CA 90069
PHONE 310-275-9366
TYPES   Commercial Talent - Film/TV Talent - Music
                         Talent - Theatre Talent
AFFILIATIONS   AFM - AGVA - DGA
REPRESENTS   Actors - Broadcast Journalists/Newscasters
                         - Composers - Directors - Teens/Young
                         Adults - Variety Artists - Voice-Over Artists

Denise Denny ....Manager

DEPAZ MANAGEMENT
2011 N. Vermont Ave.
Los Angeles, CA 90027
PHONE 323-663-3388
FAX 323-663-3365
EMAIL ....ivan@de-paz-management.com
WEB SITE ....www.de-paz-management.com
TYPES   Film/TV Talent
REPRESENTS   Actors - Teens/Young Adults

Ivan de Paz ....Manager

DETROIT COMPANY
345 N. Maple Dr., Ste. 393
Beverly Hills, CA 90210
PHONE 310-858-6858
FAX 310-271-5330
EMAIL ....patty@pattydetroit.com
TYPES   Film/TV Talent - Literary Talent
REPRESENTS   Directors - Producers - Screenwriters - TV
                         Writers

Patty Detroit ....Manager

THE DEVELOPMENT DEPARTMENT
8386 Blackburn Ave., Ste. 106
Los Angeles, CA 90048
PHONE 323-632-7319
TYPES   Film/TV Talent - Literary Talent
REPRESENTS   Actors - Directors - Producers -
                         Screenwriters - TV Writers
SUBMISSION POLICY   Established talent only
COMMENTS   Emphasis on TV writers, producers and
                         directors

Todd Johnson ....Manager

DEWALT & MUZIK MANAGEMENT
215 W. Palm Ave., Ste. 201B
Burbank, CA 91502
PHONE 818-563-1515/773-878-7521
FAX 818-563-1561
EMAIL ....suzanne@dewaltmuzik.com
SECOND EMAIL ....paula@dewaltmuzik.com
TYPES   Film/TV Talent - Theatre Talent
REPRESENTS   Actors - Children - Screenwriters -
                         Teens/Young Adults
SUBMISSION POLICY   By referral only; Via US Mail

Suzanne De Walt ....Manager
Paula Muzik ....Manager
Pat Lentz ....Assistant

BOB DIAMOND & ASSOCIATES
111 S. Kings Rd.
Los Angeles, CA 90048
PHONE 323-655-9052
TYPES   Commercial Talent - Film/TV Talent
REPRESENTS   Actors - Children - Dancers - Teens/Young
                         Adults

Bob Diamond ....Owner/Manager
Lisa M. Diamond ....VP/Manager
Charo Manansala ....VP, Talent
Nicole Rainy ....Children's Talent
Ethan Tyler ....Soaps

DIVINE MANAGEMENT
3822 Latrobe St.
Los Angeles, CA 90031
PHONE 323-221-9300
FAX 323-221-2900
EMAIL ....gayle@divinemgt.com
TYPES   Film/TV Talent - Literary Talent
REPRESENTS   Actors - Comedians - Screenwriters - TV
                         Writers

Gayle Divine ....Owner/Manager
Alex Karrys ....Manager

DIXON TALENT, INC.
432 W. 45th St., Ste. 2D
New York, NY 10036
PHONE 212-262-6033
FAX 212-262-6177
TYPES   Film/TV Talent - Literary Talent
REPRESENTS   Comedians - Producers - TV Writers

James Dixon ....Manager

DONALDSON/SANDERS ENTERTAINMENT
1640 S. Sepulveda Blvd., Ste. 530
Los Angeles, CA 90025
PHONE 310-689-9811
FAX 310-689-9801
TYPES   Literary Talent
REPRESENTS   Book Authors - Directors - Screenwriters -
                         TV Writers
COMMENTS   Also represents Comic Book Creators

Peter Donaldson ....Partner
Jay Sanders ....Partner

BONNY DORE MANAGEMENT
10940 Wilshire Blvd., Ste. 1600
Los Angeles, CA 90024
PHONE 310-443-4189
FAX 310-443-4190
EMAIL ....bonnyinc@aol.com
TYPES   Film/TV Talent - Literary Talent - Theatre
                         Talent
REPRESENTS   Actors - Book Authors - Comedians -
                         Directors - Hosts/MCs - Music Artists -
                         Musical Theatre Performers - Playwrights -
                         Speakers/Lecturers - Teens/Young Adults -
                         TV Writers - Voice-Over Artists
COMMENTS   Also affiliated with PGA

Bonny Dore ....Manager

MANAGERS

DOUGLAS MANAGEMENT GROUP
9713 Little Santa Monica Blvd., Ste. 218
Beverly Hills, CA 90210
PHONE 310-285-6090
FAX 310-285-6097
WEB SITE . . . . www.douglasmanagementgroup.com
TYPES   Literary Talent - Theatre Talent
REPRESENTS   Actors - Directors - Screenwriters - TV
                         Writers
SUBMISSION POLICY   No unsolicited material

Douglas Urbanski . . . . .Manager

DREAM TALENT
PO Box 221733
Santa Clarita, CA 91322
PHONE 818-543-1512
FAX 818-244-1642
EMAIL . . . . .info@dreamtalentmanagement.com
WEB SITE . . . . .www.dreamtalentmanagement.com
TYPES   Commercial Talent - Film/TV Talent -
                         Modeling Talent - Music Talent - Theatre
                         Talent
REPRESENTS   Actors - Children - Dancers - Infants - Print
                         Models - Runway Models - Teens/Young
                         Adults - Variety Artists - Voice-Over Artists
SUBMISSION POLICY   Hard-copy submissions only; Seeking new
                         and established talent

Karla Huff . . . . .Director
Veda Burton . . . . .Manager, Dance/Music
Emelie Jimmo . . . . .Manager, TV/Film

DREAMAKERS INC.
PO Box 5359
Crestline, CA 92325
PHONE 818-292-3090
FAX 909-338-8560
TYPES   Film/TV Talent - Literary Talent - Music
                         Talent
REPRESENTS   Actors - Comedians - Directors - Music
                         Artists - Music Producers - Producers -
                         Screenwriters

Richard Burkhart . . . . .Personal Manager

DU JOUR ENTERTAINMENT/GYPSY PRODUCTIONS
c/o Robert Miller
PO Box 4807
Chatsworth, CA 91313
PHONE 818-709-4257
FAX 818-709-4744
EMAIL . . . . .r.miller@dujourfilms.com
WEB SITE . . . . .www.dujourfilms.com
TYPES   Film/TV Talent - Literary Talent - Music
                         Talent
AFFILIATIONS   NCOPM
REPRESENTS   Actors - Book Authors - Dancers - Music
                         Artists - Print Models - Screenwriters - TV
                         Writers

Robert Miller . . . . .CEO
Charles McFadden . . . . .Promotions
Natalie Harper . . . . .Talent Management
Cynthia Busby . . . . .Project Development
Eric Stevens .Project Development
Steven Miller Esq. . . . . .Legal
Deborah Miller . . . . .Records/Research
Vern Smith . . . . .Promotions

EARTHANGELS LITERARY MANAGEMENT
6242 Warner Ave., Ste. 29G
Huntington Beach, CA 92647
PHONE 310-809-0270/714-847-8784
EMAIL . . . . .attica@anet.net
TYPES   Literary Talent
REPRESENTS   Directors - Screenwriters - TV Writers
SUBMISSION POLICY   Email or US Mail; Do not fax unsolicited
                         material; No phone calls
COMMENTS   Management and literary boutique for
                         minority and women screenwriters and
                         directors

Attica F. Peece . . . . .Primary
Cozetta Fitzgerald . . . . .Partner
Carter Hall . . . . .Partner
Martin Fong .Office Coordinator
Isabelle Laguardia . . . . .Assistant

EASTWOOD TALENT CORPORATION
208 W. 30th St., Ste. 1006
New York, NY 10001
PHONE 212-946-1175/212-631-9933
FAX 212-631-0033
WEB SITE .www.eastwoodtalent.com
TYPES   Commercial Talent - Film/TV Talent -
                         Literary Talent - Music Talent - Theatre
                         Talent
REPRESENTS   Actors - Broadcast Journalists/Newscasters
                         - Children - Comedians - Dancers - Martial
                         Artists/Stunts - Music Artists - Screenwriters
                         - Sports Personalities - Teens/Young Adults
                         - Variety Artists - Voice-Over Artists
COMMENTS   Fighters for film and TV, Professional
                         Wrestlers; Owner, Police Actors Association;
                         Provides police officers and military actors
                         for film, TV, print and music videos

Bruce Kivo . . . . .Owner

ECHO LAKE MANAGEMENT
421 S. Beverly Dr., 8th Fl.
Beverly Hills, CA 90212
PHONE 310-789-4790
FAX 310-789-4791
TYPES   Film/TV Talent - Literary Talent
REPRESENTS   Directors - Screenwriters

Michael Marcus . . . . .Manager
Amotz Zakai . . . . .Manager

ALLEN EDELMAN MANAGEMENT
5319 Ben Ave.
Valley Village, CA 91607
PHONE 818-985-8789
FAX 818-760-9637
EMAIL . . . . .aedelmanmgmt@yahoo.com
TYPES   Film/TV Talent
REPRESENTS   Actors
SUBMISSION POLICY   Send hard copies only of photos and
                         resumes; No drop-ins
COMMENTS   Looking for actors/actresses between the
                         ages of eighteen to twenty-nine years old

Allen Edelman . . . . .Manager
Quan Lo . . . . .Manager
Bert S. Weil . . . . .Manager

RONA EDWARDS PRODUCTIONS
264 S. La Cienega Blvd., Ste. 1052
Beverly Hills, CA 90211
PHONE 323-466-3013
WEB SITE . . . . .www.esentertainment.net
TYPES   Literary Talent
REPRESENTS   Screenwriters
SUBMISSION POLICY   Query letter with SASE for reply; No faxes
COMMENTS   Production; ATAS, PGA; ESE Film
                         Workshops Online

Rona Edwards . . . . .Producer/Literary Management

EIGHTH SQUARE ENTERTAINMENT
606 N. Larchmont, Ste. 307
Los Angeles, CA 90004
PHONE 323-469-1003
FAX 323-469-1516
EMAIL . . . . .eighthsq@aol.com
TYPES   Film/TV Talent - Literary Talent - Theatre
                         Talent
REPRESENTS   Actors - Comedians - Directors - Producers
                         - Screenwriters - TV Writers
SUBMISSION POLICY   By referral only

Janette Jensen 'JJ' Hoffman . . . . .No Title
Jeff Melnick . . . . .No Title

MICHAEL EINFELD MANAGEMENT
10630 Moorpark Ave., Ste. 101
Toluca Lake, CA 91602
PHONE 818-752-4238
EMAIL . . . . .mikeinfeld@aol.com
SECOND EMAIL . . . . .infeldassistant@aol.com
TYPES   Film/TV Talent - Theatre Talent
REPRESENTS   Actors - Hosts/MCs - Musical Theatre
                         Performers
COMMENTS   Represents clients on both coasts

Michael Einfeld . . . . .Manager/Producer/Packaging

EK MANAGEMENT
264 S. La Cienega Blvd., Ste. 1217
Beverly Hills, CA 90211
PHONE 310-890-9556
FAX 425-977-0548
EMAIL . . . . .ekmanagement@yahoo.com
TYPES   Literary Talent
REPRESENTS   Directors - Screenwriters

Eric Kim . . . . .Manager/Producer

ELEGANCE TALENT GROUP
4754 Aldridge Dr.
Memphis, TN 38109
PHONE 901-301-0333
FAX 901-301-0333
EMAIL . . . . .pcovington@etgmodels.com
SECOND EMAIL . . . . .talent@etgmodels.com
WEB SITE . . . . .www.elegancetalentgroup.com
TYPES   Commercial Talent - Modeling Talent -
                         Music Talent
REPRESENTS   Music Artists - Print Models - Runway
                         Models

Patrick Covington . . . . .President
Jackie Green . . . . .National Representative
Terry Hunter . . . . .Regional Representative
Shun Moore . . . . .Booking, Midwest
Eric Wooten . . . . .Point of Contact (Atlanta)
Kevin Young . . . . .Model Trainer

ELEMENTS ENTERTAINMENT
1635 North Cahuenga Blvd., 5th Fl.
Los Angeles, CA 90028
PHONE 323-461-2000
FAX 323-461-2400
TYPES   Film/TV Talent - Literary Talent
REPRESENTS   Actors - Book Authors - Comedians -
                         Directors - Screenwriters - TV Writers

Nils Larsen . . . . .Manager/Partner
Christopher Pratt .Manager/Partner
Chad Marting . . . . .Manager
Ryan Sterrenberg . . . . .Assistant
Benjamin Tacheny . . . . .Assistant

ELKINS ENTERTAINMENT CORPORATION
8306 Wilshire Blvd., Ste. 3643
Beverly Hills, CA 90211
PHONE 323-932-0400
FAX 323-932-6400
EMAIL . . . . .info@elkinsent.com
TYPES   Film/TV Talent - Theatre Talent
REPRESENTS   Actors - Composers - Directors - Musical
                         Theatre Performers - Producers -
                         Screenwriters - Seniors - Teens/Young
                         Adults - TV Writers - Variety Artists - Voice-
                         Over Artists
COMMENTS   Affiliated with AMPAS, ATVAS, PGA,
                         Dramatist Guild and AFTRA

Hillard Elkins . . . . .President
Sandi Love . . . . .VP
Diana Nunez . . . . .Assistant to Mr. Elkins

ELSBOY MANAGEMENT
1581 N. Crescent Heights Blvd.
Los Angeles, CA 90046
PHONE 323-656-3800
TYPES   Film/TV Talent - Literary Talent
REPRESENTS   Actors - Directors - Screenwriters
SUBMISSION POLICY   No submissions; By referral only

Paul Aaron . . . . .President
James Waugh . . . . .VP, Development
Matt Aldrich . . . . .Executive Assistant
Zac Sanford . . . . .Executive Assistant

ELYSIAN ENTERTAINMENT, INC.
1149 N. Gower St., Ste. 245
Hollywood, CA 90038
PHONE 323-785-2240
EMAIL . . . . .submissions@elysian-entertainment.com
WEB SITE . . . . .www.elysian-entertainment.com
TYPES   Literary Talent
REPRESENTS   Book Authors - Directors - Screenwriters
SUBMISSION POLICY   No unsolicited submissions
COMMENTS   WGA; Produces and manages emerging
                     writers and writer-directors

Sheri Fults . . . . .Producer/Manager

EMANCIPATED TALENT MANAGEMENT & CONSULTING
265 Quincy St., 1st Fl.
Brooklyn, NY 11216
PHONE 718-622-3920
FAX 501-621-7372
EMAIL . . . . .rmurphy@emancipatedtalent.com
SECOND EMAIL . . . . .joono@emancipatedtalent.com.
WEB SITE .www.emancipatedtalent.com
TYPES   Film/TV Talent - Literary Talent
REPRESENTS   Actors - Comedians - Music Artists -
                     Screenwriters

Richard J. Murphy . . . . .President
Michael 'Joono' Irving . . . . .VP
Sean Holmes . . . . .General Manager
Cliff Andrews . . . . .Music & Theatrical Coordinator
Darryl Raeburn . . . . .Music & Theatrical Coordinator

EMERALD TALENT GROUP
10 Universal City Plaza, 20th Fl.
Universal City, CA 91608
PHONE 818-753-2418
FAX 818-753-2419
EMAIL . . . . .farasr@aol.com
TYPES   Film/TV Talent - Theatre Talent
REPRESENTS   Actors - Children - Comedians -
                     Teens/Young Adults

Faras Rabadi . . . . .Owner/Manager

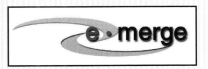

E-MERGE MANAGEMENT
6300 Wilshire Blvd., Ste. 1470
Los Angeles, CA 90048
PHONE 323-658-4233
FAX 323-658-7842
EMAIL . . . . .inquiries@e-mergemanagement.com
WEB SITE .www.e-mergemanagement.com
TYPES   Literary Talent
REPRESENTS   Book Authors - Directors - Playwrights -
                     Producers - Screenwriters - TV Writers
COMMENTS   Specializes in new media

Todd Koerner . . . . .President

ENCORE ARTISTS MANAGEMENT
A California Licensed Talent Agency
3815 W. Olive Ave., Ste. 101
Burbank, CA 91505
PHONE 818-955-8821
FAX 818-955-8833
EMAIL . . . . .lin@encorela.com
SECOND EMAIL . . . . .lin.bickelmann@talentmanagers.org
WEB SITE . . . . .www.encorela.com
SECOND WEB SITE . . . . .www.talentmanagers.org
TYPES   Commercial Talent - Film/TV Talent
AFFILIATIONS   TMA
REPRESENTS   Actors - Book Authors - Children -
                     Directors - Hosts/MCs - Print Models -
                     Producers - Screenwriters - Seniors -
                     Teens/Young Adults - TV Writers
SUBMISSION POLICY   Does not accept unsolicited email attach-
                     ments, embedded objects or unsolicited
                     faxes; Submit hard copies only; Do not call
                     to follow-up, will contact if interested
COMMENTS   Member of TMA Board of Directors

Lin Bickelmann . . . . .CEO/Talent Representative
Chris Bickelmann . . . . .CFO
Arthur Axelman . . . . .Executive VP, Literary & Packaging
Veronica James . . . . .Head, Commercials
Nicholas Day . . . . .Office Manager

ENDURANCE TALENT MANAGEMENT
2920 W. Olive Ave., Ste. 202
Burbank, CA 91505
PHONE 818-846-3547
FAX 818-846-3553
TYPES   Commercial Talent - Film/TV Talent
AFFILIATIONS   TMA
REPRESENTS   Actors - Children - Teens/Young Adults

Jamie Pease . . . . .Manager
Ben Eng . . . . .Assistant

ENDURE MANAGEMENT
12335 Santa Monica Blvd., Ste. 106
Los Angeles, CA 90025
PHONE 310-281-6859
TYPES   Literary Talent
REPRESENTS   Music Artists - Screenwriters - TV Writers
SUBMISSION POLICY   No unsolicited material accepted; No
                     phone calls

Taminika Outlaw . . . . .President/CEO

ENERGY ENTERTAINMENT
999 N. Doheny Dr., Ste. 711
Los Angeles, CA 90069
PHONE 310-274-3440
WEB SITE .www.energyentertainment.net
TYPES   Film/TV Talent - Literary Talent
REPRESENTS   Actors - Directors - Screenwriters - TV
                     Writers
COMMENTS   Also a production company

Brooklyn Weaver . . . . .Owner/Manager
Adam Marshall . . . . .Manager
Jake Wagner . . . . .Manager

ENSEMBLE ENTERTAINMENT
10474 Santa Monica Blvd., Ste. 380
Los Angeles, CA 90025
PHONE 310-882-8900
FAX 310-882-8901
TYPES   Film/TV Talent - Literary Talent
REPRESENTS   Book Authors - Directors - Screenwriters -
                        TV Writers
SUBMISSION POLICY   Industry referral preferred

Jon Brown . . . . .Partner/Manager
Jeffrey Thal . . . . .Partner/Manager
Orlando Alegret . . . . .Assistant
Patti Cummings . . . . .Assistant

ENTERTAINMENT MANAGEMENT GROUP
8265 Sunset Blvd., Ste. 203
West Hollywood, CA 90046
PHONE 323-848-3700
FAX 323-848-8665
EMAIL . . . . .emg5@sbcglobal.net
TYPES   Film/TV Talent - Literary Talent - Music
                        Talent - Theatre Talent
REPRESENTS   Actors - Music Artists
COMMENTS   Associated with SLJ Management

Robert S. Costanzo . . . . .Manager/Owner/Producer
Tanya Kacher . . . . .Manager/Producer
Roland Gotingco . . . . .Office Manager
Nick Rico . . . . .Executive Assistant to Robert S. Costanzo
Manny Trejo . . . . .Executive Assistant
Nick Rallo . . . . .Reception

ENVISION ENTERTAINMENT
9255 Sunset Blvd., Ste. 500
Los Angeles, CA 90069
PHONE 310-859-0599
FAX 310-859-0589
TYPES   Film/TV Talent
REPRESENTS   Actors

Beth Cannon . . . . .Owner/Manager
Constance Freiberg . . . . .Manager
Dominic Franceschi . . . . .Assistant

ENVOY ENTERTAINMENT
1640 S. Sepulveda Blvd., Ste. 530
Los Angeles, CA 90025
PHONE 310-689-9800
FAX 310-689-9801
TYPES   Film/TV Talent - Literary Talent
REPRESENTS   Actors - Directors - Producers -
                        Screenwriters - TV Writers

Barbara Gale . . . . .President
Amy Macnow . . . . .Manager

EPIGRAM MANAGEMENT
13636 Ventura Blvd., #508
Sherman Oaks, CA 91423
PHONE 818-461-8937
FAX 818-461-8919
EMAIL . . . . .flashforward@sbcglobal.net
TYPES   Film/TV Talent - Literary Talent
REPRESENTS   Directors - Screenwriters - TV Writers

Doug Draizin . . . . .Partner
Val McLeroy . . . . .Partner
Paula Price . . . . .Assistant

THE ESI NETWORK
6310 San Vicente Blvd., Ste. 340
Los Angeles, CA 90048
PHONE 310-888-1128/323-965-8928
FAX 310-888-1127/323-965-8927
EMAIL . . . . .info@theESInetwork.ccom
WEB SITE . . . . .www.theESInetwork.com
TYPES   Commercial Talent - Film/TV Talent -
                        Modeling Talent
REPRESENTS   Actors - Children - Infants - Print Models -
                        Seniors - Teens/Young Adults - Voice-Over
                        Artists
SUBMISSION POLICY   Young adult submissions from union talent
                        only; See Web site for submission instruc-
                        tions

Nelson Parks . . . . .CEO
Joslyn Sifuentes . . . . .Children & Seniors
Emalia Cornwell . . . . .No Title
Devin McGovern . . . . .No Title
Jason Teague . . . . .No Title

ESSENTIAL TALENT MANAGEMENT
6464 Sunset Blvd., Ste. 760
Hollywood, CA 90028
PHONE 323-469-0900
TYPES   Film/TV Talent
REPRESENTS   Actors
SUBMISSION POLICY   No unsolicitated material

Don Spradlin . . . . .Manager
Susan Yoo . . . . .Manager
T.R. Shepard . . . . .Assistant

EVANS MANAGEMENT
c/o El Capitan Ranch
8620 Copper Ridge Ave.
Las Vegas, CA 89129
PHONE 702-360-6016
FAX 702-255-2256
EMAIL . . . . .selisainc@aol.com
TYPES   Commercial Talent - Film/TV Talent -
                        Literary Talent - Music Talent - Theatre
                        Talent
AFFILIATIONS   NCOPM
REPRESENTS   Actors - Book Authors - Broadcast
                        Journalists/Newscasters - Comedians -
                        Composers - Music Artists - Sports
                        Personalities - Variety Artists - Voice-Over
                        Artists
COMMENTS   Sportscasters; Mr. Evans currently serves as
                        National Vice President, NCOPM

Stanley Evans . . . . .President
Brenda Golub . . . . .Executive Assistant

EVATOPIA
400 S. Beverly Dr., Ste. 214
Beverly Hills, CA 90212
PHONE 310-270-3868
EMAIL . . . . .submissions@evatopia.com
SECOND EMAIL . . . . .info@evatopia.com
WEB SITE . . . . .www.evatopia.com
TYPES   Literary Talent
REPRESENTS   Screenwriters
SUBMISSION POLICY   Submit via Evatopia's online form found at
                         www.evatopia.com under the link, "For Our
                         Consideration"
COMMENTS   Specializes in management of first-time
                         screenwriters; Provides individual attention
                         to clients to develop career writers;
                         Member of BAFTA

Margery Walshaw . . . . .Principal
Mary Kay . . . . .Story Editor
Jill Jones . . . . .Story Editor
Jamie Davis . . . . .Story Editor

EVERGREEN INTERNATIONAL MANAGEMENT
4988 Reforma Rd.
Woodland Hills, CA 91634
PHONE 818-224-2777
FAX 818-224-2141
EMAIL . . . . .eimanagement@yahoo.com
TYPES   Commercial Talent - Film/TV Talent -
                         Literary Talent - Music Talent
REPRESENTS   Actors - Screenwriters

Trudy Handelman . . . . .President
Larry Handelman . . . . .Assistant

EVOLUTION MANAGEMENT
901 N. Highland Ave.
Los Angeles, CA 90038
PHONE 323-850-3232
FAX 323-850-0521
TYPES   Film/TV Talent - Literary Talent
REPRESENTS   Actors - Book Authors - Directors -
                         Screenwriters - Teens/Young Adults - TV
                         Writers
SUBMISSION POLICY   No unsolicited material
COMMENTS   Production

Mark Burg . . . . .Partner
Oren Koules . . . . .Partner
Carl Mazzocone . . . . .President, Production
Laina Cohn . . . . .Talent Manager
Evan Corday .Head, TV Literary
Stephen Gates . . . . .Head, Literary Department
Brad Kaplan . . . . .Literary Manager
Tiffany Kuzon . . . . .Talent Manager
Chris Ridenhour . . . . .Literary Manager
Andrew Wilson .Literary Manager
Scott Zimmerman . . . . .Talent Manager
Chad Cole . . . . .VP, Development
Troy Begnaud . . . . .VP, Production
Justine Stevenson . . . . .General Manager
Emily Bugg . . . . .Assistant
Irma Esquibel . . . . .Assistant
Jared Ferrie . . . . .Assistant
Jason Mirch . . . . .Assistant
Oubansack Pouiphanvongxay (OP) . . . . .Assistant
Dana Sorman . . . . .Assistant
Kari Stringham . . . . .Assistant

EXILE ENTERTAINMENT
732 El Medio Ave.
Pacific Palisades, CA 90272
PHONE 310-573-1523
FAX 310-573-0109
EMAIL . . . . .exile_ent@yahoo.com
TYPES   Film/TV Talent - Literary Talent
REPRESENTS   Directors - Playwrights - Screenwriters
SUBMISSION POLICY   Send queries to exilesubs@yahoo.com

Gary Ungar . . . . .Personal Manager
Tyler Ruggeri . . . . .Assistant

FARAH FILMS & MANAGEMENT
11948 Darlington Ave., Ste. 2
Brentwood, CA 90049
PHONE 310-979-4533
EMAIL . . . . .dan@farahfilms.com
TYPES   Film/TV Talent - Literary Talent
REPRESENTS   Actors - Screenwriters - TV Writers

Dan Farah . . . . .Manager/Producer

FAST TRACK MANAGEMENT
736 N. Alta Vista Blvd.
Los Angeles, CA 90046
PHONE 323-857-1201
FAX 323-857-1211
EMAIL . . . . .bradley@fasttrackpm.com
TYPES   Film/TV Talent
REPRESENTS   Actors - Hosts/MCs - Voice-Over Artists

Bradley R. Bernstein .Manager
Alisandra M. Rand . . . . .Manager
Parker Rand . . . . .Executive Assistant

FASTBREAK MANAGEMENT, INC.
70 Clay Hill Rd.
Stamford, CT 06905
PHONE 203-329-7335
EMAIL . . . . .bfastbreak@hotmail.com
TYPES   Film/TV Talent - Literary Talent - Music
                         Talent
AFFILIATIONS   NCOPM
REPRESENTS   Actors - Comedians - Music Artists -
                         Screenwriters - TV Writers - Variety Artists -
                         Voice-Over Artists

Bud Mitchell . . . . .Manager

THE FELDMAN COMPANY
c/o The Lot
1041 N. Formosa Ave., Editorial Bldg., Rm. 213
West Hollywood, CA 90046
PHONE 323-850-2503
FAX 323-850-2506
TYPES   Film/TV Talent - Literary Talent
REPRESENTS   Actors - Book Authors - Directors -
                         Producers - Screenwriters - TV Writers

Todd Feldman . . . . .Producer/Manager
Luciano Saber . . . . .VP, Development

FELDMAN MANAGEMENT, LLC
10642 Santa Monica Blvd., Ste. 205
Los Angeles, CA 90025
PHONE 310-474-4515/310-927-8831
FAX 310-474-4876
EMAIL . . . . .cnfmgt@yahoo.com
SECOND EMAIL . . . . .feldmanmgmt@yahoo.com
TYPES   Film/TV Talent
AFFILIATIONS   DGA
REPRESENTS   Actors - Cinematographers - Producers -
                      Screenwriters - TV Writers

Caron Feldman . . . . .Manager/Producer/Owner

FESTA ENTERTAINMENT
2461 Santa Monica Blvd., Ste. 414
Santa Monica, CA 90404
PHONE 310-315-0569
EMAIL . . . . .info@festaent.com
WEB SITE . . . . .www.festaent.com
TYPES   Film/TV Talent - Literary Talent
REPRESENTS   Book Authors - Directors - Playwrights -
                      Screenwriters - TV Writers

Dannie Festa . . . . .Manager/Producer

FIELD ENTERTAINMENT
1240 N. Wetherly Dr.
Los Angeles, CA 90069
PHONE 310-271-8440
FAX 310-271-6243
EMAIL . . . . .jeff@fieldentertainment.net
TYPES   Film/TV Talent - Literary Talent
REPRESENTS   Actors - Book Authors - Directors -
                      Playwrights - Producers - Screenwriters -
                      Sports Personalities - TV Writers
SUBMISSION POLICY   No unsolicited material

Jeff Field . . . . .President/CEO

STANN FINDELLE LAW & MANAGEMENT
2029 Century Park East, Ste. 900
Los Angeles, CA 90067
PHONE 310-552-1777
FAX 310-286-1990
EMAIL . . . . .perfstanny@aol.com
TYPES   Commercial Talent - Film/TV Talent -
                      Literary Talent - Modeling Talent - Music
                      Talent
REPRESENTS   Actors - Book Authors - Broadcast
                      Journalists/Newscasters - Comedians -
                      Composers - Music Artists - Music
                      Producers - Print Models - Voice-Over
                      Artists
SUBMISSION POLICY   On approval
COMMENTS   Also represents clothing designers;
                      Member, California Bar

Stann Findelle . . . . .Attorney/Manager

FINEMAN ENTERTAINMENT
9437 Santa Monica Blvd., Ste. 206
Beverly Hills, CA 90210
PHONE 310-550-6000
FAX 310-550-7001
TYPES   Literary Talent
REPRESENTS   Actors - Directors - Producers -
                      Screenwriters - TV Writers

Ross Fineman .Manager/Producer
Samata Narra . . . . .Manager
Joanne Wozniak . . . . .Assistant

FIRE COMM MANAGEMENT
17366 Chase St.
Northridge, CA 91325
PHONE 818-343-4202
TYPES   Commercial Talent - Film/TV Talent -
                      Modeling Talent
REPRESENTS   Actors - Children - Print Models -
                      Teens/Young Adults
SUBMISSION POLICY   Seeking talent under twenty years old only

Rusty Feuer . . . . .Owner/Manager
Heather Scherer . . . . .Assistant Manager
Ron Feuer . . . . .Associate

THE FIRM, INC.
9465 Wilshire Blvd., 6th Fl.
Beverly Hills, CA 90212
PHONE 310-860-8000
FAX 310-860-8100
TYPES   Film/TV Talent - Literary Talent - Music
                      Talent - Theatre Talent
REPRESENTS   Actors - Book Authors - Comedians -
                      Composers - Directors - Music Artists -
                      Music Producers - Producers - Screenwriters
                      - Sports Personalities - TV Writers - Variety
                      Artists - Voice-Over Artists
COMMENTS   Consumer brands

Jeff Kwatinetz . . . . .Co-Chairman/CEO/Manager
Rich Frank . . . . .Chairman
Rick Yorn . . . . .Co-Chairman
Julie Yorn . . . . .Principal/President, Firm Films
Dave Baram . . . . .President/COO
Stacy Boniello . . . . .Talent Division, Film/TV
Jennifer Davisson . . . . .Manager, Film/TV
Peter Katsis . . . . .Manager
Alan Nevins . . . . .Manager, Film/TV
Michael Papale . . . . .Manager
Constance Schwartz . . . . .Strategic Marketing
Adam Shulman . . . . .Manager, Film/TV
Jennifer Sousa . . . . .Manager
Paul Frank . . . . .Executive Producer/Head, Firm Television
Lori Rischer . . . . .Promotions/Marketing, Music
Debbie Roldan . . . . .VP, Digital Music & Strategic Development

FIRST CLASS ENTERTAINMENT, INC.
483 Ridgewood Rd.
Maplewood, NJ 07040-2136
PHONE 973-763-0591
FAX 973-763-0570
EMAIL . . . . .talent@gotofirstclass.com
WEB SITE . . . . .www.gotofirstclass.com
TYPES   Music Talent
REPRESENTS   Comedians - Magicians - Music Artists -
                      Producers - Variety Artists
SUBMISSION POLICY   DVD (preferred) or Videotape (NTSC for-
                      mat), photo, bio to Attn: New Talent
                      Department
COMMENTS   Cruise ship entertainment specialists

Howard Beder Sr. . . . . .President
Howard Beder Jr. . . . . .VP

FIRST TAKE
PO Box 1071
Studio City, CA 91614
PHONE 818-286-3611
FAX 818-286-3917
EMAIL . . . . .viewfinder@adelphia.net
WEB SITE .www.viewfinder.net
TYPES   Commercial Talent - Film/TV Talent -
           Modeling Talent
REPRESENTS   Actors - Print Models - Teens/Young Adults
COMMENTS   Attends showcases

P. Michael Perez . . . . .President
C.A. Gramley . . . . .VP

FITZGERALD LITERARY MANAGEMENT
84 Monte Alto Rd.
Santa Fe, NM 87508
PHONE 505-466-1186
TYPES   Literary Talent
REPRESENTS   Book Authors - Screenwriters
SUBMISSION POLICY   No new material at this time, except by
           referral
COMMENTS   Film rights to novels

Lisa FitzGerald . . . . .Manager/Producer

ROBERT FITZPATRICK ORGANIZATION
PO Box 667
Sunset Beach, CA 90742
PHONE 714-863-4099
FAX 562-856-0597
EMAIL . . . . .fitzcorp@aol.com
WEB SITE . . . . .www.vista-ave.com
TYPES   Film/TV Talent - Music Talent - Theatre
           Talent
AFFILIATIONS   AFM
REPRESENTS   Actors - Music Artists - Music Producers -
           Teens/Young Adults
SUBMISSION POLICY   Open to submissions

Robert Fitzpatrick . . . . .No Title
Jeff Lanham . . . . .No Title
Denise Tomlinson . . . . .No Title

FIVE12 ENTERTAINMENT GROUP
14641 Magnolia Blvd., Ste. 9
Sherman Oaks, CA 91403
PHONE 818-481-8848
EMAIL . . . . .booking@five12entgroup.com
SECOND EMAIL . . . . .five12entgroup@yahoo.com
WEB SITE .www.five12entgroup.com
TYPES   Commercial Talent - Film/TV Talent -
           Modeling Talent - Music Talent
REPRESENTS   Actors - Children - Music Artists - Print
           Models - Teens/Young Adults

Starr Thompson .Talent Manager
Alicia Monique . . . . .Assistant

FLASHPOINT ENTERTAINMENT
1318 San Ysidro Dr.
Beverly Hills, CA 90210
PHONE 310-205-6300
TYPES   Literary Talent
REPRESENTS   Book Authors - Directors - Producers -
           Screenwriters
SUBMISSION POLICY   No unsolicited material

Andrew R. Tennenbaum . . . . .Manager/Producer

FLAUNT MODEL MANAGEMENT, INC.
35 W. 35th St., Ste. 901
New York, NY 10001
PHONE 212-679-9011
FAX 212-679-0938
EMAIL . . . . .flaunt@flauntmodels.com
WEB SITE .www.flauntmodels.com
TYPES   Commercial Talent - Modeling Talent
REPRESENTS   Actors - Dancers - Print Models - Runway
           Models - Seniors - Teens/Young Adults
SUBMISSION POLICY   By mail only; No phone calls; No voice-
           over submissions
COMMENTS   Affiliated with SAG and AFTRA

Gene Roseman . . . . .President
Lena Baylor . . . . .Men's Division
Millie Kelly .Talent Coordinator
Leilani A. Quinn . . . . .Fashion Division

FLAVOR UNIT ENTERTAINMENT
155 Morgan St.
Jersey City, NJ 07302
PHONE 201-333-4883
FAX 201-333-0728
TYPES   Commercial Talent - Film/TV Talent - Music
           Talent - Theatre Talent
REPRESENTS   Actors - Music Artists

Sha-Kim Compere . . . . .CEO
Queen Latifah . . . . .CEO
Dedra Tate . . . . .President/General Manager
Otis Best . . . . .General Manager/Management
Sandy Tate . . . . .Assistant

FLUTIE ENTERTAINMENT
6500 Wilshire Blvd., Ste. 2240
Los Angeles, CA 90048
PHONE 310-247-1100
FAX 310-247-1122
WEB SITE . . . . .www.flutieent.com
TYPES   Film/TV Talent - Literary Talent - Theatre
           Talent
REPRESENTS   Actors - Book Authors - Children -
           Comedians - Directors - Producers -
           Screenwriters - Sports Personalities - TV
           Writers
SUBMISSION POLICY   By US Mail or appointment only
COMMENTS   Talent branding, brand identity and brand
           management

Robert A. Flutie . . . . .Manager, Film & TV Talent
Paul M. Brown . . . . .Manager, Film & TV Talent
Amy Slomovits . . . . .Manager, Film & TV Talent
Mary McGuire . . . .Client Relations Manager/Assistant to Robert A. Flutie
Sharon King . . . . .Talent Assistant
Igal Suet . . . . .Talent Assistant

MICHAEL FLUTIE'S OFFICE (MFO)
17 Little West 12th St., Studio 333
New York, NY 10014
PHONE 212-226-7000
FAX 212-226-9791
EMAIL . . . . .info@michaelflutie.com
WEB SITE .www.michaelflutie.com
TYPES   Film/TV Talent - Modeling Talent - Music
           Talent
AFFILIATIONS   NCOPM
REPRESENTS   Actors - Hosts/MCs - Music Artists - Print
           Models - Runway Models -
           Speakers/Lecturers - Sports Personalities -
           TV Writers

Michael Flutie . . . . .Talent Brand Manager/Producer
Amit Ziv . . . . .Talent Brand Manager/Producer
Hilary Polk-Williams . . . . .Talent Brand Manager
Sean Ramsay . . . . .Talent Brand Manager

FOREMOST FILMS
205 West End Ave., Ste. 11-G
New York, NY 10023
PHONE 646-662-0829
EMAIL .jeff@foremostfilms.com
TYPES   Literary Talent
REPRESENTS   Screenwriters
SUBMISSION POLICY   Query by email only; No phone calls

Jeffrey Belkin . . . . .Manager/Producer
Mindy Finkelstein . . . . .Development Associate

MICHAEL FORMAN MANAGEMENT
409 N. Camden Dr., Ste. 205
Beverly Hills, CA 90210
PHONE 310-550-1991
FAX 310-550-1041
TYPES   Literary Talent - Theatre Talent
REPRESENTS   Actors - Book Authors - Comedians -
                         Directors - Martial Artists/Stunts - Print
                         Models - Screenwriters - Teens/Young
                         Adults - TV Writers
SUBMISSION POLICY   Accepts talent submissions; For literary sub-
                         missions, call first to discuss

Michael J. Forman . . . . .Manager/Producer
Jeff Silverberg .Creative Executive

FORSTER DELANEY MANAGEMENT
12533 Woodgreen St.
Los Angeles, CA 90066
PHONE 310-636-4477
FAX 310-636-4478
EMAIL .forsterdelaney@aol.com
TYPES   Film/TV Talent
REPRESENTS   Actors - Voice-Over Artists

Arlene Forster . . . . .Manager
Jenny Delaney . . . . .Manager
Stephanie Dozier . . . . .Assistant

FORWARD ENTERTAINMENT
9255 Sunset Blvd., Ste. 805
Los Angeles, CA 90069
PHONE 310-278-6700
FAX 310-278-6770
TYPES   Film/TV Talent
REPRESENTS   Actors - Comedians - Directors

Connie Tavel . . . . .Partner
Vera Mihailovich . . . . .Partner
Adrianne Sandoval . . . . .Executive Assistant

FOURSIGHT ENTERTAINMENT
8840 Wilshire Blvd., 2nd Fl.
Beverly Hills, CA 90211
PHONE 310-358-3150
FAX 310-358-3165
EMAIL . . . . .info@foursight.com
WEB SITE . . . . .www.foursight.com
TYPES   Literary Talent
REPRESENTS   Directors - Screenwriters
SUBMISSION POLICY   Send all queries by email

Jeremy Bell . . . . .Partner
George Heller . . . . .Partner
Michael Lasker . . . . .Partner
Clayton Sakoda . . . . .Assistant

ELIZABETH FOWLER MANAGEMENT
12400 Ventura Blvd., Ste. 306
Studio City, CA 91604
PHONE 818-980-5460
FAX 818-980-4716
EMAIL . . . . .clearpicturesinc@aol.com
TYPES   Film/TV Talent - Literary Talent
REPRESENTS   Actors - Book Authors - Directors -
                         Screenwriters
COMMENTS   A Division of Clear Pictures Entertainment
                         Inc.

Elizabeth Fowler . . . . .Manager
Paula Smith . . . . .VP, Development
Jenny Rankin . . . . .Assistant

FOX ENTERTAINMENT COMPANY
1650 Broadway
New York, NY 10019
PHONE 212-582-9072
FAX 212-956-5978
TYPES   Commercial Talent - Film/TV Talent - Music
                         Talent
REPRESENTS   Actors - Music Artists

Dick Fox . . . . .Manager/President
Jerri Bocchino . . . . .Manager
Bill Kaminer . . . . .Manager

FOX-ALBERT MANAGEMENT ENTERTAINMENT, INC.
88 Central Park West
New York, NY 10023
PHONE 212-799-9090
TYPES   Film/TV Talent - Theatre Talent
AFFILIATIONS   NCOPM
REPRESENTS   Actors
COMMENTS   Not accepting new clients

Jean Fox . . . . .President

FRAMEWORK ENTERTAINMENT
9057 Nemo St., Ste. C
West Hollywood, CA 90069
PHONE 310-858-0333/212-206-0404
FAX 310-858-1357/212-206-0409
TYPES   Film/TV Talent
REPRESENTS   Actors - Teens/Young Adults
COMMENTS   East Coast office: 129 W. 27th St., 12th Fl.
                         PH, New York, NY 10001

Peg Donegan . . . . .Manager/Producer
Maryellen Mulcahy . . . . .Manager/Producer
Howard Green . . . . .Manager
Steven Levy . . . . .Manager
Stephanie Nese . . . . .Manager
Jennifer Wiley . . . . .Manager
Laura Martinez . . . . .Associate
Robert Atwood . . . . .Associate
Justin Foran . . . . .Associate

FRENETIC MEDIA
1019 W. Edgeware Rd.
Los Angeles, CA 90026
PHONE 323-761-5959
FAX 323-761-5959
EMAIL .info@freneticmedia.com
TYPES   Literary Talent
REPRESENTS   Book Authors - Directors - Screenwriters

Steve H. Lee . . . . .Manager
Shannon Riggs . . . . .Manager

KYLE FRITZ MANAGEMENT
6325 Heather Dr.
Los Angeles, CA 90068
PHONE 323-461-5800
FAX 323-461-5808
EMAIL . . . . .kyle@kylefritz.com
WEB SITE . . . . .www.kylefritz.com
TYPES   Commercial Talent - Film/TV Talent
REPRESENTS   Actors - Teens/Young Adults - Voice-Over
                     Artists
SUBMISSION POLICY   Industry referral only

Kyle Fritz . . . . .President
Bryan Raber . . . . .Associate
Veronica Romero . . . . .Executive Assistant

THE FTL COMPANY
c/o Franklin Lett
1910 Bel Air Rd.
Los Angeles, CA 90077
PHONE 310-472-1923
FAX 310-476-5043
EMAIL . . . . .franklin@theftl.com
WEB SITE . . . . .www.theftl.com
TYPES   Commercial Talent - Film/TV Talent -
                     Literary Talent - Music Talent - Theatre
                     Talent
REPRESENTS   Actors - Book Authors - Composers - Music
                     Artists - Music Producers - Musical Theatre
                     Performers - Playwrights - Producers -
                     Variety Artists
COMMENTS   Animators

Franklin T. Lett . . . . .President
Frank T. Lett III . . . . .Director

FUEL FILMWORKS
416 Entrada Dr.
Santa Monica, CA 90402
PHONE 310-459-7800
FAX 310-459-5068
TYPES   Film/TV Talent - Literary Talent
REPRESENTS   Directors - Screenwriters - TV Writers

Cory Concoff . . . . .Manager
George Sifuentes . . . . .Jr. Manager

FULL CIRCLE MANAGEMENT
8949 Sunset Blvd., Ste. 203
West Hollywood, CA 90069
PHONE 310-289-1234
FAX 310-289-1110
TYPES   Film/TV Talent
REPRESENTS   Actors - Comedians - Hosts/MCs - Print
                     Models - Teens/Young Adults - Voice-Over
                     Artists
SUBMISSION POLICY   Air mail or email; No walk-ins

Jason M. Solomon . . . . .President/Owner (fcmgt@aol.com)
Marco Cuadros . . . . .Partner (mcfcm@aol.com)

BRIAN FUNNAGAN MANAGEMENT
7367 Hollywood Blvd., #104
Los Angeles, CA 90046
PHONE 323-876-7723
EMAIL . . . . .funnagan@sbcglobal.net
TYPES   Film/TV Talent
REPRESENTS   Actors - Comedians - Hosts/MCs -
                     Teens/Young Adults
COMMENTS   Attends showcases and workshops

Brian Funnagan . . . . .Manager/Producer
John Kiernan . . . . .Manager/Producer

ESTELLE FUSCO TALENT MANAGEMENT
72 Moriches Rd.
Lake Grove, NY 11755
PHONE 631-467-7574
FAX 631-585-2977
TYPES   Commercial Talent - Film/TV Talent -
                     Theatre Talent
REPRESENTS   Dancers - Infants - Print Models -
                     Teens/Young Adults
SUBMISSION POLICY   Pictures and resumés

Estelle Fusco . . . . .Manager

FUSE ENTERTAINMENT
1041 N. Formosa Ave., Formosa Bldg., Ste. 195
West Hollywood, CA 90046
PHONE 323-850-3873
FAX 323-850-3874
TYPES   Literary Talent
REPRESENTS   Directors - Screenwriters - TV Writers
SUBMISSION POLICY   No unsolicited submissions

Mikkel Bondesen . . . . .President/Manager
David Levine . . . . .Producer
Richard Demato . . . . .Manager
Alex Goldstone . . . . .Manager
Ben Tilden . . . . .Coordinator

LORITA GARCIA & ASSOCIATES MANAGEMENT & ENTERTAINMENT
8306 Wilshire Blvd., Ste. 941
Beverly Hills, CA 90211
PHONE 323-931-7633
FAX 323-933-1517
EMAIL . . . . .lorita_associates@sbcglobal.net
TYPES   Film/TV Talent
REPRESENTS   Actors - Comedians - Directors - Producers
                     - Teens/Young Adults - Variety Artists

Lorita James Garcia . . . . .President

GATEWAY MANAGEMENT PARTNERS
5225 Wilshire Blvd., Ste. 702
Los Angeles, CA 90036
PHONE 323-935-4141
FAX 323-935-4044
TYPES   Film/TV Talent
REPRESENTS   Actors
SUBMISSION POLICY   Not accepting submissions

Beth Colt . . . . .Manager
Amy Guenther . . . . .Manager
Emily Aaronson . . . . .Associate
Andrea Turner . . . . .Assistant

GEF ENTERTAINMENT
122 North Clark Dr., Ste. 401
West Hollywood, CA 90048
PHONE 310-888-1800
TYPES   Film/TV Talent
REPRESENTS   Actors

Geordie Frey . . . . .Manager
Sean Goodman . . . . .Assistant to Geordie Frey

MANAGERS

GEM ENTERTAINMENT GROUP, INC.
10701 Wilshire Blvd., Ste. 1202
Los Angeles, CA 90024
PHONE 310-475-4559
FAX 310-446-8465
EMAIL . . . . .info@gementertainmentgroup.com
WEB SITE . . . . .www.gementertainmentgroup.com
TYPES   Commercial Talent - Film/TV Talent -
                        Literary Talent - Modeling Talent - Theatre
                        Talent
REPRESENTS   Actors - Children - Comedians - Directors -
                        Print Models - Sports Personalities -
                        Teens/Young Adults - Variety Artists - Voice-
                        Over Artists
SUBMISSION POLICY   Via US Mail, Attention: New Talent

Gregg Edwards . . . . .President
Glenn V. Hughes III . . . . .Manager
Adam T. West . . . . .Manager

GENERATE
1545 26th St., 2nd Fl.
Santa Monica, CA 90404
PHONE 310-255-0460
FAX 310-255-0461
EMAIL . . . . .info@generatela.com
WEB SITE . . . . .www.generatela.com
TYPES   Film/TV Talent - Literary Talent - Theatre
                        Talent
REPRESENTS   Actors - Comedians - Directors -
                        Hosts/MCs - Screenwriters - Teens/Young
                        Adults - TV Writers

Jordan Levin . . . . .Partner
Kara Welker . . . . .Partner
Dave Rath . . . . .Partner
Mike Karz . . . . .Partner
Pete Aronson . . . . .Partner
Jared Hoffman . . . . .Partner
Andy Corren . . . . .Manager
Josh Weinstock . . . . .Creative Executive, Film
Terra Hoster . . . . .Management
Cori Monger . . . . .Management
Josh Goldenberg . . . . .Film
Ivana Ma . . . . .TV

M.M. GERTZ ENTERTAINMENT
3940 Laurel Canyon Blvd., Ste. 222
Studio City, CA 91604
PHONE 310-497-7212
FAX 310-656-5758
EMAIL . . . . .bam411@juno.com
TYPES   Below-the-Line Talent - Literary Talent
AFFILIATIONS   TMA
REPRESENTS   Book Authors - Screenwriters - TV Writers
SUBMISSION POLICY   Via email or US Mail
COMMENTS   ATAS

Angela S. Wells . . . . .Partner
Mathius Mack Gertz . . . . .Manager/Producer

GHETTOSUBURBIA ENTERTAINMENT
4335 Van Nuys Blvd., Ste. 116
Sherman Oaks, CA 91423
PHONE 818-774-9772
EMAIL . . . . .ghettosuburbia@yahoo.com
WEB SITE . . . . .www.ghettosuburbiaentertainment.com
TYPES   Literary Talent
REPRESENTS   Book Authors - Directors - Playwrights -
                        Screenwriters - TV Writers
SUBMISSION POLICY   See Web site; Queries via email or US
                        Mail; No phone calls; By referral only

A. Rahman Yoba . . . . .Owner/Manager/Producer/Writer
Mark B. Williams . . . . .Manager/Producer/Director/Writer (NY)
                                         (914-562-5613)

PETER GIAGNI MANAGEMENT, INC.
3835-R E. Thousand Oaks Blvd.
Westlake Village, CA 91362
PHONE 805-493-2404
FAX 805-492-9470
EMAIL . . . . .pgmgmt1@aol.com
TYPES   Film/TV Talent - Literary Talent
REPRESENTS   Actors - Directors - Screenwriters - TV
                        Writers

Peter Giagni . . . . .President
Joan Giagni . . . . .VP/Secretary

GILBERTSON-KINCAID
1334 Third St. Promenade, Ste. 201
Santa Monica, CA 90401
PHONE 310-393-8585
FAX 310-393-7085
EMAIL . . . . .gkmngmnt@aol.com
TYPES   Film/TV Talent
REPRESENTS   Actors

Gordon Gilbertson . . . . .Partner
Jo An Kincaid . . . . .Partner
Ron Del Rio . . . . .Jr. Manager

JEFF GITLIN ENTERTAINMENT
1925 Century Park East, Ste. 620
Los Angeles, CA 90067
PHONE 310-553-0951
FAX 310-553-0953
TYPES   Film/TV Talent
REPRESENTS   Actors - Comedians

Jeff Gitlin . . . . .Manager

PHILLIP B. GITTELMAN PERSONAL MANAGEMENT
1221 N. Kings Rd., PH 405
West Hollywood, CA 90069
PHONE 323-656-9215
FAX 323-656-9184
EMAIL . . . . .phildinner@adelphia.net
TYPES   Below-the-Line Talent - Commercial Talent
                        - Film/TV Talent - Literary Talent - Modeling
                        Talent - Theatre Talent
REPRESENTS   Actors - Directors - Producers
SUBMISSION POLICY   By recommendation only

Phillip B. Gittelman . . . . .Sole Owner/Operator

GLASSER BLACK MANAGEMENT
283 Cedarhurst Ave.
Cedarhurst, NY 11516
PHONE 212-947-3228/718-369-7334
FAX 516-569-9033/718-369-7335
EMAIL . . . . .gbmgrs@aol.com
SECOND EMAIL . . . . .ccbmgr@aol.com
TYPES   Film/TV Talent - Theatre Talent
REPRESENTS   Actors

Marilyn Glasser . . . . .Partner
Claudia Black . . . . .Partner

GLOBAL ENTERTAINMENT
5833 Willis Ave.
Sherman Oaks, CA 91411
PHONE 818-779-7613
FAX 818-997-1823
EMAIL . . . . .sherylabrams@sbcglobal.net
TYPES   Commercial Talent - Film/TV Talent
REPRESENTS   Actors - Children - Teens/Young Adults
SUBMISSION POLICY   Accepts submissions from actors of all ages

Sheryl Abrams . . . . .President

MARIANNE GOLAN MANAGEMENT
6528 W. 6th St.
Los Angeles, CA 90048
PHONE 323-653-1232
FAX 323-653-2326
TYPES   Film/TV Talent - Theatre Talent
REPRESENTS   Actors - Teens/Young Adults
COMMENTS   ATAS

Marianne Golan . . . . .Owner/Manager
Stefani Blumberg . . . . .Assistant

GOLD COAST MANAGEMENT
1023-1/2 Abbot Kinney Blvd.
Venice, CA 90291
PHONE 310-396-2222
FAX 310-396-1313
TYPES   Film/TV Talent
REPRESENTS   Actors

Rick Ax . . . . .Manager

DODIE GOLD MANAGEMENT, INC.
9165 Alcott St., Ste. 202
Los Angeles, CA 90035
PHONE 310-278-8585
TYPES   Film/TV Talent - Literary Talent - Theatre
                         Talent
REPRESENTS   Directors - Playwrights - Screenwriters - TV
                         Writers
SUBMISSION POLICY   No unsolicited submissions

Dodie Gold . . . . .Owner/Manager

JEFF GOLDBERG MANAGEMENT
817 Monte Leon Dr.
Beverly Hills, CA 90210
PHONE 310-271-0538
FAX 310-271-0542
EMAIL . . . . .jeffgoldbergmanagement@yahoo.com
TYPES   Commercial Talent - Literary Talent -
                         Theatre Talent
REPRESENTS   Actors - Screenwriters

Jeff Goldberg . . . . .Manager/Producer

PETER GOLDEN & ASSOCIATES, INC.
15739 Mulholland Pl.
Los Angeles, CA 90049
PHONE 818-907-9566
FAX 818-907-9567
EMAIL . . . . .broadlawn@aol.com
TYPES   Film/TV Talent - Literary Talent
REPRESENTS   Actors - Comedians - Directors -
                         Screenwriters - TV Writers
SUBMISSION POLICY   No unsolicited submissions

Peter Golden . . . . .Owner

GOLDSTAR TALENT MANAGEMENT
850 Seventh Ave., Ste. 904
New York, NY 10019
PHONE 212-315-4429
FAX 212-315-4574
TYPES   Commercial Talent - Film/TV Talent -
                         Theatre Talent
AFFILIATIONS   NCOPM
REPRESENTS   Actors - Children - Teens/Young Adults -
                         Voice-Over Artists

Sid Gold . . . . .Manager

GOLDSTEIN COMPANY, INC.
1218 N. Wetherly Dr.
Los Angeles, CA 90069
PHONE 310-285-0565
FAX 310-285-0084
TYPES   Literary Talent
REPRESENTS   Directors - Producers - Screenwriters - TV
                         Writers

Jerry Goldstein . . . . .President

THE GOTHAM GROUP, INC.
9255 Sunset Blvd., Ste. 515
Los Angeles, CA 90069
PHONE 310-285-0001
FAX 310-285-0077
TYPES   Film/TV Talent - Literary Talent
REPRESENTS   Book Authors - Directors - Producers -
                         Screenwriters - TV Writers
SUBMISSION POLICY   No unsolicited material
COMMENTS   Also represents illustrators, publishing hous-
                         es, animators and animation studios

Ellen Goldsmith-Vein . . . . .President/CEO/Manager/Producer
Julie Kane-Ritsch . . . . .Partner/Manager/Producer
Lindsay Williams . . . . .Manager/Producer
Peter McHugh . . . . .Manager/Producer
Michael Prevett . . . . .Manager/Producer
Eddie Gamarra . . . . .Manager
Ronak Kordestani . . . . .Manager
Troy Underwood . . . . .Manager
Mike Bracken . . . . .Business Affairs
Julie Nelson . . . . .Accounting
Dmitri M. Johnson . . . . .Management Trainee
Chad Steers . . . . .Management Trainee
Timothy I. Stevenson . . . . .Management Trainee
Carrie Van Hoy . . . . .Accounting
Jen Gordon . . . . .Assistant to Julie Kane-Ritsch

GRADE A ENTERTAINMENT
149 S. Barrington Ave., Ste. 719
Los Angeles, CA 90049-3310
PHONE 310-358-8600
FAX 310-919-2998
EMAIL . . . . .development@gradeaent.com
TYPES   Literary Talent
REPRESENTS   Book Authors - Directors - Screenwriters -
                         TV Writers
SUBMISSION POLICY   Queries via email only

Andy Cohen . . . . .Manager/Producer

GRAND VIEW MANAGEMENT
578 Washington Blvd., #688
Marina del Rey, CA 90292
PHONE 310-396-2500
TYPES   Film/TV Talent
REPRESENTS   Actors
SUBMISSION POLICY   By referral only

Kate Edwards . . . . .Owner/Manager

GRANT MANAGEMENT
1158 26th St., #414
Santa Monica, CA 90403
PHONE 310-586-1166
REPRESENTS   Actors

Michelle Grant . . . . .Manager

MANAGERS

GRAUP ENTERTAINMENT
3888 Willow Royal Woods Dr.
Sherman Oaks, CA 91403
PHONE 310-553-2635
EMAIL . . . . .jgraup@graupentertainment.com
TYPES   Literary Talent
REPRESENTS   Cinematographers - Directors - Producers -
                 Screenwriters - TV Writers

Jeff Graup . . . . .Owner
David Wygant . . . . .Manager

SUSAN GRAW AND ASSOCIATES
334 S. Bentley Ave., 1st Fl.
Los Angeles, CA 90049
PHONE 310-471-1681
FAX 310-472-0525
EMAIL . . . . .sgrawassoc@aol.com
SECOND EMAIL . . . . .sgassocqueries@gmail.com
TYPES   Film/TV Talent - Literary Talent
REPRESENTS   Actors - Book Authors - Directors -
                 Playwrights - Producers - Screenwriters -
                 Sports Personalities - TV Writers - Variety
                 Artists
SUBMISSION POLICY Send query letter with SASE for return of lit-
                   erary submissions

Susan Graw . . . . .Owner/President/Manager
Robert Milford . . . . .Manager
Anna B. Hausen . . . . .Executive Assistant
MC Tyler . . . . .Intern

GRAY FOX FILMS, LLC
205 S. Beverly Dr., Ste. 212
Beverly Hills, CA 90212
PHONE 323-650-1270
FAX 310-858-5858
EMAIL .grayfoxfilms@cs.com
WEB SITE . . . . .www.grayfoxfilms.com
TYPES   Literary Talent
REPRESENTS   Screenwriters
SUBMISSION POLICY Email query letter with a short paragraph
                   and script logline; No unsolicited scripts
COMMENTS   Seeking packaged screenplays

Stephen Gray . . . . .President
David Chandler .VP, Creative
Rob Seeley .Creative Director

GREEN KEY MANAGEMENT, LLC
251 W. 89th St., Ste. 4A
New York, NY 10024
PHONE 212-874-7373/310-751-3144
EMAIL . . . . .greenkeym@aol.com
WEB SITE . . . . .www.greenkeymanagement.com
TYPES   Commercial Talent - Film/TV Talent -
                 Modeling Talent - Music Talent - Theatre
                 Talent
AFFILIATIONS   NCOPM
REPRESENTS   Actors - Broadcast Journalists/Newscasters
                 - Comedians - Composers - Music Artists -
                 Print Models - Runway Models -
                 Teens/Young Adults
SUBMISSION POLICY Mail only with SASE; Send video tape only
                   upon request with SASE

Seth R. Greenky . . . . .Manager
Susan Chia . . . . .Office Manager
Boni Mollins . . . . .Associate
Nicole Valentin . . . . .Associate

JOAN GREEN MANAGEMENT
1836 Courtney Terrace
Los Angeles, CA 90046
PHONE 323-878-0484
FAX 323-878-0292
EMAIL .joangreen@pacbell.net
TYPES   Film/TV Talent
REPRESENTS   Actors - Teens/Young Adults

Joan Green . . . . .President

JULIET GREEN MANAGEMENT
9025 Wilshire Blvd., Ste. 400
Beverly Hills, CA 90211
PHONE 310-277-9090
FAX 310-385-8347
TYPES   Film/TV Talent - Literary Talent
REPRESENTS   Actors - Screenwriters - TV Writers

Juliet Green . . . . .Owner
Bill Hinkle . . . . .Assistant

MELANIE GREENE MANAGEMENT
425 N. Robertson Blvd.
Los Angeles, CA 90048
PHONE 310-858-3200
FAX 310-858-8999
TYPES   Film/TV Talent
REPRESENTS   Actors

Melanie Greene . . . . .President
Tammy Rosen . . . . .Manager
Kesha Williams . . . . .Manager
Peter McGrath . . . . .Manager
Shannon McGinnity . . . . .Jr. Manager/Assistant
Eric Deskin . . . . .Assistant
Claudia Guevara .Assistant
Danny Mancini . . . . .Assistant
Daenya McDonald . . . . .Assistant
Frank Perez . . . . .Assistant

GREENSPAN ARTIST MANAGEMENT
8748 Holloway Dr., 2nd Fl.
Los Angeles, CA 90069
PHONE 310-289-3990
FAX 310-289-8007
EMAIL .mail@greenartman.com
WEB SITE . . . . .www.greenartman.com
TYPES   Music Talent
REPRESENTS   Composers - Music Editors - Music
                 Supervisors

Anita Greenspan .President
Neil Kohan . . . . .No Title
Stacey Kelsey . . . . .No Title

GREY LINE ENTERTAINMENT, INC.
115 W. California Blvd., Ste. 310
Pasadena, CA 91105
PHONE 626-943-0950
FAX 626-943-0992
EMAIL . . . . .submissions@greyline.net
SECOND EMAIL . . . . .info@greyline.net
WEB SITE . . . . .www.greyline.net
TYPES   Literary Talent
REPRESENTS   Book Authors - Screenwriters - TV Writers
SUBMISSION POLICY   Via email; See Web site for
                         additional information

G.H. Lui . . . . .President/CEO
James Bass . . . . .VP, Development
Matthew Powers . . . . .VP, Production
Patty Anctil . . . . .Executive Director, Development
Sophie Maier . . . . .Executive Director, Sales
Colin Wright .Sales Executive
Sara Miller . . . . .Submissions Coordinator
Graham Martin . . . . .Office Coordinator
Miranda Davies . . . . .Development Executive
Serena Adams . . . . .Manager
Brent Caulfield . . . . .Manager
Adam Frye . . . . .Manager
Eric Sanders . . . . .Manager (New York)
Rick Carlisle . . . . .Manager (New York)
Carrie Long . . . . .Manager (New York)
Stewart Adams . . . . .Development Associate (Chicago)
Beth Campbell . . . . .Development Associate (London)
Alison Cheney . . . . .Development Associate (Seattle)
Thomas Foster . . . . .Development Associate (New York)
Shea Langner . . . . .Development Associate (St. Louis)
Sean O'Neil . . . . .Development Associate (Boston)
Isaak Pierce . . . . .Development Associate (Miami)
Lindsey Ryan . . . . .Development Associate (New York)
Jakob Walsh . . . . .Development Associate (Toronto)
Michael Yocum . . . . . . .Development Associate (Washington, D.C.)
Mark Kern . . . . .Editor
Reed Marconi . . . . .Editor
Stephanie Dunbar . . . . .Editor (New York)
A.J. Spencer . . . . .Editor (New York)
Naomi Holstein . . . . .Executive Assistant
Toby Panfill . . . . .Development Assistant
Paige Smith . . . . .Assistant
Rob Mathews . . . . .Intern

BRAD GROSS INC., LITERARY MANAGEMENT
6715 Hollywood Blvd., Ste. 236
Los Angeles, CA 90028
PHONE 323-461-7100
TYPES   Literary Talent
AFFILIATIONS   DGA
REPRESENTS   Directors - Screenwriters
SUBMISSION POLICY   No unsolicited material; Referral only

Brad Gross .Manager/Owner
Matt Mahler . . . . .Assistant to Brad Gross

KEN GROSS MANAGEMENT
7720 Sunset Blvd., 2nd Fl.
Los Angeles, CA 90046
PHONE 323-512-2999
FAX 323-512-2699
EMAIL . . . . .kgmla@pacbell.net
TYPES   Commercial Talent - Literary Talent
REPRESENTS   Directors - Producers - Screenwriters - TV
                         Writers
COMMENTS   Also produces

Ken Gross . . . . .President/Producer/Manager
Daryl DePollo .VP, Development

GSC MANAGEMENT
1905 N. Beverly Dr.
Beverly Hills, CA 90210-1612
PHONE 310-274-1694
TYPES   Film/TV Talent
REPRESENTS   Actors

Geraldine S. Chuchian . . . . .Manager

G.T.A., INC.
9461 Charleville Blvd., Ste. 600
Beverly Hills, CA 90212
PHONE 310-204-4412
FAX 310-471-9946
TYPES   Film/TV Talent - Music Talent
REPRESENTS   Actors - Music Artists

Jim Golden . . . . .President

SHEREE GUITAR ENTERTAINMENT
528 Palisades Dr., Ste. 133
Pacific Palisades, CA 90272
PHONE 310-454-2380
EMAIL . . . . .sheree@shereeguitarent.com
WEB SITE . . . . .www.shereeguitarent.com
TYPES   Literary Talent
REPRESENTS   Screenwriters - TV Writers
SUBMISSION POLICY   No unsolicited submissions accepted

Sheree Guitar . . . . .Literary Manager/Producer
Stephen Buehler . . . . .Reader

GUY WALKS INTO A BAR MANAGEMENT
7421 Beverly Blvd., Ste. 4
Los Angeles, CA 90036
PHONE 323-930-9935
FAX 323-930-9934
EMAIL . . . . .info@guywalks.com
WEB SITE . . . . .www.guywalks.com
TYPES   Literary Talent
REPRESENTS   Directors - Screenwriters - TV Writers
COMMENTS   Also produces

Jon Berg . . . . .Manager
Matthew Weinberg . . . . .Head, Literary Management
Ross Siegel . . . . .Director, Development
Adam Friedberg . . . . .Assistant

H2F ENTERTAINMENT
9000 Sunset Blvd., Ste. 710
West Hollywood, CA 90069
PHONE 310-275-3750
FAX 310-275-3770
TYPES   Film/TV Talent - Literary Talent
REPRESENTS   Actors - Directors - Screenwriters - TV
                         Writers

Chris Fenton . . . . .Partner
Walter Hamada . . . . .Partner
Elbert Av . . . . .No Title
Ed Corrado . . . . .No Title
Jason Hendrixson . . . . .No Title

HALPERN MANAGEMENT
10524 W. Pico St., #207
Los Angeles, CA 90064
PHONE 310-837-5566
TYPES   Film/TV Talent
REPRESENTS   Actors - Comedians - Teens/Young Adults

Joanne H. Halpern . . . . .Owner
Christopher Sherman . . . . .Theatrical

HANDPRINT ENTERTAINMENT
1100 Glendon Ave., Ste. 1000
Los Angeles, CA 90024
PHONE 310-481-4400
FAX 310-481-4419
TYPES   Film/TV Talent - Literary Talent - Music
                  Talent - Theatre Talent
REPRESENTS   Actors - Comedians - Directors -
                  Hosts/MCs - Music Artists - Producers - TV
                  Writers - Voice-Over Artists

Benny Medina . . . . .Partner
Jeff Pollack . . . . .Partner
Evan Weiss . . . . .Head, TV/Talent & Literary Manager
Michael Baum . . . . .Talent Manager
Steven Greener . . . . .Talent Manager
Jill Littman . . . . .Talent Manager
Jean Kwolek .Jr. Talent Manager
Melissa Ruderman . . . . .Jr. Music Manager

PETER HANKWITZ PRODUCTION & MANAGEMENT, INC.
14110 Riverside Dr.
Sherman Oaks, CA 91423
PHONE 818-943-2283
FAX 818-337-7444
EMAIL . . . . .info@hankwitz.com
TYPES   Literary Talent
REPRESENTS   Producers
SUBMISSION POLICY Does not accept unsolicited submissions
COMMENTS   Reps Digital Ranch Productions, Josh
                  Hancock (joshCAR), Fred Bronson & Greg
                  Evans ('Luann')

Peter Hankwitz . . . . .President/Executive Producer/Manager
Hali Simon . . . . .Head, Corporate Communications
Tom Taglang . . . . .Head, Business Development

TODD HARRIS MANAGEMENT, INC.
9229 Sunset Blvd., Ste. 405
West Hollywood, CA 90069
PHONE 310-276-7884
FAX 310-276-7894
EMAIL . . . . .th@toddharrisent.com
TYPES   Literary Talent
REPRESENTS   Directors - Producers - Screenwriters
SUBMISSION POLICY No submissions accepted

Todd Harris . . . . .President

HART ENTERTAINMENT
831 Oradell Ave.
Oradell, NJ 07649
PHONE 201-970-5402
FAX 201-221-7901
EMAIL . . . . .hartentertain@aol.com
TYPES   Literary Talent
REPRESENTS   Book Authors - Children - Dancers -
                  Teens/Young Adults

Barbara Hart . . . . .Manager

SCOTT HART ENTERTAINMENT
14622 Ventura Blvd., #746
Sherman Oaks, CA 91403
PHONE 818-906-0750
EMAIL . . . . .scotthart@aol.com
TYPES   Film/TV Talent - Literary Talent - Music
                  Talent
REPRESENTS   Actors - Directors - Music Artists
SUBMISSION POLICY No unsolicited material

Scott Hart . . . . .Manager
Michael Smith . . . . .Assistant

HART LITERARY MANAGEMENT
5686 Antelope Trail
Orcutt, CA 93455-6066
PHONE 805-937-3342
EMAIL . . . . .hartliterary@verizon.net
SUBMISSION POLICY Email queries only; Currently not accepting
                  new clients
COMMENTS   Feature length screenplays only, with com-
                  plete and original characters;
                  Autobiographical or rights-acquired true
                  stories only

Susan Hart . . . . .Owner

HART² MANAGEMENT
9255 Sunset Blvd., Ste. 600
Los Angeles, CA 90069
PHONE 310-385-0905
FAX 310-385-0908
EMAIL . . . . .rhart@hartmgmt.com
TYPES   Commercial Talent - Film/TV Talent - Music
                  Talent - Theatre Talent
AFFILIATIONS   TMA
REPRESENTS   Actors - Book Authors - Comedians - Music
                  Artists - Musical Theatre Performers -
                  Speakers/Lecturers - Teens/Young Adults -
                  Voice-Over Artists

Ronni Lynn Hart . . . . .President
Alex Evangelist . . . . .Assistant

HARVEST TALENT MANAGEMENT
132 W. 80th St., Ste. 3F
New York, NY 10024
PHONE 212-721-5756
WEB SITE .www.harvesttalent.com
TYPES   Commercial Talent - Film/TV Talent
REPRESENTS   Children - Teens/Young Adults
COMMENTS   Talent ages six to twenty-five years old only

Donnalyn Carfi . . . . .Owner

HAZEN TALENT MANAGEMENT
3500 W. Olive, Ste. 300
Burbank, CA 91505
PHONE 818-558-4072
EMAIL . . . . .hazentalent@pacbell.net
WEB SITE . . . . .www.hazentalent.biz
TYPES   Commercial Talent - Film/TV Talent -
                      Literary Talent - Modeling Talent
AFFILIATIONS   TMA
REPRESENTS   Actors - Children - Voice-Over Artists

Nan Hazen . . . . .Owner/Manager
Melinda Bassett . . . . .Owner/Manager

HEADLINE MEDIA MANAGEMENT
888 Seventh Ave., Ste. 503
New York, NY 10106
PHONE 212-728-2010
FAX 212-765-9760
EMAIL . . . . .info@headlinemedia.tv
WEB SITE . . . . .www.headlinemedia.tv
TYPES   Commercial Talent - Film/TV Talent
REPRESENTS   Broadcast Journalists/Newscasters -
                      Producers - Sports Personalities

Lou Oppenheim . . . . .CEO
Michael Glantz . . . . .President
Carol Leff . . . . .Executive VP
Janet Pawson . . . . .Executive VP
Brian Jacobs . . . . .Talent Manager
Jay Rosenstein . . . . .VP, Programming
Michelle Hall . . . . .Client Liaison
Shone Jemmott . . . . .Executive Assistant
Andrew Labovitz . . . . .Executive Assistant
Elsie Borras . . . . .Client Accounts

HEITMANN ENTERTAINMENT
1231 Fifth St., Ste. 403
Santa Monica, CA 90401
PHONE 310-699-0520
TYPES   Film/TV Talent - Literary Talent
REPRESENTS   Actors - Directors - Martial Artists/Stunts -
                      Screenwriters - TV Writers
COMMENTS   Also produces

Tarik Heitmann . . . . .Manager/Producer
Sherilyn Baird . . . . .Assistant

HERBOSCH MANAGEMENT
1035 Park Ave.
New York, NY 10028
PHONE 212-534-6558
FAX 212-534-5944
TYPES   Film/TV Talent - Theatre Talent
AFFILIATIONS   NCOPM
REPRESENTS   Actors
SUBMISSION POLICY   By mail only; No phone calls

Jano Herbosch .Manager/Owner

JOSSELYNE HERMAN & ASSOCIATES
345 E. 56th St., Ste. 3B
New York, NY 10022
PHONE 212-355-3033
FAX 212-937-5270
EMAIL . . . . .info@jhamanagement.com
WEB SITE . . . . .www.jhamanagement.com
TYPES   Commercial Talent - Film/TV Talent -
                      Modeling Talent - Music Talent - Theatre
                      Talent
AFFILIATIONS   NCOPM
REPRESENTS   Actors - Hosts/MCs - Music Artists -
                      Screenwriters - TV Writers

Josselyne Herman-Saccio . . . . .Owner/Personal Manager
David Rhee . . . . .Associate Manager
Gina Rodriguez .Associate Manager
Marie Strinden .Associate Manager

HIMBER ENTERTAINMENT, INC.
211 S. Beverly Dr., Ste. 208
Beverly Hills, CA 90212
PHONE 310-276-2500
FAX 310-276-2538
TYPES   Film/TV Talent - Theatre Talent
REPRESENTS   Actors - Directors

Steve Himber . . . . .Owner/Manager
Tracy Quinn . . . . .Manager

HINES & HUNT ENTERTAINMENT
1213 West Magnolia Blvd.
Burbank, CA 91506
PHONE 818-557-7516
FAX 818-557-7690
TYPES   Film/TV Talent - Literary Talent
REPRESENTS   Actors - Children - Hosts/MCs -
                      Teens/Young Adults - TV Writers

Terrance Hines . . . . .Manager
Charles Fulcher . . . . .No Title
Marsha Roth . . . . .No Title

HOFFLUND/POLONE
9465 Wilshire Blvd., Ste. 420
Beverly Hills, CA 90212
PHONE 310-859-1971
FAX 310-859-7250
EMAIL . . . . .lbasst@hofflundpolone.com
TYPES   Film/TV Talent - Literary Talent
REPRESENTS   Actors - Directors - Screenwriters
SUBMISSION POLICY   No unsolicited material

Judy Hofflund . . . . .Personal Manager/Producer
Gavin Polone . . . . .Personal Manager/Producer
Laura Berwick . . . . .Manager
Becca Kovacik . . . . .Manager
Robert Koslowsky . . . . .Assistant to Becca Kovacik
Gillian Singletary . . . . .Assistant to Judy Hofflund

CARY HOFFMAN MANAGEMENT
236 W. 78th St.
New York, NY 10024
PHONE 212-873-4840
FAX 212-721-2306
EMAIL . . . . .cshm99@aol.com
TYPES   Film/TV Talent - Literary Talent
REPRESENTS   Actors - Comedians - Hosts/MCs -
                         Playwrights - Screenwriters - TV Writers -
                         Voice-Over Artists
SUBMISSION POLICY   No unsolicited material

Cary Hoffman . . . . .President
Stefanie Petersen . . . . .VP, Talent

HOLDER MANAGEMENT
8322 Beverly Blvd., 3rd Fl.
Los Angeles, CA 90048
PHONE 323-651-0889
FAX 323-782-0111
EMAIL . . . . .markasst@holdermanagement.com
SECOND EMAIL . . . . .christineasst@holdermanagement.com
TYPES   Film/TV Talent - Literary Talent - Theatre
                         Talent
REPRESENTS   Actors - Directors - Producers -
                         Screenwriters - TV Writers

Mark Holder . . . . .Partner
Christine Holder . . . . .Partner

HOLLYWOOD MANAGEMENT COMPANY
8275 Fountain Ave., Ste. 1
West Hollywood, CA 90046
PHONE 310-999-4747
FAX 323-656-2766
EMAIL .jake@hollywoodmanager.biz
TYPES   Commercial Talent - Film/TV Talent
AFFILIATIONS   TMA
REPRESENTS   Actors - Comedians - Teens/Young Adults
SUBMISSION POLICY   Accepts submissions (pictures, resumé and
                         tapes with SASE) via US mail or email from
                         actors fifteen to twenty-six years old, as well
                         as actors relocating to Los Angeles; No
                         calls or visits
COMMENTS   TMA Board of Directors; Member, National
                         Association of Artists' Managers (NAAM)

Jake Azhar . . . . .Manager

HOLZMAN MANAGEMENT GROUP
6255 Sunset Blvd., Ste. 2212
Los Angeles, CA 90028
PHONE 323-467-0402
FAX 323-461-1823
TYPES   Literary Talent
REPRESENTS   Book Authors - Directors - Producers -
                         Screenwriters - Sports Personalities - TV
                         Writers
COMMENTS   Also handles brand integration, represent-
                         ing over 100 brands

Tamara Holzman . . . . .Owner/Producer/Manager

HOOK ENTERTAINMENT
26033 Mulholland Hwy.
Malibu, CA 91302
PHONE 818-871-9696
FAX 603-297-8731
EMAIL .hookent@earthlink.net
TYPES   Film/TV Talent - Modeling Talent - Music
                         Talent
AFFILIATIONS   AFM
REPRESENTS   Composers - Directors - Music Artists -
                         Music Producers - Music Supervisors - Print
                         Models - Runway Models - Screenwriters -
                         Teens/Young Adults
COMMENTS   Also affiliated with NARAS, BMI and NMPA

Jake Hooker . . . . .President
Deborah Richards . . . . .VP

HOPSCOTCH PICTURES
616 N. Robertson Blvd., Ste. B
Los Angeles, CA 90069
PHONE 310-358-0630
FAX 310-358-0631
EMAIL . . . . .asst@hopscotchpictures.com
TYPES   Literary Talent
REPRESENTS   Directors - Screenwriters
SUBMISSION POLICY   No email queries
COMMENTS   PGA

Sukee Chew . . . . .Manager/Producer
Jeff Holland . . . . .Manager
Cassandra Ehrenberg . . . . .Assistant

JOANNE HOROWITZ MANAGEMENT
9350 Wilshire Blvd., Ste. 224
Beverly Hills, CA 90212
PHONE 310-271-0719
FAX 310-271-2625
EMAIL . . . . .jhoro79301@aol.com
TYPES   Film/TV Talent
REPRESENTS   Actors
SUBMISSION POLICY   By referral only

Joanne Horowitz . . . . .President
Gunder Kehoe . . . . .Executive Assistant

HOWARD ENTERTAINMENT
10850 Wilshire Blvd., Ste. 1260
Los Angeles, CA 90024
PHONE 310-441-2701
FAX 310-441-2705
TYPES   Commercial Talent - Film/TV Talent -
                         Literary Talent - Modeling Talent - Theatre
                         Talent
REPRESENTS   Actors - Children - Comedians - Directors -
                         Producers - Screenwriters - Teens/Young
                         Adults - TV Writers
SUBMISSION POLICY   Industry referral only

Scott Howard .Manager/Principal
Eileen Stringer . . . . .Manager
Elana Dvorak . . . . .Assistant to Scott Howard

HOWELL MANAGEMENT
PO Box 2540
Merrifield, VA 22116
PHONE 703-560-1405
FAX 703-560-1406
EMAIL . . . . .info@howellmanagement.com
WEB SITE . . . . .www.howellmanagement.com
TYPES   Modeling Talent
REPRESENTS   Print Models - Runway Models

Darlene Howell . . . . .President

HYLER MANAGEMENT
20 Ocean Park Blvd., Ste. 25
Santa Monica, CA 90405
PHONE 310-264-8148/310-396-7811
FAX 310-264-8147
TYPES   Film/TV Talent - Theatre Talent
REPRESENTS   Actors
SUBMISSION POLICY   Referral only

Joan Hyler . . . . .President
Jessica Roberts . . . . .Associate
Michelle Spalter . . . . .Associate

ICM ARTISTS
Artists Acquisition, LLC
825 Eighth Ave., 26th Fl.
New York, NY 10019
PHONE 212-556-6891/212-556-5642
FAX 212-556-5677
WEB SITE . . . . .www.icmartists.com
TYPES   Dance Talent - Music Talent - Special
                         Attractions - Theatre Talent
REPRESENTS   Composers - Dancers - Music Artists -
                         Narrators - Stage Directors - Theatre
                         Companies - Variety Artists
SUBMISSION POLICY   No unsolicited material
COMMENTS   Classical, special attractions, dance, jazz,
                         world music

David V. Foster . . . . .CEO/President
Byron Gustafson . . . . .Executive VP/Managing Partner
Robert Brewer . . . . .CFO
Jenny Vogel . . . . .Executive VP/Manager, Artists & Conductors (LA)
                         (310-550-4477)
Laura Hong . . . . . .Manager, Artists & Conductors (LA) (310-550-4477)
Patricia A. Winter . . . . .Sr. VP/National Booking Director/
                         Manager, Artists & Attractions
Neil Benson . . . . .VP/National Booking Director/Manager,
                         Artists & Attractions
Seth Malasky . . . . .Associate National Booking Director
Elaine Lipcan . . . . .Booking Representative
Christina Baker . . . . .Booking Representative
Robert Berretta . . . . .Booking Representative
Andrea Johnson . . . . .Booking Representative
Caroline Woodfield . . . . .VP/Manager, Artists
Leonard Stein . . . . .VP/Director, Tour Administration
Mary Pat Buerkle . . . . .VP/Manager, Artists & Attractions
Earl Blackburn . . . . .VP/Manager, Artists & Attractions
Risë Kern . . . . .VP/Manager, Artists & Attractions
Jason Bagdade . . . . .VP/Manager, Artists & Conductors
Paul C. Bongiorno . . . . .VP/Manager, Artists & Attractions
Rachel Bowron . . . . .VP/Manager, Artists & Conductors (London)
                         (44-207-432-0800)
Jonathan Brill . . . . .VP/Manager, Artists & Conductors
Nicole Borrelli Hearn . . . . .Manager, Artists & Attractions/
                         Booking Representative
William Bowler . . . . .Associate Manager, Artists & Attractions
Danielle Bias . . . . .Publicity Manager
Deborah-Rose Andrews . . . . .Associate, Program & Travel/
                         Associate Manager, Chamber Music
James Barry . . . . .Associate, Program & Travel
Scott DeLello . . . . .Associate, Program & Travel
John Gilliand . . . . .Associate, Program & Travel
Liesl Kundert . . . . .Associate
Richard Corrado . . . . .Consultant
Stewart Warkow . . . . .Consultant
Caroline Cuss . . . . .Consultant (London) (44-207-432-0800)

ILLUMINATI ENTERTAINMENT
11901 Santa Monica Blvd., Ste. 494
Los Angeles, CA 90025
PHONE 310-820-5613
FAX 310-826-0465
WEB SITE . . . . .www.illuminatientertainment.com
TYPES   Below-the-Line Talent - Literary Talent
REPRESENTS   Book Authors - Interactive Game
                         Developers - Production Designers -
                         Screenwriters - TV Writers
COMMENTS   Specializes in clients with backgrounds in
                         video games and comic books

Ford Lytle Gilmore . . . . .President

IMG MODELS
304 Park Avenue South, 12th Fl.
New York, NY 10010
PHONE 212-253-8884
FAX 212-253-8883
EMAIL . . . . .development-ny@imgworld.com
SECOND EMAIL . . . . .modelinfo@imgworld.com
WEB SITE . . . . .www.imgmodels.com
TYPES   Modeling Talent
REPRESENTS   Print Models - Runway Models

Chuck Bennett . . . . .President
Ivan Bart . . . . .Sr. VP

IMPACT ARTISTS GROUP, LLC
244 N. California St., 1st Fl.
Burbank, CA 91505
PHONE 818-753-4040
FAX 818-753-4080
EMAIL . . . . .iag@sbcglobal.net
TYPES   Commercial Talent - Film/TV Talent -
                         Literary Talent
REPRESENTS   Actors - Directors - Hosts/MCs - Print
                         Models - Producers - Screenwriters -
                         Teens/Young Adults - TV Writers - Variety
                         Artists - Voice-Over Artists
SUBMISSION POLICY   Referral only

Peter Kluge . . . . .Manager/Partner
Coby Byerly . . . . .Associate
Tregg Nardecchia . . . . .Assistant

INCOGNITO MANAGEMENT
9440 Santa Monica Blvd., Ste. 302
Beverly Hills, CA 90210
PHONE 310-246-1500
FAX 310-246-0469
TYPES   Film/TV Talent - Literary Talent - Theatre
                         Talent
REPRESENTS   Actors - Directors - Playwrights -
                         Screenwriters - TV Writers
SUBMISSION POLICY   Referral only
COMMENTS   PGA

Lawrence Abramson . . . . .CEO
Andrew Howard . . . . .Manager
Brian Klinsport . . . . .Assistant

THE INDEPENDENT GROUP, LLC
8721 Sunset Blvd., Ste. 105
Los Angeles, CA 90069
PHONE 310-854-2300
FAX 310-854-2304
EMAIL . . . . .mail@indygroup.tv
WEB SITE . . . . .www.indygroup.tv
TYPES   Commercial Talent - Film/TV Talent -
                         Modeling Talent - Theatre Talent
REPRESENTS   Actors - Children - Hosts/MCs - Print
                         Models - Runway Models - Sports
                         Personalities - Voice-Over Artists
SUBMISSION POLICY   Mail only

Justin Evans . . . . .Manager/Partner
Steven Jensen . . . . .Manager/Producer/Partner

INDEPENDENT MOVEMENT ENTERTAINMENT
477 Madison Ave., Ste. 1200
New York, NY 10022
PHONE 212-981-4804/323-876-7995
FAX 212-308-3997
TYPES   Film/TV Talent - Literary Talent - Music
                         Talent
REPRESENTS   Actors - Comedians - Directors - Music
                         Artists
COMMENTS   West Coast office: 2700 Cahuenga Blvd.
                         East, Ste. 1401, Los Angeles, CA 90068

Jonathan Scott Shensa .No Title
Dave Lane . . . . .No Title
Max Bergur . . . . .No Title
Jon Sharp . . . . .No Title
Rob Gomez . . . . .No Title

INDUSTRY ENTERTAINMENT PARTNERS
955 S. Carrillo Dr., 3rd Fl.
Los Angeles, CA 90048
PHONE 323-954-9000
FAX 323-954-9009
TYPES   Film/TV Talent - Literary Talent
REPRESENTS   Actors - Directors - Producers -
                         Screenwriters - TV Writers

Keith Addis . . . . .Manager
Ben Browning . . . . .Production
John Baldasare . . . . .Manager
Eryn Brown . . . . .Manager
Sandra Chang . . . . .Manager
Andrew Deane . . . . .Manager
Dianne Fraser . . . . .Manager
Adam Goldworm . . . . .Manager
Helena Heyman .Manager, TV
Ira Liss . . . . .Manager
Brad Mendelsohn . . . . .Manager
Jess Rosenthal . . . . .Manager
Rosalie Swedlin . . . . .Manager

INFINITY MANAGEMENT INTERNATIONAL
7923 Hollywood Blvd.
Los Angeles, CA 90046
PHONE 323-436-2200
FAX 323-436-2201
EMAIL . . . . .infinitymgmt@juno.com
TYPES   Commercial Talent - Film/TV Talent -
                         Literary Talent - Modeling Talent - Theatre
                         Talent
AFFILIATIONS   TMA
REPRESENTS   Actors - Book Authors - Comedians -
                         Directors - Interactive Game Developers -
                         Music Artists - Playwrights - Print Models -
                         Producers - Screenwriters - TV Writers

Jon Karas . . . . .CEO
George Collins . . . . .Manager

CHERI INGRAM ENTERPRISES
256 S. Robertson Blvd., Ste. 6145
Beverly Hills, CA 90211
PHONE 310-274-8111
FAX 310-274-9333
EMAIL .cheri@cheriingram.com
WEB SITE .www.cheriingram.com
TYPES   Film/TV Talent - Music Talent - Theatre
                         Talent
REPRESENTS   Actors - Book Authors - Broadcast
                         Journalists/Newscasters - Hosts/MCs -
                         Music Artists - Screenwriters -
                         Speakers/Lecturers - Sports Personalities -
                         TV Writers - Voice-Over Artists
SUBMISSION POLICY   Established artists only
COMMENTS   Talent & Literary packaging; Specializes in
                         celebrities, media experts and public
                         speakers

Cheri Ingram .Owner/Manager
Wayne Beuhring . . . . .Director, Operations
Christine Duong . . . . .Associate Manager
Enrique Sapene . . . . .Associate Manager
David Doré . . . . .Director, Development
Martha Chaput . . . . .Production Manager

INSIGHT
1134 S. Cloverdale Ave.
Los Angeles, CA 90019
PHONE 323-932-9898
FAX 323-932-9899
EMAIL . . . . .ashibata@insightent.com
TYPES   Film/TV Talent - Modeling Talent
REPRESENTS   Actors - Directors - Print Models -
                         Producers - Teens/Young Adults
SUBMISSION POLICY   Referral only

David Ginsberg . . . . .Manager/Producer
Matthew Lesher . . . . .Manager/Producer
Todd Sharp . . . . .Manager/Producer
Akiko Shibata . . . . .Assistant to David Ginsberg & Todd Sharp

INTEGRATED FILMS & MANAGEMENT
1154 N. Wetherly Dr.
Los Angeles, CA 90069
PHONE 310-247-9655
FAX 310-247-9855
TYPES   Film/TV Talent - Literary Talent
REPRESENTS   Actors - Directors - Screenwriters - TV
                         Writers
SUBMISSION POLICY   Mail only, include SASE

Andy Trapani .Manager/Producer
Andrew Collins . . . . .Creative Executive
Chris Winvick .Creative Executive

INTELLECTUAL PROPERTY GROUP
9200 Sunset Blvd., Ste. 820
Los Angeles, CA 90069
PHONE 310-402-5152
FAX 310-402-5153
EMAIL . . . . .info@ipglm.com
WEB SITE . . . . .www.ipglm.com
TYPES   Literary Talent
REPRESENTS   Book Authors - Screenwriters
COMMENTS   Books to film and TV

Joel Gotler . . . . .Manager
Laurence S. Becsey . . . . .Manager
Leslie Conliffe . . . . .Manager
Maria Ruvalcaba Hackett .Manager
Melinda Jason . . . . .Manager
Jerry Kalajian . . . . .Manager
Justin Manask . . . . .Manager
Joshua Schechter . . . . .Manager
Danielle Konrad . . . . .Assistant to Joel Gotler
Janie Sakura Guevara . . . . .Assistant to Laurence S. Becsey
Peter Carlson-Bancroft . . . . .Assistant to Justin Manask
Samuel Goldsmith . . . . .Assistant to Joshua Schechter

INTERLINK MANAGEMENT
19528 Ventura Blvd., #113
Tarzana, CA 91356
PHONE 818-776-8686
FAX 818-776-8668
TYPES   Film/TV Talent
REPRESENTS   Actors - Comedians - Teens/Young Adults

Tracy Macom-Samuels . . . . .Manager

JAMES/LEVY MANAGEMENT, INC.
3500 W. Olive Ave., Ste. 1470
Burbank, CA 91505
PHONE 818-955-7070
FAX 818-955-7073
TYPES   Film/TV Talent
REPRESENTS   Actors - Children - Teens/Young Adults

Randall C. James . . . . .Partner
Miles D. Levy . . . . .Partner
Stephanie Gabriel . . . . .Associate
Selena Schoups . . . . .Associate

JARET ENTERTAINMENT
6973 Birdview Ave.
Malibu, CA 90265
PHONE 310-589-9600
FAX 310-589-9602
EMAIL . . . . .info@jaretentertainment.com
WEB SITE . . . . .www.jaretentertainment.com
TYPES   Literary Talent
REPRESENTS   Book Authors - Directors - Screenwriters -
                     TV Writers

Seth Jaret . . . . .CEO/Manager

JAYMES-NELSON ENTERTAINMENT
12444 Ventura Blvd., Ste. 103
Studio City, CA 91604
PHONE 818-761-7832
FAX 818-761-0082
EMAIL . . . . .jaymesjne@yahoo.com
TYPES   Film/TV Talent - Literary Talent
REPRESENTS   Actors - Book Authors - Teens/Young Adults
SUBMISSION POLICY   Industry referrals only

Cathryn Jaymes . . . . .Partner/Literary Representative
Eric J. Nelson . . . . .Partner/Theatrical Representative
Craig Becker . . . . .Literary Associate

JUDYO PRODUCTIONS
6136 Glen Holly St.
Hollywood, CA 90068
PHONE 323-462-7411
FAX 323-462-7600
WEB SITE . . . . .www.judyoproductions.com
TYPES   Film/TV Talent - Literary Talent
REPRESENTS   Actors - Directors - Hosts/MCs - Producers
                     - Screenwriters - TV Writers
SUBMISSION POLICY   No unsolicited material

Judy Orbach . . . . .Owner/Manager/Producer

KANNER ENTERTAINMENT INC.
30 W. 74th St., PH 1
New York, NY 10023
PHONE 212-496-8175
FAX 212-496-0047
EMAIL . . . . .kannerent@gmail.com
TYPES   Commercial Talent - Film/TV Talent -
                     Literary Talent
REPRESENTS   Actors - Comedians - Directors -
                     Screenwriters - TV Writers

Cathy Kanner . . . . .Partner
Zoe Moore . . . . .Assistant
Aaron Anderson . . . . .No Title

DARLENE KAPLAN ENTERTAINMENT
4450 Balboa Ave.
Encino, CA 91316
PHONE 818-981-5114
FAX 818-981-9339
EMAIL . . . . .dkentertain@aol.com
TYPES   Film/TV Talent - Theatre Talent
REPRESENTS   Actors
SUBMISSION POLICY   Referral only

Darlene Kaplan . . . . .Manager

KAPLAN PRODUCTIONS
950 Redwood Shores Pkwy., Ste. J202
Redwood Shores, CA 94065
PHONE 650-591-5055
FAX 650-591-5049
EMAIL . . . . .kapprods@aol.com
TYPES   Commercial Talent - Film/TV Talent
REPRESENTS   Actors - Comedians - Hosts/MCs

Lori Kaplan . . . . .President/Manager

KAPLAN/PERRONE ENTERTAINMENT, LLC
10202 W. Washington Blvd., Astaire Bldg., Ste. 3024
Culver City, CA 90232
PHONE 310-244-6681
FAX 310-244-2151
WEB SITE . . . . .www.kaplanperrone.com
TYPES   Film/TV Talent - Literary Talent
REPRESENTS   Directors - Screenwriters

Aaron Kaplan . . . . .Manager
Sean Perrone . . . . .Manager
Justin Killion . . . . .Manager

KARMA ENTERTAINMENT
2649 N. Beachwood Dr., Ste. 6
Hollywood, CA 90068
PHONE 323-365-4624
FAX 323-375-1535
EMAIL . . . . .james@karma-ent.com
TYPES   Film/TV Talent - Literary Talent
REPRESENTS   Actors - Directors - Producers -
                              Screenwriters
SUBMISSION POLICY   Unsolicited queries via email only
COMMENTS   Partial Client List: Sheldon Brigman -
                              Pamela Corkey - Lorena David - Matt
                              Einolf - Mark Hosack - Judith Krant -
                              James Seda

James Choi . . . . .Principal

KASS & STOKES MANAGEMENT
9229 Sunset Blvd., Ste. 504
West Hollywood, CA 90069
PHONE 310-385-8500
FAX .310-385-8501/310-385-8508
TYPES   Film/TV Talent
REPRESENTS   Actors

Robbie Kass . . . . .Partner/Manager
Bradley Stokes .Partner/Manager
Roxanna Raanan . . . . .Manager

ANN KELLY MANAGEMENT
245 W. 51st St., Ste. 411
New York, NY 10019
PHONE 646-418-5418
FAX 212-522-0077
TYPES   Commercial Talent - Film/TV Talent -
                              Theatre Talent
REPRESENTS   Actors
SUBMISSION POLICY   By mail only

Ann Kelly . . . . .Owner/President

KERSEY MANAGEMENT
1409 N. Alta Vista Blvd., Ste. 304
Los Angeles, CA 90046
PHONE 323-850-8818
EMAIL .kerseymanagement@yahoo.com
TYPES   Literary Talent
REPRESENTS   Directors - Screenwriters - TV Writers

Andrew Kersey . . . . .Literary Manager

KEY CREATIVES, LLC
9595 Wilshire Blvd., Ste. 800
Beverly Hills, CA 90212
PHONE 310-273-3004
FAX 310-273-3006
TYPES   Film/TV Talent - Literary Talent
REPRESENTS   Actors - Directors - Producers -
                              Screenwriters - TV Writers

Ken Kamins . . . . .Chairman/CEO
Jonathan Weber . . . . .Assistant to Ken Kamins
Mark Yaloff . . . . .Controller

KINESIS ENTERTAINMENT, INC.
1230 Horn Ave., Ste. 632
West Hollywood, CA 90069
PHONE 310-237-1004
FAX 310-237-1005
EMAIL . . . . .submissions@kinesisent.com
TYPES   Film/TV Talent - Literary Talent
REPRESENTS   Directors - Producers - Screenwriters - TV
                              Writers

Sean Carr . . . . .Manager
Chayton Arvin . . . . .Producer

KINETIC MANAGEMENT
24033 Calvert St.
Woodland Hills, CA 91367
PHONE 818-348-0948
FAX 818-743-7505
EMAIL . . . . .dbaird@kinetic.ws
TYPES   Literary Talent
REPRESENTS   Directors - Screenwriters
SUBMISSION POLICY   Query by email

David Baird . . . . .Manager/Producer

KING MANAGEMENT
9229 Sunset Blvd., #830
Los Angeles, CA 90069
PHONE 310-205-2800
FAX 310-205-2820
EMAIL . . . . .info@mojomail.net
TYPES   Commercial Talent - Film/TV Talent -
                              Literary Talent - Music Talent
AFFILIATIONS   DGA
REPRESENTS   Actors - Book Authors - Comedians -
                              Directors - Music Artists - Screenwriters -
                              Sports Personalities - TV Writers - Variety
                              Artists
SUBMISSION POLICY   Accepts general submissions

Marcus King . . . . .Partner/Manager/Producer
Jaime Rucker King . . . . .Partner/Manager/Producer
Shannon Bell . . . . .Assistant
Wendy Calloway . . . . .Assistant
Irwin Lee . . . . .Assistant

KINGS HIGHWAY ENTERTAINMENT
14538 Benefit St., Ste. 103
Sherman Oaks, CA 91403
PHONE 818-981-2611
TYPES   Film/TV Talent - Literary Talent
AFFILIATIONS   DGA
REPRESENTS   Actors - Directors - Screenwriters - TV
                              Writers
SUBMISSION POLICY   No unsolicited submissions
COMMENTS   Also affiliated with PGA

Barbara Price . . . . .Manager/Producer

KJAR & ASSOCIATES
10153-1/2 Riverside Dr., Ste. 255
Toluca Lake, CA 91602
PHONE 818-760-0321
TYPES   Commercial Talent - Film/TV Talent - Literary Talent
REPRESENTS   Actors - Children - Directors - Martial Artists/Stunts - Screenwriters - Teens/Young Adults - TV Writers
SUBMISSION POLICY   Mail only

Brandon Kjar . . . . .Adult/TV/Film/Equity/Literary
Maria Hanson . . . . .Literary
Ricki Lopez . . . . .Associate
Lynn Sager . . . . .Associate
Paula Singerman . . . . .Associate

DON KLEIN MANAGEMENT GROUP, INC.
8840 Wilshire Blvd., Ste. 207
Beverly Hills, CA 90211
PHONE 310-358-3240
FAX 310-358-3105
EMAIL . . . . .dylanshields@8840.net
TYPES   Film/TV Talent - Literary Talent
REPRESENTS   Directors - Producers - Screenwriters - TV Writers
SUBMISSION POLICY   Query letter only

Don Klein . . . . .President/Manager
Dylan Shields . . . . .Manager

KNIGHT LIGHT ENTERTAINMENT
PO Box 1437
Santa Monica, CA 90406
PHONE 310-476-3223
FAX 270-812-3606
EMAIL .knightlightent@aol.com
TYPES   Commercial Talent - Film/TV Talent - Modeling Talent - Music Talent
REPRESENTS   Actors - Children - Music Artists - Teens/Young Adults

Lori Noelker Knight . . . . .Owner/Manager
Mendy Edgerly . . . . .Associate

LLOYD KOLMER ENTERPRISES
65 W. 55th St.
New York, NY 10019
PHONE 212-582-4735
TYPES   Commercial Talent - Film/TV Talent
AFFILIATIONS   NCOPM
REPRESENTS   Actors
COMMENTS   Celebrity consultants to the advertising industry

Lloyd Kolmer . . . . .Manager

KOOPMAN MANAGEMENT
851 Oreo Pl.
Pacific Palisades, CA 90272
PHONE 310-573-7554
FAX 310-573-7595
EMAIL . . . . .theo@koopmanmgmt.com
TYPES   Film/TV Talent - Theatre Talent
AFFILIATIONS   AFM
REPRESENTS   Actors - Teens/Young Adults

Trice Koopman . . . . .Owner/Manager
Theo Asweriison . . . . .Manager

KRAGEN & COMPANY
14039 Aubrey Rd.
Beverly Hills, CA 90210
PHONE 310-854-4400
FAX 310-854-0238
WEB SITE . . . . .www.kenkragen.com
TYPES   Commercial Talent - Film/TV Talent - Music Talent
REPRESENTS   Actors - Book Authors - Children - Comedians - Hosts/MCs - Music Artists - Speakers/Lecturers - Variety Artists
SUBMISSION POLICY   No unsolicited material
COMMENTS   Partial client list: Smothers Brothers - Ronn Lucas - Suzanne Whang - Skip Ewing - Alisha Mullally - Liel - Collin Raye

Ken Kragen . . . . .President
Amanda Martin . . . . .Assistant to Ken Kragen

KRITZER LEVINE WILKINS ENTERTAINMENT
8840 Wilshire Blvd., Ste. 100
Beverly Hills, CA 90211
PHONE 310-358-3233
FAX 310-358-3139
TYPES   Film/TV Talent - Literary Talent - Theatre Talent
REPRESENTS   Actors - Children - Directors - Music Artists - Producers - Screenwriters - Teens/Young Adults - TV Writers

Erik Kritzer . . . . .Manager
Ben Levine . . . . .Manager
Brian Wilkins . . . . .Manager
Blake Bandy . . . . .Manager
Adam Griffin . . . . .Manager
David Katz . . . . .Assistant
Victoria Russell . . . . .Assistant
Nate Bryson . . . . .Assistant
Hunter Seidman . . . . .Assistant

BARRY KROST MANAGEMENT
9229 Sunset Blvd., Ste. 303
Los Angeles, CA 90069
PHONE 310-278-8161
FAX 310-278-8162
TYPES   Film/TV Talent - Literary Talent - Music Talent - Theatre Talent
REPRESENTS   Actors - Playwrights - Producers - Screenwriters - TV Writers

Barry Krost . . . . .Owner/Manager/Producer
John Sobanski . . . . .Head, Talent
Jean Renard . . . . .Head, Music
Sarah Baczewski . . . . .Assistant

VICTOR KRUGLOV & ASSOCIATES
7461 Beverly Blvd., Ste. 303
Los Angeles, CA 90036
PHONE 323-934-7007
EMAIL . . . . .vktalent@pacbell.net
TYPES   Commercial Talent - Film/TV Talent
REPRESENTS   Actors - Comedians - Dancers - Teens/Young Adults
COMMENTS   Represents established actors only; Non-union actors accepted for commercials

Victor Kruglov . . . . .Owner/Manager

MANAGERS

L.A. SAMMY PRODUCTIONS
4209 Burbank Blvd.
Burbank, CA 91505
PHONE 818-841-9100
FAX 818-841-4485
EMAIL . . . . .lasammy@hotmail.com
TYPES   Film/TV Talent - Music Talent
REPRESENTS   Composers - Music Producers - Producers
COMMENTS   Animated series

Samuel Oriti . . . . .Executive Producer/Manager
Don Oriolo . . . . .Executive Producer
Dana Fares . . . . .Development

LA ENTERTAINMENT
9420 Reseda Blvd., #838
Northridge, CA 91324
PHONE 818-774-1157
FAX 714-279-0053
EMAIL .livelys@sbcglobal.net
TYPES   Film/TV Talent
REPRESENTS   Children

Elain Lively . . . . .Manager

THE LANDERS GROUP
5414 Newcastle Ave., Ste. 25
Encino, CA 91316
PHONE 310-497-6054
EMAIL . . . . .roblandersgroup@aol.com
TYPES   Literary Talent - Theatre Talent
REPRESENTS   Screenwriters - TV Writers

Rob Landers . . . . .President/Manager
Niles Landers . . . . .VP
Greg Clayton . . . . .Executive Assistant

LANDIS-SIMON PRODUCTIONS & TALENT MANAGEMENT
3625 E. Thousand Oaks Blvd., #279
Thousand Oaks, CA 91362
PHONE 805-370-6387/310-281-0944
FAX 805-370-6358/310-281-0945
EMAIL .judylandis@adelphia.net
TYPES   Commercial Talent - Film/TV Talent -
                     Theatre Talent
AFFILIATIONS   TMA
REPRESENTS   Actors - Children - Musical Theatre
                     Performers - Teens/Young Adults
SUBMISSION POLICY   Include return address with submission
COMMENTS   Steven Simon's office: 8899 Beverly Blvd.,
                     Ste. 815, West Hollywood, CA 90048

Judy Landis . . . . .President/Owner
Steven Simon . . . . .President/Owner
Scott Davis . . . . .Assistant to Steven Simon

PAUL LANE ENTERTAINMENT
468 N. Camden Dr., Ste. 200
Beverly Hills, CA 90210
PHONE 310-860-7485
FAX 310-860-7400
EMAIL . . . . .info@paullane.tv
SECOND EMAIL . . . . .management@paullane.tv
TYPES   Commercial Talent - Literary Talent - Music
                     Talent
REPRESENTS   Actors - Directors - Music Artists -
                     Producers - Screenwriters

Paul Lane . . . . .Manager

LANE MANAGEMENT GROUP
13017 Woodbridge St.
Studio City, CA 91604
PHONE 818-990-6366
FAX 818-475-5000
EMAIL . . . . .lmg@lanemanagement.com
WEB SITE . . . . .www.lanemanagement.com
TYPES   Commercial Talent - Film/TV Talent -
                     Literary Talent
AFFILIATIONS   TMA
REPRESENTS   Actors - Directors - Screenwriters -
                     Teens/Young Adults
SUBMISSION POLICY   Send headshot, resumé and contact info
                     via US Mail or email

Sharon Lane . . . . .Manager
Mary Kincaid . . . . .Assistant

LANG TALENT
4605 Lankershim Blvd., Ste. 222
Universal City, CA 91602
PHONE 818-980-2900
FAX 818-980-2908
EMAIL . . . . .delang@langtalent.com
WEB SITE . . . . .www.langtalent.com
TYPES   Commercial Talent - Film/TV Talent -
                     Modeling Talent
REPRESENTS   Actors - Children - Infants - Print Models -
                     Seniors - Teens/Young Adults

De Lang King . . . . .Theatrical/Commercial
Bianca Avina . . . . .Commercial/Theatrical

THE LAUGH FACTORY MANAGEMENT
8001 Sunset Blvd.
Hollywood, CA 90046
PHONE 323-848-2800/323-656-1336
FAX 323-656-2563
EMAIL . . . . .management@laughfactory.com
WEB SITE .www.laughfactory.com
TYPES   Commercial Talent - Film/TV Talent -
                     Literary Talent - Theatre Talent
REPRESENTS   Actors - Children - Comedians -
                     Hosts/MCs - Screenwriters - Teens/Young
                     Adults - TV Writers - Variety Artists - Voice-
                     Over Artists
SUBMISSION POLICY   No unsolicited material

Jamie Masada . . . . .Founder & CEO
Elizabeth Flynn . . . . .VP, Business Development
James Harris . . . . .Creative Director
Micah Bleich .Director, New Media
Mika Hamada-Ano . . . . .Business Management

LAWRENCE INTERNATIONAL CORPORATION
8981 W. Sunset Blvd., Ste. 312
Los Angeles, CA 90069-1881
PHONE 310-246-1727
TYPES   Film/TV Talent - Music Talent - Theatre
                     Talent
REPRESENTS   Comedians - Hosts/MCs - Music Artists -
                     Variety Artists

Stan Lawrence . . . . .President/CEO
Tina Farris . . . . .Associate
Mike Flood . . . . .Associate

LAWSON ARTIST MANAGEMENT, LLC

8033 Sunset Blvd., #572
Los Angeles, CA 90046
PHONE 323-822-9108
FAX 323-822-9109
EMAIL . . . . .mikelawson@lawsonartistmanagement.com
WEB SITE . . . . .www.lawsonartistmanagement.com
TYPES   Commercial Talent - Film/TV Talent -
                        Modeling Talent - Music Talent - Theatre
                        Talent
AFFILIATIONS   TMA
REPRESENTS   Actors - Book Authors - Children -
                        Comedians - Composers - Dancers -
                        Directors - Hosts/MCs - Music Artists -
                        Music Producers - Producers - Screenwriters
                        - Teens/Young Adults - TV Writers - Variety
                        Artists - Voice-Over Artists
COMMENTS   Member of NARAS

Mike Lawson . . . . .CEO/Manager

LETNOM MANAGEMENT & PRODUCTIONS

423 W. 55th St., 2nd Fl.
New York, NY 10019
PHONE 212-830-0410, 212-830-0407/212-830-0349
FAX 212-262-4608
EMAIL . . . . .firstinitial_lastname@montelshow.com
TYPES   Below-the-Line Talent - Commercial Talent
                        - Film/TV Talent - Literary Talent - Modeling
                        Talent - Music Talent - Theatre Talent
REPRESENTS   Actors - Book Authors - Broadcast
                        Journalists/Newscasters - Children -
                        Comedians - Hosts/MCs - Music Artists -
                        Print Models - Producers -
                        Speakers/Lecturers - Teens/Young Adults -
                        TV Writers - Variety Artists - Voice-Over
                        Artists
COMMENTS   West Coast office: 13029A Victory Blvd.,
                        #371, North Hollywood, CA 91606

Montel Williams . . . . .Principal
Eric Hanson . . . . .Manager
Dan Cotoia . . . . .Manager
Nancy Goldman . . . . .Manager
Jen Roe . . . . .Manager (LA)

LEVERAGE MANAGEMENT

3030 Pennsylvania Ave.
Santa Monica, CA 90404
PHONE 310-526-0320
FAX 310-526-0321
TYPES   Film/TV Talent - Literary Talent
REPRESENTS   Actors - Book Authors - Directors -
                        Screenwriters

Michael Garnett . . . . .Manager
Stephen Levinson . . . . .Manager
Sarah Lum . . . . .Manager
Gina Marcheschi . . . . .Manager
Loch Powell . . . . .Manager
Leonard Torgan . . . . .Manager

LEVINE MANAGEMENT

9028 W. Sunset Blvd., PH 1
Los Angeles, CA 90069
PHONE 310-275-0875
FAX 310-275-1540
TYPES   Commercial Talent - Film/TV Talent -
                        Literary Talent - Theatre Talent
AFFILIATIONS   DGA
REPRESENTS   Actors - Directors - Producers -
                        Screenwriters - TV Writers

Michael Levine . . . . .President/Producer
Arnold Fram . . . . .CFO
Joanna Burish . . . . .Producer
Jance Dobrowsky . . . . .Assistant to Mr. Levine

LEVITON MANAGEMENT

1008 Indiana Ave.
Venice, CA 90291
PHONE 310-452-7400
FAX 310-452-2862
TYPES   Film/TV Talent - Literary Talent
AFFILIATIONS   NCOPM
REPRESENTS   Actors - Comedians - TV Writers

Abbe Leviton . . . . .Manager

LEVITY ENTERTAINMENT GROUP

6701 Center Drive West, Ste. 1111
Los Angeles, CA 90045
PHONE 310-417-4888
FAX 310-410-1543
WEB SITE . . . . .www.levityentertainmentgroup.com
TYPES   Film/TV Talent - Literary Talent
REPRESENTS   Actors - Comedians - Screenwriters - TV
                        Writers
COMMENTS   New Media

Robert Hartmann . . . . .Partner
Judi Brown-Marmel . . . . .Partner
Matt Schuler . . . . .Manager
Morgann Franson . . . . .Assistant
Michelle Weisbaum . . . . .Assistant

LIBERMAN ZERMAN MANAGEMENT

252 N. Larchmont Blvd., Ste. 200
Los Angeles, CA 90004
PHONE 323-464-0870
FAX 323-464-3750
TYPES   Film/TV Talent
REPRESENTS   Actors

Kay Liberman . . . . .Partner
Lenore Zerman . . . . .Partner
Geoffrey Ashley . . . . .Associate

THE LIBERTY COMPANY

Rural Route #3, Box D-13
Sundance, UT 84604
PHONE 801-226-2024
FAX 801-226-5590
TYPES   Film/TV Talent - Literary Talent
REPRESENTS   Actors - Book Authors - Directors -
                        Producers - Screenwriters

Glennis Liberty . . . . .Manager/Producer

MANAGERS

MYRNA LIEBERMAN MANAGEMENT

3001 Hollyridge Dr.
Hollywood, CA 90068
PHONE 323-463-8092
FAX 323-469-2510
TYPES   Commercial Talent - Film/TV Talent
AFFILIATIONS   TMA
REPRESENTS   Actors - Children - Teens/Young Adults
SUBMISSION POLICY   Currently accepting submissions from union and non-union actors; Children, teenagers, young adults, four to eighteen years old; Seeking character type kids and ethnic talent
COMMENTS   Newcomers welcome

Myrna Lieberman . . . . .Owner/Manager
Ashley Doss . . . . .Assistant

LIEBMAN ENTERTAINMENT

25 E. 21st St., PH
New York, NY 10010
PHONE 212-982-6666
FAX 212-982-2133
TYPES   Film/TV Talent - Literary Talent - Music Talent - Theatre Talent
REPRESENTS   Actors - Comedians - Directors - Playwrights - Screenwriters - TV Writers

Brian Liebman . . . . .Manager
Cory Richman . . . . .Manager
Rachel Klein . . . . .Assistant

LIFE MANAGEMENT

2435 Crestview Dr.
Los Angeles, CA 90046
PHONE 323-654-9772
TYPES   Film/TV Talent
REPRESENTS   Actors - Teens/Young Adults

Herb Karp . . . . .Manager

LIGHTHOUSE ENTERTAINMENT

409 N. Camden Dr., Ste. 202
Beverly Hills, CA 90210
PHONE 310-246-0499
FAX 310-246-0899
EMAIL . . . . .ssiebert@lighthousela.com
SECOND EMAIL .scott@lighthousela.com
TYPES   Film/TV Talent - Literary Talent
REPRESENTS   Actors - Directors - Screenwriters - Teens/Young Adults - TV Writers

Steven Siebert . . . . .Personal Manager/Producer
Scott Saccoccio . . . . .Assistant

LINK TALENT GROUP

4741 Laurel Canyon Blvd., Ste. 106
Valley Village, CA 91607
PHONE 818-508-0114
FAX 818-980-1637
EMAIL . . . . .kurtltg@sbcglobal.net
SECOND EMAIL .pauloltg@sbcglobal.net
WEB SITE .www.linktalentgroup.com
TYPES   Commercial Talent - Film/TV Talent - Literary Talent - Theatre Talent
REPRESENTS   Actors - Directors - Screenwriters - Teens/Young Adults
SUBMISSION POLICY   Accepting pictures and resumés
COMMENTS   Currently seeking Latino and African-American talent sixteen to twenty-three years old; Attends showcases

Paulo Andrés . . . . .Manager
Kurt Patino . . . . .Manager
Tricia Sherman . . . . .Assistant

LITTLE STARS MANAGEMENT

1874 S. Pacific Coast Hwy., Ste. 240
Redondo Beach, CA 90277
PHONE 310-326-0323
FAX 310-531-7428
EMAIL . . . . .littlestarsmgmt@gmail.com
WEB SITE .www.littlestarsmanagement.com
TYPES   Commercial Talent - Film/TV Talent - Modeling Talent - Music Talent - Theatre Talent
AFFILIATIONS   TMA
REPRESENTS   Actors - Children - Infants - Martial Artists/Stunts - Musical Theatre Performers - Print Models - Teens/Young Adults - Voice-Over Artists
SUBMISSION POLICY   Via US Mail or email only; No drop-offs
COMMENTS   Exclusively represents children, teens and young adults; Guides young talent and their parents in every aspect of the entertainment industry; Nurturing hands-on manager; Small select client list; Only works with top agencies

Annet McCroskey . . . . .Manager
Michelle Dulong . . . . .Assistant

LITTLE STUDIO FILMS
c/o Alexia Melocchi
9903 Santa Monica Blvd., Ste. 139
Beverly Hills, CA 90212
PHONE 310-552-4815/310-552-4842
EMAIL . . . . .management@littlestudiofilms.com
WEB SITE .www.littlestudiofilms.com
TYPES   Literary Talent
AFFILIATIONS   AFM
REPRESENTS   Book Authors - Directors - Producers - Screenwriters
SUBMISSION POLICY   Via email with no attachments or via US Mail with SASE
COMMENTS   Producers; Producer consultants in worldwide distribution; Represents three European media conglomerates; Affiliated with Sanger Talent Agency

Alexia Melocchi . . . . .President
Mary Ellen Morgan . . . . .CFO
Alexandra Yacovlef . . . . .Partner
Jonathan Edwards . . . . .Head, International Distribution
Andrew Ladd . . . . .Development Executive
Paul Almond . . . . .Business Affairs
Katerina Langford . . . . .Assistant to Alexia Melocchi

LLOYD ENTERTAINEMENT
9420 Wilshire Blvd., Ste. 250
Beverly Hills, CA 90212
PHONE 310-278-4800
FAX 310-278-4254
TYPES   Literary Talent
REPRESENTS   Screenwriters - TV Writers
COMMENTS   Affiliated with PGA

Lauren Lloyd .Producer/Literary Manager
Jessica Wiltgen .Manager/Creative Executive

LOLO ENTERTAINMENT CO.
12021 Wilshire Blvd., Ste. 365
Los Angeles, CA 90025-1200
PHONE 310-476-0476
TYPES   Commercial Talent - Film/TV Talent - Literary Talent - Music Talent
REPRESENTS   Actors - Comedians - Directors - Music Artists - New Media - Packaging - Producers - Screenwriters - Songwriters - TV Writers

LoEtte Loshak . . . . .Manager

JEFFREY LOSEFF MANAGEMENT
4521 Colfax Ave., Ste. 205
North Hollywood, CA 91602
PHONE 818-505-9468
FAX 818-505-9468
EMAIL . . . . .jclmgmt@aol.com
TYPES   Commercial Talent - Film/TV Talent - Modeling Talent - Theatre Talent
AFFILIATIONS   NCOPM
REPRESENTS   Actors - Comedians - Teens/Young Adults
SUBMISSION POLICY   Mail preferred to phone calls or drop-ins

Jeffrey Loseff . . . . .Owner/Manager

BONNIE LOVE MANAGEMENT
4924 Balboa Blvd., Ste. 307
Encino, CA 91316
PHONE 818-342-7100
TYPES   Film/TV Talent
REPRESENTS   Actors - Teens/Young Adults
SUBMISSION POLICY   Do not call or fax
COMMENTS   Recognizable names that need more action with their careers

Bonnie Love . . . . .Owner

LOVETT MANAGEMENT
1327 Brinkley Ave.
Los Angeles, CA 90049
PHONE 310-451-2536
FAX 310-451-0899
TYPES   Film/TV Talent - Literary Talent
REPRESENTS   Actors - Directors

Steve Lovett . . . . .President
Jason Kim . . . . .Associate

LUKEMAN LITERARY MANAGEMENT, LTD.
157 Bedford Ave.
Brooklyn, NY 11211
PHONE 718-599-8988
FAX 775-264-2189
EMAIL . . . . .noah@lukeman.com
WEB SITE . . . . .www.lukeman.com
TYPES   Literary Talent
REPRESENTS   Book Authors
SUBMISSION POLICY   No unsolicited queries

Noah Lukeman . . . . .President

LYMBEROPOULOS, INC.
PO Box 803205
Los Angeles, CA 91380
PHONE 661-297-8000
TYPES   Commercial Talent - Film/TV Talent
REPRESENTS   Actors - Broadcast Journalists/Newscasters - Children - Comedians - Hosts/MCs - Teens/Young Adults - Voice-Over Artists
SUBMISSION POLICY   Pictures, resumés and demos

Kathy Lymberopoulos .President/Manager

TAMI LYNN PRODUCTIONS
20411 Chapter Dr.
Woodland Hills, CA 91364
PHONE 818-888-8264
FAX 818-888-8267
EMAIL . . . . .tamilynn8264@aol.com
WEB SITE . . . . .www.givenachance.com/pages/tamibio.html
TYPES   Film/TV Talent - Literary Talent
REPRESENTS   Producers - Screenwriters
COMMENTS   AFTRA, SAG, WGA, WIF, PGA; Past President, COPM; Past Executive Director and Founder, NCOPM Western Division, Talent & Literary Packaging

Tami Lynn . . . . .Producer
Humaira Arsalan . . . . .Assistant to Ms. Lynn
Kassie Marriner . . . . .Assistant to Ms. Lynn

M MANAGEMENT
10 Universal City Plaza, Ste. 2000
Universal City, CA 91608
PHONE 818-753-2450
EMAIL ....kelly@mmanagement.net
TYPES   Film/TV Talent - Literary Talent - Music
                         Talent
REPRESENTS   Actors - Choreographers - Dancers -
                         Directors - Music Artists - Print Models -
                         Producers - Screenwriters - Teens/Young
                         Adults - TV Writers

Kelly McManis ....President/Manager
Brittany Mireles ....Manager
Kelli Rollins ....Assistant to Kelly McManis
Quinton Jonez ....Assistant to Brittany Mireles

MACK MUSE ENTERTAINMENT, INC.
1639 11th St., Ste. 170
Santa Monica, CA 90404
PHONE 310-450-1600
FAX 310-450-1613
WEB SITE ....www.mackmuse.com
TYPES   Commercial Talent - Film/TV Talent -
                         Literary Talent
AFFILIATIONS   TMA
REPRESENTS   Actors - Comedians - Directors - Producers
                         - Screenwriters - Teens/Young Adults - TV
                         Writers
SUBMISSION POLICY   Via US mail or email

Charlene Gorzela ....Co-President/Manager/Producer
Deborah Hildebrand ....Co-President/Producer/Manager
Karen Embry ....Manager/Producer
Trish Kane ....Manager

MACROMANAGEMENT
10795 Woodbine St., Ste. 212
Los Angeles, CA 90034
PHONE 310-559-7509
TYPES   Literary Talent
REPRESENTS   Book Authors - Directors - Screenwriters
SUBMISSION POLICY   Query letters and email limited to one
                         paragraph in length

David P. McInerney ....Literary Manager
Jameya Uhercik ....Literary Manager
Sheri Levy ....Literary Manager

MADHOUSE ENTERTAINMENT

MADHOUSE ENTERTAINMENT
8484 Wilshire Blvd., Ste. 640
Beverly Hills, CA 90211
PHONE 310-587-2200
FAX 323-782-0491
TYPES   Literary Talent
REPRESENTS   Directors - Screenwriters - TV Writers
SUBMISSION POLICY   Email queries to query@madhouseent.net;
                         Unsolicited material will be returned unread

Robyn Meisinger ....Partner/Manager/Producer
Adam Kolbrenner ....Partner/Manager/Producer
Chris Cook ....Associate Manager
Ryan Cunningham ....Story Editor

MAGENTA CREATIVE MANAGEMENT
9 N. Moore St.
New York, NY 10013
PHONE 212-226-7677
FAX 212-226-7699
WEB SITE ....www.magentamgt.com
TYPES   Commercial Talent - Film/TV Talent -
                         Modeling Talent - Theatre Talent
REPRESENTS   Actors - Directors - Hosts/MCs - Print
                         Models - Producers - Runway Models -
                         Screenwriters - TV Writers

Aaron Anderson ....CEO/Founder/Talent Manager
Alex Gradassi ....Talent Manager
Sim Lai ....Talent Manager

MAGNET MANAGEMENT
6380 Wilshire Blvd., Ste. 1606
Los Angeles, CA 90048
PHONE ....See Below
FAX 323-658-8636
EMAIL ....magnetasst@magnetmanagement.com
TYPES   Literary Talent
REPRESENTS   Directors - Screenwriters - TV Writers

Jennie Frankel ....Manager/Producer (323-658-8123)
Zach Tann ....Manager/Producer (323-658-8095)
Bob Sobhani ....Manager/Producer (323-658-8210)
Chris Mills ....Manager (323-658-8706)
Mitch Solomon ....Producer (323-456-0556)
Jane Lee ....Production Executive (323-852-1056)
Dan Hess ....Assistant (323-456-0275)

MAGNOLIA ENTERTAINMENT
9595 Wilshire Blvd., Ste. 601
Beverly Hills, CA 90212
PHONE 310-247-0450
FAX 310-247-0451
TYPES   Commercial Talent - Film/TV Talent -
                         Literary Talent
REPRESENTS   Actors - Directors - Teens/Young Adults -
                         TV Writers - Voice-Over Artists

Shelley Browning ....President/CEO/Talent & Literary Manager
Kimberlin Dalehite ....Talent Manager
Javier Contreras ....Talent & Literary Manager
Alissa Feldman ....Assistant

MAIER MANAGEMENT
9025 Wilshire Blvd., Ste. 450
Beverly Hills, CA 90211
PHONE 310-860-0099
FAX 310-860-0098
EMAIL ....maiermanagement@aol.com
WEB SITE ....www.maiermanagementgt.com
TYPES   Commercial Talent - Film/TV Talent -
                         Modeling Talent
AFFILIATIONS   TMA
REPRESENTS   Actors - Children - Hosts/MCs - Print
                         Models - Teens/Young Adults
SUBMISSION POLICY   Mail submissions: By referral only; Email
                         sumissions: Picture and resumé only; Prefer
                         actors with agents, but will develop new
                         clients

Ted Maier ....CEO/Head Manager
Tyler Madden ....Manager, Literary
Jacque Pederson ....Manager, Children

MAIN TITLE ENTERTAINMENT
5225 Wilshire Blvd., Ste. 500
Los Angeles, CA 90036
PHONE 323-964-9900
FAX 323-964-9901
TYPES   Film/TV Talent
REPRESENTS   Actors

Tracy Steinsapir . . . . .Partner
Stewart Strunk . . . . .Partner

MANAGEMENT 101
1680 North Vine St., Ste. 716
Hollywood, CA 90028
PHONE 323-467-0678
FAX 323-467-0689
TYPES   Commercial Talent - Film/TV Talent -
                         Literary Talent - Modeling Talent - Music
                         Talent - Theatre Talent
AFFILIATIONS   TMA
REPRESENTS   Actors - Book Authors - Children -
                         Comedians - Directors - Hosts/MCs -
                         Music Artists - Print Models - Producers -
                         Screenwriters - Teens/Young Adults - TV
                         Writers - Voice-Over Artists

Frederick Levy . . . . .Partner
Bryan Leder . . . . .Partner
Jay Johnson . . . . .Manager
Nelly Thompson . . . . .Assistant

MANAGEMENT 360
9111 Wilshire Blvd.
Beverly Hills, CA 90210
PHONE 310-272-7000
TYPES   Film/TV Talent - Literary Talent
REPRESENTS   Actors - Directors - Screenwriters
SUBMISSION POLICY   Industry referral

Suzan Bymel . . . . .Partner
Guymon Casady . . . . .Partner
Eric Kranzler . . . . .Partner
Evelyn O'Neill . . . . .Partner
Daniel Rappaport . . . . .Partner
David Seltzer . . . . .Partner
William Choi . . . . .Manager
Darin Friedman . . . . .Manager/Production Executive
Alex Hertzberg . . . . .Manager
Doug Johnson . . . . .Manager
Peter Kiernan . . . . .Manager
Nicole King . . . . .Manager
Christie Smith . . . . .Manager
Lainie Stolhanske . . . . .Manager
Ben Forkner .Production Executive

THE MANAGEMENT TEAM
9507 Santa Monica Blvd., Ste. 304
Beverly Hills, CA 90210
PHONE 310-276-7173
FAX 310-276-5811
TYPES   Commercial Talent - Film/TV Talent
REPRESENTS   Actors - Broadcast Journalists/Newscasters
                         - Sports Personalities

Laura Palmer . . . . .No Title
Don Edwards . . . . .No Title
Bill Shine . . . . .No Title

MANAGING ARTISTIC CONCEPTS
468 N. Camden Dr., Ste. 200
Beverly Hills, CA 90210
PHONE 310-860-5673
FAX 213-559-0647
EMAIL . . . . .tisdale@managingartisticconcepts.com
WEB SITE . . . . .www.managingartisticconcepts.com
TYPES   Below-the-Line Talent - Commercial Talent
                         - Film/TV Talent - Literary Talent - Modeling
                         Talent - Music Talent
REPRESENTS   Actors - Children - Directors - Music Artists
                         - Music Producers - Print Models -
                         Producers - Screenwriters - Teens/Young
                         Adults - TV Writers - Voice-Over Artists
SUBMISSION POLICY   Accepted in writing or by email only; No
                         phone calls; By referral only
COMMENTS   Also motion picture production

Robert Tisdale . . . . .President/CEO/Manager/Producer
Joe Jacobs . . . . .Partner/Manager/Producer
Tracy Moore . . . . .Associate Manager
Carl Tripician Esq. . . . . .Business Affairs/Consuting Producer
Jamie Slaughter . . . . .Assistant to Robert Tisdale

MANTA ENTERTAINMENT
10313 W. Jefferson Blvd.
Culver City, CA 90232
PHONE 310-839-9599
EMAIL . . . . .lou@mantaent.com
WEB SITE . . . . .www.mantaent.com
TYPES   Commercial Talent - Literary Talent - Music
                         Talent - Theatre Talent
REPRESENTS   Actors - Composers - Directors - Music
                         Artists - Music Producers - Print Models -
                         Screenwriters - Teens/Young Adults - TV
                         Writers - Variety Artists
COMMENTS   Also represents lyricists and songwriters

Lou Bond . . . . .President
Jerrold Thompson . . . . .Head, Music

MARATHON ENTERTAINMENT
8060 Melrose Ave., Ste. 400
Los Angeles, CA 90046
PHONE 323-852-1776
FAX 323-852-1777
EMAIL . . . . .ricks@marathonent.com
TYPES   Commercial Talent - Film/TV Talent -
                         Literary Talent
AFFILIATIONS   NCOPM
REPRESENTS   Actors - Broadcast Journalists/Newscasters
                         - Comedians - Directors - Hosts/MCs -
                         Producers - Screenwriters -
                         Speakers/Lecturers - TV Writers - Variety
                         Artists - Voice-Over Artists

Rick Siegel . . . . .Manager

THE MARCELLI COMPANY
11333 Moorpark, #411
Studio City, CA 91602
PHONE 818-662-8777
FAX 818-662-8899
EMAIL .rickmarcelli@aol.com
WEB SITE . . . . .www.marcellicompany.com
TYPES   Below-the-Line Talent - Film/TV Talent -
                       Modeling Talent
REPRESENTS   Actors - Book Authors - Children -
                       Choreographers - Comedians - Dancers -
                       Directors - Hosts/MCs - Magicians - Music
                       Artists - Print Models - Producers -
                       Screenwriters - Speakers/Lecturers - TV
                       Writers - Variety Artists
COMMENTS   Affiliated with ATAS and PGA

Rick Marcelli . . . . .Manager/Producer

MARKS MANAGEMENT
1030 Mission Ridge Rd.
Santa Barbara, CA 93103
PHONE 805-882-1116
FAX 805-882-9116
WEB SITE . . . . .www.marksmanagement.com
TYPES   Music Talent
REPRESENTS   Composers

Lawrence B. Marks . . . . .Owner

MARSALA MANAGEMENT
8324 Fountain Ave., Ste. B
Los Angeles, CA 90069
PHONE 323-650-3300
FAX 323-395-0903
TYPES   Film/TV Talent - Literary Talent - Theatre
                       Talent
REPRESENTS   Actors - Directors - Screenwriters -
                       Teens/Young Adults
SUBMISSION POLICY   Referrals only

Rob Marsala . . . . .President

MARSH ENTERTAINMENT
12444 Ventura Blvd., Ste. 203
Studio City, CA 91604
PHONE 818-509-1135
FAX 818-509-1137
TYPES   Film/TV Talent - Literary Talent
REPRESENTS   Actors - Directors - Screenwriters - TV
                       Writers

Sherry Marsh . . . . .Owner/Manager
Kim Olpin . . . . .Executive Assistant

THE MARSHAK/ZACHARY COMPANY
8840 Wilshire Blvd., 1st Fl.
Beverly Hills, CA 90211
PHONE 310-358-3191
FAX 310-358-3192
EMAIL . . . . .marshakzachary@aol.com
TYPES   Commercial Talent - Film/TV Talent -
                       Literary Talent - Theatre Talent
AFFILIATIONS   TMA
REPRESENTS   Actors - Comedians - Directors -
                       Playwrights - Producers - Screenwriters -
                       Teens/Young Adults - TV Writers
SUBMISSION POLICY   Referral only

Darryl Marshak . . . . .Manager/Producer/Partner
Susan Zachary . . . . .Manager/Producer/Partner
Mitch Clem . . . . .Manager
Alan Mills . . . . .Associate Manager

MARTIN LITERARY MANAGEMENT
17328 Ventura Blvd., Ste. 138
Encino, CA 91316
PHONE 818-595-1130
FAX 818-715-0418
EMAIL . . . . .sharlene@martinliterarymanagement.com
WEB SITE . . . . .www.martinliterarymanagement.com
TYPES   Literary Talent
REPRESENTS   Book Authors
SUBMISSION POLICY   Email queries preferred; No calls
COMMENTS   Represents first time and established
                       authors for nonfiction books only; No
                       screenplays; Affiliated with AAR

Sharlene Martin . . . . .Literary Manager

DAVID MARTIN MANAGEMENT
13849 Riverside Dr.
Sherman Oaks, CA 91423
PHONE 818-981-8686
FAX 818-981-0839
TYPES   Below-the-Line Talent - Commercial Talent
                       - Film/TV Talent - Music Talent - Theatre
                       Talent
AFFILIATIONS   NCOPM
REPRESENTS   Actors - Broadcast Journalists/Newscasters
                       - Comedians - Music Artists - Sports
                       Personalities - Variety Artists
SUBMISSION POLICY   Do not mail or fax resumé
COMMENTS   Established clients only

David Martin . . . . .President

MASSEI MANAGEMENT
PO Box 8178
New York, NY 10116-8178
PHONE 212-229-9767
FAX 212-627-2289/603-288-6589
EMAIL . . . . .artmassei@yahoo.com
TYPES   Commercial Talent - Film/TV Talent -
                       Theatre Talent
REPRESENTS   Actors - Teens/Young Adults

Arthur Massei . . . . .Owner

MAX FREEDMAN MANAGEMENT
11664 National Blvd., Ste. 316
Los Angeles, CA 90064
PHONE 310-429-9707
FAX 406-756-6648
EMAIL . . . . .max@mfmanage.com
WEB SITE . . . . .www.mfmanage.com
TYPES   Literary Talent
REPRESENTS   Directors - Screenwriters
SUBMISSION POLICY   Will read unproduced screenwriters' work;
                         Query letter by email only must be submit-
                         ted first; No attachments to email query
COMMENTS   Markets screenplays and finished films to
                         the industry; Offers script editing, coverage
                         and consulting services

Max Freedman . . . . .Principal/Manager/Executive Producer

DINO MAY MANAGEMENT
11262 Ventura Blvd.
Studio City, CA 91604
PHONE 818-752-3700
FAX 818-752-3701
EMAIL . . . . .dino@dinomaymanagement.com
WEB SITE . . . . .www.dinomaymanagement.com
TYPES   Commercial Talent - Film/TV Talent -
                         Modeling Talent - Music Talent
REPRESENTS   Actors - Children - Music Artists - Print
                         Models - Teens/Young Adults

Dino May . . . . .President/Manager
Harold Hafner . . . . .Manager

MBST ENTERTAINMENT
345 N. Maple Dr., Ste. 200
Beverly Hills, CA 90210
PHONE 310-385-1820
FAX 310-385-1834
TYPES   Film/TV Talent - Literary Talent - Music
                         Talent
REPRESENTS   Actors - Comedians - Directors - Music
                         Artists - Producers - Screenwriters - TV
                         Writers
SUBMISSION POLICY   Referral only

Larry Brezner . . . . .No Title
David Steinberg . . . . .No Title
Stephen Tenenbaum . . . . .No Title
Jonathan Brandstein . . . . .No Title
Meegan Kelso . . . . .No Title
Andrew D. Tenenbaum . . . . .No Title

MC TALENT
4821 Lankershim Blvd., Ste. F
North Hollywood, CA 91350
PHONE 818-487-8781
EMAIL . . . . .mctalentla@aol.com
TYPES   Commercial Talent - Film/TV Talent
REPRESENTS   Actors - Children - Print Models -
                         Teens/Young Adults
SUBMISSION POLICY   Accepted via email or US Mail only

Jamie Malone .Owner/Talent Manager
Judy Cosgrove .Owner/Talent Manager

MCGOWAN MANAGEMENT
8733 W. Sunset Blvd., Ste. 103
Los Angeles, CA 90069
PHONE 310-289-9157
FAX 310-289-0765
TYPES   Commercial Talent - Film/TV Talent -
                         Theatre Talent
REPRESENTS   Actors - Children - Voice-Over Artists

Bob McGowan . . . . .Manager
Steve Rodriguez . . . . .Manager

MCKEON-MYONES MANAGEMENT
9100 Wilshire Blvd., Ste. 350W
Beverly Hills, CA 90212
PHONE 310-288-5888
TYPES   Film/TV Talent - Literary Talent - Theatre
                         Talent
REPRESENTS   Actors - Directors - Screenwriters - TV
                         Writers
SUBMISSION POLICY   By referral only

Mary Ellen 'Mel' McKeon . . . . .Partner
Laura Myones . . . . .Partner
Robbie Stone . . . . .No Title

MCMURDO MANAGEMENT & ASSOCIATES, LLC
1274 N. Crescent Heights Blvd., #331
West Hollywood, CA 90046
PHONE 323-799-1655/323-799-1650
FAX 323-848-3073
EMAIL .mcmurdomgt@aol.com
WEB SITE . . . . .www.mcmurdomanagement.com
TYPES   Below-the-Line Talent - Commercial Talent
                         - Film/TV Talent - Literary Talent - Modeling
                         Talent - Music Talent - Theatre Talent
REPRESENTS   Actors - Book Authors - Children -
                         Comedians - Composers - Dancers -
                         Directors - Film Editors - Hosts/MCs -
                         Music Artists - Music Supervisors - Musical
                         Theatre Performers - Playwrights - Print
                         Models - Producers - Runway Models -
                         Screenwriters - Sound Editors -
                         Speakers/Lecturers - Teens/Young Adults -
                         TV Writers - Voice-Over Artists
SUBMISSION POLICY   By industry referral only

Thomas 'TJ' McMurdo . . . . .Personal Manager
Annette Robinson .Personal Manager

MEDIA FOUR
8840 Wilshire Blvd., 2nd Fl.
Beverly Hills, CA 90211
PHONE 310-358-3288
FAX 310-358-3188
EMAIL . . . . .media4ss@aol.com
TYPES   Commercial Talent - Film/TV Talent -
                         Literary Talent - Music Talent
REPRESENTS   Actors - Composers - Directors - Producers
                         - Screenwriters - Songwriters

Steve Sauer . . . . .President/CEO
Jane McKnight . . . . .Manager, Administration

MANAGERS

MEDIA TALENT GROUP
9200 Sunset Blvd., Ste. 550
West Hollywood, CA 90069
PHONE 310-275-7900
FAX 310-275-7910
TYPES   Film/TV Talent - Literary Talent
REPRESENTS   Actors - Directors - Screenwriters
SUBMISSION POLICY   Referral only
COMMENTS   Represents high-profile clients only

Geyer Kosinski . . . . .Chairman/CEO
Tucker Tooley . . . . .Producer
Chris Davey . . . . .Manager, Literary & Directors

MEG MANAGEMENT
15303 Ventura Blvd., Ste. 900
Sherman Oaks, CA 91403
PHONE 323-932-6500
FAX 323-932-6599
TYPES   Below-the-Line Talent - Film/TV Talent - Literary Talent - Modeling Talent - Music Talent
AFFILIATIONS   AFM
REPRESENTS   Actors - Comedians - Directors - Magicians - Music Artists - Music Producers - Producers - Screenwriters
SUBMISSION POLICY Always accepting submissions
COMMENTS   Currently seeking fresh talent under thirty years old, as well as very established artists; Small client base

Lawrence Miller . . . . .No Title

MICHAEL MELTZER & ASSOCIATES
12207 Riverside Dr., Ste. 208
Valley Village, CA 91607
PHONE 818-766-8339
FAX 818-766-5936
EMAIL . . . . .melmax@aol.com
TYPES   Commercial Talent - Film/TV Talent - Literary Talent
REPRESENTS   Actors - Directors - Screenwriters - Teens/Young Adults - TV Writers

Brian Berkenfeld . . . . .Manager/Partner
Michael L. Meltzer . . . . .Manager/Partner

MESSINA BAKER ENTERTAINMENT CORPORATION
955 Carrillo Dr., Ste. 100
Los Angeles, CA 90048
PHONE 323-954-8600
FAX 323-954-8111
WEB SITE .www.messinabaker.com
TYPES   Commercial Talent - Film/TV Talent - Literary Talent - Theatre Talent
REPRESENTS   Actors - Comedians - Directors - Hosts/MCs - Producers - Screenwriters - Teens/Young Adults - TV Writers - Voice-Over Artists

Rick Messina . . . . .No Title
Richard Baker . . . . .No Title
Travis Betz . . . . .No Title
Melanie Truhett-Posehn . . . . .No Title
Charlene Borja . . . . .Assistant to Melanie Truhett-Posehn
Jody Gluck .Assistant to Rick Messina
Cindy Rush . . . . .Assistant to Richard Baker

ELLEN MEYER MANAGEMENT
8899 Beverly Blvd., Ste. 612
Los Angeles, CA 90048
PHONE 310-385-8100
FAX 310-385-8108
TYPES   Film/TV Talent
REPRESENTS   Actors

Ellen Meyer . . . . .Owner/Manager
Tom Sullivan . . . . .Manager

MGA TALENT
1875 Century Park East, Ste. H-3600
Century City, CA 90067
PHONE 818-763-8400
EMAIL . . . . .rob@mgatalent.com
WEB SITE . . . . .www.mgatalent.com
TYPES   Commercial Talent - Film/TV Talent
AFFILIATIONS   TMA
SUBMISSION POLICY See submission guidelines on Web site

Robert Pafundi . . . . .Attorney/Business Development

MGC/CUSHMAN ENTERTAINMENT GROUP
10947 Bloomfield St., Ste. 209
Studio City, CA 91602
PHONE 818-980-6215
FAX 818-980-1803
EMAIL .mgc_ceg@juno.com
TYPES   Film/TV Talent
AFFILIATIONS   TMA
REPRESENTS   Actors - Teens/Young Adults
SUBMISSION POLICY Referral only; Talent should include tapes/DVDs with all submissions; Actors must be represented by an agent, be a member of SAG, and have strong co-star or guest star TV credits
COMMENTS   Past President, West Coast COPM

Micheal Cushman . . . . .President/Owner

MIDWEST TALENT MANAGEMENT, INC.
4821 Lankershim Blvd., Ste. F, PMB 149
North Hollywood, CA 91601
PHONE 818-765-3785
FAX 818-765-2903
EMAIL . . . . .talktous@midwesttalent.com
WEB SITE .www.midwesttalent.com
TYPES   Commercial Talent - Film/TV Talent - Literary Talent - Modeling Talent - Theatre Talent
AFFILIATIONS   TMA
REPRESENTS   Actors - Children - Comedians - Martial Artists/Stunts - Print Models - Teens/Young Adults - Voice-Over Artists
SUBMISSION POLICY Email submissions preferred
COMMENTS   TMA Benefits Committee

Betty McCormick Aggas . . . . .President
Mark Blake . . . . .Manager

PAMELA MIGAS MANAGEMENT (PMM)
1421 Ambassador St., Ste. 114
Los Angeles, CA 90035
PHONE 310-553-0033/310-877-0404
FAX 310-553-1952
EMAIL . . . . .pmminla@aol.com
TYPES   Commercial Talent - Film/TV Talent
REPRESENTS   Actors - Hosts/MCs

Pamela Migas . . . . .President/CEO
Vincent Sammarro . . . . .Partner

MILLENNIUM ENTERTAINMENT, INC.
9229 Sunset Blvd., Ste. 610
Los Angeles, CA 90069
PHONE 310-402-4243
EMAIL . . . . .info@ment.tv
SECOND EMAIL . . . . .submission@ment.tv
WEB SITE . . . . .www.ment.tv
TYPES   Commercial Talent - Film/TV Talent -
                         Literary Talent - Music Talent - Theatre
                         Talent
AFFILIATIONS   TMA
REPRESENTS   Actors - Comedians - Directors -
                         Hosts/MCs - Music Artists - Producers -
                         Screenwriters - TV Writers - Voice-Over
                         Artists
SUBMISSION POLICY   By email only

Dwight W. Holcomb . . . . .President
Gary Lane . . . . .CFO
Yana Zakharova . . . . .Legal Department
Sarah Gucker . . . . .Casting/Personal Appearances

MILLER AND COMPANY
9255 Sunset Blvd., Ste. 500
Los Angeles, CA 90069
PHONE 310-550-0826
FAX 310-724-8998
TYPES   Film/TV Talent
REPRESENTS   Actors

Deborah Miller . . . . .Owner/Manager
Gabe Lang . . . . .Associate

THE MILLER COMPANY
9200 Sunset Blvd., 10th Fl.
Los Angeles, CA 90069
PHONE 310-786-4900
FAX 310-777-2193
TYPES   Film/TV Talent - Literary Talent
REPRESENTS   Actors - Comedians - Directors -
                         Screenwriters - TV Writers
SUBMISSION POLICY   No unsolicited submissions

Jimmy Miller . . . . .Partner/Manager
Ilan Breil . . . . .Manager
Julie Darmody . . . . .Manager
John Elliott . . . . .Manager
Dave Fleming . . . . .Manager
Paul Nelson . . . . .Manager
Rebecca Lee . . . . .First Assistant to Jimmy Miller
Barbra Pakler . . . . .Second Assistant to Jimmy Miller
Doug Basalyga . . . . .Assistant to Ilan Breil
Shasta Cross . . . . .Assistant to John Elliott
Liz Gemmill . . . . .Assistant to Julie Darmody
Jorge Jazan . . . . .Assistant to Paul Nelson
Jana Marimpietri . . . . .Assistant to Dave Fleming

APRIL MILLS MANAGEMENT
PO Box 1983
Burbank, CA 91507
PHONE 818-667-9529
FAX 866-289-8614
EMAIL . . . . .info@aprilmillsmanagement.com
WEB SITE . . . . .www.aprilmillsmanagement.com
TYPES   Commercial Talent - Modeling Talent -
                         Theatre Talent
REPRESENTS   Actors - Children - Dancers - Print Models -
                         Teens/Young Adults - Voice-Over Artists

April Mills . . . . .Owner
Scout Michaels . . . . .Publicist

RM/M
Renée Missel Management

RENÉE MISSEL MANAGEMENT
15135 Sunset Blvd., Ste. 230
Pacific Palisades, CA 90272
PHONE 310-463-0638
FAX 805-669-4511
EMAIL . . . . .filmtao@aol.com
TYPES   Film/TV Talent - Theatre Talent
REPRESENTS   Actors - Directors

Renée Missel . . . . .Manager
Monyque Rose . . . . .Assistant

J. MITCHELL MANAGEMENT
70 W. 36th St., Ste. 1006
New York, NY 10018
PHONE 212-679-3550
WEB SITE . . . . .www.jmmtalent.com
TYPES   Commercial Talent - Film/TV Talent -
                         Theatre Talent
AFFILIATIONS   NCOPM
REPRESENTS   Actors - Book Authors - Children -
                         Teens/Young Adults - Voice-Over Artists
SUBMISSION POLICY   Kids, teens, and adults up to age twenty-
                         five can make appointment to meet online
                         at www.jmmtalent.com; Ages twenty-six and
                         older send photo and resumé by mail;
                         Include email on your submission

Jeff Mitchell . . . . .President
David Doan . . . . .Associate
Elise Koseff . . . . .Associate
Jessica Schoenholtz . . . . .Associate

MITERRE PRODUCTIONS, INC.
6221 Wilshire Blvd., Ste. 620
Los Angeles, CA 90048
PHONE 323-939-8156
FAX 323-965-0705
EMAIL . . . . .amazingsite@msn.com
WEB SITE . . . . .www.memorysite.com/miterre.htm
TYPES   Film/TV Talent - Literary Talent
AFFILIATIONS   AGVA
REPRESENTS   Book Authors - Comedians - Screenwriters
                         - Variety Artists
COMMENTS   Hypnotists, Mentalists, Kryptoman

Mike Teitelbaum . . . . .President
Helen Hopper . . . . .Talent

MANAGERS

MIXED MEDIA ENTERTAINMENT COMPANY
395 Totten Pond Rd., Ste. 301
Waltham, MA 02451
PHONE 800-597-1115/781-647-3400
FAX 781-547-0109/781-647-5574
EMAIL . . . . .showbizmanager@aol.com
TYPES   Film/TV Talent - Music Talent
AFFILIATIONS   NCOPM
REPRESENTS   Actors - Magicians - Music Artists - Variety
                         Artists
SUBMISSION POLICY   No unsolicited material

Michael Glynn . . . . .Manager

MMC ENTERTAINMENT/DANCE DIRECTIONS
PO Box 46544
Los Angeles, CA 90046
PHONE 818-769-6316
TYPES   Commercial Talent - Film/TV Talent -
                         Theatre Talent
REPRESENTS   Actors - Dancers - Musical Theatre
                         Performers - Teens/Young Adults
SUBMISSION POLICY   By referral only
COMMENTS   No children

Maureen Creigh . . . . .Owner/Manager

MODUS ENTERTAINMENT
110 S. Fairfax Ave., Ste. 250
Los Angeles, CA 90036
PHONE 323-930-6730
FAX 323-930-6736
TYPES   Film/TV Talent - Literary Talent
REPRESENTS   Actors - Broadcast Journalists/Newscasters
                         - Comedians - Directors - Screenwriters -
                         TV Writers

Lisa Blum . . . . .Manager/Producer
Coral Compagnoni . . . . .Executive Assistant/Coordinator

MOGUL MANAGEMENT
9190 W. Olympic Blvd., Ste. 210
Beverly Hills, CA 90212
PHONE 310-550-6001
FAX 310-943-3773
EMAIL . . . . .info@mogulmgmt.com
TYPES   Film/TV Talent
REPRESENTS   Actors

Armand Rabinowitz . . . . .Manager

MOMENTUM TALENT MANAGEMENT
13935 Burbank Blvd., Ste. 102
Valley Glen, CA 91401
PHONE 818-789-2033
FAX 818-789-2622
EMAIL . . . . .momentumtm@aol.com
TYPES   Film/TV Talent - Theatre Talent
REPRESENTS   Actors
SUBMISSION POLICY   Referral only

Lisa Evan Blumenthal . . . . .Owner/Manager

JAIME MONROY STUDIOS
280 S. Beverly Dr., Ste. 203
Beverly Hills, CA 90212
PHONE 310-273-6508
FAX 310-273-6728
EMAIL . . . . .info@jaimemonroystudios.com
WEB SITE .www.jaimemonroy.com
TYPES   Film/TV Talent - Modeling Talent
REPRESENTS   Actors - Print Models - Teens/Young Adults
SUBMISSION POLICY   Cover letter and headshot; Videotape upon
                         request
COMMENTS   Focus on comedic actresses; Established
                         stars, teen idols, model types with a flair for
                         comedy

Jaime Monroy . . . . .Manager/Producer
Kristen Aldridge . . . . .Host/Producer

MONSTER TALENT MANAGEMENT, INC.
5724 W. Third St., Ste. 308
Los Angeles, CA 90036
PHONE 323-965-9696
EMAIL .jgreene@monstertalentinc.com
SECOND EMAIL . . . . .bbundy@monstertalentinc.com
TYPES   Film/TV Talent
REPRESENTS   Actors - Children - Teens/Young Adults
SUBMISSION POLICY   Send photo and resumé

Robert Noll . . . . .President
Brooke Bundy . . . . .Manager
Jessie Greene . . . . .Manager
Cris Crouch . . . . .IT
Chanel Gold . . . . .Assistant

MOORE ARTISTS' MANAGEMENT
8840 Wilshire Blvd.
Beverly Hills, CA 90211
PHONE 310-578-6618
WEB SITE . . . . .www.mooreartists.com
TYPES   Commercial Talent - Film/TV Talent -
                         Literary Talent - Theatre Talent
REPRESENTS   Actors - Comedians - Directors -
                         Hosts/MCs - Producers - Screenwriters -
                         Teens/Young Adults - TV Writers - Voice-
                         Over Artists
COMMENTS   Select list of working and star actors; Select
                         list of produced writers and directors; TV
                         and film production; Packaging; Film
                         financing/funding

David B. Moore . . . . .President/CEO
Cindy Smith . . . . .Literary/Publicity
Becky McGimpsey . . . . .Head, Production/Finance

MP MANAGEMENT
18910 Mt. Castile
Fountain Valley, CA 92708
PHONE 714-965-6771
TYPES   Commercial Talent - Film/TV Talent -
                         Theatre Talent
REPRESENTS   Actors - Children - Infants - Print Models -
                         Teens/Young Adults - Voice-Over Artists
SUBMISSION POLICY   Referral only; Via US mail only with photo,
                         cover letter and resumé
COMMENTS   Full-service personal management compa-
                         ny representing children, teens and young
                         adults; Also runs Cassiopeia Theatre
                         Company, Inc.

Marlene Peroutka . . . . .President
Ce Ce Cline . . . . .VP

MSI ENTERTAINMENT, INC.
9229 Sunset Blvd., Ste. 710
Los Angeles, CA 90069
PHONE 310-300-2900
FAX 310-300-2901
TYPES   Literary Talent
REPRESENTS   Directors - Screenwriters
COMMENTS   East Coast office: 237 W. 35th St., 4th Fl.,
                         New York, NY 10001

Joel Goldstein . . . . .President

MULTI-ETHNIC TALENT
415 E. 52nd St., #6DA
New York, NY 10021
PHONE 917-689-8459
TYPES   Commercial Talent - Film/TV Talent
AFFILIATIONS   NCOPM
REPRESENTS   Actors
SUBMISSION POLICY   Referrals only
COMMENTS   Specializes in ethnic talent

Annette E. Alvarez JD . . . . .Manager
Joan C. Silverman Esq. . . . . .Manager
Todd Zeller . . . . .Manager (LA)

DEE MURA ENTERPRISES, INC.
269 W. Shore Dr.
Massapequa, NY 11758
PHONE 516-795-1616
FAX 516-795-8797
EMAIL . . . . .deemura@ix.netcom.com
TYPES   Commercial Talent - Film/TV Talent -
                         Literary Talent - Modeling Talent - Music
                         Talent - Theatre Talent
AFFILIATIONS   NCOPM
REPRESENTS   Actors - Book Authors - Broadcast
                         Journalists/Newscasters - Children -
                         Comedians - Directors - Hosts/MCs -
                         Magicians - Music Artists - Playwrights -
                         Print Models - Producers - Screenwriters -
                         Speakers/Lecturers - Sports Personalities -
                         Teens/Young Adults - TV Writers - Variety
                         Artists - Voice-Over Artists

Dee Mura . . . . .Manager
Frank Nakamura . . . . .Manager
Karen Roberts . . . . .Manager
Roberta Sokol . . . . .Manager

THE MURAVIOV COMPANY
1976 Suntree Ln., Ste. A
Simi Valley, CA 93063
PHONE 805-306-0835/818-425-5165
FAX 866-831-3136
EMAIL . . . . .themuraviovco@aol.com
TYPES   Literary Talent
REPRESENTS   Screenwriters

Kathy Muraviov . . . . .Manager

MUSIC WORLD ENTERTAINMENT
1505 Hadley St.
Houston, TX 77002
PHONE 713-772-5175
FAX 713-772-3034
WEB SITE .www.musicworldent.com
TYPES   Film/TV Talent - Music Talent
REPRESENTS   Actors - Music Artists - Music Producers

Mathew Knowles . . . . .CEO
Johnna Lister .VP/General Manager
Lin Almanza . . . . .Sr. Executive Assistant to Mathew Knowles

NANAS ENTERTAINMENT
3963 Vista Linda Dr.
Encino, CA 91316
PHONE 310-385-1204
FAX 310-385-1207
EMAIL . . . . .hnanas@aol.com
TYPES   Film/TV Talent - Literary Talent
REPRESENTS   Actors - Comedians - Directors -
                         Screenwriters
SUBMISSION POLICY   No unsolicited material

Herb Nanas . . . . .Producer
Marja Adriance . . . . .Assistant to Herb Nanas/Office Manager

NANI/SAPERSTEIN MANAGEMENT, INC.
c/o The New Yorker Hotel
16 Penn Plaza, Ste. 1575
New York, NY 10001
PHONE 212-629-4388
FAX 212-629-4218
TYPES   Commercial Talent - Film/TV Talent - Music
                         Talent - Theatre Talent
REPRESENTS   Actors - Children - Dancers - Teens/Young
                         Adults - Voice-Over Artists
SUBMISSION POLICY   Send picture and resumé, Attn: Terry
                         Saperstein

Terry Saperstein . . . . .Owner
Jermey Lange . . . . .Talent Representative

NCL TALENT
10 Universal City Plaza, Ste. 2000
Universal City, CA 91608
PHONE 818-753-2401
FAX 818-249-4934
EMAIL . . . . .ncltalent@earthlink.net
TYPES   Commercial Talent - Film/TV Talent -
                         Modeling Talent - Music Talent - Theatre
                         Talent
AFFILIATIONS   TMA
REPRESENTS   Actors - Broadcast Journalists/Newscasters
                         - Children - Comedians - Directors -
                         Hosts/MCs - Infants - Martial Artists/Stunts
                         - Music Artists - Print Models - Teens/Young
                         Adults - Variety Artists - Voice-Over Artists
SUBMISSION POLICY   No unsolicited phone calls; Accepts sub-
                         missions by email or US Mail; Referral sub-
                         missions preferred
COMMENTS   Board Member, TMA

Marco Latino . . . . .Manager
Carin Latino . . . . .Manager

NEBULA MANAGEMENT
PO Box 29490
Los Angeles, CA 90029-0490
PHONE 323-664-8244
FAX 323-372-3784
EMAIL . . . . .info@nebulamanagement.com
WEB SITE . . . . .www.nebulamanagement.com
TYPES   Commercial Talent - Film/TV Talent -
                         Literary Talent
REPRESENTS   Actors - Children - Comedians -
                         Hosts/MCs - Screenwriters - TV Writers -
                         Variety Artists - Voice-Over Artists

Renae Stuyck . . . . .Manager

NEW ENTERTAINMENT GROUP
219 S. Barrington Ave., Ste. 211
Los Angeles, CA 90049
PHONE 310-440-9759
FAX 310-440-4858
TYPES   Literary Talent
REPRESENTS   Book Authors - Producers - Screenwriters
COMMENTS   Also reps new media technology

Sonia Burda . . . . .Manager
Howard Melzman . . . . .Assistant

NEW TALENT MANAGEMENT
PO Box 2939
Beverly Hills, CA 90213
PHONE 310-275-4749
WEB SITE . . . . .www.newtalentmanagement.com
TYPES   Film/TV Talent
REPRESENTS   Actors
SUBMISSION POLICY   Do not call; See Web site

Bill Perlman . . . . .Manager

NEW WAVE ENTERTAINMENT
2660 W. Olive Ave.
Burbank, CA 91505
PHONE 818-295-5000
FAX 818-295-5099
EMAIL . . . . .bkatz@nwe.com
SECOND EMAIL . . . . .bvolk-weiss@nwe.com
WEB SITE . . . . .www.nwe.com
TYPES   Film/TV Talent - Literary Talent
REPRESENTS   Actors - Book Authors - Comedians -
                         Dancers - Directors - Hosts/MCs -
                         Magicians - Producers - Screenwriters -
                         Speakers/Lecturers - Sports Personalities -
                         Teens/Young Adults - TV Writers - Variety
                         Artists - Voice-Over Artists

Barry Katz . . . . .No Title
Brian Volk-Weiss . . . . .No Title
Mark Rousso . . . . .No Title
Justin Silvera . . . . .No Title
Anna Babbitt . . . . .Executive Assistant
Shannon Petranoff . . . . .Executive Assistant
Liz Holmes . . . . .Assistant

NEXT STOP MANAGEMENT
2923 Pearl St.
Santa Monica, CA 90405
PHONE 310-396-4959
FAX 310-399-4742
EMAIL . . . . .elizastanley@gmail.com
TYPES   Literary Talent
REPRESENTS   Directors - Screenwriters
SUBMISSION POLICY   No unsolicited submissions

Elizabeth Stanley . . . . .President

NIAD MANAGEMENT
15030 Ventura Blvd., Bldg. 19, Ste. 860
Sherman Oaks, CA 91403
PHONE 818-981-2505
FAX 818-386-2082
EMAIL . . . . .queries@niadmanagement.com
SECOND EMAIL .niad@aol.com
WEB SITE . . . . .www.niadmanagement.com
TYPES   Film/TV Talent - Literary Talent
REPRESENTS   Actors - Children - Comedians - Directors -
                         Film Editors - Hosts/MCs - Producers -
                         Screenwriters - Teens/Young Adults
SUBMISSION POLICY   Accepts queries letters but prefers referrals
                         only

Wendi Niad . . . . .Manager
Jennifer Graff . . . . .Manager

NINA SHRIEBER & ASSOCIATES
9 Desbrosses St., Ste. 307
New York, NY 10013
PHONE 212-328-0388
FAX 212-328-0391
EMAIL . . . . .info@ninashrieber.com
WEB SITE . . . . .www.ninashrieber.com

Nina Shreiber . . . . .Manager

NINE YARDS ENTERTAINMENT
8530 Wilshire Blvd., 5th Fl.
Beverly Hills, CA 90211
PHONE 310-289-1088
FAX 310-289-1288
TYPES   Film/TV Talent - Literary Talent - Music
                         Talent
AFFILIATIONS   AFM - DGA
REPRESENTS   Actors - Comedians - Directors - Music
                         Artists - Producers - Screenwriters - TV
                         Writers

Larry Schapiro .Partner/Manager
Matt Luber . . . . .Partner/Manager
Ben Feigin . . . . .Manager
Steve Crawford . . . . .Manager
Alex Cole . . . . .Manager
Kieran Maguire . . . . .Manager
Stephanie Moy . . . . .Assistant to Matt Luber
Katie Henderson . . . . .Assistant to Ben Feigin
Lauren Palotay . . . . .Assistant to Steve Crawford

OCEANSIDE ENTERTAINMENT
5749 Riverton Ave.
North Hollywood, CA 91601
PHONE 818-769-7754
EMAIL . . . . .chris@oceansideent.com
WEB SITE . . . . .www.oceansideent.com
TYPES   Film/TV Talent - Literary Talent
REPRESENTS   Screenwriters - TV Writers
SUBMISSION POLICY   By referral only
COMMENTS   Email queries okay; See Web site for details

Chris Ryan . . . . .Manager/Owner
Ziggy Mrkich . . . . .Creative Executive
Brian Vanwinkle . . . . .Associate

BARNEY OLDFIELD MANAGEMENT
PO Box 4956
New York, NY 10185
PHONE 213-840-6224/212-410-9404
FAX 213-477-2004
EMAIL . . . . .barney@angelikafilm.com
WEB SITE . . . . .www.barneyoldfield.com
TYPES   Film/TV Talent - Theatre Talent
REPRESENTS   Actors - Teens/Young Adults
SUBMISSION POLICY   Headshot and resumé
COMMENTS   Works out of New York and Los Angeles;
                     Develops film and TV projects around
                     clients; Affiliated with Angelika Film and
                     Prophet Pictures, division of Crimson
                     Screen Partners

Barney Oldfield . . . . .Manager
Thomas Bannister . . . . .Manager

ROSELLA OLSON MANAGEMENT
319 W. 105th St., Ste. 1F
New York, NY 10025
PHONE 212-864-0336
TYPES   Commercial Talent - Film/TV Talent -
                     Modeling Talent - Theatre Talent
AFFILIATIONS   NCOPM
REPRESENTS   Actors - Teens/Young Adults
SUBMISSION POLICY   Do not call
COMMENTS   Board member, National Conference of
                     Personal Managers

Rosella Olson . . . . .Manager

OMNIPOP TALENT GROUP
4605 Lankershim Blvd., Ste. 201
Toluca Lake, CA 91602
PHONE 818-980-9267/516-937-6011
FAX 818-980-9371
EMAIL . . . . .omni@omnipop.com
WEB SITE . . . . .www.omnipop.com
TYPES   Film/TV Talent - Literary Talent
REPRESENTS   Actors - Comedians - Hosts/MCs -
                     Producers - Screenwriters - TV Writers -
                     Voice-Over Artists
SUBMISSION POLICY   Referral only
COMMENTS   East Coast office: 55 W. Old Country Rd.,
                     Hicksville, NY 11801

Bruce Smith . . . . .President, West Coast Theatrical Division
Tom Ingegno . . . . .President, East Coast Theatrical Division
Ralph Asquino . . . . .President, Music Division
Simon Hopkins . . . . .VP, Music Division
Barbara Klein . . . . .VP, Corporate Division
Aaron Sacks . . . . .Director, West Coast Theatrical
Brandon Brush . . . . .West Coast Theatrical Assistant
Jenna Di Paolo . . . . .East Coast Theatrical Assistant

OMNIQUEST ENTERTAINMENT
1416 N. La Brea Ave.
Hollywood, CA 90028
PHONE 323-802-1630
FAX 323-802-1633
EMAIL .info@omniquestmedia.com
WEB SITE . . . . .www.omniquestmedia.com
TYPES   Film/TV Talent - Literary Talent
REPRESENTS   Actors - Directors - Playwrights -
                     Screenwriters - Teens/Young Adults - TV
                     Writers
SUBMISSION POLICY   Referral only
COMMENTS   East Coast office: 43 W. 24th St., 5th Fl.,
                     New York, NY 10010

Michael Kaliski . . . . .Producer/Manager
Shauna Tocchet . . . . .Manager
Laura Peterson . . . . .Creative Executive
Paul Ankenman . . . . .Assistant
Kyle Otsuki . . . . .Assistant
Tyson Sharbaugh . . . . .Assistant

OMNIUM ENTERTAINMENT GROUP
9025 Wilshire Blvd., Ste. 450
Beverly Hills, CA 90211
PHONE 310-246-2446
FAX 310-246-1879
EMAIL . . . . .omniumentertainment@gmail.com
TYPES   Commercial Talent - Film/TV Talent -
                     Theatre Talent
REPRESENTS   Actors - Children - Hosts/MCs - Seniors -
                     Teens/Young Adults
SUBMISSION POLICY   Submit headshot and resumé by US Mail

Albert Giannelli . . . . .Owner/Manager
Marissa Schulman . . . . .Assistant

ONE ENTERTAINMENT
12 W. 57th St., PH
New York, NY 10019
PHONE 212-974-3900
FAX 212-974-3977
TYPES   Film/TV Talent - Literary Talent
REPRESENTS   Actors - Children - Directors - Screenwriters
                     - TV Writers

Heather Reynolds . . . . .Owner
Jean-Louis Diamonika . . . . .Manager
Nicolas Small . . . . .Manager
Erica Tuchman . . . . .Manager

ONE TALENT MANAGEMENT
9220 Sunset Blvd., Ste. 306
Los Angeles, CA 90069
PHONE 310-550-9500
FAX 310-550-9501
TYPES   Film/TV Talent
REPRESENTS   Actors - Directors - Producers -
                     Screenwriters - Teens/Young Adults - TV
                     Writers

JJ Harris .CEO/Manager/Producer
Graciella Sanchez . . . . .Manager
Beth Kono . . . . .Manager/Producer
Priscilla Moralez . . . . .Manager
Brittany Kahan . . . . .Assistant

ONLINE TALENT GROUP/OTG TALENT
276 Fifth Ave., #204
New York, NY 10001
PHONE 212-532-5923/310-927-9157
EMAIL . . . . .otgtalent@aol.com
TYPES　　　　　　　　Below-the-Line Talent - Literary Talent
REPRESENTS　　　　　Actors - Screenwriters - Teens/Young Adults
COMMENTS　　　　　　Additional office in Los Angeles

Kim Matuka . . . . .President/Manager
Julie Chin . . . . .Manager (LA)
Vivian Reid . . . . .Manager (LA/NY)
John Rexford . . . . .Literary (LA)
Brian Roosevelt . . . . .Literary (LA)
Carla Smith . . . . .Manager (LA)
Maggie Woods . . . . .Manager

OSCARS ABRAMS ZIMEL & ASSOCIATES INC.
438 Queen St. East
Toronto, ON M5A 1T4, Canada
PHONE 416-860-1790/800-367-1582
FAX 416-860-0236
EMAIL . . . . .elaine@oazinc.com
WEB SITE . . . . .www.oscarsabramszimel.com
SECOND WEB SITE .www.oazinc.com
REPRESENTS　　　　　Voice-Over Artists

Michael Oscars . . . . .Partner
Gayle Abrams . . . . .Partner
Perry Zimel . . . . .Partner
Elaine Hamat . . . . .Voice-Overs

DIANNA OSER MANAGEMENT
269 S. Beverly Dr., #411
Beverly Hills, CA 90212
PHONE 310-788-8464
FAX 310-788-8452
TYPES　　　　　　　　Film/TV Talent - Music Talent
REPRESENTS　　　　　Actors - Directors - Hosts/MCs - Music
　　　　　　　　　　　Artists - Teens/Young Adults

Dianna Oser . . . . .Manager/Producer

OVATION MANAGEMENT
12028 National Blvd.
Los Angeles, CA 90064
PHONE 310-390-0109
FAX 310-390-2244
EMAIL . . . . .tchargin@earthlink.net
TYPES　　　　　　　　Film/TV Talent - Literary Talent - Theatre
　　　　　　　　　　　Talent
REPRESENTS　　　　　Actors - Directors - Screenwriters - TV
　　　　　　　　　　　Writers

Tony Chargin . . . . .Manager

OVERBROOK ENTERTAINMENT
450 N. Roxbury Dr., 4th Fl.
Beverly Hills, CA 90210-4218
PHONE 310-432-2400
FAX 310-432-2442
TYPES　　　　　　　　Music Talent
REPRESENTS　　　　　Music Artists

James Lassiter . . . . .President/CEO
Will Smith . . . . .Partner
Miguel Melendez . . . . .Manager

P.K.A. ENTERTAINMENT GROUP
256 S. Robertson Blvd., #3802
Beverly Hills, CA 90211
PHONE 310-358-5077/305-651-5227
FAX 413-702-2121
EMAIL . . . . .floyd@imi-world.com
SECOND EMAIL .pbfloyd1@aol.com
WEB SITE . . . . .www.hitdis.com
SECOND WEB SITE . . . . .www.imi-world.com
TYPES　　　　　　　　Commercial Talent - Literary Talent -
　　　　　　　　　　　Modeling Talent - Music Talent - Theatre
　　　　　　　　　　　Talent
REPRESENTS　　　　　Actors - Children - Cinematographers -
　　　　　　　　　　　Comedians - Composers - Dancers -
　　　　　　　　　　　Directors - Martial Artists/Stunts - Music
　　　　　　　　　　　Artists - Music Producers - Print Models -
　　　　　　　　　　　Producers - Screenwriters - Sports
　　　　　　　　　　　Personalities - TV Writers - Variety Artists -
　　　　　　　　　　　Voice-Over Artists

P.B. Floyd . . . . .Manager
Osé . . . . .Manager
Hailo . . . . .Manager

PAGE MANAGEMENT
PO Box 573040
Tarzana, CA 91357
FAX 818-883-4344
WEB SITE .www.page-management.com
TYPES　　　　　　　　Commercial Talent - Film/TV Talent -
　　　　　　　　　　　Modeling Talent
REPRESENTS　　　　　Actors - Children - Infants - Teens/Young
　　　　　　　　　　　Adults - Voice-Over Artists
COMMENTS　　　　　　Multiples

Jean Page . . . . .Director
Kathy Whisenhunt . . . . .Infants/Out of State & Northern California

PALLAS MANAGEMENT
12535 Chandler Blvd., Ste. 1
Valley Village, CA 91607
PHONE 818-506-8368
FAX 818-506-8368
EMAIL . . . . .laurapallas@sbcglobal.net
SECOND EMAIL . . . . .pallasasst1@sbcglobal.net
TYPES　　　　　　　　Commercial Talent - Film/TV Talent -
　　　　　　　　　　　Modeling Talent - Music Talent - Theatre
　　　　　　　　　　　Talent
REPRESENTS　　　　　Actors - Children - Hosts/MCs
SUBMISSION POLICY　　By US Mail or email only

Laura Pallas . . . . .Manager
Amber Davidson . . . . .Executive Assistant
K. Demarse . . . . .Executive Assistant

JUDY PALNICK ENTERTAINMENT
2401 Pearl St.
Santa Monica, CA 90405
PHONE 310-450-4136
FAX 310-450-4306
TYPES　　　　　　　　Film/TV Talent - Literary Talent - Music
　　　　　　　　　　　Talent
REPRESENTS　　　　　Actors - Cinematographers - Composers -
　　　　　　　　　　　Directors - Music Artists - Music Producers -
　　　　　　　　　　　Music Supervisors - Producers -
　　　　　　　　　　　Screenwriters - TV Writers
SUBMISSION POLICY　　No unsolicited submissions

Judy Palnick . . . . .Manager

PANACEA ENTERTAINMENT
13587 Andalusia Dr. East
Santa Rosa Valley, CA 93012
PHONE 805-491-9400
EMAIL . . . . .info@panacea-ent.com
TYPES　　　　　　　　Film/TV Talent - Music Talent
REPRESENTS　　　　　Actors - Comedians - Composers - Music
　　　　　　　　　　Artists - Music Producers
SUBMISSION POLICY　　No unsolicited submissions

Eric Gardner . . . . .Chairman/CEO

PANETTIERE & COMPANY, INC.
1841 N. Fuller Ave., Ste. 306
Los Angeles, CA 90046
PHONE 323-876-5984
FAX 323-876-5076
TYPES　　　　　　　　Below-the-Line Talent - Literary Talent
AFFILIATIONS　　　　DGA
REPRESENTS　　　　　Cinematographers - Directors - Producers -
　　　　　　　　　　Screenwriters - Sports Personalities

Vincent Panettiere . . . . .Manager

PARALLEL ENTERTAINMENT, INC.
9255 Sunset Blvd., Ste. 1040
Los Angeles, CA 90069
PHONE 310-279-1123
FAX 310-279-1147
WEB SITE . . . . .www.parallelentertainment.com
TYPES　　　　　　　　Film/TV Talent
REPRESENTS　　　　　Actors - Comedians
SUBMISSION POLICY　　No unsolicited submissions

J.P. Williams . . . . .President
Alan Blomquist . . . . .Producer
Maggie Houlehan . . . . .Manager/Publicist
Ken Madson . . . . .Manager
Jennifer Novak . . . . .Development Executive
Jeanette Hanvey . . . . .Associate
Jessica Williams . . . . .Assistant to J.P. Williams

PARK PLACE MANAGEMENT
922 S. Barrington Ave., Ste. 305
Los Angeles, CA 90049
PHONE 310-826-8126
FAX 310-861-5387
EMAIL . . . . .info@parkplace99.com
TYPES　　　　　　　　Commercial Talent - Film/TV Talent -
　　　　　　　　　　Literary Talent - Modeling Talent
REPRESENTS　　　　　Actors - Book Authors - Broadcast
　　　　　　　　　　Journalists/Newscasters - Children -
　　　　　　　　　　Comedians - Dancers - Hosts/MCs -
　　　　　　　　　　Martial Artists/Stunts - Print Models -
　　　　　　　　　　Runway Models - Screenwriters - Sports
　　　　　　　　　　Personalities - Teens/Young Adults - Variety
　　　　　　　　　　Artists

Eric W. Parkinson . . . . .Owner

PARSEGHIAN PLANCO, LLC
23 E. 22nd St., 3rd Fl.
New York, NY 10010
PHONE 212-777-7786
FAX 212-777-8642
TYPES　　　　　　　　Below-the-Line Talent - Film/TV Talent -
　　　　　　　　　　Literary Talent - Theatre Talent
REPRESENTS　　　　　Actors - Cinematographers - Directors -
　　　　　　　　　　Playwrights - Screenwriters - TV Writers
COMMENTS　　　　　See also Untitled Entertainment

Gene Parseghian . . . . .Manager
Johnnie Planco . . . . .Manager
Angela Carbonetti . . . . .Associate to Gene Parseghian
Barbara Korn . . . . .Associate to Johnnie Planco

RIA PAVIA MANAGEMENT
269 S. Beverly Dr., Ste. 214
Beverly Hills, CA 90212
PHONE 310-497-5827
EMAIL . . . . .ria@paviatalent.com
TYPES　　　　　　　　Commercial Talent - Literary Talent -
　　　　　　　　　　Theatre Talent
AFFILIATIONS　　　　TMA
REPRESENTS　　　　　Actors - Book Authors - Hosts/MCs -
　　　　　　　　　　Teens/Young Adults - Voice-Over Artists

Ria Pavia . . . . .President

PB MANAGEMENT
6449 W. Sixth St.
Los Angeles, CA 90048
PHONE 323-653-7284
FAX 323-653-5285
EMAIL . . . . .capnett@hotmail.com
TYPES　　　　　　　　Commercial Talent - Film/TV Talent -
　　　　　　　　　　Literary Talent
AFFILIATIONS　　　　TMA
REPRESENTS　　　　　Actors - Screenwriters - Teens/Young Adults
　　　　　　　　　　- TV Writers
COMMENTS　　　　　ATAS; President Emeritus, TMA

Paul Bennett . . . . .President

PEARL PICTURES MANAGEMENT
10956 Weyburn Ave., Ste. 200
Los Angeles, CA 90024
PHONE 310-443-7773
FAX 310-443-7753
EMAIL . . . . .info@pearlpics.com
TYPES　　　　　　　　Film/TV Talent - Literary Talent - Music
　　　　　　　　　　Talent
REPRESENTS　　　　　Actors - Directors - Film Editors -
　　　　　　　　　　Hosts/MCs - Screenwriters - TV Writers

Gary Pearl . . . . .No Title
J.J. Feldman . . . . .No Title

THE PHOENIX ORGANIZATION
429 Santa Monica Blvd., Ste. 470
Santa Monica, CA 90401
PHONE 310-566-5085
FAX 310-566-5098
TYPES　　　　　　　　Below-the-Line Talent - Film/TV Talent -
　　　　　　　　　　Literary Talent
REPRESENTS　　　　　Actors - Book Authors - Cinematographers
　　　　　　　　　　- Comedians - Directors - Film Editors -
　　　　　　　　　　Hosts/MCs - Producers - Screenwriters - TV
　　　　　　　　　　Writers
SUBMISSION POLICY　　Query letters only; No unsolicited material

Sean Davis . . . . .President
Kevin Demeritt . . . . .CFO
Randy Warner . . . . .Manager/Head, TV Development
Mike Wise . . . . .Manager/Head, Feature Development
Ilse Baca . . . . .Assistant

THE PITT GROUP
9465 Wilshire Blvd., Ste. 420
Beverly Hills, CA 90212
PHONE 310-246-4800
FAX 310-275-9258
TYPES   Film/TV Talent - Literary Talent
REPRESENTS   Actors - Book Authors - Directors -
                         Screenwriters - TV Writers
COMMENTS   Motion picture/TV production company

Lou Pitt ....President
Mark Wheeler ....Manager
Folayo Lasaki ....Assistant

PLUMERIA ENTERTAINMENT MANAGEMENT
726 N. Alexander St.
San Fernando, CA 91340
PHONE 818-825-0843
EMAIL ....jayenron@aol.com
TYPES   Literary Talent
REPRESENTS   Directors - Screenwriters - TV Writers
SUBMISSION POLICY   No unsolicited submissions

Rhonda Bloom ....Manager/Producer

PMA LITERARY & FILM MANAGEMENT, INC.
45 W. 21st St., 4th Fl.
New York, NY 10010
PHONE 212-929-1222
FAX 212-206-0238
EMAIL ....pmalitfilm@aol.com
WEB SITE ....www.pmalitfilm.com
TYPES   Film/TV Talent - Literary Talent
REPRESENTS   Book Authors - Directors - Producers -
                         Screenwriters
SUBMISSION POLICY   No unsolicited material will be reviewed;
                         See Web site for submission guidelines
COMMENTS   Primary focus on adult commercial fiction
                         and nonfiction with feature film and televi-
                         sion production potential

Peter Miller ....Owner/President
Kelly Skillen ....Literary Manager
Betty Ferm ....Editorial Associate
Adrienne Rosado ....Associate

MARGRIT POLAK MANAGEMENT
1954 Hillhurst Ave., #405
Los Angeles, CA 90027
PHONE 213-482-0777
TYPES   Film/TV Talent
REPRESENTS   Actors

Margrit Polak ....Manager

POLARIS ENTERTAINMENT
9171 Wilshire Blvd., Ste. 441
Beverly Hills, CA 90210
PHONE 310-271-8704
FAX 310-271-8622
EMAIL ....firstinitiallastname@polarisent.com
TYPES   Commercial Talent - Film/TV Talent -
                         Theatre Talent
AFFILIATIONS   TMA
REPRESENTS   Actors - Comedians - Directors -
                         Hosts/MCs - Producers - Screenwriters -
                         Speakers/Lecturers - Teens/Young Adults -
                         TV Writers
SUBMISSION POLICY   No unsolicited submissions; Query letter
                         only, call first; Do not use email for submis-
                         sions
COMMENTS   Formerly Saffron Management

Alan Saffron ....Manager/President
Nyle Brenner ....Manager
Jerald J. Silverhardt ....Manager
Kim Kellen ....Executive Assistant

MICHELE POMMIER MANAGEMENT
927 Lincoln Rd., Ste. 200
Miami Beach, FL 33139
PHONE 305-674-1733
FAX 305-674-7013
EMAIL ....info@michelepommier.com
WEB SITE ....www.michelepommier.com
TYPES   Modeling Talent
REPRESENTS   Print Models - Runway Models

Michele Pommier ....Principal
Candace Clapp ....Booking Agent
Donald Fatal ....Accounting

THE DEREK POWER COMPANY, INC.
818 N. Doheny Dr., Ste. 1003
West Hollywood, CA 90069
PHONE 310-550-0770
FAX 310-550-6292
EMAIL ....iampower2003@yahoo.com
SECOND EMAIL ....ikpower@pacbell.net
WEB SITE www.artists4film.com
TYPES   Film/TV Talent - Literary Talent - Music
                         Talent
REPRESENTS   Actors - Composers - Directors -
                         Screenwriters
SUBMISSION POLICY   Referral only

Derek Power ....Manager/Owner
Ilene Kahn Power ....Manager/Owner
Jeremy Kahn ....VP, New Media
Steve Fantasia ....Management Associate

PRINCIPAL ENTERTAINMENT
1964 Westwood Blvd., Ste. 400
Los Angeles, CA 90025
PHONE 310-446-1466/212-997-9191
FAX 310-446-1566/212-997-9280
TYPES   Commercial Talent - Film/TV Talent - Literary Talent
REPRESENTS   Actors - Directors - Producers - Screenwriters - Teens/Young Adults - TV Writers
COMMENTS   East Coast office: 130 W. 42nd St., Ste. 614, New York, NY 10036

Estelle Lasher . . . . .Principal/Manager
Marsha McManus . . . . .Principal/Manager
Elizabeth Robinson .Principal/Manager
Larry Taube . . . . .Principal/Manager
Meg Mortimer . . . . .Principal/Manager
Josh Kesselman . . . . .Manager/Producer
Jill Kaplan . . . . .Manager
Danny Sherman . . . . .Manager
Michael Smith . . . . .Manager
Lauren Egber . . . . .Associate
Michael Escott . . . . .Associate
Atil Singh . . . . .Associate
Josh Taylor . . . . .Associate (NY)
Colin Wilhm . . . . .Associate (NY)
Debbie Buderwitz . . . . .Bookkeeper

PRINCIPATO-YOUNG ENTERTAINMENT
9465 Wilshire Blvd., Ste. 880
Beverly Hills, CA 90212
PHONE 310-274-4474
FAX 310-274-4108
TYPES   Commercial Talent - Film/TV Talent - Literary Talent
AFFILIATIONS   TMA
REPRESENTS   Actors - Comedians - Directors - Producers - Screenwriters - TV Writers
SUBMISSION POLICY   Referral only

Peter Principato . . . . .Partner (310-274-4130)
Paul Young . . . . .Partner (310-274-4424)
Ted Bender . . . . .Manager (310-274-4457)
E. Brian Dobbins .Manager (310-274-2294)
Allen Fischer . . . . .Manager (310-274-4180)
David Gardner . . . . .Manager (310-274-4622)
Dave Rosenthal . . . . .Manager (310-432-5962)
Joel Zadak . . . . .Manager (310-274-2970)
Evan Cavic . . . . .Assistant to Peter Principato
Paige Purcell . . . . .2nd Assistant to Peter Principato
Ivy Koral . . . . .Assistant to Paul Young
Rebecca Many . . . . .2nd Assistant to Paul Young
Katie Rose Houck . . . . .Assistant to Allen Fischer
Megan Klein . . . . .Assistant to Brian Dobbins
Michael Klein . . . . .Assistant to Joel Zadak & Ted Bender
Daniel Ortega . . . . .Assistant to David Gardner

PRO AND CON PRODUCTIONS TALENT MANAGEMENT
PO Box 18376
Encino, CA 91416
PHONE 818-973-2282
EMAIL . . . . .proandconprods@yahoo.com
WEB SITE . . . . .www.geocities.com/proandconprods
TYPES   Commercial Talent - Film/TV Talent - Literary Talent - Modeling Talent - Music Talent - Theatre Talent
REPRESENTS   Actors - Comedians - Dancers - Directors - Magicians - Martial Artists/Stunts - Music Artists - Playwrights - Producers - Screenwriters - Sports Personalities - Teens/Young Adults - TV Writers - Variety Artists - Voice-Over Artists

Joshua Weisel . . . . .President

MELISSA PROPHET MANAGEMENT
15335 Morrison St., Ste. #325
Sherman Oaks, CA 91403
PHONE 818-392-8653
FAX 818-237-5690
EMAIL . . . . .mprophetmgt@aol.com
TYPES   Film/TV Talent
REPRESENTS   Actors
SUBMISSION POLICY   No unsolicited submissions; No walk-ins

Melissa Prophet . . . . .CEO/Manager
Aaron Simonoff . . . . .Assistant

PROTEGE ENTERTAINMENT
710 E. Angeleno Ave.
Burbank, CA 91501
PHONE 818-842-2000
FAX 818-526-0400
EMAIL . . . . .protegemgt@aol.com
TYPES   Commercial Talent - Film/TV Talent - Theatre Talent
REPRESENTS   Actors - Children - Teens/Young Adults - Voice-Over Artists
SUBMISSION POLICY   By referral only

David Eisenberg . . . . .Owner

PURE ARTS
1230 Montana Ave., #203
Santa Monica, CA 90403
PHONE 310-444-7383
FAX 310-394-2944
EMAIL . . . . .somers@pure-arts.com
TYPES   Film/TV Talent - Literary Talent
REPRESENTS   Actors - Directors - Producers - Screenwriters
COMMENTS   Production and management

Alan Somers . . . . .Manager/Producer

QUATTRO MEDIA
12301 Wilshire Blvd., Ste. 520
Los Angeles, CA 90025
PHONE 310-207-7100
FAX 310-207-7111
TYPES   Film/TV Talent - Literary Talent
REPRESENTS   Actors - Book Authors - Directors - Interactive Game Developers - Producers - Screenwriters - TV Writers
SUBMISSION POLICY   Referral only
COMMENTS   Also represents animators, production companies, comic book companies and video game companies; Merchandising and licensing

Aaron Berger . . . . .Partner
Russell Binder . . . . .Partner/President, Consumer Products
Peter Levin . . . . .Partner
Jim Strader . . . . .Partner
Jay Roth . . . . .CEO, Quattro Consumer Products
Billy Parks . . . . .Producer
Carina Schulze . . . . .Manager
Paulina Goldenberg . . . .Account Executive, Quattro Consumer Products

RABINER/DAMATO ENTERTAINMENT

617 N. Beverly Dr.
Beverly Hills, CA 90210
PHONE 310-925-6772
FAX 310-859-7631
EMAIL . . . . .rdentertainment@sbcglobal.net
TYPES   Film/TV Talent - Literary Talent
REPRESENTS   Actors - Directors - Screenwriters - TV
                           Writers
SUBMISSION POLICY   No unsolicited submissions

Steven Rabiner . . . . .Partner
Anne Damato . . . . .Partner

THE RADMIN COMPANY

9201 Wilshire Blvd., Ste. 102
Beverly Hills, CA 90210
PHONE 310-274-9515
FAX 310-274-0739
EMAIL . . . . .queries@radmincompany.com
TYPES   Literary Talent
REPRESENTS   Directors - Screenwriters

Linne Radmin . . . . .Manager
Becky Zoshak . . . . .Story Editor
David Langford . . . . .Story Department

VIC RAMOS MANAGEMENT

49 W. Ninth St., Ste. 5B
New York, NY 10011
PHONE 212-473-2610
FAX 212-473-2611
TYPES   Film/TV Talent
AFFILIATIONS   NCOPM
REPRESENTS   Actors
COMMENTS   NCOPM Board Member

Victor Ramos . . . . .Manager/Owner
Sandra Erickson . . . . .Manager

CHARLES RAPP ENTERPRISES, INC.

55 Broad St., 26th Fl.
New York, NY 10004
PHONE 212-247-6646
WEB SITE . . . . .www.charlesrapp.com
TYPES   Commercial Talent - Film/TV Talent -
                           Literary Talent - Music Talent
AFFILIATIONS   NCOPM
REPRESENTS   Actors - Comedians - Directors -
                           Screenwriters - TV Writers - Variety Artists -
                           Voice-Over Artists

Howard Rapp . . . . .Manager
Arnold Graham . . . . .Manager

JOSEPH RAPP ENTERPRISES, INC.

55 Broad St., 26th Fl.
New York, NY 10004
PHONE 212-265-3366
EMAIL . . . . .comedystz@aol.com
TYPES   Film/TV Talent - Music Talent
AFFILIATIONS   NCOPM
REPRESENTS   Actors - Comedians - Composers - Music
                           Artists - Variety Artists

Joseph Rapp . . . . .Manager

RAW TALENT

9615 Brighton Way, Ste. 300
Beverly Hills, CA 90210
PHONE 310-246-1100
FAX 310-246-2345
TYPES   Film/TV Talent - Literary Talent
REPRESENTS   Actors - Directors - Screenwriters - TV
                           Writers

Glenn Robbins . . . . .Manager
Doug Wald . . . . .Manager

RED BARON MANAGEMENT

c/o Manhattan Beach Studios
1600 Rosecrans Ave., Bldg. 7, 4th Fl.
Manhattan Beach, CA 90266
PHONE 310-321-7828
WEB SITE . . . . .www.redbaronfilms.com
TYPES   Film/TV Talent
AFFILIATIONS   TMA
REPRESENTS   Actors - Children - Comedians - Directors -
                           Hosts/MCs - Print Models - Producers -
                           Screenwriters - Teens/Young Adults - Voice-
                           Over Artists
COMMENTS   Production; Also represents still photogra-
                           phers and athletes

Keith Anderson . . . . .Owner
Robert Enriquez . . . . .Owner/Manager (robert@redbaronfilms.com)
Jeff Johnson . . . . .Manager (jeff@redbaronfilms.com)
Christopher Sheng . . . . .Manager (chris@redbaronfilms.com)

RED HARVEST ENTERTAINMENT

1126 Tamarind Ave.
Hollywood, CA 90038
PHONE 323-464-4230
EMAIL . . . . .info@redharvestentertainment.com
WEB SITE . . . . .www.redharvestentertainment.com
TYPES   Literary Talent
REPRESENTS   Directors - Producers - Screenwriters - TV
                           Writers
SUBMISSION POLICY   No calls; All inquiries should be made via
                           fax or email

Barry Levine . . . . .Producer

DAN REDLER ENTERTAINMENT

5303 Penfield Ave.
Woodland Hills, CA 91364
PHONE 818-999-0786
TYPES   Literary Talent
REPRESENTS   Directors - Screenwriters

Dan Redler . . . . .Manager

REEL TALENT MANAGEMENT

PO Box 491035
Los Angeles, CA 90049
PHONE 310-440-0440
EMAIL . . . . .reeltalent@aol.com
TYPES   Film/TV Talent
REPRESENTS   Actors - Children - Teens/Young Adults

Elissa Leeds . . . . .President
Michelle Broadus . . . . .Associate

REEL WORLD MANAGEMENT
591 N. Irving Blvd.
Los Angeles, CA 90004
PHONE 323-460-4090
EMAIL . . . . submissions@myreelworld.com
WEB SITE . . . . .www.myreelworld.com
TYPES   Film/TV Talent - Literary Talent
AFFILIATIONS   DGA
REPRESENTS   Directors - Producers - Screenwriters
SUBMISSION POLICY   No unsolicited material; Writers: Email log-
                         line and one paragraph synopsis, along
                         with release form on Web site, will contact
                         if interested in reviewing the script;
                         Directors: Send demo reel and CV to mail-
                         ing address along with release; Follow sub-
                         mission policy strictly
COMMENTS   Looking for writers and directors with at
                         least one feature completed; Also seeking
                         completed projects that require foreign and
                         domestic sales, specifically action thrillers,
                         horror, sci-fi and teen comedy

Roma Roth . . . . .Manager

LINDA REITMAN MANAGEMENT
820 N. San Vicente Blvd., PO Box 691736
Los Angeles, CA 90069-9736
PHONE 323-852-9091
FAX 323-852-9094
TYPES   Commercial Talent - Film/TV Talent -
                         Literary Talent - Music Talent - Theatre
                         Talent
AFFILIATIONS   TMA
REPRESENTS   Actors - Comedians - Directors - Music
                         Artists - Playwrights - Producers -
                         Screenwriters

Linda Reitman . . . . .Manager

RELEVANT ENTERTAINMENT GROUP
144 S. Beverly Dr.
Beverly Hills, CA 90212
PHONE 310-246-1212/212-431-0001
FAX 310-246-1250/212-213-2453
TYPES   Film/TV Talent - Literary Talent
REPRESENTS   Actors - Book Authors - Comedians -
                         Directors - Playwrights - Producers -
                         Screenwriters - TV Writers
COMMENTS   East Coast office: 18 W. 21st St., 6th Fl.,
                         New York, NY 10010

Michael Menchel . . . . .Partner/Manager
Jonathan Baruch . . . . .Partner/Manager
Rick Dorfman . . . . .Partner/Manager (NY)
Gina Rugolo . . . . .Manager
Beth Stine . . . . .Manager
Steve Whitney . . . . .Manager
Ali Hart . . . . .Manager (NY)
Brendan Bragg . . . . .Assistant
Sivan Gur-Arieh . . . . .Assistant
Alec Schrager . . . . .Assistant

RELEVE ENTERTAINMENT
6255 W. Sunset Blvd., Ste. 923
Los Angeles, CA 90028
PHONE 323-468-9470
FAX 323-468-9300
TYPES   Film/TV Talent - Music Talent
REPRESENTS   Actors - Music Artists

Holly Davis Carter . . . . .Manager

RIBISI ENTERTAINMENT
3278 Wilshire Blvd., Ste. 702
Los Angeles, CA 90010
PHONE 213-388-2118
FAX 213-388-2128
TYPES   Film/TV Talent
REPRESENTS   Actors
SUBMISSION POLICY   Not taking on new clients

Gay Ribisi . . . . .President

L. RICHARDSON ENTERTAINMENT
15030 Ventura Blvd., #19-545
Sherman Oaks, CA 91403
PHONE 818-990-4706
FAX 818-501-4831
EMAIL . . . . .lrichent@aol.com
WEB SITE . . . . .www.succeedinshowbiz.com
TYPES   Commercial Talent - Film/TV Talent -
                         Literary Talent
REPRESENTS   Actors - Book Authors - Children -
                         Comedians - Teens/Young Adults - Voice-
                         Over Artists
COMMENTS   ATA member

Lita Richardson . . . . .President
Garnetta Burns . . . . .Assistant
LaSalle Barnes . . . . .No Title

RIGBERG ENTERTAINMENT GROUP
1180 S. Beverly Dr., Ste. 601
Los Angeles, CA 90035
PHONE 310-712-0712
FAX 310-712-0717
TYPES   Film/TV Talent - Literary Talent
REPRESENTS   Actors - Directors - Screenwriters
SUBMISSION POLICY   No unsolicited material

Glenn Rigberg . . . . .President/Manager
John Tantillo . . . . .Producer
Lainie Kartoon . . . . .New Media Executive
Leo Bozzutto . . . . .Executive Assistant to President

THE RIGHT CONNECTION ENTERTAINMENT GROUP
PO Box 50492
Pasadena, CA 91115
PHONE 626-818-4802
EMAIL . . . . .lj4trc@yahoo.com
SECOND EMAIL . . . . .ellejai@lindalouproductions.com
WEB SITE . . . . .www.lindalouproductions.com
TYPES   Commercial Talent - Film/TV Talent -
                         Theatre Talent
AFFILIATIONS   TMA
REPRESENTS   Actors - Children - Teens/Young Adults
SUBMISSION POLICY   Mail preferred
COMMENTS   Children and young adults preferred; Up to
                         age 25 to play younger

Linda Jankins . . . . .President/CEO

RISING TALENT MANAGEMENT
405 N. Palm Dr., Ste. 102
Beverly Hills, CA 90210
PHONE 310-926-7771
FAX 310-273-3023
EMAIL . . . . .debrtm@aol.com
WEB SITE . . . . .www.risingtalent.net
TYPES   Commercial Talent - Film/TV Talent -
                          Modeling Talent
REPRESENTS   Actors - Children - Hosts/MCs - Print
                          Models - Sports Personalities - Teens/Young
                          Adults

Ed Goldstone . . . . .Manager
Debbie Entin . . . . .Manager
Emily Silverstein . . . . .Manager

RJM/RENÉE JENNETT MANAGEMENT
10028 Farragut Dr.
Culver City, CA 90232
PHONE 310-287-9979
EMAIL . . . . .reneejennett@yahoo.com
TYPES   Film/TV Talent - Literary Talent - Theatre
                          Talent
REPRESENTS   Actors - Film Editors - TV Writers
SUBMISSION POLICY   By mail and referral only

Renée Jennett . . . . .President
Harry Stern . . . . .Assistant

ROAR
9701 Wilshire Blvd., 8th Fl.
Beverly Hills, CA 90212
PHONE 310-586-8222/615-858-1282
FAX 310-586-8147/615-858-1301
TYPES   Film/TV Talent - Literary Talent - Music
                          Talent
REPRESENTS   Actors - Book Authors - Comedians -
                          Directors - Hosts/MCs - Music Artists -
                          Music Producers - Producers - Screenwriters
                          - TV Writers
SUBMISSION POLICY   No unsolicited submissions
COMMENTS   Nashville office: 1400 18th Ave. South,
                          Nashville, TN 37212

Bernard Cahill . . . . .Partner
Jay Froberg . . . . .Partner
Greg Suess . . . . .Partner
William Ward . . . . .Partner
Summers Bruno . . . . .Project Coordinator
Kim Callahan . . . . .Manager
Matt Maher . . . . .Manager
Liz Norris . . . . .Manager
Ben Tappan . . . . .Manager
Jordan Tilzer . . . . .Manager
Erik Stone . . . . .Creative Executive
Matt Bilinksy . . . . .Assistant
Matt Feick . . . . .Assistant
Brandon James . . . . .Assistant
Ashley Smith . . . . .Assistant
Caralyn Thomason . . . . .Assistant

J.C. ROBBINS MANAGEMENT
2114 Glendon Ave.
Los Angeles, CA 90025
PHONE 310-234-9595
FAX 310-234-9797
EMAIL . . . . .msthangmgt@aol.com
TYPES   Film/TV Talent - Theatre Talent
REPRESENTS   Actors - Children - Comedians -
                          Hosts/MCs - Teens/Young Adults
SUBMISSION POLICY   Send reel by mail for consideration
COMMENTS   Talent eighteen and over; Under eighteen if
                          emancipated; Star and established talent

J.C. Robbins . . . . .President/Owner
Duane Johnson . . . . .Associate Manager

MARK ROBERT MANAGEMENT
PO Box 1549
Studio City, CA 91614
PHONE 818-907-9178
WEB SITE .www.markrobertmgmt.com
TYPES   Commercial Talent - Film/TV Talent
AFFILIATIONS   TMA
REPRESENTS   Actors - Teens/Young Adults

Mark Robert . . . . .Manager

DOLORES ROBINSON ENTERTAINMENT
3815 Hughes Ave., 3rd Fl.
Culver City, CA 90232
PHONE 310-777-8777
FAX 310-841-6614
EMAIL . . . . .assistant@drobinsonent.com
TYPES   Film/TV Talent - Literary Talent
REPRESENTS   Actors - Directors - Screenwriters - TV
                          Writers

Dolores Robinson . . . . .Manager/President/Producer

BILL ROBINSON MANAGEMENT
PO Box 6284
Malibu, CA 90264
PHONE 310-457-5669
FAX 310-457-0409
EMAIL . . . . .billrmalibu@aol.com
TYPES   Film/TV Talent
REPRESENTS   Actors

Bill Robinson . . . . .No Title
Daisy Vickers . . . . .No Title

STEPHANIE ROGERS & ASSOCIATES
8737 Carlitas Joy Court
Las Vegas, NV 89117
PHONE 702-255-9999
EMAIL . . . . .sjrlion@aol.com
TYPES   Literary Talent
REPRESENTS   Book Authors - Directors - Producers -
                          Screenwriters - TV Writers
SUBMISSION POLICY   Referrals preferred; Will accept query letters
COMMENTS   Los Angeles-based literary agent for twenty
                          years; Affiliated with Philipico Pictures
                          Company and Cinemastar Partners, LLC

Stephanie Rogers . . . . .Principal/Literary
Philip Rogers . . . . .Principal/Producer

ROKLIN MANAGEMENT
8530 Wilshire Blvd., Ste. 550
Beverly Hills, CA 90211
PHONE 310-289-1088
FAX 310-289-1288
TYPES   Film/TV Talent
REPRESENTS   Actors

Lena Roklin . . . . .Manager
Gayl Leibowitz . . . . .Manager
Tim Taylor . . . . .Manager

ROSALEE PRODUCTIONS
137 W. 78th St., Apt. 1
New York, NY 10024
PHONE 212-877-5538
FAX 212-877-5641
TYPES   Film/TV Talent - Theatre Talent
AFFILIATIONS   NCOPM
REPRESENTS   Actors

Philip Rose . . . . .Manager
Jason Watkins . . . . .Associate

THE MARION ROSENBERG OFFICE
PO Box 69826
Los Angeles, CA 90069
PHONE 323-822-2793
FAX 323-388-5798
EMAIL . . . . .olivia@marionrosenberg.com
TYPES   Film/TV Talent - Literary Talent - Theatre
                         Talent
AFFILIATIONS   DGA
REPRESENTS   Actors - Book Authors - Directors -
                         Screenwriters
SUBMISSION POLICY   Referral only

Marion Rosenberg . . . . .Owner
Olivia Barham . . . . .Assistant to Marion Rosenberg

LARA ROSENSTOCK MANAGEMENT
1314 N. Hayworth Ave., Ste. 503
West Hollywood, CA 90046
PHONE 323-512-2002
TYPES   Film/TV Talent - Literary Talent
AFFILIATIONS   DGA
REPRESENTS   Actors - Directors - TV Writers

Lara Rosenstock . . . . .President

ROSENZWEIG FILMS
6399 Wilshire Blvd., Ste. 510
Los Angeles, CA 90048
PHONE 323-782-6888
FAX 323-782-6967
TYPES   Literary Talent
REPRESENTS   Screenwriters - TV Writers
SUBMISSION POLICY   Email unsolicited queries

Alison Rosenzweig . . . . .Manager

JEFF ROSS ENTERTAINMENT, INC.
14560 Benefit St., Ste. 206
Sherman Oaks, CA 91403
PHONE 818-788-6847
FAX 818-332-4023
EMAIL . . . . .jeff@jeffrossentertainment.com
TYPES   Film/TV Talent - Literary Talent
REPRESENTS   Book Authors - Directors - Playwrights -
                         Producers - Screenwriters -
                         Speakers/Lecturers - TV Writers
SUBMISSION POLICY   Query letters and industry referral only
COMMENTS   Member, TV Academy; Former board mem-
                         ber, NCOPM

Jeff Ross . . . . .President/Owner
Shareen Goon . . . . .VP

HEIDI ROTBART MANAGEMENT
1810 Malcolm Ave., Ste. 207
Los Angeles, CA 90025
PHONE 310-470-8339
FAX 310-446-8610
EMAIL . . . . .rotbartmgt@aol.com
TYPES   Commercial Talent - Film/TV Talent -
                         Literary Talent
REPRESENTS   Actors - Book Authors - Comedians -
                         Screenwriters - Teens/Young Adults - TV
                         Writers

Heidi Rotbart . . . . .President
Lori Morrison . . . . .Assistant

ROUGH DIAMOND MANAGEMENT
1424 N. Kings Rd.
Los Angeles, CA 90069
PHONE 323-848-2900
FAX 323-848-8142
EMAIL . . . . .roughdiamondmp@msn.com
TYPES   Film/TV Talent
REPRESENTS   Actors - Directors
SUBMISSION POLICY   Will consider up-and-coming talent by
                         referral only
COMMENTS   Established name talent

Julia Verdin . . . . .Owner
Bill Kravitz . . . . .Owner

RPI ENTERTAINMENT & MEDIA GROUP
PO Box 1272
Hollywood, CA 90078
PHONE 323-960-9014
FAX 775-252-6627
EMAIL . . . . .artistmgmt@rpientertainment.com
WEB SITE . . . . .www.rpientertainment.com
TYPES   Film/TV Talent
REPRESENTS   Variety Artists
COMMENTS   RPI Artists Management represents variety
                         acts for casinos, cruise ships, TV, theatrical
                         tours and revue shows

Samad Soomro . . . . .Managing Partner
Jeremy Vargus .Managing Partner
Rebecca Galo . . . . .Public Relations
Alex Scooner .Talent Representative

RPM INTERNATIONAL
9025 Wilshire Blvd., Ste. 450
Beverly Hills, CA 90211
PHONE 310-652-6220
FAX 310-246-1879
EMAIL . . . . .lrpm@ix.netcom.com
TYPES   Literary Talent
AFFILIATIONS   DGA
REPRESENTS   Directors - Producers - Screenwriters - TV
                         Writers
COMMENTS   Specializes in international talent with an
                         emphasis on the Australian and Latin film
                         industries; Also produces

Leslie Rabb . . . . .Manager/Producer
Vincent Norec . . . . .Creative Executive

SAFRAN COMPANY
9420 Wilshire Blvd., #250
Beverly Hills, CA 90212
PHONE 310-278-1450
FAX 310-278-0885
TYPES   Film/TV Talent - Literary Talent - Music
                         Talent
REPRESENTS   Actors - Directors - Music Artists -
                         Screenwriters - TV Writers

Peter Safran . . . . .Manager/Producer
Tom Drumm . . . . .Manager
Jack St. Martin . . . . .Assistant to Peter Safran

SAGER MANAGEMENT, INC.
260 S. Beverly Dr., Ste. 205
Beverly Hills, CA 90212
PHONE 310-274-4555
FAX 310-274-4353
EMAIL . . . . .felicia@sagermgmt.com
TYPES   Film/TV Talent - Theatre Talent
REPRESENTS   Actors - Children - Hosts/MCs - Runway
                         Models - Teens/Young Adults - Voice-Over
                         Artists

Felicia Sager . . . . .Manager
Amanda Sidwell . . . . .Assistant

SANDERS/ARMSTRONG MANAGEMENT
2120 Colorado Ave., Ste. 120
Santa Monica, CA 90404
PHONE 310-315-2100
FAX 310-315-2115
TYPES   Film/TV Talent - Theatre Talent
REPRESENTS   Actors
COMMENTS   Select clientele with little turnover

Nancy Sanders . . . . .Owner/Manager
Mark Armstrong . . . . .Partner/Manager
Steve Caserta . . . . .Manager
Jessica Samuel . . . . .Manager
Ruth Bornhauser . . . . .No Title
Andrew Kimble . . . . .Assistant

SANDERSON ENTERTAINMENT, INC.
9465 Wilshire Blvd., Ste. 319
Beverly Hills, CA 90212
PHONE 310-786-7887
TYPES   Film/TV Talent - Literary Talent
REPRESENTS   Actors - Comedians - Screenwriters - TV
                         Writers

Lisa Sanderson . . . . .President/CEO
Anka Brazzell . . . . .Executive Assistant

FRAN SAPERSTEIN ORGANIZATION
919 Victoria Ave.
Venice, CA 90291
PHONE 310-306-4456
FAX 310-306-4953
TYPES   Film/TV Talent - Literary Talent - Music
                         Talent
REPRESENTS   Actors - Directors - Music Artists -
                         Producers - Screenwriters

Fran Saperstein . . . . .Owner/Manager
Eric S. Saperstein . . . . .Manager
Sue Kaplan . . . . .Assistant
Mike Young . . . . .Assistant

DOROTHEA SARGENT & COMPANY
6509 Murietta Ave.
Valley Glen, CA 91401
PHONE 310-779-6848
TYPES   Commercial Talent - Film/TV Talent
REPRESENTS   Actors
SUBMISSION POLICY   Not accepting new clients

Dorothea Sargent . . . . .Owner

SAUERS ARTISTS, LLC
PO Box 146
Seal Beach, CA 90740
PHONE 310-909-4211
TYPES   Commercial Talent - Film/TV Talent
REPRESENTS   Actors - Children - Teens/Young Adults
COMMENTS   Also produces

David Sauers . . . . .Manager

SAXON ASSOCIATES MANAGEMENT
552 Norwich Dr.
West Hollywood, CA 90048
PHONE 310-657-6033
FAX 310-657-0273
EMAIL . . . . .danielsaxon@earthlink.net
TYPES   Film/TV Talent - Theatre Talent
AFFILIATIONS   TMA
REPRESENTS   Actors
SUBMISSION POLICY   By mail only; No email submissions

Daniel Saxon . . . . .President
Valerie Waraska . . . . .Associate

SCHACHTER ENTERTAINMENT
1157 S. Beverly Dr.
Los Angeles, CA 90035
PHONE 310-712-3730
FAX 310-277-6602
EMAIL .ted@schachterent.com
TYPES   Commercial Talent - Film/TV Talent -
                         Literary Talent - Theatre Talent
REPRESENTS   Actors - Children - Comedians - Directors -
                         Producers - Screenwriters - Teens/Young
                         Adults - TV Writers - Voice-Over Artists

Ted Schachter . . . . .Principal
Brantley Brown . . . . .Manager
Molly Randall . . . . .Associate

SCHUMACHER MANAGEMENT
1122 San Vicente Blvd.
Santa Monica, CA 90402
PHONE 310-458-2654
FAX 310-496-0662
EMAIL .info@schumachermgmt.com
WEB SITE .www.schumachermgmt.com
TYPES　　　　　　　　Film/TV Talent - Literary Talent
REPRESENTS　　　　　Actors - Comedians - Directors - Producers
　　　　　　　　　　　- Screenwriters - TV Writers

Mark Schumacher . . . . .Owner
Ricky Rollins . . . . .No Title

BOOH SCHUT COMPANY
11365 Sunshine Terrace
Studio City, CA 91604
PHONE 818-760-6669
TYPES　　　　　　　　Film/TV Talent - Theatre Talent
REPRESENTS　　　　　Actors
SUBMISSION POLICY　Referral; Demo reel/DVD

Booh Schut . . . . .President/Owner/Talent Manager

RICHARD SCHWARTZ MANAGEMENT
2934-1/2 Beverly Glen Circle, Ste. 107
Bel Air, CA 90077-1724
PHONE 818-783-9575
TYPES　　　　　　　　Commercial Talent - Film/TV Talent -
　　　　　　　　　　　Literary Talent - Modeling Talent
REPRESENTS　　　　　Actors - Directors - Print Models -
　　　　　　　　　　　Producers - Screenwriters - Teens/Young
　　　　　　　　　　　Adults

Richard Schwartz . . . . .Manager/Owner
Stephen Arenholz . . . . .Manager

SCORE! MEDIA VENTURES
1223 Wilshire Blvd., Ste. 470
Santa Monica, CA 90403
PHONE 310-383-0439
EMAIL . . . . .info@scoremedia.org
SECOND EMAIL . . . . .dennis@scoremedia.org
WEB SITE . . . . .www.scoremedia.org
TYPES　　　　　　　　Commercial Talent - Literary Talent
REPRESENTS　　　　　Actors - Hosts/MCs - Producers - Sports
　　　　　　　　　　　Personalities - TV Writers
COMMENTS　　　　　Offices in New York and Las Vegas; Clients
　　　　　　　　　　　include Al Bernstein (Showtime Television
　　　　　　　　　　　boxing analyst) - The North American
　　　　　　　　　　　Boxing Council - Alan Hahn (New York
　　　　　　　　　　　Newsday columnist)

Dennis Bernstein . . . . .Chairman/CEO/Manager
Fylissa Bernstein . . . . .VP, Marketing
Eric Cohen .VP, East Coast Operations
Anthony Givens . . . . .VP, Talent
Michael Hurley . . . . .VP, West Coast Operations

JERI SCOTT MANAGEMENT
211 S. Beverly Dr., Ste. 112
Beverly Hills, CA 90212
PHONE 310-887-1770
FAX 310-887-1774
TYPES　　　　　　　　Film/TV Talent
REPRESENTS　　　　　Actors
SUBMISSION POLICY　No unsolicited submissions; Referrals only

Jeri Scott . . . . .Owner

SCREEN PARTNERS, INC.
9663 Santa Monica Blvd., Ste. 639
Beverly Hills, CA 90210
PHONE 310-903-0309
FAX 310-943-2713
EMAIL . . . . .jpg@screenpartnersinc.com
WEB SITE . . . . .www.screenpartnersinc.com
TYPES　　　　　　　　Film/TV Talent - Literary Talent
REPRESENTS　　　　　Actors - Comedians - Producers
SUBMISSION POLICY　Referrals only; No unsolicited materials
COMMENTS　　　　　Does not attend showcases or workshops

Jenean Glover . . . . .Manager/Producer
Candra Palmer . . . . .Associate

SEEKERS MANAGEMENT, LLC
1850 Morton Ave.
Los Angeles, CA 90026
PHONE 818-530-8185
EMAIL . . . . .seekersmgt@yahoo.com
SECOND EMAIL . . . . .jose.fikes@talentmanagers.org
WEB SITE . . . . .www.seekersmanagement.com
TYPES　　　　　　　　Commercial Talent - Film/TV Talent -
　　　　　　　　　　　Literary Talent
AFFILIATIONS　　　　TMA
REPRESENTS　　　　　Actors - Comedians - Music Artists -
　　　　　　　　　　　Screenwriters - TV Writers
SUBMISSION POLICY　WGA writers only; Submit query letters via
　　　　　　　　　　　email

Joe Fikes . . . . .Owner/Manager

SELECT ARTISTS, LTD.
1138 12th St., Ste. 1
Santa Monica, CA 90403
PHONE 310-458-6858/818-382-4711
EMAIL . . . . .marrissa@selectartistsltd.com
SECOND EMAIL . . . . .selectartists@earthlink.net
WEB SITE .www.selectartistsltd.com
TYPES　　　　　　　　Film/TV Talent - Theatre Talent
REPRESENTS　　　　　Actors - Hosts/MCs
SUBMISSION POLICY　No unsolicited submissions of any kind; By
　　　　　　　　　　　referral only

Margarita Cannon . . . . .Valley Office
Marrissa O'Leary . . . . .Westside Office
Rebeca Gold . . . . .Valley Office
Richard Christian . . . . .Westside Office

SEVEN SUMMITS PICTURES & MANAGEMENT
8906 W. Olympic Blvd., Garden Level
Beverly Hills, CA 90211
PHONE 310-550-6777
FAX 310-550-0606
TYPES　　　　　　　　Film/TV Talent - Literary Talent - Theatre
　　　　　　　　　　　Talent
REPRESENTS　　　　　Actors - Book Authors - Directors -
　　　　　　　　　　　Producers

William Blaylock . . . . .Partner
Sarah Jackson . . . . .Partner
Nicolas Bernheim . . . . .Talent & Literary Manager
Paul Canterna . . . . .Literary Manager
Kris Koller . . . . .Assistant

MANAGERS

EARL SHANK
520 N. Kings Rd., Ste. 316
West Hollywood, CA 90048
PHONE 323-651-5241
FAX 323-651-3285
TYPES   Commercial Talent - Film/TV Talent -
                       Literary Talent
AFFILIATIONS   NCOPM
REPRESENTS   Actors - Children - Screenwriters -
                       Teens/Young Adults

Earl Shank . . . . .Manager

BURT SHAPIRO MANAGEMENT
2147 N. Beachwood Dr.
Los Angeles, CA 90068-3462
PHONE 323-469-9452
FAX 509-461-5626
EMAIL . . . . .burtjay@mail.com
WEB SITE . . . . .www.burtshapiro.com
TYPES   Commercial Talent - Film/TV Talent
REPRESENTS   Actors - Broadcast Journalists/Newscasters
                       - Children - Comedians - Hosts/MCs -
                       Producers - Sports Personalities -
                       Teens/Young Adults

Burt Shapiro . . . . .President

MARTY SHAPIRO MANAGEMENT
1010 Lexington Rd.
Beverly Hills, CA 90210
PHONE 310-859-8877
FAX 310-276-0630
EMAIL . . . . .mss@shapiro-lichtman.com
TYPES   Below-the-Line Talent - Film/TV Talent -
                       Literary Talent
AFFILIATIONS   DGA
REPRESENTS   Actors - Cinematographers - Directors -
                       Film Editors - Producers - Production
                       Designers - Screenwriters - TV Writers
SUBMISSION POLICY   Query letters only; No unsolicited material

Marty Shapiro . . . . .Manager
Susan Shapiro . . . . .Manager
Michael Shlain . . . . .Manager

SHAPIRO/WEST & ASSOCIATES, INC.
141 El Camino Dr., Ste. 205
Beverly Hills, CA 90212
PHONE 310-278-8896
FAX 310-278-7238
TYPES   Commercial Talent - Film/TV Talent -
                       Literary Talent
AFFILIATIONS   DGA
REPRESENTS   Actors - Comedians - Directors - Producers
                       - Screenwriters - Teens/Young Adults - TV
                       Writers

George Shapiro . . . . .Principal
Howard West . . . . .Principal
John Tae Lee . . . . .Manager
Tami Armitage . . . . .Manager/Assistant
Aimee Hyatt . . . . .Manager/Assistant
Shellie Turner-Banks . . . . .Office Manager

SHARK ARTISTS, INC.
PO Box 88225
Los Angeles, CA 90009
PHONE 310-503-2121
TYPES   Commercial Talent - Film/TV Talent -
                       Literary Talent - Modeling Talent - Music
                       Talent
AFFILIATIONS   NCOPM - TMA
REPRESENTS   Actors - Book Authors - Broadcast
                       Journalists/Newscasters - Composers -
                       Dancers - Directors - Music Artists - Music
                       Producers - Print Models - Producers -
                       Screenwriters - Teens/Young Adults - TV
                       Writers - Variety Artists - Voice-Over Artists
SUBMISSION POLICY   By referral only
COMMENTS   AAR

Debbie DeStefano . . . . .Partner/Personal Manager
Sam Boyd . . . . .Associate Personal Manager
Carolyn Derek . . . . .Associate Personal Manager

SHARP TALENT
117 N. Orlando Ave.
Los Angeles, CA 90048
PHONE 323-653-4104
FAX 323-653-4666
TYPES   Commercial Talent - Film/TV Talent -
                       Literary Talent - Modeling Talent - Theatre
                       Talent
REPRESENTS   Actors - Comedians - Martial Artists/Stunts
                       - Playwrights - Print Models - Teens/Young
                       Adults
SUBMISSION POLICY   Submit by referral through US Mail only;
                       No drop-offs

Melanie Sharp . . . . .Manager
Jazz Beitler . . . . .Jr. Manager/Assistant

SHARYN TALENT MANAGEMENT
PO Box 18033
Encino, CA 91416-8033
PHONE 818-609-7463
FAX 818-609-0125
EMAIL . . . . .sharyntalent@mac.com
SECOND EMAIL . . . . .sharyntalent@aol.com
TYPES   Commercial Talent - Film/TV Talent
REPRESENTS   Actors - Children - Infants - Teens/Young
                       Adults - Voice-Over Artists

Sharyn Berg . . . . .Manager
Alexis Reusser . . . . .Associate

NARELLE SHEEHAN MANAGEMENT (NSM)
PO Box 5055
Beverly Hills, CA 90209
PHONE 310-390-8125/310-385-0419
TYPES   Below-the-Line Talent - Commercial Talent
                       - Film/TV Talent
REPRESENTS   Actors - Directors - Producers - TV Writers
SUBMISSION POLICY   Not accepting talent or literary submissions
                       until further notice
COMMENTS   ATAS; Produces reality TV and infomercials;
                       Offices in London and Sydney

Narelle Sheehan . . . . .Manager/Executive Producer

SHELTER ENTERTAINMENT
9255 Sunset Blvd., Ste. 500
Los Angeles, CA 90069
PHONE 310-724-8900
FAX 310-724-8998
EMAIL .jrubin@shelterpeople.com
TYPES   Commercial Talent - Film/TV Talent -
                     Literary Talent
REPRESENTS   Actors - Comedians - Screenwriters - TV
                     Writers

Alan Lezman . . . . .President/Manager
Ray McKigney . . . . .Manager
Lynn Reynolds . . . . .Manager
Josh Rubin . . . . .Assistant

SHOELACE, INC. MANAGEMENT
1519 N. Martel Ave., #101
Los Angeles, CA 90046
PHONE 818-231-7293
FAX 323-436-0273
EMAIL . . . . .shoelaceincmgt@aol.com
TYPES   Below-the-Line Talent - Commercial Talent
                     - Film/TV Talent - Literary Talent - Modeling
                     Talent - Music Talent
REPRESENTS   Actors - Comedians - Directors - Film
                     Editors - Hosts/MCs - Producers -
                     Screenwriters - Teens/Young Adults - TV
                     Writers
COMMENTS   Specializes in the female perspective

Annaka V. Johnson . . . . .Manager

LORETTA SHREVE MODEL CENTER/
SHREVE TALENT SOURCE
2739 N. Palm Canyon Dr., Ste. 2
Palm Springs, CA 92262
PHONE 760-327-5855/760-327-5092
FAX 760-778-6557
EMAIL .shrevetalentsource@msn.com
TYPES   Commercial Talent - Modeling Talent
REPRESENTS   Dancers - Hosts/MCs - Print Models -
                     Runway Models - Seniors - Teens/Young
                     Adults - Voice-Over Artists
SUBMISSION POLICY   New clients seen by interview appointment;
                     Email, fax or call
COMMENTS   Promotional models for commercials and
                     print; Extras; Some children

Loretta Shreve . . . . .Director/Owner

THE SHUMAN COMPANY
3815 Hughes Ave., 4th Fl.
Culver City, CA 90232
PHONE 310-841-4344
FAX 310-204-3578
TYPES   Film/TV Talent - Literary Talent
REPRESENTS   Book Authors - Directors - Producers -
                     Screenwriters - TV Writers

Lawrence Shuman . . . . .Personal Manager
David Wolthoff . . . . .Consulting Elucidator
A.B. Fischer . . . . .Manager
Marc Sternberg . . . . .Development

THE SIEGAL COMPANY
9025 Wilshire Blvd., Ste. 400
Beverly Hills, CA 90211
PHONE 310-274-6088
FAX 310-385-8347
TYPES   Commercial Talent - Film/TV Talent
REPRESENTS   Actors - Hosts/MCs - Teens/Young Adults -
                     Voice-Over Artists
SUBMISSION POLICY   Accepts submissions

Sandra Siegal . . . . .President/Manager
Bill Hinkle . . . . .Manager

ALAN SIEGEL ENTERTAINMENT
345 N. Maple Dr., Ste. 375
Beverly Hills, CA 90210
PHONE 310-278-8400
FAX 310-278-8498
EMAIL . . . . .ent@alansiegel.com
TYPES   Film/TV Talent
REPRESENTS   Actors - Directors - Teens/Young Adults
SUBMISSION POLICY   No unsolicited submissions; Industry refer-
                     ral only

Alan Siegel . . . . .President, CEO
Danielle Robinson . . . . .VP

MICHAEL SIEGEL AND ASSOCIATES
3532 Hayden Ave.
Culver City, CA 90232
PHONE 310-558-6278
FAX 310-872-5525
EMAIL . . . . .mail@msalit.com
TYPES   Literary Talent
SUBMISSION POLICY   Referral only
COMMENTS   Authors, artists, literary properties

Michael Siegel . . . . .Literary Manager/Producer
Kalen Egan . . . . .Creative Executive

SILENT R MANAGEMENT
332 N. La Brea Ave.
Los Angeles, CA 90036
PHONE 323-852-6830
FAX 323-852-6831
TYPES   Film/TV Talent - Literary Talent
REPRESENTS   Directors - Screenwriters - TV Writers
SUBMISSION POLICY   Query letters

Jewerl Ross . . . . .Manager
Michael Cavaretta . . . . .Jr. Manager

BLAIR SILVER & COMPANY LLC
PO Box 3188
Manhattan Beach, CA 90266
PHONE 310-546-4669
FAX 310-545-4369
EMAIL . . . . .blair@blairsilver.com
WEB SITE . . . . .www.blairsilver.com
TYPES   Commercial Talent - Film/TV Talent -
                     Literary Talent - Modeling Talent - Theatre
                     Talent
REPRESENTS   Actors - Book Authors - Comedians -
                     Composers - Directors - Hosts/MCs -
                     Interactive Game Developers - Martial
                     Artists/Stunts - Music Artists - Music
                     Producers - Musical Theatre Performers -
                     Playwrights - Print Models - Producers -
                     Sports Personalities - TV Writers - Variety
                     Artists - Voice-Over Artists
SUBMISSION POLICY   Call office 10 am-5 pm weekdays

Blair Silver . . . . .Manager
Mark Fortier . . . . .Associate Manager

SIMMONS AND SCOTT ENTERTAINMENT, LLC
4110 W. Burbank Blvd.
Burbank, CA 91505
PHONE 818-556-3345
FAX 818-556-3315
EMAIL . . . . .publicity@simmonsandscott.com
TYPES Commercial Talent - Film/TV Talent - Music Talent - Theatre Talent
REPRESENTS Actors - Book Authors - Children - Composers - Martial Artists/Stunts - Music Artists - Music Producers - Teens/Young Adults - Voice-Over Artists
SUBMISSION POLICY Written submissions with picture, resumé and tape

Jon Simmons . . . . .Partner/Manager
Carl Scott . . . . .Partner/Manager

ANDREA SIMON ENTERTAINMENT
14011 Ventura Blvd., Ste. 101S
Sherman Oaks, CA 91423
PHONE 818-380-1901
FAX 818-380-1932
EMAIL .andreasimon@mindspring.com
TYPES Below-the-Line Talent - Film/TV Talent - Literary Talent - Theatre Talent
REPRESENTS Book Authors - Directors - Playwrights - Producers - Screenwriters - TV Writers
SUBMISSION POLICY No unsolicited material
COMMENTS Film production

Andrea Simon . . . . .Manager/Producer

SINCLAIR MANAGEMENT
95 Christopher St., Ste. 6F
New York, NY 10014
PHONE 212-366-9400
FAX 212-242-3043
TYPES Below-the-Line Talent - Commercial Talent - Film/TV Talent - Theatre Talent
AFFILIATIONS NCOPM
REPRESENTS Actors - Children - Magicians - Musical Theatre Performers - Seniors - Teens/Young Adults

Judith Lesley . . . . .Owner/Manager

SIRENSONG ENTERTAINMENT, INC.
132 E. 43rd St., #342
New York, NY 10017
PHONE 212-592-3054
EMAIL . . . . .donna@sirensongentertainment.net
WEB SITE . . . . .www.sirensongentertainment.net
TYPES Commercial Talent - Literary Talent - Theatre Talent
AFFILIATIONS NCOPM
REPRESENTS Actors - Directors - TV Writers - Voice-Over Artists

Donna DeStefano . . . . .Manager

SJV ENTERPRISES & ASSOCIATES
4025 Beethoven St.
Mar Vista, CA 90066
PHONE 310-305-0054
FAX 310-306-4517
EMAIL . . . . .sjvmanagement@msn.com
TYPES Commercial Talent
REPRESENTS Actors - Children - Print Models - Teens/Young Adults

Steve Vieira . . . . .Manager
Dolores Morgenroth . . . . .Assistant Manager
Patrick Shanahan . . . . .Assistant

DANIEL SLADEK ENTERTAINMENT CORPORATION
8306 Wilshire Blvd., PMB 510
Beverly Hills, CA 90211
PHONE 323-934-9268
FAX 323-934-7362
EMAIL . . . . .dansladek@aol.com
WEB SITE . . . . .www.danielsladek.com
TYPES Film/TV Talent
REPRESENTS Actors - Choreographers - Directors - Teens/Young Adults

Daniel Sladek . . . . .Producer/Manager

SLAMDANCE MANAGEMENT
9200 Sunset Blvd., Ste. 918
Los Angeles, CA 90069
PHONE 310-777-8200
FAX 310-777-8205
EMAIL . . . . .info@slamdancemedia.com
WEB SITE . . . . .www.slamdancemedia.com
TYPES Film/TV Talent - Literary Talent
REPRESENTS Actors - Book Authors - Producers - Screenwriters - Teens/Young Adults - TV Writers
SUBMISSION POLICY No unsolicited material; Send query letter with SASE

Robert Schwartz . . . . .CEO
George Ketvertis . . . . .Executive VP

SLEEPING GIANT ENTERTAINMENT
5225 Wilshire Blvd., Ste. 524
Los Angeles, CA 90036
PHONE 323-930-2232
TYPES Film/TV Talent - Literary Talent
REPRESENTS Actors - Directors - Screenwriters - TV Writers

Dave Brown . . . . .Principal/Manager
Scott Halle . . . . .Manager
Matt Horwitz . . . . .Assistant to Dave Brown & Scott Halle

SLJ MANAGEMENT
8265 W. Sunset Blvd., Ste. 203
West Hollywood, CA 90046
PHONE 323-848-3700
FAX 323-848-8665
EMAIL . . . . .slj@sljmanagement.com
TYPES Film/TV Talent
REPRESENTS Actors - Teens/Young Adults - Voice-Over Artists
COMMENTS Associated with Entertainment Management Group

Sandra L. Joseph . . . . .Owner
Roland Gotingco . . . . .Office Manager/Executive Assistant
Nick Rallo . . . . .Assistant
Manny Trejo . . . . .Assistant

SMART ENTERTAINMENT
9348 Civic Center Dr., Mezzanine Level
Beverly Hills, CA 90210
PHONE 310-205-6090
FAX 310-205-6093
EMAIL . . . . .submissions@smartentla.com
WEB SITE . . . . .www.smartentertainmentla.com
SECOND WEB SITE .www.smartentla.com
TYPES   Literary Talent
REPRESENTS   Book Authors - Comedians - Directors -
                         Interactive Game Developers - Producers -
                         Screenwriters - Speakers/Lecturers - TV
                         Writers - Variety Artists - Voice-Over Artists
COMMENTS   Also a production company; Committed to
                         the discovery and cultivation of new and
                         emerging talent, as well as production of
                         all genres of film and TV

John Jacobs . . . . .President/Manager/Producer
Colin O'Reilly . . . . .Manager/Producer
Zac Unterman . . . . .Story Editor

TODD SMITH & ASSOCIATES
345 N. Maple Dr., Ste. 393
Beverly Hills, CA 90210
PHONE 310-271-3911
FAX 310-271-5330
TYPES   Commercial Talent - Film/TV Talent -
                         Literary Talent
REPRESENTS   Actors - Directors - Screenwriters

Todd Smith . . . . .Manager

BETTE SMITH MANAGEMENT
499 N. Canon Dr., Ste. 216
Beverly Hills, CA 90210
PHONE 310-887-3660
FAX 310-887-3661
EMAIL . . . . .bsm@pacbell.net
TYPES   Commercial Talent - Film/TV Talent -
                         Literary Talent - Music Talent
REPRESENTS   Actors - Children - Comedians - Dancers -
                         Music Artists - Producers - Screenwriters -
                         Sports Personalities - Teens/Young Adults -
                         TV Writers - Voice-Over Artists
COMMENTS   Talent of all ages

Bette Smith . . . . .President
Sarah Price . . . . .Assistant
Rolene Thames . . . . .Receptionist/Assistant

THE SUSAN SMITH COMPANY
1344 N. Wetherly Dr.
Los Angeles, CA 90069
PHONE 310-276-4224
FAX 310-276-4343
EMAIL . . . . .susan@susansmithco.com
TYPES   Film/TV Talent
REPRESENTS   Actors
SUBMISSION POLICY   By referral only

Susan Smith . . . . .Owner

SNEAK PREVIEW ENTERTAINMENT
6705 Sunset Blvd., 2nd Fl.
Hollywood, CA 90028
PHONE 323-962-0295
FAX 323-962-0372
EMAIL . . . . .indiefilm@sneakpreviewentertain.com
WEB SITE .www.sneakpreviewentertain.com
TYPES   Commercial Talent - Film/TV Talent -
                         Literary Talent
REPRESENTS   Actors - Directors - Producers -
                         Screenwriters - TV Writers
COMMENTS   Production company

Steven J. Wolfe . . . . .Chairman/CEO/Manager
Josh Silver . . . . .Manager
Michael J. Roth . . . . .Manager
Anne McDermott . . . . .Manager, Literary
Scott Hyman . . . . .Director, Development & Production
Gints Krastins . . . . .Director, Finance Administration

CHAD SNOPEK MANAGEMENT
911 Ninth St., Ste. 107
Santa Monica, CA 90403
PHONE 310-395-4438
FAX 310-458-2947
EMAIL . . . . .cs.13@hotmail.com
TYPES   Film/TV Talent - Literary Talent
REPRESENTS   Book Authors - Directors - Playwrights -
                         Screenwriters - TV Writers

Chad Snopek . . . . .Manager/Producer

SOIREE FAIR, INC.
133 Midland Ave., Ste. 10
Montclair, NJ 07042
PHONE 973-783-9051
FAX 973-746-0426
EMAIL . . . . .soireefair@yahoo.com
WEB SITE . . . . .www.soireefair.com
TYPES   Commercial Talent - Film/TV Talent -
                         Literary Talent - Theatre Talent
AFFILIATIONS   NCOPM
REPRESENTS   Actors - Book Authors - Children - Musical
                         Theatre Performers - Playwrights -
                         Screenwriters - Sports Personalities -
                         Teens/Young Adults - Voice-Over Artists
SUBMISSION POLICY   Via mail; No returns
COMMENTS   Seeking musical theatre and commercial
                         talent of all ages; Original gay and lesbian
                         themed plays, screenplays and novels;
                         Accepting semi-pro and professional ath-
                         letes for TV and film commercials

Karen L. Gunn . . . . .President

MANAGERS

HELENE SOKOL MANAGEMENT
1425 N. Detroit St., #304
Los Angeles, CA 90046
PHONE 323-876-1425
FAX 323-876-0496
TYPES   Commercial Talent - Film/TV Talent
AFFILIATIONS   NCOPM
REPRESENTS   Actors - Children - Teens/Young Adults

Helene Sokol . . . . .Manager

SOMA MANAGEMENT
One Embarcadero Center, Ste. 2830
San Francisco, CA 94111
PHONE 415-274-7662
FAX 415-274-9962
EMAIL . . . . .ecmorgan@somamanagement.com
WEB SITE . . . . .www.somamanagement.com
TYPES   Commercial Talent - Film/TV Talent -
                           Modeling Talent
REPRESENTS   Actors - Dancers - Print Models - Producers
                           - Runway Models - Speakers/Lecturers -
                           Teens/Young Adults

Ellison Morgan . . . . .CEO/President
Karen Morgan . . . . .Creative Director

SONESTA ENTERTAINMENT, LLC
150 Ocean Park Blvd., Ste. 423
Santa Monica, CA 90405
PHONE 310-452-0778
FAX 310-452-5697
EMAIL . . . . .info@sonestaentertainment.com
TYPES   Film/TV Talent - Literary Talent - Music
                           Talent
REPRESENTS   Actors - Directors - Music Producers -
                           Screenwriters - TV Writers

Jonathan Dolin . . . . .Partner
James B. Dolin . . . . .Partner
Ryan Posen . . . . .President, Music Division
Erin Bryce . . . . .Assistant
Robin Stevens . . . . .Assistant

SPEAK SOFTLY LEGAL MANAGEMENT
13540 Ventura Blvd.
Sherman Oaks, CA 91423
PHONE 818-986-8433
FAX 818-986-8435
EMAIL . . . . .blaine@sslm.com
WEB SITE . . . . .www.sslm.com
SECOND WEB SITE . . . . .www.onthefencefilms.com
TYPES   Commercial Talent - Film/TV Talent - Music
                           Talent - Theatre Talent
REPRESENTS   Actors - Comedians - Music Artists -
                           Producers - Sports Personalities

Blaine Greenberg Esq. . . . . .President/Manager/General Counsel

LARRY SPELLMAN ENTERPRISES
1740 Camino Parocela
Palm Springs, CA 92264
PHONE 760-327-0238
FAX 760-325-2928
EMAIL . . . . .spellman.larryandcece@gte.net
TYPES   Film/TV Talent
REPRESENTS   Actors - Comedians - Variety Artists

Larry Spellman . . . . .Sole Proprietor

SPELLMAN, PAUL & WETZEL
6075 Franklin Ave., Ste. 366
Los Angeles, CA 90028
PHONE 323-871-1011/212-262-0008
FAX 323-375-0355/212-333-5180
EMAIL . . . . .cspellman126@aol.com
SECOND EMAIL . . . . .rogerpaulmgmt@aol.com
TYPES   Commercial Talent - Film/TV Talent -
                           Literary Talent - Theatre Talent
REPRESENTS   Actors - Book Authors - Children -
                           Comedians - Directors - Playwrights -
                           Screenwriters - Teens/Young Adults
COMMENTS   East Coast office: 1650 Broadway, Ste.
                           705, New York, NY 10019-6833

Christopher Spellman . . . . .No Title
Larry Spellman . . . . .No Title
Byron Wetzel . . . . .No Title
Jonathan Michaels .No Title
Roger Paul . . . . .No Title (NY)
Diana Smith .No Title (NY)

SPOT LIGHT ENTERTAINMENT
c/o Michael Andrews
PO Box 1949
Lawrenceville, GA 30046
PHONE 770-822-1036
FAX 770-822-9902
EMAIL . . . . .mandrews@slcomedy.com
WEB SITE . . . . .www.spotlightentertainment.com
SECOND WEB SITE . . . . .www.slcomedy.com
TYPES   Film/TV Talent - Literary Talent - Modeling
                           Talent - Music Talent
REPRESENTS   Actors - Book Authors - Children -
                           Comedians - Hosts/MCs - Magicians -
                           Music Artists - Music Producers -
                           Playwrights - Producers - Screenwriters -
                           Speakers/Lecturers - Sports Personalities -
                           TV Writers
SUBMISSION POLICY   No unsolicited material will be reviewed;
                           See Web site for submission guidelines
COMMENTS   Comedy show and musical concert book-
                           ings (all varieties); Concert and tour pro-
                           motion; Event planning; Film & TV produc-
                           tion

Michael Andrews . .Talent Manager/Agent, Booking & Artist Development
Renee Andrews . . . . .Marketing/Sales
Cheryle Harrison . . . . .Director, Project Development
James Hudson . . . . .Marketing/Sales/Promotions
Joy Pervis . . . . .Artist Development
Linda Thomas . . . . .Marketing/Promotions
Charles Williams . . . . .Booking/Marketing/Sales

STAR TALENT MANAGEMENT
682 N. Brookside Rd.
Allentown, PA 18106
PHONE 610-366-1700
FAX 610-366-7117
TYPES   Commercial Talent - Film/TV Talent - Music
                           Talent - Theatre Talent
AFFILIATIONS   NCOPM
REPRESENTS   Actors - Children - Dancers - Musical
                           Theatre Performers - Teens/Young Adults -
                           Voice-Over Artists
SUBMISSION POLICY   Mail photo and resumé with self-addressed
                           stamped envelope
COMMENTS   Broadway; Works in New York,
                           Philadelphia and Los Angeles; National
                           Secretary, NCOPM

Lois N. Miller . . . . .Personal Talent Manager/Owner
Stan Z. Miller . . . . .Assistant

STATION 3

8522 National Blvd., Ste. 108
Culver City, CA 90232
PHONE 310-204-4444/212-245-3250
FAX 310-204-4456/212-245-2853
TYPES   Commercial Talent - Film/TV Talent -
                        Literary Talent - Modeling Talent - Music
                        Talent - Theatre Talent
AFFILIATIONS   NCOPM
REPRESENTS   Actors - Children - Comedians - Directors -
                        Music Artists - Print Models - Producers -
                        Runway Models - Screenwriters -
                        Teens/Young Adults - TV Writers
SUBMISSION POLICY   By mail only
COMMENTS   Formerly Creative Management Group,
                        LLC; East Coast office: 850 Seventh Ave.,
                        Ste. 1100, New York, NY 10019

Edie Robb . . . . .Managing Partner (NY)
R.D. Robb . . . . .Managing Partner
Anne Woodward . . . . .Manager
Kasra Ajir . . . . .Manager
Thomas Carter . . . . .Creative Executive
Vanessa Crase . . . . .Assistant

STEIN ENTERTAINMENT GROUP

1351 N. Crescent Heights Blvd., #312
West Hollywood, CA 90046
PHONE 323-822-1400
FAX 323-822-2122
EMAIL . . . . .tstein@steinentertainment.com
WEB SITE . . . . .www.steinentertainment.com
TYPES   Commercial Talent - Film/TV Talent
REPRESENTS   Actors - Children - Teens/Young Adults -
                        Voice-Over Artists

T.J. Stein . . . . .President
Colin Harp . . . . .Assistant to T.J. Stein

STEINBERG TALENT MANAGEMENT GROUP

1560 Broadway, Ste. 405
New York, NY 10036
PHONE 212-843-3200
FAX 212-843-3470
WEB SITE . . . . .www.steinbergtalent.com
TYPES   Below-the-Line Talent - Commercial Talent
                        - Film/TV Talent - Literary Talent - Theatre
                        Talent
REPRESENTS   Actors - Book Authors - Comedians -
                        Directors - Hosts/MCs - Playwrights -
                        Producers - Screenwriters - TV Writers -
                        Variety Artists - Voice-Over Artists
SUBMISSION POLICY   No walk-ins
COMMENTS   Specializes in comedic talent

Jason Steinberg . . . . .President
Evan Steinberg . . . . .VP, Talent
Matt Gawel . . . . .Assistant

THE STERLING/WINTERS COMPANY

10900 Wilshire Blvd., Ste. 1550
Los Angeles, CA 90024
PHONE 310-557-2700
FAX 310-557-1722
TYPES   Commercial Talent - Film/TV Talent -
                        Literary Talent - Music Talent - Theatre
                        Talent
REPRESENTS   Actors - Book Authors - Comedians -
                        Directors - Hosts/MCs - Music Artists -
                        Musical Theatre Performers - Producers -
                        Speakers/Lecturers - TV Writers - Variety
                        Artists - Voice-Over Artists
COMMENTS   Marketing and branding

Erik Sterling . . . . .COO
Jason Winters . . . . .Vision Strategist
Jon Carrasco . . . . .Executive VP, Creative Director
Stephen Roseberry . . . . .Executive VP, Marketing
Steve Rosenblum . . . . .Sr. VP, Corporate
Rocco Ingemi . . . . .VP, Brand Management
Konrad Leh .VP, Talent Department
Miles Robinson . . . . .VP/Executive Assistant to Jon Carrasco
Tony Carnot . . . . .Art Director
Joel Blitz . . . . .Administration
Georgia DeCaro . . . . .Administration
Dee Rockoff . . . . .Administration
Mitch Sternard . . . . .Research & Development
Ruben Torres . . . . .Marketing Assistant to Stephen Roseberry
Zulma Ponce . . . . .Executive Assistant to Erik Sterling
Yossi Fixman . . . . .Assistant to Rocco Ingemi
Yesenia Morales . . . . .Assistant to Stephen Roseberry

HARRIET STERNBERG MANAGEMENT

4530 Gloria Ave.
Encino, CA 91436
PHONE 818-906-9600
FAX 818-906-1723
EMAIL . . . . .mgrbabe@aol.com
TYPES   Film/TV Talent - Literary Talent - Music
                        Talent
REPRESENTS   Actors - Comedians - Directors - Music
                        Artists - Songwriters - TV Writers
SUBMISSION POLICY   No unsolicited material

Harriet Sternberg . . . . .Manager

JOEL STEVENS ENTERTAINMENT COMPANY

206 S. Brand Blvd.
Glendale, CA 91204
PHONE 818-509-5700
FAX 818-509-6734
TYPES   Film/TV Talent - Literary Talent
AFFILIATIONS   TMA
REPRESENTS   Actors - Directors - Screenwriters -
                        Teens/Young Adults - TV Writers

Joel Stevens . . . . .Chairman/CEO
John S. Will . . . . .Director, Development
Ian Baca . . . . .Associate, Talent & Development

GAIL A. STOCKER PRESENTS

1025 N. Kings Rd., Ste. 113
Los Angeles, CA 90069
PHONE 323-654-4015
FAX 323-654-1150
EMAIL . . . . .gail@comedycontact.com
WEB SITE . . . . .www.comedycontact.com
TYPES   Film/TV Talent
REPRESENTS   Comedians - Hosts/MCs - Magicians -
                        Speakers/Lecturers
COMMENTS   Comedy consultant; Professional comedy
                        for corporate events; Affiliated with ATAS

Gail A. Stocker . . . . .Manager/Comedy Consultant

STONE CANYON MEDIA
10677 Somma Way
Los Angeles, CA 90077
PHONE 310-476-2882
FAX 310-476-8283
TYPES   Film/TV Talent - Literary Talent
AFFILIATIONS   DGA
REPRESENTS   Book Authors - Directors - Producers -
                         Screenwriters - TV Writers
SUBMISSION POLICY   By referral only
COMMENTS   Also affiliated with WGA

Candace Lake . . . . .Manager
Ryan Lewis . . . . .Manager

STORY ARTS MANAGEMENT
2193 Commonwealth Ave., Ste. 345
Boston, MA 02135
PHONE 617-527-2584
FAX 617-527-2358
EMAIL .janicempieroni@aol.com
WEB SITE . . . . .www.storyartsmanagement.com
TYPES   Literary Talent
REPRESENTS   Book Authors - Screenwriters - TV Writers
SUBMISSION POLICY   See Web site

Janice M. Pieroni . . . . .Founder

STRAUSS-McGARR ENTERTAINMENT
16785 123rd Terrace North
Jupiter, FL 33478
PHONE 561-746-6115
FAX 561-746-4141
EMAIL . . . . .cpm232@aol.com
WEB SITE . . . . .www.talkinganimals.net
TYPES   Film/TV Talent
REPRESENTS   Comedians - Voice-Over Artists
SUBMISSION POLICY   Call before submitting

Colleen McGarr . . . . .Manager

STUDIO TALENT GROUP
1328 12th St., Ste. 1
Santa Monica, CA 90401
PHONE 310-393-8004
FAX 310-393-2473
EMAIL . . . . .stgactor@gte.net
SECOND EMAIL . . . . .firstname@studiotalentgroup.com
WEB SITE . . . . .www.studiotalentgroup.com
TYPES   Commercial Talent - Film/TV Talent -
                         Literary Talent - Theatre Talent
AFFILIATIONS   TMA
REPRESENTS   Actors - Book Authors - Children -
                         Comedians - Print Models - Screenwriters -
                         Teens/Young Adults - TV Writers

Phil Brock . . . . .Owner
Kathryn Boole . . . . .Literary
Barry Carver . . . . .Motion Picture/TV Associate
Meghan Brown . . . . .Associate
Arloa Reston . . . . .Assistant
Mira Yellin . . . . .Assistant
Nadine Hallick . . . . .Assistant
Megan Lester . . . . .Assistant

THE SUCHIN COMPANY
12747 Riverside Dr., Ste. 208
Valley Village, CA 91607-3333
PHONE 818-505-0044
FAX 818-505-0110
TYPES   Film/TV Talent - Music Talent
REPRESENTS   Actors - Comedians - Speakers/Lecturers -
                         Sports Personalities - Teens/Young Adults -
                         Variety Artists

Milton B. Suchin . . . . .Owner

SULLIVAN TALENT GROUP
305 W. 105th St., Ste. 3-B
New York, NY 10025
PHONE 212-665-9516
FAX 212-749-0689
EMAIL . . . . .sullivantalent@aol.com
TYPES   Film/TV Talent - Theatre Talent
REPRESENTS   Actors
SUBMISSION POLICY   By mail only

Matthew Sullivan .Owner/Manager
Alyson Schwartz . . . . .Associate

SUSKIN MANAGEMENT LLC
2 Charlton St., Ste. 5K
New York, NY 10014
PHONE 212-242-2030
EMAIL . . . . .james@suskinmanagement.com
TYPES   Film/TV Talent
REPRESENTS   Actors

James Suskin . . . . .Manager

SUSSEX LTD., INC., A MANAGEMENT COMPANY
16633 Ventura Blvd., Ste. 1000
Encino, CA 91436
PHONE 818-783-0223
FAX 818-783-0335
EMAIL . . . . .berniebar@aol.com
TYPES   Film/TV Talent - Literary Talent - Music
                         Talent
REPRESENTS   Book Authors - Composers - Directors -
                         Music Artists - Music Supervisors -
                         Playwrights - Producers - Screenwriters - TV
                         Writers
SUBMISSION POLICY   Email or fax a two-page synopsis for
                         books, scripts and plays; Credits/resumés
                         for writers, authors, composers, producers
                         and directors
COMMENTS   Package presentations for TV/Films

Bernard Weitzman . . . . .President
Ruth Bruning . . . . .Associate

JEFF SUSSMAN MANAGEMENT
603 W. 115th St., #282
New York, NY 10025
PHONE 212-663-0004/310-244-3567
FAX 310-244-0347
TYPES   Film/TV Talent
AFFILIATIONS   NCOPM
REPRESENTS   Comedians
SUBMISSION POLICY   No unsolicited material

Jeff Sussman . . . . .Manager
Chandra Keyes . . . . .Manager

SUZELLE ENTERPRISES
853 Seventh Ave., Ste. 8D
New York, NY 10019
PHONE 212-397-2047
FAX 212-397-2032
WEB SITE . . . . .www.avotaynu.com/suzelle
TYPES   Commercial Talent - Film/TV Talent -
                         Modeling Talent - Theatre Talent
AFFILIATIONS   NCOPM
REPRESENTS   Actors - Broadcast Journalists/Newscasters
                         - Children - Hosts/MCs - Infants - Musical
                         Theatre Performers - Print Models - Seniors
                         - Teens/Young Adults - Voice-Over Artists
COMMENTS   Mexico City office: 21A Gonzalez de
                         Cosio, Mexico City DF03100 Mexico,
                         phone: 52-5-5523-3604

Suzanne Schachter . . . . .President
Kristyn Grasing . . . . .Assistant
Jay Mottram . . . . .Assistant

SWEENEY MANAGEMENT
8755 Lookout Mountain Ave.
Los Angeles, CA 90046
PHONE 323-822-3000
FAX 323-822-3020
EMAIL . . . . .sweedavid@aol.com
TYPES   Film/TV Talent - Literary Talent
REPRESENTS   Actors - Children - Comedians -
                         Screenwriters - Teens/Young Adults - TV
                         Writers
SUBMISSION POLICY   No unsolicited submissions

David Sweeney .Partner/Manager
Romi Schneider . . . . .Assistant

SYNCHRONICITY MANAGEMENT
9003 Saint Ives Dr.
Los Angeles, CA 90069
PHONE 310-246-1477/212-704-0515
FAX 310-274-1491/212-704-0945
TYPES   Film/TV Talent - Literary Talent - Music
                         Talent - Theatre Talent
REPRESENTS   Book Authors - Comedians - Directors -
                         Music Artists - Playwrights - Producers -
                         Screenwriters - TV Writers - Variety Artists
COMMENTS   Animation; East Coast office: 350 Fifth
                         Ave., Ste. 2716, New York, NY 10118

Adam Peck . . . . .Manager/Producer

SYNERGY MANAGEMENT, INC.
22287 Mulholland Hwy., Ste. 204
Calabasas, CA 91302
PHONE 818-703-6707
FAX 818-703-7197
TYPES   Commercial Talent - Film/TV Talent
REPRESENTS   Actors - Broadcast Journalists/Newscasters
                         - Comedians - Hosts/MCs - Voice-Over
                         Artists
COMMENTS   Also represents experts and contributors

Glen J. Clarkson . . . . .Partner/Manager
Cat Josell . . . . .Partner/Manager

THE TALENT COMPANY
501 W. Glenoaks Blvd., Ste. 446
Glendale, CA 91202
PHONE 818-242-8802
EMAIL . . . . .focustalentgroup@earthlink.net
TYPES   Commercial Talent - Film/TV Talent -
                         Modeling Talent - Theatre Talent
REPRESENTS   Actors - Teens/Young Adults
SUBMISSION POLICY   By mail or email only

Karen Renna . . . . .Manager
April Biggs . . . . .Manager

TALENT MANAGEMENT PARTNERS
PO Box 2744
Redondo Beach, CA 90278
PHONE 310-318-8868
FAX 310-318-8878
EMAIL .baybus@mindspring.com
TYPES   Commercial Talent - Film/TV Talent -
                         Literary Talent - Theatre Talent
REPRESENTS   Actors - Book Authors - Directors -
                         Screenwriters - Seniors - Teens/Young
                         Adults - TV Writers - Variety Artists - Voice-
                         Over Artists

A.T. Iorio . . . . .General Manager
Maggie Kline . . . . .Associate Manager

TALENT SCOUT INTERNATIONAL MANAGEMENT
1484-1/2 S. Robertson Blvd.
Los Angeles, CA 90035
PHONE 310-276-5160
FAX 310-276-5134
EMAIL . . . . .admin@atalentscout.com
WEB SITE . . . . .www.atalentscout.com
TYPES   Film/TV Talent - Literary Talent - Modeling
                         Talent - Theatre Talent
REPRESENTS   Actors - Book Authors - Directors -
                         Playwrights - Producers - Screenwriters - TV
                         Writers
SUBMISSION POLICY   See Web site
COMMENTS   International company; English, French and
                         German speaking talent

Alex Ross . . . . .CEO
Annette Haller . . . . .Manager
Lisa Vogel . . . . .Manager
Eok Ngo . . . . .Office Manager

TALENT SOURCE
105 Shad Row, 2nd Fl.
Piermont, NY 10968
PHONE 212-730-2701
FAX 845-359-4609
EMAIL . . . . .talentsource@tciartists.com
TYPES   Music Talent
AFFILIATIONS   AFM
REPRESENTS   Music Artists

Margo Lewis . . . . .President
Faith Fusillo . . . . .VP
Chris Tuthill . . . . .Associate

TALENTCO MODEL & TALENT MANAGEMENT
PO Box 7841
Beverly Hills, CA 90212
PHONE 604-687-0388
FAX 604-687-0308
EMAIL . . . . .talentco@canadafilm.com
WEB SITE . . . . .www.talentco.net
TYPES　　　　　　　　Commercial Talent - Film/TV Talent -
　　　　　　　　　　　Modeling Talent - Music Talent - Theatre
　　　　　　　　　　　Talent
REPRESENTS　　　　　Actors - Broadcast Journalists/Newscasters
　　　　　　　　　　　- Children - Comedians - Dancers - Infants
　　　　　　　　　　　- Martial Artists/Stunts - Print Models -
　　　　　　　　　　　Runway Models - Seniors - Sports
　　　　　　　　　　　Personalities - Teens/Young Adults - Voice-
　　　　　　　　　　　Over Artists
SUBMISSION POLICY　　By appointment only; Send photo, resumé
　　　　　　　　　　　and demo tape via US Mail
COMMENTS　　　　　　Extras; Head office: #215-209 Carrall St.
　　　　　　　　　　　(Gaoler's Mews), Vancouver BC, V6B 4K7
　　　　　　　　　　　Canada

Tania London . . . . .Principal Agent/Manager (Vancouver)
Brenda Wong . . . . .Principal Agent/Manager (Vancouver)
Anna Bonthoux . . . . .Agent/International Model Scout
Kelly James . . . . .Agent (Vancouver)
James MacLean . . . . .Manager
Lisa Nasu . . . . .Office Administrator (Vancouver)
Betsy Shimokura . . . . .Controller (Vancouver)

TALENTED MANAGERS
65 W. 90th St., Ste. 7D
New York, NY 10024
PHONE 212-579-2432
FAX 212-579-0920
EMAIL . . . . .info@talentedmanagers.com
WEB SITE . . . . .www.talentedmanagers.com
TYPES　　　　　　　　Film/TV Talent - Modeling Talent
AFFILIATIONS　　　　　NCOPM
REPRESENTS　　　　　Actors - Print Models - Runway Models -
　　　　　　　　　　　Teens/Young Adults
SUBMISSION POLICY　　Interviews by appointment only; Unsolicited
　　　　　　　　　　　materials will not be returned
COMMENTS　　　　　　See PR division Fat City Media

Michael Farkas . . . . .Manager
Marcy Sharkey . . . . .Manager

TAO MANAGEMENT & TETRAHEDRON PRODUCTIONS
2934 Beverly Glen Circle, PMB 392
Los Angeles, CA 90077
PHONE 310-289-9595
FAX 310-289-7788
TYPES　　　　　　　　Film/TV Talent - Theatre Talent
REPRESENTS　　　　　Actors
COMMENTS　　　　　　Celebrity clients only

Herb Hamsher . . . . .President
Jonathan Stoller . . . . .VP
Todd Taylor . . . . .Assistant to Mr. Hamsher & Mr. Stoller

TEITELBAUM ARTISTS GROUP
8840 Wilshire Blvd.
Beverly Hills, CA 90211
PHONE 310-358-3250
FAX 310-358-3251
TYPES　　　　　　　　Film/TV Talent - Literary Talent
REPRESENTS　　　　　Actors - Comedians - Directors -
　　　　　　　　　　　Hosts/MCs - Producers - Teens/Young
　　　　　　　　　　　Adults - TV Writers
SUBMISSION POLICY　　No unsolicited material

Mark Teitelbaum . . . . .President
Claire Burgart . . . . .Executive Assistant

TEMPTATION MANAGEMENT
8306 Wilshire Blvd., Ste. 232
Beverly Hills, CA 90211
PHONE 323-899-3752
FAX 505-213-2150
EMAIL . . . . .info@temptationmanagement.com
WEB SITE . . . . .www.temptationmanagement.com
TYPES　　　　　　　　Commercial Talent - Film/TV Talent -
　　　　　　　　　　　Literary Talent - Modeling Talent
AFFILIATIONS　　　　　TMA
REPRESENTS　　　　　Actors - Print Models - Runway Models -
　　　　　　　　　　　Teens/Young Adults

Brandon Ross .Owner/Talent Manager
Tori Arnold . . . . .Talent Manager
Gregory Quincy . . . . .Talent Manager

TERRIFIC TALENT ASSOCIATES, INC.
419 Park Ave. South, Ste. 1009
New York, NY 10016
PHONE 212-689-2800
FAX 212-481-1000
EMAIL . . . . .terrifictalent@aol.com
TYPES　　　　　　　　Commercial Talent - Film/TV Talent -
　　　　　　　　　　　Theatre Talent
AFFILIATIONS　　　　　NCOPM
REPRESENTS　　　　　Actors

Marianne Leone . . . . .Manager
Ryan Sorkin . . . . .Assistant

TGI ENTERTAINMENT CORPORATION
PO Box 476
San Francisco, CA 94104
PHONE 415-515-1923
FAX 415-346-2286
EMAIL .tgi@tgientertainment.com
WEB SITE . . . . .www.tgientertainment.com
TYPES　　　　　　　　Below-the-Line Talent - Commercial Talent
　　　　　　　　　　　- Film/TV Talent - Literary Talent - Modeling
　　　　　　　　　　　Talent - Music Talent - Theatre Talent
AFFILIATIONS　　　　　TMA
REPRESENTS　　　　　Actors - Broadcast Journalists/Newscasters
　　　　　　　　　　　- Directors - Music Artists - Music Producers
　　　　　　　　　　　- Music Supervisors - Print Models -
　　　　　　　　　　　Producers - Runway Models - Screenwriters
　　　　　　　　　　　- Sports Personalities - TV Writers - Voice-
　　　　　　　　　　　Over Artists
COMMENTS　　　　　　Publicity, production and talent manage-
　　　　　　　　　　　ment; Mailing address: 400 S. Beverly Dr.
　　　　　　　　　　　#214 Beverly Hills, CA 90212

Sam C. Houston . . . . .Chairman/CEO
Allison Gail . . . . .Vice Chairman/President
Robert Mack . . . . .CFO
David Stern . . . . .Divisional President
Curtis Smith . . . . .Production Manager
John Hobbie . . . . .Director, Artist Management/Publicity
Kelly Miller . . . . .Acquisitions

THE MICHAEL FORMAN COMPANY
409 N. Camden Dr., Ste. 205
Beverly Hills, CA 90210
PHONE 310-247-8088
EMAIL . . . . .filmtvmgmt@aol.com
TYPES　　　　　　　　Film/TV Talent - Literary Talent
REPRESENTS　　　　　Actors - Book Authors - Comedians -
　　　　　　　　　　　Directors - Screenwriters - Teens/Young
　　　　　　　　　　　Adults - TV Writers
COMMENTS　　　　　　Production company; Screenplay develop-
　　　　　　　　　　　ment

Michael Forman . . . . .President
Jeff Silverberg . . . . .Creative Executive

THIRDHILL ENTERTAINMENT
195 S. Beverly Dr., Ste. 400
Beverly Hills, CA 90212
PHONE 310-786-1936
FAX 310-786-1939
EMAIL . . . . .thirdhill@thirdhillentertainment.com
TYPES   Commercial Talent - Film/TV Talent -
                        Literary Talent - Theatre Talent
REPRESENTS   Actors - Children - Hosts/MCs -
                        Teens/Young Adults

Toni Benson . . . . .President
Amanda Hendon .Talent Manager
Stewart Bick . . . . .Talent Manager

LARRY THOMPSON ORGANIZATION
9663 Santa Monica Blvd., Ste. 801
Beverly Hills, CA 90210
PHONE 310-288-0700
FAX 310-288-0711
EMAIL .ltbeverlyhills@aol.com
WEB SITE . . . . .www.larrythompsonorg.com
SECOND WEB SITE . . . . .www.projectriseandshine.com
TYPES   Film/TV Talent
REPRESENTS   Actors - Speakers/Lecturers
SUBMISSION POLICY   No unsolicited submissions
COMMENTS   Producer

Larry Thompson . . . . .Chairman/CEO
Kelly Thompson . . . . .Director, Development
Robert G. Endara II . . . . .Director, Development

THOMPSON STREET ENTERTAINMENT
754 N. Kilkea Dr.
Los Angeles, CA 90046
PHONE 323-651-5813
TYPES   Film/TV Talent - Literary Talent
REPRESENTS   Directors - Producers - Screenwriters - TV
                        Writers
SUBMISSION POLICY   No unsolicited submissions

Susan B. Landau . . . . .Manager/Producer
Jamie Lockett . . . . .Assistant to Ms. Landau

THE ROBERT THORNE COMPANY
9654 Heather Rd.
Beverly Hills, CA 90210
PHONE 310-288-5800
FAX 310-860-1200
TYPES   Film/TV Talent
REPRESENTS   Actors

Robert Thorne . . . . .Manager
Greg Redlitz . . . . .Manager

THRIVE ENTERTAINMENT
1093 Broxton Ave., Ste. 228
Los Angeles, CA 90024
PHONE 310-209-1500
FAX 310-209-1544
EMAIL .andrew@thrive-ent.com
TYPES   Literary Talent
AFFILIATIONS   AFM - DGA
REPRESENTS   Directors - Producers - Screenwriters - TV
                        Writers
COMMENTS   Full-service literary management company

Andrew Hersh . . . . .Manager

THRULINE ENTERTAINMENT
9250 Wilshire Blvd., Ground Fl.
Beverly Hills, CA 90212
PHONE 310-595-1500
FAX 310-595-1505/310-595-1506
TYPES   Film/TV Talent - Literary Talent
REPRESENTS   Actors - Comedians - Directors -
                        Screenwriters - TV Writers
COMMENTS   Production company is Tagline
                        Entertainment; Second office: 10635 Santa
                        Monica Blvd., Ste. 180, Los Angeles, CA
                        90025, phone: 310-234-0100, fax: 310-
                        234-0200; Montréal office: 2101 St.
                        Laurent Blvd., Montréal, Quebec H2X 2T5
                        Canada, phone: 514-845-3155, fax: 514-
                        845-4140

Chris Henze .Partner/Manager
J.B. Roberts .Partner/Manager
Ron West . . . . .Partner/Manager
William Mercer . . . . .Partner/Manager
Susan Calogerakis . . . . .Manager
Marc Hamou . . . . .Manager
Ahmineh Jarnegan . . . . .Manager
Steve Kavovit . . . . .Manager
Jodi Lieberman . . . . .Manager
Alison Little . . . . .Manager
Adam Williamson . . . . .Manager
Josh Levy . . . . .Associate
David Lukan . . . . .Associate
Luke Lytar . . . . .Associate
Erin McClelland . . . . .Associate
Tony Niedert . . . . .Associate

ROZ TILLMAN MANAGEMENT
11054 Ventura Blvd., Ste. 289
Studio City, CA 91604
PHONE 818-985-3514
FAX 818-505-0481
EMAIL . . . . .roztill@pacbell.net
TYPES   Commercial Talent - Film/TV Talent -
                        Literary Talent
AFFILIATIONS   TMA
REPRESENTS   Actors - Children - Directors - Hosts/MCs -
                        Martial Artists/Stunts - Producers - Seniors -
                        Teens/Young Adults - Voice-Over Artists
SUBMISSION POLICY   No unsolicited faxes or tapes; No drop-offs
COMMENTS   Talent & Literary packaging; Past board of
                        directors, TMA

Roz Tillman . . . . .Owner/Manager

TINOCO MANAGEMENT
8033 Sunset Blvd., #573
West Hollywood, CA 90046
PHONE 323-445-9206
FAX 323-395-0965
EMAIL . . . . .tinocomanagement@yahoo.com
TYPES   Commercial Talent - Film/TV Talent -
                        Modeling Talent
REPRESENTS   Actors - Children - Comedians - Dancers -
                        Infants - Musical Theatre Performers - Print
                        Models - Teens/Young Adults - Variety
                        Artists - Voice-Over Artists
SUBMISSION POLICY   Submissions, photos and resumés by US
                        Mail or email; Mailed materials will not be
                        returned; No phone calls, faxes or walk-ins

Hector Tinoco . . . . .Manager

MANAGERS

TMT ENTERTAINMENT
648 Broadway, Ste. 1002
New York, NY 10012
PHONE 212-477-6047
FAX 212-473-3646
TYPES   Film/TV Talent - Literary Talent - Theatre
                         Talent
REPRESENTS   Actors - Directors - Screenwriters

Tina Thor . . . . .Partner
Howard Axel . . . . .Partner
Michael Gasparro . . . . .Manager

TOLTEC ARTISTS
1680 N. Vine St., Ste. 904
Hollywood, CA 90028
PHONE 323-466-1330
FAX 323-466-1340
EMAIL . . . . .tk@toltec-artists.com
TYPES   Film/TV Talent - Literary Talent
REPRESENTS   Actors - Comedians - Directors - Producers
SUBMISSION POLICY   No unsolicited submissions
COMMENTS   Animators and animation companies

Tracy Kramer . . . . .Manager

TORQUE ENTERTAINMENT
1045 Ocean Ave., PH
Santa Monica, CA 90403
PHONE 310-576-6025
FAX 310-576-6026
EMAIL . . . . .info@torque-entertainment.com
WEB SITE . . . . .www.torque-entertainment.com
TYPES   Commercial Talent - Film/TV Talent -
                         Literary Talent - Modeling Talent - Music
                         Talent - Theatre Talent
REPRESENTS   Actors - Broadcast Journalists/Newscasters
                         - Comedians - Directors - Hosts/MCs -
                         Interactive Game Developers - Musical
                         Theatre Performers - Playwrights - Print
                         Models - Runway Models - Screenwriters -
                         Seniors - Teens/Young Adults - TV Writers -
                         Voice-Over Artists

Peter Scott . . . . .Manager/Founder
Ian Roy . . . . .Literary

TRADEMARK ARTISTS MANAGEMENT
10940 Wilshire Blvd., Ste. 1600
Los Angeles, CA 90024-3944
PHONE 310-443-4135
FAX 310-557-2836
TYPES   Commercial Talent - Film/TV Talent -
                         Literary Talent - Modeling Talent - Music
                         Talent
REPRESENTS   Actors - Book Authors - Comedians - Music
                         Artists - Print Models - Producers -
                         Screenwriters - TV Writers

Marc Waddell . . . . .President
Merri Chen . . . . .VP, Operations
Erik Penn . . . . .Chief Technology Officer

TRADEMARK TALENT
338-1/2 N. Ogden Dr.
Los Angeles, CA 90036
PHONE 323-935-0003
FAX 323-935-0044
WEB SITE . . . . .www.trademarktalent.com
TYPES   Film/TV Talent - Theatre Talent
REPRESENTS   Actors - Children - Comedians -
                         Hosts/MCs - Teens/Young Adults
SUBMISSION POLICY   By mail

Devon Jackson . . . . .Manager
Vanessa Damon . . . . .Assistant

TRANCAS MANAGEMENT
1875 Century Park East, Ste. 1145
Los Angeles, CA 90067
PHONE 310-553-5599
FAX 310-553-0536
EMAIL . . . . .info@trancasfilms.com
WEB SITE . . . . .www.trancasfilms.com
TYPES   Film/TV Talent - Literary Talent
REPRESENTS   Screenwriters - TV Writers

Malek Akkad . . . . .President of Production
Sammy Montana . . . . .Story Editor
Christi Sinkus . . . . .Office Manager

TREASURE ENTERTAINMENT
468 N. Camden Dr., Ste. 200
Beverly Hills, CA 90210
PHONE 310-860-7490
FAX 310-943-1488
EMAIL . . . . .info@treasureentertainment.net
WEB SITE . . . . .www.treasureentertainment.net
TYPES   Literary Talent
REPRESENTS   Directors - Screenwriters - TV Writers
SUBMISSION POLICY   No unsolicited queries

Mark Heidelberger . . . . .Co-Chairman/CEO
Jesse Felsot . . . . .Co-Chairman/President
Ian Vishnevsky . . . . .CFO
Kevin Asbell . . . . .COO, General Counsel
Jonathan Hoffberg . . . . .VP, Business Development
Bridget McGrath . . . . .VP, Music Videos & Commercials
Andrew Yoo . . . . .VP, Corporate Finance & Operations

TRINITI MANAGEMENT
3940 Laurel Canyon Blvd., Ste. 668
Studio City, CA 91604
PHONE 818-300-0050
FAX 818-301-2532/601-510-1979
EMAIL . . . . .makenzi@trinitimanagement.com
SECOND EMAIL . . . . .marissa@trinitimanagement.com
WEB SITE . . . . .www.trinitimanagement.com
TYPES   Commercial Talent - Film/TV Talent -
                           Modeling Talent
REPRESENTS   Actors - Children - Choreographers -
                           Dancers - Hosts/MCs - Print Models -
                           Teens/Young Adults - Voice-Over Artists
SUBMISSION POLICY   Mail submissions to Attn: Seeking Rep

MaKenzi Moore . . . . .Owner
Marissa Upchurch . . . . .Owner
Christina Garvin . . . . .Assistant

TRIPLE THREAT TALENT MANAGEMENT
PO Box 665
Oxford, GA 30054
PHONE 866-756-9627
EMAIL . . . . .info@tttmanagement.com
SECOND EMAIL . . . . .tttmanagement@yahoo.com
WEB SITE .www.tttmanagement.com
TYPES   Commercial Talent - Literary Talent -
                           Modeling Talent - Music Talent
REPRESENTS   Actors - Comedians - Dancers - Music
                           Artists - Music Producers - Print Models -
                           Screenwriters - Teens/Young Adults - Voice-
                           Over Artists

Diane Knight . . . . .Manager

TRUMP MODEL MANAGEMENT
91 Fifth Ave., 3rd Fl.
New York, NY 10003
PHONE 212-924-0990
FAX 212-645-4940
EMAIL . . . . .info@tmgmt.com
WEB SITE . . . . .www.trumpmodels.com
TYPES   Modeling Talent
REPRESENTS   Print Models - Runway Models
SUBMISSION POLICY   No open calls; Photos can be submitted
                           either by email or mail
COMMENTS   Minimum height: 5'8

Corinne Nicolas . . . . .President
Valerie Boyce . . . . .Agent
Duane Gazi . . . . .Agent
Jolene Rapport . . . . .Agent
Dean Rodgers . . . . .Agent
Becky Southwick . . . . .Agent
Sanda Sperka . . . . .Agent
Jan Stewart . . . . .Agent

TRUSIK TALENT MANAGEMENT, INC.
1155 N. La Cienega Blvd., Ste. 801
West Hollywood, CA 90069-2440
PHONE 310-659-7550
FAX 310-659-7550
EMAIL . . . . .paul.trusik@talentmanagers.org
WEB SITE .www.talentmanagers.org
TYPES   Commercial Talent - Film/TV Talent -
                           Theatre Talent
AFFILIATIONS   TMA
REPRESENTS   Actors - Teens/Young Adults

Paul Trusik . . . . .Owner/Manager

TUDOR MANAGEMENT GROUP
1610 Oak St., Ste. B
Santa Monica, CA 90405
PHONE 310-392-9858
TYPES   Literary Talent - Theatre Talent
REPRESENTS   Directors - Producers - Screenwriters - TV
                           Writers
SUBMISSION POLICY   No unsolicited submissions

Mieke Berlin . . . . .Manager
Brian Aspinwall . . . . .Manager, Music
Liberty Conboy . . . . .Assistant

TURNER ARTIST MANAGEMENT
468 N. Camden Dr., Ste. 234
Beverly Hills, CA 90210
PHONE 310-860-7624
FAX 310-860-7600
EMAIL . . . . .turnerartistmgmt@aol.com
WEB SITE . . . . .www.turnerartistmanagement.com
TYPES   Below-the-Line Talent - Commercial Talent
                           - Film/TV Talent - Music Talent
REPRESENTS   Actors - Composers - Music Artists - Music
                           Producers - Sports Personalities -
                           Teens/Young Adults
COMMENTS   Separate division representing photogra-
                           phers, wardrobe stylists, hair and make-up
                           artists

David Turner . . . . .Creative Director/Owner

UNDERGROUND MANAGEMENT
447 S. Highland Ave.
Los Angeles, CA 90036
PHONE 323-930-2588
FAX 323-930-2334
WEB SITE . . . . .www.undergroundfilms.net
TYPES   Literary Talent
REPRESENTS   Book Authors - Directors - Playwrights -
                           Screenwriters - TV Writers
SUBMISSION POLICY   See Web site
COMMENTS   Also represents comic books, animators
                           and novelists

Nick Osborne . .Manager (323-930-2650, nick@undergroundfilms.net)
Trevor Engelson . . . . .Manager (323-930-2569,
                                                 trevor@undergroundfilms.net)
William Lowery . . . . .Manager (323-930-2435,
                                                 william@undergroundfilms.net)
Steven Luna . . . . .Assistant

UNIQUE TALENT GROUP
501 Santa Monica Blvd., Ste. 704
Santa Monica, CA 90401
PHONE 310-576-1954
FAX 310-451-3357
EMAIL . . . . .nick@utg-la.com
WEB SITE . . . . .www.utg-la.com
TYPES   Film/TV Talent - Literary Talent - Theatre
                       Talent
AFFILIATIONS   TMA
REPRESENTS   Actors - Children - Comedians - Directors -
                       Screenwriters - Seniors - Teens/Young
                       Adults - TV Writers
SUBMISSION POLICY   Actors: picture and resumé only; Directors:
                       demos; Writers: email query; No drop-offs
                       or calls

Ronald Bloomfield .Founder/Partner
Nicholas Terry .Partner/Manager
Sarah Halpern . . . . .Manager

UNIVERSAL MANAGEMENT GROUP (UMG)
PO Box 11421
Cincinnati, OH 45211
PHONE 513-662-6666
TYPES   Commercial Talent - Film/TV Talent -
                       Literary Talent - Modeling Talent - Music
                       Talent - Theatre Talent
REPRESENTS   Actors - Book Authors - Broadcast
                       Journalists/Newscasters - Directors -
                       Hosts/MCs - Interactive Game Developers
                       - Music Artists - Music Producers - Musical
                       Theatre Performers - Playwrights - Print
                       Models - Producers - Runway Models -
                       Screenwriters - Speakers/Lecturers - Sports
                       Personalities - TV Writers - Voice-Over
                       Artists
COMMENTS   Professional sports agency; Multi-media
                       entertainment production company;
                       Intellectual property law and rights man-
                       agement; Licensing

Brian Goldberg . . . . .Partner
Adam Limle . . . . .Partner

UNLIMITED MANAGEMENT
1640 S. Sepulveda Blvd., Ste. 515
Los Angeles, CA 90025
PHONE 310-927-1212
FAX 310-943-8099
EMAIL . . . . .info@unlimitedmanagement.net
WEB SITE . . . . .www.unlimitedmanagement.net
TYPES   Film/TV Talent - Literary Talent - Music
                       Talent
REPRESENTS   Actors - Book Authors - Directors -
                       Producers - Screenwriters - TV Writers

Paul Kelmenson . . . . .President
David Kelmenson . . . . .Producer

UNTITLED ENTERTAINMENT
331 N. Maple Dr., 3rd Fl.
Beverly Hills, CA 90210
PHONE .310-601-2100/212-777-1214
FAX 310-601-2344/212-777-1165
TYPES   Film/TV Talent - Literary Talent
REPRESENTS   Actors - Directors - Screenwriters - TV
                       Writers
SUBMISSION POLICY   No unsolicited material
COMMENTS   Features; East Coast office: 23 E. 22nd St.,
                       3rd Fl., New York, NY 10010

Jason Weinberg . . . . .Partner
Stephanie Simon . . . . .Partner
Guy Oseary . . . . .Partner
Beth Holden-Garland . . . . .Partner
Gene Parseghian . . . . .Partner (NY)
Johnnie Planco . . . . .Partner (NY)
Elise Konialian . . . . .VP (NY)
Jennifer Levine . . . . .Manager/Head, Literary
Laura Rister . . . . .Manager, Literary
Greg Clark . . . . .Manager
Mimi Di Trani . . . . .Manager
Evan Hainey . . . . .Manager
Rob Levy . . . . .Manager
Brad Marks . . . . .Manager
Jennifer Merlino . . . . .Manager
Jason Newman . . . . .Manager
Katie Rhodes . . . . .Manager
Danielle Thomas . . . . .Manager
Alissa Vradenburg . . . . .Manager
Brian Young . . . . .Manager
Matt Barbee . . . . .Assistant to Jason Weinberg
Sam Ireland . . . . .Assistant to Jason Weinberg
Edward Resetar . . . . .Assistant to Jason Weinberg & Laura Rister
Diana Seide . . . . .Assistant to Jason Weinberg
Angela Carbonetti . . . . .Assistant to Gene Parseghian
David Koth . . . . .Assistant to Beth Holden-Garland
Dwight Armstrong . . . . .Assistant to Brian Young
Deanna Beckman . . . . .Assistant to Evan Hainey
Joe Biddix . . . . .Assistant to Jason Newman
Dafna DeBasc . . . . .Assistant to Danielle Thomas
Liz Farag . . . . .Assistant to Stephanie Simon
Clara Kim . . . . .Assistant to Elise Konialian
Barbra Korn . . . . .Assistant to Johnnie Planco
Collin Mitchell . . . . .Assistant to Katie Rhodes
Erica Schillinger . . . . .Assistant to Jennifer Levine
Maryn Silverberg . . . . .Assistant to Alissa Vradenburg

V & L INTERNATIONAL, LLC
c/o Creative Talent Management Division
751 17th St.
Santa Monica, CA 90402
PHONE .310-822-1781/212-292-4228
FAX 310-822-1761/212-292-4229
EMAIL . . . . .talent@vnli.com
WEB SITE . . . . .www.vnli.com
TYPES   Commercial Talent - Film/TV Talent -
                       Literary Talent - Music Talent - Theatre
                       Talent
REPRESENTS   Actors - Book Authors - Dancers - Directors
                       - Music Artists - Music Producers -
                       Producers - Screenwriters - Voice-Over
                       Artists
SUBMISSION POLICY   Mail and email only
COMMENTS   Specializes in international talent: Linguists
                       and translators (250+ languages); East
                       Coast office: 521 Fifth Ave., Ste. 1700,
                       New York, NY 10175

Alexandra Guarnieri . . . . .Talent Manager (US)
Daniel L. Veitkus . . . . .Talent Manager (Europe)
Jennifer Sinclair . . . . .Talent Manager (Brazil)
John Coleman .Financial Manager
Gary S. Rattet . . . . .Legal Affairs
Noemi Lara . . . . .Assistant Manager (NY/LA)

VALENTINO ENTERTAINMENT

PO Box 1704
Studio City, CA 91604
PHONE 818-761-0300
FAX 818-761-0363
TYPES   Film/TV Talent - Music Talent
REPRESENTS   Actors - Music Artists - Music Producers
SUBMISSION POLICY   Send unsolicited material to: PO Box
                             1704, Studio City, CA 91604
COMMENTS   Emphasis on Latin talent

Valentino Fazzari . . . . .CEO/President
Paul Graham . . . . .Manager
Karen Medak . . . . .Manager
Rosa Montero . . . . .Office Administrator

VANGUARD MANAGEMENT GROUP

8060 Melrose Ave., 4th Fl.
Los Angeles, CA 90046
PHONE 323-655-0400/212-544-7700
FAX .323-852-1777/212-544-7800
TYPES   Film/TV Talent - Literary Talent - Music
                             Talent - Theatre Talent
REPRESENTS   Actors - Comedians - Directors -
                             Screenwriters - Teens/Young Adults - Voice-
                             Over Artists
COMMENTS   East Coast office: 220 Fifth Ave., PH West,
                             New York, NY 10001

David Guc . . . . .President
Shalin Dave . . . . .Associate
Thomas Hillard . . . . .Associate
Hedi Kim . . . . .Music Associate
Robyn Zigeler . . . . .Associate (NY)
Erica Denardo . . . . .Talent Assistant
Nick Diaz . . . . .Music Assistant (NY)

VANGUARD TALENT MANAGEMENT

1155 N. La Cienega Blvd., Ste. 502
Los Angeles, CA 90069
PHONE 310-855-0085
FAX 310-855-0083
EMAIL . . . . .s.vail@earthlink.net
TYPES   Film/TV Talent - Literary Talent
REPRESENTS   Actors - Screenwriters
SUBMISSION POLICY   By referral only

Steven Vail . . . . .Owner/Manager

VELOCITY MANAGEMENT

1855 Industrial St., Ste. 612
Los Angeles, CA 90021
PHONE 310-463-5643
FAX 310-388-0361
EMAIL . . . . .grant@velocityla.com
AFFILIATIONS   TMA
REPRESENTS   Actors - Book Authors - Directors -
                             Screenwriters - Sports Personalities - TV
                             Writers

Grant Turck . . . . .Manager

VESTA TALENT SERVICES

460 Second Ave., Ste. 11F
New York, NY 10016
PHONE 212-685-7151
FAX 212-683-4630
EMAIL . . . . .vesta460@aol.com
TYPES   Commercial Talent - Film/TV Talent
AFFILIATIONS   NCOPM
REPRESENTS   Actors - Seniors - Voice-Over Artists
SUBMISSION POLICY   By mail only
COMMENTS   Represents physically challenged performers

Jacqueline Tellalian . . . . .Manager

VIKING ENTERTAINMENT

445 W. 23rd St., Ste. 1A
New York, NY 10011
PHONE 212-620-5100
FAX 212-620-5421
TYPES   Film/TV Talent
REPRESENTS   Actors

Lisa Loosemore . . . . .Manager
Erin Butler . . . . .Assistant
Luke Boverizer . . . . .Assistant

VISION MODEL MANAGEMENT

151 Grand St., 2nd Fl.
New York, NY 10013
PHONE 212-334-7772
WEB SITE . . . . www.visionmodelmanagement.com
TYPES   Modeling Talent
REPRESENTS   Print Models

Christina Park . . . . .Owner

VISIONARY ENTERTAINMENT

1558 N. Stanley Ave.
Los Angeles, CA 90046
PHONE 323-874-4875
FAX 323-845-9722
TYPES   Film/TV Talent - Literary Talent
REPRESENTS   Actors - Directors - Screenwriters - TV
                             Writers

Tom Parziale . . . . .President
Dan Distefano . . . . .Assistant

VIVIANO FELDMAN ENTERTAINMENT

8383 Wilshire Blvd., Ste. 202
Beverly Hills, CA 90211
PHONE 323-866-0700
FAX 323-866-0704
EMAIL . . . . .viviano_feldman_entertainment@yahoo.com
TYPES   Literary Talent
REPRESENTS   Book Authors - Directors - Producers -
                             Screenwriters - TV Writers
COMMENTS   PGA

Bettina Sofia Viviano . . . . .President/Producer/Manager
Richard Feldman . . . . .President/Producer/Manager
Sarah Dale . . . . .Creative Executive

WA ENTERPRISES

343 Stuyvesant Ave.
Irvington, NJ 07111
PHONE 973-371-7668/973-819-4125
FAX 973-371-3633
EMAIL .tarrington@waenterprises.net
SECOND EMAIL . . . . .anthonyarrington2003@yahoo.com
WEB SITE . . . . .www.waenterprises.net
TYPES   Commercial Talent - Modeling Talent -
                             Music Talent
REPRESENTS   Actors - Hosts/MCs - Music Artists - Music
                             Producers - Print Models - Teens/Young
                             Adults

Anthony Arrington . . . . .President/Manager
Rayan Raymond . . . . .Manager/Web Site Administration
Richard Robinson . . . . .Research Clerk

THE ROBERT D. WACHS COMPANY
418 E. 59th St., Ste. 16B
New York, NY 10022
PHONE 212-935-9444
FAX 212-935-9229
EMAIL . . . . .wachsmgr@aol.com
TYPES   Film/TV Talent - Music Talent
REPRESENTS   Actors - Comedians - Music Artists
SUBMISSION POLICY   Talent with referral and established credits preferred
COMMENTS   Developing and producing theatrical plays and musicals for Broadway and other venues; Subsidiary: 59th Street Entertainment, Inc.

Robert Wachs . . . . .No Title

BRAD WAISBREN ENTERPRISES
PO Box 1928
Studio City, CA 91614
PHONE 818-506-3000
TYPES   Commercial Talent - Film/TV Talent
REPRESENTS   Actors - Dancers - Producers - Teens/Young Adults
SUBMISSION POLICY   Mail only; Do not call; Will not return tapes; Works with SAG and non-union new talent, ingenues and younger leading men
COMMENTS   PGA

Brad Waisbren .Manager/Producer
Marci Higer . . . . .Manager
Philip Kramer . . . . .Business Affairs

WALLACH ENTERTAINMENT
1400 Braeridge Dr.
Beverly Hills, CA 90210
PHONE 310-278-4574
FAX 310-273-0548
EMAIL .wallach1@sbcglobal.net
TYPES   Film/TV Talent
REPRESENTS   Actors - Broadcast Journalists/Newscasters - Comedians - Hosts/MCs - Sports Personalities
COMMENTS   Also produces

George Wallach . . . . .President/Personal Manager

MICHAEL WALLACH MANAGEMENT
908 Granville Ave., Ste. 300
Los Angeles, CA 90049
PHONE 310-820-9926
WEB SITE . . . . .www.howtogetarrested.com
TYPES   Film/TV Talent - Literary Talent
AFFILIATIONS   TMA
REPRESENTS   Actors - Book Authors - Broadcast Journalists/Newscasters - Producers - Sports Personalities
COMMENTS   Also represents casting directors; State-licensed talent agent; Attorney, admitted New York State bar; UCLA extension instructor 'The Business of Acting'; Author of 'How to Get Arrested'

Michael Wallach . . . . .Owner
Lisa Rosen . . . . .Assistant

WARNER ARTIST MANAGEMENT
2001 Wilshire Blvd., Ste. 210
Santa Monica, CA 90403
PHONE 310-828-2800
FAX 310-828-2877
COMMENTS   Talent representation, packaging and consulting

Douglas Warner . . . . .President

WASHINGTON SQUARE ARTS
1041 N. Formosa Ave., Writers Bldg., Ste. 305
West Hollywood, CA 90046
PHONE 323-850-2760/212-253-0333
FAX .323-850-2761/212-253-0330
WEB SITE . . . . .www.washingtonsquarearts.com
TYPES   Film/TV Talent - Literary Talent
REPRESENTS   Actors - Directors - Producers - Screenwriters - TV Writers
COMMENTS   East Coast office: 310 Bowery, 2nd Fl., New York, NY 10012

Katherine Atkinson . . . . .Talent Manager (NY)
Melissa Breaux . . . . .Talent Manager (LA)
Lynn Barstow . . . . .Assistant (LA)
Jonathan Lisiecki . . . . .Assistant (NY)

WATER STREET
5225 Wilshire Blvd., Ste. 615
Los Angeles, CA 90036
PHONE 323-939-6900
FAX 323-939-6930
TYPES   Film/TV Talent - Literary Talent
REPRESENTS   Actors - Comedians - Directors - Producers - Screenwriters - TV Writers

Michael Bircumshaw . . . . .Manager/Producer

MIMI WEBER MANAGEMENT CO.
10717 Wilshire Blvd., PH 3
Los Angeles, CA 90024
PHONE 310-470-5224
FAX 310-470-2724
TYPES   Commercial Talent - Film/TV Talent - Music Talent - Theatre Talent
AFFILIATIONS   NCOPM
REPRESENTS   Actors
SUBMISSION POLICY   No submissions by unknown talent; Working actors only
COMMENTS   Also affiliated with HRTS, AFI, ATAS and MT&R

Mimi Weber . . . . .President

DAVID WESTBERG MANAGEMENT
1604 N. Vista St.
Hollywood, CA 90046
PHONE 323-874-5544
EMAIL . . . . .dwestman@aol.com
TYPES   Commercial Talent - Film/TV Talent - Music Talent - Theatre Talent
REPRESENTS   Actors - Music Artists - Teens/Young Adults

David Westberg . . . . .Manager/Producer

WESTSIDE ARTISTS
1940 Holmby Ave.
Los Angeles, CA 90025
PHONE 310-474-4190
FAX 310-474-5943
EMAIL . . . . .talent@westside-artists.com
TYPES   Below-the-Line Talent
REPRESENTS   Cinematographers - Film Editors - Producers - Production Designers
COMMENTS   Represents costume designers

Linda Koulisis . . . . .Owner
Kerry Russell . . . . .Office Manager

WHITAKER ENTERTAINMENT
4924 Vineland Ave.
North Hollywood, CA 91601
PHONE 818-766-4441
TYPES   Commercial Talent - Film/TV Talent -
                         Literary Talent - Theatre Talent
REPRESENTS   Actors - Book Authors - Children -
                         Comedians - Hosts/MCs - Martial
                         Artists/Stunts - Producers - Screenwriters -
                         Teens/Young Adults - Voice-Over Artists

Dora Whitaker . . . . .President, Commercials/Packaging/Theatrical/
                                                       Adults/Children
Stephen Gerzeli . . .VP/Partner, Commercial/Theatrical/Literary Manager
Terrence Stone . . . . . .VP/Partner, Adult Theatrical/Commercial Manager

WILD BRIAR TALENT
7810 Isis Ave.
Los Angeles, CA 90045
PHONE 310-670-5440
TYPES   Film/TV Talent - Literary Talent
REPRESENTS   Actors - Children - Infants - Screenwriters
COMMENTS   Disabled actors; Accepting ethnic perform-
                         ers, and children; SAG only

Terre Worhach . . . . .Owner

DAN WILEY MANAGEMENT
2341 Zorada Court
Los Angeles, CA 90046-1744
PHONE 323-876-5824
FAX 323-876-5177
TYPES   Film/TV Talent
REPRESENTS   Comedians
SUBMISSION POLICY   No new submissions

Dan Wiley . . . . .Personal/Business Manager

WILHELMINA CREATIVE MANAGEMENT
300 Park Avenue South, 2nd Fl.
New York, NY 10010
PHONE 212-473-0700
EMAIL . . . . .wcm@wilhelmina.com
WEB SITE . . . . .www.wilhelmina.com
TYPES   Commercial Talent - Film/TV Talent -
                         Modeling Talent
AFFILIATIONS   NCOPM
REPRESENTS   Actors - Print Models - Teens/Young Adults
SUBMISSION POLICY   Open meet and greet the last Friday of
                         every month from 2-5 pm

Benjamin Bitonti . . . . .Director

WILHELMINA KIDS
300 Park Avenue South, 2nd Fl.
New York, NY 10010
PHONE . . . . .212-979-9797 (Talent)/212-473-1253 (Print)
FAX 212-271-1611
TYPES   Commercial Talent - Film/TV Talent -
                         Theatre Talent
AFFILIATIONS   NCOPM
REPRESENTS   Actors - Children - Teens/Young Adults
SUBMISSION POLICY   Mail only; Do not call; No drop-ins

Marlene Wallach . . . . .President
Teri Bostaji . . . . .Director

WILHELMINA MODELS
300 Park Avenue South
New York, NY 10010
PHONE 212-473-0700
FAX 212-271-1641
WEB SITE . . . . .www.wilhelmina.com
TYPES   Modeling Talent - Music Talent
REPRESENTS   Music Artists - Sports Personalities
SUBMISSION POLICY   Send photos by mail; See Web site for
                         more information
COMMENTS   Athletes, top models and music artists for
                         endorsements and personal appearances

WILL ENTERTAINMENT
1228 Romulus Dr.
Glendale, CA 91205
PHONE 818-246-4850
FAX 818-246-4520
EMAIL . . . . .garrett@willentertainment.com
TYPES   Literary Talent
REPRESENTS   Book Authors - Screenwriters - TV Writers
COMMENTS   Also represents animators, animation direc-
                         tors and book illustrators

Garrett Hicks . . . . .Manager

WILLIAMS UNLIMITED
5010 Buffalo Ave.
Sherman Oaks, CA 91423
PHONE 818-905-1058
FAX 818-995-1904
EMAIL . . . . .holly@williamsunltd.com
WEB SITE . . . . .www.williamsunltd.com
TYPES   Commercial Talent - Film/TV Talent
REPRESENTS   Children - Teens/Young Adults - Voice-
                         Over Artists
COMMENTS   NATAS; Talent 6 to 21 years old playing
                         younger

Holly Williams . . . . .President/Owner

WINDFALL MANAGEMENT
4084 Mandeville Canyon Rd.
Los Angeles, CA 90049
PHONE 310-471-6317
EMAIL . . . . .windfall1@adelphia.net
TYPES   Literary Talent
REPRESENTS   Book Authors - Screenwriters

Jeanne Field . . . . .Manager

WITT ENTERTAINMENT MANAGEMENT, INC.
800 W. First St., Ste. 505
Los Angeles, CA 90012
PHONE 213-628-9093
FAX 213-620-7095
EMAIL . . . . .addison@addisonwitt.com
WEB SITE . . . . .www.addisonwitt.com
TYPES   Commercial Talent - Film/TV Talent
REPRESENTS   Actors - Children - Infants - Teens/Young
                         Adults - Voice-Over Artists
SUBMISSION POLICY   Via email or US Mail

Addison Witt . . . . .Manager

JACKI WOLSKI LITERARY MANAGEMENT
PO Box 201
Cambria, CA 93428
PHONE 805-927-0462
EMAIL . . . . .wolskilitman@earthlink.net
TYPES   Literary Talent
REPRESENTS   Screenwriters - TV Writers
SUBMISSION POLICY   Query by email only; No unsolicited phone
                    calls or letters

Jacki Wolski . . . . .Principal

WORKING ARTISTS
9563 Langdon Ave.
North Hills, CA 91343
PHONE 818-907-1122
FAX 818-891-1293
EMAIL . . . . .info@workingartists.net
WEB SITE .www.workingartists.net
TYPES   Below-the-Line Talent - Literary Talent
AFFILIATIONS   DGA
REPRESENTS   Directors - Film Editors - Producers -
                    Screenwriters
SUBMISSION POLICY   By request only
COMMENTS   Talent & literary packaging

Debora Masterson . . . . .Principal/Literary

CHRISTOPHER WRIGHT MANAGEMENT
3207 Winnie Dr.
Los Angeles, CA 90068
PHONE 323-874-9898
FAX 323-874-9899
TYPES   Film/TV Talent
REPRESENTS   Actors
SUBMISSION POLICY   By referral only

Christopher Wright . . . . .Manager/Owner
Paul Kuszynski . . . . .Associate

W.T.A. & ASSOCIATES
3720 Lowry Rd.
Los Angeles, CA 90027
PHONE 323-661-3079
FAX 323-661-3123
TYPES   Film/TV Talent - Literary Talent
REPRESENTS   Directors - Martial Artists/Stunts -
                    Screenwriters - TV Writers

Martin Weiler . . . . .President
S. Anthony . . . . .First VP
L. Anthony . . . . .Second VP

YOUNG PERFORMERS MANAGEMENT
14429 Ventura Blvd., #111
Sherman Oaks, CA 91423
PHONE 818-335-5202/818-788-7114
EMAIL . . . . .ypsmgr@aol.com
WEB SITE .www.youngperformers.net
TYPES   Commercial Talent - Film/TV Talent -
                    Theatre Talent
REPRESENTS   Actors - Children - Teens/Young Adults
SUBMISSION POLICY   Referral preferred; Accepts submissions via
                    mail
COMMENTS   Adult division: Performers Management

Donnajeanne Goheen . . . . .Talent Manager
Karen D'Amico . . . . .Associate Manager
Jessica St. Johns . . . . .Associate Manager

YOUNG TALENT, INC.
PO Box 792
Hartsdale, NY 10530
PHONE 914-948-4744/800-947-4950
FAX 914-946-7399
TYPES   Commercial Talent - Film/TV Talent -
                    Modeling Talent - Theatre Talent
AFFILIATIONS   NCOPM
REPRESENTS   Actors - Children - Choreographers -
                    Dancers - Hosts/MCs - Musical Theatre
                    Performers - Print Models - Teens/Young
                    Adults
COMMENTS   Toddlers to young adults, three to thirty-five
                    years old

Tobe Gibson . . . . .Manager/President

BONNIE YOUNG PERSONAL MANAGEMENT
1534 N. Formosa Ave., Ste. 6
Hollywood, CA 90046
PHONE 323-969-0162
TYPES   Commercial Talent - Film/TV Talent
AFFILIATIONS   NCOPM
REPRESENTS   Actors - Teens/Young Adults - TV Writers
SUBMISSION POLICY   Union talent with agent only; Provide tape
                    for consideration

Bonnie Young . . . . .President

YUMKAS MANAGEMENT, inc.

YUMKAS MANAGEMENT
915 12th St., #1
Santa Monica, CA 90403
PHONE 310-899-9749
FAX 310-899-9769
EMAIL . . . . .carol@yumkas.com
TYPES   Film/TV Talent
REPRESENTS   Actors - Composers - Directors - Music
                    Artists - Music Producers - Musical Theatre
                    Performers - Screenwriters -
                    Speakers/Lecturers - TV Writers
SUBMISSION POLICY   Does not accept unsolicited material
COMMENTS   Partial Client List: Jason Alexander -
                    Randall Harris (Screenwriter/Director);
                    Music: Ray Herndon - Russ Kunkel - Matt
                    Rollings

Carol Yumkas . . . . .President/CEO

GENE YUSEM COMPANY
PO Box 67869
Los Angeles, CA 90067
PHONE 310-277-3330
TYPES   Film/TV Talent
REPRESENTS   Actors - Comedians - Directors -
                    Screenwriters

Gene Yusem . . . . .President

ZENITH MANAGEMENT
13801 Ventura Blvd.
Sherman Oaks, CA 91423
PHONE 323-620-2269
FAX 818-996-3458
EMAIL . . . . .aladjam@zenithmgmt.com
TYPES   Commercial Talent - Film/TV Talent -
                     Theatre Talent
REPRESENTS   Actors - Children - Dancers - Musical
                     Theatre Performers - Print Models - Seniors
                     - Teens/Young Adults - Voice-Over Artists

Laura Aladjem . . . . .Partner
Donna Miller . . . . .Partner
Jamie Hughes .Assistant to Laura Aladjem
Deven Byrnes .Assistant to Donna Miller

ZERO GRAVITY MANAGEMENT
1531 14th St.
Santa Monica, CA 90404
PHONE 310-656-9440
FAX 310-656-9441
EMAIL . . . . .zerogravity.mgmt@verizon.net
WEB SITE . . . . .www.piercewilliams.com
TYPES   Literary Talent
REPRESENTS   Directors - Screenwriters
SUBMISSION POLICY   Query letters accepted via email; No
                     phone calls

Larry Collins . . . . .VP, Development
Michael Pierce . . . . .Manager
Eric Williams . . . . .Manager
Mark C. Williams . . . . .Manager
Georgia Vestakis . . . . .Creative Associate

ZIEMBA TALENT & ASSOCIATES
13603 Marina Point Dr.
Marina del Rey, CA 90202
PHONE 310-306-1606
FAX 310-821-2807
TYPES   Film/TV Talent - Theatre Talent
REPRESENTS   Actors - Teens/Young Adults

Rob Ziemba . . . . .Owner/Manager

WORKSHEET

DATE	PROJECT	CONTACT	NOTES

WORKSHEET

FREQUENTLY CALLED PHONE NUMBERS			
NAME	COMPANY	PHONE #	FAX #

WORKSHEET

DATE	PROJECT	CONTACT	NOTES

Available online at www.hcdonline.com

WORKSHEET

FREQUENTLY CALLED PHONE NUMBERS			
NAME	**COMPANY**	**PHONE #**	**FAX #**

Hollywood Representation Directory
AGENTS AND MANAGERS

To submit your company for a free listing in the HOLLYWOOD REPRESENTATION DIRECTORY, complete and return this application form along with a <u>brief bio and/or company profile</u>. All listings are at the discretion of the Editor.

PHONE: 323-525-2376   FAX: 323-525-2393   www.hcdonline.com

COMPANY_____ C/O _____

STREET _____ CITY _____STATE_____ZIP_____

PHONE(S) _____ FAX(S)_____

PUBLISHED EMAIL _____ WEBSITE _____

NONPUBLISHED EMAIL _____ NONPUBLISHED FAX _____

AFFILIATIONS/GUILDS
(check all that apply)

- ☐ AAR
- ☐ AEA
- ☐ AFM
- ☐ AFTRA
- ☐ AGVA
- ☐ ATA
- ☐ DGA
- ☐ NCOPM
- ☐ SAG
- ☐ TMA
- ☐ WGA

YOU ARE...
(check one)

- ☐ AGENCY
- ☐ MANAGEMENT COMPANY

YOU REPRESENT...
(check all that apply)

- ☐ BELOW-THE-LINE
- ☐ MODELING
- ☐ COMMERCIAL
- ☐ FILM & TV
- ☐ MUSIC TALENT
- ☐ LITERARY
- ☐ THEATRE
- ☐ PACKAGING

TYPES OF CLIENTS REPRESENTED
(check all that apply)

- ☐ ACTORS
- ☐ ANIMALS
- ☐ BOOK AUTHORS
- ☐ BROADCAST/NEWSCASTERS
- ☐ CHILDREN
- ☐ CHOREOGRAPHERS
- ☐ CINEMATOGRAPHERS
- ☐ COMEDIANS
- ☐ COMPOSERS
- ☐ DANCERS
- ☐ DIRECTORS
- ☐ FILM EDITORS

- ☐ HOSTS/MCs
- ☐ INFANTS
- ☐ INTERACTIVE GAME DEVELOPERS
- ☐ MAGICIANS
- ☐ MARTIAL ARTISTS/STUNTS
- ☐ MUSIC ARTISTS
- ☐ MUSIC EDITORS
- ☐ MUSIC PRODUCERS
- ☐ MUSIC SUPERVISORS
- ☐ MUSICAL THEATRE PERFORMERS
- ☐ PLAYWRIGHTS
- ☐ PRINT MODELS

- ☐ PRODUCERS
- ☐ PRODUCTION DESIGNERS
- ☐ RUNWAY MODELS
- ☐ SCREENWRITERS
- ☐ SENIORS
- ☐ SOUND EDITORS
- ☐ SPEAKERS/LECTURERS
- ☐ SPORTS PERSONALITIES
- ☐ TEENS/YOUNG ADULTS
- ☐ TV WRITERS
- ☐ VARIETY ARTISTS
- ☐ VOICE-OVER ARTISTS

STAFF

NAME _____ TITLE_____

NAME _____ TITLE_____

NAME _____ TITLE_____

NAME _____ TITLE_____

NAME _____ TITLE_____

NAME _____ TITLE_____

NAME _____ TITLE_____

SUBMISSION POLICY_____

ADDITIONAL COMMENTS_____

_____

SUBMITTED BY _____ DATE _____

SECTION C

ATTORNEYS & BUSINESS AFFAIRS

- Entertainment Attorneys

- Business & Legal Affairs Departments

ABRAMS GARFINKEL MARGOLIS BERGSON LLP

9229 Sunset Blvd., Ste. 710
Los Angeles, CA 90069
PHONE 310-300-2900/212-201-1170
FAX 310-300-2901/212-201-1171
EMAIL . . . . .babrams@agmblaw.com
WEB SITE . . . . .www.agmblaw.com
PRACTICE AREAS   Full Service Representation - Arbitration &
                        Mediation - Contract Negotiation &
                        Drafting - Copyright & Trademark Matters -
                        Corporate Matters - Employment/Labor
                        Law - Financing - First Amendment Issues -
                        Intellectual Property Law - Libel & Privacy
                        Matters - Licensing - Litigation - Mergers &
                        Acquisitions - Misappropriation of Name,
                        Voice, Likeness - Motion Picture & TV Law -
                        Music Law - Partnerships/Joint Ventures -
                        Right of Publicity - Royalty Law - Tax Law -
                        Transactional Law
COMMENTS   Accounting and Management Services;
                        New York office: 237 W. 35th St., 4th Fl.,
                        New York, NY 10001; Long Island office:
                        425 Broadhollow Rd., Ste. 203, Melville,
                        NY 11747, phone: 631-777-2401, fax:
                        631-777-2402; Newport Beach office:
                        4100 Newport Pl., Ste. 830, Newport
                        Beach, CA 92660, phone: 949-250-8655,
                        x101, fax: 949-250-8656

William L. Abrams . . . . .Partner
Neil B. Garfinkel . . . . .Partner
Barry Margolis . . . . .Partner
Robert Bergson . . . . .Partner
Deron Colby . . . . .Partner
Michael J. Tulchiner . . . . .Partner
Shannon C. Hensley .Attorney
John Keating . . . . .Attorney
Caryn Kertzner . . . . .Attorney
Steve Matz . . . . .Attorney
Tina Palazzo-Fairweather . . . . .Attorney
Michael J. Twersky . . . . .Attorney
Michael J. Weiss . . . . .Attorney

IRA ABRAMS, ESQ.

5692B Fox Hollow Dr.
Boca Raton, FL 33486
PHONE 561-362-5212/828-262-9944
FAX 561-362-0245/828-262-9901
EMAIL . . . . .iraabrams@hotmail.com
PRACTICE AREAS   Arbitration & Mediation - Contract
                        Negotiation & Drafting - Copyright &
                        Trademark Matters - Intellectual Property
                        Law - Music Law - Talent Representation
COMMENTS   Music industry representation; Mediator in
                        major cases; Internet distribution

Ira Abrams . . . . .Partner

AKIN GUMP STRAUSS HAUER & FELD, LLP

2029 Century Park East, Ste. 2400
Los Angeles, CA 90067
PHONE 310-229-1000
FAX 310-229-1001
EMAIL . . . . .losangelesinfo@akingump.com
WEB SITE . . . . .www.akingump.com
PRACTICE AREAS   Full Service Representation - Copyright &
                        Trademark Matters - Corporate Matters -
                        Employment/Labor Law - Financing - First
                        Amendment Issues - Intellectual Property
                        Law - Licensing - Litigation - Mergers &
                        Acquisitions - Motion Picture & TV Law -
                        Music Law - Partnerships/Joint Ventures -
                        Tax Law
COMMENTS   Electronic games; Film and TV production;
                        Distribution and finance; Music industry live
                        event production and distribution; Fifteen
                        offices worldwide

David A. Braun . . . . .Sr. Counsel
John Burke . . . . .Partner
Howard D. Fabrick . . . . .Partner
Steve Fayne . . . . .Partner
Rex Heinke . . . . .Partner
Channing D. Johnson .Partner
Jason Karlov . . . . .Partner
Lawrence D. Levien . . . . .Partner (DC)
Scott H. Racine . . . . .Partner
Marissa Román . . . . .Partner
Cecil Shenker . . . . .Partner (San Antonio)
Wilhelm E. Liebmann . . . . .Counsel (San Antonio)
Alissa L. Morris . . . . .Associate

ALEXANDER NAU LAWRENCE FRUMES & LABOWITZ, LLP

1925 Century Park East, Ste. 850
Los Angeles, CA 90067
PHONE 310-552-0035
FAX 310-552-0135
EMAIL . . . . .walexander@anlf.com
WEB SITE . . . . .www.anlf.com
PRACTICE AREAS   Full Service Representation - Arbitration &
                        Mediation - Contract Negotiation &
                        Drafting - Corporate Matters - Financing -
                        Licensing - Mergers & Acquisitions - Motion
                        Picture & TV Law - Partnerships/Joint
                        Ventures - Talent Representation -
                        Transactional Law
COMMENTS   Financing and distribution matters;
                        Executive employment agreements;
                        Authors/publishing

Wayne Alexander . . . . .Partner
Robert Nau . . . . .Partner
Robert Lawrence . . . . .Partner
Howard Frumes . . . . .Partner
Edward Labowitz . . . . .Partner
Hope Toffel Mastras . . . . .Associate

LAW OFFICE OF JUDY ALEXANDER

1500 41st Ave., Ste. 290
Capitola, CA 95010
PHONE 831-479-3488
FAX 831-479-3498
EMAIL . . . . .ja@judyalexanderlaw.com
WEB SITE . . . . .www.judyalexanderlaw.com
PRACTICE AREAS   First Amendment Issues - Libel & Privacy
                        Matters - Misappropriation of Name, Voice,
                        Likeness - Right of Publicity - Transactional
                        Law

Judy Alexander . . . . .Attorney

ALSCHULER GROSSMAN LLP
1620 26th St., 4th Fl., North Tower
Santa Monica, CA 90404-4060
PHONE 310-907-1000
FAX 310-207-2000
EMAIL . . . . .info@alschuler.com
WEB SITE . . . . .www.alschuler.com
PRACTICE AREAS   Corporate Matters - Employment/Labor
      Law - Litigation - Talent Representation
COMMENTS   Also Institutional Representation

Daniel Alberstone . . . . .Partner
Tony D. Chen . . . . .Partner
Bruce A. Friedman . . . . .Partner
Marshall B. Grossman . . . . .Partner
Jonathan A. Loeb . . . . .Partner
Gwyn Quillen . . . . .Partner
Melissa A. Bakewell . . . . .Associate
Melissa A. Fien . . . . .Associate
Sara H. Jasper . . . . .Associate
Jason T. Riddick . . . . .Associate
Heather L. Ristau . . . . .Associate
Stacy Weinstein Harrison . . . . .Of Counsel

ALSTON & BIRD, LLP
90 Park Ave., 14th Fl.
New York, NY 10016
PHONE 212-210-9414/404-881-7965
FAX 212-210-9444/404-253-8385
WEB SITE . . . . .www.alston.com
PRACTICE AREAS   Corporate Matters - Ecommerce -
      Financing - Intellectual Property Law -
      Internet Law - Libel & Privacy Matters -
      Licensing - Litigation - Mergers &
      Acquisitions - Partnerships/Joint Ventures -
      Technology - Transactional Law
COMMENTS   Atlanta office: One Atlantic Center, 1201
      Peachtree St., Atlanta, GA 30309-3424

Aydin S. Caginalp . . . . .Partner/Head of Group/Head, New York Office
Renée Brissette . . . . .Partner
Stephanie Denkowicz .Partner
David L. Mathus . . . . .Partner
David S. Teske . . . . .Partner (Atlanta)
Mark D. Graham . . . . .Counsel
Thomas Backen . . . . .Counsel

ALTSCHUL & OLIN, LLP
16133 Ventura Blvd., Ste. 1270
Encino, CA 91436
PHONE 818-990-1800
FAX 818-990-1429/818-479-9787
PRACTICE AREAS   Contract Negotiation & Drafting -
      Copyright & Trademark Matters -
      Intellectual Property Law - Licensing - Music
      Law - Partnerships/Joint Ventures - Royalty
      Law - Talent Representation - Transactional
      Law

David E. Altschul . . . . .Partner
Milton E. Olin Jr. . . . . .Partner
Jonathan B. Altschul . . . . .Attorney
Esther M. Rubin . . . . .Executive Assistant/Office Manager
Anita Vartanian . . . . .Executive Assistant

ANAT LEVY & ASSOCIATES, PC
8840 Wilshire Blvd., 3rd Fl.
Beverly Hills, CA 90211
PHONE 310-358-3138
FAX 310-358-3104
EMAIL . . . . .alevy96@aol.com
PRACTICE AREAS   Arbitration & Mediation - Contract
      Negotiation & Drafting - Copyright &
      Trademark Matters - Motion Picture & TV
      Law - Talent Representation

Anat Levy Esq. . . . . .Attorney

LAW OFFICES OF DENNIS ANGEL
1075 Central Park Ave.
Scarsdale, NY 10583
PHONE 914-472-0820
FAX 914-472-0826
EMAIL . . . . .dangelesq@aol.com
WEB SITE . . . . .www.dangelesq.com
PRACTICE AREAS   Copyright & Trademark Matters - Motion
      Picture & TV Law
COMMENTS   Provides literary title/copyright searches and
      opinions, as well as chain of title legal
      opinions

Dennis Angel . . . . .Attorney
Robert Angel . . . . .Attorney
Rebecca Moodie . . . . .Associate

ANKER, REED, HYMES & SCHREIBER
21333 Oxnard St., 1st Fl.
Woodland Hills, CA 91367
PHONE 818-501-5800
FAX 818-501-4019
EMAIL . . . . .dschreiber@ahslawyers.com
WEB SITE . . . . .www.ahslawyers.com
PRACTICE AREAS   Arbitration & Mediation - Contract
      Negotiation & Drafting - Corporate Matters
      - Litigation - Mergers & Acquisitions -
      Partnerships/Joint Ventures - Talent
      Representation - Tax Law - Transactional
      Law
COMMENTS   Entity formation; Business and estate plan-
      ning; Wealth protection

Larry S. Hymes . . . . .Partner
Douglas K. Schreiber .Partner
Robert A. Cohen . . . . .Partner

DENNIS ARDI ATTORNEY AT LAW, PC
340 N. Camden Dr., Ste. 300
Beverly Hills, CA 90210
PHONE 310-271-6900
FAX 310-271-6963
EMAIL . . . . .da@dennisardi.com
PRACTICE AREAS   Contract Negotiation & Drafting - Licensing
      - Motion Picture & TV Law - Talent
      Representation

Dennis Ardi Esq. . . . . .Attorney at Law

ARENT FOX LLP

445 S. Figueroa St., Ste. 3750
Los Angeles, CA 90071
PHONE 213-629-7400
FAX 213-629-7401
WEB SITE . . . . .www.arentfox.com
PRACTICE AREAS   Full Service Representation - Arbitration &
                      Mediation - Communications - Contract
                      Negotiation & Drafting - Copyright &
                      Trademark Matters - Corporate Matters -
                      Ecommerce - Employment/Labor Law -
                      Intellectual Property Law - Internet Law -
                      Libel & Privacy Matters - Licensing -
                      Litigation - Misappropriation of Name,
                      Voice, Likeness - Motion Picture & TV Law -
                      Music Law - Right of Publicity - Royalty Law

Robert C. O'Brien . . .Managing Partner, Litigation & Intellectual Property,
                                                   Arbitration & Mediation
Jerrold Abeles . . . . .Partner, Litigation & Intellectual Property,
                                                   Arbitration & Mediation
Steven E. Bledsoe . . . . .Partner, Litigation
Michael S. Cryan . . . . .Partner, Arbitration & Mediation
Bela G. Lugosi . . . . .Of Counsel, Litigation & Intellectual Property/
                                                   Contract Negotiation & Drafting
Roy Z. Silva . . . . .Counsel, Litigation & Intellectual Property,
                                                   Employment/Labor Law
Antoinette Waller . . . . .Counsel, Litigation & Intellectual Property
David G. Bayles . . . . .Associate, Litigation & Intellectual Property
Amy I. Borlund . . . . .Associate, Litigation & Intellectual Property
Jon D. Holdaway . . . . .Associate, Litigation
Jennifer C. Terry . . . . .Associate, Litigation & Intellectual Property
Wayne H. Matelski . . . . .Corporate Matters
Pierre R. Prosper . . . . .Contract Negotiation & Drafting

ROGER L. ARMSTRONG, ESQ.

2574 Aspen Springs Dr.
Park City, UT 84060
PHONE 310-691-2963
FAX 310-691-8036
EMAIL . . . . .roger@rogerlarmstrong.com
WEB SITE .www.rogerlarmstrong.com
PRACTICE AREAS   Communications - Contract Negotiation &
                      Drafting - Copyright & Trademark Matters -
                      Employment/Labor Law - Financing -
                      Intellectual Property Law - Libel & Privacy
                      Matters - Licensing - Media -
                      Misappropriation of Name, Voice, Likeness
                      - Motion Picture & TV Law -
                      Partnerships/Joint Ventures - Right of
                      Publicity - Talent Representation -
                      Transactional Law

Roger L. Armstrong Esq. . . . . .Entertainment Attorney

ARNOLD & PORTER

777 S. Figueroa St.
Los Angeles, CA 90017
PHONE 213-243-4000
FAX 213-243-4199
WEB SITE . . . . .www.arnoldporter.com
PRACTICE AREAS   Contract Negotiation & Drafting -
                      Copyright & Trademark Matters -
                      Intellectual Property Law - Talent
                      Representation - Technology - Telecom
COMMENTS   New business structuring; Unfair competi-
                      tion matters; East Coast office: 399 Park
                      Ave., New York, NY 10022-4690, phone:
                      212-715-1000, fax: 212-715-1399;
                      Offices in Washington DC, Denver, San
                      Francisco, Brussells and London

James S. Blackburn . . . . .Partner
Ronald L. Johnston . . . . .Partner
Thomas McLain . . . . .Partner
Sean Morris . . . . .Partner
Regina A. Stagg . . . . .Partner
Suzanne V. Wilson . . . . .Partner
James F. Farrand . . . . .Of Counsel
Ira D. Moskatel . . . . .Of Counsel
Sol Rosenthal . . . . .Of Counsel
Harley J. Williams . . . . .Of Counsel

ART & ENTERTAINMENT LAW GROUP
OF LEBLANC & ASSOCIATES, PLC

Beauregard Centre, Beauregard Town
PO Box 3153
Baton Rouge, LA 70821-3153
PHONE 866-529-3529/310-770-4440
FAX 504-299-0193
EMAIL . . . . .info@entlawla.com
WEB SITE . . . . .www.entlawla.com
PRACTICE AREAS   Financing - Motion Picture & TV Law - Tax
                      Law - Transactional Law
REPRESENTS   Producers shooting in Louisiana, to sell
                      your tax credits without tax credit brokers
                      and assist in film financing, tax credit mon-
                      etization, and/or local production legal in
                      Louisiana; Cooperate with producers' non-
                      Louisiana entertainment attorneys
COMMENTS   Louisiana attorneys for Louisiana Pelican
                      Film Fund repped by William Morris
                      Independent to provide tax credit advances
                      for productions; Former studio/network
                      Business & Legal Affairs Executives with Fox,
                      Disney, ABC, MGM, Universal/Canal Plus
                      on over 150 productions worldwide,
                      including film finance, tax credits and
                      incentives and production legal

Michèle M. LeBlanc . . . . .Sr. Partner
Harvey Dzodin . . . . .Special International Counsel

BAKER & HOSTETLER LLP, COUNSELLORS AT LAW
333 S. Grand Ave., Ste. 1800
Los Angeles, CA 90071-1523
PHONE 213-975-1600
FAX 213-795-1740
EMAIL . . . . .info@bakerlaw.com
WEB SITE . . . . .www.bakerlaw.com
PRACTICE AREAS   Arbitration & Mediation - Employment/Labor Law - Financing - First Amendment Issues - Intellectual Property Law - Libel & Privacy Matters - Licensing - Litigation - Mergers & Acquisitions - Motion Picture & TV Law - Music Law - Partnerships/Joint Ventures - Right of Publicity - Royalty Law - Talent Representation - Tax Law - Transactional Law
COMMENTS   For a complete listing of the firm's offices, services and attorneys, please visit Web site; Main office: 3200 National City Center, 1900 E. 9th St., Cleveland, OH 44114-3485, phone: 216-621-0200, fax: 216-696-0740; East Coast office: 666 Fifth Ave., New York, NY 10103, phone: 212-589-4200, fax: 212-589-4201

Anthony S. Brill . . . . .Partner
Lisa I. Carteen . . . . .Partner
Penny M. Costa . . . . .Partner
Lawrence J. Gartner . . . . .Partner
Gary L. Gilbert . . . . .Partner
Peter W. James . . . . .Partner
Helen B. Kim . . . . .Partner
David C. Sampson . . . . .Managing Partner
Thomas Speiss . . . . .Partner
Kimberly M. Talley . . . . .Partner
Teresa R. Tracy . . . . .Partner
Robert J. Webb . . . . .Partner
Cranston J. Williams . . . . .Partner
Gary York . . . . .Partner
Naomi Young . . . . .Partner
Lisa Hinchliffe . . . . .Of Counsel
Loura L. Alaverdi . . . . .Associate
Sean A. Andrade . . . . .Associate
Scott H. Bradford . . . . .Associate
Stephen Butler . . . . .Associate
Gene A. Coppa . . . . .Associate
Stefanie M. Gushá . . . . .Associate
Tazamisha H. Imara . . . . .Associate
Lisa M. Lawrence . . . . .Associate
Lydia W. Lee . . . . .Associate
Devon K. McGranahan . . . . .Associate
Antonio Villegas . . . . .Associate
Roger M. Vinayagalingam . . . . .Associate
Felicia A. Starr . . . . .Staff Attorney

BARANOV & WITTENBERG, LLP
2049 Century Park East, Ste. 2250
Los Angeles, CA 90067
PHONE 310-229-3500
FAX 310-229-3501
WEB SITE . . . . .www.mbgwlaw.com
PRACTICE AREAS   Full Service Representation - Arbitration & Mediation - Contract Negotiation & Drafting - Corporate Matters - Employment/Labor Law - First Amendment Issues - Intellectual Property Law - Libel & Privacy Matters - Litigation - Misappropriation of Name, Voice, Likeness - Motion Picture & TV Law - Right of Publicity - Talent Representation - Transactional Law

Michael M. Baranov . . . . .Partner
Gary Wittenberg . . . . .Partner

BARNES MORRIS KLEIN MARK YORN BARNES & LEVINE
2000 Avenue of the Stars, 3rd Fl. North
Los Angeles, CA 90067
PHONE 310-319-3900
FAX 310-319-3999
WEB SITE . . . . .www.bmkylaw.com
PRACTICE AREAS   Full Service Representation

Michael Barnes . . . . .Partner
P. Kevin Morris .Managing Partner
Deborah Klein . . . . .Partner
Douglas Mark . . . . .Partner
Kevin Yorn . . . . .Managing Partner
Stephen Barnes . . . . .Partner
Jared Levine . . . . .Partner
Gregg Gellman . . . . .Partner
Pamela Hicks . . . . .Partner
Alexander Kohner . . . . .Partner
Lawrence Kopeikin . . . . .Partner
David Krintzman . . . . .Partner
Todd Rubenstein . . . . .Partner
Jeff Endlich . . . . .Attorney
Corinne Farley . . . . .Attorney
David Ferreria . . . . .Attorney
Uyen Le . . . . .Attorney
Jennifer Massey . . . . .Attorney

BARTON, KLUGMAN AND OETTING
333 S. Grand Ave., Ste. 3700
Los Angeles, CA 90071-1599
PHONE 213-621-4000
FAX 213-625-1832
WEB SITE . . . . .www.bkolaw.com
PRACTICE AREAS   Arbitration & Mediation - Contract Negotiation & Drafting - Corporate Matters - Litigation - Mergers & Acquisitions - Partnerships/Joint Ventures - Tax Law

Robert H. Klugman . . . . .Partner
Tod V. Beebe . . . . .Attorney
David J. Cartano . . . . .Attorney
Robert Louis Fisher . . . . .Attorney
Jeffrey B. Harris . . . . .Attorney
William D. Herz . . . . .Attorney
Thomas E. McCurnin . . . . .Attorney
David F. Morgan . . . . .Attorney
Mark A. Newton . . . . .Attorney
Charles J. Schufreider . . . . .Attorney
Martin J. Spear . . . . .Attorney
Ronald R. St. John . . . . .Attorney

BAUTE & TIDUS LLP
801 S. Figueroa St., Ste. 1100
Los Angeles, CA 90017
PHONE 213-630-5000
FAX 213-683-1225
EMAIL .attorneys@bautelaw.com
WEB SITE . . . . .www.bautelaw.com
PRACTICE AREAS   Full Service Representation - Arbitration & Mediation - Contract Negotiation & Drafting - Copyright & Trademark Matters - Corporate Matters - Employment/Labor Law - Intellectual Property Law - Litigation - Mergers & Acquisitions - Partnerships/Joint Ventures - Royalty Law - Transactional Law

Mark D. Baute . . . . .Partner
David P. Crochetiere . . . . .Partner
Patrick M. Maloney . . . . .Partner
Jeffrey A. Tidus . . . . .Partner
Andrea K. Diallo . . . . .Associate
Henry H. Gonzalez . . . . .Associate

HOWARD D. BEHAR

1108 Somera Rd.
Los Angeles, CA 90077
PHONE 310-476-6982
FAX 310-862-4093
EMAIL . . . . .hbehar@hdbfirm.com
PRACTICE AREAS   Contract Negotiation & Drafting -
                        Copyright & Trademark Matters -
                        Corporate Matters - Financing - Intellectual
                        Property Law - Licensing - Mergers &
                        Acquisitions - Motion Picture & TV Law -
                        Partnerships/Joint Ventures - Royalty Law -
                        Talent Representation - Transactional Law

Howard D. Behar . . . . .Attorney

BEHR ABRAMSON KALLER, LLP

9701 Wilshire Blvd., Ste. 800
Beverly Hills, CA 90212
PHONE 310-556-9200
FAX 310-556-9227
WEB SITE .www.baklawfirm.com
PRACTICE AREAS   Full Service Representation

Howard Abramson . . . . .Partner
Joel Behr . . . . .Partner
Adam Kaller . . . . .Partner
Chris Abramson . . . . .Attorney
Jennifer Levy . . . . .Attorney
Nigel McNulty . . . . .Attorney
Eric Sherman . . . . .Attorney

BEITCHMAN & ZEKIAN, PC

510 W. Sixth St., PH 1220
Los Angeles, CA 90014
PHONE 213-488-1115
FAX 213-488-1176
EMAIL . . . . .info@bzlegal.com
WEB SITE . . . . .www.bzlegal.com
PRACTICE AREAS   Full Service Representation - Arbitration &
                        Mediation - Contract Negotiation &
                        Drafting - Copyright & Trademark Matters -
                        Corporate Matters - First Amendment Issues
                        - Intellectual Property Law - Libel & Privacy
                        Matters - Licensing - Litigation -
                        Misappropriation of Name, Voice, Likeness
                        - Motion Picture & TV Law - Music Law -
                        Partnerships/Joint Ventures - Talent
                        Representation - Transactional Law
REPRESENTS   Tera Patrick - Evan Seinfeld - Michael
                        Grazaidei - Joe Henderson - Ty A. O'Neill
                        - Bill Yukich - Lars Krutak - Paul Ciolino
COMMENTS   Additional services include business forma-
                        tion, civil litigation, endorsement negotia-
                        tions and Internet/media

David P. Beitchman . . . . .Attorney
Michelle Seanez . . . . .Attorney
Todd Chvat . . . . .Attorney
Sylvia Mesropyan . . . . .Paralegal

BELDOCK LEVINE & HOFFMAN, LLP

99 Park Ave., Ste. 1600
New York, NY 10016
PHONE 212-490-0400/800-275-4977
WEB SITE . . . . .www.blhny.com
PRACTICE AREAS   Intellectual Property Law
COMMENTS   Ecommerce and computer law; Production,
                        distribution and executive employment mat-
                        ters for film, TV, radio, music, theater and
                        live events

Myron Beldock . . . . .Partner
Elliot L. Hoffman . . . . .Partner
Ray Beckerman . . . . .Partner
Jeffrey A. Greenberg . . . . .Partner
Peter S. Matorin . . . . .Partner
Cynthia Rollings . . . . .Partner
Melvin L. Wolf . . . . .Of Counsel
Daniel M. Shulman . . . . .Associate

BERGER KAHN GLADSTONE

4551 Glencoe Ave., Ste. 300
Marina del Rey, CA 90292
PHONE 310-821-9000
FAX 310-775-8775
EMAIL . . . . .info@bergerkahn.com
WEB SITE . . . . .www.bergerkahn.com
PRACTICE AREAS   Full Service Representation - Contract
                        Negotiation & Drafting - Copyright &
                        Trademark Matters - Corporate Matters -
                        Employment/Labor Law - Financing -
                        Intellectual Property Law - Licensing -
                        Litigation - Misappropriation of Name,
                        Voice, Likeness - Motion Picture & TV Law -
                        Music Law - Partnerships/Joint Ventures -
                        Royalty Law - Talent Representation -
                        Transactional Law
COMMENTS   Litigation in all entertainment law areas
                        noted above; Packaging and entertainment
                        insurance matters; Offices in Los Angeles,
                        Orange County, San Francisco Bay Area
                        and San Diego

Leon Gladstone . . . . .Principal/Founding Member
Craig Simon . . . . .Principal/Founding Member
Michael Aiken . . . . .Principal
J. Wayne Allen . . . . .Principal
Craig Aronson . . . . .Principal
Patricia Campbell . . . . .Principal
Kent Clayton . . . . .Principal
Stephan Cohn . . . . .Principal
David Ezra . . . . .Principal
Marty Florman . . . . .Principal
Steven Gentry . . . . .Principal
Arthur Grebow . . . . .Principal
James Henshall . . . . .Principal
Wayne Hersh . . . . .Principal
Ryan Hirota . . . . .Principal
Ann Johnston . . . . .Principal
Lance LaBelle . . . . .Principal
Melanie Long . . . . .Principal
Allen Michel . . . . .Principal
Jon Miller . . . . .Principal
William Mitchell . . . . .Principal
Melody Mosley . . . . .Principal
Igbo Obioha . . . . .Principal
Teresa Ponder . . . . .Principal
Owen Sloane . . . . .Principal
Sherman Spitz . . . . .Principal
Jason Wallach . . . . .Principal
Gene Weisberg . . . . .Principal
Arthur Willner . . . . .Principal
Courtney Dillaplain . . . . .Attorney

BERKOWITZ & ASSOCIATES
468 N. Camden Dr., Ste. 200
Beverly Hills, CA 90210
PHONE 310-276-9031
FAX 310-276-9272
EMAIL . . . . .barbara@berkowitzlaw.net
PRACTICE AREAS   Full Service Representation

Barbara L. Berkowitz . . . . .Attorney

BERLINER, CORCORAN & ROWE
1101 17th St. NW, Ste. 1100
Washington, DC 20036
PHONE 202-293-5555/301-570-1761
FAX 202-293-9035/301-570-4183
EMAIL . . . . .jrose13@aol.com
WEB SITE . . . . .www.bcr-dc.com
PRACTICE AREAS   Contract Negotiation & Drafting -
                      Copyright & Trademark Matters -
                      Intellectual Property Law - Music Law -
                      Talent Representation

Thomas G. Corcoran Jr. . . . . .Partner
Jay A. Rosenthal . . . . .Partner
Bridget Wimbish . . . . .Assistant to Mr. Rosenthal

GREG S. BERNSTEIN - A PROFESSIONAL CORPORATION
9601 Wilshire Blvd., Ste. 240
Beverly Hills, CA 90210
PHONE 310-247-2799
FAX 310-247-2798
EMAIL . . . . .greg@thefilmlaw.com
WEB SITE . . . . .www.thefilmlaw.com
PRACTICE AREAS   Full Service Representation - Contract
                      Negotiation & Drafting - Corporate Matters
                      - Financing - Intellectual Property Law -
                      Licensing - Motion Picture & TV Law -
                      Partnerships/Joint Ventures - Right of
                      Publicity - Talent Representation -
                      Transactional Law
REPRESENTS   Producers - Distributors - Financiers - Sales
                      Agents - Production Companies
COMMENTS   Legal production matters; Financing and
                      sales matters; Sales representation

Greg S. Bernstein . . . . .President/Attorney
Jason Dollar . . . . .Attorney

STUART BERTON - A PROFESSIONAL CORPORATION
12400 Ventura Blvd., Ste. 661
Studio City, CA 91604
PHONE 818-509-8113
FAX 818-985-1527
EMAIL . . . . .stuartberton@earthlink.net
PRACTICE AREAS   Contract Negotiation & Drafting - Talent
                      Representation
REPRESENTS   Actors - Writers - Directors - Producers -
                      Executives

Stuart Berton . . . . .Attorney

BIENSTOCK & MICHAEL, PC
250 W. 57th St., Ste. 1917
New York, NY 10107
PHONE 212-399-0099
FAX 212-399-1278
EMAIL . . . . .ronald.bienstock@musicsq.com
WEB SITE . . . . .www.musicsq.com
PRACTICE AREAS   Contract Negotiation & Drafting -
                      Copyright & Trademark Matters -
                      Corporate Matters - Intellectual Property
                      Law - Licensing - Litigation - Music Law -
                      Royalty Law

Ronald S. Bienstock . . . . .Partner
Jill A. Michael . . . . .Partner
Randall S.D. Jacobs . . . . .Of Counsel
Jeremy B. Kaplan . . . . .Associate
Daniel A. Weiss . . . . .Associate
Lindsay D. Molnar . . . . .Jr. Associate

LAW OFFICES OF PETER R. BIERSTEDT
4745 Cromwell Ave.
Los Angeles, CA 90027-1143
PHONE 323-667-2698
FAX 323-667-2699
EMAIL . . . . .peter@bierstedt.com
WEB SITE . . . . .www.bierstedt.com
PRACTICE AREAS   Mergers & Acquisitions - Arbitration &
                      Mediation - Contract Negotiation &
                      Drafting - Copyright & Trademark Matters -
                      Corporate Matters - Financing - First
                      Amendment Issues - Intellectual Property
                      Law - Libel & Privacy Matters - Licensing -
                      Motion Picture & TV Law - Music Law -
                      Partnerships/Joint Ventures - Right of
                      Publicity - Transactional Law
COMMENTS   Legal and business consulting

Peter R. Bierstedt . . . . .Principal

A. LEE BLACKMAN, PLC
16060 Ventura Blvd., Ste. 105-506
Encino, CA 91436-2761
PHONE 818-981-1332
FAX 818-688-3861
EMAIL . . . . .leandx@aol.com
WEB SITE . . . . .www.leeblackman.com
PRACTICE AREAS   Full Service Representation

A. Lee Blackman . . . . .Attorney
Anita Morris . . . . .Legal Assistant

BLACKWELL SANDERS PEPER MARTIN LLP
720 Olive St., Ste. 2400
St. Louis, MO 63101
PHONE 314-345-6255/314-345-6000
FAX 314-345-6060
EMAIL . . . . .dmathes@blackwellsanders.com
WEB SITE . . . . .www.blackwellsanders.com
PRACTICE AREAS   Full Service Representation - Contract
                      Negotiation & Drafting - Corporate Matters
                      - Financing - Intellectual Property Law -
                      Licensing - Litigation

Danica L. Mathes . . . . .Attorney
Eric F. Kayira . . . . .Attorney
Michael A. Kahn . . . . .Attorney

LAW OFFICE OF WILLIAM W. BLACKWELL
8961 W. Sunset Blvd., #2-H
West Hollywood, CA 90069
PHONE 310-777-8305
FAX 310-777-8838/310-278-2254
EMAIL . . . . .wwblackwell@hotmail.com
PRACTICE AREAS   Full Service Representation - Arbitration &
                     Mediation - Contract Negotiation &
                     Drafting - Copyright & Trademark Matters -
                     Corporate Matters - First Amendment Issues
                     - Intellectual Property Law - Libel & Privacy
                     Matters - Licensing - Litigation -
                     Misappropriation of Name, Voice, Likeness
                     - Motion Picture & TV Law - Music Law -
                     Talent Representation - Transactional Law
COMMENTS   DUI representation; Demo tapes from
                     unsigned bands and artists accepted;
                     Screenplays accepted

William W. Blackwell . . . . .Attorney
Angela Black . . . . .Talent Management

LAW OFFICES OF EDWARD BLAU
1901 Avenue of the Stars, Ste. 1900
Los Angeles, CA 90067
PHONE 310-556-8468
FAX 310-282-0579
EMAIL . . . . .edblauenlw@aol.com
PRACTICE AREAS   Contract Negotiation & Drafting - Licensing
                     - Motion Picture & TV Law - Music Law -
                     Talent Representation - Transactional Law

Edward Blau . . . . .Sole Proprietor
Dalia de la Sota . . . . .Secretary

BLECHER & COLLINS
515 S. Figueroa St., 17th Fl.
Los Angeles, CA 90071
PHONE 213-622-4222
FAX 213-622-1656/213-689-1944
EMAIL .mblecher@blechercollins.com
SECOND EMAIL . . . . .info@blechercollins.com
WEB SITE . . . . .www.blechercollins.com
PRACTICE AREAS   Litigation
COMMENTS   Complex business litigation and class
                     actions

Maxwell M. Blecher . . . . .President
Harold R. Collins Jr. . . . . .VP
John E. Andrews . . . . .No Title
Jennifer Elkayam . . . . .No Title
Ralph C. Hofer . . . . .No Title
William C. Hsu . . . . .No Title
Gary M. Joye . . . . .No Title
David W. Kesselman .No Title
James Robert Noblin .No Title
Courtney Palko . . . . .No Title
Donald R. Pepperman . . . . .No Title
Alicia G. Rosenberg .No Title

BLOOM HERGOTT DIEMER ROSENTHAL LAVIOLETTE & FELDMAN, LLP
150 S. Rodeo Dr., 3rd Fl.
Beverly Hills, CA 90212
PHONE 310-859-6800
FAX 310-859-2788
PRACTICE AREAS   Motion Picture & TV Law

Jacob A. Bloom . . . . .Partner
Alan S. Hergott . . . . .Partner
John D. Diemer . . . . .Partner
Stuart M. Rosenthal . . . . .Partner
John S. LaViolette . . . . .Partner
David B. Feldman . . . . .Partner
Candice S. Hanson . . . . .Partner
Tina J. Kahn . . . . .Partner
Leigh C. Brechen . . . . .Partner
Stephen F. Breimer . . . . .Partner
Eric M. Brooks . . . . .Partner
Michael L. Schenkman .Partner
Thomas B. Collier . . . . .Partner
Patrick M. Knapp . . . . .Partner
Carlos Goodman . . . . .Partner
Leif W. Reinstein . . . . .Partner
Brad S. Small . . . . .Partner
Ralph P. Brescia . . . . .Associate
Thomas F. Hunter . . . . .Of Counsel
Richard D. Thompson . . . . .Of Counsel

BOBBITT & ROBERTS
6100 Center Dr., Ste. 910
Los Angeles, CA 90045
PHONE 310-645-4100
FAX 310-645-5900
PRACTICE AREAS   Contract Negotiation & Drafting -
                     Intellectual Property Law - Licensing -
                     Motion Picture & TV Law - Music Law -
                     Partnerships/Joint Ventures - Talent
                     Representation - Transactional Law

Virgil Roberts . . . . .Managing Partner
Leroy Bobbitt . . . . .Partner
Diane Frazier . . . . .Office Manager, Assistant to Virgil Roberts
Kerri Taitt-Hoag . . . . .Assistant to Leroy Bobbitt

BOWEN RILEY WARNOCK & JACOBSON, PLC
1906 West End Ave.
Nashville, TN 37203
PHONE 615-320-3700
FAX 615-320-3737
EMAIL . . . . .bowenriley@bowenriley.com
WEB SITE . . . . .www.bowenriley.com
PRACTICE AREAS   Copyright & Trademark Matters -
                     Employment/Labor Law - Intellectual
                     Property Law - Music Law

Jay S. Bowen . . . . .Attorney
Steven A. Riley . . . . .Attorney
Timothy L. Warnock . . . . .Attorney
John R. Jacobson . . . . .Attorney
James N. Bowen . . . . .Attorney
William L. Campbell Jr. .Attorney
Katharine R. Cloud . . . . .Attorney
Amy J. Everhart . . . . .Attorney
Sarah Jane Glasgow . . . . .Attorney
Tim Harvey . . . . .Attorney
Salvador M. Hernandez . . . . .Attorney
Milton S. McGee III . . . . .Attorney
Amy E. Neff . . . . .Attorney
William M. Outhier . . . . .Attorney
Gregory S. Reynolds . . . . .Attorney
Steven G. Simmons . . . . .Attorney
W. Russell Taber III . . . . .Attorney
Chris L. Vlahos . . . . .Attorney

LAW OFFICES OF KATHLEEN BRAHN

15233 Ventura Blvd., PH 3
Sherman Oaks, CA 91403
PHONE 818-905-6790
FAX 818-905-6791
WEB SITE . . . . .www.brahnlaw.com
SECOND WEB SITE . . . . .www.brahnlaw.net
PRACTICE AREAS   Contract Negotiation & Drafting -
                       Financing - Intellectual Property Law - Libel
                       & Privacy Matters - Licensing -
                       Misappropriation of Name, Voice, Likeness
                       - Motion Picture & TV Law - Music Law -
                       Right of Publicity - Talent Representation
REPRESENTS   Production companies and established indi-
                       viduals
COMMENTS   Production legal, entity formation, literary
                       property, publishing and fine arts

Kathleen Brahn . . . . .Attorney/Principal

LAW OFFICES OF SAM BRASLAU

1137 S. Wooster St., Ste. 2
Los Angeles, CA 90035
PHONE 310-271-1247
EMAIL . . . . .sbraslau@msn.com
PRACTICE AREAS   Full Service Representation - Contract
                       Negotiation & Drafting - Copyright &
                       Trademark Matters - Corporate Matters -
                       Employment/Labor Law - Financing - First
                       Amendment Issues - Licensing - Litigation -
                       Mergers & Acquisitions - Misappropriation
                       of Name, Voice, Likeness - Motion Picture
                       & TV Law - Music Law - Partnerships/Joint
                       Ventures - Right of Publicity - Talent
                       Representation - Transactional Law
REPRESENTS   Toronto Films, Inc. - Independent Film
                       Center - Mesopotamian Girl, Inc. -
                       Filmwerks Inc. - Crunch Entertainment
COMMENTS   Financing for independent motion pictures;
                       Active lecturer for the Independent Film
                       Center on all aspects of motion picture dis-
                       tribution; Panel attorney for California
                       Lawyers for the Arts

Sam Braslau . . . . .Attorney

BROOKS & DISTLER

110 E. 59th St., 23rd Fl.
New York, NY 10022
PHONE 212-486-1400
FAX 212-486-2266
EMAIL . . . . .brookslaw@aol.com
WEB SITE .www.brookslawyers.com

Marsha S. Brooks . . . . .Partner
Thomas R. Distler . . . . .Partner

LAW OFFICE OF WILLIAM A. BROWN, JR.

865 S. Figueroa St., Ste. 2640
Los Angeles, CA 90017
PHONE . . . . .213-572-0661/213-910-5550 (cell)
FAX 213-572-0669
EMAIL . . . . .attywab@aol.com
PRACTICE AREAS   Contract Negotiation & Drafting -
                       Corporate Matters - Libel & Privacy Matters
                       - Litigation - Motion Picture & TV Law -
                       Music Law - Partnerships/Joint Ventures -
                       Talent Representation
REPRESENTS   Whitefire Productions, Inc. - BDP
                       Entertainment, LLC - Credo Entertainment,
                       Inc. - The Klinic Entertainment Group;
                       Screenwriters: Richard M. Johnson - Q.
                       deChambres - David Cobb - Michelle
                       Blackwell - Kay Spencer - Sandra Payne -
                       Jeffrey Moshier - Marla Cukor - James C.
                       Schlicker - Cindy Boucher - Michael
                       Wichman - Giacomo Knox
COMMENTS   Screenplay marketing; Business incorpora-
                       tion; Limited liability company (LLC) forma-
                       tion

William A. Brown Jr. . . . . .Principal/Attorney at Law

BROWNE, WOODS & GEORGE, LLP

450 N. Roxbury Dr., 7th Fl.
Beverly Hills, CA 90210-4231
PHONE 310-274-7100
FAX 310-275-5697
EMAIL . . . . .info@bwgfirm.com
WEB SITE .www.brownewoods.com
PRACTICE AREAS   Copyright & Trademark Matters - First
                       Amendment Issues - Intellectual Property
                       Law

Allan Browne . . . . .Partner
Edward A. Woods . . . . .Partner
Eric M. George . . . . .Partner
Marcy Railsback . . . . .Partner
Peter Wayne Ross . . . . .Partner
Benjamin D. Scheibe . . . . .Partner
Michael A. Bowse . . . . .Partner
Robert Broadbelt . . . . .Partner
Miles J. Feldman . . . . .Partner
Sylvia P. Lardiere . . . . .Partner
Sonia Y. Lee . . . . .Partner
Marta B. Almli . . . . .Attorney
Wayne Ball . . . . .Attorney
Ira G. Bibbero . . . . .Attorney
Warren Bleeker . . . . .Attorney
Gene F. Williams . . . . .Attorney

ENTERTAINMENT ATTORNEYS

BUCHALTER NEMER
1000 Wilshire Blvd., Ste. 1500
Los Angeles, CA 90017-2457
PHONE 213-891-0700
FAX 213-896-0400
WEB SITE . . . . www.buchalter.com
PRACTICE AREAS   Full Service Representation - Arbitration &
                        Mediation - Contract Negotiation &
                        Drafting - Copyright & Trademark Matters -
                        Corporate Matters - Ecommerce -
                        Employment/Labor Law - Financing -
                        Intellectual Property Law - Internet Law -
                        Licensing - Litigation - Mergers &
                        Acquisitions - Partnerships/Joint Ventures -
                        Royalty Law - Talent Representation -
                        Technology - Transactional Law

Donald S. Lee . . . . .Partner, Business Practices
Michael L. Wachtell . . . . .Partner, Intellectual Property
Robert A. Willner . . . . .Partner, Finance
Lisa M. Jacobsen . . . . .Of Counsel, Multimedia, Entertainment &
                                                        Communications
Douglas M. Lipstone . . . . .Sr. Counsel, Intellectual Property
Marlene Camacho Nowlin . . . .Sr. Counsel, Multimedia, Entertainment &
                                    Communications (949-760-1121)
Jason H. Fisher . . . . .Associate, Intellectual Property

BURNS & LEVINSON LLP
125 Summer St.
Boston, MA 02110
PHONE 617-345-3000
FAX 617-345-3299
WEB SITE . . . . www.burnslev.com
PRACTICE AREAS   Contract Negotiation & Drafting -
                        Copyright & Trademark Matters -
                        Intellectual Property Law - Licensing -
                        Litigation

David P. Rosenblatt . . . . .Managing Partner
George N. Tobia Jr. . . . . .Chairman, Entertainment & Media
Jerry Cohen . . . . .Co-Chairman, Intellectual Property
H. Glenn Alberich . . . . .Partner
Cornelius J. Chapman . . . . .Partner
Susan E. Stenger . . . . .Partner
Anne C. Pareti . . . . .Associate

BUSINESS AFFAIRS, INC.
10675 Santa Monica Blvd.
Los Angeles, CA 90025
PHONE 310-954-8440
FAX 310-362-8707
EMAIL . . . . .info@bizaffairs.com
WEB SITE . . . . www.bizaffairs.com
PRACTICE AREAS   Contract Negotiation & Drafting -
                        Financing - Motion Picture & TV Law -
                        Transactional Law
COMMENTS   Production counsel services

Stephen Monas . . . . .Attorney
Douglas McClure . . . . .Attorney
Bobby Garcia . . . . .Attorney
Julia Alexander . . . . .Attorney

CARROLL, GUIDO & GROFFMAN, LLP
9111 Sunset Blvd.
Los Angeles, CA 90069
PHONE 310-271-0241/212-759-2300
FAX 310-271-0775/212-759-9556
WEB SITE . . . . www.ccgglaw.com
PRACTICE AREAS   Music Law
COMMENTS   Legal services for music and new media
                        industries; No unsolicited demos; East
                        Coast office: 1790 Broadway, 20th Fl.,
                        New York, NY 10019

Rosemary Carroll . . . . .Attorney
Michael Guido . . . . .Attorney
Elliot J. Groffman . . . . .Attorney
Rob Cohen . . . . .Attorney
Jennifer L. Justice . . . . .Attorney
Gillian R. Bar . . . . .Attorney
Paul Gutman . . . . .Attorney
Renee Karalian . . . . .Attorney
Christopher Mitchell . . . . .Attorney
Janine Small . . . . .Attorney
David J. Stein . . . . .Attorney

LAW OFFICES OF JOHN A. CASE, JR.
1880 Century Park East, Ste. 516
Los Angeles, CA 90067
PHONE 310-203-3911
FAX 310-203-3915
EMAIL . . . . .jcase@caseweblaw.com
WEB SITE . . . . www.caseweblaw.com
PRACTICE AREAS   Full Service Representation - Arbitration &
                        Mediation - Contract Negotiation &
                        Drafting - Corporate Matters - Ecommerce
                        - First Amendment Issues - Intellectual
                        Property Law - Internet Law - Libel & Privacy
                        Matters - Licensing - Litigation - Media -
                        Misappropriation of Name, Voice, Likeness
                        - Partnerships/Joint Ventures - Right of
                        Publicity - Royalty Law - Technology -
                        Transactional Law

John A. Case Jr. . . . . .Attorney

LAW OFFICES OF ROBERT A. CELESTIN, ESQ.
250 W. 57th St., Ste. 2331
New York, NY 10107
PHONE 212-262-1103
FAX 212-262-1173
EMAIL . . . . .bcelestin@nyct.net
WEB SITE . . . . www.raclawfirm.com
PRACTICE AREAS   Contract Negotiation & Drafting -
                        Copyright & Trademark Matters -
                        Intellectual Property Law - Licensing -
                        Motion Picture & TV Law - Music Law -
                        Talent Representation - Transactional Law
REPRESENTS   3LW - Petey Pablo - City High - Family
                        Bond (HBO)

Robert A. Celestin Esq. . . . . .Attorney
Joel C. Barnett Esq. . . . . .Attorney
Alicia Ferriabough Esq. . . . . .Attorney
Sheena Jenkins Esq. . . . . .Attorney

CHRISTENSEN GLASER FINK JACOBS WEIL & SHAPIRO LLP
10250 Constellation Blvd., 19th Fl.
Los Angeles, CA 90067
PHONE 310-553-3000
FAX 310-556-2920
WEB SITE .www.chrisglase.com
PRACTICE AREAS   Arbitration & Mediation - Contract Negotiation & Drafting - Copyright & Trademark Matters - Corporate Matters - Employment/Labor Law - Financing - First Amendment Issues - Intellectual Property Law - Libel & Privacy Matters - Licensing - Litigation - Mergers & Acquisitions - Misappropriation of Name, Voice, Likeness - Motion Picture & TV Law - Partnerships/Joint Ventures - Right of Publicity - Royalty Law - Talent Representation - Tax Law - Transactional Law
COMMENTS   Motion picture and TV production; Finance and distribution transactions; Internet content agreements; Purchase, sale and valuation of film libraries; Merchandising; Literary property acquisitions; Litigation in all entertainment areas

Terry N. Christensen . . . . .Managing Partner
Patricia Glaser . . . . .Partner, Litigation
Barry E. Fink . . . . .Partner/Chair, Taxation, International Law
Peter M. Weil . . . . .Partner/Chair, Real Estate & Corporate
Robert L. Shapiro . . . . .Partner/Chair, Criminal Law
Nabil L. Abu-Assal . . . . .Partner, Litigation
Terry D. Avchen . . . . .Partner/Chair, Environmental Law
Leslie Lo Baugh . . . . .Partner, Environmental Law
Andrew Baum . . . . .Partner, Litigation
Mark L. Block . . . . .Partner, Litigation
Saul Breskal . . . . .Partner, Real Estate
Brett J. Cohen . . . . .Partner, Real Estate
Eric P. Early . . . . .Partner, Litigation
Joie Marie Gallo . . . . .Partner, Litigation
Miriam J. Golbert . . . . .Partner, Estate Planning & Trusts
Roger H. Howard . . . . .Partner, Real Estate
Carolyn C. Jordan . . . . .Partner, Real Estate
Jerry Katz . . . . .Partner, Real Estate
Joel Klevens . . . . .Partner, Litigation
Warren A. Koshofer . . . . .Partner, Environmental Law
Mark G. Krum . . . . .Partner, Litigation
Kevin J. Leichter .Partner, Litigation
Alisa Morgenthaler Lever . . . . .Partner, Litigation
Thomas S. Levyn .Partner, Real Estate
Caroline Mankey .Partner, Litigation
Janet S. McCloud . . . . .Partner, Corporate Securities
Timothy McOsker . . . . .Partner, Real Estate
Sean Riley . . . . .Partner, Litigation
James S. Schreier .Partner, Litigation
Peter C. Sheridan . . . . .Partner, Litigation
Gary Sommerstein . . . . .Partner/Chair, Entertainment Law
Jeffrey C. Soza . . . . .Partner, Corporate Securities & Business Law
Kerry Garvis Wright . . . . .Partner, Litigation
Stephen D. Silbert . . . .Of Counsel, Corporate Securities & Business Law
Gary N. Jacobs . . . . .Of Counsel
Greg Suess .Of Counsel, Corporate

LAW OFFICE OF DENNIS N. CLINE
1226 Oak St.
Santa Monica, CA 90405
PHONE 310-450-2000
FAX 310-450-2011
EMAIL .dnc@clineoffices.com
PRACTICE AREAS   Full Service Representation - Contract Negotiation & Drafting - Copyright & Trademark Matters - Corporate Matters - Ecommerce - Financing - First Amendment Issues - Intellectual Property Law - Internet Law - Libel & Privacy Matters - Licensing - Misappropriation of Name, Voice, Likeness - Motion Picture & TV Law - Right of Publicity - Talent Representation - Technology - Transactional Law

Dennis N. Cline . . . . .Attorney

COHEN & GARDNER, LLP
329 N. Wetherly Dr., Ste. 206
Beverly Hills, CA 90211
PHONE 310-285-7373
FAX 310-285-7374
EMAIL . . . . .admin@cohengardnerlaw.com
PRACTICE AREAS   Full Service Representation

Jeff B. Cohen . . . . .Partner
Jonathan M. Gardner . . . . .Partner
Kate McManus . . . . .Assistant

LAW OFFICE OF MICHAEL N. COHEN, PC
9025 Wilshire Blvd., Ste. 301
Beverly Hills, CA 90211
PHONE 310-288-4500
FAX 310-246-9980
EMAIL .info@patentlawip.com
WEB SITE .www.patentlawip.com
PRACTICE AREAS   Copyright & Trademark Matters - Corporate Matters - Intellectual Property Law - Internet Law - Licensing - Litigation - Misappropriation of Name, Voice, Likeness - Music Law - Right of Publicity - Technology - Transactional Law
COMMENTS   Domain name disputes

Michael N. Cohen . . . . .Owner

COLDEN & MCKUIN
141 El Camino Dr., Ste. 110
Beverly Hills, CA 90212
PHONE 310-786-8777
FAX 310-786-8756
PRACTICE AREAS   Copyright & Trademark Matters

David L. Colden . . . . .Attorney
Jeffrey Frankel . . . . .Attorney
Joel L. McKuin . . . . .Attorney

WALLACE COLLINS, ESQ.

119 Fifth Ave., 3rd Fl.
New York, NY 10003
PHONE 212-245-7300
FAX 212-586-5175
EMAIL . . . . .wallace@wallacecollins.com
WEB SITE . . . . .www.wallacecollins.com
PRACTICE AREAS   Full Service Representation - Contract
                    Negotiation & Drafting - Copyright &
                    Trademark Matters - Intellectual Property
                    Law - Internet Law - Licensing - Media -
                    Misappropriation of Name, Voice, Likeness
                    - Motion Picture & TV Law - Music Law -
                    Partnerships/Joint Ventures - Right of
                    Publicity - Royalty Law - Technology -
                    Telecom - Transactional Law
COMMENTS   Deal structuring and negotiation; Member:
                    NARAS, The Copyright Society of the U.S.A.

Wallace Collins . . . . .Attorney

LAW OFFICE OF KEITH E. COOPER, ESQ.

PO Box 691237
West Hollywood, CA 90069
PHONE 310-388-3850
FAX 310-388-3851
EMAIL . . . . .hcd@productioncounsel.com
WEB SITE .www.productioncounsel.com
PRACTICE AREAS   Arbitration & Mediation - Contract
                    Negotiation & Drafting - Copyright &
                    Trademark Matters - Corporate Matters -
                    Financing - Licensing - Motion Picture & TV
                    Law - Partnerships/Joint Ventures -
                    Transactional Law
REPRESENTS   Production Companies (Bold Films) -
                    Established Producers - Directors - Writers -
                    Feature Films (Bobby - Better Luck
                    Tomorrow)
COMMENTS   Production counsel for independent feature
                    films, from acquisition of literary property to
                    delivery of completed picture; Mediator for
                    all types of entertainment industry disputes;
                    Inquiries via law firm Web site are preferred

Keith Cooper . . . . .Attorney

BRIAN LEE CORBER, ATTORNEY AT LAW

PO Box 44212
Panorama City, CA 91412-0212
PHONE 818-786-7133
FAX 818-785-6495
EMAIL . . . . .corberlaw@aol.com
PRACTICE AREAS   Full Service Representation - Arbitration &
                    Mediation - Contract Negotiation &
                    Drafting - Copyright & Trademark Matters -
                    Corporate Matters - Intellectual Property
                    Law - Licensing - Litigation - Motion Picture
                    & TV Law - Music Law - Right of Publicity -
                    Royalty Law - Talent Representation -
                    Transactional Law
COMMENTS   Business structuring

Brian Lee Corber . . . . .Owner/Sole Proprietor

costa abrams & coate llp

COSTA ABRAMS & COATE LLP

1221 Second St., 3rd Fl.
Santa Monica, CA 90401
PHONE 310-576-6161
FAX 310-576-6160
WEB SITE . . . . .www.costalaw.com
PRACTICE AREAS   Full Service Representation - Arbitration &
                    Mediation - Contract Negotiation &
                    Drafting - Copyright & Trademark Matters -
                    Corporate Matters - Ecommerce -
                    Financing - Intellectual Property Law -
                    Internet Law - Libel & Privacy Matters -
                    Licensing - Litigation - Media - Mergers &
                    Acquisitions - Misappropriation of Name,
                    Voice, Likeness - Motion Picture & TV Law -
                    Music Law - Partnerships/Joint Ventures -
                    Right of Publicity - Talent Representation -
                    Transactional Law

Joseph P. Costa . . . . .Partner
Alan J. Abrams . . . . .Partner
Charles M. Coate . . . . .Partner
Elizabeth Floriani . . . . .Esq.
Jennifer L. Korth . . . . .Esq.
Allison Mella . . . . .Esq.
Darius Vosylius . . . . .Esq.

COVINGTON & BURLING LLP

One Front St., 35th Fl.
San Francisco, CA 94111
PHONE 415-591-6000
FAX 415-591-6091
EMAIL . . . . .kebanks@cov.com
WEB SITE . . . . .www.cov.com
PRACTICE AREAS   Full Service Representation -
                    Communications - Contract Negotiation &
                    Drafting - Copyright & Trademark Matters -
                    Corporate Matters - Intellectual Property
                    Law - Licensing - Litigation - Media -
                    Mergers & Acquisitions - Tax Law -
                    Transactional Law

Kenneth D. Ebanks . . . . .Partner

COWAN, DEBAETS, ABRAHAMS & SHEPPARD, LLP

41 Madison Ave., 34th Fl.
New York, NY 10010
PHONE 212-974-7474
FAX 212-974-8474/212-974-0912
EMAIL . . . . .cdas@cdas.com
WEB SITE . . . . .www.cdas.com
PRACTICE AREAS   Arbitration & Mediation - Contract
Negotiation & Drafting - Copyright &
Trademark Matters - Corporate Matters -
Employment/Labor Law - Financing -
Intellectual Property Law - Internet Law -
Libel & Privacy Matters - Licensing -
Litigation - Mergers & Acquisitions -
Misappropriation of Name, Voice, Likeness
- Motion Picture & TV Law - Music Law -
Partnerships/Joint Ventures - Right of
Publicity - Royalty Law - Transactional Law
COMMENTS   Correspondent firm: Donaldson & Hart,
9220 Sunset Blvd., Ste. 224, Los Angeles,
CA 90069, phone: 310-273-8394

Timothy J. DeBaets .Partner
J. Stephen Sheppard . . . . .Partner
Anne C. Baker . . . . .Partner
Frederick P. Bimbler . . . . .Partner
Toby M.J. Butterfield . . . . .Partner
Al J. Daniel Jr. . . . . .Partner
Robert I. Freedman .Partner
Mitchell E. Radin . . . . .Partner
Robert L. Seigel . . . . .Partner
Ralph J. Sutton . . . . .Partner
Kenneth N. Swezey .Partner
Robert Van Lierop . . . . .Partner
Nancy E. Wolff . . . . .Partner
Jerrold B. Gold .Of Counsel
Albert Gottesman . . . . .Of Counsel
Roger E. Kass .Of Counsel
Ellis B. Levine .Of Counsel
Michael D. Remer . . . . .Of Counsel
Lisa K. Digernes .Associate
Matthew A. Kaplan . . . . .Associate
M. Kilburg Reedy . . . . .Associate
Mason A. Weisz .Associate
Zehra Abdi .Staff Attorney
Alexis N. Mueller . . . . .Staff Attorney

CPM CREATIVE, LEGAL

8033 Sunset Blvd., Ste. 1049
Hollywood, CA 90046
PHONE 323-856-2989
FAX 323-285-5211
EMAIL . . . . .info@cpm-creative.com
WEB SITE . . . . .www.cpm-creative.com
PRACTICE AREAS   Full Service Representation
COMMENTS   Licensed to practice law in California and
New York

Christian Martinen LLM, Esq. . . . . .Attorney (NY)
Joy de Leon Esq. . . . . .Attorney

DAVENPORT LYONS

41 Madison Ave., 34th Fl.
New York, NY 10010
PHONE 212-974-7474
FAX 212-974-8474
EMAIL . . . . .jfq2@aol.com
WEB SITE .www.davenportlyons.com
PRACTICE AREAS   Full Service Representation
COMMENTS   UK office: 30 Old Burlington St., London
W1S 3NL UK, phone: 44-207-468-2600,
fax: 44-207-439-4306

Leon Morgan . . . . .Sr. Partner/Head, Media Department
Fraser Bloom .Partner, Media
Laurence Brown . . . . .Partner, Media
Sam Tatton Brown . . . . .Partner, Media
David Gore . . . . .Partner, Music & Entertainment
Martin Haines .Partner, Media
Richard Moxon . . . . .Partner, Media
Jay Quatrini . . . . .Partner, Music & Entertainment
Greg Abbott .Attorney, Media
Sandra Benoit . . . . .Attorney, Media
Elizabeth Davis . . . . .Attorney, Media
Chris Hardingham . . . . .Attorney, Media
Paul Mustafa .Attorney, Media
Guy Sheppard . . . . .Attorney, Media
Katrina Stagner . . . . .Attorney, Media
Tim Allen . . . . .Attorney, Music & Entertainment
Michelle Brown . . . . .Attorney, Music & Entertainment
Nigel Gilroy . . . . .Attorney, Music & Entertainment
Rupert Sprawson . . . . .Attorney, Music & Entertainment

DAVIS & GILBERT LLP

1740 Broadway
New York, NY 10019
PHONE 212-468-4800
FAX 212-468-4888
EMAIL . . . . .info@dglaw.com
WEB SITE . . . . .www.dglaw.com
PRACTICE AREAS   Full Service Representation
REPRESENTS   Authors - Advertising & Interactive Agencies
- Individual Artists - Industry & Trade
Associations - Motion Picture Studios -
Professional Sports Leagues - Public
Relations Firms - Television & Cable
Networks

Ronald Urbach . . . . .Partner/Co-Chair, Advertising
Lewis Rubin . . . . .Partner/Co-Chair, Corporate
Brad Schwartzberg . . . . .Partner/Co-Chair, Corporate
Mark Bokert . . . . .Partner, Benefits
Michael Ditzian . . . . .Partner, Corporate
Richard Eisert . . . . .Partner, Advertising
Martin Garbus . . . . .Partner, Litigation
Gregg Gilman . . . . .Partner, Litigation
James Johnston . . . . .Partner, Entertainment/Media
Michael Lasky . . . . .Partner/Co-Chair, Litigation
Joseph Lewczak . . . . .Partner, Advertising
Curt Myers . . . . .Partner, Corporate
Howard Rubin . . . . .Partner/Co-Chair, Litigation
Gerald Uram . . . . .Partner, Real Estate
Howard Weingrad . . . . .Partner, Advertising

DAVIS WRIGHT TREMAINE LLP
865 S. Figueroa St., Ste. 2400
Los Angeles, CA 90017
PHONE 213-633-6800
FAX 213-633-6899
EMAIL . . . . .losangeles@dwt.com
WEB SITE . . . . .www.dwt.com
PRACTICE AREAS   Full Service Representation
COMMENTS   Headquartered in Seattle, Washington,
                       Davis Wright Tremaine LLP has nine addi-
                       tional offices including: Anchorage, Alaska;
                       Bellevue, Washington; New York, New
                       York; Portland, Oregon; Los Angeles and
                       San Francisco, California; Washington,
                       D.C. and Shanghai, China

Richard D. Ellingsen . . . . .Firmwide Managing Partner
Mary Haas . . . . .Partner in Charge
William Bly . . . . .Partner
Jennifer L. Brockett . . . . .Partner
Jill R. Cohen . . . . .Partner
Dennis Diaz . . . . .Partner
Kathleen H. Drummy . . . . .Partner
James Zhi-Ying Fang . . . . .Partner
Andrew R. Hall . . . . .Partner
Marc E. Jacobowitz . . . . .Partner
Thomas E. Jeffry Jr. . . . . .Partner
John P. Krave . . . . .Partner
Robert Layton . . . . .Partner
John P. LeCrone . . . . .Partner
Kelli L. Sager . . . . .Partner
Henry J. Tashman . . . . .Partner
Andrew J. Thomas . . . . .Partner
Alonzo Wickers IV . . . . .Partner
Rochelle L. Wilcox . . . . .Partner
Camilo Echavarria . . . . .Of Counsel
Jill H. Gordon . . . . .Of Counsel
Seth D. Levy . . . . .Of Counsel
John R. Tate . . . . .Of Counsel
Robyn Aronson . . . . .Associate
Joanne Bressler . . . . .Associate
Rory Eastburg . . . . .Associate
Emilio G. Gonzalez .Associate
Janet Grumer . . . . .Associate
Karen Henry . . . . .Associate
Kristin Kosinski . . . . .Associate
Kelly S. Logue . . . . .Associate
Bruce G. McCarthy .Associate
Joshua Radis . . . . .Associate
Susan Seager . . . . .Associate
Sean D. Senn . . . . .Associate
Linda B. Truong . . . . .Associate
Wendy Wu . . . . .Associate

DEL, SHAW, MOONVES, TANAKA, FINKELSTEIN & LEZCANO
2120 Colorado Ave., Ste. 200
Santa Monica, CA 90404
PHONE 310-979-7900
FAX 310-979-7999
PRACTICE AREAS   Full Service Representation - Copyright &
                       Trademark Matters - Intellectual Property
                       Law - Misappropriation of Name, Voice,
                       Likeness - Motion Picture & TV Law -
                       Partnerships/Joint Ventures - Talent
                       Representation - Transactional Law

Ernest Del . . . . .Partner
Nina L. Shaw . . . . .Partner
Jonathan D. Moonves . . . . .Partner
Jean E. Tanaka . . . . .Partner
Jeffrey S. Finkelstein . . . . .Partner
Abel M. Lezcano . . . . .Partner
Jay Goldberg . . . . .Associate
Gordon M. Bobb . . . . .Associate
Loan T. Dang . . . . .Associate
Thomas R. Greenberg .Associate
Jeanne Bixler Way . . . . .Paralegal
Amy Parmeter . . . . .Paralegal

DIXON Q. DERN, PC
1262 Devon Ave.
Los Angeles, CA 90024
PHONE 310-557-2244
FAX 310-275-7655
EMAIL . . . . .ddern@dixlaw.com
WEB SITE . . . . .www.dixlaw.com
PRACTICE AREAS   Arbitration & Mediation - Contract
                       Negotiation & Drafting - Copyright &
                       Trademark Matters - Corporate Matters -
                       Intellectual Property Law - Motion Picture &
                       TV Law - Transactional Law

Dixon Q. Dern . . . . .Principal

DICKSTEINSHAPIRO**LLP**

DICKSTEIN SHAPIRO LLP
2049 Century Park East, Ste. 700
Los Angeles, CA 90067
PHONE 310-772-8300
FAX 310-772-8301
WEB SITE . . . . .www.dicksteinshapiro.com
PRACTICE AREAS   Full Service Representation -
                       Communications - Contract Negotiation &
                       Drafting - Copyright & Trademark Matters -
                       Corporate Matters - Employment/Labor
                       Law - Financing - First Amendment Issues -
                       Intellectual Property Law - Internet Law -
                       Libel & Privacy Matters - Licensing -
                       Litigation - Media - Mergers & Acquisitions
                       - Motion Picture & TV Law -
                       Partnerships/Joint Ventures - Tax Law -
                       Technology - Telecom - Transactional Law
REPRESENTS   Motion Picture Studios - Television
                       Networks - Production Companies -
                       Financial Institutions
COMMENTS   Washington, DC office: 202-402-2200;
                       New York office: 212-277-6500; Law serv-
                       ices also include representation in the pro-
                       duction, acquisition and sale of films and
                       TV programs, insurance coverage and risk
                       management, securities and banking

Lindsay Conner . . . . .Partner/Head, Entertainment Practice
Matthew Bergman . . . . .Partner
Eli Curi Jr. . . . . .Partner

(Continued)

DICKSTEIN SHAPIRO LLP (Continued)

Jennifer Eck . . . . .Partner
Alfred Fabricant . . . . .Partner
Howard Graff . . . . .Partner
Michael Green . . . . .Partner
Jon Grossman . . . . .Partner
Patrick Lynch . . . . .Partner
Lewis Paper . . . . .Partner
Kirk Pasich . . . . .Partner
Gabrielle Roth . . . . .Partner
Paul Taskier . . . . .Partner
Cassandra Franklin . . . . .Of Counsel
Tom Ara . . . . .Associate

DONALDSON & HART
9220 Sunset Blvd., Ste. 224
Los Angeles, CA 90069-3501
PHONE 310-273-8394/310-274-7157
FAX .310-273-5370/310-274-1437
EMAIL . . . . .staff@donaldsonhart.com
WEB SITE . . . . .www.donaldsonhart.com
PRACTICE AREAS   Full Service Representation - Arbitration & Mediation - Copyright & Trademark Matters - Intellectual Property Law - Litigation - Motion Picture & TV Law - Talent Representation
REPRESENTS   Independent Films - Writers - Directors - Producers
COMMENTS   General Counsel to Film Independent (FIND) and the Writers Guild Foundation; Former president of the International Documentary Association

Michael C. Donaldson . . . . .Attorney
Joseph F. Hart . . . . .Attorney
Lisa A. Callif . . . . .Attorney
R. Lance Belsome . . . . .Attorney
Katheleen A. Ebora . . . . .Legal Secretary to Michael C. Donaldson
Sylvia Mendoza . . . . .Assistant to Joseph F. Hart
Ryan Gooden . . . . .Legal Assistant

DOVEL & LUNER, LLP
201 Santa Monica Blvd., Ste. 600
Santa Monica, CA 90401
PHONE 310-656-7066
FAX 310-656-7069
WEB SITE . . . . .www.dovellaw.com
PRACTICE AREAS   Litigation

Julien Adams . . . . .Partner/Attorney
Greg Dovel . . . . .Partner/Attorney
Sean Luner . . . . .Partner/Attorney
Jeff Eichmann . . . . .Associate/Attorney

DOYLE & MILLER LLP
190 N. Cañon Dr., Ste. 202
Beverly Hills, CA 90210
PHONE 310-858-3700
FAX 310-858-3711
WEB SITE . . . . .www.doylemiller.com
PRACTICE AREAS   Contract Negotiation & Drafting - Copyright & Trademark Matters - First Amendment Issues - Intellectual Property Law - Libel & Privacy Matters - Misappropriation of Name, Voice, Likeness - Motion Picture & TV Law - Right of Publicity - Talent Representation

Christopher R. Doyle . . . . .Partner
Brad Miller . . . . .Partner
Marilou Mckean .Of Counsel Attorney

DREIER STEIN & KAHAN LLP

DREIER STEIN & KAHAN LLP
1620 26th St., 6th Fl., North Tower
Santa Monica, CA 90404
PHONE 310-828-9050
FAX 310-828-9101
EMAIL . . . . .info@dskllp.com
WEB SITE . . . . .www.dskllp.com
PRACTICE AREAS   Arbitration & Mediation - Copyright & Trademark Matters - First Amendment Issues - Intellectual Property Law - Internet Law - Libel & Privacy Matters - Litigation - Media - Misappropriation of Name, Voice, Likeness - Motion Picture & TV Law - Music Law - Right of Publicity - Royalty Law - Talent Representation
COMMENTS   Representation of Talent (film, television and music), distributors, production companies, managers and agents; Defamation, Labor Commission disputes

Stanton 'Larry' Stein . .Partner, Chair, Entertainment & Media Department
Yakub Hazzard . . .Partner, Co-Chair, Entertainment & Media Department
Michael J. Plonsker . . . . .Partner, Co-Chair, Entertainment & Media Department
Bennett A. Bigman . . . . .Partner
Karen L. Dillon . . . . .Partner
Daniel A. Fiore . . . . .Partner
David S. Gubman . . . . .Partner
Marcia J. Harris . . . . .Partner
Lawrence C. Hinkle II . . . . .Partner
Andrew F. Kim . . . . .Partner
Ann Loeb . . . . .Partner
Mark D. Passin . . . . .Partner
Samuel R. Pryor . . . . .Partner
Bridgette Taylor . . . . .Partner
Brooke H. Eisenhart . . . . .Associate
Jesse M. Leff . . . . .Associate
Sally S. Liu . . . . .Associate
David R. Shraga . . . . .Associate
Jonathan E. Stern . . . . .Associate

DUVAL & STACHENFELD LLP
1888 Century Park East, Ste. 2050
Los Angeles, CA 90067
PHONE 310-553-9100
FAX 310-553-9107
WEB SITE . . . . .www.dsllp.com
PRACTICE AREAS   Contract Negotiation & Drafting - Copyright & Trademark Matters - Employment/Labor Law - Financing - Licensing - Litigation - Media - Motion Picture & TV Law - Music Law - Talent Representation - Technology - Transactional Law

Matthew D. Pace . . . . .Chairman, Sports Business & Sponsorship Group
Paul I. Menes . . . . .Partner/Co-Head, Entertainment & Digital Media Practice Group
Marilyn G. Haft . . . . .Partner/Co-Head, Entertainment & Digital Media Practice Group

ECLIPSE LAW CORPORATION
9348 Civic Center Dr., Mezzanine Level
Beverly Hills, CA 90210
PHONE 310-288-5855
FAX 310-288-5853
EMAIL . . . . .rszymanski@eclipselaw.com
PRACTICE AREAS   Contract Negotiation & Drafting - Motion
                      Picture & TV Law - Talent Representation

Rob Szymanski . . . . .Partner, Entertainment Law

EDELSTEIN, LAIRD & SOBEL
9255 Sunset Blvd., Ste. 800
Los Angeles, CA 90069
PHONE 310-274-6184
FAX 310-274-6185
PRACTICE AREAS   Full Service Representation

Peter Laird . . . . .Partner
William Sobel . . . . .Partner
Gerald Edelstein . . . . .Of Counsel

LAW OFFICES OF DEMONDRE A. EDWARDS
8350 Wilshire Blvd., Ste. 200
Beverly Hills, CA 90211
PHONE 323-556-0696
FAX 323-556-0601
WEB SITE . . . . .www.dedwardslaw.com
PRACTICE AREAS   Contract Negotiation & Drafting -
                      Intellectual Property Law - Motion Picture &
                      TV Law - Music Law
REPRESENTS   Production Companies - Directors - Actors
                      - Producers - Musicians - Photographers -
                      Writers

Demondre A. Edwards .Attorney

ERIC S. ELIAS
PO Box 6671
Woodland Hills, CA 91365
PHONE 818-716-7666
PRACTICE AREAS   Full Service Representation

Eric S. Elias . . . . .Attorney

LAW OFFICES OF ROGER R. ELLIS
PO Box 3422
Westlake Village, CA 91359-0422
PHONE 310-883-5330
EMAIL . . . . .rellis@rellislaw.com
PRACTICE AREAS   Contract Negotiation & Drafting -
                      Copyright & Trademark Matters

Roger R. Ellis . . . . .Attorney
Kassy Hughes . . . . .Executive Secretary

ENGSTROM, LIPSCOMB & LACK
10100 Santa Monica Blvd., 16th Fl.
Los Angeles, CA 90067
PHONE 310-552-3800
FAX 310-552-9434
WEB SITE . . . . .www.elllaw.com
PRACTICE AREAS   Contract Negotiation & Drafting -
                      Intellectual Property Law - Litigation - Music
                      Law

Paul W. Engstrom . . . . .Partner
Lee G. Lipscomb . . . . .Partner
Walter J. Lack . . . . .Partner
Jared W. Beilke . . . . .Attorney
Robert T. Bryson . . . . .Attorney
Elizabeth Lane Crooke . . . . .Attorney
Brian D. Depew . . . . .Attorney
Brian J. Heffernan . . . . .Attorney
Elizabeth Hernandez .Attorney
Ann A. Howitt . . . . .Attorney
Richard P. Kinnan . . . . .Attorney
Brian J. Leinbach . . . . .Attorney
Steven J. Lipscomb . . . . .Attorney
Mark E. Millard . . . . .Attorney
Adam D. Miller . . . . .Attorney
Bryan C. Payne . . . . .Attorney
Thu T. Pham . . . . .Attorney
Gary A. Praglin . . . . .Attorney
Jerry A. Ramsey . . . . .Attorney
Joy L. Robertson . . . . .Attorney
Steven C. Shuman . . . . .Attorney
Alexandra J. Thompson . . . . .Attorney
Paul A. Traina . . . . .Attorney
Gregory P. Waters . . . . .Attorney
Daniel G. Whalen . . . . .Attorney
Robert J. Wolfe . . . . .Attorney
Edward P. Wolfe . . . . .Attorney

ENTERTAINMENT LAW COUNSEL, A PROFESSIONAL LAW CORP.
9171 Wilshire Blvd., Ste. 600
Beverly Hills, CA 90210
PHONE 310-860-1141
FAX 310-860-1142
EMAIL . . . . .info@entertainmentlawcounsel.com
WEB SITE . . . . .www.entertainmentlawcounsel.com
PRACTICE AREAS   Contract Negotiation & Drafting -
                      Copyright & Trademark Matters - Licensing
                      - Litigation - Motion Picture & TV Law -
                      Talent Representation - Transactional Law
REPRESENTS   Independent Film Producers/Production
                      Companies - Actors - Writers - Directors -
                      Executives - Investors

Deidra Buffington Esq. . . . . .Attorney/President

EPSTEIN, LEVINSOHN, BODINE & WEINSTEIN, LLP
1790 Broadway, 10th Fl.
New York, NY 10019-1412
PHONE 212-262-1000
FAX 212-262-5022
PRACTICE AREAS   Full Service Representation

Robert J. Epstein . . . . .Partner
Mark A. Levinsohn . . . . .Partner
James D. Arnay . . . . .Partner
Susan H. Bodine . . . . .Partner
Andrea F. Cannistraci .Partner
Alison S. Cohen . . . . .Partner
Joel H. Weinstein . . . . .Partner
Matthew L. Finkelstein . . . . .Associate
Michael P. Overn . . . . .Associate
Natalie Stanford . . . . .Attorney
Douglas C. Bernheim . . . . .Of Counsel
Benjamin C. Feldman . . . . .Of Counsel
Alan N. Skiena . . . . .Of Counsel
Brian R. Godshall . . . . .Paralegal

ESKRIDGE & ESKRIDGE LAW FIRM
100 North Main Bldg., Ste. 1036
Memphis, TN 38103-5010
PHONE 901-522-9600
FAX 901-276-3800
EMAIL . . . . .info@eskridgelaw.com
SECOND EMAIL . . . . .april@eskridgelaw.com
WEB SITE . . . . .www.eskridgelaw.com
PRACTICE AREAS   Full Service Representation

Janelle R. Eskridge . . . . .Partner
Reginald L. Eskridge . . . . .Partner
Wiley Johnson Jr. . . . . .Partner
Stanley J. Kline . . . . .Of Counsel
Hebert Rammings . . . . .Associate

FAGELBAUM & HELLER, LLP
2049 Century Park East, Ste. 4250
Los Angeles, CA 90067
PHONE 310-286-7666
FAX 310-286-7086
PRACTICE AREAS   Arbitration & Mediation - Litigation

Jerald Fagelbaum . . . . .Partner
Philip Heller . . . . .Partner
Debi Ramos . . . . .Attorney

LAW OFFICES OF GORDON P. FIREMARK
10940 Wilshire Blvd., 16th Fl.
Los Angeles, CA 90024
PHONE 310-443-4185
FAX 310-477-7676
EMAIL . . . . .gfiremark@firemark.com
WEB SITE . . . . .www.firemark.com
PRACTICE AREAS   Full Service Representation - Contract
                      Negotiation & Drafting - Copyright &
                      Trademark Matters - Internet Law -
                      Licensing - Motion Picture & TV Law -
                      Music Law - Partnerships/Joint Ventures -
                      Talent Representation
REPRESENTS   Screenwriters - Playwrights - Actors -
                      Directors - Producers - Production
                      Companies - Distributors - Theatres -
                      Agents - Managers
COMMENTS   Theatre law

Gordon P. Firemark . . . . .Attorney at Law

MARIE-ELEANA FIRST, ATTORNEY AT LAW
299 Broadway, Ste. 1505
New York, NY 10007
PHONE 212-566-3555
FAX 212-566-3555
EMAIL . . . . .mfirst@firstlawnyc.com
WEB SITE . . . . .www.firstlawnyc.com
PRACTICE AREAS   Intellectual Property Law - Music Law

Marie-Eleana First . . . . .Attorney

FISHER LAW OFFICE
124 South St., Ste. 3
Annapolis, MD 21401
PHONE 443-270-6305
FAX 443-270-6307
EMAIL . . . . .rfisher@fisherbusinesslaw.com
SECOND EMAIL . . . . .rfisher@mlrf.com
WEB SITE . . . . .www.fisherbusinesslaw.com
SECOND WEB SITE . . . . .www.mlrf.com
PRACTICE AREAS   Contract Negotiation & Drafting -
                      Copyright & Trademark Matters -
                      Corporate Matters - Mergers & Acquisitions
                      - Partnerships/Joint Ventures - Telecom

Randy Fisher . . . . .Attorney

FITELSON, LASKY, ASLAN & COUTURE
551 Fifth Avenue, Ste. 605
New York, NY 10176
PHONE 212-586-4700
FAX 212-949-6746
EMAIL . . . . .dramalex@aol.com
PRACTICE AREAS   Copyright & Trademark Matters
COMMENTS   Primarily theater representation of produc-
                      ers, authors, composers, directors, chore-
                      ographers and designers

Jerold Couture . . . . .Partner
Floria Lasky . . . . .Partner

FOLEY & LARDNER LLP
2029 Century Park East, Ste. 3500
Los Angeles, CA 90067
PHONE 310-277-2223
FAX 310-557-8475
WEB SITE . . . . .www.foley.com
PRACTICE AREAS   Full Service Representation - Arbitration &
                      Mediation - Contract Negotiation &
                      Drafting - Copyright & Trademark Matters -
                      Corporate Matters - Financing - First
                      Amendment Issues - Intellectual Property
                      Law - Libel & Privacy Matters - Licensing -
                      Litigation - Mergers & Acquisitions - Motion
                      Picture & TV Law - Music Law -
                      Partnerships/Joint Ventures - Transactional
                      Law

Paul Bargren   . . . .Partner, Litigation, Entertainment & Media (Milwaukee)
                      (414-271-2400)
Miriam Claire Beezy . .Partner/Chair, Trademark, Copyright & Advertising
                      Practice Group/Co-Chair, Entertainment & Media (LA)
Gregory S. Bruch . . .Partner, Securities Litigation, Entertainment & Media
                      (Washington, DC) (202-672-5300)
Michael M. Conway . . . .Partner, Media Law (Chicago) (312-832-4500)
Terence J. Delahunty Jr. . . .Partner, Business Law, Entertainment & Media
                      (Orlando) (407-423-7656)
Carole E. Handler . .Vice-Chair, IP Litigation, Entertainment & Media (LA)
Jarvis P. Kellogg . . . . .Partner, Business Law, Entertainment & Media
                      (Boston) (617-342-4000)
James D. Nguyen . . . . .Partner/Co-Chair, Entertainment & Media/
                      IP Litigation (LA)
Robert A. Scher . . . . . . .Partner, Litigation, Entertainment & Media (NY)
                      (212-682-7474)
Andrew B. Serwin . . . . . . .Partner, IP Litigation, Entertainment & Media
                      (San Diego) (619-234-6655)
M. Kenneth Suddleson . . . . . . .Of Counsel, Transactional & Securities,
                      Entertainment & Media (LA)

FOX SPILLANE SHAEFFER LLP
1880 Century Park East, Ste. 1004
Los Angeles, CA 90067
PHONE 310-229-9300
FAX 310-229-9380
WEB SITE .www.foxspillane.com

Gerry Fox . . . . .Partner
Jay Spillane . . . . .Partner
John Shaeffer . . . . .Partner
Donald Zachary . . . . .Partner
David Aronoff . . . . .Partner
Lincoln Bandlow . . . . .Partner
Raul Perez . . . . .Partner
Julia Ross . . . . .Of Counsel
Raphael Cung . . . . .Associate
Michele Friend . . . . .Associate
Jeff Grant . . . . .Associate
Ruth Moore . . . . .Associate
Shaheen Sheik . . . . .Associate
Garret Weinrieb . . . . .Associate
Amber Henry . . . . .Associate

JEFFERY C. FOY, A PROFESSIONAL CORPORATION
8335 Sunset Blvd., Ste. 222
West Hollywood, CA 90069
PHONE 323-337-9085
EMAIL . . . . .cfoy@cfoyesq.com
WEB SITE . . . . .www.cfoyesq.com
PRACTICE AREAS   Contract Negotiation & Drafting -
    Copyright & Trademark Matters - Financing
    - Motion Picture & TV Law -
    Partnerships/Joint Ventures - Talent
    Representation
REPRESENTS   Producers - Theatrical Talent - Distributors -
    Sales Agents
COMMENTS   Federal and state tax incentives; Production
    legal; Foreign soft money arrangements;
    Investor financing; Pick-up and presale
    financing; Section 181 tax incentive con-
    sultant; Feature film private placements; No
    unsolicited faxes

Jeffery C. Foy Esq. . . . . .President

FRANKFURT KURNIT KLEIN & SELZ
488 Madison Ave.
New York, NY 10022
PHONE 212-980-0120
FAX 212-593-9175
EMAIL . . . . .info@fkks.com
WEB SITE . . . . .www.fkks.com
PRACTICE AREAS   Full Service Representation
REPRESENTS   Producers - Distributors - Financiers -
    Executives - Writers - Directors -
    Filmmakers - Actors - Models - Musicians -
    Fine Artists - Athletes

Victoria S. Cook . . . . .Attorney
Timothy Craig . . . . .Attorney
Lisa E. Davis . . . . .Attorney
Michael Frankfurt . . . . .Attorney
Salil Gandhi . . . . .Attorney
Richard B. Heller . . . . .Attorney
Richard Hofstetter . . . . .Attorney
Ronald S. Konecky . . . . .Attorney
Mark A. Merriman . . . . .Attorney
Amy Nickin . . . . .Attorney
Andrew Patrick . . . . .Attorney
Thomas D. Selz . . . . .Attorney
Stuart Silfen . . . . .Attorney
Helen Wan . . . . .Attorney
S. Jean Ward . . . . .Attorney
Michael R. Williams . . . . .Attorney

FRANKLIN, WEINRIB, RUDELL & VASSALLO, PC
488 Madison Ave.
New York, NY 10022
PHONE 212-935-5500
FAX 212-308-0642
EMAIL . . . . .lawfirm@fwrv.com
WEB SITE . . . . .www.fwrv.com
PRACTICE AREAS   Full Service Representation - Arbitration &
    Mediation - Communications - Contract
    Negotiation & Drafting - Copyright &
    Trademark Matters - Corporate Matters -
    Ecommerce - Employment/Labor Law -
    Financing - First Amendment Issues -
    Intellectual Property Law - Internet Law -
    Libel & Privacy Matters - Licensing - Media
    - Mergers & Acquisitions - Misappropriation
    of Name, Voice, Likeness - Motion Picture
    & TV Law - Music Law - Partnerships/Joint
    Ventures - Right of Publicity - Royalty Law -
    Sports - Talent Representation - Technology
    - Telecom - Transactional Law
REPRESENTS   Actors - Authors - Recording Artists -
    Screenwriters - Production Companies -
    Directors - Theatrical Producers -
    Corporate Executives
COMMENTS   Theatre, literary publishing, record distribu-
    tion, music publishing, defamation and
    new technologies

Richard A. Beyman . . . . .Partner
Eric S. Brown . . . . .Partner
Elliot H. Brown . . . . .Partner
Jonathan Director . . . . .Partner
Nicholas Gordon . . . . .Partner
Matthew C. Lefferts . . . . .Partner
Jonathan A. Lonner . . . . .Partner
Neil J. Rosini . . . . .Partner
Michael I. Rudell . . . . .Partner
Rose H. Schwartz . . . . .Partner
John A. Vassallo . . . . .Partner
Daniel M. Wasser . . . . .Partner
Kenneth M. Weinrib . . . . .Partner
Karen M. Platt . . . . .Attorney

FRASER - ENTERTAINMENT LAW
9595 Wilshire Blvd., Ste. 900
Beverly Hills, CA 90212
PHONE 310-246-1867
EMAIL . . . . .info@fraser-elaw.com
WEB SITE . . . . .www.fraser-elaw.com
PRACTICE AREAS   Contract Negotiation & Drafting -
    Copyright & Trademark Matters -
    Corporate Matters - Ecommerce -
    Employment/Labor Law - Financing - First
    Amendment Issues - Intellectual Property
    Law - Internet Law - Libel & Privacy Matters
    - Licensing - Media - Mergers &
    Acquisitions - Misappropriation of Name,
    Voice, Likeness - Motion Picture & TV Law -
    Music Law - Partnerships/Joint Ventures -
    Right of Publicity - Royalty Law - Talent
    Representation - Transactional Law
COMMENTS   Toronto office: 980 Yonge St., Ste. 415,
    Toronto, ON M4W 3V8 Canada

Stephen Fraser . . . . .Entertainment Lawyer

FREEDMAN & TAITELMAN, LLP
1901 Avenue of the Stars, Ste. 500
Los Angeles, CA 90067-6007
PHONE 310-201-0005
FAX 310-201-0045
EMAIL . . . . .freedtait@ftllp.com
WEB SITE . . . . .www.ftllp.com
PRACTICE AREAS   Arbitration & Mediation - Contract
                      Negotiation & Drafting - Litigation

Bryan J. Freedman . . . . .Partner
Michael A. Taitelman . . . . .Partner
David M. Marmorstein . . . . .Partner
Tamara Fishbach . . . . .Associate
Gerald L. Greengard . . . . .Associate
Bradley H. Kreshek . . . . .Associate
Matthew Voss . . . . .Associate
John Vukmanovic . . . . .Associate
Jacqueline Brown . . . . .Of Counsel

FRIEDMAN, ENRIQUEZ & CARLSON, LLP
433 N. Camden Dr., Ste. 965
Beverly Hills, CA 90210
PHONE 310-273-0777
FAX 310-273-1115
EMAIL . . . . .bfriedman@go4law.com
WEB SITE www.go4law.com
PRACTICE AREAS   Full Service Representation

Barry Friedman . . . . .Partner
Paul Enriquez . . . . .Partner
Grant Carlson . . . . .Partner

FULBRIGHT & JAWORSKI
555 S. Flower St., 41st Fl.
Los Angeles, CA 90071
PHONE 213-892-9200
FAX 213-892-9494
EMAIL . . . . .info@fulbright.com
WEB SITE . . . . .www.fulbright.com
PRACTICE AREAS   Arbitration & Mediation - Copyright &
                      Trademark Matters - Financing - Intellectual
                      Property Law - Litigation - Misappropriation
                      of Name, Voice, Likeness - Music Law -
                      Right of Publicity
COMMENTS   Offices in Austin, Dallas, Hong Kong,
                      Houston, London, Minneapolis, Munich,
                      New York, San Antonio and Washington,
                      DC

C. Mark Baker . . . . .Partner (Houston)
Robert S. Bambrace . . . . .Partner (Houston)
Walter Earle Bissex . . . . .Partner (Austin)
Mary-Ellen Conway . . . . .Partner (Houston)
Stewart W. Gagnon . . . . .Partner (Houston)
Robert S. Hoffman . . . . .Partner (Houston)
Paul E. Kreiger . . . . .Partner (Houston)
Jonathan K. Newsome . . . . .Partner (Houston)
Dudley Oldham . . . . .Partner (Houston)
John Carlile Rawls . . . . .Partner
William J. Rochelle Jr. . . . . .Partner (New York)
Charles L. Strauss . . . . .Partner (Houston)
Shannon Timothy Vale . . . . .Partner (Austin)

FURGANG & ADWAR, LLP
1230 Avenue of the Americas, 7th Fl.
New York, NY 10020
PHONE 212-725-1818
FAX 212-941-9711
EMAIL . . . . .info@furgang.com
WEB SITE . . . . .www.furgang.com
PRACTICE AREAS   Contract Negotiation & Drafting -
                      Copyright & Trademark Matters -
                      Intellectual Property Law - Libel & Privacy
                      Matters - Licensing - Litigation -
                      Misappropriation of Name, Voice, Likeness
                      - Motion Picture & TV Law - Music Law -
                      Right of Publicity - Transactional Law

Stephanie Furgang Adwar . . . . .Partner
Philip Furgang . . . . .Partner
Bertrand Lanchner .Of Counsel
Sheldon Palmer . . . . .Of Counsel
Brian Scanlon . . . . .Associate

GAINES, SOLOMON LAW GROUP LLP
1901 Avenue of the Stars, Ste. 1100
Los Angeles, CA 90067
PHONE 310-556-1771
FAX 310-556-7955
PRACTICE AREAS   Full Service Representation

Frederic N. Gaines . . . . .Partner (fgaines@mggla.com)
Richard P. Solomon . . . . .Partner (rsolomon@mggla.com)

GALLET DREYER & BERKEY, LLP
845 Third Ave., 8th Fl.
New York, NY 10022-6601
PHONE 212-935-3131
FAX 212-935-4514
EMAIL . . . . .gdb@gdblaw.com
WEB SITE . . . . .www.gdblaw.com
PRACTICE AREAS   Full Service Representation - Arbitration &
                      Mediation - Contract Negotiation &
                      Drafting - Copyright & Trademark Matters -
                      Corporate Matters - Libel & Privacy Matters
                      - Litigation - Partnerships/Joint Ventures

David L. Berkey . . . . .Partner
David T. Azrin . . . . .Partner
Morrell I. Berkowitz . . . . .Partner
David S. Douglas . . . . .Partner
Jay L. Hack . . . . .Partner
Beatrice Lesser . . . . .Partner
David N. Milner . . . . .Partner
Perry L. Mintz . . . . .Partner
Seymour D. Reich . . . . .Partner
Aaron N. Wise . . . . .Partner
Joseph V. Aulicino . . . . .Associate
Lesley-Ann Maloney .Associate
Michelle P. Quinn . . . . .Associate
Scott D. Smiler . . . . .Associate
Erica J. Stein . . . . .Associate
Jerry S. Weiss . . . . .Associate
Stanley B. Dreyer . . . . .Of Counsel
Harvey Schwartz . . . . .Of Counsel

GANG, TYRE, RAMER & BROWN, INC.
132 S. Rodeo Dr.
Beverly Hills, CA 90212
PHONE 310-777-4800
FAX 310-777-4801
PRACTICE AREAS   Intellectual Property Law - Talent
                        Representation - Transactional Law

Harold A. Brown . . . . .Partner
Bruce M. Ramer . . . . .Partner
Nancy L. Boxwell . . . . .Partner
Tom R. Camp . . . . .Partner
Gregg Harrison . . . . .Partner
Jeffrey M. Mandell . . . . .Partner
Kevin S. Marks . . . . .Partner
Donald S. Passman . . . . .Partner
Lawrence D. Rose . . . . .Partner
J. Eugene Salomon Jr. . . . . .Partner
Charles A. Scott . . . . .Partner
Barbara J. Silberbusch . . . . .Partner
Cheryl M. Snow . . . . .Partner
Tara Kole . . . . .Associate
Bianca J. Levin . . . . .Associate

THOMAS F.R. GARVIN
9401 Wilshire Blvd., 9th Fl.
Beverly Hills, CA 90212
PHONE 310-278-7300
FAX 310-278-7306
PRACTICE AREAS   Full Service Representation

Thomas F.R. Garvin . . . . .Member
Carol Lynn Akiyama .Of Counsel
Peter R. Bierstedt . . . . .Of Counsel
Chris Anthony Gemignani . . . . .Of Counsel

GAULIN GROUP PLLC
730 Fifth Ave.
Crown Bldg.
New York, NY 10019
PHONE 212-582-9400
FAX 212-582-9440
EMAIL .info@gaulingroup.com
WEB SITE .www.gaulingroup.com
PRACTICE AREAS   Arbitration & Mediation - Communications
                        - Contract Negotiation & Drafting -
                        Copyright & Trademark Matters -
                        Corporate Matters - Employment/Labor
                        Law - Financing - Intellectual Property Law -
                        Licensing - Litigation - Media - Mergers &
                        Acquisitions - Misappropriation of Name,
                        Voice, Likeness - Motion Picture & TV Law -
                        Music Law - Partnerships/Joint Ventures -
                        Royalty Law - Talent Representation -
                        Transactional Law

Robert V. Gaulin . . . . .Attorney, TV & Film/Publishing/Copyright/
         Intellectual Property/Executive Employment/Acquisitions/
               Contract Negotiation & Drafting/Joint Ventures
Soren Erdmann . . . . .Attorney, Contract Negotiation & Drafting/
                                                    Licensing/Film
George T. Gilbert . . . . .Attorney, Music Law/Talent Representation
George S. Sava . . .Attorney, Litigation, Arbitration, Contract Negotiation
               & Drafting/Licensing/Sports/Talent Representation
Frederick M. Shepperd . . . . .Attorney, Acquisitions & Mergers/
               Corporate Matters, Financing/Transactional

GAVINA E. GALLIER LAW OFFICES
32 rue Pergolèse
Paris 75116, France
PHONE 33-1-4501-5281/33-6-0809-1800
FAX 33-1-4501-5281
EMAIL .ggallier@fr-legal.com
WEB SITE . . . . .www.fr-legal.com
PRACTICE AREAS   Media - Motion Picture & TV Law - Music
                        Law
REPRESENTS   19 Entertainment - TKO Music Publishing -
                        Editions d'Art YVON
COMMENTS   Provides services to French, English and
                        American clients from Paris office

Gavina Gallier . . . . .Attorney
Alexis Baumann . . . . .Sr. Counsel
Joel Gasparato . . . . .Tech Consultant

GENDLER & KELLY, APC
450 N. Roxbury Dr., PH 1000
Beverly Hills, CA 90210
PHONE 310-285-6400
FAX 310-275-7333
WEB SITE .www.gendler-kelly.com
PRACTICE AREAS   Full Service Representation - Motion Picture
                        & TV Law

Michael S. Gendler . . . . .Partner
Kevin M. Kelly . . . . .Partner
Brian E. Fortman . . . . .Attorney
Marc E. Golden . . . . .Attorney

GEORGE OLLINGER LAW FIRM
100 Rialto Pl., Ste. 700
Melbourne, FL 32901-2301
PHONE 321-728-1130
FAX 321-768-0003
EMAIL . . . . .georgeollinger@ollingerlawfirm.com
WEB SITE .www.ollingerlawfirm.com
PRACTICE AREAS   Full Service Representation

George E. Ollinger III . . . . .Attorney

GERDES LAW
8950 W. Olympic Blvd., Ste. 382
Beverly Hills, CA 90211
PHONE 310-385-9501
FAX 310-858-6703
EMAIL . . . . .ted@gerdeslaw.com
WEB SITE . . . . .www.gerdeslaw.com
PRACTICE AREAS   Copyright & Trademark Matters - First
                        Amendment Issues - Intellectual Property
                        Law - Internet Law - Libel & Privacy Matters
                        - Misappropriation of Name, Voice,
                        Likeness - Motion Picture & TV Law - Music
                        Law - Right of Publicity
REPRESENTS   Wide range of clients from individual artists
                        and small producers to Fortune 500 com-
                        panies
COMMENTS   Clearance for film, TV, Internet and adver-
                        tising

Ted F. Gerdes . . . . .Principal/Attorney

GERSH KAPLAN, LLP
15821 Ventura Blvd., Ste. 515
Encino, CA 91436
PHONE 818-536-5715/818-269-3300
FAX 818-981-4618
EMAIL ....skaplan@gershkaplanlaw.com
WEB SITE ....www.gershkaplanlaw.com
SECOND WEB SITE ....www.rainstormentertainment.com
PRACTICE AREAS   Full Service Representation - Arbitration & Mediation - Contract Negotiation & Drafting - Copyright & Trademark Matters - Corporate Matters - Ecommerce - Employment/Labor Law - Financing - Internet Law - Litigation - Motion Picture & TV Law - Music Law - Partnerships/Joint Ventures - Talent Representation - Transactional Law
REPRESENTS   Rainstorm Entertainment - Red Five Entertainment - Launchpad Releasing
COMMENTS   Also production and distribution

Steven G. Kaplan ....Attorney
James A. Sedivy ....Attorney

GIBBONS, DEL DEO, DOLAN, GRIFFINGER & VECCHIONE
One Pennsylvania Plaza, 37th Fl.
New York, NY 10119-3701
PHONE 212-613-2000
FAX 212-333-5980
WEB SITE ....www.gibbonslaw.com
PRACTICE AREAS   Intellectual Property Law

Wendy R. Stein ....Associate

GIBSON, DUNN & CRUTCHER, LLP
333 S. Grand Ave., 47th Fl.
Los Angeles, CA 90071-3197
PHONE 213-229-7000/310-552-8500
FAX 213-229-7520/310-551-8741
WEB SITE ....www.gibsondunn.com
PRACTICE AREAS   Financing - Licensing - Mergers & Acquisitions - Motion Picture & TV Law - Partnerships/Joint Ventures
COMMENTS   Second Los Angeles office: 2029 Century Park East, Ste. 4000, Los Angeles, CA 90067-3026; Offices in Dallas, Denver, Orange County, Palo Alto, New York, San Francisco, Washington DC, London, Munich, Brussels and Paris

Theodore Boutrous Jr. ....Partner, Entertainment
James P. Clark ....Partner, Entertainment
Scott Edelman ....Partner, Entertainment
Ruth Fisher ....Partner, Entertainment
Orin Snyder ....Partner, Entertainment
Lawrence Ulman ....Partner, Entertainment
William Wegner ....Partner, Entertainment

GIPSON HOFFMAN & PANCIONE
1901 Avenue of the Stars, Ste. 1100
Los Angeles, CA 90067-6002
PHONE 310-556-4660
FAX 310-556-8945
WEB SITE ....www.ghplaw.com
PRACTICE AREAS   Arbitration & Mediation - Contract Negotiation & Drafting - Copyright & Trademark Matters - Corporate Matters - Employment/Labor Law - Financing - First Amendment Issues - Intellectual Property Law - Libel & Privacy Matters - Licensing - Litigation - Mergers & Acquisitions - Misappropriation of Name, Voice, Likeness - Motion Picture & TV Law - Partnerships/Joint Ventures - Right of Publicity - Royalty Law - Tax Law - Transactional Law
COMMENTS   Film and TV distribution, finance, production and development matters

Robert E. Gipson ....Attorney
Lawrence R. Barnett ....Attorney
Jeff M. Boren ....Attorney
G. Raymond F. Gross ....Attorney
Brian M. Hoye ....Attorney
Norman S. Oberstein ....Attorney
Jonathan J. Panzer ....Attorney
Kenneth I. Sidle ....Attorney
Norm D. Sloan ....Attorney
Corey J. Spivey ....Attorney
Robert H. Steinberg ....Attorney

GIRARDI | KEESE
1126 Wilshire Blvd.
Los Angeles, CA 90017-1904
PHONE 213-977-0211/909-381-1551
FAX 213-481-1554/909-381-2566
WEB SITE ....www.girardikeese.com
PRACTICE AREAS   Intellectual Property Law - Litigation - Royalty Law
COMMENTS   Litigation of intellectual property cases and talent claims; San Bernardino office: 155 W. Hospitality Ln., Ste. 260, San Bernardino, CA 92408

Thomas V. Girardi ....Member
Robert M. Keese ....Member
David N. Bigelow ....Member
Vincent J. Carter ....Member
John K. Courtney ....Member
Robert W. Finnerty ....Member
John A. Girardi ....Member
Keith D. Griffin ....Member
Nicholas Hutchinson ....Member
Thomas Joseph Johnston ....Member
Graham B. LippSmith ....Member
David R. Lira ....Member
Shawn J. McCann ....Member
Amanda L. McClintock ....Member
Howard B. Miller ....Member
Claus F. Mory ....Member
James G. O'Callahan ....Member
V. Andre Rekte ....Member
Shahram A. Shayesteh ....Member
V. Andre Sherman ....Member
J. Paul Sizemore ....Member
Amy Fisch Solomon ....Member

GLADSTONE BAKER KELLEY
1227 - 17th Ave. South, 2nd Fl.
Nashville, TN 37212
PHONE 615-329-0900
FAX 615-329-2148
WEB SITE . . . . .www.rowlawyers.com
PRACTICE AREAS   Contract Negotiation & Drafting -
                        Copyright & Trademark Matters -
                        Corporate Matters - Employment/Labor
                        Law - Financing - Intellectual Property Law -
                        Licensing - Mergers & Acquisitions - Motion
                        Picture & TV Law - Music Law -
                        Partnerships/Joint Ventures - Royalty Law -
                        Transactional Law
COMMENTS   Entertainment industry transactions and
                        general business representation in the
                        entertainment industry; Business planning
                        and financing of entertainment ventures

Steven G. Gladstone . . . . .Partner
Robert L. Baker . . . . .Partner
D. Page Kelley III . . . . .Partner
Tyler L. Middleton . . . . .Attorney
A. Edward 'Ted' Graffam .Attorney
Tracey K. Houston . . . . .Office Manager/Executive Assistant

GLASSMAN, BROWNING & SALTSMAN, INC.
360 N. Bedford Dr., Ste. 204
Beverly Hills, CA 90210
PHONE 310-278-5100
FAX 310-271-6041
WEB SITE . . . . .www.gbslaw.com
PRACTICE AREAS   Arbitration & Mediation - Contract
                        Negotiation & Drafting - Corporate Matters
                        - Employment/Labor Law - First
                        Amendment Issues - Litigation - Mergers &
                        Acquisitions - Partnerships/Joint Ventures -
                        Right of Publicity - Transactional Law
COMMENTS   Included in practice: family law, estate
                        planning, probate, wills and trusts

Anthony M. Glassman . . . . .Partner
Amy O. Jacobs . . . . .Partner
Roger A. Browning . . . . .Partner
Jane D. Saltsman . . . . .Partner
Suzanne J. Goulet . . . . .Attorney
Richelle L. Kemler M.S.W. .Attorney
Alexander Rufas-Isaacs . . . . .Attorney

LAW OFFICES OF STEVEN J. GOLDFISHER
3115 Oakcrest Dr.
Los Angeles, CA 90068
PHONE 323-876-4300
FAX 323-876-0417
PRACTICE AREAS   Full Service Representation - Contract
                        Negotiation & Drafting - Copyright &
                        Trademark Matters - Corporate Matters -
                        Intellectual Property Law - Licensing -
                        Mergers & Acquisitions - Motion Picture &
                        TV Law - Partnerships/Joint Ventures -
                        Talent Representation - Transactional Law
REPRESENTS   Theatrical, TV and Music Production
                        Companies - Motion Picture Executives -
                        Writers - Directors - Actors - Producers -
                        Below-the-Line
COMMENTS   Authors and publishers for publication
                        rights and licensing in literary properties

Steven Goldfisher . . . . .Attorney/Owner

GOLDMAN & KAGON LAW CORPORATION
1925 Century Park East, Ste. 1050
Los Angeles, CA 90067
PHONE 310-552-1707
FAX 310-552-7938
WEB SITE . . . . .www.goldmankagon.com
PRACTICE AREAS   Contract Negotiation & Drafting

Charles D. Meyer . . . . .Attorney

GOLDRING, HERTZ, & LICHTENSTEIN, LLP
450 N. Roxbury Dr., 8th Fl.
Beverly Hills, CA 90210
PHONE 310-271-8777
FAX 310-276-8310
PRACTICE AREAS   Full Service Representation

Fred Goldring . . . . .Partner
Kenneth Hertz . . . . .Partner
Seth Lichtenstein . . . . .Partner
Jeremy Mohr . . . . .Partner
Philip Daniels . . . . .Associate
Travis Pananides . . . . .Associate
Rachel Rosoff . . . . .Associate

LAW OFFICES OF DESIREÉ GORDY
7095 Hollywood Blvd., Ste. 600
Hollywood, CA 90028
PHONE 323-874-3918
FAX 323-874-4590
PRACTICE AREAS   Contract Negotiation & Drafting - Music
                        Law

Desireé Gordy . . . . .Attorney

GRADSTEIN & LUSKIN, A PROFESSIONAL CORPORATION
10866 Wilshire Blvd., 14th Fl.
Los Angeles, CA 90024
PHONE 310-571-1700
FAX 310-571-1717
EMAIL .hgradstein@gradstein.com
WEB SITE .www.gradstein.com
PRACTICE AREAS   Full Service Representation

Henry D. Gradstein Esq. . . . . .Partner
Donna Luskin Esq. . . . . .Partner

LAW OFFICE OF BRUCE V. GRAKAL
1541 Ocean Ave., Ste. 200
Santa Monica, CA 90401
PHONE 310-917-1950
FAX 310-917-1112
PRACTICE AREAS   Contract Negotiation & Drafting - Motion
                        Picture & TV Law - Music Law -
                        Transactional Law
COMMENTS   Merchandising matters; Sponsorships

Bruce Grakal . . . . .Partner

LAW OFFICE OF JONAS M. GRANT, P.C.
11738-J Moorpark St.
Studio City, CA 91604
PHONE 818-786-4876
EMAIL . . . . .jonas@incorporatecalifornia.com
WEB SITE . . . . .www.incorporatecalifornia.com
PRACTICE AREAS   Contract Negotiation & Drafting -
                     Copyright & Trademark Matters -
                     Corporate Matters - Employment/Labor
                     Law - Intellectual Property Law - Internet
                     Law - Litigation - Motion Picture & TV Law -
                     Partnerships/Joint Ventures - Talent
                     Representation - Transactional Law
REPRESENTS   Producers - Writers - Directors - Actors -
                     Entertainment Companies
COMMENTS   Incorporation & loan-out corporations;
                     LLCs; Literary option and sale agreements
                     and related negotiations; Life rights agree-
                     ments; Releases; Motion picture and docu-
                     mentary production counsel; Private place-
                     ment memoranda; Script legal issues
                     review; Writer collaboration agreements;
                     Below-the-line employment agreements

Jonas M. Grant Esq. . . . . .Attorney/Member

LAW OFFICES OF JEFFREY L. GRAUBART
350 W. Colorado Blvd., Ste. 200
Pasadena, CA 91105-1855
PHONE 626-304-2800
FAX 626-304-2807
EMAIL . . . . .info@jlgraubart.com
WEB SITE . . . . .www.lawyers.com/entertainmentlaw
PRACTICE AREAS   Full Service Representation - Arbitration &
                     Mediation - Contract Negotiation &
                     Drafting - Copyright & Trademark Matters -
                     Corporate Matters - First Amendment Issues
                     - Intellectual Property Law - Libel & Privacy
                     Matters - Licensing - Litigation -
                     Misappropriation of Name, Voice, Likeness
                     - Motion Picture & TV Law - Music Law -
                     Partnerships/Joint Ventures - Right Of
                     Publicity - Royalty Law - Talent
                     Representation - Transactional Law
COMMENTS   Music publishing; Legitimate stage; Book
                     publishing

Jeffrey L. Graubart . . . . .Attorney

GRAY KRAUSS LLP
207 W. 25th St., 6th Fl.
New York, NY 10001
PHONE 212-966-6700
FAX 212-966-6051
EMAIL . . . . .info@indyfilmlaw.com
WEB SITE . . . . .www.indyfilmlaw.com
PRACTICE AREAS   Full Service Representation

Jonathan Gray . . . . .Attorney
Evan Krauss . . . . .Attorney
Andre Des Rochers . . . . .Attorney
Hilary Stabb . . . . .Executive Assistant

GREEN & GREEN LAW & MEDIATION OFFICES
One Embarcadero Center, Ste. 500
San Francisco, CA 94111
PHONE 415-457-8300
FAX 415-457-8757
EMAIL . . . . .bev@musiclawyer.com
WEB SITE . . . . .www.musiclawyer.com
SECOND WEB SITE . . . . .www.entertainmentlegal.com
PRACTICE AREAS   Full Service Representation - Copyright &
                     Trademark Matters - Ecommerce -
                     Intellectual Property Law - Licensing -
                     Litigation - Motion Picture & TV Law -
                     Music Law - Royalty Law
COMMENTS   Marin County office: Courthouse Square,
                     1000 Fourth St., Ste. 595, San Rafael, CA
                     94901

Beverly Robin Green .Entertainment Lawyer
Philip R. Green . . . . .Intellectual Property Law Attorney

GREENBERG GLUSKER FIELDS CLAMAN & MACHTINGER, LLP
1900 Avenue of the Stars, 21st Fl.
Los Angeles, CA 90067
PHONE 310-553-3610
FAX 310-553-0687
EMAIL . . . . .info@ggfirm.com
WEB SITE . . . . .www.ggfirm.com
PRACTICE AREAS   Copyright & Trademark Matters -
                     Intellectual Property Law - Litigation -
                     Motion Picture & TV Law - Music Law -
                     Right of Publicity - Transactional Law

Arthur N. Greenberg . . . . .Partner, Litigation
Bertram Fields . . . . .Partner, Entertainment Litigation
Stephen Claman . . . . .Partner, Real Estate, Transactional
Hillary Bibicoff . . . . .Partner, Entertainment, Transactional
Heidi Binford . . . . .Partner, Music Litigation
Robert S. Chapman . . . . .Partner, Entertainment Litigation
Bonnie E. Eskenazi . . . . .Partner, Entertainment Litigation
Jeffrey A. Krieger . . . . .Partner, Intellectual Property & Technology
Robert F. Marshall . . . . .Partner, Entertainment, Transactional
Elisabeth A. Moriarty . . . . .Partner, Entertainment Litigation
Richard E. Neff . . . . .Partner, Intellectual Property & Technology
Charles N. Shephard . . . . .Partner, Entertainment Litigation
Stephen Smith . . . . .Partner, Entertainment Litigation
Jonathan B. Sokol . . . . . .Partner, Entertainment & Music Litigation/
                            Intellectual Property & Technology
Jeffrey Spitz . . . . .Partner, Entertainment Litigation
Aaron Moss . . . . .Partner, Entertainment Litigation
Aaron Bloom . . . . .Attorney, Entertainment Litigation
Caroline H. Burgos . . . . .Attorney, Entertainment Litigation
Benita Das . . . . .Attorney, Intellectual Property & Technology
Matt Galsor . . . . .Attorney, Entertainment, Transactional
Krystal M. Hauserman . . . . .Attorney, Entertainment Litigation
Carla Roberts . . . . .Attorney, Entertainment, Transactional
Jesse Saivar . . . . .Attorney, Entertainment, Transactional
Jan M. Siok . . . . .Attorney, Intellectual Property & Technology
David Stanley . . . . .Attorney, Entertainment Litigation
Brenda Tavakoli . . . . .Attorney, Entertainment, Transactional

GREENBERG TRAURIG, LLP
2450 Colorado Ave., Ste. 400 East
Santa Monica, CA 90404
PHONE 310-586-7700
FAX 310-586-7800
EMAIL . . . . .info@gtlaw.com
WEB SITE . . . . .www.gtlaw.com
PRACTICE AREAS   Full Service Representation
COMMENTS   Thirty locations worldwide; Also provides Internet/New Media services

Ian C. Ballon . . . . .Shareholder
George M. Belfield . . . . .Shareholder
Charles Berman . . . . .Shareholder
Daniel H. Black . . . . .Shareholder
Louis J. Bovasso . . . . .Shareholder
Kenneth L. Burry . . . . .Shareholder
Vincent H. Chieffo . . . . .Shareholder
Terence J. Clark . . . . .Shareholder
Jay L. Cooper .Shareholder
Christopher Darrow . . . . .Shareholder
John Gatti . . . . .Shareholder
Mario F. Gonzalez . . . . .Shareholder
Steven Katleman . . . . .Shareholder
Joel Katz . . . . .Shareholder
Mark H. Krietzman . . . . .Shareholder
Richard I. Leher . . . . .Shareholder
M. Sean McMillan . . . . .Shareholder
Mark R. Moskowitz . . . . .Shareholder
Gregory A. Nylen . . . . .Shareholder
Randolph M. Paul . . . . .Shareholder
Carol Perrin . . . . .Shareholder
Paul D. Schindler . . . . .Shareholder
Alan Schwartz .Shareholder
Diana P. Scott .Shareholder
Jeff E. Scott . . . . .Shareholder
Todd Cooper .Of Counsel
Ira S. Epstein .Of Counsel
Michelle Lee Flores . . . . .Of Counsel
Henry W. Holmes . . . . .Of Counsel
David P. Markman . . . . .Of Counsel
Elise A. Tenen-Aoki . . . . .Of Counsel
Stephen Weizenecker . . . . .Of Counsel
Amy B. Alderfer . . . . .Associate
Marina Bonanni . . . . .Associate
Ann Clark . . . . .Associate
Anna Fudacz . . . . .Associate
Jordan D. Grotzinger . . . . .Associate
Valerie W. Ho .Associate
Lisa Nitti . . . . .Associate

GREINES, MARTIN, STEIN & RICHLAND, LLP
5700 Wilshire Blvd., Ste. 375
Los Angeles, CA 90036
PHONE 310-859-7811
FAX 310-276-5261
EMAIL . . . . .postmaster@gmsr.com
WEB SITE . . . . .www.gmsr.com
COMMENTS   Appellate law; Written advocacy

Irving H. Greines . . . . .Founding Member
Martin Stein . . . . .Founding Member
Kent L. Richland . . . . .Founding Member
Timothy T. Coates . . . . .Partner
Feris M. Greenberger . . . . .Partner
Robin Meadow .Partner
Robert A. Olson .Partner
Marc J. Poster . . . . .Partner
Barbara W. Ravitz . . . . .Partner
Alison M. Turner .Partner
Barbara S. Perry . . . . .Of Counsel
Tillman J. Breckenridge . . . . .Associate
Kent J. Bullard .Associate
Alan Diamond .Associate
Lillie Hsu . . . . .Associate
Peter O. Israel .Associate
Jens B. Koepke .Associate
Carolyn Oill . . . . .Associate
Jeffrey E. Raskin . . . . .Associate
Cynthia E. Tobisman . . . . .Associate
Edward L. Xanders . . . . .Associate

GRODSKY & OLECKI LLP
2001 Wilshire Blvd., Ste. 210
Santa Monica, CA 90403
PHONE 310-315-3009
FAX 310-315-1557
WEB SITE . . . . .www.grodsky-olecki.com
PRACTICE AREAS   Arbitration & Mediation - Copyright & Trademark Matters - Libel & Privacy Matters - Litigation - Misappropriation of Name, Voice, Likeness - Right of Publicity

Allen B. Grodsky . . . . . . .Entertainment & Intellectual Property Litigation
Michael J. Olecki . . . . .Business Litigation, Entertainment & Intellectual Property Litigation

GRUBMAN INDURSKY & SHIRE, PC
c/o Carnegie Hall Tower
152 W. 57th St.
New York, NY 10019
PHONE 212-554-0400
FAX 212-554-0444
PRACTICE AREAS   Full Service Representation - Intellectual Property Law - Motion Picture & TV Law - Music Law

Allen J. Grubman . . . . .Member
Arthur I. Indursky . . . . .Member
Lawrence Shire .Member
Joseph M. Brenner . . . . .Member
Jess H. Drabkin .Member
Jonathan A. Ehrlich . . . . .Member
Stuart J. Fried . . . . .Member
Donald R. Friedman . . . . .Member
Karen J. Gottlieb . . . . .Member
Theodore P. Harris . . . . .Member
Jonathan F. Horn . . . . .Member
Gil A. Karson . . . . .Member
Kenneth R. Meiselas . . . . .Member
Joseph D. Penachio . . . . .Member
Stuart Prager . . . . .Member
Eric D. Sacks . . . . .Member
Robert A. Strent . . . . .Member
David R. Toraya . . . . .Member
Debra A. White .Member
Alisa D. De Rosa . . . . .Associate
Peter E. Grant .Associate
Sonya W. Guardo . . . . .Associate
Grace Kim . . . . .Associate
Mira M. Kothari . . . . .Associate
Charles O. Prince . . . . .Associate
Paul H. Rothenberg . . . . .Associate
Edward H. Shapiro . . . . .Associate
David E. Wienir . . . . .Associate
Michael K. Goldsmith . . . . .Of Counsel
Bruce G. Grossberg . . . . .Of Counsel
Larry H. Schatz . . . . .Of Counsel

HAHN & BOLSON, LLP
1000 Wilshire Blvd., Ste. 1600
Los Angeles, CA 90017
PHONE 213-630-2600
FAX 213-622-6670
WEB SITE . . . . .www.hahnbolsonllp.com
PRACTICE AREAS   Arbitration & Mediation - Contract Negotiation & Drafting - Copyright & Trademark Matters - Corporate Matters - Employment/Labor Law - Intellectual Property Law - Licensing - Litigation - Mergers & Acquisitions - Partnerships/Joint Ventures - Transactional Law

Elliott J. Hahn .Partner
Jeffrey T. Bolson . . . . .Partner
Liza Kaufer . . . . .Associate
Shodai Nalcano . . . . .Associate
Amy Ikari . . . . .Director, Client Relations

HAMBURG, KARIC, EDWARDS & MARTIN LLP
1900 Avenue of the Stars, Ste. 1800
Los Angeles, CA 90067-4409
PHONE 310-552-9292
FAX 310-552-9291
EMAIL . . . . .hkem@hkemlaw.com
WEB SITE . . . . .www.hkemlaw.com
PRACTICE AREAS   Employment/Labor Law - Litigation - Music
                        Law - Partnerships/Joint Ventures

Barry G. Edwards . . . . .Partner
Sidney A. Hamburg . . . . .Partner
Steven S. Karic . . . . .Partner
Gregg A. Martin . . . . .Partner
David M. Almaraz . . . . .Associate
Fredric R. Brandfon . . . . .Associate
Ryan T. Koczara . . . . .Associate
Daniel Sanchez-Behar . . . . .Associate
Jerome B. Friedman . . . . .Of Counsel
Alan B. Grass . . . . .Of Counsel
Alfred Kim Guggenheim . . . . .Of Counsel
Mark J. Linder . . . . .Of Counsel

JONATHAN HANDEL
PO Box 69218
Los Angeles, CA 90069
PHONE 323-650-0060
FAX 323-654-5360
EMAIL . . . . .jhandel@att.net
WEB SITE . . . . .www.jhandel.com
PRACTICE AREAS   Full Service Representation - Contract
                        Negotiation & Drafting - Copyright &
                        Trademark Matters - Intellectual Property
                        Law - Internet Law - Licensing - Media -
                        Motion Picture & TV Law -
                        Partnerships/Joint Ventures - Talent
                        Representation - Technology - Transactional
                        Law
REPRESENTS   Digital Media Companies - Writers -
                        Producers - Software Developers - Internet
                        Companies
COMMENTS   Of Counsel to Troy & Gould Law Firm;
                        Previously WGA Associate Counsel;
                        Member, Business and Management
                        Advisory Board of UCLA Extension
                        Entertainment Department; Member,
                        Academy of Television Arts & Sciences

Jonathan Handel . . . . .Attorney

HANSEN, JACOBSON, TELLER, HOBERMAN, NEWMAN, WARREN & RICHMAN, LLP
450 N. Roxbury Dr., 8th Fl.
Beverly Hills, CA 90210-4222
PHONE 310-271-8777
FAX 310-550-5206
PRACTICE AREAS   Full Service Representation

Tom Hansen . . . . .Partner
Craig Jacobson . . . . .Partner
Walter Teller . . . . .Partner
Tom Hoberman . . . . .Partner
Jeanne Newman . . . . .Partner
Steve Warren . . . . .Partner
Ken Richman . . . . .Partner
John Meigs . . . . .Partner
Don Steele . . . . .Partner
Gretchen Bruggeman Rush .Partner
John Farrell . . . . .Partner
Stewart Brookman . . . . .Partner
Jason Hendler . . . . .Partner
Lev Ginsburg . . . . .Attorney
Sean Marks . . . . .Attorney

HARRIS MARTIN JONES SHRUM BRADFORD & WOMMACK
49 Music Square West, Ste. 600
Nashville, TN 37203
PHONE 615-321-5400
FAX 615-321-5469
EMAIL . . . . .info@rowlaw.org
WEB SITE . . . . .www.rowlaw.org
PRACTICE AREAS   Contract Negotiation & Drafting -
                        Copyright & Trademark Matters -
                        Corporate Matters - Litigation - Mergers &
                        Acquisitions - Music Law -
                        Partnerships/Joint Ventures

Gail S. Bradford . . . . .Attorney
James H. Harris III . . . . .Attorney
Russell A. Jones Jr. . . . . .Attorney
J. Thomas Martin . . . . .Attorney
Barry Neil Shrum . . . . .Attorney
Richard L. Wommack II . . . . .Attorney

HERRICK, FEINSTEIN LLP
2 Park Ave.
New York, NY 10016
PHONE 212-592-1400
FAX 212-592-1500
WEB SITE . . . . .www.herrick.com
PRACTICE AREAS   Corporate Matters - Employment/Labor
                        Law - Financing - Intellectual Property Law -
                        Internet Law - Litigation - Sports - Tax Law

Daniel A. Etna . . . . .Partner
Michael Heitner . . . . .Partner
Irwin A. Kishner . . . . .Partner
Ezra J. Doner . . . . .Counsel
Jeffrey M. Liebenson . . . . .Counsel
M. Darren Traub . . . . .Associate

HERTZ, SCHRAM & SARETSKY, PC
1760 S. Telegraph Rd., Ste. 300
Bloomfield Hills, MI 48302-0183
PHONE 248-335-5000
FAX 248-335-3346
EMAIL . . . . .hhertz@hsspc.com
WEB SITE . . . . .www.hsspc.com
PRACTICE AREAS   Full Service Representation
COMMENTS   Entity formation; Estate and tax planning;
                        Member: International Association of
                        Entertainment Lawyers; Board of Directors
                        & President: Motor City Music Foundation
                        (Host of the Detroit Music Awards); Board
                        of Directors: ArtServe Michigan; Member:
                        National Academy of Recording Arts &
                        Sciences, Chicago Chapter, Board of
                        Governors

Howard Hertz . . . . .Partner

HIRSCH WALLERSTEIN HAYUM MATLOF & FISHMAN
10100 Santa Monica Blvd., Ste. 1700
Los Angeles, CA 90067
PHONE 310-703-1700
FAX 310-703-1799
PRACTICE AREAS   Full Service Representation

Barry L. Hirsch . . . . .Partner
Robert S. Wallerstein . . . . .Partner
George T. Hayum . . . . .Partner
David J. Matlof . . . . .Partner
Howard A. Fishman . . . . .Partner
Ryan Nord . . . . .Associate

THE HOYT LAW GROUP, LLC
350 Fifth Ave., Ste. 7315
New York, NY 10118
PHONE 212-643-0550
EMAIL . . . . .choyt@hoytlawgroup.com
WEB SITE . . . . .www.hoytlawgroup.com
PRACTICE AREAS   Full Service Representation

Christopher Hoyt . . . . .Attorney

HUNTON & WILLIAMS
550 S. Hope St., Ste. 200
Los Angeles, CA 90071
PHONE 213-532-2000
FAX 213-532-2020
WEB SITE . . . . .www.hunton.com

Ann Marie Mortimer . . . . .Managing Partner
Lisa Brant . . . . .Partner
Belynda Reck . . . . .Partner
Daniel C. Tepstein . . . . .Partner
Tim Toohey . . . . .Partner
Steven C. Valerio . . . . .Partner

B. PAUL HUSBAND, A PROFESSIONAL CORPORATION
10 Universal City Plaza, Ste. 2000
Universal City, CA 91608
PHONE 818-753-2336
FAX 818-753-2307
EMAIL . . . . .paul.husband@husbandlaw.com
WEB SITE . . . . .www.husbandlaw.com
PRACTICE AREAS   Arbitration & Mediation - Contract
Negotiation & Drafting - Copyright &
Trademark Matters - Corporate Matters -
Employment/Labor Law - Financing -
Intellectual Property Law - Motion Picture &
TV Law - Partnerships/Joint Ventures - Right
of Publicity - Talent Representation - Tax
Law - Transactional Law
REPRESENTS   Animators - Directors - Producers - Writers
COMMENTS   Emphasis on animation; All aspects of ani-
mation business affairs and legal matters;
LLCs and other entities; International
finance

B. Paul Husband . . . . .Attorney
Fern Carpenter .Legal Assistant
Evelyn Ferrer . . . . .Entertainment Business Assistant

IDELL & SEITEL, LLP
465 California St., Ste. 300
San Francisco, CA 94104
PHONE 415-986-2400
FAX 415-392-9259
EMAIL . . . . .richard.idell@idellseitel.com
WEB SITE . . . . .www.idellseitel.com
PRACTICE AREAS   Full Service Representation - Arbitration &
Mediation - Contract Negotiation &
Drafting - Copyright & Trademark Matters -
Corporate Matters - Ecommerce -
Employment/Labor Law - First Amendment
Issues - Intellectual Property Law - Internet
Law - Licensing - Litigation - Media -
Mergers & Acquisitions - Misappropriation
of Name, Voice, Likeness - Motion Picture
& TV Law - Music Law - Partnerships/Joint
Ventures - Right of Publicity - Royalty Law -
Talent Representation - Technology -
Telecom - Transactional Law

Richard J. Idell . . . . .Partner
Owen Seitel . . . . .Partner
Patricia De Fonte . . . . .Attorney
Elizabeth J. Rest . . . . .Attorney
Ory Sandel . . . . .Attorney

IRELL & MANELLA, LLP
1800 Avenue of the Stars, Ste. 900
Los Angeles, CA 90067-4276
PHONE 310-277-1010
FAX 310-203-7199
WEB SITE . . . . .www.irell.com
PRACTICE AREAS   Contract Negotiation & Drafting -
Copyright & Trademark Matters -
Corporate Matters - Intellectual Property
Law - Libel & Privacy Matters - Licensing -
Litigation - Mergers & Acquisitions - Motion
Picture & TV Law - Right of Publicity -
Royalty Law - Talent Representation - Tax
Law
COMMENTS   Profit participation; Motion picture and TV
production

Elliot N. Brown . . . . .Partner
Richard B. Kendall . . . . .Partner
Robert Klieger . . . . .Partner
Joan Lesser . . . . .Partner
Steven A. Marenberg . . . . .Partner
Harry A. Mittleman . . . . .Partner
Matthew T. Sant . . . . .Partner
Henry Shields Jr. . . . . .Partner
Clark B. Siegel . . . . .Partner
Jane S. Wald . . . . .Partner
Bruce A. Wessel . . . . .Partner
Juliette Youngblood . . . . .Partner
David Nimmer . . . . .Of Counsel
Peter Shimamoto .Of Counsel
Uri M. Emerson-Fleming . . . . .Associate
Katharine J. Galston .Associate
Steve Hasegawa . . . . .Associate
Deborah H. Henderson . . . . .Associate
Brian E. Jones . . . . .Associate
Philip Kelly . . . . .Associate
Lee M. Liedecke . . . . .Associate
Annette G. Meyerson .Associate
Philip Miller . . . . .Associate
Kenneth J. Weatherwax . . . . .Associate

ISAACMAN, KAUFMAN & PAINTER, PC
8484 Wilshire Blvd.
Beverly Hills, CA 90211
PHONE 323-782-7700
FAX 323-782-7744
EMAIL . . . . .info@ikplaw.com
SECOND EMAIL . . . . .zucker@ikplaw.com
WEB SITE . . . . .www.ikplaw.com
PRACTICE AREAS   Full Service Representation - Contract
Negotiation & Drafting

Neil B. Fischer . . . . .No Title
Phalen G. Hurewitz .No Title
Steven R. Lowy . . . . .No Title
Robert W. Woods . . . . .No Title
Andrew Zucker . . . . .No Title

IVES LAW OFFICE
PO Box 517
Truro, MA 02666
PHONE 508-789-9383
FAX 508-413-9079
EMAIL . . . . .john@iveslawoffice.com
WEB SITE . . . . .www.iveslawoffice.com
PRACTICE AREAS   Corporate Matters - Financing - Intellectual
Property Law - Media - Motion Picture & TV
Law - Music Law
REPRESENTS   Independent and documentary filmmakers,
TV comedy and animation, writers, produc-
ers and directors
COMMENTS   Publishing Law

John G. Ives . . . . .Attorney

JACKOWAY TYERMAN WERTHEIMER AUSTEN MANDELBAUM & MORRIS
1925 Century Park East, 22nd Fl.
Los Angeles, CA 90067
PHONE 310-553-0305
FAX 310-553-5036
PRACTICE AREAS   Full Service Representation

Karl R. Austen . . . . .Attorney
Jeff A. Bernstein . . . . .Attorney
Joseph D'Onofrio . . . . .Attorney
Alan J. Epstein . . . . .Attorney
Evan E. Fitzmaurice . . . . .Attorney
Andrew L. Galker . . . . .Attorney
Robert S. Getman . . . . .Attorney
Julie M. Hunt . . . . .Attorney
James R. Jackoway . . . . .Attorney
Leon Liu . . . . .Attorney
James C. Mandelbaum . . . . .Attorney
Lisa C. McArthur . . . . .Attorney
Marcy S. Morris . . . . .Attorney
Michele M. Mulrooney . . . . .Attorney
Geoffry W. Oblath . . . . .Attorney
Darren M. Trattner . . . . .Attorney
Barry W. Tyerman . . . . .Attorney
Eric C. Weissler . . . . .Attorney
Alan S. Wertheimer . . . . .Attorney
Julian Zajfen . . . . .Attorney
Arthur O. Armstrong . . . . .Founder
Ronald J. Bass . . . . .Of Counsel

JACOBSON & COLFIN, PC
60 Madison Ave., Ste. 1026
New York, NY 10010
PHONE 212-691-5630/516-295-7689
FAX 212-645-5038/516-295-6872
EMAIL . . . . .thefirm@thefirm.com
WEB SITE . . . . .www.thefirm.com
PRACTICE AREAS   Full Service Representation - Contract
                      Negotiation & Drafting - Copyright &
                      Trademark Matters - Licensing - Litigation -
                      Misappropriation of Name, Voice, Likeness
                      - Motion Picture & TV Law - Music Law -
                      Partnerships/Joint Ventures - Right of
                      Publicity - Royalty Law - Talent
                      Representation - Transactional Law
REPRESENTS   Musicians - Record Companies - Producers
                      - Writers - Directors - Publishers -
                      Managers - Digital Creators - Magazines

Jeffrey Jacobson . . . . .Partner
Bruce Colfin . . . . .Partner
Bonnie Mohr Esq. . . . . .Of Counsel

ATTORNEY AT LAW, ERIC S. JACOBSON
3435 Wilshire Blvd., Ste. 2360
Los Angeles, CA 90010
PHONE 213-389-1131
FAX 213-380-8404
EMAIL . . . . .ejacoblaw@earthlink.net
PRACTICE AREAS   Litigation - Talent Representation -
                      Transactional Law
REPRESENTS   Independent Producers - Writers -
                      Distributors
COMMENTS   Domestic and foreign markets

Eric S. Jacobson . . . . .Attorney
Edwin M. Rosenberg . . . . .Attorney

LAW OFFICES OF LLOYD J. JASSIN
1560 Broadway, Ste. 400
New York, NY 10036
PHONE 212-354-4442
FAX 212-840-1124
EMAIL . . . . .jassin@copylaw.com
WEB SITE . . . . .www.copylaw.com
PRACTICE AREAS   Contract Negotiation & Drafting -
                      Copyright & Trademark Matters -
                      Intellectual Property Law - Internet Law -
                      Libel & Privacy Matters - Licensing - Media
                      - Misappropriation of Name, Voice,
                      Likeness - Right of Publicity - Transactional
                      Law
REPRESENTS   Miles Davis Estate - Mike Hailwood Estate -
                      Tina Louise - Pete Seeger - Publishers
                      Marketing Association (PMA) - Dr. Judith
                      Kuriansky - David Carradine - Debbie
                      Macomber
COMMENTS   Publishing Law; Book publishing; TV pro-
                      duction agreements; Co-author, *The
                      Copyright Permission and Libel Handbook*

Lloyd J. Jassin Esq. . . . . .Attorney

JEFFER MANGELS BUTLER & MARMARO, LLP
1900 Avenue of the Stars, 7th Fl.
Los Angeles, CA 90067
PHONE 310-203-8080/415-398-8080
FAX 310-203-0567/415-398-5584
EMAIL . . . . .mss@jmbm.com
WEB SITE . . . . .www.jmbm.com
PRACTICE AREAS   Full Service Representation - Arbitration &
                      Mediation - Contract Negotiation &
                      Drafting - Copyright & Trademark Matters -
                      Corporate Matters - Financing - First
                      Amendment Issues - Intellectual Property
                      Law - Libel & Privacy Matters - Licensing -
                      Litigation - Mergers & Acquisitions - Motion
                      Picture & TV Law - Music Law -
                      Partnerships/Joint Ventures - Right of
                      Publicity - Royalty Law - Talent
                      Representation - Tax Law - Transactional
                      Law
REPRESENTS   Actors - Directors - Writers - Authors -
                      Producers - Production Companies -
                      Distributors - Banks - Financiers -
                      Completion Guarantors - Agents -
                      Managers - Composers - Musicians
COMMENTS   Music and print publishing law; Business
                      entity structuring; Northern California
                      office: Two Embarcadero Center, 5th Fl.,
                      San Francisco, CA 94111

Michael S. Sherman . . .Partner/Chairman, Entertainment Practice Group
Daniel Grigsby . . . . .Partner
E. Barry Haldeman . . . . .Of Counsel
Zeke Lopez . . . . .Associate

JOHNSON & RISHWAIN, LLP
439 N. Canon Dr., Ste. 200
Beverly Hills, CA 90210
PHONE 310-975-1080
FAX 310-975-1095
EMAIL .njohnson@jrllp.com
WEB SITE . . . . .www.jrllp.com
PRACTICE AREAS   Copyright & Trademark Matters -
                     Intellectual Property Law - Libel & Privacy
                     Matters - Litigation - Misappropriation of
                     Name, Voice, Likeness - Motion Picture &
                     TV Law - Partnerships/Joint Ventures - Right
                     of Publicity
COMMENTS   Also business litigation, class action

Neville Johnson . . . . .Partner
Brian Rishwain . . . . .Partner
Douglas Johnson . . . . .Associate
Nicholas Kurtz . . . . .Associate

LAW OFFICE OF PATRICIA JOHNSON
190 N. Canon Dr., Ste. 403
Beverly Hills, CA 90210
PHONE 310-273-3105
FAX 310-273-3361
EMAIL . . . . .pjohnsonlaw@sbcglobal.net
PRACTICE AREAS   Full Service Representation - Contract
                     Negotiation & Drafting - Copyright &
                     Trademark Matters - Corporate Matters -
                     Intellectual Property Law - Libel & Privacy
                     Matters - Licensing - Litigation -
                     Misappropriation of Name, Voice, Likeness
                     - Motion Picture & TV Law - Music Law -
                     Right of Publicity - Transactional Law
COMMENTS   Also feature film production counsel

Patricia Johnson Esq. . . . . .Attorney

STEVEN M. KALB, PC
11355 W. Olympic Blvd., 4th Fl. West
Los Angeles, CA 90064
PHONE 310-479-2222/310-463-7269
FAX 310-479-4444
EMAIL .steve@kalblaw.com
PRACTICE AREAS   Contract Negotiation & Drafting -
                     Financing - Motion Picture & TV Law -
                     Talent Representation
REPRESENTS   Production Companies - Financiers -
                     Producers - Directors - Writers - Actors

Steven M. Kalb . . . . .Attorney

KAPLAN & GAMBLE, LLP
432 Park Avenue South, 2nd Fl.
New York, NY 10016
PHONE 212-684-0579
FAX 212-861-0473
EMAIL . . . . .info@kaplangamble.com
WEB SITE . . . . .www.kaplangamble.com
PRACTICE AREAS   Full Service Representation - Contract
                     Negotiation & Drafting - Copyright &
                     Trademark Matters - Corporate Matters -
                     First Amendment Issues - Intellectual
                     Property Law - Licensing - Misappropriation
                     of Name, Voice, Likeness - Motion Picture
                     & TV Law - Right of Publicity - Royalty Law -
                     Talent Representation - Transactional Law
COMMENTS   Book publishing; New media

Adam L. Kaplan . . . . .Partner
Kristi N. Gamble . . . . .Partner
Eric Ervin Esq. . . . . .Of Counsel

THE LAW OFFICE OF JUDITH R. KARFIOL
11355 W. Olympic Blvd., Ste. 300
Los Angeles, CA 90064-1632
PHONE 310-444-6345
FAX 310-444-6346
EMAIL . . . . .judith@karfiol-law.com
PRACTICE AREAS   Contract Negotiation & Drafting -
                     Copyright & Trademark Matters - Financing
                     - Motion Picture & TV Law - Transactional
                     Law
COMMENTS   In addition to film and TV contracts, servic-
                     es include production legal and employ-
                     ment agreements, including animation and
                     new media technology; Publishing contract
                     negotiation

Judith R. Karfiol Esq. . . . . .Attorney

KARPELES AND ASSOCIATES
9150 Wilshire Blvd., Ste. 270
Beverly Hills, CA 90212
PHONE 310-344-2881
FAX 310-247-9766
PRACTICE AREAS   Contract Negotiation & Drafting - Licensing
                     - Motion Picture & TV Law - Music Law -
                     Talent Representation - Transactional Law
COMMENTS   Musicians, producers, bands and man-
                     agers; Licensed to practice in California
                     and Arizona

Jason Bernstein . . . . .Attorney

LAW OFFICES OF ALLAN M. KASSIRER
4669 Del Moreno Dr.
Woodland Hills, CA 91364
PHONE 818-340-9800
FAX 818-346-5276
PRACTICE AREAS   Full Service Representation - Contract
                     Negotiation & Drafting - Copyright &
                     Trademark Matters - Ecommerce -
                     Financing - Intellectual Property Law -
                     Internet Law - Motion Picture & TV Law -
                     Talent Representation - Transactional Law
REPRESENTS   Producers - Writers - Directors - Actors

Allan M. Kassirer . . . . .Attorney

Katten Muchin Rosenman LLP

KATTEN MUCHIN ROSENMAN LLP
2029 Century Park East, Ste. 2600
Los Angeles, CA 90067-3012
PHONE 310-788-4400
FAX 310-788-4471
WEB SITE . . . . .www.kattenlaw.com
PRACTICE AREAS   Arbitration & Mediation - Contract
Negotiation & Drafting - Copyright &
Trademark Matters - Corporate Matters -
Employment/Labor Law - Financing - First
Amendment Issues - Intellectual Property
Law - Internet Law - Libel & Privacy Matters
- Mergers & Acquisitions - Misappropriation
of Name, Voice, Likeness - Motion Picture
& TV Law - Music Law - Partnerships/Joint
Ventures - Right of Publicity - Royalty Law -
Transactional Law
COMMENTS   Production matters; Offices in Charlotte,
Chicago, New York, Irving (Texas), Palo
Alto, Washington, DC and London

Melvin E. Pearl . . . . .Founding Partner (Chicago)
Melvin L. Katten . . . . .Founding Partner (Chicago)
Gail Migdal Title . . . . .Managing Partner
Howie Braun . . . . .Partner (DC)
Steve Cochran . . . . .Partner
Harrison J. Dossick . . . . .Partner
Alan Friedman . . . . .Partner (NY)
Francie Gorowitz . . . . .Partner
Susan A. Grode . . . . .Partner
David Halberstadter . . . . .Partner
Michael Hobel . . . . .Partner
Kristin L. Holland . . . . .Partner
Joyce S. Jun . . . . .Partner
John C. McBride . . . . .Partner
Zia F. Modabber . . . . .Partner
Marc S. Reisler . . . . .Partner (NY)
Rik Toulon . . . . .Partner
Joel R. Weiner . . . . .Partner
Melissa Bloom . . . . .Associate
Samantha Freedman . . . . .Associate
Ryan J. Larsen . . . . .Associate
Michael S. Poster .Associate (NY)
Scott Tenley . . . . .Associate
Shelby Weiser . . . . .Associate
Paul Burak . . . . .Of Counsel (NY)
Shelley Sadowsky . . . . .Special Counsel (DC)
Lee Shubert .Special Counsel (DC)

KATZ, GOLDEN, SULLIVAN & ROSENMAN, LLP
2001 Wilshire Blvd., Ste. 400
Santa Monica, CA 90403
PHONE 310-998-9200
FAX 310-998-9177
WEB SITE . . . . .www.kgsrlaw.com
PRACTICE AREAS   Full Service Representation - Contract
Negotiation & Drafting - Financing -
Motion Picture & TV Law - Talent
Representation

Steven Katz . . . . .Partner
Diane A. Golden . . . . .Partner
Mary E. Sullivan . . . . .Partner
Shep Rosenman . . . . .Partner
Patricia A. McVerry . . . . .Of Counsel
Suzanne Rosencrans .Of Counsel
Charles D. Silverberg . . . . .Of Counsel
Lionelle Rosenbaum . . . . .Attorney

KAUFMAN ENTERTAINMENT LAW GROUP, PC
2001 Wilshire Blvd., Ste. 400
Santa Monica, CA 90403
PHONE 310-294-1624
FAX 310-356-3234
EMAIL .pkaufman@ezbizlegal.com
WEB SITE . . . . .www.ebizlegal.com
PRACTICE AREAS   Full Service Representation - Arbitration &
Mediation - Contract Negotiation &
Drafting - Copyright & Trademark Matters -
Corporate Matters - Ecommerce -
Financing - Intellectual Property Law -
Internet Law - Licensing - Motion Picture &
TV Law - Partnerships/Joint Ventures -
Talent Representation - Transactional Law
COMMENTS   Additional office: 24025 Park Sorrento,
Ste. 240, Calabasas, CA 91302, phone:
818-224-2449

Peter L. Kaufman . . . . .Attorney

KAYE & MILLS
8840 Wilshire Blvd., 2nd Fl.
Beverly Hills, CA 90211
PHONE 310-358-3121
FAX 310-358-3175
EMAIL .kevinmills@kayemills.com
SECOND EMAIL . . . . .jessicakaye@kayemills.com
WEB SITE . . . . .www.kayemills.com
PRACTICE AREAS   Contract Negotiation & Drafting -
Copyright & Trademark Matters -
Corporate Matters - Financing - First
Amendment Issues - Intellectual Property
Law - Libel & Privacy Matters - Licensing -
Misappropriation of Name, Voice, Likeness
- Motion Picture & TV Law - Music Law -
Partnerships/Joint Ventures - Right of
Publicity - Royalty Law - Talent
Representation - Transactional Law
REPRESENTS   Production & Distribution Companies -
Writers - Directors - Producers - Actors
COMMENTS   Publishing legal services; General business

Jessica Kaye . . . . .Partner, Publishing & Author Representation
Kevin Mills . . . . .Partner, Film & TV, Business Law
Michael A. Miller . . . . .Of Counsel, Film, TV & Music

KAYE SCHOLER, LLP
1999 Avenue of the Stars, Ste. 1700
Los Angeles, CA 90067
PHONE 310-788-1000/212-836-8000
FAX 310-788-1200
WEB SITE . . . . .www.kayescholer.com
PRACTICE AREAS   Arbitration & Mediation - Contract
Negotiation & Drafting - Copyright &
Trademark Matters - Financing - Licensing -
Litigation - Mergers & Acquisitions
COMMENTS   Guild arbitration; East Coast office: 425
Park Avenue, New York, NY 10022

Stanley Pierre-Louis . . . . .Special Counsel, Litigation & Co-Chair,
Entertainment & Media
Robert Barnes . . . . .Partner, Entertainment, Media, Trademark &
Copyright Litigation
Julian Brew . . . . .Partner, Entertainment, Media, Trademark &
Copyright Litigation
Barry L. Dastin . . . . . .Partner, Entertainment, Media & Communications
Alan Friel . . . . .Counsel, Entertainment, Media & Communications
Jeffrey S. Gordon . . . . .Partner, Entertainment, Media, Trademark &
Copyright Litigation
Peter L. Haviland . . . . .Partner, Entertainment, Media, Trademark &
Copyright Litigation
Sheri Jeffrey . . . . . . .Partner, Entertainment, Media & Communications
Ken Lemberger . . . . .Counsel, Entertainment, Media & Communications
Rhonda R. Trotter . . . . .Partner, Entertainment, Media, Trademark &
Copyright Litigation

EDWARD M. KELMAN, ATTORNEY AT LAW
100 Park Ave., 20th Fl.
New York, NY 10017
PHONE 212-371-9490
FAX 212-750-1356
EMAIL . . . . .emknyc@aol.com
PRACTICE AREAS   Full Service Representation - Licensing - Motion Picture & TV Law - Talent Representation

Edward M. Kelman . . . . .Attorney at Law
Leon Ackiam . . . . .Assistant

KENOFF & MACHTINGER, LLP
1901 Avenue of the Stars, Ste. 1775
Los Angeles, CA 90067
PHONE 310-552-0808
FAX 310-277-0653
EMAIL . . . . .jay@km-entertainmentlaw.com
PRACTICE AREAS   Arbitration & Mediation - Communications - Contract Negotiation & Drafting - Copyright & Trademark Matters - Corporate Matters - Ecommerce - Employment/Labor Law - Financing - Intellectual Property Law - Internet Law - Libel & Privacy Matters - Licensing - Litigation - Media - Misappropriation of Name, Voice, Likeness - Motion Picture & TV Law - Music Law - Partnerships/Joint Ventures - Right of Publicity - Royalty Law - Talent Representation - Transactional Law
COMMENTS   Real Estate

Jay S. Kenoff .Partner, Entertainment
Leonard S. Machtinger . . . . .Partner, Entertainment & Business Litigation
Arthur L. Stashower . . . . .Of Counsel, Entertainment
Brenda S. Feigen . . . . .Of Counsel, Entertainment
Joseph B. Gourneau . . . .Associate, Entertainment & Business Litigation
Margaret Johnson . . . . .Office Manager
Lucy Kenoff . . . . .Administrator

KENYON & KENYON LLP
One Broadway
New York, NY 10004-1050
PHONE 212-425-7200
FAX 212-425-5288
EMAIL . . . . .info@kenyon.com
WEB SITE . . . . .www.kenyon.com
PRACTICE AREAS   Full Service Representation - Intellectual Property Law
COMMENTS   West Coast office: 333 W. San Carlos St., Ste. 600, San Jose, CA 95110, phone: 408-975-7500, fax: 408-975-7501; Washington, DC office: 1500 K Street NW, Washington, DC 20005-1257, phone: 202-220-4200, fax: 202-220-4201

Allen J. Baden .Partner (San Jose)
Edward T. Colbert . . . . .Partner (DC)
Dana R. Kaplan . . . . .Partner
Brian S. Mudge . . . . .Partner (DC)
Joseph F. Nicholson . . . . .Partner
Jonathan D. Reichman .Partner
James E. Rosini . . . . .Partner
Howard J. Shire . . . . .Partner
Stuart J. Sinder . . . . .Partner

KERR & WAGSTAFFE
100 Spear St., Ste. 1800
San Francisco, CA 94105-1528
PHONE 415-371-8500
FAX 415-371-0500
EMAIL . . . . .attorneys@kerrwagstaffe.com
WEB SITE .www.kerrwagstaffe.com
PRACTICE AREAS   Contract Negotiation & Drafting - Employment/Labor Law - First Amendment Issues - Intellectual Property Law - Litigation - Music Law

Keith K. Fong . . . . .Attorney
Holly Hogan . . . . .Attorney
H. Sinclair Kerr Jr. . . . . .Attorney
Ivo Labar . . . . .Attorney
Adrian J. Sawyer . . . . .Attorney
Michael von Loewwenfeldt . . . . .Attorney
James M. Wagstaffe .Attorney
Garry Pallister . . . . .Sr. Paralegal
Sarah Smoot . . . . .Paralegal
Maryann Milla . . . . .Office Management
Andrew Hanna . . . . .Legal Assistant
Kathy Kirk . . . . .Legal Assistant

KING & BALLOW
1100 Union Street Plaza
315 Union St.
Nashville, TN 37201
PHONE 615-259-3456/858-597-6000
EMAIL . . . . .comment@king-ballow.com
WEB SITE .www.kingballow.com
PRACTICE AREAS   First Amendment Issues - Intellectual Property Law - Litigation - Media - Music Law - Tax Law
COMMENTS   West Coast office: La Jolla Eastgate, 9404 Genesee Ave., Ste. 340, La Jolla, CA 92037-1355

Richard S. Busch . . . . .Partner
Paul H. Duvall . . . . .Partner (San Diego)
Mark E. Hunt . . . . .Partner
Frank S. King Jr. . . . . .Partner
Richard C. Lowe . . . . .Partner
Alan L. Marx . . . . .Partner
Douglas R. Pierce . . . . .Partner
R. Eddie Wayland . . . . .Partner
Ramona DeSalvo . . . . .Associate
Alan E. Korpady . . . . .Associate
Jo Anne Rosenblum . . . . .Associate
Tonda F. Rush . . . . .Of Counsel

KING, HOLMES, PATERNO & BERLINER, LLP
1900 Avenue of the Stars, 25th Fl.
Los Angeles, CA 90067
PHONE 310-282-8989
FAX 310-282-8903
PRACTICE AREAS   Contract Negotiation & Drafting - Litigation - Music Law - Talent Representation - Technology - Transactional Law

Howard E. King . . . . .Attorney
Keith T. Holmes . . . . .Attorney
Peter T. Paterno . . . . .Attorney
Jill H. Berliner . . . . .Attorney
Madge S. Beletsky . . . . .Attorney
Brian J. Bird . . . . .Attorney
Danna L. Cook . . . . .Attorney
Leslie E. Frank . . . . .Attorney
Michelle Jubelirer . . . . .Attorney
Seth A. Miller . . . . .Attorney
Steven J. Plinio . . . . .Attorney
Stephen D. Rothschild . . . . .Attorney
Jack Fried . . . . .Of Counsel
Jeffrey Silberman .Of Counsel
Nikki Wolontis . . . . .Of Counsel

ENTERTAINMENT ATTORNEYS

KINSELLA, WEITZMAN, ISER, KUMP & ALDISERT LLP
808 Wilshire Blvd., 3rd Fl.
Santa Monica, CA 90401
PHONE 310-566-9800
FAX 310-566-9850
WEB SITE . . . . .www.kwikalaw.com
PRACTICE AREAS   Arbitration & Mediation - Communications
                       - Copyright & Trademark Matters -
                       Ecommerce - Employment/Labor Law - First
                       Amendment Issues - Full Service Litigation -
                       Intellectual Property Law - Internet Law -
                       Libel & Privacy Matters - Licensing - Media
                       - Misappropriation of Name, Voice,
                       Likeness - Motion Picture & TV Law - Music
                       Law - Right of Publicity - Royalty Law -
                       Sports - Talent Representation - Technology
                       - Telecom

Dale F. Kinsella . . . . .Partner
Howard Weitzman . . . . .Partner
Lawrence Y. Iser . . . . .Partner
Michael J. Kump . . . . .Partner
Gregory J. Aldisert . . . . .Partner
Shawn Chapman Holley .Partner
Alan Kossoff . . . . .Partner
Patricia A. Millett . . . . .Partner
Chad R. Fitzgerald . . . . .Attorney
Gregory S. Gabriel . . . . .Attorney
Gregory P. Korn . . . . .Attorney
Jennifer J. McGrath . . . . .Attorney
Jeremiah T. Reynolds . . . . .Attorney
Kristen L. Spanier . . . . .Attorney

KIRKPATRICK & LOCKHART NICHOLSON GRAHAM LLP
10100 Santa Monica Blvd., 7th Fl.
Los Angeles, CA 90067
PHONE 310-552-5000
FAX 310-552-5001
EMAIL . . . . .info@klgates.com
WEB SITE . . . . .www.klgates.com
PRACTICE AREAS   Copyright & Trademark Matters -
                       Corporate Matters - Employment/Labor
                       Law - Financing - Intellectual Property Law -
                       Litigation - Mergers & Acquisitions
COMMENTS   22 offices in Anchorage, Beijing, Berlin,
                       Boston, Coeur D'Alene, Dallas, Harrisburg,
                       Hong Kong, Los Angeles, Miami, New
                       York, Newark, Orange County, Palo Alto,
                       Pittsburgh, Portland, San Francisco, Seattle,
                       Spokane, Taipei and Washington, DC

Jeryl A. Bowers . . . . .Partner
Kathleen O. Peterson . . . . .Partner
Thomas J. Poletti . . . . .Partner
Paul W. Sweeney Jr. . . . . .Partner

KIRTLAND & PACKARD
2361 Rosecrans Ave., 4th Fl.
El Segundo, CA 90245
PHONE 310-536-1000
FAX 310-536-1001
EMAIL . . . . .mlk@kirtlandpackard.com
WEB SITE . . . . .www.kirtlandpackard.com
PRACTICE AREAS   Libel & Privacy Matters - Litigation -
                       Misappropriation of Name, Voice, Likeness
COMMENTS   Business and entertainment litigation

Michael L. Kelly . . . . .Attorney, Entertainment & Intellectual Property
Robert M. Churella . . . . . .Attorney, Entertainment & Intellectual Property

KLEINBERG & LERNER, LLP
2049 Century Park East, Ste. 1080
Los Angeles, CA 90067
PHONE 310-557-1511
FAX 310-557-1540
EMAIL . . . . .mdiliberto@kleinberglerner.com
WEB SITE . . . . .www.kleinberglerner.com
SECOND WEB SITE . . . . .www.mrdmediation.com
PRACTICE AREAS   Full Service Representation - Arbitration &
                       Mediation - Contract Negotiation &
                       Drafting - Copyright & Trademark Matters -
                       Intellectual Property Law - Internet Law -
                       Licensing - Litigation - Misappropriation of
                       Name, Voice, Likeness - Motion Picture &
                       TV Law - Music Law

Michael R. Diliberto .Partner, Entertainment

KLEINBERG LOPEZ LANGE CUDDY & EDEL, LLP
2049 Century Park East, Ste. 3180
Los Angeles, CA 90067
PHONE 310-286-9696
FAX 310-277-7145
PRACTICE AREAS   Contract Negotiation & Drafting -
                       Copyright & Trademark Matters - Motion
                       Picture & TV Law - Music Law - Talent
                       Representation
COMMENTS   Acquisition and sale of film libraries

Kenneth Kleinberg . . . . .Partner
Peter Lopez . . . . .Partner
Robert Lange . . . . .Partner
Christine Cuddy . . . . .Partner
Scott Edel . . . . .Partner
Philip Klein . . . . .Partner
Elliott Kleinberg . . . . .Partner
Mark Kovinsky . . . . .Of Counsel
Nadia Davari . . . . .Associate
Gary Fine . . . . .Associate
Stephanie Rosenberg . . . . .Associate
Adrian Lopez . . . . .Paralegal

LAW OFFICES OF JEFFREY S. KONVITZ
1801 Century Park East, Ste. 2300
Los Angeles, CA 90067
PHONE 310-772-2800
FAX 310-789-2211
EMAIL . . . . .jkonvitz@aol.com
SECOND EMAIL . . . . .jk@konvitzlaw.com
PRACTICE AREAS   Arbitration & Mediation - Contract Negotiation & Drafting - Copyright & Trademark Matters - Corporate Matters - Financing - Intellectual Property Law - Litigation - Media - Mergers & Acquisitions - Motion Picture & TV Law - Partnerships/Joint Ventures - Talent Representation
REPRESENTS   Regent Entertainment - Blue Rider Entertainment - Apollo Promedia - Halifax Film Company - Simex - Crystal Sky Entertainment - Ave Maria Foundation - Thomas Monaghan - Imavision
COMMENTS   Also represents international co-productions

Jeffrey S. Konvitz . . . . .Owner

MATT KRIMMER & ASSOCIATES
6659 Lemonleaf Dr.
Carlsbad, CA 92011
PHONE 310-567-6428
EMAIL . . . . .matt@mattkrimmer.com
WEB SITE . . . . .www.mattkrimmer.com
PRACTICE AREAS   Full Service Representation - Copyright & Trademark Matters - Motion Picture & TV Law - Sports - Talent Representation
COMMENTS   Film & TV production services; Software licensing; Executive employment contracts

Matt Krimmer . . . . .Founder/Owner

KULIK, GOTTESMAN, MOUTON & SIEGEL
15303 Ventura Blvd., Ste. 1400
Sherman Oaks, CA 91403
PHONE 818-817-3600/310-557-9200
FAX 310-557-0224
WEB SITE . . . . .www.kgmslaw.com
PRACTICE AREAS   Motion Picture & TV Law - Music Law

Don Gottesman . . . . .Founding Partner
Glen Kulik .Founding Partner
Kent Mouton . . . . .Founding Partner
Leonard Siegel . . . . .Founding Partner
Deborah L. Feldman . . . . .Partner
David S. Olson . . . . .Partner
Thomas M. Ware II . . . . .Partner
Sharon Barber . . . . .Associate
Craig S. Berman .Associate
David A. Bernardoni . . . . .Associate
Francesca Dioguardi . . . . .Associate
Alisa Edelson . . . . .Associate
Brien Kelley . . . . .Associate
Lizzle Q. Singian . . . . .Associate
Hillary Wenner . . . . .Associate
Joseph R. Serpico . . . . .Special Counsel
Jonathan L. Smoller . . . . .Special Counsel

LAW OFFICES OF RICHARD A. KURSHNER
10950 Washington Blvd., Ste. 240
Culver City, CA 90232
PHONE 310-838-4500
FAX 310-838-4505
EMAIL .rick@kurshner.com
PRACTICE AREAS   Contract Negotiation & Drafting - Copyright & Trademark Matters - Intellectual Property Law - Licensing - Media - Motion Picture & TV Law - Music Law - Talent Representation - Transactional Law

Richard A. Kurshner . . . . .Attorney

RICHARD H. LANGAN II, ATTORNEY AT LAW
325 E. 8th St., Ste. 5-A
New York, NY 10009
PHONE 212-673-6753
EMAIL . . . . .rlangan@langan-law.com
WEB SITE . . . . .www.langan-law.com
PRACTICE AREAS   Contract Negotiation & Drafting - Copyright & Trademark Matters - Litigation - Motion Picture & TV Law - Transactional Law

Richard H. Langan II . . . . .Attorney

LAPOLT LAW, PC
9000 Sunset Blvd., Ste. 800
West Hollywood, CA 90069
PHONE 310-858-0922
FAX 310-858-0933
WEB SITE . . . . .www.lapoltlaw.com
PRACTICE AREAS   Motion Picture & TV Law - Music Law
REPRESENTS   Recording Artists - Producers - Record Company Executives - Managers - Publishers - Songwriters - Photographers - Independent Record Companies - Film Composers - Actors - Screenwriters - Producers - Film Production Companies - Directors - Authors

Dina LaPolt . . . . .Attorney
Ted Baer . . . . .Attorney
Allison Schwarz . . . . .Attorney
Heidy Vaquerano .Paralegal
Megan Myers . . . . .Administrative Assistant

LAW OFFICES OF BENJAMIN LASKI
3112 Washington Blvd.
Marina del Rey, CA 90292
PHONE 310-578-1617
FAX 310-578-1657
EMAIL .ben@laskilaw.com
WEB SITE . . . . .www.laskilaw.com
PRACTICE AREAS   Contract Negotiation & Drafting - Copyright & Trademark Matters - Intellectual Property Law - Libel & Privacy Matters - Misappropriation of Name, Voice, Likeness - Motion Picture & TV Law - Music Law - Talent Representation

Ben Laski . . . . .Attorney
Analise Vela . . . . .Assistant

ENTERTAINMENT ATTORNEYS

LAVELY & SINGER, PC
2049 Century Park East, Ste. 2400
Los Angeles, CA 90067-2906
PHONE 310-556-3501
FAX 310-556-3615
WEB SITE . . . . .www.lavelysinger.com
PRACTICE AREAS   Arbitration & Mediation - Copyright & Trademark Matters - Employment/Labor Law - Intellectual Property Law - Libel & Privacy Matters - Litigation - Misappropriation of Name, Voice, Likeness - Right of Publicity
COMMENTS   Media law; Defamation matters; Domain name matters

John H. Lavely Jr. . . . . .Partner
Martin D. Singer . . . . .Partner
Brian G. Wolf . . . . .Partner
Lynda B. Goldman . . . . .Partner
Michael D. Holtz . . . . .Partner
William J. Briggs II . . . . .Partner
Paul N. Sorrell . . . . .Partner

LAW OFFICES OF JAMES M. LEONARD
3315 Corinth Ave.
Los Angeles, CA 90066
PHONE 310-390-8120
FAX 310-391-0051
EMAIL . . . . .j-leonard@ca.rr.com
PRACTICE AREAS   Arbitration & Mediation - Contract Negotiation & Drafting - Copyright & Trademark Matters - Corporate Matters - Mergers & Acquisitions - Motion Picture & TV Law - Partnerships/Joint Ventures - Talent Representation - Transactional Law

James M. Leonard . . . . .Attorney

LEOPOLD PETRICH & SMITH
2049 Century Park East, Ste. 3110
Los Angeles, CA 90067
PHONE 310-277-3333
FAX 310-277-7444
WEB SITE . . . . .www.lpsla.com
PRACTICE AREAS   Arbitration & Mediation - Copyright & Trademark Matters - First Amendment Issues - Intellectual Property Law - Libel & Privacy Matters - Litigation - Media - Misappropriation of Name, Voice, Likeness - Motion Picture & TV Law - Right of Publicity

A. Fredric Leopold . . . . .Member
Louis P. Petrich . . . . .Member
Vincent Cox . . . . .Member
Donald R. Gordon . . . . .Member
Robert S. Gutierrez . . . . .Member
Daniel M. Mayeda . . . . .Member
Edward A. Ruttenberg . . . . .Member
Walter R. Sadler . . . . .Member
Joel M. Smith . . . . .Of Counsel
Loralee Sundra . . . . .Of Counsel
Chad O'Hara . . . . .Associate
Thomas Peistrup . . . . .Associate

LAW OFFICE OF PAUL S. LEVINE
1054 Superba Ave.
Venice, CA 90291-3940
PHONE .310-450-6711/800-742-1819
FAX 310-450-0181
EMAIL . . . . .pslevine@ix.netcom.com
WEB SITE . . . . .www.paulslevine.com
PRACTICE AREAS   Arbitration & Mediation - Contract Negotiation & Drafting - Copyright & Trademark Matters - Corporate Matters - Employment/Labor Law - Financing - First Amendment Issues - Intellectual Property Law - Libel & Privacy Matters - Litigation - Misappropriation of Name, Voice, Likeness - Motion Picture & TV Law - Music Law - Partnerships/Joint Ventures - Right of Publicity - Royalty Law - Talent Representation - Transactional Law
REPRESENTS   Writers - Producers - Directors - Musicians - Composers - Animators - Inventors - Production Companies - Distribution Companies
COMMENTS   Document preparation; Literary agent for adult, children, young adult fiction and non-fiction book authors; Book publishing law

Paul S. Levine . . . . .Attorney

LAW OFFICE OF MARK L. LEVINSON
14724 Ventura Blvd., PH
Sherman Oaks, CA 91403
PHONE 818-788-3059
FAX 818-461-1744
EMAIL . . . . .mllentlaw@aol.com
PRACTICE AREAS   Full Service Representation - Arbitration & Mediation - Contract Negotiation & Drafting - Copyright & Trademark Matters - Corporate Matters - Ecommerce - Employment/Labor Law - Intellectual Property Law - Licensing - Motion Picture & TV Law - Music Law - Royalty Law - Talent Representation - Transactional Law

Mark L. Levinson . . . . .Attorney

LEWIS BRISBOIS BISGAARD & SMITH, LLP
221 N. Figueroa St., Ste. 1200
Los Angeles, CA 90012-2601
PHONE 213-250-1800
FAX 213-250-7900
WEB SITE . . . . .www.lbbslaw.com
PRACTICE AREAS   Copyright & Trademark Matters - Employment/Labor Law - Intellectual Property Law - Litigation - Music Law - Tax Law
COMMENTS   Rights acquisition and clearance; Offices in Costa Mesa, Sacramento, San Bernardino, San Diego, San Francisco, Las Vegas, Phoenix, Tucson, Lafayette and Chicago; East Coast office: 199 Water St., Ste. 2500, New York, NY 10038

William Archer . . . . .Partner, Entertainment
Sanford Astor . . . . .Partner, Entertainment
Leo A. Bautista . . . . .Partner, Entertainment
Dan C. Decarlo . . . . .Partner, Entertainment
Steve Gibson . . . . . . .Partner, Entertainment (Las Vegas) (702-893-3383)
Alan J. Haus . . . . . . .Parnter, Entertainment (SF) (415-362-2580)
Tom C. Kiddé . . . . .Partner, Entertainment
David N. Makous . . . . .Partner, Entertainment
Jonathan Pink . . . . .Partner, Entertainment (OC) (714-545-9200)
Deborah F. Sirias . . . . .Partner, Entertainment
Glen S. Umeda . . . . .Partner, Entertainment (SF) (415-362-2580)
John S. Christopher . . . . .Associate, Entertainment
Mina F. Hamilton . . . . .Associate, Entertainment

LAW OFFICE OF TOM LEWIS
10850 Wilshire Blvd., #426
Los Angeles, CA 90024
PHONE 310-474-7588
FAX 310-470-6678
EMAIL . . . . .lawdude158@aol.com
PRACTICE AREAS   Full Service Representation - Contract Negotiation & Drafting - Copyright & Trademark Matters - Corporate Matters - Motion Picture & TV Law - Partnerships/Joint Ventures - Talent Representation - Transactional Law
COMMENTS   Works with independent producers

Tom Lewis . . . . .Attorney

LICHTER, GROSSMAN, NICHOLS & ADLER, INC.
9200 Sunset Blvd., Ste. 1200
Los Angeles, CA 90069
PHONE 310-205-6999
FAX 310-205-6990
EMAIL . . . . .cpage@lgna.com
PRACTICE AREAS   Motion Picture & TV Law - Talent Representation - Transactional Law

Linda Lichter . . . . .Partner
Peter Grossman . . . . .Partner
Peter Nichols . . . . .Partner
Michael Adler . . . . .Partner
James Feldman . . . . .Partner
Stephen P. Clark . . . . .Partner
Jonathan E. Shikora . . . . .Partner
Melissa Rogal . . . . .Partner
Annie S. Granatstein . . . . .Attorney

LINER YANKELEVITZ SUNSHINE & REGENSTREIF LLP
1100 Glendon Ave., 14th Fl.
Los Angeles, CA 90024-3503
PHONE 310-500-3500
FAX 310-500-3501
EMAIL . . . . .info@linerlaw.com
WEB SITE . . . . .www.linerlaw.com
PRACTICE AREAS   Financing - Licensing - Litigation
COMMENTS   Entertainment litigation; Entertainment-related structured financing, including slate financing; Interactive licensing

Joseph R. Taylor . . . . .Partner
Michael L. Novicoff . . . . .Partner
Edward A. Klein . . . . .Partner
Michael E. Weinsten . . . . .Partner
Randall J. Sunshine . . . . .Partner
Angela C. Agrusa . . . . .Partner
Steven A. Velkei . . . . .Partner
Joshua B. Grode . . . . .Partner
Bertha C. Willner . . . . .Partner
Teri T. Pham . . . . .Sr. Counsel
Heather H. Gilhooly . . . . .Associate
Glen A. Rothstein . . . . .Associate
Paul D. Swanson . . . . .Associate
Michael B. McCollum . . . . .Associate
Shannon H. Anderson . . . . .Associate
Alexander R. Wheeler . . . . .Associate
Tuneen E. Chisolm . . . . .Associate

MARK LITWAK & ASSOCIATES
433 N. Camden Dr., Ste. 1010
Beverly Hills, CA 90210
PHONE 310-859-9595
FAX 310-859-0806
EMAIL .law3@marklitwak.com
WEB SITE . . . . .www.marklitwak.com
PRACTICE AREAS   Full Service Representation - Arbitration & Mediation - Contract Negotiation & Drafting - Copyright & Trademark Matters - Corporate Matters - Ecommerce - Financing - Intellectual Property Law - Internet Law - Libel & Privacy Matters - Licensing - Litigation - Mergers & Acquisitions - Misappropriation of Name, Voice, Likeness - Motion Picture & TV Law - Partnerships/Joint Ventures - Right of Publicity - Royalty Law - Talent Representation - Technology - Transactional Law
REPRESENTS   Writers - Directors - Producers - Production Companies - Actors
COMMENTS   Also represents producers, entertainment and multimedia law

Mark Litwak . . . . .Attorney at Law, Entertainment
Stella Havkin . . . . .Of Counsel
Glenn Litwak . . . . .Of Counsel, Entertainment Litigation
James Talbott . . . . . . .Of Counsel, Entertainment & Intellectual Property
Peter Wilke . . . . .Of Counsel
Elizabeth Zook . . . . .Paralegal

LOEB & LOEB, LLP
10100 Santa Monica Blvd.
Los Angeles, CA 90067-4134
PHONE 310-282-2000/212-407-4000
FAX .310-282-2200/212-407-4990
EMAIL . . . . .firstinitiallastname@loeb.com
WEB SITE . . . . .www.loeb.com
PRACTICE AREAS   Full Service Representation - Mergers & Acquisitions - Arbitration & Mediation - Contract Negotiation & Drafting - Copyright & Trademark Matters - Corporate Matters - Employment/Labor Law - Financing - First Amendment Issues - Intellectual Property Law - Libel & Privacy Matters - Licensing - Litigation - Misappropriation of Name, Voice, Likeness - Motion Picture & TV Law - Music Law - Partnerships/Joint Ventures - Right of Publicity - Royalty Law - Talent Representation - Tax Law - Transactional Law
COMMENTS   Securities; Trusts & Estates; Real Estate; East Coast office: 345 Park Ave., New York, NY 10154-0037; Chicago office: 321 N. Clark St., Chicago, IL 60610-4714, ph: 312-464-3100, fax: 312-464-3111; Nashville office: 1906 Acklen Ave., Nashville, TN 37212-3740, ph: 615-749-8300, fax: 615-749-8308

Kenneth B. Anderson . . .Partner, Music, Entertainment & Media, Talent IP & Entertainment Litigation (NY) (212-407-4856)
Roger M. Arar . . . . .Partner, Entertainment & Media, Intellectual Property, Talent (NY) (212-407-4906)
Curtis W. Bajak . . .Partner, Commercial Finance, Entertainment & Media, Private Equity (LA) (310-282-2024)

(Continued)

ENTERTAINMENT ATTORNEYS

LOEB & LOEB, LLP (Continued)

Ivy Kagan Bierman . . . . . .Partner, Entertainment & Media, Advertising & Promotions, Employment & Labor, Litigation (LA) (310-282-2327)
Saul Brenner . . . . . . .Partner, IP & Entertainment Litigation, White Collar Criminal Defense, Corporate Compliance & Investigations, Entertainment & Media (LA) (310-282-2284)
Marc Chamlin . . . . .Partner, Advertising & Promotions, Branded Entertainment, Employment & Labor, Entertainment & Media, Talent (NY) (212-407-4855)
Craig A. Emanuel . . . . .Partner, Advertising & Promotions, Branded Entertainment, Entertainment & Media, Talent (LA) (310-282-2262)
Keith G. Fleer . . . . . .Partner, Entertainment & Media, Talent, Corporate Media & Entertainment, Branded Entertainment (LA) (310-282-2399)
John T. Frankenheimer . . .Partner, Entertainment & Media, Talent, Music, Private Equity (LA) (310-282-2135)
Seth D. Gelblum . . . . . .Partner, Corporate & Securities, Entertainment & Media, Intellectual Property, Theater, Trademarks & Copyrights (NY) (212-407-4931)
Carolyn Hunt . . . . .Partner, Commercial Finance, Entertainment & Media (LA) (310-282-2277)
Kenneth L. Kraus . . . . .Partner, Branded Entertainment, Entertainment & Media, Intellectual Property, Music, Trademarks & Copyrights (Nashville) (615-749-8310)
Michael A. Mayerson . . . . .Partner, Corporate Media & Entertainment, Entertainment Finance, Commercial Finance, Entertainment & Media (LA) (310-282-2165)
Nigel Pearson . . . . .Partner, Entertainment & Media, Talent, Intellectual Property, International (LA) (310-282-2332)
Stephen L. Saltzman . .Partner, Entertainment & Media, Talent, Corporate Media & Entertainment, Entertainment Finance (LA) (310-282-2127)
Paul A. Sczudio . . . . .Partner, Tax, High Net Worth Families, Entertainment & Media (310-282-2290)
James D. Taylor . . . . .Partner, Advertising & Promotions, Branded Entertainment, Entertainment & Media (NY) (212-407-4895)
Susan Z. Williams . . . . . . .Partner, Entertainment & Media, Entertainment Finance, Corporate Media & Entertainment (LA) (310-282-2063)
Scott Zolke . . . . . . .Partner, Entertainment & Media, IP & Entertainment Litigation, Talent (LA) (310-282-2299)
Leah Antonio-Ketcham . . . . .Sr. Counsel, Entertainment & Media, Intellectual Property, Talent (LA) (310-282-2383)
John C. Beiter . . . . .Of Counsel, Entertainment & Media, Intellectual Property, IP & Entertainment Litigation, Music, Trademarks & Copyrights (Nashville) (615-749-8315)
Louis Spoto . .Of Counsel, Entertainment & Media (LA) (310-282-2304)
Alison J. Dow . . . . .Associate, Advertising & Promotions, Entertainment & Media, Intellectual Property, Trademarks & Copyrights (NY) (212-407-4989)
Tiffany A. Dunn . . . . .Associate, Mergers & Acquisitions, Entertainment & Media, Trademarks & Copyrights, Music, Corporate Governance (Nashville) (615-749-8317)
Kevin Garlitz . . . . .Associate, Advertising & Promotions, Branded Entertainment, Entertainment & Media, Sports (LA) (310-282-2392)
Noah J. Leichtling . . . .Associate, Corporate & Securities, Entertainment Finance, Entertainment & Media, Mergers & Acquisitions, Private Equity (NY) (212-407-4075)
Jeff Leven . . .Associate, Branded Entertainment, Entertainment & Media, Intellectual Property, Music, Talent (LA) (310-282-2364)
Amy B. Ortner . . .Associate, Branded Entertainment, Corporate Media & Entertainment, Entertainment & Media, Intellectual Property, Music (LA) (310-282-2269)
Amanda E. Rykoff . . . . .Associate, Advertising & Promotions, Entertainment & Media, Talent (NY) (212-407-4978)
Denise M. Stevens . . . . .Associate, Music, Entertainment & Media, Intellectual Property, Trademarks & Copyrights, Branded Entertainment (Nashville) (615-749-8306)
Mark A. Streams . . . . . . .Associate, Corporate Media & Entertainment, Entertainment & Media, Mergers & Acquisitions, Private Equity (LA) (310-282-2326)
Po Yi . . . . .Associate, Advertising & Promotions, Branded Entertainment, Entertainment & Media, Intellectual Property, Music (NY) (212-407-4045)
Kenneth R. Florin . . . . .Attorney, Entertainment (NY)
Caroline Chmara . . . . .Paralegal, Entertainment & Media (LA) (310-282-2022)
Lucy Koster . . . . .Paralegal, Talent, Entertainment & Media (LA) (310-282-2268)
Leola Lanphier . . . . .Paralegal, Entertainment & Media, Entertainment Finance (LA) (310-282-2075)
Kelly M. O'Donnell . . . .Paralegal, Entertainment & Media, Advertising & Promotions (212-407-4151)

LORD, BISSELL & BROOK LLP

300 S. Grand Ave., Ste. 800
Los Angeles, CA 90071-3119
PHONE 213-485-1500
FAX 213-485-1200
WEB SITE . . . . .www.lordbissell.com
PRACTICE AREAS   Full Service Representation - Contract Negotiation & Drafting - Copyright & Trademark Matters - Intellectual Property Law - Licensing - Misappropriation of Name, Voice, Likeness - Motion Picture & TV Law - Music Law - Partnerships/Joint Ventures - Talent Representation - Technology - Transactional Law

C. Anthony Mulrain .Partner (Atlanta)
Neil Dickson . . . . .Attorney
Donald Woodard .Of Counsel (Atlanta)

LOWE LAW

11400 Olympic Blvd., Ste. 600
Los Angeles, CA 90064
PHONE 310-477-5811
FAX 310-477-7672
EMAIL . . . . .info@lowelaw.com
WEB SITE . . . . .www.lowelaw.com
PRACTICE AREAS   Contract Negotiation & Drafting - Copyright & Trademark Matters - Corporate Matters - Intellectual Property Law - Internet Law - Libel & Privacy Matters - Licensing - Litigation - Media - Misappropriation of Name, Voice, Likeness - Motion Picture & TV Law - Music Law - Partnerships/Joint Ventures - Right of Publicity - Royalty Law - Talent Representation - Transactional Law

Steven T. Lowe . . . . .Attorney
Omar S. Anorga . . . . .Associate
Loredana Nesci . . . . .Of Counsel
Tamika Tucker . . . . .Paralegal
Natasha L. Hill . . . . .Law Clerk

LAW OFFICES OF JAY W. MACINTOSH

1800 Century Park East, Ste. 600
Los Angeles, CA 90067
PHONE 310-284-3725
FAX 310-479-4629
EMAIL . . . . .macintoshj@aol.com
WEB SITE . . . . .www.jaywmacintoshlaw.com
PRACTICE AREAS   Full Service Representation - Contract Negotiation & Drafting - Copyright & Trademark Matters - Employment/Labor Law - First Amendment Issues - Intellectual Property Law - Libel & Privacy Matters - Licensing - Litigation - Motion Picture & TV Law - Music Law - Right of Publicity - Royalty Law - Transactional Law
COMMENTS   Real Estate, Bankruptcy; Former director, Board of Directors: WIF; Former chairman, Members Committee: Actors Studio; Member, Blue Ribbon Panel: ATAS; Member: SAG, AFTRA, ASCAP

Jay W. MacIntosh . . . . .Attorney at Law

LAW OFFICES OF WILLIAM E. MAGUIRE
11500 W. Olympic Blvd., Ste. 400
Los Angeles, CA 90064-1525
PHONE 310-470-2929
FAX 310-474-4710
EMAIL . . . . .maguire@artnet.net
WEB SITE . . . . .www.trademarksq.com
SECOND WEB SITE . . . . .www.copyrightesq.com
PRACTICE AREAS   Copyright & Trademark Matters -
                        Intellectual Property Law - Licensing - Right
                        of Publicity
COMMENTS   Entertainment, publishing, multimedia and
                        apparel industries

William E. Maguire . . . . .Principal

MANATT, PHELPS & PHILLIPS, LLP
11355 W. Olympic Blvd.
Los Angeles, CA 90064
PHONE 310-312-4000
FAX 310-312-4224
WEB SITE . . . . .www.manatt.com
PRACTICE AREAS   Full Service Representation
COMMENTS   See Web site for contact information on all
                        Manatt, Phelps & Phillips, LLP office loca-
                        tions

Paul H. Irving . . . . .Chairman
William T. Quicksilver . . . . .Chief Executive/Managing Partner
Edith S. Gould . . . . .Executive Director
Michael Barkow . . . . .Partner, Advertising, Marketing & Media (NY)
(212-790-4590)
Robert Becker . . . . . . .Partner, Intellectual Property (PA) (650-812-1370)
Lauren Reiter Brody . . . . .Partner, Litigation (NY) (212-790-4518)
Frances K. Browne . . . . .Partner, Litigation (NY) (212-790-4526)
Alan M. Brunswick . . . . .Partner, Employment & Labor (310-312-4213)
Gregory Clarick . . . . . . .Partner, Litigation (NY) (212-790-4500)
Christopher Cole . . . . . .Partner, Advertising, Marketing & Media (DC)
(202-585-6524)
George A. Cooke . . . . . . .Partner, Entertainment (NY) (212-790-4538)
Craig J. de Recat . . . . .Partner, Litigation (310-312-4319)
Andrew DeVore . . . . .Partner, Litigation (NY) (212-790-4500)
R. Bruce Dickson . . . . . . .Partner, Advertising, Marketing & Media (DC)
(202-585-6522)
Jeffrey S. Edelstein . . . . . .Partner, Advertising, Marketing & Media (NY)
(212-790-4533)
Gene Elerding   Partner, Advertising, Marketing & Media (310-312-4158)
Seth Gold . . . . .Partner, Intellectual Property (310-312-4371)
Linda Goldstein . . . . .Partner, Advertising, Marketing & Media (NY)
(212-790-4500)
Carl Grumer . . . . .Partner, Litigation (310-312-4149)
William M. Heberer . . . . .Partner, Advertising, Marketing & Media (NY)
(212-790-4566)
Susan E. Hollander . . .Partner, Intellectual Property (PA) (650-812-1344)
Robert Jacobs . . . . .Partner, Litigation (NY) (212-790-4550)
Matthew Kanny . . . . .Partner, Intellectual Property (310-312-4225)
Brian Kelly . . . . .Partner, Intellectual Property (310-312-4175)
Barry S. Landsberg . . . . .Partner, Litigation (310-312-4259)
Mark Lee . . . . .Partner, Intellectual Property (310-312-4128)
Stanley W. Levy . . . . . . .Partner, Employment & Labor (310-312-4379)
Mark Litvack . . . . .Partner, Litigation (310-312-4121)
Scott Lochner . . . . .Partner, Corporate & Finance (310-312-4374)
Barry E. Mallen . . . . .Partner, Litigation (310-312-4339)
Jeffrey A. Mannisto . . . . .Partner, Tax, Employee Benefits & Wealth
Management (310-312-4212)
Gerald A. Margolis . .Partner, Entertainment & Litigation (310-312-4147)
Alon Markowitz . . . . .Partner, Litigation (NY) (212-790-4565)
Laurence M. Marks . . . . .Partner, Entertainment (310-312-4154)
Charulata Pagar . . . . .Partner, Advertising, Marketing & Media
(310-312-4155)
L. Peter Parcher . . . . .Partner, Litigation (NY) (212-790-4500)
Kimo Peluso . . . . .Partner, Litigation (NY) (212-790-4500)
L. Lee Phillips . . . . .Partner, Entertainment (310-312-4111)
Jill M. Pietrini . . . . .Partner, Intellectual Property (310-312-4325)
Brad Seiling . . . . .Partner, Litigation (310-312-4234)
Robert J. Sherman   Partner, Banking & Specialty Finance (310-312-4177)
Charles Washburn, Jr. . . . . .Partner, Banking & Specialty Finance
(310-312-4372)

(Continued)

MANATT, PHELP & PHILLIPS, LLP (Continued)
Felix H. Kent . . . . . . .Sr. Counsel, Advertising, Marketing & Media (NY)
(212-790-4588)
Charles Biederman . . . . .Counsel, Entertainment (310-312-4277)
Larry Blake . . . . .Of Counsel, Entertainment (310-312-4107)
Eric J. Custer . . . . .Counsel, Entertainment (310-312-4219)
Joseph Horacek III . . . . .Counsel, Entertainment (310-312-4140)
Arnold D. Kassoy . . . . .Counsel, Tax, Employee Benefits & Global
Compensation (310-312-4314)
Melissa W. Weaver . . . . .Counsel, Entertainment (310-312-4332)
Shari Mulrooney Wollman . . . . .Counsel, Intellectual Property
(310-312-4309)
Robert Begland . . . . . . .Associate, Intellectual Property (310-312-4324)
Jordan Bromley . . . . .Associate, Entertainment (310-312-4134)
Elise Dang . . . . .Associate, Advertising, Marketing & Media (NY)
(212-790-4613)
Jennifer N. Deitch . . . .Associate, Advertising, Marketing & Media (NY)
(212-790-4595)
Shawn Hansen . . . .Associate, Intellectual Property (PA) (650-812-1367)
Angela Hurdle . . . . . . .Associate, Advertising, Marketing & Media (NY)
(212-790-4574)
Raaqim Knight . . . . . . .Associate, Intellectual Property (310-312-4323)
Christopher Koegel . . . .Associate, Advertising, Marketing & Media (DC)
(202-585-6563)
Harold McDougall . . . . .Associate, Entertainment (310-312-4180)
Lindsay M. Schoen . . . . .Associate, Advertising, Marketing & Media (NY)
(212-790-4504)
Daniel K. Stuart . . . . .Associate, Entertainment (310-312-4170)
Joy Teitel . . . . .Associate, Litigation (310-312-4264)
Paul Thomas . . . . . .Associate, Intellectual Property (PA) (650-812-1305)
Carly Van Orman . . . .Associate, Advertising, Marketing & Media (DC)
(202-585-6539)

MANNING & MARDER, KASS, ELLROD, RAMIREZ, LLP
801 S. Figueroa St., 15th Fl.
Los Angeles, CA 90017
PHONE 213-624-6900
FAX 213-624-6999
EMAIL . . . . .info@mmker.com
WEB SITE . . . . .www.mmker.com
PRACTICE AREAS   Full Service Representation - Intellectual
                        Property Law - Libel & Privacy Matters
COMMENTS   Specializes in transactional, litigational and
                        advisory services for clients in every area of
                        the entertainment industry

John A. Marder .Managing Partner
Anthony Ellrod . . . . .Partner
Jeffery M. Lenkov . . . . .Partner

MARGOLIS & TISMAN, LLP
444 S. Flower St., 6th Fl.
Los Angeles, CA 90071
PHONE 213-683-0300
FAX 213-683-0303
WEB SITE . . . . .www.winlaw.com
PRACTICE AREAS   Full Service Representation - Copyright &
                        Trademark Matters
COMMENTS   Additional offices in New York, San Diego
                        and San Francisco

Michael B. Margolis . . . . .Partner
Stephen E. Tisman . . . . .Partner
Naki M. Irvin . . . . .Attorney
Judith S. Islas . . . . .Attorney
Robert M. Lieber . . . . .Attorney
Michael D. Markovitch .Attorney
James M. Parver . . . . .Attorney
Valerie D. Ringel . . . . .Attorney
Linda M. Toutant . . . . .Attorney
Thomas M. Regele . . . . .Of Counsel

STEVEN PAUL MARK, ATTORNEY AT LAW
401 E. 80th St., Ste. 29B
New York, NY 10021
PHONE 212-717-0141
FAX 212-628-4541
EMAIL . . . . .spmlawyer@rcn.com
WEB SITE . . . . .www.spmlawyer.com
PRACTICE AREAS   Contract Negotiation & Drafting -
                     Copyright & Trademark Matters -
                     Employment/Labor Law - Intellectual
                     Property Law - Internet Law - Licensing -
                     Media - Motion Picture & TV Law - Music
                     Law - Partnerships/Joint Ventures
COMMENTS   Experience in all areas of entertainment law
                     from seller and buyer viewpoints, big and
                     small companies, especially serving those
                     just starting out

Steven Paul Mark . . . . .Attorney

MASURLAW
101 E. 15th St.
New York, NY 10003
PHONE 212-931-8220
FAX 212-931-8221
EMAIL . . . . .info@masurlaw.com
WEB SITE . . . . .www.masurlaw.com
SECOND WEB SITE .www.entmedia.com
PRACTICE AREAS   Full Service Representation - Contract
                     Negotiation & Drafting - Copyright &
                     Trademark Matters - Corporate Matters -
                     Financing - Intellectual Property Law -
                     Licensing - Mergers & Acquisitions - Motion
                     Picture & TV Law - Music Law -
                     Partnerships/Joint Ventures - Right of
                     Publicity - Transactional Law
COMMENTS   Strategic consulting

Steven Masur . . . . .Partner
Mark Anderson . . . . .Associate
Andrew McCormick . . . . .Associate
Thomas Siblo . . . . .Associate
Cheryl Wickham . . . . .Associate
Joanna Zaradkiewicz .Business Affairs
Vanessa Bonn . . . . .Assistant

MCAFEE & TAFT
Two Leadership Square, 10th Fl.
211 N. Robinson
Oklahoma City, OK 73102-7103
PHONE 405-235-9621/800-235-9621
FAX 405-235-0439
PRACTICE AREAS   Full Service Representation - Contract
                     Negotiation & Drafting - Copyright &
                     Trademark Matters - Corporate Matters -
                     Ecommerce - Employment/Labor Law -
                     Financing - Intellectual Property Law -
                     Internet Law - Licensing - Litigation -
                     Mergers & Acquisitions - Motion Picture &
                     TV Law - Music Law - Partnerships/Joint
                     Ventures - Talent Representation - Tax Law

Jay Shanker . . . . .Attorney

MCCUE, SUSSMANE & ZAPFEL
521 Fifth Ave., 28th Fl.
New York, NY 10175
PHONE 212-931-5500
FAX 212-931-5508
EMAIL . . . . .information@mszpc.com
WEB SITE . . . . .www.mszpc.com
PRACTICE AREAS   Full Service Representation - Arbitration &
                     Mediation - Contract Negotiation &
                     Drafting - Copyright & Trademark Matters -
                     Corporate Matters - Ecommerce -
                     Financing - Intellectual Property Law -
                     Internet Law - Libel & Privacy Matters -
                     Licensing - Litigation - Media - Mergers &
                     Acquisitions - Misappropriation of Name,
                     Voice, Likeness - Motion Picture & TV Law -
                     Music Law - Partnerships/Joint Ventures -
                     Right of Publicity - Royalty Law - Talent
                     Representation - Tax Law - Technology -
                     Transactional Law
REPRESENTS   Actors - Directors - Music Producers -
                     Movie Producers - Production Companies -
                     Recording Artists - Writers

John W. McCue III . . . . .Attorney
Ken S. Sussmane . . . . .Attorney
Elaine B. Zapfel . . . . .Attorney
Craig Cohen . . . . .Attorney
Craig M. Spierer . . . . .Attorney
Mathias A. Youbi . . . . .Attorney
Keith G. Sklar . . . . .Attorney

MCLANE & WONG
20501 Ventura Blvd., Ste. 217
Woodland Hills, CA 91364
PHONE 818-587-6801
FAX 818-587-6802
EMAIL . . . . .bcmclane@aol.com
WEB SITE . . . . .www.benmclane.com
PRACTICE AREAS   Contract Negotiation & Drafting -
                     Copyright & Trademark Matters -
                     Intellectual Property Law - Music Law

Ben McLane . . . . .Partner
Venice Wong . . . . .Partner

MCPHERSON & KALMANSOHN, LLP
1801 Century Park East, Ste. 2400
Los Angeles, CA 90067
PHONE 310-553-8833
FAX 310-553-9233
PRACTICE AREAS   Arbitration & Mediation - Copyright &
                     Trademark Matters - First Amendment
                     Issues - Intellectual Property Law - Libel &
                     Privacy Matters - Litigation -
                     Misappropriation of Name, Voice, Likeness
                     - Motion Picture & TV Law - Music Law -
                     Right of Publicity
COMMENTS   Guild and union disputes; Stalking control

Edwin F. McPherson . . . . .Attorney, Music, Film & TV Litigation

LAW OFFICE OF BRIAN H. MCPHERSON
PO Box 50657
Los Angeles, CA 90050-0657
PHONE 213-422-8433
FAX 323-417-4984
EMAIL .bmcpherson@prodigy.net
PRACTICE AREAS   Music Law

Brian H. McPherson . . . . .Attorney

MEDIA STRATEGIES INTERNATIONAL, INC.
814 S. Westgate Ave., Ste. 250
Los Angeles, CA 90049
PHONE 310-820-8030
FAX 310-820-8130
PRACTICE AREAS   Contract Negotiation & Drafting -
                        Financing
COMMENTS   Business affairs consultants for the
                        entertainment industry

Debra Stasson . . . . .CEO
Joan Whitehead Evans . . . . .No Title
Patricia Mayer . . . . .No Title
Clare Tully . . . . .No Title
Michael Viebrock . . . . .No Title
Dana Walker . . . . .No Title
Robert Zinser . . . . .No Title
Lois Kay . . . . .No Title
Kyndra Homuth . . . . .Business Affairs Coordinator

MILLER & PLIAKAS, LLP
9720 Wilshire Blvd., Ste. 700
Beverly Hills, CA 90212
PHONE 310-860-1313
FAX 310-860-1515
EMAIL . . . . .ddm@mp-lawfirm.com
SECOND EMAIL . . . . .rap@mp-lawfirm.com
WEB SITE . . . . .www.mp-lawfirm.com
PRACTICE AREAS   Contract Negotiation & Drafting -
                        Corporate Matters - Motion Picture & TV
                        Law - Music Law - Partnerships/Joint
                        Ventures

Darrell D. Miller Esq. . . . . .Managing Partner
Roger A. Pliakas Esq. . . . . .Partner
Jesse S. Connors Esq. .Associate

MILLER BARONDESS, LLP
1999 Avenue of the Stars, Ste. 1000
Los Angeles, CA 90067
PHONE 310-552-4400
FAX 310-552-8400
EMAIL . . . . .info@millerbarondess.com
WEB SITE . . . . .www.millerbarondess.com
PRACTICE AREAS   Contract Negotiation & Drafting -
                        Corporate Matters - Employment/Labor
                        Law - Intellectual Property Law - Litigation -
                        Mergers & Acquisitions - Partnerships/Joint
                        Ventures

Skip Miller . . . . .Partner (310-552-5251, smiller@millerbarondess.com)
Mark Barondess . . . . .Partner (310-364-3593,
                        mbarondess@millerbarondess.com)
Dan Park . . . . . . .Partner (310-552-5227, dpark@millerbarondess.com)
John Dellaverson . . . . .Of Counsel (310-552-5232,
                        jdellaverson@millerbarondess.com)
Viviane A. Abraham . . . . .Director, Admistration (310-552-5264,
                        vabraham@millerbarondess.com)

MINDFUSION LAW CORPORATION
1875 Century Park East, 6th Fl.
Los Angeles, CA 90067
PHONE 310-407-5380
FAX 310-407-5499
EMAIL . . . . .info@mindfusionlaw.com
WEB SITE . . . . .www.mindfusionlaw.com
PRACTICE AREAS   Full Service Representation

Paul Battista Esq. . . . . .Partner
Mychal A. Wilson Esq. . . . . .Partner
James Preston Fagen Esq. . . . . .Of Counsel

MITCHELL SILBERBERG & KNUPP, LLP
11377 W. Olympic Blvd.
Los Angeles, CA 90064
PHONE 310-312-2000/202-973-8109
FAX 310-312-3100/202-973-8110
EMAIL . . . . .info@msk.com
WEB SITE . . . . .www.msk.com
PRACTICE AREAS   Contract Negotiation & Drafting -
                        Copyright & Trademark Matters -
                        Corporate Matters - Employment/Labor
                        Law - Financing - First Amendment Issues -
                        Intellectual Property Law - Licensing -
                        Litigation - Mergers & Acquisitions - Motion
                        Picture & TV Law - Music Law -
                        Partnerships/Joint Ventures
COMMENTS   Domain name disputes; Defamation and
                        unfair competition matters; East Coast
                        office: 2300 M St. NW, Ste. 800,
                        Washington, DC 20037

Anthony A. Adler . . . . .Partner
Anthony J. Amendola . . . . .Partner
Patricia H. Benson . . . . .Partner
George M. Borkowski . . . . .Partner
Tracy L. Cahill . . . . .Partner
William L. Cole . . . . .Partner
Lucia E. Coyoca . . . . .Partner
Philip Davis . . . . .Partner
Larry C. Drapkin . . . . .Partner
Arthur Fine . . . . .Partner
Russell J. Frackman . . . . .Partner
Harold Friedman . . . . .Partner
Gary E. Gans . . . . .Partner
Kevin E. Gaut . . . . .Partner
Peter B. Gelblum . . . . .Partner
Eric J. German . . . . .Partner
Lawrence A. Ginsberg .Partner
Frida P. Glucoft . . . . .Partner
Lessing E. Gold . . . . .Partner
Jeffrey D. Goldman . . . . .Partner
Samantha C. Grant . . . . .Partner
Allen J. Gross . . . . .Partner
James F. Guerra .Partner (DC)
Richard S. Hessenius . . . . .Partner
Hayward J. Kaiser . . . . .Partner
Andrew E. Katz . . . . .Partner
Evan M. Kent . . . . .Partner
Deborah P. Koeffler . . . . .Partner
Thomas P. Lambert . . . . .Partner
Chester I. Lappen . . . . .Partner
Christopher B. Leonard . . . . .Partner
Adam Levin . . . . .Partner
Emma Luevano . . . . .Partner
Marc E. Mayer . . . . .Partner
Patricia Mayer . . . . .Partner
Steven J. Metalitz . . . . .Partner (DC)
Lawrence A. Michaels .Partner
Yvette Molinaro . . . . .Partner
Jean Pierre Nogues . . . . .Partner
Karen Pagnanelli . . . . .Partner
Alan L. Pepper . . . . .Partner
Seth E. Pierce . . . . .Partner
Jeffrey L. Richardson . . . . .Partner
David S. Rugendorf . . . . .Partner
Steven M. Schneider . . . . .Partner
Eric J. Schwartz .Partner (DC)
Howard D. Shapiro . . . . .Partner
Richard B. Sheldon . . . . .Partner
David A. Steinberg . . . . .Partner
Suzanne M. Steinke . . . . .Partner
Wayne R. Terry . . . . .Partner
Mark A. Wasserman . . . . .Partner
Elia Weinbach . . . . .Partner
Lucy B. Arant . . . . .Of Counsel
James I. Bang . . . . .Of Counsel
Douglas Bordewieck . . . . .Of Counsel (DC)
Robert M. Dudnik . . . . .Of Counsel
Thomas A. Freiberg Jr. . . . . .Of Counsel
Jocelyn M. Gutierrez . . . . .Of Counsel
(Continued)

MITCHELL SILBERBERG & KNUPP, LLP (Continued)

William M. Kaplan . . . . .Of Counsel
Patricia L. Laucella . . . . .Of Counsel
Ronald H. Malin . . . . .Of Counsel
Jan Powers . . . . .Of Counsel
Rob Rader . . . . .Of Counsel
Joseph G. Swan . . . . .Of Counsel
Kim H. Swartz . . . . .Of Counsel
Diana Abdulian . . . . .Associate
Andres Alvarez . . . . .Associate
Taylor Ball . . . . .Associate
Mona Banerji . . . . .Associate
Michael Chait . . . . .Associate
Robyn Cohen . . . . .Associate
Steve Foster . . . . .Associate
Wade B. Gentz . . . . .Associate
Evan Goldstein . . . . .Associate
Elaine Gonzalez . . . . .Associate
Gregory L. Goodfried . . . . .Associate
Paul Guelpa . . . . .Associate
Daniel Hayes . . . . .Associate
Stephanie B. Hess . . . . .Associate
Lauren Kim . . . . .Associate
Alexa Lewis . . . . .Associate
Frank C. Lin . . . . .Associate
Janice K. Luo . . . . .Associate
Nahla Rajan . . . . .Associate
Guy M. Roy . . . . .Associate
Jill Rubin . . . . .Associate
Valentine Shalamitski . . . . .Associate
Alexsondra Shore . . . . .Associate
Courtney M. Smith . . . . .Associate
Amber Spataro . . . . .Associate
Seth A. Stevelman . . . . .Associate
Bethanie Thau . . . . .Associate
Brett Thomas . . . . .Associate
Aaron M. Wais . . . . .Associate
Meredith Williams . . . . .Associate
Matt Williams . . . . .Associate (DC)
Sarah Taylor Wirtz . . . . .Associate

MOHAJERIAN LAW CORP.

1925 Century Park East, Ste. 500
Los Angeles, CA 90067
PHONE 310-556-3800
FAX 310-556-3817
EMAIL . . . . .lawyers@mohajerian.com
WEB SITE . . . . .www.mohajerian.com
PRACTICE AREAS   Full Service Representation - Contract
                        Negotiation & Drafting - Copyright &
                        Trademark Matters - Corporate Matters -
                        Employment/Labor Law - Intellectual
                        Property Law - Litigation - Partnerships/Joint
                        Ventures

Al Mohajerian . . . . .Attorney
Harry M. Barth . . . . .Of Counsel
Joy L. Berus . . . . .Of Counsel

MORRISON & FOERSTER, LLP

555 W. Fifth St., Ste. 3500
Los Angeles, CA 90013
PHONE 213-892-5200
FAX 213-892-5454
EMAIL . . . . .info@mofo.com
WEB SITE . . . . .www.mofo.com
PRACTICE AREAS   Arbitration & Mediation - Contract
                        Negotiation & Drafting - Copyright &
                        Trademark Matters - Corporate Matters -
                        Employment/Labor Law - Financing - First
                        Amendment Issues - Intellectual Property
                        Law - Libel & Privacy Matters - Licensing -
                        Litigation - Mergers & Acquisitions -
                        Misappropriation of Name, Voice, Likeness
                        - Motion Picture & TV Law - Music Law -
                        Partnerships/Joint Ventures - Right of
                        Publicity - Royalty Law - Talent
                        Representation - Tax Law - Transactional
                        Law
REPRESENTS   Beijing Olympic Organizing Committee for
                        the Games of the XXIX Olympiad
COMMENTS   International entertainment; Olympic
                        Games work; Collective bargaining agree-
                        ments, employment disputes and allega-
                        tions; Guild and union matters; Eighteen
                        offices worldwide

Matthew D. Berger . . . . .Partner, Entertainment & Media (Tokyo)
Sherri Blount . . . . .Partner, Entertainment & Media (Washington, DC)
Kelly Charles Crabb . . . . .Partner, Entertainment & Media
John Delaney . . . . .Partner, Entertainment & Media (New York)
Ed Gray . . . . .Partner, Entertainment & Media (Washington, DC)
Vivian Hanson . . . . .Partner, Entertainment & Media (New York)
Douglas L. Hendricks . . .Partner, Entertainment & Media (San Francisco)
Paul E. Jahn . . . . .Partner, Entertainment & Media (San Francisco)
Daniel G. McIntosh . . . . .Partner, Entertainment & Media
H. Mark Mersel . . . . . .Partner, Entertainment & Media (Orange County)
Kate O'Brien . . . . .Partner, Entertainment & Media
Jay Ponazecki . . . . .Partner, Entertainment & Media (Tokyo)
Howard Soloway . . . . .Partner, Entertainment & Media
Pauline M. Stevens . . . . .Partner, Entertainment & Media
Rosemary S. Tarlton . . . . .Partner, Entertainment & Media (San Francisco)
Russell G. Weiss . . . . .Partner, Entertainment & Media
Lisa Weiss . . . . .Partner, Entertainment & Media (New York)
Kristian E. Wiggert . . . . .Partner, Entertainment & Media (London)
Robert Woll . . . . .Partner, Entertainment & Media (Hong Kong)
Alvaro Pascotto . . . . .Of Counsel, Entertainment & Media
E. Trey Hatch . . . . .Associate, Entertainment & Media (New York)
Eve D. McCabe . . . . .Associate, Entertainment & Media
Melanie S. Tomanov . . . . .Associate, Entertainment & Media
Melody N. Torbati . . . . .Associate, Entertainment & Media
Brandon Villery . . . . .Associate, Entertainment & Media

MOSES & SINGER, LLP
The Chrysler Building
405 Lexington Ave.
New York, NY 10174-1299
PHONE 212-554-7800
FAX 212-554-7700
EMAIL . . . . .sruben@mosessinger.com
WEB SITE . . . . .www.mosessinger.com
PRACTICE AREAS   Full Service Representation - Mergers & Acquisitions - Arbitration & Mediation - Contract Negotiation & Drafting - Copyright & Trademark Matters - Corporate Matters - Employment/Labor Law - Financing - First Amendment Issues - Intellectual Property Law - Libel & Privacy Matters - Licensing - Litigation - Misappropriation of Name, Voice, Likeness - Motion Picture & TV Law - Music Law - Partnerships/Joint Ventures - Right of Publicity - Royalty Law - Tax Law - Transactional Law
COMMENTS   Serving the TV, motion picture, book publishing, recording, periodical and music publishing industries

Cathy J. Frankel . . . . .Partner, Advertising/Entertainment/ Intellectual Property/Internet/New Media
Eric P. Bergner . . . . .Partner, Entertainment/Intellectual Property/ Advertising/Internet/New Media/Privacy
Mitchell D. Bernstein . . . . . .Partner, Entertainment/Hotel & Hospitality/ Internet/New Media/Intellectual Property/Litigation
Ross J. Charap . . . . .Partner, Entertainment/Intellectual Property
Elizabeth A. Corradino . . . . .Partner, Advertising/Entertainment/ Intellectual Property/Internet/New Media/Privacy
Paul M. Fakler . . . . .Partner, Entertainment/Internet Technology/ Intellectual Property/Litigation
Howard R. Herman . . . . .Partner, Banking & Finance/Corporate/ Entertainment/Intellectual Property/Internet/New Media/Privacy
W. Drew Kastner . . . . .Partner, Entertainment/Intellectual Property/ Litigation/Internet/New Media
David Rabinowitz . . . .Partner, Privacy/Entertainment/Intellectual Property/ Internet/New Media/Litigation
Alvin H. Schulman . . . . . . .Partner, Corporate, Securities & Commercial/ Entertainment/Trusts & Estates
Abraham Y. Skoff . . .Partner, Entertainment/Intellectual Property/Litigation
Philippe A. Zimmerman . . . . .Partner, Entertainment/Intellectual Property/ Litigation

David A. Bondy . . . . .Associate
Amyt M. Eckstein . . . . .Associate
Myka W. Todman . . . . .Associate

MARC MOSES LAW
445 S. Figueroa St., Ste. 2700
Los Angeles, CA 90071
PHONE 310-940-4557
EMAIL . . . . .mmoses@marcmoseslaw.com
PRACTICE AREAS   Full Service Representation - Arbitration & Mediation - Communications - Contract Negotiation & Drafting - Copyright & Trademark Matters - Corporate Matters - Ecommerce - Employment/Labor Law - Financing - First Amendment Issues - Intellectual Property Law - Internet Law - Libel & Privacy Matters - Licensing - Litigation - Media - Misappropriation of Name, Voice, Likeness - Motion Picture & TV Law - Music Law - Partnerships/Joint Ventures - Royalty Law - Tax Law - Technology - Telecom - Transactional Law
COMMENTS   Special rates for independent film
Marc Andrew Moses . . . . .Attorney

MUNGER, TOLLES & OLSON LLP
355 S. Grand Ave., 35th Fl.
Los Angeles, CA 90071-1560
PHONE 213-683-9100/415-512-4000
FAX .213-687-3702/415-512-4077
EMAIL . . . . .info@mto.com
WEB SITE . . . . .www.mto.com
PRACTICE AREAS   Arbitration & Mediation - Contract Negotiation & Drafting - Copyright & Trademark Matters - Corporate Matters - Employment/Labor Law - Financing - First Amendment Issues - Intellectual Property Law - Libel & Privacy Matters - Licensing - Litigation - Mergers & Acquisitions - Misappropriation of Name, Voice, Likeness - Motion Picture & TV Law - Music Law - Partnerships/Joint Ventures - Right of Publicity - Royalty Law - Talent Representation - Tax Law - Transactional Law
COMMENTS   See Web site for company directory; Northern California office: 560 Mission St., 27th Fl., San Francisco, CA 91405

MUNSCH HARDT KOPF & HARR, P.C.
600 Congress Ave., Ste. 2900
Austin, TX 78701-3057
PHONE 512-391-6100
FAX 512-391-6149
EMAIL . . . . .mkneeland@munsch.com
WEB SITE . . . . .www.munsch.com
PRACTICE AREAS   Arbitration & Mediation - Contract Negotiation & Drafting - Copyright & Trademark Matters - Corporate Matters - Employment/Labor Law - Intellectual Property Law - Licensing - Litigation - Mergers & Acquisitions - Music Law - Partnerships/Joint Ventures - Tax Law - Telecom - Transactional Law

Mishell Kneeland . . . . .Attorney

MYMAN ABELL FINEMAN FOX GREENSPAN LIGHT, LLP
11601 Wilshire Blvd., Ste. 2200
Los Angeles, CA 90025-1758
PHONE 310-231-0800
FAX 310-207-2680
PRACTICE AREAS   Contract Negotiation & Drafting - Copyright & Trademark Matters - Employment/Labor Law - Licensing - Motion Picture & TV Law - Music Law - Right of Publicity - Royalty Law - Talent Representation - Transactional Law

Robert Myman . . . . .Partner/Attorney
Leslie Abell . . . . .Partner/Attorney
Tom Fineman . . . . .Partner/Attorney
Eric Greenspan . . . . .Partner/Attorney
Jeffrey T. Light . . . . .Partner/Attorney
David Fox . . . . .Partner/Attorney
Steve Younger . . . . .Partner/Attorney
Glenn Davis . . . . .Attorney
Jennifer Lynn Grega . . . . .Attorney
Laurie Megery . . . . .Attorney
Tamara Milagros-Butler .Attorney
Francois Mobasser . . . . .Attorney
Kim Stenton . . . . .Attorney
Robert Minzner .Associate, Music
Aaron Rosenberg . . . . .Associate, Music

NELSON FELKER TOCZEK DAVIS, LLP
10880 Wilshire Blvd., Ste. 2070
Los Angeles, CA 90024
PHONE 310-441-8000
FAX 310-441-8010
PRACTICE AREAS   Contract Negotiation & Drafting
COMMENTS   Distribution deal negotiation; Business
                       plans

Peter M. Nelson . . . . .Partner
Patti C. Felker . . . . .Partner
Fred D. Toczek . . . . .Partner
George M. Davis . . . . .Partner
Bruce D. Gellman . . . . .Partner
Eric A. Suddleson . . . . .Partner
Derek Kroeger . . . . .Associate
Mark J. Wetzstein .Associate

VALERIE ANN NEMETH
191 Calle Magdalena, Ste. 270
Encinitas, CA 92024-3750
PHONE 760-944-4130/310-471-7648
FAX 760-944-3325
EMAIL . . . . .vanemeth@cs.com
WEB SITE .www.entlawyer.com
PRACTICE AREAS   Contract Negotiation & Drafting -
                       Copyright & Trademark Matters -
                       Intellectual Property Law - Licensing -
                       Motion Picture & TV Law - Music Law -
                       Right of Publicity - Talent Representation -
                       Transactional Law
COMMENTS   All facets of film, TV, music and publishing
Valerie Ann Nemeth .Attorney

NIMOH LAW, PC
36 E. 20th St., 2nd Fl.
New York, NY 10003
PHONE 212-253-1545
FAX 212-591-6619
EMAIL .anita@nimohlaw.com
SECOND EMAIL . . . . .info@nimohlaw.com
WEB SITE .www.nimohlaw.com
PRACTICE AREAS   Music Law
COMMENTS   Clients in music, film, TV, theatre, advertis-
                       ing and marketing, digital media, publish-
                       ing and design

Anita Nimoh Esq. . . . . .Principal
Natalie Jean-Baptiste Esq. . . . . .Associate
Lena Kasambalides Esq. . . . . .Of Counsel

NOVIAN & NOVIAN
1801 Century Park East, Ste. 1201
Los Angeles, CA 90067
PHONE 310-553-1222
FAX 310-553-0222
EMAIL .farhad@novianlaw.com
WEB SITE .www.novianlaw.com
PRACTICE AREAS   Contract Negotiation & Drafting -
                       Copyright & Trademark Matters -
                       Corporate Matters - Employment/Labor
                       Law - First Amendment Issues - Intellectual
                       Property Law - Libel & Privacy Matters -
                       Licensing - Litigation - Mergers &
                       Acquisitions - Misappropriation of Name,
                       Voice, Likeness - Music Law - Right of
                       Publicity - Royalty Law - Talent
                       Representation - Transactional Law

Farhad Novian . . . . .Partner
David Felsenthal . . . . .Attorney
Sam Frankel . . . . .Attorney
Emily S. Levin . . . . .Attorney
Josh Mendelsohn . . . . .Attorney
William R.H. Mosher . . . . .Attorney
Susan A. Rodriguez .Attorney
Lisa Simantub . . . . .Attorney
Aaron J. Weissman .Attorney

LAW OFFICE OF CHRISTOPHER NUNES
58 W. Portal Ave., #289
San Francisco, CA 94127
PHONE 415-730-1311/323-337-9007
FAX 415-664-4392/323-337-9004
EMAIL .chris@chrisnunes.com
SECOND EMAIL . . . . .cnunes@crown-ent.com
WEB SITE .www.chrisnunes.com
PRACTICE AREAS   Contract Negotiation & Drafting -
                       Copyright & Trademark Matters -
                       Corporate Matters - Financing - Internet
                       Law - Licensing - Motion Picture & TV Law -
                       Music Law - Partnerships/Joint Ventures -
                       Royalty Law - Tax Law - Technology -
                       Telecom - Transactional Law
REPRESENTS   GreenHouse Productions - Caroline
                       D'Amore - Aguila de Oro Productions -
                       Adult Digital Entertainment - Location:SF -
                       International Short Film Association - The
                       Sippy Cups - ChickFlick Productions -
                       Character Records - DJ Sandra Collins -
                       ThunderBall - Rabbit in the Moon - Crown
                       Entertainment - Doorway Films
COMMENTS   Additional practice: Mobile; Los Angeles
                       office: 8335 Sunset Blvd., 3rd Fl.,
                       Los Angeles, CA 90069

Christopher Nunes . . . . .Founding Partner

O'DONNELL & ASSOCIATES PC
550 S. Hope St., Ste. 1000
Los Angeles, CA 90071
PHONE 213-347-0290
FAX 213-347-0299
WEB SITE . . . . .www.oslaw.com
PRACTICE AREAS   Copyright & Trademark Matters -
                       Corporate Matters - First Amendment Issues
                       - Intellectual Property Law - Licensing

Pierce O'Donnell . . . . .Partner
Jack Cairl . . . . .Partner
Mark Grady . . . . .Partner

O'MELVENY & MYERS LLP
400 S. Hope St.
Los Angeles, CA 90071-2899
PHONE 213-430-6000/212-326-2000
FAX .213-430-6407/212-326-2061
EMAIL . . . . .omminfo@omm.com
WEB SITE . . . . .www.omm.com
PRACTICE AREAS   Full Service Representation - Arbitration & Mediation - Contract Negotiation & Drafting - Copyright & Trademark Matters - Corporate Matters - Employment/Labor Law - Financing - First Amendment Issues - Intellectual Property Law - Libel & Privacy Matters - Licensing - Litigation - Mergers & Acquisitions - Misappropriation of Name, Voice, Likeness - Motion Picture & TV Law - Music Law - Partnerships/Joint Ventures - Right of Publicity - Royalty Law - Talent Representation - Tax Law - Transactional Law
COMMENTS   Century City office: 1999 Avenue of the Stars, Los Angeles, CA 90067-6035, phone: 310-553-6700, fax: 310-246-6779; New York office: Times Square Tower, 7 Times Square, New York, NY 10036-6537, phone: 212-326-2000, fax: 212-326-2061; DC office: 1625 Eye St., NW, Washington, DC 20006-4001; phone: 202-383-5300, fax: 202-383-5414

Brian M. Berliner . . . . .Partner
Christopher Brearton . . . . .Partner (Century City)
Joseph A. Calabrese . . . . .Chair, Entertainment & Media Practice (Century City)
Dale M. Cendali . . . . .Partner (NY)
Scott H. Dunham . . . . .Chair, Labor & Employment Practice
Harvey M. Eisenberg . . . . .Co-Chair, Transactions Department (NY)
David P. Enzminger . . . . .Partner
Matthew Erramouspe .Partner (Century City)
Robert Haymer . . . . .Partner (Century City)
David A. Krinsky . . .Co-Chair, Transactions Department (Newport Beach)
Mark E. Miller . . . . .Partner (SF)
David B. Murphy .Partner (Newport Beach)
Christopher C. Murray . . . . .Partner (Century City)
Kenneth R. O'Rourke . . . . .Partner
William J. Peters . . . . .Partner
Daniel M. Petrocelli .Partner (Century City)
Marvin Putnam . . . . .Partner (Century City)
Claudia E. Ray . . . . .Partner (NY)
George A. Riley . . . . .Partner (SF)
Robert A. Rizzi . . . . .Chair, Tax Practice (Washington, DC)
Richard R. Ross .Of Counsel (Century City)
Mark A. Samuels . . . . .Chair, Intellectual Property & Technology Practice
Stephen Scharf . . . . .Partner (Century City)
Robert M. Schwartz .Partner (Century City)
Robert A. Siegel . . . . .Chair, Adversarial Department
Darin W. Snyder . . . . .Partner (SF)
Brett J. Williamson . . . . .Partner (Newport Beach)
W. Mark Wood . . . . .Partner

ORRICK HERRINGTON & SUTCLIFFE LLP
777 S. Figueroa St., Ste. 3200
Los Angeles, CA 90017-5855
PHONE 213-629-2020
FAX 213-612-2499
EMAIL . . . . .pr@orrick.com
WEB SITE . . . . .www.orrick.com
PRACTICE AREAS   Full Service Representation
COMMENTS   International law firm with approximately 980 lawyers in North America, Europe, and Asia

James C. Brooks . . . . .Partner (213-612-2281)
Michael A. McAndrews . . . . .Partner (213-612-2449)
William A. Molinski . . . . .Partner (213-612-2256)
William W. Oxley . . . . .Partner (213-612-2419)
Tina M. Tran . . . . .Partner (213-612-2393)
William L. Anthony Jr. . . . . .Partner, Intellectual Property (Menlo Park) (650-614-7453)
John V. Bautista . . . . .Partner, Emerging Companies (Menlo Park) (650-614-7652)
Robert A. Cote   Partner, Intellectual Property (New York) (212-506-5279)
Ed Davis . . . . .Partner (San Francisco) (415-773-5510)
Vickie L. Feeman . . . . .Partner/Practice Group Leader (Menlo Park) (650-614-7620)
Maria Frangeskides . . . .Partner, Litigation (London) (44-20-7422-4638)
Saam Golshani . . . . .Partner (Paris) (33-1-5353-7254)
Alastair Gorrie . . . . . .Corporate Partner (London) (44-20-7422-4618)
G. Hopkins Guy III . . . . .Partner, Intellectual Property (Menlo Park) (650-614-7452)
David Halperin . . . . .Corporate Partner (Hong Kong) (852-2218-9168)
Norman C. Hile . . . . .Partner (Sacramento) (916-329-7900)
Robert M. Isackson . . . . .Partner (New York) (212-506-5280)
Fabio Marino . . . . .Partner (Menlo Park) (650-614-7353)
Thomas C. Mitchell   Partner, Bankruptcy (San Francisco) (415-773-5732)
Ira G. Rosenstein   Partner, Employment Law (New York) (212-506-5228)
Lisa T. Simpson . . . . .Partner (New York) (212-506-3767)
Neal Stender . . . . .Corporate Partner (Hong Kong) (852-2218-9199)
Michael T. Stolper . . . . .Partner (New York) (212-506-3768)
L. Mark Weeks . . . . .Partner (Tokyo) (81-3-3224-2925)
Daniel K. Yost . . . . . .Corporate Partner (Menlo Park) (650-614-7385)
Thomas H. Zellerbach . . . . .Partner (Menlo Park) (650-614-7446)
Monte Cooper . . . . .Of Counsel (Menlo Park) (650-614-7375)
Christopher S. Ruhland . . . . .Of Counsel (213-612-2274)
Samuel B. Stone . . . . . . .Of Counsel (Orange County) (949-852-7790)
Jason S. Angell . . . . .Associate (Menlo Park) (650-614-7638)
Subroto Bose . . . . .Associate, Intellectual Property (Menlo Park) (650-614-7669)
Alexandra Caminer . .Corporate Associate (London) (44-20-7422-4682)
Neel I. Chatterjee .Associate (650-614-7356)
Chester W. Day . . . . .Associate (Menlo Park) (650-614-7497)
Joshua P. Galper . . . . .Associate (Washington, DC) (202-339-8468)
P. Wayne Hale . . . . .Associate (Menlo Park) (650-614-7639)
Tarek J. Helou . . . .Associate, Litigation (San Francisco) (415-773-5838)
Jae H. Kim .Associate (213-612-2282)
Glenn M. Levy . . . . .Associate (Menlo Park) (650-614-7400)
Deepa M. Menon . . . . .Associate (Menlo Park) (650-614-7328)
Peter J. O'Rourke . . . . .Associate (Menlo Park) (650-614-7468)
Jessica R. Perry . . . . .Associate (Menlo Park) (650-614-7350)
Gabriel M. Ramsey . . . . .Associate (Menlo Park) (650-614-7361)
Theresa A. Sutton . . . . .Associate (Menlo Park) (650-614-7307)
William Benjamin Tabler III . . . . .Associate (New York) (212-506-5284)
Michael W. Trinh . . . . .Associate (Menlo Park) (650-614-7321)
Siddhartha Venkatesan . . . . . . .Associate (Menlo Park) (650-614-7456)
Marcos D. Vigil . . . . . .Associate, Litigation (New York) (212-506-3762)
Daniel J. Weinberg . . . . .Associate (Menlo Park) (650-614-7367)
Matthew D. Beckerman . . . . .Marketing Manager (213-612-2220)

THE LAW OFFICES OF MARTY O'TOOLE
1999 Avenue of the Stars, Ste. 1100
Los Angeles, CA 90067
PHONE 310-888-4000
EMAIL .mx@lawofficesofmartyotoole.com
WEB SITE . . . . .www.lawofficesofmartyotoole.com
PRACTICE AREAS   Full Service Representation - Arbitration &
                         Mediation - Contract Negotiation &
                         Drafting - Copyright & Trademark Matters -
                         Corporate Matters - First Amendment Issues
                         - Intellectual Property Law - Libel & Privacy
                         Matters - Licensing - Litigation -
                         Misappropriation of Name, Voice, Likeness
                         - Motion Picture & TV Law - Music Law -
                         Partnerships/Joint Ventures - Right of
                         Publicity - Royalty Law - Transactional Law
REPRESENTS   Musicians - Filmmakers - Screenwriters -
                         Authors
COMMENTS   Music shopping; Film packaging and pitch-
                         ing

Marty O'Toole . . . . .Attorney at Law
Adrienne Dameron . . . . .Assistant
Eric Larson . . . . .Assistant
Connor McPherson . . . . .Assistant

PAUL, HASTINGS, JANOFSKY & WALKER LLP
515 S. Flower St., 25th Fl.
Los Angeles, CA 90071
PHONE 213-683-6000
FAX 213-627-0705
WEB SITE . . . . .www.paulhastings.com
PRACTICE AREAS   Contract Negotiation & Drafting -
                         Corporate Matters - Intellectual Property
                         Law - Licensing - Talent Representation

Greg Nitzkowski . . . . .Managing Partner
Rob R. Carlson . . . . .Partner
Eve M. Coddon . . . . .Partner
Donald A. Daucher . . . . .Partner
Dennis S. Ellis . . . . .Partner
Belinda K. Orem . . . . .Partner
John E. Porter . . . . .Partner
John H. Steed . . . . .Partner
Geoffrey L. Thomas . . . . .Partner
Vincent K. Yip . . . . .Partner
Cynthia M. Cohen . . . . .Of Counsel

PAUL, WEISS, RIFKIND, WHARTON & GARRISON, LLP
1285 Avenue of the Americas
New York, NY 10019-6064
PHONE 212-373-3000/212-373-3391
FAX 212-757-3990/212-373-2092
EMAIL . . . . .jbreglio@paulweiss.com
SECOND EMAIL . . . . .mailbox@paulweiss.com
WEB SITE . . . . .www.paulweiss.com
PRACTICE AREAS   Full Service Representation - Arbitration &
                         Mediation - Contract Negotiation &
                         Drafting - Copyright & Trademark Matters -
                         Corporate Matters - Financing - First
                         Amendment Issues - Intellectual Property
                         Law - Libel & Privacy Matters - Licensing -
                         Litigation - Mergers & Acquisitions -
                         Misappropriation of Name, Voice, Likeness
                         - Motion Picture & TV Law - Music Law -
                         Partnerships/Joint Ventures - Right of
                         Publicity - Royalty Law - Talent
                         Representation - Tax Law - Transactional
                         Law
REPRESENTS   A vast array of clients, both personal and
                         institutional, involved in all aspects of the
                         entertainment industry
COMMENTS   Offices in Washington, DC, London, Paris,
                         Tokyo, Beijing, Hong Kong

John F. Breglio . . . . .Chairman/Partner, Entertainment
Peter L. Felcher . . . . .Partner, Entertainment
Charles H. Googe Jr. . . . . .Partner, Entertainment
Deborah Hartnett . . . . .Counsel, Entertainment
Helene Gaulrapp . . . . .Assistant to John F. Breglio

PEIKOFF LAW OFFICE PC
145 Avenue of the Americas, Ste. 6A
New York, NY 10013
PHONE 212-343-9600
FAX 212-343-3043
PRACTICE AREAS   Contract Negotiation & Drafting -
                         Copyright & Trademark Matters -
                         Intellectual Property Law - Licensing -
                         Motion Picture & TV Law - Talent
                         Representation - Transactional Law

Jodi Peikoff . . . . .Partner
Michael Mahan . . . . .Attorney
Nicole Marra . . . . .Attorney

PELTZ & WALKER
222 Broadway, 25th Fl.
New York, NY 10038
PHONE 212-349-6775
FAX 212-227-4002
EMAIL . . . . .apeltz@peltzwalker.com
WEB SITE . . . . .www.peltzwalker.com
PRACTICE AREAS   Arbitration & Mediation - Contract
                         Negotiation & Drafting -
                         Employment/Labor Law - Litigation -
                         Royalty Law

Alexander Peltz . . . . .Partner
Paul E. Walker . . . . .Partner
Jaymie L. Einhorn . . . . .Partner
Miles S. Reiner . . . . .Partner
Bhalinder L. Rikhye . . . . .Partner/Appellate Counsel
Edward M. Schoenman . . . . .Partner
Michael Calandra . . . . .Of Counsel
Christopher M. FitzPatrick . . . . .Associate
H. Kazuko An . . . . .Associate
L. Ruby Rey . . . . .Associate
Benjamin Shatzky . . . . .Associate
Steven M. Silverman . . . . .Associate
Wendy Tripodi . . . . .Associate

PEPPER LEGAL CONSULTING GROUP, LLC
21 E. High St.
Somerville, NJ 08876
PHONE 908-698-0330
FAX 908-248-9220
EMAIL . . . . .plcg@informationlaw.com
WEB SITE . . . . .www.informationlaw.com
PRACTICE AREAS   Full Service Representation - Arbitration &
                        Mediation - Communications - Contract
                        Negotiation & Drafting - Copyright &
                        Trademark Matters - Corporate Matters -
                        Ecommerce - Employment/Labor Law - First
                        Amendment Issues - Intellectual Property
                        Law - Internet Law - Licensing - Media -
                        Mergers & Acquisitions - Motion Picture &
                        TV Law - Music Law - Partnerships/Joint
                        Ventures - Technology - Transactional Law
REPRESENTS   13th Dream Entertainment - Buttons
                        Productions - Trans Orb Pictures -
                        Eirerobics, LLC - Watersign Creative -
                        Evolution Digital Studios - Utterance

Daniel A. Pepper Esq. . . . . .Founder

PERKINS COIE LLP
1620 26th St., 6th Fl., South Tower
Santa Monica, CA 90404-4013
PHONE 310-788-9900
FAX 310-788-3399
PRACTICE AREAS   Full Service Representation - Arbitration &
                        Mediation - Communications - Copyright &
                        Trademark Matters - Corporate Matters -
                        Ecommerce - Employment/Labor Law -
                        Financing - First Amendment Issues -
                        Intellectual Property Law - Internet Law -
                        Libel & Privacy Matters - Licensing -
                        Litigation - Media - Mergers & Acquisitions
                        - Misappropriation of Name, Voice,
                        Likeness - Music Law - Partnerships/Joint
                        Ventures - Royalty Law - Tax Law -
                        Technology - Telecom - Transactional Law

James D. DeRoche . . . . .Of Counsel
Judith B. Gitterman . . . . .Of Counsel
Paul O. Hirose . . . . .Of Counsel
David T. Biderman . . . . .Partner
Mark E. Birnbaum . . . . .Partner
Charles L. Crouch . . . . .Partner
Katherine M. Dugdale . . . . .Partner
William H. Emer . . . . .Partner
William P. Kannow . . . . .Partner
Donald E. Karl . . . . .Partner
David J. Katz . . . . .Partner
Ronald A. McIntire . . . . .Partner
Glenn E. Monroe . . . . .Partner
Audra M. Mori . . . . .Partner
Kenneth H. Ohriner . . . . .Partner
Steven G. F. Polard . . . . .Partner
Benjamin Soffer . . . . .Partner
Michael J. Wise . . . . .Partner
James J. Zhu . . . . .Partner
Sally Wilson Cano .Regional Director

PERLBERGER LAW OFFICES
515 N. Arden Dr.
Beverly Hills, CA 90210
PHONE 310-859-1511
FAX 310-859-1512
EMAIL . . . . .mpesq@perlberger.com
WEB SITE . . . . .www.perlberger.com
PRACTICE AREAS   Full Service Representation - Arbitration &
                        Mediation - Contract Negotiation &
                        Drafting - Financing - Licensing - Mergers
                        & Acquisitions - Motion Picture & TV Law -
                        Music Law - Partnerships/Joint Ventures -
                        Talent Representation - Transactional Law

Martin Perlberger . . . . .Attorney

PHILLIPS, ERLEWINE & GIVEN LLP
One Embarcadero Center, Ste. 2350
San Francisco, CA 94111
PHONE 415-398-0900
FAX 415-398-0911
WEB SITE . . . . .www.phillaw.com
PRACTICE AREAS   Full Service Representation - Contract
                        Negotiation & Drafting - Copyright &
                        Trademark Matters - Intellectual Property
                        Law - Licensing - Litigation - Royalty Law

David C. Phillips . . . . .Partner (dcp@phillaw.com)
R. Scott Erlewine . . . . .Partner (rse@phillaw.com)
David M. Given . . . . .Partner (dmg@phillaw.com)
Spencer C. Martinez . . . . .Attorney
Nicholas A. Carlin . . . . .Of Counsel
John C. Espedal . . . . .Of Counsel

TOBIAS PIENIEK, PC
515 Madison Ave.
New York, NY 10022
PHONE 212-339-8930
FAX 212-339-8927
EMAIL . . . . .tpieniek@tobylaw.com
PRACTICE AREAS   Full Service Representation - Contract
                        Negotiation & Drafting - Copyright &
                        Trademark Matters - Corporate Matters -
                        Intellectual Property Law - Licensing -
                        Motion Picture & TV Law - Music Law -
                        Partnerships/Joint Ventures - Transactional
                        Law
COMMENTS   Executive employment contracts

Tobias Pieniek . . . . .Attorney
Joan Lieberman . . . . .Attorney

PIERCE LAW GROUP, LLP
9100 Wilshire Blvd., Ste. 225E
Beverly Hills, CA 90212
PHONE 310-274-9191
FAX 310-274-9151
WEB SITE .www.piercelawgroupllp.com
PRACTICE AREAS   Full Service Representation - Contract
                        Negotiation & Drafting - Copyright &
                        Trademark Matters - Corporate Matters -
                        Employment/Labor Law - Financing -
                        Intellectual Property Law - Internet Law -
                        Libel & Privacy Matters - Licensing -
                        Litigation - Misappropriation of Name,
                        Voice, Likeness - Motion Picture & TV Law -
                        Partnerships/Joint Ventures - Right of
                        Publicity - Talent Representation -
                        Transactional Law
REPRESENTS   Primarily independent producers and pro-
                        duction companies; Partial client list:
                        Turman-Morrissey Company - World Race
                        Productions - MovieMaker Magazine -
                        Evan Astrowsky - Jeff Garlin - David
                        Arquette - The Comedy Store - Lionsgate
                        Television - Cartoon Network - Film Roman
                        - Cinamour Entertainment - Bleiberg
                        Entertainment

David Albert Pierce . . . . .Attorney, Motion Pictures/TV/Employment Law/
                                            Intellectual Property/Corporate
Don M. Hardison . . . . . .Attorney, Motion Pictures/TV/Employment Law/
                                            Intellectual Property/Corporate
Giancarlo Spolidoro . . . .Attorney, Motion Pictures/TV/Employment Law/
                                            Intellectual Property
David Himelfarb . . .Of Counsel, Motion Pictures/TV/Intellectual Property
Paul Hazen . . .Film Acquisitions Representative, Client Liasion, Paralegal
Jignasha Patel . . . . .Client Development

PILLSBURY WINTHROP SHAW PITTMAN LLP
50 Fremont St.
San Francisco, CA 94105-2228
PHONE 415-983-1000
FAX 415-983-1200
WEB SITE . . . . .www.pillsburylaw.com
PRACTICE AREAS   Full Service Representation - Arbitration &
                        Mediation - Communications - Contract
                        Negotiation & Drafting - Copyright &
                        Trademark Matters - Corporate Matters -
                        Ecommerce - Employment/Labor Law -
                        Financing - First Amendment Issues -
                        Intellectual Property Law - Internet Law -
                        Libel & Privacy Matters - Licensing -
                        Litigation - Media - Mergers & Acquisitions
                        - Misappropriation of Name, Voice,
                        Likeness - Motion Picture & TV Law - Music
                        Law - Partnerships/Joint Ventures - Right of
                        Publicity - Royalty Law - Sports - Tax Law -
                        Technology - Telecom - Transactional Law
COMMENTS   15 Offices Worldwide

Cydney Tune . . . . .Attorney (cydney.tune@pillsburylaw.com)

LAW OFFICE OF ROBERT G. PIMM
425 Market St., Ste. 2200
San Francisco, CA 94105
PHONE 415-955-2641
FAX 415-651-8817
EMAIL . . . . .bob@rgpimm.com
WEB SITE . . . . .www.rgpimm.com
PRACTICE AREAS   Contract Negotiation & Drafting -
                        Copyright & Trademark Matters -
                        Corporate Matters - Ecommerce - First
                        Amendment Issues - Intellectual Property
                        Law - Internet Law - Libel & Privacy Matters
                        - Licensing - Media - Misappropriation of
                        Name, Voice, Likeness - Motion Picture &
                        TV Law - Partnerships/Joint Ventures - Right
                        of Publicity - Royalty Law
COMMENTS   Literary Law (Book publishing)

Robert G. Pimm . . . . .Attorney

THE POINT MEDIA
10950 W. Washington Blvd., Ste. 240
Culver City, CA 90232
PHONE 310-280-9400
FAX 310-280-9484
EMAIL .hbrook@thepointmedia.com
WEB SITE . . . . .www.thepointmedia.com
PRACTICE AREAS   Full Service Representation - Contract
                        Negotiation & Drafting - Motion Picture &
                        TV Law - Talent Representation
REPRESENTS   Writers - Producers - Directors - Actors -
                        Production Companies

Harold Brook . . . . .Principal
Richard Marks . . . . .Entertainment Attorney
Jake Jacobson . . . . .Entertainment Attorney
Aviva Bergman . . . . .Entertainment Attorney
Nicholas La Terza . . . . .Entertainment Attorney
Elizabeth Zel . . . . .Entertainment Attorney
Michael Zucker . . . . .Entertainment Attorney

LAW OFFICE OF SCOTT D. POLSKY
375 Morris Rd.
Lansdale, PA 19446
PHONE 215-661-0400
FAX 215-661-0315
EMAIL . . . . .spolsky@hrmml.com
WEB SITE . . . . .www.spolskylaw.com
PRACTICE AREAS   Contract Negotiation & Drafting -
                        Corporate Matters - Financing - Mergers &
                        Acquisitions - Motion Picture & TV Law -
                        Music Law - Partnerships/Joint Ventures -
                        Talent Representation - Tax Law -
                        Transactional Law
REPRESENTS   Screenwriters - Film Producers - Film
                        Production Companies - Musicians - Music
                        Production Companies

Scott D. Polsky . . . . .Owner

PORTZ & PORTZ, ATTORNEYS AT LAW

1314 Texas Ave., Ste. 1001
Houston, TX 77002
PHONE 713-223-5299
FAX 713-223-1901
EMAIL . . . . .portznportz@yahoo.com
PRACTICE AREAS   Full Service Representation
COMMENTS   Additional services include Immigration;
                       Production and contract strategies;
                       Negotiations for rights of stories, family;
                       Injuries; Criminal, business, corporation
                       and civil; Also owns Portz Entertainment &
                       Production Co., Inc.

Charles H. Portz . . . . . . .Partner, Entertainment, Criminal & Immigration
Chuck Portz . . . . .Partner, Business, Civil & Corporate
Delia Garcia . . . . .Immigration, Family & Injuries
Craig Pena . . . . .Business, Civil, Criminal & Immigration

LAW OFFICE OF ROBERT PRESKILL

400 S. Beverly Dr., Ste. 214
Beverly Hills, CA 90212
PHONE 310-949-9234/415-377-3919
FAX 310-388-5864
EMAIL . . . . .preskilllaw@hotmail.com
WEB SITE . . . . .www.preskilllaw.com
PRACTICE AREAS   Full Service Representation - Contract
                       Negotiation & Drafting - Copyright &
                       Trademark Matters - Corporate Matters -
                       Employment/Labor Law - Financing -
                       Intellectual Property Law - Licensing -
                       Motion Picture & TV Law - Music Law -
                       Partnerships/Joint Ventures - Talent
                       Representation - Transactional Law
REPRESENTS   Authors - Animators - Start-up Music Labels
                       - Music Artists - Merchandisers - Licensers -
                       Publishers - Filmmakers - Dance Troupes -
                       Theatres - Studio Musicians

Robert Preskill . . . . .Attorney at Law

PROBSTEIN & WEINER

9696 Culver Blvd., Ste. 205
Culver City, CA 90232-2700
PHONE 310-836-1400
FAX 310-836-1420
WEB SITE . . . . .www.probsteinandweiner.com
PRACTICE AREAS   Contract Negotiation & Drafting -
                       Copyright & Trademark Matters - Licensing
                       - Litigation

Jon M. Probstein . . . . .Of Counsel/Attorney
Gerald B. Weiner . . . . .Partner/Attorney

QUINN EMANUEL URQUHART OLIVER & HEDGES, LLP

865 S. Figueroa St., 10th Fl.
Los Angeles, CA 90017
PHONE 213-443-3000/212-849-7000
FAX 213-443-3100/212-849-7100
EMAIL . . . . .johnquinn@quinnemanuel.com
WEB SITE .www.quinnemanuel.com
PRACTICE AREAS   Full Service Representation - Intellectual
                       Property Law - Litigation
COMMENTS   East Coast office: 51 Madison Ave., 22nd
                       Fl., New York, NY 10010; Offices in San
                       Francisco, Silicon Valley, Palm Springs and
                       San Diego

George R. Hedges . . . . .Partner, Entertainment
John B. Quinn . . . . .Partner, Entertainment
Eric J. Emanuel . . . . .Partner
A. William Urquhart . . . . .Partner, Entertainment
Harry A. Olivar Jr. . . . . .Partner
Timothy L. Alger . . . . .Entertainment
Jennifer Jackson Barrett . . . . .Entertainment
Harold A. Barza . . . . .Entertainment
Fred G. Bennett . . . . .Entertainment
Michael B. Carlinsky . . . . .Entertainment
Margret Caruso . . . . .Entertainment
Jeffrey A. Conciatori . . . . .Entertainment
Danielle L. Gilmore . . . . .Entertainment
Duane R. Lyons . . . . .Entertainment
Jeffrey D. McFarland . . . . .Entertainment
Jonathan B. Oblak . . . . .Entertainment
Dale H. Oliver . . . . .Entertainment
William C. Price . . . . .Entertainment
John S. Purcell . . . . .Entertainment
David W. Quinto .Entertainment
Edith Ramirez . . . . .Entertainment
Robert L. Raskopf . . . . .Entertainment
Patrick M. Shields . . . . .Entertainment
Bruce E. Van Dalsem . . . . .Entertainment
Charles Verhoeven . . . . .Entertainment
James J. Webster .Entertainment
Michael E. Williams . . . . .Entertainment
Gerald E. Hawxhurst . . . . .Of Counsel
Keith A. Meyer . . . . .Of Counsel
Sascha N. Rand . . . . .Of Counsel

LAW OFFICE OF ELSA RAMO

315 S. Beverly Dr., Ste. 508
Beverly Hills, CA 90212
PHONE 310-284-3494
FAX 310-861-5246
EMAIL . . . . .info@entertainmentattorney.biz
WEB SITE . . . . .www.entertainmentattorney.biz
PRACTICE AREAS   Contract Negotiation & Drafting -
                       Corporate Matters - Financing - Motion
                       Picture & TV Law - Music Law -
                       Transactional Law
REPRESENTS   Wingman Productions - Taurus
                       Entertainment

Elsa Ramo . . . . .Attorney/Owner
Erika Canchola . . . . .Attorney

RASKIN PETER RUBIN & SIMON

1801 Century Park East, Ste. 2300
Los Angeles, CA 90067
PHONE 310-277-0010
FAX 310-277-1980
EMAIL . . . . .graskin@raskinpeter.com
WEB SITE . . . . .www.raskinpeter.com
PRACTICE AREAS — Full Service Representation - Contract Negotiation & Drafting - Corporate Matters - Employment/Labor Law - Financing - Intellectual Property Law - Litigation - Media - Motion Picture & TV Law - Partnerships/Joint Ventures - Right of Publicity - Talent Representation - Transactional Law
REPRESENTS — Production Companies - New Media Companies - Writers - Executive Producers - Actors - Directors - Motion Picture Financiers
COMMENTS — Instructor, UCLA Entertainment Studies; Moderator and committee member, USC Entertainment Law Institute; Expert witness in television industry

Arnold P. Peter	Partner
Gary S. Raskin	Partner
Barbara M. Rubin	Partner
Jody Simon	Partner
Amy Bersch	Attorney
Tracy Roman	Attorney
Kyle Stewart	Attorney
Philip Dutton	Of Counsel
Renee Skinner	Paralegal/Firm Administrator

REED SMITH, LLP

1901 Avenue of the Stars, Ste. 700
Los Angeles, CA 90067-6078
PHONE 310-734-5200
FAX 310-734-5299
EMAIL . . . . .kpeterson@reedsmith.com
WEB SITE . . . . .www.reedsmith.com
PRACTICE AREAS — Contract Negotiation & Drafting - Copyright & Trademark Matters - Corporate Matters - First Amendment Issues - Intellectual Property Law - Libel & Privacy Matters - Litigation - Motion Picture & TV Law
COMMENTS — Offices in: London, New York, Los Angeles, San Francisco, Washington, DC, Philadelphia, Pittsburgh, Oakland, Princeton, Falls Church, Wilmington, Newark, Coventry (UK), Century City, Richmond, Harrisburg, Leesburg and Westlake Village

Stuart A. Shanus	Managing Partner
Fredric W. Ansis	Partner
Kurt C. Peterson	Partner
Denise M. Howell	Counsel (213-457-8090)
Stephen E. Sessa	Counsel
Christine M. Reilly	Associate
Rick Smith	Associate
Lena Stevens	Assistant to Kurt C. Peterson (310-734-5241)

REUBEN, RAUCHER & BLUM

1100 Glendon Ave., 10th Fl.
Los Angeles, CA 90024
PHONE 310-777-1990
FAX 310-777-1989
EMAIL .bdj@rrbattorneys.com
PRACTICE AREAS — Full Service Representation - Arbitration & Mediation - Copyright & Trademark Matters - Corporate Matters - First Amendment Issues - Intellectual Property Law - Litigation - Misappropriation of Name, Voice, Likeness - Right of Publicity
COMMENTS — Also practices family law

Timothy D. Reuben	Partner
Stephen L. Raucher	Partner
Stephanie Blum	Partner
Gregory P. Barchie	Attorney
Matthew C. Bartek	Attorney
Jami Fosgate	Attorney
Svetlana Kats	Attorney
Andrew Shupe	Attorney

RICHARDS, WATSON & GERSHON

355 S. Grand Ave., 40th Fl.
Los Angeles, CA 90071-3101
PHONE 213-626-8484
FAX 213-626-0078
WEB SITE . . . . .www.rwglaw.com
PRACTICE AREAS — Litigation
COMMENTS — Northern California office: 44 Montgomery St., Ste. 3800, San Francisco, CA 94104-4811, phone: 415-421-8484, fax: 415-421-8486; Orange County office: 1 Civic Center Circle, Brea, CA 92822-1059, phone: 714-990-0901, fax: 714-990-6230

Kayser O. Sume	Attorney, Business Litigation, Entertainment Law

RINTALA, SMOOT, JAENICKE & REES, LLP

10351 Santa Monica Blvd., Ste. 400
Los Angeles, CA 90025-6937
PHONE 310-203-0935
FAX 310-556-8921
EMAIL . . . . .rsjr@rsjr.com
WEB SITE . . . . .www.rsjr.com
PRACTICE AREAS — Copyright & Trademark Matters - Employment/Labor Law - Intellectual Property Law - Libel & Privacy Matters - Litigation - Misappropriation of Name, Voice, Likeness - Right of Publicity - Talent Representation
COMMENTS — Guild arbitrations; Cable TV litigation and franchise compliance

William T. Rintala	Partner
Peter C. Smoot	Partner
J. Larson Jaenicke	Partner
Robert A. Rees	Partner
G. Howden Fraser	Partner
Michael B. Garfinkel	Partner
Melodie K. Larsen	Partner
Anne C. Cruz	Associate
AnnMarie De Vita	Associate

ROBERTS & RITHOLZ LLP
183 Madison Ave., PH
New York, NY 10016
PHONE 212-448-1800
FAX 212-448-0020
WEB SITE .www.robritlaw.com
PRACTICE AREAS   Communications - Contract Negotiation &
                     Drafting - Copyright & Trademark Matters -
                     Corporate Matters - Ecommerce -
                     Employment/Labor Law - Financing -
                     Intellectual Property Law - Internet Law -
                     Licensing - Media - Mergers & Acquisitions
                     - Motion Picture & TV Law - Music Law -
                     Partnerships/Joint Ventures - Right of
                     Publicity - Royalty Law - Talent
                     Representation - Technology - Telecom -
                     Transactional Law

Andrew J. Bergman . . . . .Attorney
Shari R. Fallis . . . . .Attorney
Jeffrey A. Levy . . . . .Attorney
Adam E. Ritholz . . . . .Attorney
Jaimison M. Roberts . . . . .Attorney
Peter D. Rosenthal . . . . .Attorney
Jeff Sanders . . . . .Attorney
Justin Arcangel . . . . .Of Counsel
David M. Ehrlich . . . . .Of Counsel

VICKI ROBERTS, ESQ.
PO Box 642326
Los Angeles, CA 90064
PHONE 310-475-8549
FAX 310-478-6365
EMAIL . . . . .vicki@restmycase.com
WEB SITE .www.restmycase.com
PRACTICE AREAS   Full Service Representation - Contract
                     Negotiation & Drafting - Litigation - Media
                     - Talent Representation
REPRESENTS   Gary Busey - David Carradine - Jermaine
                     Jackson - Sally Kirkland - Michael Madsen
                     - Armand Assante - Michael Nouri - Bo
                     Svenson
COMMENTS   Also on-air legal commentator, consultant,
                     author and technical legal strategist

Vicki Roberts Esq. . . . . .Attorney

LAW OFFICES OF HUGH DUFF ROBERTSON, PC
1125 Gayley Ave.
Los Angeles, CA 90024
PHONE 310-824-0467
FAX 310-824-9690
EMAIL . . . . .hdr@lawhdr.com
PRACTICE AREAS   Contract Negotiation & Drafting - Litigation
                     - Tax Law - Transactional Law

Hugh Duff Robertson . . . . .Partner/Attorney
Vivian M. Lum . . . . .Attorney
Alexandra Cowie . . . . .Paralegal

RODRIGUEZ & RICCI, LLC
82 E. Allendale Rd., Ste. 2B
Saddle River, NJ 07458
PHONE 201-327-1820
FAX 201-327-1824
WEB SITE . . . . .www.rrlaw.biz
PRACTICE AREAS   Full Service Representation - Contract
                     Negotiation & Drafting - Copyright &
                     Trademark Matters - Licensing - Music Law
                     - Partnerships/Joint Ventures - Talent
                     Representation

Judith A. Ricci Esq. . . . . .Attorney
Michael A. Rodriguez Esq. . . . . .Attorney

ROHNER, WALERSTEIN & MILOKNAY
A Law Corporation
11777 San Vicente Blvd., Ste. 747
Los Angeles, CA 90049
PHONE 310-477-5001
FAX 310-826-7227
PRACTICE AREAS   Talent Representation

Franklin B. Rohner . . . . .Partner (Retired)
Donald P. Walerstein . . . . .Partner
Paul M. Miloknay . . . . .Partner
Jela Perry . . . . .Accounts Payable
Samantha Morris . . . . .Assistant
David Phillips . . . . .No Title
Joe Weiner . . . . .No Title

GLENN C. ROMANO, PC
7948 Oxford Ave.
Philadelphia, PA 19111
PHONE 215-742-0592
FAX 215-742-3892
EMAIL . . . . .glenn@glennromano.com
WEB SITE . . . . .www.glennromano.com
PRACTICE AREAS   Full Service Representation - Contract
                     Negotiation & Drafting - Copyright &
                     Trademark Matters - Corporate Matters -
                     Intellectual Property Law
COMMENTS   Business and professional legal risk man-
                     agement; Career counseling

Glenn Romano . . . . .Principal

LAW OFFICE OF HENRY W. ROOT, PC
1541 Ocean Ave., Ste. 200, Paseo del Mar
Santa Monica, CA 90401-2104
PHONE 310-395-6800
FAX 310-393-7777
EMAIL . . . . .henry@grrlaw.com
PRACTICE AREAS   Contract Negotiation & Drafting - Motion
                     Picture & TV Law - Music Law -
                     Partnerships/Joint Ventures - Transactional
                     Law

Henry W. Root . . . . .Attorney
Lynn Quarterman . . . . .Attorney
Derrick K. Lee . . . . .Attorney

ROSEN, FEIG, GOLLAND & LUNN, LLP
9454 Wilshire Blvd., Ste. 850
Beverly Hills, CA 90212
PHONE 310-275-0562
FAX 310-275-0563
EMAIL . . . . .flunn@rfgllaw.com
WEB SITE . . . . .www.rfgllaw.com
PRACTICE AREAS   Full Service Representation - Arbitration &
                     Mediation - Communications - Contract
                     Negotiation & Drafting - Copyright &
                     Trademark Matters - Corporate Matters -
                     Ecommerce - Employment/Labor Law -
                     Financing - Intellectual Property Law -
                     Internet Law - Licensing - Media - Mergers
                     & Acquisitions - Motion Picture & TV Law -
                     Music Law - Partnerships/Joint Ventures -
                     Talent Representation - Technology -
                     Telecom - Transactional Law
REPRESENTS   Writers - Producers - Composers - Actors
COMMENTS   Development, distribution, guilds and
                     unions, merchandising, Internet, publishing,
                     theatre

Adam Rosen . . . . .Partner (arosen@rfgllaw.com)
Eric Feig . . . . .Partner (efeig@rfgllaw.com)
Michael H. Golland . . . . .Parnter (mgolland@rfgllaw.com)
Frank M. Lunn . . . . .Partner (flunn@rfgllaw.com)
Sarah Conley . . . . .Of Counsel (sconley@rfgllaw.com)

ENTERTAINMENT ATTORNEYS

ROSENFELD, MEYER & SUSMAN, LLP
9601 Wilshire Blvd., Ste. 710
Beverly Hills, CA 90210
PHONE 310-858-7700
FAX 310-860-2430
EMAIL . . . . .rms@rmslaw.com
WEB SITE . . . . .www.rmslaw.com

PRACTICE AREAS	Intellectual Property Law - Licensing - Litigation - Music Law
REPRESENTS	Individual Talent - Independent Production/Distribution Companies - Music
COMMENTS	Literary material clearance; Completion guarantees

Todd W. Bonder . . . . .Partner
Lawrence Kartiganer . . . . .Partner
Burt Levitch . . . . .Partner
Jeffrey L. Nagin . . . . .Partner
Marvin B. Meyer .Of Counsel
Ron Dolecki . . . . .Sr. Counsel
W. Nathan Canby . . . . .Attorney
Renee A. Farrell . . . . .Attorney
Eric M. Greenfeld . . . . .Attorney

LAW OFFICE OF RICHARD M. ROSENTHAL, ESQ.
2940 Westwood Blvd., 2nd Fl.
Los Angeles, CA 90064
PHONE 310-474-3044
FAX 310-470-0532
EMAIL . . . . .rosenthalr@aol.com

PRACTICE AREAS	Contract Negotiation & Drafting - Intellectual Property Law - Litigation - Motion Picture & TV Law - Partnerships/Joint Ventures - Talent Representation - Transactional Law
COMMENTS	Motion picture production & distribution

Richard M. Rosenthal .Principal

ROSMAN & GERMAIN, LLP
815 Moraga Dr.
Los Angeles, CA 90049-1633
PHONE 310-440-8600
FAX 310-440-8615

PRACTICE AREAS	Full Service Representation - Intellectual Property Law

David M. Rosman . . . . .Partner
Daniel L. Germain . . . . .Partner

ROTHKEN LAW FIRM
3 Hamilton Landing, Ste. 280
San Rafael, CA 94949
PHONE 415-924-4250
EMAIL . . . . .feedback@techfirm.com
WEB SITE . . . . .www.techfirm.com

PRACTICE AREAS	Copyright & Trademark Matters - Employment/Labor Law - Intellectual Property Law - Litigation

Ira P. Rothken Esq. . . . . .Attorney

J S RUDSENSKE, PLLC
631 Woodland St.
Nashville, TN 37206
PHONE 615-244-9501
WEB SITE . . . . .www.jsrlaw.net

PRACTICE AREAS	Contract Negotiation & Drafting - Copyright & Trademark Matters - Music Law - Partnerships/Joint Ventures

J. Scott Rudenske . . . . .Attorney

SACHSE, WILLIAMS, & FALKIN, PLLC
4101 Medical Pkwy.
Heritage Park Plaza, Ste. 203
Austin, TX 78756-3734
PHONE 512-560-4950
FAX 512-532-6063
EMAIL . . . . .mark@trademarkfalkin.com
WEB SITE . . . . .www.sachsewilliams.com
SECOND WEB SITE . . . . .www.trademarkfalkin.com

Mark Falkin . . . . .Attorney
Deck Sachse . . . . .Attorney
Creede Williams . . . . .Attorney

SALTZBURG, RAY & BERGMAN, LLP
12121 Wilshire Blvd., Ste. 600
Los Angeles, CA 90025
PHONE 310-481-6700
FAX 310-481-6720
EMAIL . . . . .hls@srblaw.com
WEB SITE . . . . .www.srblaw.com

PRACTICE AREAS	Full Service Representation - Litigation - Transactional Law
COMMENTS	Bankruptcy and receivership

Henley L. Saltzburg . . . . .Partner
David L. Ray . . . . .Partner

SAUER & WAGNER, LLP
1801 Century Park East, Ste. 1150
Los Angeles, CA 90067
PHONE 310-712-8100
FAX 310-712-8108
EMAIL . . . . .sauwag@swattys.com
WEB SITE . . . . .www.swattys.com

PRACTICE AREAS	Arbitration & Mediation - Contract Negotiation & Drafting - Copyright & Trademark Matters - Employment/Labor Law - First Amendment Issues - Intellectual Property Law - Libel & Privacy Matters - Litigation - Right of Publicity
COMMENTS	Profit participation disputes

Gerald L. Sauer . . . . .Partner
Eve H. Wagner . . . . .Partner
Vina Chin . . . . .Attorney
Laurie B. Hiller . . . . .Attorney

SAYEGH & PHAM, PLC
5895 Washington Blvd.
Culver City, CA 90232
PHONE 310-895-1188
FAX 310-895-1180
EMAIL . . . . .srabin@spattorney.com
WEB SITE .www.spattorney.com
PRACTICE AREAS   Full Service Representation - Contract Negotiation & Drafting - Copyright & Trademark Matters - Corporate Matters - Employment/Labor Law - Intellectual Property Law - Licensing - Litigation - Misappropriation of Name, Voice, Likeness - Motion Picture & TV Law - Music Law - Partnerships/Joint Ventures - Right of Publicity - Talent Representation - Transactional Law
REPRESENTS   Film and music production companies, film talent and directors, music publishers, composers, recording artists, screenwriters, broadcasters, talent agencies, digital streaming and subscription services, literary authors and visual artists

F. Freddy Sayegh . . . . .Partner
Christopher Q. Pham .Partner
Susan Rabin . . . . .Of Counsel
Miguel Del Rosario . . . . .Associate
Hani Naser . . . . .Certified Mediator
Negin Saberi . . . . .Attorney
Katherine Smith . . . . .Paralegal/Notary

LAW OFFICES OF SAYSON & ASSOCIATES
3415 S. Sepulveda Blvd., Ste. 370
Los Angeles, CA 90034-6014
PHONE 310-397-2868
FAX 310-390-4533
EMAIL . . . . .jsayson@saysonlaw.com
SECOND EMAIL . . . . .info@saysonlaw.com
WEB SITE .www.saysonlaw.com
PRACTICE AREAS   Full Service Representation - Contract Negotiation & Drafting - Copyright & Trademark Matters - Ecommerce - Intellectual Property Law - Internet Law - Licensing - Litigation - Motion Picture & TV Law - Music Law - Partnerships/Joint Ventures - Talent Representation
REPRESENTS   Screenwriters - Directors - Authors - Filmmakers - Producers - Animators - Programmers - Video Game Developers
COMMENTS   Boutique law firm dedicated to serving artists, professionals, entrepreneurs, independent production companies and small-to-medium-sized businesses; Interactive video game production; Copyright infringement and associated litigation services for plaintiffs and defendants; Video game law

Joey Arnel Sayson . . . . .Attorney

SUSAN G. SCHAEFER
10940 Bellagio Rd., Ste. A
Los Angeles, CA 90077
PHONE 310-476-6543
PRACTICE AREAS   Full Service Representation - Contract Negotiation & Drafting - Corporate Matters - Mergers & Acquisitions - Motion Picture & TV Law - Partnerships/Joint Ventures - Talent Representation - Transactional Law
REPRESENTS   Production Companies - Management Companies - Distributors - Talent Agencies - Executives - Actors - Writers - Directors - Producers
COMMENTS   Production legal work

Susan G. Schaefer . . . . .Attorney
Doug Budin . . . . .Assistant
Bayne Gibby . . . . .Assistant

STEVEN C. SCHECHTER
39-26 Broadway
Fair Lawn, NJ 07410
PHONE 201-794-6660
FAX 201-880-9819
EMAIL . . . . .schechter@medialawyer.tv
WEB SITE .www.medialawyer.tv
PRACTICE AREAS   Full Service Representation - Arbitration & Mediation - Contract Negotiation & Drafting - Copyright & Trademark Matters - Corporate Matters - First Amendment Issues - Intellectual Property Law - Libel & Privacy Matters - Licensing - Litigation - Misappropriation of Name, Voice, Likeness - Motion Picture & TV Law - Partnerships/Joint Ventures - Right of Publicity - Talent Representation - Transactional Law
COMMENTS   Financing and distribution

Steven C. Schechter . . . . .Attorney

SCHLEIMER & FREUNDLICH, LLP
9100 Wilshire Blvd., Ste. 615E
Beverly Hills, CA 90212
PHONE 310-273-9807
FAX 310-273-9809
WEB SITE .www.schleimerlaw.com
PRACTICE AREAS   Copyright & Trademark Matters - Intellectual Property Law - Litigation - Right of Publicity - Royalty Law
COMMENTS   Profit participation; Artist/manager disputes; Guild and talent agency arbitrations

Joseph D. Schleimer . . . . .Partner
Kenneth D. Freundlich .Partner

SCHRECK ROSE DAPELLO & ADAMS
1790 Broadway, Ste. 20
New York, NY 10019-1412
PHONE 212-832-1977
FAX 212-832-2969
PRACTICE AREAS   Motion Picture & TV Law

Joseph J. Dapello . . . . .Partner
Nancy A. Rose . . . . .Partner
Ira Schreck . . . . .Partner
James Adams . . . . .Partner
David Berlin Esq. . . . . .Attorney
Isaac Dunham Esq. .Attorney
Jennifer Begg . . . . .Assistant to Nancy A. Rose
Marie Durkan . . . . .Assistant to Joseph J. Dapello

ENTERTAINMENT ATTORNEYS

JEREMY G. SCHUSTER
3594 Armourdale Ave.
Long Beach, CA 90808
PHONE 562-596-5900
FAX 562-431-4540
WEB SITE .www.flightlaw.com
PRACTICE AREAS   Full Service Representation - Contract
Negotiation & Drafting - Copyright &
Trademark Matters - Corporate Matters -
Intellectual Property Law - Licensing -
Litigation - Mergers & Acquisitions -
Misappropriation of Name, Voice, Likeness
- Motion Picture & TV Law -
Partnerships/Joint Ventures - Right of
Publicity - Talent Representation -
Transactional Law
COMMENTS   Production counseling

Jeremy Schuster . . . . .Sr. Attorney, Entertainment & Litigation

SEDGWICK, DETERT, MORAN & ARNOLD LLP
801 S. Figueroa St., 18th Fl.
Los Angeles, CA 90017
PHONE 213-426-6900/212-422-0202
FAX 213-426-6921/212-422-0925
EMAIL . . . . .firstname.lastname@sdma.com
WEB SITE . . . . .www.sdma.com
PRACTICE AREAS   Full Service Representation - Arbitration &
Mediation - Contract Negotiation &
Drafting - Copyright & Trademark Matters -
Corporate Matters - Employment/Labor
Law - Financing - First Amendment Issues -
Intellectual Property Law - Libel & Privacy
Matters - Licensing - Litigation -
Misappropriation of Name, Voice, Likeness
- Motion Picture & TV Law - Music Law -
Right of Publicity - Royalty Law - Talent
Representation - Transactional Law
COMMENTS   East Coast office: 125 Broad St., 39th Fl.,
New York, NY 10004-2400

Craig S. Barnes . . . . .Partner, Entertainment
Robert F. Helfing . . . . .Partner, Entertainment
James J.S. Homes . . . . .Partner, Media/Entertainment
David A. Schnider . . . . .Partner, Intellectual Property/Entertainment
John F. Stephens . . . . .Partner, Media/Entertainment
Alan C. Chen . . . . .Associate, Media/Entertainment
Aaron Rudin . . . . .Associate, Media/Entertainment
Thomas H. Vidal . . . . .Associate, Entertainment Litigation

SEDLMAYR & ASSOCIATES, PC
200 Park Avenue South, Ste. 1408
New York, NY 10003
PHONE 212-925-3456
FAX 212-925-0554
PRACTICE AREAS   Music Law

Theo Sedlmayr . . . . .Partner
Christine Calip Esq. . . . . .Attorney
Adeline B. Ferretti Esq. .Attorney
Alina Moffat Esq. . . . . .Attorney

SELVERNE, MANDELBAUM & MINTZ, LLP
1775 Broadway, Ste. 2300
New York, NY 10019
PHONE 212-259-3900
FAX 212-259-3910
PRACTICE AREAS   Copyright & Trademark Matters -
Intellectual Property Law - Music Law

Michael Selverne . . . . .Partner
Thomas I. Mandelbaum . . . . .Partner
Alan M. Mintz .Partner (Retired)
Whitney C. Broussard . . . . .Attorney
David D. Gold . . . . .Attorney
Kristin L. Daily . . . . .Associate
Stephanie R. Morris . . . . .Associate
Monika A. Tashman . . . . .Associate
Roger L. Cramer . . . . .Of Counsel

SENDROFF & BARUCH, LLP
1500 Broadway, Ste. 2001
New York, NY 10036
PHONE 212-840-6400
FAX 212-840-6401
EMAIL . . . . .msendroff@sendroffbaruch.com
WEB SITE . . . . .www.sendroffbaruch.com
PRACTICE AREAS   Contract Negotiation & Drafting -
Copyright & Trademark Matters -
Intellectual Property Law - Motion Picture &
TV Law - Music Law - Talent Representation

Mark D. Sendroff . . . . .Partner
Jason P. Baruch . . . . .Partner
Eric Goldman . . . . .Associate

SERLING ROOKS & FERRARA, LLP
119 Fifth Ave., 3rd Fl.
New York, NY 10003
PHONE 212-245-7300
FAX 212-586-5175
PRACTICE AREAS   Full Service Representation - Copyright &
Trademark Matters - Intellectual Property
Law - Music Law

Joseph Lloyd Serling .Sr. Partner
Wayne D. Rooks . . . . .Partner
Nicholas C. Ferrara . . . . .Partner
Michael L. McKoy . . . . .Partner
J. Reid Hunter . . . . .Partner
Jeffrey A. Worob . . . . .Partner
Greg W. Brooks . . . . .Associate
Ashley Collier . . . . .Associate
Nicole L. Giacco . . . . .Associate
Wallace Collins . . . . .Of Counsel
Barry Platnick . . . . .Of Counsel
Theodore D. Weis . . . . .Of Counsel

LAW OFFICE OF DEAN SHELDON SERWIN
1680 N. Vine St., Ste. 1115
Hollywood, CA 90028
PHONE 323-465-1735
FAX 323-465-1763
EMAIL . . . . .mail@deanserwin.com
WEB SITE . . . . .www.deanserwin.com
PRACTICE AREAS   Full Service Representation
COMMENTS   Additional services include music clear-
ance, Internet and video-on-demand law

Dean Sheldon Serwin . . . . .Owner
Dayna Crosby .Executive Assistant

LISA A. SHAPIRO, ESQ.
16662 Oldham Pl.
Encino, CA 91436
PHONE 818-817-0066
FAX 818-995-6200
EMAIL . . . . .lisashapiroesq@earthlink.net
PRACTICE AREAS   Full Service Representation - Contract Negotiation & Drafting - Motion Picture & TV Law - Music Law - Talent Representation - Transactional Law
REPRESENTS   Writers - Directors - Producers; Client list: Broken Sky Films - Apex Entertainment - Gold Circle Films - Evolution Entertainment - XTeam Productions - Niki Marvin Productions
COMMENTS   Full-service business affairs for small entertainment companies without in-house legal staff

Lisa Shapiro . . . . .Attorney

SHEARMAN & STERLING LLP
599 Lexington Ave.
New York, NY 10022
PHONE 212-848-4000
FAX 212-848-7179
EMAIL .rick.carpenter@shearman.com
WEB SITE . . . . .www.shearman.com
PRACTICE AREAS   Financing - Media - Mergers & Acquisitions - Partnerships/Joint Ventures

John J. Madden . . . . .Managing Partner
Rohan S. Weerasinghe . . . . .Sr. Partner

SHEPPARD MULLIN RICHTER & HAMPTON LLP
1901 Avenue of the Stars, Ste. 1600
Los Angeles, CA 90067
PHONE 310-228-3700/213-620-1780
FAX .310-228-3701/213-620-1398
WEB SITE . . . . .www.sheppardmullin.com
PRACTICE AREAS   Full Service Representation - Arbitration & Mediation - Communications - Contract Negotiation & Drafting - Copyright & Trademark Matters - Corporate Matters - Employment/Labor Law - Financing - First Amendment Issues - Intellectual Property Law - Internet Law - Libel & Privacy Matters - Licensing - Litigation - Media - Mergers & Acquisitions - Misappropriation of Name, Voice, Likeness - Motion Picture & TV Law - Music Law - Partnerships/Joint Ventures - Right of Publicity - Royalty Law - Sports - Tax Law - Technology - Transactional Law
COMMENTS   Main office: 333 S. Hope St., 48th Fl., Los Angeles, CA 90071; Additional law services include: Advertising & Branded Entertainment - Convergence & Online Technology Transactions - Strategic Alliances - Rights Acquisition

Robert A. Darwell   .Co-Chair, Entertainment, Media & Communications
Martin D. Katz . . . . .Co-Chair, Entertainment, Media & Communications
James M. Burgess . . . . .Partner
Craig Cardon . . . . .Partner
James M. Chadwick . . . . .Partner (San Francisco)
Shaun C. Clark . . . . .Partner
Guylyn Cummins . . . . .Partner (San Diego) (619-338-6645)
W. Kenneth Ferree . . . . . . .Partner (Washington, DC) (202-218-0008)
David Garcia . . . . .Partner
Robert S. Gerber . . . . .Partner (San Diego) (858-720-8907)

(Continued)

SHEPPARD MULLIN RICHTER & HAMPTON LLP (Continued)
Kevin W. Goering . . . . .Partner (New York) (212-332-3800)
Edwin Komen . . . . .Partner (Washington, DC) (202-772-5328)
Thomas Glen Leo . . . . .Partner
Linda Giunta Michaelson . . . . .Partner
Benjamin R. Mulcahy . . . . .Partner (New York) (212-332-3800)
Brian Pass . . . . .Partner
Fred R. Puglisi . . . . .Partner
Kent R. Raygor . . . . .Partner
D. Matthew Richardson . . . . .Partner
David H. Sands . . . . .Partner
Neil A. Smith . . . . .Partner (San Francisco) (415-434-9100)
Carlo F. Van den Bosch . . . . .Partner (Costa Mesa) (714-424-8215)
Louis M. Meisinger . . . . .Sr. Advisor
Richard E. Troop . . . . .Sr. Advisor
Robert J. Wynne . . . . .Sr. Advisor
Dina Appleton . . . . .Special Counsel
Kevin Straw . . . . .Sr. Associate
R. Anthony Young . . . . .Sr. Associate
Jamie Afifi . . . . .Associate
Valerie Alter . . . . .Associate
Erica Alterwitz . . . . .Associate
Brian Anderson . . . . .Associate (San Francisco) (415-434-9100)
Iddo Arad . . . . .Associate (New York) (212-332-3800)
Janene P. Bassett . . . . .Associate
Matthew W. Clanton . . . . .Associate (Washington, DC) (202-772-5312)
Richard De Lossa . . . . .Associate
Stacy Dollarhide . . . . .Associate
Erin L. Dozier . . . . .Associate (Washington, DC) (202-772-5312)
Alexis Garcia . . . . .Associate
Jonathan S. Golfman . . . . .Associate
Susan M. Hwang . . . . .Associate
Chad Levy . . . . .Associate
Scott R. Lindley . . . . .Associate
Lara Mackey . . . . .Associate
Jesse Rosenblatt . . . . .Associate
Kesari Ruzá . . . . .Associate (NY)
Demery Elizabeth Ryan . . . . .Associate
Gregory L. Slewett . . . . .Associate
Kevin Straw . . . . .Associate
Lisa N. Stutz . . . . .Associate
Christopher Tygh . . . . . . .Associate (Washington, DC) (202-218-6876)
Jade Zike . . . . .Associate

SHERMAN & NATHANSON
9454 Wilshire Blvd., Ste. 820
Beverly Hills, CA 90212
PHONE 310-246-0321
FAX 310-246-0305
EMAIL . . . . .rsherman@snmlaw.com
WEB SITE . . . . .www.snmlaw.com
PRACTICE AREAS   Arbitration & Mediation - Contract Negotiation & Drafting - Copyright & Trademark Matters - Corporate Matters - Employment/Labor Law - Intellectual Property Law - Libel & Privacy Matters - Litigation - Misappropriation of Name, Voice, Likeness - Motion Picture & TV Law - Music Law - Partnerships/Joint Ventures - Right of Publicity - Royalty Law - Talent Representation - Transactional Law

Richard Sherman . . . . .Managing Partner
Ken Nathanson . . . . .Partner
Cameron Totten . . . . .Associate

SHUKAT ARROW HAFER WEBER & HERBSMAN, LLP
111 W. 57th St., Ste. 1120
New York, NY 10019
PHONE 212-245-4580
FAX 212-956-6471
EMAIL . . . . .info@musiclaw.com
SECOND EMAIL . . . . .firstname@musiclaw.com
WEB SITE . . . . .www.musiclaw.com
PRACTICE AREAS   Full Service Representation - Contract
                     Negotiation & Drafting - Copyright &
                     Trademark Matters - Intellectual Property
                     Law - Licensing - Litigation -
                     Misappropriation of Name, Voice, Likeness
                     - Music Law - Right of Publicity - Royalty
                     Law - Talent Representation
COMMENTS   Business acquisitions and sales;
                     Employment contracts

Peter S. Shukat . . . . .Partner
Allen H. Arrow . . . . .Partner
J. Jeffrey Hafer . . . . .Partner
Dorothy M. Weber . . . . .Partner
Jonas E. Herbsman . . . . .Partner
Jason A. Finestone . . . . .Associate
Kyle D.N. Fogden . . . . .Associate
Jeanine Denzer . . . . .Assistant to Messrs. Herbsman & Fogden
Jennifer Feldman . . . . .Assistant to Mr. Shukat
Delia Green . . . . .Assistant to Ms. Weber
Natalie Hutchinson . . . . .Assistant to Mr. Arrow
Carol Lopez . . . . .Assistant to Messrs. Hafer & Finestone
Nicole Van Manen . . . . .Assistant to Mr. Shukat
Marc Deaton . . . . .Office Manager

SKRZYNIARZ & MALLEAN
9601 Wilshire Blvd., Ste. 650
Beverly Hills, CA 90210
PHONE 310-786-8876
FAX 310-786-8878
PRACTICE AREAS   Contract Negotiation & Drafting -
                     Copyright & Trademark Matters - Financing
                     - First Amendment Issues - Intellectual
                     Property Law - Libel & Privacy Matters -
                     Licensing - Misappropriation of Name,
                     Voice, Likeness - Motion Picture & TV Law -
                     Music Law - Partnerships/Joint Ventures -
                     Talent Representation
COMMENTS   Entertainment business matters

William J. Skrzyniarz .Owner, Entertainment
Tanya M. Mallean .Attorney, Entertainment

SLOANE OFFER WEBER & DERN LLP
9601 Wilshire Blvd., Ste. 500
Beverly Hills, CA 90210
PHONE 310-248-5100
FAX 310-205-9805
PRACTICE AREAS   Full Service Representation - Contract
                     Negotiation & Drafting - Talent
                     Representation

Jason Sloane . . . . .Partner
Robert Offer . . . . .Partner
David Weber . . . . .Partner
Warren Dern . . . . .Partner
Alicia De Rossett . . . . .Assistant to Robert Offer
Jaime Marchello . . . . .Assistant to David Weber
Lauren Rodriguez . . . . .Assistant to Jason Sloane
Randa Tabet . . . . .Assistant to Warren Dern

SLOSS LAW OFFICE
555 W. 25th St., 4th Fl.
New York, NY 10001
PHONE 212-627-9898
FAX 212-627-9498
EMAIL . . . . .office@slosslaw.com
WEB SITE . . . . .www.slosslaw.com
PRACTICE AREAS   Contract Negotiation & Drafting - Motion
                     Picture & TV Law - Talent Representation

John Sloss . . . . .Attorney
Paul Brennan . . . . .Attorney
Jacqueline Eckhouse . . . . .Attorney
Daniel Steinman . . . . .Attorney
Ayla Ercin . . . . .Associate
Alison Hunter . . . . .Associate
Kimberly Jaime . . . . .Associate

LAW OFFICES OF DONALD V. SMILEY
6080 Center Dr., Ste. 600
Los Angeles, CA 90045
PHONE 310-242-6754
FAX 310-915-9993
EMAIL .d.smiley@dvsmileylaw.com
PRACTICE AREAS   Full Service Representation - Arbitration &
                     Mediation - Contract Negotiation &
                     Drafting - Corporate Matters - Financing -
                     Litigation - Motion Picture & TV Law -
                     Partnerships/Joint Ventures - Talent
                     Representation - Transactional Law
REPRESENTS   Filmmakers - Talent - Producers -
                     Production Companies - Writers -
                     Management Companies - Distributors

Donald V. Smiley . . . . .Principal

SMITHAMUNDSEN, LLC
150 N. Michigan Ave., Ste. 3300
Chicago, IL 60601
PHONE . . . . .See Below
WEB SITE . . . . .www.salawus.com

Brian Rosenblatt . . . . .Partner/Co-Chair, Entertainment, Media & Privacy
                     Practice Group (312-894-3358, brosenblatt@salawus.com)
Ryan Jacobson . . . . . .Partner/Co-Chair, Entertainment, Media & Privacy
                     Practice Group (312-894-3252, rjacobson@salawus.com)
Larry Schechtman . . . . .Managing Partner (312-894-3253,
                     lschechtman@salawus.com)

SPEAK SOFTLY LEGAL MANAGEMENT
13540 Ventura Blvd.
Sherman Oaks, CA 91423
PHONE 818-986-8433
FAX 818-986-8435
EMAIL . . . . .blaine@sslm.com
WEB SITE . . . . .www.sslm.com
PRACTICE AREAS   Contract Negotiation & Drafting -
                     Employment/Labor Law - First Amendment
                     Issues - Intellectual Property Law - Internet
                     Law - Libel & Privacy Matters - Litigation -
                     Misappropriation of Name, Voice, Likeness
                     - Motion Picture & TV Law - Music Law -
                     Partnerships/Joint Ventures - Right of
                     Publicity - Talent Representation

Blaine Greenberg Esq. . . . . .President/General Counsel

THE SPENCE LAW FIRM
10 S. Fifth St., Ste. 700
Minneapolis, MN 55402
PHONE 612-375-1555
FAX 612-375-1511
WEB SITE . . . . .www.spencelawfirm.com
PRACTICE AREAS   Full Service Representation - Arbitration &
    Mediation - Contract Negotiation &
    Drafting - Copyright & Trademark Matters -
    Corporate Matters - Ecommerce -
    Employment/Labor Law - Intellectual
    Property Law - Internet Law - Libel & Privacy
    Matters - Licensing - Litigation - Media -
    Misappropriation of Name, Voice, Likeness
    - Motion Picture & TV Law - Music Law -
    Partnerships/Joint Ventures - Right of
    Publicity - Royalty Law - Talent
    Representation - Technology

Mick Spence . . . . .Attorney
Genhi Bailey . . . . .Attorney
Mary Beeman . . . . .Office Manager
Max Felsheim . . . . .Law Clerk

THE LAW OFFICE OF MAIA T. SPILMAN, LLC
535 W. 34th St., Ste. 602
New York, NY 10001
PHONE 212-678-2400
FAX 212-678-0666
EMAIL . . . . .law@maianyc.com
WEB SITE . . . . .www.maianyc.com
PRACTICE AREAS   Contract Negotiation & Drafting -
    Copyright & Trademark Matters -
    Intellectual Property Law - Licensing - Music
    Law - Transactional Law

Maia Spilman . . . . .Principal

LAW OFFICES OF MAX J. SPRECHER
5850 Canoga Ave., 4th Fl.
Woodland Hills, CA 91367
PHONE 818-996-2255
FAX 818-996-4204
EMAIL .max@sprecherlaw.com
WEB SITE .www.sprecherlaw.com
PRACTICE AREAS   Copyright & Trademark Matters -
    Intellectual Property Law - Litigation -
    Misappropriation of Name, Voice, Likeness
    - Motion Picture & TV Law - Right of
    Publicity

Max J. Sprecher . . . . .Attorney

STANKEVICH-GOCHMAN, LLP
9777 Wilshire Blvd., Ste. 550
Beverly Hills, CA 90212
PHONE 310-859-8822
PRACTICE AREAS   Full Service Representation - Talent
    Representation - Transactional Law
REPRESENTS   Actors - Writers - Directors - Media
    Companies
COMMENTS   Specialized transactional entertainment law
    firm

Mark A. Stankevich . . . . .Partner
Mark A. Gochman . . . . .Partner

STECKBAUER WEINHART JAFFE, LLP
333 S. Hope St., 36th Fl.
Los Angeles, CA 90071
PHONE 213-229-2868
FAX 213-229-2870/213-217-5490
WEB SITE . . . . .www.swjlaw.com
PRACTICE AREAS   Contract Negotiation & Drafting - Litigation
COMMENTS   East Coast office: 41 Madison Ave, 41st
    Fl., New York, NY 10010

William W. Steckbauer . . . . .Partner
Brian S. Weinhart . . . . .Partner
Robert D. Jaffe . . . . .Partner
Dawn M. Coulson . . . . .Partner
Trudi J. Lesser . . . . .Partner
Christopher Dargan . . . . .Sr. Counsel
Salvador Lavina .Sr. Counsel
Joel T. Glassman . . . . .Of Counsel
Dan Goodkin . . . . .Of Counsel
Jason J. Amoroso . . . . .Associate
Pablo Deleon . . . . .Associate
Susan M. Freedman . . . . .Associate
Robert Jenkins . . . . .Associate
Ada Katz . . . . .Associate

LAW OFFICE OF MIRIAM STERN
303 E. 83rd St.
New York, NY 10028
PHONE 212-794-1289
PRACTICE AREAS   Arbitration & Mediation - Contract
    Negotiation & Drafting - Copyright &
    Trademark Matters - Intellectual Property
    Law - Licensing - Motion Picture & TV Law -
    Music Law - Partnerships/Joint Ventures -
    Talent Representation - Transactional Law

Miriam Stern . . . . .Attorney

STONE, MEYER, GENOW, SMELKINSON & BINDER LLP
9665 Wilshire Blvd., Ste. 500
Beverly Hills, CA 90212
PHONE 310-385-9300
FAX 310-385-9333
PRACTICE AREAS   Contract Negotiation & Drafting - Motion
    Picture & TV Law - Talent Representation -
    Transactional Law

Douglas R. Stone . . . . .Partner
Neil Meyer . . . . .Partner
Rick Genow . . . . .Partner
Allison Binder . . . . .Partner
Mitch Smelkinson . . . . .Partner
Chad Christopher . . . . .Associate
Erin McPherson . . . . .Associate
Matthew Rosen . . . . .Associate
Thom Zadra . . . . .Associate
Evelyn Cheatham . . . . .Assistant to Neil Meyer
Clif Clehouse . . . . .Assistant to Chad Christopher
DeAnn Dawson . . . . .Assistant to Douglas R. Stone
Taniesha Johnson . . . . .Assistant to Mitch Smelkinson
Scott Palmason . . . . .Assistant to Allison Binder
Jordan Rojas . . . . .Assistant to Matthew Rosen
Stefanie Vann . . . . .Assistant to Rick Genow

ENTERTAINMENT ATTORNEYS

STROOCK & STROOCK & LAVAN LLP
2029 Century Park East, Ste. 1600
Los Angeles, CA 90067-3086
PHONE 310-556-5800
FAX 310-556-5959
WEB SITE . . . . .www.stroock.com
PRACTICE AREAS   Full Service Representation
COMMENTS   New York office: 180 Maiden Ln., New
                     York, NY 10038-4982, phone: 212-806-
                     5400; Miami office: 200 South Biscayne
                     Blvd., Miami, FL 33131-2385, phone:
                     305-358-9900

Barry B. Langberg . . . . .Partner
Schuyler M. Moore . . . . .Partner
Lawrence Rosenthal . . . . .Partner
Daniel A. Rozansky . . . . .Partner
Matthew C. Thompson . . . . .Partner
Deborah Drooz . . . . .Special Counsel
Mari Anzai . . . . .Associate
Eric F. Harbert . . . . .Associate
Matthew D. Moran . . . . .Associate
Michael J. Niborski . . . . .Associate
Meg E. Smith . . . . .Associate

THE STROTE LAW GROUP
4024 E. Skelton Canyon
Westlake Village, CA 91362
PHONE 818-707-1923/818-259-2939
FAX 805-707-8884/805-494-4809
EMAIL . . . . .jstrote@verizon.net
PRACTICE AREAS   Full Service Representation
COMMENTS   Music industry contract negotiation

Joel R. Strote . . . . .Principal

STUMPF CRADDOCK MASSEY FARRIMOND
1400 Post Oak Blvd., 4th Fl.
Houston, TX 77056
PHONE 713-871-0919
FAX 713-871-0408
EMAIL . . . . .hfasthoff@scmfpc.com
WEB SITE . . . . .www.scmfpc.com
PRACTICE AREAS   Copyright & Trademark Matters -
                     Corporate Matters - Ecommerce -
                     Employment/Labor Law - First Amendment
                     Issues - Intellectual Property Law - Internet
                     Law - Libel & Privacy Matters - Litigation -
                     Media - Mergers & Acquisitions -
                     Misappropriation of Name, Voice, Likeness
                     - Music Law - Partnerships/Joint Ventures -
                     Right of Publicity - Royalty Law - Tax Law -
                     Technology
REPRESENTS   Beyoncé - Destiny's Child - Music World
                     Entertainment - Chamillionaire - Rap-A-Lot
                     Records - Los Lonley Boys - Sony BMG
                     Music Entertainment

Henry J. Fasthoff IV . . . . .Attorney
C. Mark Murrah . . . . .Attorney

LAW OFFICE OF PAUL D. SUPNIK
9601 Wilshire Blvd., Ste. 828
Beverly Hills, CA 90210-5210
PHONE 310-859-0100
FAX 310-388-5645
EMAIL . . . . .info@supnik.com
WEB SITE . . . . .www.supnik.com
PRACTICE AREAS   Arbitration & Mediation - Contract
                     Negotiation & Drafting - Copyright &
                     Trademark Matters - Employment/Labor
                     Law - First Amendment Issues - Intellectual
                     Property Law - Libel & Privacy Matters -
                     Licensing - Litigation - Misappropriation of
                     Name, Voice, Likeness - Motion Picture &
                     TV Law - Right of Publicity - Royalty Law -
                     Transactional Law
REPRESENTS   Actors - Producers - Writers - Directors

Paul D. Supnik . . . . .Attorney

SURPIN, MAYERSOHN & EDELSTONE, LLP
1880 Century Park East, Ste. 618
Los Angeles, CA 90067-1606
PHONE 310-552-1808
FAX 310-553-6286
PRACTICE AREAS   Full Service Representation - Contract
                     Negotiation & Drafting - Copyright &
                     Trademark Matters - Corporate Matters -
                     Financing - Intellectual Property Law -
                     Motion Picture & TV Law -
                     Partnerships/Joint Ventures - Talent
                     Representation - Tax Law
COMMENTS   Specializes in film and TV

Shelley Surpin . . . . .Partner
Gary Edelstone . . . . .Partner
Paul Mayersohn . . . . .Partner
Katherine Shaw . . . . .Associate
Susan Andrews . . . . .Paralegal to Gary Edelstone
Kelly Billings . . . . .Assistant to Paul Mayersohn
Stephanie Stafford . . . . .Assistant to Shelley Surpin

LAW OFFICES OF NEIL SUSSMAN
10751 Densmore Ave. N.
Seattle, WA 98133
PHONE 206-363-8070
FAX 206-363-7519
EMAIL . . . . .neilsussman@mindspring.com
PRACTICE AREAS   Contract Negotiation & Drafting -
                     Copyright & Trademark Matters -
                     Corporate Matters - Intellectual Property
                     Law - Licensing - Motion Picture & TV Law -
                     Music Law - Partnerships/Joint Ventures -
                     Royalty Law - Tax Law
REPRESENTS   Honey Tongue - Nevermore - Queensrÿche
                     - The Souvenirs - The Toucans - Too Slim &
                     the Taildraggers - Second Coming
COMMENTS   Business management; Income taxes and
                     return preparation; Business Law

Neil Sussman . . . . .Entertainment Law

TANTALO & ADLER LLP

9300 Wilshire Blvd., Ste. 550
Beverly Hills, CA 90212
PHONE 310-734-8695
FAX 310-734-8696
WEB SITE . . . . .www.ta-llp.com
PRACTICE AREAS   Full Service Representation - Arbitration & Mediation - Communications - Contract Negotiation & Drafting - Copyright & Trademark Matters - Corporate Matters - Ecommerce - Employment/Labor Law - First Amendment Issues - Intellectual Property Law - Internet Law - Libel & Privacy Matters - Licensing - Litigation - Media - Misappropriation of Name, Voice, Likeness - Motion Picture & TV Law - Music Law - Right of Publicity - Royalty Law - Sports - Talent Representation - Technology - Telecom - Transactional Law

Joel Tantalo . . . . .Principal
Michael Adler . . . . .Principal

TEEPLE HALL, LLP

9255 Towne Centre Dr., Ste. 500
San Diego, CA 92121
PHONE 858-622-7878
FAX 858-622-0411
EMAIL . . . . .info@teeplehall.com
WEB SITE . . . . .www.teeplehall.com
PRACTICE AREAS   Contract Negotiation & Drafting - Intellectual Property Law - Licensing - Litigation - Mergers & Acquisitions - Music Law - Royalty Law
COMMENTS   Coordination of royalty and participation audits and settlements; Also provides entity formation, intellectual property protection, asset protection and international business services

Grant Teeple . . . . .Partner
Todd Hall . . . . .Partner
Eric Hart . . . . .Associate

MARK S. TEMPLE, A PROFESSIONAL LAW CORPORATION

10880 Wilshire Blvd., Ste. 2070
Los Angeles, CA 90024
PHONE 310-888-0044
FAX 310-470-0044
EMAIL . . . . .mst@entatty.com
PRACTICE AREAS   Full Service Representation - Contract Negotiation & Drafting - Copyright & Trademark Matters - Financing - Licensing - Motion Picture & TV Law - Partnerships/Joint Ventures - Talent Representation - Transactional Law
COMMENTS   Emphasis on transactional representation of writers, directors, actors, producers, production companies and entertainment industry executives

Mark S. Temple . . . . .Attorney
Carlton Ching . . . . .Assistant
Adam Park . . . . .Assistant

PETER M. THALL

1740 Broadway, 22nd Fl.
New York, NY 10019
PHONE 212-245-6221
FAX 212-245-6406
WEB SITE . . . . .www.thallentlaw.com
PRACTICE AREAS   Contract Negotiation & Drafting - Intellectual Property Law - Music Law

Peter M. Thall . . . . .Attorney
Jackie J. Kim . . . . .Associate
Terri F. Baker . . . . .Of Counsel
Alexander Murphy Jr. . . . . .Of Counsel

THEODORA ORINGHER MILLER & RICHMAN PC

2029 Century Park East, 6th Fl.
Los Angeles, CA 90067-2907
PHONE 310-557-2009/714-549-6200
FAX .310-551-0283/714-549-6201
EMAIL . . . . .horingher@tocounsel.com
WEB SITE . . . . .www.tocounsel.com
PRACTICE AREAS   Full Service Representation
COMMENTS   Orange County office: 535 Anton Blvd., 9th Fl., Costa Mesa, CA 92626-7109

Todd C. Theodora . . . . .Partner
Harvey T. Oringher . . . . .Partner
Dale S. Miller . . . . .Partner
David S. Richman . . . . .Partner

TISDALE & NICHOLSON, LLP

2029 Century Park East, Ste. 900
Los Angeles, CA 90067
PHONE 310-286-1260
FAX 310-286-2351
EMAIL . . . . .jtisdale@t-nlaw.com
WEB SITE . . . . .www.t-nlaw.com
PRACTICE AREAS   Full Service Representation
COMMENTS   Production, distribution and talent agreements; Finance and corporate organization work

Jeffrey A. Tisdale .Managing Partner
Guy C. Nicholson . . . . .Partner
Kevin D. Hughes . . . . .Partner
Michael D. Stein . . . . .Partner
Marc R. Staenberg . . . . .Of Counsel

LAW OFFICES OF CHARLES TOLBERT

244 Fifth Ave., Ste. 200
New York, NY 10001
PHONE 212-769-7980
FAX 212-679-2310
EMAIL . . . . .info@charlestolbert.com
WEB SITE . . . . .www.charlestolbert.com
PRACTICE AREAS   Contract Negotiation & Drafting - Copyright & Trademark Matters - Corporate Matters - Intellectual Property Law - Licensing - Motion Picture & TV Law - Music Law - Partnerships/Joint Ventures
COMMENTS   Practice also includes book publishing law, animation and photography

Charles Tolbert . . . . .Attorney
Dmitriy Dubovoy . . . . .Assistant (dmit@charlestolbert.com)

John J. Tormey III PLLC
Attorney at Law

JOHN J. TORMEY III, PLLC
217 E. 86th St., PMB 221
New York, NY 10028
PHONE .212-410-4142/845-735-9691
FAX 212-410-2380/845-735-0476
EMAIL . . . . .brightline@att.net
SECOND EMAIL . . . . .jtormey@optonline.net
WEB SITE . . . . .www.tormey.org
SECOND WEB SITE .www.tormey.net
PRACTICE AREAS   Full Service Representation - Contract
                        Negotiation & Drafting - Copyright &
                        Trademark Matters - Corporate Matters -
                        Employment/Labor Law - Financing -
                        Intellectual Property Law - Libel & Privacy
                        Matters - Licensing - Mergers &
                        Acquisitions - Misappropriation of Name,
                        Voice, Likeness - Motion Picture & TV Law -
                        Music Law - Partnerships/Joint Ventures -
                        Right of Publicity - Royalty Law - Talent
                        Representation - Transactional Law
COMMENTS   Merchandising

John J. Tormey III, Esq. . . . . .Attorney

TROY & GOULD
1801 Century Park East, 16th Fl.
Los Angeles, CA 90067
PHONE 310-553-4441
FAX 310-201-4746
WEB SITE . . . . .www.troygould.com
PRACTICE AREAS   Full Service Representation - Arbitration &
                        Mediation - Contract Negotiation &
                        Drafting - Copyright & Trademark Matters -
                        Corporate Matters - Employment/Labor
                        Law - Financing - Intellectual Property Law -
                        Internet Law - Libel & Privacy Matters -
                        Licensing - Litigation - Media - Mergers &
                        Acquisitions - Misappropriation of Name,
                        Voice, Likeness - Motion Picture & TV Law -
                        Music Law - Partnerships/Joint Ventures -
                        Right of Publicity - Royalty Law - Talent
                        Representation - Tax Law - Technology -
                        Transactional Law
REPRESENTS   Producers - Entertainment Technology
                        Companies - Talent - Studios - Digital
                        Media Companies
COMMENTS   Thirty-two lawyer, full-service firm

Gary Concoff .Member & Department Chair
Ronald S. Rosen . . . . .Member
Jonathan Handel . . . . .Of Counsel
Sharon Gold . . . . .Contract Attorney
Donald Moss . . . . .Contract Attorney
David Smith . . . . .Contract Attorney

HARRIS TULCHIN & ASSOCIATES, LTD.
11377 W. Olympic Blvd., 2nd Fl.
Los Angeles, CA 90064
PHONE 310-914-7979
FAX 310-914-7927
EMAIL . . . . .entesquire@aol.com
WEB SITE . . . . .www.medialawyer.com

Harris Tulchin . . . . .Owner/Attorney
Michelle M. Mahjobi . . . . .Director, Sales & Acquisitions
Arati Misro .Director, Sales & Acquisitions

TYRE KAMINS KATZ & GRANOF
1880 Century Park East, Ste. 300
Los Angeles, CA 90067
PHONE 310-553-6822
FAX 310-552-9024
WEB SITE . . . . .www.tyrekamins.com
PRACTICE AREAS   Full Service Representation - Arbitration &
                        Mediation - Contract Negotiation &
                        Drafting - Copyright & Trademark Matters -
                        Corporate Matters - Ecommerce -
                        Employment/Labor Law - Financing - First
                        Amendment Issues - Intellectual Property
                        Law - Internet Law - Libel & Privacy Matters
                        - Licensing - Litigation - Mergers &
                        Acquisitions - Partnerships/Joint Ventures -
                        Tax Law - Technology - Telecom -
                        Transactional Law
COMMENTS   Estate Planning, Probate & Trust, Real
                        Estate and Non-profit

Darin Margules . . . . .Partner

UNGERLAW, PC
1801 Century Park East, Ste. 1250
Los Angeles, CA 90067
PHONE 310-772-7700
FAX 310-772-7701
EMAIL . . . . .jeff@ungerlaw.com
WEB SITE . . . . .www.ungerlaw.com
SECOND WEB SITE .www.eminutes.com
PRACTICE AREAS   Corporate Matters - Partnerships/Joint
                        Ventures

Jeffrey Unger . . . . .Attorney
Bess Clark . . . . .Paralegal

VALENSI, ROSE, MAGARAM, MORRIS & MURPHY
2029 Century Park East, Ste. 2050
Los Angeles, CA 90067-3031
PHONE 310-277-8011
FAX 310-277-1706
EMAIL . . . . .mrm@vrmlaw.com
WEB SITE . . . . .www.vrmlaw.com
PRACTICE AREAS   Full Service Representation - Mergers &
                        Acquisitions - Arbitration & Mediation -
                        Contract Negotiation & Drafting -
                        Copyright & Trademark Matters -
                        Corporate Matters - Employment/Labor
                        Law - Intellectual Property Law - Licensing -
                        Litigation - Music Law - Partnerships/Joint
                        Ventures - Royalty Law - Talent
                        Representation - Tax Law

Michael R. Morris . . . . .Attorney, Music/Certified Tax Specialist
Stephen F. Moeller . . . .Attorney, Entertainment Litigation & Transactions/
                        Labor Issues
Bruce D. Sires . . . . .Attorney, Employment of Minors in the
                        Entertainment Industry/Estate Planning

VALENTE LAW
468 N. Camden Dr., Ste. 268N
Beverly Hills, CA 90210
PHONE 310-785-9531
FAX 310-694-9120
EMAIL . . . . .vl@valentelaw.net
SECOND EMAIL . . . . .pamelaf@valentelaw.net
WEB SITE .www.valentelaw.net
PRACTICE AREAS   Financing - Motion Picture & TV Law - Talent Representation - Transactional Law
COMMENTS   Talent, production and distribution; Adult and children's book publishing; Entertainment related immigration transactions

Pamela Forster . . . . .Attorney at Law

LAW OFFICES OF SUZANNE R. VAUGHAN
6848 Firmament Ave.
Van Nuys, CA 91406
PHONE 818-988-5599
FAX 818-988-5577/818-475-1903
EMAIL . . . . .srvaughan@suzyvaughan.com
WEB SITE . . . . .www.entertainmentmedialaw.com
SECOND WEB SITE . . . . .www.clearances.net
PRACTICE AREAS   Contract Negotiation & Drafting - Copyright & Trademark Matters - Intellectual Property Law - Licensing - Motion Picture & TV Law - Right of Publicity - Talent Representation
REPRESENTS   Paul Brownstein Productions - Sagittarius Pictures - Estates of Vivian Vance, Edmond O'Brien and Florence Ballard of the Supremes - Tri Crown Productions
COMMENTS   Production legal: Contracts for above-the-line talent; Consultation on clearance of film clips and music; Errors & Omissions applications; Title opinion; Copyright and title search; Script clearance

Suzanne R. Vaughan .Attorney

VENABLE LLP
2049 Century Park East, Ste. 2100
Los Angeles, CA 90067
PHONE 310-229-9900
FAX 310-229-9901
WEB SITE . . . . .www.venable.com
PRACTICE AREAS   Full Service Representation - Arbitration & Mediation - Contract Negotiation & Drafting - Copyright & Trademark Matters - Corporate Matters - Employment/Labor Law - Intellectual Property Law - Litigation - Mergers & Acquisitions - Motion Picture & TV Law - Partnerships/Joint Ventures - Talent Representation - Transactional Law
COMMENTS   Motion Picture financing and distribution arrangements

Timothy J. Gorry . . . . .Partner in Charge
Douglas C. Emhoff . . . . .Partner/Head, Litigation Department
Aaron H. Jacoby . . . . .Partner/Head, Government Department
JoAnna Esty . . . . .Partner/Head, Intellectual Property Department
David C. Meyer . . . . .Partner/Head, Transactional Department
Mark Fleischer . . . . .Of Counsel/Head, Entertainment Department
John Bronstein . . . . .Partner
Richard D. Buckley Jr. .Partner
Mitchell I. Burger . . . . .Partner
Jon-Jamison Hill . . . . .Partner
Stefan Kirchanski . . . . .Partner
Peter S. Kravitz . . . . .Partner
Christopher L. Rudd . . . . .Partner
Frank Sandelmann . . . . .Partner
Ben D. Whitwell . . . . .Partner
J. Alison Grabell . . . . .Of Counsel
Jackie M. Joseph . . . . .Of Counsel
(Continued)

VENABLE LLP (Continued)
Kenneth J. Murphy .Of Counsel
Jeffrey M. Tanzer .Of Counsel
Angel James . . . . .Associate
Melanie S. Joo . . . . .Associate
Jenna Leavitt . . . . .Associate
Bret P. Siciliano . . . . .Associate
Jennifer Whiting . . . . .Associate
Christopher T. Williams . . . . .Associate
Donald Yoo . . . . .Associate
Alice A. Park . . . . .Paralegal, Government Department
Cynthia Rubalcava . . . . .Paralegal
Damion Scheller . . . . .Paralegal
Ainsley Ahern . . . . .Sr. Docketing Specialist
Heather Briggs .Legal Assistant
Casandra Broome . . . . .Legal Assistant
LouAnn Crosby .Legal Assistant
Heather M. Edmonds . . . . .Legal Assistant
LaTanya Henry .Legal Assistant
Suzanne L. Hodel . . . . .Legal Assistant
Alethiea Taylor .Legal Assistant
Carolyn S. Simanian . . . . .Legal Assistant Coordinator
Anu M. Gupta .Office Manager
Heather Hamilton . . . . .Facilities Manager
Kara M. Barnachea . . . . .Administrative Assistant
William Smith . . . . .Offices Services Assistant
Amy L. Stark . . . . .Assistant
Kasumi Takahashi .Law Clerk
Yvette R. Tisdale .Receptionist

A. CHANDLER WARREN, JR.
7715 Sunset Blvd., Ste. 100
Los Angeles, CA 90046
PHONE 323-876-6400
FAX 323-876-3170
EMAIL . . . . .achandlerwarren@aol.com
PRACTICE AREAS   Contract Negotiation & Drafting - Licensing - Motion Picture & TV Law
COMMENTS   Practice includes theater law

A.C. Warren Jr. . . . . .Attorney

WEISCHADLE & WEISCHADLE
15 Cottage Ave., Ste. 202
Quincy, MA 02169
PHONE 617-847-4430
FAX 617-847-0050
EMAIL . . . . .dougw@wwlawfirm.net
SECOND EMAIL . . . . .davidw@wwlawfirm.net
WEB SITE . . . . .www.wwlawfirm.net
PRACTICE AREAS   Contract Negotiation & Drafting - Copyright & Trademark Matters - Corporate Matters - Intellectual Property Law - Internet Law - Licensing - Media - Misappropriation of Name, Voice, Likeness - Motion Picture & TV Law - Music Law - Partnerships/Joint Ventures
COMMENTS   Attorneys licensed in Massachusetts, New York, New Jersey, Washington DC and US Supreme Court

David E. Weischadle II Esq. . . . . .Partner
Douglas E. Weischadle Esq. . . . . .Partner

WEISSMANN, WOLFF, BERGMAN, COLEMAN, GRODIN & EVALL, LLP
9665 Wilshire Blvd., Ste. 900
Beverly Hills, CA 90212
PHONE 310-858-7888
FAX 310-550-7191
WEB SITE . . . . .www.weissmannwolff.com
PRACTICE AREAS   Full Service Representation - Arbitration & Mediation - Contract Negotiation & Drafting - Copyright & Trademark Matters - Corporate Matters - Employment/Labor Law - Financing - First Amendment Issues - Intellectual Property Law - Libel & Privacy Matters - Litigation - Media - Mergers & Acquisitions - Misappropriation of Name, Voice, Likeness - Motion Picture & TV Law - Music Law - Partnerships/Joint Ventures - Right of Publicity - Royalty Law - Talent Representation - Tax Law - Transactional Law

Eric Weissmann . . . . .Partner
Michael D. Bergman . . . . .Partner
Stanley M. Coleman . . . . .Partner
Alan L. Grodin . . . . .Partner
Mitchell Evall . . . . .Partner
Marc Benezra . . . . .Partner
Julie Ephraim . . . . .Partner
Marvin Gelfand . . . . .Partner
Steven Glaser . . . . .Partner
Nancy Harkness . . . . .Partner
Howard Hart . . . . .Partner
Wayne Kazan . . . . .Partner
Anjani Mandavia . . . . .Partner
Andrew Schmerzler . . . . .Partner
Todd Stern . . . . .Partner
Jason Poston .Attorney, Litigation
Ticci Bennet . . . . .Paralegal
Kathy Sarreal . . . . .Paralegal
Anita Sobol . . . . .Paralegal
Shannon Alexander . . . . .Associate
Brett Griffin . . . . .Associate
Adam Hagen . . . . .Associate
Thomas Mattei . . . . .Associate
Rebecca Smith . . . . .Associate
Matthew Sugarman . . . . .Associate
Peter Dekom . . . . .Of Counsel
Alan Kirios . . . . .Of Counsel
Janet Andre . . .Assistant to Mr. Bergman, Ms. Mandavia & Ms. Ephraim
Alex Collier . . . . .Assistant to Messrs. Benezra & Hagen
Pam Crawford . . . . .Assistant to Ms. Alexander & Messrs. Gelfand, Griffin & Glaser
Bo Horne . . . . .Assistant to Stanley M. Coleman
Deborah Kennedy . . . . .Assistant to Messrs. Stern & Mattei
Aida Madonato . . . . .Assistant to Eric Weissmann
Adrienne Orayton-Sarpy . . . . .Assistant to Mr. Dekom, Ms. Harkness & Ms. Smith
Rose Pedenko . . . . .Assistant to Messrs. Hart & Schmerzler
Diane Rosebud . . . . .Assistant to Mitchell Evall
Yvonne Shapiro . . . . .Assistant to Alan L. Grodin
Michele Weiss . . . . .Assistant to Messrs. Kazan & Sugarman

WENZLAU LAW GROUP, PLLC
10575 N. 114th St., Ste. 103
Scottsdale, AZ 85259
PHONE 480-344-7788
FAX 480-344-7701
EMAIL . . . . .info@arizonamusiclaw.com
WEB SITE . . . . .www.arizonamusiclaw.com
PRACTICE AREAS   Contract Negotiation & Drafting - Copyright & Trademark Matters - Corporate Matters - Employment/Labor Law - Financing - Intellectual Property Law - Licensing - Motion Picture & TV Law - Music Law
REPRESENTS   Genre Records, Ltd. - Dancesport Videos - Super Sternal Notch - Vertical Turtle Films, LLC - Door-D Entertainment, Inc.

Matthew B. Wenzlau . . . . .Sr. Attorney

LAW OFFICES OF DAVID WERCHEN
845 Third Ave., Ste. 1400
New York, NY 10022
PHONE 212-308-1999
FAX 212-593-1318
EMAIL . . . . .dw@davidwerchen.com
WEB SITE . . . . .www.davidwerchen.com
PRACTICE AREAS   Full Service Representation - Contract Negotiation & Drafting - Music Law - Royalty Law - Talent Representation - Transactional Law

David Werchen . . . . .Owner

WHITE O'CONNOR CURRY LLP
10100 Santa Monica Blvd., 23rd Fl.
Los Angeles, CA 90067
PHONE 310-712-6100
FAX 310-712-6199
EMAIL . . . . .info@whiteo.com
WEB SITE . . . . .www.whiteo.com
PRACTICE AREAS   Copyright & Trademark Matters - Employment/Labor Law - First Amendment Issues - Intellectual Property Law - Libel & Privacy Matters - Litigation - Media - Misappropriation of Name, Voice, Likeness - Motion Picture & TV Law - Music Law
COMMENTS   Also handles business, commercial and insurance litigation

Andrew M. White . . . . .Partner
Michael J. O'Connor . . . . .Partner
James E. Curry . . . . .Partner
David E. Fink . . . . .Partner
Lee S. Brenner . . . . .Partner
Keri E. Borders . . . . .Partner
Edward E. Weiman . . . . .Partner
Hajir Ardebili . . . . .Attorney
Lee-Ann S. Chae . . . . .Attorney
Dana J. Clausen . . . . .Attorney
Erin Fox . . . . .Attorney
Tami Kameda . . . . .Attorney
Amanda M. Leith . . . . .Attorney
Don A. Miller . . . . .Attorney
Brad C. Robertson . . . . .Attorney
Joshua Rodin . . . . .Attorney
Allison S. Rohrer . . . . .Attorney
Rohith Thumati . . . . .Attorney
Peter A. Travis . . . . .Attorney
Sara Wang . . . . .Attorney

PETER J. WILKE, ATTORNEY AT LAW
308 40th St., Ste. D
Manhattan Beach, CA 90266
PHONE 323-397-5380
EMAIL . . . . .petewilke@aol.com
WEB SITE . . . . .www.pwilkeindieatty.com
PRACTICE AREAS   Motion Picture & TV Law
REPRESENTS   Ginny Mule Productions - Headstone
                     Entertainment - Odyssey Pictures -
                     Symphony/New Directions Entertainment,
                     Inc. - The Creation Factory, Ltd. - Kill
                     Switch LLC - Road to Blue - Ingen
                     Technologies, Inc.
COMMENTS   Of Counsel (securities counsel) to Mark
                     Litwak, Esq. and Rosen, Feig, Golland &
                     Lunn LLP; All phases of independent film
                     production, specializing in entity formation,
                     investor documentation and compliance
                     with securities laws

Peter Wilke . . . . .Attorney
Maureen Grammar . . . . .Assistant

THE WINOGRADSKY COMPANY
11240 Magnolia Blvd., Ste. 104
North Hollywood, CA 91601
PHONE 818-761-6906
FAX 818-761-5719
EMAIL . . . . .steve@winogradsky.com
WEB SITE . . . . .www.winogradsky.com
PRACTICE AREAS   Contract Negotiation & Drafting - Licensing
                      - Motion Picture & TV Law - Music Law
REPRESENTS   Composers
COMMENTS   Also handles music clearance and publish-
                      ing administration

Steven Winogradsky Esq. . . . . .President
Alicia Blacker . . . . .Administrative Assistant

WOLF, RIFKIN, SHAPIRO & SCHULMAN, LLP
11400 W. Olympic Blvd., Ste. 900
Los Angeles, CA 90064
PHONE 310-478-4100
FAX 310-479-1422
EMAIL . . . . .mwolf@wrslawyers.com
WEB SITE . . . . .www.wrslawyers.com
PRACTICE AREAS   Arbitration & Mediation - Contract
                      Negotiation & Drafting - Copyright &
                      Trademark Matters - Corporate Matters -
                      Employment/Labor Law - Financing -
                      Intellectual Property Law - Licensing -
                      Litigation - Mergers & Acquisitions - Motion
                      Picture & TV Law - Partnerships/Joint
                      Ventures - Talent Representation - Tax Law -
                      Transactional Law
COMMENTS   Merchandising; Advertising and related
                      corporate and business matters

Roy Rifkin . . . . .Partner, Entertainment Litigation
Neal Tabachnick . . . . .Partner, Talent, Licensing & Merchandising
Michael Wolf . . . . .Partner, Transactional Matters
David Hochman . . . . .Associate, Entertainment
Joseph Petro . . . . .Associate, Licensing & Trademark

GARY S. WOLFE, A PROFESSIONAL LAW CORPORATION
9100 Wilshire Blvd., #530E
Beverly Hills, CA 90212
PHONE 310-274-8847
FAX 310-274-3118
EMAIL . . . . .gsw@gslaw.com
WEB SITE .www.gswlaw.com
PRACTICE AREAS   Tax Law
REPRESENTS   Actors - Musicians - Producers
COMMENTS   International tax planning; Asset protection
                      and audits

Gary S. Wolfe . . . . .Attorney

WOOD SMITH HENNING & BERMAN, LLP
10960 Wilshire Blvd., 18th Fl.
Los Angeles, CA 90024-3804
PHONE 310-481-7600
FAX 310-481-7650
EMAIL . . . . .lawyers@wshblaw.com
WEB SITE . . . . .www.wshblaw.com
PRACTICE AREAS   Full Service Representation -
                      Employment/Labor Law - Intellectual
                      Property Law - Litigation
COMMENTS   Offices located in Glendale, Orange
                      County, San Bernardino County, Riverside
                      County, Central California, Northern
                      California, Las Vegas and Phoenix

David F. Wood . . . . .Sr. Partner
Kevin D. Smith . . . . .Sr. Partner
Stephen J. Henning .Sr. Partner
Daniel A. Berman . . . . .Sr. Partner
Tod R. Dubow . . . . .Sr. Counsel

WYMAN & ISAACS LLP
8840 Wilshire Blvd., 2nd Fl.
Beverly Hills, CA 90211
PHONE 310-358-3221
FAX 310-358-3224
PRACTICE AREAS   Full Service Representation

Robert A. Wyman . . . . .Attorney, Entertainment Transactional
Bruce Isaacs . . . . .Attorney, Litigation
Cheryl Nelson . . . . .Attorney, Entertainment Transactional
Janna O. Smith . . . . .Attorney, Litigation
David H. Boren . . . . .Attorney, Litigation
Lee N. Rosenbaum .Of Counsel
Richard N. Blumenthal . . . . .Of Counsel
Diana Alikas . . . . .Assistant to Ms. Nelson
Marla Foreman . . . . .Assistant to Mr. Wyman
Lina Pearmain . . . . .Assistant to Mr. Isaacs

LAW OFFICE OF LARRY ZERNER
1925 Century Park East, Ste. 500
Los Angeles, CA 90067
PHONE 310-203-2299
FAX 310-388-5624
EMAIL .larry@zernerlaw.com
WEB SITE .www.zernerlaw.com
PRACTICE AREAS   Copyright & Trademark Matters -
                      Intellectual Property Law - Libel & Privacy
                      Matters - Litigation - Misappropriation of
                      Name, Voice, Likeness - Right of Publicity
REPRESENTS   Dan Ferrands - Peter Bracke - George Lutz
                      - Tai Seng Video Entertainment - Adlhoch
                      Creative - Jeff Bergquist
COMMENTS   Emphasis on copyright and trademark
                      infringement litigation

Larry Zerner . . . . .Attorney

ENTERTAINMENT ATTORNEYS

ZIFFREN, BRITTENHAM, BRANCA, FISCHER, GILBERT-LURIE, STIFFELMAN, COOK, JOHNSON, LANDE & WOLF, LLP

1801 Century Park West
Los Angeles, CA 90067
PHONE 310-552-3388
FAX 310-553-7068
PRACTICE AREAS   Full Service Representation

Ken Ziffren . . . . .Partner
Skip Brittenham . . . . .Partner
John Branca . . . . .Partner
Sam Fischer . . . . .Partner
Cliff Gilbert-Lurie . . . . .Partner
Gary Stiffelman . . . . .Partner
Melanie Cook . . . . .Partner
Matt Johnson . . . . .Partner
David Lande . . . . .Partner
Bryan Wolf . . . . .Partner
Steve Burkow . . . . .Partner
David Byrnes . . . . .Partner
Jamey Cohen . . . . .Partner
Stephen Espinoza . . . . .Partner
Kathy Hallberg . . . . .Partner
Dennis Luderer . . . . .Partner
David Nochimson . . . . .Partner
P.J. Shapiro . . . . .Partner
Mitch Tenzer . . . . .Partner
Jamie Young . . . . .Partner

ZUBER & TAILLIEU LLP

9595 Wilshire Blvd., 9th Fl.
Beverly Hills, CA 90212
PHONE 310-300-8480
FAX 310-300-8481
EMAIL . . . . .contact@ztllp.com
WEB SITE . . . . .www.zuberlaw.com
PRACTICE AREAS   Full Service Representation - Arbitration & Mediation - Contract Negotiation & Drafting - Copyright & Trademark Matters - Corporate Matters - Financing - Intellectual Property Law - Libel & Privacy Matters - Licensing - Litigation - Mergers & Acquisitions - Misappropriation of Name, Voice, Likeness - Motion Picture & TV Law - Music Law - Partnerships/Joint Ventures - Right of Publicity - Talent Representation - Transactional Law
REPRESENTS   Distribution Companies - Production Companies - Producers - Directors - Writers - Actors - Crew - Musicians - Financiers

Josh Lawler Esq. . . . . .Partner
Olivier A. Taillieu Esq. . . . . .Partner
Jeffrey J. Zuber Esq. . . . . .Partner
Thomas F. Zuber Esq. . . . . .Partner

ZUMWALT, ALMON & HAYES, PLLC

1014 16th Avenue South
Nashville, TN 37212
PHONE 615-256-7200
FAX 615-256-7106
WEB SITE . . . . .www.zahlaw.com
PRACTICE AREAS   Full Service Representation - Music Law

James G. Zumwalt . . . . .Sr. Partner
Orville Almon Jr. . . . . .Partner
Craig Hayes . . . . .Partner
Raymond G. Gonzales . . . . .Attorney
Kent Marcus . . . . .Attorney

SECTION C

BUSINESS & LEGAL AFFAIRS DEPARTMENTS

ABC ENTERTAINMENT
500 S. Buena Vista St.
Burbank, CA 91521
PHONE 818-460-7777
WEB SITE . . . . .www.abc.com

Jana Winograde . . . . . . .Executive VP/Head, Business Affairs, Primetime,
Daytime & SOAPnet
Milinda McNeely . . . . .Sr. VP, Legal Affairs
Jennifer Mayo . . . . .Sr. VP, Business Affairs
David Cohen . . . . .VP, Legal Affairs
Kerry Kennedy . . . . .VP, Business Affairs
Carlos Williams . . . . .VP, Business Affairs
Lisa Mucci . . . . .Director, Business Affairs
Traci Myman .Director, Business Affairs
Bruce Gersh . . . . .Sr. VP, Business Development
Michelle Goodman . . . . .Assistant to Kerry Kennedy
Lisa Howard . . . . .Assistant to Bruce Gersh
Kim Smith . . . . .Assistant to Jana Winograde
Solange Torres . . . . .Assistant to Jennifer Mayo

ABC TELEVISION STUDIO
500 S. Buena Vista St.
Burbank, CA 91521
PHONE 818-460-7777
WEB SITE . . . . .www.abc.com

Howard Davine . . . . .Executive VP, Touchstone Television
Jeff Frost . . . . .Sr. VP, Business Affairs
Milinda McNeely . . . . .Sr. VP, Legal Affairs
Jeff Freid . . . . .VP, Business Affairs
Veronica Gentilli . . . . .VP, Business Affairs
David Goldman .VP, Business Affairs
Jacqui Grunfeld . . . . .VP, Business Affairs
Jeff Hegedus . . . . .VP, Business Affairs
Roger Kirman . . . . .VP, Business Affairs
Sabrina Padwa .VP, Business Affairs
Mark Mazie .Executive Counsel
Stephanie Beeman . . . . .Director, Business Affairs
J. Christopher Hamilton . . . . .Director, Business Affairs
Pamela Ortiz . . . . .Assistant to Howard Davine

AGENCY FOR THE PERFORMING ARTS, INC.
99 Park Ave., Ste. 1600
New York, NY 10016
PHONE 212-972-2175
FAX 212-972-2470

Robert L. Lasky . . . . .Attorney/Business Affairs
Susan Shevlinn . . . . .Assistant to Robert L. Lasky

ARTISTS PRODUCTION GROUP (APG)
2601 Colorado Ave.
Santa Monica, CA 90404
PHONE 310-300-2400
FAX 310-300-2424

Chris George .Development Executive
Bryce Johnson . . . . .Business & Legal Affairs

BUENA VISTA HOME ENTERTAINMENT
350 S. Buena Vista St.
Burbank, CA 91521
PHONE 818-560-1000
WEB SITE . . . . .www.disney.com

Kristin McQueen . . . . .Sr. VP, Business & Legal Affairs

BUENA VISTA INTERNATIONAL, INC.
500 S. Buena Vista St.
Burbank, CA 91521
PHONE 818-560-1000
WEB SITE . . . . .www.disney.com

Lawrence J. Kaplan . . . . .Executive VP/General Manager

BUENA VISTA MOTION PICTURES GROUP
500 S. Buena Vista St.
Burbank, CA 91521
PHONE 818-560-1000
WEB SITE . . . . .www.disney.com

Bernardine Brandis . . . . .Executive VP, Business & Legal Affairs,
The Walt Disney Studios
Steve Bardwil . . . . . .Executive VP, Legal Affairs, The Walt Disney Studios
Scott Holtzman . . . . .Executive VP, Music Business Affairs
Phillip E. Muhl . . . . .Executive VP, Business & Legal Affairs
Doug Carter . . . . .Sr. VP, Business Affairs
Sylvia J. Krask . . . . .Sr. VP, Music Business & Legal Affairs
Kal Walthers . . . . .Sr. VP, Business Affairs
Judith Jecman .VP, Legal Affairs
Paige Olson . . . . .VP, Legal Affairs
David Trygstad . . . . .VP, Business Affairs
Don Welty . . . . .VP, Music Business & Legal Affairs
Kevin Monroe . . . . .Sr. Counsel
Bill Neuschaefer . . . . .Sr. Counsel
Vickie Cameron . . . . .Counsel
Chad Harris . . . . .Counsel
Gamze Onur . . . . .Counsel

BUENA VISTA PICTURES DISTRIBUTION
350 S. Buena Vista St.
Burbank, CA 91521
PHONE 818-560-1000
WEB SITE . . . . .www.disney.com

Robert Cunningham . . . . .Sr. VP/General Counsel
Denise Brown . . . . .Sr. VP, Business & Legal Affairs
Anne Moebes . . . . .Director, Business & Legal Affairs
Marste McDonald . . . . .Assistant

BUENA VISTA TELEVISION
500 S. Buena Vista St.
Burbank, CA 91521
PHONE 818-560-1000
WEB SITE . . . . .www.disney.com

Michael Thornton . . . . .Executive VP, Business & Legal Affairs
Cyndi Cruz . . . . .VP, Business Affairs
Gabrielle Davis . . . . .VP, Business Affairs
Michael Patterson .VP, Business Affairs
David Schwartz . . . . .VP, Business Affairs
Coleen Raymann . . . . .Executive Assistant to Mr. Thornton
Stan Pham . . . . .Executive Assistant to Mr. Patterson
Rita Garcia . . .Executive Assistant to Mr. Schwartz, Ms. Cruz & Ms. Davis

CBS ENTERTAINMENT
7800 Beverly Blvd.
Los Angeles, CA 90036-2188
PHONE 323-575-2345
WEB SITE . . . . .www.cbs.com
COMMENTS   East Coast office: 51 W. 52nd St., 6th Fl.,
                    New York, NY 10019

Deborah Barak . . . . .Executive VP, Business Affairs, CBS Paramount
                              Network Television Entertainment Group
Roni Mueller .Sr. VP, Business Affairs
Gary Silver . . . . .Sr. VP, Business Affairs
Joel Goldberg . . . . .VP, Business Affairs, CBS Digital Media
Sidney H. Lyons . .VP, Business Affairs, Longform Contracts & Acquisitions
Anne R. Nelson . . . . .VP, Business Affairs
Travis Pierson . . . . .VP, Business Affairs
Michael Giordano . . . . .Associate Director, Business Affairs
Cynthia Brown . . . . .Director, Business Affairs
Grant Michaelson . . . . .Director, Business Affairs
Michael Bott . . . . . . .Assistant to Gary Silver & Michael Giordano
Wai Chee Co . . . . .Assistant to Deborah Barak
Karen Deming . . . . . . .Assistant to Joel Goldberg & Jonathan Barzilay
Ileane Harustak . . . . .Assistant to Anne R. Nelson
Celeste Moore . . . . .Assistant to Grant Michaelson & Travis Pierson
Helen Rose . . . . .Assistant to Sidney H. Lyons
Shirley Sadanaga . . . . .Assistant to Roni Mueller

CBS PARAMOUNT DOMESTIC TELEVISION
5555 Melrose Ave.
Los Angeles, CA 90038-3197
PHONE 323-956-5000
WEB SITE . . . . .www.cbsparamount.com

Bruce Pottash . . . . .Executive VP, Business Affairs & Legal
Robert Sheehan . . . . .Executive VP, Business Affairs & Finance
Kim Fitzgerald . . . . .Sr. VP, Business Affairs & Legal
David Theodosopoulos . . . . .Sr. VP, Business Affairs & Legal
Peter Kane .Sr. VP, Business Affairs
Lynn Fero . . . . .VP, Business Affairs Administration
Amy Freisleben . . . . .VP, Business Affairs & Legal
Stephen Sloane . . . . .VP, Business Affairs & Legal
Joseph Jerome . . . . .VP, Legal
Cindy Teele . . . . .VP, Legal
Nicole Harris Johnson . . . . . . .Sr. Attorney, Business Affairs & Legal
Kristi Sjoholm-Sierchio Sr. Attorney, Sales Administrative & Legal Services
Teresa Youngreen . . . . .Manager, Business Affairs & Legal
Terry Carr . . . . .Assistant to Mr. Pottash
Doreen Manzetti . . . . . . .Assistant to Mr. Sloane & Ms. Harris Johnson
Lynda Skeen . . . . . .Assistant to Ms. Freisleben, Mr. Theodosopoulos &
                                                    Mr. Kane
David Trudell . . . . .Assistant to Ms. Sjoholm-Sierchio
Beverly Underwood . . . . .Assistant to Ms. Fero, Ms. Teele & Mr. Jerome
Evelyn Whitaker . . . . .Assistant to Robert Sheehan

CBS PARAMOUNT NETWORK TELEVISION
CBS Studios
4024 Radford Ave.
Studio City, CA 91604
PHONE 818-655-5000
WEB SITE . . . . .www.cbsparamount.com

David Karnes . . . . .Sr. VP, Legal Affairs (818-655-7102)
Dan Kupetz . . . . .Sr. VP, Business Affairs (818-655-7103)
Francisco Arias . . . . .VP, Business Affairs (818-655-7123)
David Lavin . . . . .VP, Business Affairs (818-655-7122)
John Phillips . . . . .VP, Business Affairs (818-655-7124)
Allison Brightman . . . . .VP, Legal (818-655-7116)
Ellen Waggoner . . . . .VP, Legal (818-655-7118)
Peilin Pratt . . . . .Director, Business Affairs (818-655-7126)
Jack Freedman . . . . .Sr. Attorney, Legal (818-655-7117)
Ray Maiello . . . . .Attorney, Legal (818-655-7115)
Rosalind Marks . . . . .Attorney, Legal (818-655-7152)
Dan Kilgore . . . .Executive Director, Legal Clearance (818-655-7113)
Catherine Ewing . . . . .Manager, Legal Clearance (818-655-7112)
Linden Garcia . . . . .Manager, Legal (818-655-7120)
Robin Samms . . . . .Paralegal (818-655-7119)
Rich Vokulich . . . .Executive Consultant, Business Affairs (818-655-7121)

CBS TELEVISION
7800 Beverly Blvd.
Los Angeles, CA 90036-2188
PHONE 323-575-2701/212-846-3787
WEB SITE . . . . .www.cbs.com
COMMENTS   East Coast office: 1515 Broadway, New
                            York, NY 10036

Jonathan H. Anschell . . . . .Executive VP/General Counsel
Mark W. Engstrom . . . . .Sr. VP/Associate General Counsel (NY)
Susanna Lowy . . . . .Sr. VP/Deputy General Counsel (NY)
Martin P. Messinger   Sr. VP/Deputy General Counsel/Stations Group (NY)
David M. Pill . . . . .Sr. VP/Associate General Counsel
Sandra K. Williams . . . . . . .Sr. VP/Deputy General Counsel/West Coast
Lura Burton . . . . .VP/Associate General Counsel
Howard F. Jaeckel . . . . .VP/Associate General Counsel (NY)
Beth Finley Jones . . . . .VP/Assistant General Counsel
Sanford I. Kryle . . . . .VP/Associate General Counsel (NY)
Douglas Edwards . . . . .Assistant General Counsel
Nicole Jaeger . . . . .Assistant General Counsel
Thomas Lane . . . . .Assistant General Counsel
Patrick Purifoy .Assistant General Counsel
Alison Wauk . . . . .Assistant General Counsel
Ray White . . . . .Assistant General Counsel
Andy Wong . . . . .Assistant General Counsel
Richard Altabef . . . . .Assistant General Counsel (NY)
Susan Anderson . . . . .Assistant General Counsel (NY)
Gigi W. Davis . . . . .Assistant General Counsel
Grace Goldblatt . . . . .Assistant General Counsel (NY)
Patricia McFarlin . . . . .Assistant General Counsel (NY)
Nicholas Poser . . . . .Assistant General Counsel (NY)
Laurie Robinson . . . . .Assistant General Counsel (NY)
Andrew Siegel . . . . .Assistant General Counsel (NY)
Jonathan Sternberg . . . . .Assistant General Counsel (NY)
Michelle Vachris . . . . .Assistant General Counsel (NY)

CBS TELEVISION DISTRIBUTION
1700 Broadway, 33rd Fl.
New York, NY 10019
PHONE 212-541-0266
FAX 212-586-7351

Jonathan Birkhahn . . . . .Executive VP, Business Affairs & Legal

CMT: COUNTRY MUSIC TELEVISION
c/o MTV Networks
2600 Colorado Ave.
Santa Monica, CA 90404
PHONE 310-752-8000
WEB SITE . . . . .www.cmt.com
COMMENTS   Nashville office: 330 Commerce St.,
                            Nashville, TN 37201, phone: 615-335-
                            8400

Jennifer R. Ortega . . . . .VP, Business & Legal Affairs (West Coast)
Jodi Carmichael . . . . . . .Sr. Counsel, Business & Legal Affairs (Nashville)
Cynthia Mangrum . . . . . . .Director, Contracts Management, Business &
                                         Legal Affairs (Nashville)
Robert L. Natter . . . . . . .Director, Business & Legal Affairs (West Coast)

COLUMBIA PICTURES - BUSINESS AFFAIRS
A Sony Pictures Entertainment Company
10202 W. Washington Blvd.
Culver City, CA 90232
PHONE 310-244-4000
WEB SITE . . . . .www.spe.sony.com

Andrew Gumpert . . . . .Sr. Executive VP, Business Affairs
Ronni Coulter . . . . .Sr. VP, Business Affairs
John Levy . . . . .Sr. VP, Business Affairs
Mark Wyman . . . . .Sr. VP, Business Affairs
Thomas Stack . . . . .VP, Business Affairs Contract Administration
Jason Lang . . . . .Assistant to Andrew Gumpert
Dorothy Rayburn . . . . .Assistant to Ronni Coulter
Rick Abercrombie . . . . .Assistant to John Levy
Dan Nowak . . . . .Assistant to Mark Wyman
Melody Grant . . . . .Assistant to Thomas Stack

COLUMBIA PICTURES - LEGAL AFFAIRS
10202 W. Washington Blvd.
Culver City, CA 90232
PHONE 310-244-4000
WEB SITE . . . . .www.spe.sony.com

Roger W. Toll . . . . .Executive VP, Legal Affairs
Eric I. Baum . . . . .Sr. VP/Associate General Counsel
Deborah D. Bruenell . . . . .Sr. VP, Legal Affairs
Luis E. Allen . . . . .VP/Associate General Counsel
Ian Wilson . . . . .VP, CTMG, Marketing, Contract Compliance
Daniel Yankelevits . . . . .VP, Legal Affairs
Lei Wagner .Assistant to Roger W. Toll
Lyle Eggleston . . . . .Assistant to Eric I. Baum & Ian Wilson
Sandra Kallander . . . . .Assistant to Deborah D. Bruenell
Tyra Taylor . . . . .Assistant to Luis E. Allen
Jane Corey . . . . .Assistant to Daniel Yankelevitz

COMEDY CENTRAL
1775 Broadway, 10th Fl.
New York, NY 10019
PHONE 212-767-8600/310-407-4700
FAX .212-767-4284/310-407-4747
WEB SITE . . . . .www.comedycentral.com
COMMENTS   West Coast office: 2049 Century Park East,
                            Ste. 4000, Los Angeles, CA 90067

Joella West . . . . .Sr. VP/General Counsel, Business & Legal Affairs
Jim Goodman . . . . .VP, Business & Legal Affairs
Genise Jackson . . . . .VP, Business & Legal Affairs
Benjamin Mauceri . . . . .VP, Business & Legal Affairs
Debbie Spander . . . . .VP, Business & Legal Affairs
Robert Guillermo . . . . .Sr. Director, Contract Administration
Timothy Brock . . . . .Director, Residuals
Andrea DeMarinis . . . . .Director, Contract Administration
Arian Sultan . . . . .Director, Business & Legal Affairs
Brian Gottlock . . . . .Counsel, Business & Legal Affairs

CREATIVE ARTISTS AGENCY - CAA
2000 Avenue of the Stars
Los Angeles, CA 90067
PHONE .424-288-2000/212-277-9000
FAX 424-288-2900

Roger Batchelder . . . . .Motion Picture, Business Affairs
Steven Brookman . . . . .Motion Picture, Business Affairs
Jenna Gambaro . . . . .Motion Picture, Business Affairs
Matthew Leaf . . . . .Motion Picture, Business Affairs
Charles Melniker . . . . .Motion Picture, Business Affairs
Glen Meredith . . . . .Motion Picture, Business Affairs
Joanna Mulas . . . . .Motion Picture, Business Affairs
Eileen Rapke . . . . .Motion Picture, Business Affairs
Keith Sears . . . . .Motion Picture, Business Affairs
Sheldon Sroloff .Motion Picture, Business Affairs
Marc Von Arx . . . . .Motion Picture, Business Affairs
Teri Eaton . . . . .TV, Business Affairs
Daniel Grover . . . . .TV, Business Affairs
Gregory Pulis . . . . .TV, Business Affairs
Jon Ringquist . . . . .TV, Business Affairs
Olivier Sultan . . . . .Theatre, Business Affairs (NY)
Angie Rho . . . . .Music, Business Affairs

CUNNINGHAM-ESCOTT-SLEVIN-DOHERTY TALENT AGENCY (LOS ANGELES)
10635 Santa Monica Blvd., Stes. 130, 135, 140
Los Angeles, CA 90025
PHONE 310-475-2111/310-475-7573
FAX 310-475-1929/310-475-3362
EMAIL . . . . .info@cesdtalent.com
WEB SITE . . . . .www.cesdtalent.com
SECOND WEB SITE . . . . .www.cesdvoices.com

Ken Slevin . . . . .President/Partner
Paul Doherty . . . . .Secretary/Treasurer/Partner
T.J. Escott . . . . .Chairman/Partner
Jo Anne Arias . . . . .Controller/VP
Vickie Weiss . . . . .Director, Business Affairs
Diane Arman . . . . .Business Affairs
Boone Jordanlee . . . . .Business Affairs
Rick Rimando . . . . .Business Affairs
Fran Ruesler . . . . .Business Affairs
Brian Foster . . . . .Assistant Controller

CUNNINGHAM-ESCOTT-SLEVIN-DOHERTY TALENT AGENCY (NEW YORK)
257 Park Ave. South, Stes. 900 & 950
New York, NY 10010
PHONE 212-477-1666
FAX 212-979-2011
EMAIL . . . . .info@cesdtalent.com
WEB SITE . . . . .www.cesdtalent.com
SECOND WEB SITE . . . . .www.cesdvoices.com

Ken Slevin . . . . .President/Partner
Paul Doherty . . . . .Secretary/Treasurer/Partner
T.J. Escott . . . . .Chairman/Partner
Jeffrey Stein . . . . .Director, Business Affairs
Alistair Heath . . . . .Assistant Director, Business Affairs
Kelley Gorden . . . . .Business Affairs
Tamika Knight . . . . .Business Affairs
Jeffrey Kronson . . . . .Business Affairs
Carla Colucci . . . . .Business Manager

THE CW TELEVISION NETWORK
4000 Warner Blvd., Bldg. 168
Burbank, CA 91522
PHONE 818-977-5000
WEB SITE . . . . .www.cwtv.com

Michael Ross . . . . .Executive VP, Business Affairs
Kelly Smith . . . . .VP, Business Affairs
Dennis Dort . . . . .VP, Legal Affairs
Jeremy Sunderland . . . . .VP/Deputy General Counsel
Ann Miyagi .Director, Business Affairs
James McGrath . . . . .Assistant to Mr. Ross
Norma Bocanegra . . . . . .Assistant to Ms. Smith, Mr. Dort & Ms. Miyagi

DIMENSION FILMS
c/o The Weinstein Company
345 Hudson St., 13th Fl.
New York, NY 10014
PHONE 646-862-3400
FAX 917-368-7000
WEB SITE . . . . .www.weinsteinco.com
SECOND WEB SITE . . . . .www.twcpublicity.com
COMMENTS   Second address: 375 Greenwich St., New
                        York, NY 10013, phone: 212-941-3800,
                        fax: 212-941-3949; West Coast office:
                        5700 Wilshire Blvd., Ste. 600, Los Angeles,
                        CA 90036, phone: 323-207-3200, fax:
                        323-954-0997

Andrew Kramer . . . . .Executive VP, Business & Legal Affairs (LA)
Lumumba Mosquera . . . . .Sr. VP, Business & Legal Affairs
Sarah Sobel . . . . .Sr. VP, Business & Legal Affairs

DISCOVERY NETWORKS, U.S.
c/o One Discovery Pl.
Silver Spring, MD 20910-3354
PHONE 240-662-2000
EMAIL . . . . .firstname_lastname@discovery.com
WEB SITE . . . . .www.discovery.com

Michael Prettyman . . . . .Sr. VP, Business Affairs
Larry Gordon . . . . .VP, Business Affairs
Rex Recka . . . . .VP, Business Affairs
Jonathan Sichel . . . . .VP, Business Affairs
Jeffrey Cross . . . . .Sr. VP, Legal Affairs
Christina Wadyka . . . . .Sr. VP, Legal Affairs
Janell Coles . . . . .VP, Legal Affairs
Carlos Gutierrez . . . . .VP, Legal Affairs
Linette Hwu . . . . .VP, Legal Affairs

BUSINESS & LEGAL AFFAIRS DEPTS.

DISNEY ABC CABLE NETWORKS GROUP
3800 W. Alameda Ave., 20th Fl.
Burbank, CA 91505
PHONE 818-569-7500
WEB SITE . . . . .www.abc.com
SECOND WEB SITE . . . . .www.disneychannel.com

Frederick Kuperberg . . . . .Executive VP, Business & Legal Affairs,
Disney-ABC Cable Networks Group
Grace Reiner . . . . .Executive VP, Business Affairs, Disney Channel
T. Scott Fain . . .Sr. VP/Deputy General Counsel, Disney Media Networks
Mark Kenchelian . . . . .Sr. VP, Business & Legal Affairs, Walt Disney
Television Animation
Jeffrey R. Lai . . .Sr. VP, Legal Affairs, Disney-ABC Cable Networks Group
Adina Savin   Sr. VP, Business Affairs, Disney-ABC Cable Networks Group
Kevin Closson . . .VP, Business Affairs, Disney-ABC Cable Networks Group
Sean Cocchia . . . .VP, Business Development, Disney Channel Worldwide
Karen Holm . . . . .VP, Legal Affairs, Disney-ABC Cable Networks Group
Chris Ryan . . . . .VP, Business Affairs, Disney-ABC Cable Networks Group
(818-973-4301)
Lori Lynem . . . . .Executive Director, Business Affairs, Disney-ABC
Cable Networks Group

THE WALT DISNEY COMPANY
500 S. Buena Vista St.
Burbank, CA 91521
PHONE 818-560-1000
WEB SITE . . . . .www.disney.com

Alan N. Braverman . . . . . . .Sr. Executive VP/General Counsel/Secretary

WALT DISNEY FEATURE ANIMATION
500 S. Buena Vista St.
Burbank, CA 91521-4866
PHONE 818-560-1000
WEB SITE . . . . .www.disney.com

John McGuire . . . . .Sr. VP, Business & Legal Affairs
Christine Chrisman . . . . .Director, Business & Legal Affairs
Eddie Khanbeigi . . . . .Director, Business & Legal Affairs
Gus Avila . . . . .Assistant to John McGuire
Angela Ontiveros . . . .Assistant to Eddie Khanbeigi & Christine Chrisman

DISNEY-ABC TELEVISION GROUP
500 S. Buena Vista St.
Burbank, CA 91521
PHONE 818-460-7777

Peter DiCecco . . . . .Sr. VP, Business & Legal Affairs, Music
Carolyn Javier . . . . .VP, Business & Legal Affairs, Music
Fera Mostow . . . . .VP, Business & Legal Affairs, Music
Meghan Crowley . . . . .Counsel
David Shea . . . . .Counsel
Candace Isaac . . . . .Assistant

DREAMWORKS SKG
100 Universal City Plaza, Ste. 5125
Universal City, CA 91608
PHONE 818-733-7000
WEB SITE . . . . .www.dreamworks.com

Brian Edwards . . . . .General Counsel
Jack Bleck . . . . .Head, Theatrical Business Affairs
Deborah Chiaramonte . . . . .Theatrical Business/Legal Affairs
Philip Goore . . . . .Theatrical Business Affairs
Rich Shuter . . . . .Network TV Business Affairs
Jamie Kershaw . . . . .Animation Business Affairs
Alison Lima .Animation Business Affairs
Alan Myerson . . . . .Animation Business Affairs
Eddie Arnez . . . . .Assistant to Jack Bleck
Marissa Stein . . . . .Assistant to Brian Edwards

E! NETWORKS
5750 Wilshire Blvd.
Los Angeles, CA 90036
PHONE 323-954-2400
WEB SITE . . . . .www.eonline.com

Sheila K. Johnson . . . . . .Sr. VP, Business Operations & General Counsel
Susan Lierle . . . . .VP, Business & Legal Affairs

ENDEAVOR AGENCY, LLC
9601 Wilshire Blvd., 3rd Fl.
Beverly Hills, CA 90210
PHONE 310-248-2000
FAX 310-248-2020

Tom McGuire . . . . .General Counsel
Catherine Sugar . . . . .Head, TV Business Affairs
Ann Du Val . . . . .Business Affairs
Vikki Karan . . . . .Business Affairs
Deb Shuwarger . . . . .Business Affairs

BUSINESS & LEGAL AFFAIRS DEPTS.

FOCUS FEATURES/ROGUE PICTURES

65 Bleecker St., 2nd Fl.
New York, NY 10012
PHONE .212-539-4000/818-777-7373
FAX 212-539-4099/818-866-4583
WEB SITE . . . . .www.focusfeatures.com
COMMENTS   West Coast office: 100 Universal City
                             Plaza, Bldg. 9128, 2nd Fl., Universal City,
                             CA 91608

Avy Eschenasy . . . . . .Executive VP, Strategic Planning, Business Affairs &
                                                    Acquisitions (LA)
Howard Meyers .Sr. VP, Business Affairs (LA)
Timothy Collins . . . . .VP, Business Affairs (LA)
Whitney Wilson . . . . .VP, Business Affairs
Alice Pope . . . . .Administrator, Business Affairs (LA)
Joanna Stoller . . . . .Manager, Business Affairs
Jennifer Towle . . . . .Manager, Music Business & Legal Affairs
Michael Bulger . . . . .Executive Assistant to Avy Eschenasy (LA)
Alex Swaekauski . . . . .Assistant, Business Affairs (LA)

FOX BROADCASTING COMPANY

10201 W. Pico Blvd.
Los Angeles, CA 90035
PHONE 310-369-1000
WEB SITE . . . . .www.fox.com
COMMENTS   Mailing address: PO Box 900, Beverly
                             Hills, CA 90213

Lee Bartlett .Executive VP, Business Affairs
Karen Fox . . . . .Sr. VP, Business Affairs
Donna Redier-Linsk . . . . .Sr. VP, Business Affairs
Minna Taylor . . . . .Sr. VP, Legal Affairs
Kathy Edrich . . . . .VP, Business Affairs
Phoebe Tisdale . . . . .VP, Production, Business Affairs
Melissa Gold .Director, Business Affairs
Connie Jones .Director, Business Affairs
Jim Lancaster . . . . .Executive Assistant to Lee Bartlett

FOX CABLE NETWORKS - CORPORATE, NEW MEDIA & DISTRIBUTION

2121 Avenue of the Stars, 17th Fl.
Los Angeles, CA 90067
PHONE 310-369-1000
WEB SITE . . . . .www.foxcable.com

Rita Tuzon . . . . .Executive VP
Jennifer Chun . . . . .Sr. VP
Scott Brown . . . . .VP
Lisa Smolinisky . . . . .Sr. Director
Matthew Bensen . . . . .Director
Adam Reiss . . . . .Director
Rodrigo Vazquez . . . . .Director
Jessica Kaveh . . . . .Manager
Susan Young . . . . .Manager
Stephanie Serpa . . . . .Contract Administrator
Tina Edwards . . . . .Executive Assistant to Rita Tuzon
Keonda Gaspard . . . . .Executive Assistant to Jennifer Chun
Ana Lisa Ruiz . . . . .Legal Assistant

FOX CABLE NETWORKS - ENTERTAINMENT

2121 Avenue of the Stars, 17th Fl.
Los Angeles, CA 90067
PHONE 310-369-1000
WEB SITE . . . . .www.foxcable.com
COMMENTS   Includes FX, Fox Movie Channel, Fox
                             Reality Channel, National Geographic and
                             the Speed Channel

Rita Tuzon . . . . .Executive VP, Business & Legal Affairs/General Counsel,
                                                    Fox Cable Networks
Michael Beller . . . .Sr. VP, Business & Legal Affairs, National Geographic
                                                        Channel (US)
Kelly Kevin Cline . . . . .Sr. VP, Business & Legal Affairs
Tony Carey . . . . .VP, Production, Business & Legal Affairs
Neil Klasky . . . . .VP, Business & Legal Affairs
Lisa Kumin . . . . .VP, Business & Legal Affairs
Darlene Lieblich Tipton . . . . .VP, Standards & Practices
Kevin Wilson . . . . .VP, Speed Channel
Jennifer Pancotto . . . . .Director, Business & Legal Affairs
Victoria Sterling . . . . .Director, Standards & Practices
Craig Sunderland . . . . .Director, Standards & Practices
Elena Mathis . . . . .Associate Director, Standards & Practices
Banafsheh Kamali-Parsee . . . . .Sr. Manager, Rights & Distribution,
                                            National Geographic Channel (US)
Terri Leftwich . . .Manager, Business & Legal Affairs, National Geographic
                                                        Channel (US)
Tony Specchierla . . . . .Manager, Standards & Practices
Brandon Slade . . . . .Coordinator, Business & Legal Affairs,
                                            National Geographic Channel (US)
Sher'ri Bell . . . . .Executive Assistant to Kelly Kevin Cline
Tina Edwards . . . . .Executive Assistant to Rita Tuzon
Vanessa Doyen . . . . .Assistant to Craig Sunderland
Tamara Kcehowski . . . . .Assistant to Neil Klasky & Jennifer Gonsky
Courtney Shearer .Assistant to Kevin Wilson
Yolanda Wilson .Assistant to Lisa Kumin

FOX CABLE NETWORKS - SPORTS

2121 Avenue of the Stars, 17th Fl.
Los Angeles, CA 90067
PHONE 310-369-1000
WEB SITE . . . . .www.foxcable.com
COMMENTS   Includes Fox Sports Net, Fox College
                             Sports, Fox Sports International and Fuel TV

Rita Tuzon . . . . .Executive VP, Business & Legal Affairs/General Counsel,
                                                    Fox Cable Networks
Karen Brodkin . . . . .Sr. VP, Fox Sports Net/Fox College Sports
Claudia Teran . . . . . .Sr. VP, Business & Legal Affairs, Fox Sports
                                                    International/Fuel TV
Leanna Einbinder . . . . .VP, Fox Sports Net/Fox College Sports
Phillip Gharabegian . . . . .VP, Fox Sports Net/Fox College Sports
David S. Wisnia . . . . .VP, Business & Legal Affairs, Fox Sports
                                                    International/Fuel TV
Peter S. Marco . . . . .Sr. Director, Business & Legal Affairs, Fox Sports
                                                    International/Fuel TV
Kai Dhaliwal . . . . .Director, Fox Sports Net/Fox College Sports
Lowell Reinstein . . . . .Director, Fox Sports Net/Fox College Sports
Suzanne Grippaldi . . . . . . .Manager, Fox Sports Net/Fox College Sports
Kris Keith . . . . .Manager, Business & Legal Affairs, Fox Sports
                                                    International/Fuel TV
Nick Cacace . . . . .Legal Assistant, Business & Legal Affairs,
                                            Fox Sports Net/Fox College Sports
Xian Douglas . . . . . .Legal Assistant, Business & Legal Affairs, Fox Sports
                                                    International/Fuel TV
Christina McGrath . . . . . . .Legal Assistant, Business & Legal Affairs,
                                            Fox Sports Net/Fox College Sports
Zabella Moore . . . . .Legal Assistant, Business & Legal Affairs, Fox Sports
                                                    International/Fuel TV
Tina Edwards . . . . .Executive Assistant to Rita Tuzon
Nakenda McKinney . . . . .Executive Assistant to Karen Brodkin
Michele Santillan . . . . .Executive Assistant, Business & Legal Affairs,
                                            Fox Sports International/Fuel TV

FOX TELEVISION STUDIOS
10201 W. Pico Blvd., Bldg. 41, Ste. 300
Los Angeles, CA 90035
PHONE 310-369-1000
FAX 310-369-7378
EMAIL . . . . firstname.lastname@fox.com
WEB SITE . . . . .www.fox.com

Jerry Longarzo . . .Executive VP, Business & Legal Affairs (310-369-0069)
Martin Carlson . . . . .VP, Business & Legal Affairs (310-369-8190)
Stacy Kreisberg . . . . .VP, Business & Legal Affairs (310-369-0552)
Cheryl Buysse Lynch . . . . . .VP, Business & Legal Affairs (310-369-5822)
James Dunn . . . . .Director, Business & Legal Affairs (310-369-1080)
Sylvie Maracci . . . . .Director, Business & Legal Affairs (310-369-5813)
Lindsay Feldman . . . .Manager, Business & Legal Affairs (310-369-4404)
Seth Rosenson . . . . .Manager, Business & Legal Affairs (310-369-3810)
Shamira Brown . . . . . . .Assistant to Stacy Kreisberg & Lindsay Feldman
Lisa Geiger . . . . .Assistant to Edward Sabin & Sylvie Maracci
Ana M. Gonzalez . . . . .Assistant to Jerry Longarzo
Jonathan Kleinman . . . . .Assistant to Martin Carlson
Wade Solomon . . . . . . .Assistant to Cheryl Buysse Lynch & James Dunn

G4 TV
12312 W. Olympic Blvd.
Los Angeles, CA 90064
PHONE 310-979-5000
FAX 310-979-5095
EMAIL . . . . .info@g4tv.com
WEB SITE www.g4tv.com

Alan Duke . . . . .Sr. VP/General Counsel
Hubert T. Smith Jr. . . . . .VP, Business & Legal Affairs
Debbie Axel . . . . .Director, Rights & Clearances
Mary Cheves . . . .Manager, Rights & Clearances/Assistant to Alan Duke
Luana Hildebrant . . . . .Assistant to Hubert T. Smith Jr.

THE GERSH AGENCY (LOS ANGELES)
232 N. Canon Dr.
Beverly Hills, CA 90210
PHONE 310-274-6611
FAX 603-506-2566
EMAIL . . . . .skravit@gershla.com

Stephen M. Kravit . . . . .Executive VP
Mevelyn Santiago . . . . .Assistant

GSN
A Sony Pictures/Liberty Media Company
2150 Colorado Ave., Ste. 100
Santa Monica, CA 90404
PHONE 310-255-6800
FAX 310-255-6810
WEB SITE . . . . .www.gsn.com
COMMENTS . . . . .The Network for Games

Michael Kohn . . . . . . .Sr. VP/General Counsel, Business & Legal Affairs
Mark Nordman . . . . .Executive Director, Business & Legal Affairs
Ann Maron . . . . .Executive Director, Business & Legal Affairs
Darlene Hopkins . . . . .Paralegal
Joan Plantenberg . . . . .Paralegal

HBO FILMS
2500 Broadway, Ste. 400
Santa Monica, CA 90404
PHONE 310-382-3000
WEB SITE . . . . .www.hbo.com/films

Jeffrey Guthrie . . . . .Sr. VP/Sr. Counsel (West Coast Programming)
Glenn Whitehead . . . . .Sr. VP, Business Affairs & Production
Susanna Felleman .VP, Business Affairs
Molly Wilson . . . . .VP/Chief Counsel (West Coast Programming)
Suzanne Young . . . . .VP, Business Affairs

HBO LATIN AMERICA GROUP
4000 Ponce de Leon Blvd., Ste. 800
Coral Gables, FL 33146
PHONE 305-648-8100
FAX 305-442-4711
WEB SITE . . . . .www.hbo-la.tv

Jose Sariego . . . . .General Counsel
Hector Almaguer . . . . .Sr. Director, Business Affairs
Rainier Lorenzo . . . . .Director, Legal Affairs

HBO, INC.
2500 Broadway, Ste. 400
Santa Monica, CA 90404
PHONE 310-382-3000/212-512-1000
WEB SITE . . . . .www.hbo.com
COMMENTS . . . . .East Coast office: 1100 Avenue of the
Americas, New York, NY 10036

Harold Akselrad . . . . .Executive VP/General Counsel, Business Affairs &
Legal (NY)
Bruce Grivetti . . . . .Executive VP, Business Affairs (NY)
Michael Lombardo . . . . .Executive VP, Business Affairs
Glenn Whitehead . . . . .Executive VP, Business Affairs
Thomas Woodbury . . . . .Executive VP, Business Affairs & Legal (NY)
Royce Battleman . . . . .Sr. VP, Business Affairs (NY)
Viviane Eisenberg . . . . .Sr. VP/Chief Counsel (NY)
Jeffrey Guthrie . . . . .Sr. VP/Chief Counsel
Eve Konstan . . . . .Sr. VP/Chief Counsel (NY)
Peter Mozarsky . . . . .Sr. VP/Sr. Counsel (NY)
Russell Schwartz . . . . .Sr. VP, Business Affairs
Sylvia Smith-Huber . . . . .VP/Sr. Counsel
Patricia Duncan . . . . .VP/Sr. Counsel
Susanna Felleman .VP, Business Affairs
Michelle Gersen .VP/Sr. Counsel (NY)
David Goodman .VP, Business Affairs
Heather Humphrey . . . . .VP, Business Affairs (NY)
Bill Isaacs . . . . .VP, Business Affairs (NY)
Elizabeth Pongracic . . . . .VP, Business Affairs
Peter Rienecker .VP/Sr. Counsel (NY)
Stephen Sapienza .VP/Sr. Counsel (NY)
Stephen Sass . . . . .VP/Sr. Counsel
Sandra Scott . . . . .VP/Sr. Counsel (NY)
Philippa Smith . . . . .VP, Business Affairs (NY)
Colette Smith .VP/Sr. Counsel (NY)
Sharon Werner . . . . .VP, Business Affairs (NY)
Elizabeth White .VP, Business Affairs
Molly Wilson . . . . .VP/Chief Counsel, Labor
Suzanne Young .VP, Business Affairs
Stephanie Abrutyn .Sr. Counsel (NY)
Tracey Barrett-Lee .Sr. Counsel (NY)
Meeka Bondy . . . . .Sr. Counsel (NY)
Robert Brofman . . . . .Sr. Counsel (NY)
Justin Brown . . . . .Sr. Counsel
Tommy Finkelstein . . . . .Sr. Counsel
Scott Jaffee . . . . .Sr. Counsel (NY)
Ole Lyngklip . . . . .Sr. Counsel (NY)
Judy McCool . . . . .Sr. Counsel (NY)
Rachel Miller . . . . .Sr. Counsel (NY)

(Continued)

BUSINESS & LEGAL AFFAIRS DEPTS.

HBO, INC. (Continued)
Natasha Shum . . . . .Sr. Counsel, Business Affairs
Gavin Wise . . . . .Sr. Counsel
Jamaal T. Lesane . . . . .Associate Counsel (NY)
Dan Dorsky . . . . .Compliance Counsel (NY)

**INTERNATIONAL CREATIVE MANAGEMENT, INC. - ICM
(LOS ANGELES)**
10250 Constellation Blvd.
Los Angeles, CA 90067
PHONE 310-550-4000
FAX 310-550-4100
WEB SITE . . . . .www.icmtalent.com

Richard B. Levy, Esq. . . . . .Chief Business Development Officer/
                                      General Counsel, Office of the Chairman
Pam Brockie . . . . .Sr. VP/Head, Motion Picture Business Affairs
Michael Tenzer . . . . .Sr. VP/Head, Business Affairs, TV
Janet Kaye . . . . .VP, Business Affairs, TV
Michael Kernan . . . . .VP, Business Affairs, TV
Anne Pedersen . . . . .VP, Business Affairs, TV
Michael Runnels . . . . .VP, Business Affairs, Motion Picture Production
Sara Stimac . . . . .VP, Legal Affairs
George Ruiz . . . . .Business Affairs, Motion Pictures
Jacqui Schock . . . . .Business Affairs, Motion Pictures
Robin Weitz . . . . .Corporate Secretary
Alison Keeny . . . . .Paralegal, Business & Legal Affairs

**INTERNATIONAL CREATIVE MANAGEMENT, INC. - ICM
(NEW YORK)**
40 W. 57th St.
New York, NY 10019
PHONE 212-556-5600
FAX 212-556-5665
WEB SITE . . . . .www.icmtalent.com

Maarten Kooij . . . . .Sr. VP, Business Affairs
John DeLaney .Business Affairs, Literary
Colin Graham . . . . .Business Affairs, Literary
Steven David . . . . .Business Affairs, Theater

LIFETIME TELEVISION
2049 Century Park East, Ste. 840
Los Angeles, CA 90067
PHONE 310-556-7500
WEB SITE . . . . .www.lifetimetv.com
COMMENTS   New York office: Worldwide Plaza, 309 W.
                     49th St., New York, NY 10019, phone:
                     212-424-7000

Pat Langer   Executive VP, Business & Legal Affairs/Human Resources (NY)
Anne Bartnett . . . . .Sr. VP, Business Affairs
Kate McCarroll . . . . .Executive Assistant to Pat Langer (NY)
Michelle Shack . . . . .Executive Assistant to Anne Bartnett

LIONSGATE

LIONSGATE
2700 Colorado Ave.
Santa Monica, CA 90404
PHONE 310-449-9200
FAX 310-255-3870
WEB SITE . . . . .www.lionsgate.com

Wayne Levin . . . . .General Counsel/Executive VP, Corporate Operations
Sandra Stern . . . . .Executive VP/COO, Lionsgate Television
James Gladstone . . . . .Executive VP, Business & Legal Affairs
Robert Melnik . . . . .Executive VP, Business Affairs/Lionsgate Films
                                      Development & Production
Jonathan Abrams . . . . .Sr. VP, Business & Legal Affairs
Adam Bialow . . . . .Sr. VP, Business & Legal Affairs, International
Wendy Jaffe . . . . .Sr. VP, Business & Legal Affairs, Acquisitions
Matthew J. Kearns . . . . .Sr. VP, Business Affairs, TV
J. David Nonaka . . . . .Sr. VP, Business & Legal Affairs
Charlyn Ware . . . . .VP, Legal Affairs & Contracts Administration
Morris Bird . . . . .Attorney, Business & Legal Affairs, International
Catherine Choate . . . . . .Attorney, Business & Legal Affairs, International
Sanjay Sharma . . . . .Attorney, Business & Legal Affairs
Hannah Knapp . . . . .Director, Business & Legal Affairs, TV
Sam Wollman . . . . .Director, Business & Legal Affairs, Acquisitions

METRO-GOLDWYN-MAYER STUDIOS, INC.
10250 Constellation Blvd.
Los Angeles, CA 90067
PHONE 310-449-3480
FAX 310-449-3006
WEB SITE . . . . .www.mgm.com/motionpictures

Darcie Denkert . . . . .President, MGM Onstage
Jay Rakow . . . . .Sr. Executive VP/General Counsel
Jonathan Bader . . . . .Executive VP, Business Affairs
Ron Sufrin . . . . .Executive VP, Home Entertainment
Barbara Van Sickle . . . . .Sr. VP/Associate General Counsel
Michael Moore . . . . .VP, Intellectual Property
Peggy Carson .Assistant to Jay Rakow
Norm Garr . . . . .Assistant to Jonathan Bader
Barbara Stelzner . . . . .Assistant to Darcie Denkert

METRO-GOLDWYN-MAYER WORLDWIDE TELEVISION
10250 Constellation Blvd.
Los Angeles, CA 90067
PHONE 310-449-3000
WEB SITE . . . . .www.mgm.com

Blake Flynn .VP, Business & Legal Affairs
Gloria Reich . . . . .VP, Business Affairs

BUSINESS & LEGAL AFFAIRS DEPTS.

MIRAMAX FILMS
161 Avenue of the Americas, 15th Fl.
New York, NY 10013-2338
PHONE 917-606-5500
FAX 917-606-5643
WEB SITE .www.miramax.com
COMMENTS   West Coast office: 8439 Sunset Blvd., West
                Hollywood, CA 90069, phone: 323-822-
                4100, fax: 323-822-4216

Michael Luisi . . . . .Executive VP, Business Affairs & Operations
Rosalind Lawton .VP, Business & Legal Affairs
Peter McPartlin .VP, Business & Legal Affairs
Christopher Brescia . . . . .VP, Business Affairs & Delivery
Julie Daccord . . . . .Director, Contracts Administration

MTV NETWORKS
1515 Broadway
New York, NY 10036
PHONE .212-846-8000/310-752-8000
FAX 212-846-1849/310-752-8808
EMAIL . . . . .firstname.lastname@mtvstaff.com
WEB SITE . . . . .www.mtv.com
COMMENTS   West Coast office: 2600 Colorado Ave.,
                4th Fl., Santa Monica, CA 90404

George Cheeks . . .Executive VP/General Counsel, MTV Music Group &
        LOGO, Co-Chief Deputy General Counsel, MTV Networks
        (212-258-8825)
Beth Matthews . . . . . .Executive VP/Deputy General Counsel, Business &
        Legal Affairs (212-846-7122)
Virginia Lazalde-McPherson . . . . .Sr. VP, Business & Legal Affairs
        (212-846-8612)
Jeffrey Schneider . . . . . .Sr. VP, Business & Legal Affairs (310-752-8476,
        jeff.schneider2@mtvstaff.com)
Koethi Zan . . . . .Sr. VP, Business & Legal Affairs (212-846-4490)
Melissa Cates . . . . .VP, Business & Legal Affairs (212-846-8368)
Lance McPherson . . . . .VP, Business & Legal Affairs (212-846-8261)
Michael Minden . . . . .VP, Business & Legal Affairs (310-752-8151)
Ken Parks . . . . .VP, Business & Legal Affairs (212-846-7020)
Erin Peyton . . . . .VP, Business & Legal Affairs (212-846-8482)
Antonious Porch . . . . .VP, Business & Legal Affairs (212-846-4654)
Jennifer Warner . . . . .VP, Business & Legal Affairs (212-846-8544)
Nadja Webb-Cogville . . . . .VP, Business & Legal Affairs (212-846-4195)
Pauline Wen . . . . .VP, Business & Legal Affairs (212-846-4423)
Jodi Carmichael . .Sr. Counsel, Business & Legal Affairs (615-335-8486)
Hillary Cohen . . . .Sr. Counsel, Business & Legal Affairs (212-846-6758)
Jason Gottlieb . . .Sr. Counsel, Business & Legal Affairs (212-846-8931)
Leigh Gross . . . . .Sr. Counsel, Business & Legal Affairs (212-846-8678)
Brian Lazarus . . . .Sr. Counsel, Business & Legal Affairs (310-752-8442)
Janet Tzou . . . . . . .Counsel, Business & Legal Affairs (212-846-3687)
Brad Hazzard . . . .Sr. Director, Business & Legal Affairs (212-258-7089)
Bahareh Kamali . . .Sr. Director, Business & Legal Affairs (212-846-7517)
Helen Nivar-Martinez . . . . .Sr. Director, Business & Legal Affairs
        (310-752-8133)
Jane Giliberto . . . . . .Director, Business & Legal Affairs (212-846-8593)
Gail Hecht . . . . .Director, Business & Legal Affairs (212-846-7921)

NBC UNIVERSAL CABLE ENTERTAINMENT
3000 W. Alameda Ave., Ste. A-250
Burbank, CA 91523-0001
PHONE 818-840-4444
FAX .818-840-3523/818-840-7673
WEB SITE . . . . .www.nbcuni.com

Beth Roberts . . .Executive VP, NBC Universal Cable Entertainment Business
        Affairs, Digital & New Business Development (818-840-3838)
Juliana Carnessale . . . . .Sr. VP, Business Affairs (818-777-0204)
Philip Matthys . . . . .VP, Business Affairs (818-777-0375)
Lauren McCollester . . . . .VP, Business Affairs (212-664-4351)
Youngmi Nash . . . . .Director, Business Affairs (818-777-2505)
Pam Schechter . . . . .Director, Business Affairs (818-840-4114)
Crissy Thomas-Taylor . . . . . .Director, Business Affairs (818-840-4573)

NBC UNIVERSAL TELEVISION DISTRIBUTION
100 Universal City Plaza
Universal City, CA 91608
PHONE 818-777-9080
FAX 818-733-4683
WEB SITE . . . . .www.nbcuni.com

Robert Fitzpatrick . . . . .Executive VP, Business & Legal Affairs (NY)
Inge Van Herle . . . . .VP, Business Affairs
Jennifer Karie . . . . .Director, Business Affairs

NBC UNIVERSAL TELEVISION STUDIO & NETWORKS
100 Universal City Plaza, Bldg. 1320, 4th Fl.
Universal City, CA 91608
PHONE 818-777-1000
WEB SITE . . . . .www.nbcuni.com

Rick Olshansky . . . . .Executive VP, NBC Universal Network &
        Studio Business Affairs
Jeremy Adell . . . . .Sr. VP, Business Affairs
Lorna Bitensky . . . . .Sr. VP, Business Affairs
Craig Kurland . . . . .Sr. VP, Business Affairs
Lee Straus .Sr. VP, Business Affairs
Masami Yamamoto . . . . .Sr. VP, Business Affairs
Kathy Bartlett . . . . .VP, Business Affairs, Administration
Pam Black . . . . .VP, Business Affairs
Peter Glawatz . . . . .VP, Business Affairs
Richard Marks . . . . .VP, Business Affairs
Beth Whelpley . . . . .VP, Business Affairs
Julie Nguyen . . . . .Director, Business Affairs
Ellen Williams . . . . .Assistant to Jeremy Adell & Craig Kurland
Louisa Wilson . . . . .Assistant to Rick Olshansky

NEW LINE CINEMA
116 N. Robertson Blvd., Ste. 200
Los Angeles, CA 90048
PHONE 310-854-5811/212-649-4900
FAX 310-854-1824/212-649-4966
WEB SITE . . . . .www.newline.com

Benjamin Zinkin . . . . .Sr. Executive VP, Business & Legal Affairs/
General Counsel
Judd Funk . . . . .Sr. Executive VP, Business & Legal Affairs
Carolyn Blackwood . . . . .Executive VP, Business & Legal Affairs
Erik Ellner . . . . .Executive VP, Business & Legal Affairs
Teri Fournier . . . . . . .Executive VP, Legal Affairs/Deputy General Counsel
Andrew Matthews . . . . . . .Executive VP, Business & Legal Affairs, Finance
Julie A. Shapiro . . . . .Executive VP, Business & Legal Affairs, TV
Craig Alexander . . . . .Sr. VP, Business & Legal Affairs
Lori Silfen . . . . .Sr. VP, Business & Legal Affairs, Music
Derek Arteta . . . . .VP, Business & Legal Affairs, Home Entertainment
Scott Kanyuck . . . . .VP, Business & Legal Affairs
Stefanie Markman . . . . .VP, Business & Legal Affairs
Carol Smithson . . . . .VP, Business & Legal Affairs
Kavita Amar . . . . .Counsel, Business & Legal Affairs
Camrin Crisci . . . . .Counsel, Business & Legal Affairs
Jeannette Hill-Yonis . . . . .Counsel, Business & Legal Affairs
Colette Kadrnka . . . . .Counsel, Business & Legal Affairs
Robyn Martin . . . . .Counsel, Business & Legal Affairs
Brian Taub . . . . .Counsel, Business & Legal Affairs, TV
John Walsh . . . . . . .Sr. VP, Business & Legal Affairs Administration, Music
Ginny Martino . . . . .VP, Business & Legal Affairs Administration
Gloria Gutierrez . . . . .Executive Director, Business & Legal Affairs
Administration, Home Entertainment
Daniel Villagomez . . . .Executive Director, Titles & Credits Administration
Susan Nezami . . . . .VP, Business & Legal Affairs
Charity Paniamogan . . . .Director, Business & Legal Affairs Administration
Robin Zlatin . . . . .Director, Business & Legal Affairs Administration
Camelia Adibi . . . . . . .Manager, Business & Legal Affairs Administration
Kimberly Baldwin . . . . .Manager, Business & Legal Affairs Administration
Lorin Green . . . . .Manager, Business & Legal Affairs Administration
Steve Kesmodel . . . . .Manager, Credits Administration
Romy Schneider . . . . . .Manager, Business & Legal Affairs Administration

NICKELODEON/MTVN KIDS & FAMILY GROUP
1515 Broadway, 38th Fl.
New York, NY 10036
PHONE 212-846-7507
FAX 212-846-1341
WEB SITE . . . . .www.nick.com
SECOND WEB SITE . . . . .www.nickatnite.com

Andra Shapiro . . . . .Executive VP/General Counsel, Nickelodeon
Melissa Polaner . . . . .Sr. VP, Business & Legal Affairs, Nickelodeon

OXYGEN MEDIA, INC.
75 Ninth Ave.
New York, NY 10011
PHONE 212-651-2000
FAX 212-651-2041
WEB SITE . . . . .www.oxygen.com

Daniel Taitz . . . . .Chief Administrative Officer/General Counsel
Fabian F. Milburn .Sr. VP, Business Operations

PARADIGM
360 N. Crescent Dr., North Bldg.
Beverly Hills, CA 90210
PHONE 310-288-8000
FAX 310-288-2000

Craig Wagner . . . . .Executive VP, Business Affairs
Shauna Emmons . . . . .Director, Business & Legal Affairs
Larry Sheffield . . . . .Executive, Business & Legal Affairs

PARAMOUNT HOME ENTERTAINMENT
5555 Melrose Ave.
Los Angeles, CA 90038-3197
PHONE 323-956-8864
FAX 323-862-2232

Marsha King . . . . .Executive VP, Business Affairs, Worldwide Home
Entertainment & Digital Distribution
Margie Pacacha . . . . .Sr. VP, Business Affairs & Legal, Worldwide
Home Entertainment

PARAMOUNT LICENSING
5555 Melrose Ave., Chevalier Bldg., #213
Los Angeles, CA 90038
PHONE 323-956-8556
FAX 323-862-1187
WEB SITE . . . . .www.viacom.com

Norman Becker . . . . .Sr. VP, Business Affairs, Legal & Operations
Eric Liang . . . . .Director, Business & Legal Affairs (323-956-2016)
Sam Jeffries . . . . .Coordinator (323-956-8527)

PARAMOUNT PICTURES DOMESTIC DISTRIBUTION
5555 Melrose Ave.
Los Angeles, CA 90038-3197
PHONE 323-956-8408
EMAIL . . . . .paul_springer@paramount.com
WEB SITE . . . . .www.paramount.com

Paul Springer . . . . .Sr. VP/Assistant General Counsel

BUSINESS & LEGAL AFFAIRS DEPTS.

PARAMOUNT PICTURES MOTION PICTURE GROUP
5555 Melrose Ave.
Los Angeles, CA 90038-3197
PHONE 323-956-5000
WEB SITE .www.paramount.com

Daniel Ferleger . . . . .Executive VP, Paramount Pictures, Business &
Legal Affairs
Paul Neinstein . . . . .Executive VP in Charge of Business Affairs
Karen Magid . . . . .Executive VP, Legal Affairs
Scott Martin . . . . .Executive VP, Intellectual Property/
Associate General Counsel
Dan Butler . . . . .Sr. VP, Business & Legal Affairs, Music
Alan Heppel . . . . .Sr. VP, Legal Affairs
Linda Wohl . . . . .Sr. VP, Legal, Music
Lindsey Bayman . . . . .Sr. VP, Business Affairs
Rona Cosgrove . . . . .Sr. VP, Business Affairs
Liz McNicoll . . . . .VP, Business Affairs, Music
Deborah Chiaramonte . . . . .VP, Legal Affairs
Robert Gasper . . . . .VP, Legal, Music
Mike Grizzi . . . . .VP, Legal Affairs
Cami Kinahan .VP, Legal Affairs
Kristen Baldwin . . . . .Attorney
Jean Chi . . . . .Attorney
Josh Deutsch . . . . .Attorney
Deborah Lintz . . . . .Attorney
Donna Roberts . . . . .Attorney
Patricia Torres . . . . .Attorney

PBS
2100 Crystal Dr.
Arlington, VA 22202-3785
PHONE 703-739-5000
FAX . . .703-739-8460 (Business Affairs)/703-837-3300 (Legal Affairs)
WEB SITE . . . . .www.pbs.org

Katherine Lauderdale . . . . .Sr. VP/General Counsel/Corporate Secretary
Jack Dougherty . . . . .VP, Program Business Affairs
Jason Dillinger   Associate General Counsel/Intellectual Property Counsel
Jill D. Patrone   Associate General Counsel/Labor & Employment Counsel
Traci L. Higgins . . . . .Assistant General Counsel
Mary L. Plantamura . . . . .Sr. Counsel/Assistant Corporate Secretary
Elizabeth Bruns . . . .Sr. Business Affairs Attorney, Program Business Affairs
Denielle Pemberton-Heard . . . . .Sr. Business Affairs Attorney,
Program Business Affairs
Eric Posner . . . . .Business Affairs Attorney/Contract Manager,
Program Business Affairs
Steve Edw. Friedman . . . . .Director, Copyright
Bradley Jones . . . . .Director, Legislative & Regulatory Affairs

SHOWTIME NETWORKS INC.
10880 Wilshire Blvd., Ste. 1600
Los Angeles, CA 90024
PHONE .310-234-5300/212-708-1600
FAX 310-234-5397
WEB SITE . . . . .www.sho.com

Melinda Benedek . . . . .Executive VP, Business Affairs & Production
Gwen H. Marcus . . . .Executive VP, Operations & General Counsel (NY)
Anne Kurrasch .Sr. VP, Business Affairs
Steve Rogers . . . . .Sr. VP, Business Affairs
Janet Stott . . . . .Sr. VP, Business Affairs

SONY ONLINE ENTERTAINMENT
8928 Terman Ct.
San Diego, CA 92121
PHONE 858-577-3100
FAX 858-577-3356
WEB SITE . . . . .www.soe.sony.com

Andrew Zaffron . . . . .Sr. VP/General Counsel
Rick Herman . . . . .VP, Business & Legal Affairs
Steven Weiss . . . . .VP, Business & Legal Affairs
Olivia Malmstrom . . . . .Assistant to Andrew Zaffron

SONY PICTURES CLASSICS
A Sony Pictures Entertainment Company
10202 W. Washington Blvd.
Culver City, CA 90232
PHONE 310-244-4000
WEB SITE . . . . .www.sonypictures.com

Diane Buck . . . . .VP, Business & Legal Affairs
Zean Bernabe . . . . .Director, Business & Legal Affairs

SONY PICTURES CONSUMER MARKETING
10202 W. Washington Blvd.
Jimmy Stewart Bldg., 3rd Fl.
Culver City, CA 90232
PHONE 310-244-4188
FAX 310-244-5563
WEB SITE . . . . .www.sonypictures.com

Gregory G. Economos . . . . .Sr. VP, Business Affairs & Operations
Christa Medeiros . . . . .Assistant to Gregory G. Economos

SONY PICTURES DIGITAL
10202 W. Washington Blvd.
Culver City, CA 90232
PHONE 310-244-4000
WEB SITE . . . . .www.sonypictures.com

Jennifer Kuo . . . . .Sr. VP, Business & Legal Affairs
Susie H. Oh . . . . .VP, Business & Legal Affairs
Sharon Sartorius . . . . .VP, Business & Legal Affairs
Jonathan Jackman . . . . .Director, Business & Legal Affairs

BUSINESS & LEGAL AFFAIRS DEPTS.

BUSINESS & LEGAL AFFAIRS DEPTS.

SONY PICTURES ENTERTAINMENT
Legal Department
10202 W. Washington Blvd.
Culver City, CA 90232
PHONE 310-244-4000
WEB SITE . . . . .www.spe.sony.com

Leah E. Weil . . . . .Executive VP/General Counsel
Corii D. Berg . . . . .Executive VP, Corporate & Distribution/
Deputy General Counsel
Jean F. Bonini . . . . .Executive VP, Legal Affairs/Chief Labor Counsel
Gregory K. Boone . . . . .Executive VP, Legal Affairs, Television
Shelly Bunge . . . . .Executive VP, Music Affairs
Jared Jussim . . . . .Executive VP, Legal Affairs, Intellectual Property
Dennis Nollette . . . . . . .Executive VP, Legal Affairs, Home Entertainment
Roger W. Toll . . . . .Executive VP, Legal Affairs, Motion Pictures
Leonard Venger . . . . .Executive VP, Litigation
Eric I. Baum . . . .Sr. VP, Legal Affairs, Worldwide & Consumer Marketing
Fran Black . . . . .Sr. VP, Legal Affairs
Sharon A. Borak . . . . .Sr. VP, Legal Affairs
Donna Brainard . . . . .Sr. VP, Script Clearance
Deborah D. Bruenell . . . . .Sr. VP, Legal Affairs
Steven W. Gerse . . . . .Sr. VP
Jennifer C. Kuo . . . . .Sr. VP, Sony Pictures Digital Productions,
Business & Legal Affairs
Gayle McDonald . . . . .Sr. VP, Rights & Title Administration
Vicki R. Solmon . . . . .Sr. VP, Trade Regulation & Copyright Protection
Larry Stephens . . . . .Sr. VP, Music Affairs
Aimee B. Wolfson . . . . .Sr. VP, Legal Affairs
Luis E. Allen . . . . .VP
Helayne Antler . . . . .VP
Diane Buck . . . . .VP, Sony Pictures Classics, Business Affairs
Mary Courtney Burke . . . . .VP
Stephen Catton . . . . .VP, Legal Affairs - Europe
Chris Elwell . . . . .VP
Paul Friedman . . . . .VP, Music Affairs
Michael Frisby . . . . .VP, Music Affairs
Eric Gaynor . . . . .VP
Steve N. Gofman . . . . .VP
Carmen Grant . . . . .VP
Maggie Heim . . . . .VP
Sarah E. Kiefer . . . . .VP
Larry Kohorn . . . . .VP, Music Affairs
Michael Kramer . . . . .VP
John R. Miller . . . . .VP
Susie Oh . . . . .VP
Suzanne P. Prete . . . . .VP
Jennifer Rick . . . . .VP, Music Affairs
Cynthia Salmen . . . . .VP, Compliance & Ethics
Sharon Sartorius . . . . .VP
David Silverman . . . . .VP
Susan Slamer . . . . .VP, Music Affairs
Melissa Taipie . . . . .VP
Susan Tyre Kirk . . . . .VP, Trademark & Immigration
Cynthia Wasney . . . . .VP
Dina Wiggins . . . . .VP
Ian Wilson . . . . .VP
Daniel Yankelevits . . . . .VP

SONY PICTURES ENTERTAINMENT - MUSIC GROUP
10202 W. Washington Blvd.
Culver City, CA 90232
PHONE 310-244-4000
WEB SITE . . . . .www.spe.sony.com

Shelly Bunge . . . . .Executive VP
Larry Kohorn . . . . .Sr. VP, Rights Management
Larry Stephens . . . . .Sr. VP, Licensing Affairs
Paul Friedman .VP, Business Affairs
Tony Scudellari . . . . .VP, TV Music Creative
Susan Slamer . . . . .VP, TV Music Licensing
Merlene Travis . . . . .VP, Music Publishing
Jamie Cyr . . . . .Director, Catalog Exploitation

SONY PICTURES HOME ENTERTAINMENT
10202 W. Washington Blvd.
Culver City, CA 90232
PHONE 310-244-4000
WEB SITE . . . . .www.spe.sony.com

Robin Russell . . . . .Sr. Executive VP/General Manager, Worldwide
Pam Kunath . . . . .Sr. VP, Business Affairs
Dennis Nollette . . . . .Sr. VP, Legal Affairs
Michael Helfand . . . . .VP, Business Affairs
Dina Wiggins . . . . .VP, Legal Affairs
Dan Primozic . . . . .Executive Director, Business Affairs

SONY PICTURES TELEVISION
10202 W. Washington Blvd.
Culver City, CA 90232
PHONE 310-244-4000
WEB SITE . . . . .www.sonypicturestelevision.com

Gregory K. Boone . . . . .Executive VP/Legal Affairs/General Counsel
Richard Frankie . . . . .Executive VP, Business Operations
Don Loughery . . . . .Executive VP, Strategic Planning
Drew Shearer . . . . .Sr. VP/CFO
Joanne Mazzu . . . . .Sr. VP, Business Affairs
J.R. McGinnis . . . . .Sr. VP, Business Affairs
Ramona Teisan . . . . .Sr. VP/Controller, TV Production
Ellen Cohen . . . . .VP, Business Affairs
Wing Hom . . . . .VP, Production Accounting
Sarah E. Kiefer . . . . .VP, Legal Affairs
Suzanne P. Prete .VP, Legal Affairs
Charles Smolsky . . . . .VP, Business Affairs
Karen Tatevosian . . . . .VP, Business Affairs
Michael Viebrock . . . . .VP, Business & Legal Affairs, SPTI
Cynthia Wasney . . . . .VP, Legal Affairs
Jeff Weiss . . . . .VP, Business Affairs
Annemarie Carretta . . . . .Sr. Counsel
Misara Shao . . . . .Attorney
Steve Maynard . . . . .Director, Business Affairs
Jennifer Stone . . . . .Manager, Business Affairs
Jeanette Arveschoug . . . . .Assistant to Mr. Loughery
Sharlynn Bose . . . . .Assistant to Ms. Mazzu
Devin Carbaugh . . . . .Assistant to Mr. McGinnis
Tony Foster . . . . .Assistant to Mr. Smolsky
Donna Hollister . . . . .Assistant to Ms. Wasney
Yolanda Lanning . . . . .Assistant to Mr. Boone
Ester Medina . . . . .Assistant to Ms. Prete & Ms. Carretta
Rose Sadler . . . . .Assistant to Mr. Frankie
Corey Saffold . . . . .Assistant to Ms. Kiefer
Stephen Shaw . . . . .Assistant to Mr. Shearer

SONY PICTURES TELEVISION INTERNATIONAL
10202 W. Washington Blvd.
Culver City, CA 90232
PHONE 310-244-4000
WEB SITE . . . . .www.sonypicturestelevision.com

Donna Cunningham . . . . .Executive VP, Operations
Sam Semon . . . . .VP, Business Affairs
Greg Rose . . . . .Executive Director, Business Affairs
Michelle Jaeger . . . . .Manager, Business Affairs
Maria Bonvicini . . . . .Administrative Assistant
Troi Moore . . . . .Administrative Assistant - Legal II

SONY PICTURES TELEVISION INTERNATIONAL NETWORKS GROUP
10202 W. Washington Blvd.
Culver City, CA 90232
PHONE 310-244-4000

Pamela Parker . . . . .VP, Business Affairs & Acquisitions
Heidi Willemsen . . . . .Director, Business Affairs
Patricia Rainwater . . . . .Manager, Contract Administration
Joseph Romero . . . . .Administrative Assistant

SPIKE TV
1775 Broadway, 10th Fl.
New York, NY 10019
PHONE 212-767-4001
FAX 212-767-8671
WEB SITE . . . . .www.spiketv.com
COMMENTS   West Coast office: 2049 Century Park East, Ste. 4000, Los Angeles, CA 90067, phone: 310-407-1200, fax: 310-407-1297

Clara Kim . . . . .Sr. VP, Business & Legal Affairs/General Counsel
Jonathan Ladd . . . . .VP, Business & Legal Affairs (LA)
Aleena Maher . . . . .VP, Business & Legal Affairs
Matt Kelman . . . . .Sr. Counsel
Kelly Wick . . . . .Sr. Counsel
Blake Wood . . . . .Executive Assistant to Clara Kim
Erin Rice . . . . .Assistant to Jonathan Ladd (LA)
Alyce Roche . . . . .Assistant to Matt Kelman & Aleena Maher
Stacy Winter . . . . .Assistant to Kelly Wick

STARZ ENTERTAINMENT
16830 Ventura Blvd., Ste. 260
Encino, CA 91436
PHONE 818-325-8820

Steve Beabout . . . . .Executive VP/General Counsel
Richard Turner . . . . .Sr. VP, Business Affairs, Programming
Richard Waysdorf . . . . .Sr. VP, Business Affairs, Distribution
Marc Barson . . . . .Deputy General Counsel, Starz Media/Sr. VP, Business Affairs, Production, Starz Entertainment
Tim Sweeney . . . . .VP, Business Affairs/Marketing
Jessie Spillane . . . . .Manager, Business Affairs, Production
Deanne Bloch . . . . .Paralegal, Business Affairs, Production
Lauren Collins . . . . .Legal Assistant, Business Affairs, Production

TBS/TURNER NETWORK TELEVISION (TNT)
3500 W. Olive Ave., 15th Fl.
Burbank, CA 91505
PHONE 818-977-5500
WEB SITE . . . . .www.tbs.tv
SECOND WEB SITE . . . . .www.tnt.tv

Patrick Kelly . . . . .VP, Business Affairs, TBS & TNT
John Palmerton . . . . .VP, Business Affairs, TBS & TNT
Mary Lawler . . . . .Sr. Director, Business Affairs, TBS & TNT
Martine Shahar . . . . .Sr. Director, Business Affairs, TBS & TNT
Clinton Wilburn . . . . .Director, Business Affairs, TBS & TNT

TURNER BROADCASTING SYSTEM, INC.
CNN Center
14 North Tower
Atlanta, GA 30303
PHONE 404-827-1008
FAX 404-827-2381
WEB SITE . . . . .www.turner.com

Louise Sams . . . . .Executive VP & General Counsel, TBS, Inc.,/President, TBS International
James McGee . . . . .Sr. Counsel, TBS/Cartoon Network (404-575-6276)

TWENTIETH CENTURY FOX
10201 W. Pico Blvd.
Los Angeles, CA 90035
PHONE 310-369-1000
WEB SITE . . . . .www.fox.com

Bob Cohen .Executive VP, Legal Affairs
Steve Plum .Executive VP, Business Affairs
Mark Resnick . . . . .Executive VP, Business Affairs
Gary D. Roberts . . . . .Executive VP, Litigation
Victoria Rossellini . . . .Executive VP, Production Finance & Business Affairs
Paul Hoffman .Sr. VP, Business Affairs
Tom Moglovkin . . . . .Sr. VP, Business Affairs
Ron Wheeler . . . . .Sr. VP, Content Protection
Chris Brock . . . . .VP, Business Affairs
Matt Dixon . . . . .VP, Business Affairs

TWENTIETH CENTURY FOX - SEARCHLIGHT PICTURES
10201 W. Pico Blvd., Bldg. 38
Los Angeles, CA 90035
PHONE 310-369-1833
FAX 310-369-3175
WEB SITE .www.foxsearchlight.com

Joseph De Marco . . . . .Executive VP
Chris Maxwell . . . . .Sr. VP, Legal Affairs
James M. Taylor . . . . .Sr. VP, Legal Affairs
Julius Galacki . . . . .Assistant to Chris Maxwell
Janie Moore . . . . .Assistant to James M. Taylor
Lolita Peralta . . . . .Assistant to Joseph De Marco

TWENTIETH CENTURY FOX TELEVISION
10201 W. Pico Blvd., Bldg. 103
Los Angeles, CA 90035
PHONE 310-369-1000

Howard Kurtzman . . . . .Executive VP, Business & Legal Affairs
Neal Baseman . . . . .Sr. VP, Business Affairs
Sam Bramhall . . . . .Sr. VP, Business Affairs
Pam Baron . . . . .Sr. VP, Business Affairs
Sandra Ortiz . . . . .Sr. VP, Business Affairs
Beth Hoffman . . . . .VP, Business Affairs
Vibiana Molina . . . . .VP, Business Affairs
UnJu Paik . . . . .Sr. VP, Legal Affairs
Jonathan Harris . . . . .VP, Legal Affairs
Wendy Bartosh . . . . .VP, Legal Affairs
Susan Bowles .Sr. Counsel, Legal Affairs
Cynthia Sakuda . . . . .Sr. Counsel, Legal Affairs

BUSINESS & LEGAL AFFAIRS DEPTS.

BUSINESS & LEGAL AFFAIRS DEPTS.

UNITED TALENT AGENCY - UTA
9560 Wilshire Blvd., Ste. 500
Beverly Hills, CA 90212
PHONE 310-273-6700
FAX 310-247-1111
WEB SITE . . . . .www.unitedtalentagency.com

Gary Gradinger . . . . .Head, Business Affairs
Thora Leiken . . . . .Business Affairs
Lauren Menkes . . . . .Business Affairs
Mike Rubi . . . . .Business Affairs
Leroy Simmons . . . . .Business Affairs
Sarah Ebrahimi . . . . .Legal Affairs

UNIVERSAL PICTURES
100 Universal City Plaza
Universal City, CA 91608
PHONE 818-777-1000
WEB SITE .www.universalstudios.com

James M. Horowitz . . . . .Co-President, Production/Executive VP,
 Universal Pictures
Nancy Eagle . . . . .Sr. VP, Business Affairs
Christopher Floyd . . . . .Sr. VP, Business Affairs
Jeff Goore . . . . .Sr. VP, Business Affairs
Helen Jorda . . . . .Sr. VP, Business Affairs
Masako Ichino .VP, Business Affairs
Anthony Zummo . . . . .Sr. VP, Legal Affairs
Grant Gullickson .VP, Legal Affairs
Carolyn Hampton . . . . .VP, Legal Affairs
Marcia Mahony .VP, Legal Affairs
Michele Moore . . . . .VP, Legal Affairs
Keith Blau .Attorney, Legal Affairs
Lisa Franklin . . . . .Attorney, Legal Affairs
Ellen Shallman . . . . .Attorney, Legal Affairs
Grace Torpoco . . . . .Attorney, Legal Affairs
Mary Ann Fortuna . . . . .Director, Title Administration
Cat Bartik-Sweeney . . . . .Assistant to Keith Blau
Hadiss DeWitt . . . . .Assistant to Helen Jorda
Mary Ann Donohue . . . . .Assistant to Michele Moore
Joseph Edwards . . . . . .Assistant to Marcia Mahony & Carolyn Hampton
Joy Evans . . . . .Assistant to Ellen Shallman & Lisa Franklin
Gwinn Ioka . . . . .Assistant to Masako Ichino
Keala Kimmons . . . . .Assistant to James M. Horowitz
Rumaisa Rahman . . . . .Assistant to Jeff Goore
Howard Rice . . . . .Assistant to Anthony Zummo
Jason Rosenbaum . . . . .Assistant to Grant Gullickson
Michelle Straubing . . . . .Assistant to Grace Torpoco
Michelle Wollmers . . . . .Assistant to Christopher Floyd

UNIVERSAL PICTURES - MUSIC BUSINESS AFFAIRS
100 Universal City Plaza, Ste. 1320 W-3
Universal City, CA 91608
PHONE 818-777-1000
FAX 818-866-1513
WEB SITE .www.universalstudios.com

Philip Cohen . . . . .Sr. VP, Music Business Affairs
Chris Saranec . . . . .Executive Director, Music Licensing
Pam Springs . . . . .Executive Director, Music Licensing
Kittie Lo . . . . .Assistant to Philip Cohen

UNIVERSAL STUDIOS HOME ENTERTAINMENT
10 Universal City Plaza, 33rd Fl.
Universal City, CA 91608
PHONE 818-777-8032
WEB SITE .www.universalstudios.com

Christine Lawton . . . . .Sr. VP, Business & Legal Affairs
Jed Lackman . . . . .VP, Business & Legal Affairs
Jean-Christophe Curelop . . . . .Director, Business & Legal Affairs
Brigitte Lifson . . . . .Director, Business & Legal Affairs
Ike Manaster . . . . .Director, Business & Legal Affairs
Linda Martinez . . . . .Director, Rights & Clearance
Daos Boonma . . . . .Manager, Legal Clearance
Maria Casteneda . . . . .Manager
Michelle Portabella . . . . .Assistant Manager, Legal Clearance

USA NETWORK
30 Rockefeller Plaza
New York, NY 10112
PHONE 212-664-4444
WEB SITE . . . . .www.usanetwork.com
COMMENTS   Oversees Sci Fi and Bravo

Beth Roberts . . . . .Executive VP, Business Affairs
Juliana Carnessale . . . . .Sr. VP, Business Affairs
Philip Matthys .VP, Business Affairs
Lauren McCollester . . . . .VP, Business Affairs
Youngmi Nash . . . . .Director, Business Affairs
Pam Schechter . . . . .Director, Business Affairs

VH1
2600 Colorado Ave.
Santa Monica, CA 90404
PHONE 310-752-8000
WEB SITE www.vh1.com

Monica Harris . . . . .VP, Business & Legal Affairs
Beck Sloca . . . . .Director, Business & Legal Affairs
Tina Perry . . . . .Counsel
Jorge Gutierrez . . . . .Executive Assistant

WARNER BROS. CONSUMER PRODUCTS
4000 Warner Blvd.
Burbank, CA 91522-0001
PHONE . . . . .See Below
FAX 818-977-6340
WEB SITE . . . . .www.warnerbros.com

Ana de Castro . . . . .Sr. VP, Business & Legal Affairs (818-977-7227)
Steve Fogelson . . . . .Sr. Attorney (818-977-5768)
Scott Whiteleather .Attorney (818-977-4599)
Oswaldo Garcia . . . . .Assistant to Ana de Castro (818-977-5095)
Natasha Jules . . . . .Assistant to Steve Fogelson & Scott Whiteleather
(818-977-5085)

WARNER BROS. DOMESTIC CABLE DISTRIBUTION
4000 Warner Blvd.
Burbank, CA 91522-0001
PHONE 818-954-6000
FAX 818-977-4222
WEB SITE . . . . .www.warnerbros.com

Ron Sunderland . . . . .Sr. VP, Legal & Business Affairs
Sandra Panattoni . . . . .Director, Legal & Business Affairs
Sara Detisch . . . . .Coordinator, Legal & Business Affairs

WARNER BROS. ENTERTAINMENT INC.
4000 Warner Blvd.
Burbank, CA 91522-0001
PHONE 818-954-6000/818-954-4223
WEB SITE . . . . .www.warnerbros.com

John A. Schulman . . . . .Executive VP/General Counsel
Sheldon Presser . . . . .Sr. VP/Deputy General Counsel
Jeremy Williams . . . . .Sr. VP/Deputy General Counsel
Leigh Chapman . . . . .Sr. VP/Chief Employment Counsel/
Deputy General Counsel
Dean Marks . . . . .Sr. VP, Intellectual Property, Corporate Business
Development & Strategy
Steve Mertz . . . . .Sr. VP/General Counsel, Europe
Zazi Pope . . . . . . .Sr. VP/Chief Litigator Counsel/Deputy General Counsel
Clarissa Weirick . . . . .Sr. VP/General Counsel, Corporate Business
Development & Strategy
Gwen Whitson . . . . .Sr. VP/Deputy General Counsel, Business
Information Systems

WARNER BROS. INTERNATIONAL TELEVISION DISTRIBUTION
4000 Warner Blvd.
Burbank, CA 91522-0001
PHONE 818-954-6000
WEB SITE . . . . .www.wbitv.com

Ron Miele   Executive VP, Business Affairs & Operations/General Counsel
Renee Wolf . . . .Sr. VP, Legal & Business Affairs/Deputy General Counsel
Robert Cooper . . . . .VP, Legal & Business Affairs
Delyth Fetherston-Dilke . . . .VP, Legal & Business Affairs, Europe (London)
Alastair McKenzie . . . . .VP, Legal & Business Affairs, Europe (London)
David Read . . . . .VP, Legal & Business Affairs
Benedict Chun . . . . .Sr. Counsel, Legal & Business Affairs
Anita McLane . . . . .Counsel, Legal & Business Affairs

WARNER BROS. PICTURES
4000 Warner Blvd.
Burbank, CA 91522-0001
PHONE 818-954-6000
WEB SITE . . . . .www.warnerbros.com

Steve Spira . . . . .President, Worldwide Business Affairs
Patti Connolly . . . . .Executive VP, Business Affairs
Keith Zajic . . . . .Executive VP, Business Affairs, Music
Dan Furie . . . . .Sr. VP, Business Affairs
Pam Kirsh .Sr. VP/Special Counsel
Richard Levin . . . . .Sr. VP/General Counsel
Jodi Levinson .Sr. VP, Business Affairs
Lisa Margolis . . . . .Sr. VP, Business & Legal Affairs, Music
David Sagal . . . . .Sr. VP/General Counsel, Business & Legal Affairs
Sandra Smokler . . . . .Sr. VP/Deputy General Counsel
Courtney Armstrong . . . . .VP, Business Affairs
Eileen Hale . . . . .VP/Deputy General Counsel
Virginia Tweedy . . . . .VP, Business Affairs Administration

WARNER BROS. PICTURES DOMESTIC DISTRIBUTION
4000 Warner Blvd.
Burbank, CA 91522-0001
PHONE 818-954-6000
WEB SITE . . . . .www.warnerbros.com

Connie Minnett . . . . .Sr. VP/General Counsel

WARNER BROS. TELEVISION
4000 Warner Blvd.
Burbank, CA 91522-0001
PHONE 818-954-6000
FAX 818-954-7367
WEB SITE . . . . .www.warnerbros.com

Brett Paul . . . . .Executive VP, Business Affairs, Operations & Finance
Karen Cease . . . . .Consultant, Business Affairs
Adam Glick . . . . .Sr. VP, Business Affairs
Sue Palladino .Sr. VP, Business Affairs
Jay Gendron . . . . .VP, Business Affairs
Dan Limerick . . . . .VP, Business Affairs
Dave Brown .Director, Business Affairs
Matthew Matzkin . . . . .Director, Business Affairs
Crystal Morales . . . . .Director, Business Affairs
Lisa Koes . . . . .Associate Director, Business Affairs
Marjorie Neufeld . . . . .Sr. VP, General Counsel
Jody Zucker . . . . .Sr. VP, Deputy General Counsel
Barbara Zuckerman . . . . .VP, Legal Affairs
Nannette Diacovo . . . . .VP, Legal Affairs
Diana O'Brien . . . . .VP, Legal Affairs
Danielle Knight . . . . .Director, Legal Affairs
Susan Parlane .Director, Legal Affairs
Sandeep Motwani . . . . .Director, Legal Affairs

WARNER HOME VIDEO
4000 Warner Blvd., Bldg. 160
Burbank, CA 91522-0001
PHONE 818-954-6000
WEB SITE . . . . .www.warnerbros.com

Beth Baier . . . . .Sr. VP, Business Affairs/General Counsel
Johnna Cho .VP, Business & Legal Affairs
Jackie Hayes .VP, Business & Legal Affairs
Julie Kelley . . . . .VP, Business & Legal Affairs
Jay Kinn . . . . .VP, Business & Legal Affairs
Dana Lira . . . . .VP, Business & Legal Affairs
Nick Macrae . . . . .VP, Business & Legal Affairs (Europe)
Octavio Pedroza . . . . .VP, Business & Legal Affairs
Louise Bagnall . . . . .Sr. Counsel, Business & Legal Affairs (Europe)
Darryl Hendrix . . . . .Sr. Counsel, Business & Legal Affairs
Cheri Kehrli . . . . .Sr. Counsel, Business & Legal Affairs
Cindy Todd . . . . .Sr. Counsel, Business & Legal Affairs
Richard Ball . . . . .Counsel, Business & Legal Affairs (Europe)
Margarita Hernandez . . . . .Counsel, Business & Legal Affairs
Yuka Kato . . . . .Counsel, Business & Legal Affairs (Asia)

BUSINESS & LEGAL AFFAIRS DEPTS.

THE WEINSTEIN COMPANY
345 Hudson St., 13th Fl.
New York, NY 10014
PHONE 646-862-3400
FAX 917-368-7000
WEB SITE . . . . .www.weinsteinco.com
SECOND WEB SITE . . . . .www.twcpublicity.com
COMMENTS   Second address: 375 Greenwich St., 3rd
                  Fl., New York, NY 10013; phone: 212-
                  941-3800; fax: 212-941-3949; West
                  Coast address: 5700 Wilshire Blvd., Ste.
                  600, Los Angeles, CA 90036; phone: 323-
                  207-3200; fax: 323-954-0997

Peter Hurwitz . . . . .General Counsel (NY)
Barry Littman . . . . .Executive VP, Business & Legal Affairs (LA)
Eric Roth . . . . .Executive VP, Business & Legal Affairs (LA)
Laine R. Kline . . . . .Sr. VP, Business & Legal Affairs (LA)
Bradley Buchanan . . . . .VP, Business & Legal Affairs (LA)
Jonathan Fuhrman . . . . .VP, Business & Legal Affairs (NY)
Clarke McCutchen . . . . .VP, Business & Legal Affairs (LA)

WILLIAM MORRIS AGENCY - WMA (LOS ANGELES)
One William Morris Pl.
Beverly Hills, CA 90212
PHONE 310-859-4000
FAX 310-859-4462
WEB SITE . . . . .www.wma.com

David Kekst . . . . .Sr. VP/General Counsel
Susan Brooks . . . . .Worldwide Head, TV Business Affairs
June Horton Van Nort . . . . .Head, Motion Picture Business Affairs
Aron Baumel . . . . .Business Affairs
Jessica Drood . . . . .Business Affairs
Ruth Engelhardt . . . . .Business Affairs
Ruth Estrada . . . . .Business Affairs
Robyn Goldman . . . . .Business Affairs
Mary Harding . . . . .Business Affairs
Angela Petillo . . . . .Business Affairs
Brian Rabolli . . . . .Business Affairs
Berkeley Reinhold .Business Affairs
David Taghioff . . . . .Business Affairs
Stuart Tenzer . . . . .Business Affairs
Kelly Weiss . . . . .Business Affairs

WILLIAM MORRIS AGENCY - WMA (NEW YORK)
1325 Avenue of the Americas
New York, NY 10019
PHONE 212-586-5100
FAX 212-246-3583
WEB SITE . . . . .www.wma.com

Don Aslan . . . . .Business Affairs
Catherine Bennett .Business Affairs
Richard Charnoff . . . . .Business Affairs
Annette Frankel . . . . .Business Affairs
David Schmerler . . . . .Business Affairs
Eric Zohn . . . . .Business Affairs

BUSINESS & LEGAL AFFAIRS DEPTS.

Hollywood Representation Directory
ENTERTAINMENT ATTORNEYS

To submit your company for a free listing in the HOLLYWOOD REPRESENTATION DIRECTORY, complete and return this application form along with a brief bio and/or company profile. All listings are at the discretion of the Editor.

PHONE: 323-525-2376   FAX: 323-525-2393   www.hcdonline.com

COMPANY _____

ADDRESS _____ CITY _____ STATE _____ ZIP _____

PHONE(S) _____ FAX(S) _____

PUBLISHED EMAIL _____ WEBSITE _____

NONPUBLISHED EMAIL _____ NONPUBLISHED FAX _____
(for internal use only)   (for internal use only)

ENTERTAINMENT LAW SERVICES

❏ FULL SERVICE REPRESENTATION

❏ ACQUISITIONS & MERGERS
❏ ARBITRATION & MEDIATION
❏ CONTRACT NEGOTIATION & DRAFTING
❏ COPYRIGHT & TRADEMARK MATTERS
❏ CORPORATE MATTERS
❏ EMPLOYMENT LABOR LAW

❏ FINANCING

❏ FIRST AMENDMENT ISSUES
❏ INTELLECTUAL PROPERTY LAW
❏ LIBEL & PRIVACY MATTERS
❏ LICENSING
❏ LITIGATION
❏ MISAPPROPRIATION OF NAME, VOICE, LIKENESS
❏ MOTION PICTURE & TV LAW

❏ MUSIC LAW
❏ PARTNERSHIPS/JOINT VENTURES
❏ RIGHT OF PUBLICITY
❏ ROYALTY LAW
❏ TALENT REPRESENTATION
❏ TAX LAW

❏ TRANSACTIONAL LAW

ADDITIONAL SERVICES _____
_____

NAME   **TITLE (include areas of specialization)**

P A R T N E R S & A T T O R N E Y S

_____   _____
_____   _____
_____   _____
_____   _____
_____   _____
_____   _____
_____   _____
_____   _____
_____   _____

ADDITIONAL COMMENTS _____
_____

SUBMITTED BY _____ DATE _____

WORKSHEET

DATE	PROJECT	CONTACT	NOTES

SECTION D

PUBLICITY COMPANIES

- Corporate
- EPK
- Film/TV Productions
- Film/TV Talent
- Marketing
- Music
- New Media
- Product Placement

11:24 DESIGN ADVERTISING, INC.

323 Culver Blvd.
Playa del Rey, CA 90293
PHONE 310-821-1775
FAX 310-821-1972
EMAIL . . . . .artsims@1124design.com
WEB SITE .www.1124design.com

TYPES	Film/TV Productions - Marketing - New Media - Promotions
RECENT ACCOUNTS	Bamboozled - Love & Basketball - The Original Kings of Comedy - Amistad - Cradle Will Rock - The Best Man
COMMENTS	Full-service multi-cultural advertising agency

Art Sims . . . . .CEO

15 MINUTES

207 W. 25th St., PH West
New York, NY 10001
PHONE 212-366-4992
FAX 212-620-3759
EMAIL . . . . .wellingtonlove@15minutespr.com

TYPES	Film/TV Productions - Marketing - Promotions
COMMENTS	Specializes in media relations for the independent film industry

Wellington Love . . . . .Founder

360 MEDIA

PO Box 725188
Atlanta, GA 31139
PHONE 404-577-8686
FAX 404-577-8644
EMAIL . . . . .info@360media.net
WEB SITE www.360media.net

TYPES	Film/TV Productions - Marketing - Music
RECENT ACCOUNTS	Taste of Atlanta - Vision Nightclub - Atlanta Jazz Festival - Atlanta Dogwood Festival - Telluride Blues & Brews Festival
COMMENTS	Entertainment, lifestyle, music and event planning

Tara Murphy . . . . .President
Paula Donner . . . . .Sr. Publicist
Anna Masters . . . . .Sr. Publicist
Jeannine Smaltz . . . . .Office & Events Manager
Katie Jones .Publicity Assistant
Ayanna Luke . . . . .Publicity Assistant
Jennifer Pirich . . . . .Assistant to President/Marketing Coordinator

42WEST

220 W. 42nd St., 12th Fl.
New York, NY 10036
PHONE 212-277-7555
EMAIL . . . . .jessieely@thedartgroup.net
SECOND EMAIL . . . . .jrjohnson@thedartgroup.net

TYPES	Film/TV Talent
COMMENTS	Los Angeles office: 1801 Century Park East, Ste. 475, Los Angeles, CA 90067, phone: 310-556-1155, fax: 310-556-1255

Leslee Dart . . . . .CEO
Robert Garlock . . . . .Partner
Amanda Lundberg . . . . .Partner
Cynthia Swartz . . . . .Partner
Allan Mayer . . . . .Strategic Communications (LA)
Michelle Benson . . . . .Publicist
Lauren Burton . . . . .Publicist
Jessie Ely . . . . .Publicist
Scott Feinstein . . . . .Publicist
Carrie Gordon . . . . .Publicist
Chanelle James . . . . .Publicist
Michael Kupferberg . . . . .Publicist
Kelly Mullens .Publicist (LA)
Tom Piechura . . . . .Publicist
Amanda Silverman .Publicist
Beau Benton . . . . .Assistant
Lea Cohen . . . . .Assistant
Seth Hyman . . . . .Assistant
JR Johnson . . . . .Assistant
Sophia Majlessi . . . . .Assistant
Meg Mcentee . . . . .Reception
Irene Rogers . . . . .Reception

AERIAL COMMUNICATIONS GROUP

970-A Eglinton Avenue West
Toronto, ON M6C 2C5, Canada
PHONE 416-787-6577
FAX 416-787-6544
EMAIL . . . . .info@aerialpr.com
WEB SITE . . . . .www.aerialpr.com

TYPES	Corporate - Film/TV Talent - Marketing - Promotions
RECENT ACCOUNTS	Paramount Home Entertainment - Dualstar Entertainment - Melbar Entertainment - Accor Hotels - Avery Dennison Office Products North America

Naomi Strasser . . . . .President
Roanne Goldsman . . . . .Director
Andrea Farnell . . . . .Account Executive
Nichola Petts . . . . .Account Executive
Stephen Shinn . . . . .Account Executive
Tamela Stillman . . . . .Account Executive

AMERICAN BLACKGUARD PUBLIC RELATIONS

PO Box 680686
Franklin, TN 37068-0686
PHONE 615-599-4032
FAX 615-599-4032
EMAIL . . . . .contact@americanblackguard.com
WEB SITE . . . . .www.americanblackguard.com

TYPES	Corporate - EPK - Film/TV Productions - Film/TV Talent - Marketing - Music - Product Placement - Promotions
RECENT ACCOUNTS	Stephen King - Mystery Writers of America - Killer Nashville (Event) - Laura Bell Bundy (Broadway Actress) - Rutledge Hill Press - Clay Stafford (Filmmaker/Author) - Christian Country Music Association - Mollye Rees (Country Music Artist) - People's Branch Theatre - Michael Smith & Associates (Artist Management) - Southeast Mystery Writers of America

Eddie Lightsey . . . . .Sr. Publicist

AMERICAN ENTERTAINMENT MARKETING
4519 Admiralty Way, Ste. D
Marina del Rey, CA 90292
PHONE 310-566-1382
EMAIL . . . . .info@aem-la.com
WEB SITE .www.aem-la.com
TYPES   Corporate - Film/TV Productions - Marketing - Promotions
RECENT ACCOUNTS   Paramount - Disney - Dimension - Miramax - Lionsgate - Sony BMG - Warner Bros.
COMMENTS   Specializes in targeting the Spanish and English speaking US Latino market

Ivette Rodriguez . . . . .President

ANGELWORKS
3142 Old Coach Dr.
Camarillo, CA 93010-1626
PHONE 888-560-3454
EMAIL . . . . .angelworks@dakotacarmel.com
WEB SITE . . . . .www.dakotacarmel.com
TYPES   EPK - Film/TV Productions - New Media
RECENT ACCOUNTS   SAG Awards - Grammy Awards - American Management Association - HarperCollins - Louis Vuitton - Rain Bird - Force of Nature - Weber-Shandwick International - Microsoft - Rodale Books - AmericaOnline - Shifter Warrior
COMMENTS   Specializes in satellite TV and radio tours; Podcasts and blogs; Party/concert/event production; Media events; National media outreach; Multiple project prices available

Elayne Angel Harbert . . . . .Principal

AR PR MARKETING FIRM
5900 Wilshire Blvd., 26th Fl.
Los Angeles, CA 90036
PHONE 323-330-0555/310-695-6452
FAX 323-330-0556
EMAIL . . . . .info@arprmarketing.com
WEB SITE . . . . .www.arprmarketing.com
TYPES   Corporate - Film/TV Talent - Marketing - Music - Product Placement - Promotions
RECENT ACCOUNTS   Sony Pictures - Universal Pictures

Arian Reed . . . . .CEO

ARTISANS PR
2530 Wilshire Blvd., Ste. 300
Santa Monica, CA 90403
PHONE 310-837-6008
FAX 310-837-2286
EMAIL .lrosner@artisanspr.com
WEB SITE . . . . .www.artisanspr.com
TYPES   Corporate - Film/TV Productions - Marketing - Music - New Media - Promotions

Keith Gayhart . . . . .Partner
Linda Rosner . . . . .Partner
Jamie Brewer . . . . .No Title

ASBURY COMMUNICATIONS
9615 Brighton Way, Ste. 201
Beverly Hills, CA 90210
PHONE 310-859-1831
FAX 310-859-9658
EMAIL . . . . .dan@asburypr.com
WEB SITE . . . . .www.asburypr.com
TYPES   Corporate - Film/TV Productions - Film/TV Talent - Marketing - Music - New Media - Promotions
COMMENTS   Post Production; Visual effects; Animation; Audio/sound design; Themed entertainment companies; Broadcast design firms; Internet sites; DVD production companies; Ad agencies; Independent feature films

Dan Harary . . . . .President
Mitch Zamarin . . . . .VP

AVID EXPOSURE LLC
PO Box 9357
North Hollywood, CA 91609
PHONE 323-465-6697
FAX 323-465-5962
EMAIL . . . . .info@avidexposure.com
WEB SITE . . . . .www.avidexposure.com
TYPES   Corporate - Film/TV Productions - Film/TV Talent - Marketing - Music - Product Placement - Promotions
RECENT ACCOUNTS   Tequan Richmond - Nicole Lyons - NASCAR - Omar Cruz/Geffen Records - Tyrese Gibson - Chris Stokes - April Scott

Laura Wright . . . . .Sr. Account Manager
Jasmine Wall . . . . .Event Producer
Jessica Petrini .Associate Publicist
Bryan Sanders .Associate Publicist

BAKER/WINOKUR/RYDER (B/W/R)
9100 Wilshire Blvd., West Tower, 6th Fl.
Beverly Hills, CA 90212
PHONE 310-550-7776/212-901-3920
FAX 310-550-1701/212-901-3995
EMAIL . . . . .firstinitiallastname@bwr-la.com
SECOND EMAIL . . . . .firstinitiallastname@bwr-ny.com
TYPES   Corporate - Film/TV Talent - Marketing - Music - Product Placement - Promotions
COMMENTS   Special events; East Coast office: 825 Eighth Ave., 15th Fl., New York, NY 10019

Larry Winokur . . . . .Founder/Co-CEO
Paul Baker . . . . .Founder/Co-CEO
Nanci Ryder .Founder/President
Cindy Guagenti . . . . .Managing Director
Paulette Kam .Managing Director

BAKER/WINOKUR/RYDER (B/W/R PPI)
9100 Wilshire Blvd., West Tower, 6th Fl.
Beverly Hills, CA 90212
PHONE 310-550-7776/310-248-6140
FAX 310-550-1701
EMAIL . . . . .mmeyerson@bwr-la.com
TYPES   Corporate - Marketing - Product Placement - Promotions
RECENT ACCOUNTS   Kasil Jeans - True Love & False Idols Clothing - Fidelity Denim - Xenergy Energy Drink - Local Celebrity - Little Ruler
COMMENTS   Product placement and brand integration division of Baker/Winokur/Ryder (B/W/R) with a focus on fashion and pop culture/youth market

Matt Meyerson . . . . .Sr. VP, Product Placement
Natasha Sirkovsky . . . . .Assistant

ED BARAN PUBLICITY
1638 Silver Lake Blvd.
Los Angeles, CA 90026
PHONE 213-482-4696
EMAIL . . . . .ed@edbaran.com
WEB SITE . . . . .www.edbaran.com
TYPES   Corporate - Film/TV Productions - Film/TV
                         Talent
RECENT ACCOUNTS   Del Shores - MTI Home Video - Ariztical
                         Entertainment - Angelo Surmelis - 5280
                         Mobile
COMMENTS   Trade and consumer publicity for special
                         events, media tours, wireless/mobile indus-
                         try, VHS/DVD releases, book releases/tours
                         and personalities

Ed Baran . . . . .Owner/President
Tracey Tiberi . . . . .Publicist (East Coast)

BARNETT MARKETING COMMUNICATIONS
420 N. Nellis Blvd., A3-276
Las Vegas, NV 89110
PHONE 702-696-1200
FAX 702-696-1211
EMAIL . . . . .ned@barnettmarcom.com
WEB SITE . . . . .www.barnettmarcom.com
TYPES   Corporate - Marketing - New Media -
                         Promotions
RECENT ACCOUNTS   The Galleon Breaks - US Air Force
                         Academy Documentary - Hollywood Bingo
                         - Strike of the Thunderbirds - Singing Santa
                         - Mutant Killer

Ned Barnett . . . . .Partner
Karolann Barnett . . . . .Partner
Daryl Toor . . . . .Partner
Joe Wheeler . . . . .Associate

THE BARRETT COMPANY
12021 Wilshire Blvd., Ste. 600
Los Angeles, CA 90025
PHONE 310-471-5764
FAX 310-478-8107
EMAIL .barcopr@earthlink.net
WEB SITE .www.thebarrettco.com
TYPES   Corporate - Film/TV Productions -
                         Marketing
RECENT ACCOUNTS   The Amazing Race - Ever Again

Charles Barrett .CEO/Chairman
Barbara Wall . . . . .President
James Carlisle . . . . .VP

BARROW/HOFFMAN PUBLIC RELATIONS
2998 Hacienda Dr.
Duarte, CA 91010
PHONE 626-357-4151
FAX 626-359-3611
EMAIL . . . . .barrowhoffman@telis.org
TYPES   Corporate

Mary Barrow . . . . .President

BENDER/HELPER IMPACT
11500 W. Olympic Blvd., Ste. 655
Los Angeles, CA 90064
PHONE 310-473-4147/212-689-6360
FAX 310-478-4727/212-689-6601
EMAIL .info@bhimpact.com
WEB SITE .www.bhimpact.com
TYPES   Corporate - Marketing - New Media -
                         Product Placement - Promotions
COMMENTS   Consumer electronics; Interactive gaming;
                         Multimedia/CD-ROM marketing; East
                         Coast office: 115 W. 30th St., Ste. 602,
                         New York, NY 10001

Dean Bender . . . . .Partner
Lee Helper . . . . .President/Partner
Shawna Lynch . . . . .Sr. VP, Home Entertainment
Adam Fenton . . . . .VP, Operations (NY)
Dana Henry . . . . .VP, Interactive Entertainment
Sarah Gumina . . . . .Director
Jonalyn Morris . . . . .Director
Melisa Rodriguez . . . . .Director
Becky Bourn . . . . .Operations Manager (LA, NY)
Dolores Aguirre-Garcia . . . . .Office Manager (NY)

BLUPRINT
8899 Beverly Blvd., Ste. 412
West Hollywood, CA 90048
PHONE 310-281-8080
FAX 310-281-8082
WEB SITE . . . . .www.blupr.com

Jill Eisenstadt-Chayet . . . . .President

HENRI BOLLINGER ASSOCIATES
PO Box 57227
Sherman Oaks, CA 91413
PHONE 818-784-0534
FAX 818-789-8862
EMAIL .info@bollingerpr.com
WEB SITE .www.bollingerpr.com
TYPES   EPK - Film/TV Productions - Marketing -
                         Music - Promotions
COMMENTS   Entertainment, leisure, communications

Henri Bollinger . . . . .Owner

BOPSTAR-PR INC.
421 Summit Ridge Pl.
Nashville, TN 37215
PHONE 615-460-7485
FAX 615-750-2313
EMAIL .info@bopstar-pr.com
WEB SITE .www.bopstar-pr.com
TYPES   Music - Promotions
RECENT ACCOUNTS   James Talley - Backbeat Books - Jazz Baby
                         - Lucia Micarelli
COMMENTS   Specializes in family entertainment, alterna-
                         tive country and folk

MaryLenore Arsenault . . . . .President/CEO

BRAGMAN NYMAN CAFARELLI (BNC)
8687 Melrose Ave., 8th Fl.
Los Angeles, CA 90069
PHONE 310-854-4800/212-253-4646
FAX 310-854-4848/212-253-4640
EMAIL . . . . .info@bncpr.com
WEB SITE . . . . .www.bncpr.com

TYPES	Corporate - Film/TV Talent - Marketing - Product Placement
RECENT ACCOUNTS	Sony Computer Entertainment - Maxim Magazine - Nike Jordans - General Motors - Cameron Diaz - Jimmy Kimmel - Eva Mendes - Kate Hudson - Jessica Alba - T-Mobile - ESPN - House - Scrubs - Dom Perignon - Extreme Home Makeover - Lip/Lift Fusion - Cadillac - The CW Network - Avon - Borders - Klipsch - New Line - Sofitel (LA) - Time Warner - Kristen Bell - Applebees - Molly Simms
COMMENTS	Sports; East Coast office: 35 E. 21st St., 4th Fl., New York, NY 10010

Michael Nyman . . . . .Chairman/CEO
Brad Cafarelli . . . . .Vice Chairman
Chris Robichaud . . . . .President/COO
John Lundy . . . . .CFO
Joe Assad . . . . .Sr. VP/General Manager (NY)
Monica Chun . . . . .Executive VP, Marketing
Doug Piwinski . . . . .Executive VP, New Business
Scott Floyd .Sr. VP, Media Relations
Lewis Kay . . . . .Sr. VP, Entertainment
Amy Glickman . . . . .VP, Entertainment
Rick Jennings . . . . .VP, Media Relations
Lauren Kucerak . . . . .VP, (NY)

BRAND CENTRAL PROMOTIONS, INC.
1223 Amethyst St.
Redondo Beach, CA 90277
PHONE 310-379-3144/800-828-1943
FAX 310-379-6034
EMAIL . . . . .info@bcpromo.com
WEB SITE . . . . .www.bcpromo.com

TYPES	Corporate - Film/TV Productions - Marketing - Music - New Media - Promotions - Outdoor Advertising
RECENT ACCOUNTS	Warner Music Group - NBC Studios - Universal Pictures - Palm, Inc. - Siemens - Rhino Entertainment - Warner Productions - Scion/Toyota
COMMENTS	High quality and custom items; Promotional give-aways, incentives, crew gifts, apparel, gift baskets

Dina Heidger . . . . .Owner/Designer
Rob Heidger . . . . .Sales Associate
Rose Garcia . . . . .Accounting

THE HOWARD BRANDY COMPANY
9514 Oakmore Rd.
Los Angeles, CA 90035
PHONE 310-839-8320
FAX 310-839-8310
EMAIL . . . . .brandypr@aol.com

TYPES	Corporate - Film/TV Productions
RECENT ACCOUNTS	Phoenix Pictures - A-Mark Films - Dan Tana's - Jeremy Thomas - Internet Song of the Year - Mark Williams - J.F. Lawton - Bill Marsilii

Julia Holmes . . . . .VP

BRICKMAN MARKETING
395 Del Monte Center, Ste. 250
Monterey, CA 93940
PHONE 831-633-4444/800-377-3739
FAX 831-633-4499
EMAIL . . . . .brickman@brickmanmarketing.com
WEB SITE . . . . .www.brickmanmarketing.com

TYPES	Film/TV Productions - Marketing
COMMENTS	Documentary, special interest and children's video/DVD publicity, marketing and distribution

Wendy Brickman . . . . .Owner

THE BRITTO AGENCY
234 W. 56th St., PH
New York, NY 10019
PHONE 212-977-6772
FAX 212-977-4350/212-977-9822
WEB SITE . . . . .www.thebrittoagency.com

TYPES	Corporate - Film/TV Talent - Marketing - Music - Product Placement
RECENT ACCOUNTS	Kim Cattrall - Angela Bassett - Star Jones - Ananda Lewis - Cuttino Mobley - Big Tigger - Motorola - Martell Cognac - Mariah Carey - Hill Harper - Rodney Jerkins
COMMENTS	Fashion, brand imaging and celebrity procurement

Marvet Britto . . . . .President/CEO

THE BROKAW COMPANY
9255 Sunset Blvd., Ste. 804
Los Angeles, CA 90069-3309
PHONE 310-273-2060
FAX 310-276-4037
EMAIL . . . . .brokawc@aol.com
WEB SITE . . . . .www.brokawcompany.com

TYPES	Corporate - Film/TV Productions - Film/TV Talent - Music

David Brokaw . . . . .No Title
Joel Brokaw . . . . .No Title
Sanford Brokaw . . . . .No Title
Kim Harjo . . . . .No Title
Diane Hadley . . . . .No Title
Teri Gustafson . . . . .No Title

NADIA BRONSON & ASSOCIATES
9220 Sunset Blvd., Ste. 210
Los Angeles, CA 90069
PHONE 310-205-4858
FAX 310-205-4860

TYPES	Corporate - Film/TV Productions - Film/TV Talent

Nadia Bronson . . . . .Contact
Thomas Castaneda . . . . .Publicity

BROWNSTEIN & ASSOCIATES, INC.
630 Ninth Ave., Ste. 215
New York, NY 10036
PHONE 212-265-3666
FAX 646-219-4340
EMAIL . . . . .amy@abrownstein.com
SECOND EMAIL . . . . .assistant@abrownstein.com
WEB SITE . . . . .www.abrownstein.com
TYPES　　　　　　　　Corporate - Film/TV Talent - Marketing - New Media
COMMENTS　　　　　Talent and corporate entertainment public relations and cause marketing; Los Angeles affiliate: Much and House Public Relations

Amy Brownstein . . . . .President
Alexis Laken . . . . .Publicity (alexis@abrownstein.com)

CATALANO PUBLIC RELATIONS & EDITORIAL SERVICES
One Central St., Ste. 8
Stoneham, MA 02180
PHONE 781-438-4640/781-226-2378
FAX 781-438-4643
EMAIL . . . . .catalanopr@aol.com
WEB SITE . . . . .www.catalanopr.com
TYPES　　　　　　　　EPK - Film/TV Productions - Film/TV Talent - Marketing - Music - New Media - Promotions
COMMENTS　　　　　Second address: PO Box 665, Winchester, MA 01890-0965

Deborah A. Catalano .Owner/President

CELEBRITY ENDEAVORS
230 Park Ave., Ste. 1000
New York, NY 10169
PHONE 212-730-8683
EMAIL . . . . .questions@celebrityendeavors.com
WEB SITE . . . . .www.celebrityendeavors.com
TYPES　　　　　　　　Film/TV Productions - Product Placement
RECENT ACCOUNTS　Bravo - Showtime - HBO - Sony Pictures - Paramount - AOL - Miramax - 20th Century Fox
COMMENTS　　　　　Inquiries by email only; Represents producers and writer/producers in the development, finance and distribution of projects; Representatives in Los Angeles, London and Sydney

David Klein . . . . .Administrator, Acquisitions & Development

THE CELEBRITY SOURCE
8033 Sunset Blvd., Ste. 2500
Los Angeles, CA 90046
PHONE 323-651-3300
FAX 323-651-3397
EMAIL . . . . .info@celebritysource.com
WEB SITE . . . . .www.celebritysource.com
TYPES　　　　　　　　Film/TV Talent
RECENT ACCOUNTS　Disney Home Entertainment - Calvin Klein Cosmetics -Toyota Motorsports - Nickelodeon - Merrill Lynch - Hallmark - Coca-Cola - Nestle Purina - Quaker Oats
COMMENTS　　　　　Procures celebrities for PR, marketing, promotional activities, special events, film premieres and fundraisers

Rita Tateel . . . . .President
Paula Greenfield . . . . .VP
Ben Scholes . . . . .Administrative Director
Maryellen Owens . . . . .Account Coordinator

CELEBRITYFOOTAGE
320 S. Almont Dr.
Beverly Hills, CA 90211
PHONE 310-360-9600
FAX 310-360-9696
EMAIL . . . . .michael@celebrityfootage.com
WEB SITE . . . . .www.celebrityfootage.com
TYPES　　　　　　　　Corporate - EPK - Film/TV Productions - Film/TV Talent - Marketing - Promotions
RECENT ACCOUNTS　New Line Cinema - Paramount Pictures - Swatch Group USA

Michael Goldberg . . . . .President

CERRELL ASSOCIATES
320 N. Larchmont Blvd.
Los Angeles, CA 90004
PHONE 323-466-3445
FAX 323-466-8653
EMAIL . . . . .info@cerrell.com
WEB SITE . . . . .www.cerrell.com
TYPES　　　　　　　　Corporate
RECENT ACCOUNTS　Western States Petroleum Association - University of Southern California - Motion Picture Association of America
COMMENTS　　　　　Media relations; Special event planning; Public affairs; Political consulting; Issues management; Government relations

Joseph R. Cerrell . . . . .Chairman
Hal Dash . . . . .President
Steve Bullock . . . . .CFO

CHASEN & COMPANY
8899 Beverly Blvd., Ste. 405
Los Angeles, CA 90048
PHONE 310-274-4400
FAX 310-274-4467
EMAIL . . . . .ronni@chasenpr.com
TYPES　　　　　　　　Corporate - Film/TV Productions - Film/TV Talent - Marketing - Music
COMMENTS　　　　　Specialties: Motion picture PR, awards campaigns, filmmaker PR, home video, soundtrack strategies and campaigns

Ronni Chasen . . . . .Owner
Jeff Sanderson . . . . .VP
Allie Lee . . . . .Account Executive
Brooke Wilcher .Account Executive

CLIFFORD PUBLIC RELATIONS
820 N. Fairfax Ave.
Los Angeles, CA 90046
PHONE 323-966-4600/212-358-0800
FAX 323-966-4601/212-358-0800
EMAIL . . . . .info@cliffordpr.com
WEB SITE . . . . .www.cliffordpr.com
TYPES　　　　　　　　Corporate - Marketing
COMMENTS　　　　　East Coast office: 286 Fifth Ave., 11th Fl., New York, NY 10001

Mike Clifford .President/CEO (NY)
Regan Phillips . . . . .Sr. VP
Niki Ostin . . . . .Account Supervisor
Kim Niadna . . . . .Account Coordinator

CLUB BEVERLY HILLS
8306 Wilshire Blvd., Ste. 279
Beverly Hills, CA 90211
PHONE 310-274-6051
FAX 310-274-7855
EMAIL . . . . .clubbeverlyhills@sbcglobal.net
SECOND EMAIL . . . . .dreams@club-beverlyhills.com
WEB SITE .www.club-beverlyhills.com
TYPES   Film/TV Productions - Film/TV Talent -
                         Marketing - Promotions
RECENT ACCOUNTS   Nothing But the Truth - Coyote Ugly -
                         Sworn to Justice - The Vanishing Women of
                         Lugu Lake - Devil's Knight - Gods and
                         Generals - If - Master Demon
COMMENTS   Photography; Management
Rose Clements . . . . .Owner
Lori Travis . . . . .President

CMG WORLDWIDE
10500 Crosspoint Blvd.
Indianapolis, IN 46256
PHONE 317-570-5000/310-651-2000
FAX 317-570-5500
WEB SITE . . . . .www.cmgworldwide.com
TYPES   Corporate - Film/TV Talent - Marketing -
                         Promotions
COMMENTS   Licensing; West Coast office: 8560 Sunset
                         Blvd., 10th Fl., Los Angeles, CA 90069
Mark Roesler . . . . .CEO
Peter Enfield . . . . .VP
Cris Piquinela . . . . .VP, Marketing & Licensing

CMPR
840 Apollo St., Ste. 213
El Segundo, CA 90245
PHONE 310-426-9900/760-438-9910
FAX .310-426-9999/760-438-9920
EMAIL . . . . .stevewebster@cmpr.net
SECOND EMAIL . . . . .info@cmpr.net
WEB SITE . . . . .www.cmpr.net
TYPES   Corporate - Film/TV Productions - Film/TV
                         Talent - Marketing - Promotions
RECENT ACCOUNTS   ESPN Original Entertainment - Mark
                         Burnett Productions - Reveille - Pete
                         Sampras - Sugar Ray Leonard
COMMENTS   Additional office: 5864 Owens Ave., Ste.
                         100, Carlsbad, CA 92008
Steve Webster . . . . .President/CEO
Rob Preston . . . . .VP, Corporate Strategy
Emily Snider . . . . .VP, National Accounts
Stephanie Reynolds . . . . .Director, National Accounts
Brad Williams . . . . .Director, Sports Accounts

CONSOLIDATED ADVERTISING DIRECTORS, INC.
8060 Melrose Ave.
Los Angeles, CA 90046
PHONE 323-653-8060
FAX 323-655-9452
EMAIL . . . . .info@psiemail.com
TYPES   Corporate - Film/TV Productions -
                         Marketing - Promotions
RECENT ACCOUNTS   All America Distributors Corporation -
                         Holloway House Publishing Company -
                         Players International Publications - National
                         Shopper Inc. - Mankind Publishing
                         Company - Knight Publishing Company -
                         Publishers Service Incorporated - Hargitay-
                         Bentley Productions - Sirkay Publishing
                         Corporation
COMMENTS   Advertising and PR for West Coast maga-
                         zine and book publishers worldwide since
                         1949
Bentley Morriss . . . . .President/CEO
Marc K. Morriss . . . . .VP
Cris Oliveros . . . . .Controller
Timothy Moroney . . . . .Art Director
Vincent Crisp . . . . .Production
Bismark Lopez . . . . .Traffic Director
Mitchell Neal . . . . .Marketing
Neal Colgrass . . . . .PR
Elaine Venezio . . . . .Promotion

COSTA COMMUNICATIONS
8265 Sunset Blvd., Ste. 101
Los Angeles, CA 90046
PHONE 323-650-3588
FAX 323-654-5207
EMAIL . . . . .rcosta@costacomm.com
WEB SITE . . . . .www.costacomm.com
TYPES   Corporate - Film/TV Productions - Film/TV
                         Talent - Marketing - Music - Promotions
COMMENTS   Oscar and other award campaigns for fea-
                         ture films; Publicity for above and below-
                         the-line talent including composers, direc-
                         tors and editors
Ray Costa . . . . .President
Richard Swift . . . . .VP
Harold Schwartz .Special Projects
Tom Kidd . . . . .Sr. Publicist

COSTELLO & COMPANY PUBLIC RELATIONS
3604 W. Clark Ave.
Burbank, CA 91505
PHONE 818-842-9604
FAX 818-558-3799
EMAIL . . . . .chrisco815@aol.com
TYPES   Corporate - Film/TV Talent - Promotions
COMMENTS   Directors, special effects, make-up, actors
                         and production companies
Chris Costello . . . . .President
Joyce Wagner . . . . .VP, Entertainment Division
Paula Lintz . . . . .Sr. Publicist
Lisa Shenkle . . . . .East Coast Representative

WARREN COWAN & ASSOCIATES
8899 Beverly Blvd., Ste. 919
Los Angeles, CA 90048
PHONE 310-275-0777
FAX 310-247-0810
EMAIL .wcowan2000@aol.com
TYPES   Corporate - Film/TV Productions - Film/TV
                         Talent - Marketing - Music - New Media -
                         Promotions

Warren Cowan . . . . .Chairman
Richard Hoffman . . . . .Sr. VP
Kevin Sasaki . . . . .Sr. VP
Jeff Sanderson . . . . .Sr. Account Executive
Daniel Bernstein . . . . .Director, Client Relations

CPR
1944 Glendon Ave., Ste. 110
Los Angeles, CA 90025
PHONE 310-441-2200
FAX 310-441-2244
EMAIL .cprpromo@verizon.net
TYPES   Corporate - Film/TV Productions -
                         Marketing - Music - New Media - Product
                         Placement - Promotions
RECENT ACCOUNTS   Music distributors and labels; TV distribu-
                         tors and production companies; Film com-
                         panies and distributors; Non-profit organi-
                         zations and events; Special projects
COMMENTS   Integrated promotions, branding and
                         strategic alliances

Carolyn Broner . . . . .President

CURRENTPR, INC.
2811 Francis Ln.
Costa Mesa, CA 92626
PHONE 714-444-9731
FAX 714-444-9733
EMAIL .alison@currentpr.com
WEB SITE . . . . .www.currentpr.com
TYPES   Corporate - Film/TV Productions -
                         Marketing - New Media
COMMENTS   Events

Alison Hill . . . . .CEO
Jim DeNuccio . . . . , ...COO
Raymond Diaz . . . . .Publicist

DONNA DANIELS PUBLIC RELATIONS
1375 Broadway, Ste. 403
New York, NY 10018
PHONE 212-869-7233
FAX 212-869-7114

Donna Daniels . . . . .Publicist
Casey Fitzpatrick . . . . .Publicist
Emily Lowe . . . . .Publicist
Lauren Schwartz . . . . .Publicist

DAVIE-BROWN ENTERTAINMENT
2225 S. Carmelina Ave.
Los Angeles, CA 90064
PHONE 310-979-1980
FAX 310-820-7277
WEB SITE . . . . .www.davie-brown.com
TYPES   Marketing - Music - New Media - Product
                         Placement - Promotions
COMMENTS   Strategic studio alliances; The Davie-Brown
                         Index (DBI)

Jim Davie . . . . .Chairman of the Board
Russell Miesels . . . . .CFO
Tom Meyer . . . . .President, Entertainment
Lori Kotarski Nelson . . . . .Executive VP
Robert Schneider .Executive VP
Adam Smith . . . . .Executive VP
Melissa Fallon . . . . .VP, TV & Emerging Media
Nancy Mammana . . . . .VP (NY)
Tim Clarke . . . . .New Business

DDA PUBLIC RELATIONS, LTD.
The Luckman Plaza
9220 Sunset Blvd., Ste. 210
Los Angeles, CA 90069
PHONE 310-205-4868
FAX 310-205-4899
EMAIL . . . . .info@ddapr.com
WEB SITE . . . . .www.ddapr.com
TYPES   Corporate - Film/TV Productions - Film/TV
                         Talent

Dennis Davidson .Chairman (London)
Fiona Searson . . . . .President (Australia)
Chris Paton . . . . .Vice Chairman (London)
Lawrence Atkinson . . . . .Executive VP
Mira Husseini . . . . .Sr. VP (London)
Graham Smith . . . . .Sr. VP (London)
Mariangela Ferrario Hall .VP
Julia Orr . . . . .Sr. Publicist

DEEP FOCUS
20 Jay St., Ste. 1110
Brooklyn, NY 11201
PHONE 718-797-3618
FAX 718-797-1577
EMAIL . . . . .info@deep-focus.net
WEB SITE . . . . .www.deep-focus.net
TYPES   Marketing - New Media - Promotions
RECENT ACCOUNTS   Miramax - Court TV - Fox Searchlight -
                         Warner Bros. - New Line Cinema -
                         Picturehouse - MTV - Sony Pictures Classics
                         - Columbia Tri-Star Home Entertainment -
                         The Weinstein Company - HBO - Twentieth
                         Century Fox - Interscope Records - Jive
                         Records - Geffen Records

Ian Schafer . . . . .CEO/Founder
Martin Marcus . . . . .VP, Finance & Operations
Erica Bulos . . . . .Assistant

DERA, ROSLAN & CAMPION, INC. PUBLIC RELATIONS

132 Nassau St., Ste. 619
New York, NY 10038
PHONE 212-966-4600
FAX 212-966-5763
EMAIL . . . . .eddie@drcpublicrelations.com
TYPES   Corporate - Film/TV Productions - Marketing - Music
RECENT ACCOUNTS   HGTV - DIY Network - Scripps Networks - National Geographic Explorer (MSNBC) - National Geographic Specials (PBS) - Chieftains - NOVA - Nelson Current Publishers
COMMENTS   Science, nature, IMAX large format films, TV specials

Joe Dera . . . . .Chief Executive
Chris Roslan . . . . .President
Eileen Campion . . . . .President
Eddie Ward . . . . .Manager, Entertainment

DEVEAUX AGENCY

12814 Victory Blvd., Ste. 173
North Hollywood, CA 91606
PHONE 310-420-9565
FAX 814-295-2174
EMAIL . . . . .tashia@deveauxagency.com
SECOND EMAIL . . . . .info@deveauxagency.com
WEB SITE .www.deveauxagency.com
TYPES   Corporate - EPK - Film/TV Productions - Film/TV Talent - Marketing - Music

Latashia DeVeaux . . . . .Principal/Sr. Publicist
Erin Jackson . . . . .Sr. Publicist
Wesley Mallette . . . . .Sr. Publicist
Danica Carroll . . . . .Mgr, Special Events

LORI DEWAAL & ASSOCIATES

7080 Hollywood Blvd., Ste. 515
Los Angeles, CA 90028
PHONE 323-462-4122
FAX 323-463-3792
EMAIL . . . . .dewaalpr@aol.com
TYPES   Corporate - Film/TV Talent
COMMENTS   Reps actors, authors, architects, designers, restaurants & non-profits

Lori DeWaal . . . . .President

DIS COMPANY

250 W. 57th St., Ste. 2428
New York, NY 10107
PHONE 212-245-5909
FAX 212-956-4126
EMAIL . . . . .dsalidorcompany@aol.com
TYPES   Film/TV Productions - Music
COMMENTS   Theater, Indie Bands

David Salidor . . . . .Owner

DOUBLE A LLC PUBLIC RELATIONS & MARKETING

2441 34th St., Ste. D
Santa Monica, CA 90405
PHONE 310-450-6890
EMAIL . . . . .alexia@doublea-pr.com
WEB SITE . . . . .www.doublea-pr.com
TYPES   Corporate - Marketing - Promotions
RECENT ACCOUNTS   Farmer's Daughter Hotel - World Festival of Sacred Music - Canon Digital Creators Contest - LA Artshow - Bus Note Press - Shade Hotel - Cabaña - Petros Greek Cuisine and Lounge - AFI's Directing Workshop for Women

Alexia Haidos . . . . .Owner

THE DOWD AGENCY

444 Park Ave., South PH
New York, NY 10016
PHONE 212-686-7777
FAX 212-686-6439
EMAIL . . . . .jim@dowdagency.com
WEB SITE . . . . .www.dowdagency.com
TYPES   Corporate - EPK - Film/TV Productions - Film/TV Talent - Marketing - New Media
RECENT ACCOUNTS   The Apprentice (NBC) - Rock Star (CBS) - On The Lot (FOX) - Gold Rush (AOL) - Dial Corporation - Triumph Pharmaceutical's SmartMouth - National Grants Conferences - The Doors - BeJane.com - World Renowned Hypnotist Paul McKenna - Chef Rocco DiSpirito - Ryan Star - Patrice Pike - Storm Large - Mig Ayesa - Yahoo! - The Trump Organization - Ace Hardware - The Apprentice - Rock Star - On the Lot - Gold Rush - Mark Burnett Productions - A&E Television Networks - Rodale - Trump University - Trump Institute - Trump Magazine - Poker Life - GoTrump.com - BeJane.com - CSA: The Confederate States of America (Sundance/IFC Film) - Downtown (Electric Wonderland Entertainment) - Bill Rancic - Dr. Randal Pinkett - Sean Yazbeck - Raj Bhakta

Jim Dowd . . . . .CEO & Founder
Stephanie Berman . . . . .Director, Accounts
Sean Martin . . . . .Sr. Account Executive
Becky Auslander . . . . .Account Executive
Jen Clark . . . . .Account Executive
Carolyn Clark . . . . .Account Executive
Mary Beth O'Toole .Account Executive
Cat Bartosevich .Publicity Coordinator

LINDA DOZORETZ COMMUNICATIONS

8033 Sunset Blvd., Ste. 996
Los Angeles, CA 90046
PHONE 323-656-4499
EMAIL . . . . .pr@ldcomm.com
TYPES   Corporate - Marketing - Music
COMMENTS   Sports, print, entertainment, public service, nonprofits

Linda Dozoretz . . . . .President

KENNETH DROZ PUBLIC RELATIONS

1330 N. Orange Dr., Ste. 111
Los Angeles, CA 90028
PHONE 323-469-9252/323-854-6858
EMAIL . . . . .kddroz@aol.com
WEB SITE . . . . .www.kendrozpr.com
TYPES   Corporate - Film/TV Productions - Film/TV Talent - Marketing - Music - New Media - Promotions
RECENT ACCOUNTS   Creative Screenwriting Expos - Phoenix Film Festival - Beverly Center/Taubman Centers, Inc. - Writers Guild Foundation - Farmers' Almanac TV - Paramount Pictures - Peninsula Films - Mitch Albom - The Romantics - Gerald Everett Jones

Ken Droz . . . . .Owner
Jessica Berger .Publicity Assistant

EISNER PUBLIC RELATIONS
1817 S. Sherbourne Dr.
Los Angeles, CA 90035
PHONE 310-839-1400
FAX 310-202-6610
EMAIL . . . . .eisnerpr@comcast.net
TYPES   Film/TV Talent
RECENT ACCOUNTS   Oxford University Press - Cause
                   Communications - Beyond Shelter -
                   Disability Rights Local Center - City of
                   Hope - Hero Entertainment, Inc.
COMMENTS   Authors, writers, composers, producers,
                   nonprofits, legal

Carol Eisner . . . . .President

EPR PUBLIC RELATIONS
551 Millwood Rd.
Toronto, ON M4S 1K7, Canada
PHONE 416-487-4464
FAX 416-487-4484
EMAIL . . . . .joefilmpr@aol.com
WEB SITE . . . . .www.epr-pr.com

Joe Everett . . . . .Director

EVOLUTIONARY MEDIA GROUP
6533 Hollywood Blvd, Ste. 200
Los Angeles, CA 90028
PHONE 323-658-8700
FAX 323-658-8750
EMAIL . . . . .jennifer@evolutionarymediagroup.com
TYPES   Corporate - Film/TV Talent - Marketing -
                         Music - Product Placement
RECENT ACCOUNTS   Suss Design - Grass Jeans - Point Du Vue
                   Salon - Roosevelt Hotel - Teddy's -
                   Tropicana Bar - Channel G - The Doors -
                   Harajuku Lovers - THe Luxe Hotel Group -
                   The Orlando Hotel - Extra Large Tech -
                   Signatures Network - Hillview - 86 - The
                   Joint - Lift - Amanda Scheer Demme -
                   Calleen Cordero - GEN ART - Downtown
                   Fashion District/The Intersection - LA
                   Fashion Awards - Golden Bridge Yoga -
                   Events Eleven - Hotel Cielo Rojo - MOCA
                   Night Vision - Nakajima - Jerry Leigh
                   Entertainment - Paper Magazine - Robins'
                   Jeans - Sweatlodge Clothing - Wasteland

Jennifer Gross . . . . .Owner

FALCO INK
850 Seventh Ave.
New York, NY 10019
PHONE 212-445-7100
FAX 212-445-0623
WEB SITE . . . . .www.falcoink.com
TYPES   Corporate - Film/TV Productions - Film/
                         TV Talent

Gary Hill . . . . .Partner
Janice Roland . . . . .Partner
Shannon Treusch . . . . .Partner

FARAONE COMMUNICATIONS, INC.
75 West End Ave., Ste. R-9A
New York, NY 10023
PHONE 212-489-1313/323-550-8732
FAX 212-489-8978/323-417-4770
EMAIL . . . . .ted.faraone@verizon.net
SECOND EMAIL . . . . .nadergroup@aol.com
WEB SITE . . . . .www.worldwidepublicrelations.com
TYPES   Corporate - Film/TV Productions - Film/TV
                         Talent - Music - New Media
COMMENTS   DVD, publishing, book authors and enter-
                   tainers; PR and media relations for the
                   entertainment, advertising, and media
                   industries; Online and ad agency clients;
                   Specializes in difficult assignments; West
                   Coast office: 4804 Laurel Canyon Blvd.,
                   Ste. 516, Valley Village, CA 91607

Ted Faraone . . . . .Principal
Randolph Nader . . . . .VP

FAT CITY MEDIA
65 W. 90th St., Ste. 7D
New York, NY 10024
PHONE 212-579-2432
FAX 212-579-0920
EMAIL . . . . .info@fatcitymedia.com
WEB SITE . . . . .www.fatcitymedia.com
TYPES   Corporate - Film/TV Talent - Marketing -
                         Product Placement
RECENT ACCOUNTS   Talented Managers - Images Model
                   Management - Bloom Model Management
                   - Cook Bros. Racing
COMMENTS   Personal management; Celebrity and prod-
                   uct branding

Michael Farkas .Founder/Account Manager

FAT DOT
87 Bedford St., Ste. 1
New York, NY 10014
PHONE 212-691-4224
FAX 212-202-7727
EMAIL . . . . .info@fatdot.net
WEB SITE . . . . .www.fatdot.net
TYPES   Corporate - EPK - Film/TV Productions -
                         Film/TV Talent - Marketing - Music - New
                         Media - Product Placement - Promotions
RECENT ACCOUNTS   The Squid and the Whale - Hoodwinked -
                   Proof - An Inconvenient Truth - Todd Field -
                   Sissy Spacek - JWT

Weiman Seid . . . . .President
Steven Carbajal . . . . .No Title
Jenny Lawhorn . . . . .No Title

FIFTEEN MINUTES
8436 W. Third St., Ste. 650
Los Angeles, CA 90048
PHONE 323-556-9700
FAX 323-556-9710
EMAIL .howard@fifteenminutes.com
WEB SITE . . . . .www.fifteenminutes.com
TYPES   Corporate - Film/TV Talent - Marketing -
                         Music

Howard Bragman . . . . .President/CEO
Ryan Croy . . . . .VP, Corporate Division
Zach Rosenfield . . . . .VP, Corporate Entertainment
Amanda Brocato . . . . .Publicist
Thea Ellis . . . . .Publicist
Gabriel Serrato . . . . .Publicist
Jordan Byrnes . . . . .No Title

FIREWORKS MARKETING & ADVERTISING

1639 11th St., Ste. 265
Santa Monica, CA 90404
PHONE 310-450-5551
FAX 310-450-8655
EMAIL .info@gofireworks.com
WEB SITE . . . . .www.gofireworks.com
TYPES   Marketing - Music - Promotions - Outdoor Advertising

John Moore . . . . .President
Mike Heat . . . . .CEO
Shani Stewart . . . . .Director, Operations
Bryan Maravilla . . . . .Creative Director
Myla Twillie . . . . .Publicity Manager

FLAG MARKETING

2420 Canyon Dr.
Hollywood, CA 90068
PHONE 323-466-5830
FAX 323-466-2357
EMAIL . . . . .christi@flagmarketing.com
WEB SITE . . . . .www.flagmarketing.com
TYPES   Film/TV Productions - Marketing - Music
COMMENTS   Street teams, Web sites, movie trailers, poster art, package design

Christi Crowe . . . . .Marketing Director
Jonathan Crowe . . . . .Art Director

FLEISHMAN-HILLARD

515 S. Flower St., 7th Fl.
Los Angeles, CA 90071
PHONE 213-629-4974
FAX 213-623-6495
WEB SITE . . . . .www.fleishman.com
TYPES   Film/TV Productions
COMMENTS   Entertainment communications; Consumer branding

Melissa Schoeb . . . . .Sr. VP/General Manager
Richard Kline . . . . .Regional President/Senior Partner

FOUNDRY COMMUNICATIONS

39 W. 19th St., Ste. 603
New York, NY 10011
PHONE 212-586-7967
FAX 866-330-5171
EMAIL . . . . .mkrause@foundrycomm.com
WEB SITE .www.foundrycomm.com
TYPES   Corporate - EPK - New Media
COMMENTS   Full-service PR; Home entertainment; Television

Michael Krause . . . . .Owner/President
Stacey Studebaker . . . . .VP
Eva Marie Damore . . . . .Sr. Account Director
Suzanne Dobson . . . . .Account Executive
Danielle Hawkes . . . . .Account Executive

ANDREW E. FREEDMAN PUBLIC RELATIONS

9127 Thrasher
Los Angeles, CA 90069
PHONE 310-271-0011
FAX 310-271-0033
EMAIL . . . . .andrew@aefpr.com
SECOND EMAIL .patty@aefpr.com
TYPES   Corporate - Film/TV Talent - Music - New Media - Product Placement - Promotions

Andrew E. Freedman . . . . .Owner

FREUD COMMUNICATIONS INC.

152 W. 57th St., Carnegie Tower, 15th Fl.
New York, NY 10019
PHONE 212-582-9795
FAX 212-582-9783
WEB SITE . . . . .www.freud.com
TYPES   Corporate - Film/TV Productions - Marketing

Matthew Hiltzik .President/CEO

FRONT PAGE PUBLICITY

2827 Columbine Place
Nashville, TN 37204
PHONE 615-383-0412
FAX 615-523-1347
EMAIL . . . . .info@frontpagepublicity.com
TYPES   Film/TV Talent - Music
RECENT ACCOUNTS   Dixie Chicks - Martina McBride - George Strait - Patty Loveless - Miranda Lambert
COMMENTS   No unsolicited materials

Kathy Best . . . . .President
Cassie McConnell . . . . .Publicist
Nicole Bourque .Administration

THE GARIS AGENCY

310 S. Twin Oaks Balley Rd., #107-200
San Marcos, CA 92078
PHONE 760-471-4807
FAX 760-454-1814
EMAIL . . . . .publicity@nationalpublicist.com
WEB SITE . . . . .www.nationalpublicist.com
TYPES   Corporate - Film/TV Talent - Marketing - Music - New Media - Product Placement - Promotions
RECENT ACCOUNTS   Kevin Allen (The Apprentice, NBC) - Nichelle Nichols (Star Trek) - Dawn Wells (Gilligan's Island/Producer) - Robert Hopcke (Author) - Joe Namath - Chris Calloway (Jazz Musician) - Danny Bonaduce - Vestin Financial (Casino & Entertainment Financiers) - Cohn Restaurant Group - World Championship of Performing Arts -Gryphon Productions (Animal Planet) - Lana Landis (Model/Spokesperson)

Dr. R. J. Garis .Agency Director
Brittany Scott . . . . .Coordinator
Mike Walters Esq. . . . . .Agency Counsel

GEM PUBLIC RELATIONS

1101 S. Robertson Blvd., #104
Beverly Hills, CA 90035
PHONE 888-575-1241
FAX 323-297-4547
EMAIL . . . . .gempublicity@gmail.com
WEB SITE . . . . .www.gem-pr.com
SECOND WEB SITE . . . . .www.toithepublicist.com
TYPES   Film/TV Talent - Marketing - Promotions
RECENT ACCOUNTS   James Francis Kelly III - David Arnold - Rodney Perry - Antonio Tarver - Doug and Jackie Christie
COMMENTS   Entertainment publicity, event planning, corporate accounts

Toi Troutman . . . . .Sr. Publicist
Jennifer Grimes . . . . .Account Manager

PAUL GENDREAU PUBLIC RELATIONS

4028 Alcove Ave.
Studio City, CA 91604
PHONE 818-985-0245
FAX 818-985-7017
EMAIL . . . . .pgpr1@roadrunner.com
TYPES   Film/TV Productions - Film/TV Talent -
                     Marketing - Promotions
RECENT ACCOUNTS   CSI: Miami - Alliance Atlantis Corporation

Paul Gendreau . . . . .Owner
Sue Francis . . . . .Publicist

BOB GOLD & ASSOCIATES

2780 Skypark Dr., Ste. 475
Torrance, CA 90505
PHONE 310-784-1040
FAX 310-784-1050
EMAIL . . . . .info@bobgoldpr.com
WEB SITE . . . . .www.bobgoldpr.com
TYPES   Corporate - Marketing - New Media

Bob Gold . . . . .President
Art Maulsby .Executive Director
Christian Dix .Account Executive
James Park . . . . .Account Executive
Todd Franke . . . . .Supervisor
Irene Fuimaono .Office Manager
Dwayna Thompkins . . . . .Sr. Account Coordinator
Louis Afrouznia . . . . .Account Coordinator
Kevin Barry . . . . .Account Coordinator

GORGEOUS PR, INC.

7551 Melrose Ave., Ste. 7
Los Angeles, CA 90046
PHONE 323-782-9000
FAX 323-658-6189
EMAIL . . . . .info@gorgeouspr.com
SECOND EMAIL . . . . .gorgeouspr@aol.com
WEB SITE . . . . .www.gorgeouspr.com
TYPES   Corporate - EPK - Film/TV Talent -
                     Marketing - Music - New Media

Versa Manos . . . . .President
Mario Martin .Account Executive
Brian McKinney . . . . .Publicity Coordinator
Kayla Isenberg . . . . .Jr. Publicist
Danielle Braden . . . . .Assistant

GREAT SCOTT P.R.ODUCTIONS

12773 Caswell Ave., Ste. 302
Los Angeles, CA 90066
PHONE 310-398-0260
FAX 310-398-0190
EMAIL . . . . .greatscottproductions@earthlink.net
WEB SITE . . . . .www.greatscottpr.com
TYPES   Corporate - Film/TV Talent - Marketing -
                     Music
RECENT ACCOUNTS   American Idol Underground - Peter White -
                     Marc Antoine - Dotsie Bausch - Earth,
                     Wind & Fire - Richard Elliot - Brian
                     Bromberg

Rick Scott . . . . .President

LIZZIE GRUBMAN PUBLIC RELATIONS

270 Lafayette St., Ste. 504
New York, NY 10012
PHONE 212-966-5000
FAX 212-966-4277
EMAIL .stacey@grubmanpr.com
WEB SITE . . . . .www.grubmanpr.com
TYPES   Corporate - Film/TV Productions - Film/TV
                     Talent - Marketing - Music - Promotions
RECENT ACCOUNTS   Macy's Kiss Book - Laurie Ann Gibson -
                     Chloe Dao - Chin Chin - Jeffrey Rackover -
                     HBO - Corcoran Group - Crush Teen
                     Nightclub - AG Jeans - Star Room - 10
                     Advertising - Jorge Posada - Tera Patrick -
                     Ambient Planet - Ciprianis - Gen Spec
                     Vitimans - Thrillist.com - Sherry Wolf
                     Handbags - Hiya Mints
COMMENTS   Full-service public relations for fashion,
                     beauty, restaurants, clubs and special
                     events

Lizzie Grubman . . . . .President/Owner
Sabrina Levine . . . . .Partner
Stacey F. Spector . . . . .CFO
Kelly Brady . . . . .Senior Account Executive
Crystal Parzik . . . . .Senior Account Executive
Jason Silber . . . . .Senior Account Executive
Leah Bignell .Account Executive
Kyle Hulcher .Account Executive
Molly Weprin .Account Executive
Anne Watkins . . . . .Assistant Account Executive

GUTTMAN ASSOCIATES

118 S. Beverly Dr., Ste. 201
Beverly Hills, CA 90212
PHONE 310-246-4600
FAX 310-246-4601
TYPES   Corporate - Film/TV Productions - Film/TV
                     Talent - Music - Product Placement -
                     Promotions
COMMENTS   Events, fashion, actors, directors

Gisela Guttman . . . . .Emeritus Chairman/CFO
Dick Guttman . . . . .President
Rona Menashe . . . . .Sr. VP
Susan Madore . . . . .Sr. Account Executive
Iris Karni . . . . .Chief Accountant
Tanya Constantino . . . . .Assistant Account Executive
Joy Huffman . . . . .Assistant Account Executive
Lauren Renschler . . . . .Assistant Account Executive
Shirin Vaklli . . . . .Assistant Account Executive

HANDS ON PUBLIC RELATIONS & MARKETING

12711 Ventura Blvd., Ste. 170
Sherman Oaks, CA 91604
PHONE 310-341-3201
EMAIL . . . . .handsonpr@aol.com
WEB SITE . . . . .www.handsonpublicrelations.com
TYPES   Corporate - Marketing - Music - New
                     Media - Promotions
COMMENTS   Entertainment related film, music and TV
                     companies; Award-winning music artists,
                     actors and actresses

Craig Melone . . . . .Chairman
Ricky Rollins . . . . .Sr. Account Executive
Francesco Aiello . . . . .Account Executive

HANSON & SCHWAM PUBLIC RELATIONS

9350 Wilshire Blvd., Ste. 315
Beverly Hills, CA 90212
PHONE 310-248-4488
FAX 310-248-4499
EMAIL . . . . .gerryporter@hspr.net
WEB SITE . . . . .www.hspr.net
TYPES   Corporate - Film/TV Productions - Film/TV Talent - Marketing - Music - New Media - Product Placement - Promotions

Gene Schwam . . . . .President/Owner
Michael Casey . . . . .Executive VP
Gerald Porter . . . . .Sr. VP (gerryporter@hspr.net)

HARRISON & SHRIFTMAN

141 W. 36th St., 12th Fl.
New York, NY 10018
PHONE 917-351-8600/310-855-1600
FAX 917-351-8601
EMAIL . . . . .contact@hs-pr.com
WEB SITE . . . . .www.hs-pr.com
TYPES   Corporate - Film/TV Talent - Marketing - Music - New Media - Product Placement - Promotions
RECENT ACCOUNTS   Grey Goose - St. Regis - H2O+ - Mercedes-Benz - W Hotels - UGG Australia - Peter Som - CORZO - Perrier - Porsche - 485 Fifth Avenue - MR CHOW - Alba - Avalon - Blackberry
COMMENTS   Miami office phone: 305-534-0008

Elizabeth Harrison . . . . .Partner
Lara Shriftman . . . . .Partner

FRANK HOLGUIN AND ASSOCIATES

79-405 Hwy. 111, Ste. 9, #441
La Quinta, CA 92253
PHONE 949-294-6001
EMAIL . . . . .frankh@fh-assoc.com
WEB SITE . . . . .www.fh-assoc.com
TYPES   Corporate - EPK - Film/TV Productions - Film/TV Talent - Marketing - Music - New Media - Product Placement - Promotions
RECENT ACCOUNTS   Peter Sherayko (Actor) - Caravan West Productions - Glenn Roland Films - Pro8mm/Pro16mm Film Production
COMMENTS   Publicity emphasis for talent, industry product introduction, studios and production companies

Frank Holguin . . . . .President
Dori Dixon . . . . .Designer/Art Director
Suzanne Hawley . . . . .Writer/Editor
Carol Dreyer . . . . .Administration

HOLLYWOOD OS

400 S. Beverly Dr., Ste. 307
Beverly Hills, CA 90212
PHONE 310-277-3001/310-277-1007
FAX 310-277-3088
EMAIL . . . . .info@hollywoodos.com
SECOND EMAIL . . . . .hollywoodos@aol.com
WEB SITE .www.hollywoodos.com
TYPES   Film/TV Productions - New Media

Angela Bertolino . . . . .CEO
Behnoosh Khalili . . . . .COO

THE HOLLYWOOD-MADISON GROUP

11684 Ventura Blvd., Ste. 258
Studio City, CA 91604
PHONE 818-762-8008
FAX 818-762-8089
EMAIL . . . . .info@hollywood-madison.com
WEB SITE . . . . .www.hollywood-madison.com
SECOND WEB SITE . . . . .www.fameindex.com
TYPES   Corporate - Film/TV Talent - Marketing - Product Placement - Promotions
RECENT ACCOUNTS   General Motors - Procter & Gamble - Sony Electronics
COMMENTS   A leading supplier of celebrities for endorsements, appearances and press campaigns

Jonathan Holiff . . . . .President

THE HONIG COMPANY, INC.

3500 W. Olive Ave., #300
Burbank, CA 91505
PHONE 818-986-4300
FAX 818-981-3141
EMAIL .info@honigcompany.com
WEB SITE . . . . .www.honigcompany.com
TYPES   Corporate - Film/TV Talent - Marketing - Promotions
RECENT ACCOUNTS   Image Entertainment - Gilbert Gottfried - Motion Picture & Television Fund - Bandai Visual

Steve Honig . . . . .President
Joe Sutton . . . . .Sr. Consultant
Emanuela Cariolagian . . . . .Press Relations
Krys Grondorf . . . . .Press Relations

HYPE

5651 Wilshire Blvd., Ste. A
Los Angeles, CA 90036
PHONE 323-938-8363
FAX 323-938-8757
EMAIL . . . . .info@hypeworld.com
WEB SITE . . . . .www.hypeworld.com
SECOND WEB SITE . . . . .www.hypefest.com
TYPES   Film/TV Productions - Marketing - New Media - Promotions
COMMENTS   Commercials, music videos and indie films

Jessie Nagel . . . . .Special Agent
Colleen O'Mara . . . . .Special Agent
Michele Lu . . . . .Publicist

I/D PUBLIC RELATIONS
155 Spring St., 6th Fl.
New York, NY 10012
PHONE .212-334-0333/323-822-4800
FAX 212-334-8444/323-822-4880
EMAIL . . . . .nyc@id-pr.com
SECOND EMAIL . . . . .la@id-pr.com
WEB SITE . . . . .www.id-pr.com
TYPES   Corporate - Film/TV Productions - Film/TV
                         Talent - Product Placement
COMMENTS   West Coast office: 8409 Santa Monica
                         Blvd., West Hollywood, CA 90069

Kelly Bush . . . . .Partner
Mara Buxbaum . . . . .Partner
Cari Ross . . . . .Partner
Ina Treciokas . . . . .Partner
Carrie Byalick . . . . .Publicist
Ed Choi . . . . .Publicist
Rebecca Feferman . . . . .Publicist
Jillian Fowkes . . . . .Publicist
Jodi Gottlieb . . . . .Publicist
Heather Greenfield . . . . .Publicist
Chris Kanavick . . . . .Publicist
Adam Keen . . . . .Publicist
Bebe Lerner . . . . .Publicist
Megan Moss . . . . .Publicist
Annick Muller . . . . .Publicist
Tamar Salup . . . . .Publicist

THE ILLUSION FACTORY
21800 Burbank Blvd., Ste. 225
Woodland Hills, CA 91367
PHONE 818-598-8400
FAX 818-598-8494
EMAIL . . . . .brian@illusionfactory.com
WEB SITE . . . . .www.illusionfactory.com
TYPES   Corporate - EPK - Film/TV Productions -
                         Marketing - New Media - Promotions -
                         Outdoor Advertising

Brian Weiner . . . . .Owner

INDIE PR
5225 Wilshire Blvd., Ste. 514
Los Angeles, CA 90036
PHONE 323-964-0700
FAX 323-964-0704
EMAIL . . . . .indiepublicity@aol.com
TYPES   Film/TV Productions - Film/TV Talent
COMMENTS   Independent films and filmmakers

Linda Brown . . . . .Owner
Jim Dobson . . . . .Owner
Karen Fried . . . . .Publicist

INFECTIOUS
1346 N. Hayworth Ave.
Los Angeles, CA 90046
PHONE 323-969-0401
FAX 323-969-8208
EMAIL . . . . .info@infectiouspublicity.com
WEB SITE . . . . .www.infectiouspublicity.com
TYPES   Music

Casey Phillips . . . . .Owner (casey@infectiouspublicity.com)
Scott Simoneaux . . . . .Owner (scott@infectiouspublicity.com)

THE IN-HOUSE WRITER
5239 Highland View Ave.
Los Angeles, CA 90041
PHONE 323-256-4950
FAX 323-375-0375
EMAIL . . . . .info@theinhousewriter.com
WEB SITE . . . . .www.theinhousewriter.com
TYPES   Corporate - Film/TV Productions -
                         Marketing - New Media
RECENT ACCOUNTS   Unversial Studios Home Entertainment -
                         International Creative Management (ICM) -
                         Disney Channel - The History Channel -
                         Warner Independent Pictures - Sony -
                         Screen Gems
COMMENTS   Provides copy for press kits, bios, releases,
                         synopses, production notes, Web copy and
                         other marketing materials

Andrew Hindes . . . . .President

INK PUBLIC RELATIONS GROUP
9229 Sunset Blvd., Ste. 525
West Hollywood, CA 90069
PHONE 310-860-0806
FAX 310-860-0805
EMAIL . . . . .courtney@inkprgroup.com
WEB SITE . . . . .www.inkprgroup.com
TYPES   Corporate - Film/TV Talent - Marketing -
                         Music - Product Placement - Promotions
RECENT ACCOUNTS   Fred Segal Cafe - Rafinity Jewelry - Charm
                         and Luck Handbags - Kim Kimble Hair
                         Care - Kate Spade - Doug Wilson - Silver
                         Cross - Calabasas Magazine

Galit Hadari . . . . .Owner
Courtney Thompson . . . . .Owner
Dan DiPietro-James . . . . .Publicist
Jenny Heller . . . . .Publicist
Marie Paulo . . . . .Publicist
Richard Pedine . . . . .Publicist
Tracy Pendleton . . . . .Publicist

IPRESSROOM CORPORATION
10801 National Blvd., Ste. 410
Los Angeles, CA 90064-4139
PHONE 310-479-0544
EMAIL . . . . .info@ipressroom.com
WEB SITE . . . . .www.ipressroom.com
TYPES   Corporate - EPK - Marketing - New Media
                         - Promotions
RECENT ACCOUNTS   Target Corporation - Trend Micro - Smith &
                         Hawken - Carmax - Bragman Nyman
                         Cafarelli - Entertainment Studios, Inc. - The
                         Hecker Law Group - American
                         Choreography Awards - Cirque du Soleil at
                         The 74th Annual Academy Awards - Salt
                         Lake 2002 Olympic Opening Ceremonies
                         - Lightforce Entertainment - Entertainment
                         Studios Inc. - The Jammx Kids - Ecast -
                         Associated Production Music - McDonald
                         Selznick Associates, Inc.

Eric Schwartzman . . . . .CEO
Chris Bechtel .VP, Products & Services
Vadim Derkach . . . . .VP, Technology
Austin Hice .Director, Digital Content

I.S.M. ENTERTAINMENT, INC.
343 Soquel Ave., Ste. 523
Santa Cruz, CA 95062
PHONE 831-475-1472
FAX 831-475-1473
EMAIL . . . . .ppinfo@ismentertainment.com
WEB SITE . . . . .www.ismentertainment.com
TYPES — Corporate - Film/TV Productions - Marketing - Product Placement - Promotions
RECENT ACCOUNTS — Bell Sports - Grand American Racing - Nature Sweet Tomatoes - Smoothie King - Zaxby's

Ian McQueen . . . . .President, Entertainment Marketing
Lori Johnson . . . . .Business Development Manager, Branded Entertainment Marketing
Danielle Killian . . . . . . .Brand Integration Director, Cause-Related Entertainment Marketing
Brett Karleen . . . . . . .Manager, Independent Film Integration
Kelly Somerville . . . . . . .Strategic Facilitator, New Business Development

JAFFE & CO., INC. STRATEGIC MEDIA
416 N. Oakhurst Dr., Ste. 305
Beverly Hills, CA 90210
PHONE 310-275-7327
FAX 310-275-7987
EMAIL .info@stevejaffepr.com
WEB SITE . . . . .www.stevejaffepr.com
TYPES — Corporate - Film/TV Productions - Film/TV Talent - New Media - Promotions
RECENT ACCOUNTS — Leonardo DiCaprio - Tony Robbins - President Bill Clinton - Koch Industries - Thierry Lhermitte - Author/Attorney Mark Lane - Dick Gregory - Galichia Medical Group - Tambar Transatlantic Theatre Fund - Russia's Channel One (ORT) - Susan Blakely Designs - Stanley Kramer Library - Rafer Johnson (Chairman, Special Olympics) - Jay Calvert, MD, FACS - Pauley Perrette - Africa Foundation for AIDS
COMMENTS — Crisis Management; Litigation Support; Legal, medical and corporate; Specializes in high-profile clients

Stephen Jaffe . . . . .Chairman

JAG ENTERTAINMENT PR
4265 Hazeltine Ave.
Sherman Oaks, CA 91423
PHONE 818-905-5511
FAX 818-501-4911
EMAIL . . . . .jgeffen@jagpr.com
WEB SITE . . . . .www.jagpr.com
TYPES — Film/TV Talent - Marketing - Music - New Media
RECENT ACCOUNTS — David Cassidy - John Lennon Songwriting Contest and Educational Tour Bus - Joshua Bell - Robin Gibb - themusicedge.com - NAMM - Sony Classical - David Sheehan - Ana Maria Martinez - Edgar Meyer - weSpark - Zade - James Galway - Corps of Compassion - Diana DeGarmo
COMMENTS — Nonprofits

Jo-Ann Geffen . . . . .President
Tracy Howard . . . . .VP
Jane Covner . . . . .Associate
Kellie Olisky . . . . .Jr. Publicist

JANE AYER PUBLIC RELATIONS
3435 Ocean Park Blvd., Ste. 107
Santa Monica, CA 90405
PHONE 310-581-1330
FAX 310-581-1335
EMAIL .jane@janeayerpr.com
WEB SITE .www.janeayerpr.com
TYPES — Corporate - Film/TV Productions - Film/TV Talent - Marketing - Music - New Media - Promotions

Jane Ayer . . . . .President
Irene Dean . . . . .VP

JENSEN COMMUNICATIONS, INC.
709 E. Colorado Blvd., Ste. 220
Pasadena, CA 91101
PHONE 626-585-9575
FAX 626-564-8920
EMAIL . . . . .info@jensencom.com
WEB SITE . . . . .www.jensencom.com
TYPES — Film/TV Productions - Marketing - Music - Promotions
RECENT ACCOUNTS — Joe Bonamassa - Spectron IQ - Herb Albert - Dave Mason - Santana - Crosby, Stills & Nash - Jackson Browne - DTS - XM Radio - Domo Records

Michael Jensen . . . . .CEO
Meghan Helsel . . . . .VP, Public Relations
Susan Stewart . . . . .VP
Jennifer Fehr . . . . .Publicist
Erin Podbereski . . . . .Publicist

LYNN ALLEN JETER & ASSOCIATES
3699 Wilshire Blvd., Ste. 850
Los Angeles, CA 90010
PHONE 323-933-8007
FAX 323-939-7361
EMAIL . . . . .lajass@ca.rr.com
SECOND EMAIL . . . . .lajassociates@yahoo.com
WEB SITE . . . . .www.lynnallenjeter.com
TYPES — Film/TV Talent - Marketing - Music - Promotions
RECENT ACCOUNTS — Companies: OneUnited Bank - The Ultimate Hustler Creator - Datari Turner - BET Awards - RNB Entertainment - South Bay Entertainment Group - Smooth Magazine; Music: Teena Marie - Yolanda Adams - DJ Battlecat - Lil' Zane - Da Brat; Actors: Wesley Jonathan - Lance Gross - Kimberly Brooks - M'fundo Morrison - Dorian Gregory - Kym Whitley - Kellita Smith; Directors: Jeff Byrd - Greg Carter - Damien Douglas
COMMENTS — Also handles events

Lynn Jeter . . . . .President
Ernie Singleton . . . . .Associate

JONAS PUBLIC RELATIONS
240 26th St., #3
Santa Monica, CA 90402
PHONE 310-656-3355
FAX 310-656-3365
TYPES — Film/TV Productions - Film/TV Talent - Marketing

Lori Jonas . . . . .Owner
Jeff Abraham . . . . .Public Relations
Jennifer Goodwin . . . . .Public Relations
Kara Rosella .Public Relations
Andi Schecter . . . . .Public Relations

JONES & O'MALLEY
10123 Camarillo St.
Toluca Lake, CA 91602
PHONE 818-762-8353
FAX 818-762-6736
TYPES   Corporate - Film/TV Talent
COMMENTS   Public relations for a variety of profession-
                         als

Jana Olson-Collins . . . . .President
Loma Collier . . . . .VP

MILTON KAHN ASSOCIATES, INC.
PO Box 50353
Santa Barbara, CA 93150
PHONE 805-969-8555
FAX 805-969-2645
EMAIL . . . . .miltonkahnpr@aol.com
WEB SITE . . . . .www.miltonkahnpr.com
TYPES   Film/TV Talent - Promotions

Milton Kahn . . . . .President

KBC MEDIA RELATIONS
316 Haddon Ave., Ste. B
Westmont, NJ 08108
PHONE 856-869-9403/856-869-9341
FAX 856-869-9342
EMAIL . . . . .kbcmedia@att.net
SECOND EMAIL .chris@kbcmedia.com
WEB SITE . . . . .www.kbcmedia.com
TYPES   Corporate - Film/TV Productions - Film/TV
                         Talent - Music - Promotions
COMMENTS   One-stop service agency; Placements
                         include all major national and international
                         media

Karen Ammond . . . . .President
Alene Ammond .Chairman of the Board
Jeff Allen . . . . .Sr. VP
Chris Barrett . . . . .VP, Film Division
Elizabeth Licorish . . . . .Assistant to the President

DAN KLORES ASSOCIATES
386 Park Ave. South, 10th Fl.
New York, NY 10016
PHONE 212-685-4300
FAX 212-685-9024
EMAIL . . . . .first_lastname@dkcnews.com
WEB SITE . . . . .www.dkcnews.com
TYPES   Corporate - Film/TV Productions - Film/TV
                         Talent
COMMENTS   New releases; Major motion pictures;
                         Integrated marketing; Crisis management

Dan Klores . . . . .President/Founding Partner
Sean Cassidy . . . . .Managing Director/President
Joe DePlasco . . . . .Managing Director
John Marino . . . . .Managing Director/Managing Partner
Matthew Traub . . . . .Managing Director/Chief of Staff

KOGER PUBLIC RELATIONS & EVENTS
11041 Santa Monica Blvd., Ste. 824
Los Angeles, CA 90025
PHONE 818-667-2316/818-795-5512
EMAIL . . . . .amber@kogerpr.com
SECOND EMAIL . . . . .dev@kogerpr.com
WEB SITE . . . . .www.kogerpr.com
TYPES   Film/TV Talent - Music - Promotions
RECENT ACCOUNTS   BET Awards - BET Comedy Awards - BET
                         25th Anniversary - ASCAP Music Awards -
                         Kirk Whalum - Kyle Eastwood - Shawn
                         Amos - Benita Hill - School of Rock
COMMENTS   Events and publicity

Amber Koger . . . . .President
Devern Fleming . . . . .VP

KRUPP KOMMUNICATIONS
130 W. 57th St., Ste. 9D
New York, NY 10019
PHONE 212-265-4704
FAX 212-265-4708
WEB SITE . . . . .www.kruppkommunications.com
TYPES   Marketing - Promotions

Heidi Krupp . . . . .President/CEO
Kelly Kimball . . . . .Sr. VP

LANDERS PR
1680 N. Vine St., Ste. 1005
Hollywood, CA 90028
PHONE 323-871-9707
FAX 323-871-9709
EMAIL . . . . .nicolel@landerspr.com
SECOND EMAIL . . . . .tracyr@landerspr.com
WEB SITE . . . . .www.landerspr.com
TYPES   Corporate - Film/TV Productions -
                         Marketing - Product Placement -
                         Promotions
RECENT ACCOUNTS   Xenon Pictures - Snoop Dogg's Hood of
                         Horror - Dark Horse Indie/Image
                         Entertainment - Splinter - My Suicidal
                         Sweetheart - Lionsgate - Dark Ride - The
                         Death of Michael Smith - Dante's Inferno -
                         Chasing the Horizon - Core Pilates - Green
                         Clean LA - Art of Tea - Mercury in
                         Retrograde (Documentary)

Nicole Landers . . . . .Founder
Laurie Gran . . . . .Publicist
Tracy Rubin . . . . .Publicist

JEFFREY LANE & ASSOCIATES
8380 Melrose Ave., Ste. 306
Los Angeles, CA 90069
PHONE 323-782-0066
FAX 323-782-0088
EMAIL . . . . .jeffrey@jeffreylane.com
WEB SITE . . . . .www.jeffreylane.com
TYPES   Corporate - Film/TV Productions - Film/TV
                         Talent - Music - Promotions
COMMENTS   Events

Jeffrey Lane . . . . .Account Executive
Roger Lane . . . . .Account Executive
Simin Adam . . . . .Account Executive

ANNE LEIGHTON MEDIA * MARKETING * MOTIVATION
3050 Decatur Ave., Ste. 1D
Bronx, NY 10467
PHONE 718-881-8183
EMAIL . . . . .leightonmedia@aol.com
WEB SITE . . . . .www.anneleighton.com
TYPES   Corporate - Film/TV Productions -
                         Marketing - Music - New Media
RECENT ACCOUNTS   Jethro Tull - Grand Funk Railroad - Jann
                         Klose - Pat DiNizio - Joe Deninzon and
                         Stratospheerius - Tower of Power - Carl
                         Palmer - Cevin Soling - David Essel
COMMENTS   Live performers and musicians; Refers other
                         publicists if not right for a project; Contacts
                         with radio promoters and retail outreach
                         firms

Anne Leighton . . . . .Owner

THE LEVERAGE GROUP
7083 Hollywood Blvd., Ste. 200
Los Angeles, CA 90028
PHONE 323-817-0044
FAX 323-817-0055
WEB SITE . . . . .www.leveragegroup.com
TYPES   Corporate - Film/TV Productions - Film/TV
                         Talent - Marketing - Music - New Media -
                         Product Placement - Promotions
RECENT ACCOUNTS   Tribeca Film Festival - Redken - U.S.A. Luge

Autumn Nazarian . . . . .Director
Kathi Sharpe-Ross . . . . .Consultant

SUSAN L. LEVIN PUBLIC RELATIONS
137 N. Larchmont Blvd., #186
Los Angeles, CA 90004
PHONE 310-503-3397
FAX 323-469-3003
EMAIL . . . . .publicity@susanlevinpr.com
WEB SITE .www.susanlevinpr.com
TYPES   Film/TV Productions - Marketing -
                         Promotions
RECENT ACCOUNTS   Mad Money - Journey to the End of Night -
                         Mozart and the Whale - Variety Academy
                         Screening Series - Walk the Line: The
                         Johnny Cash Story - The Polar Express:
                         IMAX

Susan Levin . . . . .Owner

LEVINE COMMUNICATIONS OFFICE, INC. (LCO)
1180 S. Beverly Dr., 3rd Fl.
Los Angeles, CA 90035
PHONE 310-300-0950
FAX 310-300-0951
EMAIL . . . . .info@lcoonline.com
WEB SITE . . . . .www.lcoonline.com
TYPES   Corporate - EPK - Film/TV Productions -
                         Film/TV Talent - Marketing - Music - New
                         Media - Product Placement - Promotions
RECENT ACCOUNTS   Contact office directly for account informa-
                         tion
COMMENTS   Full-service PR firm; See Web site for case
                         studies and complete list of services

Michael Levine . . . . .Founder
Dawn Miller . . . . .President/COO
Liam Collopy . . . . .VP, Literary Division
Lauren Lewis . . . . .VP, Entertainment
Donna Dillard . . . . .Operations Manager

THE LIPPIN GROUP, INC.
6100 Wilshire Blvd., Ste. 400
Los Angeles, CA 90048
PHONE 323-965-1990/212-986-7080
FAX 323-965-1993/212-986-2354
EMAIL . . . . .losangeles@lippingroup.com
WEB SITE . . . . .www.lippingroup.com
TYPES   Corporate - Film/TV Productions - Music -
                         New Media
RECENT ACCOUNTS   Architectural Digest - Victoria's Secret
                         Beauty Products - Marc Anthony Hair
                         Products - Hearts on Fire Diamonds -
                         General Electric - Kraft - Procter & Gamble
                         - Johnson & Johnson - Coke - Campbell's
                         Soup - Apple
COMMENTS   DVD, licensing, foundations, resorts, con-
                         sumer products and special events; East
                         Coast office: 369 Lexington Ave., 22nd Fl.,
                         New York, NY 10017; Corporate branding
                         unit: Brand to Hollywood

Richard Lippin .Chairman/CEO
Pam Golum . . . . .President, Entertainment, West Coast
Don Chiaramella . . . . .Executive VP
Les Eisner . . . . .Executive VP
Leah Krantzler . . . . .Executive VP
Jennifer Price . . . . .Executive VP
Robin Mesger . . . . .Sr. VP
Paul Nichols . . . . .Sr. VP
Matt Biscuiti . . . . .VP
Alex Lippin . . . . .Sr. Account Executive

LOBELINE COMMUNICATIONS
8995 Elevado Ave.
Los Angeles, CA 90069
PHONE 310-271-1551
FAX 310-271-4822
WEB SITE . . . . .www.lobeline.com
TYPES   Film/TV Talent - Marketing - Music - New
                         Media - Promotions
RECENT ACCOUNTS   Blue Man Group - David Copperfield - Bill
                         Gaither - Lipizzaner Stallions Tour

Philip Lobel . . . . .Owner (phil@lobeline.com)
Chris Kingry . . . . .No Title (chris@lobeline.com)
Michelle Avedissian . . . . .No Title (michelle@lobeline.com)

M. LORING COMMUNICATIONS PR
PO Box 1096
Agoura Hills, CA 91376
PHONE 805-231-3182
FAX 818-292-8996
EMAIL .contact@monaloring.com
WEB SITE . . . . .www.monaloring.com
TYPES   Corporate - Film/TV Talent - Music - New
                         Media - Product Placement - Promotions
RECENT ACCOUNTS   Playdate Kids Publishing - Red Van Pictures
                         - Shane Drake - Davis Mallory (Real World)
                         - Willie Herath
COMMENTS   Publishers, musicians, actors, online entre-
                         preneurs and filmmakers

Mona Loring . . . . .President
Brittany Copsey . . . . .Executive Assistant
Jordyn Borczon . . . . .Account Assistant

EDWARD LOZZI & ASSOCIATES
9454 Wilshire Blvd., Ste. 600
Beverly Hills, CA 90212-2929
PHONE 310-922-1200
EMAIL . . . . .epl@lozzipr.com
WEB SITE . . . . .www.lozzipr.com
TYPES　　　　　　　Corporate - Film/TV Talent - Marketing - Product Placement - Promotions
RECENT ACCOUNTS　30th Annual Saturn Awards - ShirleyJones.com - James Dean: Live Fast, Die Young - Monaco Forever - The Room - How It All Went Down - Night of 100 Stars Oscar Party - Jay Bernstein - Cindy Margolis
COMMENTS　　　　Public relations for books, movie premieres, home video, theatre and stage shows, campaign launches and red carpet events; Affiliate offices in New York, London and San Francisco

Edward Lozzi . . . . .President
Brian Cowan . . . . .VP
Maggie Shelton . . . . .Accounts Manager
Joseph Csongei . . . . .Red Carpet Events
Jennifer Kutner . . . . .Red Carpet Events
Pamela Moskovitz . . . . .Office Manager

LYNCH ARCHER PR ENTERTAINMENT
2221 W. Olive Ave., Ste. L
Burbank, CA 91506
PHONE 818-843-6300
EMAIL . . . . .cheryl@lyncharcher.com
WEB SITE . . . . .www.lyncharcher.com
TYPES　　　　　　　Corporate - Film/TV Talent - Marketing - Promotions

Cheryl Lynch . . . . .President

M80
2894 Rowena Ave., Ste. A
Los Angeles, CA 90039
PHONE 323-644-7800
FAX 323-644-7801
EMAIL . . . . .info@m80im.com
WEB SITE www.m80im.com
SECOND WEB SITE www.m80teams.com
TYPES　　　　　　　Corporate - Marketing - Music - New Media - Promotions
RECENT ACCOUNTS　Fox Home Entertainment - Sega America - Xbox 360 - Showtime

Dave Neupert . . . . .CEO (neup@m80im.com)
Jeff Semones . . . . .President (jeff@m80im.com)
Todd Steinman . . . . .COO (todd@m80im.com)
Joe Muran . . . . .General Manager (joey@m80im.com)

SUSAN MAGRINO AGENCY
641 Lexington Ave., 28th Fl.
New York, NY 10022
PHONE 212-957-3005
FAX 212-957-4071
EMAIL . . . . .info@smapr.com
WEB SITE . . . . .www.smapr.com
TYPES　　　　　　　Corporate - Film/TV Talent
COMMENTS　　　　Luxury leisure and lifestyle

Susan Magrino . . . . .Chairman/CEO/Founder
Allyn Magrino . . . . .President

MAKEOVER MEDIA
11138 Aqua Vista, Ste. 32
Studio City, CA 91602
PHONE 818-752-9168/818-753-9444
FAX 818-752-4953/818-688-3157
EMAIL . . . . .linda.arroz@makeovermedia.com
SECOND EMAIL . . . . .kyrian.corona@makeovermedia.com
WEB SITE . . . . .www.makeovermedia.com
TYPES　　　　　　　Corporate - Film/TV Talent - Marketing - Music - New Media - Product Placement - Promotions

Linda Arroz . . . . .Partner
Kyrian Corona . . . . .Partner

MANNING SELVAGE & LEE
1675 Broadway, 9th Fl.
New York, NY 10019
PHONE 212-468-4200
FAX 212-468-3031
EMAIL . . . . .bruce.mackenzie@mslpr.com
WEB SITE . . . . .www.mslpr.com
TYPES　　　　　　　Corporate - Film/TV Talent - Marketing - Product Placement - Promotions
RECENT ACCOUNTS　Best Buy - Heineken USA - Saab - GM - Swiffer - Mr. Clean - Vonage - Prilosec OTC - Bounce - Eli Lilly & Company - Novartis Pharmaceuticals - Philips - Home Depot - Red Bull
COMMENTS　　　　Serves as a pop culture and entertainment advocate for brands

Mark Hass . . . . .CEO
Jim Tsokanos . . . . .Executive VP
Bruce MacKenzie . . . . .Sr. VP/Director, Entertainment Marketing
Tanya Shaye . . . . .Manager, Entertainment Marketing

MANOS MANAGEMENT & PUBLIC RELATIONS
8306 Wilshire Blvd., Ste. 3500
Beverly Hills, CA 90211
PHONE 310-993-6799/818-610-3650
FAX 818-610-3637
EMAIL .manosprods@aol.com
SECOND EMAIL . . . . .manorpr@aol.com
TYPES　　　　　　　Corporate - Film/TV Productions
TERRITORY　　　　Actors - Comedians - Directors - Screenwriters - TV Writers
RECENT ACCOUNTS　XUBAZ - Hippie Ink - Bonicca Organic Bodycare - Epitome Spa & Salon - Skin Deep Magazine - ShaDang

Melinda Manos . . . . .Principal/Owner
Keith Colhane .Associate

MANTRA EMPOWERED PUBLIC RELATIONS
110 W. 26th St.
New York, NY 10001
PHONE 212-645-1600
FAX 212-989-6459
EMAIL . . . . .info@mantrapublicrelations.com
WEB SITE . . . . .www.mantrapublicrelations.com
TYPES　　　　　　　Corporate - Film/TV Productions - Film/TV Talent - Marketing - Music - New Media

Gaye Carleton .President
Christine Cassidy . . . . .Public Relations Specialist
Jan Holtzberg . . . . .Public Relations Specialist
Paul Lockwood . . . . .Public Relations Specialist
Jordyn Tyson . . . . .Public Relations Specialist

MARCELLA C PUBLIC RELATIONS, INC.
11669 Chenault St., Ste. 5
Brentwood, CA 90049
PHONE 310-471-7626/310-966-7499
FAX 310-861-1898
EMAIL . . . . .info@marcellapr.com
WEB SITE . . . . .www.marcellapr.com
TYPES   Film/TV Productions - Film/TV Talent - Music
RECENT ACCOUNTS   Rogers and Cowan - Warner Music Latina - Newmarket Films - Icon Productions - Terry Hines and Associates - BB Marketing - EMI Televisa - Xenon Pictures - Casa Nova Films- ¡Viva Tu Cine! - The Passion of The Christ - Innocent Voices - End of the Spear - Bacilos - Therese - An American Haunting - Lower City - City of Men - Rolling Family - Natasha Perez for Lady in the Water - Televisa Home Entertainment - Warner Home Video - Superman Returns (DVD) - Happy Feet (DVD) - Pedro Infante (DVD Collection)

Marcella Carlson . . . . .President/CEO
Stamatias A. De Cuenze . . . . .CFO
Antonios Cuonzo . . . . .Sr. Publicist
Sarah Morgenstein . . . . .Business Affairs/Sr. Publicist
Stephanie Carlson . . . . .PA

NORM MARSHALL & ASSOCIATES, INC.
11059 Sherman Way
Sun Valley, CA 91352
PHONE 818-982-3505
FAX 818-503-1936
EMAIL . . . . .info@normmarshall.com
WEB SITE . . . . .www.normmarshall.com
TYPES   Corporate - Film/TV Productions - Product Placement - Promotions

Norm Marshall . . . . .CEO
Devery Holmes . . . . .President/CMO
Donna Schmidt . . . . .CFO
Helene Bousel-Cohen . . . . .Sr. VP, Strategic Marketing & Client Relations
Malcolm Brooker . . . . .VP, Production Services
Caressa Lupold . . . . .VP, Branded Integration
Joe Tani . . . . .VP, International Business Development
Jeanine Ullman . . . . .VP, Client Relations
Teri Ward . . . . .VP, Client Relations
Menaka Gopinath . . . . . .Sr. Manager, Promotions & Strategic Marketing
Samantha Sarakanti . . . . .Manager, Feature Film
Julie Prentice . . . . .Sr. Director, Client Relations
Monica Jaramillo . . . . .Director, Public Relations
Tracy Merrill .Director, Branded Integration
Bailey Spencer-Jackson . . .Director, Human Resources & Business Affairs
Brett Spaulding . . . . .Production Coordinator, TV
Anne Evans . . . . .Script Supervisor

MATTER
An Edelman Company
5670 Wilshire Blvd., 22nd Fl.
Los Angeles, CA 90036
PHONE 323-857-9100
FAX 323-857-9117
EMAIL . . . . .los.angeles@edelman.com
WEB SITE . . . . .www.edelman.com
TYPES   Corporate - Film/TV Productions - Film/TV Talent - Marketing - Music - New Media - Product Placement - Promotions
RECENT ACCOUNTS   Starbucks - Xbox - Nissan - The Recording Academy - Warner Bros. Home Entertainment & Consumer Products
COMMENTS   Largest independently owned global public relations firm; 52 offices worldwide

Gail Becker . .President, Western Region/General Manager, Los Angeles/ Head, Digital Entertainment Rights & Technology

David Freeman . . .Managing Director, Entertainment Marketing Division
Andy Marks . . . . .Managing Director, Entertainment Marketing Division
Ferris Thompson . . .Managing Director, Entertainment Marketing Division

MCA PR - MINERVA COLLIER ASSOCIATES, LTD.
8721 Sunset Blvd., Ste. 215
Los Angeles, CA 90069
PHONE .310-228-1780/212-643-0627
FAX 310-652-5118
EMAIL . . . . .minerva@minervapr.com
WEB SITE . . . . .www.minervapr.com
TYPES   Corporate - Film/TV Productions - Film/TV Talent - Marketing - Music - Product Placement - Promotions
COMMENTS   Specializes in entertainment, beauty and fashion industries and high-profile celebrities; East coast address: 250 W. 57th St., New York, NY 10107

Minerva Collier . . . . .Publicist/President/CEO
Thomas A. Burgos III, Esq. . . . . .President, Business & Legal Affairs
Aneesha Williams . . . . .Publicist/VP
Edward Jones . . . . .Publicist
Jennifer Munix . . . . .Publicist
Catherine Stein . . . . .Publicist

MEDIA MONSTER COMMUNICATIONS, INC./ BRAIN GASM PRODUCTIONS ENTERTAINMENT MEDIA
11684 Ventura Blvd., Ste. 662
Studio City, CA 91604
PHONE 818-506-8675
EMAIL . . . . .mediamonster@yahoo.com
WEB SITE . . . . .www.braingasm.com
TYPES   Marketing
RECENT ACCOUNTS   Celebration of Artistic Freedome Oscar Viewing Party - Mimi Kennedy - Temecula Valley International Film and Music Festival - Heather Robertson - Michael Griffin - Back Stage West/Hollywood Reporter's Actorfest - Emmy Campaign - Oak Ridge Boys Concert - Olivia Newton-John Breast Cancer Fundraiser - Various Theatrical Productions and Music Producers/Artists

Stacey Kumagai . . . . .President

REBA MERRILL ASSOCIATES
5652 Fallbrook Ave.
Woodland Hills, CA 91367
PHONE 818-227-1200
FAX 818-227-1207
EMAIL . . . . .rmaent@earthlink.net
TYPES   Corporate - EPK - Film/TV Productions - Film/TV Talent - Marketing - Promotions
RECENT ACCOUNTS   Buena Vista International - Sony International - Warner Home Video

Reba Merrill . . . . .Producer
Cheryl Hiltzik . . . . .CEO/President
Collin Ketterer . . . . .Editor

DAVID MIRISCH ENTERPRISES
735 Fourth St.
Encinitas, CA 92024
PHONE 760-632-7770
FAX 760-632-5408
EMAIL . . . . .david@dmirisch.com
WEB SITE . . . . .www.dmirisch.com
TYPES   Promotions
RECENT ACCOUNTS   Cedars Sinai Hospital - City of Laguna
                         Niguel Victor Awards - Pageant of the
                         Masters
COMMENTS   Books celebrities and athletes for nonprofit
                         and corporate events; Fundraising for char-
                         ities needing dollars and exposure for their
                         organization or events; Also event produc-
                         tion

David Mirisch . . . . .President
Kelly McLean .Assistant to the President

MOB SCENE CREATIVE + PRODUCTIONS
421 S. Beverly Dr., 7th Fl.
Beverly Hills, CA 90212
PHONE 310-286-2233
FAX 310-286-2234
WEB SITE . . . . .www.mobscene.com
TYPES   EPK - Film/TV Productions - Marketing -
                         New Media

Brian Daly . . . . .President
Thomas Grane . . . . .President

MORRIS MARKETING, INC.
12813 La Maida St.
Valley Village, CA 91607
PHONE 818-487-9300
FAX 818-487-9303
EMAIL . . . . .sheila@morrispr.com
WEB SITE . . . . .www.morrispr.com
TYPES   Corporate - Film/TV Productions -
                         Marketing - New Media - Promotions

Sheila Morris . . . . .President/CEO

MOTION PICTURE MAGIC
3605 W. Pacific Ave.
Burbank, CA 91505
PHONE 818-953-7494
FAX 818-953-7113
EMAIL . . . . .markmills.mpm@sbcglobal.net
WEB SITE .www.motionpicturemagic.com
TYPES   Product Placement
COMMENTS   Corporate products, services, signage and
                         cleared commercials

Mark Mills . . . . .President
Tony Wilson . . . . .Director, Marketing & Operations
Carlos Garcia .Manager, Operations
Aydde Hurtado . . . . .Manager, Studio Productions & Services
Bob Romans . . . . .Manager, Logistics
Hide Sugiyama . . . . .Manager, Asia Pacific Marketing

STEVE MOYER PUBLIC RELATIONS
PO Box 5227
West Hills, CA 91308
PHONE 818-784-7027
FAX 818-784-7099
EMAIL . . . . .moyerpr@earthlink.net
TYPES   Film/TV Productions - Film/TV Talent -
                         Marketing - Music - Promotions
COMMENTS   Full-service publicity and marketing compa-
                         ny specializing in the promotion of per-
                         forming arts (music, theatre, dance), spe-
                         cial events, award shows, trade shows,
                         films, TV projects, restaurants, personalities
                         and books

Steve Moyer . . . . .Owner

MPM COMMUNICATIONS
840 N. Larrabee St., Ste. 4-303
West Hollywood, CA 90069
PHONE 310-855-9342
FAX 310-855-9372
EMAIL . . . . .mpmcomm@aol.com
SECOND EMAIL . . . . .marilee@mpmcommunications.com
WEB SITE . . . . .www.mpmcommunications.com
TYPES   Corporate - Film/TV Talent - Music -
                         Promotions
RECENT ACCOUNTS   PBS - Max Weinberg - Tonja Walker
                         Davidson - Sephora - American Academy
                         of Dermatology - Appraisal Management
                         Company - Rescue Magazine - American
                         Indian Artists, Inc.

Marilee Mahoney . . . . .President

MPRM PUBLIC RELATIONS
5670 Wilshire Blvd., Ste. 2500
Los Angeles, CA 90036
PHONE 323-933-3399
FAX 323-939-7211
EMAIL . . . . .aamman@mprm.com
WEB SITE . . . . .www.mprm.com
TYPES   Corporate - Film/TV Productions - Music -
                         New Media - Promotions
RECENT ACCOUNTS   Azureus - Amp'd Mobile - Buena Vista Blu-
                         Ray - Bridge Films - Genius Products DVD -
                         Los Angeles Ballet - Hollywood Christmas
                         Parade - Starz Media - I Have A Dream
                         Foundation - Lambda Legal Liberty Awards
                         - Spacedog - National Geographic Kids
                         Entertainment - Perfect Match - San
                         Gennaro Festival - World Series of Video
                         Games - In2TV - VOY Group - Picsel
                         Technologies
COMMENTS   Emerging media and technology, home
                         entertainment/DVD releases, feature film
                         release campaigns, cable networks, series
                         television campaigns, film directors, pro-
                         ducers and screenwriters, special events

Rachel McCallister . . . . .President
Mark Pogachefsky . . . . .President
Alan Amman . . . . .Sr. VP, General Entertainment
Michael Lawson . . . . .Sr. VP, Film & Events
Anthony Sprauve . . . . .Sr. VP, Digital Media & Technology
Ariel Carpenter . . . . .VP, Emerging Media & Technology
Jenny McIntosh . . . . .VP, Television
Shari Mesulam . . . . .VP, Events
Jennifer St. Clair . . . . .VP, Converging Media & Technology
Sarah Carragher . . . . .Director, Television
Tom Chen . . . . .Director, TV & Home Entertainment
Ariana Nash . . . . .Director, Film & Events
Ema Ostarcevic . . . . .Director, Digital Media & Technology

MUCH AND HOUSE PUBLIC RELATIONS
8075 W. Third St., Ste. 500
Los Angeles, CA 90048
PHONE 323-965-0852
FAX 323-965-0390
EMAIL . . . . .info@muchandhousepr.com
WEB SITE . . . . .www.muchandhousepr.com
TYPES   Corporate - Film/TV Productions - Film/TV
           Talent - Marketing - Product Placement
COMMENTS   All areas

Sharon House . . . . .Partner
Elizabeth Much . . . . .Partner
Alison Graham . . . . .VP
Laura Ackermann . . . . .Publicist

JULIAN MYERS PUBLIC RELATIONS
13900 Panay Way, Ste. R217
Marina del Rey, CA 90292
PHONE 310-827-9089/310-306-2290
FAX 310-827-9838
EMAIL . . . . .julian@julianmyerspr.com
WEB SITE . . . . .www.julianmyerspr.com
TYPES   Corporate - Film/TV Productions - Film/TV
           Talent - Marketing - New Media - Product
           Placement - Promotions
RECENT ACCOUNTS   AmigoDay
COMMENTS   Branding, marketing and public relations
           specialists for producers, directors, post
           production companies, filmed entertain-
           ment entities, creators; Member,
           Entertainment Publicists Professional
           Society; IATSE; Women in Film; UCLA and
           Loyola Marymount faculty

Julian Myers . . . . .Chairman

NO PROBLEM PRODUCTIONS
260 Harrison Ave., Ste. 407
Jersey City, NJ 07304
PHONE 201-433-3907
TYPES   Corporate - Music
RECENT ACCOUNTS   EMI - Sony - Penguin Books - Harmonia
           Mundi - Rykodisc - Windham Hill -
           Smithsonian/Folkways - Putumayo - Miriam
           Makeba - Jon Anderson of Yes - Tangerine
           Dream - Ladysmith Black Mambazo -
           Afropop Worldwide

Andrew Seidenfeld . . . . .Director

BLAISE NOTO & ASSOCIATES
3501 Kehala Dr.
Kihei, HI 96753
PHONE 808-879-1227/808-269-0960
FAX 808-879-2939
EMAIL . . . . .blaisenoto@hawaii.rr.com
SECOND EMAIL . . . . .blaisenoto@aol.com
TYPES   Film/TV Productions - Film/TV Talent -
           Marketing - Music - Promotions
RECENT ACCOUNTS   The Kite Runner - Apocalypto - The Passion
           of the Christ - Heart of a Dragon -
           Discovery Kids: Flight 29 Down
COMMENTS   Special events; Hollywood studio marketing
           executive for 30 years

Blaise J. Noto . . . . .President

REBECCA O'MEARA ENTERTAINMENT PUBLICITY
1517 Fern St.
New Orleans, LA 70118
PHONE 504-861-2188
EMAIL . . . . .rebeccaomeara@aol.com
TYPES   Corporate - Film/TV Talent - Marketing -
           Music - New Media - Product Placement -
           Promotions
RECENT ACCOUNTS   Atchity Entertainment - LA Wave Studio

Rebecca O'Meara . . . . .Entertainment Publicist

ON THE SCENE PRODUCTIONS
5900 Wilshire Blvd., Ste. 1400
Los Angeles, CA 90036
PHONE 323-930-1030/212-682-5200
FAX 323-930-1840/212-682-0602
EMAIL . . . . .info@onthescene.com
WEB SITE . . . . .www.onthescene.com
TYPES   Corporate - EPK - Film/TV Productions -
           Marketing - Music - New Media - Product
           Placement - Promotions
COMMENTS   New York office: 144 E. 44th St., 4th Fl.,
           New York, NY 10017; Satellite and radio
           media tours, video news releases, video
           highlights packages, Webcasting, event
           coverage, POD/VOD-casting, phonecast-
           ing

Paul Torrey . . . . .President, New Business & Product Development

ORIGINALEE MADE IN LOS ANGELES
453 S. Spring St., Ste. 941
Los Angeles, CA 90013
PHONE 213-327-0668
EMAIL . . . . .leeron@originalee.com
SECOND EMAIL . . . . .gina@originalee.com
WEB SITE . . . . .www.originalee.com
TYPES   Marketing - Product Placement -
           Promotions

Leeron Tal . . . . .Founder
Gina Goren . . . . .Founder

GIGI OTERO PUBLIC RELATIONS
1264 Ozeta Terrace, Ste. 102
West Hollywood, CA 90069
PHONE 310-386-7267
FAX 310-289-1202
EMAIL . . . . .go@gopr.biz
WEB SITE . . . . .www.gopr.biz
TYPES   Corporate - Film/TV Productions - Film/TV
           Talent - Marketing - Promotions
RECENT ACCOUNTS   ProTEL-News - ProTEL Homestead Teleport
           - MGM Networks Latin America's Casa
           Club TV - Bela Broadcasting - KBEH-TV
           Channel 63 Los Angeles - KMOH-TV
           Channel 6 Phoenix - AMP TV - GlobeCast
           America - Shepley Winnings PR - Rick Rifle
           - Mirus Entertainment
COMMENTS   Specializes in campaigns targeting general,
           US Hispanic and international markets

Gigi Otero . . . . .President

PATRICOLA/LUST PUBLIC RELATIONS
9171 Wilshire Blvd., Ste. 390
Beverly Hills, CA 90210
PHONE 323-655-5150
FAX 323-655-7223
EMAIL . . . . .susan@plpr.com
SECOND EMAIL . . . . .dlust@plpr.com
TYPES   Corporate - Film/TV Productions - Film/TV
                         Talent

Susan Patricola . . . . .Partner
David Lust . . . . .Partner
Lori Glass . . . . .Publicist
Courtney Knittel . . . . .Publicist
Jenni Weinman . . . . .Publicist
Alyse Cicora . . . . .Office Manager
Marci Coulson . . . . .Assistant to Susan Patricola
Karina Hall . . . . .Assistant to Jenni Weinman
Lisa Jammal . . . . .Assistant to David Lust
Melissa Kubrin . . . . .Assistant to Lori Glass & Courtney Knittel

PERCEPTION PUBLIC RELATIONS, LLC
3940 Laurel Canyon Blvd., #169
Studio City, CA 91604
PHONE 818-985-2190
FAX 818-985-2194
EMAIL . . . . .lea@perceptionpr.com
SECOND EMAIL . . . . .gena@perceptionpr.com
WEB SITE . . . . .www.perceptionpr.com
TYPES   Film/TV Productions - Film/TV Talent -
                         Marketing - Product Placement -
                         Promotions
RECENT ACCOUNTS   20th Century Fox - Fox Searchlight Pictures
                         - Paramount Classics
COMMENTS   Specializes in award campaigns for feature
                         films

Lea Yardum . . . . .Partner
Gena Wilder . . . . .Partner

PERSONAL PUBLICITY
12831 S. 71st St.
Tempe, AZ 85284
PHONE 480-839-9474
FAX 480-839-6575
EMAIL . . . . .dkellerpublicity@aol.com
WEB SITE . . . . .www.personalpublicity.com
TYPES   Film/TV Talent - Marketing - New Media -
                         Promotions
RECENT ACCOUNTS   Bobcat Goldthwait - Paula Poundstone -
                         Jeff Dunham - Pablo Francisco - Flip Orley
                         - The Chicago Improv

Debbie Keller . . . . .Owner
Brittney Toliver . . . . .Assistant

PLA MEDIA
1303 16th Ave. South
Nashville, TN 37212
PHONE 615-327-0100
FAX 615-320-1061
EMAIL . . . . .info@plamedia.com
WEB SITE . . . . .www.plamedia.com
TYPES   Corporate - EPK - Film/TV Productions -
                         Film/TV Talent - Marketing - Music -
                         Promotions
RECENT ACCOUNTS   The Nashville Film Festival - Warner Bros.
                         Records - Thomas Nelson Publishing
COMMENTS   Literary

Pamela Lewis . . . . .President
Kay Waggoner . . . . .Sr. Publicist
Cie Hoover . . . . .Account Executive
Derek Lefholz . . . . .Accounts/Office Coordinator
Nicole Zeller . . . . .Publicity Coordinator

PLATFORM MEDIA GROUP INC.
8335 W. Sunset Blvd., Ste. 314
Los Angeles, CA 90069
PHONE 323-337-9042
FAX 323-337-9043
EMAIL . . . . .heshelman@platformgrp.com
WEB SITE . . . . .www.platformgrp.com
TYPES   Corporate - EPK - Film/TV Productions -
                         Film/TV Talent - Marketing - Music - New
                         Media - Product Placement - Promotions -
                         Outdoor Advertising
RECENT ACCOUNTS   VW - Diageo - Wingard Spirits - Trago
                         International - Motorola - National
                         Lampoon - Capcom Entertainment
COMMENTS   Also Event Production

Henry Eshelman . . . . .Managing Director
Michele Angeloni . . . . .No Title
Hilary Carver . . . . .No Title
Will Gary . . . . .No Title
Julie Goodson . . . . .No Title

PMK/HBH PUBLIC RELATIONS
700 San Vicente Blvd., Ste. G-910
West Hollywood, CA 90069
PHONE 310-289-6200/212-582-1111
FAX 310-289-6677/212-582-6666
TYPES   Corporate - Film/TV Talent - Music
COMMENTS   East Coast office: 161 Avenue of the
                         Americas, 10th Fl., New York, NY 10013

Jennifer Allen . . . . .Managing Director
Craig Bankey . . . .(LA)
Robin Baum . . . . .Managing Director
James Dickinson . . . .(London)
Joy Fehily . . . . .VP
Jill Fritzo . . . . .VP (NY)
Andy Gelb . . . .(LA)
Erica Gray . . . .(LA)
Simon Halls . . . . .Managing Director
Victoria Harvie . . . .(LA)
Gina Hoffman . . . .(LA)
Marisa Honig . . . .(LA)
Stephen Huvane . . . . .Managing Director
Annie Jeeves . . . .(LA)
Monique Huey Jones . . . .(Chicago)
Melissa Kates . . . . .VP
Jack Ketsoyan . . . .(LA)
Pat Kingsley . . . . .Managing Director
Joy Limanon . . . .(LA)
Catherine Olim . . . . .Managing Director
Meghan Prophet . . . .(LA)
Brit Reece . . . .(LA)
Heidi Schaeffer . . . . .VP
Nate Schreiber . . . .(LA)
Heidi Slan . . . .(LA)
Danica Smith . . . .(LA)
Kelly Stephens . . . .(LA)
Dan Strickford . . . .(LA)
Ame Van Iden . . . .(LA)
Emily Yontobian . . . .(LA)
Lauren Auslander . . . .(NY)
Cindi Berger . . . . .Managing Director (NY)
Bianca Bianconi . . . .(NY)
Allen Eichhorn . . . . .Managing Director (NY)
Meridith Goldblatt . . . .(NY)
Jennifer Holiner . . . .(NY)
Eban Howell . . . .(NY)
Shea Martin . . . .(NY)
Jennifer Plante . . . .(NY)
Shawn Purdy . . . .(NY)
Ashley Schiff . . . .(NY)
Judee Sidorsky . . . .(NY)
Jonathan Streep . . . .(NY)
Victoria Varela . . . .(NY)
Stephanie Venia . . . .(NY)

FREDELL POGODIN & ASSOCIATES

7223 Beverly Blvd., Ste. 202
Los Angeles, CA 90036
PHONE 323-931-7300
FAX 323-931-7354
EMAIL . . . . .pr@fredellpogodin.com
TYPES   Corporate - Film/TV Productions
RECENT ACCOUNTS   Tsotsi (Miramax) - Y Tu Mamá También (IFC) - The Woodsman (Newmarket) - Born Into Brothels (THINKFilm) - The Story of the Weeping Camel (THINKFilm) - Enron: The Smartest Guys in the Room (Magnolia) - The Beat That My Heart Skipped (Wellspring) - Paradise Now (Warner Independent) - March of the Penguins (Warner Independent) - The Road to Guantanamo (Roadside Attractions) - Brothers of the Head - (IFC)
COMMENTS   Independent film public relations

Fredell Pogodin . . . . .Owner

PREACHER PUBLICITY & REPUTATION MANAGEMENT

1308 Factory Pl., Ste. 009
Los Angeles, CA 90013
PHONE 213-683-9701
FAX 213-683-9701
EMAIL . . . . .preacherpub@yahoo.com
WEB SITE . . . . .www.preacherpub.com
TYPES   Film/TV Productions - Film/TV Talent - Marketing - Music
COMMENTS   Post production; Print and online editing

Michael Kunkes .Press Agent/Account Manager

PREMIER PUBLIC RELATIONS

710 Seward St.
Los Angeles, CA 90038
PHONE 323-785-1020
FAX 323-785-1026
EMAIL . . . . .information@premierpr.net
WEB SITE . . . . .www.premierpr.com
TYPES   Corporate - Film/TV Productions - Film/TV Talent - Marketing
RECENT ACCOUNTS   Bauer Martinez Distribution - Buena Vista International - Focus Features - Lakeshore Entertainment - Lionsgate International - Toho-Towa - Warner Bros. International

Pamela Godwin-Austen . . . . .President
Jan Kean . . . . .VP

PREMIERE TV

429 Santa Monica Blvd., Ste. 300
Santa Monica, CA 90401
PHONE 310-899-9090
FAX 310-899-9860
EMAIL . . . . .info@premieretv.com
WEB SITE . . . . .www.premieretv.com
TYPES   EPK - Film/TV Productions - Film/TV Talent - Music
COMMENTS   Nationwide TV and radio coverage for films, TV shows, DVDs, albums or events; Satellite media tours and distribution; Event coverage; Video news releases

Shayne R. Fraeke . . . . .CEO
Eve Sharon . . . . .President

PRESS HERE PUBLICITY

138 W. 25th St., 7th Fl.
New York, NY 10001
PHONE 212-246-2640
FAX 212-582-6513
EMAIL .info@pressherepublicity.com
WEB SITE . . . . .www.pressherepublicity.com
TYPES   Music

Chloe Walsh . . . . .Publicist
Jen Appel . . . . .Publicist
Gina Schulman . . . . .Publicist
Jill Strominger . . . . .Assistant to Chloe Walsh

PRIMARY ACTION INC.

7461 Beverly Blvd., PH
Los Angeles, CA 90036
PHONE 323-692-9244
FAX 323-692-9233
EMAIL . . . . .info@primaryaction.com
WEB SITE . . . . .www.primaryaction.com
TYPES   Film/TV Talent - Marketing - Product Placement - Promotions
COMMENTS   Showroom for clients

Jeffrey Karinja . . . . .President
Jacopo Stecchini . . . . .Director, International Marketing
Linda Peluso . . . . .Sr. VP, Showroom Services
Gaia Giudi . . . . .Sr. VP, Public Relations
Emy Hovanesyan . . . . .Director, Product Placement
Adria Piaggi .VP, Marketing & Sales (Italy)
Alestar Digby . . . . .Account Executive

PRINCIPAL COMMUNICATIONS GROUP

8242 W. Third St., Ste. 200
Los Angeles, CA 90048
PHONE 323-658-1555
FAX 323-658-1556
TYPES   Corporate - Marketing - New Media

Paul Pflug . . . . .Partner
Melissa Zukerman . . . . .Partner

PRIORITY PUBLIC RELATIONS

25020 W. Avenue Stanford, Ste. 200
Valencia, CA 91355
PHONE 661-964-0333
FAX 661-964-0344
EMAIL . . . . .info@prioritypr.net
WEB SITE . . . . .www.prioritypr.net
TYPES   Corporate - Film/TV Productions - Marketing
RECENT ACCOUNTS   Promax/BDA - Promax Europe - Anime Network - Rainbow Media International - Concrete Pictures - Castalia Communications - Program Partners

Kristien Brada-Thompson . . . . .VP/Managing Director, US
Marylou Johnston . . . . .VP/Managing Director, Europe
Melissa Ford . . . . .Sr. Account Executive
Linda Eckert . . . . .Account Executive

PUBLICITY COMPANIES

PUBLIC RELATIONS ASSOCIATES
557 Norwich Dr.
Los Angeles, CA 90048
PHONE 310-659-0380
FAX 310-659-5270
EMAIL .prals@pacbell.net
TYPES   Corporate - Film/TV Productions - New
                         Media
COMMENTS   Strong international and online contacts;
                         Clients include animation studios, special
                         effects companies, post production houses
                         and the technology development industry

Lanny Sher . . . . .President/CEO

RISING STAR COMMUNICATIONS
14129 Archwood
Van Nuys, CA 91405
PHONE 818-989-5649
EMAIL . . . . .therightwriter@aol.com
TYPES   Corporate - Film/TV Productions - Film/TV
                         Talent - Marketing - Promotions
RECENT ACCOUNTS   Los Angeles Daily News - VIP Tech, Inc. -
                         Nice to Be Kneaded, Inc. - The California
                         Restaurant Association - Special Events
                         Magazine - The Pet Staff - Lee & Associates
                         - Retail Merchandiser Magazine - Norm's
                         Restaurants

Dolores Long . . . . .President

ROGERS & COWAN
Pacific Design Center
8687 Melrose Ave., 7th Fl.
Los Angeles, CA 90069
PHONE 310-854-8100
FAX 310-854-8101
EMAIL . . . . .inquiries@rogersandcowan.com
WEB SITE . . . . .www.rogersandcowan.com
TYPES   Film/TV Productions - Film/TV Talent -
                         Marketing - Music - Product Placement -
                         Promotions
COMMENTS   East Coast office: 640 Fifth Ave., 5th Fl.,
                         New York, NY 10019; London office: Fox
                         Court 14, Gray's Inn Rd., London WC1X
                         8WS, UK

Tom Tardio . . . . .CEO
Paul Bloch . . . . .Co-Chairman
Susan Ashbrook . . . . .Executive VP, Film Fashion
Fran Curtis . . . . .Executive VP, Entertainment & Lifestyles
Steve Doctrow . . . . .Executive VP, Integrated Marketing
Elliot Fischoff . . . . . . .Executive VP, Domestic Television & Film Publicity
Sandy Friedman . . . . .Executive VP, Music & Digital Entertainment
Teri Kane . . . . .Executive VP, Film & Domestic
Julie Nathanson . . . . .Executive VP, Entertainment
Alan Nierob . . . . .Executive VP, Entertainment, Personalities
Maureen O'Connor . . . . .Executive VP, Music
Sallie Olmsted . . . . .Executive VP, Convergence
Nikki Parker . . . . .Executive VP, Worldwide Film & TV
Tara Walls . . . .Executive VP, Product Placement, Entertainment Marketing
Elizabeth Hinckley . . . . .Sr. VP, Definitive Culture
Heather Krug . . . . .Sr. VP, Consumer, Sports Marketing
Cheryl Maisel . . . . .Sr. VP, Entertainment, Personalities
Ivy Mollenkamp . . . . .Sr. VP, Lifestyles & Entertainment
Holly Taylor . . . . .Sr. VP, Entertainment & Lifestyles
Wendy Zaas . . . . .Sr. VP, Video Games
Janine Azern .VP, Film (London)
Jason Padgitt . . . . .VP, Music
John Reilly .VP, Music, Latin
Karen Sundell . . . . .VP, Music
Tracy Thompson . . . . .Marketing Manager

THE ROSE GROUP
9925 Jefferson Blvd.
Culver City, CA 90232
PHONE 310-280-3710
FAX 310-280-3715
TYPES   Corporate - Film/TV Productions - Film/TV
                         Talent - Marketing - New Media
RECENT ACCOUNTS   SKYY - SKYY90 - Campari - TiVo -
                         Greenlight Financial Services - Laing Urban
                         - Diaper Dude - New Era - Greendot -
                         Playboy - Video Business - Rodmark - DWR
                         - Target Red Room - Atlantic Records -
                         Sunset Plaza - The Broad Academy - Go
                         Softwear - Meridith Jacobs - The Girls Next
                         Door - St. Andrews Grand - Tyra Banks -
                         Red Mango

Jeff Rose . . . . .Partner
Elana Weiss . . . . .Partner
Brian Rosman . . . . .VP
David Glaubke . . . . .Sr. Account Executive
Tracy Mallozzi . . . . .Sr. Account Executive
Lauren Weiss . . . . .Sr. Account Executive
Whitney Ashley . . . . .Account Executive
Brody Brown .Account Executive
Francey Grund . . . . .Account Executive
Sandy Hall . . . . .Account Executive
Laura Benetti . . . . .Account Coordinator
Jordan Kaye . . . . .Account Coordinator
Danielle Patla . . . . .Account Coordinator
Cecilia Orozco . . . . .Assistant Account Coordinator
Diane Gordon .Office Manager

STAN ROSENFIELD & ASSOCIATES
2029 Century Park East, Ste. 1190
Los Angeles, CA 90067
PHONE 310-286-7474
FAX 310-286-2255
EMAIL .stan@sra-pr.com
TYPES   Film/TV Talent

Stan Rosenfield . . . . .President
Shara Koplowitz . . . . .Head, Corporate Division/Publicist
Jennifer Shoucair .Publicist
Melissa Sun . . . . .Assistant to Stan Rosenfield
Brooke Fisher . . . . .Assistant to Shara Koplowitz
Emily Shimizu . . . . .Assistant to Jennifer Shoucair

ROUSSO/FISHER PUBLIC RELATIONS LLC
5225 Wilshire Blvd., Ste. 718
Los Angeles, CA 90036
PHONE 323-933-4646
FAX 323-933-5229
EMAIL . . . . .kirsten@roussofisher.com
WEB SITE . . . . .www.roussofisher.com
TYPES   Corporate - Film/TV Productions - Film/TV
                         Talent - Marketing - Music - New Media -
                         Product Placement - Promotions
RECENT ACCOUNTS   Levi's - La Velvet Margarita Cantina - Jim
                         Wayne Salon - Dr. Worth - Grail - Cris
                         Cashmere - Tiana - Exerstrider

Ryan Fisher . . . . .Partner
RJ Rousso . . . . .Partner
Nicole Wool . . . . .Director, Public Relations
Blair Garson . . . . .Publicity
Drew Kuhse . . . . .Publicity
Brian Stirling .Office Manager

CARL SAMROCK PUBLIC RELATIONS COMPANY
330 N. Screenland Dr., #213
Burbank, CA 91505
PHONE 818-260-0777
EMAIL .carlsamrock@cs-pr.com
TYPES   Film/TV Talent - Marketing - New Media
RECENT ACCOUNTS   DVD publicity for Warner Home Video,
                         Sony Pictures Entertainment and Buena
                         Vista Home Entertainment

Carl Samrock . . . . .President

THE MITCH SCHNEIDER ORGANIZATION (MSO)
14724 Ventura Blvd., Ste. 710
Sherman Oaks, CA 91403
PHONE 818-380-0400
FAX 818-380-0430
WEB SITE . . . . .www.msopr.com
TYPES   Music
RECENT ACCOUNTS   Ozzy Osbourne - David Bowie - The Vans
                         Warped Tour - Depeche Mode - Coachella
                         - Aerosmith

Mitch Schneider . . . . .President
Todd Brodginski . . . . .Sr. VP
Marcee Rondan . . . . .Sr. VP
Kristine Ashton-Magnuson . . . . .Sr. VP
Shazila Mohammed .Publicist
Alexandra Greenberg . . . . .Sr. Account Executive
Libby Henry . . . . .Sr. Account Executive

SCHWARTZMAN & ASSOCIATES, INC.
10801 National Blvd., Ste. 410
Los Angeles, CA 90064-4139
PHONE 310-446-8310
FAX 310-452-7031
WEB SITE .www.schwartzmanpr.com
TYPES   Corporate - EPK - Film/TV Productions -
                         Film/TV Talent - Marketing - New Media -
                         Promotions
RECENT ACCOUNTS   Cirque du Soleil - Salt Lake 2002 Olympic
                         Opening Ceremonies - Target Corporation
COMMENTS   Also podcasting and blogging

Eric Schwartzman . . . . .Managing Director
Chris Bechtel . . . . .Sr. Associate, New Media
Iris Mann . . . . .Sr. Associate
Shipherd Reed . . . . .Producer
Su-Rmi Givens . . . . .Sr. Account Executive
Jonathan Zaleski . . . . .Sr. Account Executive
Jennifer Dekel . . . . .Account Executive
Aaron Henry .Account Executive
Scott Hansen . . . . .Executive
Austin Hice . . . . .Webmaster

SELFMAN & OTHERS PUBLIC RELATIONS
PO Box 641831
Los Angeles, CA 90064
PHONE 323-653-4555
TYPES   Film/TV Productions - Film/TV Talent
COMMENTS   Actors, theatre, books, TV, events, lifestyle;
                         Proofreading and copyediting for scripts
                         and manuscripts

Flo Selfman . . . . .Principal

NANCY SELTZER & ASSOCIATES, INC.
6220 Del Valle Dr.
Los Angeles, CA 90048
PHONE 323-938-3562
FAX 323-938-0589
TYPES   Corporate - Film/TV Productions - Film/TV
                         Talent - Marketing - Music - Promotions
RECENT ACCOUNTS   Sean Connery - Shawn Ashmore - Ian
                         McShane - Garth Brooks - Whitney
                         Houston - Sara Ramirez - Kevin Zegers -
                         Placido Domingo - Taryn Rose International
                         - Rodrigo Santoro - Milos Forman - Brenda
                         Blethyn - Dan Futterman - Bridget Fonda -
                         Nora Zehetner - Ali Selim - Jessye Norman

Nancy Seltzer . . . . .Owner
Brittany Phillips . . . . .Jr. Publicist
Erin Grenz . . . . .Assistant

SET RESOURCES
3916 S. Sepulveda Blvd., Ste. 207
Culver City, CA 90230
PHONE 310-915-9180
FAX 310-388-3057
EMAIL .info@setresources.com
WEB SITE .www.setresources.com
TYPES   Marketing - Product Placement -
                         Promotions
RECENT ACCOUNTS   Hansen's - Monster - Lost - Ciao Bella -
                         Patron

John Owen . . . . .President
Aaron Gordon .New Business
Whitney Low . . . . .New Business
Phill Branch .Film Placements
Laura Leyva .TV Placements
Emille Stayner . . . . .Research

JERRY SHANDREW PUBLIC RELATIONS
1050 S. Stanley Ave.
Los Angeles, CA 90019
PHONE 323-549-9250
FAX 323-549-9254
EMAIL .shandrewpr@aol.com
SECOND EMAIL . . . . .craig@shandrewpr.com
TYPES   Corporate - Film/TV Productions - Film/TV
                         Talent - Marketing
RECENT ACCOUNTS   Sex and the City - Paramount Pictures
                         International - Sony Pictures - Nikki Ziering
                         - Chris Carmack - True Religion Jeans - Big
                         Screen Entertainment - Justin Hartley

Jerry Shandrew . . . . .Owner
Keri Hehn .Account Executive
Kevin Pearsall . . . . .Account Executive
Raul Rojas .Account Executive
Marc Vander Linden . . . . .Amsterdam/Europe
Craig Block .Office Manager

SHARP & ASSOCIATES PUBLIC RELATIONS
8721 Sunset Blvd., Ste. 208
Los Angeles, CA 90069
PHONE 310-652-7770
FAX 310-652-1037
EMAIL .sharpassociates@aol.com
SECOND EMAIL . . . . .crystalsharppr@aol.com
TYPES   Corporate - Film/TV Talent - Promotions

Pamela Sharp . . . . .Managing Director
Jeff Jones . . . . .Publicist
Crystal Kusiak . . . . .Publicist

PUBLICITY COMPANIES

SHEBA MEDIA GROUP
11152 Westheimer Rd., Ste. 299
Houston, TX 77042
PHONE 713-331-0357
FAX 713-977-4121
EMAIL . . . . .query@shebamedia.com
WEB SITE . . . . .www.shebamediagroup.com
TYPES   Corporate - Film/TV Talent - Marketing -
                          Music - New Media - Product Placement -
                          Promotions
RECENT ACCOUNTS   Love Trap Productions
COMMENTS   Books to film

Renee Byrd . . . . .Agent
Kaye P. Brooks . . . . .Literary Agent
Fanta Camara . . . . .Literary Agent
William Panyera . . . . .Literary Agent
Jeri Baylor . . . . .Head, Corporate Public Relations
Vanessa Morman .Marketing Director
Melodie Armstrong . . . . .Media Coordinator

THE SHEFRIN COMPANY
808 S. Ridgeley Dr.
Los Angeles, CA 90036
PHONE 323-931-8200
FAX 323-939-5799
EMAIL . . . . .paulshef@prodigy.net
TYPES   Film/TV Productions - Film/TV Talent -
                          Music
COMMENTS   Production companies and individuals

Paul Shefrin . . . . .President

SHEPLEY WININGS DIAMOND PUBLIC RELATIONS INC.
12725 Ventura Blvd., Ste. J
Studio City, CA 91604
PHONE 818-760-7131
FAX 818-760-2456/818-754-6769
EMAIL . . . . .info@swdpr.com
WEB SITE . . . . .www.swdpr.com
TYPES   Corporate - Film/TV Productions - Film/TV
                          Talent - Marketing - Promotions
RECENT ACCOUNTS   Sony Pictures Television - Animal Planet -
                          NBC Universal Television - Disney - Lifetime
                          Television - Telepictures - The Fine Living
                          Network - Universal Studios Pay-Per-View -
                          Game Show Network (GSN) - SoapNet -
                          PBS - Griffith Observatory - The Tennis
                          Channel - Advanta - G-Phoria - US Dance
                          Sport Championship

Michael Shepley . . . . .Partner
Bonnie Winings . . . . .President
Hope Diamond . . . . .Principal

KEITH SHERMAN & ASSOCIATES
234 W. 44th St., Ste. 1004
New York, NY 10036
PHONE 212-764-7900
FAX 212-764-0344
EMAIL . . . . .keith@ksa-pr.com
WEB SITE . . . . .www.ksa-pr.com
TYPES   Corporate - Film/TV Productions - Film/TV
                          Talent - Music
COMMENTS   Theatrical Productions; Special Events

Keith Sherman . . . . .President
Scott Klein . . . . .VP
Brett Oberman . . . . .VP

CHERYL SHUMAN, INC.
468 N. Camden Dr., Ste. 200
Beverly Hills, CA 90210
PHONE 310-285-1777/818-905-7087
FAX 310-285-1790/818-905-7087
EMAIL . . . . .cheryl@cherylshuman.com
SECOND EMAIL . . . . .cherylshumaninc@aol.com
WEB SITE . . . . .www.cherylshuman.com
TYPES   Corporate - Film/TV Productions - Film/TV
                          Talent - Marketing - Music - New Media -
                          Product Placement - Promotions
RECENT ACCOUNTS   The Academy of Television Arts and
                          Sciences
COMMENTS   Additional office: 4702 Fulton Ave., Unit
                          206, Sherman Oaks, CA 91423

Cheryl Shuman . . . . .CEO
Karen Porginski . . . . .Executive VP, Marketing
Aimee Nicole . . . . .Director, Celebrity Relations

SITRICK AND COMPANY
1840 Century Park East, Ste. 800
Los Angeles, CA 90067
PHONE 310-788-2850/212-573-6100
FAX 310-788-2855/212-573-6165
WEB SITE . . . . .www.sitrick.com
TYPES   Corporate - Film/TV Productions - Film/TV
                          Talent
COMMENTS   Also handles crisis management; East
                          Coast office: 655 Third Ave., 22nd Fl.,
                          New York, NY 10017

Michael S. Sitrick .Chairman/CEO
Seth Faison . . . . .Member of the Firm
Ross Johnson . . . . .Member of the Firm
Anita Marie Laurie . . . . .Member of the Firm
John Lippman . . . . .Member of the Firm
Tammy Taylor . . . . .Member of the Firm

SMART GIRLS PRODUCTIONS, INC.
15030 Ventura Blvd., Ste. 914
Sherman Oaks, CA 91403
PHONE 818-907-6511/818-461-0375
EMAIL . . . . .smartgirls@smartg.com
WEB SITE . . . . .www.smartgirlsproductions.com
SECOND WEB SITE . . . . .www.howtohollywood.com
TYPES   Film/TV Talent - Marketing - Promotions

Melody Jackson . . . . .Founder/CEO
Chris Bosley . . . . .Staff Writer
Virginia Young . . . . .No Title

SMOKE & MIRRORS PUBLIC RELATIONS, INC.
1825 Park Dr., Ste. 4
Los Angeles, CA 90026
PHONE 213-250-4603
EMAIL . . . . .smokemirrors@earthlink.net
WEB SITE .www.smokeandmirrorspr.com
TYPES   Corporate - Marketing - New Media
RECENT ACCOUNTS   Entertainment Technology Center at USC -
                        Thomson - Animation Mentor - Gray
                        Matter FX
COMMENTS   Full-service boutique company providing
                        event development, writing, marketing and
                        media relations services

Rochelle Winters . . . . .Principal

SOLTERS & DIGNEY
8383 Wilshire Blvd., Ste. 649
Beverly Hills, CA 90211
PHONE 323-651-9300
FAX 323-651-5944
EMAIL . . . . .lee@solterspr.com
SECOND EMAIL . . . . .jerry@solterspr.com
WEB SITE . . . . .www.solterspr.com
TYPES   Corporate - Film/TV Productions - Film/TV
                        Talent - Marketing - Music - New Media -
                        Promotions
COMMENTS   Entertainment, sports, special events, pub-
                        lishing

Lee Solters . . . . .Partner
Jerry Digney . . . . .Partner

THE SPARK FACTORY
10 E. Colorado Blvd.
Pasadena, CA 91105
PHONE 626-397-2719
FAX 626-397-2732
EMAIL .mailroom@sparkfactory.com
WEB SITE . . . . .www.sparkfactory.com
TYPES   Corporate - EPK - Film/TV Productions -
                        Marketing - New Media - Promotions
COMMENTS   Entertainment advertising for studios, net-
                        works, MSOs and independents

Tim Street . . . . .President
Rock Morehead . . . . .Sr. Writer/Producer/Editor
Shelly Alvarado . . . . .Producer/Line Producer
Jason Gottlieb . . . . .Editor/Motion Graphics Artist
Laury Santoso .Motion Graphics Artist
Drew Lindo . . . . .Assistant Editor
Sandra Salas . . . . .Production/Project Manager
Katie Ullrich . . . . .Production Coordinator/Marketing Assistant

SPASM INK
PO Box 768
North Hollywood, CA 91603-0768
PHONE 818-679-7229
FAX 818-766-4878
EMAIL . . . . .rockusa@earthlink.net
TYPES   Corporate - EPK - Film/TV Productions -
                        Film/TV Talent - Marketing - Music - New
                        Media - Promotions - Outdoor Advertising
RECENT ACCOUNTS   Movie Tunes - IndieCore - Hollywood
                        Reporter - Invasion and Matrix
                        Music/Sports Programming - Production
                        Services - Artisan News Service -
                        Entertainment Today - Metro L.A. - Rogers
                        & Cowan - Kirtland Records - KP Media -
                        Prudential John Aaroe Division
COMMENTS   Specializes in writing, editing, production
                        and content services for print, radio and
                        Internet; Provides bios and radio-show style
                        interview promotional programs, specialty
                        copy, marketing copy, ad copy, press
                        releases and press kit concepts

Darryl Morden . . . . .Owner

SPIRIT MEDIA, INC.
PO Box 43591
Phoenix, AZ 85080
PHONE 602-373-7878
EMAIL . . . . .spirit@spiritmedia.cc
WEB SITE . . . . .www.spiritmedia.cc
TYPES   Film/TV Productions - Film/TV Talent -
                        Marketing - Music - Promotions
COMMENTS   Clients include recording artists, record
                        labels, actors, film companies, athletes,
                        agents and authors

Arthur T. Phoenix . . . . .President, Management
David Goldberg . . . . .Operations Manager
Richard Berry . . . . .Legal Consultant
Kristine Phoenix . . . . .Media Relations
Weldon A. McDougal III .Consultant
Derek Bissing .Marketing & Promotions
Ramy Hosseinie . . . . .Multimedia
John J. Rust . . . . .Research Department

SSA PUBLIC RELATIONS
16027 Ventura Blvd., Ste. 206
Encino, CA 91436
PHONE 818-501-0700
FAX 818-501-7216
EMAIL . . . . .jrussel@ssapr.com
TYPES   Corporate - Film/TV Productions - Film/TV
                        Talent - Marketing - Music - New Media -
                        Promotions
COMMENTS   Domestic and international trade and con-
                        sumer publicity; Sweepstakes management
                        and design

Steve Syatt . . . . .CEO
John Russel . . . . .President

SWEPT AWAY MEDIA CORPORATION
4915 Oxford Court
Boca Raton, FL 33434
PHONE 561-241-9110/561-504-4995
FAX 561-241-4422
EMAIL . . . . .sweptawaytv@bellsouth.net
SECOND EMAIL . . . . .specialz232@sweptawaytv.com
WEB SITE . . . . .www.sweptawaytv.com
TYPES   Film/TV Productions - Film/TV Talent -
                               Marketing - Product Placement -
                               Promotions
RECENT ACCOUNTS   Universal Music and Video Distribution -
                               Paramount - Icebreakers Gum - Virgin
                               Records
COMMENTS   Youth, teen and college oriented marketing
                               firm involved in street and innovative types
                               of promotion; Works with high school, pub-
                               lic, private and charter/magnet schools

Jeff Hendler . . . . .Director
Zach Rich . . . . .VP
Amanda Rich . . . . .Business Affairs
Nancy Rich . . . . .Coordinator, Marketing

TMG INTERNATIONAL
499 N. Canon Dr., Ste. 406
Beverly Hills, CA 90210
PHONE 310-887-7077
FAX 310-887-7078
EMAIL . . . . .ck@tmginternational.com
WEB SITE . . . . .www.tmginternational.com
TYPES   Corporate - Marketing - Promotions
COMMENTS   Marketing and public relations for visual
                               effects, film releases, motion picture pre-
                               miere parties, openings

Christine King . . . . .President

TRAILER PARK INC.
1741 N. Ivar Ave.
Hollywood, CA 90028
PHONE .323-461-4232/310-845-3400
FAX 323-461-2632/310-845-3470
WEB SITE . . . . .www.trailerpark.com
TYPES   Film/TV Productions - Marketing - New
                               Media - Promotions - Outdoor Advertising
COMMENTS   Additional office: 6922 Hollywood Blvd.,
                               6th-7th Fl., Hollywood, CA 90028

Benedict Coulter . . . . .President
Tim Nett . . . . .CEO
Joel Johnston . . . . .COO
Neal Spector . . . . .Executive VP/Creative Director
Kaethy Kennedy . . . . .Executive VP, Post Production & Operations

TREVINO ENTERPRISES
10 Universal City Plaza, 20th Fl.
Universal City, CA 91608
PHONE 818-753-2455
FAX 818-753-2456
EMAIL . . . . .info@trevinoenterprises.net
WEB SITE . . . . .www.trevinoenterprises.net
TYPES   Corporate - Film/TV Talent - Marketing -
                               Music - Promotions
MARKET   Theatrical - Network TV
RECENT ACCOUNTS   ALMA Awards - Imagen Awards Press
                               Conference - Latin Grammys Post Party -
                               INDIA - Sonya Smith - Jacob Vargas -
                               Virgin Records - Universal Music
COMMENTS   Coordinates press conferences, special
                               events, wrap parties and premieres; Offers
                               publicity services to musical artists, record
                               labels and actors; Specializes in Latin mar-
                               keting and publicity

Reyna Trevino . . . . .CEO/President
David Myers . . . . .VP

TRUE PUBLIC RELATIONS
6725 Sunset Blvd., Ste. 570
Los Angeles, CA 90028
PHONE 323-957-0730
FAX 323-957-0731
TYPES   Corporate - Film/TV Productions - Film/TV
                               Talent - Music - Promotions

Marcel Pariseau . . . . .Partner
Cece Yorke . . . . .Partner
Sarah Fuller . . . . .VP

UPP ENTERTAINMENT MARKETING
3401 Winona Ave.
Burbank, CA 91504
PHONE 818-526-0111
FAX 818-526-1466
EMAIL . . . . .info@upp.net
WEB SITE . . . . .www.upp.net
TYPES   Marketing - New Media - Product
                               Placement - Promotions
COMMENTS   Branded integration, game shows, celebrity
                               outreach and lifestyle marketing

Steve Rasnick . . . . .VP

THE VELSIGNE GROUP
244 Fifth Ave., Ste. 2483
New York, NY 10001
PHONE 212-696-7441
EMAIL . . . . .info@velsignegroup.com
WEB SITE . . . . .www.velsignegroup.com
TYPES   Corporate - Film/TV Talent - Marketing -
                               Music - New Media - Promotions

Stacey Williams . . . . .President

VELVET PUBLIC RELATIONS
9701 Wilshire Blvd., 10th Fl.
Beverly Hills, CA 90212
PHONE 310-860-6103
FAX 310-388-0619
EMAIL . . . . .info@velvetpr.net
WEB SITE . . . . .www.velvetpr.net
TYPES   Film/TV Productions - Film/TV Talent
RECENT ACCOUNTS   Kiera Chaplin - Life & Death - Fashion
                            Forms - Tag Denim
COMMENTS   Fashion PR

Myriam Towmer . . . . .President
Dana Goldenberg . . . . .Publicist

THE VIARDO AGENCY
A VBX Group Company
832 N. La Brea Ave.
Los Angeles, CA 90038
PHONE 310-499-4848/323-465-0625
FAX 310-499-4848
EMAIL . . . . .info@theviardoagency.com
WEB SITE .www.theviardoagency.com
TYPES   Corporate - Film/TV Productions - Film/TV
                            Talent - Marketing - Music - New Media -
                            Product Placement - Promotions
RECENT ACCOUNTS   Christopher Knight - Adrianne Curry -
                            Oksana Baiul - Michael Lombardi - Shaun
                            Toub - Jennifer Lyon - Blu Cantrell -
                            Carolina Bacardi - Jane Wiedlin - Maverick
                            Films - Kremlin Films - Fallen Angels
                            Productions - SheDance Film Festival -
                            Back 40 Entertainment - Stage 3 Studios -
                            Magnetic Pictures - Kali Films - Sarah Kozer
                            - Carolina Bacardi - Antik Denim - Aston's
                            Nightwear - Suspect Clothing - Giantto
                            Fine Watches - Von Dutch - Joey & T -
                            Primp - Tail Bait - Good Times Charms -
                            Glow Industries - Joseph Hami Collection -
                            Spy Clothing - True Gentlemen
COMMENTS   Entertainment publicity and event produc-
                            tion; Fashion publicity and marketing;
                            Management, production, distribution and
                            financing; Product/celebrity placement and
                            celebrity gifting

Phil Viardo . . . . .President/Principal
Laurent Planeix . . . . .Managing Partner/Head, Event Production
Nina Ngo . . . . .Associate Partner
Susan Lee . . . . .Executive Assistant
Nicole Malgarini . . . . .Executive Assistant

VISTA GROUP
4561 Colorado Blvd.
Los Angeles, CA 90039
PHONE 818-551-6789
FAX 818-551-6880
EMAIL . . . . .karldahlquist@vistagroupusa.com
WEB SITE .www.vistagroupusa.com
TYPES   Film/TV Productions - Marketing - Product
                            Placement - Promotions
RECENT ACCOUNTS   Mercedes-Benz - Smart - Laurent Perrier
COMMENTS   Specializes in automotive public relations

Eric Dahlquist Jr. . . . . .Director, Client Services

W3 PUBLIC RELATIONS
5657 Wilshire Blvd., Ste. 300
Los Angeles, CA 90036
PHONE 323-934-2700
FAX 323-934-2709
EMAIL . . . . .w3pr@yahoo.com
TYPES   Corporate - Film/TV Talent - Music - New
                            Media

Sharon Weisz . . . . .President

WALLMAN PUBLIC RELATIONS
10323 Santa Monica Blvd., Ste. 109
Los Angeles, CA 90025
PHONE 310-553-8884
FAX 310-553-8885
EMAIL . . . . .asst@wallmanpr.com
TYPES   Corporate - Film/TV Productions - Film/TV
                            Talent

Lee Wallman . . . . .President
Michelle Rodriguez . . . . .Coordinator

WEBSTER & ASSOCIATES PUBLIC RELATIONS
PO Box 23015
Nashville, TN 37202
PHONE 615-777-6995
FAX 615-369-2515
EMAIL .requests@websterpr.com
WEB SITE . . . . .www.websterpr.com
TYPES   Film/TV Productions - Film/TV Talent -
                            Music
RECENT ACCOUNTS   Jim Brickman - Hootie and the Blowfish -
                            John Conlee - Crystal Gayle - Sammy
                            Kershaw - Lynyrd Skynyrd - Montgomery
                            Gentry - Jonestar - Hank Wllliams, Jr. - Kid
                            Rock - Aaron Tippin - Van Zant - Wrangler
                            - Shawn King - Charlie Daniels - Clay
                            Walker - Copley Guitars

Kirt B. Webster . . . . .President
Ebie McFarland . . . . .Publicist
Kerri Taliaferro .Manager, Operations

MURRAY WEISSMAN & ASSOCIATES
4605 Lankershim Blvd., Ste. 413
North Hollywood, CA 91602
PHONE 818-760-8995
FAX 818-760-4847
EMAIL . . . . .firstname@publicity4all.com
WEB SITE www.publicity4all.com
TYPES   Corporate - EPK - Film/TV Productions -
                            Film/TV Talent - Marketing - Music -
                            Product Placement - Promotions
RECENT ACCOUNTS   Sony - Lionsgate - Miramax - The Weinstein
                            Company - Art Directors Guild - Television
                            Academy - New Line Cinema - HATCH
                            Festival - Don Mischer Productions -
                            Paramount Pictures - Twentieth Century Fox
COMMENTS   All categories of entertainment public rela-
                            tions including film, TV, home video,
                            awards campaigns, personalities, compa-
                            nies, guilds, academies, film festivals and
                            books

Murray Weissman . . . . .President
Rick Markovitz . . . . .Executive VP
Leonard Morpurgo . . . . .VP
Jen Coyne-Hoerle . . . . .Assistant
Lindajo Loftus . . . . .Assistant

NORMAN WINTER PUBLICITY
468 N. Camden Dr.
Beverly HIlls, CA 90210
PHONE 310-858-5530
WEB SITE . . . . .www.normanwinter.com
TYPES   Corporate - Film/TV Productions - Film/TV
                        Talent - Marketing - Music - New Media
COMMENTS   Overall marketing services; Associated with
                        Garry Thompson Global Access Advisors;
                        Las Vegas office: 3003 Regency Hill Dr.,
                        Henderson, NV 89014

Norman Winter . . . . .Chairman

WOLF KASTELER & ASSOCIATES PR
335 N. Maple Dr., Ste. 351
Beverly Hills, CA 90210
PHONE 310-205-0618/212-997-9522
FAX 310-205-0879/212-957-2778
TYPES   Film/TV Talent
COMMENTS   Represents writers, producers, actors and
                        directors; East Coast office: 250 W. 57th
                        St., Ste. 521, New York, NY 10107

Annett Wolf . . . . .Partner
Lisa Kasteler . . . . .Partner
Cara Tripicchio . . . . .Associate
Nicole Caruso . . . . .VP, East Coast
Evelyn Karamanos .VP, West Coast

WORKHOUSE PUBLICITY
133 W. 25th St., No. 3W
New York, NY 10001
PHONE 212-645-8006
FAX 212-645-1950
EMAIL . . . . .info@workhousepr.com
WEB SITE . . . . .www.workhousepr.com
TYPES   Corporate - Film/TV Productions - Film/TV
                        Talent - Marketing - Music - New Media -
                        Product Placement - Promotions
RECENT ACCOUNTS   Assouline - Running Press - Bergdorf
                        Goodman - Versace - TiVo - Great
                        Performances - 24 Hour Plays - Francis
                        Ford Coppola - Tim Burton - Jared Harris -
                        David LaChapelle - ContentFilm - IFC Films
                        - Patrick McMullan - Asia Society - Gotham
                        Hall - Chocolate Bar - MAC Cosmetics -
                        Rizzoli International Publications - Soft Skull
                        Press - Joynoelle - 66° North - Philippe
                        Adec - Alison Nelson's Chocolate Bar -
                        Aroma Kitchen & Winebar - Kyotofu -
                        Kinespirit - Phil Mucci Photography - House
                        de Lux - Peter Gatien
COMMENTS   Full-service publicity; Special events, film
                        premieres and festivals

Adam Nelson . . . . .CEO
Devon Mack . . . . .CFO
Alison McGongal . . . . .VP
Gina Garza . . . . .Publicist
Kara Hughett . . . . .Publicist
Stephanie Sachs . . . . .Publicist
Lois Lo . . . . .Publicity Coordinator
Lauren Gould . . . . .Executive Assistant/Office Manager

WORKSHEET

DATE	PROJECT	CONTACT	NOTES

WORKSHEET

FREQUENTLY CALLED PHONE NUMBERS			
NAME	**COMPANY**	**PHONE #**	**FAX #**

Hollywood Representation Directory
PUBLICITY COMPANIES

To submit your company for a free listing in the HOLLYWOOD REPRESENTATION DIRECTORY, complete and return this application form along with a brief bio and/or company profile. All listings are at the discretion of the Editor.

PHONE: 323-525-2376   FAX: 323-525-2393   www.hcdonline.com

COMPANY _____

ADDRESS _____ CITY _____ STATE _____ ZIP _____

PHONE(S) _____ FAX(S) _____

PUBLISHED EMAIL _____ WEBSITE _____

NONPUBLISHED EMAIL _____ NONPUBLISHED FAX _____

TYPES
(check all that apply)

- ❑ CORPORATE
- ❑ EPK
- ❑ FILM/TV PRODUCTIONS
- ❑ FILM/TV TALENT
- ❑ MARKETING
- ❑ MUSIC
- ❑ NEW MEDIA
- ❑ OUTDOOR ADVERTISING
- ❑ PRODUCT PLACEMENT
- ❑ PROMOTIONS

RECENT ACCOUNTS

_____
_____
_____
_____
_____
_____
_____
_____

(PLEASE LIST AT LEAST ONE, IF NOT MORE, STAFF MEMBER WITH TITLE)

S T A F F

NAME _____ TITLE _____

NAME _____ TITLE _____

NAME _____ TITLE _____

NAME _____ TITLE _____

NAME _____ TITLE _____

NAME _____ TITLE _____

NAME _____ TITLE _____

ADDITIONAL COMMENTS _____

_____

SUBMITTED BY _____ DATE _____

SECTION E

CASTING DIRECTORS

- Commercials
- Film
- Industrials
- Theatre
- TV
- Voice-Overs

ABC ENTERTAINMENT CASTING (NEW YORK)
157 Columbus Ave., 2nd Fl.
New York, NY 10023
PHONE 212-456-3631
CASTS　　　　　　　TV
AFFILIATIONS　　　　CSA

Rosalie Joseph . . . . .VP, Casting
Marci Phillips . . . . .Executive Director, Casting
Janet Murphy . . . . .Executive Director, Casting & Talent Relations
Geoffrey Soffer . . . . .Manager, Casting

ABC ENTERTAINMENT CASTING (LOS ANGELES)
500 S. Buena Vista St.
Burbank, CA 91521-4651
PHONE 818-460-6308
FAX 818-460-6903
CASTS　　　　　　　TV
AFFILIATIONS　　　　CSA

Keli Lee . . . . .Executive VP, Casting, ABC Entertainment & TV
Ayo Davis . . . . .VP, Casting
Claudia Ramsumair . . . . .VP, Casting
Sandi Logan . . . . .Executive Director, Casting
Randi Chugerman . . . . .Executive Director, Casting
Lorelei Jeffers . . . . .Manager, Casting
Billy Murphy . . . . .Manager, Casting
John Villacorta . . . . .Manager, Casting
Gene Blythe . . . . .Casting Consultant

ABC FAMILY CHANNEL
3800 W. Alameda Ave., Ste. 440
Burbank, CA 91505
PHONE 818-973-4366
WEB SITE . . . . .www.abcfamily.go.com
CASTS　　　　　　　Film - TV - Voice-Over
AFFILIATIONS　　　　CSA
CREDITS　　　　　　Kyle XY - Greek - Slacker Cats - Fallen -
　　　　　　　　　Wildfire - Lincoln Heights

Elizabeth Boykewich . . . . . .Executive Director, Casting, Series & Movies
Megan Anhalt . . . . .Assistant

ABC TELEVISION STUDIO
c/o ABC Entertainment Television Group
500 S. Buena Vista St.
Burbank, CA 91521
PHONE 818-460-7777
WEB SITE . . . . .www.abc.com
SECOND WEB SITE . . . . .www.touchstonetvpress.com
CASTS　　　　　　　TV

Keli Lee . . . . .Executive VP, Casting
Ayo Davis . . . . .VP, Casting
Claudia Ramsumair . . . . .VP, Casting
Sandi Logan . . . . .Executive Director, Casting
Randi Chugerman . . . .Executive Director, Casting & Talent Development
Lorelei Jeffers . . . . .Manager, Casting
Billy Murphy . . . . .Manager, Casting
John Villacorta . . . . .Manager, Casting
Karen Noble . . . . .Casting Coordinator

LAURA ADLER
c/o Casting Society of America
606 N. Larchmont Blvd., Ste. 4B
Los Angeles, CA 90004
PHONE 323-620-1884
CASTS　　　　　　　TV
AFFILIATIONS　　　　CSA
CREDITS　　　　　　Four Kings - Twins - The Naked Truth -
　　　　　　　　　Dream On

Laura Adler . . . . .Casting Director

AIKINS/COSSEY CASTING
100 W. Pender St., Ste. 401
Vancouver, British Columbia V6B 1R8, Canada
PHONE 604-739-4612
CASTS　　　　　　　Film
AFFILIATIONS　　　　CSA
CREDITS　　　　　　Andromeda

Stuart Aikins . . . . .Casting Director
Sean Cossey . . . . .Casting Director

JANE ALDERMAN CASTING
c/o Act One Studios
640 N. La Salle St.
Chicago, IL 60610
PHONE 312-397-1182
FAX 312-397-1185
CASTS　　　　　　　Film - TV - Commercials - Theatre -
　　　　　　　　　Industrials
AFFILIATIONS　　　　CSA
SUBMISSION POLICY　Resumé upon request

Jane Alderman . . . . .Owner

SANDE ALESSI CASTING
13731 Ventura Blvd., Ste. D
Sherman Oaks, CA 91423
PHONE 818-623-7040/818-907-9799
WEB SITE . . . . .www.sandealessicasting.com
CASTS   Film - Commercials - Industrials
AFFILIATIONS   CSA
CREDITS   Entourage - Curb Your Enthusiasm - Six
                     Feet Under - Pirates of the Carribean 1-3 -
                     Zodiac - Beowulf - The Terminal - War of
                     the Worlds - Austin Powers Goldmember -
                     Fight Club - Cingular Wireless - Pepsi - Dr.
                     Pepper - Bud Light - Taco Bell
COMMENTS   Primarily background casting

Sande Alessi . . . . .Casting Director
Kristan Berona . . . . .Casting Director

A-LIST PROJECTS
132 St. Marks Pl.
New York, NY 10009
PHONE 212-533-8536
FAX 212-253-9591
EMAIL . . . . .andrew@andrewweir.net
WEB SITE . . . . .www.alistprojects.com
CASTS   Film - TV - Commercials
CREDITS   Hugo Boss - Calvin Klein - Neiman Marcus
                     - Vogue - GQ - Dolce & Gabbana - Ralph
                     Lauren - Fashion Rocks
COMMENTS   Celebrity endorsements

Andrew Weir . . . . .Casting Director
Nicole Maddox . . . . .Casting Assistant

AMVF CASTING
1901 Blue Clay Rd., Ste. G2
Wilmington, NC 28401
PHONE 910-262-2278/910-762-7171
FAX 910-762-7182
EMAIL . . . . .holland@amvfproductions.com
SECOND EMAIL . . . . .hollandstriplincasting@yahoo.com
WEB SITE . . . . .www.hollywoodeastcasting.com
CASTS   Film - TV - Commercials - Voice-Over -
                     Industrials
CREDITS   She House (WE) - Palmetto Pointe (PAX) -
                     The Apprentice - Home Run Throwback -
                     James Cameron's Expedition: Bismarck -
                     Days That Shook the World - Conspiracy
                     Theories - Champion Sportswear
COMMENTS   See Web site for list of clients and interac-
                     tive demonstration

David Schifter . . . . .Director, Casting
Holland Striplin . . . . .Director, Casting

ANDREA KENYON & ASSOCIATES CASTING
7535 Denis St.
Montreal, Quebec H2R 2E7, Canada
PHONE 514-948-2000
CASTS   Film - TV
AFFILIATIONS   CSA
CREDITS   300 - Wicker Park - The Reagans

Andrea Kenyon . . . . .Casting Director

AQUILA/WOOD CASTING
1680 Vine St., Ste. 806
Los Angeles, CA 90028
PHONE 323-460-6292
CASTS   Film
AFFILIATIONS   CSA
CREDITS   Disturbia - Evan Almighty - Fracture -
                     Catch and Release - House of Sand and
                     Fog

Deborah Aquila . . . . .Casting Director
Tricia Wood . . . . .Casting Director
Jennifer Smith . . . . .Casting Director
Samantha Finkler . . . . .Casting Associate
Erin Toner . . . . .Casting Associate

MAUREEN A. ARATA, CSA
c/o Casting Society of America
606 N. Larchmont Blvd., Ste. 4B
Los Angeles, CA 90004
PHONE 323-463-1925
CASTS   Film - TV
AFFILIATIONS   CSA

Maureen A. Arata . . . . .Casting Director

ASG CASTING, INC.
4144 Lankershim Blvd., Ste. #202
North Hollywood, CA 91602
PHONE 818-762-0200
WEB SITE . . . . .www.asgcasting.com
CASTS   TV - Commercials
AFFILIATIONS   CCDA
CREDITS   Sons & Daughters

Arlene Schuster-Goss . . . . .Casting Director
Justin Radley . . . . .Casting Director
Erin Murphy . . . . .Casting Assistant

JULIE ASHTON CASTING
6715 Hollywood Blvd., Ste. 203
Hollywood, CA 90028
PHONE 323-856-9000
FAX 323-856-9010
CASTS   Film - TV
CREDITS   Blue Collar TV - Reno 911!

Julie Ashton . . . . .Casting Director
Amanda McCann . . . . .Casting Associate

ASPEN PRODUCTION SERVICES
PO Box 8862
Aspen, CO 81612
PHONE 970-925-1031
FAX 970-925-7769
EMAIL . . . . .aspenproductions@earthlink.net
WEB SITE . . . . .www.aspenfilm.com
CASTS   Film - TV - Commercials - Industrials
CREDITS   Crossroads - Hummer - Rocawear - Evian -
                     Aero Films - Suzuki - Victoria's Secret -
                     Flying Tiger Films - State Farm - Visa
                     Olympic Campaign - Pepsi - Harley
                     Davidson - Lincoln Mercury - Comedy
                     Central - Nissan - Budweiser
COMMENTS   Print; Specializes in real people casting

Liz Long . . . . .Owner

AUTOMATIC SWEAT
5541 W. Washington Blvd.
Los Angeles, CA 90016
PHONE 323-934-5141
CASTS   Film - TV
AFFILIATIONS   CSA
CREDITS   Batman Begins - And Starring Pancho Villa
                              As Himself - Carnivàle - Lackawanna Blues
                              - Revelations

John Papsidera . . . . .Casting Director
Jennifer Cram . . . . .Casting Associate
Dylan Jury . . . . .Casting Assistant

AYC CASTING
2234 Virginia Ave., #4
Santa Monica, CA 90404
PHONE 310-314-7664/310-994-7218
FAX 310-452-3315
EMAIL .ayccasting@yahoo.com
CASTS   TV
CREDITS   Before I Do - Scariest Places on Earth -
                              Property Ladder - How Clean Is Your House
                              - Iron Chef - Pat the Bunny (DVD) - Todd
                              TV - Monster House - Breaking Up with
                              Shannen Doherty - Trash to Cash; Pilots:
                              Into the Cube - Out Foxxed - Friend or Foe
                              - The Joke's on You with Wayne Brady -
                              Your Worst Nightmare - American Family
                              Showdown
COMMENTS   Specializes in reality show casting, hidden
                              camera, family shows, kid's shows, rela-
                              tionships, single person searches, cold call-
                              ing and research

Alesia Cook . . . . .Casting Director

JEANIE BACHARACH
c/o Casting Society of America
606 N. Larchmont Blvd., Ste. 4B
Los Angeles, CA 90004
PHONE 323-463-1925
CASTS   Film - TV
CREDITS   Wanted - Judging Amy - The Guardian -
                              Close to Home - Ally McBeal

Jeanie Bacharach . . . . .Casting Director

BARRY/GREEN-KEYES CASTING
4553 Glencoe Ave., 2nd Fl., Ste. 250
Marina Del Rey, CA 90212
PHONE 310-314-9520
CASTS   Film
AFFILIATIONS   CSA
CREDITS   Alpha Dog - The Notebook - Freddy vs.
                              Jason - Friday After Next - Rush Hour 1&2
                              - Family Man

Nancy Green-Keyes . . . . .Casting Director

DEBORAH BARYLSKI
c/o Casting Society of America
606 N. Larchmont Blvd., Ste. 4B
Los Angeles, CA 90004
PHONE 323-463-1925
CASTS   TV
AFFILIATIONS   CSA
CREDITS   Life with Bonnie - Still Standing - Arrested
                              Development - Kitchen Confidential

Deborah Barylski . . . . .Casting Director

FRAN BASCOM
3400 W. Olive Ave., 3rd Fl., Ste. 315
Burbank, CA 91505
PHONE 818-295-2831
CASTS   TV - Theatre
AFFILIATIONS   CSA
CREDITS   Days of Our Lives

Fran Bascom . . . . .Casting Director
Linda Poindexter . . . . .Casting Director

PAMELA BASKER, CSA
c/o Casting Society of America
606 N. Larchmont Blvd., Ste. 4B
Los Angeles, CA 90004-1309
PHONE 818-506-6417/434-906-2373
CASTS   Film - TV - Voice-Over - Theatre
AFFILIATIONS   CSA
CREDITS   Film: The Nutty Professor 2: The Klumps -
                              Tommy Boy - Under Siege; TV: Hidden Hills
                              (NBC) - Lost at Home (ABC) - Thieves (ABC
                              Pilot) - The Fugitive (CBS Series)

Pamela Basker . . . . .Casting Director

EVE BATTAGLIA CASTING
450 E. 20 St., #9H
New York, NY 10009
PHONE 212-777-1449
CASTS   Film
AFFILIATIONS   CSA
CREDITS   Another Gay Movie - Sorry, Haters -
                              Transamerica

Eve Battaglia . . . . .Casting Director

NANCY NAYOR BATTINO CASTING
6320 Commodore Sloat Dr., 2nd Fl.
Los Angeles, CA 90048
PHONE 323-857-0151
FAX 323-954-9794
CASTS   Film - TV
AFFILIATIONS   CSA
CREDITS   Hostel - The Messengers - When a
                              Stranger Calls - The Grudge - The Moguls
                              - The Exorcisim of Emily Rose -
                              Lovewrecked - Rise - Masters of Horror -
                              Grudge 2 - Hostel 2 - One Missed Call -
                              Not Another Teen Show - The Eye -
                              Midnight Meat Train
SUBMISSION POLICY   No unsolicited submissions

Nancy Nayor Battino . . . . .Casting Director
Kelly Wagner . . . . .Casting Director
Celeste Leger . . . . .Casting Associate
Dominica Posseren . . . . .Casting Associate
Chris Gehrt . . . . .Assistant

BB CASTING & PRODUCTION SERVICES, INC.
578 Washington Blvd., #468
Marina del Rey, CA 90292
PHONE 310-963-8538/818-377-9538
FAX 310-441-5338
EMAIL . . . . .bb@bbcasting.com
WEB SITE . . . . .www.bbcasting.com
CASTS   Film - TV - Commercials - Voice-Over - Industrials
CREDITS   Film: Revolution - The Last Race - Kangaroo Jack - Diary of K.W. - Battle Plan - Cotillion '65 - Miss Supreme Queen; TV: Girlz Society - Professor Lighthead - Return to the Titanic - Petstop!; Commercials: Honda - Toyota - Sea World - Coca-Cola - Disney Home Video; Video Games: Dirty Harry - Justice League - Matrix - Spiderman 1&2 - SOCOM - DarkWatch - NBA - Xenosoga 2 - Freedom Fighters -Matrix
COMMENTS   Project manages, casts, directs, produces and provides loop groups for TV, film, voice-overs and video games

Brigitte Burdine . . . . .Owner/CEO
Raul Carrera . . . . .CFO
Keith Clark .Digital Media Supervisor
Ricky Early . . . . .Audio Engineer
Heather Rivers . . . . .Assistant to Ms. Burdine

BEACH/KATZMAN CASTING
c/o Casting Society of America
606 N. Larchmont Blvd., Ste. 311
Los Angeles, CA 90004
PHONE 323-468-6633
CASTS   Film
AFFILIATIONS   CSA
CREDITS   Film: Fred Claus - 3:10 to Yuma - The Brothers Solomon - Turistas - Little Man - Walk the Line - Red Eye - Wedding Crashers - Cursed - White Chicks - Chasing Liberty - American Wedding - Identity - The Tuxedo - About Schmidt - The Sweetest Thing - Valentine - Hanging Up - Girl, Interrupted - Teaching Mrs. Tingle - Lake Placid - Election - Jawbreaker - Disturbing Behavior - Scream 1-3 - Citizen Ruth - School Ties - Bad Influence; TV: Men in Trees

Lisa Beach . . . . .Casting Director
Sarah Katzman . . . . .Casting Director

BEECH HILL FILMS
330 W. 38th St., Ste. 1405
New York, NY 10018
PHONE 212-594-8095
FAX 212-594-8118
CASTS   Film - TV
AFFILIATIONS   CSA
CREDITS   The Black Donnellys - The Bedford Diaries - Stay - Prisoner

Alexa Fogel . . . . .Casting Director/Producer
Brendan Mason . . . . .Director, Production
Joseph Infantolino . . . . .Producer

EYDE BELASCO
c/o Western Sandblast
3780 Wilshire Blvd., 7th Fl.
Los Angeles, CA 90010
PHONE 213-388-1475
FAX 213-637-0110
CASTS   Film - TV
AFFILIATIONS   CSA
CREDITS   Film: How I Met My Boyfriend's Dead Fiancee - Numb - When a Man Falls in the Forest - Because I Said So - Lymelife - Rescue Dawn - Whisper - Half Nelson - Slither - Say Uncle - Sledge: The Untold Story - Things That Hang from Trees - Cape of Good Hope - Daredevil - Behind Enemy Lines; TV: L.A. Doctors

Eyde Belasco . . . . .Casting Director

BREANNA BENJAMIN CASTING
165 W. 46th St.
New York, NY 10036
PHONE 212-388-2347
CASTS   Film - TV - Commercials - Voice-Over - Theatre - Industrials
CREDITS   My Family Treasure - True Love
SUBMISSION POLICY   Accepts photos and resumés with return address and matching postmarks; No videotapes; Do not phone or visit

Breanna Benjamin . . . . .Casting Director
Lizz Leises . . . . .Casting Assistant

TERRY BERLAND CASTING
2329 Purdue Ave.
Los Angeles, CA 90064
PHONE 310-775-6608
WEB SITE .www.terryberlandcasting.com
CASTS   Film - TV - Commercials - Voice-Over
AFFILIATIONS   CCDA
CREDITS   Comcast - Mercedes - Alamo

Terry Berland . . . . .Casting Director
Karmen Leech . . . . .Casting Assistant

CHEMIN BERNARD CASTING
c/o Casting Society of America
606 N. Larchmont Blvd., Ste. 4B
Los Angeles, CA 90004
PHONE 213-507-7400
CASTS   Film - TV
AFFILIATIONS   CSA
CREDITS   Fat Albert - Moesha

Chemin Bernard . . . . .Casting Director

BARBARA BERSELL CASTING
2698 Greenfield Ave.
Los Angeles, CA 90064
PHONE 310-470-1670
CASTS   Film - TV - Commercials
CREDITS   Held for Ransom - The New Gods - Loser
SUBMISSION POLICY   By request; Hard copies unless specified

Barbara Bersell . . . . .Casting Director
Donna Jacobs . . . . .No Title

JUEL BESTROP & SETH YANKLEWITZ CASTING
11336 Camarillo St., Ste. 301
West Toluca Lake, CA 91602
PHONE 818-508-7451
CASTS   Film - TV
AFFILIATIONS   CSA
CREDITS   Norbit - The Heartbreak Kid - The Invisible
                      - The Break Up - The Shaggy Dog -
                      Kicking & Screaming - Are We There Yet? -
                      Surviving Christmas - I, Robot - Anchorman
                      - Dodgeball - Starsky & Hutch - The
                      Stranger - Kiss the Bride; TV: Lucky Louie -
                      Blades of Glory - Drillbit Taylor - Fool's
                      Gold

Juel Bestrop . . . . .Casting Director
Seth Yanklewitz . . . . .Casting Director
Michele Beramen . . . . .Casting Associate
Jacquelyn Palmquist . . . . .Casting Associate

BETTY MAE, INC.
1023-1/2 Abbott Kinney Blvd.
Venice, CA 90291
PHONE 310-396-6100
CASTS   Film
AFFILIATIONS   CSA
CREDITS   Bad Santa - Sin City

Mary Vernieu . . . . .Casting Director
Venus Kanani . . . . .Casting Director
JC Cantu . . . . .Casting Associate
Lindsay Graham . . . . .Casting Assistant
Julie Swistak . . . . .Casting Assistant

SHARON BIALY
16000 Ventura Blvd., #301
Encinco, CA 91436
PHONE 323-386-1894
CASTS   Film - TV
AFFILIATIONS   CSA
CREDITS   Film: Mr. Holland's Opus; TV: The Unit -
                      Bones - Medical Investigation - Skin - The
                      Mind of the Married Man

Sharon Bialy . . . . .Casting Director

BIG BAD WOLFF ENTERTAINMENT
7551 W. Sunset Blvd., #102
Los Angeles, CA 90046
PHONE 323-969-2003
FAX 323-969-2006
EMAIL . . . . .jgandcjcasting@yahoo.com
CASTS   Film - TV
AFFILIATIONS   CSA

Jan Glaser CSA . . . . .Casting Director
Christine Joyce . . . . .Casting Director

BIG HOUSE CASTING
944 N. Noble, Ste. 1
Chicago, IL 60622
PHONE 773-772-9539
EMAIL .info@bighousecasting.com
WEB SITE . . . . .www.bighousecasting.com
CASTS   Film - TV - Commercials - Voice-Over -
                      Industrials
CREDITS   Honda - IBM - Chase - McDonald's -
                      TransUnion - Best Buy - JC Penny

Kate McClanaghan . . . . .Sr. Casting Director
Priscilla Quirino . . . . .Studio Manager/Casting Director
Maya Kuper . . . . .Technical Director/Producer
Colleen Archer . . . . .Casting Director/Producer
Jon Monteverde . . . . .Chief Engineer
Ben McKinney . . . . .Studio Engineer

TAMMARA BILLIK CASTING
14044 Ventura Blvd., Ste. 309
Sherman Oaks, CA 91423
PHONE 818-789-1631
CASTS   Film - TV
AFFILIATIONS   CSA
CREDITS   Thick and Thin - Grounded for Life - Ellen -
                      Married with Children - Honey, I Shrunk the
                      Kids

Tammara Billik . . . . .Casting Director
Justine Hempe . . . . .Casting Director

JAY BINDER CASTING
321 W. 44th St., Ste. 606
New York, NY 10036
PHONE 212-586-6777
EMAIL . . . . .info@bindercasting.com
WEB SITE .www.bindercasting.com
CASTS   Film - TV - Theatre
AFFILIATIONS   CSA

Jay Binder . . . . .Casting Director
Jack Bowdan . . . . .Casting Director
Mark Brandon . . . . .Associate Casting Director
Megan Larche . . . . .Associate Casting Director
Allison Estrin . . . . .Casting Assistant
Nikole Vallins . . . . .Casting Assistant

BARBIE BLOCK
c/o Casting Society of America
606 N. Larchmont Blvd., Ste. 4B
Los Angeles, CA 90004
PHONE 323-463-1925
CASTS   Film - TV
AFFILIATIONS   CSA
CREDITS   Film: The Safety of Objects; TV: Pepper
                      Dennis - Complete Savages - Malcolm in
                      the Middle - Two Guys, a Girl and a Pizza
                      Place - The Jeff Foxworthy Show - Boy
                      Meets World

Barbie Block . . . . .Casting Director

BLUE MAN PRODUCTIONS
599 Broadway, 5th Fl.
New York, NY 10012
PHONE 212-226-6366
FAX 212-226-5923
EMAIL . . . . .casting@blueman.com
WEB SITE . . . . .www.blueman.com
CASTS   Theatre
CREDITS   Blue Man Group
SUBMISSION POLICY   Accepts headshots and resumés

Deb Burton . . . . .Casting Director
Karen Rockower .Casting Coordinator
Tascha van Auken .Casting Associate

SUSAN BLUESTEIN
c/o Casting Society of America
606 N. Larchmont Blvd., Ste. 4B
Los Angeles, CA 90004
PHONE 323-463-1925/323-468-4500
CASTS   TV
AFFILIATIONS   CSA
CREDITS   JAG - N.C.I.S.

Susan Bluestein . . . . .Casting Director

CHARLES BOGDAN
7700 Sunset Blvd., Ste. 200
Los Angeles, CA 90046
PHONE 323-969-8200
FAX 323-969-0101
EMAIL . . . . .cbcasting@yahoo.com
CASTS   Film - Commercials
CREDITS   Film: Rolling - Among the Shadows; Short
                     Films: Audit - The Translator

Charles Bogdan . . . . .Casting Director
Brian Madden . . . . .Casting Associate

JO EDNA BOLDIN CASTING
c/o Wildfire Productions
4321 Fulcrum Way NE
Rio Rancho, NM 87144
PHONE 505-867-2252
CASTS   Film - TV
AFFILIATIONS   CSA
CREDITS   The Ringer - Wildfire - The Wendell Baker
                     Story - The Missing - Buffalo Girls

Jo Edna Boldin . . . . .Casting Director

BEAU BONNEAU CASTING
84 First St.
San Francisco, CA 94105
PHONE . . . . .415-777-1142 (Producers)/415-346-2278 (Talent)
WEB SITE . . . . .www.beaubonneaucasting.com
CASTS   Film - TV - Commercials - Industrials
COMMENTS   Casts union and non-union projects; Full-
                     service agency

Theresa Benavidez . . . . .Casting Director
Colleen Renneavy . . . . .Extras Casting Director

JUDITH BOULEY
c/o Casting Society of America
606 N. Larchmont Blvd., Ste. 4B
Los Angeles, CA 90004
PHONE 323-463-1925
CASTS   Film
AFFILIATIONS   CSA
CREDITS   Deja Vu - SpongeBob: The Movie - The
                     Polar Express - Master and Commander -
                     Road to Perdition

Judith Bouley . . . . .Casting Director/Additional Casting

BOWLING/MISCIA CASTING
1775 Broadway, 10th Fl.
New York, NY 10019
PHONE 212-767-8697
CASTS   TV
AFFILIATIONS   CSA
CREDITS   Stella - The Evidence - Third Watch - The
                     West Wing - Medium - Jonny Zero

Beth Bowling . . . . .Casting Director
Kim Miscia . . . . .Casting Director
Clint Alexander . . . . .Assistant

DEEDEE BRADLEY
6767 Forest Lawn Dr., Ste. 100
Los Angeles, CA 90068
PHONE 818-977-8956
CASTS   TV
AFFILIATIONS   CSA
CREDITS   Smallville - Veronica Mars

Deedee Bradley . . . . .Casting Director
Alison Mize . . . . .Assistant

MEGAN BRANMAN
c/o Casting Society of America
606 N. Larchmont Blvd., Ste. 4B
Los Angeles, CA 90004
PHONE 323-463-1925
CASTS   TV
AFFILIATIONS   CSA
CREDITS   Big Day - How I Met Your Mother - Rock
                     Me Baby - Tarzan - LA Dragnet

Megan Branman . . . . .Casting Director

JACKIE BRISKEY
4024 Radford Ave., Admin. Bldg., Ste. 280
Studio City, CA 91604
PHONE 818-655-5601
FAX 818-655-8341
CASTS   TV
AFFILIATIONS   CSA
CREDITS   Passions
SUBMISSION POLICY   By mail only; No phone calls

Jackie Briskey . . . . .Casting Director
Dana Olson . . . . .Associate
Rachel Stoeckly . . . . .Casting Assistant

BROADCASTERS
420 Lexington Ave., 19th Fl.
New York, NY 10170
PHONE 212-986-5257/212-687-4180
FAX 212-986-5256
WEB SITE . . . . .www.hsrny.com
CASTS   TV - Commercials - Voice-Over -
                     Industrials
COMMENTS   Animation, radio and TV voice-overs; SAG,
                     AFTRA; Full-service recording studio
                     includes casting department, audio editing
                     and sound design

Stacy Seidel . . . . .Casting Director
Lisa Fischoff . . . . .Casting Director
Ian Weiss . . . . .Casting Assistant

JOHN BUCHAN CASTING, INC.
499 Sackville St.
Toronto, Ontario
M4X 1T6, Canada
PHONE 416-927-9363
CASTS   Film - TV
AFFILIATIONS   CSA
CREDITS   Where the Truth Lies - Being Julia - Clean -
                     Slings and Arrows - Ararat - American
                     Psycho 2 - The Virgin Suicides - Johnny
                     Mnemonic

John Buchan . . . . .Casting Director

BUENA VISTA MOTION PICTURES GROUP FEATURE CASTING
500 S. Buena Vista St., Team Disney Bldg., 2nd Fl.
Burbank, CA 91521
PHONE 818-560-7510
FAX 818-563-3719
CASTS   Film
AFFILIATIONS   CSA

Marcia Ross . . . . .Executive VP
Donna Morong . . . . .Sr. VP
Gail Goldberg . . . . .VP
Nadia Aleyd . . . . .Coordinator

KRISHA BULLOCK
c/o Casting Society of America
606 N. Larchmont Blvd., Ste. 4B
Los Angeles, CA 90004
PHONE 310-493-6222
CASTS   Film - TV
CREDITS   Alice - Kenan & Kel - All That - The
                              Amanda Show - Contempt - Above &
                              Beyond - Baby Huey's Great Easter
                              Adventure

Krisha Bullock . . . . .Casting Director

JACKIE BURCH
c/o Casting Society of America
606 N. Larchmont Blvd., Ste. 4B
Los Angeles, CA 90004
PHONE 323-463-1925
CASTS   Film
AFFILIATIONS   CSA
CREDITS   The Santa Clause 2 - End of Days - I Still
                              Know What You Did Last Summer

Jackie Burch . . . . .Casting Director

BURROWS/BOLAND CASTING
1337 Ocean Ave., Ste. H
Santa Monica, CA 90401
PHONE 310-587-3596
EMAIL . . . . .bbcasting@aol.com
WEB SITE .www.burrowsboland.com
CASTS   Film - TV
CREDITS   Cast Away - Hostage - The Muse - Monster
                              House - The Lord of the Rings - The Polar
                              Express - King Kong

Victoria Burrows . . . . .Casting Director
Scot Boland . . . . .Casting Director

CALLERI CASTING
133 W. 25th St., 6th Fl.
New York, NY 10001
PHONE 212-488-2190
FAX 212-488-2199
WEB SITE .www.callericasting.com
CASTS   Film - TV - Theatre
AFFILIATIONS   CSA

James Calleri . . . . .Casting Director
Paul Davis . . . . .Casting Associate
Erica Jensen . . . . .Casting Associate
Duncan Stewart . . . . .Casting Associate
Natasha Schwartz . . . . .Casting Assistant

REUBEN CANNON & ASSOCIATES
5225 Wilshire Blvd., Ste. 526
Los Angeles, CA 90036
PHONE 323-939-3190
FAX 323-939-7793
EMAIL . . . . .reubcan@aol.com
CREDITS   Johnson Family Vacation - If You Were My
                              Girl - Deliver Us from Eva - Undisputed -
                              The Brothers - Under Suspicion - John
                              Carpenter's Vampires - Down in the Delta -
                              What's Love Got to Do with It? - Who
                              Framed Roger Rabbit? - The Color Purple
SUBMISSION POLICY   By mail preferred

Reuben Cannon . . . . .Casting Director/Producer
Kim Williams . . . . .Casting Director/Producer

FERNE CASSEL
c/o Casting Society of America
606 N. Larchmont Blvd., Ste. 4B
Los Angeles, CA 90004
PHONE 323-463-1925
CASTS   Film
AFFILIATIONS   CSA
CREDITS   Monster

Ferne Cassel . . . . .Casting Director

CASTING ARTISTS, INC.
c/o Bluewater Ranch Entertainment, Inc.
1433 Sixth St.
Santa Monica, CA 90401
PHONE 310-395-1882
CASTS   Film
AFFILIATIONS   CSA

Mindy Marin . . . . .Casting Director
Kara Lipson . . . . .Casting Associate

THE CASTING COMPANY
12750 Ventura Blvd., Ste. 102
Studio City, CA 91604
PHONE 818-487-5600
WEB SITE .www.janeandjanet.com
CASTS   Film - TV
AFFILIATIONS   CSA
CREDITS   The Da Vinci Code - Poseidon -
                              Something's Gotta Give - Iron Jawed
                              Angels - A Beautiful Mind - Harry Potter
                              and the Sorcerer's Stone - Air Force One -
                              Jurassic Park 1&2 - The American President
                              - Apollo 13 - A Few Good Men - Backdraft
                              - Misery - Ghost - When Harry Met Sally -
                              Mystic Pizza - Beetlejuice - Stand By Me -
                              Home Alone - The Outsiders

Janet Hirshenson . . . . .Casting Director
Jane Jenkins . . . . .Casting Director
Michael Hirshenson . . . . .VP, Business Affairs
Michelle Lewitt Ward . . . . .Casting Director

CASTING HOUSE
5225 Wilshire Blvd., #1010
Los Angeles, CA 90036
PHONE 818-766-8797/212-965-9994
EMAIL .danny@castinghouse.net
WEB SITE .www.castinghouse.net
CASTS   Film - TV - Commercials - Voice-Over -
                              Industrials
CREDITS   Films: The Adventures of Shark Boy & Lava
                              Girl - The Amityville Horror - A New Wave
                              - A Perfect Fit - Cabbage Patch Kids - Spy:
                              The Movie - Replay - Searching for Bobby
                              DeNiro - Season of the Hunted; TV: Send
                              In the Clowns - Elimidate; Theater: The
                              World Is Round (Horizon Theater Rep.) -
                              Sea Wolf (Manhattan Ensemble) - Mercury
                              (Phil Bosakowski Theater); Short Films:
                              Standing in the Current - Ol' Man River -
                              TempTED - Augustus Fish - Angelas
                              Dungeon - Bird in Hand - The Stand Still
                              Life - Going Up - Tag - A Safe Place
COMMENTS   East Coast office: 9 Desbrosses St., 2nd
                              Fl., New York, NY 10013

Danny Roth . . . . .Casting Director/Owner
Danielle Aufiero . . . . .Casting Associate
Jessica Chappel . . . . .Casting Assistant

CASTING SOLUTIONS
PO Box 20164
New York, NY 10011
PHONE 212-875-7573
FAX 212-243-4591
EMAIL . . . . .castsolutions@msn.com
WEB SITE . . . . .www.castingsolutions.tv

CASTS	Film - TV - Commercials - Voice-Over - Theatre - Industrials
CREDITS	I Believe in America - Zombie Honeymoon - Indelible - Pop Foul
SUBMISSION POLICY	No unsolicited tapes accepted
COMMENTS	Print

Liz Ortiz-Mackes . . . . .Casting Director
Cahill Connolly . . . . .Casting Assistant

CASTING VALDES
Apartado Postal 1-281 Zona Centro
Puerto Vallarta Jalisco 48300, Mexico
PHONE 52-322-225-6023
FAX 52-322-138-5926
EMAIL . . . . .castingvaldes@yahoo.com
WEB SITE .www.mexicocasting.com

CASTS	Film - TV - Commercials
CREDITS	Nacho Libre - Puerto Vallarta Squeeze - Zapata: Sueño del Heroe - Deadly Swarm - The Heartbreak Kid - Spring Break in Bosnia - Vantage Point

Jorge Valdes Garcia . . . . .Casting Director
Sara Bachelder . . . . .Casting Associate
Stefan Anderson . . . . .Casting Assistant

CASTING WORKS LA
3601 S. Congress Ave., Ste. C-105
Austin, TX 78704
PHONE 512-485-3113
WEB SITE . . . . .www.castingworksla.com

CASTS	Film - TV - Commercials - Voice-Over - Industrials
AFFILIATIONS	CSA

Donise L. Hardy CSA . . . . .Casting Director

CBS TELEVISION CASTING
7800 Beverly Blvd., Ste. 284
Los Angeles, CA 90036
PHONE 323-575-2335/212-975-3851

CASTS	TV
AFFILIATIONS	CSA
COMMENTS	East Coast office: 51 W. 52nd St., 5th Fl., New York, NY 10019

Peter Golden . . . . .Executive VP, Talent & Casting (LA)
Lucy Cavallo . . . . .VP, Casting (LA)
Karen Church . . . . .VP, Casting (LA)
Amy Herzig . . . . .VP, Casting, East Coast (NY)
Fern Orenstein . . . . .VP, Casting (LA)
Katharina Eggman . . . . .Director, Casting (NY)
Alison Rinzel . . . . .Director, Casting (NY)
Jodi Angstreich . . . . .Assistant to Alison Rinzel
Eirinn Dimitriou . . . . .Assistant to Lucy Cavallo
Marilyn Fischer . . . . . . .Assistant to Peter Golden/Sr. Talent Coordinator
Maribeth Fox . . . . .Assistant to Amy Herzig & Katharina Eggman/ Talent Coordinator

Brittainy Roberts .Assistant to Karen Church
Erica Silverman . . . . .Assistant to Fern Orenstein

CBS/PARAMOUNT NETWORK TELEVISION CASTING
4024 Radford Ave., Admin. Bldg., Ste. 340
Studio City, CA 91604
PHONE 818-655-7100
FAX 818-655-8697

CASTS	TV
AFFILIATIONS	CSA

Sheila Guthrie . . . . .Sr. VP, Talent & Casting
Erin Rhodes . . . . .Director, Casting
Matthew Skrobalak . . . . .Director, Casting
Kristin Thomas . . . . .Manager, Casting
Brett Watson . . . . .Assistant to Sheila Guthrie
Beth Soike . . . . .Assistant to Matthew Skrobalak

CENTER THEATRE GROUP CASTING
601 W. Temple St.
Los Angeles, CA 90012
PHONE 213-972-7374
WEB SITE . . . . .www.centertheatregroup.com

CASTS	Theatre
AFFILIATIONS	CSA
COMMENTS	Casts for Mark Taper Forum, Ahmanson and Kirk Douglas Theatre

Erika Sellin . . . . .Casting Director
Bonnie Grifan . . . . .Associate Casting Director
Kendra Shay Clark . . . . .Casting Associate

CFB CASTING
846 N. Cahuenga Blvd., Bldg. B, #213
Los Angeles, CA 90038
PHONE 323-993-5473

CASTS	Film - TV
AFFILIATIONS	CSA
CREDITS	Film: Music Within - The Wild; TV: Monk - Boston Public

Corbin Bronson . . . . .Casting Director

LINDSAY CHAG
c/o Living Dreams Productions
14611 Hartsook St.
Sherman Oaks, CA 91403
PHONE 818-501-0260
FAX 818-783-4813
EMAIL . . . . .ldchag@sbcglobal.net

CASTS	Film - TV
AFFILIATIONS	CSA

Lindsay Chag . . . . .Casting Director
Martha Valentine . . . . .Assistant

DENISE CHAMIAN
c/o Casting Society of America
606 N. Larchmont Blvd., Ste. 4B
Los Angeles, CA 90004
PHONE 323-463-1925

CASTS	Film
AFFILIATIONS	CSA
CREDITS	The Island - The Mexican - Planet of the Apes - Minority Report - Big Fish
SUBMISSION POLICY	Through agents only

Denise Chamian . . . . .Casting Director

FERN CHAMPION
8255 Sunset Blvd.
Los Angeles, CA 90046
PHONE 323-650-1280
CASTS   Film - TV
AFFILIATIONS   CSA
CREDITS   Cry Wolf - Fingerprints - Pain Killer Jane -
Grandpa's Place - Back by Midnight -
Written in Blood - Momentum - Decoy -
The Mask - Beverly Hills, 90210 - Keys to
Tulsa - Babylon 5 - Mortal Kombat - Naked
Gun - Police Academy 1-6

Fern Champion . . . . .Casting Director
Paul Ruddy . . . . .Casting Director

CHANTILES/VIGNEAULT CASTING, INC.
39 W. 19th St., 12th Fl.
New York, NY 10011
PHONE 212-924-2278
CASTS   Film - TV - Commercials - Voice-Over -
Theatre - Industrials
COMMENTS   Radio, Reality TV; Host casting

Sharon Chantiles . . . . .Casting Director
Jeffrey Vigneault . . . . .Casting Director

ALETA CHAPPELLE CASTING
PO Box 1528
New York, NY 10101
PHONE 212-642-6355
AFFILIATIONS   CSA
CREDITS   Material Girls (Maverick Films) - Welcome
to America (Lionsgate) - Drumline (Fox
2000) - Introducing Dorothy Dandridge
(HBO) - The Nutty Professor - The Gregory
Hines Show - Guarding Tess - Sister Act 2 -
Boomerang - Rambling Rose

Aleta Chappelle . . . . .Casting Director

CHELSEA STUDIOS CASTING
13425 Ventura Blvd., 2nd Fl.
Sherman Oaks, CA 91423
PHONE 818-817-4350
WEB SITE . . . . .www.chelseastudios.com
CASTS   Film - TV - Commercials - Voice-Over -
Theatre - Industrials

Stanley Zucker . . . . .President
Mitch Russell . . . . .Executive VP
Vicki Goggin . . . . .Casting Director
Gayle Means . . . . .Casting Director
Lynne Quirion . . . . .Casting Director

KATHLEEN CHOPIN
c/o Casting Society of America
145 W. 28th St., Ste. 12F
New York, NY 10001
PHONE 212-244-8615
CASTS   Film
AFFILIATIONS   CSA
CREDITS   Along Came Polly - Hitch - The
Manchurian Candidate - Sweet Home
Alabama

Kathleen Chopin . . . . .Casting Director

RICH COLE
648 Broadway, Ste. 912
New York, NY 10012
PHONE 212-614-7130
CASTS   Theatre
COMMENTS   SSDC

Rich Cole . . . . .Casting Director
Bob Cline . . . . .Casting Associate

ANNELISE COLLINS CASTING
3435 Ocean Park Ave., Ste. 117
Santa Monica, CA 90405
PHONE 310-586-1936
WEB SITE . . . . .www.annelisecast.com
CASTS   Film - TV - Commercials - Voice-Over -
Industrials
AFFILIATIONS   CCDA - CSA

Annelise Collins . . . . .Casting Director

JODI COLLINS CASTING
9 Desbrosses, #520
New York, NY 10013
PHONE 212-254-3400
FAX 212-625-0116
CASTS   Film - TV - Theatre
AFFILIATIONS   CSA
CREDITS   Films: New Boobs - Nail Polish - One
Balloon - Bodies - Gabriel y Gato - One
Man's Castle - The Pink House - Shooting
Blanks - Gasline - The Pirates of Central
Park - Something Sweet - Whipped - Girl
Go Boom - Endsville - Kill by Inches - The
Curse; TV: TV Funhouse - Strangers with
Candy - The Chris Rock Show - Viva Variety

Jodi Collins . . . . .Casting Director
Stephanie Dipilla . . . . .Casting Assistant

COMPLETE CASTING
1415 Western Ave., Ste. 503
Seattle, WA 98101
PHONE 206-903-6500
EMAIL . . . . .stephen@completecasting.com
WEB SITE . . . . .www.completecasting.com
CASTS   Film - TV - Commercials - Voice-Over -
Industrials
AFFILIATIONS   CSA

Stephen Salamunovich . . . . .President/Casting Director, CSA

RUTH CONFORTE CASTING
3620 Barham Blvd., Bldg. Y, Ste. 201
Los Angeles, CA 90068
PHONE 818-771-7287
CASTS   Film - TV - Commercials - Voice-Over -
Industrials
AFFILIATIONS   CSA
COMMENTS   Also casts for corporate sales events and
reality shows

Ruth Conforte . . . . .Casting Director

SARA COOPER CASTING
7824 Martingale Ln.
Angels Camp, CA 95222
PHONE 209-785-9600/866-559-2278
FAX 815-361-5911
EMAIL ....sara@saracoopercasting.com
WEB SITE ....www.saracoopercasting.com
CASTS   Film - TV - Commercials - Industrials
CREDITS   Charles Schwab - Cinemax - California
                         Dairy Council - Running on Empty - The
                         Sorcerer
COMMENTS   Union and non-union casting

Sara Cooper ....Casting Director/Owner
Amy Campbell ....Associate
Kennedy Grace ....Associate

STEPHANIE CORSALINI CASTING
c/o Casting Society of America
606 N. Larchmont Blvd., Ste. 4B
Los Angeles, CA 90004
PHONE 323-655-7300
FAX 323-655-7300
EMAIL ....sccasting@mac.com
CASTS   Film - TV
AFFILIATIONS   CSA

Stephanie Corsalini ....Casting Director

GRETCHEN RENNELL COURT
c/o Casting Society of America
606 N. Larchmont Blvd., Ste. 4B
Los Angeles, CA 90004
PHONE 805-565-1675
CASTS   Film
AFFILIATIONS   CSA
CREDITS   Runaway Bride - The Horse Whisperer

Gretchen Rennell Court ....Casting Director

ELAINE CRAIG VOICE CASTING, INC.
6464 Sunset Blvd., Ste. 1150
Los Angeles, CA 90028
PHONE 323-469-8773
FAX 323-469-6990
EMAIL ....ecvc@elainecraig.com
WEB SITE ....www.elainecraig.com
CASTS   Voice-Over

Elaine Craig ....Executive Casting Director

CREATIVE EXTRAS CASTING
2461 Santa Monica Blvd., Ste. 501
Santa Monica, CA 90404
PHONE 310-391-9041/310-203-7860
FAX 310-391-9043
CASTS   Film - TV - Commercials
CREDITS   Dukes of Hazzard 2 - Urban Decay - Ten
                         Inch Hero - V.I.P. - Madison Heights -
                         Crocodile Dundee in LA - Home Room -
                         California Dreamin' - Mockingbirds Don't
                         Sing - NYPD Blue - Live from Baghdad -
                         The Country Bears - Calendar Girls -
                         Boston Legal - Boston Public - Blind Justice
                         - Emily's Reasons Why Not - Dirt - The
                         Wedding Planners - I Know Who Killed Me
                         - The Hottie and the Nottie - Intervention
COMMENTS   Extras

Vanessa Portillo ....Casting Director
Kim Ju ....Casting Director
Sasha Adkinson ....Casting Director

CRICKET FEET CASTING
PO Box 1417
Hollywood, CA 90028
PHONE 310-395-9540
EMAIL ....info@cricketfeet.com
WEB SITE ....www.cricketfeet.com/casting
CASTS   Film - Theatre
CREDITS   Features: Broken Windows - Teenage
                         Dirtbag - Still of the Night - How I Lost My
                         Mind - Perfect - A Dull House - Consider
                         as True - A Tree Grows Tall - Chandler Hall
                         - A New Tomorrow; Shorts: Hombre Kabuki
                         - 2 Dogs Inside - Each to Each - The Moor
                         - Queen of Cactus Cove - Salvation, Texas;
                         Theatre: Shrinks - No Mercy
COMMENTS   Specialize in low-budget SAG Indie Films

Bonnie Gillespie ....Owner

CRYSTAL SKY COMMUNICATIONS
10203 Santa Monica Blvd, 5th Fl.
Los Angeles, CA 90067
PHONE 310-843-0223
FAX 310-553-9895
CASTS   Film - TV

Dorothy Koster ....Casting Director

PATRICK CUNNINGHAM, CSA
2630 Lacy St.
Los Angeles, CA 90031
PHONE 323-222-1656
EMAIL ....pscrox@aol.com
CASTS   Film - TV
AFFILIATIONS   CSA
SUBMISSION POLICY   No phone calls or drop-offs
COMMENTS   Also affiliated with ATAS, WIF, IFP, AFP

Patrick Cunningham ....Producer/Casting Director

CURDY CURDY CASTING
2460 N. Lake Ave., Ste. 111
Altadena, CA 91001
PHONE 818-569-3055
FAX 626-798-5628
CASTS   Film - TV - Commercials - Voice-Over

Cydney McCurdy ....Casting Director
Paulara Hawkins ....Assistant

SARAH DALTON
c/o Casting Society of America
606 N. Larchmont Blvd., Ste. 4B
Los Angeles, CA 90004
PHONE 323-463-1925
CASTS   Film - TV
AFFILIATIONS   CSA
CREDITS   Even Stevens

Sarah Dalton ....Casting Director

BILLY DAMOTA
Glendale, CA 91203
PHONE 818-243-1263
EMAIL ....scooterdoestime@aol.com
WEB SITE ....www.castboy.com
CASTS   Film - TV - Commercials
AFFILIATIONS   CSA
SUBMISSION POLICY   Submit for specific projects only

Billy DaMota ....Casting Director
Rikki Diamond ....Associate

BILL DANCE CASTING
4605 Lankershim Blvd., Ste. 401
North Hollywood, CA 91602
PHONE 818-754-6634
WEB SITE . . . . .www.billdancecasting.com
CASTS   Film - TV
COMMENTS   Extras; Registration information: 818-725-4209

Bill Dance . . . . .Owner/Casting Director
Terence Harris . . . . .Casting Director
Sheri Tucker . . . . .Casting Director

DAUPHIN-BACKEL CASTING
799 Washington St., Ste. 201
New York, NY 10014
PHONE 212-897-3949
FAX 212-624-1737
EMAIL . . . . .antnewman@aol.com
CASTS   Film - TV
CREDITS   Elvis and Annabelle - The Treatment

Kathleen Backel . . . . .Casting Director
Antonia Dauphin . . . . .Casting Director

KIM DAVIS-WAGNER
11684 Ventura Blvd., Ste. 463
Studio City, CA 91604
PHONE 818-759-6796
CASTS   Film
CREDITS   Warm Blue Day - Bobby - Little Miss Sunshine - Ultraviolet - What Is It? - Breakin' All the Rules - Adaptation - Crossroads - Get Over It - Charlie's Angels 1&2 - Skipped Parts - Being John Malkovich - Never Been Kissed

Kim Davis-Wagner . . . . .Casting Director

DE LANCY-CASTRO
4741 Laurel Canyon Blvd., Ste. 100
North Hollywood, CA 91607
PHONE 818-760-7584/818-388-3222
FAX 818-760-1382
EMAIL . . . . .dccastingonline@yahoo.com
SECOND EMAIL . . . . .rdelancy@mindspring.com
CASTS   Film - TV - Commercials - Voice-Over - Theatre - Industrials
CREDITS   Ponderosa (US Casting) - Thunderdome (TNN Series) - Post Mortem (Fox) - The New Unsolved Mysteries (Lifetime) - 2002 MTV Movie Awards (Short Films) - What Should You Do? (Lifetime) - Proof Positive (SCI FI) - Facing Fame (E!) - Time in a Bottle - Breaking Vegas (History Channel) - The True Story of Alexander the Great (History Channel)
COMMENTS   Hosts; Educational; Print

Richard De Lancy . . . . .Casting Director
Eric Castro . . . . .Casting Associate

ZORA DEHORTER CASTING
c/o Casting Society of America
606 N. Larchmont Blvd., Ste. 4B
Los Angeles, CA 90004
PHONE 323-957-1657/44-0-7963-436-717
CASTS   Film - TV - Theatre
AFFILIATIONS   CSA
CREDITS   Film: Deadwater - Shamrock Boy - Kiss of the Sun - Half-Life - Loving Annabelle - Taylor - Che Guevara - Irish Eyes - Moving Alan - Southside - My Daughter's Tears - Ali G Indahouse - Did You Ever - Jane Bond - Hawaiian Gardens; TV: Dead Like Me - She Spies - Jeremiah

Zora DeHorter . . . . .Casting Director

LESLEE DENNIS
c/o Casting Society of America
606 N. Larchmont Blvd., Ste. 4B
Los Angeles, CA 90004
PHONE 323-463-1925
CASTS   TV
AFFILIATIONS   CSA
CREDITS   Deep Cover - All Souls - Charmed - Michael Hayes - Desert's Edge - Nash Bridges

Leslee Dennis . . . . .Casting Director

DONNA DESETA CASTING
525 Broadway, 3rd Fl.
New York, NY 10012
PHONE 212-274-9696
FAX 212-274-9795
WEB SITE .www.donnadesetacasting.com
CASTS   Film - TV - Commercials - Voice-Over - Theatre - Industrials
SUBMISSION POLICY   Agent submissions preferred

Donna DeSeta . . . . .Owner/Casting Director
David Cady . . . . .Casting Director
Becky Moore . . . . .Casting Director
Steve Schaefer . . . . .Casting Director
Lucy Baker . . . . .Assistant
Kyle T. Coker . . . . .Assistant

DICKSON/ARBUSTO CASTING
3875 Wilshire Blvd., Ste. 701
Los Angeles, CA 90010
PHONE 213-739-0556
FAX 213-739-3004
CASTS   Film - TV - Theatre
CREDITS   Film: Stephanie Daley - The Tao of Steve - The Business of Strangers - Bark - Interview with the Assassin; TV: Off Centre - The Mullets - The Men's Room

Joy Dickson . . . . .Casting Director
Nicole Arbusto . . . . .Casting Director

DIMENSION FILMS CASTING
375 Greenwich St.
New York, NY 10013-2338
PHONE 212-941-3800
CASTS   Film

Katrina Wolfe . . . . .Sr. VP, Production & Casting

DISNEY CHANNEL CASTING
3800 W. Alameda Ave., Ste. 2126
Burbank, CA 91505
PHONE 818-973-4086
FAX 818-973-4039
CASTS   TV

Judy Taylor . . . . .VP, Casting & Talent Relations
Cornelia Frame . . . . .Director, Casting & Talent Relations
Michelle Calderon . . . . .Casting Assistant

WALT DISNEY FEATURE ANIMATION CASTING
500 S. Buena Vista St.
Burbank, CA 91521-4970
PHONE 818-460-9565
CASTS   Film - Voice-Over
AFFILIATIONS   CSA

Jennifer Rudin Pearson . . . . .Director, Casting
Phoebe Rosenberg . . . . .Assistant, Casting

DISNEYTOON STUDIOS
500 S. Buena Vista St.
Burbank, CA 91521
PHONE 818-560-0080
CASTS   Voice-Over

Brian Mathias . . . . .Manager

PAM DIXON CASTING
10351 Santa Monica Blvd., Ste. 200
Los Angeles, CA 90025
PHONE 310-432-4852
FAX 310-432-4844
CASTS   Film
AFFILIATIONS   CSA
CREDITS   Georgia Rule - A Prairie Home Companion - Nancy Drew - The Legend of Zorro - The Craft

Pam Dixon . . . . .Casting Director
Gerald TeJada . . . . .Casting Assistant

MICHAEL DONOVAN CASTING
8170 Beverly Blvd., Ste. 105
Los Angeles, CA 90048
PHONE 323-655-9020
FAX 323-655-9021
EMAIL . . . . .mdcasting@aol.com
CASTS   Film - TV - Commercials - Theatre - Industrials
AFFILIATIONS   CCDA - CSA
COMMENTS   Over 50 features, 1,000 commercials, 100 plays and 9 TV series

Michael Donovan . . . . .Casting Director
Michelle Wade . . . . .Assistant

CHRISTY DOOLEY
c/o CBS Television City
7800 Beverly Blvd., Ste. 3371
Los Angeles, CA 90036
PHONE 323-575-4501
CASTS   TV
CREDITS   The Bold and the Beautiful
SUBMISSION POLICY   No unsolicited phone calls

Christy Dooley . . . . .Casting Director
Shannon Bradley .Casting Associate

DOWD/ROMAN CASTING
c/o The Casting Studios
200 S. La Brea Ave., 2nd Fl.
Los Angeles, CA 90036
PHONE 323-665-1776
CASTS   Commercials

Mick Dowd . . . . .Casting Director
Roman . . . . .Casting Director

MARY DOWNEY PRODUCTIONS
705 N. Kenwood St.
Burbank, CA 91505
PHONE 818-563-1200
FAX 818-563-1585
CASTS   TV
CREDITS   HGTV - Best Damn Sports Show Period (Fox Sports) - E! Entertainment

Mary Downey . . . . .Casting Director

DREAMWORKS SKG CASTING
100 Universal City Plaza
Universal City, CA 91608
PHONE 818-733-7000
FAX 818-733-6839
CASTS   Film - TV - Voice-Over
AFFILIATIONS   CSA
COMMENTS   Animation Voice-Over

Leslee Feldman . . . . .Head, Casting
Wendy Schwam . . . . .Casting Executive
Christi Soper . . . . .Casting Executive
Ania Kamieniecki . . . . .Assistant to Leslee Feldman
Sara Castaneda . . . . .Assistant

BRENNAN DUFRESNE
c/o Casting Society of America
606 N. Larchmont Blvd., Ste. 4B
Los Angeles, CA 90004
PHONE 323-463-1925
CASTS   Film - TV
AFFILIATIONS   CSA
CREDITS   CSI: NY - Garfield - The Brotherhood of Poland, N.H.

Brennan Dufresne .Casting Director

JENNIFRE' DUMONT CASTING
6430 Sunset Blvd., #1400
Los Angeles, CA 90028
EMAIL .dumontcasting@sbcglobal.net
CASTS   Film - TV - Theatre
CREDITS   Punk'd - Lovespring International - Cedric the Entertainer Presents - Free Ride - Hype - Guy Walks Into a Bar - Necessary Evil - NYPD Jew - Free Ride - Sweet Potato Queens

Jennifre' DuMont . . . . .Casting Director

DORIAN DUNAS

c/o Casting Society of America
606 N. Larchmont Blvd., Ste. 4B
Los Angeles, CA 90004
PHONE 323-463-1925
CASTS   Film - TV
AFFILIATIONS   CSA

Dorian Dunas . . . . .Casting Director

NAN DUTTON CASTING

16161 Ventura Blvd., Ste. 212
Encino, CA 91436
PHONE 818-981-3330
CASTS   TV
AFFILIATIONS   CSA
CREDITS   Drive - CSI: Miami - JAG

Nan Dutton . . . . .Casting Director

E! ENTERTAINMENT TELEVISION CASTING

5750 Wilshire Blvd., 4th Fl.
Los Angeles, CA 90036
PHONE 323-954-2400
WEB SITE . . . . .www.eonline.com
CASTS   TV
COMMENTS   24-hour entertainment network; E!
                         Entertainment Television; Style Network

Barry Nugent . . . . .Sr. VP, Talent Development & Casting
Maureen Browne . . . . .Casting Executive
Annie Roberts . . . . .Casting Director
Tiffany Reyes . . . . .Casting Coordinator
Randy Pennington . . . . .Casting Assistant

EASTSIDE STUDIOS

4626 Hollywood Blvd.
Los Angeles, CA 90027
PHONE 323-660-7874
FAX 323-660-7875
EMAIL . . . . .eastsidestudios@aol.com
WEB SITE . . . . .www.eastsidestudiosla.com
CASTS   Film - Commercials - Industrials

Doug Mangskau . . . . .Casting Director

ENGINE MEDIA GROUP

1531 14th St.
Santa Monica, CA 90404
PHONE 310-656-9366
FAX 310-656-9367
CASTS   Film - TV

Anne McCarthy . . . . .Casting Director/Producer
Jay Scully . . . . .Casting Director
Freddy Luis . . . . .Casting Director
Wayne Morse . . . . .Casting Associate
Kellie Gesell . . . . .Casting Assistant

DANIELLE ESKINAZI CASTING

1641 N. Ivar St.
Hollywood, CA 90028
PHONE 323-465-9999
EMAIL . . . . .info@daniellecasting.com
WEB SITE . . . . .www.daniellecasting.com
CASTS   Film - TV - Commercials - Theatre
AFFILIATIONS   CCDA
CREDITS   7up - Dr. Pepper - Target - Sears - Olay

Danielle Eskinazi . . . . .President
Laurie Records . . . . .Assistant

FELICIA FASANO

c/o Casting Society of America
606 N. Larchmont Blvd., Ste. 4B
Los Angeles, CA 90004
PHONE 323-463-1925
CASTS   TV
AFFILIATIONS   CSA
CREDITS   Clubhouse - The Handler

Felicia Fasano . . . . .Casting Director

MIKE FENTON

c/o Casting Society of America
606 N. Larchmont Blvd., Ste. 4B
Los Angeles, CA 90004
PHONE 323-463-1925
CASTS   Film - TV
AFFILIATIONS   CSA
CREDITS   Film: Wrinkles - Camille - Weirdsville -
                         Soul's Midnight - Surveillance - Cloud 9 -
                         The Hunt - Left Behind III: World at War -
                         Down and Derby - Last Flight Out -
                         Resistance - Blizzard - Christmas Child -
                         The 4th Tenor - Deceived - Snapshots - To
                         End All Wars - Down - Judgment; TV:
                         Dinotopia - Flatland - Just Cause - The
                         Sports Pages - The Red Phone: Manhunt -
                         Trapped

Mike Fenton . . . . .Casting Director

LISA FIELDS CASTING

c/o Casting Cafe
9000 Santa Monica Blvd.
Los Angeles, CA 90069
PHONE 310-274-9909
FAX 310-274-9919
CASTS   Film - TV - Commercials
CREDITS   Film: The Hitcher - The Texas Chainsaw
                         Massacre: The Beginning - The Amityville
                         Horror - Fearless - Blind Horizon - The
                         Texas Chainsaw Massacre - The Follow -
                         Ambush; Commercials: UPS - Vanilla Coke
                         - Microsoft MSN - M&Ms - Paine Webber -
                         Mercedes - Milk - Levi's - Nike - Bugle Boy
                         - Coke - Audi - Jeep - Lincoln - Coca-Cola
                         - Volkswagen - Mutual of Omaha - Quaker
                         Oats - Motorola

Lisa Fields . . . . .Casting Director
Emma Nelson . . . . .Casting Associate
Sean McCarthy . . . . .Casting Assistant

ALAN FILDERMAN CASTING

333 W. 39th St., Ste. 601A
New York, NY 10018
PHONE 212-695-6200
CASTS   Film - Theatre
AFFILIATIONS   CSA

Alan Filderman . . . . .Owner/Casting Director
Steve Maihack . . . . .Casting Assistant

FINCANNON & ASSOCIATES
1235 N. 23rd St.
Wilmington, NC 28405
PHONE 910-251-1500
FAX 910-251-9325
CASTS   Film - TV - Commercials
AFFILIATIONS   CSA
CREDITS   One Tree Hill - Dawson's Creek - Cold
              Mountain - Mr. 3000 - Glory Road - Ray

Craig Fincannon . . . . .Casting Director
Lisa Mae Wells Fincannon . . . . .Casting Director
Mark Fincannon . . . . .Casting Director

LEONARD FINGER CASTING
1157 Suipacha, 7 Piso
Buenos Aires 1008, Argentina
PHONE 54-11-43-93-36-34
EMAIL .leonardfinger@earthlink.net
CASTS   Film - TV
AFFILIATIONS   CSA
CREDITS   Frank Herbert's Dune Miniseries - Mr.
              Holland's Opus - Alone - Stephen King's
              Thinner - Tales from the Darkside - The
              Event
COMMENTS   International production and casting con-
              sultant

Leonard Finger . . . . .Principal

MALI FINN CASTING
303 N. Sweetzer Ave.
West Hollywood, CA 90046
PHONE 323-782-8744
CASTS   Film
AFFILIATIONS   CSA
CREDITS   Avatar - Lucky You - The Number 23 - The
              Assassination of Jesse James by the
              Coward Robert Ford - Running with Scissors
              - North Country - Dark Water - Where the
              Truth Lies - The Assassination of Richard
              Nixon - Undertow - Raising Helen - The
              Girl Next Door - The Big Bounce - Out of
              Time - Elephant - The Matrix 1-3 - All the
              Real Girls - Phone Booth - 8 Mile - K-19:
              The Widowmaker - High Crimes

Mali Finn . . . . .Casting Director
Lauren Bass . . . . .Casting Director
Elizabeth Shoai . . . . .Associate

FINN/HILLER CASTING
588 N. Larchmont Blvd., 1st Fl.
Los Angeles, CA 90004
PHONE 323-460-4530
FAX 323-460-2317
CASTS   Film - TV
AFFILIATIONS   CSA
CREDITS   Crash - Miracle - Walking Tall - A
              Cinderella Story - Coach Carter - Stealth
SUBMISSION POLICY   Via mail only

Sarah Halley Finn .Casting Director
Randi Hiller . . . . .Casting Director
Tamara Hunter . . . . .Associate
Taylor Jenkins . . . . .Assistant

BONNIE FINNEGAN CASTING
12 W. 27th St., 11th Fl.
New York, NY 10001
PHONE 212-725-3505
CASTS   Film - TV
AFFILIATIONS   CSA
CREDITS   The Safety of Objects - Queens Supreme
COMMENTS   East Coast casting consultant for
              Paramount Television

Bonnie Finnegan . . . . .Casting Director
Meghan Rafferty . . . . .Casting Associate

FIORENTINO-MANGIERI CASTING
8306 Wilshire Blvd., Ste. 1513
Beverly Hills, CA 90211
PHONE 323-671-4700
CASTS   Film - TV
AFFILIATIONS   CSA
CREDITS   E-Ring - The Shield - Close to Home (Pilot)
              - Cold Case - Catacombs

Barbara Fiorentino .Casting Director
Rebecca Mangieri . . . . .Casting Director

FIREFLY CASTING
5225 Wilshire Blvd., Ste. 502
Los Angeles, CA 90036
PHONE 323-857-1699
CASTS   Film - TV - Theatre
AFFILIATIONS   CSA
CREDITS   Film: Hairspray - Lars and the Real Girl -
              Charlie Bartlett - Deck the Halls - For Your
              Consideration - Charlotte's Web - A Mighty
              Wind - Shall We Dance - Men in Black -
              The Talented Mr. Ripley - Cold Mountain -
              Romeo+Juliet - Igby Goes Down - The
              English Patient; TV: Out of Practice - Curb
              Your Enthusiasm - The L Word

Richard Hicks . . . . .Casting Director
David Rubin . . . . .Casting Director
Stephanie Stenta . . . . .Casting Assistant

JACK FLETCHER
c/o MSI Entertainment, Inc.
9229 Sunset Blvd., Ste. 710
Los Angeles, CA 90069
PHONE 310-300-2905
FAX 310-300-2901
EMAIL . . . . .joel@groupmsi.com
CASTS   Film - TV - Commercials
CREDITS   The Chronicles of Riddick - Van Helsing -
              Princess Mononoke - Final Fantasy
COMMENTS   Animated films, shorts and games; Voice
              director

Jack Fletcher . . . . .Casting Director
Joel Goldstein . . . . .Manager

FMW CASTING
4151 Prospect Ave., Bldg. L
Los Angeles, CA 90027
PHONE 323-671-4700
CASTS   Film - TV
AFFILIATIONS   CSA
CREDITS   Factory Girl - The Good Shepherd - CSI:
                         NY - Broken Trail - Close to Home - E-Ring
                         - Cold Case - The Man - The Matador - A
                         Love Song for Bobby Long - The Cooler -
                         The Shield - Down in the Valley - Pretty
                         Persuasion - My Baby's Daddy -
                         Wonderland

Barbara Fiorentino . . . . .Casting Director
Rebecca Mangieri . . . . .Casting Director
Wendy Weidman . . . . .Casting Director

MEGAN FOLEY COMMERCIAL CASTING
11340 Moorpark St.
Studio City, CA 91602
PHONE 818-216-9350
WEB SITE .www.meganfoleycasting.com
CASTS   Film - TV - Commercials - Industrials
AFFILIATIONS   CCDA

Megan Foley . . . . .Casting Director
Chuck Marra . . . . .Casting Director

FOX BROADCASTING COMPANY CASTING
10201 W. Pico Blvd., Bldg. 100
Los Angeles, CA 90035
PHONE 310-369-1000/212-556-2400
CASTS   TV
AFFILIATIONS   CSA

Marcia Shulman . . . . .Executive VP, Casting
Bob Huber . . . . .Sr. VP, Casting
Amy Christopher . . . . .VP, East Coast Casting
Pauline O'Con . . . . .VP, Casting

EDDIE FOY III CASTING
11380 Foxglove Ln.
Corona, CA 92880
PHONE 951-272-2931/818-414-2519
FAX 951-272-2971
CASTS   Film - TV
CREDITS   Jerry Lewis Telethon

Eddie Foy III . . . . .Executive Talent Consultant

NANCY FOY
c/o Casting Society of America
606 N. Larchmont Blvd., Ste. 4B
Los Angeles, CA 90004
PHONE 323-463-1925
CASTS   Film - TV
AFFILIATIONS   CSA
CREDITS   The Ringer - Hidalgo - Miss Congeniality 2
                         - James Dean

Nancy Foy . . . . .Casting Director

JEROLD FRANKS & ASSOCIATES
84 Summit Way SW
Roanoke, VA 24014
PHONE 540-446-5878
CASTS   Film - TV
AFFILIATIONS   CSA
CREDITS   Lost

Jerold Franks . . . . .Casting Director

LISA FREIBERGER CASTING
c/o Casting Society of America
606 N. Larchmont Blvd., Ste. 4B
Los Angeles, CA 90004
PHONE 818-990-9956
CASTS   Film - TV
AFFILIATIONS   CSA
CREDITS   Nightmares & Dreamscapes - The Hades
                         Factor - Into the West - The Grid - Pirates
                         of Silicon Valley - The Last Debate -
                         Strange Justice - King of Texas - Purgatory -
                         The Last Don - Pennsylvania Miners' Story -
                         Riding the Bus with My Sister
COMMENTS   Casting consultant for Turner Network
                         Broadcasting (TNT)

Lisa Freiberger . . . . .Casting Director

GALLEGOS/CARRAFIELLO CASTING
639 N. Larchmont Blvd., Ste. 207
Los Angeles, CA 90004
PHONE 323-469-3577
EMAIL . . . . .tgccast@earthlink.net
CASTS   Film - TV - Commercials
CREDITS   Film: The Glass Jar - Two Bits & Pepper -
                         Fire and Ice; TV: Team Knight Rider - Baby
                         Talk

Dennis Gallegos . . . . .Casting Director
Meghan Carrafiello . . . . .Casting Director

NICOLE GARCIA
c/o Hollywood Center Studios
1040 N. Las Palmas, Bldg. 2
Hollywood, CA 90038
PHONE 323-860-8999
CASTS   TV
CREDITS   Mad TV

Nicole Garcia . . . . .Casting Director
Sean Earl . . . . .Associate Casting Director

RISA BRAMON GARCIA
c/o Casting Society of America
606 N. Larchmont Blvd., Ste. 4B
Los Angeles, CA 90004
PHONE 323-463-1925
CASTS   Film - TV
AFFILIATIONS   CSA
CREDITS   3 lbs. - CSI: NY - Garfield - The
                         Brotherhood of Poland, New Hampshire -
                         A Guy Thing - MDs - Like Mike - Joe
                         Somebody - Sweet November

Risa Bramon-Garcia . . . . .Casting Director

JEFF GERRARD
c/o Big House Studios
11340 Moorpark St.
Studio City, CA 91602
PHONE 818-782-9900
WEB SITE . . . . www.jeffgerrard.com
CASTS   Film - TV - Commercials - Voice-Over - Theatre - Industrials
AFFILIATIONS   CCDA
COMMENTS   Resumé available on Web site

Jeff Gerrard . . . . .Casting Director

GILMORE/MCCONNELL CASTING
c/o Casting Society of America
606 N. Larchmont Blvd., Ste. 4B
Los Angeles, CA 90004
PHONE 323-463-1925
CASTS   TV
AFFILIATIONS   CSA
CREDITS   Close to Home - The Practice - Dragnet - Head Cases

Janet Gilmore . . . . .Partner
Megan McConnell . . . . .Partner

GINSBERG/FINK CASTING
c/o Casting Society of America
606 N. Larchmont Blvd., Ste. 4B
Los Angeles, CA 90004
PHONE 323-463-1925
CASTS   Film - TV
AFFILIATIONS   CSA
CREDITS   The Sisterhood of the Traveling Pants - Sexual Life - Karen Sisco - Thirteen - Little Women

Shani Ginsberg .Casting Director
Jakki Fink . . . . .Casting Director

SUSAN GLICKSMAN CASTING
c/o Casting Society of America
606 N. Larchmont Ave., Ste. 4B
Los Angeles, CA 90004
PHONE 323-463-1925
CASTS   Film - TV
AFFILIATIONS   CSA
CREDITS   One Tree Hill - Hitler: The Rise of Evil - Behind the Camera: The Unauthorized Story of Three's Company

Susan Glicksman . . . . .President/Owner

GO CASTING
6464 Sunset Blvd., Ste. 970
Los Angeles, CA 90028
PHONE 323-469-6464
FAX 323-469-6465
CASTS   Film - TV
AFFILIATIONS   CSA
CREDITS   Film: Cursed; TV: Romy & Michele: In The Beginning - Run of the House - Shacking Up - Miss Match - Dawson's Creek - Glory Days - Grosse Pointe - Son of the Beach - Loose Cannon - The Secret Diary of Desmond - Hitz - Claude's Crib - Modern Men - Reba
COMMENTS   Various pilots

Greg Orson . . . . .Casting Director
Lesli Gelles . . . . .Casting Director
Dana Gergely . . . . .Casting Associate
Stacey Taylor . . . . .Casting Assistant

GODLOVE & COMPANY CASTING
151 W. 25th St., 11th Fl.
New York, NY 10001
PHONE 212-627-7300
EMAIL . . . . .info@godlovecasting.com
WEB SITE . . . . .www.godlovecasting.com
CASTS   Film - TV - Commercials - Voice-Over - Industrials

Linda Godlove . . . . .Owner

GAIL GOLDBERG CASTING
500 S. Buena Vista St., Frank Wells Bldg., Ste. 1088
Burbank, CA 91505
PHONE 818-560-7509
CASTS   Film
AFFILIATIONS   CSA
CREDITS   Gone, Baby, Gone - Underdog - Stick It - Annapolis - The Hot Chick - The Princess Diaries 1&2 - The Kid - 10 Things I Hate About You - Deuce Bigalow: Male Gigolo

Gail Goldberg . . . . .Casting Director

DANNY GOLDMAN & ASSOCIATES
1006 N. Cole Ave.
Los Angeles, CA 90038
PHONE 323-463-1600
FAX 323-463-3139/323 463-9566
EMAIL . . . . .dgoldcast@aol.com
WEB SITE . . . . .www.dannygoldmancasting.com
SECOND WEB SITE . . . . .www.coleavestudios.com
CASTS   Commercials - Voice-Over - Industrials
AFFILIATIONS   CCDA

Danny Goldman . . . . .No Title
Chris Devane . . . . .Studio Manager
Mariko Ballentine . . . . .Associate
Alan Kaminsky . . . . .Associate
Josh Rappaport . . . . .Associate

GOLDWASSER/MELTZER CASTING
13029-A Victory Blvd., Ste. 366
North Hollywood, CA 91606
PHONE 213-683-3742
CASTS   TV - Theatre
AFFILIATIONS   CSA
CREDITS   TV: Inferno - 3-South - The Hughleys - Family Rules - American Dad - The Freshman; Theatre: The Last Night of Ballyhoo

Carol Goldwasser . . . . .Casting Director
Howard Meltzer .Casting Director

STEPHANIE GORIN CASTING
62 Ellerbeck St.
Toronto, Ontario M4K 2V1, Canada
PHONE 416-778-6916
CASTS   Film - TV
AFFILIATIONS   CSA
CREDITS   Saw 1-3 - 1-800-Missing - Godsend - Jake 2.0 - Odyssey 5 - Degrassi: The Next Generation

Stephanie Gorin .Casting Director

AMY GOSSELS CASTING

c/o Post Ex
1382 Third Ave.
New York, NY 10021
PHONE 212-472-6981
CASTS   Film - TV - Commercials - Industrials
CREDITS   Zen and the Art of Landscaping -
        Something's Gotta Give - Godsend - The
        Floor - Walls - Perfect Disaster - The Picture
        of Dorian Gray - 5G
SUBMISSION POLICY By US Mail
COMMENTS   Also casts for print

Amy Gossels . . . . .Casting Director

JEFF GREENBERG CASTING

100 Universal City Plaza, Bldg. 3800, Ste. 100
Universal City, CA 91608
PHONE 818-526-6308
CASTS   Film - TV - Theatre
AFFILIATIONS CSA
CREDITS   According to Jim - Out of Practice -
        Stacked - Untitled Paul Reiser Project - It's
        All Relative - I'm With Her - Frasier

Jeff Greenberg . . . . .Casting Director
Allen Hooper . . . . .Casting Assistant

GREENSTEIN/DANIEL CASTING

c/o Casting Society of America
5555 Melrose Ave., Gower Mill, Ste. 117
Los Angeles, CA 90038
PHONE 323-908-3070
CASTS   Film - TV
AFFILIATIONS CSA
CREDITS   Andy Barker, P.I. - Help Me Help You - Joey
        - Situation: Comedy - The Nick & Jessica
        Variety Hour - Die, Mommie, Die! -
        According to Jim

Collin Daniel . . . . .Casting Director
Brett Greenstein . . . . .Casting Director
Paul Dinh-McCrillis .Casting Director

AARON GRIFFITH

8440 Santa Monica Blvd., Ste. 200
Los Angeles, CA 90069
PHONE 323-654-0033
EMAIL . . . . .aaron@castingdirector.nu
CASTS   Film - TV
CREDITS   Jeepers Creepers 2 - Pavilion of Women -
        Speedway Junky - George B.

Aaron Griffith . . . . .Casting Director

AL GUARINO

2118 Wilshire Blvd., Ste. 995
Santa Monica, CA 90403
PHONE 310-829-6009
CASTS   Film

Al Guarino . . . . .Casting Director

PAMELA RACK GUEST

c/o Casting Society of America
606 N. Larchmont Blvd., Ste. 4B
Los Angeles, CA 90004
PHONE 323-463-1925
CASTS   Film
AFFILIATIONS CSA

Pamela Rack Guest .Casting Director

LONNIE HAMERMAN

c/o Casting Society of America
606 N. Larchmont Ave., Ste. 4B
Los Angeles, CA 90004
PHONE 323-463-1925
CASTS   Film - TV
AFFILIATIONS CSA
CREDITS   Without a Trace - Monk - She Spies - Buffy
        the Vampire Slayer

Lonnie Hamerman . . . . .Casting Director

HAMPTON SHANNON CASTING

PO Box 900915
San Diego, CA 92190-0915
PHONE 619-582-4632
FAX 619-393-1144
EMAIL . . . . .hamptoncasting@aol.com
CASTS   Film - TV - Commercials
CREDITS   Untitled David O. Russell Project - Miriam -
        Power Rangers
COMMENTS   Universal Pictures Principal Cast, shared
        with LA Casting

Iris Hampton . . . . .Casting Director

THEODORE HANN

c/o Casting Society of America
606 N. Larchmont Blvd., Ste. 4B
Los Angeles, CA 90004
PHONE 661-478-4266
CASTS   Film - TV
AFFILIATIONS CSA
CREDITS   Mind of Mencia - Hidden Hills - Behind the
        Camera: The Unauthorized Story of
        Charlie's Angels

Theodore Hann . . . . .Casting Director

CAROL HANZEL CASTING

48 W. 21st St., 7th Fl.
New York, NY 10010
PHONE 212-242-6113
FAX 212-242-6208
CASTS   Film - TV - Commercials - Voice-Over -
        Theatre - Industrials
COMMENTS   Broadway; New York Women in Film and
        Television

Carol Hanzel . . . . .Owner/Casting

JEFF HARDWICK CASTING

3940 Laurel Canyon Blvd., Ste. 1158
Studio City, CA 91604
PHONE 818-752-9898
FAX 818-752-9890
EMAIL . . . . .jhcasting@sbcglobal.net
WEB SITE . . . . .www.jeffhardwickcasting.com
CASTS   Film - TV - Commercials - Theatre
CREDITS   Untold Stories of the ER - Monarch of the
        Moon - Adventures of Johnny Tao -
        Halfway Decent - Patient 14 - Teddy Bears'
        Picnic - The Jersey

Jeff Hardwick . . . . .Casting Director

RENE HAYNES CASTING
1314 Scott Rd.
Burbank, CA 91504
PHONE 818-842-0187
CASTS   Film
AFFILIATIONS   CSA
CREDITS   Bury My Heart at Wounded Knee - The
           New World - Into the West
COMMENTS   Area of expertise: Native American and
           First Nations projects

Rene Haynes . . . . .Casting Director

HBO FILMS CASTING
2500 Broadway, Ste. 400
Santa Monica, CA 90404
PHONE 310-382-3537
CASTS   Film
AFFILIATIONS   CSA

Carrie Frazier . . . . .Sr. VP, Feature Casting
Amy Berman . . . . .VP, Feature Casting
Liz Nauman . . . . .Executive Assistant to Carrie Frazier
Michelle Taylor . . . . .Executive Assistant to Amy Berman

HEERY CASTING, LLC
230 N. 2nd St., Ste. 1A
Philadelphia, PA 19106
PHONE 215-238-9240
CASTS   Film - TV
AFFILIATIONS   CSA
CREDITS   Rocky Balboa - Invincible - Jersey Girl -
           Hack - The Good Thief

Diane Heery . . . . .Casting Director

HELEN WHEELS PRODUCTIONS
8761 W. Villa Rita Dr.
Peoria, AZ 85382
PHONE 623-363-1543
FAX 623-476-7420
EMAIL . . . . .helenwheelsproductions@cox.net
WEB SITE . . . . .www.helenwheels.net
CASTS   Film - TV - Commercials - Voice-Over -
           Theatre - Industrials
CREDITS   Film: Forget About It - Pandemic - Denial -
           Child's Cry - RaceTrap - Turquoise Rose -
           Purgatory Arizona - A Search for Harmony;
           TV: On Set with Hunter Gomez - Forensic
           Files - ElimiDATE - Queen of Clean - Fast
           Funnies

Helen McCready . . . . .Casting Director
Wes Nobbe . . . . .Assistant

JUDY HENDERSON & ASSOCIATES CASTING
330 W. 89th St.
New York, NY 10024
PHONE 212-877-0225
CASTS   Film - TV - Commercials - Voice-Over -
           Theatre
AFFILIATIONS   CSA

Judy Henderson . . . . .Owner/Casting Director
Kimberly Graham . . . . .Associate

CATHY HENDERSON-MARTIN CASTING
201 Five Cities Dr., Ste. 134
Pismo Beach, CA 93449
PHONE 805-773-2256
CASTS   Film - TV
AFFILIATIONS   CSA
CREDITS   Check IMDB.com for current projects

Cathy Henderson-Martin CSA . . . . .Casting Director

NINA HENNINGER & ASSOCIATES CASTING
250 Columbus Ave., Ste. 204
San Francisco, CA 94133
PHONE 415-837-0847
FAX 415-333-4542
CASTS   Film - TV - Commercials - Industrials
AFFILIATIONS   CSA
CREDITS   The Pursuit of Happyness - Memoirs of a
           Geisha - What Dreams May Come - Nash
           Bridges - The Evidence - Serendipity -
           Metro - Dr. Doolittle - Jack - The
           Assassination of Richard Nixon

Nina Henninger . . . . .Casting Director

DAWN HERSHEY
c/o Casting Society of America
606 N. Larchmont Blvd., Ste. 4B
Los Angeles, CA 90004
PHONE 323-463-1925
CASTS   Film - TV - Voice-Over
AFFILIATIONS   CSA
CREDITS   Cat Tale - Drawn Together
COMMENTS   Also casts videogames

Dawn Hershey . . . . .Casting Director

RICHARD HICKS CASTING
5225 Wilshire Blvd., Ste. 502
Los Angeles, CA 90036
PHONE 323-857-1699
CASTS   Film - TV
AFFILIATIONS   CSA
CREDITS   Lars and the Real Girl - Hairspray - Charlie
           Bartlett - The L Word - Deck the Halls -
           Let's Go to Prison - For Your Consideration
           - The 4400 - Out of Practice - Shall We
           Dance - It's All Relative - A Mighty Wind -
           Curb Your Enthusiasm - Igby Goes Down -
           Dude, Where's My Car?

Richard Hicks . . . . .Casting Director

HISPANIC TALENT CASTING OF HOLLYWOOD
PO Box 46123
Los Angeles, CA 90046
PHONE 323-934-6465
WEB SITE . . . . .www.billhooey.com
CASTS   Film - TV - Commercials - Industrials
COMMENTS   Mostly casts national commercials;
           Associated with Email Casting Network
           which is open to all ethnicities

Bill Hooey . . . . .Owner

STUART HOWARD ASSOCIATES, LTD.
207 W. 25th St., Ste. 601
New York, NY 10001
PHONE 212-414-1544
CASTS   Film - TV - Commercials - Theatre
AFFILIATIONS   CSA
CREDITS   Film: Teenage Mutant Ninja Turtles:
     Coming Out of Their Shells Tour - The
     Feud - Walls of Glass; Fosse - Gypsy - In
     the Shadow of Love: A Teen AIDS Story
COMMENTS   Specializes in TV pilots, MOWs, miniseries
     and soaps

Stuart Howard .Casting Director, TV/Film
Amy Schecter .Casting Director, TV/Film
Paul Hardt .Casting Director, TV/Film

VICTORIA HUFF & ASSOCIATES
5700 Wilshire Blvd., 5 North, Ste. 5038
Los Angeles, CA 90036
PHONE 323-634-1340
CASTS   Film - TV - Theatre
AFFILIATIONS   CSA
CREDITS   Charmed - 7th Heaven - Fat Actress

Victoria Huff . . . . .Owner/Casting Director/Producer

HYPERCASTING, INC.
425 Carrall St., Ste. 405
Vancouver, British Columbia V7R 1X8, Canada
PHONE 604-639-1804
CASTS   Film - TV
AFFILIATIONS   CSA
CREDITS   Film: Hot Rod - Kickin It Old Skool - The
     Last Mimzy - Are We There Yet? - Connie
     and Carla - I Spy - Bones - Prozac Nation;
     TV: Tru Calling - Monk - The Dead Zone

Susan Taylor Brouse . . . . .Casting Director

IMPOSSIBLE CASTING
122 W. 26th St., 6th Fl.
New York, NY 10001
PHONE 212-255-3029
EMAIL . . . . .impossibleentertainment@yahoo.com
WEB SITE .www.impossiblecasting.com
CASTS   Film - TV - Commercials - Theatre
CREDITS   Converse - Disney - Head & Shoulders -
     U.S. ARMY - The Biggest Loser - Beauty &
     the Geek - Boost Mobile - Amp'd Mobile -
     Bazooka Joe - Swiss Army
COMMENTS   Specialty casting: fashion, real people,
     character types

Craig Lechner . . . . .Owner
Danny Faraq . . . . .Casting Assistant
Matthew Wulf . . . . .Casting Assistant

IVY ISENBERG CASTING
8228 Sunset Blvd., Ste. 203
West Hollywood, CA 90069
PHONE 323-654-0832
FAX 323-927-1792
EMAIL .isenberg.assistant@gmail.com

Ivy Isenberg . . . . .Casting Director

JOHN JACKSON
c/o Casting Society of America
606 N. Larchmont Blvd., Ste. 4B
Los Angeles, CA 90004
PHONE 323-463-1925
CASTS   Film - TV
AFFILIATIONS   CSA
CREDITS   Sideways - Winning the Peace - About
     Schmidt - Election - Citizen Ruth - Dead
     Dogs - Tully

John Jackson . . . . .Casting Director

ELLLEN JACOBY CASTING INTERNATIONAL
150 SE 2nd Ave., #1007
Miami, FL 33131
PHONE 305-373-0073
CASTS   Film - TV
AFFILIATIONS   CSA
CREDITS   South Beach - The Notorious Bettie Page -
     The L Word - The O.C. - CSI: Miami -
     Snow Dogs

Elllen Jacoby . . . . .Casting Director

ELISABETH JERESKI
c/o Casting Society of America
606 N. Larchmont Blvd., Ste. 4B
Los Angeles, CA 90004
PHONE 323-463-1925/310-393-3141
CASTS   Film
AFFILIATIONS   CSA

Elisabeth Jereski . . . . .Casting Director

JOEY PAUL CASTING
c/o Hollywood Center Studios
1040 N. Las Palmas, Bldg. 33, 2nd Fl.
Hollywood, CA 90038
PHONE 323-860-3306
EMAIL . . . . .dir@joeypaul.com
WEB SITE . . . . .www.joeypaul.com
CASTS   TV
CREDITS   Cory in the House - Cake - Dance
     Revolution - That's So Raven - Witch - Phil
     of the Future - Raise Your Voice

Joey Paul Jensen . . . . .Casting Director
Niner Parikh . . . . .Casting Associate
Kathryn Taylor . . . . .Casting Associate
Kim Bennink . . . . .Casting Assistant

TARA-ANNE JOHNSON
c/o Casting Society of America
606 N. Larchmont Blvd., Ste. 4B
Los Angeles, CA 90004
PHONE 818-470-1291
CASTS   TV
AFFILIATIONS   CSA
CREDITS   Nashville Star - Cattle Drive (E!) - Master
     Blasters (SCI FI) - The Ron White Show

Tara-Anne Johnson . . . . .Casting Director

SUSAN JOHNSTON CASTING

PO Box 481254
Los Angeles, CA 90048
PHONE 323-969-4800
EMAIL . . . . .susansitcom@yahoo.com
WEB SITE . . . . .www.susanjohnstoncasting.com
CASTS   Film - TV - Commercials - Voice-Over -
                     Theatre - Industrials
CREDITS   Feature: Flatland - Hollywood Kills - Mad
                     World; TV: My Life Is a Sitcom - Extreme
                     Home Makeover (Pilot) - Blind Date - Diet
                     Pepsi/Reggie Bush Campaign - LA County
                     Holiday Show (PBS) - ActorfestLA06
COMMENTS   Reality TV, music videos, webisodes
Susan Johnston .Casting Director

CHRISTINE JOYCE

7551 W. Sunset Blvd., Ste. 102
Los Angeles, CA 90046
PHONE 323-969-2003
EMAIL .bbwcasting@yahoo.com
CASTS   Film - TV
CREDITS   Ghosts of Goldfield - Pledge This! - The
                     Prince & Me 2 - Illegal Aliens - La Belle
                     Dame Sans Merci
Christine Joyce . . . . .Casting Director

TRACY KAPLAN

c/o Casting Society of America
606 N. Larchmont Blvd., Ste. 4B
Los Angeles, CA 90004
PHONE 310-559-3306
CASTS   Film - TV
AFFILIATIONS   CSA
CREDITS   Out of Practice - Without a Trace - The
                     Animal - Arlington Road
Tracy Kaplan . . . . .Casting Director

KATY CASTING INC.

1918 W. Magnolia Blvd., Ste. 206
Burbank, CA 91506
PHONE 818-563-4121
EMAIL . . . . .katywallin@earthlink.net
CASTS   Film - TV - Commercials
AFFILIATIONS   CSA
CREDITS   Film: Pransta - Finder's Fee - Pucked -
                     Descendant - Where the Red Fern Grows -
                     Outta Time - Christmas in the Clouds -
                     Trumpet of the Swan; TV: Queen - Queer
                     Eye - How to Get the Guy - Top Designer -
                     The Entertainer - The Complex: Malibu -
                     Who Wants to Marry My Dad? - Paradise
                     Hotel - Mr. Personality - Love Again
COMMENTS   Also produces; Full service casting facilities
                     for rent by day, week or month
Katy Wallin . . . . .President/Casting Director/Producer
Anita Johnson Lusk . . . . .Executive in Charge
Courtney Dubois . . . . .Director, Development
Kat Raphael . . . . .Casting Producer
Tiffany Dejillo . . . . .Coordinator

LISA MILLER KATZ

c/o Casting Society of America
606 N. Larchmont Blvd., Ste. 4B
Los Angeles, CA 90004
PHONE 323-463-1925
CASTS   TV
AFFILIATIONS   CSA
CREDITS   Everybody Loves Raymond - King of
                     Queens - According to Jim
Lisa Miller Katz . . . . .Casting Director

AVY KAUFMAN CASTING

180 Varick St., 16th Fl.
New York, NY 10014
PHONE 212-620-4256
FAX 212-620-5685
EMAIL . . . . .casting@avykaufman.com
CASTS   Film - TV - Commercials
AFFILIATIONS   CSA
CREDITS   Film: American Gangster - Marriage -
                     Awake - 10 Items or Less - Liebesleben -
                     The Return - Fields of Freedom - Off the
                     Black - All the King's Men - Whirlygirl - The
                     Architect - The Sentinel - Champions - Shut
                     Up and Sing - Syriana - Derailed - Get
                     Rich or Die Tryin' - Zathura - Everything Is
                     Illuminated - Brokeback Mountain - Capote
                     - Empire Falls - Manderlay - Dear Wendy -
                     Forty Shades of Blue; TV: Sometimes in
                     April - Lathe of Heaven
Avy Kaufman CSA . . . . .Casting Director/Owner
Elizabeth Greenberg . . . . .Casting Associate
Cody Beke . . . . .Casting Assistant
Leeba Zakharov .Casting Assistant

KEE CASTING

PO Box 3170
Guttenberg, NJ 07093
PHONE 212-725-3775
CASTS   Film - TV - Commercials - Industrials
CREDITS   Film: Music & Lyrics - The Savages - United
                     93 - Two Weeks Notice - Swimfan -
                     Hollywood Ending - Life or Something Like
                     It - The Curse of the Jade Scorpion - Down
                     - Center Stage - Coming Soon - Cruel
                     Intentions - Stepmom - Armageddon -
                     Happiness - The Object of My Affection -
                     No Looking Back - Great Expectations - As
                     Good as It Gets; TV: Hysterical Blindness -
                     Earthly Possessions - Rear Window - An
                     Unexpected Family - Garden State - The
                     Namesake - The Pleasure of Your
                     Company
COMMENTS   Specializes in background and day players
Karen E. Etcoff . . . . .Casting Director
Bill Tripician . . . . .Casting Associate

STEPHANIE KLAPPER CASTING
39 W. 19th St., 12th Fl.
New York, NY 10011
PHONE 646-486-1337
FAX 646-486-6606
CASTS   Film - TV - Theatre - Industrials
AFFILIATIONS   CSA
CREDITS   Broadway: Bells Are Ringing - It Ain't
                          Nothin' But The Blues; Off-Broadway: The
                          Unexpected Man - Dinner with Friends -
                          Dedication - Johnny Guitar - The Stendhl
                          Syndrome - String of Pearls - Uncertain
                          Terms - Roberta - 4-8-94 (The Day Kurt
                          Cobain Died); Film: Feast of the Goat

Stephanie Klapper . . . . .Casting Director

AMY KLEIN CASTING
5311 Corteen Pl., Ste. 25
Valley Village, CA 91607
PHONE 818-769-9904
EMAIL . . . . .akcasting@sbcglobal.net
CASTS   Film - TV - Commercials - Voice-Over -
                          Theatre

Amy Klein . . . . .Casting Director

THOM KLOHN
c/o Casting Society of America
606 N. Larchmont Blvd., Ste. 4B
Los Angeles, CA 90004
PHONE 323-463-1925
CASTS   Film
AFFILIATIONS   CSA

Thom Klohn . . . . .Casting Director

NANCY KLOPPER
c/o Casting Society of America
606 N. Larchmont Blvd., Ste. 4B
Los Angeles, CA 90004
PHONE 323-463-1925
CASTS   Film
AFFILIATIONS   CSA
CREDITS   Ray - Cheaper by the Dozen

Nancy Klopper . . . . .Casting Director

EILEEN MACK KNIGHT CASTING
12031 Ventura Blvd., Ste. 4
Studio City, CA 91604
PHONE 818-753-9585
CASTS   Film - TV - Voice-Over - Theatre
AFFILIATIONS   CSA
CREDITS   The Bernie Mac Show - The Proud Family -
                          Second Time Around

Eileen Mack Knight . . . . .Casting Director
Kamala A. Thomas . . . . .Associate

KOBLIN/HARDING CASTING
c/o Casting Society of America
606 N. Larchmont Ave., Ste. 4B
Los Angeles, CA 90004
PHONE 323-463-1925
CASTS   Film - TV
AFFILIATIONS   CSA
CREDITS   Film: Bob Bailey - The Girls' Guide to
                          Hunting & Fishing - Tenderness - The
                          Pleasure of Your Company - Hollow Man II
                          - Live Free or Die - Date Movie - Venom -
                          American Gun - Slow Burn - One Last
                          Thing... - Winter Solstice - Devil's Pond -
                          Dead End - Candor City Hospital -
                          Swimfan - The Touch - Emmett's Mark -
                          Stolen Summer - Offside - The Price of
                          Kissing - Scriptfellas; TV: Date Squad - The
                          Mikes

Amanda Harding . . . . .Casting Director
Amanda Koblin . . . . .Casting Director

DOROTHY KOSTER CASTING
c/o Crystal Sky Communications
10203 Santa Monica Blvd., 5th Fl.
Los Angeles, CA 90067
PHONE 310-843-0223
EMAIL . . . . .reception@crystalsky.com
WEB SITE . . . . .www.crystalsky.com
CASTS   Film - TV
CREDITS   Princess and the Bario Boy

Dorothy Koster . . . . .Casting Director

RONNA KRESS CASTING
333 S. Beverly Dr., Ste. 109
Beverly Hills, CA 90004
PHONE 310-788-0331
CASTS   Film
AFFILIATIONS   CSA
CREDITS   Pirates of the Caribbean

Ronna Kress . . . . .Casting Director

LYNN KRESSEL CASTING
23rd St. @ The Hudson River Pier 62, Rm. 304
New York, NY 10011
PHONE . . . . . . .212-414-2941/212-414-0575 (Law & Order: SVU)
CASTS   Film - TV
AFFILIATIONS   CSA
CREDITS   Law & Order - Law & Order: Criminal
                          Intent - Law & Order: Special Victims Unit -
                          Plainsong - Something The Lord Made -
                          The Five People You Meet in Heaven -
                          Warm Springs - The Grid

Lynn Kressel . . . . .Casting Director
Suzanne Ryan . . . . .Casting Director, Law & Order
Jonathan Strauss . . . . .Casting Director, Law & Order: SVU
Katharina Eggman . . . . . .Casting Director, Law & Order: Criminal Intent
                          (212-336-6374)

DEBORAH KURTZ
11751 Mississippi Ave., Ste. 140
Los Angeles, CA 90025
PHONE 310-477-6555
CASTS   Film - TV - Commercials - Voice-Over -
                          Industrials
AFFILIATIONS   CCDA
CREDITS   American Wedding - Malibu Express -
                          Modern Romance

Deborah Kurtz . . . . .Casting Director

L.A. CASTING GROUP, INC.
c/o Los Angeles Center Studios
1201 W. 5th St., Ste. F-240
Los Angeles, CA 90017
PHONE 213-534-3888
WEB SITE . . . . .www.lacgroup.com
CASTS   Film - TV - Commercials - Voice-Over -
                        Industrials
CREDITS   Grand Theft Parsons - Ascension Day -
                        King of the Ants - Suffering Man's Charity -
                        Day of the Dead: Contagium - The
                        Champagne Gang
COMMENTS   Principal and extras casting for commer-
                        cials, TV, feature films and music videos

Michael Schiavone . . . . .Casting Director
Sara Mannes . . . . .Casting Director
Emmanuel Agus . . . . .Casting Assistant
Erika Lee . . . . .Casting Assistant

ROSS LACY CASTING
c/o Casting Studios
200 S. La Brea Ave.
Los Angeles, CA 90036
PHONE 323-954-0007
WEB SITE . . . . .www.rosslacycasting.com
CASTS   Commercials

Ross Lacy . . . . .Casting Director
Johanna Weirauch . . . . .Casting Associate

DINO LADKI CASTING
8556 Rugby Dr.
West Hollywood, CA 90069
PHONE 310-289-4962
FAX 501-621-4152
EMAIL .dslcasting@gmail.com
SECOND EMAIL . . . . .roarke00@aol.com
WEB SITE .www.thecastlist.com
CASTS   Film - TV
AFFILIATIONS   CSA
CREDITS   Baby - Big Bad Wolf - Xs & Os - I Know
                        Who Killed Me - Tillamook Treasure - The
                        Lost - MTV's Undressed

Dino Ladki . . . . .Casting Director

RUTH LAMBERT
c/o Casting Society of America
606 N. Larchmont Blvd., Ste. 4B
Los Angeles, CA 90004
PHONE 323-636-9079
CASTS   TV
AFFILIATIONS   CSA
CREDITS   Game Over - Greetings From Tucson

Ruth Lambert . . . . .Casting Director

JUDY LANDAU CASTING
c/o Fifth Street Studios
1216 Fifth St.
Santa Monica, CA 90401
PHONE 310-458-1100
CASTS   Commercials - Industrials
AFFILIATIONS   CCDA

Judy Landau . . . . .Partner/Casting Director
Alan McRae . . . . .Partner/Casting Director

LANDSBURG/FIDDLEMAN CASTING
13455 Ventura Blvd., Ste. 214
Sherman Oaks, CA 91423
PHONE 818-981-4995
CASTS   Film - TV
AFFILIATIONS   CSA
CREDITS   Kevin Hill
SUBMISSION POLICY   No general submissions

Teri Fiddleman . . . . .Casting Director
Shana Landsburg . . . . .Casting Director

LAPADURA & HART CASTING
100 Universal City Plaza, Ste. 6149
Universal City, CA 91608
PHONE 818-733-4735
FAX 818-733-4726
CASTS   TV
AFFILIATIONS   CSA
CREDITS   What About Brian - Heroes - High School
                        Musical - Summerland - American Dreams
                        - Crossing Jordan - Halloweentown II:
                        Kalabar's Revenge

Jason LaPadura . . . . .Casting Director
Natalie Hart . . . . .Casting Director
Melissa Moss . . . . .Casting Associate
Keri Owens . . . . .Casting Associate
Kendra Patterson . . . . .Casting Assistant

MARILEE LEAR CASTING
1414 Hollywood Blvd.
Las Vegas, NV 89110
PHONE 702-438-9111/702-241-9401
FAX 702-453-6601
EMAIL . . . . .mlear@learenterprises.com
WEB SITE . . . . .www.nevadatalentguide.com
CASTS   Film - TV - Commercials - Voice-Over -
                        Theatre - Industrials
AFFILIATIONS   CSA
CREDITS   Film: Supercross - Road Trip - 3000 Miles
                        to Graceland - Casino - Venus & Vegas;
                        TV: Deuces Wild - 7 Days - The X-Files -
                        V.I.P. - The Net - Coronation - CSI - Las
                        Vegas - World Series of Blackjack -
                        American Dream Derby - Temptation Island
                        - Taxi Cab Confessions; Music Videos: The
                        Flaming Lips - Mack 10 - Ice Cube -
                        Diamond Rio - Nas - Terror Vision - Billy
                        Ray Cyrus

Marilee Lear . . . . .Casting Director
Parris Lane . . . . .Casting Assistant

CAROL LEFKO CASTING
PO Box 84509
Los Angeles, CA 90073
PHONE 310-888-0007
CASTS   Film - TV - Commercials - Voice-Over -
                        Theatre
CREDITS   Juggernaut - In Love, In Death - Unbroken
                        Vows - Blockbuster - Seven Below Zero -
                        Against the Wind - Trade - A Christmas Too
                        Many - Malibu Spring Break - Smile -
                        Exhibit A - The Drop - Ice Cream Sundae -
                        Downward Angel - Danny Hustle - Five
                        Stones - Dark Heart
COMMENTS   Teacher and guest lecturer

Carol Lefko . . . . .Casting Director

MIKE LEMON CASTING, CSA

413 N. 7th St., Ste. 602
Philadelphia, PA 19123
PHONE 215-627-8927
FAX 215-627-8923
EMAIL . . . . .mlcmail@mikelemoncasting.com
WEB SITE .www.mikelemoncasting.com
CASTS   Film - TV - Commercials - Voice-Over -
                         Theatre - Industrials
AFFILIATIONS   CSA
CREDITS   The Sixth Sense - Philadelphia - Annapolis -
                         In Her Shoes - Signs - Twelve Monkeys
SUBMISSION POLICY   See Web site
COMMENTS   Location casting and extras

Mike Lemon . . . . .Casting Director
Adrienne Covington .Casting Director
Rob Holt . . . . .Casting Director
Sandy Stefanowicz .Casting Director
Annette Kaplatka . . . . .Casting Director

KELLI LERNER CASTING

4735 Sepulveda Blvd., Ste. 454
Sherman Oaks, CA 91403
PHONE 310-492-5987/212-459-9293
EMAIL . . . . .kelli@kellilernercasting.com
WEB SITE . . . . .www.kellilernercasting.com
CASTS   Film - TV - Commercials - Industrials
AFFILIATIONS   CSA
COMMENTS   East Coast office: 330 W. 56th St., Ste.
                         25E, New York, NY 10019

Kelli Lerner . . . . .President/Casting Director

MATTHEW LESSALL CASTING

5225 Wilshire Blvd., Ste. 405
Los Angeles, CA 90036
PHONE 323-965-2278
WEB SITE . . . . .www.lessallcasting.com
CASTS   Film - TV
AFFILIATIONS   CSA
CREDITS   Mean Creek - Nearing Grace - Evil
                         Remains - The Poseidon Adventure (TV) -
                         Supernova (TV) - Frankenstein

Matthew Lessall CSA . . . . .Casting Director
Lynn Reinstein . . . . .Casting Director

HEIDI LEVITT CASTING

c/o Three Chapeau Productions
7201 Melrose Ave., Ste. 203
Los Angeles, CA 90046
PHONE 323-525-0800
FAX 323-525-0843
WEB SITE . . . . .www.heidilevittcasting.com
CASTS   Film
AFFILIATIONS   CSA

Heidi Levitt . . . . .Casting Director
Lauren Fernandes .Casting Associate

LIZ LEWIS CASTING PARTNERS

129A W. 20th St.
New York, NY 10011
PHONE 212-645-1500
FAX 212-645-2483
CASTS   Film - TV - Commercials - Voice-Over -
                         Theatre - Industrials
SUBMISSION POLICY   Send extra-work head shots to Angela

Liz Lewis . . . . .Casting Director
Angela Mickey . . . . .Casting Director
Erica Palgon . . . . .Casting Director
Vinnie Taylor . . . . .Casting Director/Studio Manager
Diakeim Lyles . . . . .Casting Associate
Nikki Vitale . . . . .Casting Associate

LIBERMAN/PATTON CASTING

6464 Sunset Blvd., Ste. 707
Los Angeles, CA 90028
PHONE 323-462-9175
FAX 323-462-9188
CASTS   Film - TV
AFFILIATIONS   CSA
CREDITS   Film: Firehouse Dog - Euro Trip - Straight-
                         Jacket - Masked & Anonymous - My Big
                         Fat Greek Wedding - Playing By Heart -
                         The X-Files: Fight the Future - A Rumor of
                         Angels - Cop and a Half - Without Charlie;
                         TV: Invasion - A Wrinkle in Time - Medium
                         - Las Vegas - King of Queens - Into the
                         West

Meg Liberman . . . . .Casting Director
Cami Patton . . . . .Casting Director
Irene Cagen . . . . .Casting Director
Elizabeth Barnes . . . . .Associate
Jennifer Lare . . . . .Associate
Christal Karge . . . . .Casting Associate
Erica Berger . . . . .Casting Assistant
Ben Harris . . . . .Casting Assistant
Katie Rampey . . . . .Casting Assistant

LIEN/COWAN CASTING

7461 Beverly Blvd., Ste. 203
Los Angeles, CA 90036
PHONE 323-937-0411
FAX 323-937-2070
WEB SITE . . . . .www.leancow.tv
CASTS   Commercials - Voice-Over - Industrials
AFFILIATIONS   CCDA

Michael Lien . . . . .Casting Director
Dan Cowan . . . . .Casting Director

TRACY LILIENFIELD COMPANY

c/o Casting Society of America
606 N. Larchmont Ave., Ste. 4B
Los Angeles, CA 90004
PHONE 818-784-3901
CASTS   TV
AFFILIATIONS   CSA
CREDITS   Four Kings - The New Adventures of Old
                         Christine - My Boys - Twins - The Stones -
                         Good Morning, Miami - Will & Grace

Tracy Lilienfield . . . . .Casting Director

CASTING DIRECTORS

AMY LIPPENS
c/o Casting Society of America
606 N. Larchmont Ave., Ste. 4B
Los Angeles, CA 90004
PHONE 310-840-7470
CASTS   Film - TV
AFFILIATIONS   CSA
CREDITS   Keeping Up with the Steins - House - The Wedding Album - Saw 1&2

Amy Lippens . . . . .Casting Director

ROBIN LIPPIN
c/o Casting Society of America
606 N. Larchmont Blvd., Ste. 4B
Los Angeles, CA 90004
PHONE 323-463-1925/818-553-5804
CASTS   Film - TV
AFFILIATIONS   CSA
CREDITS   Happy Family - Lizzie McGuire - State of Grace

Robin Lippin . . . . .Casting Director

MARCI LIROFF CASTING
PO Box 57948
Sherman Oaks, CA 91413
PHONE 818-784-5434
FAX 818-784-5434
CASTS   Film
CREDITS   The Spiderwick Chronicles - Just Like Heaven - Land of the Dead - Mean Girls - New York Minute - Freaky Friday - Gothika - Insomnia - Hard Ball - Iron Giant - The Spitfire Grill - Untamed Heart - The Crush - St. Elmo's Fire - Footloose - E.T. the Extra-Terrestrial - Poltergeist - Blade Runner

Marci Liroff . . . . .Casting Director

LESLIE LITT
c/o Casting Society of America
606 N. Larchmont Blvd., Ste. 4B
Los Angeles, CA 90004
PHONE 323-463-1925
CASTS   TV
AFFILIATIONS   CSA
CREDITS   Rules of Engagement - Kitchen Confidential - Friends - Listen Up

Leslie Litt . . . . .Casting Director

LONDON/STROUD CASTING
1040 N. Las Palmas, Bldg. 33, 3rd Fl.
Los Angeles, CA 90038
PHONE 323-860-3320
CASTS   Film - TV
AFFILIATIONS   CSA
CREDITS   TV: The Suite Life of Zack and Cody - Hannah Montana (Pilot) - Arli$$; Film: Grandma's Boy - Strange Wilderness

Lisa London . . . . .Casting Director
Catherine Stroud . . . . .Casting Director

BEVERLY LONG CASTING
11425 Moorpark St.
Studio City, CA 91602
PHONE 818-754-6222
FAX 818-754-6226
EMAIL . . . . .beverly@beverlylong-casting.com
WEB SITE .www.beverlylong-casting.com
CASTS   Film - TV - Commercials - Voice-Over - Industrials
AFFILIATIONS   CCDA - CSA
CREDITS   Film: Definite Maybe - Gabrielle - When a Stranger Calls; Commercials: Hallmark Cards - Minolta Camera - Heinz - Kraft Mayonnaise - Unocal - Kelloggs - NutriGrain - Bedweiser Beer - Mars Bars - Avon - Snickers - Whiskas Cat Food - Legos Toys - Head and Shoulders Shampoo - Hostess Pudding Pies - United Airlines - Gallo Wine - McDonalds - Huffy Bikes - Sprite - Subaru - Toyota - Sargents Flea Collar

Beverly Long . . . . .Casting Director
Debra-Lynn Findon . . . . .Casting Director

MOLLY LOPATA CASTING
13731 Ventura Blvd., Ste. A
Sherman Oaks, CA 91423
PHONE 818-788-0673
CASTS   TV
AFFILIATIONS   CSA
CREDITS   Pope John Paul II - The Dive from Clausen's Pier - Saving Milly - The Magic of Ordinary Days - The Perfect Husband: The Laci Peterson Story - Revenge of the Middle-Aged Woman - 10.5 - She's Too Young - Chasing Freedom - Fallen Angel - Rush of Fear - Miss Match - Profoundly Normal - Kingpin - RFK - The American Embassy - Cadet Kelly - Guilty Hearts - Fidel - Taking Back Our Town - When Billie Beat Bobby - Dune - Yesterday's Children - Come On, Get Happy: The Partridge Family Story - A Secret Affair

Molly Lopata . . . . .Casting Director

LORI WYMAN CASTING
16499 NE 19th Ave., Ste. 203
North Miami Beach, FL 33162
PHONE 305-354-3901
CASTS   Film - TV
AFFILIATIONS   CSA
CREDITS   Out of Time - 2 Fast 2 Furious - CSI: Miami - Big Trouble - All About the Benjamins - Hearts in Atlantis - The Princess Diaries

Lori Wyman . . . . .Casting Director

JUNIE LOWRY-JOHNSON CASTING
100 Universal Clty Plaza, Bungalow 5165
Universal City, CA 91608
PHONE 818-733-4384/323-850-3171
CASTS   Film - TV
AFFILIATIONS   CSA
CREDITS   Prison Break - Desperate Housewives - Big
                         Love - Ugly Betty - 12 Miles of Bad Road -
                         John from Cincinnati
COMMENTS   Second office: 1041 N. Formosa Ave.,
                         Santa Monica East Bldg., Rm. 93, West
                         Hollywood, CA 90046

Junie Lowry-Johnson . . . . .Casting Director
Scott Genkinger . . . . .Casting Director
Libby Goldstein . . . . .Casting Director
Deborah George . . . . .Casting Associate
Lisa Soltou . . . . .Casting Associate
Kevin Mockrin . . . . .Casting Assistant

LINDA LOWY CASTING
4151 Prospect Ave., The Cottages, Rm. 105
Los Angeles, CA 90027
PHONE 323-671-5438
FAX 323-671-5624
CASTS   Film - TV
AFFILIATIONS   CSA
CREDITS   Grey's Anatomy - Friday Night Lights

Linda Lowy . . . . .Casting Director
John Brace . . . . .Casting Director
Will Stewart . . . . .Casting Associate
Jonathan Piccirillo . . . . .Casting Assistant

PENNY LUDFORD CASTING
1069 Dolores Rd.
Altadena, CA 91001
PHONE 626-791-0668
CASTS   Film - TV - Commercials - Industrials
AFFILIATIONS   CSA
CREDITS   Reunion - Happy Hour - A Day Without a
                         Mexican

Penny Ludford . . . . .Casting Director

JOAN LYNN CASTING
1461 1st Ave, #355
New York, NY 10021
PHONE 212-535-5305
CASTS   Film - Commercials - Theatre
CREDITS   Sweet Land
SUBMISSION POLICY   By mail

Joan Lynn . . . . .Casting Director

MACDONALD/BULLINGTON CASTING
c/o Casting Society of America
606 N. Larchmont Blvd., Ste. 4B
Los Angeles, CA 90004
PHONE 323-463-1925
CASTS   Film
AFFILIATIONS   CSA

Perry Bullington . . . . .Casting Director
Bob MacDonald . . . . .Casting Director

MACKEY/SANDRICH CASTING
3000 W. Olympic Blvd., Bldg. 3, Rm. 2323
Santa Monica, CA 90404
PHONE .310-449-4009/212-343-3660
CASTS   Film - TV
AFFILIATIONS   CSA
CREDITS   The Good Shepherd - Hide and Seek - The
                         Cooler - Holes - The Fugitive - P.S. -
                         Unscripted
COMMENTS   East Coast office: 180 Grand St., 3rd Fl.,
                         New York, NY 10013

Amanda Mackey . . . . .Casting Director (NY)
Cathy Sandrich Gelfond . . . . .Casting Director (LA)
Kate Bulpitt . . . . .Casting Associate (NY)
Jocelyn Thomas . . . . .Casting Associate (LA)

FRANCINE MAISLER CASTING
c/o Sony Pictures
10202 W. Washington Blvd., Jimmy Stewart Bldg., Ste. 207
Culver City, CA 90232
PHONE 310-244-6945
FAX 310-244-4348
CASTS   Film
AFFILIATIONS   CSA
CREDITS   Rendition - Into the Wild - Studio 60 on the
                         Sunset Strip - Stranger Than Fiction - Miami
                         Vice - Babel - The New World - Memoirs of
                         a Geisha - Bewitched - Meet the Fockers -
                         Collateral - Connie and Carla - 21 Grams
                         - Down with Love - I Spy - Red Dragon -
                         S1m0ne - Stuart Little 2 - Spider-Man 1-3

Francine Maisler . . . . .Casting Director
Kathleen Driscoll-Mohler . . . . .Associate
Lauren Grey . . . . .Associate

MALYSZEK CASTING
2029 Century Park East, Ste. 1400
Los Angeles, CA 90067
PHONE 323-839-3821/310-772-2266, x2
FAX 310-772-2265
EMAIL . . . . .thecastinggroupinc@yahoo.com
CASTS   Film - TV - Industrials
COMMENTS   Additional office in New York

Marie Malyszek . . . . .Casting Director
Naomi Pacheco . . . . .Associate Casting Director
M. Isabel Chavez . . . . .Head Casting Coordinator

MANHATTAN THEATRE CLUB
311 W. 43rd St., 8th Fl.
New York, NY 10036
PHONE 212-399-3000
FAX 212-399-4329
CASTS   Theatre
AFFILIATIONS   CSA

Nancy Piccione . . . . .Director, Casting (x150)
David Caparelliotis . . . . .Casting Director (x157)
Jennifer McCool . . . . .Casting Assistant

CASTING DIRECTORS

MINDY MARIN
c/o Casting Artists, Inc./Bluewater Ranch
1433 6th St.
Santa Monica, CA 90401
PHONE 310-395-1882
CASTS   Film
AFFILIATIONS   CSA
CREDITS   Juno - Alien vs. Predator: AVP2 - Mr.
                     Brooks - Eragon - The Nativity Story -
                     Flicka - The Covenant - Snakes on a Plane
                     - The Family Stone - Lord of War - Thank
                     You for Smoking - Bee Season - Paycheck -
                     Open Range - Hostage - Windtalkers - The
                     Sum of All Fears

Mindy Marin . . . . .Casting Director

LIZ MARKS
PO Box 29388
Richmond, VA 23242
PHONE 804-740-0329/804-405-0416
FAX 804-749-8276
EMAIL . . . . .liz@lizmarkscasting.com
WEB SITE . . . . .www.lizmarkscasting.com
CASTS   Film - TV - Commercials - Industrials
AFFILIATIONS   CSA
COMMENTS   Iron Jawed Angels (HBO) - The Contender
                     (DreamWorks) - Legacy (UPN) - Linc's
                     (Showtime) - Paramount Parks - Busch
                     Gardens - Colonial Williamsburg

Liz Marks . . . . .Casting Director

LIZ MARX
c/o Casting Society of America
606 N. Larchmont Blvd., Ste. 4B
Los Angeles, CA 90004
PHONE 323-463-1925/310-595-1509
CASTS   TV
AFFILIATIONS   CSA
CREDITS   Psych - Quintuplets - Method & Red

Liz Marx . . . . .Casting Director

RICKI G. MASLAR CASTING
c/o Unconditional Entertainment, LLC
4130 Cahuenga Blvd., Ste. 108
Universal City, CA 91602
PHONE 818-769-6800
FAX 609-367-8986
EMAIL . . . . .rgmaslar@aol.com
CASTS   Film
CREDITS   Burden of Desire - The Tribe - Brotherhood
                     of Blood - Pandemic - Night Skies - Razor -
                     Taphephobia - Toxic - The Thirst - The Far
                     Side of Jericho

Ricki G. Maslar .Casting Director

COREEN MAYRS CASTING, INC.
555 Brooksbank Ave., Bldg. 4, Ste. 210
North Vancouver, BC V7J 3S5, Canada
PHONE 604-983-5675
CASTS   Film - TV
AFFILIATIONS   CSA
CREDITS   Antarctica - Fantastic Four - Elektra - The
                     Sisterhood of the Traveling Pants - The Five
                     People You Meet in Heaven

Coreen Mayrs . . . . .Casting Director
Heike Brandstatter . . . . .Casting Director

VALERIE MCCAFFREY CASTING
4924 Balboa Blvd., Ste. 172
Encino, CA 91316
PHONE 818-785-1886
CASTS   Film - TV - Voice-Over - Theatre
AFFILIATIONS   CSA
CREDITS   Hard Candy - What the Bleep Do We
                     Know? - American History X - Babe - Dark
                     City - Detroit Rock City - Money Talks

Valerie McCaffrey . . . . .Casting Director

MCCAFFREY GILLES CASTING
11425 Moorpark St.
Studio City, CA 91602
PHONE 818-508-1020/818-785-1886
FAX 818-782-0307
EMAIL . . . . .pam@mccaffreygilles.com
WEB SITE . . . . .www.mccaffreygilles.com
CASTS   Film - TV - Commercials - Theatre -
                     Industrials

Valerie McCaffrey . . . . .Partner
Pam Gilles . . . . .Partner

MCCANN-KNOTEK CASTING
8539 Sunset Blvd., Ste. 4-136
Los Angeles, CA 90069
PHONE 310-854-6220/310-854-0656
CASTS   Film - TV

Bob Knotek . . . . .Casting Director
Hank McCann . . . . .Casting Director

JEANNE MCCARTHY CASTING
12340 Santa Monica Blvd., Ste. 233
Los Angeles, CA 90025
PHONE 310-820-5250
FAX 310-820-5245
CASTS   Film - TV
AFFILIATIONS   CSA

Jeanne McCarthy . . . . .Casting Director
Nicole Abellera .Casting Director
Natasha Cuba . . . . .Casting Director
Joanne Bloom . . . . .Associate

JOHN MCCARTHY CASTING
1234 S. Gramercy Pl.
Los Angeles, CA 90019
PHONE 323-732-8118
CASTS   TV - Commercials - Voice-Over -
                     Industrials
AFFILIATIONS   CSA
CREDITS   South of Nowhere - 100 Deeds for Eddie
                     McDowd - The Jersey - The Journey of
                     Allan Strange - The Secret World of Alex
                     Mack

John McCarthy .Casting Director

MCCORKLE CASTING, LTD.
575 Eighth Ave., 18th Fl.
New York, NY 10018
PHONE 212-244-3899
FAX 212-244-3638
CASTS   Film - TV - Theatre
AFFILIATIONS   CSA
CREDITS   The L Word - 3 lbs. - Secret Window -
                     Basic - Chappelle's Show - Hack -
                     Rollerball

Patricia McCorkle . . . . .Casting Director

ROBERT MCGEE
c/o Casting Society of America
606 N. Larchmont Blvd., Ste. 4B
Los Angeles, CA 90004
PHONE 323-463-1925
CASTS   Film - TV
AFFILIATIONS   CSA
CREDITS   The Virgin Suicides - Game Over

Robert McGee . . . . .Casting Director

TOM MCSWEENEY CASTING
c/o Casting Society of America
606 N. Larchmont Blvd., Ste. 4B
Los Angeles, CA 90004
PHONE 323-463-1925/61-7-5588-6621
CASTS   Film - TV
AFFILIATIONS   CSA
CREDITS   House of Wax - Scooby Doo - The Great
                           Raid - Ghost Ship

Tom McSweeney . . . . .Casting Director

MEDIA CASTING & FILM PRODUCTION
4120 Douglas Blvd., Stes. 306-387
Granite Bay, CA 95746
PHONE 916-923-2131/916-224-2979
EMAIL . . . . .mediacasting@hotmail.com
WEB SITE . . . . .www.media-casting.com
CASTS   Film - TV - Commercials - Voice-Over -
                           Industrials
CREDITS   CBS & NBC MOWs - Ruby Ridge
                           (Miniseries) - A Work of Giants (BBC
                           Series) - Mad City - Life - Path to War
                           (HBO) - 8 Hallmark Channel films;
                           Independent Films: Isolated - 7eventy 5ive -
                           Her Minor Thing
COMMENTS   Starring talent, day players, background;
                           Union and non-union; Print; Covering all
                           of Northern California; Full casting facilities
                           and sound stage in Sacramento, CA

Everett Blix . . . . .Casting Director

BETH MELSKY CASTING
928 Broadway
New York, NY 10010
PHONE 212-505-5000
CASTS   Film - TV - Commercials - Voice-Over -
                           Industrials
AFFILIATIONS   CSA

Beth Melsky . . . . .Owner
Krissy Benge . . . . .Casting Director
Roger Del Pozo . . . . .Casting Director
Nancy Frigand . . . . .Casting Director
Laura Richard . . . . .Casting Director
Richard Reed . . . . .Associate
Eddie Honan . . . . .Casting Assistant
Adrian Koshy . . . . .Casting Assistant
Morgan Fischer . . . . .Video Conference & Posting
Shadd Sutton . . . . .Assistant

JOSEPH MIDDLETON
c/o Casting Society of America
606 N. Larchmont Blvd., Ste. 4B
Los Angeles, CA 90004
PHONE 323-791-7766
AFFILIATIONS   CSA
CREDITS   American Pie - The Bourne Supremacy -
                           Mr. & Mrs. Smith - Dawn of the Dead - In
                           Good Company

Joseph Middleton . . . . .Casting Director

MONIKA MIKKELSEN
c/o Casting Society of America
606 N. Larchmont Ave., Ste. 4B
Los Angeles, CA 90004
PHONE 323-653-6007
CASTS   Film
AFFILIATIONS   CSA
CREDITS   Pulse - The OH in Ohio - The Devil's
                           Rejects - The Wedding Date - Jiminy Glick
                           in Lalawood - Mindhunters - My Life
                           Without Me - Serving Sara - Love Liza -
                           Driven

Monika Mikkelsen . . . . .Casting Director

DEE MILLER/THE CASTING DIRECTORS, INC.
7300 NE 4th Ct.
Miami, FL 33138
PHONE 305-757-6055
FAX 305-757-6058
WEB SITE . . . . .www.cdcast.com
CASTS   Film - TV - Commercials - Voice-Over -
                           Industrials
AFFILIATIONS   CSA
CREDITS   See Web site
COMMENTS   Union and non-union casting services and
                           facilities since 1976

Dee Miller . . . . .President

MIMI WEBB MILLER CASTING
321 Santa Monica Blvd.
Santa Monica, CA 90401
PHONE 310-452-0863
EMAIL . . . . .mwmcasting@aol.com
CASTS   Commercials

Mimi Webb Miller . . . . .Casting Director
Lexi Mealy . . . . .Casting Associate

RICK MILLIKAN
c/o Casting Society of America
606 N. Larchmont Blvd., Ste. 4B
Los Angeles, CA 90004
PHONE 323-463-1925
CASTS   TV
AFFILIATIONS   CSA
CREDITS   Bones - CSI: Miami - The X-Files

Rick Millikan . . . . .Casting Director

LISA MIONIE
c/o Casting Society of America
606 N. Larchmont Blvd., Ste. 4B
Los Angeles, CA 90004
PHONE 323-463-1925/213-300-4905
CASTS   Film - TV
AFFILIATIONS   CSA

Lisa Mionie . . . . .Casting Director

MITCHELL/RUDOLPH CASTING
70 W. 36th St., Ste. 1006
New York, NY 10018
PHONE 212-679-3550
WEB SITE . . . . .www.mrcast.com
CASTS   Film - TV - Theatre
CREDITS   TV: Grounded for Life - American Family - Gracie's Choice (MOW) - Young Blades - Americans - The Shield - The Mountain - The Young Americans - Dante's Cove; Film: After the Sunset - The Grudge 1&2 - In the Mix - American Pie 4 - Hostel
COMMENTS   Casting sessions often open for major film and TV roles to actors without agents or managers; See company Web site to be added to email list for notification

Jeff Mitchell . . . . .Casting Director
Jennifer Rudolph .Casting Director

MJB CASTING
1335 N. La Brea Ave., #211
Hollywood, CA 90028
PHONE 323-850-8540
CASTS   Film
AFFILIATIONS   CSA
CREDITS   Garfield: A Tail of Two Kitties - Chicken Little - The Incredibles - Home on the Range - Finding Nemo - Lilo & Stitch - Monsters, Inc. - The Emperor's New Groove

Matthew Jon Beck . . . . .Casting Director

MONROE CASTING & PRODUCTION
3100 Damon Way
Burbank, CA 91505
PHONE 818-640-4770
EMAIL . . . . .pmonroecasting@aol.com
WEB SITE . . . . .www.pixiemonroecasting.com
CASTS   Film - TV - Commercials - Voice-Over - Industrials
AFFILIATIONS   CCDA
CREDITS   Film: Cries from Ramah - Black Leather Soles - Corpses - Jekyll - Flipside - Malibu Spring Break - Karma Police - Sweetwater; TV: Magic Castle After Dark; Print: Booty Boys Album
SUBMISSION POLICY   Accepted via US Mail; No phone calls, walk-ins or email
COMMENTS   Member, ATAS and EIC; Board of Directors, American Women in Radio & Television

Pixie Monroe . . . . .Casting Director
Joey Boone . . . . .Marketing
Christopher Monroe . . . . .Casting Associate

PAT MORAN & ASSOCIATES
3500 Boston St., Ste. 425
Baltimore, MD 21224
PHONE 410-558-0400
WEB SITE . . . . .www.patmoranandassociates.com
CASTS   Film - TV
AFFILIATIONS   CSA
CREDITS   The Wire - Syriana - A Dirty Shame - Wedding Crashers
SUBMISSION POLICY   By US Mail only; No phone calls or drop-bys
COMMENTS   Member, ATAS; Over 40 film and TV credits; List available upon request

Pat Moran CSA . . . . .Casting Director
Meagan Lewis . . . . .Associate
Shamos Fisher . . . . .Assistant
Sareva Racher . . . . .Assistant

BOB MORONES CASTING
c/o Sanmar Studios
4130 Cahuenga Blvd., Ste. 120
Universal City, CA 91602
PHONE 818-755-8725
FAX 818-755-8706
CASTS   Film - TV - Commercials
AFFILIATIONS   CSA
CREDITS   American Me - Resurrection Blvd. (Showtime) - Platoon - Pumpkinhead - 187 - Scarface - Kingpin

Bob Morones . . . . .Casting Director

MICHELLE MORRIS-GERTZ
c/o Casting Society of America
606 N. Larchmont Blvd., Ste. 4B
Los Angeles, CA 90004
PHONE 323-463-1925
CASTS   Film
AFFILIATIONS   CSA
CREDITS   Mr. & Mrs. Smith - Donnie Darko

Michelle Morris-Gertz . . . . .Casting Director

BARRY MOSS CASTING
484 W. 43rd St., Ste. 28-R
New York, NY 10036
PHONE 212-307-6690
CASTS   Film - TV - Theatre
AFFILIATIONS   CSA

Barry Moss CSA .Casting Director

MOVIEWORK NOW CASTING, INC.
4700 E. Thomas Rd., Ste. 104
Phoenix, AZ 85018
PHONE 602-224-5888
FAX 602-957-4070
EMAIL . . . . .patrice@movieworknow.com
WEB SITE . . . . .www.movieworknow.com
CASTS   Film - TV - Commercials - Voice-Over - Industrials
COMMENTS   Extras

Barry Farner . . . . .President
Patrice Farner . . . . .VP

MTV CASTING
2600 Colorado Ave.
Santa Monica, CA 90404
PHONE 310-752-8240
CASTS   Film - TV - Voice-Over
CREDITS   Film: Anchorman - Dodgeball - Eternal Sunshine of the Spotless Mind; TV: Nick Cannon Presents: Wild 'N Out - Punk'd

Blythe Cappello . . . . .VP, Casting, Talent & Series Development
Allison Cohn . . . . .Casting Associate
J.W. Starrett . . . . .Assistant

MTV/MTV2 TALENT
1515 Broadway, 23rd Fl.
New York, NY 10036
PHONE 212-258-8000
CASTS　　　　　　　TV

Rod Aissa .Sr. VP, Talent & Series Development
Vinnie Postestivo . . . . .Talent Director

KIMBERLY MULLEN/MARK MULLEN CASTING
4390 35th St.
Orlando, FL 32811
PHONE 407-226-1644
WEB SITE . . . . .www.mullencasting.com
CASTS　　　　　　　Film - TV - Commercials
AFFILIATIONS　　　　CSA
CREDITS　　　　　　Film: Things That Hang from Trees - The
　　　　　　　　　Hawk Is Dying - Say Yes Quickly - Jeepers
　　　　　　　　　Creepers - The Fountain - In Pieces; TV:
　　　　　　　　　South Beach - In Search of - Curse of the
　　　　　　　　　Blair Witch

Kimberly Mullen .Casting Director
Mark Mullen . . . . .Casting Director

ROGER MUSSENDEN CASTING
10202 W. Washington Blvd., Art Dept. Bldg. Rm. 23
Culver City, CA 90232
PHONE 310-244-3382
CASTS　　　　　　　Film - TV
AFFILIATIONS　　　　CSA
CREDITS　　　　　　Film: Click - Superman Returns - Scary
　　　　　　　　　Movie 4 - Deuce Bigalow: European
　　　　　　　　　Gigolo - Cellular - Blast! - 50 First Dates -
　　　　　　　　　Home of Phobia - Bring It on Again - From
　　　　　　　　　Justin to Kelly - X2 - Anger Management -
　　　　　　　　　Eight Crazy Nights - Boat Trip - The Master
　　　　　　　　　of Disguise - Mr. Deeds - Corky Romano -
　　　　　　　　　Joe Dirt - The Animal - See Spot Run - Little
　　　　　　　　　Nicky - X-Men; TV: Miss Miami - Gotta
　　　　　　　　　Kick It Up! - American Family
SUBMISSION POLICY　Do not drop off or call

Roger Mussenden . . . . .Casting Director
Pam Thomas . . . . .Casting Associate
Melissa Kostenbauder . . . . .Casting Assistant

NASSIF & BACA CASTING
c/o Casting Society of America
606 N. Larchmont Ave., Ste. 4B
Los Angeles, CA 90004
PHONE 323-463-1925
CASTS　　　　　　　Film - TV
AFFILIATIONS　　　　CSA
CREDITS　　　　　　Film: Rest Stop - Sublime - The Believers -
　　　　　　　　　Eating Out 2: Sloppy Seconds; TV: Desire -
　　　　　　　　　Fashion House
COMMENTS　　　　　Teamsters 399

Patrick Baca CSA . . . . .Casting Director
Robin S. Nassif . . . . .Casting Director

NBC ENTERTAINMENT CASTING
3000 W. Alameda Ave., Ste. 225
Burbank, CA 91523
PHONE 818-840-3774
FAX 818-840-4412
CASTS　　　　　　　TV
AFFILIATIONS　　　　CSA

Marc Hirschfeld .Executive VP, Casting
Grace Wu . . . . .Sr. VP, Casting
Brian Dorfman . . . . .VP, Casting
Jennifer McNamara . . . . .VP, Casting (NY)
Robyn Burt . . . . .Casting Coordinator
Christine Kromer . . . . .Assistant (NY)
Ani Manouchehri . . . . .Assistant
Elizabeth Moore . . . . .Assistant

NBC UNIVERSAL TELEVISION STUDIO CASTING
100 Universal City Plaza
Universal City, CA 91608
PHONE 818-840-4444
CASTS　　　　　　　TV

Nancy Perkins . . . . .Sr. VP, Casting
Steven O'Neill . . . . .VP, Casting
Patrick Dixon . . . . .Casting Coordinator for Nancy Perkins
Robert Prinz . . . . .Casting Coordinator for Steven O'Neill

DEBRA NEATHERY
4820 N. Cleon Ave.
North Hollywood, CA 91601
PHONE 818-506-5524
CASTS　　　　　　　Film - TV - Commercials - Voice-Over -
　　　　　　　　　Industrials
COMMENTS　　　　　Also Independent Films and Music Videos

Debra Neathery . . . . .Casting Director

NEW LINE CASTING
116 N. Robertson Blvd., 5th Fl.
Los Angeles, CA 90048
PHONE 310-854-5811
CASTS　　　　　　　Film

Susie Farris . . . . .Sr. VP, Casting
Corey Malanga . . . . .Casting Coordinator

BRUCE H. NEWBERG CASTING
606 N. Larchmont Blvd., Ste. 311
Los Angeles, CA 90004
PHONE 323-468-6633
FAX 323-467-6175
CASTS   Film - TV - Theatre
AFFILIATIONS   CSA
CREDITS   The Closer - The Class

Bruce H. Newberg .Casting Director
Beth Lipari . . . . .Casting Associate
Ani Avetyan . . . . .Casting Assistant
Jenny Meister . . . . .Office Manager

NICKELODEON CASTING
2600 Colorado Ave., 2nd Fl.
Santa Monica, CA 90404
PHONE 310-752-8402/212-258-8000
CASTS   TV
AFFILIATIONS   CSA
COMMENTS   Casts TV pilots/series, TV movies, program-
                               ming blocks and specials; Union/Non-
                               Union; Don't phone, fax or visit; Interviews
                               by appointment only; Accepts
                               photos/resumes by mail only; Only send
                               tapes upon request, tapes will not be
                               returned; Attends showcases; Also affiliated
                               with ATAS

Paula Kaplan .Sr. VP, Talent & Casting
Sharon Chazin Lieblein CSA . . . . .VP, Talent & Casting
Jill Greenberg Sands . . . . .VP, Talent & Casting (NY)
Shelly Sumpter Gillyard . . . . .VP, Celebrity Talent & Nick Records
Justin Antony . . . . .Director, Talent
Sarah Noonan . . .Director, Animation Talent & Casting (818-736-3000)
Leslie Zaslower . . . . .Director, Nick Jr./Noggin/Nick On Air Talent &
                               Casting (NY)
Leah Buono . . . . .Manager, Talent & Casting
Kia Riddick . . . . .Manager, The N Talent & Casting (NY)
Aszur Hill . . . . .Coordinator, The N Talent & Casting (NY)
Michelle Levitt . . . . .Coordinator, Noggin/Nick Jr. Talent & Casting (NY)
Shannon Reed . . . . .Coordinator, Animation Talent & Casting
                               (818-736-3000)
Dana Kirk . . . . .Assistant to Shelly Sumpter Gillyard
Christina Marano . . . . .Assistant to Talent & Casting (NY)
Susana Martinez . . . . .Assistant to Sharon Chazin Lieblein
Maritza Villegas . . . . .Assistant to Paula Kaplan

PATRICIA NOLAND
c/o Turner Television
4000 Warner Blvd., Bldg. 160, 11th Fl.
Burbank, CA 91522
PHONE 818-977-2335
CASTS   TV
AFFILIATIONS   CSA
CREDITS   All About Us

Patricia Noland . . . . .Casting Director

NORTH COAST CASTING
7 Fifth St.
Eureka, CA 95501
PHONE . . . . .707-442-0952 (Hotline)
EMAIL . . . . .jane@northcoastcasting.com
WEB SITE . . . . .www.northcoastcasting.com
COMMENTS   Centralized casting on the Northern
                               California Coast; Based in Humboldt
                               County; Also serving Shasta, Del Norte,
                               Mendocino, Trinity and Siskiyou Counties

Jane Morgan . . . . .Owner/Director
Zoe Ann Banker . . . . .No Title

O'HAVER + COMPANY
c/o EpoxyBox Studios
PHONE 323-650-9010/416-274-1001
WEB SITE . . . . .www.ohaver.net
CASTS   Film - TV - Commercials - Voice-Over
AFFILIATIONS   CCDA
COMMENTS   SAG and real people casting; Spanish lan-
                               guage

Jenny O'Haver . . . . .Casting Director
Robert O'Haver . . . . .Co-Owner

GILLIAN O'NEILL
c/o Casting Society of America
606 N. Larchmont Blvd., Ste. 4B
Los Angeles, CA 90004
PHONE 323-463-1925
CASTS   TV
AFFILIATIONS   CSA
CREDITS   Brothers & Sisters - Game Over - Judging
                               Amy

Gillian O'Neill . . . . .Casting Director

ORPHEUS GROUP
1560 Broadway, Ste. 405
New York, NY 10036
PHONE 212-957-8760
FAX 212-957-1320
EMAIL .orpheus.ny@verizon.net
CASTS   Film - TV - Commercials - Theatre
CREDITS   El Claiente - Choking Man - Maria Full of
                               Grace - Real Women Have Curves -
                               Girlfight

Ellyn Long Marshall . . . . .Owner
Maria E. Nelson . . . . .Owner

PAGANO/MANWILLER CASTING
21050 Lassen St.
Chatsworth, CA 91311
PHONE 818-717-5425
CASTS   TV
AFFILIATIONS   CSA
CREDITS   24

Debi Manwiller . . . . .Casting Director
Richard Pagano . . . . .Casting Director
Peggy Kennedy . . . . .Casting Director

MARVIN PAIGE CASTING
PO Box 69434
West Hollywood, CA 90069
PHONE 818-760-3040
FAX 818-766-3889
CASTS Film - TV
AFFILIATIONS CSA
CREDITS Jump - Hamal 18 - Shaka Zulu: The Last
Great Warrior - Star Trek: The Motion
Picture - General Hospital
COMMENTS Celebrity events; Production and talent con-
sultant for film and TV related documen-
taries and TV biographies, including A&E
and Turner Classic Movies; Also heads
Marvin Paige's Motion Picture & TV
Research Archive, a Hollywood and movie
history research facility

Marvin Paige . . . . .Casting Director

MARK PALADINI
c/o Casting Society of America
606 N. Larchmont Blvd., Ste. 4B
Los Angeles, CA 90004
PHONE 323-463-1925/818-613-3982
CASTS Film
AFFILIATIONS CSA
CREDITS Clarion's Call - My First Wedding

Mark Paladini . . . . .Casting Director

LINDA PHILLIPS PALO
c/o Casting Society of America
606 N. Larchmont Blvd., Ste. 4B
Los Angeles, CA 90004
PHONE 323-463-1925
CASTS Film - TV
AFFILIATIONS CSA
CREDITS Me and You and Everyone We Know -
Jeepers Creepers 2 - South of Heaven,
West of Hell - The Virgin Suicides - Don
McKay - Zero Principal - Intellectual
Property

Linda Phillips Palo . . . . .Casting Director

PARAMOUNT PICTURES FEATURES CASTING
5555 Melrose Ave., Bob Hope Bldg., Rm. 206
Hollywood, CA 90038
PHONE 323-956-5444

Gail Levin . . . . .Executive VP, Features Casting

ELLEN PARKS CASTING
349 Broadway, 4th Fl.
New York, NY 10013
PHONE 212-965-1153
CASTS Film
AFFILIATIONS CSA
CREDITS Dark Matter - Book of Love - Secretary -
Sideways

Ellen Parks . . . . .Casting Director

TIM PAYNE CASTING
9343 Culver Blvd.
Culver City, CA 90232
PHONE 310-883-3186, x101
CASTS TV
AFFILIATIONS CSA
CREDITS 10 Items or Less - Emily's Reasons Why
Not - Huff - Las Vegas - Grounded for Life

Tim Payne . . . . .Casting Director

PEMRICK/FRONK CASTING
14724 Ventura Blvd., PH
Sherman Oaks, CA 91403
PHONE 818-325-1289
WEB SITE . . . . .www.pfcast.com
CASTS Film - TV
AFFILIATIONS CSA
CREDITS Film: Troubled Waters - Four - 13 - The
Veteran - Heartstopper - The Tooth Fairy -
Pray for Morning - Tranced - The Last Sect -
Bone Dry; TV: Her Fatal Flaw - 12 Hours to
Live - Mind Games - Veiled Truth -
Presumed Dead - Lesser Evil - Double
Cross - Officer Down - Third Man Out -
The Fallen Ones

Donald Paul Pemrick . . . . .Casting Director
Dean E. Fronk . . . . .Casting Director
Elizabeth Hollywood . . . . .Casting Assistant

PERRY/REECE CASTING
500 S. Sepulveda Blvd., Ste. 310
Los Angeles, CA 90049
PHONE 310-889-1660
FAX 310-889-1670
CASTS Film - TV - Theatre

Penny Perry . . . . .Casting Director
Amy Reece . . . . .Casting Director
Christine Babayans . . . . .Associate

THE PHILADELPHIA CASTING COMPANY, INC.
114 Chestnut St., 3rd Fl.
Philadelphia, PA 19106
PHONE . . . . .215-592-7575 (Producers)/215-592-7577 (Actors)
FAX 215-592-7576
EMAIL . . . . .casting@philacast.com
WEB SITE . . . . .www.philacast.com
CASTS Film - TV - Commercials - Theatre -
Industrials
CREDITS Films: Spanish-American War Project -
Carpet One; TV: SuperNanny - PBS
KidsGo! - Cowboy University
SUBMISSION POLICY Do not fax or email pictures

Susan Gish . . . . .Casting Director
Sam Gish . . . . .Casting Director

BONNIE PIETILA
c/o Twentieth Century Fox
10201 W. Pico Blvd., Trailer 730, Rm. 2
Los Angeles, CA 90035
PHONE 310-369-3632
CASTS TV - Voice-Over
CREDITS The Simpsons

Bonnie Pietila . . . . .Casting Director

PLAYBOY TV
3030 Andrita St.
Los Angeles, CA 90065
PHONE 323-344-4500
FAX 323-344-4800
EMAIL .casting@playboy.com
WEB SITE . . . . .www.playboy.com
CASTS   Film - TV - Commercials - Voice-Over - Theatre - Industrials
CREDITS   The Weekend Flash - Jenna's American Sex Star - Night Calls - All Night Party Girls - Totally Busted

Madison Smith . . . . .Casting Director

PLAYWRIGHTS HORIZONS
416 W. 42nd St.
New York, NY 10036
PHONE 212-564-1235
FAX 212-594-0296
CASTS   Film - TV - Theatre
AFFILIATIONS   CSA
CREDITS   The Knights of Prosperity (ABC) - Playwrights Horizons - Ed (NBC) - Monk (USA) - Hope & Faith (ABC) - Heights - The White Countess - When Zachary Beaver Came to Town - Huntington Theatre Company

Alaine Alldaffer . . . . .Casting Director
Joey Cee . . . . .Casting Associate, Knights of Prosperity
Lisa Donadio . . . . .Casting Associate, Playwrights Horizons
Alyssa Biber . . . . .Casting Assistant

POWELL/MELCHER CASTING
4053 Radford
Studio City, CA 91604
PHONE 818-377-4588
CASTS   TV
AFFILIATIONS   CSA
CREDITS   Eve - One on One - Cuts - The 4400

Holly Powell . . . . .Casting Director
Elizabeth Melcher .Casting Director
Nelia Morago . . . . .Casting Director
Azja Pryor . . . . .Assistant

PRIME CASTING
6430 Sunset Blvd., Ste. 425
Hollywood, CA 90028
PHONE 323-962-0377
EMAIL .info@primecasting.com
WEB SITE . . . . .www.primecasting.com
CASTS   Film - TV - Commercials - Industrials
CREDITS   Film: Akeelah and the Bee - How to Rob a Bank - The Ripple Effect - Wild Things 2; TV: Punk'd (MTV) - Avril Lavigne Music Video - Keane Music Video; Commercial: AOL Print - AT&T Print
COMMENTS   Print, music videos; Payroll service; Casting facility

Heather Sirota . . . . .Casting Director
Peter Alwazzan . . . . .No Title

RAINBOW CASTING SERVICE
1282 Vallecita Dr.
Santa Fe, NM 87501
PHONE 505-896-9611
EMAIL . . . . .tn@teresaneptune.com
WEB SITE . . . . .www.rainbowcasting.com
CASTS   Film
CREDITS   Crazy Like the Taz - The Tao of Steve - Jennifer Monroe - Drive
SUBMISSION POLICY   Mail only
COMMENTS   Full-service; Location casting; SAG and non-union

Teresa Neptune . . . . .Casting Director

JOHANNA RAY & ASSOCIATES
1022 Palm Ave., Ste. 2
West Hollywood, CA 90069
PHONE 310-652-2511
FAX 310-652-4103
CASTS   Film
AFFILIATIONS   CSA
CREDITS   Inland Empire - The Black Dahlia - Kill Bill - Mulholland Drive

Johanna Ray .Owner/Casting Director
Jenny Jue . . . . .Casting Assistant

RDC CASTING, INC.
1004 Bathurst St.
Toronto, Ontario M5R 3G7
PHONE 416-929-6880
CASTS   Film - TV
AFFILIATIONS   CSA
CREDITS   Mr. Magorium's Wonder Emporium - Breach - Full of It - The Sentinel - 16 Blocks - The Pacifier - Assault on Precinct 13 - The Prince & Me - Confessions of a Teenage Drama Queen - Cold Creek Manor - How to Lose a Guy in 10 Days - The Tuxedo - Avenging Angelo - The Facts of Life Reunion - Jason X - The Ladies Man - Ginger Snaps

Robin D. Cook . . . . .Casting Director

TINA REAL
3108 Fifth Ave., Ste. C
San Diego, CA 92103
PHONE 619-298-0544
FAX 619-298-0389
EMAIL . . . . .tinareal1@mac.com
WEB SITE . . . . .www.tinarealcasting.com
CASTS   Film - TV - Commercials - Industrials
COMMENTS   Day players, under fives, principals and extras

Tina Real . . . . .Casting Director

ROBI REED & ASSOCIATES

6255 Sunset Blvd., #923
Los Angeles, CA 90028

PHONE	323-463-6350
CASTS	Film - TV - Commercials
CREDITS	Waist Deep - Antwone Fisher - Girlfriends - Toyota - K-Mart - Soul Food - Do the Right Thing - Malcolm X - The Tracy Morgan Show - Roc - Tuskegee Airmen - Love Jones - Gridlock'd - The Fighting Temptations - Set It Off - Pryor Offenses - Their Eyes Were Watching God - Crossover - The Gospel - Barbershop - Paradise
COMMENTS	Affiliated with the Academy of Television

Robi Reed . . . . .Casting Director/Owner
A. Doran Reed . . . . .Casting Director
Donna R. Reed .Creative Executive
Andrea Reed . . . . .Casting Director
Wil Young . . . . .Casting Coordinator

REEL TALENT/REEL KIDS

1805 E. Cabrillo Blvd., Ste. B
Santa Barbara, CA 93101

PHONE	805-969-2222/805-565-1562
FAX	805-969-9595
EMAIL	reeltalentreelkids@earthlink.net
SECOND EMAIL	reeltalent@cox.net
CASTS	Film - TV - Commercials - Voice-Over - Theatre - Industrials
COMMENTS	Casting for tri-county areas (Ventura, Santa Barbara, San Luis Obispo)

Christine Lai . . . . .Casting Director

SHARI RHODES CASTING

c/o Beverlee Dean Management
8924 Clifton Way, Ste. 103
Beverly Hills, CA 90211

PHONE	310-652-7436
FAX	209-391-5022
CASTS	Film - TV
AFFILIATIONS	CSA
CREDITS	Jump Shot - Man in the Moon - The Sand Lot - Passenger 57 - Jaws 1&2 - Close Encounters of the Third Kind

Shari Rhodes . . . . .Casting Director
Pam Frazier . . . . .Casting Director

RISINGCAST

140 S. Elm Dr.
Beverly Hills, CA 90212

PHONE	310-278-4012
EMAIL	casting@risingcast.com
WEB SITE	www.risingcast.com
CASTS	Film - TV - Voice-Over
SUBMISSION POLICY	Accepts headshot and resumé by email only; Do not mail or drop off

Gabrielle Pantera . . . . .Casting Director

RODEO CASTING

7013 Willoughby Ave.
Los Angeles, CA 90038

PHONE	323-969-9125
CASTS	Commercials - Industrials
SUBMISSION POLICY	Mail preferred; No drop-ins or phone calls
COMMENTS	Also casts for print

Britt Enggren . . . . .Casting Director

ROMANO/BENNER

c/o Casting Society of America
606 N. Larchmont Blvd., Ste. 4B
Los Angeles, CA 90004

PHONE	323-463-1925
CASTS	TV
AFFILIATIONS	CSA
CREDITS	Scrubs - Commited - One Tree Hill - What I Like About You

Debby Romano . . . . .Casting Director
Brett Benner . . . . .Casting Director

STACEY ROSEN

c/o Casting Society of America
606 N. Larchmont Blvd., Ste. 4B
Los Angeles, CA 90004

PHONE	323-463-1925
CASTS	TV
AFFILIATIONS	CSA
CREDITS	To Be Fat Like Me - The House Next Door - Murder in the Hamptons - Trump Unauthorized - Confessions of an American Bride - More Sex & the Single Mom - Berkeley - The Perfect Husband: The Laci Peterson Story - The Dead Will Tell - Perfect Romance - The Book of Ruth - A Date with Darkness: The Trial and Capture of Andrew Luster - The Stranger Beside Me - Saint Sinner - Gleason - Obsessed - Firestarter 2: Rekindled

Stacey Rosen . . . . .Casting Director

VICKI ROSENBERG & ASSOCIATES

c/o Twentieth Century Fox
10201 W. Pico Blvd., Bldg. 80, Rm. 19
Los Angeles, CA 90035

PHONE	310-369-3448
FAX	310-969-1340
CASTS	Film - TV
AFFILIATIONS	CSA
CREDITS	Bones - Judging Amy - Joan of Arcadia

Vicki Rosenberg . . . . .Casting Director
Alexis Frank Koczara . . . . .Casting Associate
Christine Smith Schevchenko . . . . .Casting Associate
Karen Morris . . . . .Casting Assistant
Beth Sekul . . . . .Casting Assistant

DONNA ROSENSTEIN

800 S. Main St., #202
Burbank, CA 91506

PHONE	818-526-4230/818-733-3581
CASTS	Film - TV
AFFILIATIONS	CSA
CREDITS	Ghost Whisperer - October Road - Wildfire
COMMENTS	Universal City office: 100 Universal City Plaza, Bldg. 5225, Rm. 168, Universal City, CA 91608

Donna Rosenstein . . . . .Casting Director
Kendra Castleberry .Casting Associate
Liz Lang . . . . .Casting Associate (Universal City)
Marlo Hughling . . . . .Casting Assistant (Universal City)

ROUNDABOUT THEATRE COMPANY
231 W. 39th, Ste. 1200
New York, NY 10018
PHONE 212-719-1073
FAX 212-642-9622
CASTS   Theatre
AFFILIATIONS   CSA

Jim Carnahan . . . . .Casting Director
Mele Nagler . . . . .Casting Director
Carrie Gardner .Sr. Casting Associate
Stephen Kopel . . . . .Casting Associate
Kate Schwabe . . . . .Casting Associate

CINDI RUSH CASTING, LTD.
27 W. 20th St., Ste. 404
New York, NY 10011
PHONE 212-414-2838
CASTS   Film - Theatre
AFFILIATIONS   CSA

Cindi Rush . . . . .Casting Director
Andrew Zerman . . . . .Casting Director
Michele Weiss . . . . .Casting Associate

MARK SAKS
c/o LA Center Studios
450 S. Bixel, Ste. M-160
Los Angeles, CA 90017
PHONE 213-534-3060
CASTS   Film - TV
AFFILIATIONS   CSA
CREDITS   Numb3rs

Mark Saks . . . . .Casting Director

GABRIELLE SCHARY
c/o Sessions West Studios
2601 Ocean Park Blvd., Ste. 120
Santa Monica, CA 90405
PHONE 310-450-0835
EMAIL . . . . .gabrielleschary@earthlink.net
WEB SITE . . . . .www.gabriellescharycasting.com
SECOND WEB SITE . . . . .www.sessionsweststudios.com
CASTS   TV - Commercials - Industrials
AFFILIATIONS   CCDA - CSA

Gabrielle Schary . . . . .Casting Director
Jenny Schmidt . . . . .Manager

BRIEN SCOTT
18034 Ventura Blvd., Ste. 275
Encino, CA 91316
PHONE 818-921-9857
CASTS   Film - TV - Commercials - Industrials
AFFILIATIONS   CCDA - CSA
CREDITS   The Boy Next Door - Summer Wind -
                         Holding onto Holden
SUBMISSION POLICY   Mail only; Send Attn: Assistant; Do not
                         phone or visit

Brien Scott . . . . .Casting Director
Amy Cohen . . . . .Associate

KEVIN SCOTT
c/o Casting Society of America
606 N. Larchmont Blvd. Suite 4B
Los Angeles, CA 90004
PHONE 323-463-1925
CASTS   TV
AFFILIATIONS   CSA
CREDITS   Half & Half - The West Wing - All About
                         the Andersons - My Wife and Kids - All of
                         Us

Kevin Scott . . . . .Casting Director

TINA SEILER
PO Box 2001
Toluca Lake, CA 91610
PHONE 818-628-1953
EMAIL . . . . .tinacasting789@yahoo.com
CASTS   Film - TV - Voice-Over - Theatre -
                         Industrials
SUBMISSION POLICY   Submit by mail
COMMENTS   Also casts for reality programming

Tina Seiler . . . . .Casting Director

LILA SELIK CASTING
PO Box 66369
Los Angeles, CA 90066
PHONE 310-556-2444
WEB SITE . . . . .www.castingbylilaselik.com
CASTS   Film - TV - Commercials - Voice-Over -
                         Industrials
AFFILIATIONS   CCDA
SUBMISSION POLICY   Only accepting submissions for unusual
                         types
COMMENTS   SAG - AFTRA

Lila Selik . . . . .Casting Director
Lourdes Regala . . . . .Casting Assistant
Debbie Haugen . . . . .Casting Assistant

AVA SHEVITT CASTING
c/o Village Studio
321 Santa Monica Blvd., #300
Santa Monica, CA 90401
PHONE 310-656-4600
CASTS   Film - TV - Commercials - Voice-Over
AFFILIATIONS   CCDA
COMMENTS   Teleconference facility

Ava Shevitt . . . . .Casting Director
Troy Shevitt . . . . .Manager
Lindsay Ravage . . . . .Casting Associate

SHOOTING FROM THE HIP CASTING
c/o Zydeco Studios
11317 Ventura Blvd.
Studio City, CA 91604
PHONE 818-506-0613
WEB SITE . . . . .www.shootingfromthehipcasting.com
CASTS   TV - Commercials
AFFILIATIONS   CCDA
CREDITS   The Naked Trucker & T-Bones (Comedy
                         Central) - Significant Others (Bravo) - Free
                         Ride (Fox) - Hollywood Vice (Fox) - Good
                         Girl, Bad Girl (Oxygen)
SUBMISSION POLICY   No calls

Francene Selkirk-Ackerman . . . . .Casting Director
Lisa Iannce . . . . .Assistant
Tiffany Maze . . . . .Assistant
Buckley Sampson . . . . .Assistant

SUSAN SHOPMAKER CASTING
545 Eighth Ave., 23rd Fl.
New York, NY 10018
PHONE 212-686-5502
FAX 646-365-3349
EMAIL . . . . .info@susanshopmakercasting.com
CASTS   Film - TV - Commercials - Theatre -
                         Industrials

Susan Shopmaker .Casting Director
Randi Glass . . . . .Casting Associate

SHOWTIME NETWORKS TALENT & CASTING
10880 Wilshire Blvd., Ste. 1600
Los Angeles, CA 90024
PHONE 310-234-5237
FAX 310-234-5390
CASTS   Film - TV

Beth Klein . . . . .Sr. VP, Talent & Casting
Trisha Debski . . . . .Casting Associate

MARK SIKES CASTING
8909 24th St.
Los Angeles, CA 90034
PHONE 818-759-7648
EMAIL . . . . .sikesmark@sbcglobal.net
WEB SITE . . . . .www.marksikes.com
CASTS   Film - TV - Commercials

Mark Sikes . . . . .Casting Director

ALYSON SILVERBERG
c/o Casting Society of America
606 N. Larchmont Blvd., Ste. 4B
Los Angeles, CA 90004
PHONE 323-463-1925
CASTS   Film - TV
AFFILIATIONS   CSA
CREDITS   Everwood - The O.C.

Alyson Silverberg .Casting Director

CLAIRE SIMON CASTING
1512 N. Fremont, Ste. 202
Chicago, IL 60622
PHONE 312-202-0124
FAX 312-202-0128
WEB SITE . . . . .www.simoncasting.com
CASTS   Film - TV - Commercials - Voice-Over -
                         Theatre
AFFILIATIONS   CSA
CREDITS   Film: Ali - Hardball - Save the Last Dance -
                         High Fidelity - A Home at the End of the
                         World; TV: What About Joan (Series) -
                         Prison Break (Pilot)

Claire Simon . . . . .Casting Director
Teresa Thoma . . . . .Casting Director, Commercials
Shelby Cherniet .Casting Associate
Chelsey Peterson .Casting Associate

CAROLINE SINCLAIR CASTING
c/o Zipper
336 W. 37th St.
New York, NY 10018
PHONE 212-279-1002
CASTS   Film - Commercials
CREDITS   The Living Wake - The House Is Burning -
                         The Dig - 2BPerfectlyHonest - Mr. Smith
                         Gets a Hustler - Particles of Truth - Music -
                         Si' Laraby - The Killing Zone - Bomb the
                         System

Caroline Sinclair .Casting Director
Bettina Bilger . . . . .Casting Associate

CLAIR SINNETT CASTING
531 Main St., Ste. 1135
El Segundo, CA 90245
PHONE 310-606-0813
FAX 310-606-0823
EMAIL . . . . .sinnett@earthlink.net
WEB SITE . . . . .www.actorsworking.com
CASTS   Film - TV - Commercials - Theatre -
                         Industrials
AFFILIATIONS   CSA
COMMENTS   Promos

Clair Sinnett . . . . .Casting Director
Aaron Revoir . . . . .Casting Assistant

MELISSA SKOFF CASTING
11684 Ventura Blvd., Ste. 5141
Studio City, CA 91604
PHONE 818-760-2058
CASTS   Film - TV
AFFILIATIONS   CSA
CREDITS   Amercian Summer - Autopsy - Augusta
                         Gone - Absolution - The Road to Christmas
                         - JAG - First Monday - Back to School
COMMENTS   Teaches cold reading classes; Private
                         coaching available

Melissa Skoff . . . . .Casting Director
Karen Harris . . . . .Casting Assistant

SLATER-BROOKSBANK CASTING
c/o USA Television
100 Universal City Plaza, Bldg. 1440, 14th Fl.
Universal City, CA 91608
PHONE 818-777-6572
CASTS   Film - TV
AFFILIATIONS   CSA
CREDITS   Commander-in-Chief - Eureka -
                         Underfunded - Baja Mil - The Redeaming
                         Season

Mary Jo Slater . . . . .Casting Director
Steve Brooksbank .Casting Director
Courtney Cleaver .Casting Assistant
Manny Fernandez .Casting Assistant

JS SNYDER & ASSOCIATES CASTING
1801 N. Kingsley Dr., Ste. 202
Los Angeles, CA 90027-3709
PHONE 323-465-4241
FAX 323-465-3446
EMAIL ....apitbull@prodigy.net
CASTS   Film - Commercials - Theatre
SUBMISSION POLICY   Accepts introductions and email submis-
                         sions from actors, but always send hard
                         copies
COMMENTS   Music videos; Acting coach/teacher

Stephen H. Snyder ....Casting Director/Partner
Bernard Abellada ....Casting Director/Partner
James Whipple ....Casting Director Associate
Marc Berg ....Casting Associate

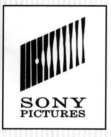

SONY PICTURES TELEVISION CASTING
9336 W. Washington Blvd., Bldg. C-207
Culver City, CA 90232
PHONE 310-202-3444/310-202-3531
CASTS   TV
AFFILIATIONS   CSA

Dawn Steinberg ....Sr. VP, Talent & Casting
Delia Frankel ....VP, Casting
Adrianna Porcaro ....Talent Coordinator, Casting

SPIKE TV CASTING
2049 Century Park East
Los Angeles, CA 90067
PHONE 310-407-1210
WEB SITE ....www.spiketv.com
CASTS   TV

Kendra Carter ....Casting Manager

CAMILLE ST. CYR CASTING
1438 N. Gower St., Bldg. 35, Ste. 156
Los Angeles, CA 90028
PHONE 323-468-4562
CASTS   TV
AFFILIATIONS   CSA
CREDITS   The Dresden Files - NCIS - Jag

Camille St. Cyr ....Casting Director

ILENE STARGER CASTING
PO Box 246, FDR Station
New York, NY 10150
PHONE 212-563-7990
CASTS   Film
AFFILIATIONS   CSA
CREDITS   Night at the Museum - The Pink Panther -
                         School of Rock - The First Wives Club -
                         Sleepy Hollow

Ilene Starger ....Casting Director
Valerie Lindquist ....Casting Associate
Zoe Rotter ....Casting Associate

STARK NAKED PRODUCTIONS (ELSIE STARK CASTING)
39 W. 19th St., 12th Fl.
New York, NY 10011
PHONE 212-366-1903
FAX 212-366-0495
EMAIL ....info@starknakedproductions.com
WEB SITE ....www.starknakedproductions.com
CASTS   Film - TV - Commercials - Voice-Over -
                         Theatre - Industrials
CREDITS   Film: The Final Patient - All Night Bodega -
                         The Blue Diner - What's Your Sign? -
                         Because of You; Theater: Four Guys
                         Named Jose. . . and Una Mujer Named
                         Maria - Latin Heat - Breaking Vegas -
                         Latinologues (Broadway)
COMMENTS   Spanish language casting and translations
                         also available

Elizabeth Gans ....Casting Associate
Joyce Baston ....Casting Associate

ADRIENNE STERN
80 Eighth Ave., Ste. 303
New York, NY 10011
PHONE 212-229-2811
CASTS   Film - TV

Adrienne Stern ....Casting Director
Tammy Porto ....Casting Associate

SALLY STINER CASTING
c/o Casting Society of America
606 N. Larchmont Blvd., Ste. 4B
Los Angeles, CA 90004
PHONE 310-392-3197
CASTS   Film - TV
AFFILIATIONS   CSA
CREDITS   Pepper Dennis - Complete Savages -
                         Malcolm in the Middle

Sally Stiner ....Casting Director
Barbie Block ....Casting Director

ANDREA STONE
c/o Casting Society of America
606 N. Larchmont Blvd., Ste. 4B
Los Angeles, CA 90004
PHONE 323-463-1925
CASTS   Film
AFFILIATIONS   CSA
CREDITS   Sex and Death 101- The Celestine
                         Prophecy - Swimming with Sharks

Andrea Stone ....Casting Director

STUART STONE
c/o Castaway Studios
8899 Beverly Blvd., Lobby Level
Los Angeles, CA 90048
PHONE 310-248-5296/323-866-1811
FAX 310-248-5297
WEB SITE . . . . .www.stonecasting.tv
CASTS   Film - TV - Commercials - Voice-Over -
                        Industrials
AFFILIATIONS   CCDA
CREDITS   Clios - Emmys
COMMENTS   Also casts for print and event hosts

Stuart Stone . . . . .Casting Director

GILDA STRATTON
c/o Casting Society of America
606 N. Larchmont Blvd., Ste. 4B
Los Angeles, CA 90004
PHONE 323-463-1925
CASTS   TV
AFFILIATIONS   CSA
CREDITS   Crumbs - Meeting the Marks - Night Court
                        - Caroline in the City

Gilda Stratton . . . . .Casting Director

ANDREW STRAUSER CASTING
1443 E. Washington Blvd., #259
Pasadena, CA 91104
PHONE 626-345-9090
EMAIL . . . . .andrew@andrewstrauser.com
WEB SITE .www.andrewstrauser.com
CASTS   TV - Commercials
CREDITS   That Yin Yang Thing (TLC) - I've Got a
                        Secret (GSN) - My Music Channel (AOL) -
                        Extreme Makeover: Home Edition - Surprise
                        by Design - Queer Eye for the Straight Girl
                        - I Wanna Be a Soap Star 1&2 - Joe
                        Millionaire 2 - From Flab to Fab

Andrew Strauser . . . . .Casting Director

STRICKMAN-RIPPS, INC.
65 N. Moore St., Ste. 3A
New York, NY 10013
PHONE 212-966-3211
CASTS   Commercials

Jill Strickman . . . . .Casting Director

STUDIO TALENT GROUP
1328 12th St., Ste. 1
Santa Monica, CA 90401
PHONE 310-393-8004
FAX 310-393-2473
EMAIL . . . . .stgactor@gte.net
WEB SITE . . . . .www.studiotalentgroup.com
CASTS   Film - TV - Industrials
SUBMISSION POLICY   Call for information
COMMENTS   Cool, independent films and shorts primari-
                        ly for FIND

Phil Brock . . . . .Casting Director

MONICA SWANN CASTING
6767 Forest Lawn Dr., Ste. 100
Los Angeles, CA 90068
PHONE 818-977-5888
CASTS   Film - TV
AFFILIATIONS   CSA
CREDITS   Cheaper by the Dozen 2 - Life Is Ruff - Roll
                        Bounce - Fat Albert - You Got Served - All
                        of Us - Soul Food - All About the
                        Andersons - Garfield 2 - The Parkers

Monica Swann . . . . .Casting Director
Bridgette Glover White . . . . .Casting Associate

DANIEL SWEE
c/o Lincoln Center Theater
150 W. 65th St.
New York, NY 10023
PHONE 212-501-3230
FAX 212-501-3141
CASTS   Film - TV - Theatre
AFFILIATIONS   CSA

Daniel Swee . . . . .Casting Director
Camille Hickman . . . . .Casting Associate

YUMI TAKADA CASTING
2105 Huntington Ln., Ste. A
Redondo Beach, CA 90278
PHONE 310-372-7287
FAX 310-937-4813
EMAIL . . . . .yumicasting@earthlink.net
CASTS   Film - TV - Commercials - Voice-Over -
                        Industrials
AFFILIATIONS   CCDA
CREDITS   Film: Letters From Iwo Jima - Gaijin 2 -
                        Haunted Freeway; TV: Movie Surfer; Print:
                        Tommy Girl; Commercials: Nissan - Pepsi -
                        AT&T; Voice-Over: Metal Gear Solid 1&2 -
                        Pax Romana
SUBMISSION POLICY   Mail only; No hand deliveries

Yumi Takada . . . . .Casting Director

BERNARD TELSEY CASTING
311 W. 43rd 10th Fl.
New York, NY 10036
PHONE 212-868-1260
CASTS   Film - TV - Commercials - Voice-Over -
                        Theatre - Industrials
AFFILIATIONS   CSA
CREDITS   Whoopi - Camp - Pieces of April; Theatre:
                        Glengarry Glen Ross - Steel Magnolias -
                        Dirty Rotten Scoundrels - Wicked (National
                        Tour) - Fat Pig - The Oldest Profession
SUBMISSION POLICY   Agent referral only; Do not phone or fax;
                        No drop-offs

Bernie Telsey . . . . .Owner
William Cantler . . . . .Casting Director

TENNER, PASKAL & RUDNICKE CASTING, INC.
10 W. Hubbard St., Ste. 2N
Chicago, IL 60610
PHONE 312-527-0665
FAX 312-527-9085
EMAIL . . . . .info@tprcasting.com
WEB SITE . . . . .www.tprcasting.com
CASTS   Film - TV - Commercials - Voice-Over -
                        Theatre - Industrials
AFFILIATIONS   CSA
CREDITS   The Break-Up - The Weather Man -
                        Stranger Than Fiction - The Amityville
                        Horror (2005) - You Are Going to Prison -
                        Drunkboat

Mickie Paskal CSA . . . . .Casting Director
Jennifer Rudnicke . . . . .Casting Director
Matt Miller . . . . .Casting Associate
Jessica Moran . . . . .Casting Associate

MARK TESCHNER CASTING
c/o ABC Television Center
4151 Prospect Ave., Stage 4, 5th Fl.
Los Angeles, CA 90027
PHONE 323-671-5542
FAX 323-671-4440
CASTS   TV
AFFILIATIONS   CSA
CREDITS   General Hospital

Mark Teschner . . . . .Casting Director
Gwen Hillier .Associate Casting Director
Kate O'Donnell . . . . .Assistant Casting Director

SHERRY THOMAS
c/o Casting Society of America
606 N. Larchmont Blvd., Ste. 4B
Los Angeles, CA 90004
PHONE 323-463-1925
CASTS   Film - TV
AFFILIATIONS   CSA
CREDITS   Medical Investigation - Skin

Sherry Thomas . . . . .Casting Director

MARK TILLMAN
c/o Casting Society of America
606 N. Larchmont Blvd., Ste. 4B
Los Angeles, CA 90004
PHONE 323-463-1925
CASTS   Film - TV
AFFILIATIONS   CSA

Mark Tillman . . . . .Casting Director

TODD/CAMPOBASSO CASTING
c/o Casting Society of America
606 N. Larchmont Blvd., Ste. 4B
Los Angeles, CA 90004
PHONE 818-503-2474
CASTS   Film - TV
AFFILIATIONS   CSA
CREDITS   Redline - Pizza With Bullets - Badland -
                        Treasure Raiders - Scenes from a Mall -
                        Someone to Watch Over Me - Demolition
                        Man - Maria's Lovers - Lock Up - Brain
                        Scan - Sky Captain and the World of
                        Tomorrow - Gods & Generals - Firetrap -
                        Tremors 3 - Moscow Heat - Forbidden
                        Warrior - Slammed - Forget About It -
                        Picket Fences - Prince of the City - Garbo
                        Talks - The Verdict - Prancer - Once Upon
                        a Time in America - Q&A - Moscow on the
                        Hudson - Gettysburg - The Godson - The
                        Silence of the Hams
COMMENTS   Teaches on-camera workshops; Also affili-
                        ated with TV Academy

Craig Campobasso . . . . .Casting Director
Joy Todd . . . . .Casting Director
Igor DeLaurentiis . . . . .Assistant
Debi Parker . . . . .Assistant

CINDY TOLAN CASTING
609 Greenwich St., Ste. 401A
New York, NY 10014
PHONE 212-430-5094
CASTS   Film
AFFILIATIONS   CSA
CREDITS   Kinsey - The Ballad of Jack and Rose -
                        Some Kind of Heaven

Cindy Tolan . . . . .Casting Director

TOTAL CASTING
816 de la Gauchetiere E.
Montreal, PQ H2L 2N2, Canada
PHONE 514-940-0514/514-845-4421
FAX 514-879-0777
EMAIL . . . . .totalcasting@canadafilm.com
SECOND EMAIL .info@totalcasting.ca
WEB SITE . . . . .www.totalcasting.ca
SECOND WEB SITE . . . . .www.agilesound.com
CASTS   Film - TV - Commercials - Voice-Over -
                        Theatre - Industrials

Helene Rousse . . . . .Casting Director
Tom Stone . . . . .Casting Assistant
Jasmine White-Gluz . . . . .Casting Assistant
Eric Webb . . . . .Marketing & Promotion

TRIBECA CASTING
451 Greenwich St., Ste. 500
New York, NY 10013
PHONE 212-966-6000
FAX 212-219-7510
WEB SITE . . . . .www.tribecacasting.com
CASTS   Film
CREDITS   See website for credits

Kerry Barden . . . . .Casting Director
Billy Hopkins . . . . .Casting Director
Paul Schnee . . . . .Casting Director
Suzanne Smith . . . . .Casting Director
Jessica Kelly . . . . .Casting Assistant

TRIBUTE PRODUCTIONS
4924 Balboa Blvd., Ste. 439
Encino, CA 91316
PHONE 818-903-7158
EMAIL . . . . .madonnadouble@hotmail.com
SECOND EMAIL . . . . .tributeproductions@earthlink.net
WEB SITE . . . . .www.tributeproductions.com
CASTS   Film - TV - Commercials - Voice-Over -
                         Theatre - Industrials
COMMENTS   Casts celebrity look-alikes, bands and
                         singers

Denise Bella-Vlasis . . . . .Casting Director

TRIPLE THREAT CASTING
11684 Ventura Blvd., Ste. 117
Studio City, CA 91604
PHONE 818-415-7450
EMAIL . . . . .tripletcasting@earthlink.net
CASTS   TV - Commercials
COMMENTS   Music Videos, Live Events, Reality TV

Susan Salgado . . . . .Casting Director

JULIE TUCKER CASTING
568 Broadway, Ste. 301
New York, NY 10012
PHONE 212-334-1167
CASTS   TV
AFFILIATIONS   CSA
CREDITS   Rescue Me - The Book of Daniel - Dexter -
                         Love Monkey - The Dresden Files - Law &
                         Order: SVU (Seasons 1 - 4) - Fort Pit (Pilot)
                         - Six Feet Under

Julie Tucker . . . . .Casting Director
Ross Meyerson . . . . .Casting Director
Kyle Crand . . . . .Casting Assistant

TWENTIETH CENTURY FOX FEATURE CASTING
10201 W. Pico Blvd., Bldg. 12, Rm. 201
Los Angeles, CA 90035
PHONE 310-369-1824
FAX 310-369-1496
CASTS   Film - Voice-Over
AFFILIATIONS   CSA
COMMENTS   Also casts for TCF, Fox 2000, Fox
                         Searchlight, Fox Animation and Fox Atomic

Donna Isaacson . . . . . . .Executive VP, Feature Casting (310-369-1824)
Christian Kaplan . . . . .Sr. VP, Feature Casting (310-369-1883)
Brehan Fitzgerald . . . . .Director, Feature Casting (310-369-5335)
Beth Hollywood . . . . .Casting Associate (310-369-5348)
Kate Horton .Casting Assistant

TWENTIETH CENTURY FOX TELEVISION CASTING
10201 W. Pico Blvd., Bldg. 103, Rm. 5118
Los Angeles, CA 90035
PHONE 310-369-2121
CASTS   TV

Sharon Klein . . . . .Sr. VP, Talent Casting
Geraldine Leder . . . . .VP, Comedy Casting
Alana Kleiman . . . . .Director, Casting
Julie Wilson . . . . .Manager, Casting

SUSAN TYLER CASTING
c/o On Your Mark Studios
13425 Ventura Blvd.
Sherman Oaks, CA 91423
PHONE 818-506-0400/310-482-6500
WEB SITE . . . . .www.tylercasting.com
CASTS   Film - TV - Commercials - Voice-Over -
                         Theatre - Industrials
AFFILIATIONS   CCDA
CREDITS   ABC Promos - Drug Free America PSA
                         (ABC) - The Stunt Man (Feature)
COMMENTS   Over 750 commercials

Susan Tyler . . . . .Casting Director
Sophia Ready . . . . .Casting Director

ULRICH/DAWSON/KRITZER CASTING
4705 Laurel Canyon Blvd., Ste. 301
Valley Village, CA 91607
PHONE 818-623-1818
CASTS   Film - TV
AFFILIATIONS   CSA
CREDITS   Mary Sunshine (Pilot) - Grace (Pilot) - Eli
                         Stone (Pilot) - Him & Us - Ops - Nip/Tuck -
                         Jack & Bobby - Eyes - The Inside (Pilot) -
                         Global Frequency (Pilot) - Missing - The
                         Dead Zone - Everwood - CSI -
                         Inconceivable - Killer Instinct - Wildfire -
                         Just Legal - Battlestar Gallactica -
                         Supernatural - I Know What You Did Last
                         Summer 3

Robert J. Ulrich . . . . .Casting Director
Eric Dawson . . . . .Casting Director
Carol Kritzer . . . . .Casting Director
Shawn Dawson . . . . .Casting Director
Liz Dean . . . . .Casting Director
Andy Henry . . . . .Associate
Alex Newman . . . . .Associate
Garrett McGuire . . . . .Associate
Sibby Kirchgessner . . . . .Associate
Hannah Cooper . . . . .Associate
Suzanne Myers . . . . .Assistant
Eric 'Stephen' Soulvere . . . . .Assistant

UNIVERSAL CASTING, LLC
1111 Lincoln Rd., Ste. 750
Miami Beach, FL 33139
PHONE 305-674-1703
FAX 305-674-1704
EMAIL . . . . .ginger@universalcast.com
SECOND EMAIL . . . . .eva@universalcast.com
WEB SITE . . . . .www.universalcast.com
CASTS   Film - TV - Commercials - Voice-Over -
                         Industrials

Carlos Rojas . . . . .Casting Director/Partner
Eva Edlund-Borges . . . . .Casting Coordinator/Partner
Ginger Wortley . . . . .Casting Coordinator/Partner

UNIVERSAL STUDIOS FEATURE FILM CASTING
100 Universal City Plaza, Bldg. 2160, Ste. 8A
Universal City, CA 91608
PHONE 818-777-8327
FAX 818-866-1403
CASTS   Film
AFFILIATIONS   CSA
CREDITS   Miami Vice - American Gangster - The
                         Break-Up - Evan Almighty - Knocked Up -
                         Charlie Wilson's War - The Bourne
                         Ultimatum

Julie Hutchinson . . . . .Sr. VP, Feature Casting
Jeffrey Gelber . . . . .Manager, Feature Casting
Nina Storm . . . . .Coordinator, Feature Casting
Damien McKay . . . . .Casting Assistant

VALKO/MILLER CASTING
12003 Guerin St.
Studio City, CA 91604
PHONE 818-754-5414
CASTS   TV
AFFILIATIONS   CSA
CREDITS   Ally McBeal - The Brotherhood of Poland,
                         N.H. - Boston Public - Two and a Half Men
                         - Joey - Boston Legal

Ken Miller . . . . .Casting Director
Nikki Valko . . . . .Casting Director
Peter Pappas . . . . .Casting Associate
Traci Moscowitz . . . . .Casting Assistant
Tara Treacy . . . . .Casting Assistant

VIDEOACTIVE TALENT
1780 Broadway, Ste. 804
New York, NY 10019
PHONE 212-541-8106
EMAIL . . . . .vworks@aol.com
WEB SITE .www.videoactiveprod.com
SECOND WEB SITE . . . . .www.joefranklin.com
CASTS   Film - TV - Commercials
CREDITS   Big Apple - Committed - Shoe Store
                         Romeo - Behind the Scenes: George
                         Benson's Absolute Benson - Behind the
                         Scenes: Diana Krall with the London
                         Symphony Orchestra at Abbey Road
                         Studios
SUBMISSION POLICY   Mail only; No phone calls or visits; No
                         children
COMMENTS   Casts for independent films, radio;
                         Produces interviews for Joe Franklin, WBBR
                         Radio

Steve Garrin . . . . .President
Emily DeGrasse . . . . .Casting Director
Louise Moore . . . . .Casting Director

THE VOICECASTER
1832 W. Burbank Blvd.
Burbank, CA 91506
PHONE 818-841-5300
FAX 818-841-2085
EMAIL . . . . .casting@voicecaster.com
WEB SITE . . . . .www.voicecaster.com
CASTS   TV - Commercials - Voice-Over -
                         Industrials

Huck Liggett . . . . .Owner/Casting Director
Martha Mayakis . . . . .Casting Director
Gary Giambo . . . . .Booth Director

VOICETRAX CASTING
1207D Bridgeway
Sausalito, CA 94965
PHONE 415-331-7267
FAX 415-331-8857
EMAIL . . . . .voicetrax@voiceover-training.com
WEB SITE . . . . .www.voiceover-training.com
CASTS   Voice-Over

Sirenetta Leoni . . . . .Casting

DEBE WAISMAN CASTING
11684 Ventura Blvd., PMB 415
Studio City, CA 91604
PHONE . . . . .818-752-7052/310-535-1325 (Extras Info)
FAX 818-752-7054
CASTS   Film - TV - Commercials - Industrials
COMMENTS   Music videos, TV pilots, print; Focus on
                         extras

Debe Waisman . . . . .Casting Director

DAVA WAITE CASTING
c/o Casting Society of America
606 N. Larchmont Blvd., Ste. 4B
Los Angeles, CA 90004
PHONE 323-463-1925/323-956-2407
CASTS   TV
AFFILIATIONS   CSA
CREDITS   My Name Is Earl - Yes, Dear

Dava Waite-Peaslee . . . . .Casting Director

ALEX WALD
c/o Casting Society of America
606 N. Larchmont Blvd., Ste. 4B
Los Angeles, CA 90004
PHONE 323-363-1147
CASTS   Film - TV
AFFILIATIONS   CSA
CREDITS   One Tree Hill

Alex Wald . . . . .Casting Director

WARNER BROS. FEATURE FILM CASTING
4000 Warner Blvd., Bldg. 103, Rm. 4
Burbank, CA 91522
PHONE 818-954-6000
CASTS   Film

Lora Kennedy .Sr. VP, Feature Casting
Kristy Carlson . . . . .VP, Feature Casting
Arlene Kiyabu .Casting Associate
Jennifer Weinstein . . . . .Casting Assistant

WARNER BROS. TELEVISION CASTING
300 Television Plaza, Bldg. 140, 1st Fl.
Burbank, CA 91522
PHONE 818-954-6000/212-636-5145
CASTS   TV
AFFILIATIONS   CSA

Mary V. Buck . . . . .Sr. VP, Casting
Tony Sepulveda . . . . .Sr. VP, Casting
Meg Simon . . . . .VP, Casting (NY)
Tony Birkley . . . . .Director, Casting
Teri Fiddleman .Director, Casting
John Power . . . . .Director, Casting
Adrienne Belai . . . . .Assistant to Meg Simon (NY)
Michael Curran . . . . .Assistant to Tony Sepulveda
Lauren Dieter . . . . .Assistant to John Power
Agnes Kim . . . . .Assistant to Tony Birkley & Teri Fiddleman
Richard Parkinson . . . . .Assistant to Mary V. Buck

WEBER & ASSOCIATES CASTING
10250 Constellation Blvd., Ste. 2060
Los Angeles, CA 90067
PHONE 310-449-3685
FAX 310-449-8749
CASTS   Film - TV
AFFILIATIONS   CSA
CREDITS   Minor Accomplishments - Jeremiah - The
                        Outer Limits - Dead Like Me - Stargate
                        Atlantis - Stargate SG-1 - She Spies
SUBMISSION POLICY No unsolicited phone calls

Paul Weber . . . . .Head Casting Director, TV

APRIL WEBSTER & ASSOCIATES
800 S. Main St., Ste. 309
Burbank, CA 91506
PHONE 818-526-4242
CASTS   Film - TV
AFFILIATIONS   CSA
CREDITS   Alias - Lost

April Webster CSA .Casting Director
Veronica C. Rooney . . . . .Casting Director
Scott David . . . . .Casting Director
Mandy Sherman .Casting Director
Gina Garcia . . . . .Casting Associate
Bonita Deneen . . . . .Casting Assistant

ROSEMARY WELDEN
c/o Casting Society of America
606 N. Larchmont Blvd., Ste. 4B
Los Angeles, CA 90004
PHONE 323-463-1925
CASTS   Film
AFFILIATIONS   CSA

Rosemary Welden .Casting Director

JOHN WELLS PRODUCTIONS
c/o Warner Bros. Studios
4000 Warner Blvd., Bldg. 1
Burbank, CA 91522-0001
PHONE 818-954-4080
CASTS   TV
AFFILIATIONS   CSA

John Levey . . . . .Sr. VP, Casting
Melanie Burgess . . . . .Associate to John Levey

KATHY WICKLINE CASTING
1080 N. Delaware Ave., Ste. 700
Philadelphia, PA 19125
PHONE 215-739-9952
FAX 215-634-6454
EMAIL .info@wicklinecasting.com
WEB SITE . . . . .www.wicklinecasting.com
CASTS   Film - TV - Commercials - Voice-Over -
                        Industrials
COMMENTS   Special events

Kathy Wickline . . . . .Casting Director
Ann Gillette . . . . .Casting Manager

GRANT WILFLEY CASTING
123 W. 18th St., 8th Fl.
New York, NY 10011
PHONE 212-685-3537
WEB SITE . . . . .www.grantwilfleycasting.com
CASTS   Film - TV - Commercials
CREDITS   Spider-Man - Eternal Sunshine of the
                        Spotless Mind - The Pink Panther - The
                        Manchurian Candidate - The Stepford
                        Wives - Law & Order - Law & Order: SVU -
                        Law & Order: CI - Third Watch - The
                        Sopranos

Grant Wilfley . . . . .Owner
Melissa Braun . . . . .Casting Director
Todd Feldman . . . . .Casting Director
Heather Reidenbach . . . . .Casting Director
Sabel . . . . .Casting Director
Dave Waldron . . . . .Casting Director

CATHERINE WILSHIRE CASTING
11684 Ventura Blvd., Ste. 118
Studio City, CA 91604
PHONE 818-623-9200/818-343-2670
FAX 818-623-0900
EMAIL . . . . .wilshirecasting@aol.com
SECOND EMAIL . . . . .zipang@aol.com
CASTS   Film - TV - Commercials
CREDITS   Film: Grave Digger - Goi - The Grove -
                    Blind Ambition - Drive-By Chronicles L.A. -
                    Devil's Knight - Island Fever - Confessions
                    of a Pit Fighter - Chinaman's Chance; TV:
                    The Eye of Dan - Unfabulous
                    (Nickelodeon) - Power Rangers (FoxTV) -
                    Wild Force (FoxTV) - Lightspeed Rescuers
                    (FoxTV) - Time Force (FoxTV) - Ned's
                    Declassified School Survival Guide
                    (Nickelodeon)
SUBMISSION POLICY   Accepts photos/resumés by mail only;
                    Interviews by appointment only; Attends
                    showcases

Catherine Wilshire . . . . .Casting Director

JASON WOOD CASTING
8205 Santa Monica Blvd.
Los Angeles, CA 90046
PHONE 323-969-9588
CASTS   Film - TV - Theatre
CREDITS   Quinceañera - Painkiller Jane - Martha
                    Behind Bars - Monk - V.I.P. - Oleanna

Jason Wood . . . . .Casting Director
Janet Markman . . . . .Associate

LIZ WOODMAN CASTING
245 W. 107th St., Ste. 8F
New York, NY 10025
PHONE 212-787-3782
CASTS   Theatre
AFFILIATIONS   CSA
CREDITS   The Full Monty - Westport County
                    Playhouse - Ford's Theatre
SUBMISSION POLICY   By agents only

Liz Woodman . . . . .Casting Director

WORLD CASTING
216 Crown St., 5th Fl.
New Haven, CT 06510
PHONE 203-781-3427
FAX 203-781-3429
CASTS   Commercials - Industrials
SUBMISSION POLICY   No unsolicited tapes of any kind

Charles Esposito . . . . .Casting Director

GERRIE WORMSER CASTING
468 S. Roxbury Dr., Apt. 104
Beverly Hills, CA 90212
PHONE 310-277-3281
COMMENTS   WIF; Talent consultant

Gerrie Wormser . . . . .Casting Director

BARBARA WRIGHT
c/o Casting Society of America
606 N. Larchmont Blvd., Ste. 4B
Los Angeles, CA 90004
PHONE 323-463-1925/818-783-6305
CASTS   Film - TV
AFFILIATIONS   CSA
CREDITS   The Wild Thornberrys Movie - Rugrats

Barbara Wright . . . . .Casting Director

RONNIE YESKEL & ASSOCIATES
c/o Casting Society of America
606 N. Larchmont Blvd., Ste. 4B
Los Angeles, CA 90004
PHONE 310-396-8004
CASTS   Film - TV
AFFILIATIONS   CSA
CREDITS   Threshold - Blade: Trinity - Igby Goes
                    Down - Curb Your Enthusiasm

Ronnie Yeskel . . . . .Casting Director

RHONDA YOUNG
c/o Casting Society of America
606 N. Larchmont Blvd., Ste. 4B
Los Angeles, CA 90004
PHONE 323-463-1925
AFFILIATIONS   CSA

Rhonda Young . . . . .Casting Director

DEBRA ZANE CASTING
9696 Culver Blvd., Ste. 110
Culver City, CA 90232
PHONE 310-558-0400
CASTS   Film
AFFILIATIONS   CSA
CREDITS   Ocean's Thirteen - Things We Lost in the
                    Fire - Dreamgirls - The Good German -
                    Fun with Dick and Jane - Jarhead - War of
                    the Worlds - Kingdom of Heaven - Ocean's
                    Twelve - The Terminal - Matchstick Men -
                    Seabiscuit - Catch Me If You Can - Solaris
                    - Full Frontal - Road to Perdition -
                    Dragonfly - Ocean's Eleven

Debra Zane . . . . .Casting Director
Tannis Vallely . . . . .Casting Associate

ZANE/PILLSBURY CASTING
585 N. Larchmont Blvd.
Los Angeles, CA 90004
PHONE 323-769-9191
CASTS   TV
AFFILIATIONS   CSA
CREDITS   The George Lopez Show - In Justice -
                    Rodney - According to Jim

Bonnie Zane . . . . .Casting Director
Gayle Pillsbury . . . . .Casting Director
Stacey Levy . . . . .Associate
Carissa Chapman . . . . .Associate

GARY ZUCKERBROD
6767 Forest Lawn Dr., Ste. 206
Los Angeles, CA 90068
PHONE 818-977-4281
CASTS   TV
AFFILIATIONS   CSA
CREDITS   Without a Trace

Gary Zuckerbrod . . . . .Casting Director
Lonnie Hammerman . . . . .Casting Associate
Becky Silverman . . . . .Casting Assistant

SECTION **F**

INDEX BY TYPE

AGENTS

Below-the-Line Talent

A...List Artists
Abrams Artists Agency (New York)
Alexa Model & Talent Management, Inc.
All Crew Agency
Doug Apatow Agency
Below The Line Artists
Boom Models & Talent
Suzanna Camejo & Associates: Artists for the Environment
Carmichael Talent
The Carson Organization, Ltd.
Casala, Ltd.
Celestine Agency
The Characters
Stacy Cheriff Agency
Clear Talent Group
The Coppage Company
The Criterion Group, Inc.
Crystal Agency
Dattner Dispoto and Associates
Digital Artists Agency (DAA)
Diverse Talent Group
Elegance Talent Agency
Esq. Management
Fosi's Modeling & Talent Agency
The Gatsby Group, Inc.
The Geller Agency
Paul Gerard Agency
The Gersh Agency (Los Angeles)
The Gersh Agency (New York)
Grant, Savic, Kopaloff and Associates
Hanns Wolters International, Inc.
Hollywood View
Hop Models & Talent Agency
Innovative Artists (Los Angeles)
International Creative Mgmt., Inc. - ICM (LA)
Jacob & Kole Agency
Lane Agency
Lemodeln Model & Talent Agency
Lenhoff & Lenhoff
Michael Lewis & Associates
M International Talent Agency
The Mack Agency
Margaret Maldonado Agency
Judy Marks Agency
Sandra Marsh Management
McDonald/Selznick Associates
The Mirisch Agency
Montana Artists Agency, Inc.
New York Office
Nicolosi & Co., Inc.
Ofrenda, Inc.
Oracle Creative Management
Orlando Management
Osbrink Talent Agency
Paradigm (Los Angeles)
The Partos Company
Peters Fraser & Dunlop (PFD)
Prime Artists
The Rappaport Agency
Michael D. Robins & Associates
Jack Scagnetti Talent & Literary Agency
The Irv Schechter Company
The Schneider Entertainment Agency
Screen Artists Agency, LLC
Sesler & Company
Shapiro-Lichtman Talent Agency, Inc.
Sheldon Prosnit Agency
The Skouras Agency
Crayton Smith Agency
The Stein Agency
Talent House Agency
Talent Trek Agency
Russell Todd Agency (RTA)
United Talent Agency - UTA
Uptown Talent, Inc.
Zenobia Agency, Inc.

Commercial Talent

ABA - Amatruda Benson & Associates
abc model/talent/sport management
About Artists Agency
Abrams Artists Agency (Los Angeles)
Abrams Artists Agency (New York)
Access Talent
Acme Talent & Literary
Actors & Others Talent Agency
Actors Etc., Inc.
Actors LA Agency
Advance LA
Affinity Model & Talent Agency
Aimée Entertainment Agency
AKA Talent Agency
Alexa Model & Talent Management, Inc.
The Alvarado Rey Agency
Michael Amato Agency
Ambassador Talent Agents, Inc.
Ambition Talent Inc.
Amsel, Eisenstadt & Frazier, Inc.
Andreadis Talent Agency, Inc.
Angel City Talent
Aqua
Arcieri & Associates, Inc.
ARIA Talent
Artist Management Agency
Artists Agency, Inc.
Associated Booking Corporation (ABC)
Atlanta Models & Talent, Inc.
Atlas Talent Agency
The Austin Agency
Donna Baldwin Talent
Baldwin Talent, Inc.
Baron Entertainment
Baskow & Associates, Inc.
Beauty Models/BC4
The Sandi Bell Talent Agency, Inc.
Berzon Talent Agency
The Bethel Agency
Beverly Hills International Talent Agency
Bicoastal Talent
Bonnie Black Talent & Literary Agency
The Blake Agency
bloc talent agency, inc.
Bobby Ball Talent Agency
Boca Talent & Model Agency
Boom Models & Talent
Brady, Brannon & Rich
Brand Model and Talent Agency, Inc.
Brass Artists & Associates
Brevard Talent Group, Inc.
BRick Entertainment
The Brogan Agency
Don Buchwald & Associates, Inc. (Los Angeles)
Don Buchwald & Associates, Inc. (New York)
Buchwald Talent Group, LLC
The Burns Agency, Inc.
Calliope Talent, Model & Artist Management, LLC
Suzanna Camejo & Associates: Artists for the Environment
The Campbell Agency
Carmichael Talent
Conan Carroll & Associates
The Carry Co.
The Carson Organization, Ltd.
Carson-Adler Agency, Inc.
Cassell-Levy, Inc. (dba Clinc)
Cast Images Talent Agency
Castle Hill Talent Agency
Cavaleri & Associates
Nancy Chaidez Agency & Associates
The Characters
Charles Talent Agency
Chateau Billings Talent Agency
Stacy Cheriff Agency
Chic Models & Talent Agency
The Christensen Group

Commercial Talent (Continued)

Ciao! Talent Agency
Circle Talent Associates
Mary Anne Claro Talent Agency, Inc.
Clear Talent Group
Colleen Cler Talent Agency
Coast To Coast Talent Group, Inc.
Commercial Talent, Inc.
The Coppage Company
Coralie Jr. Theatrical Agency
Corsa Agency
The Culbertson Group, LLC
Cunningham-Escott-Slevin-Doherty Talent (LA)
Cunningham-Escott-Slevin-Doherty Talent (NY)
Kim Dawson Talent
DDO Artists Agency
Marla Dell Talent Agency
DeSanti Talents, Inc.
Ginger Dicce Talent Agency
Dimensions III Talent Agency
Diverse Talent Group
EC Model & Talent Agency (Ent. Caterers, Inc.)
Edna Talent Management (ETM) Ltd.
Electric Talent
Elegance Talent Agency
Empire Talent Agency
Encore Talent Agency
Equinox Models/Equinox Talent/Zoo Models
Expressions Model & Talent
Sylvia Ferguson & Assoc. Talent & Literary Agency
JFA/Jaime Ferrar Agency
Film Artists Associates
Flick East-West Talents, Inc.
FORD/Robert Black Agency
Fosi's Modeling & Talent Agency
Frontier Booking International, Inc.
FRP Literary - Talent Agency
The Gage Group, Inc. (Los Angeles)
The Gage Group, Inc. (New York)
Gage Talent, Inc.
Garber Talent Agency
Dale Garrick International Agency
The Gatsby Group, Inc.
The Geddes Agency (Chicago)
Generation TV
Generations Model & Talent Agency
The Gersh Agency (Los Angeles)
The Gersh Agency (New York)
Gilla Roos, Ltd.
Michelle Gordon & Associates
Greene & Associates
Greer Lange Model & Talent Agency, Inc.
Grossman & Jack Talent
Gwyn Foxx Talent Agency (GFTA)
Neal Hamil Agency
Hanns Wolters International, Inc.
Harmony Artists
Hays Media LLC
Beverly Hecht Agency
Henderson/Hogan Agency
Hervey/Grimes Talent Agency
Daniel Hoff Agency
Hollander Talent Group
Hop Models & Talent Agency
Hot Shot Kids/Teens
Howard Talent West
The I Group Model & Talent Management
Identity Talent Agency
Image Model & Talent
IMG Models
IMG/Broadcasting
Imperium 7 Talent Agency (i7)
Independent Artists Agency, Inc.
Ingber & Associates
Innovative Artists (Chicago)
Innovative Artists (Los Angeles)
Innovative Artists (New York)
International Artists Group, Inc.

AGENTS

Commercial Talent (Continued)

International Creative Mgmt., Inc. - ICM (LA)
International Creative Mgmt., Inc. - ICM (NY)
IRISHVOX
JE Talent, LLC/JE Model, Inc.
Jet Set Management Group, Inc.
JLA Talent
Jordan, Gill & Dornbaum
JS Represents
Stanley Kaplan Talent
Kazarian/Spencer & Associates
Glyn Kennedy, Models Talent
William Kerwin Agency
Kolstein Talent Agency (KTA)
The Krasny Office, Inc.
L.A. Talent
Al Lampkin Entertainment, Inc.
Lane Agency
Le Paws
Buddy Lee Attractions, Inc.
Leighton Agency, Inc.
Lemodeln Model & Talent Agency
Lenz Agency
Sid Levin Agency
Lily's Talent Agency, Inc.
Look Talent
Jana Luker Agency
M International Talent Agency
Mademoiselle Talent & Modeling Agency
Malaky International
The Mannequin Agency
Sandra Marsh Management
Martin & Donalds Talent Agency, Inc.
McCarty Talent, Inc.
McDonald/Selznick Associates
Media Artists Group
Metropolitan Talent Agency (MTA)
MGATalent
The Gilbert Miller Agency LLC
Miramar Talent Agency
The Mirisch Agency
Model Club, Inc.
Model Team
Momentum Talent & Literary Agency
The Morgan Agency
H. David Moss & Associates
N.S. Bienstock, Inc.
Nash-Angeles, Inc.
Susan Nathe & Associates, CPC
New York Office
Nouveau Model & Talent
Nouvelle Talent Management, Inc.
NTA Talent Agency
Nu Talent Agency
NXT Entertainment, Inc.
Omnipop Talent Group
O'Neill Talent Group
Oracle Creative Management
Origin Talent
Osbrink Talent Agency
Fifi Oscard Agency, Inc.
Pacific West Artists
Dorothy Palmer Talent Agency, Inc.
Paradigm (New York)
The Paradise Group Talent Agency
Pastorini-Bosby Talent, Inc.
Peak Models & Talent
Perfectly Petite, Inc.
Periwinkle Entertainment Productions
Pinnacle Commercial Talent
Players Talent Agency
Privilege Talent Agency
PTI Talent Agency, Inc.
Q Model Management
Qualita Dell' Arte: Artists & Writers Di Qualita
Cindy Romano Modeling & Talent Agency
San Diego Model Management Talent Agency
San Francisco Top Models & Talent

Commercial Talent (Continued)

Sanger Talent Agency
The Savage Agency
Jack Scagnetti Talent & Literary Agency
Sandie Schnarr Talent
Schuller Talent/NY Kids
Screen Artists Agency, LLC
The Screen Talent Agency, Ltd.
SGM - Sara Gaynor Management
Shamon Freitas Model & Talent Agency
Sheldon Prosnit Agency
The Skouras Agency
Sky Talent Agency
The Sohl Agency
Solid Talent, Inc.
Sonja Warren Brandon's Commercials Unlimited
Special Artists Agency
Scott Stander & Associates, Inc.
Starcraft Talent Agency
Stars, The Agency
Starwil Talent
Ann Steele Agency
Steinberg's Talent Agency
Stellar Model & Talent Agency
The Stevens Group
Stewart Talent
Ivett Stone Agency
Mitchell K. Stubbs & Associates
Superior Talent Agency
Sutton, Barth & Vennari, Inc.
Tag Models
Talent & Model Land
The Talent Group
Talent Plus, Inc./Centro Models
Talent Plus/Los Latinos Talent Agency
The Talent Shop
Talent Trek Agency
Talent Unlimited, Inc.
TalentWorks
TalentWorks New York
TDN Artists (The Director's Network)
TGMD Talent Agency
The Thomas Talent Agency
Arlene Thornton & Associates
Tilmar Talent Agency
Tonry Talent
Turner Artist Management
United Talent Agency - UTA
Universal Talent Intelligence
Uptown Talent, Inc.
Vision Los Angeles
Vox, Inc.
The Wallis Agency
The Ann Waugh Talent Agency
Donna Wauhob Agency
Waving Clouds Productions
Wilhelmina West, Inc./LW1 Talent Agency
William Morris Agency - WMA (Los Angeles)
William Morris Agency - WMA (New York)
William Morris Agency - WMA (Miami Beach)
William Morris Agency - WMA (London)
William Morris Agency - WMA (Shanghai)
Shirley Wilson & Associates
World Class Sports
Ann Wright Representatives
Craig Wyckoff & Associates
Zanuck, Passon and Pace, Inc.

Film/TV Talent

ABA - Amatruda Benson & Associates
abc model/talent/sport management
About Artists Agency
Abrams Artists Agency (Los Angeles)
Abrams Artists Agency (New York)
Acme Talent & Literary
Actors & Others Talent Agency
Actors Etc., Inc.
Bret Adams, Ltd.

Film/TV Talent (Continued)

Advance LA
Affinity Model & Talent Agency
Agape Productions
Agency For the Performing Arts, Inc. (Los Angeles)
Agents For The Arts, Inc.
Aimée Entertainment Agency
AKA Talent Agency
Alexa Model & Talent Management, Inc.
The Alvarado Rey Agency
Michael Amato Agency
Ambassador Talent Agents, Inc.
Ambition Talent Inc.
American Program Bureau
Amsel, Eisenstadt & Frazier, Inc.
Beverly Anderson Agency
Andreadis Talent Agency, Inc.
Angel City Talent
Aqua
ARIA Talent
Artist Management Agency
Artists Agency, Inc.
The Artists Agency
The Artists Group, Ltd.
Associated Booking Corporation (ABC)
Atlanta Models & Talent, Inc.
The Austin Agency
Baier/Kleinman International
Donna Baldwin Talent
Baron Entertainment
Barry Haft Brown Artists Agency
Baskow & Associates, Inc.
Marc Bass Agency, Inc. (MBA)
Bauman, Redanty, & Shaul Agency
The Sandi Bell Talent Agency, Inc.
Berzon Talent Agency
The Bethel Agency
Beverly Hills International Talent Agency
Bicoastal Talent
Bonnie Black Talent & Literary Agency
The Blake Agency
bloc talent agency, inc.
Blue Ridge Entertainment
Judy Boals, Inc.
Bobby Ball Talent Agency
Boca Talent & Model Agency
The Bohrman Agency
Boom Models & Talent
Boutique
Brass Artists & Associates
Bresler Kelly & Associates
Brevard Talent Group, Inc.
BRick Entertainment
The Brogan Agency
Don Buchwald & Associates, Inc. (Los Angeles)
Don Buchwald & Associates, Inc. (New York)
Buchwald Talent Group, LLC
The Burns Agency, Inc.
Calliope Talent, Model & Artist Management, LLC
Suzanna Camejo & Associates: Artists for the
   Environment
The Campbell Agency
Carmichael Talent
Conan Carroll & Associates
The Carry Co.
The Carson Organization, Ltd.
Carson-Adler Agency, Inc.
Cast Images Talent Agency
Castle Hill Talent Agency
Cavaleri & Associates
Nancy Chaidez Agency & Associates
The Characters
Charles Talent Agency
The Chasin Agency
Chateau Billings Talent Agency
The Christensen Group
Ciao! Talent Agency
Circle Talent Associates

AGENTS

Film/TV Talent (Continued)

Mary Anne Claro Talent Agency, Inc.
Clear Talent Group
Coast To Coast Talent Group, Inc.
Contemporary Artists, Ltd.
The Coppage Company
Coralie Jr. Theatrical Agency
Cornerstone Talent Agency
Corsa Agency
Creative Artists Agency - CAA
The Criterion Group, Inc.
The Crofoot Group, Inc.
Cunningham-Escott-Slevin-Doherty Talent (LA)
Cunningham-Escott-Slevin-Doherty Talent (NY)
Curtis Brown, Ltd.
Kim Dawson Talent
DDO Artists Agency
Defining Artists
DeSanti Talents, Inc.
Ginger Dicce Talent Agency
Dimensions III Talent Agency
Diverse Talent Group
Domain
Douglas, Gorman, Rothacker & Wilhelm, Inc.
EC Model & Talent Agency (Ent. Caterers, Inc.)
Edna Talent Management (ETM) Ltd.
Dulcina Eisen Associates
Electric Talent
Elegance Talent Agency
Ellis Talent Group
Encore Talent Agency
Endeavor Agency, LLC
Esq. Management
Expressions Model & Talent
Sylvia Ferguson & Assoc. Talent & Literary Agency
JFA/Jaime Ferrar Agency
Jim Flynn Agency
FORD/Robert Black Agency
Fosi's Modeling & Talent Agency
Fresh Faces Agency, Inc.
Frontier Booking International, Inc.
FRP Literary - Talent Agency
The Gage Group, Inc. (Los Angeles)
The Gage Group, Inc. (New York)
Garber Talent Agency
Dale Garrick International Agency
The Gatsby Group, Inc.
The Geddes Agency (Chicago)
The Geddes Agency (Los Angeles)
Laya Gelff Agency
Generation TV
Generations Model & Talent Agency
Don Gerler Agency
The Gersh Agency (Los Angeles)
The Gersh Agency (New York)
Gilla Roos, Ltd.
The Glick Agency, LLC
Global Artists Agency
Michelle Gordon & Associates
Grant, Savic, Kopaloff and Associates
Greene & Associates
Greer Lange Model & Talent Agency, Inc.
Grossman & Jack Talent
GVA Talent Agency, Inc.
Gwyn Foxx Talent Agency (GFTA)
Peggy Hadley Enterprises, Ltd.
Buzz Halliday & Associates
Halpern Management
Neal Hamil Agency
Hanns Wolters International, Inc.
Harden-Curtis Associates
Harmony Artists
Hartig Hilepo Agency, Ltd.
Beverly Hecht Agency
Henderson/Hogan Agency
Hervey/Grimes Talent Agency
Daniel Hoff Agency
Hollander Talent Group

Film/TV Talent (Continued)

Hop Models & Talent Agency
Hot Shot Kids/Teens
The House of Representatives
Howard Talent West
The I Group Model & Talent Management
Identity Talent Agency
IFA Talent Agency
Image Model & Talent
IMG/Broadcasting
Impact Talent Group
Imperium 7 Talent Agency (i7)
Independent Artists Agency Inc.
Innovative Artists (Los Angeles)
Innovative Artists (New York)
International Artists Group, Inc.
International Creative Mgmt., Inc. - ICM (LA)
International Creative Mgmt., Inc. - ICM (NY)
JE Talent, LLC/JE Model, Inc.
Jet Set Management Group, Inc.
JKA Talent & Literary Agency
JLA Talent
Jordan, Gill & Dornbaum
Merrily Kane Agency
Stanley Kaplan Talent
Kazarian/Spencer & Associates
Glyn Kennedy, Models Talent
Kerin-Goldberg & Associates
William Kerwin Agency
Archer King, Ltd.
Kjar & Associates
Paul Kohner, Inc.
Kolstein Talent Agency (KTA)
The Krasny Office, Inc.
L.A. Talent
Lally Talent Agency (LTA)
Al Lampkin Entertainment, Inc.
Lane Agency
Le Paws
Leading Artists, Inc.
Buddy Lee Attractions, Inc.
Leighton Agency, Inc.
Lemodeln Model & Talent Agency
Lenz Agency
Sid Levin Agency
Bernard Liebhaber Agency
Lily's Talent Agency, Inc.
Ken Lindner & Associates, Inc.
Look Talent
The Luedtke Agency
Jana Luker Agency
M International Talent Agency
Mademoiselle Talent & Modeling Agency
Malaky International
The Mannequin Agency
Sandra Marsh Management
Martin & Donalds Talent Agency, Inc.
Max Freedman Management
Maxine's Talent Agency
The McCabe Group
McCarty Talent, Inc.
McDonald/Selznick Associates
Media Artists Group
Metropolitan Talent Agency (MTA)
MGATalent
Miramar Talent Agency
The Mirisch Agency
Model Club, Inc.
Model Team
Momentum Talent & Literary Agency
The Morgan Agency
H. David Moss & Associates
N.S. Bienstock, Inc.
Napoli Management Group
Nash-Angeles, Inc.
Nicolosi & Co., Inc.
Nouveau Model & Talent
NXT Entertainment, Inc.

Film/TV Talent (Continued)

Omnipop Talent Group
One Entertainment
O'Neill Talent Group
The Orange Grove Group, Inc.
Origin Talent
Osbrink Talent Agency
Fifi Oscard Agency, Inc.
Pakula/King & Associates
Dorothy Palmer Talent Agency, Inc.
The Meg Pantera Agency, Inc.
Pantheon
Paradigm (Los Angeles)
Paradigm (New York)
Pastorini-Bosby Talent, Inc.
Peak Models & Talent
Perfectly Petite, Inc.
Periwinkle Entertainment Productions
Phoenix Artists, Inc.
John Pierce Agency
Players Talent Agency
The Price Group LLC
Privilege Talent Agency
Professional Artists
Progressive Artists Agency
Qualita Dell' Arte: Artists & Writers Di Qualita
Rebel Entertainment Partners, Inc.
RLR Associates
Michael D. Robins & Associates
Cindy Romano Modeling & Talent Agency
San Diego Model Management Talent Agency
San Francisco Top Models & Talent
The Sarnoff Company, Inc.
The Savage Agency
Jack Scagnetti Talent & Literary Agency
The Irv Schechter Company
Schiowitz Connor Ankrum Wolf, Inc.
Sandie Schnarr Talent
Judy Schoen & Associates
Schuller Talent/NY Kids
Kathleen Schultz Associates
Screen Artists Agency, LLC
The Screen Talent Agency, Ltd.
SDB Partners, Inc.
Shamon Freitas Model & Talent Agency
Shapiro-Lichtman Talent Agency, Inc.
Sheldon Prosnit Agency
Jerome Siegel Associates
The Skouras Agency
SMA, LLC
The Susan Smith Company
SMS Talent, Inc.
The Sohl Agency
Solid Talent, Inc.
Sonja Warren Brandon's Commercials Unlimited
Scott Stander & Associates, Inc.
Starcraft Talent Agency
Stars, The Agency
Starwil Talent
Ann Steele Agency
Steinberg's Talent Agency
Stellar Model & Talent Agency
The Stevens Group
Stewart Talent
Ivett Stone Agency
Stone Manners Agency
Peter Strain & Associates, Inc. (Los Angeles)
Peter Strain & Associates, Inc. (New York)
Mitchell K. Stubbs & Associates
Summit Comedy, Inc.
Summit Talent & Literary Agency
Superior Talent Agency
Talent & Model Land
The Talent Group
Talent House Agency
Talent Plus, Inc./Centro Models
Talent Plus/Los Latinos Talent Agency
Talent Representatives, Inc.

AGENTS

Film/TV Talent (Continued)

The Talent Shop
Talent Trek Agency
Talent Unlimited, Inc.
TalentWorks
TalentWorks New York
TGMD Talent Agency
The Thomas Talent Agency
Tonry Talent
United Talent Agency - UTA
Universal Talent Intelligence
Uptown Talent, Inc.
Annette van Duren Agency
Vox, Inc.
The Wallis Agency
Warden, White & Associates
Bob Waters Agency, Inc.
The Ann Waugh Talent Agency
Donna Wauhob Agency
Waving Clouds Productions
Wilhelmina West, Inc./LW1 Talent Agency
William Morris Agency - WMA (Los Angeles)
William Morris Agency - WMA (New York)
William Morris Agency - WMA (Nashville)
William Morris Agency - WMA (Miami Beach)
William Morris Agency - WMA (London)
William Morris Agency - WMA (Shanghai)
Shirley Wilson & Associates
Ann Wright Representatives
Craig Wyckoff & Associates
Zanuck, Passon and Pace, Inc.

Literary Talent

Carole Abel Literary
Above The Line Agency
Abrams Artists Agency (Los Angeles)
Abrams Artists Agency (New York)
Acme Talent & Literary
Bret Adams, Ltd.
Agape Productions
Agency For the Performing Arts, Inc. (Los Angeles)
The Agency Group Ltd. (Los Angeles)
The Agency Group Ltd. (New York)
Aimée Entertainment Agency
The Alpern Group
Miriam Altshuler Literary Agency
Michael Amato Agency
Ambassador Talent Agents, Inc.
Ambition Talent Inc.
American Program Bureau
Marcia Amsterdam Agency
Angel City Talent
Artists Agency, Inc.
The Artists Agency
Artists Literary Group (ALG)
Loretta Barrett Books, Inc.
Baskow & Associates, Inc.
Marc Bass Agency, Inc. (MBA)
Beacon Artists Agency
Meredith Bernstein Literary Agency
Berzon Talent Agency
The Bethel Agency
Beverly Hills International Talent Agency
Bicoastal Talent
Vicky Bijur Literary Agency
Bonnie Black Talent & Literary Agency
Judy Boals, Inc.
The Bohrman Agency
Georges Borchardt, Inc.
Boutique
Brands-To-Books, Inc.
Brandt & Hochman Literary Agents
Browne & Miller Literary Associates LLC
Marcus Bryan & Associates
Don Buchwald & Associates, Inc. (Los Angeles)
Don Buchwald & Associates, Inc. (New York)
Sheree Bykofsky Associates, Inc.
The Callamaro Literary Agency

Literary Talent (Continued)

Cambridge Literary Associates, Inc.
Suzanna Camejo & Associates: Artists for the Environment
Conan Carroll & Associates
Castiglia Literary Agency
Cavaleri & Associates
Cedar Grove Agency Entertainment
The Characters
The Chasin Agency
Wm. Clark Associates
Client First Agency
Frances Collin Literary Agent
Don Congdon Associates
Contemporary Artists, Ltd.
The Coppage Company
Coralie Jr. Theatrical Agency
Cornerstone Literary, Inc.
Creative Artists Agency - CAA
The Criterion Group, Inc.
Curtis Brown, Ltd.
D4EO Literary Agency
Deiter Literary Agency
Diverse Talent Group
Dunham Literary, Inc.
The E S Agency
The Nicholas Ellison Agency
Endeavor Agency, LLC
Esq. Management
Farber Literary Agency, Inc.
Sylvia Ferguson & Assoc. Talent & Literary Agency
Folio Literary Management, LLC
Robert A. Freedman Dramatic Agency, Inc.
FRP Literary - Talent Agency
The Gage Group, Inc. (Los Angeles)
Max Gartenberg Literary Agency
The Gary-Paul Agency
The Gatsby Group, Inc.
Laya Gelff Agency
Gelfman Schneider Literary Agents, Inc.
The Gersh Agency (Los Angeles)
The Gersh Agency (New York)
Geste, Inc.
The Glick Agency, LLC
Global Artists Agency
Michelle Gordon & Associates
Graham Agency
Grant, Savic, Kopaloff and Associates
Ashley Grayson Literary Agency
Sanford J. Greenburger Associates
Brad Gross Inc., Literary Management
The Susan Gurman Agency, LLC
The Charlotte Gusay Literary Agency
The Mitchell J. Hamilburg Agency
Hanns Wolters International, Inc.
Harden-Curtis Associates
The Joy Harris Literary Agency
Hart Literary Management
John Hawkins & Associates
Hays Media LLC
Henderson/Hogan Agency
Jeff Herman Agency, LLC
Susan Herner Rights Agency
Hohman Maybank Lieb
Hollywood View
Hotchkiss & Associates
Hudson Agency
InkWell Management
Innovative Artists (Los Angeles)
International Artists Group, Inc.
International Creative Mgmt., Inc. - ICM (LA)
International Creative Mgmt., Inc. - ICM (NY)
James Peter Associates, Inc.
Janklow & Nesbit Associates
JKA Talent & Literary Agency
Merrily Kane Agency
The Kaplan-Stahler-Gumer-Braun Agency
William Kerwin Agency

Literary Talent (Continued)

Archer King, Ltd.
Kjar & Associates
Harvey Klinger, Inc.
Kneerim & Williams at Fish & Richardson, PC
Paul Kohner, Inc.
Barbara S. Kouts
Otto R. Kozak Literary & Motion Picture Agency
Cary Kozlov Literary Representation
Kristine Krupp Talent Agency
The LA Literary Agency
Lally Talent Agency (LTA)
Peter Lampack Agency, Inc.
The Lantz Office
Larchmont Literary Agency
Susanna Lea Associates
Lemodeln Model & Talent Agency
Lenhoff & Lenhoff
Levine Greenberg Literary Agency
Paul S. Levine Literary Agency
Michael Lewis & Associates
Lily's Talent Agency, Inc.
Literary and Creative Artists, Inc. (LCA, Inc.)
The Literary Group
Nancy Love Literary Agency
The Luedtke Agency
Gina Maccoby Literary Agency
Manus & Associates Literary Agency, Inc.
Max Freedman Management
Maxine's Talent Agency
McCormick & Williams
Helen McGrath & Associates
McIntosh and Otis, Inc.
Media Artists Group
Mendel Media Group LLC
Menza-Barron Agency
Metropolis
Metropolitan Talent Agency (MTA)
The Doris S. Michaels Literary Agency, Inc.
The Stuart M. Miller Co.
Momentum Talent & Literary Agency
Monteiro Rose Dravis Agency, Inc.
Montgomery West Literary Agency, LLC
N.S. Bienstock, Inc.
Jean V. Naggar Literary Agency, Inc.
Nash-Angeles, Inc.
New England Publishing Associates
New York Office
Betsy Nolan Literary Agency
Harold Ober Associates
Ofrenda, Inc.
Omnipop Talent Group
One Entertainment
The Orange Grove Group, Inc.
Original Artists
Fifi Oscard Agency, Inc.
Dorothy Palmer Talent Agency, Inc.
Pantheon
Paradigm (Los Angeles)
Paradigm (New York)
Kathi J. Paton Literary Agency
Barry Perelman Agency
L. Perkins Agency
Peters Fraser & Dunlop (PFD)
Stephen Pevner, Inc.
Phoenix Artists, Inc.
Pinder Lane & Garon-Brooke Associates, Ltd.
The Lynn Pleshette Literary Agency
Preferred Artists
Jim Preminger Agency
The Aaron M. Priest Literary Agency
Professional Artists
Susan Ann Protter Literary Agent
Qualita Dell' Arte: Artists & Writers Di Qualita
Quillco Agency
The Rabineau Wachter Sanford & Harris Literary Agency
Raines & Raines

AGENTS

Literary Talent (Continued)

read.
Reece Halsey North
Jodie Rhodes Agency
Rights Unlimited
The Angela Rinaldi Literary Agency
Ann Rittenberg Literary Agency, Inc.
RLR Associates
Michael D. Robins & Associates
The Roistacher Literary Agency
The Brant Rose Agency
The Rosenberg Group
Rosenstone/Wender
The Rothman Brecher Agency
Jane Rotrosen Agency
Peter Rubie Literary Agency
Russell & Volkening
Victoria Sanders & Associates, LLC
Sanger Talent Agency
The Sarnoff Company, Inc.
Jack Scagnetti Talent & Literary Agency
The Irv Schechter Company
Schuller Talent/NY Kids
Susan Schulman Literary Agency
The Screen Talent Agency, Ltd.
Scribblers House LLC Literary Agency
David Shapira & Associates (DSA)
Shapiro-Lichtman Talent Agency, Inc.
Ken Sherman & Associates
Bobbe Siegel Literary Agency
Jerome Siegel Associates
SMA, LLC
The Susan Smith Company
Michael H. Sommer Literary Agency
Philip G. Spitzer Literary Agency, Inc.
Stars, The Agency
The Stein Agency
Joan Stewart Agency
Stewart Talent
Stone Canyon Media
Stone Manners Agency
Marianne Strong Literary Agency
Suite A Management Talent & Literary Agency
Summit Talent & Literary Agency
Mary M. Tahan Literary Agency, LLC
Talent Representatives, Inc.
Roslyn Targ Literary Agency
S©ott Treimel NY
Trident Media Group, LLC
United Talent Agency - UTA
Universal Talent Intelligence
Annette van Duren Agency
Veritas Literary Agency
Veritas Media, Inc.
The Vicious Trend Agency
Vision Art Management
Wales Literary Agency, Inc.
Warden McKinley Literary Agency
Warden, White & Associates
Wardlow & Associates
John A. Ware Literary Agency
Watkins/Loomis Agency Inc.
Donna Wauhob Agency
Irene Webb Literary
The Wendy Weil Agency, Inc.
Weingel-Fidel Agency
William Morris Agency - WMA (Los Angeles)
William Morris Agency - WMA (New York)
William Morris Agency - WMA (Miami Beach)
William Morris Agency - WMA (London)
William Morris Agency - WMA (Shanghai)
Working Artists
Ann Wright Representatives
Writers House
Writers' Representatives, LLC
Craig Wyckoff & Associates
The Wylie Agency
Nick Yellen Creative Agency
Zachary Shuster Harmsworth Agency

Modeling Talent

abc model/talent/sport management
Abrams Artists Agency (Los Angeles)
Abrams Artists Agency (New York)
Acme Talent & Literary
Advance LA
Affinity Model & Talent Agency
Aimée Entertainment Agency
Alexa Model & Talent Management, Inc.
The Alvarado Rey Agency
Michael Amato Agency
Ambassador Talent Agents, Inc.
Aqua
Arcieri & Associates, Inc.
ARIA Talent
Artist Management Agency
Atlanta Models & Talent, Inc.
Atlas Talent Agency
Donna Baldwin Talent
Baron Entertainment
Baskow & Associates, Inc.
Beauty Models/BC4
Berzon Talent Agency
Beverly Hills International Talent Agency
Bonnie Black Talent & Literary Agency
Bleu Model Management
Bobby Ball Talent Agency
Boca Talent & Model Agency
Boom Models & Talent
Brand Model and Talent Agency, Inc.
The Brogan Agency
Don Buchwald & Associates, Inc. (Los Angeles)
Don Buchwald & Associates, Inc. (New York)
Calliope Talent, Model & Artist Management, LLC
The Campbell Agency
The Carson Organization, Ltd.
Cast Images Talent Agency
Nancy Chaidez Agency & Associates
Chateau Billings Talent Agency
Chic Models & Talent Agency
The Christensen Group
Ciao! Talent Agency
Clear Talent Group
Colleen Cler Talent Agency
Coralie Jr. Theatrical Agency
Cunningham-Escott-Slevin-Doherty Talent (LA)
Cunningham-Escott-Slevin-Doherty Talent (NY)
Kim Dawson Talent
DDO Artists Agency
Marla Dell Talent Agency
DeSanti Talents, Inc.
Dimensions III Talent Agency
Doubble Troubble Entertainment, Inc.
EC Model & Talent Agency (Ent. Caterers, Inc.)
Electric Talent
Elegance Talent Agency
Elite Model Management
Empire Talent Agency
Encore Talent Agency
Equinox Models/Equinox Talent/Zoo Models
Expressions Model & Talent
Sylvia Ferguson & Associates Talent & Literary
    Agency
Ford Models at the Raleigh Hotel
FORD/Robert Black Agency
Fosi's Modeling & Talent Agency
Gage Talent, Inc.
The Geddes Agency (Chicago)
Gilla Roos, Ltd.
Greer Lange Model & Talent Agency, Inc.
Neal Hamil Agency
Hervey/Grimes Talent Agency
Daniel Hoff Agency
Hop Models & Talent Agency
Hot Shot Kids/Teens
The I Group Model & Talent Management
Identity Talent Agency
Image Model & Talent

Modeling Talent (Continued)

IMG/Broadcasting
Independent Artists Agency, Inc.
International Artists Group, Inc.
JE Talent, LLC/JE Model, Inc.
Jet Set Management Group, Inc.
Stanley Kaplan Talent
Kazarian/Spencer & Associates
Kolstein Talent Agency (KTA)
Lane Agency
Leighton Agency, Inc.
Lemodeln Model & Talent Agency
Lenz Agency
Lily's Talent Agency, Inc.
Look Talent
M International Talent Agency
Mademoiselle Talent & Modeling Agency
Malaky International
The Mannequin Agency
Martin & Donalds Talent Agency, Inc.
McCarty Talent, Inc.
Metropolitan Talent Agency (MTA)
Miramar Talent Agency
Model Club, Inc.
Model Team
The Morgan Agency
Nouveau Model & Talent
Nouvelle Talent Management, Inc.
NTA Talent Agency
Nu Talent Agency
NXT Entertainment, Inc.
Osbrink Talent Agency
Dorothy Palmer Talent Agency, Inc.
Paradigm (New York)
The Paradise Group Talent Agency
Peak Models & Talent
Perfectly Petite, Inc.
Privilege Talent Agency
PTI Talent Agency, Inc.
Q Model Management
Q6 Model & Artist Management
Cindy Romano Modeling & Talent Agency
San Diego Model Management Talent Agency
San Francisco Top Models & Talent
The Sarnoff Company, Inc.
Jack Scagnetti Talent & Literary Agency
Schuller Talent/NY Kids
The Screen Talent Agency, Ltd.
SGM - Sara Gaynor Management
Shamon Freitas Model & Talent Agency
Sky Talent Agency
Scott Stander & Associates, Inc.
Starcraft Talent Agency
Stars, The Agency
Stellar Model & Talent Agency
The Stevens Group
Stewart Talent
Superior Talent Agency
Tag Models
The Talent Group
Talent Plus, Inc./Centro Models
Talent Plus/Los Latinos Talent Agency
The Talent Shop
Talent Trek Agency
Talent Unlimited, Inc.
TalentWorks New York
Uptown Talent, Inc.
Vision Los Angeles
Donna Wauhob Agency
Waving Clouds Productions
Wilhelmina West, Inc./LW1 Talent Agency
Zanuck, Passon and Pace, Inc.

Music Talent

abc model/talent/sport management
About Artists Agency
Abrams Artists Agency (New York)
Agape Productions

AGENTS

Music Talent (Continued)

Agency For the Performing Arts, Inc. (Los Angeles)
Agency For the Performing Arts, Inc. (Nashville)
Agency For the Performing Arts, Inc. (New York)
The Agency Group Ltd. (Los Angeles)
The Agency Group Ltd. (New York)
Agents For The Arts, Inc.
Ambassador Talent Agents, Inc.
American Program Bureau
Aqua
Irvin Arthur Associates
Associated Booking Corporation (ABC)
Baron Entertainment
Baskow & Associates, Inc.
Beachfront Bookings
The Bethel Agency
Beverly Hills International Talent Agency
Bobby Ball Talent Agency
BRick Entertainment
The Brogan Agency
Calliope Talent, Model & Artist Management, LLC
The Campbell Agency
The Carry Co.
Castle Hill Talent Agency
Cavaleri & Associates
Cedar Grove Agency Entertainment
Nancy Chaidez Agency & Associates
Coralie Jr. Theatrical Agency
Creative Artists Agency - CAA
DeSanti Talents, Inc.
EC Model & Talent Agency (Ent. Caterers, Inc.)
Encore Talent Agency
Evolution Music Partners, LLC
First Artists Management
Fresh Faces Agency, Inc.
Garber Talent Agency
The Gatsby Group, Inc.
The Gersh Agency (New York)
Gorfaine/Schwartz Agency, Inc.
The Susan Gurman Agency, LLC
Harmony Artists
Henderson/Hogan Agency
Daniel Hoff Agency
Image Model & Talent
IMG/Broadcasting
Impact Talent Group
International Creative Mgmt., Inc. - ICM (LA)
International Creative Mgmt., Inc. - ICM (NY)
Stanley Kaplan Talent
The Kaufman Agency
Archer King, Ltd.
Kraft-Engel Management
Lally Talent Agency (LTA)
Al Lampkin Entertainment, Inc.
Lane Agency
Buddy Lee Attractions, Inc.
Lemodeln Model & Talent Agency
Lily's Talent Agency, Inc.
M International Talent Agency
Malaky International
Sandra Marsh Management
Martin & Donalds Talent Agency, Inc.
Maxine's Talent Agency
The Gilbert Miller Agency LLC
The Morgan Agency
Nash-Angeles, Inc.
New York Office
NXT Entertainment, Inc.
The Orange Grove Group, Inc.
Fifi Oscard Agency, Inc.
Dorothy Palmer Talent Agency, Inc.
Paradigm (Los Angeles)
Paradigm (New York)
Perfectly Petite, Inc.
Periwinkle Entertainment Productions
Players Talent Agency
Qualita Dell' Arte: Artists & Writers Di Qualita
Michael D. Robins & Associates

Music Talent (Continued)

Sanger Talent Agency
The Savage Agency
Schuller Talent/NY Kids
Sheldon Prosnit Agency
Solid Talent, Inc.
Scott Stander & Associates, Inc.
Stars, The Agency
Talent Plus, Inc./Centro Models
The Talent Shop
Turner Artist Management
United Talent Agency - UTA
Universal Talent Intelligence
The Vicious Trend Agency
Donna Wauhob Agency
Wilhelmina Models
William Morris Agency - WMA (Los Angeles)
William Morris Agency - WMA (New York)
William Morris Agency - WMA (Nashville)
William Morris Agency - WMA (Miami Beach)
William Morris Agency - WMA (London)
William Morris Agency - WMA (Shanghai)

Talent & Literary Packaging

Abrams Artists Agency (Los Angeles)
Abrams Artists Agency (New York)
Agency For the Performing Arts, Inc. (Los Angeles)
The Agency Group Ltd. (Los Angeles)
The Agency Group Ltd. (New York)
The Alpern Group
Baskow & Associates, Inc.
Marc Bass Agency, Inc. (MBA)
Beachfront Bookings
The Bethel Agency
Beverly Hills International Talent Agency
The Blake Agency
Don Buchwald & Associates, Inc. (Los Angeles)
Don Buchwald & Associates, Inc. (New York)
Suzanna Camejo & Associates: Artists for the
   Environment
Cavaleri & Associates
The Characters
The Chasin Agency
Diverse Talent Group
The Gersh Agency (New York)
Neal Hamil Agency
Hays Media LLC
Hollywood View
Identity Talent Agency
International Artists Group, Inc.
International Creative Mgmt., Inc. - ICM (LA)
International Creative Mgmt., Inc. - ICM (NY)
JKA Talent & Literary Agency
Archer King, Ltd.
Lally Talent Agency (LTA)
Lemodeln Model & Talent Agency
Michael Lewis & Associates
The Literary Group
Metropolitan Talent Agency (MTA)
The Gilbert Miller Agency LLC
N.S. Bienstock, Inc.
Ofrenda, Inc.
The Orange Grove Group, Inc.
Original Artists
Dorothy Palmer Talent Agency, Inc.
Paradigm (Los Angeles)
Rebel Entertainment Partners, Inc.
The Brant Rose Agency
The Rothman Brecher Agency
Sanger Talent Agency
The Sarnoff Company, Inc.
Jack Scagnetti Talent & Literary Agency
The Irv Schechter Company
Ken Sherman & Associates
Stars, The Agency
Stone Manners Agency
Marianne Strong Literary Agency
Talent House Agency

Talent & Literary Packaging (Continued)

United Talent Agency - UTA
William Morris Agency - WMA (Los Angeles)
William Morris Agency - WMA (New York)
William Morris Agency - WMA (Miami Beach)
William Morris Agency - WMA (London)
William Morris Agency - WMA (Shanghai)
Writers House

Theatre Talent

About Artists Agency
Abrams Artists Agency (Los Angeles)
Abrams Artists Agency (New York)
Acme Talent & Literary
Actors Etc., Inc.
Bret Adams, Ltd.
Agency For the Performing Arts, Inc. (Los Angeles)
Agency For the Performing Arts, Inc. (New York)
The Agency Group Ltd. (Los Angeles)
The Agency Group Ltd. (New York)
Agents For The Arts, Inc.
The Alvarado Rey Agency
American Program Bureau
Beverly Anderson Agency
Andreadis Talent Agency, Inc.
Angel City Talent
Aqua
ARIA Talent
Artist Management Agency
The Artists Group, Ltd.
The Austin Agency
Baier/Kleinman International
Baron Entertainment
Barry Haft Brown Artists Agency
Marc Bass Agency, Inc. (MBA)
Bauman, Redanty, & Shaul Agency
Beachfront Bookings
Berzon Talent Agency
The Bethel Agency
Bicoastal Talent
The Blake Agency
Blue Ridge Entertainment
Judy Boals, Inc.
Bobby Ball Talent Agency
Boca Talent & Model Agency
The Bohrman Agency
Boutique
Bresler Kelly & Associates
BRick Entertainment
The Brogan Agency
Don Buchwald & Associates, Inc. (Los Angeles)
Don Buchwald & Associates, Inc. (New York)
Carmichael Talent
Conan Carroll & Associates
The Carry Co.
The Carson Organization, Ltd.
Carson-Adler Agency, Inc.
Castle Hill Talent Agency
Cavaleri & Associates
Nancy Chaidez Agency & Associates
The Characters
Charles Talent Agency
Chateau Billings Talent Agency
Stacy Cheriff Agency
Circle Talent Associates
Mary Anne Claro Talent Agency, Inc.
Clear Talent Group
Coralie Jr. Theatrical Agency
Cornerstone Talent Agency
Creative Artists Agency - CAA
The Culbertson Group, LLC
Cunningham-Escott-Slevin-Doherty Talent (NY)
DDO Artists Agency
DeSanti Talents, Inc.
Ginger Dicce Talent Agency
Doubble Troubble Entertainment, Inc.
Douglas, Gorman, Rothacker & Wilhelm, Inc.
Edna Talent Management (ETM) Ltd.

AGENTS

Theatre Talent (Continued)

Dulcina Eisen Associates
Ellis Talent Group
Empire Talent Agency
Encore Talent Agency
JFA/Jaime Ferrar Agency
Jim Flynn Agency
Fresh Faces Agency, Inc.
The Gage Group, Inc. (Los Angeles)
The Gage Group, Inc. (New York)
Garber Talent Agency
The Geddes Agency (Chicago)
The Geddes Agency (Los Angeles)
Laya Gelff Agency
Generation TV
The Gersh Agency (New York)
Global Artists Agency
Michelle Gordon & Associates
Graham Agency
Greene & Associates
Grossman & Jack Talent
The Susan Gurman Agency, LLC
GVA Talent Agency, Inc.
Peggy Hadley Enterprises, Ltd.
Buzz Halliday & Associates
Hanns Wolters International, Inc.
Harden-Curtis Associates
Harmony Artists
Hartig Hilepo Agency, Ltd.
Henderson/Hogan Agency
Hervey/Grimes Talent Agency
Daniel Hoff Agency
Hop Models & Talent Agency
Hot Shot Kids/Teens
The House of Representatives
Howard Talent West
IFA Talent Agency
Image Model & Talent
Impact Talent Group
Imperium 7 Talent Agency (i7)
Independent Artists Agency Inc.
Innovative Artists (New York)
International Artists Group, Inc.
International Creative Mgmt., Inc. - ICM (LA)
International Creative Mgmt., Inc. - ICM (NY)
IRISHVOX
JE Talent, LLC/JE Model, Inc.
Jordan, Gill & Dornbaum
Stanley Kaplan Talent

Theatre Talent (Continued)

Kazarian/Spencer & Associates
Kerin-Goldberg & Associates
William Kerwin Agency
Archer King, Ltd.
Paul Kohner, Inc.
Kolstein Talent Agency (KTA)
The Krasny Office, Inc.
L.A. Talent
Lally Talent Agency (LTA)
The Lantz Office
Leading Artists, Inc.
Buddy Lee Attractions, Inc.
Lemodeln Model & Talent Agency
Lenz Agency
Sid Levin Agency
Bernard Liebhaber Agency
Lily's Talent Agency, Inc.
Look Talent
The Luedtke Agency
M International Talent Agency
Malaky International
Martin & Donalds Talent Agency, Inc.
The McCabe Group
McDonald/Selznick Associates
Media Artists Group
Metropolitan Talent Agency (MTA)
The Gilbert Miller Agency LLC
Model Team
Momentum Talent & Literary Agency
The Morgan Agency
H. David Moss & Associates
New York Office
Nouveau Model & Talent
NXT Entertainment, Inc.
Omnipop Talent Group
Oracle Creative Management
The Orange Grove Group, Inc.
Origin Talent
Osbrink Talent Agency
Fifi Oscard Agency, Inc.
Pakula/King & Associates
The Meg Pantera Agency, Inc.
Paradigm (New York)
Perfectly Petite, Inc.
Phoenix Artists, Inc.
Players Talent Agency
Professional Artists
Progressive Artists Agency

Theatre Talent (Continued)

Qualita Dell' Arte: Artists & Writers Di Qualita
Rosenstone/Wender
San Francisco Top Models & Talent
Sanger Talent Agency
The Savage Agency
Jack Scagnetti Talent & Literary Agency
The Irv Schechter Company
Schiowitz Connor Ankrum Wolf, Inc.
Schuller Talent/NY Kids
Kathleen Schultz Associates
Screen Artists Agency, LLC
SDB Partners, Inc.
Shamon Freitas Model & Talent Agency
David Shapira & Associates (DSA)
SMS Talent, Inc.
Solid Talent, Inc.
Scott Stander & Associates, Inc.
Stars, The Agency
Starwil Talent
Ann Steele Agency
Stewart Talent
Stone Manners Agency
Peter Strain & Associates, Inc. (Los Angeles)
Peter Strain & Associates, Inc. (New York)
Mitchell K. Stubbs & Associates
Super Artists Inc.
The Talent Group
Talent House Agency
Talent Representatives, Inc.
The Talent Shop
TalentWorks New York
TDN Artists (The Director's Network)
United Talent Agency - UTA
Uptown Talent, Inc.
The Wallis Agency
Bob Waters Agency, Inc.
The Ann Waugh Talent Agency
Donna Wauhob Agency
Waving Clouds Productions
William Morris Agency - WMA (Los Angeles)
William Morris Agency - WMA (New York)
William Morris Agency - WMA (Miami Beach)
William Morris Agency - WMA (London)
William Morris Agency - WMA (Shanghai)
Ann Wright Representatives
Craig Wyckoff & Associates
Zanuck, Passon and Pace, Inc.

MANAGERS

Below-the-Line Talent

A.C.T. Management
Associated Artists PR & Management
The Bauer Company
Beaty Four Entertainment
Becker Entertainment Group
Michael Black Management, Inc.
Broom in the Moon Productions
The Coppage Company
Course Management
Cue11 Entertainment
M.M. Gertz Entertainment
Phillip B. Gittelman Personal Management
Illuminati Entertainment
Letnom Management & Productions
Managing Artistic Concepts
The Marcelli Company
David Martin Management
McMurdo Management & Associates, LLC
MEG Management
Online Talent Group/OTG Talent
Panettiere & Company, Inc.
Parseghian Planco, LLC
The Phoenix Organization

Below-the-Line Talent (Continued)

Marty Shapiro Management
Narelle Sheehan Management (NSM)
Shoelace, Inc. Management
Andrea Simon Entertainment
Sinclair Management
Steinberg Talent Management Group
TGI Entertainment Corporation
Turner Artist Management
Westside Artists
Working Artists

Commercial Talent

abc management group
Absolute Talent Management, Inc.
A.C.T. Management
A.D.S. Management
Advance LA
All That Entertainment Management
American Artists Entertainment Group
Artist International
Arts and Letters Management
Associated Artists PR & Management
Axiom Management

Commercial Talent (Continued)

Bamboo Management LLC
Bandwagon Entertainment
Beaty Four Entertainment
Bensky Entertainment
Sue Bernstein Management
Betwixt Talent Management
Blackwood Talent Management
Jane Bloom & Associates
Blubay Talent Management
Robin Brooks Management
Brown Leader Group
BSC Management
Calliope Talent Management, LLC
Candy Entertainment, Inc.
Casting Unlimited & Management
CastleBright
Central Artists
CFB Productions, Inc.
Chancellor Entertainment
Coastal Entertainment Productions
The Conversation Company, Ltd.
Cornerstone Management
Edna Cowan Management

MANAGERS

Commercial Talent (Continued)

Creative Enterprises Management
Creative Haven Entertainment
Creative Mgmt. Entertainment Group (CMEG)
Creative Talent Company
Creative Talent Management
Creative Talent Management Group (CTMG)
CTM Artists
Cue11 Entertainment
Alan David Management
Richard De Lancy & Associates Talent Agency
DEJ Management Company
Denise Denny Talent Management
Bob Diamond & Associates
Dream Talent
Eastwood Talent Corporation
Elegance Talent Group
Encore Artists Management
Endurance Talent Management
The ESI Network
Evans Management
Evergreen International Management
Stann Findelle Law & Management
Fire Comm Management
First Take
Five12 Entertainment Group
Flaunt Model Management, Inc.
Flavor Unit Entertainment
Fox Entertainment Company
Kyle Fritz Management
The FTL Company
Estelle Fusco Talent Management
Gem Entertainment Group, Inc.
Phillip B. Gittelman Personal Management
Global Entertainment
Jeff Goldberg Management
Goldstar Talent Management
Green Key Management, LLC
Ken Gross Management
Hart² Management
Harvest Talent Management
Hazen Talent Management
Headline Media Management
Josselyne Herman & Associates
Hollywood Management Company
Howard Entertainment
Impact Artists Group, LLC
The Independent Group, LLC
Infinity Management International
Kanner Entertainment Inc.
Kaplan Productions
Ann Kelly Management
King Management
Kjar & Associates
Knight Light Entertainment
Lloyd Kolmer Enterprises
Kragen & Company
Victor Kruglov & Associates
Landis-Simon Productions & Talent Management
Paul Lane Entertainment
Lane Management Group
Lang Talent
The Laugh Factory Management
Lawson Artist Management, LLC
Letnom Management & Productions
Levine Management
Myrna Lieberman Management
Link Talent Group
Little Stars Management
LoLo Entertainment Co.
Jeffrey Loseff Management
Lymberopoulos, Inc.
Mack Muse Entertainment, Inc.
Magenta Creative Management
Magnolia Entertainment
Maier Management
Management 101
The Management Team

Commercial Talent (Continued)

Managing Artistic Concepts
Manta Entertainment
Marathon Entertainment
The Marshak/Zachary Company
David Martin Management
Massei Management
Dino May Management
MC Talent
McGowan Management
McMurdo Management & Associates, LLC
Media Four
Michael Meltzer & Associates
Messina Baker Entertainment Corporation
MGATalent
Midwest Talent Management, Inc.
Pamela Migas Management (PMM)
Millennium Entertainment, Inc.
April Mills Management
J. Mitchell Management
MMC Entertainment/Dance Directions
Moore Artists' Management
MP Management
Multi-Ethnic Talent
Dee Mura Enterprises, Inc.
Nani/Saperstein Management, Inc.
NCL TALENT
Nebula Management
Rosella Olson Management
Omnium Entertainment Group
P.K.A. Entertainment Group
Page Management
Pallas Management
Park Place Management
Ria Pavia Management
PB Management
Polaris Entertainment
Principal Entertainment
Principato-Young Entertainment
Pro and Con Productions Talent Management
Protege Entertainment
Charles Rapp Enterprises, Inc.
Linda Reitman Management
L. Richardson Entertainment
The Right Connection Entertainment Group
Rising Talent Management
Mark Robert Management
Heidi Rotbart Management
Dorothea Sargent & Company
Sauers Artists, LLC
Schachter Entertainment
Richard Schwartz Management
SCORE! Media Ventures
Seekers Management, LLC
Earl Shank
Burt Shapiro Management
Shapiro/West & Associates, Inc.
Shark Artists, Inc.
Sharp Talent
Sharyn Talent Management
Narelle Sheehan Management (NSM)
Shelter Entertainment
Shoelace, Inc. Management
Loretta Shreve Model Center/Shreve Talent Source
The Siegal Company
Blair Silver & Company LLC
Simmons and Scott Entertainment, LLC
Sinclair Management
SirenSong Entertainment, Inc.
SJV Enterprises & Associates
Todd Smith & Associates
Bette Smith Management
Sneak Preview Entertainment
Soiree Fair, Inc.
Helene Sokol Management
Soma Management
Speak Softly Legal Management
Spellman, Paul & Wetzel

Commercial Talent (Continued)

Star Talent Management
Station 3
Stein Entertainment Group
Steinberg Talent Management Group
The Sterling/Winters Company
Studio Talent Group
Suzelle Enterprises
Synergy Management, Inc.
The Talent Company
Talent Management Partners
TalentCo Model & Talent Management
Temptation Management
Terrific Talent Associates, Inc.
TGI Entertainment Corporation
Thirdhill Entertainment
Roz Tillman Management
Tinoco Management
Torque Entertainment
Trademark Artists Management
Triniti Management
Triple Threat Talent Management
Trusik Talent Management, Inc.
Turner Artist Management
Universal Management Group (UMG)
V & L International, LLC
Vesta Talent Services
WA Enterprises
Brad Waisbren Enterprises
Mimi Weber Management Co.
David Westberg Management
Whitaker Entertainment
Wilhelmina Creative Management
Wilhelmina Kids
Williams Unlimited
Witt Entertainment Management, Inc.
Young Performers Management
Young Talent, Inc.
Bonnie Young Personal Management
Zenith Management

Film/TV Talent

1 Management
3 Arts Entertainment, Inc.
777 Group, LTD
A Fein Martini
A Management
abc management group
Absolute Talent Management, Inc.
ACE Media
A.C.T. Management
A.D.S. Management
Advance LA
AEI-Atchity/Entertainment International
AK Associates
Alchemy Entertainment
All That Entertainment Management
Leslie Allan-Rice Management
Allman/Rea Management
Alpha Centauri Management
AM Productions & Management
Ambitious Entertainment
American Artists Entertainment Group
American Artists Group Management
Ampersand Management Group
Anonymous Content
Anthem Entertainment
Ardent Entertainment
Art/Work Entertainment
Artist International
Artist Management
Artists International
Artists Management
Artists Only Management
Arts and Letters Management
Associated Artists PR & Management
Athena Talent Management, LLC
Marilyn Atlas Management

MANAGERS

Film/TV Talent (Continued)

Avalon Management, Inc.
Axiom Management
Bamboo Management LLC
Bandwagon Entertainment
Barking Dog Entertainment, Inc.
The Bauer Company
Beaty Four Entertainment
Becker Entertainment Group
The Beddingfield Company, Inc.
David Belenzon Management, Inc.
Carl Belfor Entertainment Management Company
Benderspink
Bensky Entertainment
Martin Berneman Management
Sue Bernstein Management
Betwixt Talent Management
Binder & Associates
Michael Black Management, Inc.
Blackwood Talent Management
Blain & Associates
Jane Bloom & Associates
Blubay Talent Management
Blue Train Entertainment
Blueprint Artist Management
Bohemia Group
Barry Bookin Management
The Braverman/Bloom Co., Inc.
Brillstein-Grey Management
Robin Brooks Management
Brookside Artist Management
Brown Leader Group
The Michael Bruno Group Los Angeles
Brustein Entertainment
BSC Management
The Burstein Company
Calliope Talent Management, LLC
Candy Entertainment, Inc.
John Carrabino Management
Central Artists
CFB Productions, Inc.
Chachkin Management
Chancellor Entertainment
Doug Chapin Management, Inc.
Joyce Chase Management
Cheatham, Greene & Company
Cine/Lit
Vincent Cirrincione Associates, Ltd.
Coastal Entertainment Productions
Cohen/Thomas Management
The Collective
Commonwealth Talent Group
The Company Artists
Concept Entertainment
Connection III Entertainment Corp.
Diane Connors Management
Contemporary Talent Partners (CTP)
The Conversation Company, Ltd.
Dan Cooper & Associates
The Coppage Company
The Core
Cornerstone Management
Cornice Entertainment
Course Management
Edna Cowan Management
Creative Enterprises Management
Creative Haven Entertainment
Creative Mgmt. Entertainment Group (CMEG)
Creative Talent Company
Creative Talent Management
Creative Talent Management Group (CTMG)
John Crosby Management
Crysis Management
CTM Artists
Cue11 Entertainment
Cutler Management
D/F Management
Marv Dauer Management

Film/TV Talent (Continued)

Alan David Management
Davila & Co.
Richard De Lancy & Associates Talent Agency
Dean Literary Concepts
Ron DeBlasio Management
DEJ Management Company
Delphinius Management
Denise Denny Talent Management
DePaz Management
Detroit Company
The Development Department
Dewalt & Muzik Management
Bob Diamond & Associates
Divine Management
dixon talent, inc.
Bonny Dore Management
Dream Talent
DreaMakers Inc.
du Jour Entertainment/Gypsy Productions
Eastwood Talent Corporation
Echo Lake Management
Allen Edelman Management
Eighth Square Entertainment
Michael Einfeld Management
Elements Entertainment
Elkins Entertainment Corporation
Elsboy Management
Emancipated Talent Management & Consulting
Emerald Talent Group
Encore Artists Management
Endurance Talent Management
Energy Entertainment
Ensemble Entertainment
Entertainment Management Group
Envision Entertainment
Envoy Entertainment
Epigram Management
The ESI Network
Essential Talent Management
Evans Management
Evergreen International Management
Evolution Management
Exile Entertainment
Farah Films & Management
Fast Track Management
Fastbreak Management, Inc.
The Feldman Company
Feldman Management, LLC
Festa Entertainment
Field Entertainment
Stann Findelle Law & Management
Fire Comm Management
The Firm, Inc.
First Take
Robert Fitzpatrick Organization
Five12 Entertainment Group
Flavor Unit Entertainment
Flutie Entertainment
Michael Flutie's Office (MFO)
Forster Delaney Management
Forward Entertainment
Elizabeth Fowler Management
Fox Entertainment Company
Fox-Albert Management Entertainment, Inc.
Framework Entertainment
Kyle Fritz Management
The FTL Company
Fuel Filmworks
Full Circle Management
Brian Funnagan Management
Estelle Fusco Talent Management
Lorita Garcia & Associates Mgmt. & Ent.
Gateway Management Partners
GEF Entertainment
Gem Entertainment Group, Inc.
Generate
Peter Giagni Management, Inc.

Film/TV Talent (Continued)

Gilbertson-Kincaid
Jeff Gitlin Entertainment
Phillip B. Gittelman Personal Management
Glasser Black Management
Global Entertainment
Marianne Golan Management
Gold Coast Management
Dodie Gold Management, Inc.
Peter Golden & Associates, Inc.
Goldstar Talent Management
The Gotham Group, Inc.
Grand View Management
Susan Graw and Associates
Green Key Management, LLC
Joan Green Management
Juliet Green Management
Melanie Greene Management
GSC Management
G.T.A., Inc.
H2F Entertainment
Halpern Management
Handprint Entertainment
Scott Hart Entertainment
Hart² Management
Harvest Talent Management
Hazen Talent Management
Headline Media Management
Heitmann Entertainment
Herbosch Management
Josselyne Herman & Associates
Himber Entertainment, Inc.
Hines & Hunt Entertainment
Hofflund/Polone
Cary Hoffman Management
Holder Management
Hollywood Management Company
Hook Entertainment
Joanne Horowitz Management
Howard Entertainment
Hyler Management
Impact Artists Group, LLC
Incognito Management
The Independent Group, LLC
Independent Movement Entertainment
Industry Entertainment Partners
Infinity Management International
Cheri Ingram Enterprises
Insight
Integrated Films & Management
Interlink Management
James/Levy Management, Inc.
Jaymes-Nelson Entertainment
JudyO Productions
Kanner Entertainment Inc.
Darlene Kaplan Entertainment
Kaplan Productions
Kaplan/Perrone Entertainment, LLC
Karma Entertainment
Kass & Stokes Management
Ann Kelly Management
Key Creatives, LLC
Kinesis Entertainment, Inc.
King Management
Kings Highway Entertainment
Kjar & Associates
Don Klein Management Group, Inc.
Knight Light Entertainment
Lloyd Kolmer Enterprises
Koopman Management
Kragen & Company
Kritzer Levine Wilkins Entertainment
Barry Krost Management
Victor Kruglov & Associates
L.A. Sammy Productions
LA Entertainment
Landis-Simon Productions & Talent Management
Lane Management Group

MANAGERS

Film/TV Talent (Continued)

Lang Talent
The Laugh Factory Management
Lawrence International Corporation
Lawson Artist Management, LLC
Letnom Management & Productions
Leverage Management
Levine Management
Leviton Management
Levity Entertainment Group
Liberman Zerman Management
The Liberty Company
Myrna Lieberman Management
Liebman Entertainment
Life Management
Lighthouse Entertainment
Link Talent Group
Little Stars Management
LoLo Entertainment Co.
Jeffrey Loseff Management
Bonnie Love Management
Lovett Management
Lymberopoulos, Inc.
Tami Lynn Productions
M Management
Mack Muse Entertainment, Inc.
Magenta Creative Management
Magnolia Entertainment
Maier Management
Main Title Entertainment
Management 101
Management 360
The Management Team
Managing Artistic Concepts
Marathon Entertainment
The Marcelli Company
Marsala Management
Marsh Entertainment
The Marshak/Zachary Company
David Martin Management
Massei Management
Dino May Management
MBST Entertainment
MC Talent
McGowan Management
McKeon-Myones Management
McMurdo Management & Associates, LLC
Media Four
Media Talent Group
MEG Management
Michael Meltzer & Associates
Messina Baker Entertainment Corporation
Ellen Meyer Management
MGATalent
MGC/Cushman Entertainment Group
Midwest Talent Management, Inc.
Pamela Migas Management (PMM)
Millennium Entertainment, Inc.
Miller and Company
The Miller Company
Renée Missel Management
J. Mitchell Management
Miterre Productions, Inc.
Mixed Media Entertainment Company
MMC Entertainment/Dance Directions
Modus Entertainment
Mogul Management
Momentum Talent Management
Jaime Monroy Studios
Monster Talent Management, Inc.
Moore Artists' Management
MP Management
Multi-Ethnic Talent
Dee Mura Enterprises, Inc.
Music World Entertainment
Nanas Entertainment
Nani/Saperstein Management, Inc.
NCL TALENT

Film/TV Talent (Continued)

Nebula Management
New Talent Management
New Wave Entertainment
Niad Management
Nine Yards Entertainment
Oceanside Entertainment
Barney Oldfield Management
Rosella Olson Management
Omnipop Talent Group
Omniquest Entertainment
Omnium Entertainment Group
One Entertainment
One Talent Management
Dianna Oser Management
Ovation Management
Page Management
Pallas Management
Judy Palnick Entertainment
Panacea Entertainment
Parallel Entertainment, Inc.
Park Place Management
Parseghian Planco, LLC
PB Management
Pearl Pictures Management
The Phoenix Organization
The Pitt Group
PMA Literary & Film Management, Inc.
Margrit Polak Management
Polaris Entertainment
The Derek Power Company, Inc.
Principal Entertainment
Principato-Young Entertainment
Pro and Con Productions Talent Management
Melissa Prophet Management
Protege Entertainment
Pure Arts
Quattro Media
Rabiner/Damato Entertainment
Vic Ramos Management
Charles Rapp Enterprises, Inc.
Joseph Rapp Enterprises, Inc.
Raw Talent
Red Baron Management
Reel Talent Management
Reel World Management
Linda Reitman Management
Relevant Entertainment Group
Releve Entertainment
Ribisi Entertainment
L. Richardson Entertainment
Rigberg Entertainment Group
The Right Connection Entertainment Group
Rising Talent Management
RJM/Renée Jennett Management
ROAR
J.C. Robbins Management
Mark Robert Management
Dolores Robinson Entertainment
Bill Robinson Management
Roklin Management
Rosalee Productions
The Marion Rosenberg Office
Lara Rosenstock Management
Jeff Ross Entertainment, Inc.
Heidi Rotbart Management
Rough Diamond Management
RPI Entertainment & Media Group
Safran Company
Sager Management, Inc.
Sanders/Armstrong Management
Sanderson Entertainment, Inc.
Fran Saperstein Organization
Dorothea Sargent & Company
Sauers Artists, LLC
Saxon Associates Management
Schachter Entertainment
Schumacher Management

Film/TV Talent (Continued)

Booh Schut Company
Richard Schwartz Management
Jeri Scott Management
Screen Partners, Inc.
Seekers Management, LLC
Select Artists, Ltd.
Seven Summits Pictures & Management
Earl Shank
Burt Shapiro Management
Marty Shapiro Management
Shapiro/West & Associates, Inc.
Shark Artists, Inc.
Sharp Talent
Sharyn Talent Management
Narelle Sheehan Management (NSM)
Shelter Entertainment
Shoelace, Inc. Management
The Shuman Company
The Siegal Company
Alan Siegel Entertainment
Silent R Management
Blair Silver & Company LLC
Simmons and Scott Entertainment, LLC
Andrea Simon Entertainment
Sinclair Management
Daniel Sladek Entertainment Corporation
Slamdance Management
Sleeping Giant Entertainment
SLJ Management
Todd Smith & Associates
Bette Smith Management
The Susan Smith Company
Sneak Preview Entertainment
Chad Snopek Management
Soiree Fair, Inc.
Helene Sokol Management
Soma Management
Sonesta Entertainment, LLC
Speak Softly Legal Management
Larry Spellman Enterprises
Spellman, Paul & Wetzel
Spot Light Entertainment
Star Talent Management
Station 3
Stein Entertainment Group
Steinberg Talent Management Group
The Sterling/Winters Company
Harriet Sternberg Management
Joel Stevens Entertainment Company
Gail A. Stocker Presents
Stone Canyon Media
Strauss-McGarr Entertainment
Studio Talent Group
The Suchin Company
Sullivan Talent Group
Suskin Management LLC
Sussex Ltd., Inc., A Management Company
Jeff Sussman Management
Suzelle Enterprises
Sweeney Management
Synchronicity Management
Synergy Management, Inc.
The Talent Company
Talent Management Partners
Talent Scout International Management
TalentCo Model & Talent Management
Talented Managers
TAO Management & Tetrahedron Productions
Teitelbaum Artists Group
Temptation Management
Terrific Talent Associates, Inc.
TGI Entertainment Corporation
The Michael Forman Company
Thirdhill Entertainment
Larry Thompson Organization
Thompson Street Entertainment
The Robert Thorne Company

MANAGERS

Film/TV Talent (Continued)

Thruline Entertainment
Roz Tillman Management
Tinoco Management
TMT Entertainment
Toltec Artists
Torque Entertainment
Trademark Artists Management
Trademark Talent
Trancas Management
Triniti Management
Troika
Trusik Talent Management, Inc.
Turner Artist Management
Unique Talent Group
Universal Management Group (UMG)
Unlimited Management
Untitled Entertainment
V & L International, LLC
Valentino Entertainment
Vanguard Management Group
Vanguard Talent Management
Vesta Talent Services
Viking Entertainment
Visionary Entertainment
The Robert D. Wachs Company
Brad Waisbren Enterprises
Wallach Entertainment
Michael Wallach Management
Washington Square Arts
Water Street
Mimi Weber Management Co.
David Westberg Management
Whitaker Entertainment
Wild Briar Talent
Dan Wiley Management
Wilhelmina Creative Management
Wilhelmina Kids
Williams Unlimited
Witt Entertainment Management, Inc.
Christopher Wright Management
W.T.A. & Associates
Young Performers Management
Young Talent, Inc.
Bonnie Young Personal Management
Yumkas Management
Gene Yusem Company
Zenith Management
Ziemba Talent & Associates

Literary Talent

3 Arts Entertainment, Inc.
6 Pictures
777 Group, LTD
A Wink and a Nod Management, Inc.
ACE Media
Acuna Entertainment
A.D.S. Management
AEI-Atchity/Entertainment International
AK Associates
Alpha Centauri Management
Ampersand Management Group
Anonymous Content
Anthem Entertainment
Archetype
Arpil Entertainment
Art/Work Entertainment
Artist International
Artist Management
Artists Only Management
Arts and Letters Management
Associated Artists PR & Management
Marilyn Atlas Management
Avalon Management, Inc.
Avery Management
Bamboo Management LLC
The Bauer Company
Baumgarten Management & Production

Literary Talent (Continued)

Beaty Four Entertainment
Becker Entertainment Group
Carl Belfor Entertainment Management Company
Benderspink
Bensky Entertainment
Michael Black Management, Inc.
Blackwood Talent Management
Blain & Associates
Blubay Talent Management
Blue Train Entertainment
Bohemia Group
Barry Bookin Management
Brand X Management
The Braverman/Bloom Co., Inc.
Bridge Falls Entertainment
Brillstein-Grey Management
Brookside Artist Management
Broom in the Moon Productions
Brustein Entertainment
BSC Management
bumberShoot Entertainment
The Burstein Company
Careyes Entertainment
Casting Unlimited & Management
CastleBright
CFB Productions, Inc.
Doug Chapin Management, Inc.
Cheatham, Greene & Company
Chic Productions & Management (CPM)
Cine/Lit
Circle of Confusion
Vincent Cirrincione Associates, Ltd.
Clark Management Company
Code
The Collective
Commonwealth Talent Group
The Company Artists
Concept Entertainment
Connection III Entertainment Corp.
Contemporary Talent Partners (CTP)
Content House
The Conversation Company, Ltd.
The Coppage Company
Cornice Entertainment
Course Management
Edna Cowan Management
Created By
Creative Convergence
Creative Enterprises Management
Creative Haven Entertainment
Creative Talent Management
Cue11 Entertainment
Marv Dauer Management
Davila & Co.
Dean Literary Concepts
DEJ Management Company
Delphinius Management
Detroit Company
The Development Department
Divine Management
dixon talent, inc.
Donaldson/Sanders Entertainment
Bonny Dore Management
Douglas Management Group
DreaMakers Inc.
du Jour Entertainment/Gypsy Productions
EarthAngels Literary Management
Eastwood Talent Corporation
Echo Lake Management
Rona Edwards Productions
Eighth Square Entertainment
EK Management
Elements Entertainment
Elsboy Management
Elysian Entertainment, Inc.
Emancipated Talent Management & Consulting
e-merge Management

Literary Talent (Continued)

Endure Management
Energy Entertainment
Ensemble Entertainment
Entertainment Management Group
Envoy Entertainment
Epigram Management
Evans Management
Evatopia
Evergreen International Management
Evolution Management
Exile Entertainment
Farah Films & Management
Fastbreak Management, Inc.
The Feldman Company
Festa Entertainment
Field Entertainment
Stann Findelle Law & Management
Fineman Entertainment
The Firm, Inc.
FitzGerald Literary Management
Flashpoint Entertainment
Flutie Entertainment
Foremost Films
Michael Forman Management
Foursight Entertainment
Elizabeth Fowler Management
Frenetic Media
The FTL Company
Fuel Filmworks
Fuse Entertainment
Gem Entertainment Group, Inc.
Generate
M.M. Gertz Entertainment
GhettoSuburbia Entertainment
Peter Giagni Management, Inc.
Phillip B. Gittelman Personal Management
Dodie Gold Management, Inc.
Jeff Goldberg Management
Peter Golden & Associates, Inc.
Goldstein Company, Inc.
The Gotham Group, Inc.
Grade A Entertainment
Graup Entertainment
Susan Graw and Associates
Gray Fox Films, LLC
Juliet Green Management
Grey Line Entertainment, Inc.
Brad Gross Inc., Literary Management
Ken Gross Management
Sheree Guitar Entertainment
Guy Walks into a Bar Management
H2F Entertainment
Handprint Entertainment
Peter Hankwitz Production & Management, Inc.
Todd Harris Management, Inc.
Hart Entertainment
Scott Hart Entertainment
Hazen Talent Management
Heitmann Entertainment
Hines & Hunt Entertainment
Hofflund/Polone
Cary Hoffman Management
Holder Management
Holzman Management Group
Hopscotch Pictures
Howard Entertainment
Illuminati Entertainment
Impact Artists Group, LLC
Incognito Management
Independent Movement Entertainment
Industry Entertainment Partners
Infinity Management International
Integrated Films & Management
Intellectual Property Group
Jaret Entertainment
Jaymes-Nelson Entertainment
JudyO Productions

MANAGERS

Literary Talent (Continued)

Kanner Entertainment Inc.
Kaplan/Perrone Entertainment, LLC
Karma Entertainment
Kersey Management
Key Creatives, LLC
Kinesis Entertainment, Inc.
Kinetic Management
King Management
Kings Highway Entertainment
Kjar & Associates
Don Klein Management Group, Inc.
Kritzer Levine Wilkins Entertainment
Barry Krost Management
The Landers Group
Paul Lane Entertainment
Lane Management Group
The Laugh Factory Management
Letnom Management & Productions
Leverage Management
Levine Management
Leviton Management
Levity Entertainment Group
The Liberty Company
Liebman Entertainment
Lighthouse Entertainment
Link Talent Group
Little Studio Films
Lloyd Entertainement
LoLo Entertainment Co.
Lovett Management
Lukeman Literary Management, Ltd.
Tami Lynn Productions
M Management
Mack Muse Entertainment, Inc.
MaCroManagement
Madhouse Entertainment
Magnet Management
Magnolia Entertainment
Management 101
Management 360
Managing Artistic Concepts
Manta Entertainment
Marathon Entertainment
Marsala Management
Marsh Entertainment
The Marshak/Zachary Company
Martin Literary Management
Max Freedman Management
MBST Entertainment
McKeon-Myones Management
McMurdo Management & Associates, LLC
Media Four
Media Talent Group
MEG Management
Michael Meltzer & Associates
Messina Baker Entertainment Corporation
Midwest Talent Management, Inc.
Millennium Entertainment, Inc.
The Miller Company
Miterre Productions, Inc.
Modus Entertainment
Moore Artists' Management
MSI Entertainment, Inc.
Dee Mura Enterprises, Inc.
The Muraviov Company
Nanas Entertainment
Nebula Management
New Entertainment Group
New Wave Entertainment
Next Stop Management
Niad Management
Nine Yards Entertainment
Oceanside Entertainment
Omnipop Talent Group
Omniquest Entertainment
One Entertainment
Online Talent Group/OTG Talent

Literary Talent (Continued)

Ovation Management
P.K.A. Entertainment Group
Judy Palnick Entertainment
Panettiere & Company, Inc.
Park Place Management
Parseghian Planco, LLC
Ria Pavia Management
PB Management
Pearl Pictures Management
Stephen Pevner, Inc.
The Phoenix Organization
The Pitt Group
Plumeria Entertainment Management
PMA Literary & Film Management, Inc.
The Derek Power Company, Inc.
Principal Entertainment
Principato-Young Entertainment
Pro and Con Productions Talent Management
Pure Arts
Quattro Media
Rabiner/Damato Entertainment
The Radmin Company
Charles Rapp Enterprises, Inc.
Raw Talent
Red Harvest Entertainment
Dan Redler Entertainment
Reel World Management
Linda Reitman Management
Relevant Entertainment Group
L. Richardson Entertainment
Rigberg Entertainment Group
RJM/Renée Jennett Management
ROAR
Dolores Robinson Entertainment
Stephanie Rogers & Associates
The Marion Rosenberg Office
Lara Rosenstock Management
Rosenzweig Films
Jeff Ross Entertainment, Inc.
Heidi Rotbart Management
RPM International
Safran Company
Sanderson Entertainment, Inc.
Fran Saperstein Organization
Schachter Entertainment
Schumacher Management
Richard Schwartz Management
SCORE! Media Ventures
Screen Partners, Inc.
Seekers Management, LLC
Seven Summits Pictures & Management
Earl Shank
Marty Shapiro Management
Shapiro/West & Associates, Inc.
Shark Artists, Inc.
Sharp Talent
Shelter Entertainment
Shoelace, Inc. Management
The Shuman Company
Michael Siegel and Associates
Silent R Management
Blair Silver & Company LLC
Andrea Simon Entertainment
SirenSong Entertainment, Inc.
Slamdance Management
Sleeping Giant Entertainment
Smart Entertainment
Todd Smith & Associates
Bette Smith Management
Sneak Preview Entertainment
Chad Snopek Management
Soiree Fair, Inc.
Sonesta Entertainment, LLC
Spellman, Paul & Wetzel
Spot Light Entertainment
Station 3
Steinberg Talent Management Group

Literary Talent (Continued)

The Sterling/Winters Company
Harriet Sternberg Management
Joel Stevens Entertainment Company
Stone Canyon Media
Story Arts Management
Studio Talent Group
Suite A Management Talent & Literary Agency
Sussex Ltd., Inc., A Management Company
Sweeney Management
Synchronicity Management
Talent Management Partners
Talent Scout International Management
Teitelbaum Artists Group
Temptation Management
TGI Entertainment Corporation
The Michael Forman Company
Thirdhill Entertainment
Thompson Street Entertainment
Thrive Entertainment
Thruline Entertainment
Roz Tillman Management
TMT Entertainment
Toltec Artists
Torque Entertainment
Trademark Artists Management
Trancas Management
Treasure Entertainment
Triple Threat Talent Management
Tudor Management Group
Underground Management
Unique Talent Group
Universal Management Group (UMG)
Unlimited Management
Untitled Entertainment
V & L International, LLC
Vanguard Management Group
Vanguard Talent Management
Visionary Entertainment
Viviano Feldman Entertainment
Michael Wallach Management
Washington Square Arts
Water Street
Whitaker Entertainment
Wild Briar Talent
Will Entertainment
Windfall Management
Jacki Wolski Literary Management
Working Artists
W.T.A. & Associates
Nick Yellen Creative Agency
Zero Gravity Management

Modeling Talent

1 Management
A Fein Martini
A.D.S. Management
All That Entertainment Management
American Artists Entertainment Group
Artist International
Artists International
Arts and Letters Management
Associated Artists PR & Management
Beaty Four Entertainment
Betwixt Talent Management
Blackwood Talent Management
Blubay Talent Management
Robin Brooks Management
Calliope Talent Management, LLC
Central Artists
Chancellor Entertainment
CTM Artists
Cue11 Entertainment
Richard De Lancy & Associates Talent Agency
DEJ Management Company
Dream Talent
Elegance Talent Group
The ESI Network

MANAGERS

Modeling Talent (Continued)

Stann Findelle Law & Management
Fire Comm Management
First Take
Five12 Entertainment Group
Flaunt Model Management, Inc.
Michael Flutie's Office (MFO)
Gem Entertainment Group, Inc.
Phillip B. Gittelman Personal Management
Green Key Management, LLC
Hazen Talent Management
Josselyne Herman & Associates
Hook Entertainment
Howard Entertainment
Howell Management
IMG Models
The Independent Group, LLC
Infinity Management International
Insight
Knight Light Entertainment
Lang Talent
Lawson Artist Management, LLC
Letnom Management & Productions
Little Stars Management
Jeffrey Loseff Management
Magenta Creative Management
Maier Management
Management 101
Managing Artistic Concepts
The Marcelli Company
Dino May Management
McMurdo Management & Associates, LLC
MEG Management
Midwest Talent Management, Inc.
April Mills Management
Jaime Monroy Studios
Dee Mura Enterprises, Inc.
NCL TALENT
Rosella Olson Management
P.K.A. Entertainment Group
Page Management
Pallas Management
Park Place Management
Michele Pommier Management
Pro and Con Productions Talent Management
Rising Talent Management
Richard Schwartz Management
Shark Artists, Inc.
Sharp Talent
Shoelace, Inc. Management
Loretta Shreve Model Center/Shreve Talent Source
Blair Silver & Company LLC
Soma Management
Spot Light Entertainment
Station 3
Suzelle Enterprises
The Talent Company
Talent Scout International Management
TalentCo Model & Talent Management
Talented Managers
Temptation Management
TGI Entertainment Corporation
Tinoco Management
Torque Entertainment
Trademark Artists Management
Triniti Management
Triple Threat Talent Management
Trump Model Management
Universal Management Group (UMG)
Vision Model Management
WA Enterprises
Wilhelmina Creative Management
Wilhelmina Models
Young Talent, Inc.

Music Talent

A Fein Martini
abc management group

Music Talent (Continued)

AM Productions & Management
American Artists Entertainment Group
Artist International
Artists Management
Associated Artists PR & Management
Beaty Four Entertainment
Becker Entertainment Group
David Belenzon Management, Inc.
Blackwood Talent Management
Barry Bookin Management
Brand X Management
Robin Brooks Management
Brookside Artist Management
Brustein Entertainment
BSC Management
Calliope Talent Management, LLC
Casting Unlimited & Management
CFB Productions, Inc.
Chachkin Management
Chancellor Entertainment
Columbia Artists Management LLC
Diane Connors Management
The Conversation Company, Ltd.
The Core
Cornerstone Management
Creative Content Management
Creative Haven Entertainment
Creative Talent Management
Creative Talent Management Group (CTMG)
Crysis Management
Cue11 Entertainment
Davila & Co.
Ron DeBlasio Management
DEJ Management Company
Delphinius Management
Denise Denny Talent Management
Dream Talent
DreaMakers Inc.
du Jour Entertainment/Gypsy Productions
Eastwood Talent Corporation
Elegance Talent Group
Entertainment Management Group
Evans Management
Evergreen International Management
Fastbreak Management, Inc.
Stann Findelle Law & Management
The Firm, Inc.
First Class Entertainment, Inc.
Robert Fitzpatrick Organization
Five12 Entertainment Group
Flavor Unit Entertainment
Michael Flutie's Office (MFO)
Fox Entertainment Company
The FTL Company
Green Key Management, LLC
Greenspan Artist Management
G.T.A., Inc.
Handprint Entertainment
Scott Hart Entertainment
Hart² Management
Josselyne Herman & Associates
Hook Entertainment
ICM Artists
Independent Movement Entertainment
Cheri Ingram Enterprises
King Management
Knight Light Entertainment
Kraft-Engel Management
Kragen & Company
Barry Krost Management
L.A. Sammy Productions
Paul Lane Entertainment
Lawrence International Corporation
Lawson Artist Management, LLC
Letnom Management & Productions
Liebman Entertainment
Little Stars Management

Music Talent (Continued)

LoLo Entertainment Co.
M Management
Management 101
Managing Artistic Concepts
Manta Entertainment
Marks Management
David Martin Management
Dino May Management
MBST Entertainment
McMurdo Management & Associates, LLC
Media Four
MEG Management
Millennium Entertainment, Inc.
Mixed Media Entertainment Company
Dee Mura Enterprises, Inc.
Music World Entertainment
Nani/Saperstein Management, Inc.
NCL TALENT
Nine Yards Entertainment
Dianna Oser Management
Overbrook Entertainment
P.K.A. Entertainment Group
Pallas Management
Judy Palnick Entertainment
Panacea Entertainment
Pearl Pictures Management
The Derek Power Company, Inc.
Pro and Con Productions Talent Management
Charles Rapp Enterprises, Inc.
Joseph Rapp Enterprises, Inc.
Linda Reitman Management
Releve Entertainment
ROAR
Safran Company
Fran Saperstein Organization
Shark Artists, Inc.
Shoelace, Inc. Management
Simmons and Scott Entertainment, LLC
Bette Smith Management
Sonesta Entertainment, LLC
Speak Softly Legal Management
Spot Light Entertainment
Star Talent Management
Station 3
The Sterling/Winters Company
Harriet Sternberg Management
The Suchin Company
Sussex Ltd., Inc., A Management Company
Synchronicity Management
Talent Source
TalentCo Model & Talent Management
TGI Entertainment Corporation
Torque Entertainment
Trademark Artists Management
Triple Threat Talent Management
Turner Artist Management
Universal Management Group (UMG)
Unlimited Management
V & L International, LLC
Valentino Entertainment
Vanguard Management Group
WA Enterprises
The Robert D. Wachs Company
Mimi Weber Management Co.
David Westberg Management
Wilhelmina Models

Theatre Talent

A Fein Martini
A.C.T. Management
A.D.S. Management
Anthem Entertainment
Archetype
Artist International
Arts and Letters Management
Associated Artists PR & Management
Bamboo Management LLC

MANAGERS

Theatre Talent (Continued)

Barking Dog Entertainment, Inc.
Baumgarten Management & Production
David Belenzon Management, Inc.
Bensky Entertainment
Michael Black Management, Inc.
Blue Train Entertainment
Blueprint Artist Management
Brookside Artist Management
Joyce Chase Management
Coastal Entertainment Productions
Columbia Artists Management LLC
Commonwealth Talent Group
Diane Connors Management
Contemporary Talent Partners (CTP)
The Conversation Company, Ltd.
The Coppage Company
Creative Talent Company
Crysis Management
Cue11 Entertainment
Alan David Management
Davila & Co.
Richard De Lancy & Associates Talent Agency
Dean Literary Concepts
DEJ Management Company
Denise Denny Talent Management
Dewalt & Muzik Management
Bonny Dore Management
Douglas Management Group
Dream Talent
Eastwood Talent Corporation
Eighth Square Entertainment
Michael Einfeld Management
Elkins Entertainment Corporation
Emerald Talent Group
Entertainment Management Group
Evans Management
The Firm, Inc.
Robert Fitzpatrick Organization
Flavor Unit Entertainment
Flutie Entertainment
Michael Forman Management
Fox-Albert Management Entertainment, Inc.
The FTL Company
Estelle Fusco Talent Management
Gem Entertainment Group, Inc.
Generate
Phillip B. Gittelman Personal Management
Glasser Black Management
Marianne Golan Management
Dodie Gold Management, Inc.
Jeff Goldberg Management
Goldstar Talent Management
Green Key Management, LLC
Handprint Entertainment
Hart² Management
Herbosch Management
Josselyne Herman & Associates
Himber Entertainment, Inc.

Theatre Talent (Continued)

Holder Management
Howard Entertainment
Hyler Management
ICM Artists
Incognito Management
The Independent Group, LLC
Infinity Management International
Cheri Ingram Enterprises
Darlene Kaplan Entertainment
Ann Kelly Management
Koopman Management
Kritzer Levine Wilkins Entertainment
Barry Krost Management
The Landers Group
Landis-Simon Productions & Talent Management
The Laugh Factory Management
Lawrence International Corporation
Lawson Artist Management, LLC
Letnom Management & Productions
Levine Management
Liebman Entertainment
Link Talent Group
Little Stars Management
Jeffrey Loseff Management
Magenta Creative Management
Management 101
Manta Entertainment
Marsala Management
The Marshak/Zachary Company
David Martin Management
Massei Management
McGowan Management
McKeon-Myones Management
McMurdo Management & Associates, LLC
Messina Baker Entertainment Corporation
Midwest Talent Management, Inc.
Millennium Entertainment, Inc.
April Mills Management
Renée Missel Management
J. Mitchell Management
MMC Entertainment/Dance Directions
Momentum Talent Management
Moore Artists' Management
MP Management
Dee Mura Enterprises, Inc.
Nani/Saperstein Management, Inc.
NCL TALENT
Barney Oldfield Management
Rosella Olson Management
Omnium Entertainment Group
Ovation Management
P.K.A. Entertainment Group
Pallas Management
Parseghian Planco, LLC
Ria Pavia Management
Polaris Entertainment
Pro and Con Productions Talent Management
Protege Entertainment

Theatre Talent (Continued)

Linda Reitman Management
The Right Connection Entertainment Group
RJM/Renée Jennett Management
J.C. Robbins Management
Rosalee Productions
The Marion Rosenberg Office
Sager Management, Inc.
Sanders/Armstrong Management
Saxon Associates Management
Schachter Entertainment
Booh Schut Company
Select Artists, Ltd.
Seven Summits Pictures & Management
Sharp Talent
Blair Silver & Company LLC
Simmons and Scott Entertainment, LLC
Andrea Simon Entertainment
Sinclair Management
SirenSong Entertainment, Inc.
Soiree Fair, Inc.
Speak Softly Legal Management
Spellman, Paul & Wetzel
Star Talent Management
Station 3
Steinberg Talent Management Group
The Sterling/Winters Company
Studio Talent Group
Sullivan Talent Group
Suzelle Enterprises
Synchronicity Management
The Talent Company
Talent Management Partners
Talent Scout International Management
TalentCo Model & Talent Management
TAO Management & Tetrahedron Productions
Terrific Talent Associates, Inc.
TGI Entertainment Corporation
Thirdhill Entertainment
TMT Entertainment
Torque Entertainment
Trademark Talent
Troika
Trusik Talent Management, Inc.
Tudor Management Group
Unique Talent Group
Universal Management Group (UMG)
V & L International, LLC
Vanguard Management Group
Mimi Weber Management Co.
David Westberg Management
Whitaker Entertainment
Wilhelmina Kids
Young Performers Management
Young Talent, Inc.
Zenith Management
Ziemba Talent & Associates

PUBLICITY COMPANIES

Corporate

Aerial Communications Group
American Blackguard Public Relations
American Entertainment Marketing
AR PR Marketing Firm
Artisans PR
Asbury Communications
Avid Exposure LLC
Baker/Winokur/Ryder (B/W/R)
Baker/Winokur/Ryder (B/W/R PPI)
Ed Baran Publicity
Barnett Marketing Communications
The Barrett Company
Barrow/Hoffman Public Relations
Bender/Helper Impact

Corporate (Continued)

Bragman Nyman Cafarelli (BNC)
Brand Central Promotions, Inc.
The Howard Brandy Company
The Britto Agency
The Brokaw Company
Nadia Bronson & Associates
Brownstein & Associates, Inc.
CelebrityFootage
Cerrell Associates
Chasen & Company
Clifford Public Relations
CMG Worldwide
CMPR
Consolidated Advertising Directors, Inc.

Corporate (Continued)

Costa Communications
Costello & Company Public Relations
Warren Cowan & Associates
CPR
CurrentPR, Inc.
Donna Daniels Public Relations
DDA Public Relations, Ltd.
Dera, Roslan & Campion, Inc. Public Relations
DeVeaux Agency
Lori DeWaal & Associates
Double A LLC Public Relations & Marketing
The Dowd Agency
Linda Dozoretz Communications
Kenneth Droz Public Relations

PUBLICITY COMPANIES

Corporate (Continued)

Evolutionary Media Group
Falco Ink
Faraone Communications, Inc.
Fat City Media
FAT DOT
Fifteen Minutes
Foundry Communications
Andrew E. Freedman Public Relations
Freud Communications Inc.
The Garis Agency
Bob Gold & Associates
Gorgeous PR, Inc.
Great Scott P.R.oductions
Lizzie Grubman Public Relations
Guttman Associates
Hands On Public Relations & Marketing
Hanson & Schwam Public Relations
Harrison & Shriftman
Frank Holguin and Associates
The Hollywood-Madison Group
The Honig Company, Inc.
I/D Public Relations
The Illusion Factory
The In-House Writer
ink Public Relations Group
iPressroom Corporation
I.S.M. Entertainment, Inc.
Jaffe & Co., Inc. Strategic Media
Jane Ayer Public Relations
Jones & O'Malley
KBC Media Relations
Dan Klores Associates
Landers PR
Jeffrey Lane & Associates
Anne Leighton Media * Marketing * Motivation
The Leverage Group
Levine Communications Office, Inc. (LCO)
The Lippin Group, Inc.
M. Loring Communications PR
Edward Lozzi & Associates
Lynch Archer PR Entertainment
M80
Susan Magrino Agency
Makeover Media
Manning Selvage & Lee
Manos Management & Public Relations
Mantra Empowered Public Relations
Norm Marshall & Associates, Inc.
Matter
MCA PR - Minerva Collier Associates, Ltd.
Reba Merrill Associates
Morris Marketing, Inc.
MPM Communications
mPRm Public Relations
Much and House Public Relations
Julian Myers Public Relations
No Problem Productions
Rebecca O'Meara Entertainment Publicity
On the Scene Productions
Gigi Otero Public Relations
Patricola/Lust Public Relations
PLA Media
Platform Media Group Inc.
PMK/HBH Public Relations
Fredell Pogodin & Associates
Premier Public Relations
Principal Communications Group
Priority Public Relations
Public Relations Associates
Rising Star Communications
The Rose Group
Rousso/Fisher Public Relations LLC
Schwartzman & Associates, Inc.
Nancy Seltzer & Associates, Inc.
Jerry Shandrew Public Relations
Sharp & Associates Public Relations
Sheba Media Group

Corporate (Continued)

Shepley Winings Diamond Public Relations Inc.
Keith Sherman & Associates
Cheryl Shuman, Inc.
Sitrick and Company
Smoke & Mirrors Public Relations, Inc.
Solters & Digney
The Spark Factory
Spasm Ink
SSA Public Relations
TMG International
Trevino Enterprises
True Public Relations
The Velsigne Group
The Viardo Agency
W3 Public Relations
Wallman Public Relations
Murray Weissman & Associates
Norman Winter Publicity
Workhouse Publicity

EPK

American Blackguard Public Relations
AngelWorks
Henri Bollinger Associates
Catalano Public Relations & Editorial Services
CelebrityFootage
DeVeaux Agency
The Dowd Agency
FAT DOT
Foundry Communications
Gorgeous PR, Inc.
Frank Holguin and Associates
The Illusion Factory
iPressroom Corporation
Levine Communications Office, Inc. (LCO)
Reba Merrill Associates
Mob Scene Creative + Productions
On the Scene Productions
PLA Media
Platform Media Group Inc.
Premiere TV
Schwartzman & Associates, Inc.
The Spark Factory
Spasm Ink
Murray Weissman & Associates

Film/TV Productions

11:24 Design Advertising, Inc.
15 Minutes
360 Media
American Blackguard Public Relations
American Entertainment Marketing
AngelWorks
Artisans PR
Asbury Communications
Avid Exposure LLC
Ed Baran Publicity
The Barrett Company
Henri Bollinger Associates
Brand Central Promotions, Inc.
The Howard Brandy Company
Brickman Marketing
The Brokaw Company
Nadia Bronson & Associates
Catalano Public Relations & Editorial Services
Celebrity Endeavors
CelebrityFootage
Chasen & Company
Club Beverly Hills
CMPR
Consolidated Advertising Directors, Inc.
Costa Communications
Warren Cowan & Associates
CPR
CurrentPR, Inc.
Donna Daniels Public Relations

Film/TV Productions (Continued)

DDA Public Relations, Ltd.
Dera, Roslan & Campion, Inc. Public Relations
DeVeaux Agency
dis COMPANY
The Dowd Agency
Kenneth Droz Public Relations
EPR Public Relations
Falco Ink
Faraone Communications, Inc.
FAT DOT
FLAG Marketing
Fleishman-Hillard
Freud Communications Inc.
Paul Gendreau Public Relations
Lizzie Grubman Public Relations
Guttman Associates
Hanson & Schwam Public Relations
Frank Holguin and Associates
Hollywood OS
Hype
I/D Public Relations
The Illusion Factory
Indie PR
The In-House Writer
I.S.M. Entertainment, Inc.
Jaffe & Co., Inc. Strategic Media
Jane Ayer Public Relations
Jensen Communications, Inc.
Jonas Public Relations
KBC Media Relations
Dan Klores Associates
Landers PR
Jeffrey Lane & Associates
Anne Leighton Media * Marketing * Motivation
The Leverage Group
Susan L. Levin Public Relations
Levine Communications Office, Inc. (LCO)
The Lippin Group, Inc.
Manos Management & Public Relations
Mantra Empowered Public Relations
Marcella C Public Relations, Inc.
Norm Marshall & Associates, Inc.
Matter
MCA PR - Minerva Collier Associates, Ltd.
Reba Merrill Associates
Mob Scene Creative + Productions
Morris Marketing, Inc.
Steve Moyer Public Relations
mPRm Public Relations
Much and House Public Relations
Julian Myers Public Relations
Blaise Noto & Associates
On the Scene Productions
Gigi Otero Public Relations
Patricola/Lust Public Relations
Perception Public Relations, LLC
PLA Media
Platform Media Group Inc.
Fredell Pogodin & Associates
Preacher Publicity & Reputation Management
Premier Public Relations
Premiere TV
Priority Public Relations
Public Relations Associates
Rising Star Communications
Rogers & Cowan
The Rose Group
Rousso/Fisher Public Relations LLC
Schwartzman & Associates, Inc.
Selfman & Others Public Relations
Nancy Seltzer & Associates, Inc.
Jerry Shandrew Public Relations
The Shefrin Company
Shepley Winings Diamond Public Relations Inc.
Keith Sherman & Associates
Cheryl Shuman, Inc.
Sitrick and Company

PUBLICITY COMPANIES

Film/TV Productions (Continued)

Solters & Digney
The Spark Factory
Spasm Ink
Spirit Media, Inc.
SSA Public Relations
Swept Away Media Corporation
Trailer Park Inc.
True Public Relations
Velvet Public Relations
The Viardo Agency
Vista Group
Wallman Public Relations
Webster & Associates Public Relations
Murray Weissman & Associates
Norman Winter Publicity
Workhouse Publicity

Film/TV Talent

42West
Aerial Communications Group
American Blackguard Public Relations
AR PR Marketing Firm
Asbury Communications
Avid Exposure LLC
Baker/Winokur/Ryder (B/W/R)
Ed Baran Publicity
Bragman Nyman Cafarelli (BNC)
The Britto Agency
The Brokaw Company
Nadia Bronson & Associates
Brownstein & Associates, Inc.
Catalano Public Relations & Editorial Services
The Celebrity Source
CelebrityFootage
Chasen & Company
Club Beverly Hills
CMG Worldwide
CMPR
Costa Communications
Costello & Company Public Relations
Warren Cowan & Associates
DDA Public Relations, Ltd.
DeVeaux Agency
Lori DeWaal & Associates
The Dowd Agency
Kenneth Droz Public Relations
Eisner Public Relations
Evolutionary Media Group
Falco Ink
Faraone Communications, Inc.
Fat City Media
FAT DOT
Fifteen Minutes
Andrew E. Freedman Public Relations
Front Page Publicity
The Garis Agency
GEM Public Relations
Paul Gendreau Public Relations
Gorgeous PR, Inc.
Great Scott P.R.oductions
Lizzie Grubman Public Relations
Guttman Associates
Hanson & Schwam Public Relations
Harrison & Shriftman
Frank Holguin and Associates
The Hollywood-Madison Group
The Honig Company, Inc.
I/D Public Relations
Indie PR
ink Public Relations Group
Jaffe & Co., Inc. Strategic Media
JAG Entertainment PR
Jane Ayer Public Relations
Lynn Allen Jeter & Associates
Jonas Public Relations
Jones & O'Malley
Milton Kahn Associates, Inc.

Film/TV Talent (Continued)

KBC Media Relations
Dan Klores Associates
Koger Public Relations & Events
Jeffrey Lane & Associates
The Leverage Group
Levine Communications Office, Inc. (LCO)
Lobeline Communications
M. Loring Communications PR
Edward Lozzi & Associates
Lynch Archer PR Entertainment
Susan Magrino Agency
Makeover Media
Manning Selvage & Lee
Mantra Empowered Public Relations
Marcella C Public Relations, Inc.
Matter
MCA PR - Minerva Collier Associates, Ltd.
Reba Merrill Associates
Steve Moyer Public Relations
MPM Communications
Much and House Public Relations
Julian Myers Public Relations
Blaise Noto & Associates
Rebecca O'Meara Entertainment Publicity
Gigi Otero Public Relations
Patricola/Lust Public Relations
Perception Public Relations, LLC
Personal Publicity
PLA Media
Platform Media Group Inc.
PMK/HBH Public Relations
Preacher Publicity & Reputation Management
Premier Public Relations
Premiere TV
Primary Action Inc.
Rising Star Communications
Rogers & Cowan
The Rose Group
Stan Rosenfield & Associates
Rousso/Fisher Public Relations LLC
Carl Samrock Public Relations Company
Schwartzman & Associates, Inc.
Selfman & Others Public Relations
Nancy Seltzer & Associates, Inc.
Jerry Shandrew Public Relations
Sharp & Associates Public Relations
Sheba Media Group
The Shefrin Company
Shepley Winings Diamond Public Relations Inc.
Keith Sherman & Associates
Cheryl Shuman, Inc.
Sitrick and Company
Smart Girls Productions, Inc.
Solters & Digney
Spasm Ink
Spirit Media, Inc.
SSA Public Relations
Swept Away Media Corporation
Trevino Enterprises
True Public Relations
The Velsigne Group
Velvet Public Relations
The Viardo Agency
W3 Public Relations
Wallman Public Relations
Webster & Associates Public Relations
Murray Weissman & Associates
Norman Winter Publicity
Wolf Kasteler & Associates PR
Workhouse Publicity

Marketing

11:24 Design Advertising, Inc.
15 Minutes
360 Media
Aerial Communications Group
American Blackguard Public Relations

Marketing (Continued)

American Entertainment Marketing
AR PR Marketing Firm
Artisans PR
Asbury Communications
Avid Exposure LLC
Baker/Winokur/Ryder (B/W/R)
Baker/Winokur/Ryder (B/W/R PPI)
Barnett Marketing Communications
The Barrett Company
Bender/Helper Impact
Henri Bollinger Associates
Bragman Nyman Cafarelli (BNC)
Brand Central Promotions, Inc.
Brickman Marketing
The Britto Agency
Brownstein & Associates, Inc.
Catalano Public Relations & Editorial Services
CelebrityFootage
Chasen & Company
Clifford Public Relations
Club Beverly Hills
CMG Worldwide
CMPR
Consolidated Advertising Directors, Inc.
Costa Communications
Warren Cowan & Associates
CPR
CurrentPR, Inc.
Davie-Brown Entertainment
Deep Focus
Dera, Roslan & Campion, Inc. Public Relations
DeVeaux Agency
Double A LLC Public Relations & Marketing
The Dowd Agency
Linda Dozoretz Communications
Kenneth Droz Public Relations
Evolutionary Media Group
Fat City Media
FAT DOT
Fifteen Minutes
Fireworks Marketing & Advertising
FLAG Marketing
Freud Communications Inc.
The Garis Agency
GEM Public Relations
Paul Gendreau Public Relations
Bob Gold & Associates
Gorgeous PR, Inc.
Great Scott P.R.oductions
Lizzie Grubman Public Relations
Hands On Public Relations & Marketing
Hanson & Schwam Public Relations
Harrison & Shriftman
Frank Holguin and Associates
The Hollywood-Madison Group
The Honig Company, Inc.
Hype
The Illusion Factory
The In-House Writer
ink Public Relations Group
iPressroom Corporation
I.S.M. Entertainment, Inc.
JAG Entertainment PR
Jane Ayer Public Relations
Jensen Communications, Inc.
Lynn Allen Jeter & Associates
Jonas Public Relations
Krupp Kommunications
Landers PR
Anne Leighton Media * Marketing * Motivation
The Leverage Group
Susan L. Levin Public Relations
Levine Communications Office, Inc. (LCO)
Lobeline Communications
Edward Lozzi & Associates
Lynch Archer PR Entertainment
M80

PUBLICITY COMPANIES

Marketing (Continued)

Makeover Media
Manning Selvage & Lee
Mantra Empowered Public Relations
Matter
MCA PR - Minerva Collier Associates, Ltd.
Media Monster Communications, Inc./
    Brain Gasm Productions Entertainment Media
Reba Merrill Associates
Mob Scene Creative + Productions
Morris Marketing, Inc.
Steve Moyer Public Relations
Much and House Public Relations
Julian Myers Public Relations
Blaise Noto & Associates
Rebecca O'Meara Entertainment Publicity
On the Scene Productions
Originalee Made in Los Angeles
Gigi Otero Public Relations
Perception Public Relations, LLC
Personal Publicity
PLA Media
Platform Media Group Inc.
Preacher Publicity & Reputation Management
Premier Public Relations
Primary Action Inc.
Principal Communications Group
Priority Public Relations
Rising Star Communications
Rogers & Cowan
The Rose Group
Rousso/Fisher Public Relations LLC
Carl Samrock Public Relations Company
Schwartzman & Associates, Inc.
Nancy Seltzer & Associates, Inc.
Set Resources
Jerry Shandrew Public Relations
Sheba Media Group
Shepley Winings Diamond Public Relations Inc.
Cheryl Shuman, Inc.
Smart Girls Productions, Inc.
Smoke & Mirrors Public Relations, Inc.
Solters & Digney
The Spark Factory
Spasm Ink
Spirit Media, Inc.
SSA Public Relations
Swept Away Media Corporation
TMG International
Trailer Park Inc.
Trevino Enterprises
UPP Entertainment Marketing
The Velsigne Group
The Viardo Agency
Vista Group
Murray Weissman & Associates
Norman Winter Publicity
Workhouse Publicity

Music

360 Media
American Blackguard Public Relations
AR PR Marketing Firm
Artisans PR
Asbury Communications
Avid Exposure LLC
Baker/Winokur/Ryder (B/W/R)
Henri Bollinger Associates
BopStar-PR Inc.
Brand Central Promotions, Inc.
The Britto Agency
The Brokaw Company
Catalano Public Relations & Editorial Services
Chasen & Company
Costa Communications
Warren Cowan & Associates
CPR
Davie-Brown Entertainment

Music (Continued)

Dera, Roslan & Campion, Inc. Public Relations
DeVeaux Agency
dis COMPANY
Linda Dozoretz Communications
Kenneth Droz Public Relations
Evolutionary Media Group
Faraone Communications, Inc.
FAT DOT
Fifteen Minutes
Fireworks Marketing & Advertising
FLAG Marketing
Andrew E. Freedman Public Relations
Front Page Publicity
The Garis Agency
Gorgeous PR, Inc.
Great Scott P.R.oductions
Lizzie Grubman Public Relations
Guttman Associates
Hands On Public Relations & Marketing
Hanson & Schwam Public Relations
Harrison & Shriftman
Frank Holguin and Associates
Infectious
ink Public Relations Group
JAG Entertainment PR
Jane Ayer Public Relations
Jensen Communications, Inc.
Lynn Allen Jeter & Associates
KBC Media Relations
Koger Public Relations & Events
Jeffrey Lane & Associates
Anne Leighton Media * Marketing * Motivation
The Leverage Group
Levine Communications Office, Inc. (LCO)
The Lippin Group, Inc.
Lobeline Communications
M. Loring Communications PR
M80
Makeover Media
Mantra Empowered Public Relations
Marcella C Public Relations, Inc.
Matter
MCA PR - Minerva Collier Associates, Ltd.
Steve Moyer Public Relations
MPM Communications
mPRm Public Relations
No Problem Productions
Blaise Noto & Associates
Rebecca O'Meara Entertainment Publicity
On the Scene Productions
PLA Media
Platform Media Group Inc.
PMK/HBH Public Relations
Preacher Publicity & Reputation Management
Premiere TV
Press Here Publicity
Rogers & Cowan
Rousso/Fisher Public Relations LLC
The Mitch Schneider Organization (MSO)
Nancy Seltzer & Associates, Inc.
Sheba Media Group
The Shefrin Company
Keith Sherman & Associates
Cheryl Shuman, Inc.
Solters & Digney
Spasm Ink
Spirit Media, Inc.
SSA Public Relations
Trevino Enterprises
True Public Relations
The Velsigne Group
The Viardo Agency
W3 Public Relations
Webster & Associates Public Relations
Murray Weissman & Associates
Norman Winter Publicity
Workhouse Publicity

New Media

11:24 Design Advertising, Inc.
AngelWorks
Artisans PR
Asbury Communications
Barnett Marketing Communications
Bender/Helper Impact
Brand Central Promotions, Inc.
Brownstein & Associates, Inc.
Catalano Public Relations & Editorial Services
Warren Cowan & Associates
CPR
CurrentPR, Inc.
Davie-Brown Entertainment
Deep Focus
The Dowd Agency
Kenneth Droz Public Relations
Faraone Communications, Inc.
FAT DOT
Foundry Communications
Andrew E. Freedman Public Relations
The Garis Agency
Bob Gold & Associates
Gorgeous PR, Inc.
Hands On Public Relations & Marketing
Hanson & Schwam Public Relations
Harrison & Shriftman
Frank Holguin and Associates
Hollywood OS
Hype
The Illusion Factory
The In-House Writer
iPressroom Corporation
Jaffe & Co., Inc. Strategic Media
JAG Entertainment PR
Jane Ayer Public Relations
Anne Leighton Media * Marketing * Motivation
The Leverage Group
Levine Communications Office, Inc. (LCO)
The Lippin Group, Inc.
Lobeline Communications
M. Loring Communications PR
M80
Makeover Media
Mantra Empowered Public Relations
Matter
Mob Scene Creative + Productions
Morris Marketing, Inc.
mPRm Public Relations
Julian Myers Public Relations
Rebecca O'Meara Entertainment Publicity
On the Scene Productions
Personal Publicity
Platform Media Group Inc.
Principal Communications Group
Public Relations Associates
The Rose Group
Rousso/Fisher Public Relations LLC
Carl Samrock Public Relations Company
Schwartzman & Associates, Inc.
Sheba Media Group
Cheryl Shuman, Inc.
Smoke & Mirrors Public Relations, Inc.
Solters & Digney
The Spark Factory
Spasm Ink
SSA Public Relations
Trailer Park Inc.
UPP Entertainment Marketing
The Velsigne Group
The Viardo Agency
W3 Public Relations
Norman Winter Publicity
Workhouse Publicity

PUBLICITY COMPANIES

Outdoor Advertising

Brand Central Promotions, Inc.
Fireworks Marketing & Advertising
The Illusion Factory
Platform Media Group Inc.
Spasm Ink
Trailer Park Inc.

Product Placement

American Blackguard Public Relations
AR PR Marketing Firm
Avid Exposure LLC
Baker/Winokur/Ryder (B/W/R)
Baker/Winokur/Ryder (B/W/R PPI)
Bender/Helper Impact
Bragman Nyman Cafarelli (BNC)
The Britto Agency
Celebrity Endeavors
CPR
Davie-Brown Entertainment
Evolutionary Media Group
Fat City Media
FAT DOT
Andrew E. Freedman Public Relations
The Garis Agency
Guttman Associates
Hanson & Schwam Public Relations
Harrison & Shriftman
Frank Holguin and Associates
The Hollywood-Madison Group
I/D Public Relations
ink Public Relations Group
I.S.M. Entertainment, Inc.
Landers PR
The Leverage Group
Levine Communications Office, Inc. (LCO)
M. Loring Communications PR
Edward Lozzi & Associates
Makeover Media
Manning Selvage & Lee
Norm Marshall & Associates, Inc.
Matter
MCA PR - Minerva Collier Associates, Ltd.
Motion Picture Magic
Much and House Public Relations
Julian Myers Public Relations
Rebecca O'Meara Entertainment Publicity
On the Scene Productions
Originalee Made in Los Angeles
Perception Public Relations, LLC
Platform Media Group Inc.
Primary Action Inc.
Rogers & Cowan
Rousso/Fisher Public Relations LLC
Set Resources
Sheba Media Group
Cheryl Shuman, Inc.
Swept Away Media Corporation
UPP Entertainment Marketing
The Viardo Agency
Vista Group
Murray Weissman & Associates
Workhouse Publicity

Promotions

11:24 Design Advertising, Inc.
15 Minutes
Aerial Communications Group
American Blackguard Public Relations
American Entertainment Marketing
AR PR Marketing Firm
Artisans PR
Asbury Communications
Avid Exposure LLC
Baker/Winokur/Ryder (B/W/R)
Baker/Winokur/Ryder (B/W/R PPI)
Barnett Marketing Communications
Bender/Helper Impact
Henri Bollinger Associates
BopStar-PR Inc.
Brand Central Promotions, Inc.
Catalano Public Relations & Editorial Services
CelebrityFootage
Club Beverly Hills
CMG Worldwide
CMPR
Consolidated Advertising Directors, Inc.
Costa Communications
Costello & Company Public Relations
Warren Cowan & Associates
CPR
Donna Daniels Public Relations
Davie-Brown Entertainment
Deep Focus
Double A LLC Public Relations & Marketing
Kenneth Droz Public Relations
FAT DOT
Fireworks Marketing & Advertising
Andrew E. Freedman Public Relations
The Garis Agency
GEM Public Relations
Paul Gendreau Public Relations
Lizzie Grubman Public Relations
Guttman Associates
Hands On Public Relations & Marketing
Hanson & Schwam Public Relations
Harrison & Shriftman
Frank Holguin and Associates
The Hollywood-Madison Group
The Honig Company, Inc.
Hype
The Illusion Factory
ink Public Relations Group
iPressroom Corporation
I.S.M. Entertainment, Inc.
Jaffe & Co., Inc. Strategic Media
Jane Ayer Public Relations
Jensen Communications, Inc.
Lynn Allen Jeter & Associates
Milton Kahn Associates, Inc.
KBC Media Relations
Koger Public Relations & Events
Krupp Kommunications
Landers PR

Promotions (Continued)

Jeffrey Lane & Associates
The Leverage Group
Susan L. Levin Public Relations
Levine Communications Office, Inc. (LCO)
Lobeline Communications
M. Loring Communications PR
Edward Lozzi & Associates
Lynch Archer PR Entertainment
M80
Makeover Media
Manning Selvage & Lee
Norm Marshall & Associates, Inc.
Matter
MCA PR - Minerva Collier Associates, Ltd.
Reba Merrill Associates
David Mirisch Enterprises
Morris Marketing, Inc.
Steve Moyer Public Relations
MPM Communications
mPRm Public Relations
Julian Myers Public Relations
Blaise Noto & Associates
Rebecca O'Meara Entertainment Publicity
On the Scene Productions
Originalee Made in Los Angeles
Gigi Otero Public Relations
Perception Public Relations, LLC
Personal Publicity
PLA Media
Platform Media Group Inc.
Primary Action Inc.
Rising Star Communications
Rogers & Cowan
Rousso/Fisher Public Relations LLC
Schwartzman & Associates, Inc.
Nancy Seltzer & Associates, Inc.
Set Resources
Sharp & Associates Public Relations
Sheba Media Group
Shepley Winings Diamond Public Relations Inc.
Cheryl Shuman, Inc.
Smart Girls Productions, Inc.
Solters & Digney
The Spark Factory
Spasm Ink
Spirit Media, Inc.
SSA Public Relations
Swept Away Media Corporation
TMG International
Trailer Park Inc.
Trevino Enterprises
True Public Relations
UPP Entertainment Marketing
The Velsigne Group
The Viardo Agency
Vista Group
Murray Weissman & Associates
Workhouse Publicity

CASTING DIRECTORS

Commercials

Jane Alderman Casting
Sande Alessi Casting
A-List Projects
AMVF Casting
ASG Casting, Inc.
Aspen Production Services
BB Casting & Production Services, Inc.
Breanna Benjamin Casting
Terry Berland Casting

Commercials (Continued)

Barbara Bersell Casting
Big House Casting
Charles Bogdan
Beau Bonneau Casting
Broadcasters
Casting House
Casting Solutions
Casting Valdes
Casting Works LA

Commercials (Continued)

Chantiles/Vigneault Casting, Inc.
Chelsea Studios Casting
Annelise Collins Casting
Complete Casting
Ruth Conforte Casting
Sara Cooper Casting
Creative Extras Casting
Curdy Curdy Casting
Billy DaMota

CASTING DIRECTORS

Commercials (Continued)

De Lancy-Castro
Donna DeSeta Casting
Michael Donovan Casting
Dowd/Roman Casting
Eastside Studios
Danielle Eskinazi Casting
Lisa Fields Casting
Fincannon & Associates
Jack Fletcher
Megan Foley Commercial Casting
Gallegos/Carrafiello Casting
Jeff Gerrard
Godlove & Company Casting
Danny Goldman & Associates
Amy Gossels Casting
Hampton Shannon Casting
Carol Hanzel Casting
Jeff Hardwick Casting
Helen Wheels Productions
Judy Henderson & Associates Casting
Nina Henninger & Associates Casting
Hispanic Talent Casting of Hollywood
Stuart Howard Associates, Ltd.
Impossible Casting
Susan Johnston Casting
Katy Casting Inc.
Avy Kaufman Casting
Kee Casting
Amy Klein Casting
Deborah Kurtz
L.A. Casting Group, Inc.
Ross Lacy Casting
Judy Landau Casting
Marilee Lear Casting
Carol Lefko Casting
Mike Lemon Casting, CSA
Kelli Lerner Casting
Liz Lewis Casting Partners
Lien/Cowan Casting
Beverly Long Casting
Penny Ludford Casting
Joan Lynn Casting
Liz Marks
McCaffrey Gilles Casting
John McCarthy Casting
Media Casting & Film Production
Beth Melsky Casting
Dee Miller/The Casting Directors, Inc.
Mimi Webb Miller Casting
Monroe Casting & Production
Bob Morones Casting
MovieWork Now Casting, Inc.
Kimberly Mullen/Mark Mullen Casting
Debra Neathery
O'Haver + Company
Orpheus Group
The Philadelphia Casting Company, Inc.
Playboy TV
Prime Casting
Tina Real
Robi Reed & Associates
Reel Talent/Reel Kids
Rodeo Casting
Gabrielle Schary
Brien Scott
Lila Selik Casting
Ava Shevitt Casting
Shooting From The Hip Casting
Susan Shopmaker Casting
Mark Sikes Casting
Claire Simon Casting
Caroline Sinclair Casting
Clair Sinnett Casting
JS Snyder & Associates Casting
Stark Naked Productions (Elsie Stark Casting)
Stuart Stone
Andrew Strauser Casting

Commercials (Continued)

Strickman-Ripps, Inc.
Yumi Takada Casting
Bernard Telsey Casting
Tenner, Paskal & Rudnicke Casting, Inc.
Total Casting
Tribute Productions
Triple Threat Casting
Susan Tyler Casting
Universal Casting, LLC
VideoActive Talent
The Voicecaster
Debe Waisman Casting
Kathy Wickline Casting
Grant Wilfley Casting
Catherine Wilshire Casting
World Casting

Film

ABC Family Channel
Aikins/Cossey Casting
Jane Alderman Casting
Sande Alessi Casting
A-List Projects
AMVF Casting
Andrea Kenyon & Associates Casting
Aquila/Wood Casting
Maureen A. Arata, CSA
Julie Ashton Casting
Aspen Production Services
automatic sweat
Jeanie Bacharach
Barry/Green-Keyes Casting
Pamela Basker, CSA
Eve Battaglia Casting
Nancy Nayor Battino Casting
BB Casting & Production Services, Inc.
Beach/Katzman Casting
Beech Hill Films
Eyde Belasco
Breanna Benjamin Casting
Terry Berland Casting
Chemin Bernard Casting
Barbara Bersell Casting
Juel Bestrop & Seth Yanklewitz Casting
Betty Mae, Inc.
Sharon Bialy
Big Bad Wolff Entertainment
Big House Casting
Tammara Billik Casting
Jay Binder Casting
Barbie Block
Charles Bogdan
Jo Edna Boldin Casting
Beau Bonneau Casting
Judith Bouley
John Buchan Casting, Inc.
Buena Vista Motion Pic. Group Feature Casting
Krisha Bullock
Jackie Burch
Burrows/Boland Casting
Calleri Casting
Ferne Cassel
Casting Artists, Inc.
The Casting Company
Casting House
Casting Solutions
Casting Valdes
Casting Works LA
CFB Casting
Lindsay Chag
Denise Chamian
Fern Champion
Chantiles/Vigneault Casting, Inc.
Chelsea Studios Casting
Kathleen Chopin
Annelise Collins Casting
Jodi Collins Casting

Film (Continued)

Complete Casting
Ruth Conforte Casting
Sara Cooper Casting
Stephanie Corsalini Casting
Gretchen Rennell Court
Creative Extras Casting
Cricket Feet Casting
Crystal Sky Communications
Patrick Cunningham, CSA
Curdy Curdy Casting
Sarah Dalton
Billy DaMota
Bill Dance Casting
Dauphin-Backel Casting
Kim Davis-Wagner
De Lancy-Castro
Zora DeHorter Casting
Donna DeSeta Casting
Dickson/Arbusto Casting
Dimension Films Casting
Walt Disney Feature Animation Casting
Pam Dixon Casting
Michael Donovan Casting
DreamWorks SKG Casting
Brennan Dufresne
Jennifre' DuMont Casting
Dorian Dunas
Eastside Studios
Engine Media Group
Danielle Eskinazi Casting
Mike Fenton
Lisa Fields Casting
Alan Filderman Casting
Fincannon & Associates
Leonard Finger Casting
Mali Finn Casting
Finn/Hiller Casting
Bonnie Finnegan Casting
Fiorentino-Mangieri Casting
Firefly Casting
Jack Fletcher
FMW Casting
Megan Foley Commercial Casting
Eddie Foy III Casting
Nancy Foy
Jerold Franks & Associates
Lisa Freiberger Casting
Gallegos/Carrafiello Casting
Risa Bramon Garcia
Jeff Gerrard
Ginsberg/Fink Casting
Susan Glicksman Casting
GO Casting
Godlove & Company Casting
Gail Goldberg Casting
Stephanie Gorin Casting
Amy Gossels Casting
Jeff Greenberg Casting
Greenstein/Daniel Casting
Aaron Griffith
Al Guarino
Pamela Rack Guest
Lonnie Hamerman
Hampton Shannon Casting
Theodore Hann
Carol Hanzel Casting
Jeff Hardwick Casting
Rene Haynes Casting
HBO Films Casting
Heery Casting, LLC
Helen Wheels Productions
Judy Henderson & Associates Casting
Cathy Henderson-Martin Casting
Nina Henninger & Associates Casting
Dawn Hershey
Richard Hicks Casting
Hispanic Talent Casting of Hollywood

CASTING DIRECTORS

Film (Continued)

Stuart Howard Associates, Ltd.
Victoria Huff & Associates
Hypercasting, Inc.
Impossible Casting
John Jackson
Elllen Jacoby Casting International
Elisabeth Jereski
Susan Johnston Casting
Christine Joyce
Tracy Kaplan
Katy Casting Inc.
Avy Kaufman Casting
Kee Casting
Stephanie Klapper Casting
Amy Klein Casting
Thom Klohn
Nancy Klopper
Eileen Mack Knight Casting
Koblin/Harding Casting
Dorothy Koster Casting
Ronna Kress Casting
Lynn Kressel Casting
Deborah Kurtz
L.A. Casting Group, Inc.
Dino Ladki Casting
Landsburg/Fiddleman Casting
Marilee Lear Casting
Carol Lefko Casting
Mike Lemon Casting, CSA
Kelli Lerner Casting
Matthew Lessall Casting
Heidi Levitt Casting
Liz Lewis Casting Partners
Liberman/Patton Casting
Amy Lippens
Robin Lippin
Marci Liroff Casting
London/Stroud Casting
Beverly Long Casting
Lori Wyman Casting
Junie Lowry-Johnson Casting
Linda Lowy Casting
Penny Ludford Casting
Joan Lynn Casting
MacDonald/Bullington Casting
Mackey/Sandrich Casting
Francine Maisler Casting
Malyszek Casting
Mindy Marin
Liz Marks
Ricki G. Maslar Casting
Coreen Mayrs Casting, Inc.
Valerie McCaffrey Casting
McCaffrey Gilles Casting
McCann-Knotek Casting
Jeanne McCarthy Casting
McCorkle Casting, Ltd.
Robert McGee
Tom McSweeney Casting
Media Casting & Film Production
Beth Melsky Casting
Monika Mikkelsen
Dee Miller/The Casting Directors, Inc.
Lisa Mionie
Mitchell/Rudolph Casting
MJB Casting
Monroe Casting & Production
Pat Moran & Associates
Bob Morones Casting
Michelle Morris-Gertz
Barry Moss Casting
MovieWork Now Casting, Inc.
MTV Casting
Kimberly Mullen/Mark Mullen Casting
Roger Mussenden Casting
Nassif & Baca Casting
Debra Neathery

Film (Continued)

New Line Casting
Bruce H. Newberg Casting
O'Haver + Company
Orpheus Group
Marvin Paige Casting
Mark Paladini
Linda Phillips Palo
Ellen Parks Casting
Pemrick/Fronk Casting
Perry/Reece Casting
The Philadelphia Casting Company, Inc.
Playboy TV
Playwrights Horizons
Prime Casting
Rainbow Casting Service
Johanna Ray & Associates
RDC Casting, Inc.
Tina Real
Robi Reed & Associates
Reel Talent/Reel Kids
Shari Rhodes Casting
RisingCast
Vicki Rosenberg & Associates
Donna Rosenstein
Cindi Rush Casting, Ltd.
Mark Saks
Brien Scott
Tina Seiler
Lila Selik Casting
Ava Shevitt Casting
Susan Shopmaker Casting
Showtime Networks Talent & Casting
Mark Sikes Casting
Alyson Silverberg
Claire Simon Casting
Caroline Sinclair Casting
Clair Sinnett Casting
Melissa Skoff Casting
Slater-Brooksbank Casting
JS Snyder & Associates Casting
Ilene Starger Casting
Stark Naked Productions (Elsie Stark Casting)
Adrienne Stern
Sally Stiner Casting
Andrea Stone
Stuart Stone
Studio Talent Group
Monica Swann Casting
Daniel Swee
Yumi Takada Casting
Bernard Telsey Casting
Tenner, Paskal & Rudnicke Casting, Inc.
Sherry Thomas
Mark Tillman
Todd/Campobasso Casting
Cindy Tolan Casting
Total Casting
Tribeca Casting
Tribute Productions
Twentieth Century Fox Feature Casting
Susan Tyler Casting
Ulrich/Dawson/Kritzer Casting
Universal Casting, LLC
Universal Studios Feature Film Casting
VideoActive Talent
Debe Waisman Casting
Alex Wald
Warner Bros. Feature Film Casting
Weber & Associates Casting
April Webster & Associates
Rosemary Welden
Kathy Wickline Casting
Grant Wilfley Casting
Catherine Wilshire Casting
Jason Wood Casting
Barbara Wright
Ronnie Yeskel & Associates
Debra Zane Casting

Industrials

Jane Alderman Casting
Sande Alessi Casting
AMVF Casting
Aspen Production Services
BB Casting & Production Services, Inc.
Breanna Benjamin Casting
Big House Casting
Beau Bonneau Casting
Broadcasters
Casting House
Casting Solutions
Casting Works LA
Chantiles/Vigneault Casting, Inc.
Chelsea Studios Casting
Annelise Collins Casting
Complete Casting
Ruth Conforte Casting
Sara Cooper Casting
De Lancy-Castro
Donna DeSeta Casting
Michael Donovan Casting
Eastside Studios
Megan Foley Commercial Casting
Jeff Gerrard
Godlove & Company Casting
Danny Goldman & Associates
Amy Gossels Casting
Carol Hanzel Casting
Helen Wheels Productions
Nina Henninger & Associates Casting
Hispanic Talent Casting of Hollywood
Susan Johnston Casting
Kee Casting
Stephanie Klapper Casting
Deborah Kurtz
L.A. Casting Group, Inc.
Judy Landau Casting
Marilee Lear Casting
Mike Lemon Casting, CSA
Kelli Lerner Casting
Liz Lewis Casting Partners
Lien/Cowan Casting
Beverly Long Casting
Penny Ludford Casting
Malyszek Casting
Liz Marks
McCaffrey Gilles Casting
John McCarthy Casting
Media Casting & Film Production
Beth Melsky Casting
Dee Miller/The Casting Directors, Inc.
Monroe Casting & Production
MovieWork Now Casting, Inc.
Debra Neathery
The Philadelphia Casting Company, Inc.
Playboy TV
Prime Casting
Tina Real
Reel Talent/Reel Kids
Rodeo Casting
Gabrielle Schary
Brien Scott
Tina Seiler
Lila Selik Casting
Susan Shopmaker Casting
Clair Sinnett Casting
Stark Naked Productions (Elsie Stark Casting)
Stuart Stone
Studio Talent Group
Yumi Takada Casting
Bernard Telsey Casting
Tenner, Paskal & Rudnicke Casting, Inc.
Total Casting
Tribute Productions
Susan Tyler Casting
Universal Casting, LLC
The Voicecaster

CASTING DIRECTORS

Industrials (Continued)

Debe Waisman Casting
Kathy Wickline Casting
World Casting

Theatre

Jane Alderman Casting
Fran Bascom
Pamela Basker, CSA
Breanna Benjamin Casting
Jay Binder Casting
Blue Man Productions
Calleri Casting
Casting Solutions
Center Theatre Group Casting
Chantiles/Vigneault Casting, Inc.
Chelsea Studios Casting
Rich Cole
Jodi Collins Casting
Cricket Feet Casting
De Lancy-Castro
Zora DeHorter Casting
Donna DeSeta Casting
Dickson/Arbusto Casting
Michael Donovan Casting
Jennifre' DuMont Casting
Danielle Eskinazi Casting
Alan Filderman Casting
Firefly Casting
Jeff Gerrard
Goldwasser/Meltzer Casting
Jeff Greenberg Casting
Carol Hanzel Casting
Jeff Hardwick Casting
Helen Wheels Productions
Judy Henderson & Associates Casting
Stuart Howard Associates, Ltd.
Victoria Huff & Associates
Impossible Casting
Susan Johnston Casting
Stephanie Klapper Casting
Amy Klein Casting
Eileen Mack Knight Casting
Marilee Lear Casting
Carol Lefko Casting
Mike Lemon Casting, CSA
Liz Lewis Casting Partners
Joan Lynn Casting
Manhattan Theatre Club
Valerie McCaffrey Casting
McCaffrey Gilles Casting
McCorkle Casting, Ltd.
Mitchell/Rudolph Casting
Barry Moss Casting
Bruce H. Newberg Casting
Orpheus Group
Perry/Reece Casting
The Philadelphia Casting Company, Inc.
Playboy TV
Playwrights Horizons
Reel Talent/Reel Kids
Roundabout Theatre Company
Cindi Rush Casting, Ltd.
Tina Seiler
Susan Shopmaker Casting
Claire Simon Casting
Clair Sinnett Casting
JS Snyder & Associates Casting
Stark Naked Productions (Elsie Stark Casting)
Daniel Swee
Bernard Telsey Casting
Tenner, Paskal & Rudnicke Casting, Inc.
Total Casting
Tribute Productions
Susan Tyler Casting
Jason Wood Casting
Liz Woodman Casting

TV

ABC Entertainment Casting (New York)
ABC Entertainment Casting (Los Angeles)
ABC Family Channel
ABC Television Studio
Laura Adler
Jane Alderman Casting
A-List Projects
AMVF Casting
Andrea Kenyon & Associates Casting
Maureen A. Arata, CSA
ASG Casting, Inc.
Julie Ashton Casting
Aspen Production Services
automatic sweat
AYC Casting
Jeanie Bacharach
Deborah Barylski
Fran Bascom
Pamela Basker, CSA
Nancy Nayor Battino Casting
BB Casting & Production Services, Inc.
Beech Hill Films
Eyde Belasco
Breanna Benjamin Casting
Terry Berland Casting
Chemin Bernard Casting
Barbara Bersell Casting
Juel Bestrop & Seth Yanklewitz Casting
Sharon Bialy
Big Bad Wolff Entertainment
Big House Casting
Tammara Billik Casting
Jay Binder Casting
Barbie Block
Susan Bluestein
Jo Edna Boldin Casting
Beau Bonneau Casting
Bowling/Miscia Casting
Deedee Bradley
Megan Branman
Jackie Briskey
Broadcasters
John Buchan Casting, Inc.
Krisha Bullock
Burrows/Boland Casting
Calleri Casting
The Casting Company
Casting House
Casting Solutions
Casting Valdes
Casting Works LA
CBS Television Casting
CBS/Paramount Network Television Casting
CFB Casting
Lindsay Chag
Fern Champion
Chantiles/Vigneault Casting, Inc.
Chelsea Studios Casting
Annelise Collins Casting
Jodi Collins Casting
Complete Casting
Ruth Conforte Casting
Sara Cooper Casting
Stephanie Corsalini Casting
Creative Extras Casting
Crystal Sky Communications
Patrick Cunningham, CSA
Curdy Curdy Casting
Sarah Dalton
Billy DaMota
Bill Dance Casting
Dauphin-Backel Casting
De Lancy-Castro
Zora DeHorter Casting
Leslee Dennis
Donna DeSeta Casting
Dickson/Arbusto Casting

TV (Continued)

Disney Channel Casting
Michael Donovan Casting
Christy Dooley
Mary Downey Productions
DreamWorks SKG Casting
Brennan Dufresne
Jennifre' DuMont Casting
Dorian Dunas
Nan Dutton Casting
E! Entertainment Television Casting
Engine Media Group
Danielle Eskinazi Casting
Felicia Fasano
Mike Fenton
Lisa Fields Casting
Fincannon & Associates
Leonard Finger Casting
Finn/Hiller Casting
Bonnie Finnegan Casting
Fiorentino-Mangieri Casting
Firefly Casting
Jack Fletcher
FMW Casting
Megan Foley Commercial Casting
Fox Broadcasting Company Casting
Eddie Foy III Casting
Nancy Foy
Jerold Franks & Associates
Lisa Freiberger Casting
Gallegos/Carrafiello Casting
Nicole Garcia
Risa Bramon Garcia
Jeff Gerrard
Gilmore/McConnell Casting
Ginsberg/Fink Casting
Susan Glicksman Casting
GO Casting
Godlove & Company Casting
Goldwasser/Meltzer Casting
Stephanie Gorin Casting
Amy Gossels Casting
Jeff Greenberg Casting
Greenstein/Daniel Casting
Aaron Griffith
Lonnie Hamerman
Hampton Shannon Casting
Theodore Hann
Carol Hanzel Casting
Jeff Hardwick Casting
Heery Casting, LLC
Helen Wheels Productions
Judy Henderson & Associates Casting
Cathy Henderson-Martin Casting
Nina Henninger & Associates Casting
Dawn Hershey
Richard Hicks Casting
Hispanic Talent Casting of Hollywood
Stuart Howard Associates, Ltd.
Victoria Huff & Associates
Hypercasting, Inc.
Impossible Casting
John Jackson
Elllen Jacoby Casting International
Joey Paul Casting
Tara-Anne Johnson
Susan Johnston Casting
Christine Joyce
Tracy Kaplan
Katy Casting Inc.
Lisa Miller Katz
Avy Kaufman Casting
Kee Casting
Stephanie Klapper Casting
Amy Klein Casting
Eileen Mack Knight Casting
Koblin/Harding Casting
Dorothy Koster Casting

CASTING DIRECTORS

TV (Continued)

Lynn Kressel Casting
Deborah Kurtz
L.A. Casting Group, Inc.
Dino Ladki Casting
Ruth Lambert
Landsburg/Fiddleman Casting
LaPadura & Hart Casting
Marilee Lear Casting
Carol Lefko Casting
Mike Lemon Casting, CSA
Kelli Lerner Casting
Matthew Lessall Casting
Liz Lewis Casting Partners
Liberman/Patton Casting
Tracy Lilienfield Company
Amy Lippens
Robin Lippin
Leslie Litt
London/Stroud Casting
Beverly Long Casting
Molly Lopata Casting
Lori Wyman Casting
Junie Lowry-Johnson Casting
Linda Lowy Casting
Penny Ludford Casting
Mackey/Sandrich Casting
Malyszek Casting
Liz Marks
Liz Marx
Coreen Mayrs Casting, Inc.
Valerie McCaffrey Casting
McCaffrey Gilles Casting
McCann-Knotek Casting
Jeanne McCarthy Casting
John McCarthy Casting
McCorkle Casting, Ltd.
Robert McGee
Tom McSweeney Casting
Media Casting & Film Production
Beth Melsky Casting
Dee Miller/The Casting Directors, Inc.
Rick Millikan
Lisa Mionie
Mitchell/Rudolph Casting
Monroe Casting & Production
Pat Moran & Associates
Bob Morones Casting
Barry Moss Casting
MovieWork Now Casting, Inc.
MTV Casting
MTV/MTV2 Talent
Kimberly Mullen/Mark Mullen Casting
Roger Mussenden Casting
Nassif & Baca Casting
NBC Entertainment Casting
NBC Universal Television Studio Casting
Debra Neathery
Bruce H. Newberg Casting
Nickelodeon Casting
Patricia Noland
O'Haver + Company
Gillian O'Neill
Orpheus Group
Pagano/Manwiller Casting
Marvin Paige Casting
Linda Phillips Palo
Tim Payne Casting
Pemrick/Fronk Casting
Perry/Reece Casting
The Philadelphia Casting Company, Inc.
Bonnie Pietila
Playboy TV
Playwrights Horizons

TV (Continued)

Powell/Melcher Casting
Prime Casting
RDC Casting, Inc.
Tina Real
Robi Reed & Associates
Reel Talent/Reel Kids
Shari Rhodes Casting
RisingCast
Romano/Benner
Stacey Rosen
Vicki Rosenberg & Associates
Donna Rosenstein
Mark Saks
Gabrielle Schary
Brien Scott
Kevin Scott
Tina Seiler
Lila Selik Casting
Ava Shevitt Casting
Shooting From The Hip Casting
Susan Shopmaker Casting
Showtime Networks Talent & Casting
Mark Sikes Casting
Alyson Silverberg
Claire Simon Casting
Clair Sinnett Casting
Melissa Skoff Casting
Slater-Brooksbank Casting
Sony Pictures Television Casting
Spike TV Casting
Camille St. Cyr Casting
Stark Naked Productions (Elsie Stark Casting)
Adrienne Stern
Sally Stiner Casting
Stuart Stone
Gilda Stratton
Andrew Strauser Casting
Studio Talent Group
Monica Swann Casting
Daniel Swee
Yumi Takada Casting
Bernard Telsey Casting
Tenner, Paskal & Rudnicke Casting, Inc.
Mark Teschner Casting
Sherry Thomas
Mark Tillman
Todd/Campobasso Casting
Total Casting
Tribute Productions
Triple Threat Casting
Julie Tucker Casting
Twentieth Century Fox Television Casting
Susan Tyler Casting
Ulrich/Dawson/Kritzer Casting
Universal Casting, LLC
Valko/Miller Casting
VideoActive Talent
The Voicecaster
Debe Waisman Casting
Dava Waite Casting
Alex Wald
Warner Bros. Television Casting
Weber & Associates Casting
April Webster & Associates
John Wells Productions
Kathy Wickline Casting
Grant Wilfley Casting
Catherine Wilshire Casting
Jason Wood Casting
Barbara Wright
Ronnie Yeskel & Associates
Zane/Pillsbury Casting
Gary Zuckerbrod

Voice-Over

ABC Family Channel
AMVF Casting
Pamela Basker, CSA
BB Casting & Production Services, Inc.
Breanna Benjamin Casting
Terry Berland Casting
Big House Casting
Broadcasters
Casting House
Casting Solutions
Casting Works LA
Chantiles/Vigneault Casting, Inc.
Chelsea Studios Casting
Annelise Collins Casting
Complete Casting
Ruth Conforte Casting
Elaine Craig Voice Casting, Inc.
Curdy Curdy Casting
De Lancy-Castro
Donna DeSeta Casting
Walt Disney Feature Animation Casting
DisneyToon Studios
DreamWorks SKG Casting
Jeff Gerrard
Godlove & Company Casting
Danny Goldman & Associates
Carol Hanzel Casting
Helen Wheels Productions
Judy Henderson & Associates Casting
Dawn Hershey
Susan Johnston Casting
Amy Klein Casting
Eileen Mack Knight Casting
Deborah Kurtz
L.A. Casting Group, Inc.
Marilee Lear Casting
Carol Lefko Casting
Mike Lemon Casting, CSA
Liz Lewis Casting Partners
Lien/Cowan Casting
Beverly Long Casting
Valerie McCaffrey Casting
John McCarthy Casting
Media Casting & Film Production
Beth Melsky Casting
Dee Miller/The Casting Directors, Inc.
Monroe Casting & Production
MovieWork Now Casting, Inc.
MTV Casting
Debra Neathery
O'Haver + Company
Bonnie Pietila
Playboy TV
Reel Talent/Reel Kids
RisingCast
Tina Seiler
Lila Selik Casting
Ava Shevitt Casting
Claire Simon Casting
Stark Naked Productions (Elsie Stark Casting)
Stuart Stone
Yumi Takada Casting
Bernard Telsey Casting
Tenner, Paskal & Rudnicke Casting, Inc.
Total Casting
Tribute Productions
Twentieth Century Fox Feature Casting
Susan Tyler Casting
Universal Casting, LLC
The Voicecaster
Voicetrax Casting
Kathy Wickline Casting

SECTION G

INDEX BY CLIENT

AGENTS

Actors

ABA - Amatruda Benson & Associates
abc model/talent/sport management
About Artists Agency
Abrams Artists Agency (Los Angeles)
Abrams Artists Agency (New York)
Acme Talent & Literary
Actors & Others Talent Agency
Actors Etc., Inc.
Actors LA Agency
Bret Adams, Ltd.
Advance LA
Affinity Model & Talent Agency
Agape Productions
Agency For the Performing Arts, Inc. (Los Angeles)
Agents For The Arts, Inc.
Aimée Entertainment Agency
AKA Talent Agency
Alexa Model & Talent Management, Inc.
The Alvarado Rey Agency
Michael Amato Agency
Ambassador Talent Agents, Inc.
Ambition Talent Inc.
American Program Bureau
Amsel, Eisenstadt & Frazier, Inc.
Beverly Anderson Agency
Andreadis Talent Agency, Inc.
Angel City Talent
Aqua
Arcieri & Associates, Inc.
ARIA Talent
Artist Management Agency
The Artists Agency
The Artists Group, Ltd.
Atlanta Models & Talent, Inc.
Atlas Talent Agency
The Austin Agency
Baier/Kleinman International
Donna Baldwin Talent
Baldwin Talent, Inc.
Baron Entertainment
Barry Haft Brown Artists Agency
Baskow & Associates, Inc.
Bauman, Redanty, & Shaul Agency
Beauty Models/BC4
The Sandi Bell Talent Agency, Inc.
Berzon Talent Agency
The Bethel Agency
Beverly Hills International Talent Agency
Bicoastal Talent
Bonnie Black Talent & Literary Agency
The Blake Agency
Blue Ridge Entertainment
Judy Boals, Inc.
Bobby Ball Talent Agency
Boca Talent & Model Agency
Boom Models & Talent
Boutique
Brady, Brannon & Rich
Brand Model and Talent Agency, Inc.
Brass Artists & Associates
Bresler Kelly & Associates
Brevard Talent Group, Inc.
BRick Entertainment
The Brogan Agency
Don Buchwald & Associates, Inc. (Los Angeles)
Don Buchwald & Associates, Inc. (New York)
Buchwald Talent Group, LLC
The Burns Agency, Inc.
Calliope Talent, Model & Artist Management, LLC
Suzanna Camejo & Associates: Artists for the Environment
The Campbell Agency
Carmichael Talent
Conan Carroll & Associates
The Carry Co.
The Carson Organization, Ltd.
Carson-Adler Agency, Inc.

Actors (Continued)

Cassell-Levy, Inc. (dba Clinc)
Cast Images Talent Agency
Castle Hill Talent Agency
Cavaleri & Associates
Celebrity Suppliers/Sports Star Suppliers
Nancy Chaidez Agency & Associates
The Characters
Charles Talent Agency
The Chasin Agency
Chateau Billings Talent Agency
Chic Models & Talent Agency
The Christensen Group
Ciao! Talent Agency
Circle Talent Associates
Mary Anne Claro Talent Agency, Inc.
Clear Talent Group
Colleen Cler Talent Agency
Coast To Coast Talent Group, Inc.
Commercial Talent, Inc.
The Coppage Company
Coralie Jr. Theatrical Agency
Cornerstone Talent Agency
Corsa Agency
Creative Artists Agency - CAA
The Culbertson Group, LLC
Cunningham-Escott-Slevin-Doherty Talent (LA)
Cunningham-Escott-Slevin-Doherty Talent (NY)
Kim Dawson Talent
DDO Artists Agency
Defining Artists
Marla Dell Talent Agency
DeSanti Talents, Inc.
Ginger Dicce Talent Agency
Dimensions III Talent Agency
Diverse Talent Group
Domain
Douglas, Gorman, Rothacker & Wilhelm, Inc.
EC Model & Talent Agency (Ent. Caterers, Inc.)
Edna Talent Management (ETM) Ltd.
Dulcina Eisen Associates
Electric Talent
Elegance Talent Agency
Ellis Talent Group
Empire Talent Agency
Encore Talent Agency
Endeavor Agency, LLC
Equinox Models/Equinox Talent/Zoo Models
Expressions Model & Talent
Sylvia Ferguson & Assoc. Talent & Literary Agency
JFA/Jaime Ferrar Agency
Film Artists Associates
Flick East-West Talents, Inc.
Jim Flynn Agency
FORD/Robert Black Agency
Fosi's Modeling & Talent Agency
Fresh Faces Agency, Inc.
Frontier Booking International, Inc.
The Gage Group, Inc. (Los Angeles)
The Gage Group, Inc. (New York)
Gage Talent, Inc.
Garber Talent Agency
Dale Garrick International Agency
The Gatsby Group, Inc.
The Geddes Agency (Chicago)
The Geddes Agency (Los Angeles)
Laya Gelff Agency
Generations Model & Talent Agency
Don Gerler Agency
The Gersh Agency (Los Angeles)
The Gersh Agency (New York)
Gilla Roos, Ltd.
The Glick Agency, LLC
Global Artists Agency
Michelle Gordon & Associates
Grant, Savic, Kopaloff and Associates
Greene & Associates
Greer Lange Model & Talent Agency, Inc.

Actors (Continued)

Grossman & Jack Talent
GVA Talent Agency, Inc.
Peggy Hadley Enterprises, Ltd.
Buzz Halliday & Associates
Halpern Management
Neal Hamil Agency
Hanns Wolters International, Inc.
Harden-Curtis Associates
Hartig Hilepo Agency, Ltd.
Beverly Hecht Agency
Henderson/Hogan Agency
Hervey/Grimes Talent Agency
Daniel Hoff Agency
Hollander Talent Group
Hop Models & Talent Agency
Hot Shot Kids/Teens
The House of Representatives
Howard Talent West
The I Group Model & Talent Management
Identity Talent Agency
IFA Talent Agency
Image Model & Talent
Impact Talent Group
Imperium 7 Talent Agency (i7)
Independent Artists Agency Inc.
Independent Artists Agency, Inc.
Ingber & Associates
Innovative Artists (Los Angeles)
Innovative Artists (New York)
International Artists Group, Inc.
International Creative Mgmt., Inc. - ICM (LA)
International Creative Mgmt., Inc. - ICM (NY)
IRISHVOX
JE Talent, LLC/JE Model, Inc.
Jet Set Management Group, Inc.
JKA Talent & Literary Agency
JLA Talent
Jordan, Gill & Dornbaum
JS Represents
Stanley Kaplan Talent
Kazarian/Spencer & Associates
Glyn Kennedy, Models Talent
Kerin-Goldberg & Associates
William Kerwin Agency
Archer King, Ltd.
Kjar & Associates
Paul Kohner, Inc.
Kolstein Talent Agency (KTA)
The Krasny Office, Inc.
L.A. Talent
Lally Talent Agency (LTA)
Lane Agency
Leading Artists, Inc.
Buddy Lee Attractions, Inc.
Leighton Agency, Inc.
Lemodeln Model & Talent Agency
Lenz Agency
Sid Levin Agency
Bernard Liebhaber Agency
Lily's Talent Agency, Inc.
Look Talent
The Luedtke Agency
Jana Luker Agency
M International Talent Agency
Mademoiselle Talent & Modeling Agency
Malaky International
The Mannequin Agency
Markham & Froggatt Ltd.
Martin & Donalds Talent Agency, Inc.
Max Freedman Management
Maxine's Talent Agency
The McCabe Group
McCarty Talent, Inc.
McDonald/Selznick Associates
Media Artists Group
Metropolitan Talent Agency (MTA)
MGATalent

AGENTS

Actors (Continued)

Miramar Talent Agency
Model Club, Inc.
Model Team
Momentum Talent & Literary Agency
The Morgan Agency
H. David Moss & Associates
Susan Nathe & Associates, CPC
Nicolosi & Co., Inc.
Nouveau Model & Talent
Nouvelle Talent Management, Inc.
NTA Talent Agency
Nu Talent Agency
NXT Entertainment, Inc.
Omnipop Talent Group
One Entertainment
O'Neill Talent Group
The Orange Grove Group, Inc.
Origin Talent
Osbrink Talent Agency
Fifi Oscard Agency, Inc.
Pacific West Artists
Pakula/King & Associates
Dorothy Palmer Talent Agency, Inc.
The Meg Pantera Agency, Inc.
Pantheon
Paradigm (Los Angeles)
Paradigm (New York)
The Paradise Group Talent Agency
Pastorini-Bosby Talent, Inc.
Peak Models & Talent
Perfectly Petite, Inc.
Phoenix Artists, Inc.
John Pierce Agency
Pinnacle Commercial Talent
Players Talent Agency
The Price Group LLC
Privilege Talent Agency
Professional Artists
Progressive Artists Agency
PTI Talent Agency, Inc.
Q Model Management
Qualita Dell' Arte: Artists & Writers Di Qualita
Rebel Entertainment Partners, Inc.
Cindy Romano Modeling & Talent Agency
San Diego Model Management Talent Agency
San Francisco Top Models & Talent
Sanger Talent Agency
The Sarnoff Company, Inc.
The Savage Agency
Jack Scagnetti Talent & Literary Agency
The Irv Schechter Company
Schiowitz Connor Ankrum Wolf, Inc.
Sandie Schnarr Talent
Judy Schoen & Associates
Schuller Talent/NY Kids
Kathleen Schultz Associates
Screen Artists Agency, LLC
SDB Partners, Inc.
SGM - Sara Gaynor Management
Shamon Freitas Model & Talent Agency
David Shapira & Associates (DSA)
Shapiro-Lichtman Talent Agency, Inc.
Jerome Siegel Associates
Sky Talent Agency
The Susan Smith Company
SMS Talent, Inc.
The Sohl Agency
Sonja Warren Brandon's Commercials Unlimited
Special Artists Agency
Scott Stander & Associates, Inc.
Starcraft Talent Agency
Stars, The Agency
Starwil Talent
Ann Steele Agency
Steinberg's Talent Agency
Stellar Model & Talent Agency
The Stevens Group

Actors (Continued)

Stewart Talent
Ivett Stone Agency
Stone Manners Agency
Peter Strain & Associates, Inc. (Los Angeles)
Peter Strain & Associates, Inc. (New York)
Mitchell K. Stubbs & Associates
Superior Talent Agency
Sutton, Barth & Vennari, Inc.
Tag Models
Talent & Model Land
The Talent Group
Talent House Agency
Talent Plus, Inc./Centro Models
Talent Plus/Los Latinos Talent Agency
Talent Representatives, Inc.
The Talent Shop
Talent Trek Agency
Talent Unlimited, Inc.
TalentWorks
TalentWorks New York
The Thomas Talent Agency
Arlene Thornton & Associates
Tonry Talent
United Talent Agency - UTA
Universal Talent Intelligence
Uptown Talent, Inc.
Vision Art Management
Vision Los Angeles
The Wallis Agency
Bob Waters Agency, Inc.
The Ann Waugh Talent Agency
Donna Wauhob Agency
Wilhelmina West, Inc./LW1 Talent Agency
William Morris Agency - WMA (Los Angeles)
William Morris Agency - WMA (New York)
William Morris Agency - WMA (Miami Beach)
William Morris Agency - WMA (London)
William Morris Agency - WMA (Shanghai)
Shirley Wilson & Associates
Ann Wright Representatives
Craig Wyckoff & Associates
Zanuck, Passon and Pace, Inc.

Animals

Ambassador Talent Agents, Inc.
The Carson Organization, Ltd.
Castle Hill Talent Agency
Coralie Jr. Theatrical Agency
Le Paws
Lemodeln Model & Talent Agency
Martin & Donalds Talent Agency, Inc.
The Gilbert Miller Agency LLC
Model Team
Oracle Creative Management
Dorothy Palmer Talent Agency, Inc.
Perfectly Petite, Inc.
Periwinkle Entertainment Productions
Cindy Romano Modeling & Talent Agency
Donna Wauhob Agency

Book Authors

Carole Abel Literary
Abrams Artists Agency (Los Angeles)
Abrams Artists Agency (New York)
Acme Talent & Literary
Agape Productions
Agency For the Performing Arts, Inc. (Los Angeles)
The Agency Group Ltd. (Los Angeles)
The Agency Group Ltd. (New York)
Aimée Entertainment Agency
Miriam Altshuler Literary Agency
Ambassador Talent Agents, Inc.
American Program Bureau
Marcia Amsterdam Agency
Artists Agency, Inc.
Artists Literary Group (ALG)

Book Authors (Continued)

Baron Entertainment
Loretta Barrett Books, Inc.
Baskow & Associates, Inc.
Meredith Bernstein Literary Agency
Berzon Talent Agency
The Bethel Agency
Beverly Hills International Talent Agency
Vicky Bijur Literary Agency
The Bohrman Agency
Georges Borchardt, Inc.
Brands-To-Books, Inc.
Brandt & Hochman Literary Agents
Browne & Miller Literary Associates LLC
Marcus Bryan & Associates
Don Buchwald & Associates, Inc. (Los Angeles)
Don Buchwald & Associates, Inc. (New York)
Sheree Bykofsky Associates, Inc.
The Callamaro Literary Agency
Cambridge Literary Associates, Inc.
Suzanna Camejo & Associates: Artists for the
  Environment
Castiglia Literary Agency
Celebrity Suppliers/Sports Star Suppliers
The Chasin Agency
Wm. Clark Associates
Coast To Coast Talent Group, Inc.
Frances Collin Literary Agent
Don Congdon Associates
Cornerstone Literary, Inc.
Course Management
Creative Artists Agency - CAA
Curtis Brown, Ltd.
D4EO Literary Agency
Deiter Literary Agency
Dunham Literary, Inc.
The E S Agency
The Nicholas Ellison Agency
Endeavor Agency, LLC
Farber Literary Agency, Inc.
Folio Literary Management, LLC
FRP Literary - Talent Agency
Max Gartenberg Literary Agency
The Gatsby Group, Inc.
Gelfman Schneider Literary Agents, Inc.
The Gersh Agency (Los Angeles)
The Gersh Agency (New York)
Ashley Grayson Literary Agency
Sanford J. Greenburger Associates
The Charlotte Gusay Literary Agency
The Mitchell J. Hamilburg Agency
The Joy Harris Literary Agency
John Hawkins & Associates
Hays Media LLC
Jeff Herman Agency, LLC
Susan Herner Rights Agency
Barbara Hogenson Agency, Inc.
Hollywood View
Hotchkiss & Associates
IMG/Broadcasting
InkWell Management
International Creative Mgmt., Inc. - ICM (LA)
International Creative Mgmt., Inc. - ICM (NY)
James Peter Associates, Inc.
Janklow & Nesbit Associates
JKA Talent & Literary Agency
Merrily Kane Agency
Archer King, Ltd.
Harvey Klinger, Inc.
Kneerim & Williams at Fish & Richardson, PC
Paul Kohner, Inc.
Barbara S. Kouts
Otto R. Kozak Literary & Motion Picture Agency
The LA Literary Agency
Lally Talent Agency (LTA)
Peter Lampack Agency, Inc.
Susanna Lea Associates
Buddy Lee Attractions, Inc.

AGENTS

Book Authors (Continued)

Lemodeln Model & Talent Agency
Lenhoff & Lenhoff
Levine Greenberg Literary Agency
Paul S. Levine Literary Agency
Literary and Creative Artists, Inc. (LCA, Inc.)
The Literary Group
Nancy Love Literary Agency
Gina Maccoby Literary Agency
Manus & Associates Literary Agency, Inc.
Max Freedman Management
Maxine's Talent Agency
Helen McGrath & Associates
McIntosh and Otis, Inc.
Mendel Media Group LLC
Menza-Barron Agency
Metropolis
Metropolitan Talent Agency (MTA)
The Stuart M. Miller Co.
Monteiro Rose Dravis Agency, Inc.
Montgomery West Literary Agency, LLC
Jean V. Naggar Literary Agency, Inc.
Nash-Angeles, Inc.
New England Publishing Associates
Betsy Nolan Literary Agency
Harold Ober Associates
Ofrenda, Inc.
Original Artists
Fifi Oscard Agency, Inc.
Dorothy Palmer Talent Agency, Inc.
Paradigm (New York)
Kathi J. Paton Literary Agency
Barry Perelman Agency
L. Perkins Agency
Peters Fraser & Dunlop (PFD)
Stephen Pevner, Inc.
Pinder Lane & Garon-Brooke Associates, Ltd.
The Aaron M. Priest Literary Agency
Susan Ann Protter Literary Agent
Qualita Dell' Arte: Artists & Writers Di Qualita
The Rabineau Wachter Sanford & Harris
   Literary Agency
Raines & Raines
Reece Halsey North
Jodie Rhodes Agency
Rights Unlimited
The Angela Rinaldi Literary Agency
Ann Rittenberg Literary Agency, Inc.
RLR Associates
Michael D. Robins & Associates
The Roistacher Literary Agency
The Rosenberg Group
Rosenstone/Wender
Jane Rotrosen Agency
Peter Rubie Literary Agency
Russell & Volkening
Victoria Sanders & Associates, LLC
Jack Scagnetti Talent & Literary Agency
The Irv Schechter Company
Susan Schulman Literary Agency
Scribblers House LLC Literary Agency
Ken Sherman & Associates
Bobbe Siegel Literary Agency
Jerome Siegel Associates
Michael H. Sommer Literary Agency
Philip G. Spitzer Literary Agency, Inc.
Stars, The Agency
Joan Stewart Agency
Marianne Strong Literary Agency
Suite A Management Talent & Literary Agency
Summit Talent & Literary Agency
Roslyn Targ Literary Agency
S©ott Treimel NY
Trident Media Group, LLC
United Talent Agency - UTA
Universal Talent Intelligence
Veritas Literary Agency
Veritas Media, Inc.

Book Authors (Continued)

Wales Literary Agency, Inc.
Warden McKinley Literary Agency
Wardlow & Associates
John A. Ware Literary Agency
Watkins/Loomis Agency Inc.
Irene Webb Literary
The Wendy Weil Agency, Inc.
Weingel-Fidel Agency
William Morris Agency - WMA (Los Angeles)
William Morris Agency - WMA (New York)
William Morris Agency - WMA (Miami Beach)
William Morris Agency - WMA (London)
William Morris Agency - WMA (Shanghai)
Ann Wright Representatives
Writers House
Writers' Representatives, LLC
The Wylie Agency
Nick Yellen Creative Agency
Zachary Shuster Harmsworth Agency

Broadcast Journalists/Newscasters

abc model/talent/sport management
Abrams Artists Agency (Los Angeles)
Abrams Artists Agency (New York)
Affinity Model & Talent Agency
Michael Amato Agency
Ambition Talent Inc.
American Program Bureau
Angel City Talent
Atlas Talent Agency
Baron Entertainment
The Bethel Agency
Boca Talent & Model Agency
Boom Models & Talent
BRick Entertainment
Don Buchwald & Associates, Inc. (Los Angeles)
Don Buchwald & Associates, Inc. (New York)
The Carry Co.
Cassell-Levy, Inc. (dba Clinc)
Celebrity Suppliers/Sports Star Suppliers
Nancy Chaidez Agency & Associates
The Characters
Chateau Billings Talent Agency
The Christensen Group
Creative Artists Agency - CAA
The Crofoot Group, Inc.
Cunningham-Escott-Slevin-Doherty Talent (LA)
Deiter Literary Agency
Garber Talent Agency
Hanns Wolters International, Inc.
The I Group Model & Talent Management
IMG/Broadcasting
Imperium 7 Talent Agency (i7)
Innovative Artists (Los Angeles)
International Artists Group, Inc.
International Creative Mgmt., Inc. - ICM (LA)
International Creative Mgmt., Inc. - ICM (NY)
Lemodeln Model & Talent Agency
Lenz Agency
Sid Levin Agency
Lily's Talent Agency, Inc.
Ken Lindner & Associates, Inc.
Malaky International
H. David Moss & Associates
N.S. Bienstock, Inc.
Napoli Management Group
Dorothy Palmer Talent Agency, Inc.
The Paradise Group Talent Agency
Pastorini-Bosby Talent, Inc.
Perfectly Petite, Inc.
Players Talent Agency
Privilege Talent Agency
Qualita Dell' Arte: Artists & Writers Di Qualita
RLR Associates
San Francisco Top Models & Talent
The Sarnoff Company, Inc.
Scott Stander & Associates, Inc.

Broadcast Journalists/Newscasters (Continued)

Stars, The Agency
Stellar Model & Talent Agency
Superior Talent Agency
The Talent Group
Talent Plus/Los Latinos Talent Agency
The Talent Shop
Talent Unlimited, Inc.
Tonry Talent
William Morris Agency - WMA (Los Angeles)
William Morris Agency - WMA (New York)
William Morris Agency - WMA (Miami Beach)
William Morris Agency - WMA (London)
William Morris Agency - WMA (Shanghai)

Children

ABA - Amatruda Benson & Associates
abc model/talent/sport management
Abrams Artists Agency (Los Angeles)
Abrams Artists Agency (New York)
Acme Talent & Literary
Actors & Others Talent Agency
Actors Etc., Inc.
Advance LA
Affinity Model & Talent Agency
Aimée Entertainment Agency
AKA Talent Agency
Alexa Model & Talent Management, Inc.
Michael Amato Agency
Ambassador Talent Agents, Inc.
Amsel, Eisenstadt & Frazier, Inc.
Andreadis Talent Agency, Inc.
Angel City Talent
Aqua
ARIA Talent
Artist Management Agency
Atlanta Models & Talent, Inc.
Donna Baldwin Talent
Baron Entertainment
Baskow & Associates, Inc.
The Sandi Bell Talent Agency, Inc.
Berzon Talent Agency
The Bethel Agency
Bicoastal Talent
Bonnie Black Talent & Literary Agency
Bobby Ball Talent Agency
Boca Talent & Model Agency
Boom Models & Talent
Brand Model and Talent Agency, Inc.
Brevard Talent Group, Inc.
BRick Entertainment
The Brogan Agency
Don Buchwald & Associates, Inc. (Los Angeles)
Don Buchwald & Associates, Inc. (New York)
Buchwald Talent Group, LLC
Calliope Talent, Model & Artist Management, LLC
The Campbell Agency
Carmichael Talent
Conan Carroll & Associates
The Carry Co.
The Carson Organization, Ltd.
Carson-Adler Agency, Inc.
Casala, Ltd.
Cassell-Levy, Inc. (dba Clinc)
Cast Images Talent Agency
Castle Hill Talent Agency
Cavaleri & Associates
Nancy Chaidez Agency & Associates
The Characters
Chateau Billings Talent Agency
Chic Models & Talent Agency
The Christensen Group
Ciao! Talent Agency
Circle Talent Associates
Mary Anne Claro Talent Agency, Inc.
Clear Talent Group
Colleen Cler Talent Agency

AGENTS

Children (Continued)

Coast To Coast Talent Group, Inc.
Commercial Talent, Inc.
Coralie Jr. Theatrical Agency
Corsa Agency
Cunningham-Escott-Slevin-Doherty Talent (LA)
Cunningham-Escott-Slevin-Doherty Talent (NY)
Kim Dawson Talent
DDO Artists Agency
Marla Dell Talent Agency
DeSanti Talents, Inc.
Dimensions III Talent Agency
Diverse Talent Group
Elegance Talent Agency
Empire Talent Agency
Encore Talent Agency
Expressions Model & Talent
Sylvia Ferguson & Assoc. Talent & Literary Agency
JFA/Jaime Ferrar Agency
Fosi's Modeling & Talent Agency
Fresh Faces Agency, Inc.
Frontier Booking International, Inc.
The Gage Group, Inc. (Los Angeles)
Dale Garrick International Agency
The Geddes Agency (Chicago)
Generation TV
Generations Model & Talent Agency
Gilla Roos, Ltd.
Grossman & Jack Talent
Neal Hamil Agency
Beverly Hecht Agency
Hervey/Grimes Talent Agency
Daniel Hoff Agency
Hollander Talent Group
Hop Models & Talent Agency
Hot Shot Kids/Teens
The House of Representatives
Howard Talent West
The I Group Model & Talent Management
Identity Talent Agency
Image Model & Talent
Impact Talent Group
Imperium 7 Talent Agency (i7)
Innovative Artists (Los Angeles)
Innovative Artists (New York)
International Artists Group, Inc.
International Creative Mgmt., Inc. - ICM (LA)
JE Talent, LLC/JE Model, Inc.
Jet Set Management Group, Inc.
JLA Talent
Jordan, Gill & Dornbaum
Stanley Kaplan Talent
Kazarian/Spencer & Associates
Glyn Kennedy, Models Talent
Kjar & Associates
L.A. Talent
Leighton Agency, Inc.
Lemodeln Model & Talent Agency
Sid Levin Agency
Lily's Talent Agency, Inc.
Jana Luker Agency
Mademoiselle Talent & Modeling Agency
Malaky International
The Mannequin Agency
Martin & Donalds Talent Agency, Inc.
Media Artists Group
MGATalent
Model Club, Inc.
Model Team
Momentum Talent & Literary Agency
The Morgan Agency
Susan Nathe & Associates, CPC
Nouveau Model & Talent
NTA Talent Agency
NXT Entertainment, Inc.
One Entertainment
Origin Talent
Osbrink Talent Agency

Children (Continued)

Dorothy Palmer Talent Agency, Inc.
Pastorini-Bosby Talent, Inc.
Perfectly Petite, Inc.
Phoenix Artists, Inc.
Privilege Talent Agency
Qualita Dell' Arte: Artists & Writers Di Qualita
Cindy Romano Modeling & Talent Agency
San Diego Model Management Talent Agency
San Francisco Top Models & Talent
Sanger Talent Agency
The Savage Agency
Schuller Talent/NY Kids
Screen Artists Agency, LLC
Shamon Freitas Model & Talent Agency
Sonja Warren Brandon's Commercials Unlimited
Scott Stander & Associates, Inc.
Starcraft Talent Agency
Stars, The Agency
Starwil Talent
Stellar Model & Talent Agency
Stewart Talent
Ivett Stone Agency
Superior Talent Agency
Tag Models
Talent & Model Land
The Talent Group
Talent Plus, Inc./Centro Models
Talent Plus/Los Latinos Talent Agency
The Talent Shop
Talent Trek Agency
Talent Unlimited, Inc.
TalentWorks
Tonry Talent
Uptown Talent, Inc.
The Ann Waugh Talent Agency
Donna Wauhob Agency
Shirley Wilson & Associates
Craig Wyckoff & Associates
Zanuck, Passon and Pace, Inc.

Choreographers

abc model/talent/sport management
Abrams Artists Agency (New York)
Bret Adams, Ltd.
Andreadis Talent Agency, Inc.
Baron Entertainment
Baskow & Associates, Inc.
Bauman, Redanty, & Shaul Agency
The Bethel Agency
bloc talent agency, inc.
Calliope Talent, Model & Artist Management, LLC
Clear Talent Group
Cunningham-Escott-Slevin-Doherty Talent (NY)
DDO Artists Agency
DeSanti Talents, Inc.
The Gage Group, Inc. (Los Angeles)
Garber Talent Agency
Neal Hamil Agency
Harden-Curtis Associates
International Creative Mgmt., Inc. - ICM (NY)
Kazarian/Spencer & Associates
Archer King, Ltd.
Lally Talent Agency (LTA)
Lily's Talent Agency, Inc.
Martin & Donalds Talent Agency, Inc.
McDonald/Selznick Associates
Paradigm (New York)
Perfectly Petite, Inc.
Rosenstone/Wender
Schuller Talent/NY Kids
Scott Stander & Associates, Inc.
Stars, The Agency
Talent House Agency
The Talent Shop
Donna Wauhob Agency
Waving Clouds Productions
William Morris Agency - WMA (Los Angeles)

Choreographers (Continued)

William Morris Agency - WMA (New York)
William Morris Agency - WMA (London)

Cinematographers

A...List Artists
All Crew Agency
Ambition Talent Inc.
Doug Apatow Agency
Below The Line Artists
Suzanna Camejo & Associates: Artists for the Environment
The Characters
Stacy Cheriff Agency
The Criterion Group, Inc.
Dattner Dispoto and Associates
Diverse Talent Group
Endeavor Agency, LLC
Esq. Management
The Gatsby Group, Inc.
The Geller Agency
Paul Gerard Agency
Grant, Savic, Kopaloff and Associates
International Creative Mgmt., Inc. - ICM (LA)
International Creative Mgmt., Inc. - ICM (NY)
Jacob & Kole Agency
Lemodeln Model & Talent Agency
Lenhoff & Lenhoff
Michael Lewis & Associates
The Mack Agency
Judy Marks Agency
Sandra Marsh Management
The Mirisch Agency
Montana Artists Agency, Inc.
New York Office
Oracle Creative Management
Orlando Management
Paradigm (Los Angeles)
The Partos Company
Prime Artists
Michael D. Robins & Associates
The Schneider Entertainment Agency
The Screen Talent Agency, Ltd.
Sesler & Company
Shapiro-Lichtman Talent Agency, Inc.
Sheldon Prosnit Agency
The Skouras Agency
The Stein Agency
TDN Artists (The Director's Network)
Russell Todd Agency (RTA)
United Talent Agency - UTA
William Morris Agency - WMA (Miami Beach)

Comedians

abc model/talent/sport management
About Artists Agency
Abrams Artists Agency (Los Angeles)
Abrams Artists Agency (New York)
Acme Talent & Literary
Actors Etc., Inc.
Advance LA
Affinity Model & Talent Agency
Agency For the Performing Arts, Inc. (Los Angeles)
Agency For the Performing Arts, Inc. (New York)
The Agency Group Ltd. (Los Angeles)
The Agency Group Ltd. (New York)
Aimée Entertainment Agency
Ambassador Talent Agents, Inc.
American Program Bureau
Amsel, Eisenstadt & Frazier, Inc.
Angel City Talent
Aqua
ARIA Talent
Irvin Arthur Associates
Associated Booking Corporation (ABC)
Donna Baldwin Talent
Baldwin Talent, Inc.

AGENTS

Comedians (Continued)

Baron Entertainment
Baskow & Associates, Inc.
Beachfront Bookings
Berzon Talent Agency
The Bethel Agency
Beverly Hills International Talent Agency
Bicoastal Talent
Bonnie Black Talent & Literary Agency
Blue Ridge Entertainment
Judy Boals, Inc.
Boca Talent & Model Agency
Boom Models & Talent
Brady, Brannon & Rich
Brass Artists & Associates
BRick Entertainment
The Brogan Agency
Don Buchwald & Associates, Inc. (Los Angeles)
Don Buchwald & Associates, Inc. (New York)
Calliope Talent, Model & Artist Management, LLC
The Campbell Agency
Carmichael Talent
The Carry Co.
The Carson Organization, Ltd.
Carson-Adler Agency, Inc.
Cassell-Levy, Inc. (dba Clinc)
Castle Hill Talent Agency
Cavaleri & Associates
Celebrity Suppliers/Sports Star Suppliers
Nancy Chaidez Agency & Associates
The Chasin Agency
The Christensen Group
Ciao! Talent Agency
Commercial Talent, Inc.
Coralie Jr. Theatrical Agency
Creative Artists Agency - CAA
Cunningham-Escott-Slevin-Doherty Talent (LA)
Cunningham-Escott-Slevin-Doherty Talent (NY)
Marla Dell Talent Agency
DeSanti Talents, Inc.
Dimensions III Talent Agency
Doubble Troubble Entertainment, Inc.
EC Model & Talent Agency (Ent. Caterers, Inc.)
Dulcina Eisen Associates
Ellis Talent Group
Encore Talent Agency
Sylvia Ferguson & Assoc. Talent & Literary Agency
JFA/Jaime Ferrar Agency
Film Artists Associates
Flick East-West Talents, Inc.
Dale Garrick International Agency
The Geddes Agency (Chicago)
The Gersh Agency (Los Angeles)
The Gersh Agency (New York)
Global Artists Agency
Greene & Associates
Grossman & Jack Talent
Halpern Management
Hanns Wolters International, Inc.
Beverly Hecht Agency
Henderson/Hogan Agency
Hervey/Grimes Talent Agency
Daniel Hoff Agency
Hop Models & Talent Agency
The House of Representatives
Howard Talent West
The I Group Model & Talent Management
Impact Talent Group
Imperium 7 Talent Agency (i7)
Independent Artists Agency Inc.
Independent Artists Agency, Inc.
International Artists Group, Inc.
International Creative Mgmt., Inc. - ICM (LA)
International Creative Mgmt., Inc. - ICM (NY)
JE Talent, LLC/JE Model, Inc.
JKA Talent & Literary Agency
Jordan, Gill & Dornbaum
Stanley Kaplan Talent

Comedians (Continued)

Kazarian/Spencer & Associates
Archer King, Ltd.
Kolstein Talent Agency (KTA)
The Krasny Office, Inc.
Al Lampkin Entertainment, Inc.
Lane Agency
Buddy Lee Attractions, Inc.
Lemodeln Model & Talent Agency
Lenz Agency
Sid Levin Agency
Lily's Talent Agency, Inc.
Look Talent
Mademoiselle Talent & Modeling Agency
Malaky International
Martin & Donalds Talent Agency, Inc.
Maxine's Talent Agency
Media Artists Group
The Gilbert Miller Agency LLC
The Morgan Agency
H. David Moss & Associates
Nicolosi & Co., Inc.
NTA Talent Agency
Nu Talent Agency
Omnipop Talent Group
Origin Talent
Pacific West Artists
Dorothy Palmer Talent Agency, Inc.
Paradigm (Los Angeles)
The Paradise Group Talent Agency
Pastorini-Bosby Talent, Inc.
Perfectly Petite, Inc.
Players Talent Agency
Privilege Talent Agency
Progressive Artists Agency
PTI Talent Agency, Inc.
Q Model Management
Qualita Dell' Arte: Artists & Writers Di Qualita
Michael D. Robins & Associates
Cindy Romano Modeling & Talent Agency
San Francisco Top Models & Talent
Sanger Talent Agency
Jack Scagnetti Talent & Literary Agency
The Irv Schechter Company
Schuller Talent/NY Kids
Sky Talent Agency
Sonja Warren Brandon's Commercials Unlimited
Scott Stander & Associates, Inc.
Starcraft Talent Agency
Stars, The Agency
Starwil Talent
Stellar Model & Talent Agency
Stewart Talent
Summit Comedy, Inc.
Super Artists Inc.
Superior Talent Agency
Talent & Model Land
Talent Plus, Inc./Centro Models
The Talent Shop
Talent Trek Agency
Talent Unlimited, Inc.
TalentWorks
TalentWorks New York
Universal Talent Intelligence
Uptown Talent, Inc.
Donna Wauhob Agency
William Morris Agency - WMA (Los Angeles)
William Morris Agency - WMA (New York)
William Morris Agency - WMA (Nashville)
William Morris Agency - WMA (Miami Beach)
William Morris Agency - WMA (London)
Shirley Wilson & Associates
Craig Wyckoff & Associates

Composers

Abrams Artists Agency (Los Angeles)
Abrams Artists Agency (New York)
Bret Adams, Ltd.

Composers (Continued)

Agape Productions
Agency For the Performing Arts, Inc. (Los Angeles)
The Agency Group Ltd. (Los Angeles)
The Agency Group Ltd. (New York)
American Program Bureau
The Bethel Agency
Beverly Hills International Talent Agency
Judy Boals, Inc.
Creative Artists Agency - CAA
Esq. Management
Evolution Music Partners, LLC
First Artists Management
Geste, Inc.
Gorfaine/Schwartz Agency, Inc.
The Susan Gurman Agency, LLC
Harden-Curtis Associates
International Creative Mgmt., Inc. - ICM (LA)
International Creative Mgmt., Inc. - ICM (NY)
The Kaufman Agency
Kazarian/Spencer & Associates
Kraft-Engel Management
The Lantz Office
Buddy Lee Attractions, Inc.
Lemodeln Model & Talent Agency
Sandra Marsh Management
The Mirisch Agency
Montana Artists Agency, Inc.
Nash-Angeles, Inc.
New York Office
Fifi Oscard Agency, Inc.
Prime Artists
Qualita Dell' Arte: Artists & Writers Di Qualita
Michael D. Robins & Associates
Sanger Talent Agency
Schuller Talent/NY Kids
The Screen Talent Agency, Ltd.
Scott Stander & Associates, Inc.
Talent Representatives, Inc.
Universal Talent Intelligence
The Vicious Trend Agency
Donna Wauhob Agency
William Morris Agency - WMA (Los Angeles)
William Morris Agency - WMA (New York)
William Morris Agency - WMA (London)
William Morris Agency - WMA (Shanghai)

Dancers

abc model/talent/sport management
About Artists Agency
Advance LA
Affinity Model & Talent Agency
Agents For The Arts, Inc.
Aimée Entertainment Agency
Ambassador Talent Agents, Inc.
American Program Bureau
Beverly Anderson Agency
Andreadis Talent Agency, Inc.
Aqua
Baron Entertainment
Baskow & Associates, Inc.
The Bethel Agency
bloc talent agency, inc.
Blue Ridge Entertainment
Judy Boals, Inc.
Boca Talent & Model Agency
Boom Models & Talent
Calliope Talent, Model & Artist Management, LLC
Carmichael Talent
The Carry Co.
The Carson Organization, Ltd.
Cassell-Levy, Inc. (dba Clinc)
Nancy Chaidez Agency & Associates
The Christensen Group
Clear Talent Group
Coralie Jr. Theatrical Agency
Cunningham-Escott-Slevin-Doherty Talent (LA)
Cunningham-Escott-Slevin-Doherty Talent (NY)

AGENTS

Dancers (Continued)

DDO Artists Agency
DeSanti Talents, Inc.
Dimensions III Talent Agency
Doubble Troubble Entertainment, Inc.
Douglas, Gorman, Rothacker & Wilhelm, Inc.
EC Model & Talent Agency (Ent. Caterers, Inc.)
Dulcina Eisen Associates
Encore Talent Agency
Sylvia Ferguson & Assoc. Talent & Literary Agency
Frontier Booking International, Inc.
Garber Talent Agency
Peggy Hadley Enterprises, Ltd.
Harden-Curtis Associates
Harmony Artists
Henderson/Hogan Agency
Daniel Hoff Agency
Howard Talent West
Image Model & Talent
Independent Artists Agency Inc.
International Artists Group, Inc.
International Creative Mgmt., Inc. - ICM (LA)
International Creative Mgmt., Inc. - ICM (NY)
Jordan, Gill & Dornbaum
Stanley Kaplan Talent
Kazarian/Spencer & Associates
Archer King, Ltd.
Lane Agency
Lemodeln Model & Talent Agency
Lenz Agency
Sid Levin Agency
Lily's Talent Agency, Inc.
Mademoiselle Talent & Modeling Agency
Malaky International
Martin & Donalds Talent Agency, Inc.
McDonald/Selznick Associates
The Gilbert Miller Agency LLC
Model Team
The Morgan Agency
NTA Talent Agency
Nu Talent Agency
NXT Entertainment, Inc.
Dorothy Palmer Talent Agency, Inc.
The Meg Pantera Agency, Inc.
Peak Models & Talent
Perfectly Petite, Inc.
The Price Group LLC
Privilege Talent Agency
Qualita Dell' Arte: Artists & Writers Di Qualita
Sanger Talent Agency
Jack Scagnetti Talent & Literary Agency
Schuller Talent/NY Kids
Stars, The Agency
Starwil Talent
Superior Talent Agency
Tag Models
Talent House Agency
The Talent Shop
Talent Trek Agency
Universal Talent Intelligence
Donna Wauhob Agency

Directors

abc model/talent/sport management
Above The Line Agency
Abrams Artists Agency (Los Angeles)
Abrams Artists Agency (New York)
Acme Talent & Literary
Bret Adams, Ltd.
Agency For the Performing Arts, Inc. (Los Angeles)
The Alpern Group
Ambition Talent Inc.
American Program Bureau
Artists Agency, Inc.
The Artists Agency
Marc Bass Agency, Inc. (MBA)
Beacon Artists Agency
The Bethel Agency

Directors (Continued)

Beverly Hills International Talent Agency
Bonnie Black Talent & Literary Agency
Judy Boals, Inc.
Bobby Ball Talent Agency
The Bohrman Agency
Don Buchwald & Associates, Inc. (Los Angeles)
Don Buchwald & Associates, Inc. (New York)
The Callamaro Literary Agency
Suzanna Camejo & Associates: Artists for the
   Environment
Cavaleri & Associates
The Characters
The Chasin Agency
Clear Talent Group
Coast To Coast Talent Group, Inc.
Contemporary Artists, Ltd.
Creative Artists Agency - CAA
The Criterion Group, Inc.
Diverse Talent Group
Douglas, Gorman, Rothacker & Wilhelm, Inc.
Endeavor Agency, LLC
Esq. Management
The Gage Group, Inc. (Los Angeles)
Garber Talent Agency
Dale Garrick International Agency
The Gatsby Group, Inc.
Laya Gelff Agency
The Geller Agency
Paul Gerard Agency
The Gersh Agency (Los Angeles)
The Gersh Agency (New York)
The Glick Agency, LLC
Global Artists Agency
Grant, Savic, Kopaloff and Associates
Brad Gross Inc., Literary Management
The Susan Gurman Agency, LLC
GVA Talent Agency, Inc.
Buzz Halliday & Associates
Hanns Wolters International, Inc.
Harden-Curtis Associates
Barbara Hogenson Agency, Inc.
Hohman Maybank Lieb
Hollywood View
Howard Talent West
IFA Talent Agency
IMG/Broadcasting
Innovative Artists (Los Angeles)
International Artists Group, Inc.
International Creative Mgmt., Inc. - ICM (LA)
International Creative Mgmt., Inc. - ICM (NY)
JKA Talent & Literary Agency
Merrily Kane Agency
The Kaplan-Stahler-Gumer-Braun Agency
Archer King, Ltd.
Paul Kohner, Inc.
Cary Kozlov Literary Representation
The Lantz Office
Larchmont Literary Agency
Lemodeln Model & Talent Agency
Lenhoff & Lenhoff
Paul S. Levine Literary Agency
Michael Lewis & Associates
The Luedtke Agency
Max Freedman Management
Metropolitan Talent Agency (MTA)
The Stuart M. Miller Co.
Natural Talent, Inc.
New York Office
NXT Entertainment, Inc.
Ofrenda, Inc.
One Entertainment
Oracle Creative Management
Original Artists
Fifi Oscard Agency, Inc.
Pantheon
Paradigm (Los Angeles)
Paradigm (New York)

Directors (Continued)

Barry Perelman Agency
Perfectly Petite, Inc.
Stephen Pevner, Inc.
Preferred Artists
Jim Preminger Agency
Prime Artists
Professional Artists
Progressive Artists Agency
Qualita Dell' Arte: Artists & Writers Di Qualita
The Rabineau Wachter Sanford & Harris
   Literary Agency
The Rappaport Agency
read.
Rebel Entertainment Partners, Inc.
RLR Associates
Michael D. Robins & Associates
The Brant Rose Agency
Rosenstone/Wender
The Rothman Brecher Agency
Sanger Talent Agency
The Sarnoff Company, Inc.
The Irv Schechter Company
The Schneider Entertainment Agency
Schuller Talent/NY Kids
The Screen Talent Agency, Ltd.
Shapiro-Lichtman Talent Agency, Inc.
Sheldon Prosnit Agency
Jerome Siegel Associates
The Skouras Agency
SMA, LLC
The Susan Smith Company
Michael H. Sommer Literary Agency
The Stein Agency
Stewart Talent
Stone Canyon Media
Stone Manners Agency
Mitchell K. Stubbs & Associates
Suite A Management Talent & Literary Agency
Summit Talent & Literary Agency
Talent Representatives, Inc.
TDN Artists (The Director's Network)
United Talent Agency - UTA
Universal Talent Intelligence
Annette van Duren Agency
Vision Art Management
Warden, White & Associates
Wardlow & Associates
Donna Wauhob Agency
Waving Clouds Productions
William Morris Agency - WMA (Los Angeles)
William Morris Agency - WMA (New York)
William Morris Agency - WMA (Miami Beach)
William Morris Agency - WMA (London)
William Morris Agency - WMA (Shanghai)
Working Artists
Craig Wyckoff & Associates
Nick Yellen Creative Agency

Film Editors

All Crew Agency
Doug Apatow Agency
Below The Line Artists
Suzanna Camejo & Associates: Artists for the
   Environment
The Characters
The Criterion Group, Inc.
Diverse Talent Group
Endeavor Agency, LLC
Esq. Management
The Geller Agency
Grant, Savic, Kopaloff and Associates
Jacob & Kole Agency
Michael Lewis & Associates
Sandra Marsh Management
The Mirisch Agency
Montana Artists Agency, Inc.
New York Office

AGENTS

Film Editors (Continued)
Prime Artists
Shapiro-Lichtman Talent Agency, Inc.
Sheldon Prosnit Agency
The Skouras Agency
The Stein Agency
United Talent Agency - UTA

Hosts/MCs
abc model/talent/sport management
About Artists Agency
Abrams Artists Agency (Los Angeles)
Abrams Artists Agency (New York)
Actors Etc., Inc.
Advance LA
Affinity Model & Talent Agency
Agency For the Performing Arts, Inc. (Los Angeles)
Agency For the Performing Arts, Inc. (Nashville)
AKA Talent Agency
The Alvarado Rey Agency
Michael Amato Agency
Ambassador Talent Agents, Inc.
Angel City Talent
Aqua
Arcieri & Associates, Inc.
ARIA Talent
Atlas Talent Agency
Baron Entertainment
Baskow & Associates, Inc.
Berzon Talent Agency
The Bethel Agency
Judy Boals, Inc.
Bobby Ball Talent Agency
Boom Models & Talent
Brady, Brannon & Rich
BRick Entertainment
The Brogan Agency
Don Buchwald & Associates, Inc. (Los Angeles)
Don Buchwald & Associates, Inc. (New York)
The Burns Agency, Inc.
Calliope Talent, Model & Artist Management, LLC
Carmichael Talent
The Carry Co.
The Carson Organization, Ltd.
Castle Hill Talent Agency
The Characters
Ciao! Talent Agency
Mary Anne Claro Talent Agency, Inc.
Coralie Jr. Theatrical Agency
Creative Artists Agency - CAA
The Crofoot Group, Inc.
Cunningham-Escott-Slevin-Doherty Talent (NY)
DDO Artists Agency
DeSanti Talents, Inc.
EC Model & Talent Agency (Ent. Caterers, Inc.)
Elegance Talent Agency
Expressions Model & Talent
Flick East-West Talents, Inc.
FORD/Robert Black Agency
Frontier Booking International, Inc.
The Gage Group, Inc. (Los Angeles)
Garber Talent Agency
The Geddes Agency (Los Angeles)
GVA Talent Agency, Inc.
Neal Hamil Agency
Hanns Wolters International, Inc.
Harmony Artists
Henderson/Hogan Agency
Hervey/Grimes Talent Agency
The House of Representatives
Howard Talent West
The I Group Model & Talent Management
Identity Talent Agency
Image Model & Talent
IMG/Broadcasting
Imperium 7 Talent Agency (i7)
International Creative Mgmt., Inc. - ICM (LA)
International Creative Mgmt., Inc. - ICM (NY)

Hosts/MCs (Continued)
JE Talent, LLC/JE Model, Inc.
Jet Set Management Group, Inc.
Stanley Kaplan Talent
Kazarian/Spencer & Associates
Kolstein Talent Agency (KTA)
Lane Agency
Buddy Lee Attractions, Inc.
Leighton Agency, Inc.
Lemodeln Model & Talent Agency
Lenz Agency
Lily's Talent Agency, Inc.
Ken Lindner & Associates, Inc.
M International Talent Agency
Malaky International
The Mannequin Agency
Martin & Donalds Talent Agency, Inc.
McCarty Talent, Inc.
The Gilbert Miller Agency LLC
The Morgan Agency
Napoli Management Group
Nouvelle Talent Management, Inc.
NTA Talent Agency
Nu Talent Agency
Omnipop Talent Group
Dorothy Palmer Talent Agency, Inc.
The Paradise Group Talent Agency
Perfectly Petite, Inc.
Players Talent Agency
Privilege Talent Agency
Rebel Entertainment Partners, Inc.
San Francisco Top Models & Talent
Sanger Talent Agency
Jack Scagnetti Talent & Literary Agency
Schuller Talent/NY Kids
SGM - Sara Gaynor Management
Shamon Freitas Model & Talent Agency
David Shapira & Associates (DSA)
Scott Stander & Associates, Inc.
Stars, The Agency
Starwil Talent
Stone Manners Agency
Summit Comedy, Inc.
Super Artists Inc.
Superior Talent Agency
Tag Models
Talent & Model Land
Talent Plus, Inc./Centro Models
The Talent Shop
Talent Trek Agency
Talent Unlimited, Inc.
TalentWorks New York
Tonry Talent
Troika
William Morris Agency - WMA (Los Angeles)
William Morris Agency - WMA (New York)
William Morris Agency - WMA (London)
William Morris Agency - WMA (Shanghai)
Zanuck, Passon and Pace, Inc.

Infants
abc model/talent/sport management
Abrams Artists Agency (Los Angeles)
Abrams Artists Agency (New York)
Actors Etc., Inc.
Advance LA
Aimée Entertainment Agency
Michael Amato Agency
Ambassador Talent Agents, Inc.
Aqua
Baron Entertainment
The Bethel Agency
Bobby Ball Talent Agency
Boom Models & Talent
Brand Model and Talent Agency, Inc.
The Brogan Agency
The Carson Organization, Ltd.
Cassell-Levy, Inc. (dba Clinc)

Infants (Continued)
Castle Hill Talent Agency
Colleen Cler Talent Agency
Kim Dawson Talent
DDO Artists Agency
Marla Dell Talent Agency
DeSanti Talents, Inc.
Sylvia Ferguson & Assoc. Talent & Literary Agency
Frontier Booking International, Inc.
The Geddes Agency (Chicago)
Generations Model & Talent Agency
Grossman & Jack Talent
Daniel Hoff Agency
Howard Talent West
The I Group Model & Talent Management
Image Model & Talent
JE Talent, LLC/JE Model, Inc.
Jet Set Management Group, Inc.
Stanley Kaplan Talent
Kazarian/Spencer & Associates
L.A. Talent
Lane Agency
Lemodeln Model & Talent Agency
Lily's Talent Agency, Inc.
The Mannequin Agency
Martin & Donalds Talent Agency, Inc.
Model Club, Inc.
Model Team
NTA Talent Agency
NXT Entertainment, Inc.
Osbrink Talent Agency
Perfectly Petite, Inc.
Privilege Talent Agency
San Diego Model Management Talent Agency
San Francisco Top Models & Talent
Schuller Talent/NY Kids
Shamon Freitas Model & Talent Agency
Sky Talent Agency
Starcraft Talent Agency
Stars, The Agency
Stellar Model & Talent Agency
Stewart Talent
Superior Talent Agency
Tag Models
Talent & Model Land
The Talent Shop
Talent Trek Agency
Talent Unlimited, Inc.
Uptown Talent, Inc.
Donna Wauhob Agency

Interactive Game Developers
The Bethel Agency
The Carson Organization, Ltd.
International Creative Mgmt., Inc. - ICM (LA)
International Creative Mgmt., Inc. - ICM (NY)
The Mack Agency
Metropolis
The Stuart M. Miller Co.
Nu Talent Agency
United Talent Agency - UTA
William Morris Agency - WMA (Los Angeles)
William Morris Agency - WMA (London)
William Morris Agency - WMA (Shanghai)

Magicians
Actors Etc., Inc.
Michael Amato Agency
Ambassador Talent Agents, Inc.
Angel City Talent
Irvin Arthur Associates
Baron Entertainment
Baskow & Associates, Inc.
The Bethel Agency
The Brogan Agency
Coralie Jr. Theatrical Agency
EC Model & Talent Agency (Ent. Caterers, Inc.)

AGENTS

Magicians (Continued)

Frontier Booking International, Inc.
Harmony Artists
Hop Models & Talent Agency
The I Group Model & Talent Management
Stanley Kaplan Talent
Al Lampkin Entertainment, Inc.
Lane Agency
Lily's Talent Agency, Inc.
Malaky International
Martin & Donalds Talent Agency, Inc.
The Gilbert Miller Agency LLC
Nouvelle Talent Management, Inc.
NTA Talent Agency
Nu Talent Agency
Dorothy Palmer Talent Agency, Inc.
Perfectly Petite, Inc.
Periwinkle Entertainment Productions
Sanger Talent Agency
Jack Scagnetti Talent & Literary Agency
Scott Stander & Associates, Inc.
Stars, The Agency
Summit Comedy, Inc.
Talent Plus, Inc./Centro Models
Talent Unlimited, Inc.

Martial Artists/Stunts

abc model/talent/sport management
Actors Etc., Inc.
Aimée Entertainment Agency
Michael Amato Agency
Angel City Talent
Aqua
Baldwin Talent, Inc.
Baron Entertainment
Berzon Talent Agency
The Bethel Agency
bloc talent agency, inc.
Bobby Ball Talent Agency
Boca Talent & Model Agency
Boom Models & Talent
BRick Entertainment
The Brogan Agency
Don Buchwald & Associates, Inc. (Los Angeles)
Don Buchwald & Associates, Inc. (New York)
Calliope Talent, Model & Artist Management, LLC
Carmichael Talent
Cassell-Levy, Inc. (dba Clinc)
Castle Hill Talent Agency
Cavaleri & Associates
Nancy Chaidez Agency & Associates
Cunningham-Escott-Slevin-Doherty Talent (NY)
EC Model & Talent Agency (Ent. Caterers, Inc.)
Encore Talent Agency
Sylvia Ferguson & Assoc. Talent & Literary Agency
Fosi's Modeling & Talent Agency
The I Group Model & Talent Management
International Artists Group, Inc.
Jet Set Management Group, Inc.
Jordan, Gill & Dornbaum
Stanley Kaplan Talent
Kazarian/Spencer & Associates
Lane Agency
Lemodeln Model & Talent Agency
Lenz Agency
Lily's Talent Agency, Inc.
Malaky International
Sandra Marsh Management
Martin & Donalds Talent Agency, Inc.
McDonald/Selznick Associates
The Gilbert Miller Agency LLC
Model Team
The Morgan Agency
NTA Talent Agency
Nu Talent Agency
Oracle Creative Management
Dorothy Palmer Talent Agency, Inc.
Perfectly Petite, Inc.

Martial Artists/Stunts (Continued)

Players Talent Agency
Privilege Talent Agency
Qualita Dell' Arte: Artists & Writers Di Qualita
Cindy Romano Modeling & Talent Agency
San Francisco Top Models & Talent
Sanger Talent Agency
Jack Scagnetti Talent & Literary Agency
Schuller Talent/NY Kids
Scott Stander & Associates, Inc.
Stars, The Agency
Stellar Model & Talent Agency
Superior Talent Agency
Talent Plus, Inc./Centro Models
The Talent Shop
Universal Talent Intelligence
Donna Wauhob Agency
Waving Clouds Productions

Music Artists

abc model/talent/sport management
About Artists Agency
Agency For the Performing Arts, Inc. (Los Angeles)
Agency For the Performing Arts, Inc. (Nashville)
Agency For the Performing Arts, Inc. (New York)
The Agency Group Ltd. (Los Angeles)
The Agency Group Ltd. (New York)
Aqua
Associated Booking Corporation (ABC)
Baskow & Associates, Inc.
Beachfront Bookings
The Bethel Agency
Beverly Hills International Talent Agency
Bobby Ball Talent Agency
The Brogan Agency
Calliope Talent, Model & Artist Management, LLC
Carmichael Talent
The Carry Co.
Carson-Adler Agency, Inc.
Cedar Grove Agency Entertainment
Celebrity Suppliers/Sports Star Suppliers
Coralie Jr. Theatrical Agency
DeSanti Talents, Inc.
Doubble Trouble Entertainment, Inc.
EC Model & Talent Agency (Ent. Caterers, Inc.)
Evolution Music Partners, LLC
Neal Hamil Agency
Harmony Artists
Daniel Hoff Agency
Imperium 7 Talent Agency (i7)
Independent Artists Agency Inc.
International Creative Mgmt., Inc. - ICM (LA)
International Creative Mgmt., Inc. - ICM (NY)
Stanley Kaplan Talent
The Kaufman Agency
Kraft-Engel Management
Lally Talent Agency (LTA)
Lane Agency
Buddy Lee Attractions, Inc.
Lemodeln Model & Talent Agency
Lily's Talent Agency, Inc.
Sandra Marsh Management
Martin & Donalds Talent Agency, Inc.
The Gilbert Miller Agency LLC
Nu Talent Agency
NXT Entertainment, Inc.
Dorothy Palmer Talent Agency, Inc.
Paradigm (Los Angeles)
Paradigm (New York)
Perfectly Petite, Inc.
Qualita Dell' Arte: Artists & Writers Di Qualita
Sanger Talent Agency
Schuller Talent/NY Kids
Scott Stander & Associates, Inc.
Talent Plus, Inc./Centro Models
The Talent Shop
TalentWorks New York
United Talent Agency - UTA

Music Artists (Continued)

The Vicious Trend Agency
Donna Wauhob Agency
William Morris Agency - WMA (Los Angeles)
William Morris Agency - WMA (Nashville)
William Morris Agency - WMA (Miami Beach)
William Morris Agency - WMA (London)
William Morris Agency - WMA (Shanghai)

Music Editors

The Agency Group Ltd. (New York)
Esq. Management
Evolution Music Partners, LLC
First Artists Management
Buddy Lee Attractions, Inc.
Lily's Talent Agency, Inc.
Sandra Marsh Management

Music Producers

abc model/talent/sport management
Agape Productions
Agency For the Performing Arts, Inc. (Los Angeles)
The Agency Group Ltd. (New York)
Baron Entertainment
The Brogan Agency
Calliope Talent, Model & Artist Management, LLC
Creative Artists Agency - CAA
Evolution Music Partners, LLC
The Gatsby Group, Inc.
Gorfaine/Schwartz Agency, Inc.
International Creative Mgmt., Inc. - ICM (LA)
International Creative Mgmt., Inc. - ICM (NY)
The Kaufman Agency
Buddy Lee Attractions, Inc.
Lemodeln Model & Talent Agency
Lily's Talent Agency, Inc.
Nash-Angeles, Inc.
Qualita Dell' Arte: Artists & Writers Di Qualita
Michael D. Robins & Associates
Sanger Talent Agency
Universal Talent Intelligence
Donna Wauhob Agency
William Morris Agency - WMA (Miami Beach)

Music Supervisors

The Agency Group Ltd. (Los Angeles)
The Agency Group Ltd. (New York)
Creative Artists Agency - CAA
Evolution Music Partners, LLC
First Artists Management
International Creative Mgmt., Inc. - ICM (LA)
International Creative Mgmt., Inc. - ICM (NY)
Kazarian/Spencer & Associates
Kraft-Engel Management
Buddy Lee Attractions, Inc.
Sandra Marsh Management
Montana Artists Agency, Inc.
Prime Artists
Sheldon Prosnit Agency
Talent House Agency

Musical Theatre Performers

About Artists Agency
Abrams Artists Agency (Los Angeles)
Abrams Artists Agency (New York)
Acme Talent & Literary
Actors Etc., Inc.
Bret Adams, Ltd.
Agents For The Arts, Inc.
Beverly Anderson Agency
Andreadis Talent Agency, Inc.
The Bethel Agency
Judy Boals, Inc.
Boutique
The Brogan Agency
Don Buchwald & Associates, Inc. (Los Angeles)

AGENTS

Musical Theatre Performers (Continued)

Don Buchwald & Associates, Inc. (New York)
Calliope Talent, Model & Artist Management, LLC
Carmichael Talent
Carson-Adler Agency, Inc.
The Characters
Creative Artists Agency - CAA
DDO Artists Agency
Marla Dell Talent Agency
Douglas, Gorman, Rothacker & Wilhelm, Inc.
Fresh Faces Agency, Inc.
The Gage Group, Inc. (Los Angeles)
The Gage Group, Inc. (New York)
Garber Talent Agency
Gilla Roos, Ltd.
Grossman & Jack Talent
Peggy Hadley Enterprises, Ltd.
Hanns Wolters International, Inc.
Harden-Curtis Associates
Harmony Artists
Henderson/Hogan Agency
Daniel Hoff Agency
Hot Shot Kids/Teens
Imperium 7 Talent Agency (i7)
International Creative Mgmt., Inc. - ICM (LA)
International Creative Mgmt., Inc. - ICM (NY)
Kazarian/Spencer & Associates
Archer King, Ltd.
Buddy Lee Attractions, Inc.
Lemodeln Model & Talent Agency
Bernard Liebhaber Agency
Lily's Talent Agency, Inc.
Martin & Donalds Talent Agency, Inc.
McDonald/Selznick Associates
H. David Moss & Associates
Nicolosi & Co., Inc.
Omnipop Talent Group
Dorothy Palmer Talent Agency, Inc.
The Meg Pantera Agency, Inc.
Perfectly Petite, Inc.
The Price Group LLC
Schuller Talent/NY Kids
The Screen Talent Agency, Ltd.
Scott Stander & Associates, Inc.
Stewart Talent
Stone Manners Agency
Super Artists Inc.
Talent House Agency
William Morris Agency - WMA (Los Angeles)
William Morris Agency - WMA (New York)
William Morris Agency - WMA (Miami Beach)
William Morris Agency - WMA (London)
William Morris Agency - WMA (Shanghai)

Playwrights

Abrams Artists Agency (Los Angeles)
Bret Adams, Ltd.
Advance LA
Agency For the Performing Arts, Inc. (Los Angeles)
Beacon Artists Agency
Berzon Talent Agency
The Bethel Agency
Judy Boals, Inc.
The Bohrman Agency
Don Buchwald & Associates, Inc. (Los Angeles)
Don Buchwald & Associates, Inc. (New York)
The Carson Organization, Ltd.
The Characters
The Coppage Company
Creative Artists Agency - CAA
Deiter Literary Agency
Diverse Talent Group
Farber Literary Agency, Inc.
Robert A. Freedman Dramatic Agency, Inc.
FRP Literary - Talent Agency
The Gage Group, Inc. (Los Angeles)
Graham Agency
The Susan Gurman Agency, LLC

Playwrights (Continued)

The Charlotte Gusay Literary Agency
Hanns Wolters International, Inc.
Harden-Curtis Associates
Barbara Hogenson Agency, Inc.
International Creative Mgmt., Inc. - ICM (LA)
International Creative Mgmt., Inc. - ICM (NY)
Merrily Kane Agency
Archer King, Ltd.
Lally Talent Agency (LTA)
The Lantz Office
Paul S. Levine Literary Agency
Lily's Talent Agency, Inc.
The Luedtke Agency
The Stuart M. Miller Co.
Fifi Oscard Agency, Inc.
Dorothy Palmer Talent Agency, Inc.
Paradigm (New York)
Stephen Pevner, Inc.
Rosenstone/Wender
Susan Schulman Literary Agency
Ken Sherman & Associates
Scott Stander & Associates, Inc.
Suite A Management Talent & Literary Agency
Talent House Agency
United Talent Agency - UTA
William Morris Agency - WMA (Los Angeles)
William Morris Agency - WMA (New York)
William Morris Agency - WMA (Miami Beach)
William Morris Agency - WMA (London)
William Morris Agency - WMA (Shanghai)
Ann Wright Representatives
Nick Yellen Creative Agency

Print Models

abc model/talent/sport management
Abrams Artists Agency (Los Angeles)
Abrams Artists Agency (New York)
Acme Talent & Literary
Actors Etc., Inc.
Actors LA Agency
Advance LA
Affinity Model & Talent Agency
Alexa Model & Talent Management, Inc.
The Alvarado Rey Agency
Michael Amato Agency
Ambassador Talent Agents, Inc.
Angel City Talent
Aqua
Arcieri & Associates, Inc.
Artist Management Agency
Atlanta Models & Talent, Inc.
Atlas Talent Agency
Donna Baldwin Talent
Baron Entertainment
Baskow & Associates, Inc.
Beauty Models/BC4
Berzon Talent Agency
Beverly Hills International Talent Agency
Bonnie Black Talent & Literary Agency
Bleu Model Management
Bobby Ball Talent Agency
Boca Talent & Model Agency
Boom Models & Talent
Brand Model and Talent Agency, Inc.
The Brogan Agency
Don Buchwald & Associates, Inc. (Los Angeles)
Don Buchwald & Associates, Inc. (New York)
Calliope Talent, Model & Artist Management, LLC
The Campbell Agency
Conan Carroll & Associates
The Carry Co.
The Carson Organization, Ltd.
Cast Images Talent Agency
Nancy Chaidez Agency & Associates
Chateau Billings Talent Agency
Chic Models & Talent Agency
The Christensen Group

Print Models (Continued)

Ciao! Talent Agency
Clear Talent Group
Colleen Cler Talent Agency
Commercial Talent, Inc.
Coralie Jr. Theatrical Agency
Crystal Talent
Cunningham-Escott-Slevin-Doherty Talent (LA)
Cunningham-Escott-Slevin-Doherty Talent (NY)
Kim Dawson Talent
DDO Artists Agency
Marla Dell Talent Agency
DeSanti Talents, Inc.
Dimensions III Talent Agency
EC Model & Talent Agency (Ent. Caterers, Inc.)
Electric Talent
Elegance Talent Agency
Elite Model Management
Empire Talent Agency
Encore Talent Agency
Equinox Models/Equinox Talent/Zoo Models
Expressions Model & Talent
Flick East-West Talents, Inc.
Ford Models at the Raleigh Hotel
FORD/Robert Black Agency
Fosi's Modeling & Talent Agency
Frontier Booking International, Inc.
Gage Talent, Inc.
The Geddes Agency (Chicago)
Generations Model & Talent Agency
Gilla Roos, Ltd.
Greer Lange Model & Talent Agency, Inc.
Grossman & Jack Talent
Neal Hamil Agency
Hervey/Grimes Talent Agency
Daniel Hoff Agency
Hop Models & Talent Agency
Hot Shot Kids/Teens
Howard Talent West
The I Group Model & Talent Management
Image Model & Talent
IMG/Broadcasting
Independent Artists Agency, Inc.
International Artists Group, Inc.
JE Talent, LLC/JE Model, Inc.
Jet Set Management Group, Inc.
Stanley Kaplan Talent
Kazarian/Spencer & Associates
Lane Agency
Leighton Agency, Inc.
Lemodeln Model & Talent Agency
Lenz Agency
Lily's Talent Agency, Inc.
Look Talent
M International Talent Agency
Mademoiselle Talent & Modeling Agency
Malaky International
The Mannequin Agency
Martin & Donalds Talent Agency, Inc.
McCarty Talent, Inc.
Miramar Talent Agency
Model Club, Inc.
Model Team
Momentum Talent & Literary Agency
The Morgan Agency
H. David Moss & Associates
Nouveau Model & Talent
Nouvelle Talent Management, Inc.
NTA Talent Agency
Nu Talent Agency
NXT Entertainment, Inc.
Osbrink Talent Agency
Paradigm (New York)
Peak Models & Talent
Perfectly Petite, Inc.
Privilege Talent Agency
PTI Talent Agency, Inc.
Q Model Management

AGENTS

Print Models (Continued)

Q6 Model & Artist Management
Qualita Dell' Arte: Artists & Writers Di Qualita
Cindy Romano Modeling & Talent Agency
San Diego Model Management Talent Agency
San Francisco Top Models & Talent
Sanger Talent Agency
The Sarnoff Company, Inc.
Schuller Talent/NY Kids
SGM - Sara Gaynor Management
Shamon Freitas Model & Talent Agency
Scott Stander & Associates, Inc.
Starcraft Talent Agency
Stars, The Agency
Starwil Talent
Stellar Model & Talent Agency
Stewart Talent
Ivett Stone Agency
Superior Talent Agency
Tag Models
The Talent Group
Talent Plus, Inc./Centro Models
Talent Plus/Los Latinos Talent Agency
The Talent Shop
Talent Trek Agency
Talent Unlimited, Inc.
TalentWorks New York
Tonry Talent
Uptown Talent, Inc.
Vision Los Angeles
Donna Wauhob Agency
Waving Clouds Productions
Wilhelmina West, Inc./LW1 Talent Agency
Zanuck, Passon and Pace, Inc.

Producers

Above The Line Agency
Acme Talent & Literary
Advance LA
Agape Productions
Agency For the Performing Arts, Inc. (Los Angeles)
All Crew Agency
The Alpern Group
Ambition Talent Inc.
American Program Bureau
Artists Agency, Inc.
The Artists Agency
Baron Entertainment
The Bethel Agency
Bonnie Black Talent & Literary Agency
The Bohrman Agency
Don Buchwald & Associates, Inc. (Los Angeles)
Don Buchwald & Associates, Inc. (New York)
Suzanna Camejo & Associates: Artists for the
    Environment
Nancy Chaidez Agency & Associates
The Characters
The Chasin Agency
Chateau Billings Talent Agency
Coast To Coast Talent Group, Inc.
Contemporary Artists, Ltd.
Creative Artists Agency - CAA
The Crofoot Group, Inc.
Dattner Dispoto and Associates
Diverse Talent Group
Endeavor Agency, LLC
The Gage Group, Inc. (Los Angeles)
The Gatsby Group, Inc.
The Gersh Agency (Los Angeles)
The Gersh Agency (New York)
Geste, Inc.
The Glick Agency, LLC
Grant, Savic, Kopaloff and Associates
Hanns Wolters International, Inc.
IMG/Broadcasting
Innovative Artists (Los Angeles)
International Creative Mgmt., Inc. - ICM (LA)
International Creative Mgmt., Inc. - ICM (NY)

Producers (Continued)

JKA Talent & Literary Agency
Merrily Kane Agency
The Kaplan-Stahler-Gumer-Braun Agency
William Kerwin Agency
Archer King, Ltd.
Kneerim & Williams at Fish & Richardson, PC
Paul Kohner, Inc.
Lemodeln Model & Talent Agency
Lenhoff & Lenhoff
Paul S. Levine Literary Agency
Michael Lewis & Associates
Lily's Talent Agency, Inc.
Ken Lindner & Associates, Inc.
The Mack Agency
Sandra Marsh Management
Martin & Donalds Talent Agency, Inc.
Max Freedman Management
McDonald/Selznick Associates
Media Artists Group
Metropolis
Metropolitan Talent Agency (MTA)
The Stuart M. Miller Co.
The Mirisch Agency
Montana Artists Agency, Inc.
Monteiro Rose Dravis Agency, Inc.
N.S. Bienstock, Inc.
Natural Talent, Inc.
New York Office
Omnipop Talent Group
Oracle Creative Management
Original Artists
Fifi Oscard Agency, Inc.
Paradigm (Los Angeles)
The Paradise Group Talent Agency
Barry Perelman Agency
Perfectly Petite, Inc.
Preferred Artists
Jim Preminger Agency
Prime Artists
Progressive Artists Agency
Qualita Dell' Arte: Artists & Writers Di Qualita
read.
Rebel Entertainment Partners, Inc.
RLR Associates
Michael D. Robins & Associates
The Brant Rose Agency
The Rothman Brecher Agency
Sanger Talent Agency
The Sarnoff Company, Inc.
The Irv Schechter Company
Schuller Talent/NY Kids
The Screen Talent Agency, Ltd.
Shapiro-Lichtman Talent Agency, Inc.
Sheldon Prosnit Agency
Ken Sherman & Associates
Jerome Siegel Associates
The Skouras Agency
SMA, LLC
Michael H. Sommer Literary Agency
Scott Stander & Associates, Inc.
The Stein Agency
Stone Canyon Media
Stone Manners Agency
Suite A Management Talent & Literary Agency
Summit Talent & Literary Agency
Talent Representatives, Inc.
United Talent Agency - UTA
Universal Talent Intelligence
Annette van Duren Agency
Vision Art Management
Warden McKinley Literary Agency
Wardlow & Associates
Waving Clouds Productions
William Morris Agency - WMA (Los Angeles)
William Morris Agency - WMA (New York)
William Morris Agency - WMA (Miami Beach)
Nick Yellen Creative Agency

Production Designers

All Crew Agency
Doug Apatow Agency
Below The Line Artists
The Bethel Agency
Suzanna Camejo & Associates: Artists for the
    Environment
The Characters
Dattner Dispoto and Associates
Diverse Talent Group
Endeavor Agency, LLC
Esq. Management
The Geller Agency
Grant, Savic, Kopaloff and Associates
International Creative Mgmt., Inc. - ICM (LA)
Jacob & Kole Agency
Michael Lewis & Associates
The Mack Agency
Sandra Marsh Management
McDonald/Selznick Associates
The Mirisch Agency
Montana Artists Agency, Inc.
New York Office
Orlando Management
Paradigm (New York)
The Partos Company
Prime Artists
Shapiro-Lichtman Talent Agency, Inc.
Sheldon Prosnit Agency
The Skouras Agency
The Stein Agency
United Talent Agency - UTA
Donna Wauhob Agency
Waving Clouds Productions

Runway Models

abc model/talent/sport management
Actors LA Agency
Advance LA
Affinity Model & Talent Agency
Alexa Model & Talent Management, Inc.
Michael Amato Agency
Ambassador Talent Agents, Inc.
Aqua
Artist Management Agency
Donna Baldwin Talent
Baron Entertainment
Baskow & Associates, Inc.
Boca Talent & Model Agency
Boom Models & Talent
Brand Model and Talent Agency, Inc.
BRick Entertainment
Calliope Talent, Model & Artist Management, LLC
The Carson Organization, Ltd.
Cast Images Talent Agency
Nancy Chaidez Agency & Associates
Chic Models & Talent Agency
The Christensen Group
Cunningham-Escott-Slevin-Doherty Talent (LA)
Kim Dawson Talent
EC Model & Talent Agency (Ent. Caterers, Inc.)
Elegance Talent Agency
Equinox Models/Equinox Talent/Zoo Models
Expressions Model & Talent
Flick East-West Talents, Inc.
FORD/Robert Black Agency
Gage Talent, Inc.
Generations Model & Talent Agency
Gilla Roos, Ltd.
Neal Hamil Agency
Daniel Hoff Agency
Hop Models & Talent Agency
Hot Shot Kids/Teens
The I Group Model & Talent Management
Image Model & Talent
IMG/Broadcasting
Independent Artists Agency Inc.
JE Talent, LLC/JE Model, Inc.

AGENTS

Runway Models (Continued)

Jet Set Management Group, Inc.
Stanley Kaplan Talent
Kazarian/Spencer & Associates
Kolstein Talent Agency (KTA)
Leighton Agency, Inc.
Lemodeln Model & Talent Agency
Lenz Agency
Lily's Talent Agency, Inc.
The Mannequin Agency
Martin & Donalds Talent Agency, Inc.
McCarty Talent, Inc.
Model Club, Inc.
Model Team
The Morgan Agency
Nouveau Model & Talent
Nouvelle Talent Management, Inc.
NTA Talent Agency
Nu Talent Agency
NXT Entertainment, Inc.
Osbrink Talent Agency
Dorothy Palmer Talent Agency, Inc.
Peak Models & Talent
Perfectly Petite, Inc.
Privilege Talent Agency
Q6 Model & Artist Management
Cindy Romano Modeling & Talent Agency
San Diego Model Management Talent Agency
SGM - Sara Gaynor Management
Shamon Freitas Model & Talent Agency
Sky Talent Agency
Scott Stander & Associates, Inc.
Starcraft Talent Agency
Stars, The Agency
Tag Models
The Talent Group
Talent Plus, Inc./Centro Models
The Talent Shop
Talent Trek Agency
Talent Unlimited, Inc.
Vision Los Angeles
Donna Wauhob Agency
Wilhelmina West, Inc./LW1 Talent Agency

Screenwriters

Above The Line Agency
Abrams Artists Agency (Los Angeles)
Abrams Artists Agency (New York)
Acme Talent & Literary
Agape Productions
Agency For the Performing Arts, Inc. (Los Angeles)
Aimée Entertainment Agency
The Alpern Group
Michael Amato Agency
Ambition Talent Inc.
The Artists Agency
Baskow & Associates, Inc.
Marc Bass Agency, Inc. (MBA)
Beacon Artists Agency
Berzon Talent Agency
The Bethel Agency
Bicoastal Talent
Bonnie Black Talent & Literary Agency
Bobby Ball Talent Agency
The Bohrman Agency
Marcus Bryan & Associates
Don Buchwald & Associates, Inc. (Los Angeles)
Don Buchwald & Associates, Inc. (New York)
The Callamaro Literary Agency
Cambridge Literary Associates, Inc.
Suzanna Camejo & Associates: Artists for the Environment
Conan Carroll & Associates
Cavaleri & Associates
Cedar Grove Agency Entertainment
The Characters
The Chasin Agency
Coast To Coast Talent Group, Inc.

Screenwriters (Continued)

Contemporary Artists, Ltd.
The Coppage Company
Coralie Jr. Theatrical Agency
Creative Artists Agency - CAA
The Criterion Group, Inc.
Curtis Brown, Ltd.
Deiter Literary Agency
Diverse Talent Group
The E S Agency
Endeavor Agency, LLC
Sylvia Ferguson & Assoc. Talent & Literary Agency
Robert A. Freedman Dramatic Agency, Inc.
FRP Literary - Talent Agency
The Gage Group, Inc. (Los Angeles)
The Gary-Paul Agency
The Gatsby Group, Inc.
Laya Gelff Agency
The Gersh Agency (Los Angeles)
The Gersh Agency (New York)
Geste, Inc.
The Glick Agency, LLC
Global Artists Agency
Michelle Gordon & Associates
Grant, Savic, Kopaloff and Associates
Brad Gross Inc., Literary Management
The Charlotte Gusay Literary Agency
GVA Talent Agency, Inc.
The Mitchell J. Hamilburg Agency
Hanns Wolters International, Inc.
Harden-Curtis Associates
Hart Literary Management
Hays Media LLC
Hohman Maybank Lieb
Hollywood View
Hotchkiss & Associates
Hudson Agency
Innovative Artists (Los Angeles)
International Artists Group, Inc.
International Creative Mgmt., Inc. - ICM (LA)
International Creative Mgmt., Inc. - ICM (NY)
JKA Talent & Literary Agency
Merrily Kane Agency
William Kerwin Agency
Archer King, Ltd.
Kjar & Associates
Kneerim & Williams at Fish & Richardson, PC
Paul Kohner, Inc.
Otto R. Kozak Literary & Motion Picture Agency
Cary Kozlov Literary Representation
Kristine Krupp Talent Agency
Lally Talent Agency (LTA)
The Lantz Office
Larchmont Literary Agency
Lemodeln Model & Talent Agency
Lenhoff & Lenhoff
Paul S. Levine Literary Agency
Michael Lewis & Associates
Lily's Talent Agency, Inc.
The Luedtke Agency
Max Freedman Management
Maxine's Talent Agency
McIntosh and Otis, Inc.
Media Artists Group
Menza-Barron Agency
Metropolis
Metropolitan Talent Agency (MTA)
The Stuart M. Miller Co.
Monteiro Rose Dravis Agency, Inc.
Montgomery West Literary Agency, LLC
Nash-Angeles, Inc.
New York Office
Ofrenda, Inc.
Omnipop Talent Group
One Entertainment
Oracle Creative Management
The Orange Grove Group, Inc.
Original Artists

Screenwriters (Continued)

Fifi Oscard Agency, Inc.
Dorothy Palmer Talent Agency, Inc.
Pantheon
Paradigm (Los Angeles)
Paradigm (New York)
Barry Perelman Agency
Stephen Pevner, Inc.
The Lynn Pleshette Literary Agency
Preferred Artists
Jim Preminger Agency
Qualita Dell' Arte: Artists & Writers Di Qualita
Quillco Agency
The Rabineau Wachter Sanford & Harris Literary Agency
Raines & Raines
read.
Michael D. Robins & Associates
Cindy Romano Modeling & Talent Agency
The Brant Rose Agency
Rosenstone/Wender
The Rothman Brecher Agency
Sanger Talent Agency
The Sarnoff Company, Inc.
Jack Scagnetti Talent & Literary Agency
The Irv Schechter Company
The Screen Talent Agency, Ltd.
Shapiro-Lichtman Talent Agency, Inc.
Ken Sherman & Associates
Jerome Siegel Associates
SMA, LLC
Michael H. Sommer Literary Agency
Stars, The Agency
The Stein Agency
Stone Canyon Media
Stone Manners Agency
Suite A Management Talent & Literary Agency
Summit Talent & Literary Agency
TDN Artists (The Director's Network)
United Talent Agency - UTA
Universal Talent Intelligence
Annette van Duren Agency
The Vicious Trend Agency
Vision Art Management
Warden McKinley Literary Agency
Warden, White & Associates
Wardlow & Associates
Donna Wauhob Agency
Waving Clouds Productions
William Morris Agency - WMA (Los Angeles)
William Morris Agency - WMA (New York)
William Morris Agency - WMA (Miami Beach)
William Morris Agency - WMA (London)
William Morris Agency - WMA (Shanghai)
Working Artists
Ann Wright Representatives
Craig Wyckoff & Associates
Nick Yellen Creative Agency

Seniors

abc model/talent/sport management
About Artists Agency
Abrams Artists Agency (Los Angeles)
Abrams Artists Agency (New York)
Actors Etc., Inc.
Agents For The Arts, Inc.
Aimée Entertainment Agency
Alexa Model & Talent Management, Inc.
Michael Amato Agency
Ambassador Talent Agents, Inc.
Beverly Anderson Agency
Andreadis Talent Agency, Inc.
Angel City Talent
Aqua
Atlanta Models & Talent, Inc.
Baldwin Talent, Inc.
Baron Entertainment
Berzon Talent Agency

AGENTS

Seniors (Continued)

The Bethel Agency
Beverly Hills International Talent Agency
Bobby Ball Talent Agency
Boca Talent & Model Agency
Boom Models & Talent
Brand Model and Talent Agency, Inc.
Brass Artists & Associates
BRick Entertainment
The Brogan Agency
Don Buchwald & Associates, Inc. (Los Angeles)
Don Buchwald & Associates, Inc. (New York)
Calliope Talent, Model & Artist Management, LLC
The Carson Organization, Ltd.
Cassell-Levy, Inc. (dba Clinc)
Castle Hill Talent Agency
Chateau Billings Talent Agency
Chic Models & Talent Agency
Circle Talent Associates
Colleen Cler Talent Agency
Commercial Talent, Inc.
Coralie Jr. Theatrical Agency
Cunningham-Escott-Slevin-Doherty Talent (NY)
DDO Artists Agency
Marla Dell Talent Agency
Elegance Talent Agency
Expressions Model & Talent
Sylvia Ferguson & Assoc. Talent & Literary Agency
JFA/Jaime Ferrar Agency
Flick East-West Talents, Inc.
Fosi's Modeling & Talent Agency
The Gage Group, Inc. (Los Angeles)
The Geddes Agency (Chicago)
The Geddes Agency (Los Angeles)
Generations Model & Talent Agency
Greer Lange Model & Talent Agency, Inc.
Peggy Hadley Enterprises, Ltd.
Hanns Wolters International, Inc.
Hervey/Grimes Talent Agency
Daniel Hoff Agency
The House of Representatives
Howard Talent West
The I Group Model & Talent Management
Identity Talent Agency
Image Model & Talent
Imperium 7 Talent Agency (i7)
Independent Artists Agency Inc.
Stanley Kaplan Talent
Kazarian/Spencer & Associates
William Kerwin Agency
Archer King, Ltd.
L.A. Talent
Leighton Agency, Inc.
Lemodeln Model & Talent Agency
Lily's Talent Agency, Inc.
Jana Luker Agency
Malaky International
The Mannequin Agency
Martin & Donalds Talent Agency, Inc.
The Gilbert Miller Agency LLC
Model Club, Inc.
Model Team
The Morgan Agency
H. David Moss & Associates
NTA Talent Agency
NXT Entertainment, Inc.
Osbrink Talent Agency
Pacific West Artists
Dorothy Palmer Talent Agency, Inc.
Perfectly Petite, Inc.
Players Talent Agency
PTI Talent Agency, Inc.
Q Model Management
Cindy Romano Modeling & Talent Agency
San Francisco Top Models & Talent
Jack Scagnetti Talent & Literary Agency
Shamon Freitas Model & Talent Agency
Sonja Warren Brandon's Commercials Unlimited

Seniors (Continued)

Scott Stander & Associates, Inc.
Starcraft Talent Agency
Stars, The Agency
Starwil Talent
The Stevens Group
Stewart Talent
Superior Talent Agency
Tag Models
Talent & Model Land
Talent Plus, Inc./Centro Models
Talent Plus/Los Latinos Talent Agency
The Talent Shop
Talent Trek Agency
Talent Unlimited, Inc.
TalentWorks New York
Tonry Talent
Uptown Talent, Inc.
The Wallis Agency
Donna Wauhob Agency

Sound Editors

Diverse Talent Group
EC Model & Talent Agency (Ent. Caterers, Inc.)
Esq. Management
Sandra Marsh Management
Sheldon Prosnit Agency

Speakers/Lecturers

abc model/talent/sport management
Abrams Artists Agency (Los Angeles)
Abrams Artists Agency (New York)
Advance LA
American Program Bureau
Angel City Talent
Irvin Arthur Associates
Baron Entertainment
Baskow & Associates, Inc.
The Bethel Agency
Bonnie Black Talent & Literary Agency
Brand Model and Talent Agency, Inc.
Calliope Talent, Model & Artist Management, LLC
Creative Artists Agency - CAA
EC Model & Talent Agency (Ent. Caterers, Inc.)
Hays Media LLC
Identity Talent Agency
IMG/Broadcasting
Imperium 7 Talent Agency (i7)
International Creative Mgmt., Inc. - ICM (LA)
International Creative Mgmt., Inc. - ICM (NY)
Jet Set Management Group, Inc.
Kolstein Talent Agency (KTA)
Buddy Lee Attractions, Inc.
Lemodeln Model & Talent Agency
Lily's Talent Agency, Inc.
The Literary Group
The Mannequin Agency
Martin & Donalds Talent Agency, Inc.
The Gilbert Miller Agency LLC
Ofrenda, Inc.
Omnipop Talent Group
Dorothy Palmer Talent Agency, Inc.
Perfectly Petite, Inc.
Sanger Talent Agency
Scott Stander & Associates, Inc.
Super Artists Inc.
Talent Plus, Inc./Centro Models
The Talent Shop
William Morris Agency - WMA (Los Angeles)
William Morris Agency - WMA (New York)
William Morris Agency - WMA (Miami Beach)
William Morris Agency - WMA (London)
William Morris Agency - WMA (Shanghai)

Sports Personalities

abc model/talent/sport management
Abrams Artists Agency (Los Angeles)
Abrams Artists Agency (New York)
Actors Etc., Inc.
Advance LA
Affinity Model & Talent Agency
The Agency Group Ltd. (Los Angeles)
The Agency Group Ltd. (New York)
Aimée Entertainment Agency
American Program Bureau
Angel City Talent
Aqua
Baldwin Talent, Inc.
Baron Entertainment
Baskow & Associates, Inc.
Berzon Talent Agency
bloc talent agency, inc.
Bobby Ball Talent Agency
Boom Models & Talent
BRick Entertainment
Don Buchwald & Associates, Inc. (Los Angeles)
Don Buchwald & Associates, Inc. (New York)
Calliope Talent, Model & Artist Management, LLC
The Carson Organization, Ltd.
Celebrity Suppliers/Sports Star Suppliers
Nancy Chaidez Agency & Associates
Coast To Coast Talent Group, Inc.
Commercial Talent, Inc.
Creative Artists Agency - CAA
The Crofoot Group, Inc.
Cunningham-Escott-Slevin-Doherty Talent (LA)
Cunningham-Escott-Slevin-Doherty Talent (NY)
DDO Artists Agency
Diverse Talent Group
Endeavor Agency, LLC
Flick East-West Talents, Inc.
The Gersh Agency (Los Angeles)
Hays Media LLC
The I Group Model & Talent Management
Identity Talent Agency
IMG/Broadcasting
Impact Talent Group
Imperium 7 Talent Agency (i7)
International Artists Group, Inc.
International Creative Mgmt., Inc. - ICM (LA)
Jet Set Management Group, Inc.
Kazarian/Spencer & Associates
Buddy Lee Attractions, Inc.
Lemodeln Model & Talent Agency
Lenz Agency
Sid Levin Agency
Ken Lindner & Associates, Inc.
The Literary Group
Media Artists Group
The Gilbert Miller Agency LLC
Model Team
Napoli Management Group
NTA Talent Agency
Nu Talent Agency
Fifi Oscard Agency, Inc.
Dorothy Palmer Talent Agency, Inc.
The Paradise Group Talent Agency
Pastorini-Bosby Talent, Inc.
Perfectly Petite, Inc.
Players Talent Agency
Privilege Talent Agency
Qualita Dell' Arte: Artists & Writers Di Qualita
RLR Associates
Cindy Romano Modeling & Talent Agency
San Francisco Top Models & Talent
The Irv Schechter Company
Stars, The Agency
The Talent Group
Talent Plus, Inc./Centro Models
The Talent Shop
United Talent Agency - UTA
Universal Talent Intelligence

AGENTS

Sports Personalities (Continued)

Donna Wauhob Agency
Waving Clouds Productions
William Morris Agency - WMA (Los Angeles)
William Morris Agency - WMA (New York)
William Morris Agency - WMA (Miami Beach)
William Morris Agency - WMA (London)
William Morris Agency - WMA (Shanghai)
World Class Sports

Teens/Young Adults

ABA - Amatruda Benson & Associates
abc model/talent/sport management
Abrams Artists Agency (Los Angeles)
Abrams Artists Agency (New York)
Acme Talent & Literary
Actors & Others Talent Agency
Actors Etc., Inc.
Actors LA Agency
Advance LA
Affinity Model & Talent Agency
Agency For the Performing Arts, Inc. (Los Angeles)
Agents For The Arts, Inc.
Aimée Entertainment Agency
AKA Talent Agency
Alexa Model & Talent Management, Inc.
Michael Amato Agency
Ambassador Talent Agents, Inc.
Amsel, Eisenstadt & Frazier, Inc.
Andreadis Talent Agency, Inc.
Angel City Talent
Aqua
ARIA Talent
Artist Management Agency
The Artists Agency
Atlanta Models & Talent, Inc.
Donna Baldwin Talent
Baldwin Talent, Inc.
Baron Entertainment
Beauty Models/BC4
The Sandi Bell Talent Agency, Inc.
Berzon Talent Agency
The Bethel Agency
Beverly Hills International Talent Agency
Bicoastal Talent
Bonnie Black Talent & Literary Agency
Bobby Ball Talent Agency
Boca Talent & Model Agency
Boom Models & Talent
Brand Model and Talent Agency, Inc.
Brass Artists & Associates
Brevard Talent Group, Inc.
The Brogan Agency
Don Buchwald & Associates, Inc. (Los Angeles)
Don Buchwald & Associates, Inc. (New York)
Buchwald Talent Group, LLC
The Burns Agency, Inc.
Calliope Talent, Model & Artist Management, LLC
Suzanna Camejo & Associates: Artists for the
   Environment
The Campbell Agency
Carmichael Talent
Conan Carroll & Associates
The Carry Co.
The Carson Organization, Ltd.
Carson-Adler Agency, Inc.
Cassell-Levy, Inc. (dba Clinc)
Cast Images Talent Agency
Castle Hill Talent Agency
Cavaleri & Associates
Nancy Chaidez Agency & Associates
The Characters
Chateau Billings Talent Agency
Chic Models & Talent Agency
The Christensen Group
Ciao! Talent Agency
Clear Talent Group
Colleen Cler Talent Agency

Teens/Young Adults (Continued)

Coast To Coast Talent Group, Inc.
Commercial Talent, Inc.
Coralie Jr. Theatrical Agency
Corsa Agency
The Culbertson Group, LLC
Cunningham-Escott-Slevin-Doherty Talent (LA)
Cunningham-Escott-Slevin-Doherty Talent (NY)
Kim Dawson Talent
DDO Artists Agency
Marla Dell Talent Agency
DeSanti Talents, Inc.
Dimensions III Talent Agency
Diverse Talent Group
Dulcina Eisen Associates
Elegance Talent Agency
Elite Model Management
Empire Talent Agency
Encore Talent Agency
Expressions Model & Talent
Sylvia Ferguson & Assoc. Talent & Literary Agency
JFA/Jaime Ferrar Agency
FORD/Robert Black Agency
Fosi's Modeling & Talent Agency
Fresh Faces Agency, Inc.
Frontier Booking International, Inc.
The Gage Group, Inc. (Los Angeles)
Dale Garrick International Agency
The Geddes Agency (Chicago)
The Geddes Agency (Los Angeles)
Generation TV
Generations Model & Talent Agency
Gilla Roos, Ltd.
Global Artists Agency
Greene & Associates
Grossman & Jack Talent
Halpern Management
Neal Hamil Agency
Hanns Wolters International, Inc.
Beverly Hecht Agency
Hervey/Grimes Talent Agency
Daniel Hoff Agency
Hop Models & Talent Agency
Hot Shot Kids/Teens
The House of Representatives
Howard Talent West
The I Group Model & Talent Management
Identity Talent Agency
Image Model & Talent
Impact Talent Group
Imperium 7 Talent Agency (i7)
Independent Artists Agency Inc.
Innovative Artists (Los Angeles)
Innovative Artists (New York)
International Creative Mgmt., Inc. - ICM (LA)
International Creative Mgmt., Inc. - ICM (NY)
JE Talent, LLC/JE Model, Inc.
Jet Set Management Group, Inc.
Jordan, Gill & Dornbaum
Stanley Kaplan Talent
Kazarian/Spencer & Associates
Glyn Kennedy, Models Talent
Archer King, Ltd.
Kjar & Associates
Kolstein Talent Agency (KTA)
L.A. Talent
Lane Agency
Leighton Agency, Inc.
Lemodeln Model & Talent Agency
Lenz Agency
Sid Levin Agency
Lily's Talent Agency, Inc.
Jana Luker Agency
M International Talent Agency
Mademoiselle Talent & Modeling Agency
Malaky International
The Mannequin Agency
Martin & Donalds Talent Agency, Inc.

Teens/Young Adults (Continued)

The McCabe Group
Media Artists Group
Metropolitan Talent Agency (MTA)
MGATalent
Model Club, Inc.
Model Team
The Morgan Agency
H. David Moss & Associates
Susan Nathe & Associates, CPC
Nicolosi & Co., Inc.
Nouveau Model & Talent
NTA Talent Agency
Nu Talent Agency
NXT Entertainment, Inc.
One Entertainment
The Orange Grove Group, Inc.
Origin Talent
Osbrink Talent Agency
Pakula/King & Associates
Dorothy Palmer Talent Agency, Inc.
Paradigm (Los Angeles)
Pastorini-Bosby Talent, Inc.
Perfectly Petite, Inc.
Phoenix Artists, Inc.
Players Talent Agency
Privilege Talent Agency
Progressive Artists Agency
PTI Talent Agency, Inc.
Q Model Management
Qualita Dell' Arte: Artists & Writers Di Qualita
Cindy Romano Modeling & Talent Agency
San Diego Model Management Talent Agency
San Francisco Top Models & Talent
Sanger Talent Agency
The Savage Agency
Judy Schoen & Associates
Schuller Talent/NY Kids
Kathleen Schultz Associates
Screen Artists Agency, LLC
SGM - Sara Gaynor Management
Shamon Freitas Model & Talent Agency
Sky Talent Agency
The Susan Smith Company
Sonja Warren Brandon's Commercials Unlimited
Scott Stander & Associates, Inc.
Starcraft Talent Agency
Stars, The Agency
Starwil Talent
Stellar Model & Talent Agency
The Stevens Group
Stewart Talent
Ivett Stone Agency
Stone Manners Agency
Peter Strain & Associates, Inc. (Los Angeles)
Peter Strain & Associates, Inc. (New York)
Mitchell K. Stubbs & Associates
Superior Talent Agency
Tag Models
Talent & Model Land
The Talent Group
Talent Plus, Inc./Centro Models
Talent Plus/Los Latinos Talent Agency
The Talent Shop
Talent Trek Agency
Talent Unlimited, Inc.
TalentWorks
The Thomas Talent Agency
Tonry Talent
Uptown Talent, Inc.
The Ann Waugh Talent Agency
Donna Wauhob Agency
William Morris Agency - WMA (Miami Beach)
Shirley Wilson & Associates
Craig Wyckoff & Associates
Zanuck, Passon and Pace, Inc.

AGENTS

TV Writers

Abrams Artists Agency (Los Angeles)
Abrams Artists Agency (New York)
Acme Talent & Literary
Bret Adams, Ltd.
Agape Productions
Agency For the Performing Arts, Inc. (Los Angeles)
The Agency Group Ltd. (Los Angeles)
The Agency Group Ltd. (New York)
The Alpern Group
Ambition Talent Inc.
Marcia Amsterdam Agency
Artists Agency, Inc.
The Artists Agency
Baskow & Associates, Inc.
Marc Bass Agency, Inc. (MBA)
Berzon Talent Agency
The Bethel Agency
Bicoastal Talent
Bonnie Black Talent & Literary Agency
The Bohrman Agency
Marcus Bryan & Associates
Don Buchwald & Associates, Inc. (Los Angeles)
Cambridge Literary Associates, Inc.
Suzanna Camejo & Associates: Artists for the
  Environment
Conan Carroll & Associates
Nancy Chaidez Agency & Associates
The Characters
Coast To Coast Talent Group, Inc.
Contemporary Artists, Ltd.
The Coppage Company
Coralie Jr. Theatrical Agency
Creative Artists Agency - CAA
Diverse Talent Group
The E S Agency
Endeavor Agency, LLC
Sylvia Ferguson & Assoc. Talent & Literary Agency
Robert A. Freedman Dramatic Agency, Inc.
FRP Literary - Talent Agency
The Gage Group, Inc. (Los Angeles)
The Gatsby Group, Inc.
Laya Gelff Agency
The Gersh Agency (Los Angeles)
The Gersh Agency (New York)
The Glick Agency, LLC
Global Artists Agency
Grant, Savic, Kopaloff and Associates
Hanns Wolters International, Inc.
Harden-Curtis Associates
Hollywood View
Innovative Artists (Los Angeles)
International Artists Group, Inc.
International Creative Mgmt., Inc. - ICM (LA)
International Creative Mgmt., Inc. - ICM (NY)
JKA Talent & Literary Agency
Merrily Kane Agency
The Kaplan-Stahler-Gumer-Braun Agency
Archer King, Ltd.
Kjar & Associates
Paul Kohner, Inc.
Otto R. Kozak Literary & Motion Picture Agency
Lemodeln Model & Talent Agency
Lenhoff & Lenhoff
Paul S. Levine Literary Agency
Michael Lewis & Associates
Lily's Talent Agency, Inc.
The Luedtke Agency
Max Freedman Management
Media Artists Group
Menza-Barron Agency
Metropolitan Talent Agency (MTA)
The Stuart M. Miller Co.
Monteiro Rose Dravis Agency, Inc.
N.S. Bienstock, Inc.
Natural Talent, Inc.
Ofrenda, Inc.
Omnipop Talent Group

TV Writers (Continued)

One Entertainment
Oracle Creative Management
The Orange Grove Group, Inc.
Original Artists
Dorothy Palmer Talent Agency, Inc.
Paradigm (Los Angeles)
Barry Perelman Agency
Preferred Artists
Jim Preminger Agency
Qualita Dell' Arte: Artists & Writers Di Qualita
Quillco Agency
read.
Michael D. Robins & Associates
Cindy Romano Modeling & Talent Agency
The Brant Rose Agency
Rosenstone/Wender
The Rothman Brecher Agency
Sanger Talent Agency
The Sarnoff Company, Inc.
Jack Scagnetti Talent & Literary Agency
The Irv Schechter Company
Susan Schulman Literary Agency
Shapiro-Lichtman Talent Agency, Inc.
Ken Sherman & Associates
SMA, LLC
Michael H. Sommer Literary Agency
Stars, The Agency
The Stein Agency
Stone Canyon Media
Stone Manners Agency
Summit Talent & Literary Agency
Talent Representatives, Inc.
United Talent Agency - UTA
Universal Talent Intelligence
Annette van Duren Agency
Vision Art Management
Warden McKinley Literary Agency
Wardlow & Associates
Donna Wauhob Agency
William Morris Agency - WMA (Los Angeles)
William Morris Agency - WMA (New York)
William Morris Agency - WMA (Miami Beach)
William Morris Agency - WMA (London)
William Morris Agency - WMA (Shanghai)
Craig Wyckoff & Associates
Nick Yellen Creative Agency

Variety Artists

abc model/talent/sport management
Actors Etc., Inc.
Agency For the Performing Arts, Inc. (Los Angeles)
Aimée Entertainment Agency
Ambassador Talent Agents, Inc.
American Program Bureau
Angel City Talent
Irvin Arthur Associates
Baron Entertainment
Baskow & Associates, Inc.
The Bethel Agency
Boca Talent & Model Agency
Boom Models & Talent
Don Buchwald & Associates, Inc. (Los Angeles)
Don Buchwald & Associates, Inc. (New York)
Calliope Talent, Model & Artist Management, LLC
Carmichael Talent
The Carson Organization, Ltd.
Castle Hill Talent Agency
Celebrity Suppliers/Sports Star Suppliers
Nancy Chaidez Agency & Associates
Clear Talent Group
Coralie Jr. Theatrical Agency
Cunningham-Escott-Slevin-Doherty Talent (LA)
Doubble Troubble Entertainment, Inc.
EC Model & Talent Agency (Ent. Caterers, Inc.)
Elegance Talent Agency
Encore Talent Agency
Sylvia Ferguson & Assoc. Talent & Literary Agency

Variety Artists (Continued)

Film Artists Associates
Hanns Wolters International, Inc.
Harmony Artists
International Creative Mgmt., Inc. - ICM (LA)
International Creative Mgmt., Inc. - ICM (NY)
Jordan, Gill & Dornbaum
Stanley Kaplan Talent
Kazarian/Spencer & Associates
Archer King, Ltd.
Al Lampkin Entertainment, Inc.
Lane Agency
Lemodeln Model & Talent Agency
Lenz Agency
Sid Levin Agency
Mademoiselle Talent & Modeling Agency
Martin & Donalds Talent Agency, Inc.
Maxine's Talent Agency
McDonald/Selznick Associates
Metropolitan Talent Agency (MTA)
The Gilbert Miller Agency LLC
The Morgan Agency
Nouvelle Talent Management, Inc.
Nu Talent Agency
Omnipop Talent Group
The Orange Grove Group, Inc.
Dorothy Palmer Talent Agency, Inc.
Perfectly Petite, Inc.
Periwinkle Entertainment Productions
Qualita Dell' Arte: Artists & Writers Di Qualita
Sanger Talent Agency
Schuller Talent/NY Kids
Scott Stander & Associates, Inc.
Stars, The Agency
Starwil Talent
Superior Talent Agency
Talent Plus, Inc./Centro Models
The Talent Shop
Talent Unlimited, Inc.
Universal Talent Intelligence
Uptown Talent, Inc.
Donna Wauhob Agency
William Morris Agency - WMA (Los Angeles)
William Morris Agency - WMA (New York)
William Morris Agency - WMA (Miami Beach)

Voice-Over Artists

abc model/talent/sport management
Abrams Artists Agency (Los Angeles)
Abrams Artists Agency (New York)
Access Talent
Acme Talent & Literary
Actors & Others Talent Agency
Actors Etc., Inc.
Agape Productions
Alexa Model & Talent Management, Inc.
Michael Amato Agency
Ambassador Talent Agents, Inc.
Angel City Talent
Arcieri & Associates, Inc.
Artist Management Agency
Atlanta Models & Talent, Inc.
Atlas Talent Agency
Donna Baldwin Talent
The Sandi Bell Talent Agency, Inc.
Berzon Talent Agency
The Bethel Agency
Boca Talent & Model Agency
Boom Models & Talent
Brady, Brannon & Rich
Brand Model and Talent Agency, Inc.
Don Buchwald & Associates, Inc. (Los Angeles)
Don Buchwald & Associates, Inc. (New York)
Buchwald Talent Group, LLC
The Burns Agency, Inc.
Calliope Talent, Model & Artist Management, LLC
The Campbell Agency
Carmichael Talent

AGENTS

Voice-Over Artists (Continued)

The Carson Organization, Ltd.
Cassell-Levy, Inc. (dba Clinc)
Cast Images Talent Agency
Castle Hill Talent Agency
Nancy Chaidez Agency & Associates
The Characters
The Christensen Group
Ciao! Talent Agency
Creative Artists Agency - CAA
Cunningham-Escott-Slevin-Doherty Talent (LA)
Cunningham-Escott-Slevin-Doherty Talent (NY)
Kim Dawson Talent
Marla Dell Talent Agency
DeSanti Talents, Inc.
Ginger Dicce Talent Agency
Dimensions III Talent Agency
Edna Talent Management (ETM) Ltd.
Elegance Talent Agency
Encore Talent Agency
Endeavor Agency, LLC
Expressions Model & Talent
FORD/Robert Black Agency
Fosi's Modeling & Talent Agency
Frontier Booking International, Inc.
FRP Literary - Talent Agency
The Gage Group, Inc. (Los Angeles)
The Geddes Agency (Chicago)
Generation TV
Generations Model & Talent Agency
Greer Lange Model & Talent Agency, Inc.
Grossman & Jack Talent
Neal Hamil Agency
Hanns Wolters International, Inc.
Hervey/Grimes Talent Agency
Daniel Hoff Agency
Hollander Talent Group
Hot Shot Kids/Teens
The I Group Model & Talent Management

Voice-Over Artists (Continued)

Image Model & Talent
Imperium 7 Talent Agency (i7)
Independent Artists Agency, Inc.
Ingber & Associates
Innovative Artists (Chicago)
Innovative Artists (Los Angeles)
Innovative Artists (New York)
International Artists Group, Inc.
International Creative Mgmt., Inc. - ICM (LA)
IRISHVOX
JE Talent, LLC/JE Model, Inc.
Stanley Kaplan Talent
Kazarian/Spencer & Associates
Kolstein Talent Agency (KTA)
Leighton Agency, Inc.
Lemodeln Model & Talent Agency
Lenz Agency
Sid Levin Agency
Lily's Talent Agency, Inc.
Look Talent
The Luedtke Agency
M International Talent Agency
Mademoiselle Talent & Modeling Agency
The Mannequin Agency
Martin & Donalds Talent Agency, Inc.
Max Freedman Management
McCarty Talent, Inc.
Nash-Angeles, Inc.
NXT Entertainment, Inc.
Omnipop Talent Group
Osbrink Talent Agency
Fifi Oscard Agency, Inc.
Dorothy Palmer Talent Agency, Inc.
Paradigm (Los Angeles)
Paradigm (New York)
Pastorini-Bosby Talent, Inc.
Peak Models & Talent
Perfectly Petite, Inc.

Voice-Over Artists (Continued)

Qualita Dell' Arte: Artists & Writers Di Qualita
Cindy Romano Modeling & Talent Agency
San Francisco Top Models & Talent
Sanger Talent Agency
Jack Scagnetti Talent & Literary Agency
Sandie Schnarr Talent
Schuller Talent/NY Kids
Shamon Freitas Model & Talent Agency
Scott Stander & Associates, Inc.
Stars, The Agency
Stellar Model & Talent Agency
Stewart Talent
Ivett Stone Agency
Superior Talent Agency
Sutton, Barth & Vennari, Inc.
Talent & Model Land
The Talent Group
Talent Plus, Inc./Centro Models
Talent Plus/Los Latinos Talent Agency
The Talent Shop
Talent Trek Agency
Talent Unlimited, Inc.
TalentWorks New York
TGMD Talent Agency
Arlene Thornton & Associates
Tonry Talent
United Talent Agency - UTA
Universal Talent Intelligence
Uptown Talent, Inc.
Vox, Inc.
The Wallis Agency
Donna Wauhob Agency
William Morris Agency - WMA (Los Angeles)
William Morris Agency - WMA (New York)
William Morris Agency - WMA (Miami Beach)
William Morris Agency - WMA (London)
Ann Wright Representatives

MANAGERS

Actors

1 Management
3 Arts Entertainment, Inc.
777 Group, LTD
A Fein Martini
A Management
abc management group
Absolute Talent Management, Inc.
ACE Media
A.C.T. Management
A.D.S. Management
Advance LA
Alchemy Entertainment
All That Entertainment Management
Leslie Allan-Rice Management
Allman/Rea Management
Alpha Centauri Management
AM Productions & Management
American Artists Entertainment Group
American Artists Group Management
Anonymous Content
Anthem Entertainment
Archetype
Ardent Entertainment
Art/Work Entertainment
Artist International
Artist Management
Artists International
Artists Only Management
Arts and Letters Management
Associated Artists PR & Management
Athena Talent Management, LLC
Marilyn Atlas Management
Avalon Management, Inc.
Axiom Management

Actors (Continued)

Bamboo Management LLC
Barking Dog Entertainment, Inc.
The Bauer Company
Becker Entertainment Group
The Beddingfield Company, Inc.
Benderspink
Bensky Entertainment
Martin Berneman Management
Sue Bernstein Management
Betwixt Talent Management
Binder & Associates
Michael Black Management, Inc.
Blackwood Talent Management
Jane Bloom & Associates
Blubay Talent Management
Blue Train Entertainment
Blueprint Artist Management
Bohemia Group
Barry Bookin Management
The Braverman/Bloom Co., Inc.
Brillstein-Grey Management
Robin Brooks Management
Brookside Artist Management
Brown Leader Group
The Michael Bruno Group Los Angeles
Brustein Entertainment
BSC Management
The Burstein Company
Calliope Talent Management, LLC
Candy Entertainment, Inc.
John Carrabino Management
CastleBright
Central Artists
Chachkin Management

Actors (Continued)

Chancellor Entertainment
Doug Chapin Management, Inc.
Joyce Chase Management
Cheatham, Greene & Company
Vincent Cirrincione Associates, Ltd.
Coastal Entertainment Productions
Cohen/Thomas Management
The Collective
Commonwealth Talent Group
The Company Artists
Connection III Entertainment Corp.
Diane Connors Management
Contemporary Talent Partners (CTP)
The Conversation Company, Ltd.
Dan Cooper & Associates
The Coppage Company
Course Management
Edna Cowan Management
Creative Enterprises Management
Creative Haven Entertainment
Creative Mgmt. Entertainment Group (CMEG)
Creative Talent Company
Creative Talent Management
Creative Talent Management Group (CTMG)
John Crosby Management
Crysis Management
CTM Artists
Cue11 Entertainment
Cutler Management
D/F Management
Marv Dauer Management
Alan David Management
Davila & Co.
Richard De Lancy & Associates Talent Agency

MANAGERS

Actors (Continued)

Ron DeBlasio Management
DEJ Management Company
Delphinius Management
Denise Denny Talent Management
DePaz Management
The Development Department
Dewalt & Muzik Management
Bob Diamond & Associates
Divine Management
Bonny Dore Management
Douglas Management Group
Dream Talent
DreaMakers Inc.
du Jour Entertainment/Gypsy Productions
Eastwood Talent Corporation
Allen Edelman Management
Eighth Square Entertainment
Michael Einfeld Management
Elements Entertainment
Elkins Entertainment Corporation
Elsboy Management
Emancipated Talent Management & Consulting
Emerald Talent Group
Encore Artists Management
Endurance Talent Management
Energy Entertainment
Entertainment Management Group
Envision Entertainment
Envoy Entertainment
The ESI Network
Essential Talent Management
Evans Management
Evergreen International Management
Evolution Management
Farah Films & Management
Fast Track Management
Fastbreak Management, Inc.
The Feldman Company
Feldman Management, LLC
Field Entertainment
Stann Findelle Law & Management
Fineman Entertainment
Fire Comm Management
The Firm, Inc.
First Take
Robert Fitzpatrick Organization
Five12 Entertainment Group
Flaunt Model Management, Inc.
Flavor Unit Entertainment
Flutie Entertainment
Michael Flutie's Office (MFO)
Michael Forman Management
Forster Delaney Management
Forward Entertainment
Elizabeth Fowler Management
Fox Entertainment Company
Fox-Albert Management Entertainment, Inc.
Framework Entertainment
Kyle Fritz Management
The FTL Company
Full Circle Management
Brian Funnagan Management
Lorita Garcia & Associates Mgmt. & Ent.
Gateway Management Partners
GEF Entertainment
Gem Entertainment Group, Inc.
Generate
Peter Giagni Management, Inc.
Gilbertson-Kincaid
Jeff Gitlin Entertainment
Phillip B. Gittelman Personal Management
Glasser Black Management
Global Entertainment
Marianne Golan Management
Gold Coast Management
Jeff Goldberg Management
Peter Golden & Associates, Inc.

Actors (Continued)

Goldstar Talent Management
Grand View Management
Grant Management
Susan Graw and Associates
Green Key Management, LLC
Joan Green Management
Juliet Green Management
Melanie Greene Management
GSC Management
G.T.A., Inc.
H2F Entertainment
Halpern Management
Handprint Entertainment
Scott Hart Entertainment
Hart² Management
Hazen Talent Management
Heitmann Entertainment
Herbosch Management
Josselyne Herman & Associates
Himber Entertainment, Inc.
Hines & Hunt Entertainment
Hofflund/Polone
Cary Hoffman Management
Holder Management
Hollywood Management Company
Joanne Horowitz Management
Howard Entertainment
Hyler Management
Impact Artists Group, LLC
Incognito Management
The Independent Group, LLC
Independent Movement Entertainment
Industry Entertainment Partners
Infinity Management International
Cheri Ingram Enterprises
Insight
Integrated Films & Management
Interlink Management
James/Levy Management, Inc.
Jaymes-Nelson Entertainment
JudyO Productions
Kanner Entertainment Inc.
Darlene Kaplan Entertainment
Kaplan Productions
Karma Entertainment
Kass & Stokes Management
Ann Kelly Management
Key Creatives, LLC
King Management
Kings Highway Entertainment
Kjar & Associates
Knight Light Entertainment
Lloyd Kolmer Enterprises
Koopman Management
Kragen & Company
Kritzer Levine Wilkins Entertainment
Barry Krost Management
Victor Kruglov & Associates
Landis-Simon Productions & Talent Management
Paul Lane Entertainment
Lane Management Group
Lang Talent
The Laugh Factory Management
Lawson Artist Management, LLC
Letnom Management & Productions
Leverage Management
Levine Management
Leviton Management
Levity Entertainment Group
Liberman Zerman Management
The Liberty Company
Myrna Lieberman Management
Liebman Entertainment
Life Management
Lighthouse Entertainment
Link Talent Group
Little Stars Management

Actors (Continued)

LoLo Entertainment Co.
Jeffrey Loseff Management
Bonnie Love Management
Lovett Management
Lymberopoulos, Inc.
M Management
Mack Muse Entertainment, Inc.
Magenta Creative Management
Magnolia Entertainment
Maier Management
Main Title Entertainment
Management 101
Management 360
The Management Team
Managing Artistic Concepts
Manta Entertainment
Marathon Entertainment
The Marcelli Company
Marsala Management
Marsh Entertainment
The Marshak/Zachary Company
David Martin Management
Massei Management
Dino May Management
MBST Entertainment
MC Talent
McGowan Management
McKeon-Myones Management
McMurdo Management & Associates, LLC
Media Four
Media Talent Group
MEG Management
Michael Meltzer & Associates
Messina Baker Entertainment Corporation
Ellen Meyer Management
MGC/Cushman Entertainment Group
Midwest Talent Management, Inc.
Pamela Migas Management (PMM)
Millennium Entertainment, Inc.
Miller and Company
The Miller Company
April Mills Management
Renée Missel Management
J. Mitchell Management
Mixed Media Entertainment Company
MMC Entertainment/Dance Directions
Modus Entertainment
Mogul Management
Momentum Talent Management
Jaime Monroy Studios
Monster Talent Management, Inc.
Moore Artists' Management
MP Management
Multi-Ethnic Talent
Dee Mura Enterprises, Inc.
Music World Entertainment
Nanas Entertainment
Nani/Saperstein Management, Inc.
NCL TALENT
Nebula Management
New Talent Management
New Wave Entertainment
Niad Management
Nine Yards Entertainment
Barney Oldfield Management
Rosella Olson Management
Omnipop Talent Group
Omniquest Entertainment
Omnium Entertainment Group
One Entertainment
One Talent Management
Online Talent Group/OTG Talent
Dianna Oser Management
Ovation Management
P.K.A. Entertainment Group
Page Management
Pallas Management

MANAGERS

Actors (Continued)

Judy Palnick Entertainment
Panacea Entertainment
Parallel Entertainment, Inc.
Park Place Management
Parseghian Planco, LLC
Ria Pavia Management
PB Management
Pearl Pictures Management
The Phoenix Organization
The Pitt Group
Margrit Polak Management
Polaris Entertainment
The Derek Power Company, Inc.
Principal Entertainment
Principato-Young Entertainment
Pro and Con Productions Talent Management
Melissa Prophet Management
Protege Entertainment
Pure Arts
Quattro Media
Rabiner/Damato Entertainment
Vic Ramos Management
Charles Rapp Enterprises, Inc.
Joseph Rapp Enterprises, Inc.
Raw Talent
Red Baron Management
Reel Talent Management
Linda Reitman Management
Relevant Entertainment Group
Releve Entertainment
Ribisi Entertainment
L. Richardson Entertainment
Rigberg Entertainment Group
The Right Connection Entertainment Group
Rising Talent Management
RJM/Renée Jennett Management
ROAR
J.C. Robbins Management
Mark Robert Management
Dolores Robinson Entertainment
Bill Robinson Management
Roklin Management
Rosalee Productions
The Marion Rosenberg Office
Lara Rosenstock Management
Heidi Rotbart Management
Rough Diamond Management
Safran Company
Sager Management, Inc.
Sanders/Armstrong Management
Sanderson Entertainment, Inc.
Fran Saperstein Organization
Dorothea Sargent & Company
Sauers Artists, LLC
Saxon Associates Management
Schachter Entertainment
Schumacher Management
Booh Schut Company
Richard Schwartz Management
SCORE! Media Ventures
Jeri Scott Management
Screen Partners, Inc.
Seekers Management, LLC
Select Artists, Ltd.
Seven Summits Pictures & Management
Earl Shank
Burt Shapiro Management
Marty Shapiro Management
Shapiro/West & Associates, Inc.
Shark Artists, Inc.
Sharp Talent
Sharyn Talent Management
Narelle Sheehan Management (NSM)
Shelter Entertainment
Shoelace, Inc. Management
The Siegal Company
Alan Siegel Entertainment

Actors (Continued)

Blair Silver & Company LLC
Simmons and Scott Entertainment, LLC
Sinclair Management
SirenSong Entertainment, Inc.
SJV Enterprises & Associates
Daniel Sladek Entertainment Corporation
Slamdance Management
Sleeping Giant Entertainment
SLJ Management
Todd Smith & Associates
Bette Smith Management
The Susan Smith Company
Sneak Preview Entertainment
Soiree Fair, Inc.
Helene Sokol Management
Soma Management
Sonesta Entertainment, LLC
Speak Softly Legal Management
Larry Spellman Enterprises
Spellman, Paul & Wetzel
Spot Light Entertainment
Star Talent Management
Station 3
Stein Entertainment Group
Steinberg Talent Management Group
The Sterling/Winters Company
Harriet Sternberg Management
Joel Stevens Entertainment Company
Studio Talent Group
The Suchin Company
Sullivan Talent Group
Suskin Management LLC
Suzelle Enterprises
Sweeney Management
Synergy Management, Inc.
The Talent Company
Talent Management Partners
Talent Scout International Management
TalentCo Model & Talent Management
Talented Managers
TAO Management & Tetrahedron Productions
Teitelbaum Artists Group
Temptation Management
Terrific Talent Associates, Inc.
TGI Entertainment Corporation
The Michael Forman Company
Thirdhill Entertainment
Larry Thompson Organization
The Robert Thorne Company
Thruline Entertainment
Roz Tillman Management
Tinoco Management
TMT Entertainment
Toltec Artists
Torque Entertainment
Trademark Artists Management
Trademark Talent
Triniti Management
Triple Threat Talent Management
Troika
Trusik Talent Management, Inc.
Turner Artist Management
Unique Talent Group
Universal Management Group (UMG)
Unlimited Management
Untitled Entertainment
V & L International, LLC
Valentino Entertainment
Vanguard Management Group
Vanguard Talent Management
Velocity Management
Vesta Talent Services
Viking Entertainment
Visionary Entertainment
WA Enterprises
The Robert D. Wachs Company
Brad Waisbren Enterprises

Actors (Continued)

Wallach Entertainment
Michael Wallach Management
Washington Square Arts
Water Street
Mimi Weber Management Co.
David Westberg Management
Whitaker Entertainment
Wild Briar Talent
Wilhelmina Creative Management
Wilhelmina Kids
Witt Entertainment Management, Inc.
Christopher Wright Management
Young Performers Management
Young Talent, Inc.
Bonnie Young Personal Management
Yumkas Management
Gene Yusem Company
Zenith Management
Ziemba Talent & Associates

Animals

Richard De Lancy & Associates Talent Agency

Book Authors

AEI-Atchity/Entertainment International
Alpha Centauri Management
Ampersand Management Group
Artist International
Avery Management
The Bauer Company
Benderspink
Bensky Entertainment
Blain & Associates
Blubay Talent Management
Barry Bookin Management
The Braverman/Bloom Co., Inc.
Brillstein-Grey Management
Brustein Entertainment
bumberShoot Entertainment
Casting Unlimited & Management
CFB Productions, Inc.
Cine/Lit
Code
Contemporary Talent Partners (CTP)
Content House
The Coppage Company
Course Management
Created By
Creative Enterprises Management
Cue11 Entertainment
Davila & Co.
DEJ Management Company
Delphinius Management
Donaldson/Sanders Entertainment
Bonny Dore Management
du Jour Entertainment/Gypsy Productions
Elements Entertainment
Elysian Entertainment, Inc.
e-merge Management
Encore Artists Management
Ensemble Entertainment
Evans Management
Evolution Management
The Feldman Company
Festa Entertainment
Field Entertainment
Stann Findelle Law & Management
The Firm, Inc.
FitzGerald Literary Management
Flashpoint Entertainment
Flutie Entertainment
Michael Forman Management
Elizabeth Fowler Management
Frenetic Media
The FTL Company
M.M. Gertz Entertainment

MANAGERS

Book Authors (Continued)

GhettoSuburbia Entertainment
The Gotham Group, Inc.
Grade A Entertainment
Susan Graw and Associates
Grey Line Entertainment, Inc.
Hart Entertainment
Hart² Management
Holzman Management Group
Illuminati Entertainment
Infinity Management International
Cheri Ingram Enterprises
Intellectual Property Group
Jaret Entertainment
Jaymes-Nelson Entertainment
King Management
Kragen & Company
Lawson Artist Management, LLC
Letnom Management & Productions
Leverage Management
The Liberty Company
Little Studio Films
Lukeman Literary Management, Ltd.
MaCroManagement
Management 101
The Marcelli Company
Martin Literary Management
McMurdo Management & Associates, LLC
J. Mitchell Management
Miterre Productions, Inc.
Dee Mura Enterprises, Inc.
New Entertainment Group
New Wave Entertainment
Park Place Management
Ria Pavia Management
Stephen Pevner, Inc.
The Phoenix Organization
The Pitt Group
PMA Literary & Film Management, Inc.
Quattro Media
Relevant Entertainment Group
L. Richardson Entertainment
ROAR
Stephanie Rogers & Associates
The Marion Rosenberg Office
Jeff Ross Entertainment, Inc.
Heidi Rotbart Management
Seven Summits Pictures & Management
Shark Artists, Inc.
The Shuman Company
Blair Silver & Company LLC
Simmons and Scott Entertainment, LLC
Andrea Simon Entertainment
Slamdance Management
Smart Entertainment
Chad Snopek Management
Soiree Fair, Inc.
Spellman, Paul & Wetzel
Spot Light Entertainment
Steinberg Talent Management Group
The Sterling/Winters Company
Stone Canyon Media
Story Arts Management
Studio Talent Group
Sussex Ltd., Inc., A Management Company
Synchronicity Management
Talent Management Partners
Talent Scout International Management
The Michael Forman Company
Trademark Artists Management
Underground Management
Universal Management Group (UMG)
Unlimited Management
V & L International, LLC
Velocity Management
Viviano Feldman Entertainment
Michael Wallach Management
Whitaker Entertainment

Book Authors (Continued)

Will Entertainment
Windfall Management

Broadcast Journalists/Newscasters

abc management group
A.D.S. Management
Bensky Entertainment
Barry Bookin Management
The Braverman/Bloom Co., Inc.
Diane Connors Management
Dan Cooper & Associates
Creative Mgmt. Entertainment Group (CMEG)
DEJ Management Company
Denise Denny Talent Management
Eastwood Talent Corporation
Evans Management
Stann Findelle Law & Management
Green Key Management, LLC
Headline Media Management
Cheri Ingram Enterprises
Letnom Management & Productions
Lymberopoulos, Inc.
The Management Team
Marathon Entertainment
David Martin Management
Modus Entertainment
Dee Mura Enterprises, Inc.
NCL TALENT
Park Place Management
Burt Shapiro Management
Shark Artists, Inc.
Suzelle Enterprises
Synergy Management, Inc.
TalentCo Model & Talent Management
TGI Entertainment Corporation
Torque Entertainment
Universal Management Group (UMG)
Wallach Entertainment
Michael Wallach Management

Children

abc management group
Absolute Talent Management, Inc.
A.C.T. Management
Advance LA
All That Entertainment Management
Leslie Allan-Rice Management
Arts and Letters Management
Bensky Entertainment
Sue Bernstein Management
Bohemia Group
Robin Brooks Management
Brown Leader Group
Calliope Talent Management, LLC
Central Artists
Connection III Entertainment Corp.
Creative Talent Company
Richard De Lancy & Associates Talent Agency
Dewalt & Muzik Management
Bob Diamond & Associates
Dream Talent
Eastwood Talent Corporation
Emerald Talent Group
Encore Artists Management
Endurance Talent Management
The ESI Network
Fire Comm Management
Five12 Entertainment Group
Flutie Entertainment
Gem Entertainment Group, Inc.
Global Entertainment
Goldstar Talent Management
Hart Entertainment
Harvest Talent Management
Hazen Talent Management
Hines & Hunt Entertainment

Children (Continued)

Howard Entertainment
The Independent Group, LLC
James/Levy Management, Inc.
Kjar & Associates
Knight Light Entertainment
Kragen & Company
Kritzer Levine Wilkins Entertainment
LA Entertainment
Landis-Simon Productions & Talent Management
Lang Talent
The Laugh Factory Management
Lawson Artist Management, LLC
Letnom Management & Productions
Myrna Lieberman Management
Little Stars Management
Lymberopoulos, Inc.
Maier Management
Management 101
Managing Artistic Concepts
The Marcelli Company
Dino May Management
MC Talent
McGowan Management
McMurdo Management & Associates, LLC
Midwest Talent Management, Inc.
April Mills Management
J. Mitchell Management
Monster Talent Management, Inc.
MP Management
Dee Mura Enterprises, Inc.
Nani/Saperstein Management, Inc.
NCL TALENT
Nebula Management
Niad Management
Omnium Entertainment Group
One Entertainment
P.K.A. Entertainment Group
Page Management
Pallas Management
Park Place Management
Protege Entertainment
Red Baron Management
Reel Talent Management
L. Richardson Entertainment
The Right Connection Entertainment Group
Rising Talent Management
J.C. Robbins Management
Sager Management, Inc.
Sauers Artists, LLC
Schachter Entertainment
Earl Shank
Burt Shapiro Management
Sharyn Talent Management
Simmons and Scott Entertainment, LLC
Sinclair Management
SJV Enterprises & Associates
Bette Smith Management
Soiree Fair, Inc.
Helene Sokol Management
Spellman, Paul & Wetzel
Spot Light Entertainment
Star Talent Management
Station 3
Stein Entertainment Group
Studio Talent Group
Suzelle Enterprises
Sweeney Management
TalentCo Model & Talent Management
Thirdhill Entertainment
Roz Tillman Management
Tinoco Management
Trademark Talent
Triniti Management
Unique Talent Group
Whitaker Entertainment
Wild Briar Talent
Wilhelmina Kids

MANAGERS

Children (Continued)

Williams Unlimited
Witt Entertainment Management, Inc.
Young Performers Management
Young Talent, Inc.
Zenith Management

Choreographers

ACE Media
A.C.T. Management
Blackwood Talent Management
Calliope Talent Management, LLC
Chachkin Management
Columbia Artists Management LLC
DEJ Management Company
M Management
The Marcelli Company
Daniel Sladek Entertainment Corporation
Triniti Management
Young Talent, Inc.

Cinematographers

Ambitious Entertainment
Associated Artists PR & Management
Becker Entertainment Group
Richard De Lancy & Associates Talent Agency
DEJ Management Company
Delphinius Management
Feldman Management, LLC
Graup Entertainment
P.K.A. Entertainment Group
Judy Palnick Entertainment
Panettiere & Company, Inc.
Parseghian Planco, LLC
The Phoenix Organization
Marty Shapiro Management
Westside Artists

Comedians

3 Arts Entertainment, Inc.
abc management group
ACE Media
A.C.T. Management
Advance LA
Alpha Centauri Management
American Artists Group Management
Artist International
Associated Artists PR & Management
Avalon Management, Inc.
Bandwagon Entertainment
Barking Dog Entertainment, Inc.
The Bauer Company
Beaty Four Entertainment
Blackwood Talent Management
Blueprint Artist Management
Bohemia Group
Barry Bookin Management
Brillstein-Grey Management
Calliope Talent Management, LLC
CFB Productions, Inc.
Cheatham, Greene & Company
Coastal Entertainment Productions
The Collective
Diane Connors Management
Contemporary Talent Partners (CTP)
The Conversation Company, Ltd.
The Core
Edna Cowan Management
Creative Mgmt. Entertainment Group (CMEG)
Creative Talent Management
Davila & Co.
Richard De Lancy & Associates Talent Agency
Ron DeBlasio Management
DEJ Management Company
Delphinius Management
Divine Management
dixon talent, inc.

Comedians (Continued)

Bonny Dore Management
DreaMakers Inc.
Eastwood Talent Corporation
Eighth Square Entertainment
Elements Entertainment
Emancipated Talent Management & Consulting
Emerald Talent Group
Evans Management
Fastbreak Management, Inc.
Stann Findelle Law & Management
The Firm, Inc.
First Class Entertainment, Inc.
Flutie Entertainment
Michael Forman Management
Forward Entertainment
Full Circle Management
Brian Funnagan Management
Lorita Garcia & Associates Mgmt. & Ent.
Gem Entertainment Group, Inc.
Generate
Jeff Gitlin Entertainment
Peter Golden & Associates, Inc.
Green Key Management, LLC
Halpern Management
Handprint Entertainment
Hart² Management
Cary Hoffman Management
Hollywood Management Company
Howard Entertainment
Independent Movement Entertainment
Infinity Management International
Interlink Management
Kanner Entertainment Inc.
Kaplan Productions
King Management
Kragen & Company
Victor Kruglov & Associates
The Laugh Factory Management
Lawrence International Corporation
Lawson Artist Management, LLC
Letnom Management & Productions
Leviton Management
Levity Entertainment Group
Liebman Entertainment
LoLo Entertainment Co.
Jeffrey Loseff Management
Lymberopoulos, Inc.
Mack Muse Entertainment, Inc.
Management 101
Marathon Entertainment
The Marcelli Company
The Marshak/Zachary Company
David Martin Management
MBST Entertainment
McMurdo Management & Associates, LLC
MEG Management
Messina Baker Entertainment Corporation
Midwest Talent Management, Inc.
Millennium Entertainment, Inc.
The Miller Company
Miterre Productions, Inc.
Modus Entertainment
Moore Artists' Management
Dee Mura Enterprises, Inc.
Nanas Entertainment
NCL TALENT
Nebula Management
New Wave Entertainment
Niad Management
Nine Yards Entertainment
Omnipop Talent Group
P.K.A. Entertainment Group
Panacea Entertainment
Parallel Entertainment, Inc.
Park Place Management
The Phoenix Organization
Polaris Entertainment

Comedians (Continued)

Principato-Young Entertainment
Pro and Con Productions Talent Management
Charles Rapp Enterprises, Inc.
Joseph Rapp Enterprises, Inc.
Red Baron Management
Linda Reitman Management
Relevant Entertainment Group
L. Richardson Entertainment
ROAR
J.C. Robbins Management
Heidi Rotbart Management
Sanderson Entertainment, Inc.
Schachter Entertainment
Schumacher Management
Screen Partners, Inc.
Seekers Management, LLC
Burt Shapiro Management
Shapiro/West & Associates, Inc.
Sharp Talent
Shelter Entertainment
Shoelace, Inc. Management
Blair Silver & Company LLC
Smart Entertainment
Bette Smith Management
Speak Softly Legal Management
Larry Spellman Enterprises
Spellman, Paul & Wetzel
Spot Light Entertainment
Station 3
Steinberg Talent Management Group
The Sterling/Winters Company
Harriet Sternberg Management
Gail A. Stocker Presents
Strauss-McGarr Entertainment
Studio Talent Group
The Suchin Company
Jeff Sussman Management
Sweeney Management
Synchronicity Management
Synergy Management, Inc.
TalentCo Model & Talent Management
Teitelbaum Artists Group
The Michael Forman Company
Thruline Entertainment
Tinoco Management
Toltec Artists
Torque Entertainment
Trademark Artists Management
Trademark Talent
Triple Threat Talent Management
Unique Talent Group
Vanguard Management Group
The Robert D. Wachs Company
Wallach Entertainment
Water Street
Whitaker Entertainment
Dan Wiley Management
Gene Yusem Company

Composers

Artist International
Artists Management
Brand X Management
Columbia Artists Management LLC
The Core
Creative Content Management
Creative Talent Management
Creative Talent Management Group (CTMG)
Cue11 Entertainment
DEJ Management Company
Delphinius Management
Denise Denny Talent Management
Elkins Entertainment Corporation
Evans Management
Stann Findelle Law & Management
The Firm, Inc.
The FTL Company

MANAGERS

Composers (Continued)

Green Key Management, LLC
Greenspan Artist Management
Hook Entertainment
ICM Artists
Kraft-Engel Management
L.A. Sammy Productions
Lawson Artist Management, LLC
Manta Entertainment
Marks Management
McMurdo Management & Associates, LLC
Media Four
P.K.A. Entertainment Group
Judy Palnick Entertainment
Panacea Entertainment
The Derek Power Company, Inc.
Joseph Rapp Enterprises, Inc.
Shark Artists, Inc.
Blair Silver & Company LLC
Simmons and Scott Entertainment, LLC
Sussex Ltd., Inc., A Management Company
Turner Artist Management
Yumkas Management

Dancers

abc management group
Blackwood Talent Management
Robin Brooks Management
Calliope Talent Management, LLC
Chancellor Entertainment
Columbia Artists Management LLC
Creative Haven Entertainment
DEJ Management Company
Bob Diamond & Associates
Dream Talent
du Jour Entertainment/Gypsy Productions
Eastwood Talent Corporation
Flaunt Model Management, Inc.
Estelle Fusco Talent Management
Hart Entertainment
ICM Artists
Victor Kruglov & Associates
Lawson Artist Management, LLC
M Management
The Marcelli Company
McMurdo Management & Associates, LLC
April Mills Management
MMC Entertainment/Dance Directions
Nani/Saperstein Management, Inc.
New Wave Entertainment
P.K.A. Entertainment Group
Park Place Management
Pro and Con Productions Talent Management
Shark Artists, Inc.
Loretta Shreve Model Center/Shreve Talent Source
Bette Smith Management
Soma Management
Star Talent Management
TalentCo Model & Talent Management
Tinoco Management
Triniti Management
Triple Threat Talent Management
V & L International, LLC
Brad Waisbren Enterprises
Young Talent, Inc.
Zenith Management

Directors

3 Arts Entertainment, Inc.
6 Pictures
777 Group, LTD
A Wink and a Nod Management, Inc.
ACE Media
A.C.T. Management
Acuna Entertainment
Ambitious Entertainment
American Artists Group Management

Directors (Continued)

Ampersand Management Group
Anonymous Content
Anthem Entertainment
Archetype
Arpil Entertainment
Art/Work Entertainment
Artist International
Artists Only Management
Arts and Letters Management
Associated Artists PR & Management
Marilyn Atlas Management
Avalon Management, Inc.
Avery Management
The Bauer Company
Baumgarten Management & Production
Becker Entertainment Group
Carl Belfor Entertainment Management Company
Benderspink
Bensky Entertainment
Martin Berneman Management
Betwixt Talent Management
Michael Black Management, Inc.
Blackwood Talent Management
Blain & Associates
Blue Train Entertainment
Blueprint Artist Management
Barry Bookin Management
Brand X Management
Brillstein-Grey Management
Brookside Artist Management
Brustein Entertainment
bumberShoot Entertainment
The Burstein Company
Careyes Entertainment
Casting Unlimited & Management
CastleBright
Doug Chapin Management, Inc.
Cheatham, Greene & Company
Chic Productions & Management (CPM)
Circle of Confusion
Vincent Cirrincione Associates, Ltd.
Code
The Collective
The Company Artists
Concept Entertainment
Connection III Entertainment Corp.
Diane Connors Management
Contemporary Talent Partners (CTP)
Content House
The Coppage Company
Cornice Entertainment
Course Management
Edna Cowan Management
Creative Convergence
Creative Enterprises Management
Creative Haven Entertainment
Creative Talent Company
Creative Talent Management
CTM Artists
Cue11 Entertainment
Marv Dauer Management
Davila & Co.
Richard De Lancy & Associates Talent Agency
DEJ Management Company
Delphinius Management
Denise Denny Talent Management
Detroit Company
The Development Department
Donaldson/Sanders Entertainment
Bonny Dore Management
Douglas Management Group
DreaMakers Inc.
EarthAngels Literary Management
Echo Lake Management
Eighth Square Entertainment
EK Management
Elements Entertainment

Directors (Continued)

Elkins Entertainment Corporation
Elsboy Management
Elysian Entertainment, Inc.
e-merge Management
Encore Artists Management
Energy Entertainment
Ensemble Entertainment
Envoy Entertainment
Epigram Management
Evolution Management
Exile Entertainment
The Feldman Company
Festa Entertainment
Field Entertainment
Fineman Entertainment
The Firm, Inc.
Flashpoint Entertainment
Flutie Entertainment
Michael Forman Management
Forward Entertainment
Foursight Entertainment
Elizabeth Fowler Management
Frenetic Media
Fuel Filmworks
Fuse Entertainment
Lorita Garcia & Associates Mgmt. & Ent.
Gem Entertainment Group, Inc.
Generate
GhettoSuburbia Entertainment
Peter Giagni Management, Inc.
Phillip B. Gittelman Personal Management
Dodie Gold Management, Inc.
Peter Golden & Associates, Inc.
Goldstein Company, Inc.
The Gotham Group, Inc.
Grade A Entertainment
Graup Entertainment
Susan Graw and Associates
Brad Gross Inc., Literary Management
Ken Gross Management
Guy Walks into a Bar Management
H2F Entertainment
Handprint Entertainment
Todd Harris Management, Inc.
Scott Hart Entertainment
Heitmann Entertainment
Himber Entertainment, Inc.
Hofflund/Polone
Holder Management
Holzman Management Group
Hook Entertainment
Hopscotch Pictures
Howard Entertainment
Impact Artists Group, LLC
Incognito Management
Independent Movement Entertainment
Industry Entertainment Partners
Infinity Management International
Insight
Integrated Films & Management
Jaret Entertainment
JudyO Productions
Kanner Entertainment Inc.
Kaplan/Perrone Entertainment, LLC
Karma Entertainment
Kersey Management
Key Creatives, LLC
Kinesis Entertainment, Inc.
Kinetic Management
King Management
Kings Highway Entertainment
Kjar & Associates
Don Klein Management Group, Inc.
Kritzer Levine Wilkins Entertainment
Paul Lane Entertainment
Lane Management Group
Lawson Artist Management, LLC

MANAGERS

Directors (Continued)

Leverage Management
Levine Management
The Liberty Company
Liebman Entertainment
Lighthouse Entertainment
Link Talent Group
Little Studio Films
LoLo Entertainment Co.
Lovett Management
M Management
Mack Muse Entertainment, Inc.
MaCroManagement
Madhouse Entertainment
Magenta Creative Management
Magnet Management
Magnolia Entertainment
Management 101
Management 360
Managing Artistic Concepts
Manta Entertainment
Marathon Entertainment
The Marcelli Company
Marsala Management
Marsh Entertainment
The Marshak/Zachary Company
Max Freedman Management
MBST Entertainment
McKeon-Myones Management
McMurdo Management & Associates, LLC
Media Four
Media Talent Group
MEG Management
Michael Meltzer & Associates
Messina Baker Entertainment Corporation
Millennium Entertainment, Inc.
The Miller Company
Renée Missel Management
Modus Entertainment
Moore Artists' Management
MSI Entertainment, Inc.
Dee Mura Enterprises, Inc.
Nanas Entertainment
NCL TALENT
New Wave Entertainment
Next Stop Management
Niad Management
Nine Yards Entertainment
Omniquest Entertainment
One Entertainment
One Talent Management
Dianna Oser Management
Ovation Management
P.K.A. Entertainment Group
Judy Palnick Entertainment
Panettiere & Company, Inc.
Parseghian Planco, LLC
Pearl Pictures Management
Stephen Pevner, Inc.
The Phoenix Organization
The Pitt Group
Plumeria Entertainment Management
PMA Literary & Film Management, Inc.
Polaris Entertainment
The Derek Power Company, Inc.
Principal Entertainment
Principato-Young Entertainment
Pro and Con Productions Talent Management
Pure Arts
Quattro Media
Rabiner/Damato Entertainment
The Radmin Company
Charles Rapp Enterprises, Inc.
Raw Talent
Red Baron Management
Red Harvest Entertainment
Dan Redler Entertainment
Reel World Management

Directors (Continued)

Linda Reitman Management
Relevant Entertainment Group
Rigberg Entertainment Group
ROAR
Dolores Robinson Entertainment
Stephanie Rogers & Associates
The Marion Rosenberg Office
Lara Rosenstock Management
Jeff Ross Entertainment, Inc.
Rough Diamond Management
RPM International
Safran Company
Fran Saperstein Organization
Schachter Entertainment
Schumacher Management
Richard Schwartz Management
Seven Summits Pictures & Management
Marty Shapiro Management
Shapiro/West & Associates, Inc.
Shark Artists, Inc.
Narelle Sheehan Management (NSM)
Shoelace, Inc. Management
The Shuman Company
Alan Siegel Entertainment
Silent R Management
Blair Silver & Company LLC
Andrea Simon Entertainment
SirenSong Entertainment, Inc.
Daniel Sladek Entertainment Corporation
Sleeping Giant Entertainment
Smart Entertainment
Todd Smith & Associates
Sneak Preview Entertainment
Chad Snopek Management
Sonesta Entertainment, LLC
Spellman, Paul & Wetzel
Station 3
Steinberg Talent Management Group
The Sterling/Winters Company
Harriet Sternberg Management
Joel Stevens Entertainment Company
Stone Canyon Media
Suite A Management Talent & Literary Agency
Sussex Ltd., Inc., A Management Company
Synchronicity Management
Talent Management Partners
Talent Scout International Management
Teitelbaum Artists Group
TGI Entertainment Corporation
The Michael Forman Company
Thompson Street Entertainment
Thrive Entertainment
Thruline Entertainment
Roz Tillman Management
TMT Entertainment
Toltec Artists
Torque Entertainment
Treasure Entertainment
Tudor Management Group
Underground Management
Unique Talent Group
Universal Management Group (UMG)
Unlimited Management
Untitled Entertainment
V & L International, LLC
Vanguard Management Group
Velocity Management
Visionary Entertainment
Viviano Feldman Entertainment
Washington Square Arts
Water Street
Working Artists
W.T.A. & Associates
Yumkas Management
Gene Yusem Company
Zero Gravity Management

Film Editors

The Bauer Company
Creative Haven Entertainment
DEJ Management Company
Delphinius Management
McMurdo Management & Associates, LLC
Niad Management
Pearl Pictures Management
The Phoenix Organization
RJM/Renée Jennett Management
Marty Shapiro Management
Shoelace, Inc. Management
Westside Artists
Working Artists

Hosts/MCs

abc management group
A.C.T. Management
A.D.S. Management
Alpha Centauri Management
American Artists Group Management
Artist International
Associated Artists PR & Management
Avalon Management, Inc.
Axiom Management
The Bauer Company
David Belenzon Management, Inc.
Blueprint Artist Management
Barry Bookin Management
The Braverman/Bloom Co., Inc.
Brown Leader Group
Calliope Talent Management, LLC
Chancellor Entertainment
Coastal Entertainment Productions
Dan Cooper & Associates
The Core
Creative Haven Entertainment
Creative Mgmt. Entertainment Group (CMEG)
Creative Talent Company
Cue11 Entertainment
Richard De Lancy & Associates Talent Agency
DEJ Management Company
Delphinius Management
Bonny Dore Management
Michael Einfeld Management
Encore Artists Management
Fast Track Management
Michael Flutie's Office (MFO)
Full Circle Management
Brian Funnagan Management
Generate
Handprint Entertainment
Josselyne Herman & Associates
Hines & Hunt Entertainment
Cary Hoffman Management
Impact Artists Group, LLC
The Independent Group, LLC
Cheri Ingram Enterprises
JudyO Productions
Kaplan Productions
Kragen & Company
The Laugh Factory Management
Lawrence International Corporation
Lawson Artist Management, LLC
Letnom Management & Productions
Lymberopoulos, Inc.
Magenta Creative Management
Maier Management
Management 101
Marathon Entertainment
The Marcelli Company
McMurdo Management & Associates, LLC
Messina Baker Entertainment Corporation
Pamela Migas Management (PMM)
Millennium Entertainment, Inc.
Moore Artists' Management
Dee Mura Enterprises, Inc.
NCL TALENT

MANAGERS

Hosts/MCs (Continued)

Nebula Management
New Wave Entertainment
Niad Management
Omnipop Talent Group
Omnium Entertainment Group
Dianna Oser Management
Pallas Management
Park Place Management
Ria Pavia Management
Pearl Pictures Management
The Phoenix Organization
Polaris Entertainment
Red Baron Management
Rising Talent Management
ROAR
J.C. Robbins Management
Sager Management, Inc.
SCORE! Media Ventures
Select Artists, Ltd.
Burt Shapiro Management
Shoelace, Inc. Management
Loretta Shreve Model Center/Shreve Talent Source
The Siegal Company
Blair Silver & Company LLC
Spot Light Entertainment
Steinberg Talent Management Group
The Sterling/Winters Company
Gail A. Stocker Presents
Suzelle Enterprises
Synergy Management, Inc.
Teitelbaum Artists Group
Thirdhill Entertainment
Roz Tillman Management
Torque Entertainment
Trademark Talent
Triniti Management
Universal Management Group (UMG)
WA Enterprises
Wallach Entertainment
Whitaker Entertainment
Young Talent, Inc.

Infants

Robin Brooks Management
Dream Talent
The ESI Network
Estelle Fusco Talent Management
Lang Talent
Little Stars Management
MP Management
NCL TALENT
Page Management
Sharyn Talent Management
Suzelle Enterprises
TalentCo Model & Talent Management
Tinoco Management
Wild Briar Talent
Witt Entertainment Management, Inc.

Interactive Game Developers

Delphinius Management
Illuminati Entertainment
Infinity Management International
Quattro Media
Blair Silver & Company LLC
Smart Entertainment
Torque Entertainment
Universal Management Group (UMG)

Magicians

Alpha Centauri Management
Barry Bookin Management
First Class Entertainment, Inc.
The Marcelli Company
MEG Management
Mixed Media Entertainment Company

Magicians (Continued)

Dee Mura Enterprises, Inc.
New Wave Entertainment
Pro and Con Productions Talent Management
Sinclair Management
Spot Light Entertainment
Gail A. Stocker Presents

Martial Artists/Stunts

abc management group
ACE Media
A.D.S. Management
Advance LA
Associated Artists PR & Management
The Braverman/Bloom Co., Inc.
Calliope Talent Management, LLC
Eastwood Talent Corporation
Michael Forman Management
Heitmann Entertainment
Kjar & Associates
Little Stars Management
Midwest Talent Management, Inc.
NCL TALENT
P.K.A. Entertainment Group
Park Place Management
Pro and Con Productions Talent Management
Sharp Talent
Blair Silver & Company LLC
Simmons and Scott Entertainment, LLC
TalentCo Model & Talent Management
Roz Tillman Management
Whitaker Entertainment
W.T.A. & Associates

Music Artists

1 Management
A Fein Martini
abc management group
All That Entertainment Management
AM Productions & Management
American Artists Entertainment Group
Artist International
Associated Artists PR & Management
Beaty Four Entertainment
Becker Entertainment Group
David Belenzon Management, Inc.
Blackwood Talent Management
Bohemia Group
Barry Bookin Management
Brand X Management
Robin Brooks Management
Brookside Artist Management
Brustein Entertainment
BSC Management
Calliope Talent Management, LLC
Casting Unlimited & Management
CFB Productions, Inc.
Chancellor Entertainment
Columbia Artists Management LLC
Diane Connors Management
The Conversation Company, Ltd.
The Core
Cornerstone Management
Creative Content Management
Creative Talent Management
Creative Talent Management Group (CTMG)
Cue11 Entertainment
Davila & Co.
Richard De Lancy & Associates Talent Agency
Ron DeBlasio Management
DEJ Management Company
Delphinius Management
Bonny Dore Management
DreaMakers Inc.
du Jour Entertainment/Gypsy Productions
Eastwood Talent Corporation
Elegance Talent Group

Music Artists (Continued)

Emancipated Talent Management & Consulting
Endure Management
Entertainment Management Group
Evans Management
Fastbreak Management, Inc.
Stann Findelle Law & Management
The Firm, Inc.
First Class Entertainment, Inc.
Robert Fitzpatrick Organization
Five12 Entertainment Group
Flavor Unit Entertainment
Michael Flutie's Office (MFO)
Fox Entertainment Company
The FTL Company
Green Key Management, LLC
G.T.A., Inc.
Handprint Entertainment
Scott Hart Entertainment
Hart[2] Management
Josselyne Herman & Associates
Hook Entertainment
ICM Artists
Independent Movement Entertainment
Infinity Management International
Cheri Ingram Enterprises
King Management
Knight Light Entertainment
Kragen & Company
Kritzer Levine Wilkins Entertainment
Paul Lane Entertainment
Lawrence International Corporation
Lawson Artist Management, LLC
Letnom Management & Productions
LoLo Entertainment Co.
M Management
Management 101
Managing Artistic Concepts
Manta Entertainment
The Marcelli Company
David Martin Management
Dino May Management
MBST Entertainment
McMurdo Management & Associates, LLC
MEG Management
Millennium Entertainment, Inc.
Mixed Media Entertainment Company
Dee Mura Enterprises, Inc.
Music World Entertainment
NCL TALENT
Nine Yards Entertainment
Dianna Oser Management
Overbrook Entertainment
P.K.A. Entertainment Group
Judy Palnick Entertainment
Panacea Entertainment
Pro and Con Productions Talent Management
Joseph Rapp Enterprises, Inc.
Linda Reitman Management
Releve Entertainment
ROAR
Safran Company
Fran Saperstein Organization
Seekers Management, LLC
Shark Artists, Inc.
Blair Silver & Company LLC
Simmons and Scott Entertainment, LLC
Bette Smith Management
Speak Softly Legal Management
Spot Light Entertainment
Station 3
The Sterling/Winters Company
Harriet Sternberg Management
Sussex Ltd., Inc., A Management Company
Synchronicity Management
Talent Source
TGI Entertainment Corporation
Trademark Artists Management

MANAGERS

Music Artists (Continued)
Triple Threat Talent Management
Turner Artist Management
Universal Management Group (UMG)
V & L International, LLC
Valentino Entertainment
WA Enterprises
The Robert D. Wachs Company
David Westberg Management
Wilhelmina Models
Yumkas Management

Music Editors
Cue11 Entertainment
Delphinius Management
Greenspan Artist Management

Music Producers
abc management group
American Artists Entertainment Group
Artist International
Artists Management
Beaty Four Entertainment
Blackwood Talent Management
Brand X Management
Calliope Talent Management, LLC
Casting Unlimited & Management
Chachkin Management
Chancellor Entertainment
Diane Connors Management
Creative Content Management
Creative Talent Management Group (CTMG)
Cue11 Entertainment
DEJ Management Company
Delphinius Management
DreaMakers Inc.
Stann Findelle Law & Management
The Firm, Inc.
Robert Fitzpatrick Organization
The FTL Company
Hook Entertainment
L.A. Sammy Productions
Lawson Artist Management, LLC
Managing Artistic Concepts
Manta Entertainment
MEG Management
Music World Entertainment
P.K.A. Entertainment Group
Judy Palnick Entertainment
Panacea Entertainment
ROAR
Shark Artists, Inc.
Blair Silver & Company LLC
Simmons and Scott Entertainment, LLC
Sonesta Entertainment, LLC
Spot Light Entertainment
TGI Entertainment Corporation
Triple Threat Talent Management
Turner Artist Management
Universal Management Group (UMG)
V & L International, LLC
Valentino Entertainment
WA Enterprises
Yumkas Management

Music Supervisors
Cue11 Entertainment
DEJ Management Company
Delphinius Management
Greenspan Artist Management
Hook Entertainment
McMurdo Management & Associates, LLC
Judy Palnick Entertainment
Sussex Ltd., Inc., A Management Company
TGI Entertainment Corporation

Musical Theatre Performers
A.C.T. Management
A.D.S. Management
Associated Artists PR & Management
Blueprint Artist Management
Brookside Artist Management
Coastal Entertainment Productions
Columbia Artists Management LLC
Creative Talent Company
Cue11 Entertainment
Davila & Co.
DEJ Management Company
Bonny Dore Management
Michael Einfeld Management
Elkins Entertainment Corporation
The FTL Company
Hart² Management
Landis-Simon Productions & Talent Management
Little Stars Management
McMurdo Management & Associates, LLC
MMC Entertainment/Dance Directions
Blair Silver & Company LLC
Sinclair Management
Soiree Fair, Inc.
Star Talent Management
The Sterling/Winters Company
Suzelle Enterprises
Tinoco Management
Torque Entertainment
Universal Management Group (UMG)
Young Talent, Inc.
Yumkas Management
Zenith Management

Playwrights
A.C.T. Management
Ampersand Management Group
Associated Artists PR & Management
Brookside Artist Management
The Coppage Company
Creative Haven Entertainment
Davila & Co.
Dean Literary Concepts
DEJ Management Company
Delphinius Management
Bonny Dore Management
e-merge Management
Exile Entertainment
Festa Entertainment
Field Entertainment
The FTL Company
GhettoSuburbia Entertainment
Dodie Gold Management, Inc.
Susan Graw and Associates
Cary Hoffman Management
Incognito Management
Infinity Management International
Barry Krost Management
Liebman Entertainment
The Marshak/Zachary Company
McMurdo Management & Associates, LLC
Dee Mura Enterprises, Inc.
Omniquest Entertainment
Parseghian Planco, LLC
Pro and Con Productions Talent Management
Linda Reitman Management
Relevant Entertainment Group
Jeff Ross Entertainment, Inc.
Sharp Talent
Blair Silver & Company LLC
Andrea Simon Entertainment
Chad Snopek Management
Soiree Fair, Inc.
Spellman, Paul & Wetzel
Spot Light Entertainment
Steinberg Talent Management Group
Sussex Ltd., Inc., A Management Company
Synchronicity Management

Playwrights (Continued)
Talent Scout International Management
Torque Entertainment
Underground Management
Universal Management Group (UMG)
Nick Yellen Creative Agency

Print Models
1 Management
abc management group
Absolute Talent Management, Inc.
A.D.S. Management
All That Entertainment Management
American Artists Entertainment Group
Artist International
Arts and Letters Management
Associated Artists PR & Management
Betwixt Talent Management
Blackwood Talent Management
Blubay Talent Management
Robin Brooks Management
Calliope Talent Management, LLC
Central Artists
Chancellor Entertainment
Cue11 Entertainment
Richard De Lancy & Associates Talent Agency
DEJ Management Company
Dream Talent
du Jour Entertainment/Gypsy Productions
Elegance Talent Group
Encore Artists Management
The ESI Network
Stann Findelle Law & Management
Fire Comm Management
First Take
Five12 Entertainment Group
Flaunt Model Management, Inc.
Michael Flutie's Office (MFO)
Michael Forman Management
Full Circle Management
Estelle Fusco Talent Management
Gem Entertainment Group, Inc.
Green Key Management, LLC
Hook Entertainment
Howell Management
IMG Models
Impact Artists Group, LLC
The Independent Group, LLC
Infinity Management International
Insight
Lang Talent
Letnom Management & Productions
Little Stars Management
M Management
Magenta Creative Management
Maier Management
Management 101
Managing Artistic Concepts
Manta Entertainment
The Marcelli Company
Dino May Management
MC Talent
McMurdo Management & Associates, LLC
Midwest Talent Management, Inc.
April Mills Management
Jaime Monroy Studios
MP Management
Dee Mura Enterprises, Inc.
NCL TALENT
P.K.A. Entertainment Group
Park Place Management
Michele Pommier Management
Red Baron Management
Rising Talent Management
Richard Schwartz Management
Shark Artists, Inc.
Sharp Talent
Loretta Shreve Model Center/Shreve Talent Source

MANAGERS

Print Models (Continued)

Blair Silver & Company LLC
SJV Enterprises & Associates
Soma Management
Station 3
Studio Talent Group
Suzelle Enterprises
TalentCo Model & Talent Management
Talented Managers
Temptation Management
TGI Entertainment Corporation
Tinoco Management
Torque Entertainment
Trademark Artists Management
Triniti Management
Triple Threat Talent Management
Trump Model Management
Universal Management Group (UMG)
Vision Model Management
WA Enterprises
Wilhelmina Creative Management
Young Talent, Inc.
Zenith Management

Producers

777 Group, LTD
A Wink and a Nod Management, Inc.
A.C.T. Management
A.D.S. Management
AK Associates
Ambitious Entertainment
American Artists Entertainment Group
American Artists Group Management
Ardent Entertainment
Artist International
Associated Artists PR & Management
Avalon Management, Inc.
Avery Management
The Bauer Company
Becker Entertainment Group
David Belenzon Management, Inc.
Carl Belfor Entertainment Management Company
Bensky Entertainment
Michael Black Management, Inc.
Blubay Talent Management
Blue Train Entertainment
Blueprint Artist Management
Barry Bookin Management
Brand X Management
The Braverman/Bloom Co., Inc.
Brillstein-Grey Management
Broom in the Moon Productions
Brustein Entertainment
BSC Management
Careyes Entertainment
CastleBright
Doug Chapin Management, Inc.
Circle of Confusion
The Collective
Diane Connors Management
Contemporary Talent Partners (CTP)
The Coppage Company
Course Management
Creative Content Management
Creative Enterprises Management
Creative Haven Entertainment
Creative Talent Management
Cue11 Entertainment
Alan David Management
DEJ Management Company
Delphinius Management
Detroit Company
The Development Department
dixon talent, inc.
DreaMakers Inc.
Eighth Square Entertainment
Elkins Entertainment Corporation
e-merge Management

Producers (Continued)

Encore Artists Management
Envoy Entertainment
The Feldman Company
Feldman Management, LLC
Field Entertainment
Fineman Entertainment
The Firm, Inc.
First Class Entertainment, Inc.
Flashpoint Entertainment
Flutie Entertainment
The FTL Company
Lorita Garcia & Associates Mgmt. & Ent.
Phillip B. Gittelman Personal Management
Goldstein Company, Inc.
The Gotham Group, Inc.
Graup Entertainment
Susan Graw and Associates
Ken Gross Management
Handprint Entertainment
Peter Hankwitz Production & Management, Inc.
Todd Harris Management, Inc.
Headline Media Management
Holder Management
Holzman Management Group
Howard Entertainment
Impact Artists Group, LLC
Industry Entertainment Partners
Infinity Management International
Insight
JudyO Productions
Karma Entertainment
Key Creatives, LLC
Kinesis Entertainment, Inc.
Don Klein Management Group, Inc.
Kritzer Levine Wilkins Entertainment
Barry Krost Management
L.A. Sammy Productions
Paul Lane Entertainment
Lawson Artist Management, LLC
Letnom Management & Productions
Levine Management
The Liberty Company
Little Studio Films
LoLo Entertainment Co.
Tami Lynn Productions
M Management
Mack Muse Entertainment, Inc.
Magenta Creative Management
Management 101
Managing Artistic Concepts
Marathon Entertainment
The Marcelli Company
The Marshak/Zachary Company
MBST Entertainment
McMurdo Management & Associates, LLC
Media Four
MEG Management
Messina Baker Entertainment Corporation
Millennium Entertainment, Inc.
Moore Artists' Management
Dee Mura Enterprises, Inc.
New Entertainment Group
New Wave Entertainment
Niad Management
Nine Yards Entertainment
Omnipop Talent Group
One Talent Management
P.K.A. Entertainment Group
Judy Palnick Entertainment
Panettiere & Company, Inc.
The Phoenix Organization
PMA Literary & Film Management, Inc.
Polaris Entertainment
Principal Entertainment
Principato-Young Entertainment
Pro and Con Productions Talent Management
Pure Arts

Producers (Continued)

Quattro Media
Red Baron Management
Red Harvest Entertainment
Reel World Management
Linda Reitman Management
Relevant Entertainment Group
ROAR
Stephanie Rogers & Associates
Jeff Ross Entertainment, Inc.
RPM International
Fran Saperstein Organization
Schachter Entertainment
Schumacher Management
Richard Schwartz Management
SCORE! Media Ventures
Screen Partners, Inc.
Seven Summits Pictures & Management
Burt Shapiro Management
Marty Shapiro Management
Shapiro/West & Associates, Inc.
Shark Artists, Inc.
Narelle Sheehan Management (NSM)
Shoelace, Inc. Management
The Shuman Company
Blair Silver & Company LLC
Andrea Simon Entertainment
Slamdance Management
Smart Entertainment
Bette Smith Management
Sneak Preview Entertainment
Soma Management
Speak Softly Legal Management
Spot Light Entertainment
Station 3
Steinberg Talent Management Group
The Sterling/Winters Company
Stone Canyon Media
Suite A Management Talent & Literary Agency
Sussex Ltd., Inc., A Management Company
Synchronicity Management
Talent Scout International Management
Teitelbaum Artists Group
TGI Entertainment Corporation
Thompson Street Entertainment
Thrive Entertainment
Roz Tillman Management
Toltec Artists
Trademark Artists Management
Tudor Management Group
Universal Management Group (UMG)
Unlimited Management
V & L International, LLC
Viviano Feldman Entertainment
Brad Waisbren Enterprises
Michael Wallach Management
Washington Square Arts
Water Street
Westside Artists
Whitaker Entertainment
Working Artists
Nick Yellen Creative Agency

Production Designers

Ambitious Entertainment
Columbia Artists Management LLC
Creative Haven Entertainment
DEJ Management Company
Illuminati Entertainment
Marty Shapiro Management
Westside Artists

Runway Models

All That Entertainment Management
American Artists Entertainment Group
Betwixt Talent Management
Blubay Talent Management

MANAGERS

Runway Models (Continued)

Calliope Talent Management, LLC
Chancellor Entertainment
Cue11 Entertainment
Richard De Lancy & Associates Talent Agency
DEJ Management Company
Dream Talent
Elegance Talent Group
Flaunt Model Management, Inc.
Michael Flutie's Office (MFO)
Green Key Management, LLC
Hook Entertainment
Howell Management
IMG Models
The Independent Group, LLC
Magenta Creative Management
McMurdo Management & Associates, LLC
Park Place Management
Michele Pommier Management
Sager Management, Inc.
Loretta Shreve Model Center/Shreve Talent Source
Soma Management
Station 3
TalentCo Model & Talent Management
Talented Managers
Temptation Management
TGI Entertainment Corporation
Torque Entertainment
Trump Model Management
Universal Management Group (UMG)

Screenwriters

3 Arts Entertainment, Inc.
6 Pictures
777 Group, LTD
A Wink and a Nod Management, Inc.
ACE Media
A.C.T. Management
Acuna Entertainment
AEI-Atchity/Entertainment International
AK Associates
Alpha Centauri Management
Ampersand Management Group
Anonymous Content
Anthem Entertainment
Archetype
Arpil Entertainment
Art/Work Entertainment
Artist International
Artists Only Management
Arts and Letters Management
Associated Artists PR & Management
Marilyn Atlas Management
Avalon Management, Inc.
Avery Management
Bamboo Management LLC
The Bauer Company
Baumgarten Management & Production
Beaty Four Entertainment
Becker Entertainment Group
Carl Belfor Entertainment Management Company
Benderspink
Bensky Entertainment
Michael Black Management, Inc.
Blackwood Talent Management
Blain & Associates
Blubay Talent Management
Blue Train Entertainment
Bohemia Group
Barry Bookin Management
Brand X Management
The Braverman/Bloom Co., Inc.
Bridge Falls Entertainment
Brookside Artist Management
Broom in the Moon Productions
Brustein Entertainment
bumberShoot Entertainment
The Burstein Company

Screenwriters (Continued)

Careyes Entertainment
Casting Unlimited & Management
CastleBright
Doug Chapin Management, Inc.
Chic Productions & Management (CPM)
Circle of Confusion
Vincent Cirrincione Associates, Ltd.
Clark Management Company
Code
The Collective
Commonwealth Talent Group
The Company Artists
Concept Entertainment
Connection III Entertainment Corp.
Contemporary Talent Partners (CTP)
Content House
The Conversation Company, Ltd.
The Coppage Company
Cornice Entertainment
Course Management
Creative Convergence
Creative Enterprises Management
Creative Haven Entertainment
Creative Talent Management
Cue11 Entertainment
Marv Dauer Management
Davila & Co.
Dean Literary Concepts
DEJ Management Company
Delphinius Management
Detroit Company
The Development Department
Dewalt & Muzik Management
Divine Management
Donaldson/Sanders Entertainment
Douglas Management Group
DreaMakers Inc.
du Jour Entertainment/Gypsy Productions
EarthAngels Literary Management
Eastwood Talent Corporation
Echo Lake Management
Rona Edwards Productions
Eighth Square Entertainment
EK Management
Elements Entertainment
Elkins Entertainment Corporation
Elsboy Management
Elysian Entertainment, Inc.
Emancipated Talent Management & Consulting
e-merge Management
Encore Artists Management
Endure Management
Energy Entertainment
Ensemble Entertainment
Envoy Entertainment
Epigram Management
Evatopia
Evergreen International Management
Evolution Management
Exile Entertainment
Farah Films & Management
Fastbreak Management, Inc.
The Feldman Company
Feldman Management, LLC
Festa Entertainment
Field Entertainment
Fineman Entertainment
The Firm, Inc.
FitzGerald Literary Management
Flashpoint Entertainment
Flutie Entertainment
Foremost Films
Michael Forman Management
Foursight Entertainment
Elizabeth Fowler Management
Frenetic Media
Fuel Filmworks

Screenwriters (Continued)

Fuse Entertainment
Generate
M.M. Gertz Entertainment
GhettoSuburbia Entertainment
Peter Giagni Management, Inc.
Dodie Gold Management, Inc.
Jeff Goldberg Management
Peter Golden & Associates, Inc.
Goldstein Company, Inc.
The Gotham Group, Inc.
Grade A Entertainment
Graup Entertainment
Susan Graw and Associates
Gray Fox Films, LLC
Juliet Green Management
Grey Line Entertainment, Inc.
Brad Gross Inc., Literary Management
Ken Gross Management
Sheree Guitar Entertainment
Guy Walks into a Bar Management
H2F Entertainment
Todd Harris Management, Inc.
Heitmann Entertainment
Josselyne Herman & Associates
Hofflund/Polone
Cary Hoffman Management
Holder Management
Holzman Management Group
Hook Entertainment
Hopscotch Pictures
Howard Entertainment
Illuminati Entertainment
Impact Artists Group, LLC
Incognito Management
Industry Entertainment Partners
Infinity Management International
Cheri Ingram Enterprises
Integrated Films & Management
Intellectual Property Group
Jaret Entertainment
JudyO Productions
Kanner Entertainment Inc.
Kaplan/Perrone Entertainment, LLC
Karma Entertainment
Kersey Management
Key Creatives, LLC
Kinesis Entertainment, Inc.
Kinetic Management
King Management
Kings Highway Entertainment
Kjar & Associates
Don Klein Management Group, Inc.
Kritzer Levine Wilkins Entertainment
Barry Krost Management
The Landers Group
Paul Lane Entertainment
Lane Management Group
The Laugh Factory Management
Lawson Artist Management, LLC
Leverage Management
Levine Management
Levity Entertainment Group
The Liberty Company
Liebman Entertainment
Lighthouse Entertainment
Link Talent Group
Little Studio Films
Lloyd Entertainement
LoLo Entertainment Co.
Tami Lynn Productions
M Management
Mack Muse Entertainment, Inc.
MaCroManagement
Madhouse Entertainment
Magenta Creative Management
Magnet Management
Management 101

MANAGERS

Screenwriters (Continued)

Management 360
Managing Artistic Concepts
Manta Entertainment
Marathon Entertainment
The Marcelli Company
Marsala Management
Marsh Entertainment
The Marshak/Zachary Company
Max Freedman Management
MBST Entertainment
McKeon-Myones Management
McMurdo Management & Associates, LLC
Media Four
Media Talent Group
MEG Management
Michael Meltzer & Associates
Messina Baker Entertainment Corporation
Millennium Entertainment, Inc.
The Miller Company
Miterre Productions, Inc.
Modus Entertainment
Moore Artists' Management
MSI Entertainment, Inc.
Dee Mura Enterprises, Inc.
The Muraviov Company
Nanas Entertainment
Nebula Management
New Entertainment Group
New Wave Entertainment
Next Stop Management
Niad Management
Nine Yards Entertainment
Oceanside Entertainment
Omnipop Talent Group
Omniquest Entertainment
One Entertainment
One Talent Management
Online Talent Group/OTG Talent
Ovation Management
P.K.A. Entertainment Group
Judy Palnick Entertainment
Panettiere & Company, Inc.
Park Place Management
Parseghian Planco, LLC
PB Management
Pearl Pictures Management
Stephen Pevner, Inc.
The Phoenix Organization
The Pitt Group
Plumeria Entertainment Management
PMA Literary & Film Management, Inc.
Polaris Entertainment
The Derek Power Company, Inc.
Principal Entertainment
Principato-Young Entertainment
Pro and Con Productions Talent Management
Pure Arts
Quattro Media
Rabiner/Damato Entertainment
The Radmin Company
Charles Rapp Enterprises, Inc.
Raw Talent
Red Baron Management
Red Harvest Entertainment
Dan Redler Entertainment
Reel World Management
Linda Reitman Management
Relevant Entertainment Group
Rigberg Entertainment Group
ROAR
Dolores Robinson Entertainment
Stephanie Rogers & Associates
The Marion Rosenberg Office
Rosenzweig Films
Jeff Ross Entertainment, Inc.
Heidi Rotbart Management
RPM International

Screenwriters (Continued)

Safran Company
Sanderson Entertainment, Inc.
Fran Saperstein Organization
Schachter Entertainment
Schumacher Management
Richard Schwartz Management
Seekers Management, LLC
Earl Shank
Marty Shapiro Management
Shapiro/West & Associates, Inc.
Shark Artists, Inc.
Shelter Entertainment
Shoelace, Inc. Management
The Shuman Company
Silent R Management
Andrea Simon Entertainment
Slamdance Management
Sleeping Giant Entertainment
Smart Entertainment
Todd Smith & Associates
Bette Smith Management
Sneak Preview Entertainment
Chad Snopek Management
Soiree Fair, Inc.
Sonesta Entertainment, LLC
Spellman, Paul & Wetzel
Spot Light Entertainment
Station 3
Steinberg Talent Management Group
Joel Stevens Entertainment Company
Stone Canyon Media
Story Arts Management
Studio Talent Group
Sussex Ltd., Inc., A Management Company
Sweeney Management
Synchronicity Management
Talent Management Partners
Talent Scout International Management
TGI Entertainment Corporation
The Michael Forman Company
Thompson Street Entertainment
Thrive Entertainment
Thruline Entertainment
TMT Entertainment
Torque Entertainment
Trademark Artists Management
Trancas Management
Treasure Entertainment
Triple Threat Talent Management
Tudor Management Group
Underground Management
Unique Talent Group
Universal Management Group (UMG)
Unlimited Management
Untitled Entertainment
V & L International, LLC
Vanguard Management Group
Vanguard Talent Management
Velocity Management
Visionary Entertainment
Viviano Feldman Entertainment
Washington Square Arts
Water Street
Whitaker Entertainment
Wild Briar Talent
Will Entertainment
Windfall Management
Jacki Wolski Literary Management
Working Artists
W.T.A. & Associates
Nick Yellen Creative Agency
Yumkas Management
Gene Yusem Company
Zero Gravity Management

Seniors

A.D.S. Management
Associated Artists PR & Management
Calliope Talent Management, LLC
Central Artists
Richard De Lancy & Associates Talent Agency
DEJ Management Company
Elkins Entertainment Corporation
Encore Artists Management
The ESI Network
Flaunt Model Management, Inc.
Lang Talent
Omnium Entertainment Group
Loretta Shreve Model Center/Shreve Talent Source
Sinclair Management
Suzelle Enterprises
Talent Management Partners
TalentCo Model & Talent Management
Roz Tillman Management
Torque Entertainment
Unique Talent Group
Vesta Talent Services
Zenith Management

Sound Editors

McMurdo Management & Associates, LLC

Speakers/Lecturers

abc management group
A.C.T. Management
A.D.S. Management
Beaty Four Entertainment
David Belenzon Management, Inc.
Barry Bookin Management
Calliope Talent Management, LLC
Cue11 Entertainment
DEJ Management Company
Delphinius Management
Bonny Dore Management
Michael Flutie's Office (MFO)
Hart^2 Management
Cheri Ingram Enterprises
Kragen & Company
Letnom Management & Productions
Marathon Entertainment
The Marcelli Company
McMurdo Management & Associates, LLC
Dee Mura Enterprises, Inc.
New Wave Entertainment
Polaris Entertainment
Jeff Ross Entertainment, Inc.
Smart Entertainment
Soma Management
Spot Light Entertainment
The Sterling/Winters Company
Gail A. Stocker Presents
The Suchin Company
Larry Thompson Organization
Universal Management Group (UMG)
Yumkas Management

Sports Personalities

abc management group
A.D.S. Management
Arias & Associates International
Artist International
Axiom Management
Blain & Associates
Blubay Talent Management
Barry Bookin Management
The Braverman/Bloom Co., Inc.
Calliope Talent Management, LLC
Casting Unlimited & Management
Central Artists
Diane Connors Management
Cornerstone Management
Creative Enterprises Management

MANAGERS

Sports Personalities (Continued)

Creative Mgmt. Entertainment Group (CMEG)
Cue11 Entertainment
DEJ Management Company
Eastwood Talent Corporation
Evans Management
Field Entertainment
The Firm, Inc.
Flutie Entertainment
Michael Flutie's Office (MFO)
Gem Entertainment Group, Inc.
Susan Graw and Associates
Headline Media Management
Holzman Management Group
The Independent Group, LLC
Cheri Ingram Enterprises
King Management
The Management Team
David Martin Management
Dee Mura Enterprises, Inc.
New Wave Entertainment
P.K.A. Entertainment Group
Panettiere & Company, Inc.
Park Place Management
Pro and Con Productions Talent Management
Rising Talent Management
SCORE! Media Ventures
Burt Shapiro Management
Blair Silver & Company LLC
Bette Smith Management
Soiree Fair, Inc.
Speak Softly Legal Management
Spot Light Entertainment
The Suchin Company
TalentCo Model & Talent Management
TGI Entertainment Corporation
Turner Artist Management
Universal Management Group (UMG)
Velocity Management
Wallach Entertainment
Michael Wallach Management
Wilhelmina Models

Teens/Young Adults

A Fein Martini
A Management
abc management group
Absolute Talent Management, Inc.
Advance LA
Leslie Allan-Rice Management
American Artists Group Management
Anthem Entertainment
Artist International
Artists International
Artists Only Management
Arts and Letters Management
Marilyn Atlas Management
Axiom Management
Bamboo Management LLC
Bensky Entertainment
Blackwood Talent Management
Jane Bloom & Associates
Blueprint Artist Management
Bohemia Group
Robin Brooks Management
Brookside Artist Management
Brown Leader Group
BSC Management
Calliope Talent Management, LLC
Central Artists
Chancellor Entertainment
Cheatham, Greene & Company
The Collective
Connection III Entertainment Corp.
Creative Mgmt. Entertainment Group (CMEG)
Creative Talent Company
Cue11 Entertainment
Richard De Lancy & Associates Talent Agency

Teens/Young Adults (Continued)

Denise Denny Talent Management
DePaz Management
Dewalt & Muzik Management
Bob Diamond & Associates
Bonny Dore Management
Dream Talent
Eastwood Talent Corporation
Elkins Entertainment Corporation
Emerald Talent Group
Encore Artists Management
Endurance Talent Management
The ESI Network
Evolution Management
Fire Comm Management
First Take
Robert Fitzpatrick Organization
Five12 Entertainment Group
Flaunt Model Management, Inc.
Michael Forman Management
Framework Entertainment
Kyle Fritz Management
Full Circle Management
Brian Funnagan Management
Estelle Fusco Talent Management
Lorita Garcia & Associates Mgmt. & Ent.
Gem Entertainment Group, Inc.
Generate
Global Entertainment
Marianne Golan Management
Goldstar Talent Management
Green Key Management, LLC
Joan Green Management
Halpern Management
Hart Entertainment
Hart² Management
Harvest Talent Management
Hines & Hunt Entertainment
Hollywood Management Company
Hook Entertainment
Howard Entertainment
Impact Artists Group, LLC
Insight
Interlink Management
James/Levy Management, Inc.
Jaymes-Nelson Entertainment
Kjar & Associates
Knight Light Entertainment
Koopman Management
Kritzer Levine Wilkins Entertainment
Victor Kruglov & Associates
Landis-Simon Productions & Talent Management
Lane Management Group
Lang Talent
The Laugh Factory Management
Lawson Artist Management, LLC
Letnom Management & Productions
Myrna Lieberman Management
Life Management
Lighthouse Entertainment
Link Talent Group
Little Stars Management
Jeffrey Loseff Management
Bonnie Love Management
Lymberopoulos, Inc.
M Management
Mack Muse Entertainment, Inc.
Magnolia Entertainment
Maier Management
Management 101
Managing Artistic Concepts
Manta Entertainment
Marsala Management
The Marshak/Zachary Company
Massei Management
Dino May Management
MC Talent
McMurdo Management & Associates, LLC

Teens/Young Adults (Continued)

Michael Meltzer & Associates
Messina Baker Entertainment Corporation
MGC/Cushman Entertainment Group
Midwest Talent Management, Inc.
April Mills Management
J. Mitchell Management
MMC Entertainment/Dance Directions
Jaime Monroy Studios
Monster Talent Management, Inc.
Moore Artists' Management
MP Management
Dee Mura Enterprises, Inc.
Nani/Saperstein Management, Inc.
NCL TALENT
New Wave Entertainment
Niad Management
Barney Oldfield Management
Rosella Olson Management
Omniquest Entertainment
Omnium Entertainment Group
One Talent Management
Online Talent Group/OTG Talent
Dianna Oser Management
Page Management
Park Place Management
Ria Pavia Management
PB Management
Polaris Entertainment
Principal Entertainment
Pro and Con Productions Talent Management
Protege Entertainment
Red Baron Management
Reel Talent Management
L. Richardson Entertainment
The Right Connection Entertainment Group
Rising Talent Management
J.C. Robbins Management
Mark Robert Management
Heidi Rotbart Management
Sager Management, Inc.
Sauers Artists, LLC
Schachter Entertainment
Richard Schwartz Management
Earl Shank
Burt Shapiro Management
Shapiro/West & Associates, Inc.
Shark Artists, Inc.
Sharp Talent
Sharyn Talent Management
Shoelace, Inc. Management
Loretta Shreve Model Center/Shreve Talent Source
The Siegal Company
Alan Siegel Entertainment
Simmons and Scott Entertainment, LLC
Sinclair Management
SJV Enterprises & Associates
Daniel Sladek Entertainment Corporation
Slamdance Management
SLJ Management
Bette Smith Management
Soiree Fair, Inc.
Helene Sokol Management
Soma Management
Spellman, Paul & Wetzel
Star Talent Management
Station 3
Stein Entertainment Group
Joel Stevens Entertainment Company
Studio Talent Group
The Suchin Company
Suzelle Enterprises
Sweeney Management
The Talent Company
Talent Management Partners
TalentCo Model & Talent Management
Talented Managers
Teitelbaum Artists Group

MANAGERS

Teens/Young Adults (Continued)

Temptation Management
The Michael Forman Company
Thirdhill Entertainment
Roz Tillman Management
Tinoco Management
Torque Entertainment
Trademark Talent
Triniti Management
Triple Threat Talent Management
Trusik Talent Management, Inc.
Turner Artist Management
Unique Talent Group
Vanguard Management Group
WA Enterprises
Brad Waisbren Enterprises
David Westberg Management
Whitaker Entertainment
Wilhelmina Creative Management
Wilhelmina Kids
Williams Unlimited
Witt Entertainment Management, Inc.
Young Performers Management
Young Talent, Inc.
Bonnie Young Personal Management
Zenith Management
Ziemba Talent & Associates

TV Writers

3 Arts Entertainment, Inc.
777 Group, LTD
ACE Media
A.C.T. Management
Acuna Entertainment
AEI-Atchity/Entertainment International
AK Associates
Alpha Centauri Management
Ampersand Management Group
Anonymous Content
Archetype
Art/Work Entertainment
Artist International
Associated Artists PR & Management
Marilyn Atlas Management
Avalon Management, Inc.
Avery Management
Bamboo Management LLC
The Bauer Company
Baumgarten Management & Production
Carl Belfor Entertainment Management Company
Benderspink
Bensky Entertainment
Michael Black Management, Inc.
Blackwood Talent Management
Blain & Associates
The Braverman/Bloom Co., Inc.
Bridge Falls Entertainment
Brillstein-Grey Management
Brookside Artist Management
Broom in the Moon Productions
Brustein Entertainment
bumberShoot Entertainment
The Burstein Company
Casting Unlimited & Management
Cheatham, Greene & Company
Circle of Confusion
Code
The Collective
Concept Entertainment
Contemporary Talent Partners (CTP)
Content House
The Conversation Company, Ltd.
The Coppage Company
Cornice Entertainment
Course Management
Edna Cowan Management
Creative Convergence
Creative Enterprises Management

TV Writers (Continued)

Creative Haven Entertainment
Cue11 Entertainment
Davila & Co.
DEJ Management Company
Delphinius Management
Detroit Company
The Development Department
Divine Management
dixon talent, inc.
Donaldson/Sanders Entertainment
Bonny Dore Management
Douglas Management Group
du Jour Entertainment/Gypsy Productions
EarthAngels Literary Management
Eighth Square Entertainment
Elements Entertainment
Elkins Entertainment Corporation
e-merge Management
Encore Artists Management
Endure Management
Energy Entertainment
Ensemble Entertainment
Envoy Entertainment
Epigram Management
Evolution Management
Farah Films & Management
Fastbreak Management, Inc.
The Feldman Company
Feldman Management, LLC
Festa Entertainment
Field Entertainment
Fineman Entertainment
The Firm, Inc.
Flutie Entertainment
Michael Flutie's Office (MFO)
Michael Forman Management
Fuel Filmworks
Fuse Entertainment
Generate
M.M. Gertz Entertainment
GhettoSuburbia Entertainment
Peter Giagni Management, Inc.
Dodie Gold Management, Inc.
Peter Golden & Associates, Inc.
Goldstein Company, Inc.
The Gotham Group, Inc.
Grade A Entertainment
Graup Entertainment
Susan Graw and Associates
Juliet Green Management
Grey Line Entertainment, Inc.
Ken Gross Management
Sheree Guitar Entertainment
Guy Walks into a Bar Management
H2F Entertainment
Handprint Entertainment
Heitmann Entertainment
Josselyne Herman & Associates
Hines & Hunt Entertainment
Cary Hoffman Management
Holder Management
Holzman Management Group
Howard Entertainment
Illuminati Entertainment
Impact Artists Group, LLC
Incognito Management
Industry Entertainment Partners
Infinity Management International
Cheri Ingram Enterprises
Integrated Films & Management
Jaret Entertainment
JudyO Productions
Kanner Entertainment Inc.
Kersey Management
Key Creatives, LLC
Kinesis Entertainment, Inc.
King Management

TV Writers (Continued)

Kings Highway Entertainment
Kjar & Associates
Don Klein Management Group, Inc.
Kritzer Levine Wilkins Entertainment
Barry Krost Management
The Landers Group
The Laugh Factory Management
Lawson Artist Management, LLC
Letnom Management & Productions
Levine Management
Leviton Management
Levity Entertainment Group
Liebman Entertainment
Lighthouse Entertainment
Lloyd Entertainement
LoLo Entertainment Co.
M Management
Mack Muse Entertainment, Inc.
Madhouse Entertainment
Magenta Creative Management
Magnet Management
Magnolia Entertainment
Management 101
Managing Artistic Concepts
Manta Entertainment
Marathon Entertainment
The Marcelli Company
Marsh Entertainment
The Marshak/Zachary Company
MBST Entertainment
McKeon-Myones Management
McMurdo Management & Associates, LLC
Michael Meltzer & Associates
Messina Baker Entertainment Corporation
Millennium Entertainment, Inc.
The Miller Company
Modus Entertainment
Moore Artists' Management
Dee Mura Enterprises, Inc.
Nebula Management
New Wave Entertainment
Nine Yards Entertainment
Oceanside Entertainment
Omnipop Talent Group
Omniquest Entertainment
One Entertainment
One Talent Management
Ovation Management
P.K.A. Entertainment Group
Judy Palnick Entertainment
Parseghian Planco, LLC
PB Management
Pearl Pictures Management
The Phoenix Organization
The Pitt Group
Plumeria Entertainment Management
Polaris Entertainment
Principal Entertainment
Principato-Young Entertainment
Pro and Con Productions Talent Management
Quattro Media
Rabiner/Damato Entertainment
Charles Rapp Enterprises, Inc.
Raw Talent
Red Harvest Entertainment
Relevant Entertainment Group
RJM/Renée Jennett Management
ROAR
Dolores Robinson Entertainment
Stephanie Rogers & Associates
Lara Rosenstock Management
Rosenzweig Films
Jeff Ross Entertainment, Inc.
Heidi Rotbart Management
RPM International
Safran Company
Sanderson Entertainment, Inc.

MANAGERS

TV Writers (Continued)

Schachter Entertainment
Schumacher Management
SCORE! Media Ventures
Seekers Management, LLC
Marty Shapiro Management
Shapiro/West & Associates, Inc.
Shark Artists, Inc.
Narelle Sheehan Management (NSM)
Shelter Entertainment
Shoelace, Inc. Management
The Shuman Company
Silent R Management
Blair Silver & Company LLC
Andrea Simon Entertainment
SirenSong Entertainment, Inc.
Slamdance Management
Sleeping Giant Entertainment
Smart Entertainment
Bette Smith Management
Sneak Preview Entertainment
Chad Snopek Management
Sonesta Entertainment, LLC
Spot Light Entertainment
Station 3
Steinberg Talent Management Group
The Sterling/Winters Company
Harriet Sternberg Management
Joel Stevens Entertainment Company
Stone Canyon Media
Story Arts Management
Studio Talent Group
Sussex Ltd., Inc., A Management Company
Sweeney Management
Synchronicity Management
Talent Management Partners
Talent Scout International Management
Teitelbaum Artists Group
TGI Entertainment Corporation
The Michael Forman Company
Thompson Street Entertainment
Thrive Entertainment
Thruline Entertainment
Torque Entertainment
Trademark Artists Management
Trancas Management
Treasure Entertainment
Tudor Management Group
Underground Management
Unique Talent Group
Universal Management Group (UMG)
Unlimited Management
Untitled Entertainment
Velocity Management
Visionary Entertainment
Viviano Feldman Entertainment
Washington Square Arts
Water Street
Will Entertainment
Jacki Wolski Literary Management
W.T.A. & Associates
Nick Yellen Creative Agency
Bonnie Young Personal Management
Yumkas Management

Variety Artists

A.C.T. Management
Advance LA
Alpha Centauri Management
Avalon Management, Inc.
David Belenzon Management, Inc.
The Braverman/Bloom Co., Inc.
Brustein Entertainment
BSC Management
Calliope Talent Management, LLC
CFB Productions, Inc.
Coastal Entertainment Productions
The Collective

Variety Artists (Continued)

Columbia Artists Management LLC
Diane Connors Management
The Conversation Company, Ltd.
Edna Cowan Management
Cue11 Entertainment
DEJ Management Company
Delphinius Management
Denise Denny Talent Management
Dream Talent
Eastwood Talent Corporation
Elkins Entertainment Corporation
Evans Management
Fastbreak Management, Inc.
The Firm, Inc.
First Class Entertainment, Inc.
The FTL Company
Lorita Garcia & Associates Mgmt. & Ent.
Gem Entertainment Group, Inc.
Susan Graw and Associates
ICM Artists
Impact Artists Group, LLC
King Management
Kragen & Company
The Laugh Factory Management
Lawrence International Corporation
Lawson Artist Management, LLC
Letnom Management & Productions
Manta Entertainment
Marathon Entertainment
The Marcelli Company
David Martin Management
Miterre Productions, Inc.
Mixed Media Entertainment Company
Dee Mura Enterprises, Inc.
NCL TALENT
Nebula Management
New Wave Entertainment
P.K.A. Entertainment Group
Park Place Management
Pro and Con Productions Talent Management
Charles Rapp Enterprises, Inc.
Joseph Rapp Enterprises, Inc.
RPI Entertainment & Media Group
Shark Artists, Inc.
Blair Silver & Company LLC
Smart Entertainment
Larry Spellman Enterprises
Steinberg Talent Management Group
The Sterling/Winters Company
The Suchin Company
Synchronicity Management
Talent Management Partners
Tinoco Management

Voice-Over Artists

abc management group
Absolute Talent Management, Inc.
A.C.T. Management
A.D.S. Management
Advance LA
Anthem Entertainment
Arts and Letters Management
Associated Artists PR & Management
Marilyn Atlas Management
Bamboo Management LLC
The Bauer Company
Bensky Entertainment
Blackwood Talent Management
Robin Brooks Management
The Burstein Company
Calliope Talent Management, LLC
Doug Chapin Management, Inc.
Coastal Entertainment Productions
Diane Connors Management
The Conversation Company, Ltd.
Creative Mgmt. Entertainment Group (CMEG)
Creative Talent Company

Voice-Over Artists (Continued)

Creative Talent Management
CTM Artists
Cue11 Entertainment
Cutler Management
Alan David Management
Richard De Lancy & Associates Talent Agency
DEJ Management Company
Delphinius Management
Denise Denny Talent Management
Bonny Dore Management
Dream Talent
Eastwood Talent Corporation
Elkins Entertainment Corporation
The ESI Network
Evans Management
Fast Track Management
Fastbreak Management, Inc.
Stann Findelle Law & Management
The Firm, Inc.
Forster Delaney Management
Kyle Fritz Management
Full Circle Management
Gem Entertainment Group, Inc.
Goldstar Talent Management
Handprint Entertainment
Hart[2] Management
Hazen Talent Management
Cary Hoffman Management
Impact Artists Group, LLC
The Independent Group, LLC
Cheri Ingram Enterprises
The Laugh Factory Management
Lawson Artist Management, LLC
Letnom Management & Productions
Little Stars Management
Lymberopoulos, Inc.
Magnolia Entertainment
Management 101
Managing Artistic Concepts
Marathon Entertainment
McGowan Management
McMurdo Management & Associates, LLC
Messina Baker Entertainment Corporation
Midwest Talent Management, Inc.
Millennium Entertainment, Inc.
April Mills Management
J. Mitchell Management
Moore Artists' Management
MP Management
Dee Mura Enterprises, Inc.
Nani/Saperstein Management, Inc.
NCL TALENT
Nebula Management
New Wave Entertainment
Omnipop Talent Group
Oscars Abrams Zimel & Associates Inc.
P.K.A. Entertainment Group
Page Management
Ria Pavia Management
Pro and Con Productions Talent Management
Protege Entertainment
Charles Rapp Enterprises, Inc.
Red Baron Management
L. Richardson Entertainment
Sager Management, Inc.
Schachter Entertainment
Shark Artists, Inc.
Sharyn Talent Management
Loretta Shreve Model Center/Shreve Talent Source
The Siegal Company
Blair Silver & Company LLC
Simmons and Scott Entertainment, LLC
SirenSong Entertainment, Inc.
SLJ Management
Smart Entertainment
Bette Smith Management
Soiree Fair, Inc.

MANAGERS

Voice-Over Artists (Continued)
Star Talent Management
Stein Entertainment Group
Steinberg Talent Management Group
The Sterling/Winters Company
Strauss-McGarr Entertainment
Suzelle Enterprises
Synergy Management, Inc.
Talent Management Partners

Voice-Over Artists (Continued)
TalentCo Model & Talent Management
TGI Entertainment Corporation
Roz Tillman Management
Tinoco Management
Torque Entertainment
Triniti Management
Triple Threat Talent Management
Universal Management Group (UMG)

Voice-Over Artists (Continued)
V & L International, LLC
Vanguard Management Group
Vesta Talent Services
Whitaker Entertainment
Williams Unlimited
Witt Entertainment Management, Inc.
Zenith Management

SECTION **H**

INDEX BY NAME